THE LIVING TORAH

The Five Books of Moses

A new translation based on traditional Jewish sources,
with notes, introduction, maps, tables, charts, bibliography
and index

by

Rabbi Aryeh Kaplan

MAZNAIM PUBLISHING CORPORATION
NEW YORK / JERUSALEM

To my children:
Yosef Menachem Yisrael Meir, Avigail Faiga,
Devorah Rivkah, Eliezer Michah, Rochel Louiza,
Reuven Yehudah, Shimeon Yitzhak, and Haim Simhah;
and to their mother

Copyright © 1981 by Rabbi Aryeh Kaplan

For information write:

Maznaim Publishing Corporation
4304 12th Avenue
Brooklyn, New York 11219

Second Edition

ISBN 0-940118-29-7

Photocompostion by Simcha Graphic Associates

Printed and bound in Jerusalem, Israel
by Vagshal Ltd.

This third edition of The Living Torah *is dedicated to the memory of Rabbi Aryeh Kaplan, zt'l, whose writings inspired many. May his works continue to bring Torah into every home.*

TRANSLATOR'S INTRODUCTION

It is with great trepidation that one begins a translation of the Torah. It is the book most sacred to Judaism; every single word has infinite significance and depth. From the beginning, the translator knows that most of this will be lost in translation. Yet, at the same time, the translator has the responsibility to preserve as much of the Torah's depth and meaning as humanly possible.

Moreover, it is much easier to translate a book that has never been translated. The Torah, however, has been translated dozens of times. What justification is there for a new translation? What will this one have that others have lacked?

Most previous translations of the Torah can be divided into two categories. The "traditional" ones are, for the most part, based on the King James translation. Although a superb scholarly work, this translation is not rooted in Jewish sources, and often goes against traditional Jewish teachings. Furthermore, the language is archaic and difficult for the modern reader. Both of these shortcomings remain in most "traditional" translations.

Although the modern translations may be more readable, they are often even more divorced from Judaic sources than the others. While archeological and linguistic discoveries may be extremely interesting, they are not part of an unbroken tradition. Many Jewish traditions regarding how to translate the Torah date no more than a thousand years after its writing. Since change was slow to come in ancient times, one would expect these traditions to have a high degree of reliability.

Even more important, these traditions form a fundamental area of Jewish faith. No less than the Torah itself, the Talmud and its cognate works are part of Jewish tradition. A translation that disregards the teachings of the ancient sages will appear strange, almost alien, to the modern Jewish reader.

Therefore, the philosophy of this translation has been to treat the Torah as a living document. Our sages teach that "every day the Torah should be as new."[1] This indicates that even a translator may not treat the Torah as an archaic document. It also implies that archaic or obsolete language must not be used when translating the Torah, because this language gives the impression of the Torah being old, not new.

Thus, for example, many purists still insist on translating the second person singular as "thee," because Hebrew distinguishes between the second person singular and plural. It is obvious that this would, indeed, make the translation more "accurate." But, on the other hand, it would also give the text an archaic flavor, no matter how modern the rest of the language. For this reason, expressions such as this one were not used.

More important is the use of idiomatic language in the Torah. The greatest mistake any translator could make would be to translate an idiom literally. Imagine an expression such as, "I have a frog in my throat," translated into another language, in which its idiomatic meaning is not known.

It is obvious that the Torah contains much idiomatic usage, and translating it literally (as do most translations) distorts the meaning of the text. To a large degree, the "Oral Torah" consists of a tradition as to how to render the idiomatic language of the Torah. Thus, the Oral Tradition teaches that the expression literally translated, "between the eyes" (Exodus 13:9), is actually an idiom denoting the center of the head just above the hairline.[2] To translate it literally would not only go against tradition, but would be incorrect.

The Talmud itself warns of this. In one of the most important teachings regarding translation, the Talmud states, "One who translates a verse literally is misrepresenting the text. But one who adds anything of his own is a blasphemer."[3]

---

1. Rashi on Deuteronomy 27:15.
2. This is obvious from Deuteronomy 14:1.
3. *Kiddushin* 49a; *Tosefta, Megillah* 3:21.

The Talmud realizes that one who translates literally will often find himself translating idiomatic language, and to do so literally is the cardinal sin of translation. One must clearly understand what is to be taken literally and what is to be taken idiomatically. However, one may not add anything of his own. Any such judgment must be based firmly on tradition.

Another problem in translating the Torah is that of sentence structure. Clearly, the sentence structure of the Hebrew of three thousand years ago bears little, if any, resemblance to that of any modern language. Therefore, if one slavishly adheres to the original sentence structure in translating, he will often produce a result very different from that intended by the original. At best, many passages will be difficult, if not impossible, to understand.

This problem was recognized by Maimonides, and his advice should be engraved in every translator's mind. In his own words:[4]

> One who wishes to translate from one language to another, and tries to translate word by word, maintaining the order of both the subject and the words, will find his work very difficult, and will ultimately end up with a translation that is highly questionable and confusing.
>
> Rather, one who translates from one language to another must first understand the concept. Then he should relate and explain the subject according to his understanding, providing a clear exposition in the language [into which he is translating]. This is impossible without transposing the order of words.
>
> Moreover, the translator will sometimes have to use many words to translate a single word, while at other times he will have to use a single word to translate many. He will have to add and delete words so that the concept may be clearly expressed in the language into which he is translating.

This rule places great responsibility on the translator. When one translates literally, word for word, ambiguities in the original may be preserved, if not aggravated. But if the translator must understand the text, he also has the responsibility to interpret it. To do so correctly, he must not only analyze the text very carefully, but he must also study all the works that interpret it.

A good example is the Torah's description of the Tabernacle and Priestly vestments. Many passages are highly ambiguous, and without help from the tradition, it is very difficult to picture these items. If the translator does not begin with a picture, the translation will be even more difficult to understand than the original. The reader will complete the text having little idea as to what is actually meant.

On the other hand, if the translator has a good mental image of the Tabernacle, it will come across in his translation. The ambiguities (which most probably stem from our lack of knowledge of Biblical idiom) vanish, and a clear picture emerges. If actual illustrations and diagrams can be added to the text, clarity is enhanced all the more.

This approach is particularly important where Torah law is concerned. A literal approach will often convey an impression that is diametrically opposed to the way that the law was carried out in practice. At best, unless the translator is completely familiar with the law, the result will be ambiguous and difficult to understand. But if the structure of the law is well-known to the translator, it can be presented clearly in the translation.

This is particularly important in the Book of Leviticus, which deals with sacrifice and Levitical purity. In most translations, the reader ends up confused, with little, if any, idea how the sacrificial system worked. What we have tried to do is present the laws as they were practiced and as they appear in the codes, so that a clear picture emerges from the text.

The narratives of the Torah were meant to read like a story, and this too must be preserved in translation. In telling a story, there is no room for heavy language or complex sentence structure. Sometimes one Hebrew sentence will be broken up into a number of sentences in English; at other times, two Hebrew sentences may be joined into one in the translation. The final goal is always clarity and readability.

An example of idiom is the manner in which the Torah handles dialogue. In English, this is

4. Letter to Sh'muel ibn Tibbon.

handled by setting each statement in quotation marks and beginning it as a new paragraph. There is then no need to repeat the name of the person speaking. In Hebrew, the same goal is attained by repeating the expression, "And he said" before each statement. Translating this literally can be very awkward and repetitive. What we have done in a number of places is simply to translate "And he said" with a set of quotation marks.

Another frequent area of difficulty involves the various names of God. The convention, following the Septuagint, is to translate the Tetragrammaton as "the Lord," and *Elohim* as "God." This, however, often produces strained results, and somehow, referring to God as "the Lord" has a distinctly un-Jewish flavor. We have therefore consistently used "God" as the favored name, since it is the most often used. "Lord" has been used secondarily. This also reduces wordiness, since instead of "the Lord our God," we translate such a passage as "God our Lord."

Since the Torah is the subject of literally thousands of commentaries, a major problem in translation arises where there is a disagreement as to the meaning of a passage. In simple terms, which commentary should the translator use? The easiest approach would be consistently to follow a single commentary. However, this would lead to many places where clarity would have to be sacrificed, or where lengthy explanations would be needed. Furthermore, it would involve the translator in making value judgments as to the merits of the various major commentators.

Therefore, whenever there is a dispute regarding the meaning of a passage, the decision as to which interpretation to use has been based primarily on literary judgment. The fact that one opinion is favored over another is not meant to imply that we consider that opinion the most accurate. We are far from being in a position to judge the major commentators. If we have chosen the opinion of one commentator, it is only because his interpretation provides the simplest and clearest translation.

The only exception to this rule has been where Torah law is concerned. Here, we have consistently translated the passages so that they reflect the final decision in Jewish law. For the most part, this means following Maimonides' code (the *Yad*). Where law is concerned, literary considerations are secondary.

In many cases, the major alternative interpretations of a verse are presented in the notes. Where some highly ambiguous verses are concerned, this might mean presenting as many as a dozen different opinions. Rather than discuss each opinion, we have translated the verse according to each authority in the notes.

In the notes, we have also tried to identify each person and place to the best of our ability. Both parallel texts from the Scripture, and Talmudic and Midrashic works have been widely consulted. Where geographical places are concerned, modern geographers too have been consulted.

Although the notes were not meant as a commentary, they are intended to help the reader understand the text. Where the text does not provide all the information needed for comprehension, it has been supplied in the notes. It is hoped that the notes will help even those of limited background gain insight into the depth of the Torah.

In short, what we have attempted to provide is a translation of Judaism's most important Book, that is accurate, clear, modern, readable, and above all, in consonance with the living tradition of Judaism. While most of the translation will be understandable even to a young teenager, there is considerable material that even the advanced scholar will find of interest. It is meant to be a book that can be given to a boy on the day of his Bar Mitzvah, and yet remain the subject of lifelong study.

As if by divine providence, this translation took me exactly nine months to complete, and in a sense, it is my tenth child. If anything, one's love for the Torah can transcend that of any mere human being.

It is my prayer that this translation bring the word of God to the millions of Jews to whom the Hebrew original is still a closed book. May they see not only the text itself, but the infinitude of depth that lies beneath it. And for those familiar with the original sources, may it also open new vistas and provide new insights. May it be a small step in bringing our people back to their heritage, and may it be a small contribution in bringing about the final redemption.

Aryeh Kaplan

23 Tammuz, 5740

USING THIS VOLUME

The Living Torah is a volume that is meant to be read and enjoyed. The language has been kept simple enough for even a fairly young child to understand the text and enjoy the stories. For the person who wishes to delve deeper, there are extensive notes, explaining most areas where questions are likely to occur. References to the notes are indicated in the text by an asterisk (*). The asterisk therefore tells the reader that there is a note on the word or phrase that he is reading.

The volume is rounded out with maps, illustrations, diagrams and charts—everything needed to make it more understandable. No effort has been spared in making this the most comprehensive one volume translation of the Torah available.

In the original, the Torah's text is broken into natural divisions known as *parshioth*. In this volume, every *parshah* has been numbered and captioned. This will provide the reader with a feeling for the original text, as it existed before the scripture was broken into chapter and verse. The captions also serve to break up the text and give the reader a frame of reference.

This system has also been incorporated into the Table of Contents, which is the first ever to list each *parshah* of the Torah. This can serve as a ready reference where one can quickly find any idea in the Torah. The reader will also find the Table of Contents useful insofar as it will enable him to see the general structure of the Torah.

In parentheses, immediately after each *parshah* heading in the Table of Contents is the chapter and verse with which the *parshah* begins.

The text is also divided according to the weekly portions read from the Torah in synagogue, *sidroth* in Hebrew. The names of these *sidroth* are usually taken from the first words in the Hebrew original of each portion. The *sidra* names are also included in the Table of Contents, and in the running head on the top of the inside left hand page.

Chapter and verse are noted in a number of ways. The chapter number is always placed in the outside margin, while the verse is in superscripts preceding the text. When a new chapter begins, it is indicated in the margin in somewhat larger type. The chapter and verse with which the open page begins is also indicated in the running heads at the top of the right hand page.

This volume also contains an extensive bibliography, listing virtually every work cited in the notes. For the most part, traditional Jewish sources have been used. In some cases, Jewish sources that are not considered part of the mainstream tradition have been cited, but these are always sources that are, at least on occasion, quoted in mainstream traditional sources. Although some ancient classical non-Jewish sources have been quoted, they are used mainly to clarify questions of geography or history, and not to explain the text.

An important feature of this volume is a comprehensive index, which is in itself a major work. Every name, place, law, idea, and concept that appear either in the text or the notes has been indexed. The index therefore opens up the text and makes it possible to find anything at a glance. Those who have spent hours trying to find an obscure reference will immediately welcome this feature.

In general, we have tried to produce a volume that could be used and enjoyed by a young child, and yet, at the same time, remain an important source and tool to him, no matter how far he advances in his studies. Simple enough for a child, this volume is comprehensive enough to be valuable to even the most advanced scholar. It is a volume that can be extremely valuable to the layperson and specialist alike. It will make studying the Torah a living experience for all.

CONTENTS

PLATES

בְּרֵאשִׁת

GENESIS

Bereshith

[1. Creation, the First Day]

¹ In the beginning God created heaven and earth.* ² The earth was without **1** form and empty, with darkness on the face of the depths, but God's spirit* moved on the water's surface. ³ God said, "There shall be light," and light came into existence. ⁴ God saw that the light was good, and God divided between the light and the darkness. ⁵ God named the light "Day," and the darkness He named "Night." It was evening and it was morning, one day.

[2. The Second Day]

⁶ God said, "There shall be a sky* in the middle of the water, and it shall divide between water and water." ⁷ God [thus] made the sky, and it* separated the water below the sky from the water above the sky. It remained that way.* ⁸ God named the sky "Heaven." It was evening and it was morning, a second day.

[3. The Third Day]

⁹ God said, "The waters under the heaven shall be gathered to one place, and dry land shall be seen." It happened. ¹⁰ God named the dry land "Earth," and the gatherings of water, He named "Seas." God saw that it was good.

¹¹ God said, "The earth shall send forth vegetation. Seedbearing plants and fruit trees that produce their own kinds of fruits with seeds shall be on the earth." It happened. ¹² The earth sent forth vegetation, plants bearing their own kinds of seeds, and trees producing fruits containing their own kinds of seeds.* God saw that it was good. ¹³ It was evening and it was morning, a third day.

[4. The Fourth Day]

¹⁴ God said, "There shall be lights in the heavenly sky* to divide between

---

1:1   **In the beginning . . .** Others translate this, "In the beginning of God's creation of heaven and earth, the earth was without form and empty . . ." (Rashi). Still others combine the first three verses: "In the beginning of God's creation . . . when the earth was without form and empty . . . God said, "Let there be light." (*Bereshith Rabbah*)

1:2   **God's spirit.** Others: "God's wind."

1:6   **sky.** (Saadia) *Rakia* in Hebrew, literally "spread" or "expanse." Usually translated as "firmament."

1:7   **it separated.** Or "He divided" (Septuagint).

—   **It remained that way.** Usually translated, "It was so." Later, we translate this as, "It happened."

1:12   **trees producing fruits . . .** Or, "specific species of trees that produce fruits with seeds." See 1:21, 1:24.

1:14   **heavenly sky.** Literally "the firmament of the heaven."

3

day and night. They shall serve as omens [and define] festivals, days and years. [15] They shall be lights in the heavenly sky, to shine on the earth." It happened. [16] God [thus] made the two large lights, the greater light to rule the day, and the smaller light to rule the night. [He also made] the stars. [17] God placed them in the heavenly sky to shine on the earth, [18] to rule by day and by night, and to divide between the light and the darkness. God saw that it was good. [19] It was evening and it was morning, a fourth day.

[5. The Fifth Day]

[20] God said, "The water shall teem with swarms of living creatures. Flying creatures shall fly over the land, on the face of the heavenly sky." [21] God [thus] created the great sea monsters,* along with every particular species of living thing that crawls, with which the waters teem, and every particular species of winged flying creature. God saw that it was good. [22] God blessed them, saying, "Be fruitful and become many, and fill the waters of the seas. Let the flying creatures multiply on the land." [23] It was evening and it was morning, a fifth day.

[6. The Sixth Day]

[24] God said, "The earth shall bring forth particular species of living creatures, particular species of livestock, land animals,* and beasts of the earth." It happened. [25] God [thus] made particular species of beasts of the earth, particular species of livestock, and particular species of animals that walk the land. God saw that it was good.

[26] God said, "Let us* make man with our image and likeness.* Let him dominate the fish of the sea, the birds of the sky, the livestock animals, and all the earth—and every land animal that walks the earth." [27] God [thus] created man with His image. In the image of God, He created him, male and female He created them. [28] God blessed them. God said to them, "Be fertile and

---

1:21   **sea monsters.** Or "whales," or "dragons." *Taninim* in Hebrew; see Exodus 7:9. The Midrash states that it alludes to a pair of particularly great sea creatures, the Leviathan and its mate. See Isaiah 27:1, Psalms 74:14, 104:26, Job 3:8, 40:25.

1:24   **land animals.** (Ramban, from Genesis 7:27). Others translate this as "creeping things." *Remes* in Hebrew.

1:26   **Let us . . .** God was speaking to all the forces of creation that He had brought into existence (cf. *Targum Yonathan*; Ramban). Now that all the ingredients of creation had essentially been completed, all would participate in the creation of man, the crown of creation. Others interpret "we" in the majestic sense, and translate the verse, "I will make man in My image" (*Emunoth veDeyoth* 2:9; Ibn Ezra).

—   **in our image and likeness.** Man is thus a microcosm of all the forces of creation. A major part of the Kabbalah deals with explaining exactly how this is so (see *Nefesh HaChaim* 1:1). Moreover, of all creation, only man resembles God in having free will (Maimonides, *Yad, Teshuvah* 5:1). Others explain "image" and "likeness" here to refer to a sort of conceptual archetype, model, or blueprint that God had previously made for man (Rashi). This "model" is seen as the primeval man" (*Adam Kadmon*).

become many.* Fill the land and conquer it. Dominate the fish of the sea, the   1
birds of the sky, and every beast that walks the land.

²⁹ God said, "Behold, I have given you every seedbearing plant on the face
of the earth, and every tree that has seedbearing fruit. It shall be to you for
food. ³⁰ For every beast of the field, every bird of the sky, and everything that
walks the land, that has in it a living soul, all plant vegetation shall be food."
It remained that way. ³¹ God saw all that he had made, and behold, it was very
good. It was evening and it was morning, the sixth day.

[7. The Sabbath]

¹ Heaven and earth, and all their components, were [thus] completed   2
² With the seventh day, God finished all the work that He had done. He [thus]
ceased* on the seventh day from all the work that He had been doing. ³ God
blessed the seventh day, and He declared it to be holy, for it was on this day
that God ceased from all the work that He had been creating [so that it would
continue] to function.

[8. Man]

⁴ These are the chronicles of heaven and earth when they were created, on
the day God* completed* earth and heaven.

⁵ All the wild shrubs* did not yet exist on the earth, and all the wild plants
had not yet sprouted. This was because God had not brought rain on the
earth, and there was no man to work the ground. ⁶ A mist rose up from the
earth, and it watered the entire surface of the ground. ⁷ God formed man out
of dust of the ground,* and breathed into his nostrils a breath* of life. Man
[thus] became a living creature. ⁸ God planted a garden in Eden* to the east.
There He placed the man that He had formed. ⁹ God made grow out of the
ground every tree that is pleasant to look at and good to eat, [including] the

---

1:28 **Be fertile** . . . Some say that this is a commandment (cf. *Chinukh*), while other maintain that it is a blessing
(see *Tosafoth, Yevamoth* 65b, s.v. *VeLo*; Maharsha, *Sanhedrin* 59b, s.v. *VeHarey*).

2:2 **ceased.** (Hirsch). *Shavath* in Hebrew. Usually translated as "rested."

2:4 **God.** For the rest of this chapter, the Torah uses two names, *Adonoy Elohim*, usually translated as "the
Lord God." In the earlier chapters, only the name *Elohim* (usually translated "God") was used. According to tradition, *Elohim* denoted a creation with unmitigated justice, whereas the name *Adonoy* denotes
an admixture of mercy. Since there is no simple, contemporary way to translate *Adonoy Elohim*, we translate it as "God."

— **completed.** Literally "made," *Assah* in Hebrew. This word, however, is often seen denoting completion.

2:5 **wild shrubs.** Literally "shrubs of the field." In Hebrew, the association with field denotes wildness in
contrast to domesticity.

2:7 **ground.** *Adamah* in Hebrew, related to *Adam*, the Hebrew word for man. Both words are also cognate to
adom, meaning red, and *dam* meaning blood.

— **breath** (Septuagint). Or, "soul" (cf. Targum).

2:8 **Eden.** Delight in Hebrew.

2   Tree of Life in the middle of the garden, and the Tree of Knowledge of good
and evil.

[10] A river flowed out of Eden to water the garden. From there it divided
and became four major rivers. [11] The name of the first is Pishon.* It surrounds
the entire land of Ḥavilah* where gold is found. [12] The gold of that land is
[especially] good. Also found there are pearls* and precious stones.* [13] The
name of the second river is Giḥon.* It surrounds the land of Cush.* [14] The
name of the third river is the Tigris* which flows to the east of Assyria. The
fourth river is the Euphrates.*

[15] God took the man and placed him in the Garden of Eden to work it and
watch it. [16] God gave the man a commandment, saying, "You may definitely
eat from every tree of the garden. [17] But from the Tree of Knowledge of good
and evil, do not eat, for on the day you eat from it, you will definitely die."

[18] God said, "It is not good for man to be alone. I will make a compatible
helper for him." [19] God had formed every wild beast and every bird of heaven
out of the ground. He [now] brought [them] to the man to see what he would
name each one. Whatever the man called each living thing [would] remain its
name. [20] The man named every livestock animal and bird of the sky, as well as

---

2:11   **Pishon.** Some identify the Pishon with the Nile (Rashi). Others say that it is the Ganges or the Indus
(Josephus, Abarbanel), see next note. Rabbi Aaron Marcus identifies it with the Karun, which flows
through Iran into the Persian Gulf (*Keseth HaSofer* 121a). He also notes that the flow of these rivers could
have been changed drastically by the Great Flood.

—   **Ḥavilah.** Some identify this with India (Josephus, *Antiquities* 1:1:3; *Targum Yonathan*). Marcus, however,
identifies it with an area on the Persian Gulf. See Genesis 10:7, 10:29, 25:18, 1 Samuel 15:7. See note on
10:7. Significantly, there is a city Havelian on the upper Indus river, between Kashmir and Pakistan.

2:12   **pearls.** (Saadia Gaon, ibn Janach, ibn Ezra, Radak). *Bedolach* in Hebrew. See
Targum on 1 Chronicles 1:23. Others translate it as crystal (Rashi on Numbers
11:7). Most translations follow Aquila's Greek translation, and render it
"bdellium." This is a gum resin, very much like myrrh, obtained from various
trees of the genus Commiphora of the Burseraceae family. The Midrash,
however, states explicitly that it is not this herbal material (*Bereshith Rabbah*). In
the Septuagint, it is translated as anthrax (literally, "burning coal"), most
probably a red mineral such as the carbuncle, ruby, garnet or red sapphire.

—   **precious stones.** *Shoham* stones in Hebrew. Translated as beryl (*Targum*), onyx,
lapis lazuli, or sardonex. See Exodus 25:7, Ezekiel 28:13, Job 28:16.

2:13   **Gihon.** Josephus identifies it with the Nile (*Antiquities* 1:1:3). Rabbi Aaron
Marcus says that some identify it with the Amu-dar'ya, which flows from
Afghanistan into the Aral Sea in Russia, and once flowed into the Caspian Sea
(*Keseth HaSofer* 61a, 62a). He says that it also might be the Qezal Owzan River,

Bdellium

which flows northward through Iran into the Caspian Sea, or the Khabur, a tributary of the Euphrates
flowing through Syria.

—   **Cush.** Usually translated as Ethiopia. Marcus identifies it with the land of Kassites, in the near east. The
Kassites were an ancient dynastic family who lived in Babylonia, and are known to have ruled between
1761 and 1185 b.c.e. See note on 10:6.

2:14   **Tigris.** *Ḥiddekel* in Hebrew. In Arabic, the Tigris is the Dicle or Dijla (cf. *Targum*). See Daniel 10:4.

—   **Euphrates.** *P'rath* in Hebrew. In Arabic, the Euphrates is currently known as the Firat, al Farat, and al
Furat.

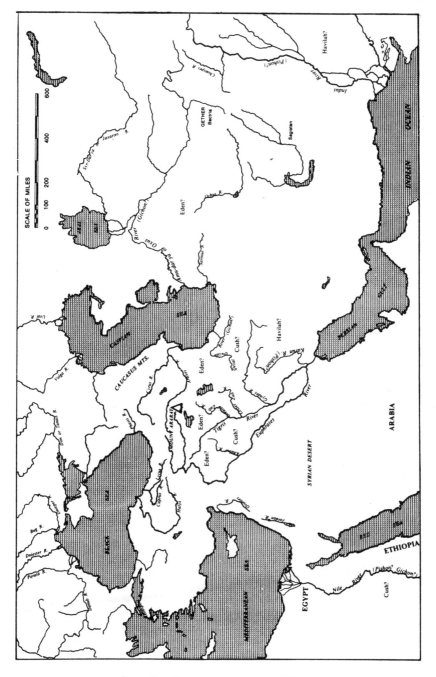

PLATE 1.   RIVERS OF THE ANCIENT WORLD

2 all the wild beasts. But the man did not find a helper who was compatible for him.

²¹ God then made the man fall into a deep state of unconsciousness, and he slept. He took one of his ribs* and closed the flesh in its place. ²² God built the rib that he took from the man into a woman, and He brought her to the man. ²³ The man said, "Now this is bone from my bones and flesh from my flesh.* She shall be called Woman (*Ishah*) because she was taken from man (*ish*)." ²⁴ A man shall therefore leave his father and mother and be united with his wife, and they shall become one flesh.

²⁵ The man and his wife were both naked, but they were not embarrassed by one another.

3 ¹ The serpent was the most cunning of all the wild beasts that God had made. [The serpent] asked the woman, "Did God really say that you may not eat from any of the trees of the garden?"

² The woman replied to the serpent, "We may eat from the fruit of the trees of the garden. ³ But of the fruit of the tree that is in the middle of the garden, God said, 'Do not eat it, and do not [even] touch it, or else you will die.'"

⁴ The serpent said to the woman, "You will certainly not die! ⁵ Really, God knows that on the day you eat from it, your eyes will be opened, and you will be like God,* knowing good and evil."

⁶ The woman saw that the tree was good to eat and desirable to the eyes,* and that the tree was attractive as a means to gain intelligence. She took some of its fruit and ate [it]. She also gave some to her husband, and he ate [it]. ⁷ The eyes of both of them were opened, and they realized that they were naked. They sewed together fig leaves, and made themselves loincloths.

⁸ They heard God's voice moving about* in the garden with the wind of the day.* The man and his wife hid themselves from God among the trees of the garden. ⁹ God called to the man, and He said, "Where are you [trying to hide]?"

¹⁰ "I heard Your voice in the garden," replied [the man], "and I was afraid because I was naked, so I hid."

2:21 **ribs.** Or "sides" (Rashi).
2:23 **bone from my bones . . .** An expression meaning "my flesh and blood," see Genesis 29:14.
3:5   **like God.** (Rashi). Others, however, have "like the great," or "like the great angels" (*Targum; Targum Yonathan.* Cf. Ibn Ezra). The word *Elohim* used here denotes any superior power or powers. and can refer to God, angels, judges or rulers (*Moreh Nevukhim* 1:2).
3:6   **to the eyes.** Or "for the eyes" (Rashi).
3:8   **moving about.** Literally "walking." The commentaries explain that it was the voice that was moving, not God.
—   **wind of the day.** Literally. Some translate it, "the cool of the day." Others, "the direction of the [conclusion of] the day," namely the west (Rashi). Hence the teaching that "the Divine Presence is in the west."

¹¹ [God] asked, "Who told you that you are naked? Did you eat from the tree which I commanded you not to eat?"

¹² The man replied, "The woman that you gave to be with me—she gave me what I ate from the tree."

¹³ God said to the woman, "What is this that you have done?"
The woman replied, "The serpent seduced me and I ate [it]."

¹⁴ God said to the serpent, "Because you did this, cursed are you more than all the livestock and all the wild beasts. On your belly you shall crawl, and dust you shall eat, all the days of your life. ¹⁵ I will plant hatred between you and the woman, and between your offspring and her offspring. He will strike you in the head, and you will strike him in the heel."

[9. The Woman's Curse]

¹⁶ To the woman He said, "I will greatly increase your anguish and your pregnancy. It will be with anguish that you will give birth to children. Your passion will be to your husband, and he will dominate you."

[10. Man's Curse]

¹⁷ To Adam* He said, "You listened to your wife, and ate from the tree regarding which I specifically gave you orders, saying, 'Do not eat from it.' The ground will therefore be cursed because of you. You will derive food from it with anguish all the days of your life. ¹⁸ It will bring forth thorns and thistles for you, and you will eat the grass of the field. ¹⁹ By the sweat of your brow you will eat bread. Finally* you will return to the ground, for it was from [the ground] that you were taken. You are dust, and to dust you shall return."

²⁰ The man named his wife Eve,* because she was the mother of all life.

²¹ God made leather garments* for Adam and his wife and He clothed them.

[11. The Expulsion]

²² God said, "Man has now become like one of us in knowing good and evil. Now he must be prevented from putting forth his hand and also taking from the Tree of Life. He [can] eat it and live forever!" ²³ God banished [man] from the Garden of Eden, to work the ground from which he was taken. ²⁴ He

3:17 **Adam.** Or "man."
3:19 **Finally.** Or "until."
3:20 **Eve.** *Chavah* in Hebrew, cognate to the word *chai*, meaning life.
3:21 **leather garments.** Some translate this "shrouds of skin," denoting the growth of the male foreskin and female hymen (*Maaseh HaShem*; from *Sanhedrin* 38b, *Eruvin* 100b).

3 drove away the man, and stationed the cherubim* at the east of Eden, along
with the revolving sword blade,* to guard the path of the Tree of Life.

[12. Cain and Abel]

4 ¹ The man knew* his wife Eve. She conceived and gave birth to Cain. She
said, "I have gained* a man with God." ² She gave birth again, this time to his
brother Abel.* Abel became a shepherd, while Cain was a worker of the soil.

³ An era ended.* Cain brought some of his crops as an offering to God.
⁴ Abel also offered some of the firstborn of his flock, from the fattest ones.*
God paid heed to Abel and his offering, ⁵ but to Cain and his offering, He
paid no heed. Cain became very furious and depressed.* ⁶ God said to Cain,
"Why are you so furious? Why are you depressed? ⁷ If you do good, will there
not be special privilege? And if you do not do good, sin is crouching at the
door. It lusts after you, but you can dominate it."

⁸ Cain said [something] to his brother Abel. Then, when they happened to
be in the field, Cain rose up against his brother Abel, and killed him. ⁹ God
asked Cain, "Where is your brother Abel?"

"I do not know," replied [Cain]. "Am I my brother's keeper?"

¹⁰ God said, "What have you done? The voice of your brother's blood is
screaming to Me from the ground. ¹¹ Now you are cursed from the ground
that opened its mouth to take your brother's blood from your hand. ¹² When
you work the ground, it will no longer give you of its strength. You will be
restless and isolated* in the world.

¹³ Cain said, "My sin is too great to bear!* ¹⁴ Behold, today You have

---

3:24 **cherubim.** Rashi notes that they are angels of destruction. Man is told that he must eventually die and is
banished from paradise. He can only return to paradise after death, and before doing so, he must pass
by these angels of purgatory (Bachya). The prophet must also pass these angels to approach the Tree of
Life and obtain a vision. This is the significance of the cherubim on the Ark (Exodus 25:18), and those
seen in Ezekiel's vision (Ezekiel 1:5, 10:15). (Rambam on Exodus 25:18).

— **revolving sword blade.** (*Targum;* see Radak, *Sherashim* s.v. *Lahat*). Others have, "a flaming sword that
revolves." See note on Exodus 7:11.

4:1 **knew.** Mentioned after they ate from the Tree of Knowledge. Rashi notes that Cain and Abel were born
before the sin.

— **gained.** Literally "bought." In Hebrew this is *kanah,* from which the name Cain (*Kayin* in Hebrew) is
derived.

4:2 **Abel.** *Hevel* in Hebrew, literally a breath or vanity. He was called this because he never lived to have children (*Midrash HaGadol;* Cf. Ramban).

4:3 **An era ended.** Literally, "It was the end of days." It is significant that this same expression is used to
denote the Messianic era, when the present era will end. It possibly refers to the expulsion from Eden,
whereupon a new era began, see note on 4:1. Most sources render this, "in the course of time."

4:4 **from the fattest ones.** (*Zevachim* 116a; Radak). Or "from their fats."

4:5 **depressed.** (Hirsch). Literally, "his face fell."

4:12 **isolated.** *Nad* in Hebrew, from *nadah,* to be isolated or banished (cf. Hirsch). Others, "a wanderer,"
from *nadad.*

4:13 **My sin . . .** (Ralbag). Or, "My punishment is too great . . ." (Ibn Ezra; Chizzkuni); or, "Is my sin then
too great to forgive?" (Rashi; Chizzkuni).

banished me from the face of the earth, and I am to be hidden from Your face. **4** I am to be restless and isolated in the world, and whoever finds me will kill me."

¹⁵ God said to him, "Indeed!* Whoever kills Cain will be punished seven times as much.*" God placed a mark on Cain so that whoever would find him would not kill him. ¹⁶ Cain went out from before God's presence. He settled in the land of Nod,* to the east of Eden.

¹⁷ Cain knew his wife. She conceived and gave birth to Enoch.* [Cain] was building a city, and he named the city Enoch, after his son.

¹⁸ Enoch had a son Irad. Irad had a son Mechuyael. Mechuyael had a son Methushael. Methushael had a son Lemekh.

¹⁹ Lemekh married two women. The first one's name was Adah, and the second one's name was Tzillah. ²⁰ Adah gave birth to Yaval. He was the ancestor of all those who live in tents and keep herds. ²¹ His brother's name was Yuval. He was the ancestor of all who play the harp and flute. ²² Tzillah also had a son, Tuval Cain, a maker of all copper and iron implements.* Tuval Cain's sister was Naamah.*

²³ Lemekh said to his wives, "Adah and Tzillah, hear my voice; wives of Lemekh, listen to my speech. I have killed a man by wounding [him], and a child by bruising [him].* ²⁴ If Cain shall be revenged seven times, then for Lemekh it shall be seventy-seven times."

²⁵ Adam knew his wife again, and she gave birth to a son. She named him Seth*—"Because God has granted (*shath*) me other offspring in place of Abel, whom Cain had killed."

²⁶ A son was also born to Seth, and [Seth] named him Enosh. It was then initiated to pray with God's name.*

[13. The First and Second Generations]

¹ This is the book of the Chronicles of Adam:* **5**

4:15 **Indeed.** (cf. Rashi). *La-khen* in Hebrew, literally "to yes." The word is usually translated as "therefore."
— **Seven times as much.** Or, "Do not dare kill Cain! He will be punished after seven [generations]" (Rashi). Indeed, Cain was killed after seven generations by Tuval Cain (see note on 4:23).
4:16 **Nod.** Hebrew for isolation or wandering, see note to 4:12.
4:17 **Enoch.** *Chanokh* in Hebrew, from the root *chanakh*, to train or to educate.
4:22 **a maker . . .** (*Targum*). Hirsch has, "who sharpened everything that cuts copper and iron." (See Radak, *Sherashim*, s.v. *Latash, Charash*).
— **Naamah.** According to some traditions, she was Noah's wife. In the Midrash, however, this is disputed, and other ancient sources state that Noah married his niece, Amzarach, daughter of Rakh'el (*Sefer HaYov'loth* 4:33). (Regarding *Sefer HaYov'loth*, see Bibliography.)
4:23 **I have killed . . .** According to traditions, Lemekh had just killed Cain and Tuval Cain.
4:25 **Seth.** *Sheth* in Hebrew, from the Hebrew *shath*, "placing" or "granting."
4:26 **pray.** (*Targum*). Literally "call in the name of God." Others have, "to profane God's name," indicating the rise of idolatry (Rashi).
5:1 **chronicles of Adam** (*Targum; Saadia*). Or, "chronicles of man" (Sforno; Septuagint).

5   On the day that God created man, He made him in the likeness of God. ² He created them male and female. He blessed them and named them Man (*Adam*) on the day that they were created.

³ Adam lived 130 years, and he had a son in his likeness and form. He named him Seth. ⁴ Adam lived 800 years after he had Seth, and he had sons and daughters. ⁵ All the days that Adam lived were 930 years, and he died.

[14. The Third Generation]

⁶ Seth lived 105 years, and he had a son Enosh. ⁷ Seth lived 807 years after he had Enosh, and he had sons and daughters. ⁸ All of Seth's days were 912 years, and he died.

[15. The Fourth Generation]

⁹ Enosh lived 90 years, and he had a son Kenan. ¹⁰ Enosh lived 815 years after he had Kenan, and he had sons and daughters. ¹¹ All of Enosh's days were 905 years, and he died.

[16. The Fifth Generation]

¹² Kenan lived 70 years, and he had a son Mahalalel. ¹³ Kenan lived 840 years after he had Mahalalel, and he had sons and daughters. ¹⁴ All of Kenan's days were 910 years, and he died.

[17. The Sixth Generation]

¹⁵ Mahalalel lived 65 years, and he had a son Yered. ¹⁶ Mahalalel lived 830 years after he had Yered, and he had sons and daughters. ¹⁷ All of Mahalalel's days were 895 years, and he died.

[18. The Seventh Generation]

¹⁸ Yered lived 162 years, and he had a son Enoch.* ¹⁹ Yered lived 800 years after he had Enoch, and he had sons and daughters. ²⁰ All of Yered's days were 962 years, and he died.

[19. The Eighth Generation]

²¹ Enoch lived 65 years, and he had a son Methuselah.* ²² Enoch walked with God for 300 years after he had Methuselah, and he had sons and daughters. ²³ All of Enoch's days were 365 years. ²⁴ Enoch walked with God, and he was no more, because God had taken him.*

5:18 **Enoch.** *Chanokh* in Hebrew. See note on 4:17.
5:21 **Methuselah.** *Methushelach* in Hebrew.
5:24 **God had taken him.** According to tradition, he entered paradise without dying. See note on 3:24.

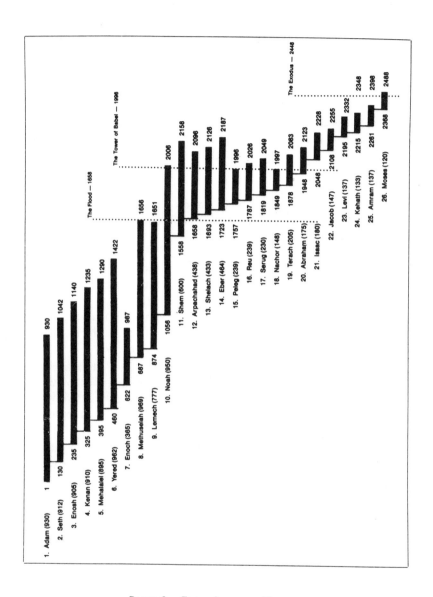

PLATE 2. FROM ADAM TO MOSES

5

[20. The Ninth Generation]

²⁵ Methuselah lived 187 years, and he had a son Lemekh. ²⁶ Methuselah lived 782 years after he had Lemekh, and he had sons and daughters. ²⁷ All of Methuselah's days were 969 years, and he died.

[21. The Tenth Generation]

²⁸ Lemekh lived 182 years, and he had a son. ²⁹ He named him Noah,* saying, "This one will bring us relief from our work and the anguish of our hands, from the soil that God has cursed." ³⁰ Lemekh lived 595 years after he had Noah, and he had sons and daughters. ³¹ All of Lemekh's days were 777 years, and he died.

[22. Noah's Children and the Titans]

³² Noah was 500 years old, and Noah fathered Shem, Ham, and Yefeth.*

6 ¹ Man began to increase on the face of the earth, and daughters were born to them. ² The sons of God* saw that the daughters of man were good, and they took themselves wives from whomever they chose. ³ God said, "My spirit will not continue to judge man forever, since he is nothing but flesh. His days shall be 120 years."

⁴ The titans* were on the earth in those days and also later. The sons of God had come to the daughters of man and had fathered them. [The titans] were the mightiest ones who ever existed, men of renown.

[23. The Decree]

⁵ God saw that man's wickedness on earth was increasing. Every impulse of his innermost thought was only for evil, all day long. ⁶ God regretted that He had made man on earth, and He was pained to His very core. ⁷ God said, "I will obliterate humanity that I have created from the face of the earth—man, livestock, land animals, and birds of the sky. I regret that I created them." ⁸ But Noah found favor in God's eyes.

5:29 **Noah.** *Noach* in Hebrew, meaning rest. Also related to the word *nacham,* meaning "to bring relief" or "comfort."

5:32 **Yefeth.** Japheth in English. See note on 9:27.

6:2 **sons of God.** According to some, these were the fallen angels (Josephus 1:3:1, see next note). Others translate this as "sons of the rulers" or "judges" (*Targum,* Rashi. See note on 3:5). Still others say that the "sons of God" are the descendants of Seth, while the "sons of man" are the descendants of Cain (Ibn Ezra).

6:4 **titans.** *Nefilim* in Hebrew, literally "fallen ones." They were called this because they were the sons of the fallen angels (*Targum Yonathan*). See Numbers 13:33.

Noah   נֹחַ   6

[24. Noah and his Times]

⁹ These are the chronicles of Noah:
Noah was a righteous man, faultless* in his generation. Noah walked with
God. ¹⁰ Noah fathered three sons: Shem, Ham and Yefeth.
¹¹ The world was corrupt* before God, and the land was filled with crime.*
¹² God saw the world, and it was corrupted. All flesh had perverted its way on
the earth.

[25. The Great Flood]

¹³ God said to Noah, "The end of all flesh has come before Me. The world
is filled with [man's] crime. I will therefore destroy them with the earth.
¹⁴ "Make yourself an ark* of cypress* wood. Divide the ark into compart-
ments. Caulk the inside and outside with pitch.* ¹⁵ This is how you shall con-
struct it: The ark's length shall be 300 cubits, its width 50 cubits, and its height
30 cubits.* ¹⁶ Make a skylight* for the ark. Make it slanted, so that it is one
cubit [wide] on top.* Place the ark's door on its side. Make a first, second and
third [deck].
¹⁷ "I Myself am bringing the flood.* Water shall be on the earth to destroy
from under the heavens all flesh having in it a breath of life. All that is on land

---

6:9   **faultless.** *Tamim* in Hebrew. The word can be translated as whole, unblemished, perfect, innocent, pious,
        or honest.
6:11   **Corrupt.** From the Hebrew root *shachath.* The word has the connotation of decadence, perversion,
        destruction, and damage. It is especially used to denote sexual immorality and idolatry (Rashi).
—   **crime** (Rashi). *Chamath* in Hebrew. The word also denotes immorality, violence, oppression, cruelty, and
        outrage.
6:14   **ark.** *Tevah* in Hebrew, literally a box. This indicates that it did not have the shape of a boat (Abarbanel).
—   **cypress.** *Gopher* in Hebrew. This word is usually translated as cypress, since it is
        assumed that the greek word for cypress, *kyparissos* (from *kaphar* or *gaphar*), is derived
        from the Hebrew. The commentaries also state that it is a species of pine (Abar-
        banel), or boxwood (ibn Janach, based on Saadia Gaon). The *Targum* renders it as
        kadrom or *kadros,* which the Talmud defines as a species of cedar (*Rosh HaShanah*
        23a). The Talmud itself translates *gopher* as *mabliga* or *golmish,* both species of cedar
        (*Sanhedrin* 108b, *Rosh HaShanah* 23a; cf. *Arukh* s.v. *Adar*). The Septuagint, however,
        translates it as "squared timber."   Cypress
—   **pitch.** *Kofer* in Hebrew. The word also denotes asphalt or bitumen. See below, 11:3.
6:15   **cubits.** A cubit is approximately 18 inches, so the dimensions of the ark would have been 450 feet long,
        75 feet wide, and 45 feet high. Some authorities maintain that the cubit is as much as 24 inches.
6:16   **skylight.** *Tzohar* in Hebrew. Others say that it was a luminous stone (Rashi).
—   **Make it slanted . . .** Literally, "finish it to a cubit on top."
6:17   **flood.** *Mabul* in Hebrew. This word is used only to denote the Great Flood in the time of Noah. Some
        say that it comes from the root *naval,* denoting death (as in *nevalah*); and hence, a *mabul* is a killing agent
        (Radak, *Sherashim,* s.v. *Naval;* Hirsch). Others maintain that it comes from the roots *balah* (to wear out,
        grind down), *balbal* (to confuse, mix up), or *yaval* (to transport). It is also related to the root *balal,* to mix
        or stir.

6   will die. ¹⁸ But I will keep My pledge* that you will come into the ark. You will
be together with your sons, your wife, and your sons' wives.

¹⁹ "From all life, all flesh, bring two of each kind into the ark to live with
you. They shall be male and female. ²⁰ From each separate species of bird,
from each separate species of livestock, and from each separate species of land
animals, bring to yourself two of each kind to live. ²¹ Take with you all the
food that will be eaten, and keep it in storage. It shall be food for you and [the
animals]."

²² Noah did all that God had commanded him. He did it [exactly].*

7   ¹ God said to Noah, "Come into the ark, you and your family. I have seen
that you are righteous before Me in this generation. ² Take seven pairs of every
clean animal,* each consisting of a male and its mate. Of every animal that is
not clean, take two, a male and its mate. ³ Of the birds of the heaven also take
seven pairs, each consisting of a male and its mate. Let them keep seed alive
on the face of all the earth, ⁴ because in another seven days, I will bring rain
on the earth for forty days and forty nights. I will obliterate every organism
that I have made from the face of the earth."

⁵ Noah did all that God had commanded. ⁶ Noah was 600 years old* when
the flood occurred; water was on the earth. ⁷ Noah, along with his sons, his
wife, and his sons' wives, came into the ark ahead of* the waters of the flood.
⁸ The clean animals, the animals which were not clean, the birds, and all that
walked the earth ⁹ came two by two to Noah, to the ark. They were male and
female, as God had commanded Noah.

¹⁰ Seven days passed, and the flood waters were on the earth. ¹¹ It was in
the 600th year of Noah's life, in the second month,* on the 17th of the month.
On that day all the wellsprings of the great deep burst forth and the floodgates
of the heavens were opened. ¹² It would continue to rain on the earth for forty
days and forty nights.

6:18   **pledge.** *B'rith* in Hebrew, usually translated as covenant.
6:22   **exactly.** Not in text, but implied (Ramban).
7:2   **seven pairs** . . . (*Bereshith Rabbah;* Radak, Malbim. See 7:9). Literally, "seven by seven." This is a detail
not mentioned earlier in 6:19. Earlier, when the Torah uses God's name *Elohim,* which denotes justice,
only two animals are mentioned. Accepting a sacrifice is an act of mercy, which pertains to God's name
Adonoy (see commentaries on Leviticus 1:2). In the verse here, the name *Adonoy* is used, and seven pairs
are required, the extra ones for sacrifice (Rashi). See below 8:20.
7:6   **600 years old.** From the genealogies in Genesis 5, we can easily determine that Noah was born in the
year 1056 after Adam's creation. The flood therefore occurred in the year 1656.
7:6   **ahead of.** Or "because of."
7:11   **second month.** In the Talmud, there is a dispute as to whether the months are counted from Tishrei, and
the second month is Marcheshvan, or from Nissan (cf. Exodus 12:2), and the second month is Iyyar (*Rosh
HaShanah* 11a). Other ancient sources state unequivocally that this was Marcheshvan (*Targum Yonathan;*
Josephus, *Antiquities* 1:3:1). According to tradition, 17 Marcheshvan, 1656 would have fallen on October
27, 2106 b.c.e.

¹³ On that very day,* Noah boarded the ark along with his* sons, Shem,   **7**
Ham and Yefeth. Noah's wife and the three wives of his sons were with them.
¹⁴ They [came] along with every separate kind of beast, every separate kind of
livestock, every separate kind of land animal, and every separate kind of flying
creature—every bird [and] every winged animal. ¹⁵ Of all flesh that has in it a
breath of life, they came to Noah, to the ark, two by two. ¹⁶ Those who came
were male and female. Of all flesh they came, as God had commanded
[Noah]. God then sealed him inside.

¹⁷ There was a flood on the earth for forty days. The waters increased, lifting the ark, and it rose from on the ground. ¹⁸ The waters surged* and
increased very much, and the ark began to drift on the surface of the water.
¹⁹ The waters on the earth surged [upward] very, very much, and all the high
mountains under the heavens were covered. ²⁰ The waters had surged upward
fifteen cubits* and all the mountains were covered.

²¹ All flesh that walked the earth perished: birds, livestock, wild beasts, and
every lower animal that swarmed on the land, as well as every human being.
²² Everything on dry land whose life was sustained by breathing* died. ²³ [The
flood] thus obliterated every organism that had been on the face of the land:
humanity, livestock, land animals, and birds of the heaven. They were obliterated from the earth. Only Noah and those with him in the ark survived.

²⁴ The waters surged on the earth for 150 days.

¹ God gave special thought* to Noah, and to all the beasts and livestock   **8**
with him in the ark. God made a wind blow on the earth, and the waters
began to subside. ² The wellsprings of the deep and the floodgates of heaven
were sealed. The downpour from the heavens thus stopped. ³ The waters
receded from the earth. They continued to recede, and at the end of 150 days,
the water had [visibly] diminished.*

⁴ In the seventh month, on the 17th day of the month,* the ark came to rest

---

7:13   **on that very day.** Or, "in broad daylight" (Rashi).
—   **his.** Literally "Noah's." We omit the repetition of the name.
7:18   **surged.** Literally "became strong."
7:20   **upward fifteen cubits.** Between 23 and 30 feet (see note on 6:15). Some say that this means that the water
       was so deep that it covered the mountains by 15 cubits (*Yoma* 76a; Rashi). There is, however, another
       opinion that the powerful currents caused the water to surge over the mountains (*Bereshith Rabbah* 32).
7:22   **life was sustained by breathing.** Literally, "all that has a breath of the spirit of life," or "all that has in it a
       lifegiving breath."
8:1   **gave special thought to.** Literally, "remembered."
8:3   **visibly diminished** (Malbim). This can also be translated, "began to evaporate." According to Rashi, the
       waters stopped raging after 150 days, and then began to diminish.
8:4   **17th day of the month.** According to the standard chronology, this was 17 Nissan (*Targum Yonathan;*
       Ramban). Other sources, however, maintain that this was the seventh month after the rain ended (which
       was Kislev), and hence, this was 17 Sivan (*Seder Olam* 4, *Bereshith Rabbah;* Rashi). This would have been
       May 23.

8   on the Ararat Mountains.* ⁵ The waters continued to diminish [visibly] until the tenth month. In the tenth month, on the first of the month,* the mountain peaks became visible.

⁶ After forty days, Noah opened the window he had made in the ark. ⁷ He sent out the raven, and it departed. It went back and forth until the water had dried up from the land's surface.

⁸ He then sent out the dove to see if the water had subsided from the land's surface. ⁹ The dove could not find any place to rest its feet, and it returned to him, to the ark. There was still water over all the earth's surface. [Noah] stretched out his hand, and brought it to him in the ark.

¹⁰ He waited another seven days, and once again sent the dove out from the ark. ¹¹ The dove returned to him toward evening, and there was a freshly-plucked olive leaf in its beak. Noah then knew that the water had subsided from the earth. ¹² He waited yet another seven days and sent out the dove [again]. This time it did not return to him any more.

¹³ In the 601st year [of Noah's life], in the first [month], on the first of the month,* the land was drained off and Noah removed the ark's hatch. He saw that the land's surface was beginning to dry. ¹⁴ By the second month, on the 27th day of the month,* the land was completely dry.

[26. Aftermath of the Flood]

¹⁵ God spoke to Noah saying, "Leave the ark—you, along with your wife, your sons, and your son's wives. ¹⁶ Take out with you every living creature from all flesh: birds, livestock, and all land animals that walk the earth. Let them swarm on the land. They shall breed* and multiply on the earth."

¹⁸ Noah left the ark along with his sons, his wife, and his sons' wives.

Ararat Mountains. Ancient sources state that it is a mountain in Armenia (*Targum Yonathan;* Josephus, *Antiquities* 1:3:5). This would point to the currently known Mount Ararat in Turkey, near Russia and Iran, some 200 miles southeast of the Black Sea. Some sources render Ararat as *Kardu* or *Kardunia* (*Targum Onkelos; Bereshith Rabbah*), denoting the Cordyne Mountains in Kurdistan, which is the area in Turkey where Mt. Ararat stands. Josephus also writes that the Armenians called that place Apobaterion, "the place of descent." He notes that Berosus the Chaldean (circa. 330–250 b.c.e.) mentions that parts of this ship still exist in the Cordyne Mountains in Armenia, and that people carry off pieces for good luck (cf. *Sanhedrin* 76a). He also quotes Nickolas of Damascus (born 64 b.c.e.; Book 96), that it was in the land near Minyas, on a mountain known as Baris. Cf. Jeremiah 51:27. Also see 2 Kings 19:37, Jeremiah 37:38. "Mount Ararat" consists of two mountains, Great Ararat, 16,916 feet high, and Little Ararat, 12,840 feet high. It is significant to note that Mt. Ararat is very close to the Murat River, which is one of the headwaters of the Euphrates. This may indicate that Noah had not been carried very far from where he started out.

8:5   **In the tenth month.** This is 1 Tammuz (*Targum Yonathan;* Ramban). According to the other opinion (see note on 8:4), this was 1 Av (July 5).

8:13   **In the 601st year.** This was 1 Tishrei, 1657 (September 2). It was Rosh HaShanah, the Hebrew New Year.

8:14   **second Month.** This was 27 Marcheshvan. It occurred on October 27, exactly one solar year after the flood had begun (Rashi).

8:16   **breed.** Literally, "be fruitful."

[19] Every beast, every land animal, and every bird—all that walk the land—left 8
the ark by families.

[20] Noah built an altar to God. He took a few of all the clean livestock and
all the clean birds,* and he sacrificed completely-burned offerings* on the
altar. [21] God smelled the appeasing fragrance,* and God said to Himself,
"Never again will I curse the soil because of man, for the inclination of man's
heart is evil from his youth. I will never again strike down all life as I have just
done. [22] As long as the earth lasts, seedtime and harvest, cold and heat, summer and winter, and day and night, shall never again cease [to exist]."

[1] God blessed Noah and his children. He said to them, "Be fruitful and 9
multiply,* and fill the earth. [2] There shall be a fear and dread of you instilled
in all the wild beasts of the earth, and all the birds of the sky, in all that will
walk the land, and in all the fish of the sea. I have placed them in your hands.

[3] "Every moving thing that lives shall be to you as food. Like plant vegetation, I have [now] given you everything.* [4] But nevertheless, you may not eat
flesh of a creature that is still alive.*

[5] "Only of the blood of your own lives will I demand an account.* I will
demand [such] an account from the hand of every wild beast. From the hand
of man—[even] from the hand of a man's own brother—I will demand an
account of [every] human life. [6] He who spills human blood shall have his own
blood spilled by man, for God made man with His own image.*

[7] "Now be fruitful and multiply, swarm all over the earth and become
populous on it."

[27. The Rainbow]

[8] God said to Noah and his sons with him, [9] "I Myself am making a covenant with you and with your offspring after you. [10] [It will also include] every
living creature that is with you among the birds, the livestock, and all the

---

8:20   **clean livestock** . . . See note on 7:2.
—   **completely burned offerings.** *Oloth* in Hebrew, literally, offerings that ascend, since the entire offering
     ascends when it is burned. Usually translated as "burnt offerings." Others, however, interpret it as
     "uplifting offerings" (Hirsch). Also see Genesis 22:2, Exodus 18:12, 24:5.
8:21   **appeasing fragrance.** *Nicho'ach* in Hebrew, related to the name Noach (Noah). Others translate this as
     "pleasant fragrance," "scent of satisfaction," or "expression of compliance" (Hirsch). It means that God
     was pleased with the sacrifice (Ibn Ezra). See Leviticus 1:9.
9:1   **Be fruitful and multiply.** The same expression is used in 1:22, 1:28, 8:16.
9:3   **like plant vegetation.** Previously only plants had been permitted (1:30); now meat was equally permitted.
9:4   **creatures that are still alive.** Literally, "flesh whose blood is in its soul." As long as an animal is alive, its
     blood is seen as being attached to its soul (Hirsch. Cf. Deuteronomy 12:23). This commandment is
     meant to forbid flesh from a living animal.
9:5   **only of the blood** . . . This is seen as a commandment against suicide (*Bereshith Rabbah;* Rashi. Cf. *Bava
     Kama* 91b).
9:6   **for God made man** . . . See Genesis 1:26,27, 5:1. This prescribes capital punishment for murder, even
     for gentiles.

9 beasts of the earth with you—all who left the ark, including every animal on
earth. ¹¹ I will make My covenant with you, and all life will never be cut short
by the waters of a flood. There will never again be a flood to destroy the
earth."

¹² God said, "This is the sign that I am providing for the covenant between
Me, you, and every living creature that is with you, for everlasting generations: ¹³ I have placed My rainbow in the clouds, and it shall be a sign of the
covenant between Me and the earth. ¹⁴ When I bring clouds over the earth, the
rainbow will be seen among the clouds. ¹⁵ I will then recall the covenant that
exists between Me, you and every living soul in all flesh. ¹⁶ The rainbow will be
in the clouds, and I will see it to recall the eternal covenant between God and
every living soul in all flesh that is on the earth."

¹⁷ God said to Noah, "This is the sign of the covenant that I have made
between Me and all flesh on the earth."

[28. Canaan is Cursed]

¹⁸ The sons of Noah who emerged from the ark were Shem, Ham and
Yefeth. Ham was the father of Canaan. ¹⁹ These three were Noah's sons, and
from them, the whole world was repopulated.

²⁰ Noah began to be a man of the soil, and he planted a vineyard. ²¹ He
drank some of the wine, making himself drunk, and uncovered himself in the
tent. ²² Ham, the father of Canaan, saw his father naked, and he told it to his
two brothers outside. ²³ Shem and Yefeth took a cloak and placed it on both
their shoulders. Walking backwards, they then covered their father's nakedness. They faced away from him and did not see their father naked.

²⁴ Noah awoke from his wine-induced sleep, and he realized what his
youngest son* had done to him. ²⁵ He said, "Cursed is Canaan!* He shall be a
slave's slave to his brothers!"

²⁶ He then said, "Blessed be God, the Lord of Shem! Canaan shall be his
slave! ²⁷ May God expand* Yefeth, but may He dwell in the tents of Shem. Let
Canaan be their slave!"

9:24   **youngest son.** According to some authorities, the order of birth was Yefeth, Shem, Ham; thus Ham was
the youngest (Ramban on 6:10; cf. *Sefer HaYashar*). In the Talmud, however, the order of birth is Yefeth,
Ham, Shem (*Sanhedrin* 69b), and this is also the order in which the genealogies are presented (Genesis
11). Therefore Ham is not the youngest son, but the "least son," that is, the lowliest and least significant
(Rashi). Others say that the "youngest son" refers to Shem, and that Noah knew about the good deed
that he did (Chizzkuni). Other ancient sources, however, state that the order of birth was Shem, Ham,
Yefeth (*Yoveloth* 4:33; see below, note on 10:21).

9:25   **Cursed is Canaan.** Or, "Cursed is Canaan's father" (Saadia).

9:27   **expand.** *Yaph't* in Hebrew, a play on the name Yefeth. The word is from the root *pathah*, meaning to
expand (Radak, *Sherashim*). This means that Yefeth was blessed that his descendants would be very populous and would have extensive lands (Bachya). Others note that the root *pathah* is used primarily in a
psychological sense; therefore, the word denotes expansion and enlargement of the mind. The blessing

²⁸ Noah lived 350 years after the flood. ²⁹ All of Noah's days were 950   9
years, and he died.

[29. Descendants of Yefeth and Ham]

¹ These are the chronicles of Noah's sons, Shem, Ham and Yefeth. Chil-   **10**
dren were born to them after the flood.
² The sons of Yefeth* were Gomer,* Magog,* Madai,* Yavan,* Tuval,*
Meshekh,* and Tiras.*

would then be that Yefeth's descendants would have great intellectual accomplishments, and since
Greece (Yavan) descended from Yefeth, this would allude to Greek philosophy (Hirsch).

10:2   **Yefeth.** All the following nations belong to the Indo-European language group. Some have identified
Yefeth with the Greek *Iapetus.*

—   **Gomer.** Most probably the Celts (cf. Herodotus 2:33), the Franks, or the Gauls, all of whom were closely
related. Early sources translate this as *Afrikey* (*Targum Yonathan.* Cf. *Targum* on 1 Kings 20:22, 22:49, where
this is the translation of Tarshish; see 10:4). This *Afrikey*, however, is not Africa, but Frikia or Phrygia
(*Arukh HaShalem;* Buber on *Pesikta Zutratha* 26a. See **Togarma** below in note on 10:3). The Phrygians
were an ancient nation who lived to the south of the Black Sea (cf. *Iliad* 2:862; Herodotus 7:30,31). They
were originally known as Brigians (Herodotus 7:73). Linguistically, the Phrygians were related to the
Armenians, but they may have also been related to the Franks, since there is a resemblance between the
two names. Indeed, there are ancient sources that identify Gomer with the Franks (*Sefer HaYashar*, p. 26;
Tol'doth Yitzchak).
        The Phrygians were pushed out of their general land in the 8th century b.c.e. by the Cimerians, a
people who originally lived in southern Russia (Crimea), to the north of the Black Sea (cf. Herodotus
4:11, 1:16, 1:103). It is therefore significant that the Talmud identifies Gomer with Germamia (*Yoma*
10a; *Yerushalmi, Megillah* 1:9). Germamia denotes Cimeria rather than Germany (cf. *Arukh HaShalem*). In
ancient Assyrian, the Cimerians were indeed known as the Gimerrai, cognate to Gomer (in other places,
however this is the translation of Togarma, see *Targum* on Ezekiel 27:14, 38:6). The Cimerians were seen
as originally having been a Nordic people (*Odyssey* 11:12–19). Some sources identify them with the
Cimbri of Jutland (around Denmark), a nation of Teutonized Celts.
        Josephus writes that Gomer was the founder of the nation known as the Galatians (*Antiquities* 16:1;
cf. Abarbanel). Galatia was in the same area as Phrygia and Cimeria, but it was renamed Galatia (from
Gaul) when it was conquered by the Celts of Gaul.
        Other ancient sources agree with this, writing that Gomer lived to the east of the Tina (Halys, cf.
Herodotus 1:6) River (*Sefer HaYov'loth* 9:8).

—   **Magog.** Most probably a Teutonic people, living to the north of the Holy Land (cf. Ezekiel 38:2). Some
sources identify Magog with Germania (*Targum Yonathan; Targum* on 1 Chronicles 1:5; *Pesikta Zutratha*).
Others identify them with the Goths (*Yerushalmi, Megillah* 1:9). These were a Teutonic people who
migrated to Scythia, in what is now southern Russia.
        It is therefore not contradictory when some sources identify Magog with Scythia (Josephus; *Yoma*
10a, according to Rabbenu Chananel; *Arukh* s.v. *Germamia*). Ancient histories state that the Scythians
came from Asia, driven by the Massagetae (cf. *Meshekh*), and settling near the Cimerians (Herodotus
4:11; see above note). Linguistically, the Scythians were related to the Iranians, and hence, to the Persians and the Medes. It is therefore significant that there was a Persian tribe known as the Germanians
(Herodotus 1:125).
        Other sources note that Magog may denote the Mongols, whose very name may be a corruption of
Magog. Indeed, Arab writers referred to the Great Wall of China as the "wall of al Magog" (Rabbi
Aaron Marcus, *Kesseth HaSofer*, p. 112a).
        Other ancient sources agree with the identification of Magog as living to the north of the Black Sea
(*Yov'loth* 9:8).

—   **Madai.** Ancestor of the Medes (Josephus; *Yerushalmi, Megillah* 1:9). This is also the opinion of the Talmud
(*Yoma* 10a, cf. *Hagahoth Beth Chadash*, Rabbenu Chananel ad loc; *Eyn Yaakov* ibid.). Another source translates Madai as Chamadai (*Targum* on 1 Chronicles 1:5), possibly referring to Hamadan, an ancient
Medean capital. An ancient source states that Madai is to the west of Gomer and Magog, on the shores
and the islands (*Yov'loth* 9:9). (See Herodotus 7:62).

10   ⁵ The sons of Gomer were Ashkenaz,* Riphath,* and Togarmah.*

— **Yavan.** *Yawan* in ancient Hebrew, denoting Ionia (cf. Josephus. Also see Herodotus 7:94). Other sources state that Yavan is Macedonia (*Targum Yonathan; Yoma* 10a, see previous note). Others translate it as Ovisos (*Yerushalmi, Megillah* 1:9), denoting Ephisus, an ancient Greek city in Lydia, founded by the Ionians around 1050 b.c.e. An ancient source states that Yavan lived on the islands and the shore of Lydia (*Yov'loth* 9:10), where indeed the Ionians lived.

— **Tuval.** A northern country, see Ezekiel 38:2, 27:13. This is usually identified with Bithynia (*Targum Yonathan; Targum* on 1 Chronicles 1:5; *Yerushalmi, Megillah* 1:9). The Talmud also refers to it as Beth-unyaki, which is the Talmudic term for Bithynia (*Yoma* 10a). This is in the area to the east of the Bospherus (*Yov'loth* 9:11). Josephus, however, says that the Tuvalites were the Ibers. Some say that these were the people of the Iberian Peninsula, and hence they were the original Spaniards. Indeed, one source says that this is why the Spanish refer to themselves as *cen-tuvales* (*gentualla*), literally "people of Tuval" (Abarbanel). However, there was also an Iberian people who lived to the east of the Black Sea.

— **Meshekh.** A northern kingdom; cf. Ezekiel 38:2, 27:13; Psalms 120:5. Most Talmudic sources identify Meshekh with Mysia (see *Targum Yonathan; Targum* on 1 Chronicles 1:5; *Yerushalmi, Megillah* 1:9; *Yoma* 10a; Buber on *Pesikta Zutratha* 26a). This was the land to the west of Bithynia, along the Dardanelles (Hellespont) and Marmara Sea (cf. *Yov'loth* 9:12; Herodotus 7:42,74). They might possibly be associated with Mycenae, an ancient city in Greece. Josephus, however, associates Meshekh with Cappadocia, whose capital is Mazaka, in what is now central Turkey (see Herodotus 1:72). It is very close to Galatia (see Gomer). Another possibility would be to identify Meshekh with the Massagatae, an ancient people who lived in Russia to the east of the Aral Sea (cf. Herodotus 1:201). It was these people who drove the Scythians into Cimeria (Ibid. 4:11). It is also possible to identify Meshekh with the Moschians mentioned in ancient sources (Herodotus 7:78). The name may be related to the Muskeva River, and hence to Moscow. Indeed, there are sources that say the Meshekh was the forerunner of the Slavs (*Kesseth Ha-Sofer*).

— **Tiras.** The *Targum* identifies this as Tarkey (*Targum Yonathan*), which is identified as Thrace. Josephus likewise states that Tiras is Thrace. This is a people who lived in the Balkans, in what is now European Turkey and Bulgaria. Indeed (as we see in the *Targum*) Turkey derives its name from Thrace. Linguistically Thracian is related to Albanian. There is also a possible relationship with the Etruscans. It is notable that there was a Tearus (Tiras) River going through Thrace (Herodotus 4:89).

   In the Talmud, however, there is a dispute as to the identity of Tiras, with some saying that it is Thrace, while others say that it is Persia (*Yoma* 10a; *Yerushalmi, Megillah* 1:9). The Persians, however, received their name from Perseus, whose kingdom was originally Tiryns (Herodotus 7:61). Moreover, one of the original Persian tribes was the Terusieans or Derusieans (*Ibid.* 1:125).

   Another ancient source identifies Tiras with the larger Mediterranean islands (*Yov'loth* 9:14).

10:3 **Ashkenaz.** This is a nation associated with the Ararat area; Jeremiah 51:27. In Talmudic sources, it is rendered as Asia (*Targum Yonathan; Targum* on 1 Chronicles 1:6; *Yerushalmi, Megillah* 1:9). In ancient times, besides denoting the entire continent, Asia also referred to what is now the western part of Asiatic Turkey, bordering on the Aegean Sea. However, there was also a tribe of Asies living in the area of Sardis (the modern Sart), the captial of Lydia (Herodotus 4:45). Both are the same area.

   Josephus, on the other hand, says that the Ashkenazites are the Reginians. Some associate this with Rhegium (the modern Regga), on the tip of the Italian peninsula (cf. Herodotus 1:167). However, there was also a Rhagae or Rages that was a major city in Medea (cf. *Tobit* 4:1). This was a bit south of the present Teheran, due south of the Caspean sea (cf. *Arukh HaShalem*, s.v. *Asia*). The Medes indeed were known to descend from the race of the Achemenids (Herodotus 7:61).

   More logical, however, would be to associate the "Reginia" of Josephus with Regnum Polemonis, to the south-east of the Black Sea, immediately in the Ararat area. The "Asia" mentioned in Talmudic sources could then be Amasia, a city in that area.

   By the tenth century, the term Ashkenaz was used to refer to Germany (*Siddur Rav Amram Gaon*). This may be because, as we have seen, Gomer, the father of Ashkenaz, was associated with "Germania." But according to this, the "Reginia" mentioned in Josephus may have been the Rennus or Rhine area. There are other sources that relate Ashkenaz to the Ashkuza mentioned in ancient writings, or to the Scythians.

— **Riphath.** In 1 Chronicles 1:6, however, the reading is Diphath (cf. Rashi ad loc.). Josephus identifies these people with the Paphlagonians, an ancient people who lived on the Rifas River (see *Kesseth HaSofer* 113a. Cf. Herodotus 7:72; *Iliad* 2:851). Other sources identify it with Parkhvan, Parkvi or Parsvey (*Targum Yonathan; Targum* on 1 Chronicles 1:6), most probably Parkvi, a country in Northern Ariana (in Per-

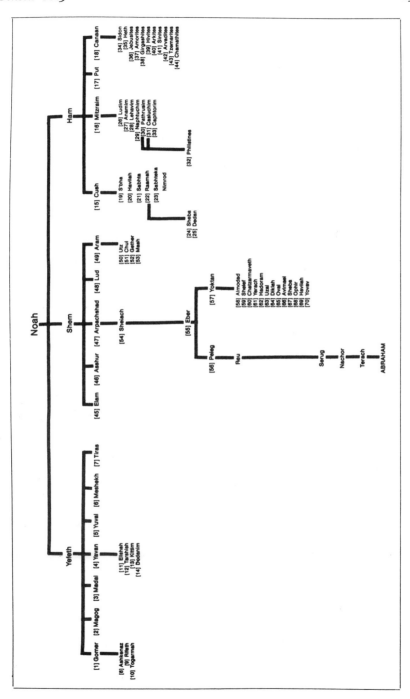

PLATE 3. DESCENDANTS OF NOAH

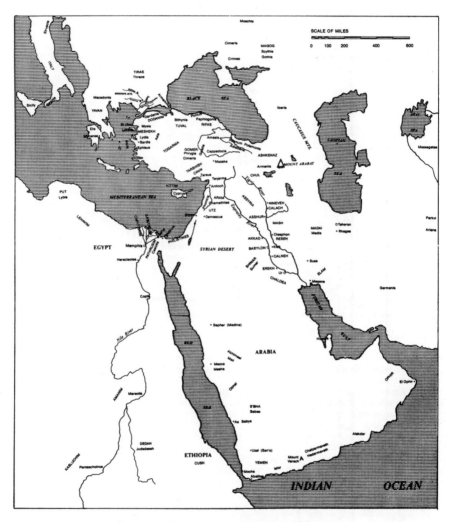

PLATE 4.   NATIONS OF THE ANCIENT WORLD

⁴ The sons of Yavan were Elishah,* Tarshish,* Kittim,* and Dodanim.*   **10**
⁵ From these the isolated nations* branched out into their lands. Each had
its own language for its families in its nations.
⁶ The sons of Ham were Cush,* Mitzraim,* Put,* and Canaan.*

sia). Still others identify it with Chadiv or Hadiath (*Yerushalmi, Megillah* 1:9; *Bereshith Rabbah* 37). The cor-
rect reading is most probably Hadiyv, which is identified with Adiebena, a district in Assyria between the
Lycus and Caprus rivers. Abarbanel identifies these people with the Etruscans, who settled in Italy,
Venice and France.

— **Togarmah.** A northern people; see Ezekiel 27:14, 38:6. Josephus identifies these people with the Phrygians (*see* Gomer). Other sources have Barberia (*Targum Yonathan; Targum* on Chronicles 1:6), which some
identify as Germania, Barbara, or Britannia. Indeed there are sources that render Togarmah as Ger-
maniki or Germania (*Yerushalmi, Megillah* 1:9; *Bereshith Rabbah* 37; *Targum* on Ezekiel 38:6). There are
other sources that identify Togarmah with the Armenians (*Keseth HaSofer*) or Turks (Abarbanel). Indeed,
in a modern sense, Togarmah is used for Turkey. The name Togarmah corresponds to Tegarma, found
in cuneiform inscriptions, referring to an area near Carchemish in Armenia.

10:4   **Elisha.** This is seen as an island; see Ezekiel 27:7. Josephus identifies it with the Aeolians (*Antiquities*
1:6:1), who were known to have inhabited the island of Lesbos (Herodotus 1:151). Others, however,
identify it with Sicily (Abarbanel). This is supported by the *Targum* which renders it Italia (*Targum* on
Ezekiel 27:7).
Talmudic sources identify Elisha with Alsu or Elis (*Yerushalmi, Megillah* 1:9; *Bereshith Rabbah* 37). This
may be identified with Elis, an ancient land in Peloponnesus (southern Greece) along the Ionian Sea (see
Iliad 2:615). A small village, Ilis or Eleis, currently remains on the site of the city of Elis. In the interior of
the country was the sanctuary and valley of Olympia, where the quadrennial Olympic games were held
for over 1000 years.
Others identify this Talmudic source with Hellas, since the Greeks called themselves Hellas or Ellis
(*Kesseth HaSofer*). This was indeed an ancient appelation for a Greek tribe (cf. *Iliad* 2:681; but see
Thucydides 1:3). It may also be associated with the Halys River, which separated the Greek-dominated
area from the Asiatic. The name Helles is also found in the Hellespont, the channel that currently separates Europe from Asia (the modern Dardanelles).

— **Tarshish.** In 1 Chronicles 1:7, it is Tarshishah. It was famed for its ships, see 1 Kings 10:22, 22:49, etc.
Also see Isaiah 23:10, 66:19, Ezekiel 38:13, Jonah 1:3. Josephus identifies it with Cilicia, whose capital
was Tarsus. The identification with Tarsus is also upheld in Talmudic sources (*Targum Yonathan; Yerushalmi, Megillah* 1:9). Some associate it with Tuscany, Lombardi, Florence and Milan (Abarbanel. Cf. *Sefer
HaYashar*).

— **Kittim.** An island people; cf. Jeremiah 2:10, Ezekiel 27:6. Also see Numbers 24:24, Isaiah 23:1, 23:12,
Daniel 11:30. Josephus identifies it with Cyprus, whose main city was Citius (cf. Abarbanel). The *Targum*,
however identifies it with Italy (*Italion, Italia*), and hence, it is seen as the source of the Italian and
Romans (cf. *Targum* on Numbers 24:24).

— **Dodanim.** In 1 Chronicles 1:7 it is Rodanim (cf. *Bereshith Rabbah* 37:1). The Dodonians were known to be
an ancient people (cf. *Iliad* 2:748; Herodotus 2:52–57). The *Targum* renders it as Dardania, a city on the
Dardanelles, after which the strait was named (cf. Herodotus 1:189, 7:43; *Iliad* 2:819). The *Targum*
(*Yonathan*) also adds Ridos, Chamen and Antioch. Ridos is identified with Rhodes (Abarbanel). Others
identify the Dodanim with the Bohemians (*Tol'doth Yitzchak;* cf. *Sefer HaYashar*).

10:5   **isolated nations** (Cf. Hirsch; *Kesseth HaSofer*). Literally "islands."
10:6   **Cush.** See note on 2:13. There was also an ancient city of Kish 8 miles east of Babylon. Other ancient
sources also indicate that it was to the east of the Holy Land (cf. *Yov'loth* 9:1). The *Targum* however,
renders it as Arabia (*Targum Yonathan; Targum* on 1 Chronicles 1:8). This, however, may also have
referred to an area in Africa on the upper Nile (cf. Herodotus 2:19). Josephus identifies Cush here with
Ethiopia.

— **Mitzraim.** The Hebrew name for Egypt. Regarding the origin of the name "Egypt," see Josephus, *Contra
Apion* 1:15.

— **Put.** See Jeremiah 46:9, Ezekiel 27:10, 38:5, Nahum 3:9. Josephus identifies it with Lybyos or Lybia in
North Africa. In Coptic (ancient Egyptian), Lybia is also known as Phiait. The *Targum*, however, renders
it as Alichrok, possibly Heracleotes. Other ancient sources state that it is to the east of the Holy Land
(*Yov'loth* 9:1).

10   ⁷ The sons of Cush were S'bha,* Havilah,* Sabhta,* Raamah* and
Sabht'ka.*
The sons of Raamah were Sheba* and Dedan.*
⁸ Cush was the father of Nimrod,* who was the first to amass power in the
world. ⁹ He was a mighty trapper before God. There is thus a saying, "Like
Nimrod, a mighty trapper before God!" ¹⁰ The beginning of his kingdom was
Babylon,* along with Erekh,* Akkad* and Calneh,* in the land of Shinar.*
¹¹ Asshur* left that land, and he built Nineveh,* Rechovoth Ir* and Calach,*

—   **Canaan.** Aborigine tribe of the Holy Land. See below 10:15–19.
10:7   **S'bha,** usually transliterated as Seba. Cf. Isaiah 43:3, 45:14, Psalms 72:10. Josephus identifies this with
        the Sabeans, a people living in southern Arabia. The name may still be preserved in the town of As
        Sabya. The *Targum* renders it Sinirai or Sinidai. In the Talmud, this nation is identified with Sakistan or
        Sagistan (*Yoma* 10a). Sagistan is a district in Drangonia in the Persian Empire, occupied by Scythians.
—   **Havilah.** See note on 2:11. The *Targum* has India. Josephus, however, has Getuli.
—   **Sabhta.** Usually transliterated Sabta. Josephus identifies this nation with the Astaborans. The Talmud
        identifies it with outer Takistan, see S'bha. The *Targum* renders it S'midai, Smadai or Samrai, a Cushite
        tribe, possibly the Sabrata of North Africa.
—   **Raamah.** They were traders in spices, precious stones and gold; Ezekiel 27:22. Here the *Targum* has
        Lubai, the Lybians. The second time Raamah is mentioned in this verse, however, the *Targum* (*Yonathan*)
        has Mavryatinos, which is Mauretania, a district in northwest Africa. (cf. *Yevamoth* 63a; *Sifri*, Deutero-
        nomy 320).
—   **Sabht'ka.** Usually transliterated as Sabteca. The *Targum* renders it Zingain, possibly the African Zeugis.
—   **Sheba.** Actually Sh'bha. See 1 Kings 10:1, Genesis 10:28, 25:3. Josephus identifies these with the
        Sabeans, as he does to S'bha. The *Targum* renders it Zamdugad, Zamrugad (on Genesis) or Zmargad and
        Dmargad (on Chronicles).
—   **Dedan.** Josephus identifies this nation with the Judadeans of western Etheopia. The *Targum* has M'zag,
        perhaps the Mazices of northern Africa.
10:8   **Nimrod.** See Micah 5:5. He is credited as being the first Babylonian king and the builder of the Tower,
        see below 11:1–9 (*Sefer HaYashar;* Josephus 1:4:3. Cf. *Targum Yonathan* on 10:11). See note on 14:1,
        25:29.
10:10   **Babylon.** *Babel* or *Babhel* in Hebrew. See below 11:9.
—   **Erekh.** See Ezra 4:9, Rashi *ad loc.* This was a city near Ur, on the lower Euphrates River. The Talmud
        (*Yoma* 10a) identifies it with Urikhuth, or Arkhath. This is identified with Uruk, an ancient name for
        Erekh. The *Targum* had Hadas, which may be identified with Edessa. The Midrash identifies it with
        Charan (*Bereshith Rabbah* 37).
—   **Akkad.** This was the royal city of Accad, which was the capital of northern Babylonia. The exact site of
        the city is unknown, although it was near Sippar, and about 30 miles north of Babylon. The *Targum*
        renders this as Netzivim (*Targum Yonathan; Bereshith Rabbah* 37). This was a city in the northeast end of
        Mesopotamia (cf. *Shabbath* 32b).
—   **Calneh.** The Talmud identifies this as Nofar-Ninfi (*Yoma* 10a). This is Nippur, midway between Erekh
        and Babylon on the Euphrates River. It is the modern Niffer. Other sources identify it with Ctesphon, a
        city on the eastern bank of the Tigris (*Targum Yonathan; Bereshith Rabbah* 37).
—   **Shinar.** Usually identified with Sumer. The *Targum* calls it the land of Pontus (*Targum Yonathan*). This is
        obviously not Pontus, which was a land to the south of the Black Sea. Rather, it is the Latin word *pontus,*
        meaning sea. Hence, Pontus was the "land of the sea," that is the land toward the Persian Gulf. See note
        on 14:1.
10:11   **Asshur.** See 10:22. Hebrew for Assyria. It also denotes a city on the Tigris River, some 50 miles south of
        Nineveh. The Talmud (*Yoma* 10a) identifies it with Selik, that is Seleucia. See Genesis 2:14.
—   **Nineveh.** The ancient capital of Assyria, on the Tigris River. See Jonah 1:2, 2 Kings 19:36.
—   **Rechovoth Ir.** Literally "broad places of the city," or "avenues of the city." The Talmud says that it is
        Euphrates of Mishan (*Yoma* 10a). Meshan or Mesene is the island formed by Euphrates, the Tigris and
        the Royal Canal. The *Targum,* however, translates it, "avenues of the city." Thus, it would not be a place
        name, but would denote the fact that Asshur built Nineveh as a city with avenues.

as well as Resen,* between Nineveh and Calach. [Nineveh] is a great city.*   **10**
 ¹³ Mitzraim fathered the Ludim,* the Anamim,* the Lehabhim,* the Naf-
tuchim,* ¹⁴ the Pathrusim* and the Casluchim* (from whom the Philistines*
descended) and the Caphtorim.*

[30. Descendants of Canaan]

¹⁵ Canaan fathered Sidon* (his firstborn) and Heth,* ¹⁶ as well as the Jebu-
sites,* the Amorites,* the Girgashites,* ¹⁷ the Hivites,* the Arkites,* the Sinites,*

—   **Calach.** This is a city a few miles south of Nineveh. Its modern name is Nimrud! The Talmud states that
    it is "Borsof on the Euphrates" (*Yoma* 10a). This is Borsif or Borsippa, some 20 miles south of Babylon
    on the Euphrates. It is, however, a long distance from Nineveh. The *Targum* renders it Pariyoth of Char-
    yoth, probably denoting Chadiyath in Assyria.
—   **Resen.** The Talmud identifies Resen with Aktispon or Ctesphon (*Yoma* 10a; cf. Tosafoth, *Gittin* 6a, s.v.
    U'MiBhey). See comment on Calneh. The *Targum* renders it Talsar or Talasar, see *Targum* on Isaiah 37:12,
    2 Kings 19:12.
—   **great city.** This refers to Nineveh (*Yoma* 10a; Rashi).
10:13 **Ludim.** The *Targum* renders this Givatai. This appears to be related to the name Gipt or Egypt, and also
    to the word Coptic, which denotes the ancient language of Egypt (cf. *Megillah* 18a, *Sanhedrin* 115a).
    Josephus, however, states that all the nations in this verse are unidentifiable.
—   **Anamim.** The *Targum* renders this Martiorti or Mariotai. These are the people of Mareotis, a district in
    lower Egypt containing the town of Marea.
—   **Lehabhim.** Literally "fire people," since their faces are like fire (Rashi). The *Targum* translates this name
    as Livvakai or Livkai, possibly a Lybian tribe. Josephus states that they are Lybians. See note on 10:6
    regarding Put.
—   **Naftuchim.** The *Targum* translates this as Pontsikhnai or Pantsekhyaanaei, probably denoting Pen-
    taschoinos. This is a district in Egypt later referred to as Dodekaschoinos.
10:14 **Pathrusim.** See Isaiah 11:11, Jeremiah 44:1, 44:15, Ezekiel 29:14, 30:14. The *Targum* translates it as
    Nasyotai or Gasyotai, denoting Casiotis, the district surrounding Mount Casius, east of Pelusium in
    Egypt. The *Targum* on 1 Chronicles 1:12 reverses the definition of Pathrusim and Casluchim. In the
    Midrash it is rendered as Parvitoth (*Bereshith Rabbah* 37).
—   **Casluchim.** The *Targum* renders this as Pentpoletai, most probably Pentapolis, an Egyptian district also
    called Cyrenaica. In the Midrash it is rendered Pekosim (*Bereshith Rabbah* 37). Saadia Gaon identifies it
    with Sa'id on the upper Nile.
—   **Philistines.** *Pelishtim* in Hebrew. These people lived on the shore of the Mediterranean between the Holy
    Land and Egypt (cf. Exodus 13:17).
—   **Caphtorim.** See Deuteronomy 2:23, Amos 9:7. It is identified as an island, Jeremiah 47:4. From the con-
    text, it appears to be an island on the Nile Delta. However, the Septuagint, and the *Targum* (*Yonathan*)
    translate it as Cappadocia, Kaputkai or Kapudka. This was an area south of the Black Sea (see note on
    10:2 regarding Meshekh). This does not seem to be a possible explanation, since from the context, these
    are an Egyptian people. Saadia Gaon identifies it with Damyat or Shafchu, to the west of Port Sa'id (Cf.
    Masa'oth Rabbi Binyamin 24). According to the Midrash, the Caphtorim were pygmies, and were
    descendants of the Pathrusim and the Casluchim (*Bereshith Rabbah* 37). Accordingly, this verse should be,
    "and the Pathrusim and Casluchim, from whom there descended the Philistines and Caphtorim."
10:15 **Sidon.** *Tzidon* in Hebrew, to the north of the Holy Land, see 10:19. This was the captial of Phoenicia.
    However, according to the *Targum* (on 1 Chronicles 1:13), Canaan's first-born was Bothnias (or
    Cothnias), who was the founder of Sidon.
—   **Heth.** *Cheth* in Hebrew, father of the Hittites, one of the tribes living in the Holy Land; cf. Genesis 15:20.
    They lived to the west of the Dead Sea around Hebron; Genesis 23:5. Both the Hittites and Amorites
    were associated with the Jerusalem area; Ezekiel 16:3,45.
10:16 **Jebusites.** *Yebhusi* in Hebrew. Jebus (*Yebhus*) is identified with Jerusalem; Judges 19:10, 1 Chronicles
    11:4; Joshua 15:63, Judges 1:21. The Jebusites therefore lived in the Jerusalem area. Later, however,
    this area was settled by the Hittites (*Pirkey Rabbi Eliezer* 36; Rashi on Deuteronomy 12:17).
—   **Amorites.** A people who originally lived on the west of the Dead Sea, but were driven out (Genesis 14:7).

10   ¹⁸ the Arvadites,* the Tzemarites,* and the Chamathites.* Later the families of
the Canaanites became scattered.

¹⁹ The Canaanite borders extended from Sidon toward Gerar* until
Gaza,* and toward Sodom, Gomorrah,* Admah and Tzevoyim,* until Lasha.*

²⁰ These are the descendants of Ham, according to their families and languages, by their lands and nations.

[31. Descendants of Shem]

²¹ Sons were also born to Shem. He was the ancestor of the Hebrews,*
[and] the brother of Yefeth, the eldest.*

They lived around Hebron, where they allied with Abraham (Genesis 14:13). They also lived around
Shechem (Genesis 48:22). Later, they settled the land on the east bank along the Arnon River, near
Moab (Numbers 21:13). They also lived in Gilead (Numbers 32:39). They later invaded the Holy Land
again (Judges 1:34).

—   **Girgashite.** Inhabitants of the Holy Land (Genesis 15:21). According to tradition, they left the Holy
Land before the Israelite invasion and settled in Africa (*Yerushalmi, Shabbath* 6:31; Rashi on Exodus 33:2,
34:11).

10:17 **Hivites.** *Chivi* in Hebrew. They lived in the central part of the Holy Land near Shechem (Genesis 34:2).
They also lived in Gibeon, and survived the conquest of the Holy Land (Joshua 9:3,7, 11:19). They lived
in the north, near Mount Lebanon, from Hermon to Chamath (Judges 3:3). Some identify them with the
people of Tripoli (*Targum Yerushalmi*). The Midrash apparently notes that they were cave dwellers
(*Chaldun; Bereshith Rabbah* 37). They were also adept at testing soil by taste (*Shabbath* 85a, but see *Tosefoth
ad loc.* s.v. *Chivi*). See note on 36:3.

—   **Arkites.** They are identified as the residents of Arce, a city at the northwest foot of Mount Lebanon
(Josephus; *Bereshith Rabbah* 37. Cf. *Bekhoroth* 57b).

—   **Sinites** (cf. Isaiah 49:12, Radak ad loc.). Josephus states that their identity is unknown. Others, however,
identify them with the Antusai (*Targum Onkelos; Targum Yonathan; Bereshith Rabbah* 37). This is most probably associated with the city of Orhosia, a Phoenician seaport, south of the Eleutheros River. Other
sources identify the Sinites with the Kafruseans (*Targum Yerushalmi*).

10:18 **Arvadites.** These are identified as the inhabitants of the island of Aradus on the Phoenician coast (Josephus; *Yerushalmi, Megillah* 1:9, *Bereshith Rabbah* 37). Others identify them with the town of Antridanai,
that is, Antarados, a town opposite the island of Arados (*Targum Yerushalmi*). Another source identifies
them with the Lutsai, probably the inhabitants of Arethusia, between Epiphania and Emasa.

—   **Tzemarites.** Literally "wool people," possibly because they sold or worked with wool (*Bereshith Rabbah*
37). Talmudic sources render their area as Chametz, Chomtzia, Chamitai and Chumtzai (*Targum
Yonathan; Yerushalmi, Megillah* 1:9; *Bereshith Rabbah* 37). This is identified with Emasa (the modern Hums)
a city of Syria on the eastern bank of the Orontes River. See note on 36:36.

—   **Chamathites.** This is to the north near Mount Hermon; Judges 3:3. Also see Numbers 13:21, 34:8,
Amos 6:14, Ezekiel 47:17. It is on the Orontes River. Josephus states that it is the place called Amathe,
although the Macedoneans call it Ephania (cf. *Bereshith Rabbah* 37). It is also identified with Antioch
(*Targum Yonathan*).

10:19 **Gerar.** Capital of the Philistine nation, toward the south of the Holy Land, near the coast (Genesis 20:1,
26:1).

—   **Gaza.** *Aza* in Hebrew. City on the south of Holy Land along the Mediterranean shore.

—   **Gomorrah.** *Amorah* in Hebrew.

—   **Tzevoyim.** These four cities were in what is now the southern end of the Dead Sea (Genesis 14:2,3). They
were destroyed by God for their wickedness (Genesis 19:24,25). These cities formed the southeast border
of the Canaanite territory.

—   **Lasha.** Or Lesha. This is identified with Caldahi (*Targum Yonathan; Bereshith Rabbah* 37). This is most
probably Callirohoe, a resort city on the eastern shore of the Dead Sea.

10:21 **Hebrews** (Cf. *Targum Yonathan;* Ibn Ezra). Literally, "the sons of Eber" (see 10:24, 11:14). In Hebrew,

22 The sons of Shem were Elam,* Asshur,* Arpachshad,* Lud,* and Aram.* **10**
23 The sons of Aram were Utz,* Chul,* Gether,* and Mash.*
24 Arpachshad had a son Shelach. Shelach had a son Eber.*
25 Eber had two sons. The name of the first was Peleg, because the world became divided in his days.* His brother's name was Yoktan.*
26 Yoktan was the father of Almodad,* Shelef,* Chatzarmaveth,* Yerach,*
27 Hadoram,* Uzal,* Diklah,* 28 Obhal,* Abhimael,* Sh'bha,* 29 Ophir,* Havi-

---

"Hebrews" are *Ivri'im,* literally, "Eberites," or "Sons of Eber." Others, however, translate this verse, "sons of all who live on the other side of the river" (Rashi; Ramban).

— **the eldest.** This refers to Yefeth (see note on 9:24). However, according to those who maintain that Shem was the eldest, the verse should be translated, "the older brother of Yefeth."

10:22 Elam. See Genesis 14:19. It is associated with Media (Isaiah 21:2, Jeremiah 25:25). We thus find that the capital city of Shushan (Susa) was in the province of Elam on the Ulai River (Daniel 8:2). Josephus thus writes that Elam was the ancestor of the Persians. It is thus described as the territory between Shushan and Media (Saadia Gaon). Other sources identify it with the area between the Tigris and India (*Yov'loth* 9:2).

— **Asshur.** Identified with Assyria (cf. Josephus). See 2:14, 10:11. Their territory was basically east of the Tigris.

— **Arpachshad.** He was the ancestor of Abraham (see 11:10). Josephus states that he was the ancestor of the Chaldeans, who lived on the lower Euphrates. In Hebrew, the Chaldeans were known as *Casdim* (see note on 11:28). They lived near the Persian Gulf (*Yov'loth* 9:4). The *Targum* translates the name as Arphasdai (*Targum* on 1 Chronicles 1:17,18). See Herodotus 6:5.

— **Lud.** Josephus identifies this with Lydia, south of the Black Sea (see Herodotus 7:74).

— **Aram.** Ancestor of Aramaea (from where the language Aramaic comes), to the northeast of the Holy Land, approximately where Syria is now. Josephus states that the Greeks called the Aramaeans Syrians. Its capital was Damascus (Isaiah 7:8). It also included the area between the Tigris and Euphrates rivers (*Yov'loth* 9:5). Laban was thus called an Aramaean (Genesis 22:20, 24:4, cf. Deuteronomy 26:5). Aram was important because of its association with Abraham's family.

10:23 Utz. Cf. Jeremiah 25:20, Job 1:1. Josephus writes that Utz founded the cities of Trachnitis and Damascus, and settled the lands between the Holy Land and Celesyria (*Antiquities* 1:6:4). Other sources identify Utz with Armatyai (*Targum* on 1 Chronicles 1:17), which is most probably the modern Armannia (Romania, near Constantinople). See *Targum* on Lamentations 4:21, 1 Chronicles 1:42, Job 1:1. See note on Chul.

— **Chul.** Josephus states that Chul founded Armenia, a land to the south of the eastern Black Sea. See Herodotus 7:73.

— **Gether.** According to Josephus, the founder of the Bactrian nation.

— **Mash.** In 1 Chronicles 1:17 it is Meshekh (see 10:2). Josephus identifies it with Charax Spanisi. Other sources state that it is the land in the area of Mount Mash in Mesopotamia, north of Netzivim (*Kesseth HaSofer*).

10:24 Eber. Ancestor of the Hebrews. See note on 10:21. He was a prophet (Rashi).

10:25 world became divided. This refers to the split occurring after the destruction of the Tower of Babel (see 11:8). This took place in the year that Peleg died (*Seder Olam;* Rashi). According to the chronologies (see 11:19), this was in the year 1996, when Abraham was 48 years old.

— **Yoktan.** Josephus states that he and his children lived near the Cophon River in India. In Arabian traditions, he is Kochton, the founder of Yemen (see *Kesseth HaSofer,* 123a).

10:26 Almodad. Some identify him with the founder of Morad in Yemen (*Kesseth HaSofer*). Others say that it is Allumaeoltae mentioned in Ptolemy's *Geography.*

— **Shelef.** Possibly Shalepynoi mentioned by Ptolemy (*Geography* 6:7, p. 154).

— **Chatzarmaveth.** Literally "Courtyard of Death." Some identify this with Hadarmaveth in southern Arabia (*Kesseth HaSofer* 122a).

— **Yerach.** To the west of Hadarmaveth, there is a Mount Varach (*Kesseth HaSofer*).

10:27 Hadarom. Some interpret this as denoting "the south." This was a fortress to the south of San'a (*Kesseth HaSofer*). See 1 Chronicles 18:10; Zechariah 12:11.

— **Uzal.** This was the ancient Arabic name for San'a, the capital of Yemen (*Kesseth HaSofer*).

10 lah,* and Yovav.* All these were the sons of Yoktan. ³⁰ Their settlements*
extended from Meshah* toward Sepher,* the eastern mountain.*
   ³¹ These are the descendants of Shem,* according to their families and languages, by their lands and nations.
   ³² Such were the families of Noah's sons, according to their chronicles in
their nations.* From these, the nations spread over the earth after the flood.

[32. The Tower of Babel]

11   ¹ The entire earth had one language with uniform words. ² When [the
people] migrated from the east, they found a valley in the land of Shinar,* and
they settled there. ³ They said to one another, "Come, let us mold bricks and
fire them." They then had bricks to use as stone, and asphalt* for mortar.
⁴ They said, "Come, let us build ourselves a city, and a tower whose top shall
reach the sky. Let us make ourselves a name, so that we will not be scattered
all over the face of the earth."

— **Diklah.** Literally a palm tree. Some say that it is an area in Mina, abundant in palm trees (cf. Pliny 6:28).

10:28 **Obhal.** Some identify this with Avalitae on the Ethiopian Coast.

— **Abhimael.** Literally "Father of Mael." Some identify this with the Mali, a tribe living in the Mecca area, described by Theophrastus (*Enquiry into Plants* 9:4). This is the Minaei described by Strabo.

— **Sh'bha.** Or Sheba. See 10:7, 25:3.

10:29 **Ophir.** The place from which King Solomon brought gold; 1 Kings 9:28, 10:11. Cf. Psalms 45:9, Isaiah 13:12. From the context, it is a place on the Arabian peninsula. Some identify it with El Ophir, a town in Oman. Josephus, however, identifies Ophir with Aurea Chersonesus, belonging to India (*Antiquities* 8:6:4). The Septuagint translates Ophir as Sophia, which is Coptic for India. There was indeed an ancient city known as Soupara or Ouppara in the vicinity of Goa on the western coast of India. Later authors identified Ophir with the New World (Rabbi Azzaria de Rossi, *Meor Eynaim, Imrey Binah* 11; David Gans, *Nechmad VeNaim* 3:75; *Tzemach David* 2:1533; *Seder HaDoroth* 5254).

— **Havilah.** See notes on 10:7, 2:11. Some identify this with Chavlotai, an area on the Persian Gulf described in ancient geographies (Strabo 16:728). This is Huvaila in Bahrein. Others state that it is Avalitae on the Avalite Bay (now Zeila), a city on the Sea of Adan south of Bab el Mandeb. There is also a Nagar Havili in India, on the Arabian Sea, some 80 miles north of Bombay. There is also a town Chwala on the Caspian Sea, and therefore in Russian the Caspian Sea is called *Chwalinskoje More*. The name Havilah in the Torah may refer to more than one place.

— **Yovav.** This is identified as Yovevitai or Yoveritai mentioned by Ptolemy, along the Salachitis Gulf (Gulf of Oman).

10:30 **Their settlements.** This refers to the children of Yoktan. According to some authorities, however, it refers to all the children of Shem (Cf. Ramban on 11:12).

— **Mesha.** This is identified with Mecca (Saadia). Others say that it is Mocha (Al Mukha) in Yemen (cf. Ptolemy, *Geography* 6:7, 14a, 74b). Others identify it with Mesene (Khowr-e Musa) at the mouth of the Tigris, where it flows into the Persian Gulf.

— **Sepher.** Some sources identify this with Medina (Saadia Gaon). The Midrash states that it is T'phari or Taphar (*Bereshith Rabbah* 37). Others identify it with Isfor in southern Arabia.

— **eastern mountain.** Some identify this with Alakdar in eastern Arabia, on the Indian Ocean (*Kesseth HaSofer*).

10:31 **Shem.** The descendants of Shem are known as the Semites. Theirs is the Semitic language group.

10:32 **nations.** There are seventy nations mentioned in this chapter. These are the seventy nations or seventy languages often mentioned in Talmudic literature.

11:2 **Shinar.** See note on 10:10.

11:3 **asphalt.** See 14:10, Exodus 2:3. In ancient times, asphalt was often used as a mortar. The *Targum Yonathan*, however, renders the word *chemar* here as clay.

⁵ God descended* to see the city and the tower that the sons of man had   **11**
built. ⁶ God said, "They are a single people, all having one language, and this
is the first thing they do! Now nothing they plan to do will be unattainable for
them! ⁷ Come, let us* descend and confuse their speech, so that one person
will not understand another's speech."

⁸ From that place, God scattered them all over the face of the earth, and
they stopped building the city. ⁹ He named it Babel,* because this was the
place where God confused* the world's language. It was from there that God
dispersed [humanity] over all the face of earth.

[33. The Eleventh Generation]

¹⁰ These are the chronicles of Shem:

Shem was 100 years old when he had a son Arpachshad,* two years after
the flood. ¹¹ Shem lived 500 years after he had Arpachshad, and he had sons
and daughters.

[34. The Twelfth Generation]

¹² Arpachshad was 35 years old when he had a son Shelach. ¹³ Arpachshad
lived 403 years after he had Shelach, and he had sons and daughters.

[35. The Thirteenth Generation]

¹⁴Shelach was 30 years old when he had a son Eber. ¹⁵ Shelach lived 403
years after he had Eber, and he had sons and daughters.

[36. The Fourteenth Generation]

¹⁶ Eber was 34 years old when he had a son Peleg. ¹⁷ Eber lived 430 years
after he had Peleg, and he had sons and daughters.

[37. The Fifteenth Generation]

¹⁸ Peleg was 30 years old when he had a son Reu. ¹⁹ Peleg lived 209 years
after he had Reu, and he had sons and daughters.

[38. The Sixteenth Generation]

²⁰ Reu was 32 years old when he had a son Serug. ²¹ Reu lived 207 years
after he had Serug, and he had sons and daughters.

11:5   **descended.** An anthropomorphism denoting special attention, especially for the purpose of punishing
the wicked (*Moreh Nevukhim* 1:10).
11:16 **us.** God was speaking to the angels, or to the forces of creation (Rashi; Ibn Ezra). See note on Genesis
1:26.
11:9   **Babel.** Hebrew for Babylonia or Babylon.
—   **Confused.** *Balal* in Hebrew, cognate to Babel.
11:10 **Arpachshad.** See 10:24.

11

²² Serug was 30 years old when he had a son Nachor. ²³ Serug lived 200 years after he had Nachor, and he had sons and daughters.

[40. The Eighteenth Generation]

²⁴ Nachor was 29 years old when he had a son Terach. ²⁵ Nachor lived 119 years after he had Terach, and he had sons and daughters.

[41. Abram]

²⁶ Terach was 70 years old when he fathered Abram, Nachor and Haran. ²⁷ These are the chronicles of Terach:
Terach fathered Abram, Nachor and Haran.
Haran had a son Lot. ²⁸ Haran died during the lifetime of his father Terach, in the land of his birth, Ur Casdim.*
²⁹ Abram and Nachor married. The name of Abram's wife was Sarai. The name of Nachor's wife was Milcah, the daughter of Haran (who was the father of Milcah and Yiscah*). ³⁰ Sarai was sterile; she had no children.
³¹ Terach took his son Abram, his grandson Lot (Haran's son), and his daughter-in-law Sarai (Abram's wife). With them, he left Ur Casdim, heading toward the land of Canaan. They came as far as Charan* and settled there.
³² All of Terach's days were 205 years, and Terach died in Charan.

Lekh Lekha   לֶךְ לְךָ

[42. Abram's Call and Migration]

12

¹ God said to Abram, "Go away from your land, from your birthplace, and from your father's house, to the land that I will show you. ² I will make you into a great nation. I will bless you and make you great. You shall become a blessing. ³ I will bless those who bless you, and he who curses you, I will curse. All the families of the earth will be blessed through you."
⁴ Abram went as God had directed him, and Lot* went with him. Abram

---

11:28 **Ur Casdim.** Often translated Ur of the Chaldeans. Some say that the Casdim derived their name from Arpachshad, which is Arp-casad. Others say that the name came from Kesed (22:22), and was not used until after Abraham's time (Radak). (See *Yov'loth* 11:3).

11:29 **Yiscah.** Usually identified with Sarah (Rashi; *Targum Yonathan*; Josephus, *Antiquities* 1:6:5). In English, this is sometimes rendered as Jessica.

11:31 **Charan.** A city in Mesopotamia, some 400 miles northeast of the Holy Land. The journey from Ur to Charan was close to 600 miles.

12:4 **Lot.** See 11:31, 37:25. Also see note on Exodus 7:22.

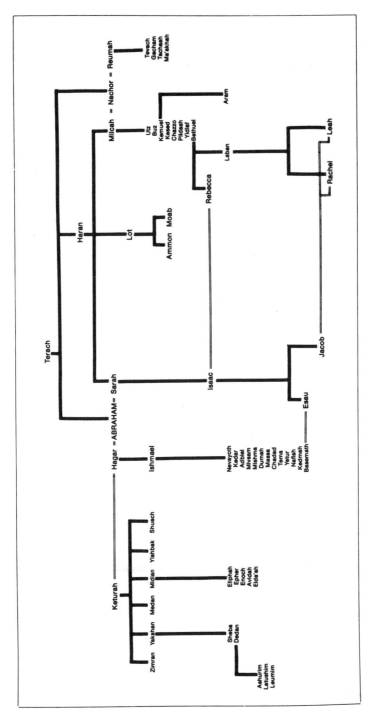

PLATE 5.   ABRAHAM'S FAMILY

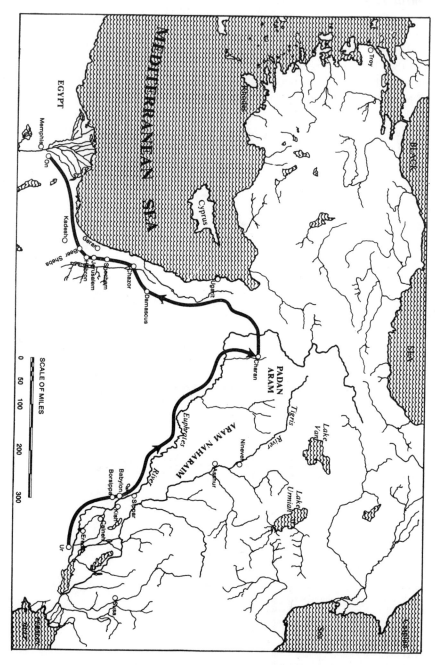

PLATE 6.   ABRAHAM'S JOURNEY

was 75 years old when he left Charan.* ⁵ Abram took his wife Sarai, his   12
nephew Lot, and all their belongings, as well as the people they had gathered,*
and they left, heading toward Canaan. When they came to Canaan, ⁶ Abram
traveled through the land as far as the area of Shechem,* coming to the Plain
of Moreh.* The Canaanites were then in the land.

⁷ God appeared to Abram and said, "I will give this land to your offspring." [Abram] built an altar there to God who had appeared to him.

⁸ From there, [Abram] moved on to the mountains east of Bethel.* He set
up his tent with Bethel to the west and Ai* to the east. He built an altar there
and called in God's name. ⁹ Abram then continued on his way, moving steadi-
ly toward the south.*

[43. Troubles]

¹⁰ There was a famine in the land. Abram headed south* to Egypt to stay
there for a while, since the famine had grown very severe in the land. ¹¹As they
approached Egypt, he said to his wife Sarai, "I realize that you are a good-
looking woman. ¹² When the Egyptians see you, they will assume that you are
my wife* and kill me, allowing you to live. ¹³ If you would, say that you are my
sister. They will then be good to me for your sake, and through your efforts,
my life will be spared."

¹⁴ When Abram came to Egypt, the Egyptians saw that his wife* was very

12:5   **75 years old** . . . According to the genealogies, Abram was born in 1948, so this was the year 2023.
—   **the people they had gathered.** Literally, "the soul that they had made," or "the souls that they had
       made." It can be interpreted to mean the servants they had acquired (Rashi), or the people that they had
       converted to God's cause (Rashi; Ibn Ezra). It can also denote the spiritual gifts that they had acquired
       (*Sefer Yetzirah* 6; Raavad *ad loc.*)
12:6   **Shechem.** A city near the center of the Holy Land, in the vicinity of the
       present Nablus.
—   **Plain of Moreh.** (*Targum;* Rashi). *Elon Moreh* in Hebrew. See Deuteron-
       omy 11:30. Other sources translate it as "the Terebinth of Moreh" (Ibn
       Ezra; Ramban on 14:6). The terebinth of the Torah is a large tree (*Pistacia
       atlantica*) of the sumac family, also related to the pistachio. It is also
       sometimes identified with the oak. The terebinth could live for over a
       thousand years, and was often as much as twenty feet in diameter. The
       Terebinth of Moreh would have been a particularly large tree that served
       as a landmark in the area. See Genesis 35:4, Judges 9:6.

Terebinth

12:8   **Bethel.** *Beth El* in Hebrew, literally, "the house of God." This was a city
       some 20 miles south of Shechem. It is identified with the modern Beitin,
       some 10 miles north of Jerusalem.
—   **Ai.** A town a little less than two miles east of Bethel. Identified with the modern Haiyin.
12:9   **south.** Negev in Hebrew, literally the drylands.
12:10 **headed south.** Literally, "went down."
12:12 **they will assume.** Literally, "They will say, 'This is his wife.'"
12:14 **his wife.** Literally, "the woman."

12 beautiful. ¹⁵ Pharaoh's officials saw her, and spoke highly of her to Pharaoh.* The woman was taken to Pharaoh's palace. ¹⁶ He treated Abram well because of her, and [Abram] thus acquired sheep, cattle, donkeys, male and female slaves, she-donkeys, and camels.

¹⁷ God struck Pharaoh and his palace* with severe plagues because of Abram's wife Sarai. ¹⁸ Pharaoh summoned Abram and said, "How could you do this to me*? Why didn't you tell me that she was your wife? ¹⁹ Why did you say that she was your sister* so that I should take her to myself as a wife? Now here is your wife! Take her and go!"

²⁰ Pharaoh put men in charge* of [Abram], and they sent him on his way along with his wife and all that was his.

13 ¹ Abram headed northward* to the Negev along with his wife and all that was his, including Lot. ² Abram was very rich, with livestock, silver and gold. ³ He continued on his travels, from the Negev toward Bethel, until [he came to] the place where he originally had his tent, between Bethel and Ai, ⁴ the site of the altar that he had built there at first. Abram called in God's name.

⁵ Lot, who accompanied Abram, also had sheep, cattle and tents. ⁶ The land could not support them living together; their wealth was so great that they could not stay together. ⁷ Friction developed between the herdsmen of Abram's flocks and those of Lot. The Canaanites and Perizites* were then living in the land.

⁸ Abram said to Lot, "Let's not have friction between me and you, and between my herdsmen and yours. After all, we're brothers. ⁹ All the land is before you. Why not separate from me*? If you [go to] the left, I will go to the right; if to the right, I will take the left."

12:15 Pharaoh. A generic name for Egyptian kings (Josephus, *Antiquities* 8:6:2), coming from the Egyptian *par ao,* the "Great House." This event occurred in 2023 (1737 b.c.e.), during the Second Intermediate Period, where the pharaohs are not known by name. However, there is a possible 163 year disparity in chronologies (see note on Exodus 2:23), so that this Pharaoh may be the one who is assumed to have reigned in 1900 b.c.e. This would be Amenemhet II of the 12th Dynasty.

Pharaoh

12:17 palace. Or, "household." Literally, "house."

12:18 How could you . . . Literally, "What is this that you have done to me?"

12:19 Why did you . . . Literally, "Why did you say, 'She is not my wife.' " In the Hebrew idiom, a direct quote would be used where English uses an indirect quote.

12:20 put men in charge. Or, "gave men orders regarding him."

13:1 headed northward. Literally, "went up."

13:7 Perizites. This is the first mention of this nation, which is later mentioned together with the other Canaanite nations (see 15:20; Exodus 3:8, 3:17, 23:23, etc.). They most probably lived between Bethel and Shechem (cf. Genesis 34:30), especially around Bezek (Khirbet Ibzik) (Judges 1:4). They lived near the Amorite, Hittite and Yebusite (Joshua 11:3), as well as in the forests near the Rephaim (Joshua 17:15). Some say that they were called Perizim because they lived in unwalled cities (*Perazoth*) (*Kesseth HaSofer*).

13:9 Why not . . . The Hebrew word *na* makes an imperative into a request rather than a demand. It is often translated as "Please," or "if you would," but here we translate it as "why not." In many places, we leave it untranslated.

¹⁰ Lot looked up and saw that the entire Jordan Plain,* all the way to   13
Tzoar* had plenty of water. (This was before God destroyed Sodom and
Gomorrah.*) It was like God's own garden, like the land of Egypt. ¹¹Lot chose
for himself the entire Jordan Plain. He headed eastward,* and the two separated. ¹² Abram lived in the land of Canaan, while Lot dwelt in the cities of the
Plain,* having migrated* as far as Sodom. ¹³ But the people of Sodom were
very wicked, and they sinned against God.*

¹⁴ After Lot left him, God said to Abram, "Raise your eyes, and, from the
place where you are now [standing], look to the north, to the south, to the
east, and to the west. ¹⁵ For all the land that you see, I will give to you and to
your offspring forever. ¹⁶ I will make your offspring like the dust of the earth;
if a man will be able to count [all] the grains of dust in the world, then your
offspring also will be countable. ¹⁷ Rise, walk the land, through its length and
breadth, for I will give it [all] to you."

¹⁸ Abram moved on.* He came and settled in the Plains* of Mamre,* in
Hebron,* and there he built an altar to God.

[44. The War]

¹ It was around this time* that Amraphel* king of Shinar,* Ariokh* king   **14**

13:10 **Plain.** *Kikar* in Hebrew, literally a flat cake or circle of Jordan. This was a flat oval area in what is now the
southern part of the Dead Sea. See below 19:25. It seems that the Jordan then had underground chan-
nels through which it could flow, so the water did not collect in the area. See *Targum Yonathan* on 14:3.
—   **Tzoar.** A city originally known as Bela, associated with Sodom and Gomorrah (14:2). Also see 19:22,
Deuteronomy 34:3. According to tradition, Tzoar was settled later than the other four cities (*Shabbath*
10b; Rashi on 19:20). From the context, it would seem that Tzoar was the southernmost of these cities,
possibly on the southern bank of what is now the Dead Sea. (see Josephus, *Wars* 4:8:4).
       According to context, this phrase fits here. However, the verse literally ends, "Like the land of Egypt,
as one comes to Tzoar." Accordingly, this "Tzoar" may not be the one associated with Sodom, but an
ancient Egyptian frontier fortress.
—   **Sodom and Gomorrah.** See below 19:24. Also see 10:19.
13:11 **eastward.** (The verse literally says, "from the east," but from the context, this must be interpreted as
"eastward," since the Jordan is to the east of Bethel (Radak. See Rashi; Ibn Ezra).
13:12 **cities of the plain.** Sodom and its associated cities.
—   **migrated.** Literally, "having moved his tents" (Radak, *Sherashim*). Others translate it, "pitching his tents
until Sodom," or "setting up his tents near Sodom." See above, 10:19.
13:13 **were very wicked and. . .** (Ralbag; Septuagint). Or, "were very evil and sinful to God" (following cantellation). "This was the sin of your sister Sodom: pride, lots of bread, and the careless ease that she and
her sattelites had. She did not support the poor and those in need" (Ezekiel 16:49).
13:18 **moved on.** Literally, "moved his tents." See 13:12.
—   **Plains.** *Eloney Mamre* in Hebrew. Others translate it, "Terebinths of Mamre."
       See note on 12:6. Josephus states that it was by an oak called Ogyges (Ancient
       One) (*Antiquities* 1:10:4; *Wars* 4:9:7).
—   **Mamre.** An Amorite who was Abram's ally (14:13). This area was later known
       as Kiryath HaArba (35:27).
—   **Hebron.** A well known city, some 18 miles west of the Dead Sea, not very far   Abraham's Oak
       from Sodom. This would mean that Abram migrated some 28 miles southward from Bethel.
14:1   **It was around this time . . .** (Rabenu Meyuchas). Literally, "It was in the days of Amraphel," or "It was
       in the days when Amraphel . . ."

14 of Ellasar,* Chedorlaomer* king of Elam,* and Tidal* king of Goyim*
² waged war against Bera king of Sodom, Birsha king of Gomorrah, Shinav
king of Admah, Shemever king of Tzevoyim,* and the king of Bela (now
Tzoar*).
³ All of these had come together* in Siddim Valley* (now the Dead Sea*).
⁴ They* had served Chedorlaomer for twelve years, but in the thirteenth year*
they rebelled. ⁵ In the fourteenth year, Chedorlaomer and his allied kings
came. They defeated* the Rephaim* in Ashteroth Karnaim,* the Zuzim* in

- **Amraphel.** Talmudic sources identify him with Nimrod (above, 10:8; cf. *Targum Yonathan; Eruvin* 53a; Rashi). Some identify him with the famed Hammurabi, who in ancient writings is referred to as Ammurapi. This may have occurred at the beginning of his reign, before he had built his famed empire, and hence, the leading king is seen as Chedorlaomer (14:4,5,9). However, since he later became famous, the age is identified with him.
- **Shinar.** This is identified with Sumer. The *Targum Yonathan* renders it as Pontus (see note on 10:10). In some manuscripts, however, the reading is Bogtos, denoting Baghdad.
- **Ariokh.** A king of Larsa by the name of Eriaku is found in ancient writings. It was later also a popular name (cf. Daniel 2:14).
- **Ellasar.** This is the same as Larsa, a city just south of Erekh, and 100 miles south of Babylon. It was a major power center in ancient times. See note on 10:10.
- **Chedorlaomer.** *K'darla'omer* in Hebrew. Some sources indicate that he was originally one of Amraphel's generals, who rebelled and established an independent kingdom (*Sefer HaYashar*). The name itself is a Hebraicized form of *Kudur* (servant of) and *Lagamar,* the name of an Elamite deity.
- **Elam.** A city-state in the area of Shushan. See note on 10:22.
- **Tidal.** He can be identified with the Tudghala or Tudhaliya of cuniform texts, who was king of the Northern Kurdish or Hittite nations.
- **Goyim.** Literally "nations" or "hordes" (see *Targum*). This might indicate that he was the king over a number of nations, or perhaps, a barbaric king. Others, interpret Goyim as a place name (Rashi). It may be identified with Gutium in Kurdistan. See Joshua 12:23.
- 14:2 **Sodom . . . Tzevoyim.** See above, 10:19. Also see Deuteronomy 24:22, Hosea 11:8.
- **Tzoar.** See note on 13:10. The name was changed after the other cities were destroyed (19:22). Bela was still used as a name (36:32).
- 14:3 **had come together.** That is, the kings of Sodom and its sattelites had made a treaty to serve Chedorlaomer, and this treaty was made in Siddim Valley (Rashi). Others say that the five cities of the plain had made a mutual defense pact in this valley. Another possible explanation is that they gathered for war in Siddim Valley (see 14:8).
- **Siddim Valley.** After the destruction, this area was submerged to become the Dead Sea. The name Siddim is from the root *sadad* (cf. Isaiah 28:24, Hosea 10:11), which is also the root of the word *sadeh,* a field (Radak). Hence, Onkelos translates it, "Field Valley," or "Valley of Fields." *Targum Yonathan* renders it, "Orchard Valley," but, since the word for orchard is *pardes,* it can also be rendered "Paradise Valley" (see *Bereshith Rabbah* 42).
- **Dead Sea.** *Yam HaMelach* in Hebrew, literally the Salt Sea. In Moses' time, Siddim Valley was no longer known, and it had to be identified. This plain was in what is now the southern part of the Dead Sea, which is much shallower and more recent geologically than the northern part.
- 14:4 **They.** That is, the five cities of the plain.
- **thirteenth year.** According to others, "then for 13 years they rebelled" (*Bereshith Rabbah* 42). According to some, the servitude began immediately after the Tower of Babel (*Seder Olam Rabbah* 1; cf. *Shabbath* 11a, Rashi *ad loc.* s.v. *Esrim*).
- 14:5 **defeated.** Literally "struck." It can also mean "killed," "attacked," or "conquered."
- **Rephaim.** The *Targum* has "mighty ones," or "giants," cf. Deuteronomy 2:11, 2:21. Their land was promised to Abraham (15:20), and part of it was given to Lot's descendants (Deuteronomy 2:20). Og, a giant reputed to be over ten feet tall, was reputed to be one of the survivors of the Rephaim (Deuteronomy 3:11; Joshua 12:4, 13:12). Their land was later called Bashan, to the east of the Jordan (Deuteronomy 3:13). They were associated with the Perizites (Joshua 17:15, see Genesis 15:20). Some sources identify them with the Hivites (*Bereshith Rabbah* 44).

Ham,* the Emim* in Shaveh Kiryathaim,* ⁶ and the Horites* in the hill coun-   **14**
try of Seir,* as far as Eyl Paran,* which borders the desert.* ⁷ They then turned
back and came to Eyn Mishpat* (now Kadesh*), and they conquered the
entire field of the Amalekites,* as well as the Amorites* who lived in Chatzatzon Tamar.*

⁸ The kings of Sodom, Gomorrah, Admah, Tzevoyim and Bela (Tzoar)
marched forth. They set up battle lines in Siddim Valley, ⁹ against Chedorlaomer king of Elam, Tidal king of Goyim, Amraphel king of Shinar, and
Arioch king of Ellasar. There were four kings against the five. ¹⁰ Siddim Valley

---

- **Ashteroth Karnayim.** Ancient twin cities, some 22 miles east of the Sea of Galilee (Kinereth Sea), on what is now the Golan Heights. Actually Karnayim was a little over two miles northeast of Ashteroth. Later, Og lived near there (Joshua 9:10, 12:4, 13:12) in Edrei (Deuteronomy 1:4. Cf. Rashi on Deuteronomy 1:4). Ashteroth was also the name of a Sidonite deity (cf. 1 Kings 11:5 etc.). Karnayim literally means "twin horns" (Radak).
- **Zuzim.** These are identical with the Zumzumim of Deuteronomy 2:20 (Rashi). Zumzumim was the name given to this race of giants by the Amonites (Deuteronomy 2:20). The *Targum* renders it *takifin*, literally "the powerful ones."
- **Ham.** A city 14 miles to the east of the Jordan River, and 25 miles southwest of Ashteroth Karnayim. We thus see that the attackers were coming from the north and heading south. Some sources, however, render this verse, "the Zuzim among them" (*Bereshith Rabbah* 42). This follows from Deuteronomy 2:20, where the Zuzim are identified with the Raphaim.
- **Emim.** Literally, "fearsome ones" (*Targum*), a name given to the Rephaim (giants) by the Moabites (Deuteronomy 2:11). They lived in what was later Moabite territory (see next note).
- **Shaveh Kiryathaim.** An ancient city, 8 miles east of the Dead Sea, 5 miles north of the Arnon River, and 67 miles south of Ham. It is literally, "the plain of two cities." It was on the frontier of Moab (Ezekiel 25:9; cf. Jeremiah 48:1,2,23,24). It later became part of Reuben's territory (Numbers 32:37, Joshua 13:19).
- **14:6** **Horites.** *Chorites* in Hebrew. These were the original inhabitants of Seir who were later driven out and destroyed by Esau's descendants (Deuteronomy 2:12, 2:22; cf. Genesis 36:8). Seir may have been named later, after Seir the Horite (cf. Genesis 36:27). See note on 36:2.
- **Seir.** The area later occupied by Esau (Genesis 36:8). Seir is the hill country to the south of the Dead Sea. This means that the invaders swung around the Dead Sea and headed west.
- **Eyl Paran.** To the west of Seir. Eyl is translated "plain" in the *Targum*. According to this, it might be associated with the plain known as Arabah directly south of the Dead Sea (see below). Other sources render this "Terebinth of Paran" (Ramban; Septuagint), indicating a grove or oasis. It would then be related to the word *elon* (see note on 12:6). See Rashi, *Targum* on Ezekiel 31:14.
  Paran was the area settled by Ishmael (21:21). It was on the way from Sinai (Numbers 10:12), from where the spies were sent out, heading through the Tzin Desert (Numbers 13:3,21). The Arabah is between Paran and Tophel (Deuteronomy 1:1).
- **the desert.** Probably the Tzin Desert, see above.
- **14:7** **Eyn Mishpat.** Literally, "Well of Decision," or "Well of Judgment."
- **Kadesh.** This is Kadesh Barnea (compare Numbers 13:26 and 32:8). The *Targum* renders this Rekem, which is identified as Petra, 43 miles due south of the Dead Sea (cf. 16:14, 20:1). Others say that it is an area some 55 miles southwest of the Dead Sea. (Cf. *Tosafoth, Gittin* 2a, s.v. *Ashkelon*).
- **Amalekites.** These were not the descendants of Esau (Genesis 36:12), since the latter were born much later and named after this earlier tribe (Ramban). Otherwise, it may denote the field where the Amalekites later lived (Radak; Ramban).
- **Amorites.** See note on 10:16.
- **Chatzatzon Tamar.** This is Eyn Gedi on the western shore of the Dead Sea (2 Chronicles 20:2; *Targum;* Rashi). See Judges 1:16, note on 15:19 below, regarding the Kenite.

14   was full of tar pits,* and when the kings of Sodom and Gomorrah tried to flee,
     they fell into them. The others fled to the mountains.*
        ¹¹ [The victors] seized all the goods of Sodom and Gomorrah, and all the
     food, and they departed. ¹² When they left, they [also] took Abram's nephew
     Lot and his possessions, since he had been living in Sodom. ¹³ Those who
     escaped* came and brought the news to Abram the Hebrew,* who was living
     undisturbed* in the plains of Mamre the Amorite,* brother of Eshkol and
     Aner. They were Abram's allies.
        ¹⁴ When Abram heard that his kinsman had been taken captive, he called
     out* all his 318 fighting men* who had been born in his house. He hurried
     after [the invaders], catching up with them in Dan.* ¹⁵ He divided [his forces]
     against them [and attacked] that night—he and his servants. He attacked, and
     pursued [the invaders] as far as Chovah,* which is to the left of Damascus.*
        ¹⁶ [Abram] brought back all the property. He also brought back his kins-
     man Lot and all his goods, along with the women and the [other] people.
     ¹⁷ After he returned from his victory over Chedorlaomer and his allied kings,
     the king of Sodom came out to greet him in Level Valley* (now King's
     Valley.*)
        ¹⁸ Malkhi-tzedek* king of Salem* brought forth bread and wine. He was a

---

14:10 **tar pits.** Even now, asphalt is found in the Dead Sea region. The Romans referred to it as *Mer Asphaltitis*,
       the Asphalt Sea, and it was known to cast up lumps of asphalt (Josephus, *Wars* 4:8:4; Tacitus, *Histories*
       5:6).
—   **mountains.** That is, to the mountains on the west of the Dead Sea, toward Hebron, where Abram was
       living.
14:13 **Those who escaped.** Some have it in the singular, "the refugee."
—   **Hebrew.** See note on 10:21.
—   **living undisturbed.** See Hirsch.
—   **Amorite.** One of the defeated nations. See 14:7.
14:14 **called out.** Or "hurried" (*Targum*), or "armed" (Ibn Ezra).
—   **fighting men** (Ibn Ezra). Or "students" (Rashi).
—   **Dan.** A city at the northern end of the Holy Land, 12 miles north of Lake Hula, and 120 miles north of
       Hebron. It may have been called that since it would later be named Dan, or else there may have been an
       ancient city there by that name (Radak). *Targum Yonathan* identifies it as Dan of Ceasarea, since Ceasarea
       was some three miles to the east of Dan. See Joshua 19:47, Judges 18:29). Saadia identifies it with the
       Banias River.
            This indicates that the invaders had a head start, and Abraham did not catch up with them until Dan.
—   **Chovah.** See Judith 4:4, 15:4. This is unidentified, but since they were heading northeast, it would be to
       the northwest of Damascus, possibly in the valley where the Albana River comes through the mountains.
       The *Targum* has "north of Damascus."
—   **Damascus.** The capital of Syria, 42 miles northeast of Dan. This was probably as far as they could pursue
       in a single day. See note on 30:36.
14:17 **Level Valley.** *Emek Shavé* in Hebrew.
—   **Kings Valley.** *Emek HaMelekh.* It was probably near Jerusalem; see 2 Samuel 18:18.
14:18 **Malkhi-tzedek.** Usually transliterated Melchizedek, literally "Righteous King" or "King of Tzedek." See
       Psalms 110:4. He is identified as Shem, the son of Noah (*Targum Yonathan; Nedarim* 32b; Rashi. However,
       see 2 *Enoch* 23:26). Tzedek was a name of Jerusalem, and Malkhi-tzedek was the title given its king, like
       Pharaoh in Egypt (Radak, Ralbag on Joshua 10:1; cf. Isaiah 1:26).
—   **Salem.** Jerusalem, cf. Psalms 76:3 (*Targum;* Rashi; Josephus, *Antiquities* 1:10:2).

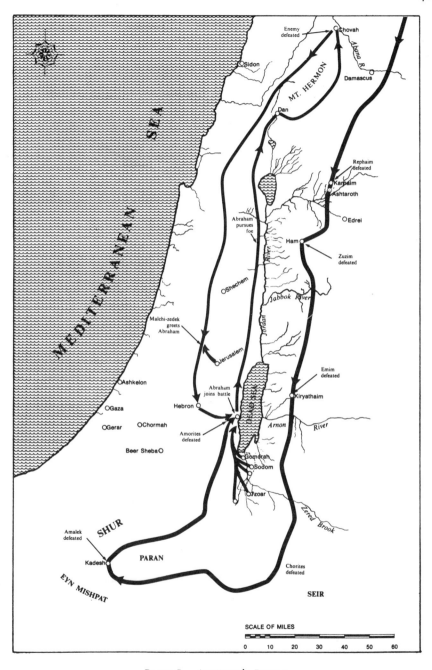

PLATE 7. ABRAHAM'S BATTLE

14 priest to God, the Most High. ¹⁹ He blessed [Abram], and said, "Blessed be
Abram to God Most High, Possessor of heaven and earth. ²⁰ And blessed be
God Most High, who delivered your enemies into your hand." [Abram then]
gave him a tenth* of everything.

²¹ The king of Sodom said to Abram, "Give me the people. You can keep
the goods."

²² Abram replied to the king of Sodom, "I have lifted my hand [in an oath]
to God Most High, Possessor of heaven and earth! ²³ Not a thread nor a shoelace*! I will not take anything that is yours! You should not be able to say, 'It
was I who made Abram rich.' ²⁴ The only exception* is what the young men
have eaten, and the portion of the men who went with me, Aner, Eshkol and
Mamre. Let them take their share."

[45. The Pact Between Halves]

15 ¹ After these events, God's word came to Abram in a vision, saying, "Fear
not Abram, I am your shield. Your reward is very great."

² Abram said, "O Lord, God, what will you give me if I remain childless?
The heir* to my household will be Damascus Eliezer.*"

³ Abram continued, "You have given me no children. A member of my
household will inherit what is mine."

⁴ Suddenly* God's word came to him: "That one will not be your heir!
One born from your own body will inherit what is yours." ⁵ He then took
[Abram] outside and said, "Look at the sky and count the stars. See if you can
count them." [God] then said to him, "That is how [numerous] your descendants will be."

⁶ [Abram] believed in God, and He counted it as righteousness.*

⁷ [God] said to him, "I am God who took you out of Ur Casdim to give
you this land as a possession.*"

14:20 **tenth.** *Maaser* in Hebrew, literally a tithe. See Genesis 28:22, Deuteronomy 14:22.
14:23 **shoelace.** Or "shoestrap." Cf. Isaiah 5:27.
14:24 **The only exception.** See Radak, *Sherashim;* Ibn Ezra.
15:2 **heir.** *Ben meshek* in Hebrew. It can also denote a steward or caretaker. (See Radak, *Sherashim,* s.v. *Meshek, Shakak*).
— **Damascus Eliezer.** He may have been called this because he was from Damascus, or because he led the chase to Damascus (*Bereshith Rabbah* 44). In Hebrew it is *Dameshek,* and some say it is a title given to the one in charge of a household or a teacher (*Yoma* 28b; cf. Amos 3:12).
15:4 **Suddenly.** The word *hiney* used here is untranslatable. It is often rendered as "here" or "behold," but this is an approximation of an expression that has no equivalent in the Indo-European languages. For this reason, it is often left untranslated. In general, it serves to intensify a statement and to provide emphasis. Here, the intensity denotes that it was a sudden or intense experience.
15:6 **righteousness.** *Tzedakah* in Hebrew, also meaning charity. Others interpret it, "and he (Abraham) count-ed it as charity" (Ramban).
15:7 **possession.** Literally, "to inherit it."

⁸ "O Lord, God," replied [Abram], "How can I really know that it will be 15 mine?"

⁹ [God] said to him, "Bring for Me a prime* heifer, a prime goat, a prime ram, a dove and a young pigeon.*"

¹⁰ [Abram] brought all these for Him. He split them in half, and placed one half opposite the other.* The birds, however, he did not split.* ¹¹ Vultures descended on the carcasses, but Abram drove them away.

¹² When the sun was setting, Abram fell into a trance, and he was stricken by a deep dark dread. ¹³ [God] said to Abram, "Know for sure that your descendants will be foreigners in a land that is not theirs for 400 years.* They will be enslaved and oppressed.* ¹⁴ But I will finally bring judgment against the nation who enslaves them, and they will then leave with great wealth. ¹⁵ You shall join your fathers in peace, and you will be buried at a good old age. ¹⁶ The fourth generation* will return here, since the Amorite's sin will not have run its course until then."

¹⁷ The sun set, and it became very dark. A smoking furnace and a flaming torch passed between the halves of the animals. ¹⁸ On that day, God made a covenant with Abram, saying, "To your descendants I have given this land, from the Egyptian River* as far as the great river, the Euphrates*; ¹⁹ [the lands of] the Kenites,* the Kenizites,* the Kadmonites,* ²⁰ the Hittites,* the Perizites,*

15:9 **prime.** *Meshulesheth* in Hebrew, literally "threefold," "triplet," or "third grade." This denotes the best quality (*Tosafoth, Gittin* 56a, s.v. Egla; *Chizzkuni*). Others interpret it to mean "third-born" (Rashi, *Pesachim* 68a, *Shabbath* 11a). Another interpretation is that the animals were to be three years old (*Targum Yonathan;* Ibn Ezra). Others say that they were to be part of a triplet (Ramban). Finally, there are some who maintain that three of each animal were to be brought (Onkelos; Rashi).

— **dove and . . .** All these species, and none other, would be used later for sacrifice. The four types here may represent the 400 years (15:13) and the four generations (15:16) mentioned later (cf. Hirsch).

15:10 **split them . . .** This was the way of making a covenant (Rashi). Indeed, the words *b'rith* (covenant) and *bathar* (split) appear to be closely related (cf. Radak, *Sherashim,* s.v. *Barath*). It symbolized that just as the two halves of the animal were really one, so were the two people making the covenant. Moreover, just as one side cannot live without the other, so the two cannot live without each other (Ralbag; *Ikkarim* 4:45). It was also seen as a malediction; anyone violating the oath would be torn asunder like the animals (Bachya).

— **did not split.** Cf. Leviticus 1:17. (*Bereshith Rabbah* 44)

15:13 **400 years.** This occurs at the end of the verse, but from context, it belongs here. The 400 years were counted from Isaac's birth, since he never lived in his own land. It lasted until the Exodus (*Seder Olam Rabbah;* Rashi).

— **They will be . . .** literally, "they (the others) will enslave and oppress them."

15:16 **fourth generation.** Levi came to Egypt. The four generations were then Levi, Kohath, Amram, Moses (cf. Rashi).

15:18 **Egyptian River.** Some say that it is the Nile (*Targum Yonathan*), but this is a minority opinion. Ibn Ezra says that it is the Shichur River (cf. Joshua 13:3, Jeremiah 2:18), which is identified with Wadi el Arish, on the border of the Holy Land, some 90 miles east of the present Suez Canal (see note on Exodus 23:31). See Numbers 34:5.

— **Euphrates.** This is the limit reached in the days of Solomon (1 Kings 5:1).

15:19 **Kenites.** It seems that they lived near Moab, to the west of the Dead Sea (cf. Numbers 24:21; *Bava Bathra* 56a). They lived in *Ir HaTamarim* (Palm City) (Judges 1:16), which may be identified with Chatzatzon

15   the Rephaim,* ²¹ the Amorites,* the Canaanites,* the Girgashites and the Yebusites.*

[46. Birth of Ishmael]

16   ¹ Abram's wife Sarai had not borne him any children. She had an Egyptian slave-girl by the name of Hagar. ² Sarai said to Abram, "God has kept me from having children. Come* to my slave, and hopefully I will have sons* through her." Abram heeded Sarai.

³ After Abram had lived in Canaan for ten years,* his wife Sarai took Hagar the Egyptian her slave, and gave her to her husband Abram as a wife. ⁴ [Abram] came to her, and she conceived. When she realized that she was pregnant, she looked at her mistress with contempt. ⁵ Sarai said to Abram, "It's all your fault! I myself placed my slave in your arms*! Now that she sees herself pregnant, she looks at me with disrespect. Let God judge between me and you!"

⁶ Abram replied to Sarai, "Your slave is in your hands. Do with her as you see fit." Sarai abused her, and [Hagar] ran away from her.

⁷ An angel of God encountered her by a spring in the desert, in the oasis* on the road to Shur.* ⁸ [The angel] said, "Hagar, maid of Sarai! From where are you coming, and where are you going?"

Tamar (above, 14:7), to the west of the Dead Sea. The *Targum* translates Keni as Shaalmite, an Arabic tribe (cf. *Bava Bathra* 56a; *Yerushalmi, Shevi'ith* 6:1; *Yerushalmi, Kiddushin* 1:8; *Bereshith Rabbah* 44).

—   **Kenizites.** They are identified as the Nebatians, a tribe that lived to the southeast of the Holy Land, near Edom (see above-mentioned sources; cf. *Targum Yonathan* on Numbers 11:22; *Targum* on Isaiah 60:7, Ezekiel 27:21).

—   **Kadmonites.** Identified simply as Arabs, living in the area of Ammon, to the northeast of the Dead Sea (above sources). Literally, "the Easterner" cf. 1 Samuel 24:14. The Dead Sea was also known as the "Eastern Sea" or "Kadmoni Sea" (Ezekiel 47:18, Joel 2:20, Zechariah 38:17).

15:20 **Hittites.** Living around Hebron. See note on 10:15.

—   **Perizites.** See note on 13:7.

—   **Rephaim.** See note on 14:5.

15:21 **Amorite.** See note on 10:16.

—   **Canaanite.** A generic name, since by this time, many of the tribes had intermingled. Possibly associated with Sidon (10:15).

—   **Girgashite and Yebusite.** See 10:16.

16:2 **Come.** Denoting intimacy, as in *biyah* (ibn Janach).

—   **I will have sons.** Or, "I will be built up."

16:3 **ten years.** That is, when Abraham was 85 years old; see 12:4. This, then, was in the year 2033.

16:5 **in your arms.** Literally, "in your bosom," or "in your lap."

16:7 **oasis.** *Eyin* in Hebrew, as distinguished from *eyn ha-mayim* which we translate as well or spring.

—   **road to Shur.** This was a well known road to Egypt, some 50 miles south of the Mediterranean coast. It is obvious that Hagar was returning to Egypt, her homeland (cf. 16:1).

The *Targum* translates Shur as Chagra, a city on the border of the Holy Land, possibly on the "River of Egypt" (Wadi el Arish, see above, 15:18). This would place it near the present Al Qusayma, approximately 100 miles southwest of Hebron. The name Shur is still found in the area in such places as Jebel es-Sur in the et-Tih desert.

"I am running away from my mistress, Sarai," she replied.   **16**

⁹ The angel of God said to her, "Return to your mistress, and submit yourself to her."

¹⁰ [Another*] angel said in God's name,* "I will grant you many descendants. They will be so many that they will be uncountable."

¹¹ [Still another] angel of God said to her, "You are pregnant, and will give birth to a son. You must name him Ishmael,* for God has heard your prayer.* ¹² He will be a rebel.* His hand will be against everyone, and everyone's hand will be against him. Still, he will dwell undisturbed* near all his brothers.*"

¹³ [Hagar] gave a name to God* who had spoken to her, [saying], "You are a Vision God,*" for she said, "Didn't I [still] see here after my vision*?" ¹⁴ She therefore named the oasis, "Oasis to Life my Vision"* (*Be'er LaChai Ro'i*). It is between Kadesh* and Bered.*

¹⁵ Hagar bore Abram's son. Abram gave the name Ishmael to his son, who had been born to Hagar. ¹⁶ He was 86 years old* when Hagar bore his son Ishmael.

[47. Circumcision]

¹Abram was 99 years old.* God appeared to him and said, "I am God   **17**

Josephus identifies Shur with Pelusium on the Mediterranean coast near Egypt (*Antiquities* 6:7:3). Saadia Gaon states that it is Jifar. Also see note on 16:14.

The angel therefore encountered Hagar just as she was leaving the Holy Land.

16:10 **Another.** Cf. Rashi on 16:9.
—   **in God's name.** Literally, "An angel of God said to her," but obviously it was God making the promise, and not the angel (cf. Radak; Rashi on 18:10).
16:11 **Ishmael.** *Yishmael* in Hebrew, literally, "God will hear."
—   **prayer.** (*Targum*). Literally, "suffering."
16:12 **rebel.** (*Targum;* cf. Ibn Ezra). *Perè Adam* in Hebrew. *Perè* is a wild donkey (cf. Isaiah 32:14, Hosea 8:9, Job 6:5, 11:12, 24:5) and hence, it can be translated, "a wild donkey of a man" (*Targum Yonathan;* Ramban). Rashi interprets it to mean an "outdoor man" or "a man who will live in Paran."
—   **dwell undisturbed.** See note on 14:13. Cf. *Targum Yonathan.*
—   **near all his brothers.** Or, "He will dwell over all his brothers," (cf. Rashi).
16:13 **gave a name...** Or, "prayed to God" (*Targum*).
—   **Vision God.** Or, "God of vision" (Ibn Ezra).
—   **Didn't I . . .** (cf. *Targum;* Rashi). Or, "Wasn't I able to see after my vision?" or "Did I not have a vision after He saw me?" (Ibn Ezra).
16:14 **Oasis to Life my Vision.** Or "Well of the lifegiving vision," (*HaKethav VeHaKabbalah*); "Well of the vision of the Living One" (Rashi; *Targum*); or "Well to the Living One who sees me" (Ibn Ezra). Ibn Ezra identifies this with Zimum (or in other versions, Zimzum), where the Arabs hold an annual festival. This is Zemzem near Mecca. According to this, however, Hagar headed into the Arabian Peninsula rather than toward Egypt.
—   **Kadesh.** See note on 14:7.
—   **Bered.** Or Bared. The *Targum* renders this Chagra, the same as it does for Shur; see above, note on 16:7. *Targum Yonathan,* however, has Chalutzah. Kadesh and Bered were some 20 miles apart, and the oasis was between them on the Shur Road.
16:16 **86 years old.** See note on 16:3. This was the year 2034.
17:1 **99 years old.** Thirteen years after Ishmael was born, in the year 2047. See below, 17:25. The vision did not come until Ishmael was legally an adult.

17   Almighty.* Walk before Me and be perfect.* ² I will make a covenant between
       Me and you, and I will increase your numbers very much.''

       ³ Abram fell on his face. God spoke to him [again], saying, ⁴ "As far as I
       am concerned, here is My covenant with you: You shall be the father of a
       horde of nations. ⁵ No longer shall you be called Abram. Your name shall
       become Abraham,* for I have set you up as the father of a horde of nations. ⁶ I
       will increase your numbers very, very much, and I will make you into
       nations—kings will be your descendants. ⁷ I will sustain My covenant between
       Me and between you and your descendants after you throughout their genera-
       tions, an eternal covenant; I will be a God to you and to your offspring after
       you. ⁸ To you and your offspring I will give the land where you are now living
       as a foreigner. The whole land of Canaan shall be [your] eternal heritage, and
       I will be a God to [your descendants].''

       ⁹ God [then] said to Abraham, "As far as you are concerned, you must
       keep My covenant—you and your offspring throughout their generations.
       ¹⁰ This is My covenant between Me, and between you and your offspring that
       you must keep: You must circumcise every male. ¹¹ You shall be circumcised*
       through the flesh of your foreskin. This shall be the mark of the covenant
       between Me and you.

       ¹² "Throughout all generations, every male shall be circumcised when he
       is eight days old.* [This shall include] those born in your house,* as well as
       [slaves] bought with cash from an outsider, who is not your descendant. ¹³ [All
       slaves,] both houseborn and purchased with your money must be circumcised.
       This shall be My covenant in your flesh, an eternal covenant. ¹⁴ The uncircum-
       cised male whose foreskin has not been circumcised, shall have his soul cut off
       from his people*; he has broken My covenant.''

[48. Fulfillment]

       ¹⁵ God said to Abraham, "Sarai your wife—do not call her by the name
       Sarai, for Sarah is her name. ¹⁶ I will bless her, and make her bear you a son. I
       will bless her so that she will be [the mother] of entire nations—kings will be
       her descendants.''

—   **God Almighty.** *El Shaddai* in Hebrew. *Shaddai* is interpreted as being the same as *she-dai,* "He who has
     sufficient [power]" (Rashi).
—   **perfect.** *Tamim* in Hebrew. See note on 6:9.
17:5 **Abraham.** *Avraham* in Hebrew. It is related to *Av Ham,* the "father of hordes," but the "r" is retained.
17:11 **You shall be circumcised. . .** (Radak; *Sherashim*; Chizzkuni; Septuagint). Or, "When you are circum-
     cised" (Saadia); or, "You shall cut off the flesh of your foreskin" (Targum; Rashi).
17:12 **Eight days old.** Cf. Leviticus 12:3.
—   **born in your house.** Some say that this denotes homeborn slaves (*Shabbath* 135b; Rashi).
17:14 **cut off from his people.** This denotes being cut off from one's spiritual source. It also denotes premature
     death and childlessness (see above, 9:11).

¹⁷ Abraham fell on his face and he laughed.* He said to himself, "Can a **17** hundred-year-old man have children? Can Sarah, who is ninety, give birth?"
¹⁸ To God, Abraham said, "May it be granted that Ishmael live before you!"
¹⁹ God said, "Still, your wife Sarah will give birth to a son. You must name him Isaac.* I will keep My covenant with him as an eternal treaty, for his descendants after him. ²⁰ I have also heard you with regard to Ishmael. I will bless him, and make him fruitful, increasing his numbers very greatly. He will father twelve princes,* and I will make him into a great nation. ²¹ But I will keep my covenant with Isaac, whom Sarah will bear to you this time next year."
²² When He finished speaking to him, God went up,* [leaving] Abraham.
²³ Abraham took his son Ishmael, everyone born in his house, and every [slave] bought for money—every male in his household—and he circumcised the flesh of their foreskins. [It was] on the very day* that God had spoken to him.
²⁴ Abraham was 99 years old when he was circumcised on the flesh of his foreskin. ²⁵ His son Ishmael was thirteen years old when the flesh of his foreskin was circumcised. ²⁶ On the very day that Abraham and his son Ishmael were circumcised, ²⁷ all the men of the household, both homeborn and bought for cash from a stranger, were circumcised with him.

VaYera   וַיֵּרָא

[49. The Visitors]

¹ God appeared to [Abraham] in the Plains of Mamre while he was sitting **18** at the entrance of the tent in the hottest part of the day. ² [Abraham] lifted his eyes and he saw three strangers* standing a short distance from him. When he saw [them] from the entrance of his tent, he ran to greet them, bowing down to the ground.

17:17 **laughed.** *Yitzchak* in Hebrew, equivalent to Isaac (see next note). Some interpret the word *tzachak* here literally as "laughed" (Abarbanel; Septuagint), while others interpret it as "rejoiced" (Targum; Saadia; Rashi).
17:19 **Isaac.** *Yitzchak* in Hebrew. Literally, "He will laugh," or "he laughed."
17:20 **twelve princes.** Enumerated in 25:13–15.
17:22 **went up.** This indicates that the prophetic vision ended (*Moreh Nevukhim* 1:10). See note on 11:5.
17:23 **on the very day.** Literally, "on that very day" (cf. Rashi). Others have, "in broad daylight" (*Pirkey Rabbi Eliezer* 29; see note on 7:13). Some say that this took place on Yom Kippur (*ibid.*). According to others, it was on Passover (cf. Rashi on 19:3).
18:2 **strangers.** Literally, anonymous "men;" see below, 24:29. They were actually angels in disguise (Rashi). See below, 19:1.

18   ³ He said, "Sir,* if you would,* do not go on without stopping by me.*
⁴ Let some water be brought, and wash your feet. Rest under the tree. ⁵ I will
get a morsel of bread for you to refresh yourselves. Then you can continue on
your way. After all,* you are passing by my house."

"All right," they replied. "Do as you say."

⁶ Abraham rushed to Sarah's tent and said, "Hurry! Three measures* of
the finest flour! Knead it and make rolls."

⁷ Abraham ran to the cattle, and chose a tender, choice calf. He gave it to a
young man who rushed to prepare it. ⁸ [Abraham] fetched some cottage
cheese* and milk, and the calf that he prepared, and he placed it before [his
guests]. He stood over them as they ate under the tree.

⁹ They asked him, "Where is your wife Sarah?"

"Here in the tent," he replied.

¹⁰ "I will return to you this time next year," said [one of the men], "and
your wife Sarah will have a son."

Sarah was listening behind the entrance of the tent, and he was on the
other side. ¹¹ Abraham and Sarah were already old, well on in years, and
Sarah no longer had female periods. ¹² She laughed to herself, saying, "Now
that I am worn out, shall I have my heart's desire*? My husband is old!"

¹³ God said to Abraham, "Why did Sarah laugh and say, 'Can I really have
a child when I am so old?' ¹⁴ Is anything too difficult for God? At the designated time, I will return, and Sarah will have a son."

¹⁵ Sarah was afraid and she denied it. "I did not laugh," she said.
[Abraham]* said, "You did laugh."

¹⁶ The strangers got up from their places and gazed at Sodom. Abraham
went with them to send them on their way.

¹⁷ God said, "Shall I hide from Abraham what I am going to do? ¹⁸ Abra-

---

18:3   **Sir.** Literally, "My lords." According to others, "O God." According to the second opinion, Abraham
was asking God not to break off the prophecy (*Shevuoth* 35b; Rashi). See 18:13.

—   **if you would.** Literally, "If I have found favor in your eyes."

—   **go on . . .** Literally, "go on from your servant." This form of address, however, is not used in the current
English idiom. Therefore, wherever "your servant" is used in this manner, it is usually translated as
"me."

18:5   **After all.** Literally, "because therefore." See below 19:8, 33:10. Others have, "Because it is for this
reason that you have passed by your servant" (cf. Ramban).

18:6   **measures.** *Se'im* in Hebrew, plural of *sa'ah*, a measure equivalent to 7.3 liters or 7.7 quarts. The three
sa'ahs that she took were therefore equivalent to around 30 cups or 8 pounds of flour.

18:8   **cottage cheese.** *Chemah* in Hebrew, usually translated as curd. It is something that can be eaten alone; see
Isaiah 7:15, 7:22; cf. Proverbs 30:33. Others interpret it to denote a kind of leben or yoghurt. According
to Rashi, the word *chemah* denotes cream. (cf. *Targum* and Judges 5:25). The Septuagint, on the other
hand, translates it as butter. Indeed, in Middle Eastern lands, it was the custom to eat butter alone.

18:12 **heart's desire** (Ibn Ezra). Or, "shall I once again regain my youth" (Rashi).

18:15 **Abraham** (Ramban; Sforno). According to others, God was speaking (*Yerushalmi, Sotah* 7:1; *Bereshith Rabbah* 48).

ham is about to become a great and mighty nation, and through him all the   18
nations of the world will be blessed.* ¹⁹ I have given him special attention* so
that he will command his children and his household after him, and they will
keep God's way, doing charity and justice. God will then bring about for
Abraham everything He promised."

²⁰ God [then] said, "The outcry against* Sodom is so great, and their sin*
is so very grave. ²¹ I will descend* and see. Have they done everything implied
by the outcry that is coming before Me? If not, I will know."

²² The men turned from where they were, and headed toward Sodom.
Abraham was still standing before God.

²³ He came forward and said, "Will You actually wipe out the innocent
together with the guilty? ²⁴ Suppose there are fifty innocent people in the city.
Would You still destroy it, and not spare the place for the sake of the fifty good
people inside it? ²⁵ It would be sacrilege even to ascribe such an act to You—
to kill the innocent with the guilty, letting the righteous and the wicked fare
alike. It would be sacrilege to ascribe this to You! Shall the whole world's
Judge not act justly?"

²⁶ God said, "If I find fifty innocent people in Sodom, I will spare the
entire area for their sake."

²⁷ Abraham spoke up and said, "I have already said too much* before my
Lord! I am mere dust and ashes! ²⁸ But suppose that there are five missing
from the fifty innocent? Will You destroy the entire city because of the five?"

"I will not destroy it if I find forty-five there," replied God.

²⁹ [Abraham] persisted* and said, "Suppose there are forty there?"

"I will not act for the sake of the forty."

³⁰ "Let not my Lord be angry, but I [must] speak up. What if there are
thirty there?"

"I will not act if I find thirty there."

³¹ "I have already spoken too much now before my Lord! But what if
twenty are found there?"

"I will not destroy for the sake of the twenty."

³² "Let my Lord not become angry, but I will speak just once more. Suppose ten are found there?"

18:18 **will be blessed.** See 12:3.
18:19 **given him special attention.** Literally, "have known him because." Cf. Rashi.
18:20 **against.** Or, "the cry of Sodom," indicating the cry of its victims. (See Ramban, Ibn Ezra; Radak).
— **their sin.** See note on 13:13.
18:21 **descend.** See note on 11:5.
18:27 **said too much** (Onkelos). Others, "I have begun to speak" (*Targum Yonathan;* Rashi); "I have desired to
speak" (Ibn Ezra); or "I have dared to speak" (*HaKethav VeHaKabbalah*).
18:29 **persisted.** Literally, "spoke to Him again."

18   "I will not destroy for the sake of the ten."

³³ When He finished speaking with Abraham, God left [him]. Abraham then returned home.

19   ¹ The two angels* came to Sodom in the evening, while Lot was sitting at the city gate. Lot saw them and got up to greet them, bowing with his face to the ground. ² He said, "Please, my lords, turn aside to my house. Spend the night, bathe your feet, and then continue on your way early in the morning."

"No," they replied, "we will spend the night in the square."

³ [Lot] kept urging them until they finally turned aside to him and came to his house. He made a feast for them and baked matzah,* and they ate.

⁴ They had not yet gone to bed when the townspeople, the men of Sodom, surrounded the house—young and old alike—all the people* from every quarter. ⁵ They called out to Lot and said, "Where are the strangers who came to you tonight? Bring them out to us so that we may know* them!"

⁶ Lot went out to them in front of the entrance, shutting the door behind him. ⁷ He said, "My brothers, don't do such an evil thing! ⁸ I have two daughters who have never known a man. I will bring them out to you. Do as you please with them. But don't do anything to these men. After all, they have come under my roof*!"

⁹ "Get out of the way*!" they shouted.

They were saying, "This one man came here as an immigrant, and now all of a sudden, he has set himself up as a judge! We'll give it to you worse than to them!"

They pushed against Lot very much, and tried to break down the door. ¹⁰ The strangers [inside] reached out and pulled Lot to them into the house, closing the door. ¹¹ They struck the men who were standing at the entrance with blindness*—young and old alike—and [the Sodomites] tried in vain to find the door.

¹² The strangers said to Lot, "Who else do you have here? A son-in-law? Your own sons? Your daughters? If you have anyone in the city, get them out of the area. ¹³ We are about to destroy this place, for [the people's] outcry is great before God. God has sent us to destroy it."

19:1   **two angels.** These were two of the three who had visited Abraham (18:2). One had had the mission of announcing that Abraham would have a son (18:10), and had left after having finished the mission. See below 19:5,10, where these angels are also referred to as men.
19:3   **matzah.** Unleavened bread. This was something that could be baked in a few minutes. It is from here, however, that there is a tradition that this episode occurred on Passover (Rashi. See note on 17:23).
19:4   **all the people.** There were no innocent ones (Rashbam).
19:5   **know.** Hence, the term sodomy.
19:8   **under my roof.** Literally, "they have come in the shadow of my rafters." See above, 18:5.
19:9   **Get out of the way.** Literally, "Come close over there," or "Move aside" (Rashi). Others have, "Push up closer" (Hirsch).
19:11   **blindness.** Or, "hallucinations" (Malbim).

¹⁴ Lot went out and spoke to his sons-in-law, who were betrothed* to his   19
daughters. He said, "Get moving! Get out of this area! God is about to
destroy the city!" To his sons-in-law, it was all a big joke.
¹⁵ As dawn was breaking, the two angels hurried Lot. "Get moving!" they
said. "Take your wife and two daughters who are here! You don't want to be
swept away because of the city's sin!"
¹⁶ He hesitated. The strangers grabbed him, his wife, and his two
daughters by the hand, leading them out, and left them on the outskirts of the
city. God had shown pity on [Lot]. ¹⁷ When [the angel] had led them out, he
said, "Run for your life! Do not look back! Do not stop anywhere in the
valley! Flee to the hills, so that you not be swept away!"
¹⁸ Lot said to them, "O God,* no! ¹⁹ I have found favor in your eyes, and
you have been very kind in saving my life! But I cannot reach the hills to
escape. The evil will overtake me and I will die! ²⁰ Please, there is a city here
close enough for refuge. It is insignificant*! I will flee there—isn't it insignificant?—and I will survive."
²¹ [The angel] replied to him, "I will also give you special consideration*
in this matter. I will not overturn the city you mentioned. ²² But hurry! Run
there! I can do nothing until you get there."
The city was henceforth known as Tzoar (Insignificant).*
²³ The sun had risen by the time that Lot arrived in Tzoar. ²⁴ God made
sulphur and fire rain down on Sodom and Gomorrah—it came from God,
out of the sky. ²⁵ He overturned these cities along with the entire plain,
[destroying] everyone who lived in the cities and [all] that was growing from
the ground.
²⁶ [Lot's] wife looked behind him, and she was turned into a pillar of salt.*
²⁷ Abraham woke up early in the morning, [hurrying back] to the place
where he had stood before God. ²⁸ He stared at Sodom and Gomorrah and
the whole area of the plain, and all he saw was heavy smoke rising from the
earth, like the smoke of a lime kiln.*

19:14 betrothed. (Rashi; Josephus, *Antiquities* 1:12:4).
19:18 O God. (*Targum*). Others, "Please sir, no!" (Ibn Ezra).
19:20 insignificant. *Mi-tzar* in Hebrew. See 19:22.
19:21 give you special consideration. Literally, "lift your face," an idiom.
19:22 Tzo'ar. Its original name was Bela (14:2). It was south of the present Dead Sea (see note on 13:10).
19:26 pillar of salt. Josephus states that in his time, this pillar could still be seen (*Antiquities* 1:11:4). It was also
    known in Talmudic times (*Berakhoth* 54b). Significantly, at the southern end of the Dead Sea, there is a
    mountain of salt called Jebel Usdum (Sodom Mountain), 6 miles long, 3 miles wide, and some 1000 feet
    thick. Although it is now covered with a layer of earth several feet thick, the rest of the mountain is solid
    salt. This also supports the contention that Lot and his family were heading *south* toward Tzoar. A rain of
    salt was part of the upheaval (see Ibn Ezra here and Deuteronomy 29:22).
19:28 lime kiln. Lime produces prodigious quantities of smoke when it is slaked.

19   ²⁹ When God had destroyed the cities of the plain, God had remembered Abraham. Thus, when He overturned the cities in which Lot lived, He allowed Lot to escape the upheaval.

³⁰ Lot went up from Tzoar, and settled in the hills together with his two daughters, since he was afraid to remain in Tzoar. He lived in a cave alone with his two daughters.

³¹ The older girl said to the younger, "Our father is growing old, and there is no other man left in the world to marry us in a normal manner. ³² Come, let's get our father drunk with wine, and sleep with him. We will then survive through children from our father."

³³ That night, they got their father drunk with wine, and the older girl went and slept with her father. He was not aware that she had lain down or gotten up.

³⁴ The next day, the older girl said to the younger, "Last night it was I who slept with my father. Tonight, let's get him drunk with wine again. You go sleep with him, and we will survive through children from our father."

³⁵ That night, they again made their father drunk with wine. The younger girl got up and she slept with him. He was not aware that she had lain down or gotten up.

³⁶ Lot's two daughters became pregnant from their father. ³⁷ The older girl had a son, and she named him Moab.* He is the ancestor of [the nation] Moab that exists today.

³⁸ The younger girl also had a son, and she named him Ben-Ami.* He is the ancestor of the people of Ammon* who exist today.

[50. Sarah and Abimelekh]

20   ¹ Abraham migrated from there to the land of the Negev, and he settled between Kadesh and Shur.* He would often visit Gerar.* ² [There] he announced that his wife Sarah was his sister, and Abimelekh,* king of Gerar, sent messengers and took Sarah.

19:37 Moab. *Moav* in Hebrew. A form of *me-av,* meaning "from a father. The nation of Moab lived to the southeast of the Dead Sea, probably not far from where Moab was born. Significantly, Ruth came from Moab, and she was the ancestress of King David, and hence, of the Messiah.

19:38 Ben-Ami. Literally, "son of my people," or "son of my kin."

— **Ammon.** An ancient nation who lived to the northeast of the Dead Sea.

20:1 Kadesh and Shur. This would be the area around Beer Lachai Roi, see note on 16:14.

— **Gerar.** On the southwest border of the Holy Land, see note on 10:19. The Midrash identifies it as Gerdike or Gerarike (*Bereshith Rabbah* 52), which is this Gerar. It is a city some 55 miles north of Kadesh, so although Abraham's primary dwelling was to the south, he would often visit Gerar, perhaps for supplies (cf. Radak). Some, however, suggest that this Gerar was Wadi Gerur, some 13 miles southwest of Kadesh, literally between Kadesh and Shur. See below, 26:17. (Also see *Yov'loth* 16:10).

20:2 Abimelekh. Literally, "father-king." This was a title given to Philistine kings, much like Pharaoh was given to Egyptian monarchs (Psalms 34:1, Rashi ad loc.; cf. *Sefer HaYashar* 65,66). Persian kings were

³ God came to Abimelekh in a dream that night. "You will die because of 20
the woman you took," He said. "She is already married."

⁴ Abimelekh had not come near her. He said, "O Lord, will You even kill
an innocent nation*? ⁵ Didn't [her husband] tell me that she was his sister? She
also claimed that he was her brother. If I did something, it was with an innocent heart and clean hands."

⁶ God said to him in the dream, "I also realize that you have done this
with an innocent heart. That is why I prevented you from sinning against Me,
not giving you an opportunity to touch her. ⁷ Now return the man's wife, for
he is a prophet. He will pray for you, and you will live. But if you do not
return [her], you can be sure that you will die—you and all that is yours."

⁸ Abimelekh got up early in the morning, and he summoned all his servants. He discreetly* repeated all these words to them, and the men were very
frightened. ⁹ Abimelekh summoned Abraham and said to him, "How could
you do this to us? What terrible thing did I do to you that you brought such
great guilt upon me and my people? The thing you did to me is simply not
done!"

¹⁰ Abimelekh then asked Abraham, "What did you see to make you do
such a thing?"

¹¹ Abraham replied, "I realized that the one thing missing here is the fear
of God. I could be killed because of my wife. ¹² In any case, she really is my
sister.* She is the daughter of my father,* but not the daughter of my mother.
She [later] became my wife. ¹³ When God made me wander from my father's
house, I asked her to do me a favor. Wherever we came, she was to say that I
was her brother.*"

¹⁴ Abimelekh took sheep, cattle, and male and female slaves, and he gave
[them] to Abraham. He [also] returned [Abraham's] wife Sarah to him.
¹⁵ Abimelekh said, "My whole land is before you. Settle wherever you see fit.*"

given the title *Padi-shach,* which also means "father-king." In Hebrew, *av* means master as well as father.
So the designation Avi-melekh may mean "master-king" or arch-king. See note on 41:43.

20:4 **innocent nation.** The guilty nation was Sodom.

20:8 **discreetly.** Literally, "in their ears" (see 44:18). Or "publicly," see 23:10,13.

20:12 **sister.** Also denotes any close relative. See 13:8.

— **daughter of my father.** He actually meant, "granddaughter of my father," since Sarah was a granddaughter of Terach. Sarah was the daughter of Abraham's brother Haran (see note on 11:29). (cf. Rashi).

20:13 **she was to say . . .** There are three nested direct quotations in this verse, but following the English idiom,
the two inner ones are rendered as indirect quotations. Literally, the verse reads, "I said to her, 'This is
the favor that I want you to do for me: Wherever we come, say of me, "He is my brother."'"

20:15 **Settle . . .** According to many opinions, Abraham therefore decided to settle in Beer-sheba, which was
the border of the Philistine territory (cf. Ramban on 21:32; *Matnath Kehunah* on *Bereshith Rabbah* 54:2).
This is also supported in other ancient sources (*Yov'loth* 16:11). See below, 21:14. Others, however,
maintain that Abraham remained in Gerar (Ibn Ezra; Radak).

20   ¹⁶ To Sarah he said, "I am giving* your 'brother' a thousand pieces of silver.
Let it be compensation* for you and all who are with you for all that has been
done.* You can stand up tall.*"

        ¹⁷ Abraham prayed to God, and God healed Abimelekh, as well as his wife
and slavegirls, so that they were able to have children. ¹⁸ God had previously
sealed up every womb in Abimelekh's house, because of Abraham's wife
Sarah.

                        [51. Isaac and Ishmael]

21   ¹ God granted special providence* to Sarah as He said He would, and
God did what He promised for Sarah. ² Sarah became pregnant, and she gave
birth to Abraham's son in his old age. It was at the exact time that God had
promised it to him. ³ Abraham gave the name Isaac* to the son he had, to
whom Sarah had just given birth. ⁴ When his son Isaac was eight days old,
Abraham circumcised him, as God had commanded.

        ⁵ Abraham was 100 years old when his son Isaac was born. ⁶ Sarah said,
"God has given me laughter. All who hear about it will laugh* for me." ⁷ She
said, "Who would have even suggested to Abraham that Sarah would be nursing children? But here I have given birth to a son in his old age!"

        ⁸ The child grew and was weaned. Abraham made a great feast on the day
that Isaac was weaned. ⁹ But Sarah saw the son that Hagar had born to Abraham playing.* ¹⁰ She said to Abraham, "Drive away this slave together with
her son. The son of this slave will not share the inheritance with my son
Isaac!"

        ¹¹ This troubled Abraham very much because it involved his son. ¹² But

---

20:16 **am giving.** Literally, "have given." (See *HaKethav VeHaKabbalah*).
—   **compensation.** A difficult idiom, literally translated as "an eye covering." Thus, "something to prevent
        you from seeing any more evil" (cf. Ibn Ezra; Rashi). Others interpret it as a vindication, something that
        will cover other people's eyes and prevent them from seeing wrong (Rashbam). Another interpretation is
        that "[the money] will cover people's eyes and prevent them from looking at you wantonly" (Ramban).
        Other commentators take it literally, as a veil to show that Sarah was a properly married woman (*Ha-
        Kethav VeHaKabbalah*). Still other sources translate *eynayim* as "colors" rather than "eyes," and render the
        phrase, "let [the money] be used to buy you a colorful cloak" (Radak). Finally, some make the subject of
        the phrase Abraham: "[Abraham] shall be for you as an eye-covering," however the latter expression is
        translated (Ibn Ezra).
—   **for all that has been done** (Rashi). Others connect it to the end of the verse, "Before everyone you stand
        tall" (Ibn Ezra).
—   **stand up tall** (cf. Rashi). Others have, "You should have learned a lesson from all this" (*Targum;* Ibn
        Ezra). Since this entire sentence involves ancient idioms, it is extremely difficult to interpret and
        translate.
21:1   **granted special providence.** *Pakad* in Hebrew (see Hirsch). Usually translated as "remembered" or
        "visited."
21:3   **Isaac.** *Yitzchak* in Hebrew. See above, 17:19.
21:6   **will laugh.** *Yitzachak* in Hebrew, a play on Yitzchak. It means "to be happy for me" (Rashi).
21:9   **playing** (Ibn Ezra; *Yov'loth* 17:4). Others have "scoffing" or "sporting" (Sforno; Rashi). The verse may
        also be read, "Sarah saw that the son . . . was a scoffer" (Hirsch).

God said to Abraham, "Do not be troubled because of the boy and your slave.   21
Do everything that Sarah tells you. It is through Isaac that you will gain posterity.* ¹³ But still, I will also make the slave's son into a nation, for he is your
child."

¹⁴ Abraham got up early in the morning. He took bread and a skin* of
water, and gave it to Hagar, placing it on her shoulder. He sent her away with
the boy. She left and roamed aimlessly in the Beer-sheba desert.* ¹⁵ When the
water in the skin was used up, she set the boy under one of the bushes. ¹⁶ She
walked away, and sat down facing him, about a bowshot away. She said, "Let
me not see the boy die." She sat there facing him, and she wept in a loud
voice.

¹⁷ God heard the boy weeping. God's angel called Hagar from heaven and
said to her, "What's the matter Hagar? Do not be afraid. God has heard the
boy's voice there where he is. ¹⁸ Go and lift up the boy. Keep your hand strong
on him,* for I will make of him a great nation."

¹⁹ God opened her eyes, and she saw a well of water. She went and filled
the skin with water, giving the boy some to drink.

²⁰ God was with the boy. [The boy] grew up and lived in the desert, where
he became an expert archer.* ²¹ He settled in the Paran Desert,* and his
mother got him a wife from Egypt.*

[52. The Treaty at Beer-sheba]

²² Around that time, Abimelekh and his general Pikhol* made a declaration to Abraham, saying, "God is with you* in all that you do. ²³ Now swear to
me here by God that you will not deal falsely with me, with my children, or
with my grandchildren. Show to me and the land where you were an immigrant the same kindness that I have shown to you."

²⁴ "I will swear," replied Abraham.

²⁵ Abraham then complained to Abimelekh about the well that Abimelekh's servants had taken by force. ²⁶ Abimelekh said, "I don't know who

---

21:12 **gain posterity.** Literally, "you will be said to have offspring," or, "offspring will be considered yours."
21:14 **skin.** Or a wooden container (cf. Ibn Ezra).
— **Beer-sheba desert.** She may have begun heading toward Egypt from Beer-sheba where Abraham lived
(see notes on 20:15, 16:7). This is the first mention of Beer-sheba in the Torah. It is some 25 miles east of
Gerar, connected by a wadi. See below, 26:17.
21:18 **keep your hand** (Hirsch). Others, "hold him tight."
21:20 **archer.** See 21:16.
21:21 **Paran Desert.** South of Beer Lachai Roi. See notes on 14:6, 16:12.
— **Egypt.** Her homeland, above 16:1 (*Bereshith Rabbah* 53; Rashi). The *Targum Yonathan* states that the wife's
name was Fatima.
21:22 **Pikhol.** According to some, this is a title rather than a proper name (see *Bereshith Rabbah* 54). In ancient
Egyptian, *Pakhel* means "the spokesman."
— **God is with you.** See 26:28.

21 could have done such a thing. You never told me. I heard nothing about it until today."

²⁷ Abraham took sheep and cattle and gave them to Abimelekh, and the two of them made a treaty. ²⁸ Abraham then put seven female sheep* aside by themselves. ²⁹ Abimelekh asked Abraham, "What is the meaning of these seven ewes that you have set aside?"

"Take these seven ewes from my hand," replied [Abraham]. "It will be my proof that I dug this well."

³¹ That area was therefore called Beer-sheba,* since the two had made an oath there. ³² They thus made a treaty in Beer-sheba. Abimelekh and his general Pikhol then left, and they returned to the land of the Philistines.

³³ [Abraham] planted a tamarisk* tree in Beer-sheba, and there he called in the name of God, Lord of the Universe.* ³⁴ Abraham lived [there] in the land of the Philistines* for many days.

[53. The Test]

22   ¹ After these events, God tested Abraham.

"Abraham!" He said.

"Yes.*"

² "Take your son, the only one you love—Isaac—and go away to the Moriah* area. Bring him as an all-burned offering* on one of the mountains that I will designate to you."

³ Abraham got up early in the morning and saddled his donkey. He took

21:28 **seven female sheep.** In Hebrew, seven is *sheva,* having the same root as *shevua,* an oath. An oath thus obligates a person through everything that was made in the seven days of creation (Hirsch). It also obligates a person through the power of all the seven Noachide commandments (*Midrash HaGadol*). See note on 21:31.

21:31 **Beer-sheba.** *Beer Sheva* in Hebrew, literally, "Well of the Seven," alluding to the seven ewes (*Midrash HaGadol*). See note on 28:28. See above, notes on 20:15, 21:14.

21:33 **tamarisk.** *Eshel* in Hebrew (see Ibn Janach; Radak, *Sherashim*). Also see 1 Samuel 22:6, 31:13. The *Targum* also renders it as a tree. The tamarisk is a wide tree of the *Tamarix* family, with small leaves like a cypress. Some identify it with the *shittim* wood used in the Tabernacle (Exodus 25:5; cf. *Bereshith Rabbah* 94; *Tanchuma, Terumah* 9). In the Talmud, however, the *eshel* is identified as an orchard or an inn for wayfarers (*Sotah* 10a; Rashi).

—   **Lord of the Universe.** Or "Eternal Lord."

21:34 **Philistines.** Beer-sheba was on the border of the Philistine lands (see note on 20:15).

22:1 **Yes.** Literally, "Here I am," or "I am here." It is, however, an idiom denoting an answer to a summons; see 27:1, 31:1, 37:13, Exodus 3:4, 1 Samuel 3:4, 2 Samuel 1:7. See note on 15:4.

22:2 **Moriah.** This was the Temple Mount; 2 Chronicles 3:1. Some say that it was called Moriah because the Amorites lived there (Rashbam; see Syrian version of *Yov'loth* 18:2). It is in Jerusalem, 43 miles north of Beer-sheba.

—   **all-burned offering.** See note on 8:20.

Tamarisk

his two men with him, along with his son Isaac. He cut wood for the offering,   22
and set out, heading for the place that God had designated.

⁴ On the third day, Abraham looked up, and saw the place from afar.
⁵ Abraham said to his young men, "Stay here with the donkey. The boy and I
will go to that place. We will worship* and then return to you."

⁶ Abraham took the offering wood and placed it on [the shoulders of] his
son Isaac. He himself took the fire* and the slaughter knife, and the two of
them went together. ⁷ Isaac spoke up to Abraham.

"Father."

"Yes, my son."

"Here is the fire and the wood. But where is the lamb for the offering?"
⁸ "God will see to a lamb for an offering, my son," replied Abraham.
The two of them continued together. ⁹ When they finally came to the place
designated by God, Abraham built the altar there, and arranged the wood. He
then bound his son Isaac, and placed him on the altar on top of the wood.
¹⁰ Abraham reached out and took the slaughter knife to slit his son's throat.

¹¹ God's angel called to him from heaven and said, "Abraham!
Abraham!"

"Yes."

¹² "Do not harm* the boy. Do not do anything to him. For now I know
that you fear God. You have not withheld your only son from Him.*"

¹³ Abraham then* looked up and saw a ram caught by its horns in a
thicket. He went and got the ram, sacrificing it as an all-burned offering in his
son's place. ¹⁴ Abraham named the place "God will See" (*Adonoy Yir'eh*).*
Today, it is therefore said, "On God's Mountain, He will be seen."

¹⁵ God's angel called to Abraham from heaven a second time, ¹⁶ and said,
"God declares, 'I have sworn by My own Essence, that because you performed
this act, and did not hold back your only son, ¹⁷ I will bless you greatly, and
increase your offspring like the stars of the sky and the sand on the seashore.
Your offspring shall inherit* their enemies' gate. ¹⁸ All the nations of the
world shall be blessed through your descendants*—all because you obeyed
My voice.'"

22:5 **worship.** Literally, "prostrate ourselves."
22:6 **fire.** Either a fire bucket or flints for making fire.
22:12 **harm.** Literally, "put forth your hand," an idiom for "harm."
—   **Him.** Literally, "Me." But the angel is speaking in God's name.
22:13 **then.** (*Targum;* Rashi). Or, "saw a ram after it had been caught," or "after which it was caught;" (Hirsch; *HaKethav VeHaKabbalah*).
22:14 **Yireh.** As we have seen, the original name of the place was Salem (14:18). With *yireh* added to it, it became *Yeru-shalem* or Jerusalem (*Midrash Tehillim* 76).
22:17 **inherit.** Or "possess," or "conquer." Seizing the gate was symbolic of conquering the entire city.
22:18 **shall be blessed.** See above, 12:3, 18:18.

22   ¹⁹ Abraham returned to his young men, and together they set out and went
to Beer-sheba. Abraham remained in Beer-sheba.*

[54. Rebecca]

²⁰ After this, Abraham received a message: "Milcah has also had children
from your brother Nachor*: ²¹ Utz,* his first-born; Buz,* his brother, Kemuel
(father of Aram*), ²² Kesed,* Chazo, Pildash, Yidlaf and Bethuel. ²³ Bethuel
has had a daughter Rebecca.*'"

Milcah bore the above eight [sons] to Abraham's brother Nachor.
²⁴ [Nachor's] concubine* was named Reumah. She also had children: Tevach,
Gacham, Tachash* and Ma'akhah.*

Chayay Sarah   חַיֵּי שָׂרָה

[55. Sarah Dies]

23   ¹ Sarah had lived to be* 127 years old. [These were] the years of Sarah's
life. ² Sarah died in Kiryath Arba,* also known as Hebron,* in the land of

---

22:19   **in Beer-sheba.** See notes on 20:15, 21:34. According to Rashi, however, Abraham now lived in Hebron,
        and he only stopped in Beer-sheba for a short while. See note on 23:2.
22:20   **Milcah . . . Nachor.** See above, 11:29.
22:21   **Utz.** See 10:23, 36:28, Jeremiah 25:20, Lamentations 4:21. The Talmud identifies him with Job accord-
        ing to one opinion (*Yerushalmi, Sotah* 5:6). Others say that the land of Utz where Job lived was founded by
        this Utz (Ibn Ezra on Job 1:1).
—   **Buz.** Cf. Jeremiah 25:23. Some say that this was the grandfather of Elihu ben Barachel the Buzite (Ibn
        Ezra on Job 32:2; cf. *Sefer HaYashar* p. 58).
—   **Aram.** Significantly, there is another Aram identified with Utz (above, 10:23). It is possible that they were
        named after the earlier ones (Radak on 10:23). This would indicate that there were two Aramaean nations,
        one descended directly from Shem, and a second, younger one descended from Nachor. One
        source states that this Aram was the founder of Aram Naharaim (*Sefer HaYashar*, p. 58. See 24:10, Deu-
        teronomy 23:5). The word *avi* however, can be translated as "leader" rather than father, indicating that
        Kemuel was the leader of Aram. *Targum Yonathan* thus renders this verse, "Kemuel, the great magician of
        the Aramaeans."
22:22   **Kesed.** Possibly the ancestor of the Casdim (Radak; *Sefer HaYashar* p. 58).
22:23   **Bethuel . . . Rebecca.** See below, 24:45,47, 25:20.
22:24   **Concubine.** A common-law wife.
—   **Tachash.** Associated with the *tachash*, whose skins were used for the Tabernacle (Exodus 25:5; Zohar
        2:139a, 2:147b).
—   **Ma'akhah.** He is significant because he was the founder of a tribe whose land was captured by Manasseh
        (Deuteronomy 3:14), and who was later allowed to live with the Israelites (Joshua 13:13). Also see 2
        Samuel 10:6. There was a city Aram Ma'akhah (1 Chronicles 19:6) and Avel Beth Ma'akhah (1 Kings
        15:20, 2 Kings 15:29; 2 Samuel 20:14). On Deuteronomy 3:14 and elsewhere, the *Targum* identifies
        Ma'akhah with Epicoerus, between Calirrhoe and Livias, to the northeast of the Dead Sea (see Ptolemy,
        Geography 5:16:9). Avel Beth Ma'akhah, however, is 12 miles north of Lake Hula. Ma'akhah is generally
        believed to have lived in the Mount Hermon area.
23:1   **Sarah had lived . . .** Literally, "The life of Sarah was . . ."
23:2   **Kiryath Arba.** See 35:27. This was the original name for Hebron; see Joshua 14:15, Judges 1:10. Also see
        Joshua 15:54, 20:7. The name Kiryath Arba literally means "City of the Four," or "City of Arba." Some

Canaan. Abraham came to eulogize Sarah and to weep for her.   23

³ Abraham rose from beside his dead, and he spoke to the children of Heth.* ⁴ "I am an immigrant and a resident among you," he said. "Sell me property for a burial place with you so that I can bury my dead, [and not have her here] right in front of me."

⁵ The children of Heth replied to Abraham, saying to him, ⁶ "Listen to us, Sir. You are a prince of God in our midst. Take our best burial site* to bury your dead. No one among us will deny you his burial site to bury your dead."

⁷ Abraham rose, and he bowed down to the local people,* the children of Heth. ⁸ He spoke to them and said, "If you really want to help me bury my dead and [put her out of] my presence, listen to me, and speak up for me to Ephron* son of Tzohar. ⁹ Let him sell me the Makhpelah Cave,* which belongs to him, at the edge of his field. Let him sell it to me in your presence for its full price, as a burial property."

¹⁰ Ephron was then sitting among the children of Heth. Ephron the Hittite replied to Abraham in the presence of the children of Heth, so that all who came to the city gate could hear. ¹¹ "No, my lord," he said." "Listen to me. I have already given you the field. I have [also] given you the cave that is there. Here, in the presence of my countrymen, I have given it to you. Bury your dead."

¹² Abraham bowed down before the local people. ¹³ He spoke to Ephron so that all the local people could hear. "If you will only listen to me," he said.

---

say that Arba was the father of a number of giants who lived there (Joshua 15:13, 21:11), and according to this, Arba was the greatest of the Anak-giants (Ibn Ezra here; Joshua 14:15, Rashi ad loc.). It also could have been called "City of the Four" because four giants lived there, Sheshai, Achiman, Talmi, and their father (Rashi here; Numbers 13:22, Joshua 15:14, Judges 1:10. See Artscroll commentary). Others say that it was given this name because of the four pairs buried there: Adam and Eve, Abraham and Sarah, Isaac and Rebecca, and Jacob and Leah (*Bereshith Rabbah* 58; Rashi). According to the Talmud, the giant mentioned in Joshua 14:15 is Abraham (*Yerushalmi, Shabbath* 16:1), and hence "City of the Four" might have referred to the four allies, Abraham, Aner, Eshkol and Mamre (14:13, 14:24; *Bereshith Rabbah* 58). This name was still retained in later times; Nehemiah 11:25.

—   **Hebron.** This would appear to indicate that they lived in Hebron at the time. According to Talmudic tradition, Sarah died right after the Test (chapter 22), and they had lived in Hebron for the past 12 years. Thus, on the way back from Moriah, Abraham only stopped in Beer-sheba for a short while (see note on 22:19). According to other sources, they lived in Beer-sheba at this time, but Sarah was heading north toward Jerusalem to inquire about her husband and son when she died in Hebron (*Sefer HaYashar*, p. 64).

23:3   **children of Heth.** That is, the Hittites. See note on 10:15.

23:6   **burial site.** Or grave, tomb, or cemetery.

23:7   **local people.** Literally, "the people of the land."

23:8   **Ephron.** Significantly, there is a Mount Ephron some 6 miles northwest of Jerusalem (Joshua 15:9, 2 Chronicles 13:19).

23:9   **Makhpelah Cave.** Literally, "Doubler Cave." It was so named because it had two levels (*Targum; Eruvin* 53a; Rashi). The name also applied to the entire area; below 23:17,19. According to tradition, Adam and Eve had been buried there (*Yerushalmi, Taanith* 4:2). It can still be visited today.

23   "I am giving you the money for the field. Take it from me, and I will bury my
dead there."

¹⁴ Ephron replied to Abraham, saying to him, ¹⁵ "My lord, listen to me.
What's 400 silver shekels* worth of land between you and me? Bury your
dead."

¹⁶ Abraham understood what Ephron meant. He weighed out for Ephron
the silver that had been mentioned in the presence of the children of Heth,
400 shekels in negotiable currency.

¹⁷ Ephron's field in Makhpelah adjoining Mamre* thus became [Abra-
ham's] uncontested property. [This included] the field, its cave, and every tree
within its circumference. ¹⁸ It was Abraham's purchase with all the children of
Heth who came to the city gate as eyewitnesses. ¹⁹ Abraham then buried his
wife Sarah in the cave of Makhpelah Field, which adjoins Mamre (also known
as Hebron), in the land of Canaan.

²⁰ This is how the field and its cave became the uncontested property of
Abraham as a burial site, purchased from the children of Heth.

[56. A Wife for Isaac]

24   ¹ Abraham was old, well advanced in years, and God had blessed Abraham with everything. ² He said to the senior servant* of his household, who
was in charge of all that he owned, "Place your hand under my thigh.* ³ I
will bind you by an oath to God, Lord of heaven and earth, that you will not
take a wife for my son from the daughters of the Canaanites among whom I
live. ⁴ Instead, you must go to my native land, to my birthplace, and obtain a
wife for my son Isaac."

⁵ "But what if the girl does not want to come back with me to this land?"

23:15 **shekels.** A shekel was a unit of weight, equal to 22.8 grams or 0.8 ounces. A silver shekel was therefore a
little smaller than a silver dollar, and worth around $1.00. Abraham therefore paid 20 pounds of silver,
or about $400 for the cave. Considering land values at the time, this was highly excessive. Thus, for
example, King Omri paid only 6000 shekels for the entire territory of Samaria (1 Kings 16:25), and
Jeremiah paid only 17 shekels for a property that was at least as large as Makhpelah Field (Jeremiah
32:9). For comparison, according to the Hammurabi Code of that time, a year's wage for a working man
was between six and eight shekels.
23:17 **adjoining Mamre** (Chizzkuni). See above, 13:18. Josephus notes that the "Tree of Mamre" is approximately one half mile (6 furlongs) from Hebron proper (*Wars* 4:9:7).
24:2 **senior servant.** According to Talmudic tradition, this anonymous servant was Eliezer (above, 15:2; *Targum Yonathan; Yoma* 28b; Rashi).
—   **under my thigh.** This was a form often used for an oath; see below 47:29. According to Biblical idiom,
children issue from the "thigh" of the father (Genesis 46:26, Exodus 1:5, Judges 8:30), and hence, it is a
euphemism for the procreative organ. According to Talmudic tradition, the servant was to place his
hand near (Saadia; cf. Abarbanel) the holy sign of the covenant, just as in later times an oath would be
made on a Torah scroll (*Shevuoth* 38b; *Targum Yonathan;* Rashi). According to some, it was a sign of
obedience (Ibn Ezra).

asked the servant. "Shall I bring your son back to the land that you left?"   24

⁶ "Be most careful in this respect," replied Abraham. "Do not bring my son back there! ⁷ God, the Lord of heaven, took me away from my father's house and the land of my birth. He spoke to me and made an oath. 'To your offspring I will give this land.*' He will send His angel before you, and you will indeed find a wife there for my son. ⁸ If the girl does not want to come back with you, then you shall be absolved of my oath. But [no matter what,] do not bring my son back there!"

⁹ The servant placed his hand under the thigh of Abraham his master, and he took an oath regarding this. ¹⁰ The servant then took ten of his master's camels, bringing along the best things his master owned. He set off and went to Aram Naharayim,* to the city of Nachor.*

¹¹ [When he arrived,] he let the camels rest on their knees outside the city, beside the well. It was in the evening when women go out to draw water.

¹² He prayed, "O God, Lord of my master Abraham: Be with me today, and grant a favor to my master Abraham. ¹³ I am standing here by the well, and the daughters of the townsmen are coming out to draw water. ¹⁴ If I say to a girl, 'Tip over your jug and let me have a drink,' and she replies, 'Drink, and I will also water your camels,' she will be the one whom You have designated* for Your servant Isaac. [If there is such a girl,] I will know that You have granted a favor for my master."

¹⁵ He had not yet finished speaking, when Rebecca appeared. She had been born to Bethuel, the son of Milcah, the wife of Abraham's brother Nachor.* Her jug was on her shoulder. ¹⁶ The girl was extremely good-looking, [and] she was a virgin untouched by any man. The girl went down, filled her jug, and then came up again.

¹⁷ The servant ran toward her. "If you would, let me sip a little water from your jug," he said.

¹⁸ "Drink, Sir," she replied. She quickly lowered her jug to her hand and gave him a drink. ¹⁹ When he had finished drinking, she said, "Let me draw

---

24:7 **to your offspring** . . . See 12:7, 15:18 (Rashi).

24:10 **Aram Naharayim.** Literally, "Aram of the Rivers." It was called this because it was between the Euphrates and Tigris Rivers (Rashi). The area is thought to be in the great bend of the Euphrates. See next note.

— **city of Nachor.** Some say that this is Charan, where Abraham's brother Nachor (11:27,31) now lived (Ramban on 11:28; see note on 22:20). We thus find that Rebecca's brother Laban lived in Charan (27:43, 28:10, 29:4). This is approximately 450 miles north of Hebron. However, there is a city Nahur mentioned in ancient Mari documents, and this may have been a suburb of Charan.

24:14 **designated.** Or "indicated," "determined," or "selected." There is a question as to whether Torah law allows a person to ask for a sign of this type (see *Yad, Avodath Kokhavim* 11:4; Raavad *ad loc.*; *Yoreh Deah* 179:4 in *Hagah*).

24:15 **she had been born** . . . See 22:20.

24 water for your camels, so they can [also] drink their fill." ²⁰ She quickly emptied her jug into the trough and ran to the well again to draw water. She drew water for all his camels.

²¹ The man stood there gaping at her. But he remained silent, waiting to determine for certain whether or not God had made his journey successful.

²² When the camels had finished drinking, he took a gold ring* weighing half a shekel,* and two gold bracelets, weighing ten gold shekels,* for her arms. ²³ "Whose daughter are you?" he asked. "If you would, tell me if there is a place in your father's house for us to spend the night."

²⁴ She replied, "I am the daughter of Bethuel, son of Milcah, whom she bore to Nachor." ²⁵ She then said, "We have plenty of straw and fodder, as well as a place for people to spend the night."

²⁶ The man bowed low and prostrated himself to God. ²⁷ He said, "Blessed be God, Lord of my master Abraham, who has not withdrawn the kindness and truth that He grants to my master. Here I am, still on the road, and God has led me to the house of my master's close relatives!"

²⁸ The girl ran to her mother's quarters* and told her what had happened.

²⁹ Rebecca had a brother named Laban. He ran outside to the stranger,* to the well. ³⁰ He had seen the ring, and the bracelets on his sister's arms, and had heard his sister Rebecca relating what the man had said to her. He came to the stranger, who was still standing beside the camels near the well, ³¹ and said, "Come! [You're a man] blessed by God! Why are you still standing there outside? I have cleaned the house and prepared a place for the camels."

³² The stranger came into the house and unmuzzled the camels. [Laban] gave the camels straw and fodder, and provided water [for the stranger] and the men with him to wash their feet. ³³ Food was served, but [the stranger] said, "I will not eat until I have spoken my piece."

"Speak," replied [the host].

³⁴ [The stranger] said, "I am Abraham's servant. ³⁵ God granted my master a very great blessing, and he prospered. [God] granted him sheep, cattle, silver, gold, slaves, slavegirls, camels and donkeys. ³⁶ Finally, my master's

---

24:22 **ring.** *Nezem* in Hebrew. Here it is a nose ring (24:47). The word *nezem* itself, however, can denote either an ear ring (Genesis 35:4, Exodus 32:2) or a nose ring (Isaiah 3:21, Ezekiel 16:12; cf. Ibn Ezra). Some say that a *nezem* is an open ring.

— **half shekel.** *Beka* in Hebrew, equivalent to half a shekel (Exodus 38:26, Rashi *ad loc.*). The ring weighed a little less than half an ounce.

— **ten shekels.** Around 8 ounces. See note on 23:15.

24:28 **mother's quarters** (cf. *Bereshith Rabbah* 60; *Kethuvoth* 102b; Rashi). Literally, "[she] told it to her mother's house."

24:29 **stranger.** Literally, an anonymous "man." See 18:2.

Nezem

wife Sarah gave birth to a son for my master after she had grown very old, and [my master] gave him all that he owned. 24

[37] "My master bound me by an oath: 'Do not take a wife for my son from the daughters of the Canaanites, in whose land I live. [37] Instead, you must go to my father's house, to my family, and there you shall get a wife for my son.'

[39] "I said to my master, 'But what if the girl will not come back with me?' [40] He said to me, 'God, before whom I have walked, will send His angel with you and make your mission successful. But you must find a wife for my son from my family and from my father's house. [41] There is only one way that you can be free of my dread oath.* If you go to my family and they do not give you a girl, you will be released from my dread oath.'

[42] "Now today I came to the well, and I prayed, 'O God, Lord of my master Abraham, if You will, grant success to this mission that I am undertaking. [43] I am now standing by the town well. When a girl comes out to draw water, I will say to her, "Let me drink some water from your jug." [44] If she answers, "Not only may you drink, but I will also draw water for your camels," then she is the wife designated by God for my master's son.'

[45] "I had not yet finished speaking to myself, when Rebecca suddenly came out, carrying her jug on her shoulder. When she went down to the well and drew water, I said to her, 'Please give me a drink.' [46] She immediately lowered her jug and said, 'Drink! I will also water your camels.' I took a drink, and she also gave the camels water.

[47] "I questioned her and asked, 'Whose daughter are you?' She replied, 'I am a daughter of Bethuel, son of Nachor, whom Milcah bore to him.' I then placed a ring on her nose, and bracelets on her arms. [48] I bowed low and prostrated myself to God. I blessed God, Lord of my master Abraham, who led me on a true path to get a niece of my master for his son.

[49] "Now if you want to do what is kind and right to my master, tell me. If not, say so, and I will go to the right or to the left."

[50] Laban and Bethuel [both] spoke up. "It is something from God!" they said. "We cannot say anything to you, bad or good. [51] Rebecca is right here in front of you. Take her and go. Let her be a wife for your master's son, as God has spoken."

[52] When Abraham's servant heard these words, he prostrated himself on the ground to God.

[53] The servant brought out gold and silver jewelry, as well as articles of clothing, and gave them to Rebecca. He also gave precious gifts* to her

---

24:41 dread oath. *Alah* in Hebrew, also meaning a curse. It is thus an oath accompanied by a curse for not fulfilling it, as distinguished from a *shevuah* (see note on 21:28).
24:53 precious gifts (Ibn Ezra; Ibn Janach). Or "delicious fruits" (Rashi; cf. Radak, *Sherashim,* s.v. *Meged*).

24   brother and mother. ⁵⁴ He and his men then ate and drank, and they spent the night.

When they got up in the morning, [the servant] said, "Let me go back to my master."

⁵⁵ [The girl's] brother and mother replied, "[At least] let the girl remain with us for another year or ten [months].* Then she can go."

⁵⁶ "Do not delay me," said [the servant]. "God has already shown my mission to be successful. Let me leave, so that I can go to my master."

⁵⁷ "Let's call the girl and ask her personally," they replied.

They summoned Rebecca and said to her, "Do you want to go with this man?"

"I will go," she replied.

⁵⁹ They let their relative Rebecca go,* along with her attendant,* Abraham's servant, and his men. ⁶⁰ They blessed Rebecca and said to her, "Our sister, grow into thousands of myriads. May your descendants inherit the gate of their foes.*"

⁶¹ Rebecca set off with her girls, and they rode on the camels, following the stranger. The servant thus took Rebecca and left.

⁶² Isaac was on his way, coming from* Beer LaChai Roi.* He was then living in the Negev area. ⁶³ Isaac went out to meditate in the field toward evening. He raised his eyes, and saw camels approaching.

⁶⁴ When Rebecca looked up and saw Isaac, she fell* from the camel. ⁶⁵ She asked the servant, "Who is this man coming toward us in the field?"

"That is my master," replied the servant. [Rebecca] took her veil and covered herself.

⁶⁶ The servant told Isaac all that had happened. ⁶⁷ Isaac brought [the girl] into his mother Sarah's tent, and he married Rebecca. She became his wife, and he loved her. Isaac was then consoled for the loss of his mother.

24:55 **a year or ten months** (*Targum Yonathan; Kethuvoth* 57b; Rashi; Radak). Or, "a week or ten days" (cf. *Bereshith Rabbah* 60).

24:59 **let . . . go.** (cf. Exodus 5:1). It can also mean "sent off," "bid farewell," or "escorted."

—   **attendant.** Literally, "nurse." This may have been Deborah (35:8). It may also denote "childhood companions," see 24:61.

24:60 **inherit.** Or "conquer." See note on 22:17. This is a blessing given to brides to this very day.

24:62 **on his way, coming . . .** Literally, "came from coming." Others translate it, "Isaac was coming from his usual journeys to . . ." (*Targum;* Ramban; Rashbam; Radak).

—   **Beer LaChai Roi.** See 16:14. Isaac later lived there (25:11). Some say that he prayed there because this was where an angel had been seen (Ramban). Others maintain that he had gone to visit Hagar (*Bereshith Rabbah* 60; Rashi).

24:64 **fell.** Or, "almost fell" (Saadia).

[57. Abraham's Last Days]

25

¹ Abraham married another woman whose name was Keturah.* ² She bore him Zimran,* Yakshan, Medan,* Midian,* Yishbak and Shuach.* ³ Yakshan fathered Sheba and Dedan.* The sons of Dedan were the Ashurim, Letushim and Leumim.* ⁴ The sons of Midian* were Eiphah,* Epher,* Enoch,* Avidah and Elda'ah. All these were Keturah's descendants.

⁵ Abraham gave all that he owned to Isaac. ⁶ To the sons of the concubines that he had taken, Abraham [also] gave gifts. Then, while he was still alive, he sent them to the country of the East,* away from his son Isaac.

⁷ This, then, is the account of Abraham's years.* He lived a total of 175 years.* ⁸ Abraham breathed his last and died at a good age, old and satisfied, and he was gathered to his people.* ⁹ His sons, Isaac and Ishmael, buried him

---

25:1   **Keturah.** A concubine (1 Chronicles 1:32). Some sources identify her with Hagar (*Targum Yonathan; Bereshith Rabbah* 61; Rashi). Others, however, maintain that she was a third wife (*Bereshith Rabbah* 57; *Zohar* 1:133b; Ibn Ezra; Rashbam; Ramban on 25:6). One ancient source states that Hagar was already dead at this time (*Yov'loth* 19:13).

25:2   **Zimran.** See Radak on Jeremiah 25:25. Some identify him with Zabram, a major city between Mecca and Medina mentioned in Ptolemy's *Geography*. Josephus renders the name Zambran.

—   **Medan.** See 37:36. Possibly associated with Medina.

—   **Midian.** A well known nation, living to the northeast of the Gulf of Aqaba on the Arabian Peninsula, in what is now southern Jordan. See below, 37:28, 36:25. They were often involved with the Israelites; Numbers 22:4, Judges 7:12, 6:1, etc. Most significantly, Moses married a Midianite woman (Exodus 2:16).

—   **Shuach.** Job's friend in the land of Utz (10:23, 22:21) was Bildad from Shuach (Job 2:11, Ibn Ezra ad loc.). In ancient times there was a nation by the name of Sachia in western Arabia, to the east of Batanaea (Ptolemy, *Geography* 5:15).

25:3   **Sheba and Dedan.** See 10:7 and 10:28. The *Targum* on 1 Chronicles 1:32 translates these as Zmargad and M'zag, the same as on 1 Chronicles 1:9, and above 10:7 (see note there). Since the *Targum* relates them, the verse may be speaking of groups that lived in specific places, and not individuals. Josephus renders Sheba here as Shabathan.

—   **Ashurim . . .** A nation (Rashi; Josephus). See above 2:14, 10:11; below, note on 25:18. Possibly associated with Shur or Asir in Yemen. These are omitted in Chronicles. The *Targum* translates the three names here as, "caravan drivers, traders and colonists" (cf. *Targum Yonathan; Bereshith Rabbah* 61; Rashi; see *Targum* on 46:3).

25:4   **sons of Midian.** Midian had five kings, for each of these five nations; Numbers 31:8.

—   **Eiphah.** An Arabian tribe mentioned as bringing gold and incense in caravans from Sheba; Isaiah 60:6 (Rashi ad loc). The *Targum* on Isaiah 60:6 renders it Halad, while the *Targum* on 1 Chronicles 1:33 renders it Chavaled.

—   **Epher.** From which Africa received its name according to Josephus. He also quotes Alexander Polyhistor (c. 100–40 b.c.e.) that this Epher conquered Libya and gave it his name, Africa (*Antiquities* 1:15:1).

—   **Enoch.** *Chanokh* in Hebrew. See above, 4:17, 5:18.

25:6   **countries of the East.** It seems that all these lived in the Arabian peninsula, and Josephus supports this. He also writes that they took over the lands of the Troglodytes, an ancient people living along the Red Sea (*Antiquities* 1:15:1; see Herodotus 4:183; Didorus 3:31; Strabo 17:771).

25:7   **This then . . .** Literally, "These are the days of the years of Abraham's life that he lived;" see below 25:17. We interpret "days" here as being idiomatic for "account."

—   **175 years.** It can easily be seen from the dates given in scripture here that Isaac was 75 years old, and Ishmael 88 when Abraham died. Jacob and Esau were 15; see below, note on 25:29.

25:8   **gathered to his people.** A clear indication of immortality of the soul. See above; 15:15.

25 in Makhpelah Cave, in the field of Ephron son of Tzohar the Hittite, which borders Mamre. ¹⁰ The field that Abraham purchased from the children of Heth is thus where Abraham and his wife Sarah were buried.

¹¹ After Abraham died, God blessed Isaac, his son. Isaac lived in the vicinity of Beer LaChai Roi.*

[58. Ishmael]

¹² These are the chronicles of Ishmael son of Abraham, whom Hagar the Egyptian, Sarah's slave, bore to Abraham:

¹³ These are the names of Ishmael's sons in order of their birth: Nebayoth* (Ishmael's first-born), Kedar,* Adbiel,* Mibsam, ¹⁴ Mishma, Duma,* Masa,* ¹⁵ Chadad, Tema,* Yetur,* Nafish* and Kedmah. ¹⁶ These were Ishmael's sons, and these names were given to their towns and encampments. There were twelve princes* for their nations.

¹⁷ This is the account of Ishmael's years. He lived a total of 137 years. He breathed his last and died, and he was gathered to his people.

25:11 **Beer LaChai Roi.** See note on 24:62.

25:13 **Nebayoth.** *Nevayoth* in Hebrew. The Torah later specifies that it was his sister who married Esau (28:9, 36:3). It appears that the people of Nebayoth were nomads engaged in sheep-raising (Isaiah 16:7; Radak ad loc.). They are identified with the Nabateans, who lived in northern Arabia, to the south of the Dead Sea (*Targum* on 1 Chronicles 1:29; Josephus, *Antiquities* 1:12:4. See 1 Maccabees 5:25, 9:35; 2 Maccabees 5:8; Strabo 16:4; Pliny 12:37). Their capital was Petra, the ancient site of Kadesh (Strabo 16:799, 17:803; Pliny 6:32). Also see Josephus, *Antiquities* 14:3:3, 14:6:4.

— **Kedar.** The *Targum* renders this as Arabia; cf. Ezekiel 27:21. This was a well known nation; see Isaiah 21:16,17, 42:11, Jeremiah 2:10. They were an eastern tribe (Jeremiah 49:28), raising and dealing in sheep (Isaiah 60:17, Ezekiel 27:21), living in black tents (Song of Songs 1:5), and they were hostile (Psalms 120:5). They were associated with a city Chatzor (Jeremiah 49:28). Some identify them with the Kidru found in Assyrian writings, and with the Cedrei in ancient geographies (Pliny 5:11).

— **Adbiel.** The name is found in ancient Assyrian writings.

25:14 **Duma.** See Isaiah 21:11 (Radak, Ibn Ezra, ad loc., but see Rashi). Josephus renders it Idumas, perhaps relating it to Idumia. There was a place on the Syrian-Arabian border known as Duma or Dumath Algandel. There is also a Duma in Syria, some 10 miles east of Damascus. Domita is mentioned by Ptolemy (5:19).

— **Masa.** See Genesis 10:30, Exodus 17:7. The name is found in ancient Assyrian writings.

25:15 **Tema.** It is associated with Arabia (Isaiah 21:14), especially with Dedan and Buz (Jeremiah 25:23). This was also a people who had caravans associated with Sheba (Job 6:19). It was a nation that lived in the northern Arabian desert. It may be associated with the present city of Tayma in Saudi Arabia. The *Targum* on 1 Chronicles 1:30 renders it Adroma, literally "the south." There is an area known as Hadramut in southern Arabia.

— **Yetur.** Yetur and Nafish were driven out of the area east of the Jordan by Reuben, Gad and Manasseh (1 Chronicles 5:19; Rashi ad loc.). This is in the exact area of Ituraea, northeast of Lake Hula (see Strabo 16:755; Pliny 5:19). They originally came from another area named Ituraea in the Arabian Desert (Strabo 16:756). They then settled in the mountain range to the north and south of Damascus, in regions where it was difficult to reach them. During the time of the Second Temple, the Hasmonean King Aristoblus forced the people of Ituraea to convert to Judaism and annexed their territory to Judea (Josephus, *Antiquities* 13:11:3). The area was later annexed to Syria by the Romans (Tacticus, *Annals* 12:23).

— **Nafish.** See above note, from 1 Chronicles 5:19.

25:16 **twelve princes.** See above 17:20.

¹⁸ [His descendants] lived in the area from Havilah* to Shur* (which   25
borders on Egypt), all the way to Assyria.* They overran all their brethren.*

Toledoth   תּוֹלְדוֹת

[59. Jacob and Esau]

¹⁹ These are the chronicles of Isaac son of Abraham:

Abraham was Isaac's father. ²⁰ When Isaac was 40 years old, he married
Rebecca, daughter of Bethuel the Aramaean of Padan Aram* and sister of
Laban the Aramaean.

²¹ His wife was sterile, and Isaac pleaded with God for her sake. God
granted his plea, and Rebecca became pregnant. ²² But the children clashed
inside her, and when this occurred,* she asked, "Why is this happening to
me?" She went to seek a message from God.

²³ God's word to her was, "Two nations are in your womb. Two governments will separate from inside you. The upper hand will go from one
government to the other. The greater one will serve the younger.*'"

²⁴ When the time came for her to give birth, there were twins in her womb.
²⁵ The first one came out reddish,* as hairy* as a fur coat. They named him

---

25:18 Havilah. See above, 2:11, 10:7, 10:29. Saul also pursued the Amelikes between Shur and Havilah; 1
Samuel 15:7. Others interpret this expression as Havilah-by-Shur to distinguish from other places
known as Havilah.
— **Shur.** See above; 16:7, 20:1.
— **Assyria.** All the way to the north; see above, 2:14, 10:11. Some associate this with Asshurim mentioned
in 25:3.
— **They overran. . .** (Cf. Rashi; Hirsch). See 16:12. This would mean that the Ishmaelite Arabs would take
over the territory of Abraham's other sons, dominating the entire Middle East. Literally, "on the face of
all his brethren he fell." Others interpret it, "He traveled among all his brothers" as a nomad (Ibn Ezra).
Another interpretation is, "He died in the presence of all his brethren" (Ibn Ezra). See note on 37:28.
25:20 Padan Aram. Some sources state that this is identical with Aram Naharaim mentioned above in 24:10
(Radak). Others write that *padan* means a yoke or field, and that this is the Field of Aram (Hosea 12:13),
the area between Aram Naharaim and Aram Tzova (Allepo) (Rashi; Ibn Ezra). Charan is about 100 miles
northeast of Allepo. The word *padan* is found to mean a pair (*Targum* on 1 Samuel 11:7). The area is
sometimes simply called Padan alone (Genesis 48:7). Also see Daniel 11:45.
25:22 when this occurred . . . (Hirsch). Otherwise, the expression here is very ambiguous: "If so, why am I
thus?" Some interpret it; "If this is the way it must be, why go on?" (Ramban; cf. *Bereshith Rabbah* 63).
Other interpretations are, "If [there is such pain], why did we pray for children?" (Rashi); "Why am I
having such an unusual pregnancy?" (Ibn Ezra; Radak); or, "If I am upright, why is this happening?"
(*HaKethav VeHaKabbalah*).
25:23 The greater one . . . Rebecca thus knew that Jacob would be the chosen one. This explains 25:28 and
28:5.
25:25 reddish. Either with a ruddy complexion (Ibn Janach; cf. *Midrash HaGadol*) or with red hair (cf. *Torah
Sh'lemah* 131). Cf. 1 Samuel 16:12. Others translate *admoni* as "manly" (*Chizzkuni*; cf. Josephus, *Antiquities* 1:18:1). In any case, the word is a play on Edom, see below, 25:30.
— **hair.** *Se'ar* in Hebrew, from which Seir is derived (cf. 32:4; see Josephus, *Antiquities* 1:18:1; *Torah Sh'lemah*
141). See below, 27:11.

25 Esau.* ²⁶ His brother then emerged, and his hand was grasping Esau's heel. [Isaac*] named him Jacob.* Isaac was 60 years old* when [Rebecca] gave birth to them.

²⁷ The boys grew up. Esau became a skilled trapper, a man of the field. Jacob was a scholarly* man who remained with the tents. ²⁸ Isaac enjoyed eating Esau's game and favored him,* but Rebecca favored Jacob.*

²⁹ Jacob was once simmering a stew,* when Esau came home exhausted from the field.* ³⁰ Esau said to Jacob, "Give me a swallow of that red stuff! I'm famished!" (He was therefore given the name Edom*).

³¹ "First sell me your birthright,*" replied Jacob.

³² "Here I'm about to die!" exclaimed Esau. "What good is a birthright to me?"

³³ "Make an oath to me right now," said Jacob.

He made the oath, and sold his birthright to Jacob. ³⁴ Jacob then gave Esau bread and lentil stew. [Esau] ate it, drank, got up and left. He thus rejected the birthright.

[60. Isaac and the Philistines]

26 ¹ There was a famine in the land, aside from the first famine in the time of Abraham.* Isaac went to Abimelekh* king of the Philistines in Gerar.*

— **Esau.** *Esav* in Hebrew; literally "made" or "completed" (Rashbam; cf. *Lekach Tov*).
25:26 Isaac. (cf. Rashi; *Yerushalmi, Berakhoth* 1:6). According to others, it was God who named him (Rashi).
— **Jacob.** *Yaakov* in Hebrew, literally "he will heel," because he was grasping Esau's heel. See below, 27:36. Also see Hosea 12:4.
— **60 years old.** Jacob and Esau were therefore born in the year 2108.
25:27 scholarly (cf. Rashi; *Targum Yonathan;* Saadia). *Tam.* in Hebrew, also meaning simple, plain, quiet, perfect (*Targum*), or single-minded (Hirsch). See note on 6:9.
25:28 Isaac favored . . . Isaac saw that Esau was careful to honor his parents, and could therefore be trusted to keep the tradition from previous generations (see note on 27:4). Others interpret this sentence, "Isaac loved Esau because he was a trapper with his mouth," that is, a smooth talker (*Tanchuma* 8; Rashi; Hirsch).
— **Rebecca favored Jacob.** See note on 25:23.
25:29 Jacob . . . According to tradition, this was the consolation meal prepared after Abraham's death (*Targum Yonathan; Bava Bathra* 16b). See *Yov'loth* 24:3.
— **Esau came . . .** There is a tradition that he had just killed Nimrod (above, 10:8. See *Baaley Tosafoth.* Also see Rashi, *Pesachim* 54b s.v. *Bigdo*).
25:30 Edom. Literally red. See above, 25:25. Also see below 32:4, 36:1, 36:8, 36:19, etc. In later times, the Greeks called Edom, Idumia (Josephus, *Antiquities* 2:1:1).
25:31 birthright. This meant that Jacob would now be the primary heir and would also serve as the family priest (Rashi).
26:1 first famine. Above, 12:10. This chapter is the only place where we see Isaac without Abraham or Jacob, and it is here that we see Isaac's life literally as a carbon copy of Abraham's (see 26:18). While it had been Abraham's task to blaze spiritual trails, it was Isaac's mission to consolidate them.
— **Abimelekh.** Probably not the same as the one involved with Abraham; see note on 20:2. According to one source, this was the previous Abimelekh's son (*Targum* on 26:28).
— **Gerar.** See above, 20:1. It was on the boundary of the Holy Land, 10:19. From the context, it seems that Isaac was headed toward Egypt. This is difficult to understand, since Isaac lived in Beer Lachai Roi

[2] God appeared to [Isaac] and said, "Do not go down to Egypt. Remain **26** undisturbed in the land that I shall designate to you. [3] Remain an immigrant in this land. I will be with you and bless you, since it will be to you and your offspring that I will give all these lands. I will thus keep the oath that I made to your father Abraham. [4] I will make your descendants as numerous as the stars of the sky,* and grant them all these lands. All the nations on earth shall be blessed through your descendants.* [5] All this is because Abraham obeyed My voice, and kept My charge, My commandments, My decrees, and My laws."

[6] Isaac thus settled in Gerar. [7] When the local men asked about his wife, he told them that she was his sister. He was afraid to say that she was his wife. Rebecca was so good-looking that the local men could have killed him because of her.

[8] Once, after [Isaac] had been there for some time, Abimelekh, king of the Philistines, was looking out the window, and he saw Isaac enjoying himself with his wife Rebecca. [9] Abimelekh summoned Isaac. "But she is your wife!" he said. "How could you have said that she is your sister?"

"I was afraid that I would die because of her," replied Isaac.

[10] "What have you done to us?" demanded Abimelekh. "One of the people could easily have slept with your wife! You would have made us commit a terrible crime!"

[11] Abimelekh issued an order to all the people: "Whoever touches this man or his wife shall die."

[12] Isaac farmed in the area. That year, he reaped a hundred times [as much as he sowed], for God had blessed him. [13] This was the beginning of his prosperity. He then continued to prosper until he became extremely wealthy. [14] He had flocks of sheep, herds of cattle, and a large retinue of slaves.

The Philistines became jealous of him. [15] They plugged up all the wells that his father's servants had dug while Abraham was still alive, and they filled them with earth.

[16] Abimelekh said to Isaac, "Go away from us. You have become much more powerful than we are."

[17] Isaac left the area and camped in the Gerar Valley,* intending to settle there. [18] He redug the wells that had been dug in the days of his father Abra-

(25:11), which is to the west of Gerar, on the way to Egypt. It is possible that Isaac went to Gerar because of Abraham's previous treaty (cf. Ramban). Alternatively, this is connected to the following sentence, and Isaac went to Gerar at God's command (Josephus, *Antiquities* 1:18:2). However, see note on 20:1.

26:4 **stars of the sky.** See above, 15:5, 22:17.

— **shall be blessed . . .** See above, 12:3, 22:18.

26:17 **Gerar Valley.** or Gerar Wadi (Saadia). A wadi is a stream or river that flows primarily during the rainy season. There is such a wadi connecting Gerar and Beer-sheba, flowing to the south. See note on 20:1.

26   ham, which had been plugged up by the Philistines after Abraham's death. He
gave them the same names that his father had given them.

[19] Isaac's servants then dug in the valley, and found a new well, brimming
over with fresh water. [20] The shepherds of Gerar disputed with Isaac's
shepherds, claiming that the water was theirs. [Isaac] named the well Challenge (*Esek*), because they had challenged him.

[21] They dug another well, and it was also disputed. [Isaac] named it
Accusation (*Sitnah**).

[22] He then moved away from there and dug another well. This time it was
not disputed, so he named it Wide Spaces (*Rechovoth**). "Now God will grant
us wide open spaces," he said. "We can be fruitful in the land."

[23] From there, [Isaac] went up to Beer-sheba. [24] God appeared to him that
night and said, "I am God of your father Abraham. Do not be afraid, for I am
with you. I will bless you and grant you very many descendants because of My
servant Abraham."

[25] [Isaac] built an altar there and called in God's name. He set up his tents
there, and his servants dug a well in the area.

[26] Abimelekh came to [Isaac] from Gerar, along with a group of friends
and his general Pikhol.* [27] "Why have you come to me?" asked Isaac. "You
hate me; you drove me away from you!"

[28] "We have indeed seen that God is with you," they replied. "We propose
that there now be a dread oath between you and us. Let us make a treaty with
you, [29] that just as we did not touch you, you will do no harm to us. We did
only good to you and let you leave in peace. Now you are the one who is
blessed by God."

[30] [Isaac] prepared a feast for them, and they ate and drank. [31] They got up
early in the morning, and made a mutual oath. Isaac then bid them farewell,
and they left in peace.

[32] On that very day, Isaac's servants came and told him about the well they
had been digging. "We have found water!" they announced. [33] [Isaac] named
the well Shibah.* The city is therefore called Beer-sheba* to this very day.

26:21 **Sitnah.** See Ezra 4:6. This has the same root as Satan.
26:22 **Rechovoth.** There is a well known as Rehueibeh 20 miles southwest of Beer-sheba, equidistant between
  Beer-sheba and the site of Gerar. We thus see that Isaac was following the wadi from Gerar to Beer-
  sheba.
26:26 **Pikhol.** Probably a title, see note on 21:22. This was some 75 years after Abimelekh and Pikhol had
  made a similar treaty with Abraham, above 21:22-32.
26:33 **Shibah.** *Shivah* in Hebrew. This is the masculine for seven, while Sheba (*sheva*) is the feminine. See above,
  note on 21:31. Some say that this was the well that Abraham dug in Beer-sheba (21:25), which had been
  plugged up by the Philistines (Ramban), while others maintain that it was a new well (Rashbam).
— **Beer-sheba.** Abraham had given the name only to the well or the district (see 21:14), while Isaac gave it

[61. Esau Marries]

³⁴ When Esau was forty years old,* he married Judith* daughter of Beeri* 26
the Hittite,* and Basemath* daughter of Elon the Hittite. ³⁵ [His wives]
became a source of spiritual bitterness to Isaac and Rebecca.

[62. The Blessing]

¹ Isaac had grown old and his eyesight was fading. He summoned his elder **27**
son Esau.

"My son."

"Yes."

² "I am old and I have no idea when I will die. ³ Now take your equipment, your dangler* and bow, and go out in the field to trap me some game.
⁴ Make it into a tasty dish, the way I like it,* and bring it to me to eat. My soul
will then bless you before I die."

⁵ Rebecca had been listening while Isaac was speaking to Esau, his son.
Esau went out to the field to trap some game and bring it home.

⁶ Rebecca said to her son Jacob, "I just heard your father speaking to your
brother Esau. He said, ⁷ 'Bring me some game and prepare it into something
tasty. I will eat it and bless you in God's presence before I die.' ⁸ Now, my son,
listen to me. Heed my instructions carefully. ⁹ Go to the sheep and take two
choice young kids. I will prepare them with a tasty recipe, just the way your
father likes them. ¹⁰ You must then bring it to your father, so that he will eat it
and bless you before he dies.*'"

¹¹ "But my brother Esau is hairy," replied Jacob. "I am smooth-skinned.

to the city that subsequently sprung up in the area (Radak). Moreover, Isaac's designation became the
place's permanent name (Rabbi Menasheh ben Yisroel, *Conciliator* 48).
26:34 40 years old. Emulating his father Isaac (25:20; *Bereshith Rabbah* 65; Rashi).
— **Judith.** *Yehudith* in Hebrew, a name that subsequently became popular among Jews. Some say that Esau
    did not have any children by this Judith. Others identify her with Oholibamah in 36:2, (see Rashi ad
    loc.; Josephus, *Antiquities* 1:18:4).
— **Beeri.** The name is also found in Hosea 1:1.
— **Hittite.** See above, 10:15, 15:20, 23:5.
— **Basemath.** Some say that she was the Adah bath Elon in 36:2 (Ibn Ezra here, Rashi on 36:2. Also see
    36:10,13,17). Some say that Esau's wives were from the land of Seir (*Sefer HaYashar*, p. 73). The fathers of
    Esau's wives were great lords among the Canaanites (Radak; Josephus).
27:2 dangler. *Teli* in Hebrew, variously translated as sword (Onkelos; Rashi) or quiver (*Targum Yonathan;*
    Rashbam; Radak, Ibn Ezra). The word, however, suggests something hanging, like a bolo or lasso, that
    would be used to *trap* game.
27:4 the way I like it. See above, 25:28. Isaac wanted Esau to have the merit of parental honor, since this
    would make him worthy of a spiritual blessing (Sforno). Isaac may have known of Esau's shortcomings,
    but felt that the blessing would improve him (Radak). Isaac was not aware of the prophecy (25:23) or of
    the fact that the birthright legally belonged to Jacob (25:33), and hence the blessing would automatically
    go to Esau (Ramban).
27:10 you must bring . . . Rebecca was aware that the blessing was rightfully Jacob's (see previous note). With-
    out this ruse, however, it might have been impossible for Jacob to obtain it.

27 ¹² Suppose my father touches me. He will realize that I am an imposter! I will gain a curse rather than a blessing!"

¹³ "Let any curse be on me, my son," said the mother. "But listen to me. Go, bring me what I asked."

¹⁴ [Jacob] went and fetched what his mother had requested. She took [the kids] and prepared them, using the tasty recipe that [Jacob's] father liked best. ¹⁵ Rebecca then took her older son Esau's best clothing, which she had in her keeping, and put them on her younger son Jacob. ¹⁶ She [also] placed the young goats' skins on his arms and on the hairless parts of his neck.

¹⁷ Rebecca handed to her son Jacob the delicacy, and the bread she had baked. ¹⁸ He came to his father.

"Father."

"Yes. Who are you, my son?"

¹⁹ "It is I, Esau, your first-born," said Jacob. "I have done as you asked. Sit up, and eat the game I trapped, so that your soul will bless me."

²⁰ "How did you find it so quickly, my son?" asked Isaac.

"God your Lord was with me."

²¹ "Come closer to me," said Isaac to Jacob. "Let me touch you, my son. Are you really Esau or not?"

²² Jacob came closer to his father Isaac, and [Isaac] touched him. He said, "The voice is Jacob's voice, but the hands are the hands of Esau." ²³ He did not realize who it was because there was hair on [Jacob's] arms, just like those of his brother Esau. [Isaac] was about to bless him.

²⁴ "But are you *really* my son Esau?"

"I am."

²⁵ "Then serve me [the food]. I will eat the game that my son trapped, so that my soul may bless you."

[Jacob] served it, and [Isaac] ate. He then brought [Isaac] some wine, and he drank it.

²⁶ His father Isaac said to him, "Come closer and kiss me, my son."

²⁷ [Jacob] approached and kissed him. [Isaac] smelled the fragrance of his garments, and blessed him.

He said, "See, my son's fragrance is like the perfume of a field blessed by God.

²⁸ "May God grant you the dew of heaven and the fat of the earth, much grain and wine. ²⁹ Nations will serve you; governments will bow down to you. You shall be like a lord over your brother; your mother's children will prostrate themselves to you. Those who curse you are cursed, and those who bless you are blessed.*"

27:29 those who curse you . . . See 12:3.

³⁰ Isaac had finished blessing Jacob, and Jacob had just left his father **27** Isaac, when his brother Esau came back from his hunt. ³¹ He had also prepared a delicacy and brought it to his father. "Let my father get up and eat his son's venison," he said, "so that your soul may bless me."

³² "Who are you?" asked his father Isaac.

"I am your first-born, Esau," he replied.

³³ Isaac was seized with a violent fit of trembling. "Who . . . where . . . is the one who trapped game and just served it to me? I ate it all before you came and I blessed him. The blessing will remain his.*"

³⁴ When Esau heard his father's words, he let out a most loud and bitter scream. "Bless me too, Father," he pleaded.

³⁵ "Your brother came with deceit, and he already took your blessing."

³⁶ "Isn't he truly named Jacob (*Ya'akov*)! He went behind my back (*akav*) twice. First he took my birthright, and now he took my blessing!"

[Esau] pleaded, "Couldn't you have saved me a blessing too?"

³⁷ Isaac tried to answer. "But I made him like a lord over you," he said. "I have given him all his brothers as slaves. I have associated him* with the grain and the wine. Where . . . what . . . can I do for you, my son?"

³⁸ Esau said to his father, "Is there only one blessing that you have, my father? Father! Bless me too!" Esau raised his voice and began to weep.

³⁹ His father Isaac then replied and said, "The fat places of the earth can still be your dwelling, and [you can still have] the dew of heaven. ⁴⁰ But you shall live by your sword. You may have to serve your brother, but when your complaints mount up, you will throw his yoke off your neck."

⁴¹ Esau was furious at Jacob because of the blessing that his father had given him. He said to himself, "The days of mourning for my father will be here soon. I will then be able to kill my brother Jacob."

⁴² Her older son's plans were reported to Rebecca. She sent word and summoned her younger son Jacob. "Your brother Esau is consoling himself by planning to kill you," she said. ⁴³ "Now, my son, listen to me. Set out and flee to my brother Laban in Charan. ⁴⁴ Remain with him awhile until your brother's anger has subsided. ⁴⁵ When your brother has calmed down from his rage against you, and has forgotten what you have done to him, I will send word and summon you home. But why should I lose you both on the same day?"

⁴⁶ Rebecca said to Isaac, "I am disgusted with life because of those Hittite

---

27:33 The blessing will remain his. Literally, "He will also be blessed." Isaac realized that since the blessing had been granted with divine inspiration, it was valid, and Jacob was the one chosen by God (*Bereshith Rabbah* 67; Sforno).

27:37 I have associated him. "I have placed him close" (Radak), or "I have supported him with" (*Targum*).

women.* If Jacob marries such a Hittite girl, from the daughters of this land, why should I go on living?"

28   ¹ Isaac summoned Jacob and gave him a blessing and a charge. "Do not marry a Canaanite girl,*" he said. ² "Set out and go to Padan Aram, to the house of your maternal grandfather Bethuel. Marry a daughter of your uncle Laban. ³ God Almighty will then bless you, make you fruitful, and increase your numbers. You will become an assembly of nations.* ⁴ He will grant Abraham's blessing to you and your descendants, so that you will take over the land which God gave to Abraham, where you previously lived only as a foreigner."

⁵ Isaac then sent Jacob on his way. [Jacob] headed toward Padan Aram, to Laban son of Bethuel the Aramaean, the brother of Rebecca, Jacob and Esau's mother.

⁶ Esau saw that Isaac had blessed Jacob and sent him to Padan Aram to find a wife, including in his blessing the charge, "Do not marry a Canaanite girl." ⁷ [He also knew that] Jacob had obeyed his father and mother, and had gone to Padan Aram. ⁸ Esau understood that the Canaanite girls were displeasing to his father Isaac.

⁹ Esau therefore went to Ishmael and married Machlath* daughter of Abraham's son Ishmael, a sister of Nebayoth,* in addition to his other wives.*

VaYetze   וַיֵּצֵא

[63. Jacob's Journey]

¹⁰ Jacob left Beer-sheba* and headed toward Charan.* ¹¹ He came to a familiar place and spent the night there because the sun had already set. Taking some stones, he placed them at his head and lay down to sleep there.

¹² He had a vision in a dream. A ladder was standing on the ground, and

---

27:46 **Hittite women.** See 26:34.
28:1   **Do not marry . . .** See 24:3.
28:3   **assembly of nations.** See 17:5.
28:9   **Machlath.** Not mentioned again. Some say that she is the Basemath mentioned in 36:3 (*Yerushalmi, Bikkurim* 3:3; cf. Josephus, *Antiquities* 1:18:8).
—   **sister of Nebayoth.** See above 25:13. Some say that Nebayoth is mentioned because Ishmael had more than one wife (Ibn Ezra). There is a tradition that Ishmael died at this point, and Nebayoth gave his sister to Esau (*Megillah* 14a; Rashi).
—   **in addition to . . .** See 26:34.
28:10 **Beer-sheba.** Where Isaac lived, above 26:33. However, some say that Isaac then lived in Hebron (see 35:27), and that Jacob had gone to Beer-sheba to pray (Ramban on 28:17). Others maintain that Isaac moved to Hebron later (*Yov'loth* 29:19).
—   **Charan.** See above, 11:31, note on 24:10.

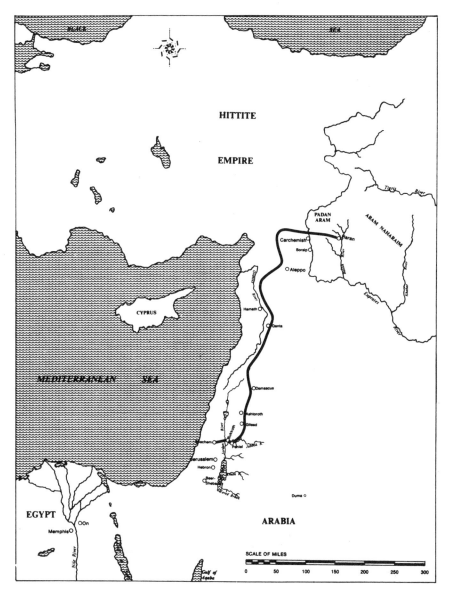

PLATE 8.   JACOB'S JOURNEY

28 its top reached up toward heaven.* God's angels were going up and down on
it. [13] Suddenly he saw God standing over him.*

[God] said, "I am God, Lord of Abraham your father, and Lord of Isaac. I
will give to you and your descendants the land upon which you are lying.
[14] Your descendants will be like the dust of the earth.* You shall spread out to
the west, to the east, to the north, and to the south. All the families on earth
will be blessed through you and your descendants.* [15] I am with you. I will
protect you wherever you go and bring you back to this soil. I will not turn
aside from you until I have fully kept this promise to you."

[16] Jacob awoke from his sleep. "God is truly in this place," he said, "but I
did not know it." [17] He was frightened. "How awe-inspiring this place is!" he
exclaimed. "It must be God's temple. It is the gate to heaven!"

[18] Jacob got up early in the morning and took the stone that he had placed
under his head. He stood it up as a pillar and poured oil on top of it. [19] He
named the place God's Temple (Beth El*). The town's original name, however,
had been Luz.*

[20] Jacob made a vow. "If God will be with me," he said, "if He will protect
me on the journey that I am taking, if He gives me bread to eat and clothing
to wear, [21] and if I return in peace to my father's house, then I will dedicate
myself totally to God.* [22] Let this stone that I have set up as a pillar become a
temple to God.* Of all that You give me, I will set aside a tenth* to You."

29   [1] Jacob set off briskly, and headed toward the land of the people of the
East. [2] [He came to a place] where he saw a well in a field. Three flocks of
sheep were lying beside it, since it was from this well that the flocks were
watered. The top of the well was covered with a large stone. [3] When all the
flocks would come together there, [the shepherds] would roll the stone from

---

28:12 **ladder** . . . The ladder represented all the spiritual levels, which would now be given to Jacob and his descendants. It was shown to him now, when Jacob was about to start a family.

28:13 **over him** (Saadia). Or, "near him" (cf. Exodus 18:13). Or, "on top of it (the ladder)" (*Bereshith Rabbah*
69). See note on Deuteronomy 27:12.

28:14 **dust of the earth.** See above, 13:16, 15:5, 22:17.

—   **all the families** . . . Above, 12:3, 18:18, 22:18, 26:4.

28:19 **God's Temple.** We render this Beth El instead of Bethel. According to many authorities, Jacob was lying
on the place of the Holy of Holies in Jerusalem (*Pesachim* 88a; *Pirkey Rabbi Eliezer* 35; Ramban). Hence, it
was literally the "gate of heaven" (see *Jerusalem, Eye of the Universe*, p. 50). From Beer-sheba to Jerusalem
is 42 miles, a good day's journey (see note on 30:36). According to others, however, this was the Bethel
which was Abraham's first home in the Holy Land (12:8).

—   **Luz.** See 35:6, 48:3; Rashi on Joshua 16:2, 18:13, Judges 1:23. Also see Judges 1:26. According to those
who say that Beth El is in Jerusalem, there were two villages there, Salem (14:18) and Luz.

28:21 **I will dedicate myself** . . . Literally, "God will be my Lord" (cf. Ramban; Sforno; Hirsch). Others have it
as part of the condition: "and if God will be my Lord"—that is, "If God will be uniquely associated
with me and my children forever" (Rashi).

28:22 **temple** . . . It was later the place of the Holy of Holies (see note on 22:19).

—   **tenth.** Literally a tithe. See note on 14:20.

the top of the well and water the sheep. Then they would replace the stone on the well.

⁴ [Some shepherds were there.] "From where do you come, brothers?" asked Jacob.

"We are from Charan."

⁵ "Do you know Nachor's grandson, Laban?"

"We know him."

⁶ "Is he doing well?"

"Well enough! Here's his daughter Rachel, coming with the sheep."

⁷ "But it's still the middle of the day. It's not yet time to bring the livestock together. Why not water the sheep and go on grazing?"

⁸ "We can't until all the flocks have come together. [All of us] then roll the stone from the top of the well. Only then can we water the sheep."

⁹ While he was still conversing with them, Rachel appeared with her father's sheep. She was the shepherdess. ¹⁰ Jacob looked at his cousin Rachel who was with his uncle Laban's sheep. He stepped forward, and rolled the stone from the top of the well, watering his uncle Laban's sheep.

¹¹ Jacob kissed Rachel and wept aloud. ¹² He told her that he was Rebecca's son, and thus related to her father. She ran to tell her father.

¹³ When Laban heard the news that Jacob had arrived, he ran to greet him. He embraced and kissed him, and brought him home. [Jacob] told Laban all that had happened. ¹⁴ "Yes indeed, you are my own flesh and blood,*" said Laban.

Jacob remained with him for a month. ¹⁵ Laban then said to Jacob, "Just because you are my close relative, does it mean that you must work for me for nothing? Tell me what you want to be paid."

¹⁶ Laban had two daughters. The older one's name was Leah, and the younger one's name was Rachel. ¹⁷ Leah had lovely eyes,* while Rachel was shapely and beautiful.

¹⁸ Jacob had fallen in love with Rachel. "I will work for you seven years for Rachel, your younger daughter," he said.

¹⁹ "Better I should give her to you than to another man," replied Laban. "You can stay with me."

²⁰ Jacob worked seven years for Rachel. But he loved her so much, it seemed like no more than a few days. ²¹ Finally Jacob said to Laban, "The time is up. Give me my bride and let me marry her."

²² [Laban] invited all the local people and made a wedding feast. ²³ In the

---

29:14 **flesh and blood.** Literally, "bone and flesh;" see 2:23.
29:17 **lovely eyes.** (*Targum;* Tur). Others have "weak eyes," or "sensitive eyes."

29 evening, he took his daughter Leah and brought her to [Jacob] who consummated the marriage with her. [24] Laban had also given his servant Zilpah to his daughter Leah to be her handmaid.*

[25] In the morning, [Jacob discovered that] it was Leah. He said to Laban, "How could you do this to me? Didn't I work with you for Rachel? Why did you cheat me?"

[26] "In our country it is something that is simply not done!" replied Laban. "[We never] give a younger daughter in marriage before the first-born. [27] But wait until this week [of wedding celebrations*] for [Leah] is over. Then we will give you the other girl—in return for the work that you will do for me for another seven years."

[28] Jacob complied and completed the week of celebration for [Leah]. [Laban] then gave him his daughter Rachel as a wife.* [29] To his daughter Rachel, Laban gave his servant Bilhah* as a handmaid.

[30] [Jacob] thus also married Rachel, and he loved Rachel more than Leah. He worked for [Laban] another seven years.

[31] [God saw that Leah was unloved, and He opened her womb. Rachel remained barren.

[32] Leah became pregnant and gave birth to a son. She named him Reuben.* "God has seen my troubles," she said. "Now my husband will love me."

[33] She became pregnant again and had a son. "God has heard (shama) that I was unloved," she said, "and He also gave me this son." She named the child Simeon (Shim'on).

[34] She became pregnant again and had a son. "Now my husband will become attached* (lavah) to me," she said, "because I have given him three sons." [Jacob] therefore named the child Levi.

[35] She became pregnant again and had a son. She said, "This time let me praise (odeh) God," and named the child Judah (Yehudah). She then stopped having children.

30 [1] Rachel realized that she was not bearing any children to Jacob. She was jealous of her sister and said to Jacob, "Give me children! If not, let me die!"

29:24 **handmaid.** A servant rather than a slave (Lekach Tov; Josephus, Antiquities 1:19:8).

29:27 **week [of wedding celebrations].** (Rashi; Yov'loth 28:28). See Judges 14:12,17. From here is derived the custom of making seven days of feasts for a bride and groom (sheva berakhoth) even today (Pirkey Rabbi Eliezer 16).

29:28 **his daughter Rachel** . . . After the Torah was given, it was forbidden to marry two sisters (Leviticus 18:18).

29:29 **Bilhah.** Some say that she was Zilpah's sister (Yov'loth 28:9; Tzavaath Naphtali 1:11). Others say that both Bilhah and Zilpah were also Laban's daughters (Targum Yonathan on 29:24,29; Pirkey Rabbi Eliezer 36).

29:32 **Reuben.** Reuven in Hebrew. The name can be broken into reu ben, "see a son," or "a son of seeing." It may also be short for ra'ah be-onyi—"[God] saw my troubles."

29:34 **attached.** Or "indebted" (Hirsch).

² Jacob became furious with Rachel. "Shall I take God's place?" he said.   30
"It is He who is holding back the fruit of your womb."

³ [Rachel] said, "Here is my handmaid Bilhah. Come to her and let her
give birth on my lap.* Through her I will then also have a son.*'"

⁴ She gave him her handmaid Bilhah as a wife, and Jacob came to her.
⁵ Bilhah became pregnant and gave birth to Jacob's son. ⁵ Rachel said, "God
has judged (*dan*) me and has also heard my prayer. He has finally given me a
son!" She therefore named the child Dan.

⁷ Rachel's handmaid Bilhah became pregnant again and had a second son
by Jacob. ⁸ Rachel said, "I have been twisted around with my sister through
all of God's roundabout ways (*naphtuley*), but I have finally won.*'" She therefore named the child Naphtali.

⁹ Leah realized that she was no longer having children. She took her handmaid Zilpah and gave her to Jacob as a wife. ¹⁰ Leah's handmaid Zilpah bore
Jacob a son. ¹¹ "Good fortune* (*gad*) has come!" exclaimed Leah. She named
the child Gad.

¹² Leah's handmaid Zilpah bore a second son to Jacob. "It's my happiness
(*asher*)," said Leah. "Young girls will consider me happy!" She named the
child Asher.

¹⁴ Reuben took a walk during the wheat harvest* and he found mandrakes* in the field. He brought them to his mother Leah.

30:3 **on my lap.** Literally, "on my knees." This denotes that the child born would be considered hers. The
woman giving birth would sit on the lap of the foster mother, using the lap like a birthstool (see Exodus
1:16). The child would then appear to emerge between the legs of the foster mother.
— **have a son.** See 16:2.
30:8 **I have been twisted . . .** (Rashi). A difficult phrase, also interpreted, "I have offered many prayers to God
regarding my sister, and I have been answered" (*Targum;* Rashi); "With divine bonds I have been bound
to my sister" (Menachem ben Seruk in Rashi); "With divine struggles I have struggled with my sister"
(Ibn Ezra); or "Divine mysteries have been hidden from me regarding my sister" (Malbim).
30:11 **good fortune.** Or "success." (*Targum Yonathan;* Rashi; Josephus). Others render it, "A troop has come,"
(Ibn Ezra), that is, "she (Leah) has had a troop of sons," or "let him be considered as many children."
Also see below, 49:19. Or, "I have been vindicated" (Saadia).
30:14 **wheat harvest.** In the late spring.
— **mandrakes** (*Targum;* Ibn Ezra; Radak, *Sherashim;* Josephus).
Dudaim in Hebrew, from the word *dodim* denoting passion
or carnal love (Radak, *Sherashim;* cf. Ezekiel 16:8, 23:17,
Proverbs 7:16). It was called this because of its use as an
aphrodisiac and fertility potion (*Midrash Ne'elam, Zohar*
1:134b). The mandrake (*mandragora officinarum*) is an herb
of the beladonna or potato family. It has a thick perrenial
root, often split down the middle, like the lower limbs of
the human body. Stalkless, it has large leaves that straddle
the ground and violet flowers (cf. Rashi). In the spring, its
yellow fruit, the size of a tomato, ripens. This fruit can
have an intoxicating fragrance (Song of Songs 7:14).

Mandrake

The variety found by Reuben was a rare, extinct species that gives off deadly fumes when pulled from
the ground (*Midrash Aggadah* on Genesis 49:14, quoted in *Tzeror HaMor* as *Midrash HaGaluy; Toledoth Yitz-*

30   Rachel said to Leah, "Please give me some of your son's mandrakes."

15 "Isn't it enough that you have taken away my husband?" retorted Leah. "Now you even want to take my son's mandrakes!"

"All right," replied Rachel. "[Jacob] will sleep with you tonight in exchange for your son's mandrakes."

16 When Jacob came home from the field that evening, Leah went out to meet him. "You will come to me," she said. "I have paid for your services with my son's mandrakes." He slept with her that night.

17 God heard Leah's [prayer], and she became pregnant, giving birth to a fifth son to Jacob. 18 Leah said, "God has given me my reward (sakhar) because I have given my handmaid to my husband." She named the child Issachar.*

19 Leah became pregnant again, and she bore Jacob a sixth son. 20 "God has given me a wonderful gift (zeved)," said Leah. "Now let my husband make his permanent home (zevul) with me." She named the child Zebulun (Zevulun). 21 Leah then had a daughter, and she named her Dinah.*

22 God gave special consideration* to Rachel. He heard her [prayer] and opened her womb. 23 She became pregnant and gave birth to a son. "God has gathered away (asaph) my humiliation," she said. 24 She named the child Joseph (Yoseph), saying, "May God grant another (yoseph) son to me."

25 After Rachel had given birth to Joseph, Jacob said to Laban, "Let me leave.* I would like to go home to my own land. 26 Let me have my wives and children, since I have earned them by working for you, and I will go. You are well aware of the service that I rendered you."

27 "Haven't I earned your friendship*?" replied Laban. "I have made use of divination* and have learned that it is because of you that God has blessed me."

28 "Just name your price!" said [Laban]. "I will give it!"

29 "You know full well how I worked for you," replied [Jacob], "and how your livestock fared with me. 30 You had very little before I came, but since

chak on 49:14. Cf. Niddah 31a; Josephus, Wars 7:6:3). In the Talmud, there appears to be a dispute as to whether Reuben brought home the violet flowers, the fruits or the root (Sanhedrin 99b). Other sources indicate that he brought home two fruits (Tzava'ath Yissachar 1:3,5,7; Josephus, Antiquities 1:19:8).

Obviously, the Patriarchs and Matriarchs knew how to use these plants in mystical ways (30:37). Still, Rachel did not bear children because of the mandrakes, but because of her prayers (30:2, 30:22; cf. Zohar 1:157b). According to one ancient source, Rachel did not eat the mandrakes, but offered them to God (Tzava'ath Yissachar 2:6).

30:18 Issachar. Yissakhar in Hebrew. The name can be interpreted as yesh sekhar—"there is reward" (Radak). The name also alludes to Leah's paying for Jacob's services (30:16).

30:21 Dinah. Some say that Dinah was Zebulun's twin sister (Ibn Ezra; Tol'doth Yitzchak; Yov'loth 28:23).

30:22 special consideration. See note on 8:1.

30:25 Let me leave. Some say that Rebecca had sent the promised word (27:45) to him (Sefer HaYashar).

30:27 Haven't I earned your friendship? Literally, "If I have found favor in your eyes."

—   divination. See note on 31:19.

then it has increased and become very substantial. God blessed you with my   **30** coming. But when will I do something to build my own estate?"

³¹ "What shall I give you?"

"Do not *give* me anything. Just do this one thing for me. I will come back and tend your sheep, giving them the best care.* ³² I will go through all your flocks [with you] today. Remove every lamb that is spotted or streaked, every sheep that has dark markings. [Also remove] every goat that is streaked or spotted. It is with that kind that I will be paid.

³³ "In the future, this will be a sign of my honesty. I will let you inspect all that I have taken as my pay. Any goat that is not spotted or streaked, or any sheep without dark markings, that is in my possession can be considered stolen."

³⁴ "Agreed!" replied Laban. "May your words only come true!"

³⁵ That day, [Laban] removed the ringed and streaked he-goats, and all the spotted and streaked she-goats—every one with a trace of white.* [He also removed] every sheep with dark markings. These he gave to his sons. ³⁶ He then separated himself from Jacob by the distance of a three day journey.* Jacob was left tending Laban's remaining sheep.

³⁷ Jacob took wands of fresh storax,* almond* and plane.* He peeled white

---

30:31 giving them the best care. Or "waiting" (*HaKethav VeHaKabbalah*).

30:35 trace of white. In the ancient middle east, goats usually were completely black.

30:36 three day journey. According to the Talmud (*Pesachim* 93b), a day's journey is 10 parsangs or approximately 34 miles. (The Talmud thus defines the distance between Jerusalem and Mod'in, a distance of 17 miles, as being 15 *mil* or 5 parsangs). A three day journey was therefore 102 miles.

30:37 storax. (Ibn Janach; Radak, *Sherashim*; Septuagint). *Livneh* in Hebrew, a "white tree." It was believed to have occult powers, and was sacred to idolators (Hosea 4:13). The storax (*styrax*) has white blossoms (cf. *Targum Yonathan*), and its bark yields a brown, vanilla-scented resin when it is peeled. Others, however, identify the *livneh* as the white poplar (*populus alba*), a tree having white bark (Rashi on Hosea 4:13; cf. Septuagint there). Here Rashi translates it as *tremble*, French for aspen, a species of poplar. Others translate it as elm (Radak on Hosea 4:13). A possible allusion to Laban.

                              Storax   **Poplar**

—   **almond** (Saadia Gaon, quoted in Radak, *Sherashim*; cf. *Targum* on 17:23). *Luz* in Hebrew; see above 28:19. In Arabic, an almond is *loz*. Others, however, translate *luz* as hazel. Rashi thus translates it as *coudre* (*coudrier*), French for hazel, and Radak (*Sherashim*) translates it as *avelanier* (*alveane*), Spanish for hazel. (See *Tosafoth, Bekhoroth* 8a, s.v. *Tarnegoleth*).

—   **plane.** *Armon* in Hebrew. The Septuagint translates it as *platanes*, the plane tree. It is called *armon* because its bark peels off the trunk, leaving it naked (*arum*). There might also be an allusion to Laban's trickery (*armah; Lekach Tov*). The reference is to the oriental plane (*planatus orientalis*). This is a tall tree, with a trunk as great as 18 feet in diameter, having a lofty crest (cf. Ezekiel 31:8). It is like the sycamore, and was very common in the Middle East. Later sources, however, identify the *armon* as the chestnut tree (Rashi;

30 stripes in them by uncovering the white layer under the wands' [bark].*

³⁸ He set up the wands that he peeled near the watering troughs where the flocks came to drink, facing the animals. It was when they came to drink that they usually mated. ³⁹ The animals mated in the presence of the wands, and the young they bore were ringed, spotted and streaked.

⁴⁰ Jacob segregated the young animals. Still, he made the animals in Laban's flocks look at the ringed ones and all those with dark markings. But he bred his own flocks separately, and did not let them breed with Laban's flocks.

⁴¹ Whenever the stronger animals mated, Jacob placed the wands before their eyes at the troughs, so that they would mate facing the wands. ⁴² But when the sheep were feeble, he did not place [the wands]. The feeble ones thus went to Laban, while Jacob got the stronger ones.

⁴³ In this manner, the man became tremendously wealthy. He had many sheep and goats,* as well as slaves, slave-girls, camels and donkeys.

31 ¹ [Jacob] began to hear that Laban's sons were saying, "Jacob has taken everything belonging to our father. He has become rich by taking our father's property!" ² When Jacob saw Laban in person, [Laban also] did not behave to him as he did before.

³ God said to Jacob, "Go back to your birthplace in the land of your fathers. I will be with you."

⁴ Jacob sent word and summoned Rachel and Leah to the field where his flock was. ⁵ "I saw your father's face," he said. "He is not acting the same with me as he used to. But the God of my father has been with me.

⁶ "You know full well that I served your father with all my strength. ⁷ Your father swindled me and changed his mind about my pay at least ten times, but God would not let him harm me. ⁸ If he said, 'Your pay will be the spotted ones,' then all the animals gave birth to spotted young. If he said, 'Ringed ones will be your wage,' then all the animals dropped ringed ones. ⁹ God thus eroded your father's livestock and gave it to me.

Radak, *Sherashim*). This is difficult to understand, since the chestnut did not grow in Mesopotamia where Jacob was (Also see *Tosafoth, Rosh HaShanah* 23a, s.v. *Armonim, Sukkah* 32b, s.v. *Dulba, Bava Bathra* 81a, s.v. *Armonim*).

— **he peeled . . .** It appears that by deep meditation on the wands, Jacob was able to direct spiritual energy and actually to change the genetic structure of the sheep (*Bereshith Rabbah* 73; *Midrash Tehillim* 8:6; *Tanchuma* B 24; *Midrash HaGadol*). Kabbalistic sources note that at this time, Jacob was manipulating some of the highest spiritual forces that exist (*Zohar* 161a, 163a; *Etz Chaim, Shaar HaAkudim*). See below, 31:12.

30:43 **sheep and goats.** The Hebrew word *tzon* denotes small domestic animals, including both sheep and goats, as we see from context here (cf. Rashi on Exodus 12:5). We usually translate it here as "flocks" or "animals."

Plane

¹⁰ "During the breeding season, I suddenly* had a vision.* I saw that the **31** bucks mounting the sheep were ringed, spotted and flecked.

¹¹ "An angel called to me in God's name,* 'Jacob!'—and I replied 'Yes.' ¹² He said, 'Raise your eyes, and you will see that the bucks mounting the sheep are ringed, spotted and flecked. Let this be a sign that I have seen all that Laban is doing to you. ¹³ I am the God of Beth El,* where you anointed a pillar and made an oath to Me. Now set out and leave this land. Return to the land where you were born.' "

¹⁴ Rachel and Leah both spoke up. "Do we then still have a portion and an inheritance in our father's estate?" they exclaimed. "Why, he treats us like strangers! ¹⁵ He has sold us and spent the money! All the wealth that God has taken from our father actually belongs to us and our children. Now, whatever God has said to you, do it!"

¹⁷ Jacob began the journey, placing his children and wives on the camels. ¹⁸ He led away all his livestock, and took all the goods he had acquired, including everything that he had bought in Padan Aram. He was heading to see his father Isaac in the land of Canaan.

¹⁹ Meanwhile, Laban was away, shearing his sheep. Rachel stole* the fetishes* that belonged to her father.

²⁰ Jacob decided to go behind the back of Laban the Aramaean, and did not tell him that he was leaving. ²¹ He thus fled with all he owned. He set out and crossed the Euphrates,* heading in the direction of the Gilead Mountains.*

31:10 **suddenly** . . . Literally, "I lifted my eyes and saw in a dream." The phrase, "lifting eyes," in general, is usually translated as raising eyes or looking up. This is very difficult here, since why would one look up to see a dream? Therefore, it seems to be an idiom denoting seeing with new concentration or in a new light (see above, 13:10, 18:2,24,63, 22:4,13, 33:1, 43:29, etc.). If taken literally, the verse here would be interpreted, "I lifted my eyes and saw a vision [in the sky]." The expression of "lifting eyes" can also denote concentration, contemplation and meditation: "I contemplated the scene and had a vision." It is surprising that none of the commentaries discuss this. See 31:12.

—   **vision.** Literally a dream.

31:11 **an angel** . . . See note on 16:10.

31:13 **Beth El.** See 28:19.

31:19 **Rachel stole** . . . Some say that it was to prevent her father from worshipping them (*Bereshith Rabbah* 74; Rashi). Others maintain that it was to prevent him from using them in divination to find Jacob (*Tanchuma* 12; Rashbam; Ibn Ezra; cf. 30:27; Hosea 3:4, Zechariah 10:2). Still others maintain that Rachel took them to gain her father's pardon (Josephus, 1:19:9).

—   **fetishes.** *Teraphim* in Hebrew, sexual images, from the word *turpha* (*Tanchuma* 12; *Zohar* 164a). These were images having human form (cf. 1 Samuel 19:13). In some cases, they were made out of the shrunken head of a first-born infant (*Targum Yonathan; Tanchuma* 12). They were not necessarily idols (Rambam, from 1 Samuel 19:13; Judges 17:5, 18:5), but here they were used for idolatrous purposes (31:30; *Zohar*). In general, they were used as a meditative device to obtain messages (Hosea 3:4, Zechariah 10:2; Ibn Ezra; Radak; Ralbag; Rashi on Ezekiel 21:26). The *teraphim* would be tapped, inducing a relaxed, meditative state (*Zohar* 164a, from 2 Samuel 24:16; cf. *Yad, Avodath Kokhavim* 11:6; *Chinukh* 510).

31:21 **Euphrates.** Literally "river." See *Targum.* At this point, the Euphrates was 70 miles south of Charan on the way to the Holy Land.

Teraphim

31   **22** On the third day,* Laban was informed that Jacob had fled. **23** He took
along his kinsmen and pursued [Jacob] for seven days,* intercepting him in
the Gilead Mountains.

24 God appeared to Laban the Aramaean that night in a dream, and said,
"Be very careful not to say anything, good or bad, to Jacob."

25 Laban then overtook Jacob. Jacob had set up his tents on a hill, while
Laban had stationed his kinsmen on Mount Gilead.

26 Laban said to Jacob, "How could you do this? You went behind my
back and led my daughters away like prisoners of war! **27** Why did you have to
leave so secretly? You went behind my back and told me nothing! Why, I
would have sent you off with celebration and song, with drum and lyre! **28** You
didn't even let me kiss my grandsons and daughters goodby.

"What you did was very foolish. **29** I have it in my power to do you great
harm. But your father's God spoke to me last night and said, 'Be very careful
not to say anything, good or bad, to Jacob.'

30 "I realize that you left because you missed your parents' home. But why
did you have to steal my gods?"

31 Jacob spoke up. "[I left this way] because I was afraid," he said. "I
thought that you might take your daughters away from me by force. **32** If you
find your gods with anyone here, let him not live! Let all our close relatives
here be witnesses. See if there is anything belonging to you and take it back."
Jacob did not realize that Rachel had stolen them.*

33 Laban went into the tents of Jacob, Leah, and the two handmaids, but
he found nothing. When he left Leah's tent, he went into Rachel's. **34** Rachel
had taken the fetishes and placed them inside a camel cushion, sitting down
on them. Laban inspected the entire tent, and found nothing. **35** [Rachel] said
to her father, "Do not be angry, my lord, but I cannot get up for you. I have
my female period." Laban searched, but he did not find the fetishes.

36 Jacob was angry, and he argued with Laban, asserting himself. "What is
my crime?" he exclaimed. "What terrible thing did I do that you came chasing me like this? **37** You inspected all my things—what did you find from your
house? Place it right here! In front of my relatives and yours! Let them determine which of us is right!

—   **Gilead mountains.** These were the mountains to the east of the Jordan and north of the Jabbok River,
     some 300 miles south of the Euphrates. Jacob was thus heading south through Damascus. This area is
     identified with the land of the Rephaim (14:5; Yov'loth 29:9). Jacob was thus taking the same route as the
     four invading kings in the time of Abraham.
31:22 **third day.** See 30:36.
31:23 **seven days.** See note on 30:36. The normal distance covered would be 238 miles, but if rushing, the
     entire distance of 370 miles could have been covered (see notes on 14:15, 28:19). In ten days, Jacob
     could easily have covered the distance.
31:32 **Rachel had stolen them.** Jacob's curse came true (35:18).

31

[38] "Twenty years I worked for you! All that time, your sheep and goats never lost their young. Not once did I ever take a ram from your flocks as food. [39] I never brought you an animal that had been attacked—I took the blame myself. You made me make it good whether it was carried off by day or by night.*

[40] "By day I was consumed by the scorching heat, and at night by the frost, when sleep was snatched from my eyes. [41] Twenty years now I have worked for you in your estate—fourteen years for your two daughters, and six years for some of your flocks. You changed my wages ten times!

[42] "If the God of my fathers—the God of Abraham and the Dread* of Isaac—had not been with me, you would have sent me away empty-handed! But God saw my plight and the work of my hands. Last night, He rendered judgment*!'"

[43] Laban interrupted Jacob. "The daughters are my daughters! The sons are my sons! The flocks are my flocks! All that you see is mine! But my daughters . . . what can I do to them today? Or to the children they have born? [44] Now come! Let's make a treaty—you and I. Let there be a tangible evidence of it between you and me."

[45] Jacob took a boulder and raised it as a pillar. [46] "Gather stones!" he said to his relatives. They took stones and made a large mound. They ate there on top of the mound.*

[47] Laban called it Witness Mound (*Yegar Sahadutha**), but Jacob named it Gal'ed.*

[48] "This mound shall be a witness between you and me today," said Laban. "That's why it is called Gal'ed. [49] [Let the pillar be called*] Watchpost (*Mitzpah.**) Let it be said that God will keep watch between you and me when we are out of each other's sight. [50] If you degrade my daughters, or marry other women in addition to them, there may be no one with us, but you must always realize that God is the Witness between you and me."

[51] Laban then said, "Here is the mound and here is the pillar that I have set up between us. [52] The mound shall be a witness, and the pillar shall be a

---

31:39 **carried off** . . . Or "stolen." See Exodus 22:12.
31:42 **Dread.** See 31:53. Since Isaac was still alive, Jacob would not call Him "God of Isaac."
— **He rendered judgment** (Ramban). Or, "He reprimanded you last night" (Rashi).
31:46 **on top of the mound.** Or, "by the mound." Cf. 24:13. (Artscroll).
31:47 **Yegar Sahadutha.** Witness Mound in Aramaic, Laban's language.
— **Gal'ed.** The same in Hebrew.
31:49 **Let the pillar be** . . . (*Lekach Tov*).
— **Mitzpah.** Some sources see this as a proper noun (Ramban). See Judges 10:17, 11:11, 11:34, Hosea 5:1. Others, however, do not see it as a proper name (*Targum;* Rashi), and would interpret the verse, "There was a watchpost, regarding which he said . . ." Some identify this place with Ramath Gilead in 1 Kings 22:3. This is 24 miles north of the Jabbok, and 25 miles east of the Jordan. See note on 32:3.

31 witness. I am not to go beyond the mound with bad intentions, and you are not to go beyond the mound and pillar. ⁵³ May the God of Abraham, the god of Nachor, and the god of their fathers be our judge."

Jacob swore by the Dread of his father Isaac. ⁵⁴ He then butchered an animal on the hill, and invited his relatives to break bread. They had a meal and spent the night on the hill.

32 ¹ Laban got up early the next morning and kissed his grandsons and daughters goodby. He then blessed them and left to return home.

² Jacob also continued on his way. He encountered angels of God.* ³ When Jacob saw them, he said, "This is God's camp." He named the place Twin Camps* (*Machanaim**).

VaYishlach   וַיִּשְׁלַח

[64. Jacob Meets Esau]

⁴ Jacob sent messengers ahead of him to his brother Esau, to Edom's Field* in the Seir area.* ⁵ He instructed them to deliver the following message:

"To my lord Esau. Your humble servant Jacob says: I have been staying with Laban, and have delayed my return until now. ⁶ I have acquired cattle, donkeys, sheep, slaves and slave-girls, and am now sending word to tell my lord, to gain favor in your eyes."

⁷ The messengers returned to Jacob with the report: "We came to your brother Esau, and he is also heading toward you. He has 400 men with him."

⁸ Jacob was very frightened and distressed. He divided the people accompanying him into two camps, along with the sheep, cattle and camels. ⁹ He said, "If Esau comes and attacks one camp, at least the other camp will survive."

32:2   **angels . . .** According to others, "divine messengers," a welcoming committee sent by Rebecca (*Sefer HaYashar*, p. 82).

32:3   **Twin Camps.** That is, Jacob's camp and the divine camp (Ramban).

—   **Machanaim.** It was a city on the border between Gad and Manasseh, associated with Ramath-Mitzpeh (Joshua 13:26, 13:30). Also see Joshua 21:38, 1 Chronicles 6:65; 2 Samuel 2:8, 2:12, 2:29, 17:24,27. Some identify Machanaim with Khirbath al-Makhna, 2.5 miles north of Aijalon, which would place it 14 miles north of the Jabbok River, and 10 miles east of the Jordan. Jacob was thus apparently headed toward the juncture of the Jordan and the Jabbok. According to others, however, Machanaim was actually on the Jabbok River.

32:4   **Edom's Field.** See 25:30. The area was apparently named for Esau.

—   **Seir-area.** See above, 14:6. This seems to contradict the statement that Esau did not settle in Seir until after Jacob's arrival (36:8). Some say that Esau did not actually live in Seir now, but only visited it regularly (Ramban on 36:6; Sforno; Chizzkuni). Others say that this was not Mount Seir, and that the area was named for Esau (Josephus 2:2:1; see notes on 25:25, 26:20). It appears that Esau now lived in the plains near Seir. and later invaded the hill country (see *Aggadath Bereshith*).

In general, Seir is the area south of the Zered Brook and the Dead Sea. The messengers were therefore sent a distance of 90 miles from Machanaim.

[10] Jacob prayed: "O God of my father Abraham and God of my father 32
Isaac. You Yourself told me, 'Return to the land where you were born, and I
will make things go well with you.*' [11] I am unworthy of all the kindness and
faith that You have shown me. [When I left home,] I crossed the Jordan with
[only] my staff, and now I have enough for two camps. [12] Rescue me, I pray,
from the hand of my brother—from the hand of Esau. I am afraid of him, for
he can come and kill us all—mothers and children alike. [13] You once said, 'I
will make things go well with you, and make your descendants like the sand
grains of the sea, which are too numerous to count.*' "

[14] After spending the night there, he selected a tribute for his brother Esau
from what he had with him. [15] [The tribute consisted of] 200 female goats, 20
male goats, 200 ewes, 20 rams, [16] 30 nursing camels with their young, 40 cows,
10 bulls, 20 female donkeys, and 10 male donkeys.

[17] These he gave to his servants, each herd by itself. He said to his servants,
"Go on ahead of me. Keep a space between one herd and the next."

[18] He gave the first group instructions: "When my brother Esau
encounters you, he will ask, 'To whom do you belong? Where are you going?
Who owns all this that is with you?' [19] You must reply, 'It belongs to your servant Jacob. It is a tribute to my master Esau. [Jacob] himself is right behind
us.' "

[20] He gave similar instructions to the second group, to the third, and to all
who went after the herd. "You must [all] say the same thing to Esau when you
meet him," he said. [21] "You must also say, 'Your servant Jacob is right behind
us.' "

[Jacob] said [to himself], "I will win him over with the gifts that are being
sent ahead, and then I will face him. Hopefully, he will forgive me."

[22] He sent the gifts ahead of him, and spent the night in the camp. [23] In the
middle of the night he got up, and took his two wives, his two handmaids, and
his eleven sons, and sent them across the Jabbok River* shallows. [24] After he
had taken them and sent them across, he also sent across all his possessions.

[25] Jacob remained alone. A stranger* [appeared and] wrestled with him
until just before daybreak. [26] When [the stranger] saw that he could not defeat

---

32:10 Return to the land ... See 31:3, 31:13.
32:13 like the sand grains ... See 28:14.
32:23 Jabbok River. An eastern tributary of the Jordan, about midway between the Kinnereth and the Dead
Sea.
32:25 stranger. According to tradition, this was Samael, guardian angel of Esau and the incarnation of Evil
(*Bereshith Rabbah* 77; *Rashi*; *Zohar*). See Hosea 12:4,5. Jacob's wrestling with him would symbolize the
struggle with evil that he and his descendants would have from this time forth (*Bachya*; See *Handbook of
Jewish Thought* 4:29). According to others, it was a holy angel, symbolizing Jacob's future struggles with
the spiritual (*Targum Yonathan*; *Tanchuma*).

32   him, he touched the upper joint of [Jacob's] thigh.* Jacob's hip joint became dislocated as he wrestled with [the stranger].

²⁷ "Let me leave!" said [the stranger]. "Dawn is breaking."

"I will not let you leave unless you bless me."

²⁸ "What is your name?"

"Jacob."

²⁹ "Your name will no longer be said to be Jacob, but Israel (*Yisra'el**). You have become great (*sar*) before God and man.* You have won."

³⁰ Jacob returned the question. "If you would," he said, "tell me what *your* name is."

"Why do you ask my name*?" replied [the stranger]. He then blessed [Jacob].

³¹ Jacob named the place Divine Face (*Peniel*). [He said,] "I have seen the Divine face to face, and my soul has withstood it.*" ³² The sun rose and was shining on him as he left Penuel.* He was limping because of his thigh.

³³ The Israelites* therefore do not eat the displaced nerve* on the hip joint to this very day. This is because [the stranger] touched Jacob's thigh on the displaced nerve.

33   ¹ Jacob looked up and saw Esau approaching with 400 men. He divided the children among Leah, Rachel and the two handmaids. ² He placed the

---

32:26 **thigh.** Or "hip socket," i.e. where the thigh joins the hip. See note on 24:3. This denotes that although Jacob was victorious in his struggles, his children would suffer. See 34:2.

32:29 **Israel.** This was later reaffirmed by God (35:10). Also see 1 Kings 18:31, 2 Kings 17:34.

—   **You have become great . . .** (*Targum*). Or, "You have become a prince (*sar*) among the angels and man" (Ralbag). Others have, "You have fought (or struggled) with a divine being and you have won" (*Bereshith Rabbah;* Josephus 1:2:2; Septuagint; cf. Hosea 4:5). The root of the word *sari-tha* here is thus *sarah*, meaning to contend or "fight to win" (Radak, *Sherashim.* cf. Hosea 9:6). It is related to the root *sarar*, to rule; cf. Numbers 16:13, Esther 1:22, Proverbs 8:16. Also see Judges 9:22, Hosea 8:4.
      Israel (*Yisrael*) thus means, "he who will be great [before] God," or "he who will struggle with the divine."

32:30 **Why do you ask . . .** See Judges 13:18.

32:31 **I have seen the Divine . . .** See Judges 6:22, 13:22, Isaiah 6:5.

32:32 **Penuel.** Although Jacob named it Peniel, it was later known as Penuel; see 1 Kings 12:25. It is near Sukkoth; below 33:16, Judges 8:8. It is usually identified with Tulul edh dhahab, on the south bank of the Jabbok, near the bend, about 10 miles east of the Jordan. However, from the context here, it seems that Peniel was on the north bank of the Jabbok, where another ancient mount (*tel*) is found. It may be that Jacob named the northern area Peniel, and then left the southern area, which was later known as Penuel. This is some 15 miles south of Machanaim (see note on 32:3).

32:33 **Israelites.** Literally, "children of Israel." This is the first time that this expression is used.

—   **displaced nerve.** *Gid ha-nasheh* in Hebrew. This is the sciatic nerve, the large main nerve of the lower extremity, running down the back of the leg. Therefore, before the hindquarter of any animal can be eaten, this nerve, with all its branches, must be carefully removed. Since it is very difficult to do this, hindquarters are usually not eaten by Jews. The nerve touched by the angel is seen as the place where evil has strong influence (*Zohar*).

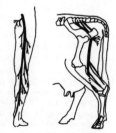

Sciatic Nerve

handmaids and their children in front, Leah and their sons behind them, and   33
Rachel and Joseph to the rear. ⁵ [Jacob] then went ahead of them, and he
prostrated himself seven times as he approached his brother.

⁴ Esau ran to meet them. He hugged [Jacob], and throwing himself on his
shoulders,* kissed him. They [both] wept. ⁵ Esau looked up and saw the
women and children. "Who are these to you?" he asked.

"They are the children whom God has been kind enough to grant me,"
replied [Jacob].

⁶ The handmaids approached along with their children, and [the women]
bowed down. ⁷ Leah and her children also approached and bowed down.
Finally, Joseph and Rachel came forward and bowed down.

⁸ "What did you have to do with that whole camp that came to greet me?"
asked [Esau].

"It was to gain favor in your eyes," replied [Jacob].

⁹ "I have plenty, my brother," said Esau. "Let what is yours remain
yours."

¹⁰ "Please! No!" said Jacob. "If I have gained favor with you, please
accept this gift from me. After all,* seeing your face is like seeing the face of
the Divine,* you have received me so favorably. ¹¹ Please accept my welcoming gift* as it has been brought to you. God has been kind to me, and I have
all [I need]." [Jacob thus] urged him, and [Esau finally] took it.

¹² "Let's get going and move on," said [Esau]. "I will travel alongside
you."

¹³ "My lord," replied Jacob, "you know that the children are weak, and I
have responsibility for the nursing sheep and cattle. If they are driven hard for
even one day, all the sheep will die. ¹⁴ Please go ahead of me, my lord. I will
lead my group slowly, following the pace of the work* that I have ahead of
me, and the pace of the children. I will eventually come to [you], my lord, in
Seir."

¹⁵ "Let me put some of my people at your disposal," said Esau.

"What for?" replied Jacob. "Just let me remain on friendly terms with
you."

¹⁶ On that day, Esau returned along the way to Seir. ¹⁷ Jacob went to Suk-

---

33:4 **throwing himself on his shoulders.** A sign of emotion, see 45:14,15. Literally, "falling on his neck," but
"neck" here denotes the shoulders (Sh'muel ben Chofni Gaon on 45:14).
33:10 **After all.** See note on 18:5.
— **face of the Divine.** See 33:31 (*Bereshith Rabbah* 77).
33:11 **welcoming gift.** Literally, "blessing." But in Hebrew, "welcome" is "blessed is he who comes" (cf.
Rashi).
33:14 **work.** (Ibn Ezra). Others, "caravan" or "drove" (cf. Rashi; Radak), or "possessions" (Saadia).

33 koth.* There, he built himself a house, and made shelters for his livestock. He
therefore named the place Sukkoth (Shelters).

[65. Arrival at Shechem]

[18] When Jacob came from Padan Aram and entered the boundaries of
Canaan, he arrived safely* in the vicinity of Shechem.* He set up camp in view
of the city. [19] He bought the piece of open land upon which he set up his tent
for 100 kesitahs* from the sons of Chamor, chief of Shechem.* [20] He erected
an altar there, and named it God-is-Israel's-Lord (*El Elohey Yisrael*).

[66. The Affair of Dinah]

34 [1] Leah's daughter Dinah,* whom she had borne to Jacob, went out to visit
some of the local girls. [2] She was seen by Shechem, son of the chief of the
region, Chamor the Hivite.* He seduced her, slept with her, and [then] raped
her.* [3] Becoming deeply attached to Jacob's daughter Dinah, he fell in love
with the girl, and tried to make up with her. [4] Shechem said to his father
Chamor, "Get me this young girl as a wife."

[5] Jacob learned that his daughter Dinah had been defiled. His sons were in
the field with the livestock, and Jacob remained silent until they came home.
[6] Meanwhile, Shechem's father, Chamor, came to Jacob to speak with him.
[7] Jacob's sons returned from the field. When they heard what had happened,
the men were shocked and they seethed with anger. [Shechem] had committed
an outrage against Israel, sleeping with a daughter of Jacob! Such an act
could not be tolerated!

[8] Chamor tried to reason with them. "My son Shechem is deeply in love

---

33:17 **Sukkoth.** A locality on the East Bank of the Jordan, cf. Joshua 13:27, Judges 8:4,5. It is associated with Shechem; Psalms 60:8, 108:8. It is thought to be Tel Deir Alla on the Jabbok River, 2.5 miles east of the Jordan.

33:18 **safely.** (*Targum;* Rashi; Josephus 1:21:1). *Shalem* in Hebrew. Others maintain that Shalem (Salem) is the name of a city near Shechem (*Sefer HaYashar* p. 87; Rashbam; Bachya; Chizzkuni; Abarbanel). Indeed, there is a city known as Salaam some 5 miles east of Shechem (cf. *Yov'loth* 30:1). See I Samuel 9:4. Although Jerusalem was also known as Shalem or Salem (14:18), this is a different city (Chizzkuni).

—   **Shechem.** This was also Abraham's first stop in the Holy Land (12:6).

33:19 **kesitahs.** In the Talmud, Rabbi Akiba notes that in Africa (or Phrygia, see 10:2) a *kesitah* is equivalent to a *ma'ah* (*Rosh HaShanah* 26a). A *ma'ah* is usually seen as one twenty-fourth of a shekel (*Tosefta, Bava Bathra* 5:4), and hence the 100 kesitahs would be around 4.17 shekels. Other sources state that a *ma'ah* is one twentieth of a shekel (*Targum* on Exodus 30:13), and hence the 100 kesitahs would be 5 shekels (*Sefer HaYashar*). According to others, the kesitah is equivalent to a sela or two shekels, and hence the price was 200 shekels (*Bereshith Rabbah* 79; Ralbag; *MeAm Lo'ez/The Torah Anthology* 3:155). See Job 42:11.
        This was later Joseph's burial place; Joshua 24:32.

—   **chief of Shechem** (ibn Caspi). Or, "father of Shechem." See below, 34:19.

34:1   **Dinah.** Some say she was 12 years old (*Yov'loth* 30:3).

34:2   **Hivite.** See 10:17, 36:3.

—   **raped her.** see Ramban; Ralbag.

with your daughter," he said. "If you would, let him marry her. ⁹ Intermarry **34**
with us. You can give us your daughters, and we will give you ours. ¹⁰ You will
be able to live with us, and the land will be open before you. Settle down, do
business here, and [the land] will become your property."

¹¹ Shechem [also] spoke to [Dinah's] father and brothers. "I will do anything to regain your favor. I will give you whatever you ask. ¹² Set the bridal
payment and gifts as high as you like—I will give whatever you demand of me.
Just let me have the girl as my wife."

¹³ When Jacob's sons replied to Shechem and his father Chamor, it was
with an ulterior motive. After all, they were speaking to the one who had
defiled their sister Dinah.

¹⁴ "We can't do that," they said. "Giving our sister to an uncircumcised
man would be a disgrace to us. ¹⁵ The only way we can possibly agree is if you
will be like us and circumcise every male. ¹⁶ Only then will we give you our
daughters and take your daughters for ourselves. We will be able to live
together with you and [both of us] will become a single nation. ¹⁷ But if you do
not accept our terms and agree to be circumcised, we will take our daughter
and go."

¹⁸ Their terms seemed fair to Chamor and his son Shechem. ¹⁹ Since he
desired Jacob's daughter, the young man lost no time in doing it. He was the
most respected person in his father's house.

²⁰ Chamor and his son Shechem came to the city gate, and they spoke to
the citizens of their city. ²¹ "These men are friendly toward us," they said.
"They live on the land and support themselves profitably from it. The land
has more than ample room for them. We will marry their daughters, and give
them ours. ²² But it is only if their terms are met that these men will consent to
live with us and become one nation. Every male among us must first be circumcised, just as they are circumcised. ²³ Won't their livestock, their possessions, and all their animals eventually be ours? Just let us agree to their condition and live with them."

²⁴ All the people who came out to the city gate agreed with Chamor and
his son Shechem. The males who passed through the city gate all allowed
themselves to be circumcised.

²⁵ On the third day, when [the people] were in agony, two of Jacob's sons,
Simeon and Levi, Dinah's brothers, took up their swords. They came to the
city without arousing suspicion and killed every male.* ²⁶ They also killed

---

34:25 killed every male. Since the citizens did not penalize Shechem for his crime, they were considered
accomplices (Maimonides, *Yad, Melakhim* 9:14). Furthermore, the people of Shechem were planning to
attack Jacob and plunder him (*Sefer HaYashar;* see above 34:23). Besides this, the city deserved divine
punishment, since they were notorious for seducing and raping the daughters of strangers (*Tzava'ath Levi*
6:8–11; cf. Ramban).

34 Chamor and his son Shechem by the sword, and took Dinah from Shechem's house. Then they left.

²⁷ Jacob's sons came upon the dead, and plundered the city that had defiled their sister. ²⁸ They took the sheep, cattle, donkeys, and whatever else was in the city and the field. ²⁹ They also took the women and all the children as captives. They took everything from the houses, plundering all the [city's] wealth.

³⁰ Jacob said to Simeon and Levi,* "You have gotten me in trouble, giving me a bad reputation among the Canaanites and Perizites* who live in the land. I have only a small number of men. They can band together and attack me, and my family and I will be wiped out."

³¹ "Should he have been allowed to treat our sister like a prostitute?" they replied.

[67. Preparations for Beth El]

35 ¹ God said to Jacob, "Set out and go up to Beth El.* Remain there and make an altar to [Me], the God who appeared to you when you were fleeing from your brother Esau."

² Jacob said to his family and everyone with him, "Get rid of the idolatrous artifacts* that you have. Purify yourselves and change your clothes. ³ We are setting out and going up to Beth El. There I will make an altar to God, who answered me in my time of trouble, and who has been with me on the journey that I have taken."

⁴ They gave Jacob all the idolatrous artifacts that they had, even the rings in their ears. Jacob buried them under the terebinth tree near Shechem.*

⁵ They began their journey. The terror of God was felt in all the cities around them, and they did not pursue Jacob's sons.

⁶ Jacob and all the people with him came to Luz in the land of Canaan—that is, to Beth El. ⁷ He built an altar there, and he named the place Beth El's God (*El Beth El*), since this was the place where God was revealed to him when he was fleeing from his brother.

34:30 **Jacob said** . . . See 49:6.
— **Perizites.** See 13:7.
35:1 **Beth El.** See 28:19. Jerusalem was 32 miles south of Shechem, while Bethel was 19 miles south. The expression "go up" is used since Jerusalem is higher than Shechem.
35:2 **idolatrous artifacts.** Literally "foreign gods," or "alien gods." Others render it "alienated gods" or "alienating gods" (cf. Hirsch). Some say that these were the artifacts plundered from Shechem (*Targum Yonathan;* Rashi). According to others, Jacob had discovered the teraphim that Rachel had taken (above 31:19; Josephus 1:20:2; *Yov'loth* 31:2).
35:4 **terebinth tree** . . . See note on 12:6. It was under this tree that Joshua later set up a stone (Joshua 24:26; Rashi *ad loc.*).

8 Rebecca's nurse Deborah* died, and she was buried in the valley of Beth   35
El, under the oak.* It was named Weeping Oak (*Alon Bakhuth*).

[68. Beth El]

9 Now that Jacob had returned from Padan Aram, God appeared to him
again and blessed him. 10 God said to him, "Your name is Jacob. But your
name will not be only Jacob; you will also have Israel as a name." [God thus]
named him Israel.*

11 God said to him, "I am God Almighty. Be fruitful and increase.* A
nation and a community of nations will come into existence from you.* Kings
will be born from your loins.* 12 I will grant you the land that I gave to Abraham and Isaac.* I will also give the land to your descendants who will follow
you."

13 God went up* and left [Jacob] in the place where He had spoken to him.
14 Jacob had set up a pillar* in the place that God had spoken to him. He
[now] offered a libation* on it, and then poured oil on it. 15 Jacob had named
the place where God had spoken to him Beth El (God's Temple).*

16 They moved on from Beth El, and were some distance* from Ephrath*
when Rachel began to give birth. Her labor was extremely difficult. 17 When
her labor was at its worst, the midwife said to her, "Don't be afraid. This one
will also be a son* for you." 18 She was dying, and as she breathed her last, she
named the child Ben-oni (My Sorrow's Son). His father called him Benjamin.*

35:8 Deborah. See above, 24:59. This was a name that would later become famous through a prophetess by
the same name (Judges 4:4). Some say that Rebecca had sent Deborah to inform Jacob that it was safe to
return home (Rashi; *Lekach Tov; Sefer HaYashar* p. 79. See note on 30:25). According to others, Jacob had
stopped at his parents' home and had picked up Deborah (*Yov'loth* 31:30).

—   **oak.** *Alon* in Hebrew. (see *Targum Yonathan*). There is a difference between an *eleh* (terebinth) and an *alon*
(cf. Isaiah 6:13). Others translate *alon* here as "plain" (Onkelos; Rashi). Benjamin of Toledo identifies
the Valley of Alon with Val de Luna, 5 miles from Mount Gilboa (*Massoth Binyamin* 8).

35:10 Israel. See above, 32:29.

35:11 Be fruitful . . . See above, 1:22, 1:28, 8:17, 9:1, 9:7. This is seen as a commandment to have children
(*Yevamoth* 65b).

—   **community of nations . . .** See above 17:5, 17:16, 28:3. Also see 48:4.

—   **Kings will be born . . .** Above, 17:6, 17:16.

35:12 I will grant you the land . . . Above, 12:7, 13:15, 26:3,4, 28:13.

35:13 went up. See note on 17:22.

35:14 pillar. This is the one mentioned in 28:18 (Ibn Ezra; Ramban).

—   **libation.** *Nesekh* in Hebrew. Jacob poured water and/or wine on the pillar to purify it (Ibn Ezra; Ramban). It was also to dedicate it as a place of future sacrifice (*Targum Yonathan*). Such libations would later
be an integral part of the service; see Exodus 29:40, Leviticus 23:13, Numbers 15:5, etc.

35:15 Beth El. See above, 28:19.

35:16 some distance. About half a mile (*Maasoth Binyamin* 10). It was to the north of Ephrath or Bethlehem.

—   **Ephrath.** Bethlehem (35:19). See 48:7. Also see 1 Samuel 17:12, Micah 5:1, Psalms 132:6, Ruth 1:2,
4:11, 1 Chronicles 2:24. It is 5 miles south of Jerusalem, and 16 miles from Bethel.

35:17 also be a son. See 30:24.

35:18 Benjamin. *Binyamin* in Hebrew, literally "son of the right." Some interpret this as "son of the right

35   [19] Rachel died and was buried on the road to Ephrath, now known as
Bethlehem.* [20] Jacob set up a monument* on her grave. This is the monument
that is on Rachel's grave to this very day.*
        [21] Israel traveled on, and he set up his tent beyond Herd Tower (*Migdal
Eder*).* [22] While Jacob was living undisturbed in the area, Reuben went and
disturbed the sleeping arrangements* of Bilhah, his father's concubine. Jacob
heard about it.

[69. Jacob's Sons; Isaac's Death]

Jacob had twelve sons.
        [23] The sons of Leah were Reuben (Jacob's first-born), Simeon, Levi,
Judah, Issachar, and Zebulun.
        [24] The sons of Rachel were Joseph and Benjamin.
        [25] The sons of Rachel's handmaid Bilhah were Dan and Naphtali.
        [26] The sons of Leah's handmaid Zilpah were Gad and Asher.
These are the sons born to Jacob in Padan Aram.
        [27] Jacob thus came to his father Isaac in Mamre, at Kiryath Arba, better
known as Hebron.* This is where Abraham and Isaac had resided.
        [28] Isaac lived to be 180 years old. [29] He breathed his last and died, and was
gathered to his people, old and in the fullness of his years. His sons, Esau and
Jacob, buried him.*

hand," meaning a son of strength (Ramban). Others state that it means "son of the south," since Benjamin was the only son born in the Holy Land, which is to the south of Aramaea (Rashi; *Sefer HaYashar*
p. 96). There is also an opinion that it is the same as *ben yamim*, son of days, or son of old age (Rashi;
Rashbam; *Tzava'ath Binyamin* 1:6; Philo, *De Nominum Mutatione* 3:92).

35:19   **Bethlehem.** *Beth Lechem* in Hebrew, literally "House of Bread." It is 5 miles south of Jerusalem.

35:20   **monument.** Hence, the custom to place gravestones by the dead (*Bereshith Rabbah* 82).

—   **to this very day.** See 1 Samuel 10:2, Jeremiah 31:15. It is a famous site even today. The tomb is described
as consisting of 11 stones, placed there by the 11 brothers, and a large stone on top, put there by Jacob
(*Lekach Tov; Massoth Binyamin* 10. Cf. *Tosafoth, Sanhedrin* 47b, s.v. *KeSheYistom*). A structure was built
around it in the 1700's. This is the familiar Rachel's Tomb.

35:21   **Migdal Eder.** It is on a hill (Micah 4:2; Rashbam). See *Shekalim* 7:4. It is halfway between Bethlehem and
Hebron (cf. *Tzava'ath Reuven* 3:13). There is a tradition that the Messiah will arive there (*Targum Yonathan*).

35:22   **disturbed the sleeping arrangements.** According to Talmudic tradition, after Rachel's death, Jacob
moved his bed to the tent of Rachel's handmaid Bilhah. Reuven moved Jacob's bed and placed it in
Leah's tent (*Shabbath* 55a,b; *Targum Yonathan;* Rashi). The Hebrew word here, *shakhav*, literally means to
lie down or to make bedding arrangements, but it is often used as a euphemism for sex. Some say that
Reuben actually desired Bilhah and lay next to her (*You'loth* 33:2,4). At the time Bilhah was drunk
(*Tzava'ath Reuven* 4:13). In any case, Reuven lost the birthright because of this. See 49:4; 1 Chronicles
5:1. See 2 Samuel 16:22, 20:3.

35:27   **Hebron.** See above regarding Mamre (13:8) and Kiryath Arba (23:2). As to whether Isaac had moved
there or had lived there all along, see note on 28:10.

35:29   **buried him.** In Makhpelah, see 49:31.

[70. Esau's Line]

¹ These are the chronicles of Esau, also known as Edom.

36

² Esau took wives from the daughters of Canaan. These were Adah, daughter of Elon the Hittite,* and Oholibamah,* daughter of Anah, daughter of Tziv'on* the Hivite.* ³ [He also married] Basemath,* daughter of Ishmael [and] sister of Nebayoth.*

⁴ Adah bore Esau's son Eliphaz.*
Basemath bore Reuel.*

⁵ Oholibamah bore Yeush,* Yalam, and Korach.*
The above are Esau's sons who were born in the land of Canaan.

⁶ Esau took his wives, his sons, his daughters, all the members of his household, his livestock animals, and all the possessions that he had acquired in the land of Canaan, and he moved to another area, away from his brother Jacob. ⁷ This was because they had too much property to be able to live together.* Because of all their livestock, the land where they were staying could not support them. ⁸ Esau therefore settled in the hill country of Seir.* There Esau became [the nation of] Edom.*

36:2 **Adah** . . . Some say that she was Basemath daughter of Elon; see note on 26:34. Others say that she may have been her sister (Ramban).

— **Oholibamah.** Or Aholibamah. Some say that she is Judith daughter of Beeri (Rashi; see note on 26:34). Many, however, dispute this (Rashbam; Ramban; see *Sefer HaYashar*). See 36:41.

— **daughter of Anah, daughter of Tziv'on.** Most probably, "daughter of Anah, granddaughter of Tziv'on" (Ibn Ezra; Ramban on 36:25). We thus see that Oholibamah was the daughter of Anah, who was the son of Tziv'on (36:24,25). According to the Midrash, however, Oholibamah was the daughter of both Anah and Tzivon, since Anah committed incest with his mother (*Bereshith Rabbah* 82; Rashi). According to others, Anah was a woman, the daughter of Tziv'on (*Tosafoth, Bava Bathra* 115b, s.v. *Melamed;* cf. Rashba ibid.; Ritva on *Eyn Yaakov*). According to this, her father could indeed have been Beeri the Hittite.

— **Hivite.** See note on 10:17. This is somewhat difficult, since Tziv'on and Anah are later described as Horites (36:20,24). Some say that Hivite here does not denote a nationality, but rather, an agricultural talent (*Tosafoth, Shabbath* 85a s.v. *Chivi*). Hence, the verse here should be translated, "Tziv'on the agriculturist." Others say that the Horites are descended from the Hivites (*Sefer HaYashar* p. 27), and hence the two tribes are essentially identical (Ramban on Deuteronomy 2:10).

36:3 **Basemath.** Some say that she is identical with Machlath; see note on 28:9. She may have taken the name of Esau's original wife, Basemath (26:34).

— **Nebayoth.** See 38:9.

36:4 **Eliphaz.** See 36:10. He was the father of Amalek (36:11). Some identify him with Job's friend Eliphaz (*Sekhel Tov;* Rashi on Job 4:1; Ibn Ezra on Job 2:11). There is a tradition that Eliphaz had been sent by Esau to kill Jacob, but because Eliphaz had been raised by Isaac, he spared Jacob (Rashi on 29:11).

— **Reuel.** See 36:10,13,17, 1 Chronicles 1:35. Cf. Exodus 2:18, Numbers 10:29.

36:5 **Yeush.** See 36:14,18.

— **Korach.** Although Korach was a son of Oholibamah, some identify him with Chief Korach, son of Eliphaz, a son of Adah (36:16). This would be because Eliphaz fathered Korach by committing adultery with Oholibamah (*Bereshith Rabbah* 82; Rashi). Others say that there were two individuals with the name Korach (Rashi, *Sotah* 13a, s.v. *Shloshim;* Rashbam on 36:16. Cf. Ibn Ezra).

36:7 **too much property** . . . See 13:6.

36:8 **settled in** . . . See note on 32:4. Although Esau may have lived in Seir earlier, he could have now inherited the Hebron area, but he chose to settle in Seir (cf. Josephus 2:1:1). Other sources speak of a war between Esau and Jacob (*Sefer HaYashar; Yov'loth* 38:10).

— **There Esau** . . . Cf. Josephus 2:1:1.

36   ⁹ These are the chronicles of Esau, the ancestor of Edom, in the hill
country of Seir:

   ¹⁰ These are the names of Esau's sons:
      Eliphaz, son of Esau's wife Adah;
      Reuel, son of Esau's wife Basemath.*
   ¹¹ The sons of Eliphaz were Teman,* Omar,* Tzefo,* Gatam,* and Kenaz.*
¹² Timna* became the concubine of Esau's son Eliphaz, and she bore Eliphaz's son Amalek.* All these are the descendants of Esau's wife Adah.

   ¹³ These are the sons of Reuel: Nachath,* Zerach,* Shamah, and Mizzah.
These are the descendants of Esau's wife Basemath.

   ¹⁴ These are the sons of Esau's wife Oholibamah, daughter of Anah,
daughter of Tziv'on: By Esau she had Yeush, Yalam, and Korach.*

   ¹⁵ These are the [original] tribal chiefs* among the children of Esau:

The sons of Esau's firstborn Eliphaz: Chief Teman,* Chief Omar, Chief
Tzefo, Chief Kenaz, ¹⁶ Chief Korach,* Chief Gatam,* Chief Amalek.* These
were the tribal chiefs from Eliphaz in the land of Edom. The above were
descendants of Adah.

   ¹⁷ These are the tribal chiefs among the children of Esau's son Reuel:

36:10 Eliphaz . . . Reuel. See 36:4.

36:11 Teman. See 36:15,42, 1 Chronicles 1:53. Also see 36:34. Teman was a city some 50 miles to the south of
the Dead sea, near Petra. It might also be identified with Yemen (see note on 36:34). See Jeremiah
49:7,20, Ezekiel 25:13, Amos 1:12, Habakkuk 3:3. From the verses, Teman appears to be an area to the
south of Seir; Obadiah 1:9; Ramban on 36:34. Job's friend Eliphaz was from Teman; Job 2:11, see note
on 36:4.

—   **Omar.** See 36:15.

—   **Tzefo.** See 36:15. In 1 Chronicles 1:36, the name is given as Tzefi. There is a tradition that Tzefo was the
military leader of Edom, and possibly one of the early settlers of Rome (*Sefer HaYashar*, pp. 163, 169,
175; *Yossipon* 2; *MeAm Lo'ez/The Torah Anthology* 3:551, 588, 4:8,24,233; Ramban on 49:31; Bachya on
50:9). See note on 36:43.

—   **Gatam.** See 36:16. Josephus renders this as Gotham.

—   **Kenaz.** See 36:15,42. Also see 15:19.

36:12 Timna. She was the daughter of Seir the Horite; 36:22. Although she was a princess, she was content to
be a concubine in Abraham's family (*Sanhedrin* 99b; Rashi). In 1 Chronicles 1:36, however, Timna is
seen as a daughter of Eliphaz. According to Talmudic tradition, Eliphaz fathered Timna by committing
adultery with Seir's wife, and then he married her (*Tanchuma, VaYeshev* 2; Rashi; *BaMidbar Rabbah* 14:10).
Others say that the Timna in Chronicles is a different individual (Radak on Chronicles; Ramban). See
Lekach Tov; Rashbam, here. This may be the Timna in 36:40, and she may have been a woman (See
Rashba, *Bava Bathra 115b*).

—   **Amalek.** Israel's arch-enemy; Exodus 17:16, Deuteronomy 25:19. See 36:16.

36:13 Nachath . . . See 36:5,18.

—   **Zerach.** See 36:33.

36:14 Yeush, Yalam . . . See 36:5,18.

36:15 tribal chiefs. Kings without a crown (*Sanhedrin* 99b; see Ramban on 36:40, Numbers 20:14). These might
have ruled before the kings, or concurrently, see Exodus 15:15.

—   **Chief Teman.** See 36:11.

36:16 Korach. See note on 36:5. Some say that this is the Timna in 1 Chronicles 1:36 (Rashbam; see *BaMidbar
Rabbah* 14:10).

—   **Gatam.** See 36:11.

—   **Amalek.** See 36:12.

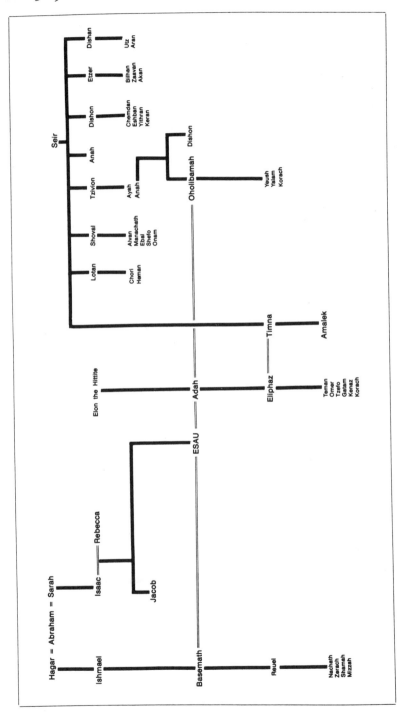

PLATE 9. ESAU'S FAMILY

36 Chief Nachath, Chief Zerach, Chief Shamah, Chief Mizzah.* These are the
tribal chiefs from Reuel in the land of Edom. The above were descendants of
Esau's wife Basemath.
    ¹⁸ These are the sons of Esau's wife Oholibamah: Chief Yeush, Chief
Yalam, Chief Korach.* These are the tribal chiefs from Esau's wife Oholibamah, daughter of Anah.
    ¹⁹ These are the sons of Esau, and these are their tribal chiefs. This is what
constitutes Edom.

[71. Seir's Line]

    ²⁰ These are the children of Seir the Horite,* the [original] inhabitants of
the land: Lotan,* Shoval,* Tziv'on,* Anah,* ²¹ Dishon,* Etzer,* Dishan.* These
were the tribal chiefs of the Horites among the sons of Seir in the land of
Edom.
    ²² The sons of Lotan were Chori* and Hemam. Lotan's sister was Timna.*
    ²³ These are the sons of Shoval: Alvan,* Manachath, Ebhal, Shefo,* and
Onam.
    ²⁴ These are the children of Tziv'on: Ayah* and Anah.* Anah was the one
who discovered [how to breed] mules* in the desert when he was tending the
donkeys for his father Tziv'on.

36:17 Nachath . . . See 36:13.
36:18 Yeush . . .See 36:5,14.
36:20 Horite. See notes on 14:6, 36:2. See also 36:22. However, some maintain that the term *chori* here does
not denote a nation, but rather nobility (*Targum Yonathan;* Ibn Ezra, from Jeremiah 27:20). Thus, the
verse would be translated, "These are the sons of the noble Seir," or "these are the sons of Seir the free-
man." Others translate the verse, "These are the sons of the Horite lineage in the land of Seir" (Ramban; cf. Josephus 2:1:1). Seir then denotes Esau, see note on 25:25. Some say that Seir's lineage was:
Ham, Canaan, Chivi, Chur, Seir (*Sefer HaYashar,* p. 27).
—   **Lotan.** See 36:22,29.
—   **Shoval.** See 36:29.
—   **Tziv'on.** See 36:2,29.
—   **Anah.** See note on 36:2. Here Anah is seen as a son of Seir, while in 36:24, he is a son of Tziv'on.
According to Talmudic tradition, Tziv'on fathered Anah by committing incest with his mother
(*Pesachim* 54a; Rashi on 36:24).
36:21 Dishon. See 36:26,30. Also see 36:25.
—   **Etzer.** See 36:27,30.
—   **Dishan.** See 36:38,30.
36:22 Chori. Or Hori. It is possible that he was the one to give the name to the Horites.
—   **Timna.** See note on 36:12.
36:23 Alvan. In 1 Chronicles 1:40, it is Alyan. See 36:40.
—   **Shefo.** In 1 Chronicles 1:40 it is Shefi (cf. Ralbag there).
36:24 Ayah. See 1 Chronicles 1:40. Others, however, have the name here as V'ayah or Fayah (Rashbam; Ibn
Ezra).
—   **Anah.** See notes on 36:2, 36:24.
—   **mules.** (*Pesachim* 54b; *Chullin* 7b; *Yerushalmi Berakhoth* 8:5; Rashi). The mule is a crossbreed between a
horse and a donkey. *Yemim* in Hebrew. Others identify the *Yemim* with the Emim (14:5), and translate the
verse, "who encountered giants" (Onkelos; cf. Ibn Ezra, Ramban. Also see *Sefer HaYashar,* p. 97). The
Vulgate translates *yemim* as "hot springs," and the Syriac renders it as water or springs, but there is no

²⁵ These are the children of Anah*: Dishon* and Oholibamah daughter of **36** Anah.

²⁶ These are the sons of Dishon*: Chemdan,* Eshban, Yithran* and Keran.

²⁷ These are the sons of Etzer: Bilhan, Zaavan, and Akan.*

²⁸ These are the sons of Dishan: Utz* and Aran.

²⁹ These are the tribal chiefs of the Horites: Chief Lotan, Chief Shoval, Chief Tziv'on, Chief Anah, ³⁰ Chief Dishon, Chief Etzer, Chief Dishan. These are tribes* of the Horites according to their chiefs in the land of Seir.

[72. Kings of Edom]

³¹ These are the kings who ruled in the land of Edom before any king reigned over the Israelites.*

³² Bela son of Beor* became king of Edom, and the name of his capital* was Dinhava.*

---

support for this in Judaic sources. (Also see *Or Yashar, Siddur Ramak, Amud HaTorah* 11). The Septuagint leaves the word untranslated.

36:25 Anah. If Anah son of Seir and Anah son of Tziv'on are two different individuals, this is most probably the former.

— **Dishon.** See 36:21.

— **Oholibamah.** Esau's wife; 36:2.

36:26 Dishon. Dishan in the text, but from the context, and order in 36:21, this is Dishon. This is also the way it is in 1 Chronicles 1:41 (see Radak *ad loc.*). Some say that Dishan died and Dishon took his name (*Lekach Tov*).

— **Chemdan.** In 1 Chronicles 1:41 it is Chamran.

— **Yithran.** Possibly Yetheth in 36:40.

36:27 Akan. In 1 Chronicles 1:42 it is Yaakan.

36:28 Utz. See above 10:23, 22:21. The *Targum* on 1 Chronicles 1:42 renders it Armanyus; see *Targum* on 1 Chronicles 1:17; note on 10:23.

36:30 tribes. See note on 36:40.

36:31 before any king . . . Simply, this means that these kings reigned long before there was a king in Israel. Many commentaries, however, state that the first king of Israel alluded to in this verse is Moses (cf. Deuteronomy 33:5; Rashbam; Ibn Ezra; Ralbag). We do, however, find that there were Edomite kings contemporary to Moses (Numbers 20:14). Therefore, it must be said that Moses was not considered a king until the concept of a king was given to the Israelites (Deuteronomy 17:15). It also appears that the chiefs (*alufim*) ruled over Edom right after the Exodus (cf. Exodus 15:15), but the kings may have reigned concurrently (see *Mekhilta* on Exodus 15:14; but see Ramban on 36:40). Of course, if the *alufim* are seen as tribes (see 36:40), this does not present any problem.

There is a tradition that the Edomite kings began to reign 550 years before the first Israelite king (Rabenu Chananel, quoted in Bachya on 32:16). Since Saul, the first king of Israel, took his throne in 2882 (879 b.c.e.), this would mean that Edom's kingdom began 550 years earlier in 2332 (1429 b.c.e.). This was the year that Levi died, and it is well established that Levi was the last of Jacob's sons to die. Thus, there may have been a tradition that Esau's kingdom did not begin during the lifetime of any of Jacob's sons.

There is, however, a conflicting tradition that the reign of Bela (36:32) began in 2258, twenty years after Jacob came to Egypt (see note on 36:32).

36:32 Bela son of Beor. According to one tradition (see above note), his reign began in 2258, twenty years after Jacob came to Egypt (*Sefer HaYashor*, p. 167). He reigned for 30 years, until 2288 (*ibid.*). Other sources, however, identify Bela with Balaam son of Beor (Numbers 22:5; *Targum* on 1 Chronicles 1:43; but see

36   ³³ Bela died, and he was succeeded as king by Yovev* son of Zerach* from Botzrah.*

³⁴ Yovav died, and he was succeeded as king by Chusham* from the land of the Temanites.*

³⁵ Chusham died, and he was succeeded as king by Hadad son of Badad,* who defeated Midian in the field of Moab.* The name of his capital was Avith.

³⁶ Hadad died, and he was succeeded as king by Samlah* of Masrekah.*

³⁷ Samlah died, and he was succeeded as king by Saul* from Rechovoth-on-the-River (*Rechovoth HaNahar*).*

³⁸ Saul died, and he was succeeded as king by Baal Chanan* son of Akhbor.

Ibn Ezra here). This would be very difficult to reconcile with a chronology that places all these kings before Moses' death, since Balaam was not killed until the 40th year after the Exodus (Numbers 31:8).

— **capital** (*Targum Yonathan*). Others state that this is the city of his birth (*Shemoth Rabbah* 37; Rashi; cf. Ramban). According to the second opinion, the cities mentioned in this section are not in Edom.

— **Dinhava.** According to the first opinion in the previous note, this is an unidentified city in Edom. According to the second opinion, it is a city in Africa (*Sefer HaYashar*, p. 169). Some sources identify it with Carthage or a nearby city (*Yossipun* 2). Around this time, Carthage (still known as Cambe) was ruled by colonists from Sidon (see *The Torah Anthology*, Volume 3, p. 666, note 68). It was invaded by the Phoenicians in 814 b.c.e. when its name was changed to Carthage.

36:33 **Yovav.** He reigned for 10 years, from 2288 to 2298 (*Sefer HaYashar*, p. 168). See above 10:29, Joshua 11:4.

— **Zerach.** See 36:13.

— **Botzrah.** Some say that this was a city in Edom (Ramban); cf. Isaiah 34:6, 63:1. This can be identified as Buseirah, 20 miles south of the Dead Sea in Seir (cf. *BaMidbar Rabbah* 14:10; Ptolemy, *Geography* 5:17). Others say that it is the city in Moab mentioned in Jeremiah 48:24 (Rashi; cf. *Bereshith Rabbah* 83). This is a city in Gilead some 15 miles east of the Kinneret Sea, later known as Bostra or Busra-Eski Sham (cf. 1 Maccabees 5:26). Also see Jeremiah 49:13, 49:22, Amos 1:12, Micah 2:12. The *Targum* (on 1 Chronicles 1:44) renders it Bevatra. The dispute as to whether it was in Edom or Moab would follow the question as to whether the cities mentioned here are Edomite capitals, or the birthplaces of the Edomite kings.

36:34 **Chusham.** He reigned for 20 years, from 2298 to 2318 (*Sefer HaYashar*, pp. 168, 173). He died around the same time as Dan.

— **Temanites.** Teman is associated with Botzrah (Amos 1:12). It is therefore a capital city of Esau (Obadiah 1:9; Bachya; *BaMidbar Rabbah* 14:10). This is identified with a city a mile or two east of Petra, some 50 miles south of the Dead Sea. Others identify it with Mocha, a city in Yemen, and hence, Yemen is known as Teman (*MeAm Lo'ez/The Torah Anthology* 3:209). The *Targum* simply renders it as "South."

36:35 **Hadad son of Badad.** He reigned 35 years, from 2318 to 2353, and died in the same year as Kohath son of Levi (*Sefer Hayashar*, p. 173). Hadad was the name of a Syrian storm god, and was hence a common name. See 1 Kings 11:14, 15:18. (cf. Ibn Ezra on 36:31).

— **who defeated . . .** This took place before the Exodus (*Sefer HaYashar*, p. 174). Later Midian and Moab made peace out of fear of the Israelites (Rashi; *Sifri*, Rashi, on Numbers 22:4; *BaMidbar Rabbah* 20:5). These sources would also contradict the teaching that Bela was Balaam (note on 36:32).

36:36 **Samlah.** He reigned 18 years, from 2353 to 2371 (*Sefer HaYashar*, pp. 182, 188).

— **Masrekah.** Some associate this with the Tzemari mentioned in 10:18 (*Sekhel Tov*).

36:37 **Saul.** *Sha'ul* in Hebrew, like the Israelite King Saul. He reigned 40 years, from 2371 to 2411 (*Sefer Ha-Yashar*, p. 188).

— **Rechovoth HaNahar.** The *Targum* renders it Rechovoth on the Euphrates, following the tradition that this was the home town of the king, not a city in Edom. It may be associated with Rechovoth Ir (10:11). Other sources translate it as "Avenues on the River" (*Targum* on 1 Chronicles 1:48). It is also identified with Pethorah (Balaam's city; Numbers 22:5, Deuteronomy 23:5; *Sefer HaYashar*, p. 188). According to those who maintain that the cities are in Edom, the "river" here would probably be the Zered Brook which formed the northern boundary of Edom.

36:38 **Baal Chanan.** He reigned 38 years, from 2411 to 2449 (*Sefer HaYashar*, pp. 188, 196). According to this,

³⁹ Baal Chanan son of Akhbor died, and he was succeeded as king by **36** Hadar.* The name of his capital was Pau.* His wife's name was Meheitaval, daughter of Matred, daughter of May Zahav.*

⁴⁰ These are the names of the tribes* of Esau, according to their families in their respective areas, named after [individuals]*: The tribe of Timna,* the tribe of Alvah,* the tribe of Yetheth,* ⁴¹ the tribe of Oholibamah,* the tribe of Elah,* the tribe of Pinon,* ⁴² the tribe of Kenaz,* the tribe of Teman,* the tribe of Mibtzar,* ⁴³ the tribe of Magdiel,* the tribe of Iram.*

he was king at the time of the Exodus in 2448. From the *Sefer HaYashar* (p. 203), however, it seems that he died before the Exodus. Therefore, some sources amend the reading and state that he reigned 35 years, from 2411 to 2446 (note on *Seder HaDoroth* 2444; see note on 36:39). The name Baal Chanan may be interpreted to mean "Baal is merciful" (the same as Hannibal cf. *Sekhel Tov*). Others say that Chanan was his city, and the name means "Master of Chanan" (Ramban; *Tur*).

36:39 Hadar. In 1 Chronicles 1:50 it is Hadad. He was from Aramaea and reigned for 48 years, from 2446 to 2493/4. He was defeated and killed 5 years after the death of Moses (*Sefer HaYashar* 203, 228). Since the Torah was written while he was still alive, there is no mention of his death here, but it is mentioned in 1 Chronicles 1:50 (Malbim on Chronicles). He was the king who refused the Israelites passage through his land (Numbers 20:14).

— **Pau.** In 1 Chronicles 1:50 it is Pa'i (Radak ad loc.).

— **May Zahav.** Literally Water of Gold or Gold-water. The verse appears to indicate that Meheitaval was the daughter of both Matred and May Zahav (cf. 36:2). Thus, May Zahav may have been her grandfather. Alternatively, Matred and May Zahav were her father and mother (Ibn Ezra). Other sources say that May Zahav was Matred's nickname, because he could pour gold like water (*Lekach Tov;* Bachya; cf. *Targum Yonathan*). Others say that he was a refiner of gold, melting gold like water (*Targum Onkelos;* Saadia).

36:40 tribes. The same word, *aluf,* is used here as above, but here the meaning is somewhat different. If *aluf* above would be translated as "duke," here it would be translated as "dukedom" (cf. Rashi; Ibn Ezra). Some say that these are the chiefs that ruled after the period of the kings (Ramban; Ralbag; Radak; cf. 1 Chronicles 1:51, *Targum* ad loc.). This, however, would be impossible to reconcile with the above chronology, since these chiefs would have lived after the Torah was given (see note on 36:31). According to this second opinion, the *alufim* mentioned here may be individuals. They also may be the tribes that survived until the end of the period of kings, and existed in the time of Moses (cf. Rashbam).

— **according to their families** ... cf. 10:5,31.

— **Timna.** Possibly a son of Eliphaz; cf. 1 Chronicles 1:36 (see *Lekach Tov; Sekhel Tov;* Rashbam; on 36:12). Timna was also the name of Eliphaz' concubine (36:12,22), and the Timna here may have been a woman (Rashba, *Bava Bathra* 115b; cf. *BaMidbar Rabbah* 14:10; Ibn Ezra). Others say that this Timna was a son of Yeush (36:14; *Sefer HaYashar,* p. 97).

— **Alvah.** Possibly the same as Alvan (36:23). Others say that these were sons of Timna, and hence, tribes of Amalek (36:12; Ibn Ezra). Another opinion is that Alvah was a son of Yeush (*Sefer HaYashar, loc. cit.*).

— **Yetheth.** Possibly Yithran (36:26). Others say that Yetheth was a son of Yeush (*Sefer HaYashar*).

36:41 Oholibamah. This was the name of Esau's wife (36:2,5,14). It is possible that she had a tribe named after her, particularly since she is treated specially with regard to the chiefs (36:18). Some say that this Oholibamah was a woman chief (Rashba, *Bava Bathra* 115b). According to others, it was a man with this name (Ibn Ezra). Some say that he was a son of Yalam, son of Oholibamah (36:14; *Sefer HaYashar*).

— **Elah.** Possibly a son of Yalam (*Sefer HaYashar*). Some identify this tribe with the city of Elat (1 Samuel 17:2; cf. Deuteronomy 2:8, 2 Kings 14:22, 16:6).

— **Pinon.** Also a son of Yalam (*Sefer HaYashar*). This is associated with Punan in the Tzalmona area (Numbers 33:42; *Sekhel Tov*).

36:42 Kenaz. A son of Eliphaz (36:11,15; *Sekhel Tov*). According to others, a son of Yalam (*Sefer HaYashar*). See 15:19.

— **Teman.** A son of Eliphaz (36:11,15; *Sekhel Tov*). According to others, a son of Korach (36:14; *Sefer HaYashar*).

— **Mibtzar.** See Psalms 118:11 (cf. *Sekhel Tov*). A son of Korach (*Sefer HaYashar*).

36:43 Magdiel. Some say that this is the tribe that founded Rome (*Pirkey Rabbi Eliezer* 38; Rashi; cf. *Bereshith*

36   These are the tribes of Esau, each with its own settlements in its hereditary lands. This is how Esau was the ancestor of the Edomites.

VaYeshev   וַיֵּשֶׁב

[73. Joseph is Sold]

37   [1] Meanwhile, Jacob settled in the area* where his father had lived in the land of Canaan.
[2] These are the chronicles of Jacob:
Joseph was 17 years old. As a lad, he would tend the sheep with his brothers, the sons of Bilhah and Zilpah, his father's wives. Joseph brought his father a bad report about them.
[3] Israel loved Joseph more than any of his other sons, since he was the child of his old age. He made [Joseph] a long colorful coat.* [4] When his brothers realized that their father loved him more than all the rest, they began to hate him. They could not say a peaceful word to him.
[5] Then Joseph had a dream, and when he told it to his brothers, they hated him all the more. [6] "Listen to the dream I had," he said to them. [7] "We were binding sheaves in the field, when my sheaf suddenly stood up erect. Your sheaves formed a circle around my sheaf, and bowed down to it."
[8] "Do you want to be our king?" retorted the brothers. "Do you intend to rule over us?" Because of his dreams and words, they hated him even more.
[9] He had another dream and told it to his brothers. "I just had another dream," he said. "The sun, the moon, and eleven stars were bowing down to me."
[10] When he told it to his father and brothers, his father scolded him and said, "What kind of dream did you have? Do you want me, your mother, and your brothers to come and prostrate ourselves on the ground to you?" [11] His

Rabbah 83). Some say that Magdiel was a son of Korach (*Sefer HaYashar*). There are also traditions that Eliphaz's son Tzefo (36:11) founded Rome or settled the area (*Yosippun* 2; *Yalamdenu* 72, in *Batey Midrashim* 1:160). He became king over the Italians in 2316, and this was 78 years after Jacob arrived in Egypt (*Sefer HaYashar* pp. 172, 175).
—   **Iram.** Also a son of Korach (*Sefer HaYashar*, p. 97). There is a tradition that he will bring gifts to the Messiah (*Bereshith Rabbah* 83).
37:1 settled in the area. Hebron; 37:14. Also see 35:27.
37:3 long colorful coat. *Kethoneth passim* in Hebrew. It was a royal garment; 2 Samuel 13:18 (cf. Ralbag *ad loc.*). The word *passim* can be translated as "colorful" (Radak; Septuagint), embroidered (Ibn Ezra; Bachya; Ramban on Exodus 28:2), striped (Ibn Janach; Radak, *Sherashim*), or with pictures (*Targum Yonathan*). It can also denote a long garment, coming down to the palms of the hands (Rashbam; Ibn Ezra; Baaley Tosafoth; *Bereshith Rabbah* 84), and the feet (*Lekach Tov*). Alternatively, the word denotes the material out of which the coat was made, which was fine wool (Rashi) or silk (Ibn Janach). Hence, *kethoneth passim,* may be translated as "a full-sleeved robe," "a coat of many colors," "a coat reaching to his feet," "an ornamented tunic," "a silk robe," or "a fine woolen cloak."

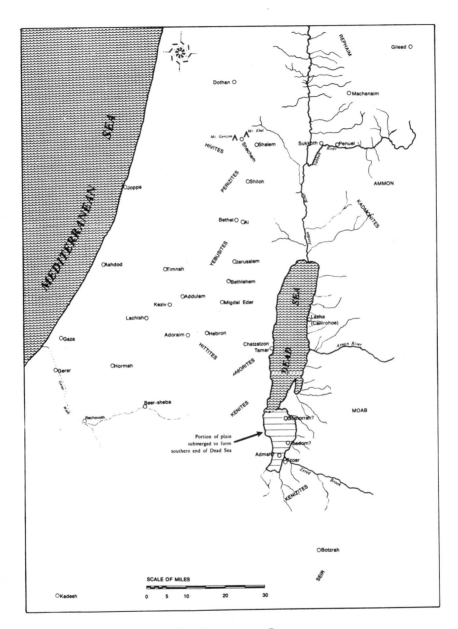

PLATE 10.   LAND OF THE PATRIARCHS

37 brothers became very jealous of him, but his father suspended judgment.*

¹² [Joseph's] brothers left to tend their father's sheep in Shechem.* ¹³ Israel said to Joseph, "I believe* your brothers are keeping the sheep in Shechem. I would like you to go to them."

"I'm ready," replied [Joseph].

¹⁴ "Then see how your brothers and the sheep are doing," said [Israel]. "Bring me a report."

[Israel] thus sent him from the Hebron valley, and [Joseph] arrived in Shechem. ¹⁵ A stranger* found him blundering about in the fields. "What are you looking for?" asked the stranger.

¹⁶ "I'm looking for my brothers," replied [Joseph]. "Perhaps you can tell me where they are tending the sheep."

¹⁷ "They already left this area," said the man. "I heard them planning to go to Dothan.*"

Joseph went after his brothers and found them in Dothan. ¹⁸ They saw him in the distance, and before he reached them, they were plotting to kill him.

¹⁹ "Here comes the dreamer!" they said to one another.* "Now we have the chance! Let's kill him and throw him into one of the wells. We can say that a wild beast ate him. Then let's see what will become of his dreams!"

²¹ Reuben heard these words and tried to rescue [Joseph]. "Let's not kill him!" he said.

²² Reuben tried to reason with his brothers. "Don't commit bloodshed. You can throw him into this well* in the desert, and you won't have to lay a hand on him." His plan was to rescue [Joseph] from [his brothers] and bring him back to his father.

²³ When Joseph came to his brothers, they stripped him of the long colorful coat that he was wearing. ²⁴ They took* him and threw him into the well. The well was empty; there was no water in it.

37:11 **suspended judgment.** Or, "pondered the matter," "kept the matter in mind" or, "his father waited to see the result" (Rashi). Literally, "his father watched the word."

37:12 **Shechem.** See 12:6, 33:18, 48:22. Shechem is some 48 miles north of Hebron.

37:13 **I believe . . .** This is actually posed as a question, "Aren't your brothers . . .?" In many cases, however, the question is rhetorical, and is more accurately translated as a statment. See 40:8.

37:15 **stranger.** A traveler (Ibn Ezra). Others say that it was Gabriel (*Targum Yonathan;* Rashi).

37:17 **Dothan.** Tell Dothna, a city some 15 miles north of Shechem. It later became part of the territory of Joseph (Manasseh); see 2 Kings 6:13.

37:19 **to one another.** According to Talmudic tradition, the main plotters were Simeon and Levi (*Targum Yonathan*). See 49:6. It is for this reason that, of the older brothers, only Reuben and Judah spoke up to spare Joseph. According to other sources, Simeon, Dan and Gad were the main plotters (*Tzava'ath Zebulun* 2:1).

37:22 **well.** A well that had been dug, but had come out dry (*Tzava'ath Zebulun* 2:7). Alternatively "pit" or "cistern."

37:24 **they took.** Written, "he took." Some say that it was Simeon who threw Joseph into the pit (*Bereshith Rabbah* 84). It was for this reason that Simeon was later singled out for special punishment by Joseph

²⁵ The [brothers] sat down and ate a meal. When they looked up, they saw an Arab* caravan coming from Gilead.* The camels were carrying gum,* balsam,* and resin,* transporting them to Egypt.   **37**

²⁶ Judah said to his brothers, "What will we gain if we kill our brother and cover his blood? ²⁷ Let's sell him to the Arabs and not harm him with our own hands. After all, he's our brother, our own flesh and blood." His brothers agreed.

²⁸ The strangers, who turned out to be Midianite traders* approached, and [the brothers*] pulled Joseph out of the well. They sold him to the Arabs for twenty pieces of silver. [These Midianite Arabs] were to bring Joseph to Egypt.

²⁹ When Reuben returned to the well, Joseph was no longer there.

(42:24). According to others, it was Reuben who gently lowered Joseph into the pit (Josephus, *Antiquities* 2:3:2).

37:25 **Arab.** (*Targum;* Saadia). Literally, Ishmaelites. See 1 Chronicles 2:17, 27:30. Also see note on 37:28.

— **Gilead.** Gilead was to the northeast of the Holy Land, on the trade route from Mesopotamia to Egypt, as we see in the case of Jacob above (31:21). This route passed through Dothan. It was famous for its spices, see following notes.

— **gum.** *Nekhoth* in Hebrew. See 43:11. The *Targum* renders it as *sh'af,* a kind of wax or gum (Rashi; cf. *Bereshith Rabbah* 91). On the basis of Semitic cognates, it is usually identified with tragacanth, the aromatic sap of a species of *Astragalus,* a short prickly shrub of the family Papilionaceae (cf.Septuagint). Others say that it comes from the member of the carob family (*Lekach Tov;* Ibn Janach; Radak, *Sherashim*). Rashi says that *nekhoth* is a generic word for spices.

— **balsam.** *Tzeri* or *Tzori* in Hebrew. Balsam is a gum extracted from the sap of the tree *Commiphora apobasamum,* and it is used for incense and perfume. Gilead was a famed source of balsam (Jeremiah 8:22, 46:11).

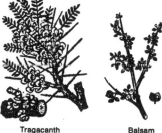

Tragacanth   Balsam

— **resin.** *Lot* in Hebrew. See 43:11. On the basis of Semitic cognates, it is usually identified as labdanum or laudanum, a soft, dark resin derived from various bushes known as rockroses, of the genus *cistus.* It is used for making perfume. The Midrash defines it as mastic (*Bereshith Rabbah* 91), the resin of the mastic tree, *Pistacia lenticus,* a member of the pistachio family (cf. Septuagint). The *Targum* renders it *letum,* a species mentioned in the Mishnah (*Shevi'ith* 7:6), and identified as a chestnut (Rambam *ad loc.;* Ibn Janach) or pine extract (Ibn Janach; cf. Radak, *Sherashim*). Rashi identifies it as aristolocia, the birthwort. (See *Otzar Maasoth,* p. 95).

Rock Rose   Mastic

37:28 **Midianite traders.** These were the Arabs mentioned above. When they approached, they were recognizable as Midianites (Ibn Ezra; Radak; cf. Josephus 2:3:3; *Yov'loth* 34:11). We thus see that the Midianites are called "Arabs" (Ishmaelites; Judges 8:24). This might have been because Ishmael was identified with all his brothers (25:18). Others say that the Ishmaelites and Midianites were two different groups, see next note.

— **the brothers** (Rashi). There is a tradition that they bought shoes with the money that they got for Joseph (*Tanchuma* 2; cf. *Tzava'ath Zebulun* 3:2). Some say that the brothers sold Joseph to the Ishmaelites, and the Ishmaelites to the Midianites (Rashi). According to others, it was the Midianites who took Joseph from the pit (*Sefer HaYashar;* Rashbam; Bachya). There is a tradition that Joseph was sold on Yom Kippur (*Yov'loth* 34:13).

37 [Reuben] tore his clothes in grief. [30] He returned to his brothers. "The boy is gone!" he exclaimed. "And I—where can I go?"

[31] [The brothers] took Joseph's coat. They slaughtered a goat and dipped the coat in the blood. [32] They sent the long colorful coat, and it was brought to their father. "We found this," explained [the brothers when they returned]. "Try to identify it. Is it your son's coat or not?"

[33] [Jacob immediately] recognized it. "It is my son's coat!" he cried. "A wild beast must have eaten him! My Joseph has been torn to pieces!" [34] He tore his robes in grief and put on sackcloth. He kept himself in mourning for many days. [35] All his sons and daughters* tried to console him, but he refused to be comforted. "I will go down to the grave mourning for my son," he said. He wept for [his son] as only a father could.*

[36] The Midanites* sold [Joseph] in Egypt to Potiphar,* one of Pharaoh's officers, captain of the guard.*

[74. Judah and Tamar]

38 [1] Around this time, Judah left his brothers. He became friends* with a man of Adullam* by the name of Chirah.* [2] There Judah met the daughter*

37:35 daughters. This is the first mention of Jacob's daughters. These may be previously unmentioned daughters, or alternatively, Jacob's daughters-in-law (*Targum Yonathan; Bereshith Rabbah* 84; Rashi), or granddaughters (Ibn Ezra).

— **as only a father . . .** Literally, "his father wept for him." Some translate, "Thus his father wept for him." According to others, it was Isaac who wept for Jacob (*Targum Yonathan; Bereshith Rabbah* 84; Rashi; Ibn Ezra). On the basis of the chronology in the Torah, Isaac did not die until Joseph was 29 years old, 12 years after he was sold.

37:36 Midanites. Actually, the Midanites and Midianites were separate tribes (25:2). Some say that the Midianites sold Joseph to the Midanites (*Bereshith Rabbah* 84; see *Sefer HaYashar*). Others, however, state that the Midanites here are the same as the Midianites (*Targum*). Moreover, from the context, it seems obvious that the Midianites are the same as the Arabs or Ishmaelites (see 39:1; Ramban).

— **Potiphar.** This is an Egyptian name, *Pa-diu-par*, meaning "given of the house" in ancient Egyptian, hence denoting a steward. *Par* is ancient Egyptian for house, as in Par-aoh (above, 12:15). It can also be related to the name found in ancient inscriptions. *Pa-diu-ap-Ra*, literally, "one whom Ra has given," where Ra is the Egyptian sun god. This is also the meaning of Poti Phera, below, 41:45.

— **captain of the guard.** Cf. 2 Kings 25:8, Jeremiah 39:9. The royal prison was therefore in his house; below 40:13. Some say that he was the chief executioner (*Targum*; Saadia; Ramban; cf. Daniel 2:14). Others say that he was the chief butcher (Rashi; cf. Ibn Ezra) or chief cook (Josephus 2:4:1; cf. 1 Samuel 9:23,24). He was the third most powerful man in the kingdom (*Tzav'ath Yosef* 13:5). Some say that he was the priest of Elev (*Yov'loth* 34:11), while others identify him with Poti Phera (see 41:45).

38:1 became friends with . . . See 38:12,20. Others, "He camped around until he came to . . ." (Redak).

— **Adullam.** This is a city some 41 miles south of Shechem, and 11 miles northwest of Hebron. It is identified with Tel esh-Sheikh Madhkur. See Joshua 12:15, 15:35, 1 Samuel 22:1, 2 Samuel 23:13, Micah 1:15, Nehemiah 11:30.

— **Chirah.** He was the foreman of Judah's shepherds (below, 38:12; *Tzava'ath Yehudah* 8:1). From the expression, "his name was Chirah," we see that he was a righteous person. There is a tradition that whenever the expression, "his name was," precedes the actual name, the person in question was righteous (*BaMidbar Rabbah* 10; *Esther Rabbah* 6:2).

38:2 daughter. Some say that her name was Alyath (*Sefer HaYashar*, p. 126). Other sources give her name as Bath Shua (*Yov'loth* 34:20; cf. 38:12; 1 Chronicles 2:3).

of a merchant* named Shua.* He married her and came to her. **38**
³ She became pregnant and had a son. He named the child Er. ⁴ She
became pregnant again, and had another son. She named him Onan. ⁵ She
gave birth once again to a son, and she named him Shelah. [Judah] was in
Keziv* when she gave birth to [this child].

⁶ Judah took a wife for Er his first-born, and her name was Tamar.*
⁷ Judah's first-born Er was evil in God's eyes, and God made him die. ⁸ Judah
said to Onan, "Marry your brother's wife, and thus fulfill the duty of a
brother-in-law* to her. You will then raise children to keep your brother's
[name] alive.*" ⁹ Onan, however, realized* that the children would not carry
his name. Therefore, whenever he came to his brother's wife, he let [the seed]
go to waste on the ground,* so as not to have children in his brother's name.
¹⁰ What he did was evil in God's eyes, and He also made him die.

¹¹ Judah said to his daughter-in-law Tamar, "Live as a widow in your
father's house until my son Shelah is grown." He was putting her off* because
he was concerned that [Shelah], too, would die like his brothers. Tamar left
and lived in her father's house.

¹² A long time passed, and Judah's wife, the daughter of Shua, died. Judah
sought consolation, and he went to supervise his sheep shearers in Timna,*
together with his friend, Chirah the Adullamite. ¹³ Tamar was told that her
father-in-law was going to Timna to shear his sheep. ¹⁴ She took off her
widow's garb, and covered herself with a veil. Thus disguised, she sat at the

---

— **merchant.** (*Targum; Pesachim* 50a; Rashi). Literally, a "Canaanite." The word "Canaanite," however, is used to denote a merchant; see Isaiah 23:8, Hosea 12:8, Zechariah 14:21; Proverbs 26:24, Job 40:50. It can come from the word *kana*, meaning to drive down and hence denote a bargainer or haggler (Ramban; Radak, *Sherashim*). The Holy Land may have thus been known as the "Land of Canaan" or "Trade Land" because it was on the trade route from Mesopotamia to Egypt.
　Others, however, say that Shua was actually a Canaanite (Saadia; Ibn Ezra; *Sefer HaYashar*, p. 126; *Yov'loth* 34:20). See 1 Chronicles 2:3 (*Targum*; Malbim *ad loc.*).
— **Shua.** Shoa is a nation in Babylonia (Isaiah 22:5, Ezekiel 23:23), and if he was not a Canaanite, this may have been his place of origin. The expression, "his name was Shua" would indicate that he was a righteous man (*Sekhel Tov;* see note on 38:1). Some say that he was king of Adullam (*Tzava'ath Yehudah* 8:2).
38:5 Keziv. Most probably Akhziv or Achziv (Joshua 15:44, Micah 1:14) or Kezeba (1 Chronicles 4:22), a town some 3 miles southwest of Adullam. It is identified as Tel el-Beida.
38:6 Tamar. Literally a "palm tree." This is a name that would recur in David's family (1 Samuel 13:1), since he was a descendant of Tamar (see note on 38:29). Since it says "her name was Tamar," we see that she was righteous. Some say that she was from Aram Naharaim (*Tzava'ath Yehudah* 10:1; *Yov'loth* 41:1).
38:8 duty of a brother-in-law. *Yibum* in Hebrew; see Deuteronomy 25:5; Ruth 1:15. Some say that this was instituted by Judah (*Bereshith Rabbah* 85).
— **You will then . . .** Literally, "you will then raise up seed for your brother."
38:9 realized. On the basis of what his father had told him (*Sekhel Tov Yov'loth* 41:5). Other sources indicate that his mother did not want him to have children by Tamar (*Tzava'ath Yehudah* 10:6).
— **let the seed go to waste . . .** It is from here that all the discussions regarding birth control and masturbation are derived (*Yevamoth* 34b; *Niddah* 13a; *Bereshith Rabbah* 85).
38:11 putting her off (Rashi; *Sefer HaYashar*, p. 128). Literally, "he said."
38:12 Timna. A city 4 miles northeast of Adullam, now known as Tibna. See Joshua 15:57, 2 Chronicles 28:18.

38   entrance of Twin Wells (*Eynayim**) on the road to Timna. She had seen that
     Shelah had grown, and she had not been given to him as a wife.
        ¹⁵ Judah saw her, and because she had covered her face,* he assumed that
     she was a prostitute.* ¹⁶ He turned aside to her on the road, not realizing that
     she was his own daughter-in-law.
        "Hello there," he said. "Let me come to you."
        "What will you give me if you come to me?"
        ¹⁷ "I will send you a kid from the flock."
        "But you must give me something for security until you send it."
        ¹⁸ "What do you want for security?"
        "Your seal, your wrap,* and the staff in your hand," she replied.
        He gave them to her and came to her, making her pregnant. ¹⁹ She got up
     and left, taking off her veil and putting her widow's garb back on.
        ²⁰ Judah sent the young kid with his friend the Adullamite in order to get
     the security back from the woman, but [his friend] could not find her. ²¹ [The
     friend] asked the local people, "where is the religious prostitute*? She was
     near Twin Wells (*Eynayim*), alongside the road."
        "There was no religious prostitute here," they replied.
        ²² He returned to Judah and said, "I could not find [the woman]. The local
     men said that there was no sacred prostitute there."
        ²³ "Let her keep [the security]," replied Judah. "We don't want to become
     a laughingstock. I tried to send her the kid, but you couldn't find her."
        ²⁴ Some three months passed, and Judah was told, "Your daughter-in-law
     has been behaving loosely. She has become pregnant from her looseness."

38:14 Eynayim. Twin Wells or Twin Springs or Eyes. Some identify Eynayim with Enam in Joshua 15:34. See
   below 38:21, where it is also referred to as Eynayim. Others say that it denotes two wells with a gate
   between them (Ibn Ezra), or a fork in the road by a well (Rashi). Others interpret it as "open eyes," and
   state that it denotes an open, visible place (Rashbam; Radak; cf. *Targum; Lekach Tov; Sekhel Tov*).
38:15 covered her face. It was the custom for sacred prostitutes to cover their faces (Ramban; Bachya). Ancient
   sources describe this as being like a wreath of string covering the head and face (Herodotus 1:199).
—   **prostitute.** See note on 38:21.
38:18 wrap. *Pethilah* in Hebrew. This is alternatively translated as a cloak (*Targum;* Rashi), a belt (Saadia; Rashbam), a hood (Radak), or the special shawl worn by aristocrats (Ramban; cf. *Tzava'ath Yehudah* 12:4).
   Ancient sources note that in the Middle East, people usually wore a long tunic reaching to the feet, with
   a short white cloak thrown around them, and besides this, people would always carry a seal and a walking stick with an elaborately carved top (Herodotus 1:195). The *pethilah* would then be the white cloak.
   Other sources indicate that the seal and string (*pethilah*) were to bind the sheep, and the staff was the
   shepherd's crook (*Sekhel Tov*).
38:21 religious prostitute. *Kedeshah* in Hebrew. See Deuteronomy 23:18 which seems to indicate that the pagan
   custom was to use the hire of such prostitutes for sacrifice. The *kedeshah* is also associated with sacrifice in
   Hosea 4:14. See Numbers 25:1,2. Ancient sources state that among the Amorites it was a custom that
   girls would have to sit seven days as prostitutes before being married (*Tzava'ath Yehudah* 12:2; cf. Herodotus 1:199; also see *Kethuboth* 3b). Judah had no interest in her as a sacred prostitute, and, therefore,
   above (38:15), the word *zonah* denoting a simple prostitute, is used.

"Take her out and have her burned,*" said Judah. 	38

²⁵ When she was being taken out, she sent [the security] to her father-in-law with the message, "I am pregnant by the man who is the owner of these articles." [When Judah came to her,]* she said, "If you would, identify [these objects]. Who is the owner of this seal, this wrap, and this staff?"

²⁶ Judah immediately recognized them. "She is more innocent than I am!" he said. "She did it because I did not give her to my son Shelah." He was not intimate with her anymore.

²⁷ When the time came for her to give birth, there were twins in her womb. ²⁸ As she was in labor, one of them put out an arm. The midwife grasped it and tied a crimson thread* on it. "This one came out first," she announced.

²⁹ He pulled his hand back, and then his brother came out. "You have asserted yourself with such pushiness (*peretz*)!" she said. [Judah] named the child Peretz.*

³⁰ His brother, with the crimson thread on his hand, was then born. [Judah] named him Zerach.*

[75. Joseph's Temptation]

¹ Joseph had been brought down to Egypt, and Potiphar, one of 	39
Pharaoh's Egyptian officers, the captain of the guard, had purchased him from the Arabs who had brought him there. ² God was with Joseph, and He made him very successful. Soon he was working in his master's own house.* ³ His master realized that God was with [Joseph], and that God granted success to everything he did.

⁴ Joseph gained favor with [his master] and before long, he was appointed as [his master's] personal servant.* [His master] placed him in charge of his household, giving him responsibility for everything he owned. ⁵ And as soon as [his master] had placed him in charge of his household and possessions,

---

38:24 **burned.** It seems that there was no legal justification to burn her, but Judah was using the discretionary power given to the courts to prevent immorality by imposing particularly harsh punishments (Mizrachi; *Or HaChaim;* cf. Ramban; *Sanhedrin* 46a). Moreover, if it were the prescribed penalty, how could Judah later refrain from imposing it? Some say that Judah was punishing her for undermining the morality of the Israelites (*Yov'loth* 41:17), or as revenge (*Tzava'ath Yehudah* 12:5). According to other sources, "burning" here denotes branding and not a death penalty (*Tur*).

38:25 **When she was being taken out . . .** (cf. *Yov'loth* 41:18; Rashbam). Alternatively, "She sent word to her father-in-law, 'I am pregnant by the man who is the owner of certain articles.' She said, 'Please identify them . . .'"

38:28 **crimson thread.** See Exodus 25:4.

38:29 **Peretz.** He was the ancestor of King David; see Ruth 4:18–22. Compare note on 19:36. See 1 Chronicles 2:5, 2:9 ff.

38:30 **Zerach.** Literally, "shining forth." See 1 Chronicles 2:6.

39:2 **Soon . . .** (Sforno).

39:4 **personal servant** (Sforno).

39 God blessed the Egyptian because of Joseph. God's blessing was in all [the Egyptian] had, both in the house and the field.

⁶ [His master] left all his affairs in Joseph's hands, except for the food he himself ate.* He did not concern himself with anything [Joseph] did. Meanwhile, Joseph grew to be* well built and handsome.

⁷ In the course of time,* his master's wife* cast her eyes on Joseph. "Sleep with me," she said.

⁸ He adamantly refused. He reasoned with his master's wife. "My master does not even know what I do in the house. He has entrusted me with everything he owns. ⁹ No one in this house has more power than I have. He has not kept back anything at all from me, except for you—his wife. How could I do such a great wrong? It would be a sin before God!"

¹⁰ She spoke to Joseph every day, but he would not pay attention to her. He would not even lie next to her or spend time with her.

¹¹ One such day, [Joseph] came to the house to do his work. None of the household staff was inside. ¹² [The woman] grabbed him by his cloak. "Sleep with me!" she pleaded. He ran away from her, leaving his cloak in her hand, and fled outside.

¹³ When she realized that he had left his cloak in her hand and fled outside, ¹⁴ she called her household servants. "See!" she said. "He brought us a Hebrew man to play games* with us! He came to rape me, but I screamed as loud as I could! When he heard me scream and call for help, he ran outside and left his cloak with me!"

¹⁶ She kept [Joseph's] cloak with her until his master came home, ¹⁷ and she told him the same story. "The Hebrew slave that you brought us came to play games with me! ¹⁸ When I screamed and called for help, he fled outside, leaving his cloak with me!"

¹⁹ When her husband heard his wife's story and her description of the incident, he became furious. ²⁰ Joseph's master had him arrested, and placed him in the dungeon where the king's prisoners were kept. He was to remain in that dungeon.

39:6 **except for the food . . .** From context, the final clause modifies the first part of the sentence. Literally, "He did not concern himself with anything regarding him except for the food he ate." This is because the Egyptians considered food touched by foreigners to be contaminated (see below, 43:32; Ibn Ezra; Radak; cf. Herodotus 2:41). Others say that it refers to the food that Joseph ate, indicating that Joseph was given a special diet, better than that of the other slaves (Josephus 2:4:1). According to others, this is a euphemism for intimacy with his wife (compare 39:9; *Targum Yerushalmi*; Rashi; Sh'muel ben Chofni Gaon).

—   **grew to be . . .** Or "remained." Cf. 29:17.

39:7 **In the course of time.** Literally, "after these events." See 40:1.

—   **wife.** Some say that her name was Zelikhah (*Sefer HaYashar*, p. 126; cf. *Tzava'ath Yosef* 3:6).

39:14 **play games.** Or "mock us" or "insult us" or "have pleasure with us." The word means to laugh or play.

²¹ God was with Joseph, and He showed him kindness, making him find favor with the warden of the dungeon. ²² Soon, the warden had placed all the prisoners in the dungeon under Joseph's charge. [Joseph] took care of everything that had to be done. ²³ The warden did not have to look after anything that was under [Joseph's] care. God was with [Joseph], and God granted him success in everything he did.

[76. The Prisoners' Dreams]

40

¹ Soon after this,* the Egyptian king's wine steward and baker offended* their master, who was the king of Egypt. ² Pharaoh was incensed at his two courtiers, the chief steward and chief baker, ³ and he had them arrested. They were placed in the house of the captain of the guard,* in the same dungeon where Joseph was imprisoned. ⁴ They were under arrest for a long period of time, and the captain assigned Joseph to look after them.

⁵ One night, the two of them dreamed. The Egyptian king's steward and baker, who were imprisoned in the dungeon, each had a dream that seemed to have a special meaning.* ⁶ When Joseph came to them in the morning, he saw that they were upset. ⁷ He tried to find out what was wrong with Pharaoh's courtiers who were his fellow prisoners in his master's house. "Why do you look so worried today?" he asked.

⁸ "We [each] had a dream," they replied, "and there is no one [here] to interpret it."

"Interpretations are God's business," replied Joseph. "If you want to, tell me about [your dreams]."

⁹ The chief steward related his dream to Joseph. "In my dream," he said, "there was a grape vine right there in front of me. ¹⁰ The vine had three branches. As soon as its buds formed, its blossoms bloomed, and its clusters ripened into grapes. ¹¹ Pharaoh's cup was in my hand. I took the grapes and squeezed them into Pharaoh's cup. Then I placed the cup in Pharaoh's hand."

¹² Joseph said to him, "This is the interpretation: The three branches are three days. ¹³ In three days, Pharaoh will lift your head* and give you back

---

40:1 **Soon after this.** Literally, "after these events." See 39:7.
— **offended.** According to Midrashic tradition, there was a fly in the wine and a pebble in the bread (*Bereshith Rabbah* 88; Rashi). Others state that they tried to assassinate the king with poison (*Targum Yonathan*) or that they tried to seduce his daughter (*Bereshith Rabbah*).
40:3 **captain of the guard.** Potiphar. See 37:36.
40:5 **special meaning.** Literally, "each one like the interpretation of the dream." This means that the dream had a special meaning (Rashbam). Others, "a portentous dream" (Rashi), or "a dream with its interpretation" (Ibn Ezra; *Bereshith Rabbah* 88). Some translate it, "a dream with personal significance," or "a dream needing interpretation."
40:13 **lift your head.** Idiom for "single you out," or "give you special consideration."

40 your position. You will place Pharaoh's cup in his hand, just as you did before, when you were his steward.

14 "But when things go well for you, just remember that I was with you. Do me a favor and say something about me to Pharaoh. Perhaps you will be able to get me out of this place. 15 I was originally kidnapped from the land of the Hebrews, and when I came here, I did not do anything to deserve being thrown in the dungeon."

16 The chief baker saw that [Joseph] was able to give a good interpretation. He said to Joseph, "I also saw myself in my dream.* There were three baskets of fine white bread* on my head. 17 In the top basket, there were all kinds of baked goods that Pharaoh eats. But birds were eating it from the basket on my head!"

18 Joseph replied, "This is its interpretation: The three baskets are three days. 19 In three days, Pharaoh will lift your head—right off your body! He will hang you on a gallows, and the birds will eat your flesh."

20 The third day was Pharaoh's birthday, and he made a feast for all his servants. Among his servants, he gave special attention* to the chief wine steward and the chief baker. 21 He restored the chief steward to his position, and allowed him to place the cup in Pharaoh's hand. 22 The chief baker, however, was hanged, just as Joseph had predicted.

23 The chief steward did not remember Joseph. He forgot all about him.

MiKetz   מִקֵּץ

[77. Joseph's Vindication]

41   1 Two full years passed. Then Pharaoh* had a dream. He was standing

---

40:16 **saw myself** . . . (Hirsch).

— **fine white bread.** (*Targum Yonathan; Yerushalmi, Betza* 2:6; Rambam on Eduyoth 3:10; Ibn Ezra; Ramban; cf. Septuagint; Josephus 2:5:3). *Chori* in Hebrew, probably something white. Others interpret it as "baskets of biscuits" (Radak, *Sherashim*); "baskets of twigs" (Rashi); "white baskets (Ibn Janach); or "perforated baskets" (Rashbam). In ancient Egyptian, *khara* means woven.

40:20 **gave special attention.** Literally, "lifted the heads of," see above, 40:13.

41:1 **Pharaoh.** According to tradition, this occurred in the year 2230 (1532 b.c.e.). Some say that it was the year that Isaac died (*Yov'loth* 40:12). According to Talmudic tradition, the dream occurred on Rosh HaShanah, the New Year (*Rosh HaShanah* 10b, end).

According to this chronology, the king of Egypt at the time was probably Amenhotep I of the 18th Dynasty, who ruled from 1545–1525 b.c.e.

However, it may be necessary to correct the chronology by 18 years (see *The Torah Anthology* 4:240), so the king would then be Ahmose (1552–1527 b.c.e.), the first king of the 18th Dynasty. It was he who drove the Hyksos out of Egypt. According to conventional chronologies, the reign of Ahmose was from 1570 to 1545 b.c.e.

As mentioned above, however, it may be necessary to make a correction by as much as 163 years (note on 12:15). The Pharaoh would then be the one who, according to conventional chronologies, reigned in 1695 b.c.e. This would place the Pharaoh in the 14th Dynasty, which was when Egypt was

near the Nile, ² when suddenly seven handsome, healthy-looking cows   41
emerged from the Nile, and grazed in the marsh grass.* ³ Then another seven,
ugly, lean cows emerged from the Nile, and stood next to the cows already on
the river bank. ⁴ The ugly, lean cows ate up the seven handsome, fat cows.
Pharaoh then woke up.

⁵ He fell asleep again and had a second dream. He saw seven fat, good ears
of grain growing on a single stalk. ⁶ Then, suddenly, another seven ears of
grain grew behind them, thin and scorched by the [hot] east wind. ⁷ The seven
thin ears swallowed up the seven fat, full ears. Pharaoh woke up and realized
that it had been a dream.

⁸ In the morning he was very upset. He sent word, summoning all the
symbolists* and wise men of Egypt. Pharaoh told them his dreams, but there
was no one who could provide a satisfactory interpretation.

⁹ The chief wine steward spoke to Pharaoh. "I must recall my crimes
today," he said. ¹⁰ "Pharaoh was angry at us, and he placed me under arrest in
the house of the captain of the guard, along with the chief baker. We dreamed
one night—he and I each had a dream that seemed to have its own special
meaning. ¹¹ There was a young Hebrew man with us, a slave of the captain of
the guard. We told him our dreams, and he interpreted them. He provided
each of us with an interpretation, ¹² and things worked out just as he said they
would. I was given back my position, while [the baker] was hanged."

¹⁴ Pharaoh sent messengers and had Joseph summoned. They rushed him
from the dungeon. He got a haircut* and changed clothes, and then came to
Pharaoh.

¹⁵ Pharaoh said to Joseph, "I had a dream, and there is no one who can
interpret it. I heard that when you hear a dream, you can explain it."

¹⁶ Joseph answered Pharaoh, "It is not by my own power. But God may
provide an answer concerning Pharaoh's fortune.*"

¹⁷ Pharaoh related it to Joseph: "In my dream, I was standing on the bank

---

under the rule of the Hyksos. Since very little is known historically of that period, it would explain why
there are no historic records of Joseph. Josephus also writes that the Israelites lived in Egypt during the
reign of the Hyksos (*Contra Apion* 1:14).

41:2 **marsh grass** (Ramban). *Achu* in the Hebrew, from the Egyptian *Akhi*. See Job 8:11, Ben Sirah 40:16. This
is usually identified with a type of bullrushes or papyrus (cf. *Targum Yonathan;* Saadia). Others translate it
as marsh (Rashi; Josephus 2:5:5; Septuagint).

41:8 **symbolists.** or hieroglyphists. *Chartumim* in Hebrew, probably from the ancient Egyptian *cher themu*,
chief writer (cf. Ibn Ezra). See Exodus 7:11 (and Hirsch *ad. loc.*), Daniel 1:20. Inscriptions were thought
to have magic power, and were used for divination. Others say that they used the bones of the dead for
their incantations (Rashi).

41:14 **haircut** (*Targum*). Literally, "he shaved."

41:16 **It is not by my own power** . . . (Rashi). Or, "No matter how I [interpret it], let God make it come out
good for you" (Ibn Ezra); or, "I cannot do it by myself, but God will tell you what it means" (Rashbam).

41 of the Nile. [18] Suddenly, seven fat, handsome cows emerged from the Nile, and grazed in the marsh grass. [19] Then, just as suddenly, seven other cows emerged after them, very badly formed and emaciated. I never saw such bad ones in all Egypt. [20] The emaciated, bad cows proceeded to eat the first seven, healthy cows. [21] These were completely swallowed by the [emaciated cows], but there was no way of telling that they were inside. The cows looked just as bad as they had at first. Then I woke up.

[22] "Then I had another dream. There were seven full, good ears of grain growing on one stalk. [23] Suddenly, seven other ears of grain grew behind them. [The second ones] were shriveled, thin, and scorched by the east [desert] wind. [24] The thin ears swallowed up the seven good ears.

"I told this to the symbolists, but none of them could interpret it for me."

[25] Joseph said to Pharaoh, "Pharaoh's dream has a single meaning. God has told Pharaoh what He is about to do. [26] The seven good cows are seven years. The seven good ears are [the same] seven years. It is one dream.

[27] "The seven emaciated, bad cows who came up after [the first ones] are also seven years. The seven empty, wind-scorched ears will [likewise] be seven years of famine.

[28] "It is as I have told Pharaoh—God has shown Pharaoh what He is about to do. [29] Seven years are coming, during which there will be a great surplus of food all over Egypt. [30] These will be followed by seven years of famine, when all the surplus in Egypt will be forgotten. The famine will ravage the land. [31] The ensuing famine will be so terrible that there will be no way of telling that there was once a surplus in the land.

[32] "The reason that Pharaoh had the same dream twice is because the process has already been set in motion by God, and God is rushing to do it.

[33] "Now Pharaoh must seek out a man with insight and wisdom, and place him in charge of Egypt. [34] Pharaoh must then take further action, and appoint officials over the land. A rationing system will have to be set up* over Egypt during the seven years of surplus.

[35] Let [the officials] collect all the food during these coming good years, and let them store the grain under Pharaoh's control. The food will be kept in the cities under guard. [36] The food can then be held in reserve for the land when the seven famine years come to Egypt. The land will then not be depopulated by the famine."

41:34 **A rationing system** . . . (Saadia; cf. Josephus 2:5:7). *Chimesh* in Hebrew. Others have "alert Egypt" (Rashi; cf. Exodus 13:18, Joshua 1:14, 4:12, Judges 7:11), or, "collect a fifth of Egypt's produce" (*Targum Yonathan;* Rashbam; Ibn Ezra; Radak; see 47:24). Some say, "Divide Egypt into five administrative districts" (cf. Isaiah 19:18).

³⁷ Pharaoh and all his advisors considered it an excellent plan. ³⁸ Pharaoh **41** said to his advisors, "Can there be another person who has God's spirit in him as this man does?"

³⁹ Pharaoh said to Joseph, "Since God has informed you about all this, there can be no one with as much insight and wisdom as you. ⁴⁰ You shall be in charge of my government,* and food will be distributed* to my people by your orders. Only by the throne will I outrank you."

⁴¹ Pharaoh then formally declared* to Joseph, "I am placing you in charge of the entire land of Egypt." ⁴² Pharaoh took his ring off his own hand and placed it on the hand of Joseph. He had him dressed in the finest linen garments, and placed a gold chain around his neck. ⁴³ He had [Joseph] ride in his second royal chariot,* and [those going] ahead of him announced, "The Viceroy*!" [Joseph] was thus given authority over all Egypt.

⁴⁴ Pharaoh said to Joseph, "I am Pharaoh. Without your say, no man will lift a hand or foot in all Egypt." ⁴⁵ Pharaoh gave Joseph the name Tzaphnath Paaneach.* He gave him Asenath,* daughter of Poti Phera,* the priest* of

---

41:40 government. Literally, "house."

— **food will be distributed** (Rashi; *Targum*). Or, "by your word, the people will be organized" (Rashbam); or, "all the people will kiss you as their master" (Radak, *Sherashim*).

41:41 formally declared. Literally, "said."

41:43 second royal chariot (Rashi; Ramban; Ralbag; *Sefer HaYashar*). Or, "the chariot of the second in command" (Rashbam; Ibn Ezra).

— **The Viceroy.** (*Targum*). *Avrekh* in Hebrew. Since *rekh* can mean king (see 2 Samuel 3:39, Radak *ad loc.*), this word can be interpreted as "father of the king" or "arch-ruler" (*Sifri* on Deuteronomy 1:1; *Bava Bathra* 4a; Rashi; Rashbam. See 45:8; note on 20:2). It may also be related to the Akadian word *abarakhu*, denoting the chief steward of the royal house. Others define *Avrekh* as "merciful father" (Sh'muel ben Chofni). Still others see it as a command, "bow down" (Ibn Janach; Radak, *Sherashim;* Sforno). It may thus be related to the Egyptian expression *a-bor-k*, "prostrate yourself," or *aprek*, "head bowed." Others see it as related to the Egyptian *ibrek*, "attention," *aabrek* "to the left" or "stand aside," *ap-rekh-u*, "head of the wise," *ab-rek*, "rejoice!" or *abu-rek*, "your command is our desire."

According to other sources, *Avrekh* was the public name given to Joseph, while *Tzaphnath Paaneach* (41:45) was the private name used in the palace (*Agadath Bereshith* 73). Others interpret the verse, "as he passed [the people] called out, 'I will bow down'" (Ibn Ezra).

41:45 Tzaphnath Paaneach. Many authorities state that this is a Hebrew translation of the Egyptian name that he was given, and that it means "revealer of secrets" (*Targum;* Rashi; Septuagint; Josephus 2:6:1). Others say that it is an Egyptian name (Ibn

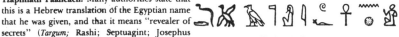

Tzafanath Paaneach

Ezra; Radak, *Sherashim*). In Egyptian, Tzaphnath is *tza-pa-neth* meaning, "the Neth speaks" or "the god speaks." Paaneach is *pa-anakh*, meaning "the life," where *anach* or *ankh* is the symbol of life. Hence the name can be translated as, "Lord of life," "Neth speaks life," or "The God speaks and [this man] lives."

— **Asenath.** There is a tradition that she was actually Dinah's daughter by Shechem (34:2), and after being brought to Egypt, she was adopted by Poti Phera (*Targum Yonathan;* Pirkey Rabbi Eliezer 38). According to this, the name Asenath comes from a Hebraic root, possibly from *S'neh* (a bush), since she was hidden under a bush (*Chizzkuni*). It is also possible that Asenath is an Egyptian name, since in Egyptian *ase-nath* means "Belonging to God" or "Belonging to Neth," where Neth is an Egyptian goddess. Some say that Asenath was an Egyptian (*Midrash Tadshe* 21, *Yalkut Shimoni* 2:9).

Asenath

41 On,* as a wife. Joseph thus went out to oversee Egypt. ⁴⁶ When he stood before Pharaoh, Joseph was 30 years old.*

Joseph left Pharaoh's court, and he made an inspection tour of the entire land of Egypt. ⁴⁷ During the seven years of surplus, the land produced loads* of grain. ⁴⁸ [Joseph] collected the food during the seven years that Egypt was now enjoying, and he placed the food in the cities. The food growing in the fields around each city was placed inside [the city]. ⁴⁹ Joseph accumulated so much grain, it was like the sand of the sea. They had to give up counting it, since there was too much to count.

⁵⁰ Joseph had two sons before the famine years came, borne to him by Asenath, daughter of Poti Phera, priest of On. ⁵¹ Joseph named the first-born Manasseh (*Me-nasheh*)—"because God has made me forget (*nasheh*) all my troubles—and even my father's house." ⁵² He named his second son Ephraim—"Because God has made me fruitful* (*p'ri*) in the land of my suffering."

⁵³ The seven years of surplus that Egypt was enjoying finally came to an end. ⁵⁴ The seven years of famine then began, just as Joseph had predicted. There was famine in all the other lands, but in Egypt there was bread. ⁵⁵ Eventually, however, all of Egypt also began to feel the famine, and the people cried out to Pharaoh for bread. Pharaoh announced to all Egypt, "Go to Joseph. Do whatever he tells you."

⁵⁶ The famine spread over the entire area. Joseph opened all the storehouses, and he rationed supplies to Egypt. But the famine was growing worse in Egypt. ⁵⁷ The famine was [also] growing more severe in the entire area, and [people from] all over the area came to Egypt to obtain rations from Joseph.

42 ¹ Jacob learned that there were provisions in Egypt, and he said to his sons, "Why are you fantasizing*?" ² "I have heard that there are supplies in

---

— **Poti Phera.** This is also an Egyptian name, *Pa-diu Per-Ra,* meaning "given of the House of Ra," where "House of Ra" is the sacred name for On (see below). It may also be seen as having the same meaning as Potiphar; see note on 37:36. Some say that Poti Phera was the same person as Potiphar (*Sotah* 13a; *Targum Yonathan;* Rashi; *You'loth* 40:10).

Pote Phera

— **priest.** Either high priest (*Targum;* Rashbam) or one of the priests (Josephus 2:6:1).

— **On.** *Ionu* in ancient Egyptian, the center of worship of the sun-god Ra. Its sacred name was *Per-Ra,* "House of Ra" (see notes on 12:15, 37:36), which was translated into Greek as Heliopolis. It is 7 miles north of the present Cairo, and "Cleopatra's Needle" which stands in Central Park came from there. Poti Per-Ra which means "given of Per-Ra," can thus literally mean "the priest of On." See 41:50, 46:20; Radak on Ezekiel 30:17. Also see Jeremiah 43:13.

41:46 **30 years old.** Thus, he had been in Egypt for 13 years; see 37:2.

41:47 **loads** (*Targum*). Or "by the handful" (Rashi), indicating that each ear produced a handful of grain (Rashbam).

41:52 **fruitful.** Or "restored" (Josephus).

42:1 **fantasizing** (Radak). Or, "why are you looking at one another" (Septuagint); or, "Why are you showing off" (Rashi; Rashbam; *Taanith* 10b); or, "Why are you afraid" (*Targum Yonathan*).

Egypt," he explained. "You can go there and buy food. Let us live and not   42
die."

⁸ Joseph's ten brothers went to buy grain in Egypt. ⁴ But Jacob did not
send Joseph's brother Benjamin along with the others. "Something might
happen to him," he said.

⁵ Israel's sons came to buy rations along with the others who came because
of the famine in Canaan. ⁶ Joseph was like a dictator over the land, since he
was the only one who rationed out food for all the people. When Joseph's
brothers arrived, they prostrated themselves to him, with their faces to the
ground.

⁷ Joseph recognized his brothers as soon as he saw them. But he behaved
like a stranger and spoke harshly to them. "Where are you from?" he asked.

"From the land of Canaan—to buy food," they replied.

⁸ Joseph recognized his brothers, but they did not recognize him. ⁹ He
remembered what he had dreamed about them.* "You are spies!" he said to
them. "You have come to see where the land is exposed to attack.*"

¹⁰ "No my lord!" they replied. "We are your servants who have come only
to buy food. ¹¹ We are all the sons of the same man. We are honorable men.
We would never think of being spies!"

¹² "No!" retorted [Joseph]. "You have come to see where the land is
exposed."

¹³ "We are twelve brothers," they pleaded. "We are the sons of one man
who is in Canaan. Right now the youngest brother is with our father, and one
brother is gone."

¹⁴ "I still say* that you are spies," replied Joseph. ¹⁵ "There is only one
way that you can convince me. By Pharaoh's life, [all of] you will not leave this
place unless your youngest brother comes here. ¹⁶ Let one of you go back and
bring your brother. The rest will remain here under arrest. This will test your
claim and determine if you are telling the truth. If not, by Pharaoh's life, you
will be considered spies."

¹⁷ Joseph had them placed under arrest for three days. ¹⁸ On the third day,
Joseph said to them, "If you do as I say, you will live. I fear the God. ¹⁹ We will
see if you are really being candid. One of you will be held hostage in the same
building where you were kept under arrest. The rest can go and bring supplies
to your hungry families. ²⁰ Bring your youngest brother here, and your claim
will be substantiated. Then you will not die."

42:9 **dreamed** . . . See 37:7,9, 42:6.
— **exposed** . . . Literally, "the nakedness of the land." They spoke Hebrew rather than Canaanite (a language related to Egyptian), and hence, the story that they came from Canaan could be suspect.
42:14 **I still say.** Literally, "It is as I have said."

42   They agreed to this, [21] but they said to one another, "We deserve to be punished because of what we did to our brother. We saw him suffering when he pleaded with us, but we would not listen. That's why this great misfortune has come upon us now."

[22] Reuben interrupted them. "Didn't I tell you not to commit a crime against the boy?" he said. "You wouldn't listen. Now a [divine] accounting is being demanded for his blood*!"

[23] Meanwhile, they did not realize that Joseph was listening, since they [had spoken to him] through a translator. [24] Joseph left them and wept. When he returned, he spoke to them sternly again. He had Simeon* taken from them and placed in chains before their eyes.

[25] Joseph gave orders that when their bags were filled with grain, each one's money should also be placed in his sack. They were also to be given provisions for the journey. This was done. [26] [The brothers] then loaded the food they bought on their donkeys, and they departed.

[27] When they came to the place where they spent the night, one of them* opened his sack to feed his donkey. He saw his money right there at the top of his pack. [28] "My money has been returned!" he exclaimed to his brothers. "It's in my pack!"

Their hearts sank. "What is this that God has done to us?" they asked each other with trembling voices.

[29] When they came to their father Jacob in the land of Canaan, they told him about all that had happened to them. [30] "The man who was the lord of the land spoke to us harshly," they said, "and he charged us with spying on the land. [31] We said to him, 'We are honorable men. We have never been spies. [32] We are twelve brothers, all of the same father. One of us has been lost, and the youngest is now with our father in Canaan.'

[33] "The man who was the lord of the land said to us, 'I have a way of knowing if you are honorable. Leave one of your brothers with me, take [what you need] for your hungry families, and go. [34] Bring your youngest brother back to me, and then I will know that you are honorable men, and not spies. I will give your brother back to you, and you will be able to do business in [our] land.'"

[35] They began emptying their sacks, and each one's money was [found to be] in his sack. [The brothers] and their father saw the money-bags and they were afraid.

42:22 a divine accounting . . . See 9:5.
42:24 Simeon. See note on 37:24.
42:27 one of them. Levi (*Targum Yonathan; Bereshith Rabbah* 91; Rashi).

³⁶ Their father Jacob said to them, "You're making me lose my children! Joseph is gone! Simeon is gone! And now you want to take Benjamin! Everything is happening to me!"

³⁷ Reuben tried to reason with his father. "If I do not bring [Benjamin] back to you," he said, "you can put my two sons* to death. Let him be my responsibility, and I will bring him back to you."

³⁸ "My son will not go with you!" replied Jacob. "His brother is dead, and he is all I have left. Something may happen to him along the way, and you will bring my white head down to the grave in misery!" ,

¹ The famine became worse in the area. ² When they had used up all the supplies that they had brought from Egypt, their father said to them, "Go back and get us a little food."

³ Judah tried to reason with him. He said, "The man warned us, 'Do not appear before me unless your brother is with you.' ⁴ If you consent to send our brother with us, we will go and get you food. ⁵ But if you will not send [him], we cannot go. The man told us, 'Do not appear before me unless your brother is with you.'"

⁶ Israel said, "Why did you do such a terrible thing to me, telling the man that you had another brother?"

⁷ [The brothers] replied, "The man kept asking about us and our family. He asked, 'Is your father still alive? Do you have another brother?' We simply answered his questions. How were we to know that he would demand that we bring our brother there?"

⁸ "Send the boy with me," said Judah to his father Israel. "Let us set out and get going. Let's live and not die—we, you, and also our children. ⁹ I myself will be responsible for him. You can demand him from my own hand. If I do not bring him back and have him stand here before you, I will have sinned for all time. ¹⁰ But if we had not waited so long, we could have been there and back twice by now!"

¹¹ Their father Israel said to them, "If that's the way it must be, this is what you must do. Take some of the land's famous products in your baggage, a little balsam,* a little honey, and some gum, resin,* pistachio nuts and almonds. ¹² Take along twice as much money, so that you will be able to return the money that was put at the tops of your packs—it might have been an oversight. ¹³ And your brother—take him. Go and return to the man.

42:37 two sons. Chanokh and Palu (46:9). Reuben actually had four sons.

43:11 balsam. See above, 37:25. We see there that it was valuable, since special caravans brought it to Egypt. It is ironic that the gift should have consisted of the same substances that were in the caravan that brought Joseph to Egypt.

—   **gum, resin.** Tragacanth and Labdanum, see notes on 37:25.

43 ¹⁴ May God Almighty grant that the man have pity on you and let you go along with your other brother and Benjamin. If I must lose my children, then I will lose them."

¹⁵ The brothers* took the gift and also brought along twice as much money [as was needed]. They set out with Benjamin and went to Egypt. [Once again] they stood before Joseph. ¹⁶ When Joseph saw Benjamin with them, he said to the overseer of his household, "Bring these men to the palace. Butcher an animal and prepare it. These men will be eating lunch with me."

¹⁷ The man did as Joseph said, and he escorted the brothers to Joseph's palace. ¹⁸ When the men [realized that] they were being brought to Joseph's palace, they were terrified. They said, "We are being brought here because of the money that was put back in our packs the last time. We will be framed and convicted. Our donkeys can be confiscated, and we can even be taken as slaves.*"

¹⁹ When they were at the door of Joseph's palace, they went over to the overseer and spoke to him. ²⁰ "If you please, sir," they said, "we originally came down to buy food. ²¹ Then, when we came to the place where we spent the night, we opened our packs, and each man's* money was at the top of the pack. It was our own money, in its exact weight. We have brought it back with us. ²² We have also brought along other money to buy food. We have no idea who put the money back in our packs!"

²³ "Everything is fine as far as you are concerned," replied [the overseer]. "Don't be afraid. The God you and your father worship must have placed a hidden gift in your packs. I received the money you paid." With that, he brought Simeon out to them.

²⁴ The man brought the brothers into Joseph's palace. He gave them water so they could wash their feet, and had fodder given to their donkeys. ²⁵ They got their gifts ready for when Joseph would come at noon, since they heard that they would be eating with him.

²⁵ When Joseph arrived home, they presented him with the gifts they had brought. They prostrated themselves on the ground to him.

²⁶ He inquired as to their welfare. "Is your old father at peace?" he asked. "Remember, you told me about him. Is he still alive?"

²⁸ "Your servant our father is at peace," they replied, "He is still alive." They bowed their heads and prostrated themselves.

43:15 brothers. Literally, "men."

43:18 donkeys . . . From context. Literally, "take us for slaves along with our donkeys." They might have been as concerned for their animals as themselves (cf. *Moreh Nevukhim* 3:40), since even if they could escape, without animals to transport the grain, their families would die of starvation (Ramban; *MeAm Lo'ez/The Torah Anthology* 3:412).

43:21 each man's. This is not what actually happened (42:27,35), but they simplified the account (*Sekhel Tov*).

²⁹ [Joseph] looked up and saw his brother Benjamin, his mother's son. He   **43**
said, "This must be your youngest brother, about whom you told me." [To
Benjamin] he said, "God be gracious to you, my son."
³⁰ Joseph rushed out. His emotions had been aroused by his brother, and
he had to weep. He went to a room and there he wept. ³¹ He washed his face
and came out. Holding in his emotions, he said, "Serve the meal."
³² [Joseph] was served by himself, and [the brothers] by themselves. The
Egyptians who were eating with them [were also] segregated. The Egyptians
could not eat with the Hebrews, since this was taboo to the Egyptians.*
³³ When [the brothers] were seated before [Joseph], they were placed in
order of age, from the oldest to the youngest. The brothers looked at each
other in amazement. ³⁴ [Joseph] sent them portions from his table,* giving
Benjamin five times as much as the rest. They drank with him and became
intoxicated.
¹ Joseph gave his overseer special instructions. "Fill the men's packs with   **44**
as much food as they can carry," he said. "Place each man's money at the top
of his pack. ² And my chalice—the silver chalice—place it on top of the
youngest one's pack—along with the money for his food." [The overseer] did
exactly as Joseph instructed him.
³ With the first morning light, the brothers took their donkeys and were
sent on their way. ⁴ They had just left the city* and had not gone far, when
Joseph said to his overseer, "Set out and pursue those men. Catch up with
them and say to them, 'Why did you repay good with evil? ⁵ It's [the cup] from
which my master drinks, and he uses it for divination. You did a terrible
thing.'"
⁶ [The overseer] caught up with them, and repeated exactly those words to
them. ⁷ They said to him, "Why do you say such things? Heaven forbid that
we should do such a thing! ⁸ After all, we brought you back the money we
found at the top of our packs—all the way from Canaan. How could we steal
silver or gold from your master's house? If any of us has it in his possession,
he shall die. You can take the rest of us for slaves."
¹⁰ "It *should* be as you declare," he replied. "But only the one with whom it

43:32 **this was taboo . . .** The Egyptians were very careful about eating with strangers (see note on 39:6). This
was because the Hebrews ate sheep, and hence their mouths and utensils were considered contaminated,
since sheep were sacred to the Egyptians (*Targum; Sekhel Tov*). Cf. 46:34, Exodus 8:22. Actually, only the
female animals were sacred (Herodotus 2:41).

43:34 **from his table.** (*Targum Yonathan*).

44:4 **the city.** This was Memphis, the ancient capital of Egypt. It was also the city where Joseph lived with
Potiphar (cf. *Tzava'ath Yosef* 4:6). It was on the west bank of the Nile, some 12 miles south of the present
Cairo, and some 25 miles south of On (41:45). In Hebrew, Memphis is known as Moph (Hosea 9:6) or
Noph (Isaiah 19:13, Jeremiah 2:16, Ezekiel 30:13, etc.). However, if this was during the time of the
Hyksos, the capital might have been Tanis.

44 is found will be my slave. The rest will be able to go free."

¹¹ Each one quickly lowered his pack to the ground, and they all opened their packs. ¹² [The overseer] inspected each one, beginning with the oldest and ending with the youngest. The chalice was found in Benjamin's pack.

¹³ [The brothers] tore their clothes in grief. Each one reloaded his donkey, and they returned to the city. ¹⁴ When Judah and his brothers came to Joseph's palace, he was still there. They threw themselves on the ground before him. ¹⁵ Joseph said to them, "What did you think you were doing? Don't you realize that a person like me can determine the truth by divination?"

¹⁶ "What can we say to my lord?" replied Judah. "How can we speak? How can we prove our innocence? God has uncovered our old guilt. Let us be your slaves—we and the one in whose possession the chalice was found."

¹⁷ "Heaven forbid that I do that!" said [Joseph]. "The one in whose possession the chalice was found shall be my slave. [The rest of] you can go in peace to your father."

VaYigash   וַיִּגַּשׁ

[78. Joseph Reveals Himself]

¹⁸ Judah walked up to [Joseph] and said, "Please, your highness, let me say something to you personally.* Do not be angry with me, even though you are just like Pharaoh.

¹⁹ "You asked if we still had a father or another brother. ²⁰ We told you, 'We have a father who is very old, and the youngest [brother] is a child of his old age. He had a brother who died, and thus, he is the only one of his mother's children still alive. His father loves him.'

²¹ "You said to us, 'Bring him to me, so that I may set my eyes on him.' ²² We told you, 'The lad cannot leave his father. If he left him, his father would die.' ²³ You replied, 'If your youngest brother does not come with you, you shall not see my face again.'

²⁴ "We went to your servant our father and told him what you said. ²⁵ When our father told us to go back and get some food, ²⁶ we replied, 'We cannot go. We can go only if our youngest brother is with us. If he is not with us, we cannot even see the man [in charge].'

²⁷ "Your servant our father said, 'You know that my wife [Rachel] bore me

---

44:18 **let me say** . . . Literally, "Let me speak a word in my lord's ear." The usual expressions here are "your servant" and "my lord" in place of "I" and "you," representing the old court language, that was even used in Europe. Since it is confusing to the modern reader, here it is replaced with "I" and "you."

two sons. ²⁸ One has already left me, and I assume that he was torn to pieces **44** by wild animals. I have seen nothing of him until now. ²⁹ Now you want to take this one from me too! If something were to happen to him, you will have brought my white head down to the grave in evil misery.'

³⁰ "And now, when I come to your servant our father, the lad will not be with us. His soul is bound up with [the lad's] soul! ³¹ When he sees that the lad is not there, he will die! I will have brought your servant our father's white head down to the grave in misery. ³² Besides, I offered myself to my father as a guarantee for the lad, and I said, 'If I do not bring him back to you, I will have sinned to my father for all time.'

³³ "So now let *me* remain as your slave in place of the lad. Let the lad go back with his brothers! ³⁴ For how can I go back to my father if the lad is not with me? I cannot bear to see the evil misery that my father would suffer!"

¹ Joseph could not hold in his emotions. Since all his attendants were **45** present,* he cried out, "Have everyone leave my presence!" Thus, no one else was with him when Joseph revealed himself to his brothers. ² He began to weep with such loud sobs that the Egyptians could hear it. The news [of these strange happenings] reached Pharaoh's palace.

³ Joseph said to his brothers, "I am Joseph! Is my father still alive?" His brothers were so startled, they could not respond.

⁴ "Please, come close to me," said Joseph to his brothers.

When they came closer, he said, "I am Joseph your brother! You sold me to Egypt. ⁵ Now don't worry or feel guilty because you sold me. Look! God has sent me ahead of you to save lives! ⁶ There has been a famine in the area for two years, and for another five years there will be no plowing or harvest. ⁷ God has sent me ahead of you to insure that you survive in the land and to keep you alive through such extraordinary means.*

⁸ "Now it is not you who sent me here, but God. He has made me Pharaoh's vizier,* director of his entire government, and dictator of all Egypt.

⁹ "Hurry, go back to my father, and give him the message: Your son Joseph says, 'God has made me master of all Egypt. Come to me without delay. ¹⁰ You will be able to settle in the Goshen district* and be close to me—

45:1 **Since all . . .** (Radak). Or, "He could not tolerate everyone standing over him (Rashi).
45:7 **extraordinary means.** Literally, "through great deliverance" (Septuagint). It can also be read, "To keep alive for you a great survival," which means, "to insure that a great many of you survive" (*Yov'loth* 43:18).
45:8 **Pharaoh's vizier.** Literally, "a father to Pharaoh." See note on 41:43. "Pharaoh's father" was an ancient term for the royal vizier.
45:10 **Goshen district.** This is an area in the eastern Nile delta, west of what is now the northern Suez Canal. It was close to the capital, and thus close to where Joseph was living. It was also the part of Egypt close to Canaan (46:29). It is usually said to be the area between Tanis (Onomed) and Memphis (Judith 1:9,10). Josephus identifies it with the Heliopolis region (*Antiquities* 2:7:6, see below 47:11). The Septuagint (on

Goshen

45 you, your children, your grandchildren, your sheep, your cattle, and all that you own. [11] I will fully provide for you there, since there will still be another five years of famine. I do not want you to become destitute, along with your family and all that is yours.'

[12] "You and my brother Benjamin can see with your own eyes that I myself am speaking to you. [13] Tell Father all about my high position in Egypt, and about all that you saw. You must hurry and bring Father here."

[14] [With that, Joseph] fell on the shoulders* of his brother Benjamin, and he wept. Benjamin [also] wept on [Joseph's] shoulders. [15] [Joseph] then kissed all his brothers and wept on their [shoulders]. After that, his brothers conversed with him.

[16] News spread to Pharaoh's palace that Joseph's brothers had shown up. Pharaoh and his advisors were pleased.

[17] Pharaoh told Joseph to instruct his brothers, "This is what you must do: Load your beasts and go directly to Canaan. [18] Bring your father and your families and come to me. I will give you the best land in Egypt. You will eat the fat of the land. [19] Now you are instructed to do the following: Take wagons from Egypt for your small children and wives, and also use them for your father. Come [20] and do not be concerned with your belongings, for the best of Egypt will be yours."

[21] Israel's sons agreed to do this. Joseph gave them wagons according to Pharaoh's instructions, and he also provided them with food for the journey. [22] He gave each of [his brothers] an outfit of clothes. To Benjamin, however, he gave 300 pieces of silver and five outfits.

[23] [Joseph] sent the following to his father: Ten male donkeys, loaded with Egypt's finest products, as well as ten female donkeys, loaded with grain, bread, and food for his father's journey.

[24] He sent his brothers on their way. As they were leaving, he said to them, "Have a pleasant journey*!"

[25] [The brothers] headed north from Egypt, and they came to their father Jacob in Canaan. [26] They broke the news to him: "Joseph is still alive. He is the ruler of all Egypt."

46:28) renders Goshen as Hero-opolis, which is south of Pelusium and northeast of Cairo (Ptolemy, *Geography* 4:5). Elsewhere, the Septuagint speaks of it as "the Arab land of Gesem" (on 46:34). The area to the east of the Nile was known as the Arabian territory (Herodotus 2:8).
45:14 shoulders (Sh'muel ben Chofni Gaon). See above 33:4.
45:24 Have a pleasant journey. Literally, "Do not have agitation (or anger) on the way." This can be interpreted as "do not have any discomfort on the way (Ibn Janach; Radak; Hirsch), or "have a pleasant journey." Alternatively, the expression can be interpreted, "Do not have any fear on the way" (*Bekhor Shor*); "Do not worry while you're gone" (Rashbam); "Do not quarrel on the way" (Rashi; Ibn Ezra; Septuagint); "Don't get in trouble on the way" (*Targum Yonathan*); "Don't get too involved on the way" (*Taanith* 10a; Rashi); or "Don't rush too much on the way" (*Bereshith Rabbah* 94).

²⁶ [Jacob's] heart became numb,* for he could not believe them. ²⁷ Then **45**
they related all the words that Joseph had spoken to them, and he saw the
wagons that Joseph had sent to transport him. The spirit of their father Jacob
was then revived.

²⁸ "It's too much!" said Israel. "My son Joseph is alive! I must go and see
him before I die!"

¹ Israel began the journey, taking all his possessions, and he arrived in **46**
Beer-sheba.* He offered sacrifices to the God of his father Isaac. ² God spoke
to Israel in a night vision, and said, "Jacob! Jacob!"

"Yes," replied [Jacob].

³ [God] said, "I am the Omnipotent* God of your father. Do not be afraid
to go to Egypt, for it is there that I will make you into a great nation. ⁴ I will
go to Egypt with you, and I will also bring you back again. Joseph will place
his hands on your eyes.*"

⁵ Jacob set out from Beer-sheba. Israel's sons transported their father,
along with their children and wives, on the wagons that Pharaoh had sent to
carry them. ⁶ They took their livestock and all the possessions that they had
acquired in Canaan. Jacob came to Egypt with all his descendants. ⁷ His sons
and grandsons were with him. He also brought his daughters,* his granddaughters, and all his offspring to Egypt with him.

[79. Jacob's Family]

⁸ These are the names of the Israelites* who came to Egypt:
Jacob and his sons.*
Reuben was Jacob's first-born. ⁹ Reuben's sons* were Enoch (*Chanokh*),*
Palu, Chetzron and Carmi.

¹⁰ Simeon's sons*: Yemuel,* Yamin, Ohad, Yakhin,* Tzochar,* as well as
Saul (*Shaul*)* son of the Canaanite woman.*

45:26 **became numb** (cf. Ibn Ezra; Hirsch). Or, "He doubted it in his heart" (Rashi; Rashbam; cf. *Targum*).
46:1 **Beer-sheba.** South of Hebron where Jacob lived (*Yov'loth* 44:1), and hence, on the way to Egypt.
46:3 **Omnipotent** (see Saadia Gaon on *Sefer Yetzirah* 1:1 (p. 35, note 2); Radak, *Sherashim*, s.v. AYL.)
46:4 **Joseph will place . . .** When a man dies, it was the custom for the son to close his eyes (*Zohar* 226a; Ibn
Ezra; *Lekach Tov;* cf. *Shabbath* 77a). Or, "Joseph will take care of your concerns" (Rashbam; Sforno; cf.
Job 9:33).
46:7 **daughters.** See above, 37:35.
46:8 **Israelites.** See above, 32:33. Here, *beney Yisrael* cannot mean "children of Israel" in the literal sense, since
Jacob is counted among them, as we shall see. See *Targum.*
— **Jacob and his sons.** Jacob is thus the first person counted. See note on 46:15.
46:9 **Reuben's sons.** See Exodus 6:14, Numbers 26:5,6, 1 Chronicles 5:3.
— **Enoch.** The name was used for earlier people (4:17, 5:18, 25:4).
46:10 **Simeon's sons.** See Exodus 6:15, Numbers 26:12,13, 1 Chronicles 4:24.
— **Yemuel.** In Exodus 6:15 it is also Yemuel. However, in Numbers and Chronicles it is Nemuel. It is pos-
sible that the name was changed after they were in Egypt (cf. Sh'muel ben Chofni Gaon; *Sekhel Tov;*
Lekach Tov on Numbers; Ramban *ibid.; Teshuvoth Rashba* 12, end).

46   ¹¹ Levi's sons*: Gershon, Kehath* and Merari.

¹² Judah's sons*: Er, Onan,* Shelah, Peretz and Zerach.* Er and Onan died in Canaan. The sons of Peretz were Chetzron and Chamul.

¹³ Issachar's sons*: Tolah, Puvah,* Yov* and Shimron.

¹⁴ Zebulun's sons*: Sered, Elon and Yachle'el.

¹⁵ All the above were [from] the sons that Leah bore to Jacob in Padan Aram. Besides this, there was also [Jacob's] daughter Dinah. The tally [so far, including*] his sons and daughters, is 33.

¹⁶ Gad's sons*: Tzifion,* Chagi, Shuni, Etzbon,* Eri, Arodi,* and Areli.

¹⁷ Asher's sons*: Yimnah, Yishvah, Yishvi and Beriah. There was also their sister Serach.* The sons of Beriah were Chever and Malkiel.

¹⁸ The above are [from] the sons of Zilpah. Laban gave her to his daughter Leah, and she bore these sons to Jacob. Here there are 16 in all.

¹⁹ The sons of Jacob's wife Rachel were Joseph and Benjamin.

— **Ohad, Yakhin.** These two are mentioned in Exodus, but not in Numbers. It appears that these tribes became extinct after the sin at Baal Peor (Numbers 25:9; cf. Rashi on Numbers 26:13; *Bereshith Rabbah* 99:7). In Chronicles, Yariv is substituted for Ohad and Yakhin. It is possible that the remnants of these two sub-tribes united to form a new group.

— **Tzochar.** Identical to Zerach in Numbers and Chronicles (Rashi, Numbers; *Teshuvoth Rashba loc. cit.*).

— **Saul.** He had the same name as King Saul. Some say that this Saul was an ancestor of Zimri (Numbers 25:14; *Targum Yonathan; Sanhedrin* 82b; *HaKethav VeHaKabbalah*).

— **Canaanite woman.** Some say that this is mentioned because Simeon was the only one of the brothers to marry a Canaanite (Ibn Ezra; Radak). According to some ancient sources, her name was Adiva, and after Saul was born, Simeon took a wife from Aramaea like his other brothers (*Yov'loth* 34:20, 21). According to other sources, Saul was the son of Dinah and Shechem, and he had been adopted by Simeon (Bertenoro; *Bereshith Rabbah* 80; Rashi; cf. Hirsch). Others translate it as, "Saul who acted like the son of a Canaanite" (*Sanhedrin* 82b; *Targum Yonathan*).

46:11 Levi's sons. See Exodus 6:16; 1 Chronicles 6:1.

— **Kehath.** Sometimes spelled Kohath. He was the grandfather of Moses.

46:12 Judah's sons. See Numbers 26:20; 1 Chronicles 2:3, 4:21.

— **Er, Onan.** See above, 38:3-8.

— **Peretz and Zerach.** Above, 38:29,30.

46:13 Issachar's sons. See Numbers 26:23,24, 1 Chronicles 7:1.

— **Puvah.** Puah in 1 Chronicles 7:1.

— **Yov.** Yashuv in Numbers and Chronicles (Rashi on Numbers). The name was changed in Egypt when Yov devoted himself to study (*Sekhel Tov;* Rashi on Chronicles).

46:14 Zebulun's. Numbers 26:26.

46:15 including . . . There are only 32 names listed here, so Jacob must be included in the tally (Ibn Ezra on 46:23; Radak). According to others, the total of 33 is completed by Levi's daughter Yochebed (Numbers 26:59; Rashi; *Bava Bathra* 123a,b).

46:16 Gad's sons. Numbers 26:15.

— **Tzifion.** In Numbers it is Tzefon.

— **Etzbon.** Azni in Numbers (Rashi *ibid.*).

— **Arodi.** Arod in Numbers.

46:17 Asher's sons. 1 Chronicles 7:30. In Numbers 26:44, Yishva is omitted (*Sifethey Chakhamim* on Numbers 26:13).

— **Serach.** See Numbers 26:46. Some say that she was Asher's step-daughter (Ramban on Numbers; *Ba'aley Tosafoth ibid.*). According to Midrashic tradition, she attained immortality for telling Jacob that Joseph was still alive (*Targum Yonathan* here and on Numbers; Rashi on Numbers; *Pirkey Rabbi Eliezer* 48).

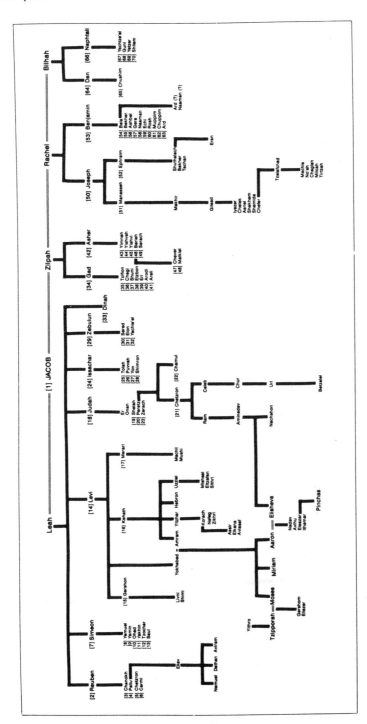

PLATE 11. JACOB'S DESCENDANTS

46   ²⁰ In Egypt, Joseph had sons born to him by Asenath, daughter of Poti
Phera, priest of On: Manasseh and Ephraim.*
        ²¹ Benjamin's sons*: Bela,* Bekher,* Ashbel,* Gera,* Naaman,* Echi,*
Rosh,* Muppim,* Chuppim* and Ard.*
        ²² The above are [from] the sons that Rachel bore to Jacob. There are 14 in
all.
        ²³ Dan's sons*: Chushim.*
        ²⁴ Naphtali's sons*: Yachtze'el, Guni, Yetzer and Shilem.*
        ²⁵ The above are [from] the sons of Bilhah. Laban gave her to his daughter
Rachel, and she bore these sons to Jacob. Here there are 7 in all.
        ²⁶ Thus, the number of people who came to Egypt with Jacob, who were
his blood descendants,* was 66, not counting the wives of Jacob's sons.

46:20 Manasseh, Ephraim. See above, 41:51,52.

46:21 Benjamin's sons. In Numbers 26:38, they are listed as Bela, Ashbel, Achiram, Shefufam and Chupam (see Rashi; Ibn Ezra on Numbers 26:12). There is a still different count in 1 Chronicles 8:1 (see Radak, Ralbag ad loc.). Some say that the Benjamin mentioned in 1 Chronicles 7:6 is not Jacob's son (Radak; Malbim). Cf. 1 Chronicles 7:10, Ezra 10:22, Nehemiah 3:23.

— **Bela.** Mentioned in Numbers 26:38, 1 Chronicles 7:6, 8:1.

— **Bekher.** Also in 1 Chronicles 7:6, but not in Numbers or 1 Chronicles 8:1. Some say that he was a grandchild of Benjamin (Radak on 1 Chronicles 8:1). See 2 Samuel 20:1. Also see Numbers 26:35.

— **Ashbel.** Also in Numbers. In 1 Chronicles 8:1 he is counted as Benjamin's second son. Some say that he is the Yediel in 1 Chronicles 7:6 (Rashi, Radak).

— **Gera.** It is possible that he was a son of Bela and thus a grandson of Benjamin; cf. 1 Chronicles 8:3, 8:5 (Ralbag). Also see 1 Chronicles 8:7, Judges 3:15, 2 Samuel 16:5.

— **Naaman.** Also a son of Bela, and a grandson of Benjamin; Numbers 26:40 (Ibn Ezra here; Rashi, Ramban, on Numbers (26:24). Also see 1 Chronicles 8:4,7.

— **Echi.** Achiram in Numbers 26:38 (Rashi, Ibn Ezra ibid.). Possibly Achiyah in 1 Chronicles 8:7 and Acho'ach in 1 Chronicles 8:5. Cf. 2 Samuel 23:9, 23:28. He may also be called Echud in 1 Chronicles 8:6. Significantly, Josephus refers to him as Yess (*Antiquities* 2:7:4).

— **Rosh.** Not mentioned elsewhere. But see 2 Samuel 15:32, 16:1.

— **Muppim.** Shefufam or Shufam in Numbers 26:39 (Rashi, Ibn Ezra *ibid.*). Also Shefufan in 1 Chronicles 8:5 (Ralbag), and Shupim in 1 Chronicles 7:12,15.

— **Chuppim.** Also in 1 Chronicles 7:12,15. In Numbers 26:38 it is Chupam (Ibn Ezra *ibid.*).

— **Ard.** A son of Bela; Numbers 26:40. Possibly the Adar in 1 Chronicles 8:3. (see Sh'muel ben Chofni).

46:23 Dan's sons. Although there was only one son, this is a formulaic usage (*Bava Bathra* 143b). See Numbers 26:8, 1 Chronicles 2:7, 2:8, 3:22, 4:13, 4:15, 7:17, 2 Samuel 23:32 (Sh'muel ben Chofni Gaon). However, some say that Dan had other sons who died (Ibn Ezra). Indeed, ancient sources state that Dan had four other sons, Shimon, Asudi, Yocha, and Sh'lomo, but they died the year he came to Egypt (*Yov'loth* 44:28,29). According to others, he had more sons later (*Tosafoth, Bava Bathra* 143b, s.v. *She-hayu*).

    Many of the discrepancies may be explained in this manner, since it is possible that the individuals named here died childless, while others were born later and are mentioned in Numbers and Chronicles. Sub-tribes could have also become extinct or changed their names. Obviously, a complete analysis is beyond the scope of these notes.

— **Chushim.** Shucham in Numbers 26:42. See 1 Chronicles 7:12. According to Talmudic tradition, Chushim was deaf (*Sotah* 13a) and extremely powerful (*Bereshith Rabbah* 93). It was he who killed Esau (*Sotah* 13a).

46:24 Naphtali's sons. See Numbers 26:48,49, 1 Chronicles 7:13. According to ancient sources, Naphtali had another son Ivi, who died (*Yov'loth* 44:31).

— **Shilem.** Also in Numbers 26:49. But in Chronicles, it is Shalum.

46:26 blood descendants. Literally, "emanating from his 'thigh.'" See note on 24:3, 32:26.

²⁷ Joseph's sons, born to him in Egypt, added another two individuals. [Adding it all up,] the number of individuals in Jacob's family who came to Egypt was 70. **46**

[80. Jacob Arrives in Egypt]

²⁸ [Jacob] sent Judah ahead of him to make preparations in Goshen. They then arrived in the Goshen district. ²⁹ Joseph [personally] harnessed his chariot, and he went to greet his father Israel in Goshen. He presented himself to [his father], and threw himself on his shoulders, weeping on his shoulders for a long time. ³¹ "Now I can die," said Israel to Joseph. "I have seen your face, and you are still alive."

³¹ To his brothers and his father's family, Joseph said, "I will go and tell Pharaoh. I will say the following to him: 'My brothers and my father's family have come to me from Canaan. ³² These men deal in livestock and are tenders of sheep. They have brought along their sheep, their cattle, and all their possessions.'

³³ "When Pharaoh summons you and inquires as to your occupation, ³⁴ you must say, 'We and our fathers have dealt in livestock all our lives.*' You will then be able to settle in the Goshen district, since all shepherds are taboo* in Egypt."

¹ Joseph went and told Pharaoh. He said, "My father and brothers have come from Canaan, along with their sheep, their cattle, and all their belongings. They are now in the Goshen district." ² From among his brothers, he selected five men* and presented them to Pharaoh. **47**

³ Pharaoh asked [Joseph's] brothers, "What is your occupation?"

"We are shepherds," they replied to Pharaoh, "we and our fathers before us."

⁴ "We have come to stay awhile in your land," they explained to Pharaoh, "because there is no grazing for our flocks, so severe is the famine in Canaan. If you allow us, we will settle in the Goshen district."

⁵ Pharaoh said to Joseph, "Your father and brothers have now come to

---

46:34 **We and our fathers.** Literally, "Your servants have been livestock men from our youth until now; also us, also our fathers."

— **shepherds are taboo.** Some say that this was because sheep were sacred to Egyptians, and hence, those who raised them for food were considered an abomination (Rashi; see above, 43:32). Others say that the Egyptians were vegetarians (Ibn Ezra). If this was after the Hyksos were driven out, it might have been a reaction against the Hyksos, who were "shepherd kings" (Josephus, *Contra Apion* 1:14). Others say that it was a social taboo (Rashbam). According to others, the fact that shepherding was taboo was an advantage, since the Israelites would not be competing with the Egyptians (Josephus *Antiquities* 2:7:5).

47:2 **five men.** Some say that these were Reuben, Simeon, Levi, Issachar, and Benjamin, the weakest of the brothers (*Bereshith Rabbah* 95; Rashi). According to others, they were the strongest of the brothers: Zebulun, Dan, Naphtali, Gad and Asher (*Targum Yonathan; Bava Kama* 92a).

47 you. ⁶ The land of Egypt is at your disposal. Settle your father and brothers in the best area. Let them settle in the Goshen district. If you have capable men among them, you can appoint them as livestock officers over my [cattle]."

⁷ Joseph brought his father Jacob and presented him to Pharaoh. Jacob blessed Pharaoh. ⁸ "How old are you?" asked Pharaoh of Jacob.

⁹ "My journey through life* has lasted 130 years,*" replied Jacob. "The days of my life have been few and hard. I did not live as long as my fathers did during their pilgrimage through life." ¹⁰ With that, Jacob blessed Pharaoh and left his presence.

¹¹ Joseph found a place for his father and brothers to live. He gave them an estate in the Rameses* region, in the best area, as Pharaoh had ordered. ¹² Joseph provided all the needs of his father, his brothers, and all his father's family, down to the very youngest.*

¹³ There was no bread in the entire area, since the famine was very severe. [The people of] Egypt and Canaan* became weak with hunger. ¹⁴ Joseph collected all the money in Egypt and Canaan in payment for the food [the people] were buying. Joseph brought [all] the money to Pharaoh's treasury.

¹⁵ When the money in Egypt and Canaan was used up, Egyptians from all over* came to Joseph. "Give us bread!" they cried. "Why should we die before you just because there is no money?"

¹⁶ "Bring your livestock," replied Joseph. "If there is no more money, I will give you [what you need] in exchange for your animals."

¹⁷ They brought their livestock to Joseph, and Joseph gave them bread in

---

47:9 **journey through life** . . . Literally, "the days of the years of my wandering."

— **130 years.** Since Jacob was born in 2108 (25:26), the year was now 2238 (1523 b.c.e.).

47:11 **Rameses region.** This was in Goshen (Rashi; Ibn Ezra on 46:1). Some sources identify it with Pelusium, a city at the extreme northeast of the Nile delta (*Targum Yonathan;* see note on Exodus 1:11). Others identify it with Hero-opolis (cf. 45:10; Septuagint on 46:28), which may be Avaris, the ancient Hyksos capital (Josephus, *Contra Apion* 1:14), identified with Typho's City (*Ibid.* 1:26). Josephus himself, however, clearly identifies Rameses with Heliopolis (*Antiquities* 2:7:6), and this opinion is shared by Saadia Gaon (on Exodus 1:11).

Etymologically, Rameses comes from the Egyptian *Ra-meses* "born of Ra," where *meses* (born of) is also the root of the name Moses (*Moshe*) (see Exodus 2:10). Hence, it would be logical that the area around Heliopolis (or On, see note on 41:50) should be known as

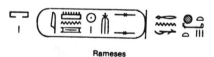

Rameses

Rameses. The name was later also adopted by a number of Pharaohs.

Other sources identify Rameses with Tanis, Qantir or San el-Chagar.

47:12 **down to the very youngest.** Literally, "bread according to the children" (cf. Rashi; Radak).

47:13 **Egypt and Canaan.** Here we see the extent of the famine. This would be highly unusual, since crops in Canaan depended on rain, while those in Egypt depended on the Nile, which was fed by precipitation in central Africa, an entirely different weather system.

47:15 **Egyptians from all over.** Literally, "All Egypt."

exchange for horses, flocks of sheep, herds of cattle,* and donkeys. He saw   **47**
them through that year with bread in exchange for all their livestock.

¹⁸ The year came to an end. They came to him the next year, and said, "We
are not holding anything back from you, your highness. But since the money
and animal stocks are used up, there is nothing left for you besides our dried-
up bodies and our land. ¹⁹ Why should we die before your very eyes—us and
our land? Buy our bodies and our land in exchange for bread. Let us become
Pharaoh's serfs, and let our land [also be his]. Give us seed grain! Let us live
and not die! Let the land not become desolate."

²⁰ Joseph [thus] bought up all the farm land in Egypt for Pharaoh. Every
man in Egypt had sold his field, for the famine was too much for them, and
the land became Pharaoh's property. ²¹ [Joseph] moved the people to tne
cities* in all Egypt's borders, from one end to the other.

²² The only land he did not buy up was that of the priests, since the priests
had a [food] allotment from Pharaoh. They ate the [food] allotment that
Pharaoh gave them, and did not have to sell their lands.

²³ Joseph announced to the people, "Today I have purchased your
[bodies] and your lands for Pharaoh. Here is seed grain for you. Plant your
fields. ²⁴ When it produces grain, you will have to give a fifth to Pharaoh.* The
other four parts will be yours, as seed grain for your fields, and as food for
you, your wives and your children."

²⁵ "You have saved our lives," they responded. "Just let us find favor in
your eyes, and we will be Pharaoh's serfs."

²⁶ Joseph set down a decree (that is in force until today*) that one-fifth of
[whatever grows on] the farm land of Egypt belonged to Pharaoh. Only the
priestly lands did not belong to Pharaoh.

²⁷ Meanwhile, [the fledgling nation of] Israel lived in Egypt, in the Goshen
district. They acquired property there, and were fertile, with their population
increasing very rapidly.

VaYechi   וַיְחִי

[81. Jacob's Last Days]

²⁸ Jacob made Egypt his home for 17 years. He lived to be 147 years old.*

47:17 flocks of sheep . . . Literally, "possession of sheep and possession of cattle" (cf. Hirsch). It might mean
that sheep and cattle were signed over rather than actually given, while horses and donkeys were actually
given over.
47:21 moved the people . . . Since they no longer owned the land.
47:24 a fifth . . . See note on 41:34.
47:26 until today. i.e. when the Torah was written.
47:28 He lived to be . . . Literally, "Jacob's days, the years of his life were . . ."

47 ²⁹ When Israel realized that he would soon die,* he called for his son Joseph. "If you really want to do me a kindness,*" he said, "place your hand under my thigh.* Act toward me with truth and kindness, and do not bury me in Egypt. ³⁰ Let me lie with my fathers. Carry me out of Egypt, and bury me in their grave."

"I will do as you say," replied [Joseph].

³¹ "Swear to me," said [Jacob].

[Joseph] made an oath to him, and, from where he was on the bed, Israel bowed.*

48 ¹ A short time after this, Joseph was told that his father was sick. [Joseph went to his father,] taking his two sons, Manasseh and Ephraim, along with him. ² When Jacob was told that Joseph was coming to him, Israel summoned his strength and sat up in bed.

³ Jacob said to Joseph, "God Almighty once appeared to me in Luz, in the land of Canaan. He blessed me, ⁴ and said to me, 'I will make you fruitful and numerous, and have you give rise to an assembly of nations. I will give this land to you and your descendants as their property forever.*'

⁵ "Now, the two sons who were born to you in Egypt before I came here shall be considered as mine. Ephraim and Manasseh shall be just like Reuben and Simeon to me. ⁶ Any children that you have after them, however, shall be considered yours. They shall inherit only through their [older] brothers.

⁷ "When I was coming from Padan, [your mother] Rachel died on me. It was in Canaan, a short distance before we came to Ephrath.* I buried her there along the road to Ephrath (Bethlehem)."

⁸ Israel saw Joseph's sons. "Who are these?" he asked.

⁹ "They are the sons that God gave me here," replied Joseph to his father.

"If you would, bring them to me," said [Jacob]. "I will give them a blessing."

¹⁰ Israel's eyes were heavy with age, and he could not see. When [Joseph] brought [his sons] near him, [Israel] kissed them and hugged them. ¹¹ "I never even hoped to see your face," said Israel to Joseph. "But now God has even let me see your children."

47:29 **When Israel realized** . . . Literally, "The days grew near for Israel to die."
— **If you want to do me a kindness.** Literally, "If I have found favor in your eyes." Here it is obvious that Jacob does not mean it literally, since he is speaking to his son. It is possible that this expression has the same idiomatic meaning above 18:3, 19:19, 30:27, 33:10, 33:15, 34:11, 39:4. The expression may have been used both literally and idiomatically (cf. Hirsch).
47:31 **from where he was on the bed** . . . Or, "he bowed, leaning on his staff" (Shmuel ben Chofni Gaon; Septuagint). See above 37:10 (*Lekach Tov*).
48:4 **I will make you** . . . Above 35:11,12. Also see 28:13.
48:7 **Rachel died** . . . See 35:16–19.

¹² Joseph took [the boys] from near his [father's] lap,* and he bowed down   **48**
to the ground.

¹³ Joseph then took the two boys. He placed Ephraim to his right (to
Israel's left), and Manasseh to his left (to Israel's right). He then came close to
[his father]. ¹⁴ Israel reached out with his right hand and placed it on Ephraim's head [even though] he was the younger son. He [placed] his left hand
on Manasseh's head. He deliberately crossed his hands, even though Manasseh was the firstborn.

¹⁵ [Jacob] gave Joseph a blessing. He said, "The God before whom my
fathers, Abraham and Isaac, walked, is the God who has been my Shepherd
from as far back as I can remember until this day, ¹⁶ [sending] an angel* to
deliver me from all evil. May He bless the lads, and let them carry my name,
along with the names of my fathers, Abraham and Isaac. May they increase in
the land like fish."

¹⁷ When Joseph saw that his father had placed his right hand on Ephraim's
head, he was displeased. He tried to lift his father's hand from Ephraim's
head and place it on Manasseh's. ¹⁸ "That's not the way it should be done,
Father," said Joseph. "The other one is the firstborn. Place your right hand on
his head."

¹⁹ His father refused and said, "I know, my son, I know. [The older one]
will also become a nation. He too will attain greatness. But his younger
brother will become even greater, and his descendants will become full-
fledged nations.*"

²⁰ On that day [Jacob] blessed them. He said, "[In time to come] Israel will
use you as a blessing. They will say, 'May God make you like Ephraim and
Manasseh.*'" He [deliberately] put Ephraim before Manasseh.

²¹ Israel said to Joseph, "I am dying. God will be with you, and He will
bring you back to your ancestral land. ²² In addition to what your brothers
shall share, I am giving you Shechem,* which I took from the Amorite* with
my sword and bow.*"

48:12 **his father's lap** (*Sekhel Tov;* Sforno). Or, "from between his [own] knees" (Radak; Hirsch. Cf. *Lekach Tov;*
  Sh'muel ben Chofni Gaon).
48:16 **sending an angel.** (Saadia Gaon; Shmuel ben Chofni Gaon). Or, "The angel who delivered me . . ."
  (Rashi; Abarbanel). Some say that the "Angel" denotes God's providence (Shmuel ben Chofni Gaon;
  Ralbag; *HaKethav VeHaKabbalah*).
48:19 **full-fledged nations** (Saadia). Or, "famous nations;" "many nations" (*Targum Yonathan;* Ibn Ezra);
  "world-filling nations" (Rashi; Radak); "rulers of nations" (Onkelos); "destroyers of nations" (*Lekach
  Tov*); or "famous among nations."
48:20 **May God make you . . .** This blessing is still used today.
48:22 **Shechem.** See above 12:6, 33:18. (*Targum Yonathan;* Rashi; Ibn Ezra). See Joshua 24:32. Others translate
  the word *shechem* here as "a portion" (Onkelos; Rashi). The word literally means a "shoulder," and
  some interpret it to mean a hill.
—   **Amorite.** See above, 10:16, 14:7, 15:16, 15:21. Some take "Amorite" as a generic term for all the tribes
  of Canaan (Ibn Ezra).

[82. Blessings: Reuben, Simeon, Levi]

49   ¹ Jacob called for his sons. [When they came,] he said, "Come together, and I will tell you what will happen in the course of time.* ² Come and listen, sons of Jacob; listen to your father Israel.

³ "Reuben, you are my firstborn, my strength and the beginning of my manhood, first in rank and first in power. ⁴ [But because you were] unstable as water, you will no longer be first. This is because you moved* your father's beds, committing a profane act. He moved my bed*!

⁵ "Simeon and Levi are a pair*; instruments of crime are their wares.* ⁶ Let my soul not enter their plot; let my spirit* not unite with their meeting—for they have killed men* with anger, maimed bulls with will.* ⁷ Cursed be their rage, for it is fierce, and their fury, for it is cruel. I will disperse them in Jacob, scatter them in Israel.

[83. Judah]

⁸ "Judah, your brothers shall submit (*yodu*) to you.* Your hand shall be on your enemies' necks; your father's sons shall bow to you.

⁹ "Young lion, Judah, you have risen from prey, my son. He crouches, lies like a lion, like an awesome lion,* who will dare rouse him?

— **sword and bow.** This may allude to the wars that Jacob's sons fought against the Amorites after the Shechem massacre (*Targum Yonathan; Bereshith Rabbah* 97. Cf. *You'loth* 34; *Tzavaath Yehudah* 3; *Sefer Ha-Yashar,* p. 98ff; *Midrash VaYisu; MeAm Lo'ez/The Torah Anthology* 3:219ff.). According to others, it may allude to the Shechem massacre itself (Sh'muel ben Chofni Gaon; Ibn Ezra). Others render the Hebrew as "with my prayer and supplication" (Onkelos; *Mekhilta, BeShalach* 2; Rashi).

49:1 **in the course of time.** Literally, "at the end of days." Compare Moses' blessing; Deuteronomy 33.

49:4 **you moved** . . . (Sh'muel ben Chofni; Radak; *Sherashim;* Ibn Ezra; *Bereshith Rabbah* 98). See 1 Chronicles 5:1, that as a result of this, Reuben lost the birthright. There is a question as to whether this refers to the episode with the mandrakes (30:14) or that with Bilhah (35:22) (*Bereshith Rabbah* 98). The Hebrew can also be translated, "he went up [on] his father's bed." See next note.

— **He moved my bed!** (Ralbag; following cantellation notes). Literally, "then you profaned my couch—went up." Variously interpreted, "You profaned that which went up on my couch" (Rashi); "You profaned my couch, [but] went up [and repented]" (*Lekach Tov*); "You profaned my exalted couch" (*Saadia; Sekhel Tov*); "You profaned my couch; it is cut off" (Radak, *Sherashim,* s.v. *Alah;* Ibn Ezra; *Bereshith Rabbah* 98); "You profaned my couch by removing it" (translation of Sh'muel ben Chofni); or "[Your instability] arose when you profaned my couch" (Radak, *Sherashim*).

49:5 **a pair** (*Bereshith Rabbah* 98; Rashi). Literally, "brothers."

— **wares** (Saadia; Sh'muel ben Chofni; Ibn Ezra). Or "weapons" (Rashi); "brother" (Rashbam); "companions" (*Sekhel Tov*); "food" (Sh'muel ben Chofni); "troops" (ibn Janach). Others translate the verse, "They are at home with instruments of crime" (Rashi; Ralbag; *Bereshith Rabbah* 98); or "They plot with instruments of violence" (Septuagint).

49:6 **spirit** (Radak; cf. Psalms 16:9). The Hebrew word *kavod* here usually means honor.

— **killed men.** Referring to Shechem; see 34:26.

— **maimed bulls** . . . Literally, "maimed a bull." Some say that this refers to Joseph (*Targum Yonathan; Lekach Tov;* Rashi; see Deuteronomy 33:17); see note on 37:19,24. Some translate the verse, "they tore down a wall with their will" (Ibn Ezra).

49:8 **submit** (Rashbam; Sforno). Or "praise" (Rashi; Ibn Ezra; Ralbag).

49:9 **awesome lion.** See *Avoth deRabbi Nathan* B 43. Cf. Hirsch. See Numbers 24:9.

¹⁰ "The scepter will not depart from Judah, nor legislation* from his **49**
descendants.* Nations will submit to him* until the final tranquility* comes.

¹¹ "He loads down his donkey with a [single] grapevine, his young donkey
with a single vine branch.* He even washes his clothes in wine, his cloak in the
blood of grapes. ¹² But his eyes are more sparkling than the wine,* his teeth
whiter than milk.*

[84. Zebulun]

¹³ "Zebulun shall settle the seashores; he will be a harbor for ships; his
border shall reach Sidon.*

[85. Issachar]

¹⁴ "Issachar is a strong-boned donkey,* stretching out between the
saddlebags.* ¹⁵ But he sees that the resting place is good, and that the land is
pleasant, so he will bend his back to the load, working like a slave.*

49:10 **legislation** (Sh'muel ben Chofni; Radak; Ralbag; cf. Psalms 60:9, 105:9). The Hebrew *me-chokek* has the
connotation of both law and writing. Hence, others translate it as "the scribe's pen" (*Sekhel Tov;* Ibn
Ezra); "the scribe" (*Bereshith Rabbah* 98; Radak, *Sherashim*); or "the law inscribing pen" (Hirsch).

— **from his descendants.** (*Targum*). A euphemism, literally, "from between his legs." Others, "the scribal
pen will not depart from his lap" (Ibn Ezra), or "the scribe will not depart from near his feet" (*Bereshith
Rabbah* 98).

— **submit to him** (*Targum;* Ibn Ezra; Radak, *Sherashim, s.v. Yikah;* cf. Proverbs 30:17). Others, "He will
gather nations" (Ramban; *Bereshith Rabbah* 99); "He will have a gathering of nations" (Rashi; Rashbam);
or "He will make nations gnash their teeth" (*Bereshith Rabbah* 99).

— **tranquility** (Sforno; *Torah Sh'lemah* 157; cf. Jeremiah 12:1, Job 3:26). This may be seen as referring to the
Messianic age. Others write that the Hebrew word *shiloh* here is from the root *nashal,* and translate the
verse, "until the exile comes" (Sh'muel ben Chofni; cf. Deuteronomy 7:1, 19:5, Job 27:8). Or, it can be
taken as a form of *she-lo* (that which is his), and the verse is then rendered, "until that which is [rightly]
his comes" (*Targum;* Septuagint; *Bereshith Rabbah* 99; cf. Ezekiel 21:32). Or, it can be seen as two words
shai lo (a gift to him), and the verse is, "until a gift is brought to him" (Rashi; Lekach Tov; cf. Isaiah
18:7). Or, *shiloh* can denote a special descendant; "Until he has a special descendant" (*Targum Yonathan;
Lekach Tov;* Ibn Ezra; Ralbag Sh'muel ben Chofni; cf. Deuteronomy 28:57). Or, "until it reaches its final
nadir" (Hirsch). Others see Shiloh as a proper noun, possibly a name of the Messiah (*Sanhedrin* 98b;
Bereshith Rabbah 99). Of course, Shiloh was also the name of the site of the Tabernacle before the Temple
was built in Jerusalem (Joshua 18:1, 1 Samuel 1:3 etc.). Hence, some translate the verse, "The scepter
will not begin (*yasar*) in Judah . . . until Shiloh comes to an end" (*Sekhel Tov; Ba'aley Tosafoth; Toledoth Yitzchak*).

49:11 **He loads down . . .** (*Kethuvoth* 111b; Rashi).

49:12 **his eyes are more sparkling . . .** (Saadia Gaon; Sh'muel ben Chofni; ibn Janach; Hirsch). Or, "his eyes
are red from wine" (Rashi; cf. *Tzava'ath Yehudah* 14); "his face is redder than wine" (Radak; c.f. *Baaley
Tosafoth*); "his mountains are red like (from) wine" (*Targum;* Rashi); "his springs sparkle like (are red
from) wine" (Rashi; *Sekhel Tov*).

— **his teeth . . .** Or, "his teeth white from milk" (Rashi); or "His valleys are white [with sheep] with milk"
(*Targum;* Rashi).

49:13 **Sidon.** The northwest boundary of the Holy Land; above, 10:19. Cf. 10:15. Also see *Tzava'ath Zebulun* 6.

49:14 **strong-boned donkey** (Rashi; Ibn Ezra). Or, "Issachar has a powerful body" (Saadia; Shmuel ben
Chofni), "Issachar shall haul by donkey" (in contrast to Zebulun; *Bereshith Rabbah* 99); or "Issachar was
caused by a donkey" (*Niddah* 31a; *Bereshith Rabbah* 98). According to one opinion, a donkey found the
mandrakes and died (above, 30:14; *Midrash Aggadah,* quoted *Tzeror HaMor* as *Midrash HaGaluy*).

— **saddlebags** (Radak; Sforno). Or, "resting between stops" (Rashi; *Targum*); or "lying between the
extremes [of the land]" (Sh'muel ben Chofni; cf. Ibn Janach).

[86. Dan]

49   ¹⁶ "Dan shall fight for (*dan*)* his people, like any one of the tribes of Israel.* ¹⁷ Let Dan be a snake on the road, a viper* on the path, biting the horse's heel, so the rider falls backward. ¹⁸ I pray that God will help you.*

[87. Gad]

¹⁹ "Raiders (*gad*) shall raid Gad, but he will raid at [their] heel.*

[88. Asher]

²⁰ "From Asher shall come the richest foods; he shall provide the king's delights.*

[89. Naphtali]

²¹ "Naphtali is a deer* running free*; he delivers* words of beauty.*

49:15 But he sees . . . (Ibn Ezra; Sh'muel ben Chofni). Cf. *Tzava'ath Yessachar* 3:1, 5:5.

49:16 fight for . . . Or "avenge" (Rashi), or "judge" (Radak).

—   **like any one of the tribes** . . . Although he was the son of a handmaid (Radak). Others, "like the unique tribe of Israel" (Rashi); or "the tribes of Israel will be united" (Rashi).

49:17 viper. *Shefifon* in Hebrew, occurring only here. The Septuagint and Vulgate render it as *Cerastes*. On the basis of Semitic cognates, it is most probably the black and red horned viper, *Pseudocerastes fieldi*, that lives in the Holy Land. The Hebrew name comes from its rustling of scales. This snake digs into the sand with only his long thin horns protruding (cf. *Yerushalmi, Terumah* 8:3), and when birds take these horns for worms and peck at them, the snake kills them. Hence, this is seen as an indication that Dan will engage in guerilla warfare. In Talmudic tradition, this is seen as a prediction of Samson's career.

Horned Viper

49:18 I pray . . . (*Chizzkuni; HaKethav VeHaKabbalah*). Or, "I hope for your deliverance, O God" (Ramban).

49:19 Raiders shall raid Gad . . . (Ibn Ezra; Radak; Ralbag; *Yerushalmi, Sotah* 8:10; cf. Sh'muel ben Chofni). Literally, "Gad, a troop (*gedud*) shall raid him (*ye-gud-enu*), and he shall raid (*ya-gud*) heel." Others have, "Gad shall provide a raiding troop, and his troop shall return on his path" (Rashi; *Lekach Tov*); "Troops shall follow Gad, and then he shall bring up the rear" (*Targum;* Rashbam); "Gad shall go forward and attack (in contrast to Dan), and he shall attack [the enemy's] heel" (Sforno); "Gad shall constantly be attacked, but he will pursue his foes" (Ramban); "Raiders will attack Gad, but he will cut off their heel" (Sh'muel ben Chofni; Bachya; *Tur*); "Plunderers shall cut at Gad, but he will cut at their heel" (Hirsch); "Gad shall overflow with troops . . ." (*Lekach Tov*); ". . . and he will have the final victory" (*Tanchuma* 12; Abarbanel); "Gad's masses will come together, and he will remain together in the end" (Abarbanel); "Gad will attack head-on, and he will [also] attack from the rear" (Malbim); or "Good fortune will pursue Gad, and he will have good fortune in the end" (cf. 30:10).

49:20 the king's delights. Or "sweetmeats fit for a king."

49:21 deer. Literally, a "she-deer" or "hind". Others, "gazelle." It can also be translated as a tree or plain (see below).

—   **running free.** Or "sent." Or, "a gazelle-like messenger" (Hirsch); or, "A hind sent as a gift" (Ibn Ezra). Cf. *Tzava'ath Naphtali* 2:1. See below.

—   **he delivers** (Rashi; Rashbam). Or, "which delivers" (Ramban).

—   **words of beauty** (Rashi; Ibn Ezra; Radak). Or, "words of victory" (Rashbam). Others translate this verse, "Naphtali is a spreading tree, that puts out beautiful branches (*Baaley Tosafoth;* Malbim); or "Naphtali is a full-bearing field, that bears beautiful trees (*Chizzkuni; HaKethav VeHaKabbalah;* cf. *Targum*). Possibly, "beautiful foals" (cf. *Targum* on 30:32; *Eruvin* 53b).

[90. Joseph]

²² "Joseph is a fruitful son,* [like] a fruitful vine* by the fountain,* with   49
branches* running* over the wall.*
²³ "[People] made his life bitter* and attacked him*; masters of strife*
made him their target.* ²⁴ But his resolution* remained firm,* and his arms
were [eventually] bedecked with gold.* This was from Jacob's Champion, and
from then on, he became a shepherd,* a builder* of Israel.
²⁵ "[This was] from your father's God, who will [still] help you, and [from]

49:22 fruitful son. Although in Hebrew the phrase *ben porath* is used twice, the first time it is translated as
"fruitful son," and the second time, "a fruitful vine" (*Targum;* Saadia Gaon; Sh'muel ben Chofni).
Others see it as a repetition (Rashbam; Ibn Ezra).

— **fruitful vine.** Or "branch" or "bough" (*Targum;* Saadia Gaon; Ibn Ezra; Ramban; Sforno; cf. Psalms
80:16). Or, "a handsome son" (Rashi); "a noble, distinguished son" (Hirsch); "a vine sending forth
shoots" (Ibn Ezra); "a young bull" (*Bereshith Rabbah* 98; cf. Deuteronomy 33:17); "a son of cows" (referring to Pharaoh's dream; 41:2; *Bereshith Rabbah* 98); "a young interpreter [of dreams]" (*Aggadath Bereshith* 73; *Midrash Aggadah*); "a son suffering from treachery" (*Bereshith Rabbah* 78); or, "a royal son (*Tzeror
HaMor*). In ancient Egyptian, *porath* or *pereth* is grain.

— **fountain.** Or "well" or "spring" (*Targum*). Or, "like a fountain" (*Lekach Tov*); "to the eye" (Rashi); "away
from the eye" (*Berakhoth* 20a).

— **branches** (Ibn Ezra). Or "daughters" (see below).

— **running.** Literally, "striding" or "strutting." Some translate the two words as "running branches" (Ibn
Ezra). On the basis of Semitic cognates, some translate these two words as "a wild colt," but there is no
traditional basis for this.

— **wall** (Rashi). Or, "to see" (Rashi).
    The verse can thus be rendered, "Joseph is a handsome son, a son handsome to the eye; girls strode
out to see him" (*Bereshith Rabbah* 98; Rashi); or "young girls strode out on the wall [to see him]" (*Targum
Yonathan; Pirkey Rabbi Eliezer* 39). Or, "[Your] daughters will walk the boundaries [of their own lands]"
(*Tanchuma, Pinchas* 9; *BaMidbar Rabbah* 14:7, 21:12; alluding to the fact that among Joseph's descendants,
women will be the first to inherit land; see Numbers 27:1, Joshua 17:6).

49:23 made his life bitter (Rashi). Or, "made him their target" (Ibn Ezra); or "were treacherous to him" (*Bereshith Rabbah* 98).

— **attacked.** Or "quarreled" (*Targum;* Rashi). Or, "shot at him" (*Sekhel Tov;* Ibn Ezra).

— **masters of strife** (*Targum;*Rashi; cf. Rashbam). Cf. Jeremiah 9:7, Proverbs 26:18,19. Or, "expert bowmen" or "masters of arrows" (Ibn Ezra).

— **made him their target** (Hirsch). Or "attacked him" or "were furious at him" (cf. 27:41). The verse can
also be translated, "Master bowmen hated him, they made him their target and shot at him" (Ibn Ezra);
or "Archers bitterly attacked him, they shot him and harrassed him."

49:24 resolution. Or "power" (*Targum;* Rashi). Or, "his bow" (*Sekhel Tov;* Ibn Ezra; Radak).

— **remained firm** (*Targum;* Rashi). Or, "he drew his bow with strength" (Rashbam); "his strength returned
as before" (*Targum Yonathan; Sotah* 36b); or, "He held back his desires" (referring to Potiphar's wife,
above, 39:8; Rashi; see next note).

— **his arms were bedecked with gold** (*Targum;* Rashi; cf. 41:42). Or, "he bent his arm" (Rashbam), "his arm
was strong" (Ibn Ezra; Radak); "his arm conquered" (Sh'muel ben Chofni). Others render this phrase,
"his sperm-ducts were let loose" (*Yerushalmi, Horayoth* 2:5; *Pirkey Rabbi Eliezer* 39; Rashi); and hence, the
entire verse is translated, "He held back his desires [with Potiphar's wife], but his seed was spilled"
(*Ibid.*).

— **he became a shepherd** (*Targum Yonathan;* Rashi); referring to Joseph. Others have, "This was from
Jacob's Champion, from the Shepherd, the Rock of Israel" (cf. Septuagint). Or, "from there was
shepherded . . ." (Hirsch).

— **builder** (cf. *Targum;* Rashi; Rashbam). Literally, "stone" or "rock." (Radak). Some translate it as
"essence" (Saadia Gaon; Sh'muel ben Chofni). Some say that this is an allusion to the Messiah coming
from Joseph (Sh'muel ben Chofni; Ralbag; *Tzeror HaMor;* cf. *Midrash Aggadah; Sukkah* 52b; *Torah Sh'lemah*
330).

49   the Almighty,* who will bless you. [Yours will be] the blessings of heaven
      above, the blessing of the water lying beneath,* the blessing of breast* and
      womb.
        ²⁶ "May your father's blessing add to* the blessing of my parents, lasting
      as long as* the eternal hills. May they be for Joseph's head, for the brow* of
      the elect* of his brothers.

                              [91. Benjamin; Conclusion]

        ²⁷ "Benjamin is a vicious wolf. He eats a portion in the morning, and
      divides his prey in the evening."

        ²⁸ All these are the tribes of Israel, twelve in all, and this is what their father
      said to them when he blessed them. He gave each one his own special blessing.
        ²⁹ [Jacob] then gave [his sons] his final instructions. "I am going to join my
      people [in death]," he said. "Bring me to my fathers, to be buried in the cave
      in the field of Ephron the Hittite.* ³⁰ [This is] the cave in Makhpelah Field,
      bordering Mamre, in the land of Canaan. Abraham bought it along with the
      field from Ephron the Hittite as burial property. ³¹ This is where Abraham
      and his wife Sarah are buried*; this is where Isaac and his wife Rebecca are
      buried*; and this is where I buried Leah.* ³² The purchase of the field and its
      cave from the children of Heth [is still recognized]."
        ³³ Jacob thus concluded his instructions to his sons. He drew his feet back
      onto the bed, breathed his last, and was brought back to his people.

50   ¹ Joseph fell on his father's face. He wept there and kissed [his father].

49:25 and from the Almighty . . . (Ibn Ezra). Or, "and [you were] with the Almighty (*Targum Yonathan;* Rashi).
— **lying beneath.** Literally, "the abyss (subterranean water) crouching below" (cf. Radak).
— **breast** . . . Literally "breasts" (Rashbam). Or, "blessings of father and mother" (*Targum;* Rashi); or, "blessings of food and children" (*Lekach Tov*).
49:26 add to. Or, "be in addition to" (*Targum;* Rashi). Or, "stronger than" (*Sekhel Tov*).
— **as long as** . . . (Rashi). Or, "until the heights of the eternal hills" (Ibn Ezra). More literally, "desires" (Saadia; *Bereshith Rabbah* 98). Some interpret the phrase, "as long as the eternal mountains exist" (Radak).
— **brow.** More accurately, the top of the head, the place where an infant's head is soft (Radak, *Sherashim*). See Deuteronomy 28:35, 2 Samuel 14:25, Job 2:7. Cf. *Targum.*
— **elect.** Cf. Deuteronomy 33:16. This can mean "one set apart" (*Targum;* Rashi; *Bereshith Rabbah* 98); "most consecrated" (Sforno); "king" (Rashbam; Radak); or "crown" (Ibn Ezra; Radak, *Sherashim*). The Hebrew word, *nazir,* here also denotes a Nazirite (Numbers 6:2), and some sources state that Joseph actually took a Nazirite vow (*Bereshith Rabbah* 98).
49:29 cave in the field . . . See above, 23:9.
49:31 Abraham and Sarah . . . See above, 23:19, 25:9.
— **Isaac and Rebecca** . . . Above, 35:29. There, however, it does not mention that Isaac was buried in Makhpelah.
— **buried Leah.** The burial of Rebecca and Leah is not mentioned previously. An ancient source states that Leah was buried "near Rebecca, to the left of Sarah" (*Yov'loth* 36:21). For a discussion of how the graves were arranged, see *MeAm Lo'ez/The Torah Anthology* 3:549.

² Joseph then ordered his servants, the physicians, to embalm* his father. The 50 physicians thus embalmed Israel. ³ It took forty days, since that was the time required for embalming. Egypt mourned [Jacob] for seventy days.*

⁴ When the period of mourning for Jacob was over, Joseph addressed Pharaoh's court and said, "If you would do me a favor, give the following personal message to Pharaoh: ⁵ 'My father bound me by an oath and he declared, "I am dying. You must bury me in the grave that I prepared* for myself in the land of Canaan." Now, if you allow me, I will head north and bury my father. I will return.'"

⁶ "Go bury your father," said Pharaoh, "just as he had you swear."

⁷ Joseph headed north to bury his father, and with him went all of Pharaoh's courtiers who were his palace elders, as well as all the [other] elders of Egypt. ⁸ All of Joseph's household, his brothers, and his father's family [also went]. All they left behind in Goshen were their small children, their sheep and their cattle. ⁹ A chariot brigade and horsemen also went with them. It was a very imposing retinue.

¹⁰ They came to Bramble Barn* (*Goren HaAtad*) on the bank* of the Jordan, and there they conducted a great, imposing funeral. [Joseph] observed a

---

50:2 **embalm.** However, Jews do not practice embalming today. The embalming process consisted of infusing and soaking the body with balsam or cedar oil and natrum, a form of native sodium carbonate, found in a lake in the Lybian desert (*Zohar* 1:250b, 2:141b; Sh'muel ben Chofni; Abarbanel. Cf. Herodotus 2:87; Diodorus Siculus 1:91). It appears that he was prepared as a mummy (Sh'muel ben Chofni).

50:3 **seventy days.** Forty for embalming, and thirty for mourning; (Rashi); cf. Numbers 20:29, Deuteronomy 34:8. Although embalming normally required 70 days (Herodotus *loc. cit.*), Jacob was only given a partial embalming, for 40 days. Nevertheless, the normal waiting period would still be 70 days (Sh'muel ben Chofni; cf. *Midrash Aggadah*).

50:5 **prepared** (*Targum*). Literally "dug."

50:10 **Bramble Barn.** Or "Bramble Threshing Floor" (see Judges 9:14, Psalms 58:10; *Targum* on Genesis 2:18; *Shevi'ith* 7:5). On the basis of the Septuagint and cognate Semitic words, the *atad* here is identified as the Box Thorn (*Lycium europaeum*), which is known to grow on the bank of the Jordan. As Maimonides notes (on *Shevi'ith* 7:5; cf. Saadia), it has black edible seeds (*Sherashim*). The Septuagint and the Vulgate translate it as Rhammus; while the Radak renders it in Spanish as *cardon*, the spurge.

Rhammus   Thorn

— **bank.** Literally, "on the other side of the Jordan." Usually, this is given with relation to the Holy Land, so this would be the east bank of the Jordan (Rabbenu Meyuchas). Cf. Numbers 32:19, Deuteronomy 1:1, 3:8, 4:49, 11:30; Joshua 1:14. This would indicate that instead of coming to Canaan along the coastal route, Joseph took the King's Highway (Numbers 20:17, 21:22), which lead to the trans-Jordan region. This was the route of the Exodus. According to others, however, "the other side" here denotes the west bank of the Jordan (*Sekhel Tov; Chizzkuni*).

50 seven day mourning period* for his father. [11] When the Canaanites living in the area saw the mourning in Bramble Barn, they said, "Egypt is in deep mourning here." The place on the bank of the Jordan was therefore called Egypt's Mourning (*Avel Mitzraim*).*

[12] [Jacob's] sons did as he had instructed them. [13] His sons carried him to Canaan, and they buried him in the cave of Makhpelah Field, bordering Mamre. [This is] the field that Abraham bought for burial property from Ephron the Hittite.

[14] After he buried his father, Joseph returned to Egypt along with his brothers and all those who went with him to his father's burial. [15] Joseph's brothers began to realize [the implications] of their father's death. "What if Joseph is still holding a grudge against us?" they said. "He is likely to pay us back for all the evil we did him."

[16] They instructed [messengers] to tell Joseph: "Before he died, your father gave us final instructions. He said, [17] 'This is what you must say to Joseph: Forgive the spiteful deed and the sin your brothers committed when they did evil to you.' Now forgive the spiteful deed that [we], the servants of your father's God, have done."

As [the messengers*] spoke to him, Joseph wept.

[18] His brothers then came and threw themselves at his feet. "Here!" they said, "We are your slaves!"

[19] "Don't be afraid," said Joseph to them. "Shall I then take God's place*? [20] You might have meant to do me harm, [but] God made it come out good. [He made] it come out as it actually did, where the life of a great nation has been preserved. [21] Now don't worry. I will fully provide for you and your children." He thus comforted them and tried to make up.*

[22] Joseph remained in Egypt along with his father's family. He lived to be 110 years old. [23] Joseph saw Ephraim's grandchildren,* and the children of Manasseh's son Makhir* were also born on Joseph's lap.

---

seven day mourning period. Cf. 1 Samuel 31:13, Job 2:13. According to some sources, this is the source of the practice of sitting seven days in mourning (*shiva*) (*Yerushalmi, Mo'ed Katan* 3:5; *Pirkey Rabbi Eliezer* 17).

50:11 Avel Mitzraim. Or "plain of Egypt" (cf. Rashi on 14:6 and on Numbers 33:49). On geographical grounds, this may be identified with Evel Shittim (Numbers 33:49).

50:17 the messengers (*Lekach Tov*).

50:19 Shall I then take . . . See above, 30:2. Jacob used the exact same words to Joseph's mother, Rachel.

50:21 tried to make up. See 34:3.

50:23 grandchildren. Literally, "third generation." Actually, the term can be interpreted to indicate Ephraim's children (the third generation from Joseph; Sh'muel ben Chofni); Ephraim's grandchildren (Sh'muel ben Chofni); or Ephraim's great-grandchildren (Ralbag). The generations were: Ephraim, Shuthelach, Eran (Numbers 25:35,36; cf. 1 Chronicles 7:20).

children of Manasseh's son Makhir. Most notably Gilead (Numbers 26:29. See 1 Chronicles 7:14,16; Numbers 27:1, 32:29, 36:1, Joshua 17:3).

²⁴ Joseph said to his close family,* "I am dying. God is sure to grant you   50
special providence* and bring you out of this land, to the land that he swore
to Abraham, Isaac and Jacob."

²⁵ Joseph then bound the Israelites by an oath: "When God grants you
[this] special providence, you must bring my remains out of this place."

²⁶ Joseph died at the age of 110 years. He was embalmed and placed in a
sarcophagus in Egypt.

50:24 **close family.** Literally, "brothers."
—   **special providence.** See above, 21:1.

שְׁמוֹת

EXODUS

Sh'moth

שְׁמוֹת

[1. Israel's Growth]

¹ These are the names of Israel's sons who came to Egypt with Jacob, each **1** with his family: ² Reuben, Simeon, Levi, Judah, ³ Issachar, Zebulun, Benjamin, ⁴ Dan, Naphtali, Gad and Asher. ⁵ The [original] number of Jacob's direct descendants,* including Joseph who was in Egypt, was seventy.*

⁶ Joseph, his brothers, and [everyone else in] that generation died. ⁷ The Israelites were fertile and prolific, and their population increased. They became so numerous that the land was filled with them.

[2. The New Order]

⁸ A new king,* who did not know of Joseph, came into power over Egypt. ⁹ He announced to his people, "The Israelites are becoming too numerous and strong for us. ¹⁰ We must deal wisely with them. Otherwise, they may increase so much, that if there is war, they will join our enemies and fight against us, driving [us] from the land.*"

¹¹ [The Egyptians] appointed conscription officers over [the Israelites] to crush their spirits with hard labor. [The Israelites] were to build up the cities of Pithom* and Ra'amses* as supply centers for Pharaoh. ¹² But the more [the

---

1:5 **direct descendants.** Literally, "souls emanating from Jacob's thigh." See Genesis 46:26; note on Genesis 24:2.
— **seventy.** See Genesis 46:27.
1:8 **A new king.** Or, "regime" or "dynasty." According to tradition, this occurred around the time of Miriam's birth, which was 2361 (1400 b.c.e.). Hence, the name Miriam denotes bitterness (*Seder Olam Rabbah* 3). The "new king" would then be Thutmose IV, who reigned 1411–1397 b.c.e.
    If we accept the 163 year discrepancy (see note on Genesis 12:15), then this occurred around what would be considered 1563 b.c.e. The New Kingdom, starting with the 18th Dynasty, is known to have begun in 1575 b.c.e. This started with Ahmose (*Ach-moshe*), who drove the Hyksos out of Egypt. Although the Israelites were not driven out at this time, the Hyksos were a Semitic tribe, and therefore the changed political climate would have adversely affected the Israelites. A new surge of nationalism would also have resulted in prejudice against foreign elements. (cf. Josephus, *Contra Apion* 1:14,26. Also see *You'loth* 46:11).
1:10 **driving us from the land.** Literally, "they will [make us] go up from the land" (*Sotah* 11a; Rashi; Saadia Gaon; Syriac). Or, "they will leave the land" (Rashi; Ibn Ezra).
1:11 **Pithom.** According to tradition, this is Tanis (*Targum Yonathan*). Tanis was an ancient Egyptian city on the north-east delta of the Nile. It was the chief commercial center of Egypt, and the capital of the Hyksos. It might have been razed when the Hyksos were expelled, and now it had to be rebuilt. Although the Hyksos had been driven to the north, supply depots would be necessary if a new campaign were required.
    It might be possible to identify Pithom with Patumus, which is mentioned in ancient histories as being to the north of the Suez Canal (Herodotus 2:158). It may also be the Per-atum (house of the god Atum), a city near Tjeku (Sukkoth?) mentioned in ancient sources (*Papyrus Anastasi* 4:4:56). This is identified with Tell el Maskhutah, on the eastern edge of Wadi Tumilat.

Pithom

    The name Pithom may come from the Egyptian *pi tem*, "the place of crying out."

1 Egyptians] oppressed them, the more [the Israelites] proliferated and spread. [The Egyptians] came to dread the Israelites.

¹³ The Egyptians started to make the Israelites do labor designated to break their bodies. ¹⁴ They made the lives of [the Israelites] miserable with harsh labor involving mortar and bricks, as well as all kinds of work in the field. All the work they made them do was intended to break them.

¹⁵ The king of Egypt spoke to the [chief*] Hebrew midwives, whose names were Shifra and Puah. ¹⁶ He said, "When you deliver Hebrew women, you must look carefully at the birthstool.* If [the infant] is a boy, kill it; but if it is a girl, let it live."

¹⁷ The midwives feared God, and did not do as the Egyptian king had ordered them. They allowed the infant boys to live. ¹⁸ The king of Egypt summoned the midwives and demanded, "Why did you do this? You let the infant boys live!"

¹⁹ "The Hebrew women are not like the Egyptians," replied the midwives to Pharaoh. "They know how to deliver. They can give birth before a midwife even gets to them."

²⁰ God was good to the midwives, and the people increased and became very numerous. ²¹ Because the midwives feared God, He gave them great families* [of their own].

²² Pharaoh then gave orders to *all* his people: "Every boy who is born must be cast into the Nile, but every girl shall be allowed to live."

[3. Moses]

2 ¹ A man of the house of Levi* went and married Levi's daughter.* ² The

---

— **Ra'amses.** See Genesis 47:11. There, however, the area was named Rameses, while here it is Ra'amses (cf. Ibn Ezra). It is identified as Pelusium commanding the entrance to Egypt (see note on Genesis 47:11) (Herodotus 2:141). Others identify it as Qantir.

Ra'amses

1:15 **chief** (Ibn Ezra; cf. Sforno). Some say that these midwives were Israelites (Rashbam), and Talmudic tradition associates them with Yokhebed and Miriam or Elisheva (*Sotah* 11b). Others say that the midwives were Egyptian (Malbim; Josephus, *Antiquities* 2:9:2) hence, the verse would be translated "the midwives in charge of the Hebrews." One source states that the midwives were proselytes (*Midrash Tadshe* 21; *Yalkut Shimoni, Yehoshua* 9).

1:16 **birthstool.** *Avnayim* in Hebrew, literally, "twin stones." In those days, women gave birth sitting up, so that when the baby was delivered between the "twin stones" of the birthstool, it would be held by the midwife. Others translate the verse "you must look between their rigid (stone-like) legs" (*Sotah* 11b; *Sh'moth Rabbah* 1:14, 18); or, "you will see them in heavy labor" (Hirsch).

1:21 **gave them great families** (*Targum Yonathan;* Rashi; Ibn Ezra). Literally, "He made them houses." According to others, "[Pharaoh] set up clinics for them" (so that the Hebrew women would not be able to deliver at home; *Lekach Tov;* Rashbam; Tur).

2:1 **man.** This was Amram, son of Kehoth, son of Levi (6:18; Numbers 3:18, 26:58, 1 Chronicles 5:29, 23:13). Amram was an important Israelite leader (*Sotah* 12a; Josephus 2:9:3). According to one ancient source, he had spent a number of years in the Holy Land (*Yov'loth* 46:10).

— **Levi's daughter.** Yokhebed (6:20; Numbers 26:59).

woman became pregnant and had a son.* She realized how extraordinary [the   2 child] was, and she kept him hidden for three months. ³ When she could no longer hide him, she took a papyrus* box, coating it with asphalt* and pitch, and she placed the child in it. She placed it in the rushes* near the bank of the Nile. ⁴ [The child's] sister* stood herself at a distance to see what would happen to him.

⁵ Pharaoh's daughter* went to bathe in the Nile, while her maids walked along the Nile's edge. She saw the box in the rushes, and sent her slave-girl* to fetch it. ⁶ Opening [the box] she saw the boy. The infant began to cry, and she had pity on it. "It is one of the Hebrew boys," she said.

⁷ [The infant's] sister said to Pharaoh's daughter, "Shall I go and call a Hebrew woman to nurse the child for you?"

⁸ "Go," replied Pharaoh's daughter. The young girl went and got the child's own mother.

⁹ "Take this child and nurse it," said Pharaoh's daughter to [the mother]. "I will pay you a fee." The woman took the child and nursed it.

¹⁰ When the child matured,* [his mother] brought him to Pharaoh's daughter. She adopted him as her own son, and named him Moses (*Moshe*).* "I bore (*mashe*)* him from the water," she said.

2:2   **son.** This was actually her third child, since Miriam was the eldest (2:4), and Aaron, his brother, was older than Moses by three years (7:7).

2:3   **papyrus** (Septuagint). *Cyperus papyrus. Gomeh* in Hebrew, from the ancient Egyptian word *gom.* (see Isaiah 18:2, Job 8:11, 35:7). It is known that the ancient Egyptians used to make boats of bundles of papyrus (cf. Ibn Janach; Radak, *Sherashim*). In the Talmud it is referred to as *gemi.* Rashi translates it as *jonc,* French for cane.

—   **asphalt** (Radak, *Sherashim;* Septuagint), *Chemar* in Hebrew; see Genesis 11:3, 14:10. Others write that it is a red clay (Ibn Ezra; ibn Janach; cf. Ralbag). (See Josephus, *Wars* 4:8:4)

Papyrus

—   **rushes.** *Sof* in Hebrew, from *thuf,* the ancient Egyptian word for uncut papyrus (cf. Radak, *Sherashim;* Ralbag). See Isaiah 19:6, Jonah 2:6. Others identify it with the bulrush or cat-tail, *Typha angustata.* Rashi translates it as *resel,* French for reeds. Significantly, in Ethiopian, *supho* denotes a red-topped kind of reed. This might explain the etymology of the Red Sea (see below, 10:19).

2:4   **sister.** Miriam (15:20; Numbers 26:59, 1 Chronicles 5:29).

2:5   **Pharaoh's daughter.** According to Talmudic tradition, she is the Bithiah mentioned in 1 Chronicles 4:18 (*Targum ad loc.; Sanhedrin* 19b; *Pirkey Rabbi Eliezer* 48). Other sources, however, appear to indicate that Bithiah was Solomon's wife (*BeMidbar Rabbah* 10:4). Today, this name is usually pronounced Bathyah. (Significantly, the name Bati is found in ancient Egyptian texts). Other ancient sources state that the name of Pharaoh's daughter was Tarmuth (*Yov'loth* 47:5) or Thermuthis (Josephus, *Antiquities* 2:9:5). This would be Ne-termut, in ancient Egyptian texts. Still earlier sources state that her name was Merris, (Meres in Egyptian) and that Moses' foster father was Khenefiris (Artapanus [2nd Century b.c.e.], quoted in Eusobius, *Preparation Evangelica* 9:27). Khenefiris or Kha-neph Ra (Sebek-hetep IV) was a king of the 13th Dynasty. Some say that she could not have children of her own (Philo, *De Vita Moses* 2:201; *Wisdom* 19:6).

—   **sent her slave-girl.** (Rashi; Ibn Ezra). Or, "stretched out her arm" (*Targum;* Rashi). Both opinions are cited in the Talmud (*Sotah* 12b).

2:10   **matured.** He was two years old (*Sh'moth Rabbah* 1:31).

—   **Moses.** In Egyptian, *Moshe* means a son. Thus, his naming is prefaced by a phrase that is literally translated, "he became to her as a son" (cf. Ibn Ezra; *Hadar Zekenim*). Significantly, the suffix *moshe* is found

2   ¹¹ When Moses was grown,* he began to go out to his own people, and he saw their hard labor. [One day] he saw an Egyptian kill* one of his fellow Hebrews.* ¹² [Moses] looked all around, and when he saw that no one was [watching], he killed the Egyptian and hid his body in the sand.

¹³ Moses went out the next day, and he saw two Hebrew men* fighting. "Why are you beating your brother?" he demanded of the one who was in the wrong.

¹⁴ "Who made you our prince and judge?" retorted [the other]. "Do you mean to kill me as you killed the Egyptian?"

Moses was frightened. "The incident is known," he said. ¹⁵ When Pharaoh heard about the affair, he took steps to have Moses put to death. Moses fled from Pharaoh, and ended up in the land of Midian.*

[Moses] was sitting near the well. ¹⁶ The sheik* of Midian had seven daughters, who came to draw water. As they were beginning to fill the troughs and water their father's sheep, ¹⁷ other shepherds came and tried to chase them away. Moses got up and came to their aid, and then watered their sheep.

¹⁸ When they came to their patriarch Reuel,* he asked them, "How did you get to come home so early today?"

(and exclusively so) in the names of many Pharaohs of the 18th Dynasty, such as Ka-moshe ("son of [Ra's] majesty"), Ach-moshe (Ahmose; "son of the moon," or "the moon is born") and Toth-moshe (Thutmose; "son of Toth"). The word *moshe* may indeed be of Semitic origin (see next note), introduced by the Semitic Hyksos.

    According to other ancient sources, the name Moses comes from the Egyptian *mo* (water) and *uses* (drawn from) (Josephus, *Antiquities* 2:9:6, *Contra Apion* 1:31; Philo *De Vita Moses* 2:17; Malbim).

    Some sources state that Moses' Egyptian name was Monius (Ibn Ezra; cf. Abarbanel; Josephus, *Contra Apion* 1:26, 28). Other ancient sources claim that Moses' name was preserved among the Gentiles as the legendary Musaeus, teacher of Orpheus, from whom the Muses obtained their name (Artapanus, in Eusebius, *Preparatio Evangelica* 9:27).

— **bore.** See 2 Samuel 22:17, Psalms 18:12; note on Genesis 47:11. In Egyptian, *mase* or *mashe* means to give birth. Others see the word as related to the Hebraic *mush,* and of Semitic origin (Rashi; Chizzkuni; Tur; see previous note).

2:11 **grown.** According to various opinions, he was 12 (*Sh'moth Rabbah* 5:1), 18 (*Sefer HaYashar*), 20 (*Sh'moth Rabbah* 1), 21 (*Yov'loth* 47:10), 29 (*Shalsheleth HaKabbalah*), 32 (*BeMidbar Rabbah* 14:40), 40 (*Sh'moth Rabbah* 1), 50 (Artapanus, *loc. cit.*), or 60 years old (Rabbi Moshe HaDarshan, *Bereshith Rabathai,* p. 13) at the time.

— **kill** (*Sh'moth Rabbah* 1:32). Or "beating."

— **fellow Hebrews.** According to tradition, the Hebrew was the husband of Shelomith, daughter of Dibri of Dan, mentioned in Leviticus 24:10,11 (*Sh'moth Rabbah* 1:32; *Tanchuma* 9). According to others, he was a fellow member of Moses' sub-tribe, Kehoth (*Pirkey Rabbi Eliezer* 48).

2:13 **two Hebrew men.** According to tradition, Dathan and Aviram, mentioned in Numbers 16:1, 26:9 (*Nedarim* 64b).

2:15 **Midian.** See Genesis 25:2. Ironically, the same Midianites who sold Joseph to Egypt (Genesis 37:28) now sheltered the one who would lead his people out of Egypt. Midian was north-east of the Gulf of Aqaba, and therefore Moses fled along the trade route that crossed the Sinai Peninsula, a distance of some 250 miles.

2:16 **sheik** (*Lekach Tov; Targum*). Or, "priest," the usual connotation of the word *cohen* used here. Both opinions are found in the *Mekhilta* (on 18:1).

2:18 **Reuel.** Some say that he was their grandfather (cf. Numbers 10:29; *Targum Yonathan;* Rashbam; Ibn Ezra; Radak, *Sherashim,* s.v. *Chathan*). Others identify Reuel with Jethro (see 3:1; *Mekhilta,* Rashi, on 18:1;

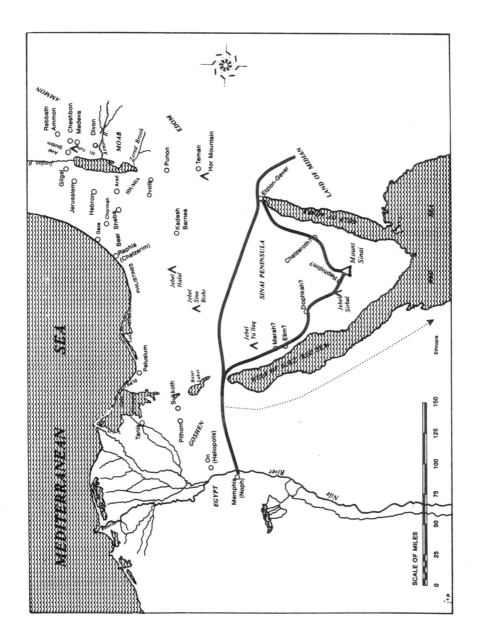

PLATE 12.　MOSES' JOURNEY

2   ¹⁹ "An Egyptian stranger rescued us from some shepherds," they replied.
"He also drew water for us and watered our sheep."

²⁰ "And where is he now?" he asked his daughters. "Why did you
abandon the stranger? Call him, and let him have something to eat."

²¹ Moses decided to live with the man. He gave Moses his daughter Tzipporah* as a wife. ²² When she gave birth to a son, [Moses] named him
Gershom.* "I have been a foreigner (*ger*) in a strange land," he said.

[4. New Oppression]

²³ A long time then passed, and the king of Egypt died.* The Israelites were
still groaning because of their subjugation. When they cried out because of
their slavery, their pleas went up before God. ²⁴ God heard their cries, and He
remembered His covenant with Abraham, Isaac and Jacob.* ²⁵ God saw the
Israelites, and He was about to show concern.*

[5. The Burning Bush]

3   ¹ Moses tended the sheep of his father-in-law Jethro,* sheik of Midian. He
led the flock to the edge of the desert, and he came to God's Mountain, in the
Horeb area.*

Josephus 2:12:1; see *Sifri* on Numbers 10:29). The name Reuel is also found in Genesis 36:4.
2:21   **Tzipporah.** Literally, "Lady-bird."
2:22   **Gershom.** *Ger Sham,* "a foreigner there."
2:23   **king of Egypt died.** According to the usual chronology, this refers to the death of Ay in 2444 (1317
       b.c.e.), when Horemheb (1317–1290 b.c.e.) came into power (see *The Torah Anthology* 4:240). The Pharaoh
       of the Exodus would then have been Horemheb, and the cataclysm of the Exodus would have brought
       about the end of the 18th Dynasty.
            If we accept the 163 year discrepancy, then this would indicate the death of Thutmose II in 1490
       b.c.e. (2434), and the powerful Thutmose III (1490–1436 b.c.e.) would have been the Pharaoh of the
       Exodus. The Exodus and ensuing events may then have given rise to the apparent monotheism of
       Ikhnaton, a century later.
            Incidentally, the 163 discrepancy is evident from the fact that Pharaoh Necho who, in usual
       chronologies reigned from 609 to 495 b.c.e., defeated King Josiah in 3316 or 443 b.c.e. (2 Kings 23:29;
       Seder HaDoroth).
2:24   **with Abraham, Isaac and Jacob.** With Abraham (Genesis 15:14), Isaac (Genesis 17:21, 26:3), and Jacob
       (Genesis 46:4). See Genesis 50:24.
2:25   **about to show concern** (cf. *Targum;* Rashi).
3:1   **Jethro.** Yithro in Hebrew. See 18:1; note on 2:18.
—   **Horeb area.** (Ramban on Deuteronomy 1:6). This was the area around Sinai (17:6, Deuteronomy 1:6,
       4:10; cf. Ben Sirah 48:7). Sinai is thus sometimes referred to as "the mountain of Horeb (33:6). Others,
       however, say that Horeb was the lower of the two peaks of Sinai (cf. Ibn Ezra on Deuteronomy 1:6).
       Most early sources identify Mount Sinai with Jebel Musa or Mount Catherine on the southern Sinai
       peninsula, a five day journey (200 miles) from Egypt, and some 40 miles from the Red Sea (*Ma'asoth Bin-
       yamin* 24; *Masa Rabbi Obadiah Bertenoro* 3). According to this, Moses had traveled approximately 100
       miles along the west coast of the Gulf of Aqaba.
            There are some difficulties, with this, however, since this "Mountain of God" seems to have been on
       a direct route between Midian and Egypt (4:27), and not more than a three day journey (some 120 miles)
       from where the Israelites lived (3:18). On the basis of this, it may be conjectured that Mount Sinai was
       Jebel Ya'llaq (some 32 miles from the northern end of the Gulf of Suez) or Jebel Sinn Bishr (60 miles due

² God's angel appeared to [Moses] in the heart* of a fire, in the middle of a   3
thorn-bush.* As he looked, [Moses] realized that the bush was on fire, but was
not being consumed. ³ Moses said [to himself], "I must go over there and
investigate this wonderful phenomenon. Why doesn't the bush burn?"

⁴ When God saw that [Moses] was going to investigate, He called to him
from the middle of the bush.

"Moses, Moses!" He said.

"Yes," replied [Moses].

⁵ "Do not come any closer," said [God]. "Take your shoes off your feet.
The place upon which you are standing is holy ground."

⁶ [God then] said, "I am the God of your father, the God of Abraham,
God of Isaac, and God of Jacob."

Moses hid his face, since he was afraid to look* at the Divine.

⁷ God said, "I have indeed seen the suffering of My people in Egypt. I have
heard how they cry out because of what their slave-drivers [do], and I am
aware of their pain. ⁸ I have come down* to rescue them from Egypt's power.
I will bring them out of that land, to a good, spacious land, to a land flowing
with milk and honey, the territory of the Canaanites, Hittites, Amorites, Perizzites, Hivites and Yebusites.*

⁹ "Right now the cry of the Israelites is coming to Me. I also see the pressure to which Egypt is subjecting them. ¹⁰ Now go. I am sending you to
Pharaoh. Bring My people, the Israelites, out of Egypt."

¹¹ "Who am I that I should go to Pharaoh?" said Moses to God. "And
how can I possibly get the Israelites out of Egypt?"

¹² "Because I will be with you," replied [God]. "Proof that I have sent you
will come when you get the people out of Egypt. All of you will then become
God's servants* on this mountain."

---

east of Bitter Lakes). Obviously, this question is very important in determining the route of the Exodus.
The area was called Horeb (*Chorebh*) because of its dryness (Ibn Ezra). See note on 3:2.

3:2   heart. (*Tanchuma* 14: Ibn Ezra; *Moreh Nevukhim* 1:39; Radak, *Sherashim*, s.v. Lavav). Or "flame" (*Targum*;
Rashi; *Sekhel Tov*), or "essence" (Ibn Janach).

—   thorn-bush. *S'neh* in Hebrew. This is most probably the black raspberry (*rubus sanctus*), which has berries
that turn red and then black (*Yerushalmi, Ma'asroth* 1:2, 3a; cf. Septuagint; Vulgate). The Midrash also
identifies it as a species of thorn-bush (*Sh'moth Rabbah* 1:9, 2:9). Others identify it as the sana plant (*Casia
obovata*), the shurbu (*Colutea istria*) of the wild juju (*Zizyphus spina*).
    It is most probable that the name Sinai is derived from this word *S'neh* (Ramban on Deuteronomy
6:1; Radak, *Sherashim*, s.v. *S'neh*). Some note that the rocks of Sinai have crystalline markings looking
like a s'neh-bush (Rabbi Moshe of Narbonne on *Moreh Nevukhim* 1:66). Cf. 1 Samuel 14:4.

3:6   afraid to look. See note on Genesis 32:31.

3:8   come down. See note on Genesis 11:7.

—   Canaanites . . . See Genesis 15:19–21. The Kenite, Kenizite, Kadmonite, Rephaim and Girgashite mentioned there are not here, and the Hivite here is not mentioned there (see *Lekach Tov*). See 13:5, Genesis
10:15–18.

3:12   become God's servants (Hirsch). Or "serve God," or "worship God" (cf. Ramban).

3   13 Moses said to God, "So I will go to the Israelites and say, 'Your fathers'
God sent me to you.' They will immediately ask me what His name is. What
shall I say to them?"

   14 "I Will Be Who I Will Be,*" replied God to Moses.

[God then] explained, "This is what you must say to the Israelites: '*I Will
Be* sent me to you.'"

   15 God then said to Moses, "You must [then] say to the Israelites, 'YHVH,*
the God of your fathers, the God of Abraham, Isaac and Jacob, sent me to
you.' This is My eternal name,* and this is how I am to be recalled for all
generations.

   16 "Go, gather the elders of Israel,* and say to them, 'YHVH, the God of
your fathers, appeared to me—the God of Abraham, Isaac and Jacob. He
said, "I have granted you special providence* regarding what is happening to
you in Egypt. 17 I declare that I will bring you out of the wretchedness of
Egypt, to the land of the Canaanites, Hittites, Amorites, Perizzites, Hivites and
Yebusites—to a land flowing with milk and honey."'

   18 "They will take what you say seriously. You and the elders of Israel will
then go to the king of Egypt. You must tell him, 'YHVH, God of the Hebrews,
revealed Himself to us. Now we request that you allow us to take a three day
journey* into the desert, to sacrifice to YHVH our God.'

   19 "I know in advance that the Egyptian king will not allow you to leave
unless he is forced to do so.* 20 I will then display My power* and demolish

---

3:14   I Will Be . . . *Ehyeh Asher Ehyeh* in Hebrew. This is a Divine Name (*Shevuoth* 35a), and it is therefore not
       translated by the *Targum.* It denotes that God has absolute existence (*Moreh Nevukhim* 1:63; cf. Septu-
       agint), and that He is outside the realm of time (Sforno). According to the Kabbalists, this Name denotes
       the Crown (*Kether*) of creation, that is, the very first thought and impulse of Will that initiated the creative
       process. Hence it is "I will be," since at the time of that impulse, everything was in the future. This first
       thought is identified with the idea of Israel (*Bereshith Rabbah* 1:5; *Berakhoth* 6a; *Tikkuney Zohar* 17a; see *God
       Man and Tefillin,* p. 35 ff.). This name was revealed now that God was about to create the nation Israel.
3:15   YHVH. This is the Tetragrammaton which may not be pronounced under any circumstances (cf. *San-
       hedrin* 90a; Philo, *De Vida Moses* 3:519, 529). If this section is read out loud, this name should be read as
       "Lord" (cf. Septuagint). This name denotes God's utter transcendence (*Kuzari* 2:2; *Moreh Nevukhim*
       1:61). This name also denotes the creative power that constantly sustains the universe. God is telling
       Moses that not only is the initial purpose of creation now being fulfilled, but also the process that will
       insure its continual existence.
—   eternal name. The Tetragrammaton denotes the level where past, present and future are the same (*Tur,
       Orach Chaim* 5; Rabbi Eliezer of Garmiza on *Sefer Yetzirah* 1:1).
3:16   elders of Israel. The 70 elders (24:1,9; Numbers 11:16,24) which would later constitute the Great San-
       hedrin. Like any other prophet, Moses would first have to establish his credentials with the Sanhedrin
       (Hai Gaon, in *Teshuvoth HaGeonim, Shaarey Teshuvah* 14).
—   special providence. The same words used by Joseph (Genesis 50:24,25).
3:18   three day journey. Around 120 miles. See note on 3:1.
3:19   unless he is forced . . . (Ralbag; Septuagint). Literally, "and not with a strong hand." Alternatively,
       "and not even by threat of force" (Ramban; Hirsch); "even after a show of force" (Chizzkuni; Sforno);
       "but not because of his strength" (Rashi; Rashbam); "even after My miracles" (Abarbanel); or "and
       most emphatically so."
3:20   display My power. Literally, "I will send forth My Hand."

Egypt through all the miraculous deeds that I will perform in their land. Then 3 [Pharaoh] will let you leave.

²¹ "I will give the people status among the Egyptians, and when you all finally leave, you will not go empty-handed.* ²² Every woman shall borrow articles of silver and gold, as well as clothing, from her neighbor or from the woman living with her. You shall load this on your sons and daughters, and you will thus drain Egypt [of its wealth]."

¹ When Moses [was able to] reply, he said, "But they will not believe me. 4 They will not listen to me. They will say, 'God did not appear to you.'"

² "What is that in your hand?" asked God.

"A staff."

³ "Throw it on the ground."

When [Moses] threw it on the ground, it turned into a snake, and Moses ran away from it.

⁴ God said to Moses, "Reach out and grasp its tail." When [Moses] reached out and grasped [the snake], it turned back into a staff in his hand.

⁵ "This is so that they will believe that God appeared to you," [He said]. "The God of their fathers, the God of Abraham, Isaac and Jacob."

⁶ God then said to Moses, "Place your hand [on your chest] inside your robe."

When [Moses] placed his hand in his robe and removed it from his chest, it was leprous, [as white] as snow.

⁷ "Place your hand in your robe again," said [God].

[Moses] placed his hand [back] into his robe, and when he removed it from his chest, his skin had returned to normal.

⁸ "If they do not believe you," [said God], "and they do not pay attention to the first miraculous sign, then they will believe the evidence of the second sign.

⁹ "And if they also do not believe these two signs, and still do not take you seriously, then you shall take some water from the Nile and spill it on the ground. The water that you will take from the Nile will turn into blood on the ground."

¹⁰ Moses pleaded with God. "I beg you, O God, I am not a man of words—not yesterday, not the day before—not from the very first time You spoke to me.* I find it difficult to speak and find the right language.*"

3:21 **not go empty-handed.** See Genesis 15:14.

3:22 **load.** Or, "dress your children with them" (*Targum Yonathan*).

4:10 **first time You spoke to me.** This indicates either that Moses had heard God's voice before, or that he had spent quite a while near the Burning Bush (Rashi; *Seder Olam Rabbah* 5). Or, "even after You spoke to me" (Ramban; *Lekach Tov*), or, "because You have spoken to me" and I am so immersed in prophecy (Ralbag).

4   "Who gave man a mouth?" replied God. "Who makes a person dumb
or deaf? Who gives a person sight or makes him blind? Is it not I—God?
¹² Now go! I will be with your mouth and teach you what to say."

¹³ "I beg you O Lord!" exclaimed [Moses]. "Please! Send someone more
appropriate*!"

¹⁴ God displayed anger toward Moses. "Is not Aaron the Levite your
brother?" He said. "I know that *he* knows how to speak! He is setting out to
meet you, and when he sees you, his heart will be glad. ¹⁵ You will be able to
speak to him, and place the words in his mouth. I will then be with your
mouth and his mouth, and I will teach you what to do. ¹⁶ He will speak to the
people for you. He will be your spokesman,* and you will be his guide.*
¹⁷ Take this staff in your hand. With it, you will perform the miracles."

[6. Moses Leaves Midian]

¹⁸ Moses left and returned to his father-in-law Jether.* He said, "I would
like to leave and return to my people in Egypt, to see if they are still alive."

"Go in peace," said Jethro to Moses.

¹⁹ While Moses was still in Midian, God said to him, "Go return to Egypt.
All the men who seek your life have died."

²⁰ Moses took his wife and sons* and, putting them on a donkey, set out to
return to Egypt. He also took the divine staff in his hand.

²¹ God said to Moses, "On your way back to Egypt, keep in mind all the
wondrous powers that I have placed in your hand. You will use them before
Pharaoh. But I will make him obstinate,* and he will not allow the people to
leave. ²² You must say to Pharaoh, 'This is what God says: Israel is My son, My
firstborn. ²³ I have told you to let My son go and serve Me. If you refuse to let
him leave, I will [ultimately] kill your own first-born son.'"

²⁴ When they were in the place where they spent the night along the way,

—   I find it difficult to speak . . . (Rashbam; *Lekach Tov;* Chizzkuni;Ralbag). Literally, "I am heavy of mouth
and heavy of tongue." Others write that it denotes a speech defect (Rashi; Ibn Ezra; Ralbag; Bachya,
quoting Rabbenu Chananel).
4:13 Send someone more appropriate. (*Targum;* Sforno). Literally, "send by the one You will send." Or,
"Send whomever else You wish" (Rashi; Rashbam); or, "Send [Aaron], the one You usually send"
(Rashi).
4:16 spokesman. Literally, "mouth."
—   guide (Ralbag). Literally, "God" or "judge." Or, "master" (*Targum;* Rashi; Rashbam).
4:18 Jether. *Yether* in Hebrew, another form of Jethro (3:1). Some say that the name was changed to Jethro
when he became a believer (Rashi on 18:1). Here, we see that it was at this point, when he spoke to
Moses, who had just returned from Sinai.
4:20 sons. This indicates that Moses' second son, Eliezer (18:4) had already been born. He might have just
been born, and since it was before his circumcision, not yet named. See 4:24.
4:21 make him obstinate. Literally, "harden his heart."

God confronted Moses and wanted to kill him.* ²⁵ Tzipporah took a stone　4
knife and cut off her son's* foreskin, throwing it down* at [Moses'] feet.* "As
far as I am concerned, you're married* to blood,*" she said [to the child].*

²⁶ [God] then spared [Moses]. "[You were] married to blood because of
circumcision," she said.

[7. First Confrontations]

²⁷ God said to Aaron,* "Go meet Moses in the desert."

[Aaron] went, and when he met [Moses] near God's Mountain,* he kissed
him. ²⁸ Moses described to Aaron everything that God had told him about his
mission, as well as the miraculous proofs that He had instructed him to
display.

²⁹ Moses and Aaron went [to Egypt], and they gathered all the elders of
Israel. ³⁰ Aaron related all the words that God had told Moses, and he
demonstrated the miraculous proofs before the people.

³¹ The people believed. They accepted the message that God had granted
special providence to the Israelites, and that He had seen their misery. They
bowed their heads and prostrated themselves.

¹ Moses and Aaron then went to Pharaoh and said, "This is what YHVH,　5
God of the Hebrews, declares: 'Let My people leave, so they can sacrifice* to
Me in the desert.'"

4:24　**wanted to kill him.** Moses, for not circumcising his son. According to others, it was for delaying (see
　　　4:27; Rashbam cf. *Nedarim* 34a). Some say that God wanted to kill the uncircumcised infant (*Nedarim*
　　　32a).
4:25　**her son's is.** Some say that it was her newborn son Eliezer (*Sh'moth Rabbah;* Rashi; Ibn Ezra). According to
　　　others, it was the older son, Gershom, who was not yet circumcised (*Targum Yonathan; Sefer HaYashar*).
—　　**throwing it down** (Rashi). Literally, "touching;" see next note.
—　　**Moses' feet** (Rashi; Rashbam; Ibn Ezra). In the Talmud, one opinion is that it was at Moses' feet, another
　　　that it was at the child's feet, and a third, that it was at the feet of the angel who wanted to kill him (*Yeru-
　　　shalmi, Nedarim* 3:9). Others have, "the blood ran down [the child's] feet" (Ralbag); or, "She peeled back
　　　[the foreskin] toward his legs" (Malbim).
—　　**married.** Literally, "a bridegroom of blood." Some interpret the Hebrew word *chathan* here to denote a
　　　newly circumcised child (Ibn Ezra), because the child is being initiated into new joy (Radak, *Sherashim*).
—　　**married to blood.** Or, "you are like a murderer to me" (Ibn Ezra; Radak, *Sherashim; Tur*); "you are the
　　　murderer of my husband" (Rashi); or "You are bleeding so much" (Ralbag). According to the opinion
　　　that she was addressing Moses (see next note), she said, "Through this bloody child you will remain
　　　mine [and live]" (Rashbam; *Targum Yonathan*); or, "Your marriage to me requires this blood" (Sforno;
　　　Chizzkuni; Tur; cf. *Targum*). Or, "the circumcision blood of [my son] is staunched" (Septuagint).
—　　**to the child.** In the Talmud there is a debate as to whether she was addressing Moses or the child (*Yeru-
　　　shalmi, Nedarim* 3:9).
4:27　**to Aaron.** Who was then in Egypt.
—　　**God's mountain.** See note on 3:1, that this appears to indicate that Sinai was on a direct route between
　　　Egypt and Midian. However, God may have been angry with Moses for taking this indirect route
　　　through the southern Sinai (see note on 4:24).
5:1　　**sacrifice** (Ibn Ezra; Radak, *Sherashim;* Ralbag). Or, "celebrate a festival to Me" (*Targum Yonathan*). In the
　　　Talmud both opinions are cited (*Chagigah* 10b).

5   ² Pharaoh replied, "Who is YHVH that I should obey Him and let Israel
go? I do not recognize YHVH. Nor will I let Israel leave."

³ "The God of the Hebrews has revealed Himself to us," said [Moses and
Aaron]. "Please, allow us to take a three day journey into the desert, and let us
sacrifice to YHVH our God. Otherwise, He may strike us down with the
plague or the sword."

⁴ The Egyptian king said to them, "Moses and Aaron, why are you dis-
tracting the people from their work? Get back to your own business!"

⁵ "The peasants are becoming more numerous," said Pharaoh, "and you
want them to take a vacation from their work!"

⁶ That day, Pharaoh gave new orders to the people's administrators and
foremen. He said, ⁷ "Do not give the people straw for bricks* as before. Let
them go and gather their own straw. ⁸ Meanwhile, you must require them to
make the same quota of bricks as before. Do not reduce it. They are lazy, and
are protesting that they want to go sacrifice to their God. ⁹ Make the work
heavier for the men, and make sure they do it. Then they will stop paying
attention to false ideas."

¹⁰ The administrators and foremen went out and told the people,
"Pharaoh has said that he will no longer give you straw. ¹¹ You must go and
get your own straw wherever you can find it. Meanwhile, you may not reduce
the amount of work you must complete."

¹² The people spread out all over Egypt to gather grain stalks for straw.
¹³ The administrators pressured them and said, "You must complete your
daily work quota, just as before when there was straw." ¹⁴ The Israelite foremen, whom Pharaoh's administrators had appointed, were flogged. They
were told, "Yesterday and today you did not complete your quotas. Why
didn't you make as many bricks as before?"

¹⁵ The Israelite foremen came and protested to Pharaoh. "Why are you
doing this to us?" they said. ¹⁶ "We are no longer given straw, but we are told
to make bricks. We are the ones being flogged, but it is your people's fault.*"

¹⁷ "You are lazy!" retorted Pharaoh. "Lazy! That's why you are saying that
you want to sacrifice to God. ¹⁸ Now go! Get to work! You will not be given
any straw, but you must deliver your quota of bricks."

¹⁹ The Israelite foremen realized that they were in serious trouble. They
had been clearly told that they could not reduce their daily brick quota.

²⁰ When they were leaving Pharaoh, [the foremen] encountered Moses and
Aaron waiting to meet them. ²¹ "Let God look at you and be your Judge,"

5:7   **straw for bricks.** Unbaked mud bricks were used, and these had to be held together with straw. Such
         bricks can still be found.
5:16   **but it is your people's fault.** Or, "and it is a sin for your people" (*Targum Yonathan*; Rashi; Rashbam).

they said. "You have destroyed our reputation* with Pharaoh and his   5
advisors. You have placed a sword to kill us in their hands."

²² Moses returned to God and said, "O Lord, why do You mistreat Your
people? Why did You send me? ²³ As soon as I came to Pharaoh to speak in
Your name, he made things worse for these people. You have done nothing to
help Your people."

¹ God said to Moses, "Now you will begin to see what I will do to   **6**
Pharaoh. He will be forced* to let them go. [Not only that, but] he will be
forced to drive them out of his land."

VaEra   וָאֵרָא

[8. Reassurance]

² God spoke to Moses and said to him, "I am YHVH.* ³ I revealed Myself
to Abraham, Isaac and Jacob as God Almighty (*El Shaddai*),* and did not allow
them to know Me by My name YHVH.* ⁴ I also made My covenant with them,
[promising] to give them the land of Canaan, the land of their pilgrimage,
where they lived as foreigners. ⁵ I have also heard the groaning of the Israelites, whom the Egyptians are holding as slaves, and I have remembered My
covenant.

⁶ "Therefore say to the Israelites [in My name], 'I am God. I will take you
away from your forced labor in Egypt and free you from their slavery. I will
liberate you with a demonstration of My power,* and with great acts of judgment. ⁷ I will take you to Myself as a nation, and I will be to you as a God. You
will know that I am God your Lord, the One who is bringing you out from
under the Egyptian subjugation. ⁸ I will bring you to the land regarding which
I raised My hand,* [swearing] that I would give it to Abraham, Isaac and

---

5:21   **destroyed our reputation.** Literally, "making our aroma stink in the eyes of Pharaoh." See Genesis
       34:30.
6:1   **he will be forced.** Literally, "with a strong hand." See 3:19.
6:2   **I am YHVH.** To be pronounced "Lord" or "God." See note on 3:15.
6:3   **God Almighty.** See Genesis 17:1, 35:11, 48:3, 28:7.
—   **did not allow them** . . . Actually, God did use the Tetragrammaton (YHVH) in speaking to Abraham
       (Genesis 15:7) and Jacob (Genesis 28:13). The name was also used by angels (Genesis 16:11, 19:13,14,
       18:14), by the Patriarchs themselves (Genesis 14:22, 15:2, 15:8, 16:2, 16:5, 22:14, 24:27, 24:31, 24:40,
       24:44, 24:48, 26:22, 27:7, 27:27, 28:31, 29:32, 33:35, 30:24, 30:30, 32:10, 49:18), and even by gentiles
       (Genesis 24:3, 24:31, 26:28,29, 30:27, 31:49). It is true, however, that the Tetragrammaton was never
       used in speech before the time of the Patriarchs. Among the Patriarchs, the Tetragrammaton was known,
       but not its inner significance (Ramban; Ibn Ezar). This was because the Patriarchs received their proph-
       ecy from the level associated with the name *El Shaddai*, while only Moses received it from the level asso-
       ciated with the Tetragrammaton (*Moreh Nevukhim* 2:35; Ralbag; *Milchamoth HaShem* 6). Knowing God's
       name in the true sense is something great, as we see in Isaiah 52:6, Jeremiah 31:33, Psalms 83:19.
6:6   **demonstration of My power.** Literally, "outstretched arm."
6:8   **raised My hand.** An idiom for an oath; see Genesis 14:22.

6 Jacob. I will give it to you as an inheritance. I am God.'"

⁹ Moses related this to the Israelites, but because of their disappointment*
and hard work, they would no longer listen to him.

[9. Moses Demures]

¹⁰ God spoke to Moses, saying,* ¹¹ "Go,* speak to Pharaoh, king of Egypt,
and he will let the Israelites leave his land."

¹² Moses spoke, interrupting the revelation.* "Even the Israelites will not
listen to me," he said. "How can I expect Pharaoh to listen to me? I have no
self-confidence when I speak.*"

[10. Aaron is Included]

¹³ God [then] spoke to [both] Moses and Aaron. He gave them instructions
regarding the Israelites and Pharaoh, king of Egypt, so they would be able to
get the Israelites out of Egypt.

[11. Genealogy]

¹⁴ These are the heads of their extended families*:

The sons of Israel's first-born, Reuben: Enoch (*Chanokh*), Pallu, Chetzron
and Carmi. These are the families of Reuben.*

¹⁵ The sons of Simeon*: Yemuel, Yamin, Ohad, Yakhin and Tzochar, as
well as Saul, son of the Canaanite woman. These are the families of Simeon.

¹⁶ According to their family records,* these are the names of Levi's sons*:
Gershon, Kehoth and Merari. Levi lived to be 137 years old.

¹⁷ The families descending from Gershon*: Livni* and Shimi.*

6:9   **disappointment.** Literally "short spirit." Alternatively, "impatience," or "broken spirit." See Numbers
       21:4, Micah 2:7, Proverbs 14:29.
6:10   **God spoke . . .** This is the first time that this expression is used. It is the expression used to introduce
       most of the commandments.
6:11   **Go.** Literally, "come." Since God is omnipresent, He does not tell Moses to "go." Alternatively, this
       may be an idiomatic use of the word come.
6:12   **interrupting the revelation.** Literally, "Moses spoke before God."
—   **I have no self-confidence . . .** (Cf. Rashi; Ralbag) . . . Literally, "I have uncircumcised lips." The expres-
       sion may also be interpreted, "I can hardly speak," or "I have a speech defect." See 4:10.
6:14   **extended families.** Or, "clans," or "paternal clanheads." Literally, "heads of the house of their fathers."
       See below, 12:3.
—   **sons of . . . Reuben.** See Genesis 46:9.
6:15   **sons of Simeon.** Genesis 46:10.
6:16   **family records.** (cf. *Targum Yonathan*).
—   **Levi's sons.** Genesis 46:11, 1 Chronicles 5:27.
6:17   **from Gershon.** See Numbers 3:18, 1 Chronicles 6:2.
—   **Livni.** Numbers 26:58, 1 Chronicles 6:5, 6:14.
—   **Shimi.** Not mentioned in Numbers 26. It appears that there was also a Shimi who was a great-grandson
       of Levi (1 Chronicles 6:27, see Malbim ibid. 6:5). Also see Zechariah 12:13, 1 Chronicles 23:9, 25:17.

¹⁸ The sons of Kehoth*: Amram,* Yitzhar,* Hebron (*Chevron*),* and Uzziel.* **6**
Kehoth lived to be 133 years old.
¹⁹ The sons of Merari*: Machli* and Mushi.*
According to their family records, the above are the families of Levi.
²⁰ Amram married his aunt* Yokhebed,* and she bore him Aaron and
Moses. Amram lived to be 137 years old.
²¹ The sons of Yitzhar*: Korach,* Nefeg and Zikhri.
²² The sons of Uzziel*: Mishael,* Eltzafan* and Sithri.
²³ Aaron married Nachshon's* sister, Elisheva* daughter of Aminadav.*
She bore him* Nadav, Avihu,* Eleazar* and Ithamar.*
²⁴ The sons of Korach*: Assir,* Elkana* and Aviasaf.* These are the
families of the Korachites.

6:18   **sons of Kehoth.** See Numbers 3:19, 1 Chronicles 5:28, 6:3, 23:12.
—   **Amram.** Moses' father; see below 6:20, Numbers 26:59. See Numbers 3:27, 1 Chronicles 26:23.
—   **Yitzhar.** See below, 6:21, 1 Chronicles 6:23. In 1 Chronicles 6:7, he is referred to as Aminadav (cf. Radak, Ralbag *ad loc.*).
—   **Hebron.** Numbers 3:27, 26:58, 1 Chronicles 15:9, 23:19, 26:23,30,31. The name is the same as that of the city.
—   **Uzziel.** See below 6:22.
6:19   **Sons of Merari.** Numbers 3:20, 3:33, 1 Chronicles 6:4, 6:14, 23:21, 24:26.
—   **Machli.** Cf. Numbers 3:33, 26:58, Ezra 8:18. Also see 1 Chronicles 6:32, 23:21. There was also a Machli who was the son of Mushi; 1 Chronicles 6:32, 23:23, 24:30.
—   **Mushi.** Numbers 3:33, 26:58, 1 Chronicles 6:32, 23:23, 24:30.
6:20   **his aunt.** See above, 2:1. After the Torah was given, it was forbidden for a man to marry his aunt; Leviticus 18:12, 20:19 (see *Yerushalmi, Yevamoth* 11:2; Chizzkuni). Some ancient sources indicate that Yokhebed was not Amram's aunt, but his cousin (*Septuagint; Syriac*). According to this she would be a granddaughter rather than a daughter of Levi.
—   **Yokhebed.** See Numbers 26:59. Josephus (2:9:4), gives her name as Yokhabel.
6:21   **sons of Yitzhar.** See 1 Chronicles 6:23; 23:18.
—   **Korach.** Below, 6:24. He was the one who was to lead the rebellion against Moses, Numbers 16:1. See 1 Chronicles 6:22,23.
6:22   **sons of Uzziel.** Leviticus 10:4.
—   **Mishael.** Leviticus 10:4.
—   **Eltzafan.** Leviticus 10:4, Numbers 3:30.
6:23   **Nachshon.** He was a prince of the tribe of Judah (Numbers 1:7, 2:3), and an ancestor of King David (Ruth 4:20, 1 Chronicles 2:10).
—   **Elisheva.** In the *Septuagint*, her name is given as Elizabeth.
—   **Aminadav.** A great-grandson of Judah's son Peretz (Genesis 38:29): Peretz, Chetzron (Genesis 46:12), Ram, Aminadav (Ruth 4:18-20, 1 Chronicles 2:9,10).
—   **she bore him.** See Numbers 3:2, 26:60, 1 Chronicles 5:29, 24:1.
—   **Nadav, Avihu.** They had been chosen as the next generation of leaders (24:1, 24:9, 28:1), but they died because of improper sacrifice (Leviticus 10:1, Numbers 3:4, 26:61, 1 Chronicles 24:2).
—   **Eleazar.** El'azar in Hebrew. See below 6:25. Eleazar was groomed for the High Priesthood before Aaron's death (Numbers 3:32, 4:16, 17:2, 19:3). He then held this position (Numbers 20:26, 26:1, Deuteronomy 10:2). He led the Israelites along with Joshua (Numbers 32:28, 34:17, Joshua 14:1), and he outlived Joshua by several years (Joshua 24:33).
—   **Ithamar.** He was later to keep the accounts of the Tabernacle (Exodus 38:21), and was in charge of transporting it (Numbers 4:28,33, 7:8). Cf. Ezra 8:2, 1 Chronicles 24:3-6.
6:24   **sons of Korach.** See 6:21. His sons did not die when he rebelled (Numbers 26:11). They are credited with writing Psalms 42, 44-48, 84, 87.
—   **Assir.** See 1 Chronicles 6:7. There was also an Assir who was a son of Aviasaf; 1 Chronicles 6:22.

6   25 Aaron's son, Eleazar, married one of the daughters of Putiel,* and she
bore him Pinchas.*

The above are the heads of the Levite clans according to their families.

26 This then [is the lineage] of Moses and Aaron, to whom God said,
"Bring the Israelites out of Egypt *en masse.*"* 27 They are the ones who spoke to
Pharaoh, king of Egypt, in order to get the Israelites out of Egypt. It [involved
both] Moses and Aaron. 28 Still, on that day in Egypt, God spoke [only*] to
Moses.

[12. Second Demurral]

29 God spoke to Moses* and said, "I am God. Relate to Pharaoh, king of
Egypt, all that I am saying to you."

30 Interrupting the revelation,* Moses said, "I do not have the self-confidence* to speak. How will Pharaoh ever pay attention to me?"

[13. Moses Told What to Expect]

7   1 God said to Moses, "Observe! I will be making you like a god* to
Pharaoh, and your brother Aaron will be your prophet.* 2 You must
announce* all that I order you to, and your brother Aaron will relate it to
Pharaoh. He will then let the Israelites leave his land.

3 "I will make Pharaoh obstinate,* and will thus have the opportunity to

---

—   **Elkana.** 1 Chronicles 6:8, 6:10.
—   **Aviasaf.** 1 Chronicles 6:8, 6:22, 9:19.
6:25   **Putiel.** Talmudic tradition identifies him with Jethro (*Bava Bathra* 109b; *Sotah* 43a; *Mekhilta,* Rashi, on
        18:1). Possibly from the Egyptian *Poti,* "the one belonging to" (see notes on Genesis 37:36, 41:45), and
        the Hebrew *El,* "God" hence, "One devoted to God." Indeed, there are traditions that Jethro was an
        advisor to Pharaoh for a while. Some say that Putiel was an Israelite (Ibn Ezra).
—   **Pinchas.** Or Phinehas. The name Pinchas may be from the Egyptian *Pi-neches,* meaning "the dark one,"
        "the one who aroused himself," "the incantator," or "the covered one." (Others derive it from a semitic
        root; cf. *Sekhel Tov).* See Ezra 7:5, 8:2, 1 Chronicles 5:30, 6:35. Pinchas stood up to stop assimilation in
        Moab (Numbers 25:7), and was given eternal priesthood (Numbers 25:11). He was the priest of war
        (Numbers 31:6, Joshua 22:13), and later an important leader (Joshua 22:30–32, Judges 20:28,
        1 Chronicles 9:20).
6:26   **en masse.** Literally, "by their armies." Or, "in organized groups."
6:28   **only.** (Ramban; Cf. *Sifra* on Leviticus 1:1). Or, "Still, by day . . . God spoke [only] to Moses" (cf. Num-
        bers 12:6; *VaYikra Rabbah* 1:13; *K'li Yekar).* Others connect it to the next verse, "On that day in Egypt,
        when God spoke to Moses, 29 God spoke to Moses saying . . ." (Rashi; Ibn Ezra).
6:29   **God spoke to Moses.** A second time (Bachya; *HeKethav VeHaKabbalah).* According to some, this is a
        repetition of 6:10–12; (Rashi, Rashbam).
6:30   **Interrupting the revelation.** See 6:12.
—   **I do not have the self-confidence.** See 6:12.
7:1   **like a god.** (*Targum Yonathan;* Baaley Tosafoth). Or, "a judge" (Rashi); "a master" (Onkelos); "like an
        angel" (Ibn Ezra). The word *Elohim* used here has all these connotations. See 4:16.
—   **prophet.** Or "spokesman" (*Targum).* See 4:16.
7:2   **announce** (Rashi). Or, "tell [Aaron]" (*Targum Yonathan;* Ibn Ezra).
7:3   **make . . . obstinate.** Literally, "harden Pharaoh's heart" (above 4:21).

display many miraculous signs and wonders in Egypt. ⁴ This is why Pharaoh   7
will not pay attention to you. But then I will display My power* against Egypt,
and with great acts of judgment, I will bring forth from Egypt My armies—My
people, the Israelites. ⁵ When I display My power* and bring the Israelites out
from among them, Egypt will know that I am God."

⁶ Moses and Aaron did this. They did exactly* as God had instructed
them.

⁷ When they spoke to Pharaoh, Moses was 80 years old, and Aaron was 83
years old.

[14. The Staff Becomes a Serpent]

⁸ God said to Moses and Aaron, ⁹ "When Pharaoh speaks to you, he will
tell you to prove yourself with a miraculous sign. You [Moses] must then tell
Aaron, 'Take your staff and throw it down before Pharaoh. Let it become* a
viper*!'" ¹⁰ Moses and Aaron came to Pharaoh. They did exactly as God had
said. Aaron threw his staff down before Pharaoh, and it became a viper.

¹¹ Pharaoh summoned his scholars and magicians. The master symbolists*
were able to do the same thing with their magic tricks.* ¹² When each one
threw down his staff, [the staffs] all turned into vipers.

Aaron's staff then swallowed up their staffs. ¹³ But Pharaoh remained
obstinate and did not pay attention to them, just as God had predicted.

[15. Warning for the First Plague]

¹⁴ God said to Moses, "Pharaoh is obstinate and he refuses to let the
people leave. ¹⁵ Pay a call on Pharaoh in the morning, when he goes out to the
water. Stand where you will meet him on the bank of the Nile. Take in your
hand the staff that was transformed into a snake.

7:4   **display My power.** Literally, "send forth My hand."
7:5   **display My power.** Same.
7:6   **exactly.** (*Lekach Tov;* cf. *Mekhilta* on 19:7). See Genesis 6:22.
7:9   **let it become.** A command, cf. Genesis 1:3.
—   **viper.** *Tanin* in Hebrew. Some say that this is the same snake (*nachash*) that it became at the Burning Bush
      (4:3), see below 7:15 (Rashi; *Lekach Tov;* Radak, *Sherashim,* s.v. *tanan*). Others say that by the Burning
      Bush, God gave Moses a sign for the Israelites, but before Pharaoh, the staff turned into a crocodile (Ibn
      Ezra; *K'li Yekar*), and that this was Aaron's staff and not Moses' (*K'li Yekar,* cf. *Zohar*). Others say that
      Moses gave his staff to Aaron (Ibn Ezra).
7:11 **master symbolists.** See Genesis 41:8. Some say that they were astrologers (*Targum Yonathan* on 7:22).
—   **magic tricks.** *Lahat* in Hebrew. Some say that this has the connotation of speed, and hence denotes
      sleight of hand (Ibn Ezra; Ralbag; Hirsch). Others say that it is a kind of hypnotism (Bachya), possibly
      involving a sword (Radak, *Sherashim;* cf. Genesis 3:24). According to other opinions, since the word *lahat*
      usually denotes fire or flame, this is a kind of fire magic (Ramban). Significantly, in Egyptian, the same
      word (*reka*) denotes both fire and magic. According to the Talmud (*Sanhedrin* 67b; Rashi), this was magic
      involving the sword at the entrance of Eden (Genesis 3:24). It did not involve the "Tree of Life," but the
      forces of evil that form a shell around the tree. Other sources state that *lahat* is another form of *lat* mean-
      ing "hidden arts" (below 7:22; Ibn Janach; Ralbag).

7   ¹⁶ "Say to him: God, Lord of the Hebrews, has sent me to you with the
message, 'Let My people leave, and let them worship Me in the desert.' So far,
you have not paid attention. ¹⁷ God [now] says, 'Through this you will know
that I am God.' I will strike the water of the Nile with the staff in my hand, and
[the water] will turn into blood. ¹⁸ The fish in the Nile will die, and the river
will become putrid. The Egyptians will have to stop drinking water from the
Nile."

[16. Blood: The First Plague]

¹⁹ God said to Moses, "Tell Aaron to take his staff and extend his hand
over the waters of Egypt—over their rivers, their canals,* their reservoirs,* and
every place where water is kept*—and [the water] shall turn into blood. There
will be blood throughout all Egypt, even in wooden [barrels] and stone
[jars].*"

²⁰ Moses and Aaron did exactly as God had instructed. [Aaron] held the
staff up, and then struck the Nile's water in the presence of Pharaoh and his
officials. The Nile's water was transformed into blood. ²¹ The fish in the Nile
died, and the river became so polluted that the Egyptians were no longer able
to drink the Nile's water. There was blood everywhere in Egypt.

²² However, when the master symbolists of Egypt were able to produce the
same effect with their hidden arts,* Pharaoh became obstinate. He would not
pay attention to [Moses and Aaron], just as God had predicted. ²³ Pharaoh
turned his back to them and went to his palace. Even to this [miracle], he
would not pay attention.

²⁴ The Egyptians dug around the Nile for drinking water, since they could
not drink any water from the river. ²⁵ After God struck the Nile, [it remained
that way] for seven full days.

7:19   **canals** (Rashi; *Targum*). *Y'orim* in Hebrew (Cf. Daniel 12:5). Or, "streams." The word is usually assumed
to denote irrigation canals (Radak, *Sherashim; Sekhel Tov*), because they flow from the Nile, which is
known as the *Y'or* (Ibn Janach). The term usually refers to Egyptian canals (2 Kings 19:24, Isaiah 7:18,
19:6, 37:25). The word *y'or* is thought to be related to the ancient Egyptian *iaur* or *aur,* a canal, stream, or
arm of the Nile. In Coptic, the word is *eiero* or *eioor*.

—   **reservoirs.** *Agam-im* in Hebrew. It is thus translated in Old French as *astonc* (Rashi), and in Spanish as
estanque (Radak, *Sherashim*). It can also denote a lake or pool (*palude* in Spanish; Radak, *Sherashim*).
Others write that this is any gathering of rain water (Ibn Ezra). The word may therefore be related to the
Egyptian, since *ag* is a flood, and *agem* or *agep* is rain.

—   **where water is kept.** Literally, "gatherings of water." These denote cisterns and wells (Ibn Ezra).

—   **wooden barrels** . . . (*Targum;* Rashi; Ibn Ezra). In ancient Semitic texts, a similar expression means
"woods and fields." It is questionable whether or not this last sentence is part of what Moses was to tell
Aaron.

7:22   **hidden arts.** (Ibn Ezra). From the root *lut,* meaning to hide or conceal. See note on 7:11. According to
some, this involved a form of demonology (*Sanhedrin* 67b).

[*17. Frogs: The Second Plague*]   7

²⁶ God said to Moses, "Go to Pharaoh and say to him in My name,* "Let My people leave so they can serve Me. ²⁷ If you refuse to let them leave, I will strike all your territories with frogs. ²⁸ The Nile will swarm with frogs, and when they emerge, they will be in your palace, in your bedroom, and [even] in your bed. [They will also be in] the homes of your officials and people, even in your ovens and kneading bowls. ²⁹ When the frogs emerge, they will be all over you, your people, and your officials."

¹ God said to Moses, "Tell Aaron to point the staff in his hand at the rivers,   8 canals and reservoirs, and he will make frogs emerge upon Egypt."

² Aaron held his hand out over the waters of Egypt, and the frogs emerged, covering Egypt. ³ The master symbolists were able to produce the same effect with their hidden arts, making frogs emerge on Egyptian land.

⁴ Pharaoh summoned Moses and Aaron, and said, "Pray to God! Let Him get the frogs away from me and my people. I will let the people leave and sacrifice to God."

⁵ "Try and test me,*" replied Moses. "Exactly when shall I pray for you, your officials and your people? The frogs will [immediately] depart from you and your homes, remaining only in the Nile."

⁶ "Tomorrow!" said [Pharaoh].

"As you say," replied [Moses]. "You will then know that there is none like God our Lord. ⁷ The frogs will depart from you, as well as from your houses, your officials and your people. They will remain only in the Nile."

⁸ Moses and Aaron left Pharaoh, and Moses cried out to God concerning the frogs that He had brought upon Pharaoh. ⁹ God did just as Moses said, and the frogs in the houses, courtyards and fields died. ¹⁰ [The Egyptians] gathered them into great heaps, and the land stank.

¹¹ When Pharaoh saw that there had been a respite, he hardened his heart and would not listen to them, just as God had predicted.

[*18. Lice: The Third Plague*]

¹² God said to Moses, "Tell Aaron to hold out his staff and strike the dust of the earth. It will turn into lice all over Egypt."

¹³ They did this. Aaron held out his hand with his staff, and struck the dust

---

7:26   **in My name.** Literally, "This is what God says: . . ." See note on Genesis 20:13.
8:5   **Try and test me.** (Rashbam). Or, "try and show off" (*Targum Yonathan;* Rashi); "let me give you the honor," (*Sekhel Tov;* Ibn Ezra); "demonstrate your status to me" (Radak, *Sherashim;* cf. *Targum*); or "give me the order" (Ibn Janach).

8   of the earth. The lice appeared, attacking man and beast. Throughout all
     Egypt, the dust had turned into lice.

     ¹⁴ The master symbolists tried to produce lice with their hidden arts, but
     they could not. [Meanwhile], the lice were attacking man and beast alike. ¹⁵ "It
     is the finger* of God," said the master symbolists to Pharaoh. But Pharaoh
     remained obstinate and would not listen, just as God had predicted.

[19. Harmful Creatures: The Fourth Plague]

     ¹⁶ God said to Moses, "Get up early in the morning, and confront
     Pharaoh when he goes out to the water. Say to him in My name,* 'Let My
     people leave and serve Me. ¹⁷ If you do not let My people leave, I will send
     swarms of harmful creatures* [to attack] you, your officials, your people, and
     your homes. The houses of Egypt, and even the ground upon which they
     stand, will be filled with these creatures.

     ¹⁸ "On that day, I will miraculously set apart the Goshen area, where My
     people remain, so that there will not be any harmful creatures there. You will
     then realize that I am God, right here on earth. ¹⁹ I will therefore make a dis-
     tinction* between My people and your people. This miraculous sign will take
     place tomorrow.'"

     ²⁰ God did this, and huge throngs of creatures attacked the palaces of
     Pharaoh and his officials. Throughout all Egypt, the land was devastated by
     the creatures.

     ²¹ Pharaoh summoned Moses and Aaron. "Go!" he said. "[You have
     permission to] sacrifice to your God here in [our] land."

     ²² "That would hardly be suitable," replied Moses. "What we will sacrifice

---

8:15   **finger.** *Etzba* in Hebrew. In ancient Egyptian, the word *etzba* or *tzeba* also denotes a finger, but it also
        denotes retribution. The Egyptian occultists may have also been saying, "It is God's retribution."
8:16   **in My name.** Literally, "This is what God says: . . ."
8:17   **harmful creatures.** *Arov* in Hebrew. In the Midrash there is a dispute. Rabbi Nechemia says that *arov*
        denotes flies, and Rabbi Yehudah states that it denotes a mixture of wild animals (*Sh'moth Rabbah* 11:4).
        Most Midrashim accept the interpretation that *arov* is wild animals, and this opinion is reflected in most
        later commentaries (*Targum Yonathan;* Rashi; Ibn Ezra; Radak, *Sherashim;* Ibn Janach; Josephus,
        Antiquities 2:14:3). This would make the verse, "He sent the *arov* and it ate them" (Psalms 78:11) in its
        most literal sense. However, even here, some say that the animals only ate their food (Ralbag).
              Still, there are many sources that interpret *arov* as flies (cf. *Haggadah, Minhag Teiman* 42; *Midrash Or
        HaAfelah,* quoted in *Torah Sh'lemah* 65). Some ancient sources identify the *arov* as dog-flies (Septuagint;
        Ethiopic edition of *Yov'loth* 48:5), or blood-suckers (Philo, *De Vita Mosis* 2:101). Another source states
        that it is a mixture of insects and snakes (*Sefer HaYashar*). It is also possible that the Hebrew *arov* is related
        to the ancient Egyptian *a'ov,* denoting beetles, specifically the scarab or dung beetle.
              Other sources identify the *arov* as an invasion of a specific kind of animal, either wolves (Rashbam),
        panthers (*Midrash Tehillim* 78:45), eagles or other birds (*Ibid.*), or even giant squid (*silonith* in Hebrew;
        Ibid.; Sefer HaYashar p. 207; *Sekhel Tov; Midrash Aggadah; Midrash VaYosha;* see *The Torah Anthology* 4:254,
        note 18). See *Wisdom of Solomon* 11:15–18.
8:19   **distinction.** (Rashbam; Ibn Ezra) *Peduth* in Hebrew, literally, "redemption," or "sign of redemption."

to God our Lord is sacred* to the Egyptians. Could we sacrifice the sacred   8
animal of the Egyptians before their very eyes and not have them stone us?
²³ What we must do is make a three day journey into the desert. There we will
be able to sacrifice to God our Lord, just as He told us."

²⁴ "I will let you leave," said Pharaoh, "as long as you do not go too far
away. You can sacrifice to God your Lord in the desert. But pray for me!"

²⁵ Moses answered, "When I leave your presence, I will pray to God.
Tomorrow, the creatures will go away from Pharaoh,* his servants, and his
people. But let Pharaoh never again deceive us, refusing to let the people sacrifice to God."

²⁶ Moses left Pharaoh's presence and prayed to God. ²⁷ Doing as Moses
requested, God caused the creatures to leave Pharaoh, his servants and his
people. Not a single one remained. ²⁸ But this time again, Pharaoh made himself obstinate, and he would not let the people leave.

[20. Epidemic: The Fifth Plague]

¹ God told Moses to go to Pharaoh, and in the name of* God, Lord of the   9
Hebrews, say to him, "Let My people leave and serve Me. ² For if you refuse to
let them leave, and continue holding them, ³ God's power* will be directed
against your livestock in the field. The horses, donkeys, camels, cattle and
sheep [will die from] a very serious epidemic.

⁴ "God will [again] make a miraculous distinction, [this time] between
Israel's livestock and that of Egypt. Not a single [animal] belonging to the
Israelites will die. ⁵ God has set a fixed time, and has announced that He will
strike* the land with this tomorrow."

⁶ On the next day, God did this, and all the livestock in Egypt died. Of the
Israelites' livestock, however, not a single one was affected. ⁷ Pharaoh sent
word and discovered that among the Israelites' livestock, not a single [animal]
had died. But Pharaoh remained obstinate and would not let the people leave.

[21. Boils: The Sixth Plague]

⁸ God said to Moses and Aaron, "Take a handful* of furnace soot* and

---

8:22 **sacred.** (*Targum Yonathan;* Rashi). See notes on Genesis 39:6, 43:32. Others say that the sheep was disgusting to the Egyptians (Rashbam; cf. Ibn Ezra).
8:25 **Pharaoh.** Since Pharaoh had shown respect for God, Moses uses the respectful third person.
9:1 **in the name of** . . . Literally, "and say to him, 'this is what God . . . ' "
9:3 **power.** Literally, "hand."
9:5 **strike.** Literally, "do."
9:8 **handful.** A double handful, where both hands are placed together and filled (cf. Leviticus 16:12; Ibn
Ezra *ad loc.;* Rashi here translates it as *joinchiez,* a "joined handful."
—   **soot.** (Rashi; Hirsch; *Septuagint*). Or, "ashes" (*Targum Yonathan; Vulgate*), or "cinders" or "embers"

9 throw it up in the air before Pharaoh's eyes. ⁹ It will settle as dust on all Egypt, and when it falls on man or beast anywhere in Egypt, it will cause a rash breaking out into boils.*' "

¹⁰ They took the furnace soot and stood before Pharaoh. Moses threw it up in the air, and it caused a rash, which broke into boils, in man and beasts. ¹¹ The master symbolists could not stand before Moses as a result of the rash, since the rash had attacked the symbolists [along with] the rest of Egypt.

¹² [Now it was] God who made Pharaoh obstinate. He did not listen to [Moses and Aaron], just as God had predicted.

[22. Warning]

¹³ God told Moses to get up early in the morning and confront Pharaoh, saying to him in the name of God, Lord of the Hebrews,* "Let My people leave and serve Me. ¹⁴ This time, I am prepared to send all My catastrophes against your very heart. [They will strike] your officials and your people, so that you will know that there is none like Me in all the world.

¹⁵ "I could have unleashed My power,* killing you and your people with the epidemic [sent against the animals], and you would have been obliterated from the world. ¹⁶ The only reason I let you survive was to show you My strength, so that My name will be discussed all over the world.

¹⁷ "But now you are still lording it over* My people, refusing to let them leave. ¹⁸ At this time tomorrow, I will bring a very heavy hail. Never before in Egypt, since the day it was founded, has there been anything like it.

¹⁹ "Now send word and make arrangements to shelter your livestock and everything else you have in the field. Any man or beast who remains in the field, and does not come indoors, will be pelted by the hail and will die."

²⁰ Some of* Pharaoh's subjects feared God's word, and they made their slaves and livestock flee indoors. ²¹ But those who did not fear God's word left their slaves and livestock in the field.

[23. Hail: The Seventh Plague]

²² God said to Moses, "Stretch out your hand toward the sky, and there

---

(*rescoldo* in Spanish; Radak, *Sherashim*). Some sources state that it is the white ash that forms on burning embers (*Lekach Tov; Sekhel Tov*).

9:9 **boils.** (Hirsch). Or "blisters" (*Sekhel Tov*). Others have, "boils breaking into open sores" (*Septuagint*). (See *Bava Kama* 8ob).

9:13 **in the name** . . . Literally, "Say to him: this is what God . . . says: . . ."

9:15 **unleashed My power.** Literally, "extend My hand."

9:17 **lording it over** . . . (Ibn Ezra; Radak, *Sherashim*). Or, "oppressing" (*Targum;* Rashi; Rashbam).

9:20 **Some of** . . . This is not part of Moses' speech (*Targum Yonathan*). According to some, however, it is (cf. Sforno).

will be hail throughout all Egypt. [It will fall] on man and beast, and on all 9 outdoor plants* all over Egypt.

²³ Moses pointed his staff at the sky, and God caused it to thunder and hail, with lightning striking the ground.* God then made it hail on the land of Egypt. ²⁴ There was hail, with lightning flashing* among the hailstones. It was extremely heavy, unlike anything Egypt had experienced since it became a nation.

²⁵ Throughout all Egypt, the hail killed every man and animal who was outdoors. The hail destroyed all the outdoor plants, and smashed every tree in the fields. ²⁶ Only in Goshen, where the Israelites lived, there was no hail.

²⁷ Pharaoh sent word and summoned Moses and Aaron. He said to them, "This time I am guilty! God is Just! It is I and my people who are in the wrong! ²⁸ Pray to God. There has been enough of this supernatural* thunder and hail. I will let you leave. You will not be delayed again."

²⁹ Moses said to him, "When I go out of the city,* I will spread my hands [in prayer] to God. The thunder will then stop, and there will not be any more hail. You will then know that the whole world belongs to God.

³⁰ "I realize that you and your subjects still do not fear God. ³¹ The flax* and barley have been destroyed, since the barley was ripe, and the flax had formed stalks. ³² But the wheat and spelt* have not been destroyed, since they are late in sprouting.*"

9:22 **outdoor plants.** Literally, "grass of the field." See Genesis 1:11, 2:5.

9:23 **lightning striking the ground** (Ralbag; Sforno; Hirsch). Or, "fire flashing" (*Targum Yonathan*), or "fire streaming to the ground" (Ibn Ezra). Cf. Psalms 78:48, 105:32, 148:8.

9:24 **flashing** (*Targum*). Or "fire darting," or "fire jumping" (*Targum Yonathan; Sekhel Tov*); "deadly fire" (*Sh'moth Rabbah*); or "self-contained fire" (Hirsch), or "fire holding itself to the hail" (Malbim). Cf. Ezekiel 1:4. The expression can also be translated, "lightning flashes in close succession," "incessant fire," "a mass of fire," or "forked lightning." Some say that it denotes a meteorite shower (Ibn Ezra, *Sefer HaAtzamim*).

9:28 **supernatural** (cf. Ralbag). Literally, "God's thunder." (cf. *Targum; Targum Yonathan*).

9:29 **city.** Possibly Memphis (see note on Genesis 44:4). If this was during the 18th Dynasty, the Capital city would have been Thebes.

9:31 **The flax** . . . This is still part of Moses' speech (Saadia Gaon; Rashbam; Ramban; Tur; Hirsch). According to others, this is the Torah's comment (Ibn Ezra).

9:32 **spelt.** (Septuagint; *espelta* in Spanish, Radak, *Sherashim;* Bertonoro on *Kilayim* 1:1), otherwise known as *Dinkel* (*Tifereth Yisroel* on *Kilayim* 1:1). This is a species of wheat (*Pesachim* 35a) known as *triticum spelta*. Maimonides, however, writes that it is a kind of desert wheat (commentary on *Kilayim* 1:1). Since no evidence of spelt has been found in Biblical times, some identify the *kusemeth* here as Emmer wheat (*triticum dicoccum*), which is found in ancient Egyptian tombs. Others say that it is *triticum dioccoides*, which grows wild in the Holy Land. Thus, in Hebrew there are two types of wheat, *chita*, and *kusemeth,* and in ancient Egyptian, these may correspond to *chetzt* or *khent* and *kamut*.

— **late in sprouting.** And still not emerged from the ground (Ibn Ezra; Radak, *Sherashim*). Or, "still yielding" (Rashi; *Lekach Tov;* Saadia; both explanations are found in *Sekhel Tov*).

Spelt

9　　　³³ Moses left Pharaoh's presence, and went out of the city. As soon as he spread his hands out to God, the thunder ceased, and the hail and rain stopped falling to the ground. ³⁴ But when Pharaoh saw that there was no longer any rain, hail or thunder, he continued in his sinful ways. He and his officials continued to make themselves obstinate. ³⁵ Pharaoh hardened his heart and did not let the Israelites leave, just as God had predicted through Moses.

Bo　　　　　　　　　　　　　　　　　　　　　בֹּא

[24. Warning]

10　　　¹ God said to Moses, "Go* to Pharaoh. I have made him and his advisors stubborn, so that I will be able to demonstrate these miraculous signs among them. ² You will then be able to confide* to your children and grandchildren how I made fools* of the Egyptians, and how I performed miraculous signs among them. You will then fully realize that I am God."

³ Moses and Aaron came to Pharaoh. In the name of God, Lord of the Hebrews, they said to him, "How long will you refuse to submit to Me? Let My people leave and serve Me. ⁴ If you refuse to let My people leave, I will bring locusts to your territories tomorrow. ⁵ They will cover every visible speck of land, so that you will not be able to see the ground, and they will eat all that was spared for you by the hail, devouring every tree growing in the field. ⁶ They will fill your palaces, as well as the houses of your officials and of all Egypt. It will be something that your fathers and your fathers' fathers have never seen, since the day they were in the land."

With that, [Moses] turned his back and left Pharaoh.

⁷ Pharaoh's officials said to him, "How long will this [man] continue to be a menace to us? Let the men go, and let them serve God their Lord. Don't you yet realize that Egypt is being destroyed?"

⁸ Moses and Aaron were brought back to Pharaoh. "Go serve God your Lord," he said. "But exactly who will be going?"

⁹ "Young and old alike will go," replied Moses. "We will go with our sons and our daughters, with our sheep and cattle. It is a festival to God for [all of*] us."

10:1　**Go.** See note on 6:11.
10:2　**confide.** Literally, "place in the ear of." See note on Genesis 20:8.
—　　**made fools of.** Or, "amused Myself with" (Rashi); "dealt wantonly with (Ibn Ezra); or, "did fearsome acts with" (Radak, *Sherashim; Targum*).
10:9　**all of.** (Ibn Ezra).

¹⁰ "May God only be with you just as I will let you leave with your chil-   10
dren*!" replied Pharaoh. "You must realize that you will be confronted* by
evil.* ¹¹ But that's not the way it will be. Let the males go and worship God, if
that's really what you want!" With that, he had them expelled from his
presence.

[25. Locusts: The Eighth Plague]

¹² God said to Moses, "Extend your hand over Egypt [to bring] the locusts,
and they will emerge on Egypt. They will eat all the foliage in the land that was
spared by the hail."

¹³ Moses raised his hand over Egypt, and all that day and night, God made
an east wind blow over the land. When morning came, the east wind* was
carrying the locusts. ¹⁴ The locusts invaded Egypt, settling on all Egyptian territory. It was a very severe [plague]. Never before had there been such a locust
plague, and never again [would the like be seen].

¹⁵ The [locusts] covered the entire surface of the land, making the ground
black. They ate all the plants on the ground and all the fruit on the trees,
whatever had been spared by the hail. Nothing green remained on the trees
and plants throughout all Egypt.

¹⁶ Pharaoh hastily summoned Moses and Aaron. "I have committed a
crime," he said, "both to God your Lord and to you. ¹⁷ Now forgive my
offense just this one more time. Pray to God your Lord! Just take this death
away from me!"

¹⁸ [Moses] left Pharaoh's presence and prayed to God. ¹⁹ God turned the
wind around, [transforming it into] a very strong west wind. It carried away
the locusts, and plunged them* into the Red Sea.* Not a single locust

---

10:10 **May God only . . .** (Ralbag). Or, "Even if God is with you when I send you, evil will confront you"
(Rashi).

— **you will be confronted** (Ibn Ezra). Literally, "evil is before your face." Possibly, "the evil will come back
on you" (Ramban), or "Your intentions are evil" (Rashbam; cf. *Targum*). See next note.

— **evil.** *Ra* in Hebrew. According to some, however, this is speaking of Ra, the Egyptian sun god (cf. Rashi;
Yalkut Shimoni 392). See below, 32:12. Some sources identify this with Baal Tzafon (below, 14:2; *Lekach
Tov*).

10:13 **east wind.** The east wind would often blow across the desert from Arabia, or even from Iran, Pakistan or
India, carrying locusts (cf. Diodorus Siculus 3:29; Orosius 4:11; Livy 42:2; Aelien, *Of the Nature of
Animals* 3:12)

10:19 **plunged them . . .** Locust swarms were often carried away by the wind into the sea (cf. Joel 2:20; Pliny
11:35).

— **Red Sea.** Or "Erythrean Sea" (*Septuagint* cf. original Greek of *1 Maccabees* 4:9; *Wisdom of Solomon* 10:18,
19:7). *Yam Suf* in Hebrew, literally, "Sea of Reeds" (Rashi on 13:18; see note on 2:3) or "End Sea." (Ibn
Ezra on 13:18). This probably denotes the Gulf of Suez, which separates Egypt from the Sinai Peninsula.
See note on 13:18.

In ancient times, the term "Red Sea" or "Erythrean Sea" referred to what is now the Red Sea as well
as its two arms, the Gulf of Suez and the Gulf of Aqaba (cf. Rashi; Herodotus 2:11). However, it also

10 remained within all Egypt's borders. [20] But once again, God made Pharaoh obstinate, and he would not let the Israelites leave.

[26. Darkness: The Ninth Plague]

[21] God said to Moses, "Reach out toward the sky with your hand, and there will be darkness in Egypt. The darkness will be palpable.*"

[22] Moses lifted his hand toward the sky, and there was an opaque darkness in all Egypt, lasting for three days. [23] People could not see each other, and no one left his place for three days. The Israelites, however, had light in the areas where they lived.

[24] Pharaoh summoned Moses. "Go!" he said. "Worship God! Even your children can go with you. Just leave your sheep and cattle behind."

[25] "Will you then provide us* with sacrifices and burnt offerings* so that we will be able to offer them to God our Lord?" replied Moses. [26] "Our livestock must also go along with us. Not a single hoof can be left behind. We must take them to serve God our Lord, since we do not know what we will need to worship God until we get there."

[27] God made Pharaoh obstinate, and he was no longer willing to let [the Israelites] leave. [28] "Leave my presence!" said Pharaoh to [Moses]. "Don't dare see my face again! The day you appear before me, you will die!"

[29] "As you say," replied Moses. "I will not see your face again."

[27. Preparations for the Final Plague]

11 [1] God said to Moses, "There is one more plague that I will send against Pharaoh and Egypt. After that, he will let you leave this place. When he lets you leave, he will actually drive you out of here. [2] Now speak to the people discreetly,* and let each man request* from his friend gold and silver articles. Let every woman make [the same] request of her friends."

---

included the rest of the waters to the south of Asia Minor, such as the Persian Gulf and the Indian Ocean (Josephus, *Antiquities* 1:1:3; Herodotus 4:37; Pliny 6:28; Strabo 16:765).

Some say that it is called the Red Sea because of the color of its reeds (see note on 2:3), the corals in its waters, the color of the mountains bordering its coasts, or the glow of the sky reflected in it. Others say that its name is derived from the ancient nation of Erythria, so named because its inhabitants painted their faces red (Dio Cassius 68:28; Philostratus, *Apollonius* 3:50; Arrian, *Indica* 37). It is possible that the name may also be associated with Edom (see Genesis 25:30), which means red. It is also said that it is called the "Red Sea" because it lies to the south, and the south is called the "red zone" (cf. Photius 250:717).

10:21 **palpable** (*Sh'moth Rabbah* 14:1; Rashi; Ibn Ezra; Ramban). Alternatively, "the darkness was opaque" (Radak, *Sherashim; Septuagint;* cf. *Wisdom of Solomon* 17:5); or "intense darkness" (Rashi; Rashbam).

10:25 **Will you then provide us** . . . (Abarbanel). Or, "you should also be giving us . . ." (Rashi; Ibn Ezra; Ramban).

— **burnt offerings.** See note on Genesis 8:20.

11:2 **discreetly.** (cf. Septuagint) Literally, "in the ears of." See note on 10:2, Genesis 20:8.

— **let each man request.** See 3:22, 12:35.

³ God gave the people status among the Egyptians. Moses was also very ¹¹ highly respected in Egypt, both by Pharaoh's officials and by the people.

[28. Death of the First-Born]

⁴ Moses said [to Pharaoh] in God's name,* "Around midnight, I will go out in the midst of Egypt. ⁵ Every first-born in Egypt will die, from the first-born of Pharaoh sitting on his throne, to the first-born of the slave girl behind the millstones. Every first-born animal [will also die].

⁶ "There will be a great cry of anguish throughout all Egypt. Never before has there been anything like it, and never again will there be the like. ⁷ But among the Israelites, a dog will not even whine* because of man or beast. You will then realize that God is making a miraculous distinction between Egypt and Israel.

⁸ "All your officials here will come and bow down to me. They will say, 'Leave! You and all your followers!' Only then will I leave." He left Pharaoh in great anger.

[29. Final Reassurance]

⁹ God said to Moses, "Pharaoh will not listen to you. This is so that I will be able to do all the more wonders in Egypt."

¹⁰ Moses and Aaron had done all these wonders before Pharaoh. Still, because God had made Pharaoh obstinate, he would not let the Israelites leave his land.

[30. The Passover Described]

¹ God said to Moses and Aaron in Egypt: ² This month* shall be the head ¹²
month to you. It shall be the first month of the year.*

³ Speak to the entire community of Israel, saying: On the tenth of this month,* every man must take a lamb* for each extended family,* a lamb for each household. ⁴ If the household is too small for a lamb, then he and a close

---

11:4 **in God's name.** Literally, "This is what God says . . ."
11:7 **not even whine** . . . (*Targum Yonathan;* Rosh; Chizzkuni). Or, "growl at man or beast" (*Targum;* Ibn Ezra; Septuagint), "bark at . . ." or "bite" (Ibn Ezra; Ralbag). Literally, "not sharpen his tongue" (Rashi), or "not wag its tongue" (Ibn Janach; Radak, *Sherashim*). Cf. Joshua 10:21.
12:2 **This month** . . . Nissan. This occurs in March and April.
— **first month of the year.** This is seen as a commandment to maintain a calendar (*Rosh HaShanah* 18a; *Sanhedrin* 11a; *Sefer HaMitzvoth;* Positive Commandment 193). The calendar is lunar in nature, with an occasional leap-month added to keep it in conformity with the solar year.
12:3 **tenth of this month.** This was only required for the first Passover in Egypt, but not subsequently (*Pesachim* 96a; Rashi).
— **lamb.** The Hebrew word *seh* here can denote any young of the small ruminants, and can thus refer either to a lamb or to a kid, as we see in 12:5.
— **extended family.** See 6:14, Numbers 1:2, 17:17 (*Mekhilta; Pesachim* 96a; Rashi; Hirsch).

12 neighbor can obtain a [lamb together], as long as it is for specifically designated individuals.* Individuals shall be designated for a lamb according to
how much each one will eat.

⁵ You must have a flawless young animal, a one-year-old male. You can
take it from the sheep or from the goats. ⁶ Hold it in safekeeping until the
fourteenth day of this month.

The entire community of Israel shall then slaughter [their sacrifices] in the
afternoon.* ⁷ They must take the blood and place it on the two doorposts and
on the beam above the door of the houses in which they will eat [the sacri-
fice].*

⁸ Eat the [sacrificial] meat during the night, roasted over fire. Eat it with
matzah* and bitter herbs.*

⁹ Do not eat it raw or cooked in water, but only roasted over fire, including* its head, its legs, and its internal organs.

¹⁰ Do not leave any of it over until morning. Anything that is left over until
morning must be burned in fire.

¹¹ You must eat it with your waist belted, your shoes on your feet, and your
staff in your hand,* and you must eat it in haste. It is the Passover (*Pesach*)*
offering to God.

¹² I will pass through Egypt on that night, and I will kill every first-born in
Egypt, man and beast. I will perform acts of judgment against all the gods of
Egypt. I [alone] am God.

¹³ The blood will be a sign for you on the houses where you are staying. I
will see the blood and pass you by (*pasach*). There will not be any deadly
plague among you when I strike Egypt.

¹⁴ This day must be one that you will remember. You must keep it as a
festival to God for all generations. It is a law for all time that you must celebrate it.

¹⁵ Eat matzahs for seven days. By the first day, you must have your homes

---

12:4   **designated individuals.** That is, those who will partake in a specific lamb must be designated beforehand
(*Pesachim* 81a).

12:6   **in the afternoon** (*Pesachim* 61a; Rashi). Literally, "between the evenings."

12:7   **take the blood** . . . This was done only for the first Passover in Egypt. In subsequent years, the blood
would be placed on the altar, just like the blood of other sacrifices (*Tosefta, Pesachim* 8).

12:8   **matzah.** Unleavened bread. Even though the Passover sacrifice is not offered now that the Temple does
not exist, matzah is still eaten on the Seder night.

—   **bitter herbs.** These are also still eaten at the Seder. The bitter herb can consist of horseradish, romaine
lettuce, endives, palm ivy (?) or succory (?) (*Pesachim* 39a).

12:9   **including** . . . (Rashi). Or, "with its head on its knees" (Ralbag; *Kedushath Levi*). (cf. *Mekhilta; Pesachim*
74a; *Yerushalmi, Pesachim* 7:1).

12:11 **You must eat it** . . . This was true only on that first Passover (*Mekhilta; Pesachim* 96a).

—   **Passover.** See 12:13.

cleared of all leaven.* Whoever eats leaven from the first day until the seventh day will have his soul cut off from Israel.* 12

¹⁶ The first day shall be a sacred holiday, and the seventh day shall [also] be a sacred holiday. No work may be done on these [days]. The only [work] that you may do is that which is needed so that everyone will be able to eat.*

¹⁷ Be careful regarding the matzahs, for on this very day I will have brought your masses out of Egypt. You must carefully keep this day for all generations; it is a law for all times. ¹⁸ From the 14th day of the first month in the evening,* until the night of the 21st day of the month, you must eat [only] matzahs. ¹⁹ During [these] seven days, no leaven may be found in your homes. If someone eats anything leavened his soul shall be cut off from the community of Israel. [This is true] whether he is a proselyte or a person born into the nation.* ²⁰ You must not eat anything leavened. In all the areas where you live, eat matzahs.

[31. Passover Preparations]

²¹ Moses summoned the elders of Israel,* and said to them, "Gather [the people]* and get yourselves sheep for your families, so that you will be able to slaughter the Passover sacrifice.

²² "You will then have to take a bunch of hyssop* and dip it into the blood that [will be placed] in a basin. Touch the beam over the door and the two doorposts with some of the blood in the basin. Not a single one of you may go out the door of his house until morning.

²³ "God will then pass through to strike Egypt. When he sees the blood

---

12:15 you must have your homes cleared . . . This is a commandment to remove leaven (*chametz*) before the Passover, and it is the reason that we search for leaven the night before (*Pesachim* 5a; *Sefer HaMitzvoth*, Positive Commandment 156).

— have his soul cut off . . . See note on Genesis 17:14.

12:16 the only work . . . Work on festivals is forbidden, just as on the Sabbath, but it is permitted to make a fire, to cook and to carry, since these acts are needed to prepare food.

12:18 in the evening. From here we see that festivals begin in the evening and end at sunset (Ralbag).

12:19 person born into the nation. Literally, "a native born in the land."

12:21 elders of Israel. See note on 3:16.

— Gather the people. (Radak, *Sherashim;* cf. Judges 4:6). Or, "go forth" (Hirsch); "Remove [idolatry]" (*Targum Yonathan; Mekhilta*); or, "Lead or buy sheep" (Rashi).

12:22 hyssop. (*Septuagint;* Bertenoro, Rabbi Yitzchak ben Malkhi-tzedek, on *Shevi'ith* 8:1). *Ezov* in Hebrew, cognate to the English. This is a form of wild middle eastern marjoram (*marjorna syriaca* or *origanum maru*). It is a low plant, a little over a foot high, with blue blossoms. The Mishnah describes it as having woody lower parts, with branches growing sideways, containing at least three buds on top (*Parah* 11:8,9). Although it grew wild, it was also cultivated as a spice (*Maasroth* 3:9). It is an aromatic spice with deodorizing properties (Ibn Ezra). Some authorities identify the *ezov* with the caper plant (*caparis spinosa*), or with wild thyme or oregano (Rambam on *Shevi'ith* 8:1, *Nega'im* 14:6; *MeAm Loez;* cf. *Shabbath* 109b; *Arukh*).

Hyssop

12 over the door and on the two doorposts, God will pass over that door, and
not let the force of destruction* enter your houses to strike.

²⁴ "You must keep this ritual as a law, for you and your children forever.
²⁵ When you come to the land that God will give you, as He promised, you
must [also] keep this service. ²⁶ Your children may [then] ask you, 'What is this
service to you?' ²⁷ You must answer, 'It is the Passover service to God. He
passed over the houses of the Israelites in Egypt when He struck the Egyptians, sparing our homes.'"

The people bent their heads and prostrated themselves. ²⁸ The Israelites
went and did as God had instructed Moses and Aaron. They did it exactly.

[32. The Final Plague]

²⁹ It was midnight. God killed every first-born in Egypt, from the first-
born of Pharaoh, sitting on his throne, to the first-born of the prisoner in the
dungeon, as well as every first-born animal.

³⁰ Pharaoh stayed up that night, along with all his officials and all the rest
of Egypt. There was a great outcry, since there was no house where there were
no dead.

³¹ [Pharaoh] sent for Moses and Aaron during the night. "Get moving!"
he said. "Get out from among my people—you and the Israelites! Go! Worship God just as you demanded! ³² Take your sheep and cattle, just as you
said! Go! Bless me too!"

³³ The Egyptians were also urging the people to hurry and leave the land.
"We are all dead men!" they were saying.

³⁴ The people took their dough before it could rise. Their leftover dough*
was wrapped in their robes [and placed] on their shoulders. ³⁵ The Israelites
[also] did as Moses had said.* They requested silver and gold articles and
clothing from the Egyptians. God made the Egyptians respect the people, and
they granted their request. [The Israelites] thus drained Egypt of its wealth.

[33. The Exodus]

³⁷ The Israelites traveled from Rameses* toward Sukkoth.* There were

---

12:23 **force of destruction.** *Mash'chith* in Hebrew, literally "the destroyer." *Targum Yonathan* translates it,
"angels of destruction." See 1 Samuel 13:17, 2 Samuel 24:16, Jeremiah 51:25.
12:34 **leftover dough** (*Targum; Mekhilta;* Rashi). Or, "masses of dough" (Radak, *Sherashim*); or "kneading pans"
(Saadia Gaon; Rashbam; Ibn Ezra; Septuagint).
12:35 **as Moses had said.** See above, 11:2, 3:22.
12:37 **Rameses.** See Genesis 47:11. This is distinct from Ra'amses mentioned in 1:11.

about 600,000 adult males* on foot,* besides the children.* ³⁸ A great mixture   12
[of nationalities] left with them.* There were [also] sheep and cattle, a huge
amount of livestock.

³⁹ [The Israelites] baked the dough that they had brought out of Egypt into
unleavened (matzah) cakes, since it had not risen. They had been driven out of
Egypt and could not delay, and they had not prepared any other provisions.
⁴⁰ The lifestyle* that the Israelites endured in Egypt had thus lasted 430
years. ⁴¹ At the end of the 430 years, all of God's armies left Egypt in broad
daylight.* ⁴² There was a night of vigil for God, [preparing] to bring them out
of Egypt. This night remains for the Israelites a vigil to God for all generations.

[34. Passover Laws]

⁴³ God said to Moses and Aaron, "This is the law of the Passover sacrifice:
"No outsider may eat it. ⁴⁴ If a man buys a slave for cash and circumcises

—   **Sukkoth.** Cf. 13:30, Numbers 33:5. Some say that this is the Egyptian Tjek or
Sekhut (see note on 1:11), capital of the Nome Heroopolites, and site of the village
of Naville. Josephus identifies it with Letopolis, which was rebuilt as Babel when
Cambyses laid Egypt waste (*Antiquities* 2:15:1). This is apparently the same as Fostat
or Cairo (cf. Strabo 17:807).

Sukkoth

       According to Talmudic tradition, Sukkoth was 120 (Rashi; *Ba'aley Tosafoth*) or 130 (*Targum Yonathan;
Lekach Tov*) Hebrew miles from Rameses. This is 102 or 110 miles. If it is assumed that Rameses was
identical with Heliopolos, then this would set Sukkoth along the Gulf of Suez or in the northern Sinai
Peninsula. If Rameses is Pelusium, it could be in approximately the same area. In general, this is a three
day journey (see note on Genesis 30:36).
—   **600,000 adult males.** Over 20 years old, see below, 38:26, Numbers 1:46, 11:21, 26:51.
—   **on foot.** (*Targum Yonathan;* Radak, *Sherashim;* Septuagint). Or, "able-bodied men" (*Midrash HaGadol;*
Josephus 2:15:1). See Numbers 11:21, Judges 20:2, 1 Samuel 4:10, 15:4, Jeremiah 12:5, etc.
—   **besides the children.** In all, some three million people participated in the Exodus (*Targum Yonathan*).
12:38   **A great mixture** . . . See Numbers 11:4. Also see Nehemiah 13:3, Jeremiah 25:20, 50:37. This group
numbered well over a million (*Targum Yonathan; Mekhilta*).
12:40   **lifestyle** (Hirsch; cf. *Mekhilta; Megillah* 9a). Since the 400 years (Genesis 15:13) were counted from Isaac's
birth, and Isaac was born when Abraham was 100 years old (Genesis 21:5), the 430 years had to have
begun when Abraham was 70 years old. Abraham was 75 years old when he left Charan (Genesis 12:4),
so this was five years earlier. Some say that this is counted from the time of the Covenant Between Halves
(Genesis 15:13), which occurred before Abraham left Charan (see *Mekhilta; Seder Olam;* Gra *ad loc.;*
Rashi). Others say that Abraham began his life of wandering as a foreigner when he was 70 years old,
and this lifestyle endured for 430 years (cf. Gra *loc. cit.;* Rambam) Others state that Canaan was under
Egyptian domination, and therefore the Israelites and their ancestors had been under Egyptian domination for 430 years (cf. *Torah Sh'lemah* 421).
       If we assume that 400 years elapsed between Isaac's birth and the Exodus, then, since Isaac was 60
when Jacob was born (Genesis 25:26), and Jacob was 130 when he came to Egypt (Genesis 47:9), the
total number of years the Israelites were in Egypt was actually 210 (*Seder Olam; Pirkey Rabbi Eliezer* 48).
       Josephus, however, states that the Israelites were in Egypt for a total of 215 years (*Antiquities* 2:15:2;
cf. Septuagint; *Pirkey Rabbi Eliezer* 48). According to this, the 430 years were counted from the time that
Abraham was 75 years old, when he left Charan. The 400 years would then have begun when Isaac was
five years old.
12:41   **in broad daylight.** Or, "on that very day"; cf. Genesis 7:13.

12 him, then [the slave] can eat it. ⁴⁵ [But if a gentile is] a temporary resident or a hired hand, he may not eat [the Passover sacrifice].

⁴⁶ "It must be eaten by a single group.* Do not bring any of its meat out of the group. Do not break any of its bones.

⁴⁷ "The entire community of Israel must keep [this ritual]. ⁴⁸ When a proselyte joins you and wants to offer the Passover sacrifice to God, every male [in his household] must be circumcised. He may then join in the observance, and be like a native-born [Israelite]. But no uncircumcised man may eat [the sacrifice]. ⁴⁹ The same law shall apply both for the native-born [Israelite] and for the proselyte who joins you."

⁵⁰ All the Israelites did as God had instructed Moses and Aaron. They did it exactly.

[35. Leaving Egypt]

⁵¹ On that very day, God took the Israelites out of Egypt in organized groups.

[36. Commemorating the Exodus]

13   ¹ God spoke to Moses, saying, ² "Sanctify to Me every first-born that initiates the womb among the Israelites. Among both man and beast, it is Mine."

³ Moses said to the people: Remember this day as [the time] you left Egypt, the place of slavery, when God brought you out of here with a show of force.* No leaven may be eaten. ⁴ You left this day, in the month of standing grain.*

⁵ There will come a time when God will bring you to the land of the Canaanites, Hittites, Amorites, Hivites and Yebusites.* He swore to your ancestors that He would give it to you—a land flowing with milk and honey. [There too] you will have to keep this service. ⁶ Eat matzahs for seven days, and make the seventh day a festival to God. ⁷ Since matzahs must be eaten for [these] seven days, no leaven may be seen in your possession. No leaven may be seen in all your territories.

⁸ On that day, you must tell your child, "It is because of this that God acted for me when I left Egypt."

12:46 **single group** (*Mekhilta;* Saadia; Rashi). Literally, "in one house."

13:3 **show of force.** Literally, "a strong hand." See 6:1.

13:4 **month of standing grain** (Rashbam; see above, 9:31). Some say that Aviv was the original name of this month. See below 23:15, 34:18, Deuteronomy 16:1. Later, the Babylonian name, Nissan, was used for this month (Esther 3:7, Nehemiah 2:1; *Yerushalmi, Rosh HaShanah* 1:2).

13:5 **Canaanites** . . . See note on 3:8. Only the nations whose lands were considered to be "flowing with milk and honey" are mentioned here (*Mekhilta;* Ramban).

⁹ [These words]* must also be a sign on your arm and a reminder in the   13
center of your head.*

God's Torah will then be on your tongue.* It was with a show of strength
that God brought you out of Egypt. ¹⁰ This law must therefore be kept at its
designated time from year to year.

[37. Consecration of the First-Born]

¹¹ There will come a time when God will have brought you to the land of
the Canaanites, which he promised you and your ancestors, and he will have
given it to you. ¹² You will then bring to God every [first-born] that initiates
the womb. Whenever you have a young* firstling animal, the males belong to
God.*

¹³ Every firstling donkey must be redeemed with a sheep. If it is not
redeemed, you must decapitate it.*

You must [also] redeem every first-born among your sons.*

¹⁴ Your child may later ask you, "What is this?" You must answer him,
"With a show of power, God brought us out of Egypt, the place of slavery.
¹⁵ When Pharaoh stubbornly refused to let us leave, God killed all the first-
born in Egypt, man and beast alike. I therefore sacrifice to God all male firstling [animals], and redeem all the first-born of my sons."

¹⁶ [These words] shall [also] be a sign on your arm* and an insignia* in the
center of your head.

[All this] is because God brought us out of Egypt with a show of strength.

13:9 **These words.** This indicates that this Hebrew chapter must be included in the Tefillin, which are worn on
the arm and head. The other three sections are mentioned in 13:16, and in Deuteronomy 6:8, and
11:18. Hence, there are four chapters of the Torah, written on parchment, in the Tefillin.

— **center of your head.** Literally, "between your eyes," an idiom denoting the center of the head, just above
the hairline (cf. Deuteronomy 14:1; Radak, s.v. *Tataf*). See below, 13:16.

— **on your tongue.** Literally, "in your mouth."

13:12 **young.** *Sheger* in Hebrew. Cf. Deuteronomy 7:13 (Rashbam; Radak, *Sherashim*). See *Ecclesiasticus* 40:19.

— **the males belong to God.** See 34:19,20, Leviticus 27:26, Deuteronomy 15:19.

13:13 **decapitate it** (Rashi; Ibn Ezra; Bertenoro on *Bekhoroth* 1:7). The word *araf* here apparently means to sever
the spinal column. The animal is struck on the back of the neck with a cleaver (*Bekhoroth* 10b, 13a) with
enough force to sever the spinal column, the gullet and the windpipe (*Yerushalmi, Sotah* 9:5, 43a; cf. *Sotah*
46b). See 34:20. Also see Deuteronomy 21:4, Isaiah 66:3, Hosea 10:2.

— **redeem every first-born . . .** For five shekels; Numbers 3:47, 18:15. See 22:28, Leviticus 8:16.

13:16 **arm.** According to Talmudic tradition, the weak arm, that is, the left arm (*Menachoth* 37a).

— **insignia.** Or, "frontlets" (Ibn Janach, Radak, s.v. *Tataf*; cf. *Targum* on 2 Samuel 1:10; *Shabbath* 57a,b;
Tosafoth, *Menachoth* 34b; Ramban). *Totafoth* in Hebrew. The *Targum* renders this word as Tefillin, having
the connotation of prayer, judgment and testimony (Tosafoth, *Menachoth* 34b, s.v. *LeTotafoth*). In Greek
they were also known as phylacteries, from the root *phylassin*, meaning to watch or to guard. (See
Josephus, *Antiquities* 4:8:13 commentaries on Ezekiel 24:17).

According to Talmudic tradition, the word *totafoth* alludes to the four boxes in the head Tefillin, since
tot in a Caspian dialect is two and *foth* or *poth* is two in African or Phrygian (see note on Genesis 10:2;
Menachoth 34b). The word *tot* appears to be cognate to "two," and possibly also to the latin *totas*, and

BeShalach בְּשַׁלַּח

[38. The Route from Egypt]

[17] When Pharaoh let the people leave, God did not lead them along the Philistine Highway,* although it was the shorter route. God's consideration was that if the people encountered armed resistance, they would lose heart and return to Egypt. [18] God therefore made the people take a roundabout path, by way of the desert* to the Red Sea.* The Israelites were well prepared* when they left Egypt.

[19] Moses took Joseph's remains with him. Joseph had bound the Israelites by an oath: "God will grant you* special providence, and you must then bring my remains out of here with you."

[20] [The Israelites] moved on from Sukkoth,* and they camped in Etham,* at the edge of the desert.

---

hence the English "total." *Poth* is cognate to the Gothic *bothe*, the English "both," and the Sanscrit *botto*.

    Significantly in ancient Egyptian, *ftu* or *fot* means four, while *tot* can denote a gathering, resemblance, divine, or hard leather. Hence, *totafoth* may have had the connotation of a fourfold amulet, made of leather, as the Tefillin indeed are. Others note that in Egyptian, *tot* or *otat* denotes the brain, where the head Tefillin are placed (Abarbanel).

13:17 Philistine Highway. Literally, "Way of the land of the Philistines." Josephus refers to this as the "Palestine Highway" (*Antiquities* 2:15:3). This is the usual route to Egypt, along the Mediterranean coast through Philistine territory (cf. Herodotus 3:5). There was an ancient enmity between the Israelites and the Philistines (*Targum Yonathan; Mekhilta;* Rashi; Josephus 2:15:3). See Genesis 10:14, 21:32, 26:14; 1 Chronicles 7:21, *Targum ad loc.*

13:18 by way of the desert (*Targum;* Saadia; Rashi). Or, "by way of the Red Sea desert" (*Targum Yonathan;* Ibn Ezra).

— **Red Sea.** See note on 10:19 that this was most probably the Gulf of Suez. Literally, however, *Yom Suf* is the Sea of Reeds (Rashi), and not necessarily identified with the Red Sea. Some sources seem to indicate that it was at the mouth of the Nile (*Sotah* 12a, Rabbi Yoshia Pinto [Riph in *Eyn Yaakov*] *ad loc.; Sh'moth Rabbah* 1:21; Radak on *Pirkey Rabbi Eliezer* 48:41). The "Sea of Reeds" would then be Lake Manzaleh at the eastern mouth of the Nile. This would also agree with the opinion that "Freedom Valley," the site of the crossing, was Tanis (see note on 14:2), a city just off Lake Manzaleh. Others maintain that the crossing occurred at Lake Sirbonis (see Avraham Corman, *Yetziath Mitzraim U'Mattan Torah*, p. 334).

    Significantly, in ancient Egyptian, *Sufi* or *Thufi* is the word for the swampy districts of the Delta. However, there was also an area known as Sau, which was a district west of the Red Sea (cf. Ibn Ezra here).

— **well prepared.** Or "provisioned" (Ibn Ezra; see Genesis 41:34). Or, "with eagerness" or "with enthusiasm" (*Targum; Mekhilta*); "well armed" (*Mekhilta;* Rashi; Rashbam; Ramban; but see Josephus 2:15:3); or "the fifth generation" (*Midrash HaGadol;* Septuagint; see Genesis 15:16); "in five groups" (*Targum Yonathan*); or "one out of five" (*Mekhilta;* Rashi; cf. Demetrius in Eusbius, *Prepatoria Evengelica* 9:29).

13:19 God will grant you. See Genesis 50:25.

13:20 Sukkoth. See above, 12:37.

— **Etham.** See Numbers 33:6,7. In Numbers 33:8, we see that after crossing the Red Sea, the Israelites were again in Etham. If we say that the "Red Sea" is the Gulf of Suez, this would indicate that Etham was to the north-east of the gulf. The Israelites went into this area, and then turned back (see 14:1) and went along the west coast of the gulf, crossing the sea back to Etham. Some identify Etham with the Shur Desert (Ibn Ezra; see 15:22). Significantly, in ancient Egyptian, *etam* means "seashore." Some identify Etham with the Egyptian *Chetem*, which denotes a fortress. There was a Chetem near Pelusium, just west of Lake Sirbonis.

²¹ God went before them by day with a pillar of cloud, to guide them **13** along the way. By night it appeared as a pillar of fire, providing them with light. They could thus travel day and night. ²² The pillar of cloud by day and the pillar of fire at night never left [their position] in front of the people.

[39. Egypt Pursues]

¹ God spoke to Moses, saying, ² "Speak to the Israelites and tell them to **14** turn back and camp before Freedom Valley,* between Tower* and the sea, facing Lord-of-the-North.* Camp opposite it, near the sea. ³ Pharaoh will then say that the Israelites are lost in the area and trapped in the desert. ⁴ I will harden Pharaoh's heart and he will come after them. I will triumph* over Pharaoh and his entire army, and Egypt will know that I am God."

[The Israelites] did as [they had been instructed].

⁵ Meanwhile, the king of Egypt received the news that the people were escaping. Pharaoh and his officials changed their minds regarding the people, and said, "What have we done? How could we have released Israel from doing our work?"

⁶ [Pharaoh] harnessed* his chariot, and summoned his people to go with him. ⁷ He took 600 chariots with chosen crews, as well as* the entire chariot

---

14:2 **Freedom Valley.** (Rashi). *Pi HaChiroth* in Hebrew. See 14:9; Numbers 33:7,9. Literally, "The mouth of freedom," possibly "Freedom Bay." The Hebrew *Pi* can also denote the mouth of a river (cf. Isaiah 19:7). Talmudic sources identify Pi HaChiroth with Pithom (*Mekhilta*), which is said to be on the site of Tanis (*Targum Yonathan;* see 1:11). This would indicate that the crossing was along the Mediterranean, possibly at Lake Manzaleh or Lake Sirbonis (see 13:18). Pi HaChiruth would then be a delta tributary of the Nile. Indeed there is a town Per Chet Cher mentioned in ancient texts as being near Tanis. Per Cheru was also the name of a canal and a generic name for the temples of Horus. Another town in the delta was Per Ari.

Some say that Pi HaChiruth was the mouth of Suez (Abarbanel). Other sources indicate that it was a narrow valley where the Israelites were completely boxed in (*Mekhilta; Sekhel Tov*), or a narrow beach between cliffs and the sea (Josephus 2:15:3).

— **Tower.** *Migdal* in Hebrew. See Jeremiah 44:1, 46:14, Ezekiel 29:10, 30:6.

— **Lord of the North.** *Baal Tzafon* in Hebrew. According to Talmudic sources, this was a huge idol (*Mekhilta;* Rashi; Ibn Ezra). Some say that this was to the south of Egypt, along the Red Sea (Josephus 2:15:1; *MeAm Lo'ez/The Torah Anthology* 5:166). Egyptian sources from the Hellenistic period speak of the *Megdal pef Bla Tzapnu* (Cairo Papyrus 31169), which is identified as Jebu al Chasan, some 8 miles north of Suez. (This would indicate that the crossing was near the Bitter Lakes, where the Gulf of Suez was thought to have extended in ancient times). It may have been called Lord-of-the-North because it was at the northern end of the Suez Gulf.

Those who favor a northern crossing, identify Tzafon with Dafne or Tachpanchas (Jeremiah 2:16, 43:7, Ezekiel 30:18), near Pelusium and Lake Serbonis. Others identify it as the sanctuary of Zeus Casius, a small hill on the western extremity of Lake Serbonis, known as Machmudiyya. Still others say that it is Rus Kasrun near the Serbonic Lake, the site of the Hellenistic-Roman city of Casius.

14:4 **triumph.** Literally, "I will be glorified."

14:6 **harnessed** (*Mekhilta;* Rashi). Or, "had [someone] harness" (Ibn Ezra).

— **as well as** (Rashi).

— **infantry** (*Mekhilta;* see below, 14:9). Others, "third-ranked officers (*Targum;* Ibn Ezra); "a third horse" (besides the regular two; *Targum Yonathan*). Josephus writes that besides the 600 war chariots, there were 50,000 horsemen, and 200,000 foot soldiers (*Antiquities* 2:15:3).

14   corps of Egypt, with supporting infantry* for them all. [8] God hardened the
      heart of Pharaoh, king of Egypt, and he went after the Israelites. Meanwhile,
      the Israelites were leaving in triumph.*

      [9] Setting out after [the Israelites], the Egyptians overtook them while they
      were camping by the sea, at Freedom Valley, opposite Lord-of-the-North.
      All of Pharaoh's chariot horses, cavalry and infantry were there. [10] As Pharaoh
      came close, the Israelites looked up. They saw the Egyptians marching at their
      rear, and the people became very frightened.

      The Israelites cried out to God. [11] They said to Moses, "Weren't there
      enough graves in Egypt? Why did you have to bring us out here to die in the
      desert? How could you do such a thing to us, bringing us out of Egypt?
      [12] Didn't we tell you in Egypt to leave us alone and let us work for the Egyp-
      tians? It would have been better to be slaves in Egypt than to die [here] in the
      desert!"

      [13] "Don't be afraid," replied Moses to the people. "Stand firm and you
      will see what God will do to rescue you today. You might be seeing the Egyp-
      tians today, but you will never see them again. [14] God will fight for you, but
      you must remain silent.*"

                              [40. Crossing the Sea]

      [15] God said to Moses, "Why are you crying out to Me? Speak to the Israel-
      ites, and let them start moving. [16] Raise your staff and extend your hand over
      the sea. You will split the sea, and the Israelites will be able to cross over on
      dry land.

      [17] "I will harden the hearts of the Egyptians, and they will follow you.
      Thus I will triumph over Pharaoh and his entire army, his chariot corps and
      his cavalry. [18] When I have this triumph over Pharaoh, his chariot corps and
      cavalry, Egypt will know that I am God."

      [19] God's angel had been traveling in front of the Israelite camp, but now it
      moved and went behind them. The pillar of cloud thus moved from in front
      of them and stood at their rear. [20] It came between the Egyptian and the
      Israelite camps. There was cloud and darkness that night, blocking out all
      visibility.* All that night [the Egyptians and Israelites] could not approach one
      another.

      [21] Moses extended his hand over the sea. During the entire night, God
      drove back the sea with a powerful east wind, transforming the sea bed into

---

14:8   triumph. Literally, "with a high hand" (cf. *Targum*).
14:14 but you must . . . (Ibn Ezra).
14:20 blocking out all visibility (*Sekhel Tov;* Saadia; Ibn Janach; Rosh, *Hadar Zekenim;* Septuagint; *Pesachim* 2a;
       cf. Ibn Ezra). Or, "[and the pillar of fire] illuminated the night" (Rashbam; Ibn Ezra).

dry land. The waters were divided. ²² The Israelites entered the sea bed on dry 14
land. The water was on their right and left like [two] walls.*

²³ The Egyptians gave chase and came after [the Israelites]. All of
Pharaoh's horses, chariot corps and cavalry went into the middle of the sea.
²⁴ Toward the end of the night* God struck* at the Egyptian army* with the
pillar of fire and cloud. He panicked the Egyptian army. ²⁵ The chariot wheels
became bogged down,* and they could move only with great difficulty. The
Egyptians cried out, "Let us flee from Israel! God is fighting for them against
Egypt!"

[41. The Egyptians' Downfall]

²⁶ God said to Moses, "Extend your hand over the sea. The waters will
come back over the Egyptians, covering their chariot corps and cavalry."

²⁷ Just before morning, Moses extended his hand over the sea, and the sea
returned to its normal condition. The Egyptians were fleeing [the water],* but
God swamped the Egyptians in the middle of the sea. ²⁸ The waters came back
and covered the cavalry and chariots. Of all Pharaoh's army that had followed
[the Israelites] into the sea, not a single one remained.

²⁹ Meanwhile,* the Israelites were walking in the midst of the sea on dry
land. The water was on their right and on their left like [two] walls.

³⁰ Thus, on that day, God rescued the Israelites from Egypt. The Israelites
saw the Egyptians dead on the seashore. ³¹ The Israelites saw the great power*
that God had unleashed against Egypt, and the people were in awe of God.
They believed in God and in his servant Moses.

[42. The Song]

¹ Moses and the Israelites then sang this song* to God. It went: 15

14:22 **like two walls.** Here we clearly see that it was not merely a low tide. The place of the crossing was
apparently known in Talmudical times, since there is a special blessing said when one sees it (*Berakhoth*
54a; cf. *Nesiath Rabbi Ovadiah MeBertenoro* 3)

14:24 **toward the end of the night.** Literally, "the morning watch." This is the last third of the night, around 2
a.m. (Rashi; cf. *Berakhoth* 3a). Others say that it was around the first dawn or sunrise (*Mekhilta*; HaGra *ad
loc.*)

— **struck** (Radak, *Sherashim*; Genesis 41:6). Or "gazed at" (Rashi). This is the thunder, lightning and rain
that struck the Egyptians (Psalms 77:18,19; *Targum Yonathan; Mekhilta; Yerushalmi, Sotah* 8:3; Rashbam;
Josephus 2:16:3).

— **army.** Or, "camp."

14:25 **bogged down** (Septuagint; from root *asar;* cf. Ecclesiastes 4:14). Or, "they tried to turn the chariots'
wheels" (Rashbam; Ibn Ezra; Chizzkuni); or "[God] made the chariot wheels fall off" (*Targum;* Rashi).

14:27 **fleeing.** (Septuagint) Or, literally, "fleeing toward [the water in confusion]" (*Shemoth Rabbah;* Rashi).

14:29 **Meanwhile** (Ibn Ezra). Or, "But the Israelites" (Rashbam).

14:31 **power.** Literally, "hand."

15:1 **this song.** This song is part of the daily liturgy.

15   I will sing to God for His great victory,*
Horse and rider He threw in the sea.
² My strength and song is God*
And this is my deliverance;
This is my God, I will enshrine Him*
My father's God, I will exalt Him.
³ God is the Master of* war,
God is His name.
⁴ Pharaoh's chariots and army
He cast in the sea;
His very best officers
Were drowned in the Red Sea.
⁵ The depths covered them;
They sank to the bottom
Like a stone.
⁶ Your right Hand, O God
Is awesome in power;
Your right Hand, O God
crushes the foe.
⁷ In Your great Majesty
You broke Your opponents;
You sent forth Your wrath
It devoured them like straw.
⁸ At the blast of Your Nostrils
the waters towered.
Flowing water stood like a wall.
The depths congealed
In the heart of the sea.
⁹ The enemy said, "I will give chase;
I will overtake, divide the spoils,
I will satisfy myself.
I will draw my sword;
My hand will demolish them."

—   **His great victory** (cf. Rashbam). Or, "He has triumphed over the proud (*Targum;* Rashi); or "He has shown His pride" (Ibn Ezra).

15:2   **My strength** . . . (*Targum;* Ibn Ezra; Radak, *Sherashim*). Or, "God's strength and cutting power was my deliverance" (Rashi).

—   **I will enshrine Him** (*Targum;* Radak, *Sherashim*). Or, "I will glorify Him" (Rashi; Rashbam; cf. *Shabbath* 133b), or, "I will try to emulate Him" (*Shabbath* 133b).

15:3   **master** (Rashi). Literally, "man."

¹⁰ You made Your wind blow;
The sea covered them.
They sank like lead
In the mighty waters.*
¹¹ Who is like You among powers, God?
Who is like You, majestic in holiness,
Awesome in praise, doing wonders?
¹² You put forth Your right Hand;
The earth swallowed them.
¹³ With love, You led
the people You redeemed;
With might, You led [them]
to Your holy shrine.
¹⁴ Nations heard and shuddered;
Terror gripped those who dwell in Philistia.
¹⁵ Edom's chiefs* then panicked;
Moab's heroes were seized with trembling;
Canaan's residents melted away.
¹⁶ Fear and dread fell upon them.
At the greatness of Your Arm
They are still as stone.
Until Your people crossed, O God,
Until the people You gained crossed over.
¹⁷ O bring them and plant them
On the mount You possess.
The place You dwell in
Is Your accomplishment, God.
The shrine of God
Your Hands have founded.
¹⁸ God will reign forever and ever.

¹⁹ [This song was sung] when* Pharaoh's horse came into the sea, along

---

15:10 **mighty waters.** Or, "the mighty sank like lead in the waters" (cf. *Menachoth* 53a).
15:15 **chiefs.** See Genesis 36:15.
15:19 **This song was sung** . . . Many authorities maintain that this verse is not part of the song (Ramban; Abudarham, p. 63; cf. *Zohar* 3:168a). Others, however, maintain that it is an integral part of the song (*Midrash HaGadol*; Ibn Ezra). It would then be translated, "For Pharaoh's horse came. . ." (cf. Saadia; Rashi, *Gittin* 90a s.v. *Ki*).

15   with his chariot corps and cavalry, and God made the sea come back on them. The Israelites had walked on dry land in the midst of the sea.

[43. Miriam's Song]

²⁰ Miriam* the prophetess, Aaron's sister, took the drum* in her hand, and all the women followed her with drums and dancing.* ²¹ Miriam led them in the response, "Sing to God for His great victory, horse and rider He cast in the sea.*"

[44. The Bitter Waters]

²² Moses led the Israelites away from the Red Sea, and they went out into the Shur Desert.* They traveled for three days in the desert without finding any water. ²³ Finally they came to Marah,* but they could not drink any water there. The water was bitter (*marah*), and that was why the place was called Marah. ²⁴ The people complained to Moses. "What shall we drink?" they demanded.

²⁵ When [Moses] cried out to God, He showed him a certain tree.* [Moses] threw it into the water, and the water became drinkable.

It was there that [God] taught them survival techniques and methods,* and there He tested them. ²⁶ He said, "If you obey God your Lord and do what is upright in His eyes, carefully heeding all His commandments and keeping all His decrees, then I will not strike you with any of the sicknesses that I brought on Egypt. I am God who heals you."

15:20 **Miriam.** The first mention of her name. See 2:4.
— **drum.** *Tof* in Hebrew; see Genesis 31:27. The word is thought to denote a small flat hand drum. See *Kanim* 3:6.
— **dancing.** (*Targum;* Septuagint). Others say that the *mechol* mentioned here is a musical instrument (*Mekhilta; Pirkey Rabbi Eliezer* 42; Radak *ad loc.* 42:68). This is described as somewhat larger than a *tof* and played with sticks (Saadia Gaon). Others maintain that it is a percussion instrument somewhat like a tambourine.

Machol

15:21 **Sing to God. . .** See 15:1. Some say that they sang the entire song (Saadia; *Chizzkuni*), and that they sang it along with the men (Philo, *De Vida Musa;* cf. *Mekhilta*).
15:22 **Shur Desert.** See Genesis 16:7, 20:1, 25:18. (cf. *Targum; Targum Yonathan*). Josephus identifies this with the Pelusian Desert (*Antiquities* 6:7:3). Saadia, on the other hand identifies it with Jifur, an old name for Es Sur, south-west of the desert of Et-tih (Etham?) near Egypt. A number of sources identify Shur with Etham mentioned above (13:20; see Numbers 33:8; Ibn Ezra; Bachya).
     Along the eastern shore of the Gulf of Suez, there is a strip of level land. The northern part of this is known as Shur, extending toward the Mediterranean, while the southern part is the Sin Desert (16:1). Local traditions identify the first stop with Ayun Musa (the Springs of Moses), on the east side of the Gulf, 9 miles south of Suez and 1.5 miles from the coast.
15:23 **Marah.** See Numbers 33:8. This is usually identified with Bir Huwara or Eyn Chawara, some 60 miles south of Suez, and 47 miles south of Ayun Musa, 7 miles from the coast. Others identify Marah with Ain Naba (also known as el-Churkudeh), a fountain with a large flow of brackish water, some 10 miles south-east of Suez.
15:25 **tree.** Or a piece of wood (Josephus 2:3:2). It is said to be fig, pomegranate, or oleander (*Mekhilta; MeAm Lo'ez*). Josephus writes that they also purged the well by pouring out large amounts of water from it.
— **survival techniques** . . . (Ramban; *Tur*). Or, "a decree and a law" (*Mekhilta;* Rashi).

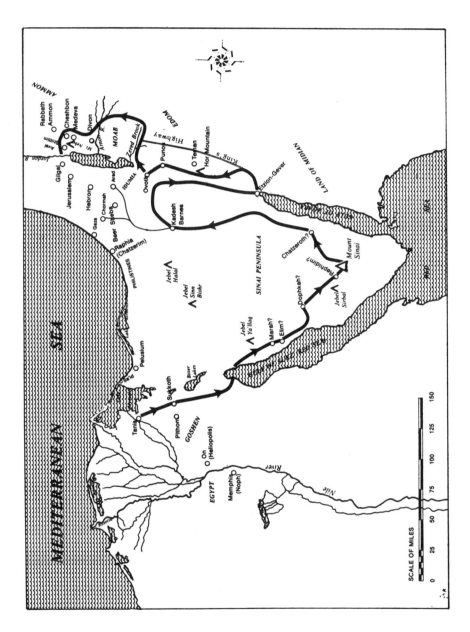

PLATE 13. THE EXODUS

15   *[45. Elim and Sin]*

[27] Then they came to Elim.* Here there were twelve springs of water and seventy date palms. They [then] camped by the water.*

16   [1] They moved on from Elim, and the entire community of Israel came to the Sin Desert,* between Elim and Sinai. It was the 15th of the second month* after they had left Egypt.

[2] There in the desert, the entire Israelite community began to complain against Moses and Aaron. [3] The Israelites said to them, "If only we had died by God's hand in Egypt! There at least we could sit by pots of meat and eat our fill of bread! But you had to bring us out to this desert, to kill the entire community by starvation!"

[46. Promise of Food]

[4] God said to Moses, "I will make bread rain down to you from the sky. The people will go out and gather enough for each day. I will test them to see whether or not they will keep My law. [5] On Friday,* they will have to prepare* what they bring home. It will be twice as much as they gather every other day."

[6] Moses and Aaron said to the Israelites, "When evening comes, you will know that it was God who took you out of Egypt; [7] and in the morning, you will see God's glory. He has heard your complaints, which are against God. After all, what are we that you should complain against us?"

[8] Moses said, "In the evening, God will give you meat to eat, and in the morning, there will be enough bread to fill you up. God has heard your complaints, which you are actually addressing against Him. What are we? Your complaints are not against us, but against God!"

[9] Moses said to Aaron, "Tell the entire Israelite community to gather before God,* for He has heard your complaints."

15:27 **Elim.** See Numbers 33:9. Possibly, "Place of Terebinths." This is usually identified with Wadi Gharandel, the next oasis on this route, some 10 miles south of Marah. In medieval times, there was a city in this area known as Ailom (*Mas'aoth Rabbi Binyamin* 24). Some say that this was a very good resting place (*Mekhilta*), while according to others, the trees and wells were insufficient for the huge number of people (Josephus 3:1:3).

—   **by the water.** Possibly along the Red Sea; cf. Numbers 33:10.

16:1   **Sin Desert.** See note on 15:22; Numbers 11:33; Ezekiel 30:15,16. This is the plain along the edge of the Sinai plateau called Debbet er-Ramleh.

—   **the 15th** . . . This was 30 days after the Exodus (see 12:6). Some say that this occurred in Alush (Numbers 33:13; *Seder Olam Rabbah* 5; Ramban). See note on 17:1.

16:5   **Friday.** Literally, "the sixth day." There are no day names in Hebrew.

—   **they will have to prepare** . . . Since food cannot be prepared on the Sabbath; see below, 16:23 (cf. *Betza* 2b; *Pesachim* 74b).

16:9   **gather before God.** See below, 16:33.

[10] When Aaron spoke to the entire Israelite community, they turned **16** toward the desert. God's glory was visible in the clouds.

[47. The Manna]

[11] God spoke to Moses, saying [12] "I have heard the complaints of the Israelites. Speak to them and say, 'In the afternoon you will eat meat, and in the morning, you will have your fill of bread. You will then know that I am God your Lord.'"

[13] That evening, a flock of quail* came and covered the camp. Then in the morning, there was a layer of dew around the camp. [14] When the layer of dew evaporated, there were little grains* all over the surface of the desert. It looked like fine frost* on the ground.

[15] The Israelites looked at it, and had no idea what it was. "What is it*?" they asked one another.

Moses said to them, "This is the bread that God is giving you to eat. [16] God's instructions are that each man shall take as much as he needs. There shall be an omer* for each person, according to the number of people each man has in his tent."

[17] When the Israelites went to do this, some gathered more and some less. [18] But when they measured it with an omer, the one who had taken more did not have any extra, and the one who had taken less did not have too little. They had gathered exactly enough for each one to eat.

[19] Moses announced to them, "Let no man leave any over until morning."

16:13 **quail** (Septuagint). Cf. Numbers 11:31,32, Psalms 105:40. The *s'lav* here is usually identified with *Teturnix Xeturnix,* the smallest member of the quail family, which is particularly abundant in the Red Sea area during the migratory season. They come up in immense numbers from Arabia and the other countries. Unlike the manna, the quails were only available this one time (Abarbanel).

Quail

16:14 **grains.** *Mechuspas* in Hebrew. Or, "small round balls" (Ibn Ezra; Saadia; Ibn Janach; Radak, *Sherashim*); see 16:31 (Sforno; Septuagint). Others, "like hailstones" (Rashbam; *gresle* in French); "flakes" (*Targum;* Ramban); "a sandwich" (Rashi); or "something sticky" (*Yoma* 75b; Josephus 3:1:6).

— **fine frost.** Or fine chalky frost (*Targum;* Rashi). Cf. Psalms 147:16, Job 38:29.

16:15 **What is it?** *Man hu* in Hebrew, which can also be translated, "it is *man,*" or "it is manna" (see 16:31). The word *man* here is taken to be a form of *mah* meaning what (*Targum; Mekhilta;* Ibn Janach s.v. *Min;* Josephus 3:1:6). Some say that it is an Egyptian expression (Rashbam; Ibn Ezra; *Lekach Tov*). Actually, in ancient Egyptian, "what is this" would be *ma nu,* which would sound like *man hu.*

According to others the word *man* here means food (Rashi; Saadia; Ibn Ezra; Ibn Janach; cf. *Sukkah* 39b), possibly from the Egyptian (*Sekhel Tov*). The verse would then be translated, "They did not know what it was, but when Moses said . . . they said, 'It is food!'" Others say that *man* is a gift, from the root *manah* (Radak, *Sherashim*).

In ancient Egyptian, the word *man* can mean a gift, something coming from the sky, or so . . . *thing* coming every day. Significantly *mem* or *man* also denotes coriander (see 16:31).

16:16 **omer.** A measure equal to around 2 quarts.

16   **20** Some men did not listen to Moses and left a portion over for the morning. It became putrid and maggoty with worms. Moses was angry with [these people].

21 [The people] gathered it each morning, according to what each person would eat. Then, when the sun became hot, it melted.

22 When Friday came, what they gathered turned out to be* a double portion of food, two omers for each person. All the leaders* of the community came and reported it to Moses.

23 [Moses] said to them, "This is what God has said: Tomorrow is a day of rest, God's holy Sabbath. Bake what you want to bake, and cook what you want to cook [today].* Whatever you have left over, put aside carefully until morning."

24 They put it way until [Saturday] morning, as Moses had instructed. It was not putrid, and there were no maggots in it.

25 Moses announced, "Eat it today, for today is God's Sabbath. You will not find [anything] in the field today. **26** You are to gather [this food] during the six weekdays, but the seventh day is the Sabbath, and on that [day] there will not be any."

27 Still, some people went out to gather [food] on Saturday,* but they found nothing.

[48. The Sabbath]

28 God told Moses [to say to the Israelites],* "How long will you refuse to keep My commandments and My law? **29** You must realize that God has given you the Sabbath, and that is why I gave you food for two days on Friday. [On the Sabbath] every person must remain in his designated place.* One may not leave his home [to gather food]* on Saturday."

30 The people rested on Saturday.* **31** The family of Israel* called [the food]

16:22 **turned out to be.** (*Mekhilta;* Rashi).

— **leaders.** These were apparently the leaders of the tribes; see 35:27; Numbers 1:44, 2:3 ff.

16:23 **Bake what you want . . .** Since cooking is forbidden on the Sabbath (Rashi; Ramban; see 16:5).

16:27 **Saturday.** Literally, "the seventh day."

16:28 **to say . . .** (Ibn Ezra).

16:29 **designated place.** This indicates that it was forbidden to leave the environs of the camp and go more than 2000 cubits away from it (Cf. *Eruvin* 48a; *Yerushalmi, Eruvin* 1:10; *Mekhilta* on 21:13).

— **to gather food** (Ibn Ezra; cf. *Targum Yonathan*). This is because carrying outdoors is considered a violation of the Sabbath (*Eruvin* 17b; cf. Numbers 15:32 f).

16:30 **rested on Saturday.** This was the first Sabbath. It is from the manna that the Sabbath of creation became known.

16:31 **family of Israel.** Or, literally, "the house of Israel." Some say that this designates the women (Hirsch; *Targum Yonathan, Mekhilta,* Rashi, on 19:3).

manna.* It looked like coriander* seed, [except that it was] white.* It tasted **16**
like a honey doughnut.*

³² Moses said, "This is what God has commanded: Fill an omer measure
with [the manna] as a keepsake for your descendants. They will then see the
food that I fed you in the desert when I brought you out of Egypt."

³³ Moses said to Aaron, "Take an urn* and fill it with an omer of manna.
Place it before God* as a keepsake for your descendants."

³⁴ As God commanded Moses, Aaron [later]* placed it before the [Ark of]
Testimony* as a keepsake. ³⁵ The Israelites were to eat the manna for 40
years,* until they came to inhabited territory. They ate the manna until they
came to the edge of the land of Canaan.*

³⁶ An omer is a tenth of an ephah.*

[49. Water from the Rock]

¹ The entire Israelite community moved on from the Sin Desert, traveling **17**
according to God's instructions* until they camped in Rephidim.* There was

---

—   **manna.** *Man* in Hebrew. See note on 16:15.

—   **coriander** (Rashi; Saadia; Ibn Janach; Ibn Ezra). Coriander is an old world herb,
Coriandrum sativum of the carrot family. Its aromatic black seeds are used for season-
ing. Others translate *gad* here to denote mustard seed (Ibn Ezra; cf. *Sekhel Tov*).

—   **except that . . .** (Rashi; *Mekhilta; Radak, Sherashim*). It looked like mother of pearl
(*Yoma* 75a). See Numbers 11:7.

—   **doughnut** (*Me'am Loez, Bilmuelos* in Ladino) or pancake (Saadia; Ibn Janach;
Abarbanel). Talmudic sources state that *tzefichath* was made from a poured batter
rather than a dough (*Makhshirin* 5:9, Rashi, Bertenoro *ad loc.*; Rash on *Challah* 1:4;
Sekhel Tov). Others, "like dough prepared with honey" (Rashi), or "honey wafers"
(Saadia; Ibn Ezra; Septuagint). From other sources, however, it appears that
tzefichath denotes a honeycomb (Rashi, *Sotah* 48b, s.v. *Ha-tzefichath; Shabbath* 43b, **Coriander**
Betza 36a, s.v. *Sh'tey Challoth*). See *Wisdom of Solomon* 15:20,21.

16:33   **urn.** A large clay jar (*Mekhilta; Targum Yonathan;* Rashi). According to others, the word *tzintzeneth* denotes
a glass jar, so that the manna could be seen (Rabbenu Chananel; Abarbanel; HaGra on *Mekhilta;
Minchah Belulah*). It might also have been a gold vessel (one possible translation of the *Septuagint*). In
Egyptian, *tzenat* is a vase, and *snu* is a jar, while *serbet* is a vessel of silver-gold alloy. *Sen* is a kind of
precious stone.

—   **before God.** After the Tabernacle would be erected (*Mekhilta;* Rashi). But see above, 16:9.

16:34   **later.** When the Tabernacle was made (see previous note).

—   **Ark of Testimony** (Rashi; see 25:10).

16:35   **40 years.** See Numbers 14:33.

—   **edge of land of Canaan.** Joshua 5:12.

16:36   **ephah.** A measure, equal to 5 gallons or 22 liters.

17:1   **traveling . . .** Some say that this alludes to the stops in Dophkah and Alush, mentioned in Numbers
33:12,13 (Ibn Ezra; cf. Ramban).

—   **Rephidim.** This is usually thought to be Wadi Refayad, some 10 miles west of Mount Sinai (Jebal Musa)
(cf. Ramban on 17:5). It is a day's journey from Sinai, and 2 days from Elim (*Masa'oth Rabbi Binyamin* 24).
Others say that it is the upper part of the oasis of Feiran, the broad long oasis that is the most fertile part
of Sinai, or alternatively, the narrow defile, el-Watiya, 27 miles beyond Feiran.

17   no water for the people to drink. ² The people began to quarrel with Moses. "Give us water to drink!" they exclaimed.

"Why are you quarreling with me?" asked Moses. "Are you trying to test God?"

³ The people began to suffer thirst because [of the lack] of water, and they began demonstrating against Moses. "Why did you bring us out of Egypt?" demanded [the leader]. "Do you want to make me, my children and my livestock die of thirst?"

⁴ Moses cried out to God. "What shall I do for this people?" he said. "Before long they will stone me!"

⁵ God said to Moses, "March in front of the people* along with the elders of Israel. Take in your hand the staff with which you struck the Nile, and go. ⁶ I will stand before you there on the rock at Horeb.* You must strike the rock, and water will come out of it for the people to drink." Moses did this in the presence of the elders of Israel.

⁷ [Moses] named the place Testing-and-Argument* because the people had argued and had tested God. They had asked, "Is God with us or not?"

[50. Amalek]

⁸ Amalek* arrived and attacked Israel there in Rephidim. ⁹ Moses said to Joshua,* "Choose men for us, and prepare for battle against Amalek. Tomorrow, I will stand on top of the hill with the staff of God in my hand."

¹⁰ Joshua did as Moses had told him, engaging Amalek in battle. Moses, Aaron and Chur* went up to the top of the hill. ¹¹ As long as Moses held his hands up, Israel would be winning, but as soon as he let his hands down, the

---

17:5   **march in front** . . . (Rashi; Sforno). Or "go ahead of the people" (Ramban; see Genesis 18:5, 32:17, 33:3).

17:6   **Horeb.** See 3:1. Apparently, Horeb was in the Horeb section. This was apparently a large boulder sitting in the desert, that was known in later times (cf. Josephus 3:1:7).

17:7   **Testing-and-Argument.** *Massa U'Merivah* in Hebrew. See Deuteronomy 6:16, 9:22, 33:8, Psalms 95:8.

17:8   **Amalek.** A tribe descended from Esau, see Genesis 36:12. Amalek came from around Gobolitis and Petra, to the north of Sinai (Josephus 3:2:1). See Numbers 24:20.

17:9   **Joshua.** Joshua was a grandson of Elishama son of Amihud, the prince of the tribe of Ephraim (1 Chronicles 7:27; Numbers 1:10). Since the Ephraimites were direct descendants of Joseph, they were never enslaved (*Sifethey Cohen* on Exodus 14:3). The Ephraimites retained a strong militaristic tradition (1 Chronicles 7:21; *Targum Yonathan* on 3:17; *Pirkey* Rabbi Eliezer 48), and Joshua's father Nun or Non was an important general (*Yalkut Shimoni* on Chronicles 1177). Joshua was Moses' assistant even in Egypt (cf. *Sh'moth Rabbah* 19:5), and it was at that time that Moses changed his name from Hoshea to Joshua (Numbers 13:16, Rashbam *ad loc.*; Ramban here).

17:10   **Chur.** Or *Hur.* He was an important leader with Aaron (24:14) of the tribe of Judah (31:2). His genealogy was Judah, Peretz, Chetzron, Caleb, Chur (1 Chronicles 2:18,19; cf. Genesis 46:12). According to tradition, the Ephrath in 1 Chronicles 2:19 who was Caleb's wife was Miriam, and therefore, Chur was Miriam's son (Rashi; *Sh'moth Rabbah* 40:4; *Targum* on 1 Chronicles 2:19). Others say that Chur was Miriam's husband (Josephus 3:2:4). Talmudic tradition states that Chur was killed when he tried to prevent the worship of the Golden Calf (*Sanhedrin* 7a; *Targum Yonathan*, Rashi, on Exodus 32:5).

battle would go in Amalek's favor. ¹² When Moses' hands became weary, they   17
took a stone and placed it under him, so that he would be able to sit on it.
Aaron and Chur then held his hands, one on each side, and his hands
remained steady until sunset. ¹³ Joshua was thus able to break the ranks* of
Amalek and his allies* with the sword.

[51. Divine Vengeance]

¹⁴ God said to Moses, "Write this as a reminder in the Book* and repeat it
carefully* to Joshua. I will totally obliterate the memory of Amalek from
under the heavens.*"
¹⁵ Moses built an altar, and he named it God-is-my-Banner.* ¹⁶ He said,
"The Hand is on God's Throne.* God shall be at war with Amalek for all
generations."

Yithro   יִתְרוֹ

[52. Jethro's Advice]

¹ Moses' father-in-law, Jethro,* sheik of Midian, heard about all that God   18
had done for Moses and His people Israel when He brought Israel out of
Egypt. ² Jethro* brought along Moses' wife, Tzipporah,* who had been sent
home earlier,* ³ and her two sons. The name of the [first] one was Gershom,
because [Moses] had declared, "I was a foreigner (ger) in a strange land.*"
⁴ The name of the [other] one was Eliezer, because, "My father's God (El) was
my Helper (ezer), rescuing me from Pharaoh's sword.*"

17:13 **break the ranks** (*Targum Yonathan;* Ibn Janach). Or, literally, "weaken."
— **allies.** Amalek had allied with other nations to attack the Israelites (*Mekhilta;* Josephus 3:2:1).
17:14 **book.** The Torah. See 24:4,7, 34:27.
— **carefully.** Literally, "in his ears." See note on Genesis 20:8.
— **I will totally obliterate** . . . See Deuteronomy 25:19.
17:15 **God is my Banner.** (Rashbam). *Adonoy Nissi* in Hebrew. Or, "God is my Miracle" (Targum; Rashi); or,
"God has raised me up" (Saadia Gaon).
17:16 **The Hand is on God's Throne.** This denotes a divine oath (*Targum; Mekhilta;* Rashi). Or, "When the
divine throne [of Israel] is established, then God shall be at war . . ." (*Mekhilta;* Rashbam; Ramban). Or,
"With a secret hand, God wages war . . ." (Septuagint).
18:1 **Jethro.** See notes on 2:18, 3:1. According to some authorities, Jethro was Moses' brother-in-law (Ibn
Ezra on Numbers 10:29).
  There is a question as to whether or not the Torah is in chronological order here. According to some,
Jethro came before the giving of the Ten Commandments, while according to others, he came afterward
(*Zevachim* 116a; Ramban).
18:2 **Jethro.** Actually, "Jethro, father-in-law of Moses." The same is true in 18:5 and 18:12, but for the sake
of simplicity, it is abbreviated.
— **Tzipporah.** See 2:21.
— **sent home earlier.** At Aaron's advice (*Mekhilta;* Rashi), soon after the episode of the circumcision (4:25).
18:3 **Gershom** . . . See 2:22.
18:4 **Eliezer** . . . See note on 4:20; 2:15.

18   ⁵ Jethro came together with [Moses'] wife and sons to the desert, where
Moses was staying, near God's mountain.* ⁶ He sent word to Moses: "I, your
father-in-law Jethro, am on my way to you, along with your wife. Her two
sons are with her."

⁷ Moses went out to greet his father-in-law, bowing down low and kissing
him. They asked about each other's welfare and went into the tent. ⁸ Moses
told his father-in-law about all that God had done to Pharaoh and Egypt for
the sake of Israel, as well as all the frustrations* they had encountered on the
way, and [how] God had rescued them.

⁹ Jethro expressed joy because of all the good that God had done for
Israel, rescuing them from Egypt's power. ¹⁰ He said, "Praised* be God, who
rescued you from the power of Egypt and Pharaoh—who liberated the people
from Egypt's power. ¹¹ Now I know that God is the greatest of all deities.
Through their very plots, He rose above them.*"

¹² Jethro brought burnt offerings* and [other] sacrifices to God. Aaron
and all the elders of Israel came to share the meal with Moses' father-in-law
before God.*

¹³ The next day,* Moses sat to judge the people. They stood around Moses
from morning to evening. ¹⁴ When Moses' father-in-law saw all that [Moses]
was doing for the people, he said, "What are you doing to the people? Why
are you sitting by yourself and letting all the people stand around you from
morning until evening?"

¹⁵ "The people come to me to seek God,*" replied Moses to his father-in-
law. ¹⁶ "Whenever they have a problem, they come to me. I judge between
man and his neighbor, and I teach God's decrees and laws."

¹⁷ Moses' father-in-law said to him, "What you are doing is not good.
¹⁸ You are going to wear yourself out, along with this nation that is with you.

18:5   **God's Mountain.** See 3:1 (Ibn Ezra; Abarbanel).

18:8   **frustrations** (Radak, *Sherashim*). *T'la'ah* in Hebrew. Or, "hardships."

18:10 **Praised.** Literally, "blessed."

18:11 **Through their very plots** . . . (*Targum;* Rashi; Septuagint). Literally, "Because in the thing that they
        plotted on them." Alternatively, "The very thing they plotted came on them" (Abarbanel); "Through
        their very plots, He amused Himself with them" (Rashbam, cf. 10:2); "I am aware of how the
        [Egyptians] plotted against [the Israelites" (Ramban; Chizzkuni). Or, "He saved the people from Egypt's
        power despite all their plots against them" (Ralbag).

18:12 **burnt offerings.** See note on Genesis 8:20.

—   **before God.** Aware of God's presence (Ralbag; Hirsch). Others say that "before God" denotes that they
        were in front of the altar Moses had built (17:15; Sforno; Abarbanel), the burning bush (Josephus 3:3),
        Mount Sinai (Ralbag), or Moses' tent (Ibn Ezra; *Sekhel Tov*). Or, "of what was offered before God"
        (Chizzkuni).

18:13 **the next day.** Simply, the day after Jethro had come (Ibn Ezra; Ramban; Josephus 3:4:1). There is how-
        ever, a tradition, that this was on the day after Yom Kippur, right after Moses came down with the
        second set of Tablets (*Mekhilta; Targum Yonathan;* Rashi; see below, 34:29, Deuteronomy 10:5).

18:15 **to seek God.** (Ibn Ezra). Or, "to learn God's will" (*Targum;* Rashi).

Your responsibility is too great. You cannot do it all alone. **18**

¹⁹ "Now listen to me. I will give you advice, and God will be with you. You must be God's representative for the people, and bring [their] concerns to God. ²⁰ Clarify* the decrees and laws for [the people]. Show them the path they must take, and the things they must do.

²¹ "But you must [also] seek out from among all the people capable,* God-fearing men—men of truth, who hate injustice.* You must then appoint them over [the people] as leaders of thousands, leaders of hundreds, leaders of fifties, and leaders of tens.*

²² "Let them administer justice for the people on a regular basis.* Of course, they will have to bring every major case to you, but they can judge the minor cases by themselves. They will then share the burden, making things easier for you. ²³ If you agree to this, and God concurs,* you will be able to survive. This entire nation will then also be able to attain its goal of peace.*"

²⁴ Moses took his father-in-law's advice, and did all that he said. ²⁵ He chose capable men from all Israel, and he appointed them as administrators over the people, leaders of thousands, leaders of hundreds, leaders of fifties, and leaders of tens. ²⁶ They administered justice on a regular basis, bringing the difficult cases to Moses, and judging the simple cases by themselves.

²⁷ Moses let his father-in-law depart, and he went away to his homeland.*

[53. The Ten Commandments]

¹ In the third month after the Israelites left Egypt, on the first of the month,* they came to the desert of Sinai.* ² They had departed from Rephi- **19**

18:20 **clarify** (Hirsch; cf. Saadia Gaon). Or, "warn" (Ibn Ezra).
18:21 **capable.** *Chayal* in Hebrew. See Genesis 47:6, 1 Kings 1:42, Proverbs 12:4, 31:10, Ruth 3:11. Or, "competent," or "resourceful" (Hirsch). Alternatively, "men with leadership qualities" (Ramban), "efficient men" (Ramban), "strong men" (Ibn Janach); "stronghearted" or "confident men" (*Tanchuma* 2; Ralbag); "men with initiative" (*Divrey Sh'lomo; MeAm Lo'ez*); "men of status" (Rashbam), or, "wealthy men" (*Mekhilta;* Rashi; *Sekhel Tov;* cf. Genesis 34:29, Isaiah 8:4, 30:6, Jeremiah 16:3). Or, "superior men," implying self-control, moral superiority and leadership (*Yad, Sanhedrin* 2:7).
— **injustice.** *Betza* in Hebrew. Cf. Ezekiel 22:12; Judges 5:19, Micah 4:13. Or, "robbery" (Ramban; Bachya; *MeAm Lo'ez*); "improper gain" (Rashbam), or "gain" (Rashi, Ibn Ezra). There is actually a Talmudic dispute regarding the last two explanations (*Kethuboth* 105b; *Mekhilta*).
— **leaders** . . . Cf. Deuteronomy 1:15.
18:22 **on a regular basis.** Literally, "at all times." Or, "on a permanent basis."
18:23 **concurs.** (*Mekhilta;* Rashi; Ibn Ezra; Ralbag). Or, "when God orders you [to judge them]" (Rashbam); or, "then God will be able to give you the commandments" (*Targum Yonathan; Sekhel Tov;* Abarbanel; *Div'rey Shalom;* Hirsch; Josephus 3:4:1).
— **its goal of peace** (Hirsch). Literally, "will be able to come to its place in peace." Or, "all the people will be able to go home in peace" (Rashbam; Ibn Ezra; *Sekhel Tov;* Ramban).
18:27 **and he went away** . . . See Numbers 10:29–32.
19:1 **first of the month** (*Shabbath* 86b; *Mekhilta; Targum Yonathan;* Rashi; cf. Ibn Ezra). Literally, "on that day." This was the first of the Hebrew month of Sivan, around June.

19 dim* and had arrived in the Sinai Desert, camping in the wilderness. Israel camped opposite the mountain.

³ Moses went up to God.* God called to him from the mountain and said, "This is what you must say to the family of Jacob* and tell the Israelites: ⁴ 'You saw what I did in Egypt, carrying you on eagles' wings and bringing you to Me. ⁵ Now if you obey Me and keep My covenant, you shall be My special treasure* among all nations, even though* all the world is Mine. ⁶ You will be a kingdom of priests and a holy nation to Me.' These are the words that you must relate to the Israelites."

⁷ Moses came [back] and summoned the elders of the people, conveying to them all that God had said. ⁸ All the people answered as one and said, "All that God has spoken, we will do."

Moses brought the people's reply back to God. ⁹ God said to Moses, "I will come to you in thick cloud, so that all the people will hear when I speak to you. They will then believe in you forever."

Moses told God the people's response [to that].* ¹⁰ God said to Moses, "Go to the people, and sanctify them today and tomorrow. Let them [even]* immerse* their clothing. ¹¹ They will then be ready for the third day,* for on the third day, God will descend* on Mount Sinai in the sight of all the people.

¹² "Set a boundary for the people around [the mountain], and tell them to be careful not to climb the mountain, or [even] to touch its edge. Anyone touching the mountain will be put to death. ¹³ You will not have to lay a hand on him,* for he will be stoned or cast down.* Neither man nor beast will be

---

—   **desert of Sinai.** This might have occurred before Jethro came; see 18:5. Alternatively, they may still have been in Rephidim, but since Jethro was coming from the east, he may have sent word to Moses when he arrived at "God's Mountain."

19:2 **Rephidim.** See 17:1,8.

19:3 **up to God.** Through meditation (Abarbanel. Cf. *Moreh Nevukhim* 1:10).

—   **family of Jacob.** See note on 16:31.

19:5 **special treasure.** (Rashi; Ibn Ezra; Septuagint). Cf. Ecclesiastes 2:8, 1 Chronicles 29:3. The word is often used to denote Israel's special status as a chosen people; Deuteronomy 7:6, 14:2, 26:18. Or "beloved" (*Targum*). Alternatively, "then you must belong to Me exclusively" (Hirsch).

—   **even though** (Ibn Ezra). Or, "because all the world is Mine" (cf. Rashbam); Or, "among all the nations that are on the face of the earth" (*Targum Yonathan*).

19:9 **the people's response . . .** (Rashi).

19:10 **even.** They must also immerse their bodies (*Mekhilta;* Ramban; Chizzkuni; cf. Leviticus 17:16). See 19:14. Along with circumcision (12:48), this was part of the conversion process through which the Israelites entered the covenant of the Torah (*Yevamoth* 46b).

—   **immerse.** In Torah law, "washing" always denotes immersion in a *mikvah* or other natural body of water (cf. 2 Kings 5:10,14).

19:11 **third day.** This was said on the 4th of Sivan, and the Commandments would be given on the 6th.

—   **descend.** Reveal Himself to people who are otherwise unworthy (cf. *Moreh Nevukhim* 1:10).

19:13 **You will not have to . . .** (*Targum Yonathan*). Or, "Do not touch him with your hand" (*Lekach Tov;* Rashbam; Ibn Ezra; Baaley Tosafoth). Or, "Let no hand touch [the mountain]" (*Mekhilta*).

—   **cast down.** (*Sanhedrin* 45a; Rashi; *MeAm Lo'ez;* cf. Malbim; Hirsch). Or, "he shall be stoned or shot [with an arrow]" (Rashbam; Ibn Ezra; Bachya; Abarbanel; cf. 2 Chronicles 26:15) or, "He will be stoned or

allowed to live. But when the trumpet* is sounded with a long blast, they will   **19** then be allowed to climb the mountain."

¹⁴ Moses went down from the mountain to the people. He sanctified them, and they immersed [themselves and] their clothing. ¹⁵ Moses said to the people, "Keep yourselves in readiness for three days. Do not come near a woman.*"

¹⁶ The third day arrived. There was thunder* and lightning in the morning, with a heavy cloud on the mountain, and an extremely loud blast of a ram's horn. The people in the camp trembled. ¹⁷ Moses led the people out of the camp toward the Divine Presence.* They stood transfixed at the foot of the mountain.

¹⁸ Mount Sinai was all in smoke because of the Presence that had come down on it. God was in the fire, and its smoke went up like the smoke of a lime kiln.* The entire mountain trembled violently. ¹⁹ There was the sound of a ram's horn, increasing in volume to a great degree. Moses spoke, and God replied with a Voice.

²⁰ God came down on Mount Sinai, to the peak of the mountain. He summoned Moses to the mountain peak, and Moses climbed up. ²¹ God said to Moses, "Go back down and warn* the people that they must not cross the boundary in order to see the Divine, because this will cause many to die. ²² The priests, who [usually] come near the Divine must also sanctify themselves, or else God will send destruction among them."

²³ Moses replied to God, "The people cannot climb Mount Sinai. You already warned them to set a boundary around the mountain and to declare it sacred."

²⁴ God said to him, "Go down. You can then come [back] up along with Aaron.* But the priests and the [other] people must not violate the boundary to go up to the Divine; if they do, He will send destruction among them."

²⁵ Moses went down to the people and conveyed this to them.

---

killed with lightning bolts" (*Targum Yonathan*). Others, "Let no man touch [the mountain] with his hand, for he must then be put to death by stoning [after being] thrown down" (*Mekhilta; Sanhedrin* 45a) See 21:31, Leviticus 4:23.

—   **trumpet.** *Yovel* in Hebrew. The ram's horn mentioned below 19:16 (Rashi; Ibn Ezra; *Targum*). See Joshua 6:5. Also see Leviticus 25:10.

19:15 Do not come near . . . Some say that the narrative continues with 24:1.

19:16 thunder. Or "noises." See 20:15. There was also a heavy rain and great winds (Judges 5:4, Psalms 68:9, 77:18; Josephus 3:5:2).

19:17 Divine Presence. (cf. *Targum; Mekhilta;* Rashi). Literally "God."

19:18 lime kiln. (Rashi). See Genesis 19:28.

19:21 warn (Rashi). Literally, "bear witness." See 19:23.

19:24 come back up . . . See 24:12.

[54. The First Two Commandments]

20   ¹ God spoke all these words, saying*:

² I am God your Lord, who brought you out of Egypt, from the place of slavery.*

³ Do not have any other gods before Me. ⁴ Do not represent [such gods]* by any carved statue or picture of anything in the heaven above, on the earth below, or in the water below the land. ⁵ Do not bow down to [such gods] or worship them. I am God your Lord, a God who demands exclusive worship.* Where My enemies are concerned, I keep in mind the sin of the fathers for [their] descendants,* to the third and fourth [generation]. ⁶ But for those who love Me and keep My commandments, I show love for thousands [of generations].*

[55. The Third Commandment]

⁷ Do not take the name of God* your Lord in vain.* God will not allow the one who takes His name in vain to go unpunished.

[56. The Fourth Commandment]

⁸ Remember the Sabbath to keep it holy. ⁹ You can work during the six weekdays and do all your tasks. ¹⁰ But Saturday* is the Sabbath to God your Lord. Do not do anything that constitutes work.* [This includes] you, your son, your daughter, your slave, your maid, your animal, and the foreigner* in

---

20:1   **God spoke** . . . The Ten Commandments are repeated in Deuteronomy 5:6–18.

20:2   **I am God** . . . This is a commandment to believe in God (*Sefer HaMitzvoth,* Positive Commandment 1; see Josephus 3:5:5; Philo, *Decalogue* 1:385). Others, however, state that belief in God is too basic to be an actual commandment (Ramban on *Sefer HaMitzvoth,* loc. cit.)

20:4   **Do not represent** . . . (*Sefer HaMitzvoth,* Negative Commandment 2; *Yad, Avodath Kokhavim* 3:9). Literally, "do not make." See 20:20.

20:5   **who demands** . . . (Hirsch). *Kana* in Hebrew, used exclusively with relation to God; 34:14, Deuteronomy 4:24, 5:9, 6:15; cf. Joshua 24:19, Nahum 1:2. On the basis of the verbal form, "jealous," "zealous," or "vengeful" (*Mekhilta;* Rashi), but more accurately, "acting to punish" (*Moreh Nevukhim* 1:44; cf. Saadia Gaon).

—   **for their descendants.** But only if they follow their fathers' ways; cf. Deuteronomy 24:16 (*Berakhoth* 7a).

20:6   **generations.** (*Targum;* Rashi).

20:7   **name of God.** The sense is changed from the first to the third person. Some therefore say that only the first two commandments were given directly by God (*Makkoth* 24a; *Shir HaShirim Rabbah* 1:13; Ramban). See note on 20:16.

—   **in vain.** Or, "illegally" (cf. 23:1). This commandment primarily forbids false and trivial oaths (*Mekhilta; Shevuoth* 21a; *Targum Yonathan;* Rashi). However, it also prohibits all unnecessary use of God's name (Ramban; *Berakhoth* 33a).

20:10 **Saturday.** Literally, "the seventh day," but this is the Hebrew expression for Saturday.

—   **work.** By tradition, there are 39 categories of work (*Shabbath* 73a). These include carrying (16:29), cooking and other food preparation (16:23), lighting fires (35:3), and all agricultural activities (34:21). By tradition, all such activities as writing, making cloth, sewing, making leather, building, laundering, and assembling articles are also forbidden.

—   **foreigner** (cf. Ramban). Especially a gentile employee (Ralbag) or, "proselyte" (*Mekhilta*), even a minor (Ralbag). See 23:12.

your gates. ¹¹ It was during the six weekdays that God made the heaven, the   20
earth, the sea, and all that is in them, but he rested on Saturday. God therefore blessed the Sabbath day and made it holy.

[57. The Fifth Commandment]

¹² Honor your father and mother. You will then live long on the land that
God your Lord is giving you.

[58. The Sixth Commandment]

¹³ Do not commit murder.

[59. The Seventh Commandment]

Do not commit adultery.

[60. The Eighth Commandment]

Do not steal.*

[61. The Ninth Commandment]

Do not testify* as a false witness against your neighbor.*

[62. The Tenth Commandment]

¹⁴ Do not be envious of your neighbor's house.

[63. Envy]

Do not be envious* of your neighbor's wife, his slave, his maid, his ox, his
donkey, or anything else that is your neighbor's.

[64. Aftermath]

¹⁵ All the people saw* the sounds, the flames,* the blast of the ram's horn,
and the mountain smoking. The people trembled when they saw it, keeping

---

20:13 **Do not steal.** This is primarily a commandment against kidnapping (21:16; *Mekhilta;* Rashi). However, it
also forbids all sorts of dishonesty (*Targum Yonathan*).
— **testify.** The Hebrew *anah* can also mean answer, respond, or speak up. However, it is also used specifically for testimony, see 1 Samuel 12:3, 2 Samuel 1:16, Isaiah 3:9, 59:12, Micah 6:3, Job 15:6, Numbers 35:30.
— **neighbor.** Or, "countryman."
20:14 **Do not be envious.** This is a continuation of the Tenth Commandment.
20:15 **saw.** Some say that it was an experience of synesthesia, where they actually saw sounds (*Mekhilta;* Rashi;
Ibn Ezra; *Moreh Nevukhim* 1:46)
— **the sounds, the flames** (Rashi). Or, "the thunder and lightning" (*Maaseh HaShem, Maaseh Torah* 7; cf.
Ramban).

20 their distance. [16] They said to Moses,* "You speak to us, and we will listen. But let God not speak with us any more, for we will die if He does."

[17] "Do not be afraid," replied Moses to the people. "God only came to raise you up.* His fear will then be on your faces, and you will not sin."

[18] The people kept their distance while Moses entered the mist* where the Divine was [revealed].*

[65. Concluding Rules]

[19] God said to Moses: This is what you must tell the Israelites:

You have seen that I spoke to you from heaven. [20] Do not make a representation of anything that is with Me.* Do not make silver or gold gods for yourselves.

[21] Make an earthen altar for Me. You can sacrifice your burnt offerings,* your peace offerings,* your sheep and your cattle on it. Wherever I allow My name to be mentioned,* I will come to you and bless you.

[22] When* you eventually build a stone altar for Me, do not build it out of cut stone. Your sword will have been lifted against it, you will have profaned it. [23] Do not climb up to My altar with steps,* so that your nakedness not be revealed on it.

Mishpatim   מִשְׁפָּטִים

[66. The Hebrew Slave]

21   [1] These are the laws that you must set before [the Israelites]:

20:16 **They said to Moses** . . . According to many, this is in chronological order, and they asked Moses after the giving of the Ten Commandments (*Mekhilta;* Rashbam; Ibn Ezra, Abarbanel, on 20:15). Others say that this was before the Ten Commandments (Ramban). According to others, the people said this to Moses after the Second Commandment, and the rest were given through Moses (Chizzkuni; see note on 20:7).

20:17 **raise you up** (Mekhilta; Rashi). Or, "test" or "prove you" (Saadia; Ibn Ezra; Hirsch; cf. 16:4); "admonish you" (Rashbam), "refine you" (Ramban); "train you" or "accustom you [to prophecy]" (*Moreh Nevukhim* 3:24; Sforno; Ramban; cf. Ibn Janach. See Deuteronomy 8:16.

20:18 **mist.** Some say that this is the heavy cloud in 19:9 (Rashi). *Araphel* in Hebrew. Or, "opaque darkness" (Hirsch; Radak, *Sherashim;* cf. Isaiah 60:2, Jeremiah 13:16, Joel 2:2). According to others, "glowing mist" (Bachya; *MeAm Lo'ez*), or "blinding light" (*HaKethav VeHaKabbalah*).

— **where the Divine was revealed.** The narrative continues in 24:1.

20:20 **Do not make a representation** Literally, "Do not make with me." This is a commandment not to make a statue of anything associated with God, such as angels. It also extends to making replicas of articles used in the Holy Temple (*Avodah Zarah* 43a,b; *Yad, Avodath Kokhavim* 3:10; *Sefer HaMitzvoth,* Negative Commandment 4).

20:21 **burnt offerings.** See note on Genesis 8:20. Also see below, 24:5.

— **peace offerings.** See Leviticus 3:1. Also see below 24:5, 32:6. Or, "fellowship offerings."

— **Wherever I allow** . . . That is, in the Holy Temple, where the Tetragrammaton was used in prayers and blessings (*Sotah* 38a; Rashi).

20:22 **When** . . . This is saying that a permanent stone altar would have to be built eventually, for the Holy Temple. It was built of stone and filled with earth (*Mekhilta;* Rashi). See 27:1.

20:23 **with steps.** Instead, it had a ramp (*Mekhilta;* Rashi).

² If you buy a Hebrew slave,* he shall serve for six years, but in the seventh 21 year, he is to be set free without liability. ³ If he was unmarried when he entered service, he shall leave by himself. But if he was a married man, his wife shall leave with him.

⁴ If his master gives him a wife,* and she bears sons or daughters, the woman and her children shall remain her master's property. [The slave] shall leave by himself.

⁵ If the slave declares, "I am fond of my master, my wife and my children; I do not want to go free," ⁶ his master must bring him to the courts.* Standing [the slave] next to the door or doorpost, his master shall pierce his ear with an awl.* [The slave] shall then serve [his master] forever.*

[67. The Hebrew Maidservant]

⁷ If a man sells his daughter as a maidservant,* she shall not be freed as male servants are released. ⁸ Her master should* provisionally designate her as his bride, and if she is not pleasing to him, he must let her be redeemed. He* is considered to have broken faith with her, and he therefore does not have the right to sell her to anyone else.*

⁹ If [the master] designates her as a bride for his son, she must be treated exactly the same as any other girl.

¹⁰ [Similarly], if [the master]* marries another wife,* he may not diminish [this one's] allowance, clothing or conjugal rights.

21:2 **Hebrew slave.** One who was sold for robbery; see 22:2 (*Mekhilta;* Rashi). See Leviticus 25:39, Deuteronomy 15:12.
21:4 **wife.** A gentile slave woman (*Mekhilta;* Rashi).
21:6 **the courts** (*Targum; Mekhilta;* Rashi). The word *Elohim* denotes God, but it also denotes judges or courts; see 22:7, 22:8, 22:27, 1 Samuel 2:25, Judges 5:8, Psalms 82:1,6, 138:1. In this case, a court composed of three judges is required (*Yad, Avadim* 3:9).
— **Standing the slave** . . . The master must pierce the ear into the door; Deuteronomy 15:17 (see *Lechem Mishneh* on *Yad, Avadim* 3:9).
— **forever.** Until the jubilee; Leviticus 25:40 (*Mekhilta; Targum Yonathan; Kiddushin* 21b; Rashi).
21:7 **maidservant.** This can only be done with a minor girl (*Mekhilta;* Rashi). It was permitted for a man to sell his minor daughter only when he was absolutely destitute with no possible means of support (*Kiddushin* 20a; *Yad, Avadim* 4:2).
21:8 **should.** (*Kiddushin* 19a). The master does this by declaring, "you are my designated bride" (*Yad, Avadim* 4:7).
— **He.** The master. Also, her father may not sell her again (Hirsch; *Torah Temimah*). See next note.
— **anyone else** (Rashi; *Yad, Avadim* 4:10). Literally, "to a foreign nation" (*Mekhilta;* Ramban). It can also denote, "to someone unsuitable for marriage" (Hirsch). It would then be a general commandment that the father is not permitted to sell his daughter to a gentile or to anyone else who could not possibly marry her.
21:10 **the master.** Or, "the son."
— **another wife.** Polygamy was permitted by Torah Law. It was only forbidden later by a ban pronounced by all European rabbis under the leadership of Rabbenu Gershom (*circa* 965-1028).

21   ¹¹ If none of the above three* are done to [the girl], then she shall be released without liability or payment.

[68. Manslaughter]

¹² If one person strikes another and [the victim] dies, [the murderer] must be put to death.*

¹³ If he did not plan to kill [his victim], but God caused it to happen, then I will provide a place where [the killer] can find refuge.*

[69. Murder]

¹⁴ If a person plots against his neighbor to kill him intentionally,* then you must even take him from My altar* to put him to death.

[70. Injuring a Parent]

¹⁵ Whoever intentionally injures* his father or mother shall be put to death.

[71. Kidnapping]

¹⁶ If one person kidnaps and sells another, and [the victim] is seen* in his hand, then [the kidnapper] shall be put to death.

[72. Cursing a Parent]

¹⁷ Whoever curses* his father or mother shall be put to death.

[73. Personal Injury]

¹⁸ [This is the law] when two men fight, and one hits the other with a stone or with [his] fist.* If [the victim] does not die, but becomes bedridden, ¹⁹ and

---

21:11 above three. Redemption, marriage, or marriage to a son (Rashi). The girl then must be released automatically when she reaches puberty.

21:12 the murderer ... See Genesis 9:6, Leviticus 24:17, Numbers 35:30.

21:13 I will provide a place ... See Numbers 35:10–34, Deuteronomy 19:1–13, Joshua 20:1–9.

21:14 intentionally (Hirsch). Or, "by foul play," "with premeditation," or "with guile."

—   **from My altar.** And such a murderer can certainly be removed from any refuge city (Ibn Ezra; Chizzkuni). Even if the murderer is a priest offering sacrifice, he can be taken from the altar (*Mekhilta;* Rashi).
      Some say that in the desert, before the refuge cities were selected, the altar served as a refuge for the accidental murderer (Sforno). According to others, the altar served as sanctuary for unpremeditated murder, but not for the premeditated crime (Abarbanel; *Akedath Yitzchak; MeAm Lo'ez*). See 1 Kings 2:28, 32.

21:15 injures. Causing bleeding (*Sanhedrin* 84b).

21:16 seen. By witnesses (*Mekhilta;* Rashi). Literally, "found." Cf. Deuteronomy 24:7.

21:17 whoever curses. See Leviticus 20:9.

21:18 fist (Ramban; Ibn Ezra; Septuagint; cf. *Kelim* 17:12; *Bava Kama* 90b; Isaiah 58:4). Or, "something hard" (Saadia; Ibn Janach); "a clod of earth" (Radak, *Sherashim;* Ibn Ezra on Isaiah 58:4); "thrown stone or brick" (Rashbam; *Arukh* s.v. *kurmiza,* from *Targum*); or "club" (*Arukh HaShalem* s.v. *kurmiza*).

then gets up and can walk under his own power,* the one who struck him shall 21
be acquitted. Still, he must pay for [the victim's] loss of work, and must provide for his complete cure.

[74. Killing of Slaves]

²⁰ If a man strikes his male or female slave* with a rod, and [the slave] dies under his hand, [the death] must be avenged.* ²¹ However, if [the slave] survives for a day or two, then, since he is [his master's] property, [his death] shall not be avenged.

[75. Personal Damages]

²² [This is the law] when two men fight and [accidentally] harm a pregnant woman, causing her to miscarry. If there is no fatal injury [to the woman], then [the guilty party] must pay a [monetary] penalty. The woman's husband must sue for it,* and [the amount] is then determined by the courts.
²³ However, if there is a fatal injury [to the woman], then he must pay full compensation for her life.*
²⁴ Full compensation must be paid for the loss of an eye, a tooth, a hand or a foot.* ²⁵ Full compensation must [also] be paid for a burn, a wound,* or a bruise.*

[76. Injury to Slaves]

²⁶ If a person strikes his male or female slave* in the eye and blinds it,* he shall set [the slave] free in compensation for his eye.
²⁷ [Similarly,] if he knocks out the tooth of his male or female slave, he must set [the slave] free in compensation for his tooth.

21:19 **his own power** (*Targum; Mekhilta;* Rashi; *Yad, Rotzeach* 7:4). Or, "and can walk with his cane" (cf. Ramban).
21:20 **slave.** A gentile bought as a slave (*Mekhilta;* Rashi).
— **avenged.** Implying a death penalty for the master (*Sanhedrin* 52b; Rashi).
21:22 **must sue for it** (*Bava Kama* 43a; Rashi).
21:23 **must pay full compensation** . . . This is speaking of a case where the woman's assailant did not intend to kill the man with whom he was fighting (*Chidushey HaRan, Sanhedrin* 79b; cf. *Yad, Rotze'ach* 4:1). Literally, "you must give a soul for a soul." According to some, this is speaking of a case where the woman's assailant intended to kill the other man, and there is a dispute as to whether this expression implies the death penalty or monetary payment (*Sanhedrin* 79a,b).
21:24 **Full compensation** . . . (*Mekhilta; Targum Yonathan; Bava Kama* 84a; Rashi). Literally, "an eye for an eye, a tooth for a tooth, a hand for a hand, a foot for a foot." These expressions, however, are meant idiomatically and not literally. See Leviticus 24:19,20, Deuteronomy 19:21.
— **a bruise** (Rashi). Or, "a wound" (Saadia; Ibn Janach); or, "a scrape" (Radak, *Sherashim*).
21:25 **a wound.** Or, "cut" (Rashi; Radak, *Sherashim*).
21:26 **slave.** A gentile bought as a slave (*Mekhilta;* Rashi).
— **blinds it** (see *Bava Kama* 98a; *Yad, Avadim* 5:8,9). Literally, "and destroys it."

21   *[77. The Killer Ox]*

²⁸ If an ox* gores a man or woman, and [the victim] dies, the ox must be
stoned to death, and its flesh may not be eaten. The owner of the ox, however,
shall not be punished.

²⁹ But if the ox was in the habit of goring on previous occasions, and the
owner was warned but did not take precautions, then, if it kills a man or
woman, the ox must be stoned, and its owner shall also [deserve to] die.*
³⁰ Nevertheless,* an atonement fine must be imposed on him, and he must pay
whatever is imposed on him as a redemption for his life.

³¹ This law also applies if [the ox] gores a minor boy or a minor girl.

³² If the ox gores a male or female slave, [its owner] must give thirty silver
shekels* to [the slave's] master, and the bull must be stoned.

                                   [78. A Hole in the Ground]

³³ [This is the law] if a person digs a hole in the ground, or uncovers a hole,
and does not cover it over. If an ox or donkey falls into it, ³⁴ the one responsible for the hole must make restitution, restoring the full value [of the animal]
to its owner. The dead animal remains the property [of its owner].*

                                   [79. Damage by Goring]

³⁵ If one person's ox injures the ox of another person, and it dies, they
shall sell the live ox and divide the money received for it. They shall also
divide the dead animal.

³⁶ However, if the ox was known to be in the habit of goring on previous
occasions, and its owner did not take precautions, then he must pay the full
value of [the dead] ox. The dead animal remains the property of [its owner].*

                                   [80. Penalties for Stealing]

³⁷ If a person steals an ox or sheep and then slaughters or sells it, he must
repay five oxen for each ox, and four sheep* for each sheep.

22   ¹ If a burglar is caught in the act of breaking in,* and is struck and killed, it

---

21:28 **ox.** Any bovine animal.
21:29 **deserve to die.** By God's hand (*Mekhilta;* Rashi).
21:30 **Nevertheless** (Rashi; *Bava Kama* 40a; *Yad, Nizkey Mamon* 10:4). Literally, "if." Cf. Numbers 35:31.
21:32 **30 silver shekels.** Around $30.
21:34 **of its owner.** (*Mekhilta;* Rashi; *Yad, Niz'key Mamon* 7:13).
21:36 **of its owner.** (*Bava Kama* 10b; *Mekhilta*). In both these cases, the value of the dead carcass is therefore
       deducted from the amount of compensation that must be paid.
21:37 **four sheep.** See 2 Samuel 12:6.
22:1   **breaking in** (Hirsch). Cf. Jeremiah 2:34, Ezekiel 8:8, Amos 9:2, Job 24:16. Or, "digging in" (Radak,
       Sherashim); or, "with deadly intent" (Rashbam).

is not considered an act of murder.* ² However, if he robs in broad daylight,* 22 then it is an act of murder [to kill him].

[A thief] must make full restitution. If he does not have the means, he must be sold [as a slave to make restitution] for his theft.

³ If the stolen article is found in his possession, and it is a living ox, donkey or sheep, he must make double restitution.

[81. Damage by Grazing]

⁴ If a person grazes a field or a vineyard, and lets his livestock loose so that it grazes in another person's field, he must make restitution with the best of his field and the best of his vineyard.

[82. Damage by Fire]

⁵ If fire gets out of control and spreads through weeds,* and [then] consumes bound or standing grain or a field, the one who started the fire must make restitution.

[83. The Unpaid Custodian]

⁶ If one person gives another money or articles to watch,* and they are stolen from the house of the person [keeping them], then if the thief is found, [the thief]* must make [the usual] double restitution.

⁷ If the thief is not found, the owner of the house shall be brought to the courts, [where he must swear] that he did not lay a hand on* his neighbor's property.

⁸ In every case of dishonesty,* whether it involves an ox, a donkey, a sheep, a garment, or anything else that was [allegedly] lost, and [witnesses]* testify

---

—   **not considered an act of murder.** Literally, "he has no blood."

22:2   **in broad daylight** (Rashbam; Ibn Ezra; cf. Saadia). Literally, "if the sun shines on him," an idiom. Or, "if it is clear (that he has no deadly intent" (*Mekhilta; Sanhedrin* 72a; Rashi); or "if it is done publicly [in the presence of witnesses]" (*Targum*; Ramban).

22:5   **weeds.** or "thorns" (Rashi).

22:6   **to watch.** Without paying for their being watched (*Targum Yonathan; Bava Metzia* 94a). These are items that are usually watched without fee (Ramban; *Tosafoth, Bava Metzia* 41b, s.v. *Karna*).

—   **the thief** (*Bava Kama* 63b; Rashi). See 22:3.

22:7   **lay a hand on.** That he did not hide the missing article (Rashbam; Ramban). Or, "that he did not make personal use of the article" (*Bava Metzia* 41a). Since the custodian has no right to make personal use of the articles in his safekeeping, as soon as he does so, he becomes like a thief, and thus has full responsibility for any loss. See 22:10.

22:8   **In every case . . .** (following Rashi; *Yad, Genevah* 4:1). Or, "In every case of liability" (*Targum;* Rashbam); or, "In every case of negligence" (*Bava Kama* 107b; *Targum Yonathan;* Radak, *Sherashim,* s.v. *Pesha*); or, "In every case of denied guilt" (Saadia).

—   **witnesses** (Rashi; *Yad, loc. cit.;* cf. *Bava Kama* 108b). Or, "[where the keeper] says [part of the claim is true" (*Kiddushin* 65b, Rashi *ad loc.*)

22   that it was seen,* both parties' claims must be brought to the courts.* The person whom the courts declare guilty must then make double restitution to the other.

[84. The Paid Custodian]

⁹ If one person gives another a donkey, an ox, a sheep, or any other animal to watch,* and it dies, is maimed, or is carried off in a raid, without eye witnesses, ¹⁰ then the case between the two must be decided on the basis of an oath to God. If [the person keeping the animal] did not make use of* the other's property, the owner must accept it,* and [the person keeping the animal] need not pay.

¹¹ However, if it was stolen from [the keeper], then he must make restitution to [the animal's] owner.

¹² If [the animal] was killed by a wild beast and [the keeper] can provide evidence,* he need not make restitution for the attacked animal.

[85. The Borrowed Article]

¹³ If a person borrows something from another, and it becomes broken or dies,* and the owner is not involved* with [the borrower], then [the borrower] must make full restitution.

¹⁴ However, if the owner was involved with him, then [the borrower] need not make restitution.

If the article was hired, [the loss] is covered by the rental price.*

[86. Seduction]

¹⁵ If a man seduces a virgin who is not betrothed,* he must pay a dowry

---

- **that it was seen.** See above note. Literally, "which he says, that this is it."
- **to the courts.** See note on 21:6.
- **22:9 to watch.** For pay. See note on 22:6.
- **22:10 make use of.** Literally, "lay a hand on." See note on 22:7. (*Mekhilta;* Rashi; cf. *Bava Metzia* 41a).
- **it.** The dead animal (*Mekhilta; Adereth Eliahu*). Or, "the owner must accept the oath" (Rashi; Rashbam; see *Bava Kama* 106a; *Shevuoth* 45a).
- **22:12 evidence.** Witnesses (Rashi; Sforno). In every case where it is possible to provide witnesses, this is what must be done (*Yad, Sekhiruth* 1:2; see above, 22:9). According to some, other evidence that the animal was killed, such as part of the body is also acceptable (Rashbam; Ibn Ezra. This point is debated in *Bava Kama* 10b, 11a; *Mekhilta;* cf. *Targum Yonathan*). If there are no witnesses or evidence, he may swear and be exempt from liability (*Bava Metzia* 83a; *Yad, Sekhiruth* 1:2).
- **22:13 broken or dies.** Even by accident (Rashi).
- **involved.** But if the owner is working for the borrower in any manner whatever, there is no liability (*Mekhilta; Bava Metzia* 94a; Rashi; *Yad, Sho'el* 2:1). Where the owner is working for the borrower, it is assumed that the owner has some benefit in lending the article (Hirsch). Literally, "and its owner is not with it." This can also be interpreted, "the owner is not there at the time" (Ibn Ezra on 22:14), or, "the owner was not [working] with [the article]" (Rashbam).
- **22:14 If the article . . .** (*Mekhilta;* Rashi). Or, "If [the owner] is an employee [of the borrower], then [the loss] is covered by his wages" (*Yad, Sekhiruth* 1:3; *Sekhel Tov; Bekhor Shor;* Chizzkuni; Abarbanel; *Adereth Eliahu*).
- **22:15 betrothed.** Betrothal rights (*erusin*) is the first step in marriage, where the couple are legally married, and

and must marry her. ¹⁶ If her father* refuses to allow him to marry her, then 22
he must pay [the father] the usual dowry money for virgins.*

[87. Occult Practices]

¹⁷ Do not allow a sorceress to live.*
¹⁸ Whoever lies with an animal must be put to death.*

[88. Idolatry and Oppression]

¹⁹ Whoever sacrifices to any deity other than God alone must be condemned to death.*
²⁰ Do not hurt the feelings of a foreigner* or oppress him, for you were foreigners in Egypt.
²¹ Do not mistreat a widow or an orphan. ²² If you mistreat them,* and they cry out to Me, I will hear their cry. ²³ I will [then] display My anger and kill you by the sword, so that your wives will be widows, and your children, orphans.

[89. Lending Money]

²⁴ When you lend money to My people, to the poor man among you, do not press him for repayment.* [Also] do not take interest* from him.
²⁵ If you take your neighbor's garment as security [for a loan], you must return it to him before sunset.* ²⁶ This alone is his covering, the garment for

---

the marriage can only be dissolved by an official bill of divorce. Today, the giving of the ring is the betrothal ceremony. Adultery with a betrothed girl is a crime punishable by death. Deuteronomy 22:23 f (Rashbam). The second step of marriage is when the husband brings the bride into his domain (*nesuin*).

22:16 **her father.** And certainly if she herself refuses (*Kethuvoth* 39b; *Kiddushin* 46a).

— **usual dowry.** 50 silver shekels (Deuteronomy 22:29; *Kethuvoth* 29b; Rashi). Since there are 4 *zuzim* to a shekel, this is equal to 200 zuzim (*Sekhel Tov*). This is also the amount that is written in a woman's marriage contract (*kethuvah*) upon marriage (*Kethuvoth* 10a). It was enough for a person to live on for a year (*Peah* 8:8; Rash, Bertenoro ad loc.)

22:17 **Do not allow** . . . See Deuteronomy 18:10,11; Leviticus 19:26,31.

22:18 **Whoever** . . . See Leviticus 18:23, 20:15,16, Deuteronomy 27:21. This was done for occult practices (*Sanhedrin* 105a,b).

22:19 **condemned to death.** See Deuteronomy 17:7.

22:20 **foreigner.** In general, anyone from another country (Rashi; *MeAm Lo'ez*). Specifically, a proselyte (Ralbag; *Sefer HaMitzvoth*, Negative Commandment 253; *Chinukh* 63). See 23:9, Leviticus 19:33,34, Deuteronomy 24:17,18, 27:19.

22:22 **them.** Literally, "him."

22:24 **do not press him** . . . (*Bava Metzia* 75b; *Yad, Malveh* 1:3). Literally, "do not behave like a creditor toward him" (Rashi; Ramban). Or, "do not act as if you have power over him" (*Targum*); or, "do not demand special consideration from him" (Ibn Ezra).

— **interest.** The word *neshekh* used here specifically denotes prepaid interest (*Bava Metzia* 60b; Ralbag). See Leviticus 25:35-38, Deuteronomy 15:7-11, 23:19,20.

22:25 **before sunset** (*Targum Yonathan;* see Deuteronomy 24:13). Or, "at sunset" (Saadia). In the Talmud, this opinion is cited, as well as another which would translate the verse, "you must return it [and allow him to wear it] until sunset" (*Bava Metzia* 114b).

22 his skin. With what shall he sleep? Therefore, if he cries out to Me, I will
listen, for I am compassionate.

[90. Accepting Authority]

²⁷ Do not curse the judges.* Do not curse* a leader of your people.
²⁸ Do not delay* your offerings of newly ripened produce* and your agricultural offerings.*
Give me the first-born of your sons.*
²⁹ You must also do likewise with your ox and sheep.* It must remain with

---

22:27 the judges. (*Targum*). *Elohim* in Hebrew. Or, "God" (Septuagint). See note on 21:6. Some sources cite both interpretations (*Mekhilta; Sanhedrin* 66a; Rashi: *Sefer HaMitzvoth*, Negative Commandment 60).

— **curse.** The first "curse" in this verse is *kalal*, while the second is *arar*. *Kalal* is a curse that someone should lose his status, while *arar* is one that he should dry up and not have any blessing. *Kalal* is motivated by defiance, while *arar* is motivated by envy (Hirsch; *Chothem Takhnith*, p. 125). Some say that *arar* is a curse that one should be cast down (*yarah*) or shut out from divine light (*or*). (*Yerioth Sh'lomo*, Volume 1, 3:13, p. 88c).

22:28 delay. More specifically "transpose" (*Terumah* 3:6; *Sefer HaMitzvoth*, Negative Commandment 154; *Yad, Terumah* 3:23). One may not give these offerings in the wrong order.

— **offerings of newly ripened produce.** (Rashi, *Terumah* 4a; Bertenoro, *Terumah* 3:6). Denoting the first fruits or *bikkurim* (*Targum; Mekhilta; Terumah* 4a). See below 23:19. Some say that it is called *mele'ah* from the root *malea* meaning full or ripe, since it must be given as soon as the fruit ripens (Rashi; Radak, *Sherashim*). Others say that fruit that is "full" because no tithes or offerings have as yet been removed from it (Rabbenu Gershom, *Terumah* 4a). Cf. Numbers 18:27, Deuteronomy 22:9.
The Septuagint translates this as "the first fruits of your *alonos*", where the Greek *alonos* can denote threshing floor, garden, vineyard, or orchard. Saadia likewise translates it "the first fruits of your wine and grain."
According to others, *mele'ah* is that which is gathered in at harvest (Ramban). Still others take it as a word for wine (Ibn Ezra). It can also mean rain (Rashbam).

— **agricultural offerings.** This is the agricultural offering that is given to the cohen-priest, later known as *terumah* (*Mekhilta; Terumah* 4a; Rashi; cf. Numbers 15:19, 18:8,24). The word *dema* used here is unique, but it is seen as a synonym for *terumah* (*Mekhilta*; Rambam on *Damai* 1:3; *Oholoth* 16:4, *Taharoth* 2:3, Rambam, Rash *ad loc.*). Significantly, in ancient Egyptian, the word *dema* denotes something upon which a special title has been bestowed, or something with a special status. It may be that this was the word used for *terumah* before Aaron's sons were chosen as the priests.
Many see the word *dema* as being related to *dim'ah*, the word for tears. Hence, it denotes juices squeezed from the fruit, particularly wine and olive oil (Radak, *Sherashim*; Ramban; Abarbanel). Others see it specifically denoting olive oil (Saadia; Ibn Janach; Rashbam; cf. Pliny 11:6) or wine (*Targum Yonathan*). Others also include winnowed grain, since it is removed from the husk like a tear from the eye (Malbim). The Septuagint translates it as *lynou*, a vat, and specifically a wine vat.
Some see this as also being a connotation for *terumah* since *terumah* is separated primarily after the work on the crops is completed, and thus, after the grapes and olives are pressed (Ralbag; cf. Deuteronomy 18:4; *Tosefta, Terumah* 3:10,11,12; *Yad, Terumoth* 5:5,6). Others say that it is because, unlike the first fruits, *terumah* must also be brought from liquids such as wine and oil (Tosafoth, *Terumah* 4a, s.v. *mele'athekha*; cf. *Terumah* 1:8).
According to other authorities, the primary connotation of *dema* is that of a mixture (Raavad, *Tum'ath Meth* 9:9; cf. *Orlah* 2:4; *Gittin* 52b). According to this, as soon as the obligation to separate *terumah* falls on produce, it is considered to be mixed (*damah*) with the *terumah*. *Terumah* is therefore called *dema* because it is separated from a mixture (Rabbenu Gershom, *Terumah* 4a; Rashi ibid.). Significantly, in ancient Egyptian, *dema* also denotes a mixture.

— **first born . . . sons.** See above 13:2,13.

22:29 do likewise . . . See 13:12.

its mother for seven days,* but on the eighth day, you must give it to Me. 22
³⁰ Be holy people to Me. Do not eat flesh torn off in the field by a predator.* Cast it to the dogs.

[91. Justice]

¹ Do not accept* a false report.*   23
Do not join forces with a wicked person to be a corrupt witness.*
² Do not follow the majority to do evil.*
Do not speak up in a trial to pervert justice.* A case must be decided on the
basis of the majority.*
³ Do not favor [even] the poorest man in his lawsuit.

[92. Strayed Animals]

⁴ If you come across your enemy's ox or donkey going astray, bring it back
to him.*

— **seven days.** See Leviticus 22:27.
22:30 **flesh torn off** . . . This, specifically forbids flesh from a living animal (*Targum; Chullin* 73b; *Yerushalmi,*
Nazir 6:1; *Sefer HaMitzvoth,* Negative Commandment 182.) See Genesis 9:4. Or, "the flesh of an animal
attacked by a predator in the field" (*Chullin* 102b; *Mekhilta; Rashi*). See Leviticus 22:8. It includes any
animal that has a lesion or wound that will eventually kill it (*Chullin* 3:1). See Ezekiel 4:14, 44:31.
23:1 **accept.** (*Targum; Rashi; cf. Pesachim* 118a; *Sanhedrin* 7a). Or, "do not spread false rumors" (Ibn Ezra).
— **false report** (*Targum; Rashi*). Or, "an illegal report" (see 20:7). This prohibits the courts from accepting
illegal testimony, specifically when the defendant or opposing party is not present (*Sanhedrin* 7a; *Yad,*
Sanhedrin 21:7; *Sefer HaMitzvoth,* Negative Commandment 281). Or, "a trivial report." This is seen as a
commandment against listening to malicious gossip (*lashon ha-ra*) when not necessary, even if it is true
(*Pesachim* 118a).
— **to be a corrupt witness.** Since two witnesses are always needed (Numbers 35:30, Deuteronomy 17:6,
19:15), and a wicked person is not a valid witness, it is forbidden to join with him to make a pair
(*Mekhilta;* Saadia; *Yad, Eduth* 10:1; Ibn Ezra; Sforno). Or "Do not join forces with a wicked person to be
a false witness" (*Targum; Rashi*).
23:2 **do not follow** (*Targum;* Rashbam; Ibn Ezra; Bachya). Or, "Do not follow a majority [of one] to impose a
[death] penalty" (*Mekhilta; Yad, Sanhedrin* 8:1).
— **to pervert justice** (Ibn Ezra; Tur; Abarbanel). See 23:6; Deuteronomy 27:19, Malachi 3:5. The form
li-n'toth here denotes "to turn [oneself] aside" (cf. Numbers 22:26; 2 Kings 20:10; Psalms 17:11). Hence,
it is also translated, "do not speak up [in a trial] to bend yourself [to follow the consensus]" (*Sefer*
HaMitzvoth, Negative Commandment 183; cf. Rashbam; Saadia, *Yad, Sanhedrin* 10:1). Or, "Do not
speak up to bend yourself [and change your mind about your verdict]" (*Yad, Sanhedrin* 10:2; *Sefer*
HaMitzvoth loc. cit.). See next note.
    Others translate this, "Do not speak up in a lawsuit [to coach either party]" (Bachya; cf. *Yad, San-*
hedrin 21:10; *Choshen Mishpat* 17:8).
    Since the verb *anah* has the connotation of testimony (20:13), the verse can also say, "do not testify at
a trial to pervert justice."
— **A case must be decided** . . . (*Chullin* 11a; *Bava Metzia* 49b; Saadia; *Sefer HaMitzvoth,* Positive 175). This is
a general rule that we must follow a majority in all cases.
    Some put the entire second part of the verse together, "Do not speak up in a trial, leaning toward the
majority to pervert justice"(*Mekhilta;* Rashbam; Abarbanel). The form *le-hatoth* used here has the connotation of perverting justice; Isaiah 10:2, Proverbs 17:23, 18:5, Lamentations 3:35. It also has the
connotation of turning aside another (Numbers 22:23, 1 Kings 8:58). Hence, "Do not speak up in a trial
to turn aside, following a majority to change someone else's decision" (Chizzkuni).
23:4 **If you come across** . . . See Deuteronomy 22:1.

23

[93. The Fallen Animal]

⁵ If you see the donkey of someone you hate lying under its load, you might want to refrain from helping him,* but [instead] you must make every effort to help* him [unload it].*

[94. Justice and Festivals]

⁶ Do not pervert justice for your degraded countryman* in his lawsuit.
⁷ Keep away from anything false.

Do not kill a person who has not been proven guilty* or one who has been acquitted.* [Ultimately] I will not let a guilty person escape punishment.*

⁸ Do not accept bribery.* Bribery blinds the clear-sighted and twists the words of the just.*

⁹ Do not oppress a foreigner.* You know how it feels to be a foreigner, for you were foreigners in Egypt.

¹⁰ You may plant your land for six years and gather its crops. ¹¹ But during the seventh year, you must leave it alone* and withdraw* from it. The needy among you will then be able to eat [from your fields] just as you do, and whatever is left over can be eaten by wild animals. This also applies to your vineyard and your olive grove.

¹² You may do whatever you must during the six week days, but you must stop on Saturday.* Your donkey and ox must then be able to rest, and your

---

23:5 **you might want to refrain** (*Targum*).
— **make every effort to help.** (*Targum;* Rashi).
— **unload it.** (*Bava Metzia* 32a; *Mekhilta; Yad, Rotzeach* 13:1; *Sefer HaMitzvoth,* Positive Commandment 202). Some see the verb *azav* here as denoting unloading rather than helping (Ibn Ezra). Others see it as denoting loading (Ibn Janach; Radak, *Sherashim*).
23:6 **degraded.** Or, "worthless." Therefore, justice must be administered fairly even to the worst criminal (*Mekhilta; Yad, Sanhedrin* 20:5; *Sefer HaMitzvoth,* Negative Commandment 278). The word literally means "one who desires" (Rashi; Radak, *Sherashim*), and hence also denotes a poor person (*Targum*).
23:7 **not been proven guilty.** Literally, "guiltless." This teaches that it is forbidden for the courts to impose a death penalty on the basis of circumstantial evidence (*Mekhilta; Yad, Sanhedrin* 20:1; *Sefer HaMitzvoth,* Negative Commandment 290). It also teaches that it is forbidden to impose the death penalty as long as anyone has evidence to present in the accused's favor (*Mekhilta; Sanhedrin* 33b; Rashi).
— **or one who has been acquitted.** Once a suspect has been acquitted, the death penalty cannot be imposed no matter how much evidence against him is found. This prohibits double jeopardy (*Ibid.*) Some count these as two separate commandments (Ramban on *Sefer HaMitzvoth loc. cit; Chinukh* 82).
— **Ultimately . . .** (*Mekhilta;* Rashi).
23:8 **Do not accept bribery.** See Deuteronomy 16:19.
— **words of the just.** (Rashbam; Hirsch). Or, "words of the innocent" (Ibn Ezra); or, "just claims" (*Targum;* Saadia; Rashi).
23:9 **foreigner.** Or "proselyte." See above 22:20. Here the Torah is speaking specifically to judges (Ralbag; Chizzkuni; *Bekhor Shor*).
23:10 **leave it alone.** (Rashi; Rashbam; Radak, *Sherashim*). Or, "let it be public" (Saadia; Ralbag). See Leviticus 25:1-7.
— **withdraw from it.** Not eating any of its produce (*Mekhilta;* Rashi).
— **wild animals.** Literally, "animals of the field" (see note on Genesis 2:5).
23:12 **Saturday.** Literally, "the seventh day." See above, 20:9,10.

maid's son and the foreigner* must be able to relax.   23

¹³ Be very careful to keep everything I have said to you.

Do not pronounce the name of another deity. You must not let it be heard through your mouth.

¹⁴ Offer a sacrifice* to Me three times* each year.

¹⁵ Keep the Festival of Matzahs.* Eat matzahs for seven days, as I commanded you, during the prescribed time in the month of standing grain, since this is when you left Egypt.

Do not appear before Me empty-handed.*

¹⁶ [Also keep] the Reaping Festival,* through the first fruits of your produce that you planted in the field.* [There is also] the Harvest Festival* [right after]* the end of the year, when you gather your produce from the field.

¹⁷ Three times each year, every male among you must appear before God,* Master [of the universe].*

¹⁸ Do not sacrifice the blood of My [Passover] offering in the presence of leavened bread.*

Do not allow the fat* of My offering* to remain overnight until morning.

¹⁹ Bring your first fruits to the Temple of God your Lord.*

Do not cook meat* in milk,* [even]* that of its mother.

—   **foreigner.** (Hirsch). See note on 20:10.

23:14   **Offer a sacrifice.** Or, "celebrate" (see *Chagigah* 10b). See next note.

—   **three times** (*Targum;* Rashi; Radak, *Sherashim*). Or, "Celebrate three pilgrimage festivals to Me each year" (Ibn Ezra; cf. *Sefer HaMitzvoth*, Positive Commandment 52). See 34:23, Deuteronomy 16:16.

23:15   **festival of matzahs.** Or, "festival of unleavened bread." See 12:15, 13:6, 34:18, Leviticus 23:6, Deuteronomy 16:16.

—   **Do not appear before Me . . .** See 34:20, Deuteronomy 16:16.

23:16   **reaping festival.** This is Shavuoth (Rashi). See 34:22, Deuteronomy 16:10, 16:16.

—   **through the first fruits . . .** See Numbers 28:26. See below 23:19.

—   **harvest festival.** This is Sukkoth (Rashi). See Leviticus 23:34, Deuteronomy 16:13,16.

—   **right after** (Ibn Ezra). Sukkoth falls two weeks after the new year (*Rosh HaShanah*).

23:17   **Three times each year . . .** See note on 23:14.

—   **Master of the Universe** (*Targum*).

23:18   **Do not sacrifice . . .** See 34:25, Deuteronomy 16:4.

—   **fat.** This was the part that was to be burned on the altar. See Leviticus 3:16, 17:6. Also see below 29:13, Leviticus 3:3, 7:31, etc.

—   **offering.** Or, "festival offering" (see *Chagigah* 10b). See 34:25, Deuteronomy 16:4. This is speaking specifically of the Passover offering (Rashbam), but applies to all offerings and sacrifices (*Sefer HaMitzvoth*, Negative Commandment 116). Above (12:10), there was a commandment not to leave over the edible portions; here there is a commandment not to leave over the portions that are to be burned on the altar.

23:19   **Bring your first fruits . . .** See Deuteronomy 26:2 f. Also see 26:2, 34:22,26, Leviticus 2:14, 23:17, Numbers 18:13.

—   **meat.** Literally, "kid," denoting any young animal (Hirsch; cf. *Chullin* 114a; *Midrash HaGadol*).

—   **in milk.** See 34:26, Deuteronomy 14:21. This commandment forbids us to eat meat cooked in milk (*Sefer HaMitzvoth, Negative* Commandment 187; *Yad, Maakholoth Assuroth* 9:3).

     One reason for this law is that meat represents death (the slaughter of the animal), while milk represents new life, and it is not proper to mix life and death (Recanti; *Tzeror HaMor; Zohar* 2:124b). It is also forbidden because eating meat cooked in milk was an idolatrous practice, especially on festivals (*Moreh Nevukhim* 3:48; Ralbag).

—   **even.** (Cf. *Chullin* 114a, Ramban *ad loc.;* Hirsch).

23

[*95. Promises and Instructions*]

²⁰ I will send an angel* before you to safeguard you on the way, and bring you to the place that I have prepared. ²¹ Be careful in his presence and heed his voice. Do not rebel against him, since My name is with him.* He will not pardon your disobedience.

²² But if you obey him and do all that I say, then I will hate your enemies and attack your foes. ²³ My angel will go before you and bring you among the Amorites, Hittites, Perizzites, Canaanites, Hivites and Yebusites,* and I will [then] annihilate them.

²⁴ Do not bow down to their gods and do not serve them. Do not follow the ways of [these nations]. You must tear down [their idols] and break their sacred pillars.*

²⁵ You will then serve God your Lord, and He will bless your bread and your water. I will banish sickness from among you.

[*96. The Land*]

²⁶ In your land, no woman will suffer miscarriage or remain childless. I will make you live out full lives.

²⁷ I will cause [the people] who are in your path to be terrified of Me,* and I will throw all the people among whom you are coming into a panic. I will make all your enemies turn their backs [and flee] from you.

²⁸ I will send deadly wasps* ahead of you, and they will drive out the Hivites, Canaanites and Hittites before you.* ²⁹ I will not drive them out in a single year, however, lest the land become depopulated, and the wild animals become too many for you [to contend with]. ³⁰ I will drive [the inhabitants]

23:20 **angel.** See Joshua 5:14 (*Shemoth Rabbah* 32:3; Rashbam; Abarbanel). Some say that this angel was necessary since all prophets other than Moses could only receive their prophecy through an angel (*Moreh Nevukhim* 3:34). Others say that the "messenger" here denotes a prophet (Ralbag). See 32:34.

23:21 **since ...** (Rashi; Abarbanel). Literally, "He will not pardon ... since My name is with him." This means, "My commandment is with him" (*Moreh Nevukhim* 1:64). Some translate this, "He will not forgive you, even though My name [indicating mercy] is in him" (Saadia); or, "He will not forgive you, since he is [merely] My representative" (Ralbag).

23:23 **Amorites ...** See note on 3:8.

23:24 **sacred pillars.** See Genesis 28:18, 35:14, Deuteronomy 16:22.

23:27 **I will cause ...** Literally, "I will send My terror ahead of you."

23:28 **deadly wasps.** Some authorities identify the *tzir'ah* here with the hornet, *Vespa Orientalis*, a species that is known to multiply in time of war. It was known as a honey-producing insect (*Makh'shirim* 6:4), and in Talmudic times, was known to be dangerous (*Shabbath* 80b; *Taanith* 14a). Also see Deuteronomy 7:20, Joshua 24:12; *Wisdom of Solomon* 12:8.

Hornet

According to others, *tzir'ah* denotes a type of plague (Saadia; Ibn Janach; Radak, *Sherashim*), perhaps related to leprosy (Ibn Ezra).

— **Hivites ...** Only the nations to the east of the Jordan (Rashi). Cf. Joshua 24:12.

out little by little, giving you a chance to increase and [fully] occupy the land. 23
³¹ I will set your borders from the Red Sea* to the Philistine Sea,* from the desert* to the river.* I will give the land's inhabitants into your hand, and you will drive them before you.
³² Do not make a treaty with [these nations] or with their gods. ³³ Do not allow them to reside in your land, since they may then make you sin to Me. You may even end up worshiping their gods, and it will be a fatal trap to you.

[97. Sealing the Covenant]

¹ [God]* said to Moses, "Go up to God along with Aaron, Nadav and 24
Avihu,* and seventy of the elders of Israel.* [All of] you must bow down at a distance. ² Only Moses shall then approach God. The others may not come close, and the people may not go up with him.
³ Moses came and told the people all of God's words and all the laws. The people all responded with a single voice, "We will keep every word that God has spoken."
⁴ Moses wrote down all of God's words. He got up early in the morning, and built an altar* at the foot of the mountain, along with twelve pillars for the twelve tribes of Israel.* ⁵ He sent the [consecrated] young men* among the Israelites, and they offered oxen* as burnt offerings* and peace offerings* to God.

23:31 **Red Sea.** The Gulf of Aqaba, which is the eastern arm of the Red Sea (Rashi on 10:19). Others say that this is the Gulf of Suez, which is the western arm of the Red Sea (*Midrash HaGadol*).
— **Philistine Sea.** The southern Mediterranean, near the land of the Philistines (Rashbam).
— **desert.** Some say that this is the desert to the south of the Holy Land (Rashbam), while others say that it is to the east (*Midrash HaGadol*).
— **river.** The Euphrates (*Targum Yonathan;* Rashi). Others, however, identify it with the "River of Egypt" in Genesis 15:18. (*Torah Sh'lemah* 19:311). This is identified as Wadi el Arish (Saadia on Numbers 34:4; *Chamra VeChayay, Sanhedrin* 11b; *Teshuvoth Radbaz* 6:2206; cf. *Kuzari* 2:14).
24:1 **God.** (Ramban; *Lekach Tov;* Ralbag). Or "an angel" (*Sanhedrin* 38b; *Targum Yonathan;* Malbim). Some say that it is the angel mentioned in 23:20 (Abarbanel).
    According to many authorities, this is in chronological order, and Moses was now called after the Ten Commandments (Ibn Ezra; Ramban; *Targum Yonathan*). According to others, this was before the Ten Commandments, on the fourth day (Rashi; *Mekhilta* on 19:10; *Lekach Tov; Midrash HaGadol*).
— **Nadav and Avihu.** Aaron's sons, see 6:23.
— **and seventy . . .** See note on 3:16.
24:4 **altar.** See 20:21–23.
— **twelve pillars. . .** To demonstrate the unity of Israel (Rashbam; Chizzkuni). Some say that the blood was sprinkled on these twelve pillars for the people's sake (Abarbanel on 24:8). See 1 Kings 18:31.
24:5 **consecrated young men.** These were the first-born, who served as priests before Aaron's sons were chosen (*Zevachim* 115b; *Targum Yonathan;* Rashi). See Numbers 4:8, 3:45; Note on Genesis 25:31.
— **oxen.** (Ramban; Recanti; Bachya; Ralbag). Or, "they offered burnt offerings and oxen as peace offerings" (both possibilities are discussed in *Chagigah* 6b; *Yoma* 52b).
— **burnt offerings.** See note on Genesis 8:20.
— **peace offerings.** See note on 20:21. These sacrifices were an integral part of the covenant, and along with circumcision and immersion (19:10), they were part of the conversion process for a proselyte in the time of the Temple (*Kerithoth* 8b). Some say that only a burnt offering (*olah*) is required (*Yad, Issurey Biyah* 13:5;

24   ⁶ Moses took half the blood [of these offerings], and put it into large bowls.
The other half he sprinkled on the altar.
          ⁷ He took the book of the covenant* and read it aloud to the people. They
replied, "We will do and obey all that God has declared."
          ⁸ Moses then took [the rest of] the blood and sprinkled it on the people.*
He said, "This is the blood of the covenant that God is making with you
regarding all these words."
          ⁹ Moses then went up, along with Aaron, Nadav and Avihu, and seventy of
Israel's elders. ¹⁰ They saw a vision* of the God of Israel, and under His feet*
was something like a sapphire* brick,* like the essence of a clear [blue] sky.*
          ¹¹ [God] did not unleash His power* against the leaders* of the Israelites.
They had a vision of the Divine, and they ate and drank.*

  Mechusar Kapparah 1:2), but one may bring a peace offering and a burnt offering (*Yad, Maaseh HaKorbanoth*
  1:6).

24:7 **book of the covenant.** Some say that this includes all of Genesis and Exodus up to the giving of the Ten
  Commandments (Rashi; *Mekhilta* on 19:10). According to others, it was all the laws discussed up until
  this point (*Mekhilta loc. cit.*), particularly 21:1–23:19 (Ramban; Ibn Ezra on 23:4; Hirsch), or the admoni-
  tions in Leviticus 25:1–26:46 (*Mekhilta;* Chizzkuni). Others say that it was the Ten Commandments
  (Rabbi Yehudah HaChasid, quoted in *Paneach Raza*) or the verse, Exodus 19:5 (*Midrash HaGadol;*
  Bachya). See 34:28, 2 Kings 23:2.

24:8 **on the people.** Or, "on behalf of the people [on the altar]" (*Targum*). Some say that it was sprinkled on
  the 12 pillars (Abarbanel, see 24:4).

24:10 **saw a vision** (Ibn Ezra; *Emunoth VeDeyoth* 2:12). See 1 Kings 22:19, 2 Chronicles 18:18, Isaiah 6:1.

— **under His feet.** Just as feet come in contact with the ground, so allegorically, God's "feet" are the
  attribute that comes in contact with the level below. They are therefore seen as the means of prophecy
  (*Zohar* 2:104b, 2:169b, 3:53b, 3:68a). Others say that God's "feet" denote the ultimate essence of
  creation (*Moreh Nevukhim* 1:28). Others say that their vision consisted of the feet of the Throne of Glory
  (*Targum; Emunoth VeDeyoth* 2:9). See Isaiah 6:1, Ezekiel 1:26.

— **sapphire.** See 28:18. The Throne of Glory was seen as made of sapphire (Ezekiel 1:26, 10:1). The sapphire is blue, and it may be that they saw a vision of the sky as being below God. Others say that the
  sapphire mentioned here is ultimately transparent (Sforno; see *Yad, Yesodey HaTorah* 3:1). This stone is
  related to wisdom (Bachya on 28:18), and the Hebrew word *sappir* is related to *sefer*, a book (Tzioni). It is
  also related to vision (Bachya *loc. cit.*). Some say that this "sapphire" is like a "third eye," through which
  mystical vision is attained (Raavad on *Sefer Yetzirah* 1:1), and indeed, this third eye is associated with a
  sapphire blue color. It involves meditating on a single point (*Tikkuney Zohar* 7a) and complete quietness
  of mind (cf. *Likutey Moharan* 6:5).

— **brick** (Rashi; Ibn Ezra; Ramban; Septuagint). According to some, this brick showed God's closeness to
  Israel, since the brick symbolized that He had in mind the bricks that the Israelites had been forced to
  make (*Targum Yonathan;* Rashi). According to others, this was the brick out of which the Tablets of the
  Law would be carved (*Sifri, BeHaAlothekha* 101). Some say that they saw brickworking tools (*Yerushalmi,
  Sukkah* 4:3).
    Others translate this verse, "something like the whiteness of sapphire" (Saadia, Ibn Janach; cf. Ibn
  Ezra; Rashbam; Chizzkuni; *Lekach Tov*), or "transparency of sapphire" (Sforno; *Moreh Nevukhim* 1:28;
  see above note). See Joshua 19:26. Their vision may have been that of pure empty space (Ralbag), the
  primeval formless matter or hyle (*Maaseh HaShem, Maaseh Torah* 10), or a pure spiritual essence (*Avodath
  HaKodesh* 3:36; Abarbanel).

— **like the essence . . .** (Rashbam; *Bekhor Shor*). Or, "Like the essence of heaven in purity;" or, "transparent
  as the sky itself."

24:11 **unleash His power** (*Targum Yonathan;* Saadia; Rashi; Rashbam; Ibn Ezra; Ramban). Literally, "send
  forth His hand." Or, "did not send forth His hand [to grant prophecy" (*Lekach Tov; Tzeror HaMor;*

[98. Moses Ascends]

¹² God said to Moses,* "Come up to Me, to the mountain, and remain there. I will give you the stone tablets,* the Torah and the commandment that I have written for [the people's] instruction."

¹³ Moses and his aid Joshua* set out. Moses went up on God's Mountain. ¹⁴ He said to the elders, "Wait for us here until we return to you. Aaron and Chur* will remain with you. Whoever has a problem can go to them."

¹⁵ As soon as Moses reached the mountain top, the cloud covered the mountain. ¹⁶ God's glory rested on Mount Sinai, and it* was covered by the cloud for six days. On the seventh day, He called to Moses from the midst of the cloud.

¹⁷ To the Israelites, the appearance of God's glory on the mountain top was like a devouring flame. ¹⁸ Moses went into the cloud, and climbed to the mountain top.* Moses was to remain on the mountain for forty days and forty nights.*

Terumah   תְּרוּמָה

[99. The Offering]

¹ God spoke to Moses, saying*: ² Speak to the Israelites and have them   **25**

Sforno; Hirsch; Malbim); or, "did not send forth His hand [to conceal Himself]" (Baaley Tosafoth).

— **leaders.** Those who went with Moses (*Targum Yonathan;* Rashi). Or possibly, those lower in stature (Abarbanel).

— **ate and drank.** Some say that this was disrespectful (Rashi), or that they lacked true meditation (*Moreh Nevukhim* 1:5; Ralbag). Others state that they did not need meditation (Abarbanel). Still others say that they made a feast later to celebrate (Ramban; Sforno), possibly eating the peace offerings (Ibn Ezra).
     According to others, "They saw the Divine, but they could still eat and drink" (Malbim). Or, unlike Moses who went forty days without food when he saw the Divine (34:28), they had to eat and drink (*Tanchuma B. Acharey* 13a; *Midrash Agadah* on Leviticus 16:1; Ibn Ezra). Others say that the vision of the Divine nourished them like food (*Zohar* 1:135a,b; cf. *VaYikra Rabbah* 20:10; *Berakhoth* 17a; *Targum; Lekach Tov*).

24:12 **God said . . .** There is a dispute as to whether this is in chronological order, or whether it was before the Ten Commandments (*Yoma* 4a).

— **stone tablets.** See 31:18, 32:15, Deuteronomy 4:13, 5:19. These may have been made of the sapphire brick the Israelites saw, see note on 24:10.

24:13 **Joshua.** See 17:9.

24:14 **Chur.** See 17:10.

24:15 **it.** The mountain (Rashi), Or, "and Moses was covered" (Ibn Ezra). Both are opinions found in the Talmud (*Yoma* 4b).

24:18 **mountain top** (Ibn Ezra). Literally "mountain."

— **forty days.** . . . The narrative continues in 31:18.

25:1 **God spoke to Moses . . .** Some say that this was said to Moses during the 40 days on the mountain (*Tanna DeBei Eliahu Rabbah* 17; *Lekach Tov* on 35:1; Ibn Ezra; *Baaley Tosafoth; Zohar* 2:194a, 224a). According to others, it was said after the Golden Calf, when Moses went up for the second set of tablets (34:29; *Seder Olam Rabbah* 6 from Exodus 34:32; *Tanchuma* 8; Rashi on 31:18, 33:11). See notes on 25:16, 26:30.

25   bring Me an offering.* Take My offering from everyone whose heart impels
     him to give.
         ³ The offering that you take from them shall consist of the following:
     Gold, silver, copper,* ⁴ sky-blue* [wool],* dark red* [wool], [wool dyed with]

25:2   **offering.** *Terumah* in Hebrew, literally, something that is uplifted or elevated (to a higher status).

25:3   **copper.** Or, "bronze." The Septuagint thus translates the word as *xalkos* which can denote copper or
bronze, and the *MeAm Lo'ez*, also, translates it as *alambre* which is Spanish for copper or bronze. There is
some indication that the Hebrew word *nechosheth* used here indicates pure unalloyed copper (Deuteronomy 8:9; Radak on 1 Kings 7:45). Others, however, state that the Temple vessels were made of brass,
which has the same color as gold (Ezra 8:27, Ibn Ezra *ad loc.;* Radak, s.v. *Tzahav;* Rambam on *Middoth*
2:3), and the Talmud clearly states that the vessels made by Moses consisted of this material (*Arkhin* 10b).
Josephus writes that the brass altar looked like gold (*Antiquities* 3:6:8; see below 27:2). Perhaps it was an
alloy of copper and silver or gold.

25:4   **sky-blue** (Saadia; *Yad, Tzitzith* 2:1; Josephus 3:6:4).
Tekheleth in Hebrew. According to others, it was
greenish blue or aquamarine (Rashi; Ibn Ezra; cf.
Yerushalmi, *Berakhoth* 1:5), deep blue, the color of
the evening sky (Menachem, quoted in Rashi on
Numbers 15:38), azure or ultramarine (Radak,
Sherashim) or hyacinth blue (Septuagint; cf. *Arukh s.v.*
Teynun). The Talmud states that it resembled indigo
(*Menachoth* 42b).

Indigo   Cuttlefish

     This blue dye was taken from an animal known
as the *chilazon* (*Tosefta, Menachoth* 9:6). It is a boneless invertebrate (*Yerushalmi, Shabbath* 1:3), having a shell
that grows with it (*Devarim Rabbah* 7:11). It is thus identified with a snail of the *purpura* family (Ravya on
Berakhoth 3b; *Mossef HeArukh*, s.v. *Purpura*). The Septuagint also occasionally translates *tekheleth* as *olopor-*
phoros, which indicates that it was made from the pure dye of the purpura (see next note).
     There were some who identified the *chilazon* with the common cuttlefish, *Sephia officinalis* (*Eyn*
Tekheleth, p. 29), but most evidence contradicts this.
     It is known that the ancient Tyrians were skilled in making this sky-blue dye (2 Chronicles 2:6; cf.
Ezekiel 27:16), and that the snails from which it was made were found on the coast of northern Israel
and Phoenecia (*Targum Yonathan* on Deuteronomy 33:19; *Shabbath* 26a; Strabo 16:757). This indicates
that it was the famed Tyrian blue. Around the ancient Tyrian dyeworks, shells of *Murex trunculus* and
Murex brandaris are found. These dyes were also made in Greece and Italy, (Ezekiel 27:7, *Targum ad loc.;*
cf. *Iliad* 4:141; Aristotle, *History of Animals* 5:15), and remains of these ancient dyeworks have been found
in Athens and Pompeii. The shells found there were the *Purpura haemastoma* and *Murex brandaris* (cf. Pliny
9:61).

     Some have identified the *chilazon* with *Janthina pallia*
or *Janthina bicolor*, deep water snails which produce a
light violet-blue (hyacinth) dye (Rabbi Yitzchak Isaac
HaLevi Herzog; *The Dying of Purple in Ancient Israel*,
Unpublished, 1919). In ancient times, animals such as
these were renowned for their dyes (Pliny 9:60,61).
     The dye is removed from a cyst near the head of

Purpura   Janthina

the snail, preferably while the animal is still alive
(*Shabbath* 75a; Aristotle, *History of Animals* 5:15). It is boiled with alum as a clarifyer (*Menachoth* 42b, Rashi
ad loc.; cf. Rashi, *Avodah Zarah* 33b) to produce the dye. The wool is then grounded with alkanat root or
aloe wood in order for it to take the dye well (*Yad, Tzitzith* 2:2; Pliny 9:63).
     Only a few drops of dye could be obtained from each snail (Pliny 9:61), and according to one
modern researcher, over 8000 snails would be needed to make a single cubic centimeter of the dye. This
explains its high cost and its restriction to royalty. See note on Numbers 15:38.

—   **wool.** (*Yevamoth* 4b; Rashi). Nothing other than wool or linen could be used for the priestly vestments
(*Kelayim* 9:1). Some say that the verse here is speaking of dyed silk (Abarbanel; cf. Ibn Ezra), but this goes
against Talmudic tradition (Bachya; *Sedey Chemed, Chanukah* 14, 8:52).

crimson worm,* linen,* goats' wool,* ⁵ reddened* rams' skins, blue-processed   25
skins,* acacia* wood, ⁶ oil for the lamp,* spices for the anointing oil* and the

—   **dark red** (Ibn Ezra; Ibn Janach; *Pesikta Rabathai* 20:3, 86a). *Argaman* in Hebrew. Others state that it is similar to lake, a purplish red dye extracted from lac (Radak, *Sherashim;* Rambam on *Kelayim* 9:1; cf. *Yad, Kley HaMikdash* 8:13). Although the Septuagint translates *argaman* as *porphura* or *porphoreus,* which means purple, in ancient times, "purple" denoted a deep crimson, most notably the dye obtained from the purpura snail. Ancient sources indicate that it was close to the color of fresh blood (Iliad 4:141).

     Talmudic sources state that *argaman* was obtained from a living creature (*Yerushalmi, Kelayim* 9:1), and other sources indicate that it was an aquatic creature (*1 Maccabees* 4:23; Abarbanel on 25:10). Like *tekheleth* it was obtained from Tyre (*2 Chronicles* 2:6, cf. Ezekiel 27:16) as well as Greece or Italy (Ezekiel 27:7, *Targum ad loc.*).

     This dye was therefore most probably derived from a species of the murex or purpura snail. The Septuagint translation, *porphura,* also denotes the purpura snail. Ancient sources indicate that snails caught in the north yielded a blue dye, while those from the south yielded a reddish dye (Aristotle, *History of Animals* 5:15). *Argaman* was most probably obtained from the "red purpura," *Purpura haemastoma,* known to the ancients as the *buccinum* (Pliny 9:61; see *Reshith Limudim* 1:6).

     In ancient times, material dyed with this color was extremely valuable (cf. *Shabbath* 90a; *Kelim* 27:12), and it was weighed as carefully as gold (*Kelim* 29:4).

     The Hebrew word *argaman* is obscure, but it is thought to be related to *ragman,* Sanskrit for red. Others say that it is related to the root *arag,* meaning "to weave" (*BeMidbar Rabbah* 4:17, 12:4). Some therefore say that it consisted of two types of thread or three colors woven together (Raavad, *Kley HaMikdash* 8:13). Some say that it is an irridescent dye, having greenish overtones (*Zohar* 2:139a; *Tikkuney Zohar* 70, 127b, top, 124a, top; *Maaseh Choshev* 3:2).

—   **crimson worm** (Saadia; Radak, *Sherashim;* Ramban on Parah 3:10; Septuagint). *Tolaath shani* in Hebrew. Some sources indicate that it was close to orange (*Pesikta Rabathai* 20:3, Radal *ad loc.* 36) or pink (*Zohar* 2:139a as quoted in *Maaseh Choshev* 3:2).

     The dye is produced by a mountain worm (*Tosefta, Menachoth* 9:16) that looks like a red pea (Rashi on Isaiah 1:18; *Yad, Parah Adumah* 3:2). This is the *Kermes biblicus,* known as *kermez* in Arabic (cf. Saadia; Ralbag translates it as *grana,* Spanish for conchineal), the conchineal insect, or shield louse, that lives on oak trees in the Holy Land (cf. Pliny 21:22). There are two species, *Kermes nahalali* and *Kermes greeni.* In the early spring, when the females are filled with red eggs and become pea-shaped, the red dye can be squeezed out of them (*MeAm Lo'ez*). See Leviticus 14:4–6, Numbers 19:6.

—   **linen.** *Shesh* in Hebrew, literally, "six," indicating a six ply linen thread (*Yoma* 71b). For this purpose, Egyptian linen, which was particularly silk-like, was used (Saadia; Ibn Ezra).

—   **goats' wool.** Like angora (Saadia; Rashi; Abarbanel) or mohair (*MeAm Lo'ez, tiptik* in Turkish). Or, "goats' hair" (Rashbam; Ibn Ezra).

25:5   **reddened . . .** Dyed red (Saadia; Rashi). Or, according to others, reddened by some process while the animal is still alive (cf. *Tosefta, Shabbath* 91:13; *Yerushalmi, Shabbath* 7:2).

—   **blue processed skins** (Rabbi Yehudah, *Yerushalmi, Shabbath* 2:3; *Arukh s.v. Teynun; Koheleth Rabbah* 1:9; Josephus 3:6:1, 3:6:4; Septuagint; Aquilla). *Tachash* in Hebrew. Others have "black leather" (Saadia; Ibn Janach), that is, leather worked in such a manner as to come out dark and waterproof (Avraham ben HaRambam). In ancient Egyptian, *tachash* also denotes a kind of specially worked leather. See Ezekiel 16:10.

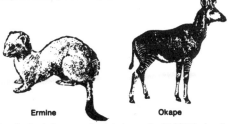

Ermine   Okape

     Other sources identify *tachash* as a species of animal. Some say that it is the ermine (Rabbi Nechemia, *Yerushalmi, loc. cit.; Arukh,* s.v. *glaksinon*). The word *galy axeinon* denotes the ermine, a member of the weasel family imported by the Axenoi (see Jastrow). Others state that it is a member of the badger family (Rashi on Ezekiel 16:10).

     Others say that it is a colorful one-horned animal known as a keresh (*Yerushalmi, loc. cit.; Shabbath*

25   sweet-smelling incense,* [7] and sardonyxes* and other precious stones* for the
     ephod* and breastplate.*
       [8] They shall make Me a sanctuary, and I will dwell among them.
       [9] You must make the tabernacle and all its furnishings following the plan
     that I am showing you.

                              [*100. The Ark*]

       [10] Make an ark* of acacia wood, 2½ cubits long, 1½ cubits wide, and 1½
     cubits high.* [11] Cover it with a layer* of pure gold on the inside and outside,
     and make a gold rim* all around its top.

28b;   Tanchuma   6;
Rashi; cf. Chullin 59b).
Some say that this is a
species   of   wild   ram
(Ralbag),   possibly   an
antelope, okape or gi-
raffe. Some see the one-

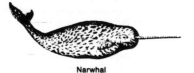
Narwhal

Dugong

horned creature as the narwhal (*Mondon monoceros*) which has its left tooth developed into a single long
horn-like appendage. This animal, which can grow to be over 16 feet long, is occasionally found on the
southern Sinai shores.
    In Arabic, *tukhush* denotes the sea cow or dugong (*Dugong hempirchi*) an aquatic mammal which is
found on the shores of the Sinai. Some thus say that the *tachash* is a type of seal, since its skins were used
for the tabernacle's roof, and sealskins were often used for this purpose (cf. Pliny 2:56).

—   **acacia** (Saadia, *shant* in Arabic). *Shittim* in Hebrew, *shittah* in the
    singular (Isaiah 41:19). The *shittah* is probably *Acacia albida*, a tall
    tree with a thick trunk, now growing only in Migdal Tzavo'aya. The
    wood is very light and hard (cf. Abarbanel; Chizzkuni) and it does
    not absorb moisture. The Talmud states that it is a member of the
    cedar family (*Rosh HaShanah* 28a; Ralbag Radak s.v. *Shut*). The
    Septuagint translates it as "decay-proof wood" (cf. Josephus
    3:6:1; Philo, *Questions and Answers* 53), and this is supported by Tal-
    mudic tradition (Yoma 72a, Rashi *ad loc.* from 26:15).

25:6   **oil for the lamp.** See below, 27:20.
—   **anointing oil.** See 30:23-33.
—   **incense.** See 30:34-38.
25:7   **sardonyxes.** See below, 28:20. Also see Genesis 2:12.   Acacia
—   **precious stones.** Perfectly formed (Ramban). Or, "stones meant to be set" (Rashi; Rashbam; cf. Abar-
       banel).
—   **ephod.** See 28:6-12.
—   **breastplate.** See 28:15-30.
25:10 **ark.** *Aron* in Hebrew. See 37:1-9. A simple box without legs (Rashi). Others, however, state that it had
       legs (Ibn Ezra on 25:12) or a lower rim (cf. Yoma 72b).
—   **2½ cubits . . .** The dimensions of the ark were thus 3' 9" x 2' 3" x 2'
       3". According to others, the cubits here were only of 5 hand-
       breadths, and the ark's dimensions were 3' 1.5" x 1' 10.5" x 1'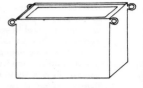
       10.5".
         Some say that the walls of the ark were a handbreadth (3 inches)
       thick (Yoma 72b, Rabbenu Chananel *ad. loc.*; Abarbanel; *Maaseh
       Choshev* 8:2). According to others, it was one half handbreadth
       (1.5 inches) or a fingerbreadth (0.75 inches) thick (*Bava Bathra* 14a;
       Bareitha Melekheth HaMishkan 6.)
25:11 **layer.** Some say that this was like a thin box of gold around the wooden box (Yoma 72b; Ralbag). Accord-
       ing to others, the box was gilded with gold leaf (*Yerushalmi, Shekalim* 6:1. See note on 30:3.

¹² Cast* four gold rings for [the ark], and place them on its four corners,* two rings on one side, and two on the other side.*
¹³ Make two carrying poles of acacia wood and cover them with a layer of gold. ¹⁴ Place the poles in the rings on the sides of the ark,* so that the ark can be carried with them. ¹⁵ The poles must remain in the ark's rings and not be removed.
¹⁶ It is in this ark that you will place the testimony* that I will give you.*
¹⁷ Make a golden cover* for the ark, 2½ cubits long and 1½ cubits wide.*

25

— **rim.** Or "crown," *zer* in Hebrew. According to the first opinion above (previous note), the outer gold box extended a little more than a handbreadth above the wooden core of the ark, so as to protrude slightly above the cover when it was placed on the ark (*Yoma* 72b; Rashi; *Midrash Agadah*). Others say that this implies that the edges of the wooden core should also be covered (Chizzkuni).
    Some say that the purpose of this rim was to hold the ark-cover (Rashi; Ralbag). Josephus (3:6:5), however, states that the cover was held on with hinges.

25:12 Cast. Some say that the rings were cast separately, and then attached to the ark (Ralbag; Abarbanel; cf. 37:13). According to others, the rings were cast together with the outer shell or welded onto it (Rashbam). Some say that the carrying poles actually went through the walls of the ark, and that these rings were like re-inforcements (Josephus 3:6:5; cf. *Bava Bathra* 14a).

— **corners.** (*Targum;* Radak, *Sherashim*). Some say that the rings were at the very top of the ark (Rashi). According to others, they were 2½ handbreadths (7 inches) from the top of the ark (*Shabbath* 92a, Rashi *ad loc.*). Still others state that the rings were at the very bottom of the ark (Ramban; Bachya). According to those who maintain that the ark had legs, the rings were on its feet (Ibn Ezra; Abarbanel).

— **two rings** . . . Thus, the ark had only four rings, one on each corner (Rashi; Rashbam; *Lekach Tov;* Ralbag; Abarbanel). Others maintain that the ark had eight rings, two on each corner, and translate the verse, "place [the first four rings] on [the ark's] four corners, and then place [another] two rings on one side, and two on the other" (*Tosafoth, Yoma* 72a, s.v. *Kethiv*). According to one opinion, the rings on the corners were to move the ark by hand, while the second set of rings for the poles were on the ark's sides, and not on its corners (Rosh: *Tur*). Others maintain that each ring affixed to the ark held a second movable ring through which the poles were placed, translating the verse, "Weld four rings onto the four corners of the ark, and [place in these rings] two rings on one side, and two rings on the other" (*Bekhor Shor;* Chizzkuni; *Or HaChaim*) (A). According to the opinion that the ark had legs, the verse would be translated "place [the first four rings] on [the ark's] four feet, and [place] two rings on one side [of the ark itself], and two rings on the other side," indicating that the first set of rings was on the ark's feet, and the second set on its sides (Ibn Ezra).

A

25:14 in the rings . . . The poles were parallel to the shorter ends of the ark, so that there were 2½ cubits between the two poles (*Menachoth* 98a,b; Rashi; Rashbam; Ramban) (A). However, other sources indicate that the poles went along the length of the ark (Josephus 3:6:5) (B).

25:16 testimony. Some say that this denotes the Tablets of the Ten Commandments (Rashbam; Ibn Ezra; cf. 1 Kings 8:9). Others say that it also includes the entire Torah (Rashi; Abarbanel; *Tzeror HaMor;* Introduction to *Yad*). This point is debated in the Talmud (*Bava Bathra* 14a). The dispute is related to the dispute as to when the commandment was given (see next note).

A

— **I will give you.** If the command was given while Moses was on the mountain, then "testimonies" can denote the tablets, which were yet to be given. However, if the command was given after Moses came down with the tablets (see note on 25:1), then "testimony" must denote the Torah that was yet to be given.

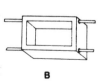

25:17 cover. (Saadia; Rashi; Rashbam). *Kapporeth* in Hebrew. The Septuagint translates it as *ilastyrion*, which denotes reconciliation, propitiation, appeasement and atonement (*Kapparah;* cf. *Tanchuma* 10) *Tzeror HaMor*). Philo translates it as "throne of mercy" or "mercy seat" (*Questions and Answers* 60; cf. *Tanchuma, VaYakhel* 7).

B

— **2½ cubits** . . . 3' 9" x 2' 3", like the dimensions of the ark (25:10). The Talmud states that the ark cover

25   **18** Make two* golden cherubs,* hammering them out from the two ends*
of the cover. **19** One cherub shall be on one end, and one on the other. Make
the cherubs from [the same piece of gold] as the cover itself,* on its two ends.
20 The cherubs shall spread their wings upward* so that their wings shield the
cover.* The cherubs shall face one another,* but their faces shall [also be
inclined downward] toward the cover.*

       21 Place the cover on top of the ark [after]* you place into the ark the testi-
mony that I will give you.

       22 I will commune* with you there, speaking to you from above the ark-
cover, from between the two cherubs that are on the Ark of Testimony. [In this
manner] I will give you instructions for the Israelites.

[101. The Table]

       23 Make a table* out of acacia wood, 2 cubits long, one cubit wide, and 1½
cubits high.* **24** Cover it with a layer of pure gold,* and make a gold rim* all

---

was one handbreadth (3 inches) thick (*Sukkah* 5a). It can easily be calculated that if it were solid gold, it
would weigh (without the cherubs), some 2500 pounds, or 17 talents (see note on 25:39). Some sources
thus state that the ark cover was considerably thinner (*Tur*), since we find that the ark had to be light
enough to be carried easily (Baaley Tosafoth on 25:11). One source states that the ark-cover weighed
one talent (150 pounds), just like the menorah (25:39; Saadia Gaon, quoted in Ibn Ezra on 38:24). The
ark cover would therefore have been around 3/16 inch thick, or, if the cherubs are taken into account,
more likely around 1/8 inch thick. It may have been made like an inverted open box, so that its sides
were one handbreadth thick on the outside.

25:18 **two.** Paralleling God's two names, the Tetragrammaton and *Elohim* (*Paneach Raza; Midrash Tadshe* 2). See
25:20.

— **cherubs.** See note on Genesis 3:24. The cherubs were creatures like birds (*Or HaAfelah;* Rashbam; Chizzkuni; Philo, *De Vide Mose* 2:99) with wings (25:20) and faces like human infants (*Chagigah* 13b; Ralbag).
Some say that one was male and the other was female (Rashi on 1 Chronicles 3:10; Bachya, from *Yoma*
54a; cf. *Zohar* 3:59a). See Ezekiel 10:7-15.

— **ends.** Lengthwise (Rashbam; Ibn Ezra) at the very edges of the cover (*Haamek Davar*).

25:19 **from the same piece** . . . (Saadia; Rashi; Ibn Ezra; Rashi on 25:18).

25:20 **upward.** Parallel to their heads (Rashi; Rashbam), as if they were taking off (Ralbag).

— **shield the cover.** Their wings were 10 handbreadths (30 inches) over the ark-cover (*Sukkah* 5b). This was
the height of the cherubs (Rashi *ad loc.*).

— **face one another.** Directly. Others say that they faced toward the east, toward the opening of the Holy of
Holies, with their heads inclined toward each other (*Bava Bathra* 99a). Others say that their bodies faced
toward the east, but their heads faced each other (*Chokhmath HaMishkan; Maaseh Choshev* 8:5). They faced
each other so that they would not appear to be gods (*Moreh Nevukhim* 3:45).

— **inclined downward** . . . (*Baaley Tosafoth;* Ibn Ezra). Or, "The cherubs shall face one another, with their
faces toward the middle of the ark-cover" (Rashbam).

25:21 **after** (Saadia; Rashi; Ibn Ezra; Ralbag; Abarbanel). Or, "because you will place the testimony . . . in the
ark" (Ramban; cf. *Yerushalmi, Shekalim* 6:1). Others, "Place the cover . . . and then you will be able to
place the testimony" (Chizzkuni).

25:22 **commune** (Ibn Janach; cf. *Targum*). Or, "I will meet with you at set times" (Rashi; Radak, *Sherashim*).

25:23 **table.** See 37:10-16.

— **2 cubits** . . . Its dimensions were thus 36" x 18" x 27". According to others, it was 30" x 15" x 22.5"
(*Menachoth* 96a; *Bareitha* 8). The height included the legs and the thickness of the table's upper board
(Rashi; Ibn Ezra; cf. *Pesachim* 109b). The top of the table consisted of a perfectly flat slab of wood
(*Menachoth* 96b), that was not attached to the legs (*Pesachim* 109a). The legs were described as resembling
those the Dorians use on their beds (Josephus 3:6:6)

around it. ²⁵ Make a frame* a handbreadth wide all around the table, and on   25
the frame all around, the golden rim shall be placed.*

²⁶ Make four gold rings* for [the table], and place the rings on the four
corners of its four legs. ²⁷ The rings shall be adjacent to* the frame, [and] they
shall be receptacles for the poles with which the table is carried. ²⁸ The poles
shall be made of acacia wood and covered with a layer of gold. They will be
used to carry the table.

²⁹ For [the table] make* bread forms,* incense bowls,* and side frames,* as

25:24 Cover it . . . Some say that the table was covered with gold only on the outside (*Paaneach Raza* on 25:11).
Others, however, maintain that it was gilded on all sides (Abarbanel; cf. Tosafoth *Chagigah* 26b, s.v.
Kaan).

— **gold rim.** See 25:11. Or "crown" (cf. Rashi).

25:25 frame. This frame held the table's legs together, and the top
board of the table was placed upon it (Tosefta, *Menachoth* 11:3;
Menachoth 96b; Ralbag; Radak s.v. *Zer*) (A). Others maintain
that this was a wooden rim around the top of the table upon
which the crown was placed (Ibid.; Chizzkuni) (B). According
to this opinion, the frame was to the sides of the table, so that

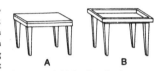

the entire top was exposed (*Menachoth* 96b). Some say that this frame was held in place by the crown
around the top of the table board (Abarbanel), but this seems to go against the Talmud. According to
some, the rim was directly on the edge of the table, protruding above the flat surface and attached to the
legs (Josephus 3:6:6).

— **and on the frame** . . . Since the table only had a single golden rim, and not two (Rashi; cf. *Yoma* 72b).
According to the opinion that the frame was below the table top, the rim ran around the frame, and
extended somewhat above the table top, possibly to hold it in place (Ralbag; *Maaseh Choshev* 7:2).
According to those who maintain that the frame was above the table top, the crown was on the frame
(Chizzkuni). There are, however, some who maintain that there were two rims, one on the table top to
hold the frame, and another on the frame itself (Abarbanel).

25:26 gold rings. These were also cast (37:13). Some say that these were half rings, with one end in the legs and
the other in the frame (Josephus 3:6:6). Others say that each fixed ring had a movable ring attached to it
to hold the poles, just like the ark (Or HaChaim).

25:27 adjacent to. But not in the frame (*Lekach Tov*; Abarbanel). Some say that they were directly below the
frame (Rashbam). According to others, the rings were completely or partly in the frame itself (Ralbag; cf.
Josephus 3:6:6).

25:29 make. See below 37:10–12. Numbers 4:6, 1 Chronicles 28:17.

— **bread forms.** (*Menachoth* 97a; Rashi) These were used to form the showbread (25:30). There were three
sets of bread forms, one for the dough, one for baking, and one to place the bread in after it was baked
so that it would not be damaged (*Menachoth* 94a; *Yad, Temidin* 5:8). Some say that all these were made of
gold (*Ibid.*), while others say that the forms for baking were made of iron (Rashi). However, some say
that no iron was used in the tabernacle (Ibn Ezra on 25:3; cf. 27:19, Deuteronomy 27:5). Regarding the
shape of the bread, see 25:30.

The Hebrew word *ka'aroth* used here literally means plates. Some say that plates were actually placed
on the table, as if to set it for a meal (Philo, *Questions and Answers* 72).

— **incense bowls** (*Menachoth* 97a; Rashi). For the frankincense (Leviticus 24:7). Some say that these were like
small boxes (Saadia). There is a question as to whether they were placed in the center of the table
between the loaves, or on top of the loaves (*Menachoth* 96a; see note on 25:30).

The word *kappoth* used here often is used to denote spoons. Philo (*loc. cit.*) writes that they were part of
the table setting.

— **side frames** (*Menachoth* 97a.) *Kesavoth* in Hebrew. Some say that the function of these was to support the
breads from the side, so that the loaves would not crumble (Tosafoth, *Menachoth* 94b, s.v. *Hayinu; Or
HaAfelah; Yad, Temidin* 5:9), or to prevent them from falling when the table was lifted (*Menachoth* 96b).
They were needed, since there were twelve loaves, six in each stack (Leviticus 24:5,6). According to this
opinion, the loaves were stacked directly one on top of the other.

25 well as the half tubes* that will serve as dividers* [between the loaves of bread]. All these shall be made of pure gold.

³⁰It is on this table that showbread* shall be placed before Me at all times.

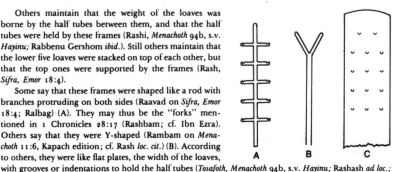

Others maintain that the weight of the loaves was borne by the half tubes between them, and that the half tubes were held by these frames (Rashi, *Menachoth* 94b, s.v. *Hayinu;* Rabbenu Gershom *ibid.*). Still others maintain that the lower five loaves were stacked on top of each other, but that the top ones were supported by the frames (Rash, *Sifra, Emor* 18:4).

Some say that these frames were shaped like a rod with branches protruding on both sides (Raavad on *Sifra, Emor* 18:4; Ralbag) (A). They may thus be the "forks" mentioned in 1 Chronicles 28:17 (Rashbam; cf. Ibn Ezra). Others say that they were Y-shaped (Rambam on *Menachoth* 11:6, Kapach edition; cf. Rash *loc. cit.*) (B). According to others, they were like flat plates, the width of the loaves, with grooves or indentations to hold the half tubes (*Tosafoth, Menachoth* 94b, s.v. *Hayinu;* Rashash *ad loc.; Maaseh Choshev* 7:3) (C).

Some say that these frames rested on the ground, while others maintain that they rested on the table top (*Menachoth* 94b).

According to some, the *kesavoth* here were not the side frames, but the half tubes (see next note).

There is also an opinion that there were no side supports at all, but that the breads were held in place by the frame (Rabbi Yosi, *Menachoth* 96b, cf. Tosafoth ad loc.). This may agree with the Septuagint, which translates the *kesoth* or *kesavoth* (37:16) as spondeon, denoting libation cups (cf. Ibn Janach; also see Philo, *Questions and Answers* 72). Others say that they were pans to hold water to knead the bread (Chizzkuni).

— **half tubes** (*Menachoth* 97a; *Yad, Beth HaBechirah* 3:14) (D). Menakiyoth in Hebrew, cf. Jeremiah 52:19. These were placed between the breads to allow air to circulate between them, and possibly to support them (*Menachoth* 96a; see previous note). There were 28 such half tubes in all,

14 for each side, so that 3 were placed between each loaf, except for the two upper ones, where only 2 were placed between them (*Menachoth* 97a; *Yad, Beth HaBechirah* 3:14).

Some reverse these two and maintain that the *kesoth* were the half tubes and the *menakiyoth* were the frames (Rashi; Radak, s.v. *Nasakh;* cf. *Tosafoth, Menachoth* 96b, s.v. *Lo*).

The Septuagint translates *menakioth* as *kuathoi,* Greek for the cups used for drawing wine out of the *krator* or bowl, (cf. Philo *loc. cit.*). Others state that they were ladles or spoons (Saadia; Ibn Janach), measuring cups (Ramban), or implements to clean the ovens (Chizzkuni).

— **serve as dividers** (Rashbam; Rashi; cf. Numbers 4:7). Or, "to cover the bread" if it refers to the frames which were gold plates concealing the bread (cf. 37:16). If the above utensils were cups and bowls, this is then translated "with which they are poured" (Septuagint; c.f. Ibn Ezra).

25:30 showbread. *Lechem ha-panim* in Hebrew, literally, "bread of the face." See Leviticus 24:5–8.

The loaves were rectangular, a cubit long, and 5 handbreadths wide (18" x 15"). They thus covered the entire table, leaving two handbreadths (6") in the middle for the pans of frankincense (Leviticus 24:7). (*Menachoth* 96a; *Yad, Temidin* 5:9) (A). According to others, the loaves covered the entire table, and the frankincense was placed on top of the stack (*Menachoth* 96a) (B).

Each loaf was made of 2/10 ephah of flour (Leviticus 24:5; see below). It was rolled into a loaf 5 handbreadths wide and 10 handbreadths long (15" x 30").

Before it was baked (*Melekheth Sh'lomoh* on *Menachoth* 11:5), the sides were bent up 2 handbreadths (6") on each side. This would give the bread its final square shape where its base was 5 x 6 handbreadths (*Menachoth* 96a). The loaves would have the shape of a box with both ends removed (*Menachoth* 96b). According to others, their shape was more like that of a boat (*Ibid.*).

In order to strengthen the walls of the loaves, pieces of dough 7 fingerbreadths (5¼") by one hand-

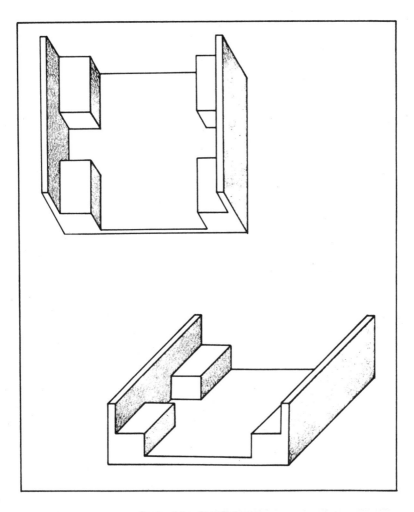

PLATE 14. THE SHOWBREAD

25

[*102. The Lamp*]

³¹ Make a menorah* out of pure gold. The menorah shall be formed by hammering it. Its base,* stem, and [decorative] cups,* spheres* and flowers* must be hammered out of a [single piece of gold].

³² Six branches* shall extend from its sides, three branches on one side of the menorah, and three branches on the other side.

breadth (3″) were placed on the corners (Rashi, *Menachoth* 96a, s.v. *VeKarno-theha; Tifereth Yisrael, Chomer BaKodesh* 2:51).

The loaves themselves were like unperforated matzah (*Pesachim* 37a; Josephus 3:10:7) around a half inch thick. [This is a simple calculation. The volume of the loaf was 2 tenths of an ephah, and since an ephah is 3 saah, the volume was 0.6 saah. The Talmud notes that 3 cubic cubits is equal to 40 saah (*Eruvin* 4b); and, since there are 6 handbreadths to a cubit, 1 saah is 16.2 cubic handbreadths. Since the volume of each loaf was 0.6 saah, it was 9.72 cubic handbreadths. Then, since the loaf was 5 x 10 handbreadths in size, its area was 50 square handbreadths. Dividing by this, the thickness of each loaf comes out to be 0.194 handbreadth or 0.58 inch] (Ralbag; *Tifereth Yisrael loc. cit.*)

Although the Talmud states that the breads were a handbreadth thick (*Pesachim* 37a), it is impossible to say that this was the thickness of the entire loaf. Rather, it was the thickness of the sides (Rashi; *Teshuvoth Tashbatz* 1:134), that is, the pieces of dough placed in the corners (*Tifereth Yisrael loc. cit;* see above).

25:31 **menorah.** A seven branched lamp. See 37:17-24, Numbers 8:4.

— **base.** Some say that this was like a triangular box with three legs (Rashi; *Baaley Tosafoth*) (A). In his commentary on the Mishnah, however, Maimonides draws the base as being like a hemisphere with three legs (*Menachoth* 3:7, see Kapach edition) (B). Other ancient drawings show the menorah

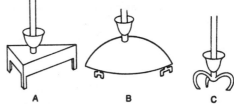

A   B   C

as having three legs extending directly from its base (cf. *Yad, Beth HaBechirah* 3:2; *Bareitha* 9; Ralbag) (C). Josephus (3:6:7), however, does not mention any legs.

Above the base there was a flower (from Numbers 8:4). The base and the flower together took up 3 handbreadths (9″) (*Menachoth* 28b).

— **cups.** Like "Alexandrian goblets" (*Menachoth* 28b). Wide with a narrow bottom, like the top of a champagne goblet (*Yad, Beth HaBechirah* 3:9; Rashi has *medirness* in French, a wine goblet) (D). Some sources state that the cups were to catch any dripping oil (Chizzkuni). Other sources, however, state that they were solid (Rambam on *Menachoth* 3:7), or merely impressed into the stem (Rashbam on 25:32). Some sources appear to indicate that the cups were inverted, with the wide side downward (Ralbag; Picture in Rambam *loc. cit.;* see Kapach's note).

— **spheres.** *Kaphtorim* in Hebrew, see Amos 9:1, Zephaniah 2:14. Some say that they were egg-shaped (*Yad, Beth HaBechirah* 3:9; cf. *Arukh* s.v. *Tapuach*).

— **flowers.** Like the flowers on a column (*Menachoth* 28b). These were like bowls with the edges bent outward (*Yad, Beth HaBechirah* 3:9) (E).

25:32 **branches.** Some say that they were hollow (Ibn Ezra). However, the majority maintain that they were solid (Abarbanel). Some maintain that this is implied by the word "hammered" (*mikshah*) (*Evven HaAzel, Beth HaBechirah* 3:4), but this is impossible, since the trumpets were *mikshah* (Numbers 10:2).

Some say that the branches were curved and extended on both sides like semicircles (Ibn Ezra on 25:37, 27:21; *Chokhmath HaMishkan* 4b; *Maaseh Choshev* 7:7), and most ancient pictures have it in this form. Others, however, say that the branches were straight

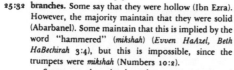

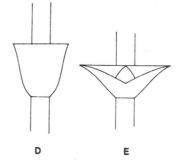

D   E

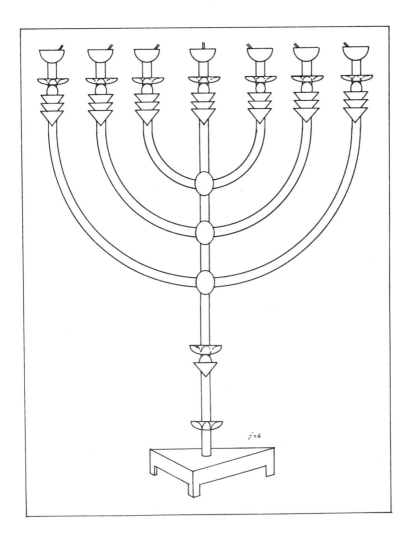

PLATE 15.   THE MENORAH

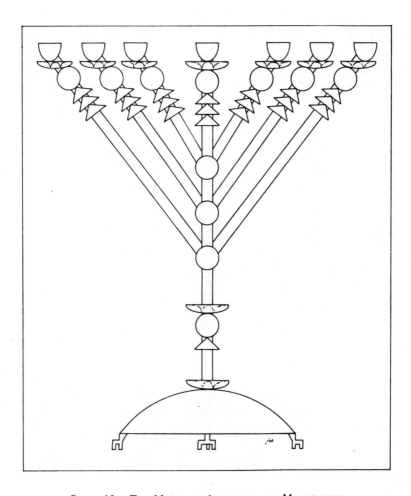

PLATE 16.   THE MENORAH ACCORDING TO MAIMONIDES

³³ There shall be three embossed* cups, as well as a sphere and a flower on each and every one of the branches. All six branches extending from the menorah's [stem] must be the same in this respect.

³⁴ The [shaft of the] menorah shall have four embossed cups* along with its spheres and flowers.* ³⁵ A sphere shall serve as a base* for each pair of branches extending from [the shaft]. This shall be true for all six branches extending from the [stem of] the menorah. ³⁶ The spheres and branches shall be an integral part of [the menorah]. They shall all be hammered out of a single piece of pure gold.

³⁷ Make seven lamps* on [the menorah]. Its lamps shall be lit so that they shine [primarily] toward its center.*

³⁸ [The menorah's] wick tongs* and ash scoops* shall [also] be made out of pure gold.

25

and extended diagonally upward, making the menorah look like a Y (Rashi; Avraham ben HaRambam; Rambam on *Menachoth* 3:7, picture in original manuscript, reproduced in Kapach edition).

25:33 **embossed** (*Targum; Yad, Beth HaBechirah* 3:2). Rashi states that this is niello, a word used also in English to denote an art of decorating metal with incised designs and black antiquing. Others say that it is a kind of beaten work (Ibn Ezra, from Proverbs 8:34). Others say that the Hebrew word *me-shukad-im* comes from the word *shaked*, as almond. It can thus mean almond-shaped (Saadia), decorated with almonds (Rashbam), or engraved like almonds (Radak, *Sherashim;* Ibn Janach). Others say that the metal is beaten in such a way that the surface appears like a pattern of tiny almonds (Rambam on *Menachoth* 3:7).

25:34 **four embossed cups** (Saadia; cf. *Yoma* 52b). One of these was below the branches, and three were above, paralleling the cups on the branches (*Menachoth* 28b; Rashi).

— **spheres and flowers.** Above the cups (*Menachoth* 28b).

25:35 **as a base.** Since the branches extended out of the sphere (*Menachoth* 28b). Literally, "under the branches."

The form of the menorah was then (*Menachoth* 28b);

3 hb.	9"	base and flower (25:31)
2 hb.	6"	smooth
1 hb.	3"	cup, sphere and flower
2 hb.	3"	smooth
1 hb.	3"	sphere with two branches
1 hb.	3"	smooth
1 hb.	3"	sphere with two branches
1 hb.	3"	smooth
1 hb.	3"	sphere with two branches
2 hb.	6"	smooth
3 hb.	9"	three cups, sphere, flower, lamp

The entire menorah was thus 18 handbreadths (4' 6") tall (see Rashi on 25:35; *Maaseh Choshev* 7:9).

25:37 **lamps.** Bowls or cups to hold oil (Rashi). Each of these cups held ½ log (6.8 ounces or 200 c.c.) of oil (*Menachoth* 88b; *Yad, Temidim* 3:11). If the cups were hemispherical in shape, they would be 3.6 inches (9.14 cm.) in diameter. These cups were an integral part of the menorah (*Yad, Beth HaBechirah* 3:6), but there are some who dispute this, and maintain that they were removable (*Menachoth* 88b).

— **toward its center.** Some say that this means that the wicks should face the center shaft (Rashi on Numbers 8:2; Rashbam; Ralbag) (A). Others maintain that the lamps themselves were tilted toward the center (*Menachoth* 98b; *Yad, Beth HaBechirah* 3:8) (B). This may mean that the side of the lamps toward the center slanted inward (Yehudah HaChasid).

25:38 **wick tongs.** *Malkachaim* in Hebrew, tongs or tweezers to insert and adjust the wicks (Rashi; Rashbam; Ralbag). Others say that they

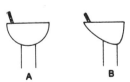

A   B

25   **39** [The menorah], including all its parts,* shall be made of a talent* of pure gold.

40 Carefully observe the pattern that you will be shown on the mountain and make [the menorah] in that manner.

[103. The Tabernacle]

26   **1** Make the tabernacle* out of ten large tapestries consisting of twined linen,* and sky-blue, dark red, and crimson [wool], with a pattern of cherubs* woven into* them. **2** Each tapestry shall be 28 cubits long and 4 cubits wide,* with each tapestry the same size.

3 The [first] five tapestries shall be sewn* together, and the [second] five shall [also] be sewn together.

4 Make loops of sky-blue wool at the edge of the innermost tapestry of the first group. Do the same on the edge of the innermost tapestry of the second group. **5** Place 50 loops on the one tapestry, and 50 on the edge of the tapestry in the second group. [The two sets of loops shall be made so that] the loops are exactly opposite one another.

6 Make 50 golden fasteners.* The two [groups of] tapestries will then be

---

were "wick holders," built into the menorah, possibly as plates over the oil holders (Ramban).

— **ash scoops.** *Machtoth* in Hebrew, small scoops to remove the ashes from the cups each day (Rashi; Rashbam; Ralbag). Others say that these were "ash catchers", small pans around each lamp to catch sparks and ashes, built into the menorah (Ramban).

25:39 all its parts. Literally, "all its utensils." However, the tongs and scoops were not included in the talent (*Menachoth* 88b; *Yad, Beth HaBechirah* 3:6).

— **talent.** *Kikar* in Hebrew. A talent is equal to 3000 shekels (see below 38:26, Rashi *ad loc.;* Rashi here) or 150 pounds (68.4 kg.). It can therefore easily be calculated that the diameter of the stem and branches of the menorah was around 1-1/8 inches (3 cm.).

[The weight of the menorah was 68.4 kg., and since the specific gravity of gold is 19.2, the volume of the menorah was 3562 cc. The combined length of the stem and all seven branches can be calculated to be around 200 inches (500 cm.). Therefore, the cross section of the branches was 7 square centimeters, and their diameter was 3 cm.]

26:1 tabernacle. These tapestries constituted the tabernacle proper. See 36:8 ff.

— **twined linen.** The threads were made of six thinner threads twisted together. The colored wools were also twined together with the linen to form a single thread, with various colors dominating (*Yad, Kley HaMikdash* 8:14).

— **cherubs.** See note on 25:18. Some say that there was a pattern of cherubs (*Midrash HaGadol*), while others maintain that there were two cherubs on each curtain (Rabbenu Meyuchas).

— **woven into.** So that the form could be seen on both sides of the tapestry (*Yoma* 72b; Rashi; *Yad, Kley HaMikdash* 8:15).

26:2 28 cubits long . . . Each curtain was 42' x 6'. This was the maximum width that could be woven practically.

26:3 sewn (Rashi; Rashbam; cf. *Shabbath* 99a, Rashi *ad loc.* s.v. *VeNere'in*). Literally, "attached."

26:6 fasteners. *Keres* in Hebrew. Some say that they were shaped like knees (Ibn Ezra from Isaiah 46:1) (A); they were therefore angular in shape, something like a staple (*Maaseh Choshev* 4:2) (B). Others say that they had hooks at both ends to go through the loops (Radak, *Sherashim*) (C). Still others describe them as being ¼ fingerbreadth long (3/8"), with bulbs at both ends to go through the loops (Rabbenu Meyuchas) (D).

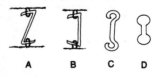

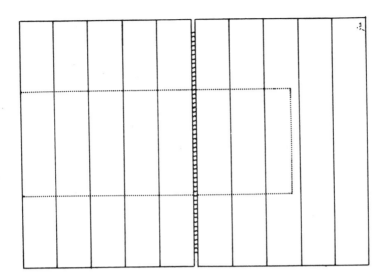

PLATE 17A.   THE TAPESTRIES OVER THE TABERNACLES

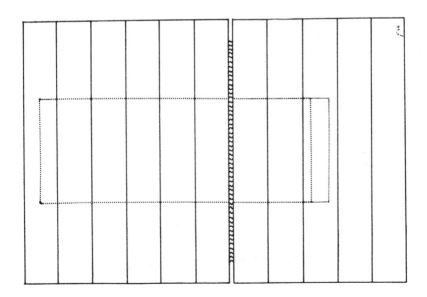

PLATE 17B.   THE SHEETS OF GOATS' WOOL

26 able to be joined together, so that the tabernacle will be one piece.*

⁷ Make sheets of goat's wool to serve as a tent over the tabernacle. There shall be 11 such sheets, ⁸ and each sheet shall be 30 cubits long, and 4 cubits wide.* All 11 sheets must be the same size.

⁹ Sew together the [first] five sheets by themselves, and the [other] six sheets by themselves. Half of the sixth sheet shall hang over* the front* of the tent.

¹⁰ Make 50 loops* on the edge of the innermost sheet of the first group, and 50 loops on the edge of the innermost sheet of the second group. ¹¹ Make 50 copper fasteners. Place the fasteners in the loops, bringing the tent together and making it one.

¹² There will then remain an extra portion from what is left over in [the breadth] of the sheets of the tent. The extra half sheet shall trail behind* the back* of the tabernacle.

—   **one piece.** The entire array was therefore 28 x 40 cubits (42' x 60'). As we shall soon see, the interior of the tabernacle was 10 x 30 cubits. Since the beams were one cubit thick, the exterior dimensions were 12 x 31 cubits. The height of the tabernacle was 10 cubits (26:16). Therefore, when the tapestries were placed over the beams, they left the lower 2 cubits of the beams exposed on the sides, and the lower cubit exposed in the back.

There is another opinion (see 26:24) that the beams were wedge-shaped, only one fingerbreadth (3/4") on top. According to this, the outer dimension of the beams on top was only 10 x 30 cubits, and only the lower cubit of the beams was exposed on the sides. This was the part of the beams covered with the bases. In the back of the tabernacle, even the bases were covered (*Shabbath* 98b).

According to another opinion, only the bottom cubit was exposed all around (Josephus 3:6:4).

26:8 **30 cubits . . .** Each curtain was 45' x 6'. These sheets were 2 cubits longer than the tapestries. They therefore hung down on the sides one cubit below the tapestries. Regarding the back, see below.

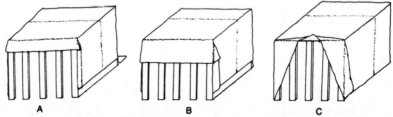

A   **B**   **C**

26:9 **shall hang over** (Rashbam; Rashi, *Shabbath* 98b, s.v. *Tartey*). Thus, the goats' wool sheet hung down 2 cubits (3 feet) over the front of the tabernacle (A). According to others, the pillars in front of the tabernacle (36:37) took up another cubit, so that the sheet hung down only one cubit (18") (*Maaseh Choshev* 4:5).

The verse can also be translated (more literally), "fold the sixth sheet down over the opening of the tent." According to this, the entire sixth sheet was over the front of the tent (*Bareitha Melekheth HaMishkan* 3) (B). According to this second opinion, the fasteners of the goats' wool sheets would be directly over those of the tapestries (cf. Rashi on 26:5).

According to one opinion, the corners of this overhanging curtain were folded back, giving the entrance a triangular appearance (Josephus 3:6:4) (C).

—   **front.** The eastern side.

26:10 **loops.** From goats' wool, like the sheets themselves (Abarbanel; *Maaseh Choshev* 4:4). One opinion maintains that the loops were of blue wool (*Torah Sh'lemah* 26:18).

26:12 **The extra half sheet . . .** Since there were 11 sheets, and half a sheet hung down over the front of the

13 The extra cubit on both sides in the length of the tent's sheets shall hang 26 down over the sides of the [tapestries of the] tabernacle to cover them on both sides.

14 Make a roof* for the tent out of reddened rams' skins. Above it* make a roof out of the blue processed hides.

[104. The Beams]

15 Make upright beams for the tabernacle out of acacia wood. 16 Each beam shall be 10 cubits long,* and 1½ cubits wide.

17 Each beam shall have two matching* square pegs* [carved out at the bottom]. All the beams for the tabernacle must be made in this manner.

18 Make 20 beams* for the southern side of the tabernacle. 19 Place 40

tabernacle (26:9). This half sheet was 2 cubits wide. According to the one who holds that the beams were a cubit wide on top, (see 26:6, 26:24), one cubit covered the bases, and one cubit trailed on the ground behind the tabernacle. According to the one who holds that the beams were narrow on top, two cubits trailed behind (*Shabbath* 98b). Some say that the curtains did not actually trail on the ground, but were held away from the tabernacle by the stakes (*Bekhor Shor;* Chizzkuni).

As mentioned above, (26:9), there is an opinion that the entire sixth sheet hung over the front of the tabernacle. This would follow the opinion that the beams were narrow on top, and that the covering hung down a full 10 cubits in the back. This verse would then be translated, "The remainder of the tent's sheets shall hang down. Half of [the first group] of remaining sheets shall hang down over the rear of the tabernacle." The group of 5 sheets was 20 cubits wide, and half of it would be the 10 cubits of the height of the tabernacle.

— **back.** The west side.

26:14 roof. Literally "covering."

— **Above it.** This is disputed; according to some, there was a single covering, made of the red and blue hides (*Bareitha* 3).

26:16 10 cubits . . . The beams were therefore 15′ x 2′ 3″. They were one cubit thick (A). According to some, they were wedge-shaped, a cubit thick on the bottom, and one fingerbreadth (¾″) on top (*Shabbath* 98b) (B). Other sources indicate that they were a handbreadth (3″) thick (Josephus 3:6:3; cf. Abarbanel).

26:17 matching (Rashbam), or "parallel" (Radak, *Sherashim,* cf. 1 Kings 7:28), or "tapered" (Rashi).

Others translate the verse, "Each beam shall have two pegs, [and they shall also] be plugged into one another." This indicates that on the sides of the beams there were pegs and holes to receive them (Ramban; *Bareitha* 1) (C). These pegs were 3¾ cubits (5′ 7¼″) from each end of the beams (*Maaseh Choshev* 2:7).

— **square pegs.** These were 1 cubit long so that they were covered by the bases (26:19). These pegs were formed by carving around ¼ inch (0.9 cm) all around the beam, and a notch twice as thick in the center (Ramban; see note on 26:18) (A). According to others, each peg was ¼ x ¼ cubit (9″ x 4½″), and was made by carving out ¼ cubit all around the beam, and ¼ cubit in the middle (Rashi; *Maaseh Choshev* 4:8) (B,C).

26:18 20 beams. Since each beam was 1½ cubits wide, the wall was 30 cubits (45′) long.

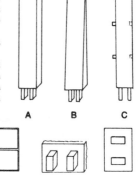

A   B   C

A   B   C

26 silver bases* under the 20 beams. There shall be two bases under each beam, one [to hold] each peg.

²⁰ For the second side of the tabernacle to the north, there shall [likewise] be 20 beams ²¹ and 40 silver bases. [Here too] there shall be two sockets under each and every beam.

²² Make six beams* for the west side of the tabernacle, ²³ and place [another] two beams at the corners.*

²⁴ [All the beams] must be exactly next to each other on the bottom. [Every pair] shall also be [joined] together evenly* on top with a [square] ring.* This shall also be done with the two [beams] on the two corners.

²⁵ Thus, [on the west side] there will be [a total of] eight beams and 16 silver bases, two bases under each and every beam.

²⁶ Make crossbars out of acacia wood. There shall be five* for the beams of the first side of the tabernacle [to the south]. ²⁷ [There shall also be] five for the beams of the second side [to the north], and five for the beams of the tabernacle on the western wall. ²⁸ [Of these], the center crossbar shall go through

—   **silver bases.** The outer dimensions of each base were one cubit high, one cubit thick, and ¾ wide, one half the width of a beam. It is simple to calculate that the walls of the bases could have been no more than around ⅓ inch (0.9 cm.) thick (A).

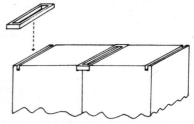

A   B

[Each base weighed one talent (38:27), which is 150 pounds or 68.4 kg (see note on 25:39). Since silver has a specific gravity of 10.5, each base had a volume of 6514 cc. The circumference of each base was 3½ cubits or 160 cm. and its height was one cubit or 45.72 cm. By simple division, the width of a wall comes out to be 0.9 cm thick.]

According to the opinion that the walls of the bases were ¼ cubit thick (Rashi on 26:17) (B), we must say that the bases were hollow. (If they were solid, each base would weigh 627 kg. or over 9 talents, in contradiction to an explicit verse stating that each one weighed only one talent).

26:22 six beams. For a width of 9 cubits.

26:23 two beams . . . Adding another 3 cubits, making the outside of the western wall 12 cubits (18') long. According to the opinion that the beams were tapered on top, the corner beams were special, since they came to a point on top (*Shabbath* 98b). According to the opinion that the beams were only a handbreadth thick, these corner beams were a cubit square (Josephus 4:6:3).

26:24 joined together evenly. According to the opinion that the beams were as wide on top as they were on the bottom. According to the opinion that the beams were wedge-shaped, this verse is translated, "they shall be tapered on top, [with each pair joined] by a single ring" (*Shabbath* 98b).

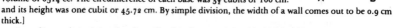

—   **square ring.** (*Maaseh Choshev* 2:6). These rings fitted into slots on the tops of the beams, joining each pair together (Rashi; *Bareitha* 1) (see figure). Some sources, however indicate that the rings here are those through which the crossbars (26:26) passed (*Bareitha* 1; Ramban).

26:26 five. Four of these, for the top and bottom, were half the length of the wall, while the fifth, for the center (26:28), was the entire length of the wall (Rashi; *Bareitha* 1). One source states that these crossbars consisted of sections 5 cubits (7½') long that plugged into one another (Josephus 4:6:3). They were placed through rings, one fourth of the way from the top and bottom of the beams (*Maaseh Choshev* 2:3).

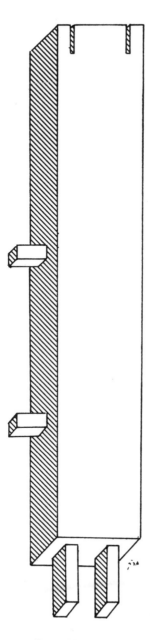

PLATE 18. A BEAM

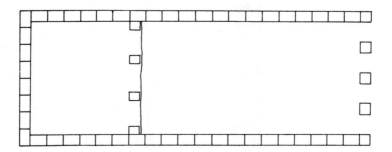

PLATE 19A.   THE TABERNACLE, TOP VIEW

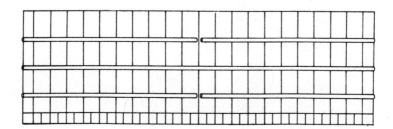

PLATE 19B.   THE TABERNACLE, SIDE VIEW

the middle of the beams, from one end [of the tabernacle] to the other. 26

²⁹ Cover the beams with a layer of gold. Also make gold rings* [on the beams] to hold the crossbars. The crossbars shall also be covered with a layer of gold.

³⁰ You will then be ready to set up the tabernacle in the proper manner, as you were shown on the mountain.*

[105. The Partition]

³¹ Make a cloth partition* out of sky-blue, dark red and crimson [wool, woven together] with twined linen. Cherubs shall be woven into it [so that they can be seen on both sides]. ³² Place it on four gold-covered acacia pillars* having gold hooks. [The pillars shall be] set in four silver sockets.

³³ Place the cloth partition directly under the fastenings* [holding the tapestries together].

Into the space behind this curtain you will bring the Ark of Testimony. This curtain will thus divide between the Sanctuary and the Holy of Holies. ³⁴ You will then place the cover on the Ark of Testimony in the Holy of Holies.

³⁵ Place the table outside the curtain, toward the northern wall of the tabernacle. The menorah shall be opposite the table, toward the southern wall of the tabernacle.

³⁶ Make a drape for the entrance of the tent, out of sky-blue, dark red and crimson wool, and twined linen. It shall be embroidered* work. ³⁷ Make five acacia pillars* to hold the drape. Cover them with a layer of gold and place golden hooks on them. Cast five copper bases for [the pillars].

[106. The Altar]

¹ Make the altar out of acacia wood. The altar shall be square, 5 cubits by 5 **27**

26:29 **rings.** Round rings (*Maaseh Choshev* 2:3). Some say that they were open on top, to take the crossbars (Abarbanel).

26:30 **as you were shown** . . . This would indicate that the commandment came after the 40 days (see note on 25:1).

26:31 **cloth partition.** *Parocheth* in Hebrew. The same word is now used for the covering of the Torah ark.

26:32 **pillars.** These were one cubit by ¾ cubit (18″ x 13¼″), half the width of the pillars on the outside, and the exact size to fit a single base (*Maaseh Choshev* 3:1). Others say that these pillars were the same as the ones on the outside (Abarbanel).

26:33 **under the fastenings.** This was 10 cubits from the inner wall. The Holy of Holies was therefore 10 x 10 cubits (15′ x 15′). It was perfectly cubical in shape. (*Bareitha* 4).

26:36 **embroidered.** (*Yoma* 72a).

26:37 **pillars.** These pillars had a cross section of one cubit square (*Bareitha of 49 Middoth,* in *Yalkut Shimoni* 422; *Maaseh Choshev* 3:3).

27:1 **5 cubits** . . . The dimensions of the altar were thus 7½′ x 7½′ x 4½′ (Rabbi Yosé, *Zevachim* 59b; Josephus 3:6:8). According to others, the altar also had a base that was 7 cubits high, and therefore, it stood 10 cubits (15′) high (Rabbi Yehudah, *Ibid.*; *Yad, Beth HaBechirah* 2:5).

27 cubits, and 3 cubits high.* ² Make protrusions* on all four sides as an integral part of [the altar]. Then cover it with a layer of copper.*

³ Make pots to remove its greasy ashes, as well as scoops,* sacrificial basins,* flesh pokers,* and fire pans* [for the altar]. All these instruments shall be made of copper.

⁴ Make a screen* out of copper net to go around [the altar]. Place four copper rings on the four corners of the screen. ⁵ The screen shall be placed below the decorative border* of the altar, extending downward until the middle of the altar.

⁶ Make carrying poles for the altar out of acacia wood covered with a layer of copper. ⁷ Place the poles in the rings* so that the poles will be on the two sides of the altar when it is carried.

⁸ [The altar] shall be a hollow structure made out of boards.* You must make it as you were shown on the mountain.

[107. The Enclosure]

⁹ Make the enclosure for the tabernacle in this manner:
On the south side, there shall be hangings* made of twined linen. [Like all

---

27:2 **protrusions.** Literally "horns." These were hollow boxes, one cubit square, and 5 handbreadths high (18" x 18" x 15") (*Zevachim* 54a; *Yad, Beth HaBechirah* 2:8; *Maaseh Choshev* 6:3). Others say that while this was true of the altar in the Temple, it may not have been true of the altar in the desert (Ralbag), and there the "horns" may have been round and horn-shaped (Avraham ben HaRambam).

— **copper.** Or "brass" that shone like gold (Josephus 3:6:8).

27:3 **scoops** (Rashi, *videl* in French). These were used to scoop up the ashes.

— **sacrificial basins.** To catch the blood of sacrifices and splash it on the altar (Rashi; Rashbam).

— **flesh pokers.** To turn over the sacrifices on the altar. They were in the shape of curved hooks (Rashi). Others say that they were like pitchforks (*Or HaAfelah*) or rakes (Ralbag).

— **fire pans.** To carry fire to the inside altar (Rashi). Some say that they were like large spoons (Ralbag). According to others, they were pokers for the ashes on the altar (Rashbam; *Midrash HaGadol*).

27:4 **screen.** This was one cubit wide, covering the space directly above the middle of the altar (*Maaseh Choshev* 6:5). According to the opinion that the altar was 3 cubits high, it began 1¼ cubits (27") above the ground, and extended upward to 2¼ cubits above   **Flesh Hooks** the ground. Some say that it protruded to catch any stray coals falling from the altar (*Targum Yonathan* on 27:5).

However, the Septuagint translates *mikhbar* here as *esxapon*, a hearth or place for offerings. It was made out of heavy copper netting to provide draft for the fire (cf. Josephus 3:7:8).

27:5 **decorative border.** Or "molding" (*Zevachim* 62a). According to those who maintained that the altar was 3 cubits high, this would be directly below the top of the altar. According to those who maintain that it was 10 cubits high, it was 3 cubits from the top of the altar.

The Septuagint translates *karkov* here as *pureon*, the place where the fire burns. Hence, the verse would then be translated, "The [copper net] hearth shall be placed under the place where the fire burns."

27:7 **rings.** The rings on the screen (Rashi). See 38:5.

27:8 **hollow structure . . .** It was filled with earth when the altar was used (20:21, *Mekhilta*, Rashi, ad loc.).

27:9 **hangings.** Woven like fine netting (Rashi).

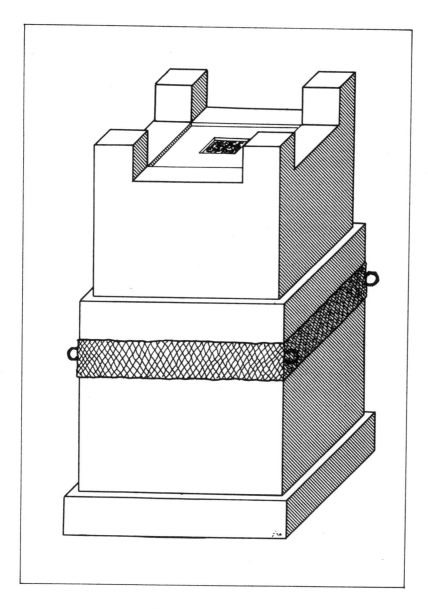

PLATE 20. THE ALTAR

27 the other] sides, it shall be 100 cubits long. [10] It shall have 20 pillars* and 20 copper bases.* The hooks and bands* for the pillars shall be made of silver.

[11] The same shall be done on the north side. The hangings shall be 100 cubits long, with 20 pillars and 20 copper bases, with silver hooks and bands for the pillars.

[12] The width of the hangings at the western end of the enclosure shall be 50 cubits, and it shall have 10 pillars and 10 bases.

[13] The width of the enclosure at its eastern end shall [also] be 50 cubits. [14] [Of this,] the hangings on one side of [the entrance] shall be 15 cubits long, with 3 pillars and 3 bases. [15] On the other side, the hangings shall [also] be 15 [cubits long], with 3 pillars and 3 bases. [16] The entrance of the enclosure shall [be covered] with a 20 cubit embroidered* drape made of sky-blue, dark red, and crimson wool together with twisted linen. It shall have 4 pillars* and 4 bases.

[17] All the pillars of the outer enclosure shall have silver hoops, silver hooks, and copper bases.

[18] The length of the enclosure shall be 100 cubits, and its width shall be 50 cubits.* [The pillars holding the hangings] of twined linen shall be 5 cubits high,* and their bases shall be made of copper.

[19] All the equipment used to make the tabernacle shall be made out of copper. The stakes [for the tabernacle itself], and all the stakes* for the enclosure shall also be made of copper.

27:10 pillars. These pillars had a cross section one cubit (18″) square, and may have been round (*Maaseh Choshev* 5:4,5). Some say that they were covered with copper (*Ibid.; Yalkut Shimoni* 425). Others say that they were copper poles (Josephus 3:6:2).

— **bases.** Some say that these were imbedded in the ground like spears (Josephus 3:6:2).

27:11 bands. Decorative bands going around the pillars (Rashi; Sforno). Some say that these bands held the hooks to the poles (Ibn Ezra). Others translate *chashuk* here as "decorations" (Septuagint; Ibn Janach) or "melted inlays" (Saadia). Besides these, the poles also had silver caps (38:17; *Maaseh Choshev* 5:4; Josephus 3:6:2).

27:16 embroidered. With pictures of animals (Josephus).

— **pillars.** Some say that these were like all the others (*Maaseh Choshev* 5:8). Other sources state that they were covered with silver (Josephus).

27:18 50 cubits. Literally, "50 x 50 cubits." Some say that this indicates that the open space in front of the Tabernacle was 50 x 50 cubits (Rashi).

— **5 cubits.** 7½ feet. This was the width of the hangings, and the height of the poles holding them (Rashi; Josephus). There is another opinion that they were 5 cubits taller than the tabernacle, and therefore a total of 15 cubits (22½″) high (*Zevachim* 59b, 60a; *Maaseh Choshev* 5:2; see below, 38:14).

27:19 stakes. The bottoms of the curtains were tied to these stakes with ropes so that they would not blow in the wind (*Bareitha* 5; Rashi; Rashbam; Chizzkuni). Other sources indicate that ropes were attached to these pegs or stakes, and tied to the upper ends of the beams to prevent them from swaying in the wind (Josephus 3:6:2).

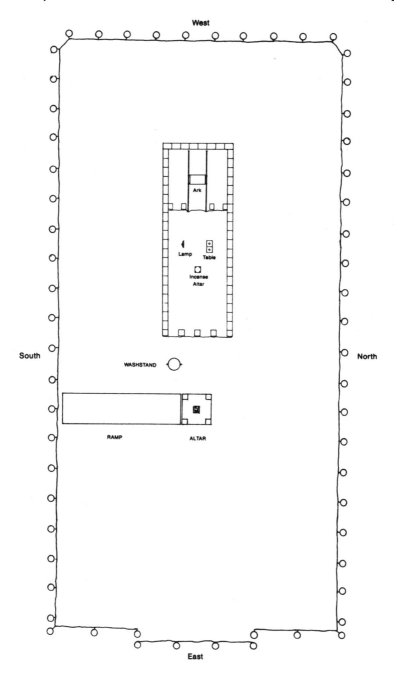

PLATE 21. THE TABERNACLE AND ENCLOSURE

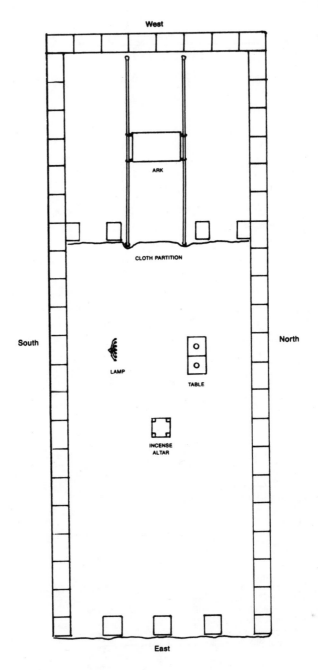

PLATE 22. THE TABERNACLE AND ITS FURNITURE

Tetzaveh

[108. Oil for the Lamp]

²⁰ You, [Moses], must command the Israelites to bring you clear illuminating oil, made from hand crushed* olives, to keep the lamp constantly burning. ²¹ Aaron and his sons shall arrange for [the lamps to burn] from evening until morning in God's presence, in the Communion Tent,* outside the cloth partition that conceals the [Ark of] Testimony.* It is a rule for all time that [this oil shall come] from the Israelites.

[109. The Vestments]

¹ [Separate] your brother Aaron and his sons from among the Israelites, **28**
[and] bring them close to you so that Aaron, and his sons, Nadav, Avihu, Eleazar and Ithamar,* can become priests to Me.

² Make sacred vestments that are both dignified and beautiful for your brother Aaron.

³ Speak to everyone who is naturally talented,* to whom I have granted a spirit of wisdom, and let them make Aaron's vestments. These [vestments] will then be used to consecrate him and make him a priest to Me.*

⁴ These are the vestments that they shall make: a breastplate, an ephod, a robe, a knitted* tunic, a turban, and a sash. Make them as sacred vestments for Aaron and his sons so that they will be able to be priests to Me.

⁵ [The skilled workers]* shall take the gold, the sky-blue, dark red and crimson wool, and the linen.

[110. The Ephod]

⁶ [These workers] shall make the ephod* out of gold [thread],* sky-blue,

---

27:20 **hand crushed** . . . In a mortar (*Menachoth* 86b; Rashi).
27:21 **Communion Tent.** See note on 25:22, 33:7. Or, "meeting tent," since the Israelites would gather around it (Radak, s.v. *ya'ad*). The Hebrew word *mo'ed* here can also be related to *eduth,* since both share the same root, and hence it can be translated, "Testimony Tent." Following the usual meaning of the word *mo'ed,* the expression can also be rendered, "Festive Tent."
— **Testimony.** See above, 25:16. The word *eduth* which we translated as "testimony" can also be translated as "communion" or "token of communion." See above note.
28:1 **Nadav, Avihu** . . . See above, 6:23.
28:3 **naturally talented.** Literally, "wise of heart."
— **These vestments** . . . See below, 29:29,30.
28:4 **knitted.** See note on 28:39.
28:5 **The skilled workers.** (Rashi; *Lekach Tov*).
— **sky-blue** . . . See notes on 25:4.
28:6 **ephod.** See below, 39:1 ff. There are several opinions as to how the ephod was made.

28   dark red and crimson wool, together with twined linen, in a patterned bro-
     cade.* ⁷ It shall have two attached shoulder pieces* at its two corners, and
     [these] shall be sewn* [to it]. ⁸ The ephod's belt* which is made in the same

Some say that the ephod was essentially like a half-cape, as wide as the body, reaching from just below the elbows to the heel. It had a belt which was long enough to be tied in front, right over the solar plexus. It also had two shoulder straps ("shoulder pieces") that were

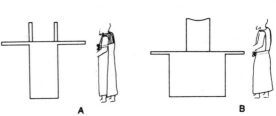

A   B

sewn onto the belt right over the upper corners of the cape. These straps were long enough to reach slightly over the shoulders. At the ends of these straps on the shoulders, the settings for the sardonyx stones were attached (Rashi on 28:4,6; *Yad, Kley HaMikdash* 9:9; Ralbag; Sforno; *Akedath Yitzchak; Midrash HaGadol*) (A).

Others agree that it was a long garment, but say that it was more like a skirt, from the waist to the heels, covering the high priest in front and back. It also had a section covering the entire back up to the neck, and the corners of this section are referred to as the "shoulder pieces," to which the sardonyx stones were attached (Rashbam) (B).

Still others also agree that it was long, but maintain that it was much simpler in construction. They see it as a kind of cape made of a single rectangular piece of cloth, draped over the shoulders like a large tallith, and hanging down to the feet in back. At the waist, it had a belt to hold it. It is described as being like the robes used by Greek priests, most probably the *mandyas* (Rabbenu Meyuchas) (C).

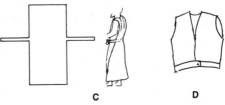

C   D

There are, however, a number of authorities who maintain that it was not a long garment at all, but rather like a vest with a belt around its lower edge, tied in front (Chizzkuni on 28:27) (D). Others see it as a kind of backwards vest, tied in the back, with an opening in front to hold the breastplate (*Siddur of Saadia Gaon*, p. 271) (E).

Josephus describes the ephod as being a sleeved garment. The main part was a cubit square, with an opening for the breastplate, worn over the front of the body. It had straps, most probably going around the neck, which buttoned on to the sardonyxes on the opposite sides to hold the ephod in place (*Antiquities* 3:7:5; *Wars* 5:5:7) (F).

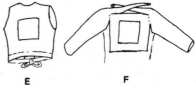

E   F

— **gold thread.** The gold would be beaten into thin sheets and then cut into fine threads (Rashi; see 39:3). One thread of gold was mixed with six threads of each of the other materials, the sky-blue, dark red and crimson wool, and linen. This would produce 4 seven-ply threads, which were then twined together to produce a single 28-ply thread. (*Yad, Kley HaMikdash* 9:5, from *Yoma* 72a). Josephus notes that the ephod itself contained more gold than its belt (*Wars* 5:5:7).

— **patterned brocade.** *Choshev* in Hebrew; see note on 26:1. Josephus describes the belt as having a striped pattern of gold, sky blue, crimson, white and dark red, and states that the ephod had the same pattern, but with more gold (*Wars* 5:5:7).

28:7 **shoulder pieces.** Straps (Rashi), cords (Chizzkuni), the upper corner of the garment (Rabbenu Meyuchas; Rashbam), or sleeves (Josephus).

— **sewn** (Rashi; see 26:3). Literally, "attached," or "of one piece with it" (see note on 28:6).

28:8 **ephod's belt** (Saadia). Others translate *cheshev aphuda-tho* as "interwoven belt" (Rabbenu Meyuchas), "belt of adornment" (Rashi), or "band for a belt" (Ibn Janach; Radak, *Sherashim*). Some say that the belt

manner [as the ephod itself] shall be [woven] together with it* out of gold 28
[thread], sky-blue, dark red, and crimson wool, and twined linen.

⁹ Take two sardonyx* stones,* and engrave* on them the names of Israel's
sons. ¹⁰ There shall be six names on one stone, and the remaining six names
on the second stone [inscribed] in the order of their birth.* ¹¹ The names of

was worn just below the chest (*Yad, Kley Mikdash* 9:11), while others maintain that it was tied over the
navel (Raavad *ad loc.*).
— **woven together with it** (Rashi). Or, "of the same material as it." This latter interpretation seems to be
that of Josephus, who maintains that the belt was not part of the ephod, but a separate garment,
attached to the breastplate. It was looped around the back, and then around the front again (*Antiquities*
3:7:5; *Wars* 5:5:7).
28:9 **sardonyx** (Josephus; *loc. cit.*; the same word is used in Greek cf. Septuagint). Sardonyx is a type of cryptocrystalline quartz, related to agate, with alternating red and white bands. Thus, these stones may have
born a strong resemblance to Levi's banner, which was divided into thirds, white, black and red
(*BeMidbar Rabbah* 2:7). These might have been rare sardonyxes which also had these exact divisions of
color.
   Other sources translate *shoham* here as beryl (*Targum*). Beryl is a silicate of beryllium and aluminum,
$Be_3Al_2(SiO_3)_6$, that is bluish-green in color. Since the ancients did not classify stones according to
chemical composition, it can denote any bluish-green stone. See notes on 28:18,20.
   Shoham was one of the stones of Eden (Genesis 2:12).
— **stones.** Some say that the stones were square in shape (*Yad, Kley HaMikdash* 9:9; *Midrash HaGadol*).
According to some ancient sources, however, they were hemispherical in shape (Philo, *Questions and
Answers* 109). Some later sources say that they were round (Ibn Ezra, short version).
— **engrave.** (*Targum*). In Hebrew, the root *patach* means to open, but in ancient Egyptian, *petech* means to
engrave.
— **in the order of their birth.** Some take this literally (Rashi; Josephus, *Antiquities* 3:7:5; cf. Genesis
29:31-30:24). The names were therefore:

   right: Reuben, Simeon, Levi, Judah, Dan, Naphtali
   left: Gad, Asher, Issachar, Zebulun, Joseph, Benjamin.

   According to others, the verse is interpreted, "Six names shall be on the first stone, while on the
other stone, there shall be six names in the order of their birth." According to this, the names are in
order of birth only on the second stone, but on the first stone, Judah comes first (*Sotah* 36a, Rashi *ad loc.*
s.v. KeToldatham):

   right: Judah, Reuben, Simeon, Levi, Dan, Naphtali
   left: Gad, Asher, Issachar, Zebulun, Joseph, Benjamin.

   Others, however, do not translate *ke-tolda-tham* here as "in order of their birth," but as, "according
to their chronicles." According to one opinion, they are listed in the same manner as they are at the
beginning of the Book of Exodus (1:2-5) (*Sotah* 36b, Rashi *ad loc.* s.v. *Be-Chumash*):

   right: Reuben, Simeon, Levi, Judah, Issachar, Zebulun.
   left: Benjamin, Dan, Naphtali, Gad, Asher, Joseph.

   Others basically agree with this interpretation, but maintain that the names follow the order of their
mothers with Leah first and Rachel last. (*Baaley Tosafoth;* cf. *BeMidbar Rabbah* 2:7; see note on 25:21). The
order is then:

   right: Reuben, Simeon, Levi, Judah, Issachar, Zebulun.
   left: Dan, Naphtali, Gad, Asher, Joseph, Benjamin.

   Other sources agree with this ordering, except that they have the names alternate from one stone to
the other, and transpose Dan and Naphtali (*Yad, Kley HaMikdash* 9:9; Avraham ben HaRambam; Ralbag; *Or HaChaim; Get Pashut* 129:127; *Teshuvoth Kenesseth Yechezkel* 1):

   right: Reuben, Levi, Issachar, Naftali, Gad, Joseph.
   left: Simeon, Judah, Zebulun, Dan, Asher, Benjamin.

28 Israel's sons shall be engraved by a skilled jeweler, [and it shall appear] like the engraving on a signet ring.

[These stones] shall then be placed in gold settings.* ¹² Place the two stones on the two shoulder pieces of the ephod as remembrance stones for Israel's sons.* Aaron shall carry their names on his two shoulders before God as a remembrance.

[111. The Settings]

¹³ Make gold settings.* ¹⁴ [Also] make matched* cables* of pure gold, braided like cords.* The braided cables shall then be attached to the settings.

[112. The Breastplate]

¹⁵ Make a decision* breastplate. It shall be a patterned brocade* like the ephod. Make it out of gold [thread], sky-blue, dark red and crimson wool,

---

There is another opinion that the tribes on the sardonyx stones were divided in exactly the same manner as they were at Mount Gerizim and Eval (Deuteronomy 27:13; Rav Kahanah, *Sotah* 36a):

> right: Simeon, Levi, Judah, Issachar, Joseph, Benjamin.
> left: Reuben, Gad, Asher, Zebulun, Dan, Naphtali.

Finally, there are some who omit Levi and Joseph, and substitute Manasseh and Ephraim (*Teshuvoth HaGeonim, Harkevy,* 4; *Otzar HaGaonim, Yoma* 70; cf. Rashi, *Sotah* 36b, s.v. *Lo*).

> right: Reuben, Simeon, Judah, Dan, Naphtali, Gad.
> left: Asher, Issachar, Zebulun, Manasseh, Ephraim, Benjamin.

There is a tradition that there were 25 letters in each of these stones (*Sotah* 36a).

28:11 **settings** (Rashi; *Yad, Kley HaMikdash* 9:9). *Mishbetzoth* in Hebrew. Others translate the word as "rosettes" or "gold mesh settings," because they were made of knitted or braided gold (Saadia; Ibn Janach; Radak, *Sherashim;* Ralbag). Josephus describes these settings as buttons resembling small shields (*Wars* 5:5:7), and the Septuagint likewise translates *mishbetzoth* as *aspidiskos,* "small shieldlike discs." Other ancient Greek sources translate it as *sphigkteras,* "bands" or "straps" (Aquilla).

28:12 **for Israel's sons.** Or, "for the Israelites." Some say that these letters on the right sardonyx shone as a sign that a sacrifice was accepted (Josephus, *Antiquities* 8:8:9).

28:13 **settings.** These are the ones mentioned in 28:11 (cf. Rashi; Mizrachi). Some say that these settings had attached rings through which the cables were passed (*Yad, Kley HaMikdash* 9:9; Avraham ben Ha-Rambam; *Midrash HaGadol;* cf. Josephus, *Antiquities* 3:7:5).

28:14 **matched** (Ibn Janach; Radak, *Sherashim*). *Migbaloth* in Hebrew. Or "medium-sized" (Saadia), or "at the edges" (Rashi) or "attached" (Septuagint).

— **cables** or "chains", *sharsheroth* in Hebrew. Some say that they were attached to the settings like roots (*shoresh*) of a tree (Rashi on 28:22) (see figure). According to one opinion, the cables mentioned here were merely decorative (Yehudah HaChasid), but others maintain that they were to hold the breastplate (Rashi; see below 28:22-24).

— **braided** . . . (Rashi; Radak, *Sherashim,* quoting his father). Or, "twisted like rope" (Rashbam; Saadia; Ibn Janach). Some apparently describe these cables as being made of a bunch of gold threads held together by a gold thread wound around them (*Targum;* Radak, *Sherashim,* from 1 Kings 7:17; cf. *Menachoth* 39a) cf. Deuteronomy 22:12. See note on 28:28.

28:15 **decision** . . . (Rashi). Or, "judgment breastplate" (*Targum*). See 39:8-21.

— **patterned brocade.** Here again, the pattern is not described. However, in one place, this type of work is described as having a lion on one side of the cloth and an eagle on the other (*Yerushalmi, Shekalim* 8:2). See note on 28:30.

and twined linen. [16] When folded over, it shall be a span* long and a span   28
wide.

[17] Set it with four rows of mounted stones.*
The first of these rows shall contain a carnelian,* an emerald* and a topaz.*
[18] The second row: carbuncle,* sapphire,* beryl.*

28:16 span. This is the distance between the tips of the thumb and pinky in a spread hand, and it is equivalent to ¼ cubit or 9″ (*Tosefta, Kelim, Bava Metzia* 6:4; *Eruvin* 21a; *Yad, Kley HaMikdash* 9:6; Josephus, *Antiquities* 3:7:5). The breastplate was thus made out of a brocade one cubit by ¼ cubit, and then folded over.

According to others, a span is the distance between the extended thumb and forefinger, and is half of a 5-handbreadth cubit, or 7½″ (*Teshuvoth Rashbam* 9:10; *Sefer Chasidim,* Mekitzey Nirdamim edition, 692). Others say that a span is ¼ cubit or 6″ (Kalir, quoted in Tosafoth, *Eruvin* 21a, s.v. *Echad*). Finally, some say that a span is equal to a handbreadth, 3″ (Philo, *Questions and Answers* 111; cf. *Targum Yerushalmi*).

28:17 stones. Here too there is a question as to whether the stones were square or round, see note on 28:9 (cf. *Mishneh LaMelekh, Kley HaMikdash* 9:6).

—   **carnelian** (*Shiltey Gibborim* 46; *Midrash Talpioth,* s.v. *Evven*). *Odem* in Hebrew. The carnelian is a variety of flesh-colored (*carne*) cryptocrystalline quartz, having a color similar to a ruby due to traces of ferrous oxide. Ancient Greek sources translate it as sardion (Septuagint; Josephus, *Wars* 5:5:7). The sardion, sardine or sard was a deep orange-red variety of carnelian which was found near Sardis, the capital of ancient Lydia.

Most sources agree that it was a red stone (*Targum; BeMidbar Rabbah* 2:7). Some sources state that the *odem* here was a ruby (Bachya; *MeAm Lo'ez*). However, in ancient nomenclature, the name given to a stone is denoted its visual appearance rather than chemical composition, and hence, the "ruby" could be any bright red stone.

According to most authorities, the *odem* was the stone of Reuben (*Targum Yonathan; BeMidbar Rabbah* 2:7; see note on 28:21). According to some, however, it was the stone of Judah (Tzioni, *BeMidbar*). See Ezekiel 28:13.

—   **emerald** (Saadia; Ibn Janach; Radak, *Sherashim;* Chizzkuni; *MeAm Lo'ez*). *Pidtah* in Hebrew. Most other sources also indicate that it was a green stone (*Targum; BeMidbar Rabbah* 2:7). One early source identifies it as *prasma,* Spanish for prase, a dark green variety of cryptocrystalline quartz (Bachya). It can also denote chrysoprase, an apple-green variety, or plasma, a leek green or emerald green type.

Ancient Greek sources translate *pitdah* as topaz (see next note), where the sequence is "sardion, topaz, emerald" (Septuagint; Josephus, *Antiquities* 3:7:5, *Wars* 5:5:7). However, it appears that the mainstream tradition had a reading in the Septuagint, "sardion, emerald, topaz" (cf. Chizzkuni). Hence, the *pitdah* would be translated as *smaragdos,* Greek for emerald or malachite (cf. Pliny 37:16). Nonetheless, there are a number of later sources that identify the *pitdah* with topaz (*Shiltey Gibborim* 46; cf. *Sh'moth Rabbah* 38:8). There are, however, some indications that the "topaz" of the ancients was actually green (Pliny 37:32). The *pitdah* was the stone of Simeon (*Targum Yonathan; BeMidbar Rabbah* 2:7). Others say that it was the stone of Issachar (Tzioni, *BeMidbar*). See Ezekiel 28:13, Job 28:19.

—   **topaz** (Chizzkuni). *Bareketh* in Hebrew. Numerous sources indicate that it was a stone that was yellow (Saadia; Ibn Janach) or saffron-colored (*Lekach Tov; Targum* on Song of Songs 5:14). If it is assumed that the Septuagint transposes this stone with the one above (see previous note), then it would also translate this as *topazion,* Greek for topaz or similar yellow gemstones (cf. Strabo 16:770; Diodurus Siculus 3:39).

There is, however, a question as to whether or not the topaz mentioned in ancient sources is the same as the present topaz. It may denote citrine, a yellow variety of quartz, or peridot, a yellow-green variety of chrysolite (see note on 28:20). Some sources appear to indicate that *bareketh* is actually a gold lustered pyrite (Radak, *Sherashim;* cf. *Targum*).

According to current version of the Septuagint and Josephus (*Antiquities* 3:7:5; *Wars* 5:5:7), the *bareketh* here is the emerald. Other sources state that it was a bluish stone (*Shiltey Giborim* 46; *Shemoth Rabbah* 38:8 [*dyknithin*] according to *Arukh* s.v. *yaknatin,* which translates it as blue hyacinth).

There are some sources that transpose this with the next stone, and translate it as carbuncle (Bachya; cf. King James translation). Other sources say that it contained red, white and black stripes (*BeMidbar Rabbah* 2:7).

The *bareketh* was the stone of Levi (*Targum Yonathan,* etc.). Others state that it was the stone of Zebulun (Tzioni, *BeMidbar*). See Ezekiel 28:13.

28:18 carbuncle (Chizzkuni; *Shiltey Gibborim* 46; *MeAm Lo'ez*). *Nophekh* in Hebrew. Ancient Greek sources trans-

28   19 The third row: jacinth,* agate,* amethyst.*

late *nophek* as *anthrax* denoting coal (Septuagint; Josephus *loc. cit.*). This is usually interpreted to mean a mineral that is red, the color of burning coal (Pliny 37:25; Theophrastus, *On Stones* 18). It is hence rendered as carbuncle (Vulgate), from *carbo*, latin for coal. This denotes a particularly brilliant red garnet, but can also denote a ruby or ruby spinel.

Some sources, however, take "coal" in its literal sense and state that *nophekh* was a black stone (Ibn Janach; Radak, *Sherashim*). The Midrash (*BeMidbar Rabbah* 2:7) states that the colors of the stones on this row were "sky-blue, black, white." There is evidence (see next note), that the first two colors are transposed, and the reading should be "black, sky-blue, white," so that this would agree that the *nophekh* was black. Some say that it is related to *pukh* meaning stibium, a black powder (Ibn Ezra on 28:9, from 2 Kings 9:30).

There are sources, however, which indicate that the *nophekh* was indeed a blue stone (Saadia; *Lekach Tov; Targum* on Song of Songs 5:14). Those sources which would transpose the Septuagint translation with the previous stone (see previous note), would also render this as emerald (*Targum;* Bachya; cf. King James).

The *nophekh* was the stone of Judah (*Targum Yonathan*, etc.) Others say that it was the stone of Reuben (Tzioni, *BeMidbar*). See Ezekiel 27:16, 28:13.

—   **sapphire:** *Sapir* in Hebrew. In Greek it is also translated as *sappheiros* (Septuagint). This, however, denotes any blue stone, and some say that the sapphire of the ancients was really the lapis-lazuli (cf. Pliny 37:39). Some sources, however, state that the Biblical sapphire was actually a clear colorless stone, identified either as crystal (Radak, *Sherashim*) or diamond (ibid.; Ibn Janach; Saadia; see note on 24:10).

Some sources identify the *sapir* with the emerald (*Lekach Tov; Targum* on Song of Songs 5:14), but this appears to be a transposition with the previous word. The same is true of the Midrash (*BeMidbar Rabbah* 2:7), which has it as being a black stone. Some sources would have it as being a red stone (Ibn Ezra here on 24:10, from Lamentations 4:7). Josephus renders it as jasper, but this is probably a transposition with the next stone in the Septuagint, which in turn is a transposition with the last stone (see next note).

The sapphire was the stone of Issachar (*Targum Yerushalmi; BeMidbar Rabbah* 2:7). Other sources, however, state that it was the stone of Dan (*Targum Yonathan*), whose banner and stone were blue. A third opinion is that it was the stone of Simeon (Tzioni, *BeMidbar*).

—   **beryl** (Bachya; cf. Chizzkuni; Douai-Rheims translation). *Yahalom* in Hebrew. This is a bluish-green precious stone, midway between the emerald and aquamarine in color.

The Septuagint has *iastis*, which, if a transposition is assumed, is rendered by Josephus as *iaspis,* denoting jasper (cf. Vulgate). However, since jasper is usually identified with *yashpeh* (28:20), it can safely be assumed that the translation of the last stone in this line was transposed with the last stone of the fourth line (see Josephus, *Antiquities* 3:7:5). The correct translation in the Septuagint here would therefore be *byrilion*, (which in our editions of the Septuagint is the translation for *shoham*, cf. Josephus, *Wars* 5:5:7, but in Josephus, *Antiquities* 3:7:5, is the translation of *yashpeh*). The beryl of the ancients is described as being a yellowish blue-green (cf. Pliny 37:20). It is surmised that the word may denote a type of precious jade.

Some say that the *burla* mentioned in ancient sources (Bachya) is the pearl (*Toledoth Yitzchak; MeAm Lo'ez*).

Many sources however, identify the *yahalom* with the diamond (Ibn Ezra on 28:9; Radak, *Sherashim; Shiltey Gibborim* 46). The Midrash also identifies it as a white or clear gem (*BeMidbar Rabbah* 2:7). Others say that this is the chalcedony.

The *yahalom* was the stone of Zebulun (*Targum Yerushalmi; BeMidbar Rabbah* 2:7). Others say that it was the stone of Naphtali (*Targum Yonathan*), which was greyish. A third opinion is that it was Gad's stone (Tzioni). See Ezekiel 28:13.

28:19   jacinth. *Leshem* in Hebrew. Greek sources translate this as *ligurion* (Septuagint; Josephus, *Antiquities*). This is a bright orange stone like the jacinth, often likened to the carbuncle (Pliny 8:57) or amber (*ibid.* 37:11). Many other sources have it resembling the topaz in color (Ibn Janach; Radak, *Sherashim;* Cf. Bachya; *MeAm Lo'ez*).

Other sources, however, see it as a blue stone (*BeMidbar Rabbah* 2:7; *Shemoth Rabbah* 38:8). Thus, some sources identify it with turquoise (*Shiltey Gibborim*) or beryl (*Lekach Tov; Targum* on Song of Songs 5:14).

While the order in our versions of the Septuagint is "ligure, agate, amethyst," in one place Josephus has "agate, amethyst, ligure" (*Wars* 5:5:7). Other sources also appear to agree that the *leshem* is an agate (cf. Saadia). The *Targum* renders it *kankirey* which is seen as coming from the Greek *kegchri*, grains, because it is a stone with a granular pattern (*Arukh*, s.v. *kanker*).

²⁰ The fourth row: chrysolite,* onyx,* jasper.*   **28**

The *leshem* was the stone of Dan (*Targum Yerushalmi; BeMidbar Rabbah* 2:7). This stone was given to him because Leshem was an important city in Dan (Joshua 19:47; *Shiltey Gibborim* 46). Others say that it was the stone of Gad (*Targum Yonathan*) or Ephraim (Tzioni).

— **agate.** *Sh'vo* in Hebrew; *achatis* in Greek (Septuagint). This is a type of striped or variegated chalcedon (cf. Pliny 37:54). The Midrash also sees this as a grey stone (*BeMidbar Rabbah* 2:7).

As noted above, the order in the Septuagint on this line is "ligure, agate, amethyst." Josephus, however, has "ligure, amethyst, agate" (*Antiquities*), or "agate, amethyst, ligure" (*Wars*). Hence, according to his reading, the *sh'vo* would be the amethyst (see next note).

The *Targum* translates *sh''vo* as *tarkia* which some identify as the turquoise (*Arukh*, s.v. *Trika;* cf. *Bachya; Toledoth Yitzchak; MeAm Lo'ez*). It is hence seen as a sapphire-like blue stone (*Lekach Tov; Targum* on Song of Songs 5:14). Others see *tarkia* as related to *anthrax*, Greek for coal (see note on 28:18), and hence a black-stone (Saadia; Radak, *Sherashim*). Others see it as a red, carbuncle-like stone, and render it as jacinth (Shiltey Gibborim), an orange-red stone.

The *sh'vo* was the stone of Naphtali (*Targum Yerushalmi*, etc.) or, according to some, of Asher (*Targum Yonathan*) or Manasseh (Tzioni).

— **amethyst.** *Achlamah* in Hebrew; *amithysos* in Greek (Septuagint). This is a violet or purple stone, that was thought by the ancients to be an antidote for drunkenness (cf. Pliny 37:40). The Midrash also states that it was the color of diluted wine (*BeMidbar Rabbah* 2:7). The Greek word comes from *a-* "not", and *mithysos* drunken, and may be related to the Hebrew *achlamah*, which has the connotation of a dream.

The amethyst has the property of turning yellow when heated. Hence, some sources see it as a (partially?) yellow stone (Saadia; Ibn Janach). It may thus be related to the word *chelmon*, the yellow of an egg.

The *Targum* translates this word as "calf's eye." This is taken to be a kind of onyx (*Shiltey Gibborim*) or agate (Josephus, *Antiquities*). It is also possible that it was an amethyst heated on the edges to give it a yellow border and an eye-like appearance. Some sources translate *achlamah* as crystal (Bachya; *Toledoth Yitzchak; MeAm Lo'ez*).

The *achlamah* was the stone of Gad (*Targum Yerushalmi* etc.) According to others, it was the stone of Issachar (*Targum Yonathan*) or Benjamin (Tzioni).

28:20 **chrysolite.** *Tarshish* in Hebrew; *chrysolithos* in Greek (Septuagint; Josephus, *Antiquities;* Bachya; *Shiltey Gibborim*). The chrysolite of antiquity is described as being a yellowish stone, the color of amber (Pliny 37:11, 42). Traditional sources identify it with the color of pure olive oil (*BeMidbar Rabbah* 2:7; Bachya; *Toledoth Yitzchak*). These sources maintain that the *tarshish* was the stone of Asher, whose blessing was oil (*BeMidbar Rabbah* 2:7; cf. Genesis 49:20).

Other sources, however, maintain that the *tarshish* is the aquamarine, a brilliant blue-green stone (*Targum; Arukh;* Saadia; Ibn Janach; Radak; cf. King James). These sources would identify the stone with Zebulun, whose blessing was to live by the sea (*Targum Yonathan;* Bachya cf. Genesis 49:13). Others maintain that this was the stone of Joseph (Tzioni).

— **onyx.** *Shoham* in Hebrew; see notes on 28:9, Genesis 2:12. *Onyx* in Greek (Josephus, *Antiquities* 3:7:5; Vulgate; Chizzkuni; Bachya; *MeAm Lo'ez*). This is a stone having bands of black, white, and red or other colors. On 28:9, the Septuagint translates *shoham* as *sard-onyx* as does Josephus.

It is therefore reasonable that the order of this line is "chrysolite, onyx, beryl," as given by Josephus in one place (*Antiquities* 3:7:5; cf. Vulgate). In another place, however, he has the order as, "onyx, beryl, chrysolite" (*Wars* 5:5:7). In our versions of the Septuagint, the order is, "chrysolite, beryl, onyx."

According to the last two readings, the *shoham* would be the beryl, and this view is shared by many other sources (*Targum;* Radak, *Sherashim*). This is seen, perhaps, as an emerald colored jade (cf. *Shiltey Gibborim*). The Septuagint on Genesis 2:12 translates as prase. Others see it as a black stone (*BeMidbar Rabbah* 2:7), or a reflective white stone (Saadia; Ibn Ezra on 28:9), perhaps a white form of beryl.

The *shoham* was the stone of Joseph (*Targum Yerushalmi; Targum Yonathan*). Others say that it was Asher's stone (Tzioni).

— **jasper.** (Saadia; Radak; Ibn Janach; Chizzkuni; Bachya; *Me'Am Lo'ez;* King James). *Yaspeh* in Hebrew. The Hebrew is apparently cognate to the English. Although the Greek versions have either onyx, beryl, or chrysolite (see previous note), there is probably a transposition between this word and *sapir* or *yahalom* (*q.v.*).

The *Targum* renders this as *panterey*, which some sources translate as striped or spotted (*Arukh*, s.v. *panther, apantir*). However, the word may be related to the Greek *pante*, "all," and thus means "all-

28   These stones shall be placed in gold settings.*

    [21] The stones shall contain the names of the twelve sons of Israel,* one for each of the twelve [stones]. Each one's name shall be engraved as on a signet ring, to represent the twelve tribes.

colored." This Midrash also says that the *yashpeh* is of all colors (*BeMidbar Rabbah* 2:7). This suggests a type of opal.

    The *yashpeh* was the stone of Benjamin (*Targum Yerushalmi; Targum Yonathan*). Some say that it was the stone of Naphtali (Tzioni).

—   **settings.** Some say that the stones fit exactly into indentations, "filling" the settings (Rashi; *Yad, Kley HaMikdash* 9:6). Others maintain that the stones were held in the settings with three prongs (Ramban on 25:7). Other sources indicate that the stones were perforated and woven into the breastplate (*Lekach Tov*; Rabbi Avraham ben Azriel, *Arugath HaBosem*, p. 281; cf. Josephus, *Antiquities* 3:7:5).

28:21 The stones shall contain . . . See note on 28:9. Some say that the names were simply in order of birth (*Targum Yonathan; Midrash HaGadol*, except that Issachar and Naphtali are transposed). The order is then (actually, it is reversed here, since Hebrew reads from right to left):

Reuben	Simeon	Levi
Judah	Dan	Naphtali
Gad	Asher	Issachar
Zebulun	Joseph	Benjamin

    Others say that Jacob's sons were divided according to their mothers, with Leah's sons first, and Rachel's last (*Shemoth Rabbah* 38:10; *Targum* on Song of Songs 5:14; Bachya; Chizzkuni; *Tur*). This is favored because *leshem* then comes out as Dan's stone (*Baaley Tosafoth* on 28:10; Rashi on Judges (18:29). The order is then:

Reuben	Simeon	Levi
Judah	Issachar	Zebulun
Dan	Naphtali	Gad
Asher	Joseph	Benjamin

    According to some authorities, the names were ordered downward in columns rather than across in the rows (*Minchath Chinukh* 99).

    The Midrash that discusses the colors of the stones (*BeMidbar Rabbah* 2:7) also has the same order, except that Gad and Naphtali are transposed (cf. Rashash *ad loc.*). This is the opinion used earlier.

    Finally, there is an opinion that the tribes were in the same order as they camped in the desert (Numbers 2; Tzioni, *BeMidbar; Otzar HaGeonim*, Yoma 70; *Targum Yonathan*, Numbers 2:3; *Zohar* 2:230a; Siddur Rav Saadia Gaon, p. 271; Abarbanel):

Judah	Issachar	Zebulun
Reuben	Simeon	Gad
Ephraim	Manasseh	Benjamin
Dan	Asher	Naphtali

    If alternate rows are transposed, the order becomes very much like that of the earlier opinions, and Dan's stone remains the *leshem* (cf. *Peliah*, p. 32a).

Reuben	Simeon	Gad
Judah	Issachar	Zebulun
Dan	Asher	Naphtali
Ephraim	Manasseh	Benjamin

    In order for the breastplate to contain all the letters of the Hebrew alphabet, the names of the Patriarchs, Abraham, Isaac and Jacob were added, as well as the words *shiv'tey Yeshurun*, or "tribes of Jeshurun" (*Yoma* 73b). Other sources give these last words as *Shiv'tey Yah* (*Yad, K'ley HaMikdash* 10:11; cf. Psalms 122:4), or *Shiv'tey Yisrael* (*Yerushalmi*, Yoma 1:3).

    Some say that "Abraham Isaac Jacob" were written on the first stone, and the other words on the last (*Shemoth Rabbah* 38:11; *Yad, K'ley HaMikdash* 9:7). Others maintain that they were divided among the stones so that there were six letters on each stone (Chizzkuni; Bachya). There were thus a total of 72 letters on the breastplate (Ibid.; *Raziel HaMalakh*, p. 44).

²² Make matched cables out of pure gold, braided like cords, for the   **28**
breastplate.* ²³ Make two gold rings for the breastplate, and attach them to
the two [upper]* corners of the breastplate. ²⁴ Attach the two gold braids to
the two rings on the two corners of the breastplate. ²⁵ Attach the two braids on
the two corners to the two settings,* and they shall [thus] be attached to the
[two] shoulder pieces* of the ephod, toward the front.

²⁶ Make two gold rings, and attach them to the two [lower]* corners of the
breastplate, on the edge that is toward the inside* of the ephod. ²⁷ Make
[another] two gold rings, and attach them to the bottoms of the two shoulder
pieces,* toward the front where they are sewn on, above the ephod's belt.*
²⁸ Lace* the [lower] rings of the breastplate to the [lower]* rings of the ephod
with a twist* of sky-blue wool, so that [the breastplate] shall remain directly
above the ephod's belt.

²⁹ Aaron will thus carry the names of Israel's sons on the decision breastplate over his heart when he comes into the sanctuary.* It shall be a constant
remembrance before God.

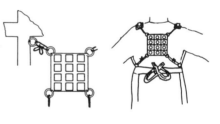

28:22 **for the breastplate** (Rashi). According to this, these
are the same ones mentioned above (28:14).
Others translate this verse, "attach matched cables
. . . to the breastplate." See 39:15 (see figure).
According to this, these were a second set of
cables, fixed to the breastplate and then attached
to the ephod's shoulder settings. This opinion
maintains that there were two cables on each
upper corner of the breastplate, one coming down
from the ephod, and one going up from the
breastplate itself (*Midrash HaGadol;* Avraham ben
HaRambam; cf. Josephus, *Antiquities* 3:7:5).

28:23 **upper** (Rashi; Rashbam).

28:25 **settings.** See 28:13.

—   **shoulder pieces** . . . (see figure) Or, "they shall be attached to the two sleeves of the ephod toward the
neck" (see note on 28:6).

28:26 **lower.** (Rashi).

—   **inside.** Where the ephod comes around the body somewhat.

28:27 **bottoms of the two shoulder pieces.** Or, "bottoms of the sleeves" (see note on 28:6). These rings were
near the breasts, under the armpits (*Yad, Kley HaMikdash* 9:8, 9:11).

—   **above the ephod's belt.** According to those who maintain that the shoulder pieces were straps, they were
sewn on the back above the ephod's belt (see note on 28:6).

28:28 **lace.** Or "bind" (Rashi; Rashbam). *Rakhas* in Hebrew. Or, "unite" (Onkelos), or "tighten" (Ibn Janach;
Lekach Tov on 38:28). Or, "they shall raise the breastplate so that its rings are near the rings of the ephod"
(Radak, *Sherashim*). Or, "fill in the space between the breastplate's rings and the ephod's rings with twist-
ed thread of blue wool" (Josephus, *Antiquities* 3:7:5; cf. *Targum Yonathan*). See Isaiah 40:4, Psalms 31:21.

—   **lower** (Rashi on 28:6; *Yad, Kley HaMikdash* 9:11; Meiri, *Yoma* 72b). Josephus, however, maintains that the
entire space between all four rings was interwoven with blue thread (*Antiquities* 3:7:5, see previous note).

—   **twist.** This can denote either two strands twisted together, or a thread doubled over. It can also denote a
bunch of threads bound together by another thread wound around them. See note on Numbers 15:38.
Also see Genesis 38:18, below, 28:37.

28:29 **sanctuary.** See 26:34.

28   ³⁰ Place the Urim and Thumim* in* the decision breastplate, and they shall be over Aaron's heart when he comes before God. Aaron will then carry the decision-making device for the Israelites before God at all times.

[113. The Robe]

³¹ Make the robe* that is [worn under]* the ephod completely out of sky-

---

28:30 **Urim and Thumim.** Usually translated as "lightings and perfections," since the message shone forth and was then perfected by the High Priest. The Urim and Thumim would be consulted like an oracle; the High Priest would meditate on the stones until he reached a level of divine inspiration. He would see the breastplate with inspired vision, and the letters containing the answer would appear to light up or stand out. With his divine inspiration, the High Priest would then be able to combine the letters to spell out the answer (*Yoma* 73b; Ramban; Bachya on Numbers 28:21; cf. *Handbook of Jewish Thought* 6:36).

Some say that the word Thumim has the connotation of pairing, since it was the inspiration that allowed the priest to arrange the letters to spell out a message (Bachya on Numbers 28:21). Others say that the message was called *Thumim* (perfect) because it was irrevocable (*Midrash HaGadol;* cf. *Yoma* 73b).

Josephus writes that when the Israelites went to battle, the stones would shine forth with great splendor as a sign of victory (*Antiquities* 3:8:9).

The Septuagint translates Urim and Thumim as *dylosis khai alytheia,* where *dylosis* denotes pointing out, manifestation, or explanation, and *alytheia* means truth. According to this, the root of *Urim* may be *yarah,* to teach.

As far as the nature of the "Urim and Thumim" that were placed in the breastplate, some say that they consisted of mystical divine names of God (*Targum Yonathan;* Rashi; Rashbam; Ramban; *Zohar* 2:234b). Some say that these names were placed inside the fold of the breastplate (Rashi). Others, however, maintain that they were placed on the outside of the breastplate, and that the priest would meditate on these names to attain inspiration (*Me'or Eynayim* 46).

According to others, the Urim and Thumim were the engraved stones themselves (*Lekach Tov;* Ralbag; *Otzar HaGeonim, Berakhoth* 6; cf. Josephus, *Antiquities* 3:8:9), but some emphatically reject this (Radak, *Sherashim*). Some maintain that the *Urim and Thumim* were the borders of the tribes (*Bekhor Shor; Hadar Zekenim*) or astrological signs (Ibn Ezra; cf. Ramban, Ralbag).

Philo (*Vide de Muse* 2:152) writes that the Urim and Thumim were two *agalmatophory* representing revelation and truth. The word *agalmatophory* is taken from *agalma,* an image or portrait, and *phory,* an ornament. The two images may have been the lion and eagle woven into the breastplate itself (see note on 28:15).

—   **in.** (*Targum*). Literally, "to."

28:31 **robe.** *Meil* in Hebrew. Some say that it had sleeves (Raavad, *Kley HaMikdash* 9:3; Rabbenu Meyuchas; *Siddur Rav Saadia Gaon,* p. 271; cf. Rashi on 29:4) while others maintain that it was sleeveless (*Yad, Kley HaMikdash* 9:3; *Midrash HaGadol;* cf. Josephus, *Antiquities* 3:7:4).

According to many, the *meil* was a closed robe that was slipped over the head (Rashi; Rashbam; Rabbenu MeYuchas) (A). It was woven as a single

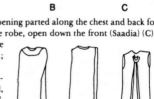

A   B   C

garment without seams (Josephus, *Wars* 5:5:7), and had an opening parted along the chest and back for the head (*Antiquities* 3:7:4) (B). Others say that it was a simple robe, open down the front (Saadia) (C).

Others, however, maintained that it was open in front like a large sleeveless cape, and only closed at the neck (Ramban; *Lekach Tov;* see Avraham ben HaRambam) (D).

According to another opinion, the *meil* was a long rectangular piece of cloth with a hole in the middle for the head, very much like a long *tallith katan* (Ralbag; *Tifereth Yisrael, Kelelay Bigdey Kodesh*). According to some, it hung in front and back (*ibid.*) (E), while others maintain that it hung on both sides (Radbaz on *Yad, Kley HaMikdash* 9:3) (F).

D   E   F

blue wool.* ³² It shall have an opening for the head in the middle, and this   28
opening shall have a woven border all around it, like there is around the head
opening of a coat of mail. [The neck] shall thus not be left open.*

³³ On the bottom [of the robe], place pomegranates* made of sky-blue,
dark red, and crimson wool, all along its lower border. In between* [these
pomegranates] all around, there shall be gold bells. ³⁴ Thus, there shall be a
gold bell and a pomegranate, a gold bell and a pomegranate, all around the
lower edge of the robe.

³⁵ Aaron shall wear [this robe] when he performs the divine service. The
sound [of the bells] shall be heard when he enters the sanctuary before God,
and when he goes out, so that he not die.

[114. The Other Vestments]

³⁶ Make a forehead-plate* of pure gold, and engrave on it in the same
manner as a signet ring, [the words], "Holy to God.*" ³⁷ Attach a twist* of

The *meil* came down to the priest's feet (Josephus, *Antiquities* 3:7:4; *Wars* 5:5:7; Philo, *De Vida Musa* 2:118–121).

— **worn under.** (Rashi; *Midrash HaGadol; Yad, Kley HaMikdash* 10:3).

— **completely out of** . . . (Rashi; Radak, *Sherashim; Zevachim* 88b). Or, "woven in one piece" (cf. *Targum Yonathan;* Josephus *Wars* 5:5:7).

28:32 **not be left open** (Rashbam; Chizzkuni). Or, "so that it not be torn" (Rashi). Or, "Do not tear it," implying a negative commandment (*Yoma* 72a; *Yad, Kley HaMikdash* 9:3).

28:33 **pomegranates.** Hollow spheres in the shape of pomegranates (Rashi; *Zevachim* 88b). Josephus, however, states that the "pomegranates" here were pomegranate-colored threads or fringes (*Antiquities* 3:7:4).

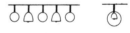

A   B

In the Talmud it is debated as to whether there were 72 or 36 such pomegranates (*Zevachim* 88b). Other sources indicate that there were 70 (*Lekach Tov; Zohar* 3:203a,b).

— **In between.** So that the bells and pomegranates alternated all around the bottom of the *meil* (Rashi; Chizzkuni; cf. Josephus, *Antiquities* 3:7:4) (A). Others say that the bells were inside the hollow pomegranates (Ramban; Bachya; cf. Ibn Ezra; *Tosefoth Yom Tov, Kanim* 3:6) (B). Josephus apparently holds that the bells were hung from the "pomegranates" (*Wars* 5:5:7), but in a special manner so that the two alternated (*Antiquities* 3:7:4).

28:36 **forehead-plate.** This was a thin gold plate, 2 fingerbreadths (1¼") wide, and extending from ear to ear (*Shabbath* 63b).

— **Holy to God.** Or, "consecrated to God," *Kodesh le-YHVH* in Hebrew. The letters were made so they protruded from the front of the plate, like letters on a coin (*Gittin* 20a; cf. *Yad, Kley HaMikdash* 9:3, Raavad *ad loc.*).

28:37 **twist.** *Pethil* in Hebrew. See note on 28:28. Some say that this was a twisted thread attached to holes in both ends of the plate to tie it to the head (*Yad, Kley HaMikdash* 9:3; Ramban) (A). Others maintain that there was a third thread going through a hole in the middle of the

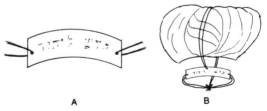

A   B

plate and over the turban, and then tied to the other two threads in the back (Rashi; Raavad, on *Yad. loc. cit.*) (B).

28   sky-blue wool to it, so that it can be [worn] next to the turban. It must be [worn] right near the front of the turban.

    38 [This plate] shall be worn on Aaron's forehead. Aaron shall thus carry the device that expiates [errors]* in the sacred offerings that the Israelites consecrate as holy gifts. It shall be on his forehead at all times to make [these offerings] acceptable for [the Israelites] before God.

    39 Knit* the tunic out of linen.

    [Also] make the turban* out of linen and an embroidered sash.*

    40 For Aaron's sons,* make tunics* and sashes.* Also make them hats* that are both dignified and beautiful.

According to another opinion, the *pethil* here was a 1½–2 inch band attached to the plate, going around the head (*Chullin* 138a, according to Rabbenu Chananel, Meiri, *Shabbath* 57b; Rif 26b; *Arukh*, s.v. *Kippah;* cf. Genesis 38:18). Some say that this band was (also?) under the plate to protect the head from the hard metal (Rambam on *Shabbath* 6:1) (C).

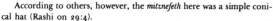

    Others, however, say that the cap mentioned in the Talmud (*Chullin* 138a) was a blue cap that went over the turban (Josephus, *Antiquities* 3:7:6; *Wars* 5:5:7). See note on 28:39, 39:28.

C

28:38 errors. Specifically, ritual uncleanliness (*Menachoth* 25a; Rashi).

28:39 knit. (cf. *Midrash HaGadol*). This was a patterned weave that could best be attained by knitting (however, see *Yad, Kley Mikdash* 8:19). Some write that it had a pattern of depressions, like settings for precious stones, (Rashi on 28:4). Others say that it was a diamond-shaped pattern, like an array of small eyes (Saadia; Ibn Janach; cf. Ibn Ezra). According to another opinion, it was a hexagonal pattern, like a honeycomb or the lining of a cow's second stomach (*Yad, Kley HaMikdash* 8:16).

    This *kethoneth* had arm-length sleeves that were made separately and sewn on (*Ibid.*). It sat close to the body, and came down to the feet (*Ibid.* 8:17; Josephus *Antiquities* 3:7:2). The sleeves were tied at the wrists (Josephus) (see figure).

—   turban (Ibn Janach; Radak, *Sherashim*). This consisted of a strip of linen 16 cubits (24′) long, which was wound around the top of the priest's head (*Yad, Kley HaMikdash* 8:19).

    Josephus notes that after being wound around, it was sewn, and then covered with a piece of fine linen to hide the seams. This was true for both the high priest and the common priests (*Antiquities* 3:7:3). In the case of the High Priest, however, this linen turban was covered with a layer of sky-blue wool (see note on 28:37). Over this was a crown consisting of three horizontal golden bands, with a sort of flower or cup on top. The crown was open in the front to allow for the forehead-plate (*Antiquities* 3:7:6) (see figure).

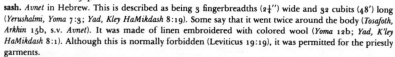

    According to others, however, the *mitznefeth* here was a simple conical hat (Rashi on 29:4).

—   sash. *Avnet* in Hebrew. This is described as being 3 fingerbreadths (2¼″) wide and 32 cubits (48′) long (*Yerushalmi, Yoma* 7:3; *Yad, Kley HaMikdash* 8:19). Some say that it went twice around the body (*Tosafoth, Arkhin* 15b, s.v. *Avnet*). It was made of linen embroidered with colored wool (*Yoma* 12b; *Yad, K'ley HaMikdash* 8:1). Although this is normally forbidden (Leviticus 19:19), it was permitted for the priestly garments.

    Josephus (*Antiquities* 3:7:2) describes the sash as being worn over the heart, slightly above the elbows. It was four fingers wide and loosely woven, so that it appeared like the skin of a snake. Its main body was linen, and it was embroidered with a floral design of linen and blue, dark-red and crimson wool. When it was worn, its ends were allowed to hang down to the ankles, except during the service, when the ends were thrown over the left shoulder.

28:40 Aaron's sons. These served as the common priests, as opposed to Aaron himself, who was High Priest. The tunic, sash and hat mentioned here, along with the pants (28:42), were the vestments of the common priest.

⁴¹ Place these [vestments] on Aaron and his sons. Then anoint* them, and **28**
install* them, sanctifying them to be priests to Me.

⁴² Also make linen pants* to cover their nakedness, reaching from their
waists to their thighs.

⁴³ [All these vestments]* must be worn by Aaron and his sons whenever
they enter the Communion Tent or offer sacrifice on the altar, performing the
divine service in the sanctuary; otherwise they will have committed a sin and
they will die. This shall be a law for [Aaron] and his descendants after him for
all time.

[115. Consecration of the Priests]

¹ This is what you, [Moses] must do to consecrate [Aaron and his sons] as **29**
priests to Me.

Take a young bull,* two unblemished rams,* ² loaves of unleavened
bread,* unleavened loaves kneaded with olive oil,* and flat matzahs brushed

---

—   **tunics.** These were exactly the same as the tunic of the High Priest (28:39; *Yoma* 12b; *Yad, Kley HaMikdash*
8:16; Ramban on 39:27; Josephus, *Antiquities* 3:7:4). Some, however, question whether or not the common priest's tunic was made with a textured pattern (*tashbetz*) like that of the High Priest (Ibn Ezra on
28:39; *Mishneh LaMelekh, Kley HaMikdash* 8:16).

—   **sashes.** Some say that the sashes were exactly the same as that of the High Priest, while others maintain
that the common priest's sash was of plain linen (*Yoma* 12b). Josephus (*Antiquities* 3:7:2) holds that they
were the same.

—   **hats.** *Migba'oth* in Hebrew. Some say that this is exactly the same as the High Priest's turban (Rashi; cf.
Yoma 25a, *Tosafoth ad loc.* s.v. *Notel*). Josephus also notes that both are the same, except that the High
Priest's is covered with blue and a gold crown (see above). Others say that they are the same in form, but
that the common priest's is put on, while the High Priest's is wound on (*Yad, Kley HaMikdash* 8:1).

According to others, however, the two differed
in shape, with the turban of the High Priest being
narrow, and the common priest's being wider (*Tosafoth, Yoma* 12b, s.v. *Eleh;* Ibn Ezra) (A). Another
opinion is that the High Priest's *mitznefeth* was a turban, while the *migba'ath* of the common priest was a
conical hat (*Raavad, Kley HaMikdash* 8:1), shaped
perhaps like an inverted goblet (cf. Ibn Janach) (B).

                                                            A   **B**

According to others, the *migba'ath* was a cap that went under the turban, both for ordinary priests
and the High Priest (*Lekach Tov* on 28:37) (C). See 39:28.

28:41   **anoint.** See 30:22–30.

—   **install.** Literally, "fill hands." See 29:24.

28:42   **pants.** These were closed pants, reaching from the waist to the
knees (*Niddah* 13b; *Yad, Kley HaMikdash* 8:18). They had laces
around the knees where they could be tied (*Ibid.;* Josephus,
Antiquities 3:7:1). Others, however, maintain that it was tied at
the waist (*Tifereth Yisrael, Kelelay Bigdey Kodesh*). The common
priest thus had a total of four vestments, and the High Priest
eight (Rashi).

28:43   **All these** . . . (Rashi). Or, "the pants" (Ramban).

29:1   **young bull.** In its second year (*Parah* 1:2; *Yad, Maaseh Korbanoth*
1:14). See Leviticus 8:2.

—   **rams.** Also in their second year (*Parah* 1:3).

29:2   **unleavened bread.** This is the *revukhah* or *murbekheth* mentioned in Leviticus 7:12 (Rashi; *Menachoth* 78a).

29   with olive oil.* All [the cakes] must be made of fine wheat flour. ³ Place [all the cakes] in a basket, and bring them in the basket along with the young bull and the two rams.

⁴ Bring Aaron and his sons to the door of the Communion Tent, and immerse* them in a mikvah.*

⁵ Take the vestments and place the tunic, the ephod's robe, the ephod and the breastplate on Aaron. Bind him with the ephod's belt. ⁶ Then place the turban on his head, and place the sacred plate [below] the turban.

⁷ Take the anointing oil, pour [a little] on [Aaron's] head, and anoint* him.

⁸ Bring forth [Aaron's] sons and dress them with the [linen] tunics. ⁹ His sons shall wear belts, just like Aaron,* and they shall also wear hats. You shall thus install Aaron and his sons [as priests, and this procedure] shall remain a law for all time.

¹⁰ Bring the young bull before the Communion Tent,* and have Aaron and his sons place their hands on the bull's head. ¹¹ Slaughter the bull before God, at the door of the Communion Tent. ¹² Take the bull's blood and place it on the altar's protrusions* with your finger. Spill all the [remaining] blood on the altar's foundation.*

¹³ Take all the fat that covers the inner organs,* as well as the lobe* of the liver, and the two kidneys with the fat around them, and burn them on the altar. ¹⁴ You must burn the bull's flesh, along with its skin and the food in its intestines,* outside the camp. It is a sin offering.

It consists of dough, cooked in boiling water, baked, and then fried (*Yad, Maaseh Korbanoth* 9:19; *Sifra* on Leviticus 7:12). See Leviticus 6:14.

— **unleavened loaves** . . . These were loaves kneaded with warm water and olive oil (*Yad, Maaseh Korbanoth* 13:8¹).

— **flat matzahs** . . . Brushed with oil after baking (*Yad. loc. cit.*).

29:4 **immerse.** (Rashi; *Targum Yonathan; Midrash HaGadol;* cf. Josephus, *Antiquities* 3:8:6). See note on 19:10; Leviticus 15:16.

— **mikvah.** A specially constructed pool containing 40 *sa'ah* (80–180 gallons) of water (*Targum Yonathan*). The Torah here literally says, "he shall wash in *the* water," indicating the special water of the mikvah (*Rashi. Chagigah* 11a, s.v. *BaMayim*).

29:7 **anoint.** After pouring the oil on the priest's head, he would make an X-like mark with it on the priest's forehead (*Kerithoth* 5b; *Yad, Kley HaMikdash* 1:9; see *Tifereth Yisrael* on *Zevachim* 10:6; *Torah Sh'lemah* 23:194 ff).

29:9 **just like Aaron.** See note on 28:40.

29:10 **Bring** . . . See Leviticus 8:14 ff.

29:12 **protrusions.** Or "horns." See 27:2. This is standard procedure for a sin offering, Leviticus 4:30).

— **foundation.** This was a slight protrusion a cubit above the ground (Rashi; *Zevachim* 59b).

29:13 **all the fat** . . . That is, all the fat in the body cavity (Rambam, introduction to *Kadshim*). See Leviticus 3:3.

— **lobe** (Ibid.; Septuagint; Abarbanel; *Sefer Halttur* 2, *Asereth HaDibroth* 44, p. 3b). Or, "the Diaphragm along with some of the liver" (*Targum;* Rashi; Radak, *Sherashim; HaKethav VeHaKabbalah*). These were the usual parts burnt with such an offering; Leviticus 3:4, etc.

29:14 **food in its intestines** (Radak, *Sherashim*). *Peresh* in Hebrew. (cf. *Targum; Targum Yonathan*).

¹⁵ Take the first ram and have Aaron and his sons place their hands on its 29
head. ¹⁶ When you then slaughter the ram, take its blood and sprinkle it on all
sides of the altar.* ¹⁷ Cut the ram into pieces. Then wash* off its intestines*
and legs, and place them together with* the cut up pieces [of the ram] and its
head. ¹⁸ Burn the entire ram on the altar; it is a burnt offering* to God. It
shall thus be an appeasing fragrance,* a fire-offering to God.

¹⁹ Take the second ram, and have Aaron and his sons place their hands on
its head. ²⁰ When you then slaughter the ram, take its blood and place some of
it on the right ear lobe* of Aaron and his sons, as well as on their right
thumbs* and right big toes. Sprinkle the [remaining] blood on all sides of the
altar.

²¹ Collect the blood that is on the altar, and [together] with the anointing
oil, sprinkle it on Aaron and his vestments, as well as on his sons and their
vestments. This will consecrate [Aaron] and his vestments, as well as his sons
and their vestments.

²² Take the [intestinal] fat* of the [second] ram, along with its broad tail,*
the fatty layer covering the stomachs,* the lobe of the liver, the two kidneys
together with their fat, and the right hind leg, since this ram is an installation
[offering].* ²³ [Also take] one cake of [unleavened] bread, one loaf of oil bread,
and one flat cake from the basket of unleavened bread that is before God.

²⁴ Place all [these items] onto the open hands of Aaron and his sons, and
have them wave [these items] in the prescribed motions* of a wave offering
before God. ²⁵ Then take [these items] from their hands and burn them on the
altar after* the [first ram which is a] burnt offering. Let it be an appeasing
fragrance before God, since it is a fire offering to God.

²⁶ Take the breast of Aaron's installation ram, and wave it in the motions

---

29:16 **all sides** . . . This is done by sprinkling blood on the two opposite corners of the altar, so that the blood
reaches all four sides of the altar (Rashi). See Leviticus 1:5.
29:17 **wash.** See Leviticus 1:9, 1:13.
— **intestines** (*Targum Yonathan*). Or, "body cavity"(*Targum*).
— **together with** (Rashi; Mizrachi).
29:18 **burnt offering.** See Leviticus 1:3 ff.
— **appeasing fragrance.** See note on Genesis 8:21.
29:20 **lobe.** The helix or upper part of the ear (*Targum; Midrash HaGadol*). See Leviticus 8:24, 14:14.
— **thumbs.** On the middle joint (Rashi). See Leviticus 8:24.
29:22 **intestinal fat.** The fat on the stomachs. See Leviticus 3:3.
— **broad tail.** On sheep, the tail grows long and very fat.
— **stomachs.** See Leviticus 3:3.
— **installation offering.** It is offered like a peace offering, see Leviticus 3.
29:23 **Also take** . . . See 29:2.
29:24 **prescribed motions.** It is waved back and forth in the four compass directions, and then up and down
(*Menachoth* 62a; Rashi). Some say that the order, with the individual facing east, is right, left, front, up,
down, back.
29:25 **after.** (Rashi; Mizrachi). Literally, "on."

29   prescribed for a wave offering. This shall be your portion, [Moses].

     ²⁷ Sanctify the breast of the wave offering and the hind leg of the uplifted
offering* [for all time]. These are the parts of the installation ram of Aaron
and his sons that were waved with the prescribed horizontal and vertical*
motions. ²⁸ It shall be a law for all times that this be an offering for Aaron and
his sons from the Israelites, taken from their peace offerings as a priestly offering to God.*

     ²⁹ Aaron's sacred vestments shall [also] be passed down to his descendants
after him* to give them special status* and to install them. ³⁰ The descendant
who takes [Aaron's] place to enter the Communion Tent and perform the
divine service in the [inner]* sanctuary must [first] put on [these vestments] for
seven [consecutive] days.*

     ³¹ Take the [rest of the] installation ram and cook its flesh in a sanctified
area.* ³² Aaron and his sons shall eat the ram's meat along with the bread in
the basket near the entrance of the Communion Tent. ³³ They will gain
atonement by eating [these offerings], and they will thus be installed to their
consecrated rank.

     [These offerings] are sacred, and therefore may not be eaten by any out-
sider.* ³⁴ If any meat of the installation offering or any of the bread is left over
until morning, you must burn the leftovers in the fire. Since it is consecrated,
it may not be eaten.

     ³⁵ Do exactly as I have instructed you for Aaron and his sons. Their instal-
lation shall take seven days.*

     ³⁶ Sacrifice a young bull as a sin offering* each day* for atonement. By
sprinkling* [the blood of this offering] on the altar, you will atone for [any
misdeed associated with making] it,* and by anointing it you will sanctify it.
³⁷ For [all] seven days, you shall make such atonement for the altar and sanc-
tify it, thus making the altar holy of holies. Anything that touches the altar will
therefore become sanctified.

29:27 **uplifted offering.** *Terumah* in Hebrew, the usual word for the offering given to priests.
—   **horizontal and vertical.** (cf. Rashi).
29:28 **taken from their peace offerings** . . . See Leviticus 7:31,32.
29:29 **after him.** That is, future high priests (Rashi).
—   **to give them special status** (*Targum;* Rashi). Or, "to anoint them in" (Saadia; Radak, *Sherashim*).
29:30 **inner** (Rashi).
—   **consecutive days** (*Yad, Kley HaMikdash* 4:13).
29:31 **sanctified area.** The enclosure around the tabernacle (Rashi).
29:35 **seven days.** During which they may not leave the enclosure (Leviticus 8:35).
29:36 **sin offering.** See Leviticus 4.
—   **each day** (Ibn Ezra; *Lekach Tov;* Ralbag). Cf. Ezekiel 43:22.
—   **By sprinkling** (Rashi). Or "atoning" (Radak, *Sherashim*).
—   **for any misdeed** . . . (cf. Rashi).

[116. Consecrating the Altar]

³⁸ This is what you must do for the altar:
[Offer] two yearling sheep each day consecutively. ³⁹ The first sheep shall be offered in the morning, and the second sheep in the afternoon.

⁴⁰ Offer 1/10 ephah* fine flour mixed with 1/4 hin* pressed olive oil, and a libation of 1/4 hin wine, with the first sheep. ⁴¹ Offer the second sheep in the afternoon along with a meal offering and libation just like that of [the sheep] offered in the morning. It shall then be an appeasing fragrance to God.

⁴² This shall also be the continual burnt offering for all generations.* [It shall be offered] before God at the entrance of the Communion Tent, the place where I commune* with [all the people]* by speaking with you there.*

⁴³ It is there that I will commune with the Israelites, and [the tabernacle]* will thus be sanctified with My glory. ⁴⁴ I will sanctify the Communion Tent and the altar, and I will also sanctify Aaron and his sons to be priests to Me.

⁴⁵ I will make My presence felt* among the Israelites, and I will be a God for them. ⁴⁶ They will realize that I, God their Lord, brought them out of Egypt to make My presence felt among them. I am God their Lord.

[117. The Incense Altar]

¹ Make an altar to burn incense out of acacia wood. ² It shall be square, a cubit long and a cubit wide, and 2 cubits high,* including its horns.* ³ Cover it with a layer of pure gold,* on its top, its walls all around, and its horns. Make a gold rim all around it.

⁴ Place two gold rings under [the altar's] rim on its two opposite sides* as

---

29:40 **1/10 ephah.** Around 2 quarts (2.2 liters).

— **¼ hin.** Around 1 quart.

29:42 **for all generations.** See Numbers 28:2-8.

— **commune.** See 25:22.

— **all the people.** Literally, "you" in plural.

— **by speaking** . . . Some say that prophecy could also come from the altar, just as from between the cherubs (*Bareitha Melekheth HaMishkan* 14). Simply, however, this is speaking of the tabernacle in general.

29:43 **the tabernacle** (Rashi; Ibn Ezra).

29:45 **make My presence felt** (*Moreh Nevukhim* 1:25). Literally, "dwell."

30:2 **a cubit long** . . . It was therefore 18" x 18" x 36". Some say that it was 15" x 15" x 30" (*Eruvin* 4a; *Maaseh Choshev* 7:1). It appears that it was made of solid wood (cf. 27:8), although some say that it was like an inverted box (*Maaseh Choshev* 7:1).

— **horns.** Or "protrusions" (see 27:2). Some say that these protrusions were small cubes, three fingerbreadths (2¼") on each side (*Maaseh Choshev* 7:1). Others, however, maintain that they were horn-like protrusions. See note on 27:2.

30:3 **layer** . . . The Talmud notes that this layer was as thick as a dinar (*Eruvin* 19a). See note on 38:24.

30:4 **two gold rings** . . . Some say that they were on opposite corners of the altar (*Maaseh Choshev* 7:1). Others say that it had four rings, one on each corner (Abarbanel; cf. Baaley Tosafoth).

30 receptacles to hold the poles with which it is carried. ⁵ Make the carrying poles out of acacia wood and cover them with a layer of gold.

⁶ Place [this altar] in front of the cloth partition* concealing the Testimony Ark—before the cloth partition concealing the testimony* area where I commune with you.

Aaron shall burn incense on [this altar] each morning when he cleans out the lamps. ⁸ He shall [also] burn [incense] before evening when he lights the lamps. Thus, for all generations, there will be incense before God at all times.

⁹ Do not burn any unauthorized* incense on it. Furthermore, do not offer any animal sacrifice,* meal offering, or libation on it.

¹⁰ [Furthermore,] once each year* Aaron shall make atonement* on the horns of [this altar]. For all generations, he shall make atonement with the blood of the atonement sacrifice once each year. [This altar] shall be a holy of holies to God.

Ki Thisa   כִּי תִשָּׂא

[118. Instructions for a Census]

¹¹ God spoke to Moses saying*:

¹² When you take a census* of the Israelites to determine their numbers,* each one shall be counted by giving an atonement offering for his life. In this manner, they will not be stricken by the plague when they are counted. ¹³ Everyone included in the census must give a half shekel. This shall be by the sanctuary standard,* where a shekel is 20 gerahs.* It is half of such a shekel that must be given as an offering to God.

¹⁴ Every man over 20 years old shall be included in this census and give this offering to God. ¹⁵ The rich may not give more, and the poor may not give

---

30:6   **in front of the cloth partition.** Between the table and the lamp (see 26:34; *Yoma* 33b; *Yad, Beth HaBechirah* 3:17).

—   **testimony.** *Eduth* in Hebrew. Or, "communion place."

30:9   **unauthorized.** Donated by an individual and not made special for this purpose (Rashi). Or, made with unauthorized ingredients (Ibn Ezra; Ramban).

—   **animal sacrifice.** Literally, "burnt offering."

30:10 **once each year.** On Yom Kippur (Rashi; *Yoma* 61a). See Leviticus 16:18. See Leviticus 4:7.

—   **make atonement.** By placing blood (Rashi).

30:11 **God spoke . . .** Some say that this was after the sin of the Golden Calf (*Yerushalmi, Shekalim* 2:3).

30:12 **take a census** (*Targum;* Saadia). Literally, "when you lift the head." See Genesis 40:13,20.

—   **to determine their numbers.** Or, "to count each one separately (Saadia). *Pakad* in Hebrew. See Genesis 21:1.

30:13 **sanctuary standard.** Literally, "sanctuary shekel" or "holy shekel."

—   **a shekel is 20 gerahs.** A *gerah* is the same as a *ma'ah* (*Targum*), a weight equivalent to 1.14 grams. Hence, a shekel is 22:8 grams or 0.8 ounces. Josephus notes that it is around 4 drachmas (*Antiquities* 3:8:2). A half shekel was a silver coin around the size of a half dollar.

less than this half shekel. It is an offering to God to atone for your lives.   30
¹⁶ You will take this atonement money from the Israelites and use it for making the Communion Tent. It will thus be a remembrance for the Israelites before God to atone for your lives.

[119. The Washstand]

¹⁷ God spoke to Moses saying:
¹⁸ Make a copper washstand* along with a copper base* for it. Place it between the altar and the Communion Tent, and fill it with water for washing.
¹⁹ Aaron and his sons must wash their hands and feet from [this washstand]. ²⁰ If they are not to die, they must wash with the water [of this washstand] before entering the Communion Tent or approaching the altar to perform the divine service, presenting a fire offering to God. ²¹ If they are not to deserve death, they must first wash their hands and feet. This shall be for [Aaron] and his descendants a law for all time, for all generations.

[120. The Anointing Oil]

²² God spoke to Moses, saying:
²³ You must take the finest fragrances, 500 [shekels]* of distilled* myrrh,*

30:18 washstand. *Kiyyor* in Hebrew. It looked like a large kettle with two spigots for washing (Rashi; *Maaseh Choshev* 6:8; *Yoma* 37a). According to others, it was apparently like a basin with spigots (Radak, *Sherashim*, who says it was like a *cuenca*, Spanish for basin). It was later made with 12 spigots (*Yoma* 37a). See 1 Samuel 2:14.

— **base** (*Targum;* Rashi; Ibn Janach; Radak, *Sherashim*). *Kan* in Hebrew. See 1 Kings 7:38, 2 Chronicles 4:14 (cf. Ibn Ezra). In shape, the base was somewhat like an inverted pot (Tosafoth, *Zevachim* 22a, s.v. *Kal VeChomer; Maaseh Choshev* 6:9), or like an open box (Tosafoth). Some say that it was 3 handbreadths (9″) high (Rabbenu Meyuchas).

    Later, this base was made to include a mechanism to fill the washstand with water (*Yad, Beth Ha-Bechirah* 3:18), as well as machinery to lower the entire washstand into a well (Raavad *ibid.; Yoma* 37a; *Zevachim* 20a; *Yad, Biyyath HaMikdash* 5:14). A similar mechanism may have existed in the Tabernacle (See *Torah Sh'lemah* 38:6).

30:23 500 shekels. Around 25 pounds.

— **distilled.** (Septuagint). *Deror* in Hebrew. Or, "free of impurities" (Ibn Janach; Radak, *Sherashim*); or "wild" (Ramban; Bachya). On the basis of Semitic cognates, some suggest "flowing" or "congealed into pearls."

— **myrrh** (Raavad, *Kley HaMikdash* 1:3; Ramban; Bachya; Septuagint). *Mor* in Hebrew. Myrrh is a gum resin produced by trees and shrubs of the family *Burseracea*, most notably *Commiphora myrrha*, *Commiphora abysinica*, and *Commiphora schimperi*. The resin is obtained from Arabia and adjacent Africa, and is taken from the small, prickly, gray-barked trees. Pearls of myrrh are brown, red or yellow, with an oily texture, becoming hard and brittle with age. It has a pleasing fragrance, very much like balsam, and a lasting, bitter, aromatic taste, hence the name *mor*, which signifies bitterness.

Myrrh   Musk Deer

    According to many authorities, however, the *mur* here is not myrrh but musk (Saadia; *Yad, Kley*

30   [two] half portions,* each consisting of 250 [shekels] of fragrant cinnamon*
      and 250 [shekels] of fragrant cane,* ²⁴ and 500 shekels of cassia,* all measured

HaMikdash 1:3; Abarbanel; cf. Radak, *Sherashim;* Ibn Janach). This is an extract taken from the musk
deer (*Moschus moschiferus*) which lives in Nepal and Tibet (see Ibn Ezra).

— **two half portions** (Rashi, *Kerithoth* 5a; Bachya; Ralbag; cf. *Yad, Kley HaMikdash* 1:2). According to
Josephus, however, it would be translated, "a half portion . . ." (*Antiquities* 3:8:3).

— **fragrant cinnamon** (Rashi; Septuagint; Abarbanel,
Canela in Spanish; Ibn Janach; Rambam on
Kerithoth 1:1, but see Ramban on 31:34). *Kinman* in
Hebrew. This is the dried bark of the cinnamon
tree, *Cinnamomum zeylanicum*, a species of laurel
cultivated mainly in Ceylon (cf. *Yad, Kley Ha-
Mikdash* 1:3; cf. Theophrastus, *Plants* 9:7;
Herodatus 3:111).

Cinnamon   Alloe

According to others, however, the *kinman* of
the Bible is aloeswood or lignum aloes (Radak,
Sherashim; cf. Saadia; see Ramban on 31:34). This
is the resinous hartwood, *Aquilaria agallocha* of the
family *Thymalaeaceae,* which grows in the East Indies and tropical Southeast Asia, and is still used for
incense and perfumes.

According to other ancient sources, the "cinnamon" of antiquity was not the Ceylonese product, but
an herb coming from Arabia (Theophrastus, *History of Plants* 9:4; Strabo 16:778; Diodorus Sicculus
2:49, 3:46) or Ethiopia (Pliny 12:42). Some identify it with "Mecca Straw" (*paja de Mecca* in old Spanish;
Ramban; Abarbanel), which was used as fodder for camels (*Shir HaShirim Rabbah* on 4:4). There are also
indications that the "cinnamon" of antiquity grew in the Holy Land (*Yerushalmi, Peah* 7:4; *Bereshith
Rabbah* 65:17; see *Kaftor VaPherach* 10, 31a).

— **fragrant cane.** *Keneh bosem* in Hebrew.
Ancient sources identify this with the
sweet calamus (Septuagint; Rambam
on Kerithoth 1:1; Saadia; Ibn
Janach). This is the sweetflag or flag-
root, *Acoras calamus* which grows in
Europe. It appears that a similar
species grew in the Holy Land, in the
Hula   region   in   ancient   times
(Theophrastus, *History of Plants* 9:7).
Other sources apparently indicate
that it was the Indian plant, *Cympopogan martini,* which has the form of
red straw (*Yad, Kley HaMikdash* 1:3).

Canna   Cympopogan   Hemp

On the basis of cognate pronunciation and Septuagint readings, some identify *Keneh bosem* with the English and Greek cannabis, the hemp plant.

There are, however, some authorities who identify the "sweet cane" with cinnamon bark (Radak,
Sherashim). Some say that *kinman* is the wood, and *keneh bosem* is the bark (Abarbanel).

30:24 **cassia** (Radak, *Sherashim; Peshita;* Vulgate). *Kidah* in Hebrew; *ketzia* in Aramaic (*Targum;*
Rambam on *Kelayim* 1:8). Cassia is the common name for the bark of the tree *Cin-
namomum cassia* or *Cassia lignea* belonging to the laurel family, which grows in China.
(*Pachad Yitzchak,* s.v. *Ketoreth;* cf. Pliny 12:43; Theophrastus, *History of Plants* 9:7;
Diodorus Siculus 3:46; Herodatus 3:110).

There are some, however, who identify the "cassia" of the ancients, and hence *kidah*
here, with costus, known as *kosh't* in the Talmud (*Yad, Kley HaMikdash* 1:3; Saadia; Ibn
Janach; cf. Rashi). Costus is the root of the annual herb, *Sausurea lappa,* which grows on   Cassia
the mountain slopes of Kashmir, and is used for incense and perfume.

The Septuagint translates *kidah* here as *iris,* possibly *Castus speciosus.* Others suggest that it is kitto or
mosylon, a plant very much like cassia, coming from Meuzel on the African coast (cf. Dioscorides, *De
Materia Medica* 1:13).

by the sanctuary standard, along with a gallon* of olive oil.

30

²⁵ Make it into sacred anointing oil. It shall be a blended compound,* as made by a skilled perfumer, [made especially for] the sacred anointing oil.

²⁶ Then use it to anoint the Communion Tent, the Ark of Testimony, ²⁷ the table and all its utensils, the menorah and its utensils, the incense altar, ²⁸ the sacrificial altar and all its utensils, the washstand and its base. ²⁹ You will thus sanctify them, making them holy of holies, so that anything touching them becomes sanctified.

³⁰ You must also anoint Aaron and his sons, sanctifying them as priests to Me.

³¹ Speak to the Israelites and tell them, "This shall be the sacred anointing oil to Me for all generations. ³² Do not pour it on the skin of any [unauthorized] person, and do not duplicate it with a similar formula. It is holy, and it must remain sacred to you. ³³ If a person blends a similar formula, or places it on an unauthorized person, he shall be cut off* [spiritually] from his people.

[121. The Incense]

³⁴ God said to Moses: Take fragrances such as balsam,* onycha,* gal-

---

— **gallon.** *Hin* in Hebrew. Actually 0.97 gallon, or 3.6 liter.

30:25 blended compound. The anointing oil was made by soaking the aromatic substances in water until the essential essences are extracted. The oil is then placed over the water, and the water slowly cooked away, allowing the essences to mix with the oil (*Yad, Kley HaMikdash* 1:2; from *Kerithoth* 5a). According to another opinion, the oil was cooked with the aromatic herbs, and then filtered out (*Ibid.*).

30:33 cut off. See note on Genesis 17:14.

30:34 balsam (*Yad, Kley HaMikdash* 2:4; cf. *Kerithoth* 6a; Rashi; Radak, *Sherashim;* Saadia; Rambam on *Kerithoth* 1:1). *Nataf* in Hebrew. Some say that *nataf* denotes the wood of the balsam, rather than the sap (Ramban). Balsam is also known as *tzori* in Hebrew (see Genesis 37:25). It is derived from the balsam tree, *Commiphora opobalsamum,* known as *kataf* in the Talmud, which grows wild in Yemen and around Mecca.

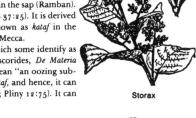

Storax

The Septuagint translates *nataf* here as *stacte,* which some identify as storax gum (*Pachad Yitzchak,* s.v. *Ketoreth;* cf. Dioscorides, *De Materia Medica* 1:79). However, the Greek word can also mean "an oozing substance", very much like the basic connotation of *nataf,* and hence, it can denote any gum (thus, *stacte* can also denote myrrh; Pliny 12:75). It can thus denote balsam gum as well.

— **onycha.** *Shecheleth* in Hebrew. The *Targum* translates this as *tufra,* the Talmud as *tziporen* (*Kerithoth* 6a), and the Septuagint as *onyx,* all denoting "fingernail." Some maintain that this is a spice actually prepared from human fingernails (cf. *Arukh* s.v. *Tziporen*), but most authorities see it as coming from an aquatic animal (*Mossef HeArukh ibid.;* Ramban). It is therefore usually identified as onycha (Hirsch; King James) or blatta byzantia (Abarbanel; *Shiltey Gibborim* 85), the fingernail-like operculum or closing flap of certain snails of the murex family, such as the *Onyx marinus, Strom-*

Strombus   Onycha

30 banum,* and pure frankincense,* all of the same weight,* as well as [other specified] fragrances.* ³⁵ Make [the mixture] into incense, as compounded by a

bus lentiginosus, or *Unguis Odaratus* (*Tifereth Yisrael, Chomer Bakodesh* 2:67; Cf. Ben Sirah 24:15; Dioscorides, *De Materia Medica* 2:10). This emits a very pleasant smell when burned.

Other sources, however, state that *shecheleth* is a kind of root (Rashi). The Talmud also appears to indicate that it came from an annual plant (*Kerithoth* 6b). Some identify this plant with a species of rockrose, *Cistus ladaniferus,* which has fingernail-like petals.

The onycha was rubbed with an alkali solution prepared from the bitter vetch (*Vicia sativa*) (cf. Rambam on *Maaser Sheni* 2:4) to remove all impurities. It was then soaked in the fermented juice of the caper berry (*Caparis spinosa*) (see *Tosafoth, Betza* 25b, s.v. *VeTzalaf*) or strong white wine to enhance its fragrance (*Kerithoth* 6a; *Yad, Kley HaMikdash* 2:5).

— **galbanum** (Rashi; Septuagint). *Chelbanah* in Hebrew. It is a yellow-brown gum resin obtained from the Persian plant, *Ferula galbaniflua* (Pliny 12:56,24,13; Dioscorides, *De Materia Medica* 3:97). Alone it had a pungent, almost unpleasant odor (*Kerithoth* 6b).

According to some, the *chelbanah* here is the gum of the common storax tree (Rambam on *Kerithoth* 1:1).

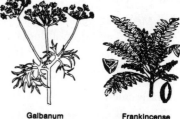

Galbanum　　　Frankincense

— **frankincense.** Or oliban. (Septuagint). *Levonah* in Hebrew. This is a gum resin from trees of the genus *boswellia,* most notably *Boswellia carterii* and *Boswellia frereana* from Arabia, and *Boswellia serratae* from India. The gum is yellowish and semi-transparent, with a bitter nauseous taste. It is hard and capable of being pulverized, producing a strong aromatic odor when burned.

— **all of the same weight** (*Targum; Kerithoth* 5a; Rashi; Saadia). Or, "each ground separately" (Ibn Ezra; cf. *Yad, Kley HaMikdash* 2:5).

— **other specified fragrances.** By tradition, an additional 7 fragrances were added, besides the four mentioned here, to give a total of eleven.

The formula for the incense was given in terms of the *maneh* which was 100 shekels or 5 pounds. It was

70 maneh	350 lb.	Balsam
70 maneh	350 lb.	Onycha
70 maneh	350 lb.	Galbanum
70 maneh	350 lb.	Frankincense
16 maneh	80 lb.	Myrrh
16 maneh	80 lb.	Cassia
16 maneh	80 lb.	Spikanard (*shiboleth nard*)
16 maneh	80 lb.	Saffron (*karkom*)
12 maneh	60 lb.	Costus (*kosh't*)
9 maneh	45 lb.	Cinnamon
3 maneh	15 lb.	Cinnamon bark

Spikanard　　　Saffron

365

The total amount was 365 maneh, so that one maneh (5 lb) could be burned each day of the solar year.

Besides these ingredients, ¼ kav (1 cup) of Sodom salt (nitrate) and small amounts of *maaleh ashan* (probably *Leptadenia pyrotechnica,* which contains nitric acid) and *kippath ha-yardan* (probably cyclamen) were added. Besides this, 9 quarts (*kab*) of vetch lye (*borith karshina*) and 21 quarts (3 *saah* and 3 *kab*) of caper wine were used to prepare the onycha.

Cyclamen

master perfumer, well-blended,* pure and holy. ³⁶ Grind it very finely, and 30
place it before the [Ark of] Testimony in the Communion Tent where I commune with you. It shall be holy of holies to you.

³⁷ Do not duplicate the formula of the incense that you are making for
personal use, since it must remain sacred to God. ³⁸ If a person makes it to
enjoy its fragrance, he shall be cut off [spiritually] from his people.

[122. The Architects]

¹ God spoke* to Moses, saying: 31
² I have selected Betzalel son of Uri son of Chur,* of the tribe of Judah, by
name. ³ I have filled him with a divine spirit, with wisdom, understanding and
knowledge, and with [the talent for] all types of craftsmanship. ⁴ He will be
able to devise plans* as well as work in gold, silver and copper, ⁵ cut stones to
be set, carve wood, and do other work.

⁶ I have also given him Oholiav son of Achisamakh of the tribe of Dan [as
an assistant]. [Besides this], I have placed wisdom in the heart of every
naturally talented* person.

They will thus make all that I have ordered, ⁷ the Communion Tent, the
Ark for the Testimony, the ark cover to go on it, all the utensils for the tent,
⁸ the table and its utensils, the pure [gold] menorah and all its utensils, the
incense altar, ⁹ the sacrificial altar and all its utensils, the washstand and its
base, ¹⁰ the packing cloths,* the sacred vestments for Aaron the priest, the
vestments that his sons wear to serve, ¹¹ the anointing óil, and the incense for
the sanctuary. They will thus do all that I command.

[123. The Sabbath]

¹² God told Moses ¹³ to speak to the Israelites and say to them:
You must still* keep My sabbaths. It is a sign between Me and you for all
generations, to make you realize that I, God, am making you holy. ¹⁴ [There-
fore] keep the Sabbath as something sacred to you. Anyone doing work [on
the Sabbath] shall be cut off spiritually from his people, and therefore, anyone
violating it shall be put to death. ¹⁵ Do your work during the six week days,

---

30:35 **well-blended** (*Targum;* Rashi; Radak, *Sherashim;* Saadia) Or, "salted" (Ibn Ezra; cf. Ibn Janach), referring
to the Sodom salt that was added, Or, "finely ground" (Ramban).
31:1 **God spoke** . . . See 35:30–36:1.
31:2 **Betzalel** . . . son of Chur. See note on 17:10. Betzalel was thus Miriam's grandson.
31:4 **devise plans** (*Targum Yonathan; Lekach Tov*). Or, "weave designs" (Rashi).
31:6 **naturally talented.** Literally, "wise of heart". See 28:3.
31:10 **packing cloths** (Rashi; Ibn Ezra). Or, "unique vestments" (Ramban).
31:13 **still.** Even while building the Tabernacle (*Mekhilta;* Rashi).

31 but keep Saturday* as a Sabbath of sabbaths, holy to God. Whoever does any
work on Saturday shall be put to death.

    ¹⁶ The Israelites shall thus keep the Sabbath, making it a day of rest for all
generations, as an eternal covenant. ¹⁷ It is a sign between Me and the Israelites that during the six weekdays God made heaven and earth, but on Saturday, He ceased working and withdrew to the spiritual.*

[124. The Golden Calf]

    ¹⁸ When [God] finished speaking to Moses on Mount Sinai, He gave him
two tablets* of the Testimony. They were stone tablets, written with God's
finger.*

32   ¹ Meanwhile, the people began to realize that Moses was taking a long time
to come down from the mountain. They gathered around Aaron and said to
him, "Make us an oracle* to lead us. We have no idea what happened to
Moses, the man who brought us out of Egypt."

    ² "Take the rings off the ears of your wives and children," replied Aaron.
"Bring them to me."

    ³ All the people took off their earrings and brought them to Aaron. ⁴ He
took [the rings] from the people, and had someone form [the gold] in a mold,*
casting it into a calf. [Some of the people* began to] say, "This, Israel, is your
god, who brought you out of Egypt."

    ⁵ When Aaron saw [this],* he built an altar before [the calf]. Aaron made
an announcement and said, "Tomorrow, there will be a festival* to God."

    ⁶ Getting up early the next morning, [the people] sacrificed burnt offerings
and brought peace offerings. The people sat down to eat and drink, and then
got up to enjoy themselves.

[125. Moses' Response]

    ⁷ God declared to Moses,* "Go down, for the people whom you brought

---

31:15 **Saturday.** Literally, "the seventh day." See note on 16:5.

31:17 **withdrew to the spiritual** (cf. *Bahir* 57; Ramban on Genesis 2:7). *Nafash* in Hebrew. Or, "withdrew to
Himself" (Hirsch); or, "finished accomplishing what He intended" (*Moreh Nevukhim* 1:67); or, "rested"
(*Targum;* Rashi; Radak, *Sherashim*).

31:18 **tablets.** According to tradition the tablets were square, 6 x 6 x 3 handbreadths (18″ x 18″ x 9″) (*Bava
Bathra* 14a). They were made of sapphire (*Lekach Tov;* see note on 24:10).

—   **finger.** "Instrument" (*Moreh Nevukhim* 1:66). See above, 8:15 (cf. *Midrash HaGadol*).

32:1 **oracle** (Rashbam; Ralbag; cf. Ramban; Ibn Ezra; *Kuzari* 1:96). Or, "god" (*Targum*).

32:4 **form . . . in a mold** (Saadia; Ibn Ezra; Ibn Janach; Radak, *Sherashim*). Or, "formed it with a goldsmith's
tool" (Rashi), or "bound in a sheet" (Rashi).

—   **Some of the people . . .** (see Rashi).

32:5 **this.** According to some, he saw Chur (see 17:10, 31:2) being killed for trying to prevent the making of
the Golden Calf, (*Sanhedrin* 7a; *Targum Yonathan;* Rashi).

—   **festival.** Or, "sacrifice" (See note on 23:18).

32:7 **God declared . . .** This occurred on 17 Tammuz, a day that would later be a time of mourning (*Seder
Olam* 6; *Taanith* 26b).

out of Egypt have become corrupt. **8** They have been quick to leave the way   **32**
that I ordered them to follow, and they have made themselves a cast-metal
calf. They have bowed down and offered sacrifice to it, exclaiming, 'This,
Israel, is your god, who brought you out of Egypt.'"

9 God then said to Moses, "I have observed the people, and they are an
unbending* group. **10** Now do not try to stop Me when I unleash my wrath
against them to destroy them. I will then make you into a great nation."

11 Moses began to plead before God his Lord. He said, "O God, why
unleash Your wrath against Your people, whom you brought out of Egypt
with great power and a show of force*? **12** Why should Egypt be able to say
that* You took them out with evil intentions,* to kill them in the hill country
and wipe them out from the face of the earth. Withdraw Your display of anger,
and refrain from doing evil to Your people.

13 "Remember Your servants, Abraham, Isaac and Jacob. You swore to
them by Your very essence, and declared that* You would make their descendants as numerous as the stars of the sky, giving their descendants the land
You promised, so that they would be able to occupy it forever."

14 God refrained from doing the evil that He planned for His people.

[126. Moses Descends]

15 Moses turned around, and began going down the mountain with the
two Tablets of Testimony in his hand. They were tablets written on both sides,
with the writing visible from either side. **16** The Tablets were made by God and
written with God's script engraved on the Tablets.

17 Joshua* heard the sound of the people rejoicing, and he said to Moses,
"It sounds as though there is a battle going on in the camp!"

18 "It is not the song* of victory," replied [Moses],* "nor the dirge of the
defeated. What I hear is just plain singing."

19 As he approached the camp and saw the calf and the dancing,* Moses
displayed anger, and threw down the tablets that were in his hand, shattering
them at the foot of the mountain. **20** He took the calf that the [people] had
made, and burned it in fire, grinding it into fine powder. He then scattered it
on the water,* and made the Israelites drink it.*

32:9   **unbending.** Literally, "stiff-necked."
32:11 **show of force.** Literally, "mighty hand" (see 6:1).
32:12 **that.** Actually, there is a direct quote here.
—   **with evil intentions.** Or, "against the power of Ra" (see note on 10:10).
32:13 **that.** Actually a direct quote.
32:17 **Joshua.** See 24:13.
32:18 **song** (Radak, *Sherashim*). Or, "shout" (Rashi).
—   **replied [Moses]** (*Shemoth Rabbah* 41:1; Ramban). Or, "continued Joshua" (Saadia; Ibn Ezra).
32:19 **dancing.** Or, "drums" (see note on 15:20).
32:20 **water.** Of the brook (Deuteronomy 9:21).

32   ²¹ Moses said to Aaron, "What did the people do to you, that you allowed them to commit such a great sin?"

²² "Do not be angry, my lord," replied Aaron, "but you must realize that the people have bad tendencies.* ²³ They said to me, 'Make an oracle* to lead us, since we do not know what happened to Moses, the man who took us out of Egypt.' ²⁴ When I responded to them, 'Who has gold?' they took it off and gave it to me. I threw the gold into the fire and the result was this calf."

²⁵ Moses realized that the people had actually been restrained.* Aaron had restrained them, doing only a small part* of what the outspoken ones* [had demanded].*

²⁶ Moses stood up at the camp's entrance and announced, "Whoever is for God, join me!" All the Levites gathered around him.

²⁷ He said to them, "This is what God, Lord of Israel, says: Let each man put on his sword, and go from one gate to the other in the camp. Let each one kill [all those involved in the idolatry],* even his own brother, close friend, or relative."

²⁸ The Levites did as Moses had ordered, and approximately 3000 people were killed that day. ²⁹ Moses said, "Today you can be ordained* [as a tribe dedicated] to God with a special blessing. Men have [been willing to kill even] their own sons and brothers [at God's command]."

³⁰ The next day, Moses said to the people, "You have committed a terrible sin. Now I will go back up to God and try to gain atonement for your crime."

³¹ Moses went back up to God,* and he said, "The people have committed

---

—   **made the Israelites drink it.** Like a suspected adulteress; Numbers 5:24 ff.

32:22 **have bad tendencies** (Rashi). Or, "are among evildoers" (Ibn Ezra, end of 31:18).

32:23 **oracle.** See note on 32:1.

32:25 **been restrained** (Ralbag). Or, "exposed" (Rashi; Sforno; Ibn Janach); "exposed to harm" (Abarbanel); "undisciplined" (Rashbam; Chizzkuni); "unrestrained" (Hirsch); "going the wrong way" (Ibn Janach; Radak, *Sherashim*).

—   **doing only a small part** (Ralbag; Hirsch; cf. *Shabbath* 119a). Or, "so as to be derided" (Radak, *Sherashim;* Rashi).

—   **outspoken ones** (Ralbag; Hirsch). Or, "enemies" (Rashi; Ibn Ezra; Radak, *Sherashim*to7).

—   **had demanded** (Ralbag). Or, "Moses saw that the people had been exposed; for Aaron had exposed them and they could be the subject of derision to their enemies" (Rashi). Or, "Moses saw that the people were unrestrained, since Aaron had shown their lack of restraint to some degree when they stood up against him" (Hirsch). Or, "Moses saw that the people were going the wrong way, because Aaron had allowed them to revert . . ." (Ibn Janach; Radak, *Sherashim*).

32:27 **all those involved** . . . (*Targum Yonathan*).

32:29 **"be ordained"** (Rashi; Sforno). Literally, "fill your hands;" see above, 28:41. Or, "inaugurate yourselves with a sacrifice" (Onkelos); "bring a sacrifice as atonement [for the act of killing]" *(Targum Yonathan)*; or, "fulfill your obligation, since you must still kill your own sons and brothers" (Saadia). It is here that the Levites gained their special status (Rashi).

32:31 **went back up** . . . This was on 18 Tammuz (*Seder Olam* 6) or 19 Tammuz (Rashi on 33:11). Moses then remained on the mountain for an additional 40 days (cf. Deuteronomy 9:25). According to some, however, Moses ascended for only a short while, and then prayed for 40 days in the camp (*Pirkey Rabbi Eliezer* 46; Radal *ad loc.* 46:13; Ramban on 33:11).

a terrible sin by making a golden idol. [32] Now, if You would, please forgive 32
their sin. If not, You can blot me out from the book* that You have written.''

[33] God replied to Moses, "I will blot out from My book those who have
sinned against Me. [34] Now go; you still have to lead the people to [the place]
that I described to you. I will send My angel before you.* Still, when I grant
special providence to the people, I will take this sin of theirs into account.''

[35] God then struck the people with a plague because of the calf that Aaron
had made.

[127. Moses and the Decree]

[1] God declared to Moses, "You and the people you took out of Egypt will 33
have to leave this place and go to the land regarding which I swore to Abraham, Isaac and Jacob that I would give it to their descendants. [2] I will send an
angel* ahead of you, and drive out the Canaanites, Amorites, Hittites, Perizites, Hivites and Yebusites.*

[3] "[You will thus go to] a land flowing with milk and honey. However, I
will not go with you, since you are an unbending* people, and I may destroy
you along the way.''

[4] When they heard this bad news, the people began to mourn. They
stopped wearing jewelry.*

[5] God told Moses to say to the Israelites, "You are an unbending people.
In just one second I can go among you and utterly destroy you. Now take off
your jewelry and I will know what to do with you.''

[6] From [that time at] Mount Horeb on, the people no longer wore their
jewelry.*

[7] Moses took [his]* tent and set it up outside the camp at a distance. He
called it the Meeting Tent.* [Later],* whoever sought God would go to the
Meeting Tent outside the camp.

32:32 **the book.** An allegory meaning, "erase me from Your memory" (*Moreh Nevukhim* 2:47), or, "blot me out
from all creation" (Ralbag). Others see it as meaning, "blot me out from the book of life," that is, "kill
me" (Abarbanel; cf. *Targum Yonathan; Rosh HaShanah* 16b). Alternatively, the "book" denotes the Torah
itself (Rashi).

32:34 **I will send My angel** . . . See note on 23:20.

33:2 **angel.** See previous note.

— **Canaanites.** . . See note on 3:8.

33:3 **unbending.** Literally, "stiff-necked."

33:4 **stopped wearing jewelry.** See 32:2. Some say that the "jewelry" here denotes the spiritual gifts that
the Israelites received at Sinai (*Shabbath* 88a; *Targum Yonathan;* Rashi).

33:6 **From that time** . . . (Saadia). Or, "The people took off the jewelry that they had on from Mount Horeb"
(Rashi). See note on 3:1.

33:7 **his** (Rashi). Literally, "the tent." Or, "Moses took to the tent" (*Targum Yonathan*).

— **Meeting Tent.** Or, "Tent of Study" (Onkelos). Although the same term, *Ohel Moed,* is used, it is not the
Communion Tent mentioned earlier. Or, "communion tent," since God communed with Moses in that
tent until the Tabernacle was erected (Ibn Ezra). Or, "He took the Tabernacle . . ." before the enclosure

33 ⁸ Whenever Moses went out to the tent, all the people would rise, and each person would stand near his own tent, gazing at Moses until he would come to his tent. ⁹ When Moses went into the tent, the pillar of cloud would descend and stand at the tent's entrance, and [God] would speak to Moses. ¹⁰ When the people saw the pillar of cloud standing at the tent's entrance, the people would rise, and each one would bow down at the entrance of his tent.

¹¹ God would speak to Moses face to face, just as a person speaks to a close friend. [Moses] would then return to the camp. But his aid, the young man,* Joshua son of Nun,* did not leave the tent.

[128. Moses' Plea]

¹² Moses said to God, "You told me to bring these people [to the Promised Land], but You did not tell me whom You would send with me. You also said that You know me by name and that You are pleased with me.*

¹³ "Now, if You are indeed pleased with me, allow me to know Your ways, so that I will know how to [remain] pleasing to You. [Also], You must confirm* that this nation is Your people."

¹⁴ "My presence* will go and lead you," replied [God].

¹⁵ [Moses] said, "If Your presence does not accompany [us], do not make us leave this place. ¹⁶ Unless You accompany us, how can it be known that I and Your people are pleasing to You? [But if You do,] I and your people will be distinguished from every nation on the face of the earth."

[129. The Divine Glory]

¹⁷ God said to Moses, "Since you have been pleasing to Me and I know you by name, I will also fulfill this request of yours."

¹⁸ "Please let me have a vision* of Your Glory," begged [Moses].

¹⁹ [God] replied, "I will make all My good pass before you, and reveal the

---

was set up (*Ibid.*). Moses was in the "Meeting Tent" from Yom Kippur until the Tabernacle was erected (Rashi). Some say that he was there 40 days from 18 Tammuz on (Ramban).

—   **Later** . . . (Ramban).

33:11 young man. Joshua was 42 at the time (*Seder Olam* 12; Rashi on Judges 11:26). Others say that he was 56 (Ibn Ezra). He was a young man compared to Moses, who was 80 (Ramban).

—   **Joshua** . . . See above, 17:9, 24:13, 32:17. Joshua was therefore worthy of becoming the next leader of the Israelites (see Numbers 27:18).

33:12 pleased with me. Literally, "I have found favor in Your eyes."

33:13 confirm. (See Ramban on Genesis 1:4).

33:14 My presence. And not the angel (see above 33:3,4).

33:18 have a vision (*Emunoth VeDeyoth* 2:12). Or, "Let me comprehend Your unique nature" (*Yad, Yesodey HaTorah* 1:10).

Divine Name in your presence. [But still,] I will have mercy and show kindness   33
to whomever I desire.*"

²⁰ [God then] explained, "You cannot have a vision of My Presence. A man
cannot have a vision of Me and still exist.*"

²¹ God then said, "I have a special place* where you can stand* on the
rocky mountain. ²² When My glory passes by, I will place you in a crevice in
the mountain,* protecting you with My power* until I pass by. ²³ I will then
remove My protective power,* and you will have a vision of what follows from
My existence.* My essence itself,* however, will not be seen."

[130. The Second Tablets]

¹ God said to Moses,* "Carve out two tablets for yourself, just like the first   34
ones. I will write on those tablets the same words that were on the first tablets
that you broke. ² Be ready in the morning, so that you will be able to climb
Mount Sinai in the morning and stand waiting for Me on the mountain peak.
³ No man may climb up with you, and no one else may appear on the entire
mountain. Even the cattle and sheep may not graze near the mountain."

⁴ Moses carved out two stone tablets like the first. He then got up early in
the morning and climbed Mount Sinai, as God had commanded him, taking
the two stone tablets in his hand.

⁵ God revealed Himself* in a cloud, and it stood there with [Moses].*
[Moses] called out in God's name.*

33:19 **But still** . . . (see *Berakhoth* 7a). Or, "I will let you know to whom I will show mercy and kindness" (Rashbam; Ramban).

33:20 **and still exist.** Literally, "and live." Or, "No man nor any other living creature can see Me" (Ralbag).

33:21 **I have a special place** (Rashi). Or, "All space is under My domain" (Rashi; Baaley Tosafoth). Or, "There is a way of reaching up to Me" (*Moreh Nevukhim* 1:8).

— **where you can stand.** Literally. Some take this expression idiomatically, and render it, "You must remain in contemplation of the origin of all things" (*Moreh Nevukhim* 1:16; Abarbanel).

33:22 **When My glory passes by** . . . (Literally). Or, "When [you try] to pass over the boundaries [toward] My glory, I will let you reach the limit of your powers" (Abarbanel).

— **protecting you with My power** (cf. *Targum*). Literally, "placing My hand over you." Or, "protecting you with My cloud" (*Emunoth VeDeyoth* 2:12; see 34:5).

33:23 **My protective power** (cf. *Targum*). Literally, "My hand."

— **of what follows from My existence** (Hirsch; cf. *Moreh Nevukhim* 1:34; *Avodath HaKodesh* 3:40). Literally, "My back." Or, "a glimmer of My essence" (*Emunoth VeDeyoth* 2:12); or, "a partial realization of My uniqueness" (*Yad, Yesodey HaTorah* 1:10).

— **My essence** . . . Literally, "My face."

34:1 **God said** . . . This was on 1 Elul (*Seder Olam* 6). Moses would remain on the mountain for a third period of 40 days (34:28; Deuteronomy 10:10), finally coming down with the second Tablets on Yom Kippur.

34:5 **revealed Himself** (*Targum*). Literally, "descended." See note on Genesis 11:7, Exodus 19:11.

— **it** . . . The cloud (Ibn Ezra; Avraham ben HaRambam). Or, "[God] stood with [Moses]" (Ramban; *Emunoth VeDeyoth* 2:12); or, "[Moses] stood there with [God]" (*Targum Yonathan;* Sforno).

— **Moses called** . . . (*Targum Yonathan;* Mizrachi). Or, "[God] proclaimed the Divine Name" (*Lekach Tov;* Ibn Ezra).

34   ⁶ God passed by before [Moses] and proclaimed,* "God, God, Omnipotent,* merciful and kind, slow to anger, with tremendous [resources of] love
and truth. ⁷ He remembers deeds of love for thousands [of generations],* forgiving sin, rebellion and error.* He does not clear [those who do not repent],*
but keeps in mind the sins of the fathers to their children and grandchildren,
to the third and fourth generation.*"

⁸ Moses quickly bowed his head and prostrated himself. ⁹ He said, "If You
are indeed pleased with me, O God, let my Lord go among us. This nation
may be unbending, but forgive our sins and errors, and make us Your own.*"

¹⁰ God said: I will make a covenant before all your people, and will do
miracles that have never been brought into existence in all the world, among
any nation. All the people among whom you [dwell] will see how fearsome are
the deeds that I, God, am doing with you.

¹¹ Be very careful with regard to what I am instructing you today. I will
drive the Amorites, Canaanites, Hivites, Perizzites, Hittites and Yebusites out
before you. ¹² Be most careful not to make a treaty with the people who live in
the land where you are coming, since they can be a fatal trap to you.* ¹³ You
must shatter their altars, break down their sacred pillars, and cut down their
Asherah trees.* ¹⁴ Do not bow down to any other god, for God is known as
one who demands exclusive worship, and He does indeed demand it.

¹⁵ [Be careful] that you not make a treaty with [the people] who live in the
land. When they practice their religion and sacrifice to their gods, they will
invite you, and you will end up eating their sacrifice. ¹⁶ You will then allow
their daughters to marry your sons, and when their daughters worship their
gods, they will lead your sons to follow their religion.

¹⁷ Do not make any cast metal idols.

¹⁸ Keep the Festival of Matzahs. Eat matzahs for seven days as I command-

---

34:6   **and proclaimed** (Rashbam; Ibn Ezra; Sforno). Or, "and [Moses] prayed" (*Targum Yerushalmi; Pirkey Rabbi
Eliezer* 46; Mizrachi).
—   **Omnipotent** (Saadia). Or, "the merciful and kind God" (*Targum*).
34:7   **of generations** (*Targum*). See 20:6.
—   **sin, rebellion and error** (See *Yoma* 36b).
—   **those who do not repent** (*Targum; Yoma* 88a; Rashi). Or, "He does not completely destroy" (cf. Jeremiah
30:11).
—   **third and fourth generation.** See 20:5.
34:9   **make us Your own.** Literally, "make us Your inheritance" (Saadia; Radak, *Sherashim*). Or, "grant us an
inheritance" (Rashi).
34:12   **Be most careful . . .** See 23:32,33. This is virtually a repetition of that chapter, see note on 34:27.
34:13   **Asherah trees.** These were sacred trees or poles (Rashi). See Deuteronomy 16:21. Asherah was a popular
fertility goddess in the near east, worshiped by Sidon (1 Kings 11:5,33), Tyre (Josephus, *Contra Apion*
1:18), and the Philistines (1 Samuel 31:10). She is often identified with Astarte and Aphrodite (Septuagint; Herodianus 5:6:10). While stone pillars were erected in honor of Baal, wooden poles or pillars
were erected in honor of Asherah.

ed, in the designated time in the month of standing grain. It was in the month 34
of standing grain that you left Egypt.

¹⁹ The first-born initiating every womb is Mine. Among all your livestock,
you must separate out the males* of the first-born cattle and sheep. ²⁰ The
first-born of a donkey must be redeemed with a sheep, and if it is not
redeemed, you must decapitate* it. You must [also] redeem every first-born
among your sons.

Do not appear before Me empty-handed.

²¹ You may work during the six weekdays, but on Saturday, you must stop
working, ceasing from all plowing and reaping.*

²² Keep the Festival of Shavuoth* through the first fruits of your wheat
harvest. Also keep the Harvest Festival soon after the year changes.*

²³ Three times each year, all your males shall thus present themselves
before God the Master, Lord of Israel. ²⁴ When I expel the other nations
before you and extend your boundaries, no one will be envious of your land
when you go to be seen in God's presence three times each year.

²⁵ Do not slaughter the Passover sacrifice with leaven in your possession.
Do not allow the Passover sacrifice to remain overnight until morning.*

²⁶ Bring the first fruits of your land to the Temple of God your Lord.
Do not [eat]* meat cooked in milk, [even that of] its own mother.*

[131. Moses Returns]

²⁷ God said to Moses, "Write these words down for yourself, since it is
through these words that I have made a covenant with you and Israel.*"

²⁸ [Moses] remained there with God [on the mountain] for 40 days and 40
nights* without eating bread nor drinking water. [God] wrote* the words of
the covenant, consisting of the Ten Commandments,* on the Tablets.

34:19 **separate out the males** (see Ibn Janach; Radak, *Sherashim*).
34:20 **decapitate.** See 13:13.
34:21 **from all plowng and reaping** (*Lekach Tov;* Rashbam; Ibn Ezra). Or, "[even] during plowing and planting
season" (Saadia).
34:22 **Shavuoth.** Literally, "Weeks." See 23:16.
— **Harvest festival** . . . Sukkoth. See 23:16.
34:25 **Do not slaughter** . . . See 23:18.
34:26 **Do not eat** . . . (Saadia; *Chullin* 115b).
— **even that of** . . . See 23:19.
34:27 **Write these words** . . . Because of the Golden Calf, the covenant now had to be renewed (Ramban). The
above verses, 34:11-26, are virtually a repetition of 23:10-23, which may have been the original "book
of the covenant" (24:7).
34:28 **40 days** . . . From 1 Elul until Yom Kippur (*Seder Olam* 6).
— **God wrote** . . . (Rashbam; Ibn Ezra; see 34:1). However, according to others, "[Moses] wrote" (*Lekach
Tov* on 34:27; Abarbanel).
— **Ten Commandments.** *Assereth HaDevarim* in Hebrew, literally, "ten statements."

34   ²⁹ Moses came down from Mount Sinai with the two Tablets of the Testimony in his hand. As Moses descended from the mountain, he did not realize that the skin of his face had become luminous* when [God] had spoken to him.

³⁰ When Aaron and all the Israelites saw that the skin of Moses' face was shining with a brilliant light, they were afraid to come close to him. ³¹ Moses summoned them, and when Aaron and all the community leaders returned to him, Moses spoke to them. ³² After that, all the Israelites approached, and [Moses] gave them instructions regarding all that God had told him on Mount Sinai.*

³³ When Moses finished speaking with them, he placed a hood* over his face.

³⁴ Whenever Moses came before God to speak with Him, he would remove the hood until he was ready to leave. He would then go out and speak to the Israelites, [telling them] what he had been commanded. ³⁵ The Israelites would see that the skin of Moses' face was glowing brilliantly. Moses would then replace the hood over his face until he would [once again] speak with God.

VaYakhel   וַיַּקְהֵל

[132. The Sabbath]

35   ¹ Moses assembled the entire Israelite community and said to them, "These are the words that God has commanded for [you] to do*:

² "You may do work during the six weekdays, but Saturday must be kept holy as a Sabbath of Sabbaths to God. Whoever does any work on [that day] shall be put to death. ³ Do not ignite any fire on the Sabbath, no matter where you may live."

[133. Materials for the Tabernacle]

⁴ Moses said to the entire Israelite community, "This is the word that God has commanded*:

34:29 **had become luminous.** *Karan* in Hebrew. Literally, "was giving off rays ('horns') of light" (Ibn Ezra).
34:32 **Moses gave them instructions** . . . Some say that this relates to 35:4-17, which was told to him during the last 40 days (see note on 25:1).
34:33 **hood** (*Targum Yonathan*). Or, "mask" (Rashi; *Targum*); or "veil" (*Lekach Tov*; Radak, *Sherashim*).
35:1 **These are the words** . . . See above, 31:12-17.
35:4 **This is the word** . . . See 25:1-7.

5 "Collect among yourselves an elevated offering to God. If a person feels 35 like giving an offering to God, he can bring any of the following: gold, silver, copper, 6 sky-blue [wool], dark red [wool], [wool died with] the crimson worm, fine linen, goats' wool, 7 reddened ram's skins, blue processed hides, acacia wood, 8 oil for the lamp, fragrances for the anointing oil and perfume incense, 9 as well as sardonyxes and other precious stones for the ephod and the breastplate.

10 "Every naturally talented individual among you shall come forth and make all that God has ordered: 11 The tabernacle along with its over-tent, roof, fasteners, beams, crossbars and pillars; 12 the ark and its carrying poles, the ark cover, the cloth partition; 13 the table along with its carrying poles, all its utensils and the showbread; 14 the menorah lamp along with its utensils, lights and illuminating oil; 15 the incense altar and its carrying poles; the anointing oil, the perfumed incense, the drape for the tabernacle's entrance; 16 the sacrificial altar along with its carrying poles and all its utensils; the washstand and its base; 17 the hangings for the enclosure, its pillars and bases, the drape for the enclosure's entrance; 18 the stakes for the tent, the stakes for the enclosure, the tying ropes*; 19 the packing cloths* for sacred use, the sacred vestments for Aaron the priest, and the vestments that his sons will wear to serve."

20 The entire Israelite community left Moses' presence. 21 Each person who was ready to volunteer* then came forward. [Also] each one who wanted to give brought a donation to God for the making of the Communion Tent, all its necessities, and the sacred vestments.

22 The men accompanied the women, and those who wanted to make a donation brought bracelets,* earrings,* finger rings,* and body ornaments,*

35:18 **tying ropes.** To tie the stakes to the poles and hangings (Rashi). See above 27:19. Also see Numbers 3:26,37, 4:26,32.
35:19 **packing cloths.** See above, 31:10.
35:21 **who was ready to volunteer.** (*Targum;* Ibn Janach). Literally, "whose heart lifted him up." Or, "whose natural talents were awakened" (Ibn Ezra; Ramban; see 35:26). Or, "each person brought according to the dictates of his heart" (Saadia).
35:22 **bracelets** (Rashi; *Midrash HaGadol*). *Chach* in Hebrew. Or, "earrings" (Ibn Ezra; Ibn Janach; Chizzkuni), "nose rings" (Rabbenu Meyuchas, from Isaiah 37:29), "lip rings" (Radak, *Sherashim,* from Ezekiel 38:4, or "brooch" (*Minchah Belulah; MeAm Lo'ez;* Hirsch). Some say that a *chach* is a plain gold ring, while the "earrings" and "finger rings" mentioned below are ornamented (*Lekach Tov*).

Bracelet   Anklet   Nezem

— **earrings** (Rabbenu Meyuchas, from 32:2). *Nezem* in Hebrew. Or, "nose rings" (Ibn Ezra; *Lekach Tov;* from Genesis 24:47, Isaiah 3:21).
— **finger rings** (*Midrash HaGadol*).

35 all made of gold. There were also all the ones who donated a wave offering* of gold to God. ²³ Every person who had sky-blue wool, dark red wool, crimson wool, fine linen, goats' wool, reddened rams' skins or blue processed hides, brought these items. ²⁴ Whoever donated silver or copper brought it as a divine offering, and anyone who had acacia wood that could be used for the dedicated work, also brought it.

²⁵ Every skilled woman put her hand to spinning, and they [all] brought the spun yarn of sky-blue wool, dark red wool, crimson wool and fine linen. ²⁶ Highly skilled women volunteers also spun the goats' wool.

²⁷ The tribal leaders* brought the sardonyxes and other precious stones for the ephod and breastplate, ²⁸ as well as the fragrances and olive oil for the lamp, the anointing oil, and the perfumed incense.

²⁹ Every man and woman among the Israelites who felt an urge to give something for all the work that God had ordered through Moses, brought a donation for God.

[134. Appointing the Architects]

³⁰ Moses said to the Israelites*: "God has selected Betzalel son of Uri son of Chur, of the tribe of Judah, ³¹ and has filled him with a divine spirit of wisdom, understanding, knowledge, and [a talent for] all types of craftsmanship. ³² [He will thus be able] to devise plans, work in gold, silver and copper, ³³ cut stones to be set, and do carpentry and other skilled work.*

³⁴ "[God] also gave to him and Oholiav son of Achisamakh, of the tribe of Dan, the ability to teach [others]. ³⁵ He has granted them a natural talent for

— **body ornaments.** *Kumaz* in Hebrew. According to some, a jeweled belt (Saadia; *Peshitah*). According to others, a gold genital shield for women (*Shabbath* 84a; Rashi), possibly a chastity belt (Rabbenu Ephraim; *Maskil LeDavid; Maaseh Toviah, Gan Naul* 3). Others say that it is a gold brassiere (*Yerushalmi, Shabbath* 6:4), an arm band (Chizzkuni), or a pornographic sculpture (Rabbi Aaron Alrabi, *Kenzal*). The Septuagint translates *kumaz* as *emplokion*, something that holds a garment, possibly a brooch or belt (cf. Hirsch; Pliny 11:50; Diodorus Siclus 3:44).

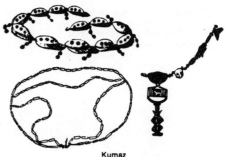

Kumaz

— **wave offering.** See above, 29:24 (cf. Sforno). This consisted of gold coins and bullion (Ramban).

35:27 **tribal leaders.** See above, 16:22.

35:30 **Moses said . . .** Quoting 31:2–11.

35:33 **skilled work** (*Targum;* Rashi, *Betza* 13b). *Malekheth machasheveth* in Hebrew. Or, "carefully planned work" (*Chagigah* 10b, top).

all craftsmanship, to form materials, to brocade or embroider patterns with   35
sky-blue, dark red and crimson wool and fine linen, and to weave. They will
thus be able to do all the necessary work and planning.*
    ¹ "Betzalel shall thus do all that God commanded, along with Oholiav and   36
every other skilled individual, to whom God has granted the wisdom and
understanding to know how to do all the work necessary for the sacred task."
    ² Moses summoned Betzalel, Oholiav, and all the other skilled individuals
upon whom God had bestowed a natural talent, all who volunteered to dedicate themselves to completing the task. ³ In Moses' presence, they took the
entire donation that the Israelites had brought to complete the work on the
sacred task.
    Meanwhile, [the Israelites]* were bringing more gifts each morning. ⁴ All
the craftsmen engaged in the sacred work [left] the work* they were doing,
and came [to Moses]. ⁵ They said to Moses, "The people are bringing much
more than is needed for the work that God commanded to do."
    ⁶ Moses gave orders to make an announcement in the camp, "Let no man
or woman bring any more material* for the sacred offering."
    The people stopped bringing, ⁷ but the materials were more than enough
for all the work that had to be done.

[135. Making the Tabernacle]

    ⁸ All the most talented craftsmen worked on the tabernacle itself,* which
consisted of ten tapestries made of twined linen, together with sky-blue, dark
red and crimson wool, brocaded with cherubs.
    ⁹ All the tapestries were the same size, 28 cubits long and 4 cubits wide.
¹⁰ The [first] five tapestries were sewn* together, as were the other five.
¹¹ Loops of sky-blue wool were made on the innermost tapestry of the second
group [of five]. ¹² There were 50 loops on the first tapestry, and 50 on its
counterpart on the second group, with all the loops [on one side] parallel to
those [on the other side]. ¹³ Fifty gold fasteners were made to attach [the sets
of] tapestries together to make the tabernacle into a single unit.

35:35 **They will thus be able** . . . (Hirsch). Or, "along with everyone who did work and planning" (*Targum*); or,
"doing ordinary work and skilled craftsmanship" (Malbim).
36:3 **the Israelites.** (Ramban; Ibn Ezra). Or, "the workers" (Abarbanel; *HaNothen Imrey Shefer; Tzeror HaMor*).
36:4 **left the work.** Or, "left the materials with which they were working (see note on 36:6). Or, "brought the
work they were doing" (*Midrash HaGadol*).
36:6 **any more material** (Ramban). Literally, "Let no man or woman do any more work." This teaches that
carrying is considered work (*Yerushalmi, Shabbath* 1:1; Chizzkuni).
36:8 **All the most talented** . . . Following 26:1–37.
36:10 **were sewn.** Literally, "he sewed." Some say that "he" denotes Betzalel (Ibn Ezra on 37:1), indicating that
he oversaw all the work (*Tanchuma* 7). According to others, it denotes Moses (*Tanchuma* 10; *Midrash
HaGadol*) or the skilled craftsmen (Bachya on 37:1). This is true of all the passive statements here.

[136. Making the Over-tent]

¹⁴ They* made sheets out of goats' wool for the over-tent covering the tabernacle. There were 11 such sheets, ¹⁵ and all 11 were the same size, 30 cubits long, and 4 cubits wide.

¹⁶ Five sheets were sewn together to form one group, and six to form the [second] group. ¹⁵ Fifty loops were made on the innermost sheet of the [first] group, and [another] fifty on the innermost sheet of the second group. ¹⁸ They made 50 copper fasteners to join the over-tent together and make it a single unit.

¹⁹ They made a roof for the tabernacle out of reddened rams' skins, and [another] roof above it out of blue processed hides.

[137. Making the Beams]

²⁰ They made the upright beams for the tabernacle out of acacia wood. ²¹ Each beam was 10 cubits long and 1½ cubits wide, ²² with two matching square pegs [on the bottom]. All the tabernacle's beams were made in this manner.

²³ They made 20 beams for the southern wall of the tabernacle, ²⁴ along with 40 silver bases to go under the 20 beams. There were two bases under each beam, one base going under each of the two square pegs [on the bottom] of each beam.

²⁵ On the second wall of the tabernacle to the north, they [also] made 20 beams, ²⁶ along with 40 silver bases, two bases under each of a beam's two pegs.

²⁷ For the western wall of the tabernacle, they made 6 beams, ²⁸ along with two finishing beams for the corners of the tabernacle.

²⁹ At the bottom, all the [beams] were joined next to one another exactly, and on top, every pair was joined with a [square] ring. This was [also] true of the two [beams] on the two corners.

³⁰ Thus, [on the west side,] there was a total of 8 beams, along with 16 bases, two bases for each beam.

³¹ They made 5 crossbars of acacia wood for the first wall of the tabernacle [to the south], ³² [a second set of] 5 crossbars for the second wall of the tabernacle [to the north], and 5 similar crossbars for the western wall of the tabernacle. ³³ The middle crossbar was made to go through the center of the beams from one end to the other.

³⁴ They covered the beams with a layer of gold. They also made the rings

36:14 **They.** Literally, "he made." See previous note.

that would hold the crossbars out of gold, and they covered the crossbars 36
themselves with a layer of gold. ³⁵ They made the cloth partition out of sky-blue, dark red and crimson
wool and twined linen, brocaded with cherubs. ³⁶ They made four acacia poles
to hold it, covering [the poles] with a layer of gold with gold hooks [attached].
They also cast four silver bases [for these poles].

³⁷ They made an embroidered drape for the tent's entrance out of sky-
blue, dark red and crimson wool and twined linen. ³⁸ There were five poles to
hold it, along with gold hooks, caps* and bands. There were also five copper
bases for [these poles].

[138. Making the Ark]

¹ Betzalel made* the ark of acacia wood, 2½ cubits long, 1½ cubits wide, 37
and 1½ cubits high. ² He covered it with a layer of pure gold on the inside, and
made a gold rim for it all around. ³ He cast four gold rings for its four
corners, two rings for one side, and two for the other.

⁴ He made carrying poles of acacia wood and covered them with a layer of
gold. ⁵ He then placed the carrying poles in the rings on the ark's sides, so that
the ark could be carried with them.

⁶ He made a pure gold cover, 2½ cubits long and 1½ cubits wide. ⁷ He
made two golden cherubs, hammering them out from the two ends of the
cover. ⁸ The cherubs were made on both ends from the same piece of metal as
the cover itself, one cherub on one end, and one on the other. ⁹ The cherubs
had their wings outstretched upward so as to shield the ark-cover with their
wings. They faced one another, with their faces [somewhat inclined down-
ward] toward the cover.

[139. Making the Table]

¹⁰ He made the table out of acacia wood, 2 cubits long, one cubit wide,
and 1½ cubits high. ¹¹ He covered it with a layer of pure gold, and made it a
gold rim all around. ¹² He made a frame for it, one handbreadth wide, and
placed [the] gold rim on the frame.

¹³ He cast* four gold rings for [the table], placing the rings on the corners
of its four legs. ¹⁴ The rings were adjacent to the frame, and were meant to

---

36:38 **caps.** These are not mentioned for the pillars in 26:37 (see Chizzkuni). See note on 38:17. Some translate
this as "their hooks, with the coating for their ends and their hoops made out of gold," indicating that
the hooks were made of silver, but their ends were covered with gold (*Teshuvoth Meir Nethivim* 75; cf.
Zohar 2:227a).
37:1 **Betzalel made.** This, and the next two sections parallel 25:10-40.
37:13 **cast.** A detail not mentioned in 25:26.

37 hold the poles used to carry the table. ¹⁵ He made acacia poles to carry the
table, and covered them with a layer of gold.

¹⁶ He made the utensils to go on the table,* bread forms and incense
bowls, as well as half tubes and side frames* to serve as dividers [for the
bread], all out of pure gold.

[140. Making the Lamp]

¹⁷ He made the menorah out of pure gold, hammering the menorah along
with its base, stem, and decorative cups, spheres and flowers, out of a single
piece of metal.

¹⁸ Six branches extended from the menorah's sides, three on one and three
on the other. ¹⁹ There were three embossed cups, a sphere, and a flower on
each branch. This was true of all six branches extending from the menorah.

²⁰ The menorah's [shaft] had four embossed cups, along with its own
spheres and flowers. ²¹ There was a sphere at the base of each of the three pairs
of branches extending from [the stem]. This was true of all six of [the
menorah's] branches. ²² The spheres and branches were all made from the
same [ingot] as the [menorah itself]. It was all hammered from a single piece
of pure gold.

²³ He thus made the menorah with seven lamps. [He also made] its wick
tongs and ash scoops out of pure gold. ²⁴ The [menorah] and all its parts were
made from a talent of gold.

[141. Making the Incense Altar]

²⁵ He made the incense altar* of acacia wood, one cubit square, and,
including its horns, two cubits high. ²⁶ He covered its top, its walls all around,
and its horns, with a layer of pure gold, and made it a gold rim all around.

²⁷ He made two rings [for the altar] below its rim on its two opposite sides,
so as to hold the poles with which [the altar] was carried. ²⁸ He made the
carrying poles out of acacia wood, and covered them with a layer of gold.

²⁹ Using the techniques of a perfumer, he made the sacred anointing oil
and the pure perfume incense.

[142. Making the Sacrificial Altar]

38   ¹ He made the sacrificial altar* out of acacia wood, five cubits square, and
three cubits high. ² He made the protrusions on all four corners as an integral

---

37:16 **to go on the table.** A detail not mentioned in 25:29.
—   **half tubes.** Note that the order in 25:19 is transposed.
37:25 **He made** . . . Paralleling 30:1–6.
38:1   **He made** . . . Paralleling 27:1–8.

part of [the altar's] structure, and then covered [the entire structure] with a   38
layer of copper.

⁵ He made all the altar's utensils, pots, scoops, sacrificial basins, flesh
pokers, and fire pans. They were all made out of copper.

⁴ He made a screen out of copper mesh, and placed it below the [altar's]
decorative border, extending downward until the middle of the altar.   ⁵ He
cast* four rings on the copper screen to hold* the carrying poles.   ⁶ He made
acacia carrying poles and covered them with a layer of copper.   ⁷ He placed the
carrying poles in the rings on the altar's corners, so that it could be carried.

He constructed [the altar] as a hollow structure made out of boards.

[143. Making the Washstand]

⁸ He made the copper washstand* and its copper base out of the mirrors*
of the dedicated women who congregated* at the entrance of the Communion
Tent.

[144. Making the Enclosure]

⁹ He made the enclosure [for the tabernacle].*   On the south side, the
twined linen hangings were 100 cubits long,   ¹⁰ held by 20 poles, with 20 copper bases and silver pole hooks and bands.

¹¹ On the north side, it was also 100 cubits long, held by 20 poles, with 20
copper bases and silver pole hooks and bands.   ¹² On the west side, the curtains were 50 cubits, held by 10 poles, with 10 bases and silver pole hooks and
bands.

¹³ The east side was [also] 50 cubits [wide].   ¹⁴ The hangings on one side, [of
the enclosure] were 15 cubits long, held by three poles with three bases.   ¹⁴ The
same was true of the other side of the enclosure's entrance, so that the hangings there were [also] 15 cubits [wide], held by three poles with three bases.

¹⁶ All the enclosure's hangings were made of twined linen.   ¹⁷ The bases for
the poles were made of copper, while the pole hooks and bands were made of
silver. All the enclosure's poles [also] had silver caps,* and the [poles them-
selves] were ringed* with silver.

38:5   **cast.** A detail not mentioned in 27:4.
—   **to hold** . . . Here we clearly see that the rings on the screen were to carry the altar. See note on 27:7.
38:8   **washstand.** See 30:18.
—   **mirrors.** This might support the contention that the "copper" mentioned here is actually brass (cf.
          Abarbanel). See note on 25:3.
—   **dedicated women who congregated** (Rashi). Some say to worship (*Targum*). Or, "celebrated" (Ibn
          Janach), or "exiled themselves" (Avraham ben HaRambam). Or, "the craftswomen" (Ibn Ezra, short
          version).
38:9   **He made** . . . Paralleling 27:9-19.
38:17 **silver caps.** A detail not mentioned above. See note on 27:11.
—   **ringed** (see Radak, *Sherashim*). Or, "since they were inlayed with silver" (Saadia).

38   ¹⁸ The drape for the enclosure's entrance was embroidered out of sky-
blue, dark red and crimson wool, together with twined linen. It was 20 cubits
long, and 5 cubits wide (or high), just like the [other] hangings of the
enclosure. ¹⁹ It was held with four poles, having four copper bases, and silver
hooks, caps and bands.

²⁰ All the stakes used for the tabernacle itself and the surrounding en-
closure were made of copper.

Pekudey   פְּקוּדֵי

[145. The Accounting]

²¹ These are the accounts of the Tabernacle (the Tabernacle of Testimony),
which were calculated by Moses' order by the Levites* under Ithamar,* son of
Aaron the priest.

²² Betzalel son of Uri son of Chur, of the tribe of Judah, [used these
materials] to make all that God had commanded Moses. ²³ With him was
Oholiav son of Achisamakh, of the tribe of Dan, who was a skilled carpenter,
and [was also expert in] brocading and embroidering with sky-blue, dark red
and crimson wool, and fine linen.

[146. The Materials]

²⁴ All the gold was used in the work to complete the sacred task. The
amount of gold donated as a wave offering* was 29 talents and 730 shekels* by
the sanctuary standard.

²⁵ The silver census money [collected from] the community came out to
100 talents and 1775 shekels* by the sanctuary standard. ²⁶ This consisted of a

---

38:21 **by the Levites** (Rashi; Ralbag). Or, ". . . the accounts of the Tabernacle . . . which would be carried by
the Levites" (Ibn Ezra).

—   **Ithamar.** Aaron's youngest son (6:23).

38:24 **wave offering.** See above, 35:22.

—   **29 talents and 730 shekels.** Since a talent is 3000 shekels,this was a total of 87,730 shekels, 1/7 shekel for
each person counted. It was a total of $4386\frac{1}{4}$ pounds of gold.

According to Saadia Gaon (quoted in Ibn Ezra, *Perush HaKitzur*), $\frac{1}{2}$ talent was used to plate each of
the 48 beams of the Tabernacle, accounting for 24 talents. Another 2 talents was used for the four pillars
holding the cloth partition; 1 talent for the menorah; 1 talent for the ark and its cover, and 1 talent for
the table and golden altar. This accounts for the 29 talents. The additional 730 shekels (36.5 pounds)
were used for such items as the fasteners and clothing.

Since $\frac{1}{2}$ talent was used for each pillar, which was 10 cubits high, and $1\frac{1}{2}$ cubits wide, it can easily be
calculated that the thickness of the gold on the pillars was approximately 1/100 inch.

If it is assumed that the same thickness was used all around the incense altar, it can be calculated that
the top of the altar had a gold layer around $\frac{1}{4}$ inch thick.

38:25 **100 talents and 1775 shekels.** This is 301,775 shekels, or 15,088.75 pounds.

beka, which was a half shekel by sanctuary standards, for each of the 603,550 **38**
men* over 20 years old included in the census.
²⁷ The 100 talents were used to cast the bases for the sanctuary and the
cloth partition. There were a total of 100 bases* made out of the 100 talents,
one talent for each base. ²⁸ Out of the remaining 1775 shekels,* the hooks,
caps and inlaid hoops* for the pillars were made.
²⁹ The copper donated as a wave offering came out to 70 talents and 2400
shekels.* ³⁰ It was used to make the bases* for the Communion Tent's
entrance, the copper altar along with its copper screen and all the altar's
utensils, ³¹ the bases for the surrounding enclosure, the bases for the enclosure's entrance, the stakes for the tabernacle, and the stakes for the surrounding enclosure.*
¹ From the sky-blue, dark red and crimson wool, they made the packing **39**
cloths for sacred use.
They [also] made the sacred vestments for Aaron, as God had commanded
Moses.

[147. Making the Ephod]

² He* made the ephod* out of gold [thread], sky-blue, dark red and crimson wool, and twined linen.
³ They beat out thin sheets* of gold, and cut them into threads, which were
[then] included in the sky-blue, dark red and crimson wool, and the fine linen.
[The ephod was made] as a patterned brocade.* ⁴ They made shoulder
pieces for it, sewn to its two corners. ⁵ The ephod's attached belt, [woven]

— **603,550 men.** See 12:37; Numbers 1:46, 26:51.
38:27 100 bases. There were 20 beams on both the north and south walls of the Tabernacle, and 8 beams on
the west, making a total of 48. Thus, there were a total of 96 bases for the 48 beams, and an additional 4
bases for the four beams holding the cloth partition (Rashi).
38:28 1775 shekels. 88.75 pounds.
— **the hooks, caps** . . . Since there were a total of 60 poles holding the enclosure's hangings, there was
around 1⅓ pounds of silver for each pole.
38:29 70 talents and 2400 shekels. A total of 212,400 shekels or 10,620 pounds, around ⅓ shekel for each person counted. However, some say that the talent used to measure the copper was larger than that used to
measure precious metals (Saadia).
38:30 bases. There were 60 bases for the sixty poles for the enclosure, and another five for the drape at the
tabernacle's entrance. Some say that each base weighed one talent (Chizzkuni).
38:31 and the stakes . . . Since the washstand is not mentioned, some say that the copper to make it was not
included in this reckoning.
39:2 He. See note on 36:10.
— **made the ephod.** The next few sections parallel 28:6-43.
39:3 thin sheets. See Numbers 17:3 (Radak, *Sherashim*).
— **brocade.** Some say that gold threads were also interwoven in the tapestries for the Tabernacle (*Baraitha of
49 Middoth*).

39   together* with it, was made in the same manner, [also] out of gold [thread],
      sky-blue, dark red and crimson wool, and twined linen. [It was thus made] as
      God had commanded Moses.

[148. Setting the Sardonyxes]

⁶ They prepared the sardonyx stones to be placed in the settings. The
[stones] were engraved as on a signet ring with the names of Israel's sons. ⁷ He
placed them on the ephod's shoulder pieces as remembrance stones for
Israel's sons. [It was done] as God had commanded Moses.

[149. Making the Breastplate]

⁸ He made the breastplate out of brocaded work, just like the ephod. [It
was also] made from gold [thread], sky-blue, dark red and crimson wool, and
twined linen. ⁹ The breastplate was made to be a square when folded over. It
was a span long, and, when folded over,* a span wide.

¹⁰ [The breastplate] was set with four rows of precious stones:
The first row: carnelian, emerald, topaz.
¹¹ The second row: carbuncle, sapphire, beryl.
¹² The third row: jacinth, agate, amethyst.
¹³ The fourth row: chrysolite, onyx, jasper.
¹⁴ The stones contained the names of Israel's sons. There were twelve
names, engraved as on a signet ring, one for each of the twelve tribes.

¹⁵ Matched pure gold cables, braided like cords, were attached to* the
breastplate. ¹⁶ They made two gold settings and two gold rings, and they
placed the two rings on the breastplate's two [upper] corners. ¹⁷ The two gold
braids were then attached to the two rings on the breastplate's corners. ¹⁸ The
two braids on the two corners were attached to the two settings, and they were
thus attached to the ephod's shoulder pieces toward the front.

¹⁹ They made two gold rings and placed them on the breastplate's two
[lower] corners, on the edge toward the inside of the ephod. ²⁰ They made two
gold rings, and placed them on the bottoms of the ephod's two shoulder
pieces toward the front, near where they were attached, above the ephod's
belt. ²¹ They laced the breastplate by its rings to the rings of the ephod with a

---

39:5   **woven together.** Two expressions. Two words in 28:8 are transposed, giving the verse a slightly different
       meaning.
39:9   **when folded over.** A detail not mentioned in 28:16. It appears that it was folded over in the width and
       not in the length.
39:15 **attached to.** In 28:22 the verse has "for" instead (cf. Chizzkuni).

twist of sky-blue wool, so that the breastplate would remain above the ephod's belt. The breastplate would thus not be displaced from the ephod. [All this was done] as God had commanded Moses.

[150. Making the Robe]

²² He made the robe for the ephod, weaving it* completely out of sky-blue wool. ²³ The robe's opening was in the middle, like the opening of a coat of mail, with a border all around so that it not be left open.

²⁴ On the skirt of the robe, they made pomegranates out of twined* sky-blue, dark red and crimson wool. ²⁵ They made pure gold bells, and placed the bells between the pomegranates. [The bells] were thus all around on the bottom of the robe between the pomegranates. ²⁶ There was a bell and a pomegranate, a bell and a pomegranate, all around the bottom of the robe.

[It was thus made] for the divine service, as God had commanded Moses.

[151. Making the Other Vestments]

²⁷ They made the tunics for Aaron and his sons by weaving them out of fine linen.

²⁸ [They made] the linen turban, the fine* linen hats, and the linen pants, [all out of] twined linen.

²⁹ [They made] the belt, embroidered out of twined linen, and sky-blue, dark red and crimson wool.

[It was all done] as God had commanded Moses.

[152. Making the Head-plate]

³⁰ They made the head-plate as a sacred coronet, out of pure gold. Written on it, in the same manner as a signet ring's engraving, were [the words], "Holy to God."

³¹ They placed a twist of sky-blue wool on [the head-plate], so that it could be placed over the turban.* [It was all done] as God had commanded Moses.

39:22 **weaving it.** A detail not mentioned in 28:31 (cf. *Yoma* 72b; *Zevachim* 88a).

39:24 **twined.** A detail not mentioned in 28:33.

39:28 **fine** (Rashi; Ibn Janach; Radak, *Sherashim*). *P'er* in Hebrew. Or, "the turban hats" (Ramban; cf. Isaiah 3:20, Ezekiel 44:18). Or, "the buttons on top of the hats" (Hai Gaon, quoted in Chizzkuni). Or, "the knob on the side of the hat [to hold the turban]" (*Lekach Tov*). According to Jospehus, this might be the cloth placed over the turbans (see note on 28:39).

39:31 **over the turban.** Thus, some say that either one thread went over the turban, or the cap went over the turban (see note on 28:37). Or, "to place it near the turban, which is above it (*Targum Yonathan*).

39   *[153. The Tabernacle is Completed]*

³² All the work on the Communion Tent Tabernacle was thus completed.* The Israelites did exactly as God had commanded Moses.

[154. Moses Approves]

³³ They brought the Tabernacle to Moses.* [There was] the Communion Tent along with its equipment, its fastenings, beams, crossbars, pillars and bases; ³⁴ the roof of reddened rams' hides, the roof of blue processed hides, the cloth partition; ³⁵ the Ark of Testimony and its carrying poles, the ark cover, ³⁶ the table and its equipment, the showbread, ³⁷ the pure [gold] menorah along with its prescribed lamps,* all its utensils, and the illuminating oil; ³⁸ the golden altar, the anointing oil, the perfumed incense, the Communion Tent's drape; ³⁹ the copper altar along with its carrying poles and all its equipment; the washstand and its base; ⁴⁰ the hangings for the enclosure, its poles and bases, the drape for the enclosure's entrance, its tying ropes and stakes, all the equipment used in the Communion Tent Tabernacle's service, ⁴¹ the packing cloths for sacred use, the sacred vestments for Aaron the priest, and the vestments that his sons would wear to serve.

⁴² The Israelites had done all the work exactly in the manner that God had commanded Moses.

⁴³ When Moses saw that all the work had been done exactly as God had ordered, he blessed [all the workers].

[155. Orders for Erecting the Tabernacle]

40   ¹ God spoke to Moses, saying:

² On the first day of the first month,* you shall erect the Communion Tent Tabernacle. ³ Place the Ark of Testimony there, and shield the ark with the cloth partition. ⁴ Bring in the table and set it up, and bring in the menorah and light its lamps. ⁵ Place the gold incense altar [directly] in front of the Ark of Testimony, and then set up the drape at the Tabernacle's entrance.

⁶ Place the sacrificial altar in front of the entrance of the Communion Tent Tabernacle. ⁷ [Then] place the washstand between the Communion Tent and the altar, and fill it with water. ⁸ Set up the enclosure all around, and place the drape over the enclosure's entrance.

39:32 was thus completed. This was on 25 Kislev, which would later be the first day of Chanukah (*BeMidbar Rabbah* 13:2; Chizzkuni). Nevertheless, the Tabernacle was not erected until 1 Nissan (see 40:2).
39:33 They brought . . . See above, 35:11–19.
39:37 prescribed lamps (Ramban). Or, "lamps to be lit" (Chizzkuni).
40:2 On the first day . . . 1 Nissan, almost a year after the Exodus. See 40:17.

⁹ Take the anointing oil, and anoint the tabernacle and everything in it.*   40
You will thus sanctify it and all its equipment making it holy.

¹⁰ Anoint the sacrificial altar and all its equipment. You will thus sanctify the altar, and it will be holy of holies.

¹¹ Anoint the washstand and its basin, and make them holy.

¹² Bring Aaron and his sons to the Communion Tent's entrance, and have them immerse in a mikvah.* ¹³ Then have Aaron put on the sacred vestments, and anoint him, thus sanctifying him as a priest to Me.

¹⁴ Bring forth Aaron's sons and place the tunics on them. ¹⁵ Then anoint them, just as you anointed their father, so that they will be priests to Me. It will be done so that their anointing will make them an eternal [hereditary]* priesthood for all generations.

¹⁶ Moses proceeded to do exactly as God had commanded him.

[156. The Tabernacle is Erected]

¹⁷ In the first month of the second year [of the Exodus], on the first of the month, the Tabernacle was erected.

¹⁸ Moses erected* the Tabernacle. He [did this by] setting up the bases, placing the beams [in them], and [fastening them together] with the crossbars. He [then] set up the pillars. ¹⁹ He spread the tent over the tabernacle, and placed the tent's roof* over it. [It was all done] as God had commanded Moses.

[157. Placing the Ark]

²⁰ He took the [Tablets of] Testimony* and placed them in the Ark. He then placed the carrying poles in the ark, and set the cover on top of the ark. ²¹ He brought the ark into the Tabernacle, and set up the cloth partition so that it would shield the Ark of Testimony. [It was all done] as God had commanded Moses.

[158. Placing the Table]

²² He placed the table in the Communion Tent,* outside the cloth parti-

---

40:9 and anoint . . . Some say that this was done by placing the anointing oil on the four fingers of the hand, and rubbing it on the inside and outside of each article (*Or HaAfelah* on 30:26).

40:12 have them immerse . . . See note on 29:4.

40:15 hereditary (Ralbag; Saadia; Cf. *Yad, Kley HaMikdash* 1:7).

40:18 erected. Or, "supervised the erection" (*Haamek Davar*).

40:19 roof. Just one roof is mentioned. See note on 26:14.

40:20 Tablets of Testimony (*Targum Yonathan;* Rashi). He took them from a plain box in his own tent, and brought them to the golden ark (Ramban; see Deuteronomy 10:1,3).

40:22 Communion Tent. From here it appears that the area outside the Holy of Holies was called the Communion Tent (*Ohel Moed*).

40 tion,* on the north side of the Tabernacle. ²³ Then he placed the prescribed
arrangement of bread on it before God. [It was all done] as God had commanded Moses.

[159. Placing the Lamp]

²⁴ He placed the menorah in the Communion Tent directly across from the
table, on the southern side of the Tabernacle. ²⁵ He then lit the lamps before
God. [It was all done] as God had commanded Moses.

[160. Placing the Incense Altar]

²⁶ He placed the golden altar in the Communion Tent in front of the cloth
partition. ²⁷ Then he burned perfume incense on it. [It was all done] as God
had commanded Moses.

[161. The Drape and Altar]

²⁸ He placed the drape over the Tabernacle's entrance.

²⁹ He [then] placed the sacrificial altar in front of the entrance of the
Communion Tent Tabernacle, and he sacrificed the burnt offering and meal
offering* on it. [It was all done] as God had commanded Moses.

[162. Placing the Washstand]

³⁰ He set the washstand between the Communion Tent and the altar, and
he filled it* with water for washing. ³¹ Moses,* Aaron, and [Aaron's] sons,
washed their hands and feet from it. ³² They would wash [in this manner]
whenever they came to the Communion Tent or offered sacrifice on the altar.
[It was all done] as God had commanded Moses.

[163. Setting up the Enclosure]

³³ He set up the enclosure surrounding the tabernacle and altar, and he
placed the drape over the enclosure's entrance. With this, Moses completed all
the work.

[164. The Cloud]

³⁴ The cloud covered the Communion Tent, and God's glory* filled the

---

—   **outside** . . . Near the partition (*Midrash HaGadol;* cf. *Yoma* 33b).
40:29 **burnt offering and meal offering.** See 29:40.
40:30 **filled it.** Literally, "placed water there."
40:31 **Moses.** He, too, was functioning as a priest at that time (Rashi).
40:34 **God's glory.** Either a feeling of holiness (cf. Ramban) or an actual physical glow (*Moreh Nevukhim* 1:44).
        In any case, God's presence was evident in the Tabernacle (*Moreh Nevukhim* 1:19).

Tabernacle. ³⁵ Moses could not come into the Communion Tent, since the 40
cloud had rested on it, and God's glory filled the Tabernacle.

³⁵ [Later], when the cloud would rise up from the Tabernacle, it [would be
a signal] for the Israelites to move on, [and this was true] in all their travels.
³⁷ Whenever the cloud did not rise, they would not move on, [waiting] until
the day it did. ³⁸ God's cloud would then remain on the Tabernacle by day,
and fire was in it by night.* This was visible to the entire family of Israel, in all
their travels.

40:38 God's cloud . . . See 13:22; Numbers 9:15-23.

וַיִּקְרָא

LEVITICUS

VaYikra

וַיִּקְרָא

[1. Burnt Offerings of Cattle]

1 God called to Moses,* speaking to him from the Communion Tent.* He **1** said: 2 Speak to the Israelites, and tell them the following:

When one of you brings a mammal as an offering to God, the sacrifice must be taken from the cattle, sheep or goats.*

3 If the sacrifice is a burnt offering* taken from the cattle, it must be an unblemished* male. One must bring it of his own free will to the entrance of the Communion Tent, before God. 4 He shall press his hands on the head of the burnt offering, and it shall then be accepted as an atonement for him.

5 He shall have the young bull slaughtered* before God*. Aaron's sons, the priests, shall then bring forth the blood, dashing* it on all sides* of the altar that is in front of the Communion Tent's entrance.

6 He shall have the burnt offering skinned and cut into pieces. 7 Aaron's sons shall place fire on the altar, and arrange wood on the fire. 8 Aaron's sons shall then arrange the cut pieces, the head, and the fatty intestinal membrane* on top of the wood that is on the altar fire. 9 The inner organs* and legs, however, must [first]* be scrubbed with water.*

The priest* shall thus burn the entire [animal] on the altar as a completely burnt fire offering to God, an appeasing fragrance.*

1:1   **God called . . .** Because Moses had been unable to enter the sanctuary (Exodus 40:35).
—   **speaking to him . . .** The narrative continues on 8:1.
1:2   **sheep or goats.** The Hebrew word, *tzon*, used here is generic, including all smaller ungulates such as sheep and goats.
1:3   **burnt offering.** *Olah* in Hebrew. This was an offering that was completely burned, and was the first sacrifice mentioned by name in the Bible. See Genesis 8:20. Also see Genesis 4:4.
—   **unblemished.** See 22:18-25.
1:5   **slaughtered.** By slitting its throat in the prescribed manner.
—   **before God.** In the enclosure of the Tabernacle, later in the Temple grounds.
—   **dashing.** Or "splashing" (cf. Malbim).
—   **on all sides.** The blood was dashed on the two opposite corners so that the blood would reach all sides of the altar (Rashi). The blood was splashed on the north-east and south-west corners of the altar (*Tamid* 30b; Rashi, *Zevachim* 53b; *Yad, Maaseh HaKarbanoth* 5:6).
1:8   **fatty intestinal membrane** (Ramban). *Padar* in Hebrew. This is the membrane dividing the intestines from the stomachs. Others translate *padar* or *peder* as fat in general (Rashbam; Ibn Ezra; Radak, *Sherashim;* Septuagint). According to others, *padar* denotes the chest organs, the lungs, the windpipe, and everything attached to them (Saadia); according to some, even including the heart and liver (Ibn Janach; see *Tamid* 4:3; *Yad, Maaseh Hakorbanoth* 6:7).
        The *padar* is placed over the animal's neck to cover the cut where the animal was slaughtered (*Yoma* 26a; Rashi).
1:9   **inner organs.** Intestines (*Lekach Tov;* cf. *Moreh Nevukhim* 3:46).
—   **first.** Before any part was burned (Ramban).
—   **scrubbed . . .** Or "washed" (see *Tamid* 4:2; *Yad, Maaseh Hakorbanoth* 6:4 Chizzkuni).
—   **priest.** *Cohen* in Hebrew. A descendant of Aaron.
—   **appeasing fragrance.** See note on Genesis 8:21. Some have, "a hint of a desire to be pleasing [to God]"

1

[2. Burnt Offerings of Smaller Animals]

¹⁰ If one's burnt offering is a smaller animal, it shall be taken from the sheep or goats; and one must [likewise] present an unblemished male. ¹¹ He shall have it slaughtered on the north side* of the altar before God, and the priests who are Aaron's descendants shall dash its blood on all sides of the altar.

¹² [The animal] shall be cut into pieces, and the priest shall arrange them, along with the head and intestinal membrane, on top of the wood on the altar fire. ¹³ The internal organs and feet shall [first] be washed with water, and the priest shall then offer everything, burning it on the altar. It is a completely burnt fire offering, an appeasing fragrance to God.

[3. Burnt Offering of Birds]

¹⁴ If one's burnt offering is a bird, he must bring a turtle dove* or a young* common dove. ¹⁵ The priest shall bring it to the altar and nip off* its head. [After] draining [the bird's] blood* on the altar's wall,* he shall burn [the head]* on the altar.

(Hirsch, *HaKethav VeHaKabbalah* on Genesis 8:21). Or, "a fragrance that brings down [spiritual energy]" (*Bahir* 109; Recanti, *Tetzaveh* 15a; Bachya on Genesis 8:21; *Avodath HaKodesh* 1:6). The Hebrew word *nicho'ach* here may also be related to the root *nachah* denoting rest and serenity, so that it may be translated, "a fragrance inducing serenity," or "inducing a meditative state." The most simple meaning, however, of *re'ach nicho'ach* here is, "an acceptable sacrifice" (Targum on Ezekiel 20:41).

1:11   **north** . . . Opposite the altar's ramp, which was to the south.

1:14   **turtle dove.** *Tor* in Hebrew (from word tur-tle here is derived). This is identified as *Streptopelia turtur* (cf. Saadia), a smaller variety of dove. It is a beautiful bird with bright stripes on its neck. When the bird matures, the feathers on its neck become an irridescent red (Rashi on *Chullin* 22b), and only then can the bird be offered as a sacrifice

Dove   Turtle Dove

(*Chullin* 22b; *Yad, Issurey HaMizbeach* 3:2). Some note that this is a wild variety of bird (Ralbag). See Genesis 15:9.

—   **young.** These can only be sacrificed before the feathers begin to glisten (*Ibid*).

—   **common dove.** The domesticated dove, *Columba domestica* (see *Chullin* 62a).

1:15   **nip off.** *Malak* in Hebrew; see 5:8. The priest would allow the fingernail on his thumb to grow long. Holding the bird in his hand, he would drive this fingernail through the back of the bird's neck, severing the spine, along with both the gullet and the windpipe. He would have to be careful, however, not to cut through the majority of the flesh of the neck (*Zevachim* 65b; *Chullin* 21a; Rashi; *Yad, Maaseh HaKorbanoth* 6:23). According to others, however, only the gullet *or* the windpipe had to be severed (Ibn Janach). There is another opinion that after the spine was severed with the priest's fingernail, the bird's throat would be slit with a knife (Saadia Gaon, quoted in *Mebhaser HaBavil*, p. 87; Rabbi Yehuda HaChasid).

—   **After** . . . (see Rashi; *Sifra; Zevachim* 64b; Ramban).

—   **altar's wall.** On the upper half of the south-east corner (*Yad, Maaseh HaKorbanoth* 6:20).

—   **the head.** After the bird was slaughtered, the head would be cut off and burned separately (Ramban;

¹⁶ He shall remove [the bird's] crop* along with its [adjacent] feathers* and cast them into the place of the fatty ashes,* directly to the east of the altar. ¹⁷ He shall split the bird apart by its wings* without tearing it completely in half.* The priest shall then burn it on the altar, on the wood that is on the fire. It is a burnt offering, a fire offering that is an appeasing fragrance to God.

[4. The Meal Offering]

¹ If an individual presents a meal offering* to God, his offering must consist of the best grade of wheat meal.* On it, he shall pour olive oil* and place frankincense.*

² He shall bring it to the priests who are Aaron's descendants, and [a priest] shall scoop out three fingers full* of its meal and oil, [and then take] all

Rambam on *Zevachim* 6:5; *Yad, Maaseh HaKorbanoth* 6:21; Radak, *Sherashim*). According to others, however, the head was left attached to the bird's body when it was burned on the altar (Rashi, *Zevachim* 64b, s.v. *U'Mavdil; Chullin* 21b, s.v. *Af*; Chizzkuni). The verse would then be translated, "He shall burn [the entire bird] on the altar, ¹⁶ [but first] he shall. . . ." (Rashi).

1:16   **crop** (Rashi; Saadia; Ibn Janach). *Murah* in Hebrew. Or, "entrails" (Ramban; Hirsch).

 —   **adjacent feathers** (Ramban; Ibn Ezra, Radak, *Sherashim*; Rambam, Bertenoro, on Zevachim 6:5). *Notzah* in Hebrew. Or, "intestines" (Rashi), "food in crop" (Targum), or "gizzard" (Saadia; Ibn Janach; cf. *Zevachim* 65a).

 —   **fatty ashes.** *Deshen* in Hebrew. This was the place where the altar's ashes were placed each morning, see below 6:3 (Rashi).

Crop

1:17   **by its wings** (Targum). Or, "above its wings" (Saadia; Ramban). Or, "he shall split it apart with its feathers" (without plucking it; *Yereyim HaShalem* 319; cf. Rashi).

 —   **without tearing it . . .** Or, "without tearing off [its wings]" (*Targum Yonathan*). This means that it is not necessary to separate it (*Yad, Maaseh HaKorbanoth* 6:22).

2:1   **meal offering.** *Minchah* in Hebrew. See Genesis 4:3. Some say that it comes from the root *nachah* denoting lowness, and thus translating it "homage gift" (Hirsch; *HaKethav VeHaKabbalah*; cf. Genesis 32:14). It can also be related to the word *nicho'ach*, see above 1:9. Or, it can come from the root *nachah* in the sense that it denotes rest; hence a *minchah* can denote an "inanimate offering," an offering taken from the vegetable kingdom.

 —   **wheat meal.** *Soleth* in Hebrew. This was wheat meal (*Sifra*; Rashi; from Exodus 29:2). It was the best grade of meal, perfectly clean of all bran (Saadia; Ibn Ezra; cf. *Kiddushin* 69b). The *soleth* used for meal offerings was a coarsely ground meal (Rashi, *Menachoth* 66a, s.v. *Shel Gerosoth*; Radak, *Sherashim*, from *Avoth* 5:15, cf. Meiri *ad loc.*). It had to be carefully sifted to remove all the fine flour (*Menachoth* 85a; *Yad, Issurey Mizbeach* 6:12).

     The amount of such an offering was 1/10 ephah or around 2 quarts (Rashi; *Yad, Maaseh HaKorbanoth* 13:3).

 —   **olive oil.** At least 1 *log* (300 cc. or 10 fl. oz.) (*Menachoth* 51a, 88a; *Yad, Maaseh HaKorbanoth* 13:7, Ralbag).

 —   **frankincense.** *Levonah* in Hebrew. See Exodus 31:34. The amount of frankincense placed on the offering was one handful (*Sifra*; *Yad, Maaseh HaKorbanoth* 13:7).

2:2   **three fingers full.** The priest scooped out the flour with the three middle fingers of the hand, using the thumb and pinky to rub off any flour sticking out at the ends (*Menachoth* 11a. Rashi; Radak, *Sherashim*). According to others, however, the *kemitzah* was a complete handful (*Yad, Maaseh HaKorbanoth* 13:13, see *Kesef Mishneh ad loc.*; Ralbag). The priest would have to scoop up at least an amount the size of two olives (around 100 c.c. or 3½ fluid ounces) (*Yad, loc.cit.*).

     Before scooping up the flour, the frankincense would be put to the side, so that only flour and oil would be scooped up (*Sotah* 14b; *Yad, Maaseh HaKorbanoth* 13:12).

2   the·frankincense.* The priest shall then burn [this] memorial portion* on the altar as a fire offering, an appeasing fragrance to God.

³ The rest of the meal offering shall belong to Aaron and his descendants. It is holy of holies among the fire offerings to God.

[5. The Baked Offering]

⁴ If he brings a meal offering that was baked in an oven, it shall consist [either] of unleavened loaves* made of wheat meal mixed with olive oil,* or* flat matzahs saturated* with olive oil.

[6. The Pan Offering]

⁵ If the sacrifice is a pan fried offering,* it shall be made of wheat meal mixed with olive oil, and it shall remain unleavened.

⁶ Break it into little pieces,* and pour olive oil on it. [In this respect] it is [like every other] meal offering.*

[7. The Deep Fried Offering]

⁷ If your sacrifice is a meal offering prepared in a deep pot,* it shall be made of wheat meal in olive oil.*

Scooping the portion from a meal offering was in place of slaughter of an animal (Rambam on *Menachoth* 1:1).

— **and then take** . . . The frankincense would then be removed separately, and placed on the scooped flour (*Ibid.*; Rashi; *Sifra*).

— **memorial portion** (Ibn Ezra; Radak, *Sherashim*). *Azkarah* in Hebrew. Or, "burned portion" (Saadia, from Psalms 20:4; cf. Ibn Janach).

2:4   **loaves.** *Challoth* in Hebrew. This denotes thick, and possibly round, loaves (Ibn Ezra). See note on 2:6.

— **mixed with olive oil.** Together with warm water (*Yad, Maaseh HaKorbanoth* 13:8). All meal offerings were kneaded with warm water (*Menachoth* 55a; *Yad, Maaseh HaKorbanoth* 12:21) Some say that this made a better quality loaf (*Tifereth Yisrael, Menachoth* 5:8), especially since the offerings were made with coarse meal. According to others, warm water was used so that additional care would be taken that the offering not begin to ferment (*Likutey Halakhoth, Zevach Todah, Menachoth*, p. 22a,b; *Metzafeh Ethan* on *Menachoth* 53a; cf. Rashi, *Menachoth* 53a, s.v. *Menayin*).

— **or** . . . (*Menachoth* 63a; Rashi). Literally "and."

— **saturated.** Literally, "anointed." A *log* (10 oz.) of oil was taken, and rubbed on the unperforated matzahs until it was all absorbed (*Yad, Maaseh HaKorbanoth* 13:9). According to others, the matzahs were anointed with the oil in the form of an X (see Exodus 29:7), and the rest of the oil could be consumed by the priests (cf. Rashi; *Menachoth* 74b, 75a).

Some say that the matzahs were oiled after they were baked (*Yad, Maaseh HaKorbanoth* 13:8), but others question this and state that they may have been oiled before baking (Ralbag).

2:5   **pan fried** . . . Literally, "meal offering on a pan" (see *Menachoth* 63a; Rashi.) *Machbath* in Hebrew. Cf. Ezekiel 4:3. The oil was first placed in the pan (2:7), and then the meal was placed on it. More oil was then mixed with the meal, and it was kneaded with warm water (*Yad, Maaseh HaKorbanoth* 13:6; cf. Rashi, *Menachoth* 74b, s.v. *Matan Shemen*).

2:6   **break it** . . . In all these offerings, the 1/10 ephah of flour was baked into ten loaves (*Menachoth* 76a; *Yad, Maaseh HaKorbanoth* 13:10; Rashi). Each of these loaves would then be broken into four pieces, each approximately the size of an olive (*Sifra; Menachoth* 75a,b; *Yad, loc. cit.*). Some say that any pieces larger than olive size must be broken up further (Rashi, *Menachoth* 75b; Rambam on *Menachoth* 6:4).

— **In this respect** . . . This was done to all meal offerings that were baked or fried (*Menachoth* 75a; Rashi; *Yad, Maaseh HaKorbanoth* 13:6).

2:7   **deep pot** (Rashi; *Menachoth* 63a; Saadia). *Marchesheth* in Hebrew.

⁸ You may thus bring a meal offering in any of these ways* [as an offering] 2
to God. It shall be presented to the priest and brought to the altar. ⁹ The
priest shall then lift out* the memorial portion from the meal offering, and
burn it on the altar. It is a fire offering, an appeasing fragrance to God.

¹⁰ The remainder of the meal offering then belongs to Aaron and his
descendants. It is holy of holies, one of God's fire offerings.

¹¹ Do not make any meal offering that is sacrificed to God out of leavened
dough. This is because you may not burn anything fermented* or sweet* as a
fire offering to God. ¹² Although these may be brought as a first-fruit offering* to God, they may not be offered on the altar as an appeasing fragrance.

¹³ Moreover, you must salt every meal offering. Do not leave out the salt of
your God's covenant from your meal offerings. [Furthermore,] you must
[also] offer salt with your animal sacrifices.*

[8. First Grain Offerings]

¹⁴ When you bring an offering of the first grain,* it should be [brought] as
soon as it ripens on the stalk.* Your first grain offering shall consist of fresh
kernels* [of barley],* roasted in a perforated pan,* [and then* ground into]
coarse meal.*

¹⁵ Place olive oil and frankincense on it, just like for any other meal offer-

---

— **in olive oil.** Oil was placed in the pot first (*Menachoth* 74b, 75a).

2:8 **these ways.** Baked in an oven, on a pan, or in a deep pot (Rashi).

2:9 **lift out.** Or, "raise to a higher status." *Harem* in Hebrew, related to the word *terumah*. See 6:8. After the loaf was broken into pieces (2:6), the priest would scoop out three fingers full as above 2:2 (*Menachoth* 61a; Rashi).

2:11 **fermented.** Or "leavened" (cf. Ibn Ezra).

— **sweet.** *Devash* in Hebrew, usually translated as honey. Here it denotes any fruit juice (Rashi), especially date extract (Rashbam; cf. *Menachoth* 84a; Yerushalmi, *Bikkurim* 1:3). Others, however, take this literally to mean honey (*Yad, Issurey Hamizbeach* 5:1; *Mishneh LaMelekh ad loc.*; *Sefer Hamitzvoth*, Negative 98; cf. *Makhshirim* 6:4).

2:12 **first fruit offering.** Which was not offered on the altar (*Menachoth* 84b; Rashi). See 23:17, Numbers 28:26 (*Sifra*).

2:13 **you must [also] offer salt . . .** That is, the sacrifices were salted before being placed on the altar (*Menachoth* 21a,b; *Yad, Issurey HaMizbeach* 5:11).See Numbers 18:19.

2:14 **first grain.** This was the omer, mentioned in 23:10-14 (*Menachoth* 68b, 84a; *Yad, Temidim* 7:12; Rashi).

— **as soon as it ripens . . .** (Radak, *Sherashim*; Hirsch). *Aviv* in Hebrew. Some say that it denotes barley (*Menachoth* 61b; cf. Exodus 9:31), especially when it is ripe enough to be eaten (Saadia; Ibn Janach). According to others, it refers to the early grain (Rashi, *Menachoth* 66a, s.v. *aviv*). Still others maintain that it denotes grain roasted in a perforated vessel (*Targum Yonathan*; cf. *Menachoth* 66a; *Yad, Tamidim* 7:22).

— **fresh kernels.** *Karmel* in Hebrew. (*Menachoth* 84a; see Rashi, *Menachoth* 64b, s.v. *Karmel*; *Yad, Temidim* 7:9). These were grains that were not yet dry and hard (*Menachoth* 66b; Rashi; Radak, *Sherashim*).

— **of barley** (See *Yad, Temidim* 7:11; see earlier notes).

— **roasted in . . .** (*Menachoth* 66b; *Yad, Temidim* 7:12). *Kaluy* in Hebrew.

— **and then** (*Menachoth* 66b; *Yad, Temidim* 7:12).

— **ground into coarse meal** (Rashi 66a, s.v. *Ve-gerusaoth*;) or "cracked grains" (Saadia; Radak, *Sherashim*; Ibn Janach). This was the best grade of barley meal, equivalent to *soleth* made of wheat (Rashi, *Menachoth* 66a, s.v. *Shel Gerosoth*, 27a s.v. *Geresh*, 69b s.v. *Ve-Lo*; *Sotah* 14a).

2 ing. [16] As a fire offering to God, the priest shall then burn the memorial portion taken from its coarse meal and oil, as well as all its frankincense.

[9. Peace Offerings of Cattle]

3 [1] If one's sacrifice is a peace offering* and it is from the cattle, he may offer either an unblemished male or an unblemished female before God. [2] He shall press his hands on the head of the sacrifice, and have it slaughtered at the entrance of the Communion Tent. The priests who are Aaron's descendants shall dash its blood on all sides of the altar.

[3] The portion of the peace offerings that must be presented as a fire offering to God must include the layer of fat covering the stomachs* and all the other fat attached to the stomachs.* [4] The two kidneys along with the fat on them* along the flanks,* and the lobe* over the liver near the kidneys* must [also] be removed.

[5] Aaron's descendants shall burn this on the altar, along with* the burnt offering which is on the wood on the fire. It is a fire offering, an appeasing fragrance to God.

3:1   **peace offering.** *Shelamim* in Hebrew, *shelem* in the singular (Amos 5:22). See Exodus 24:5. From the word *shalom*, meaning peace. Or, "fellowship offering" (*Sifra*; Radak, *Sherashim; HaKethav VeHaKabbalah*), "repayment offering" (Rashbam; *HaKethav VeHaKabbalah*), or "perfection offering" (Ibn Janach). Some say that it is the "offering of a whole person" since it is not brought for sin (Ramban; *Lekach Tov; Midrash HaGadol; HaKethav VeHaKabbalah*).

3:3   **layer of fat . . .** This is particularly the layer of fat that covers the animal's two stomachs, the omasum (*hemses*) and the reticulum (*beth ha-kosoth*) (*Chullin* 93a; *Yad, Maakhaloth Assuroth* 7:6; *Yoreh Deah* 64:8). Some also include the fat on the paunch or rumen (*keres*) (*Tosefta, Chullin* 9:3; *Hagahoth Maimonioth, Maachaloth Assuroth* 7:6; *Yoreh Deah* 64:9). This is often identified as the viscal peritoneum.
         Specifically not included, however, is the fat attached to the abdominal cavity (*Sifra*). Also not included is the fat on the intestines (*Yad, Maachaloth Assuroth* 7:9; see next note). See note on 3:17.

—   **all the other fat . . .** This, specifically, is the fat on the maw (*keva*) (*Chullin* 49b; *Yad, Maakhaloth Assuroth* 7:6; *Yoreh Deah* 64:14). This is usually identified with the grain-like protrusions of peritoneal fat now designated as appendices epiploicae (*chitte de-karkashta; Chullin* 49b). Some authorities also include the fat on the intestines (Rabbi Akiba, *Chullin* 49b). The fat on the spleen is also included (*Chullin* 93a; *Yoreh Deah* 64:10). This includes fat that is actually attached to these organs (Ralbag).

3:4   **the fat on them . . .** This is primarily the fatty capsule covering the kidneys (*Chullin* 93a; *Yoreh Deah* 64:12).

—   **along the flanks** (Rashi; Radak, *Sherashim*). *Kesalim* in Hebrew. This is the fat in the body cavity over the hind legs (*Chullin* 93a; *Yad, Maakhaloth Assuroth* 7:6,7). Some translate *kesalim* as inner organs (Saadia; cf. Ibn Janach).

—   **lobe** (Rambam, Introduction to *Zevachim*; Abarbanel; *Sefer Halttur* 2, *Assereth HaDibroth* 44, p. 3b; Septuagint; cf. Ralbag; *Tamid* 4:2). *Yothereth* in Hebrew. See Exodus 29:13. This is usually identified as the caudate lobe of the liver, which in ruminants, rests on the right kidney (see next note).
         Others, however, translate *yothereth* as the diaphragm (Rashi; Radak, *Sherashim; HaKethav VeHaKabbalah* on Exodus 29:19). This is derived from the Targum, which renders *yothereth* as *chatzra.* However, there are others who identify the *chatzra* with the lobe of the liver (Hai Gaon, quoted in *Arukh HaShalem*; cf. *Beth Yosef, Yoreh Deah,* 41, s.v. *Kathav Behag*).

—   **near the kidneys** Or "on the kidneys". However, according to those who translate *yothereth* as diaphragm, they render the verse, "the diaphragm over the liver, along with the kidneys" (Rashi; Ibn Ezra).

3:5   **along with** (Rashi). Literally "on". See Exodus 29:25.

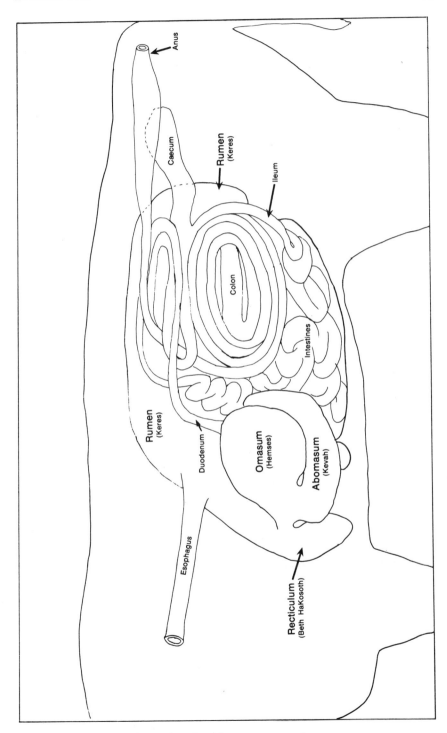

PLATE 23. THE STOMACHS OF A COW

3

[10. Peace Offerings of Sheep]

⁶ If one's sacrifice for a peace offering to God is taken from the smaller animals, he may [also] present an unblemished male or female animal.

⁷ If he brings a sheep as his sacrifice, he shall present it before God. ⁸ He shall press his hands on the head of the sacrifice and have it slaughtered in front of the Communion Tent. Aaron's descendants shall then dash its blood on all sides of the altar.

⁹ He shall present the choicest parts* of his peace offering as a fire offering to God, removing the broad tail up to the backbone,* along with the layer of fat covering the stomachs and all the other fat attached to the stomachs. ¹⁰ The two kidneys along with the fat on them along the flanks, and the lobe over the liver near the kidneys, must [also] be removed. ¹¹ The priest shall burn them on the altar, to be consumed* as a fire offering to God.

[11. Peace Offerings of Goats]

¹² If his sacrifice is a goat, he shall present it before God. ¹³ He shall press his hands on its head, and have it slaughtered before the Communion Tent. Aaron's descendants shall then dash its blood on all sides of the altar.

¹⁴ As his fire offering sacrifice to God, he shall present the layer of fat that covers the stomachs, and all the other fat attached to the stomachs. ¹⁵ The two kidneys along with the fat on them along the flanks, and the lobe over the liver near the kidneys, shall also be removed. ¹⁶ The priests shall burn them on the altar, to be consumed as a fire offering, an appeasing fragrance.

All the prescribed internal fat thus belongs to God. ¹⁷ It shall be an eternal law, for all your generations, that you are not to eat any internal fat [that is normally sacrificed]* nor any blood, no matter where you may live.

[12. Sin Offerings for the High Priest]

4   ¹ God spoke to Moses with instructions to speak to the Israelites and tell them the following:

3:9   **choicest parts** (Rashi; *Targum Yonathan; Yad, Maakhaloth* 7:5; cf. Ramban). See Genesis 4:4. Or, "the fat broad tail" (Ibn Ezra), or "the fat and broad tail" (Saadia). See Exodus 29:22.

—   **backbone.** *Atzeh* or *etzah* in Hebrew. The bone over the kidney (*Chullin* 11a; Rashi; Saadia; Ibn Janach; Radak, *Sherashim; Yad, Maaseh HaKorbanoth* 1:8; *Yoreh Deah* 64:13 in *Hagah*). This is usually identified as the *os cruris* or the *os caudae coccygisve.*

3:11   **to be consumed.** Literally "bread," *lechem* in Hebrew. Some say that this denotes something acceptable before God (Saadia). According to others it denotes "food" (Ibn Ezra), "flesh" (Ibn Janach; Radak), or "fuel for the fire" (Rashi; Hirsch). It might be called a "bread offering" because part of it was eaten; but see Numbers 28:2. It may also denote "spiritual food."

3:17   **normally sacrificed** (cf. *Chullin* 93a; *Yad, Maakhaloth Assuroth* 7:5).

² [This is the law] if an individual commits an inadvertent sin by violating   **4** certain [specified]* prohibitory commandments of God.

³ If the anointed priest* commits an [inadvertent] violation, bringing guilt to his people, the sacrifice for his violation shall be an unblemished young bull* as a sin offering to God. ⁴ He shall bring the bull before God to the entrance of the Communion Tent, and press his hands on the bull's head. He shall then slaughter the bull before God.

⁵ The anointed priest shall take the bull's blood and bring it into the Communion Tent. ⁶ The priest shall dip his finger into the blood, and sprinkle it seven times before God toward* the cloth partition in the sanctuary. ⁷ The priest shall then place some of the blood on the horns of the incense altar which is before God in the Communion Tent. He shall then spill out all the [rest of the] bull's blood at the base of the sacrificial altar, which is in front of the Communion Tent's entrance.

⁸ He shall separate out all the fat of the sin offering bull, [taking] the layer of fat covering the stomachs, and all the fat attached to the stomachs. ⁹ The two kidneys, the fat on them along the flanks, and the lobe on the liver near the kidneys, shall [also] be removed. [All these] are the same as the [parts] removed from the peace offering. The priest shall then burn them on the sacrificial altar.

¹¹ [He shall take] the bull's skin and all its flesh, from head to toe, as well as the food in its intestines.* ¹² The entire bull shall thus be removed to the ritually pure place outside the camp, where the altar's ashes are deposited.* It shall be burned in fire on the wood in the place where the ashes are deposited.

[13. Sin Offerings for the Community]

¹³ If the entire community of Israel commits an inadvertent [violation] as a result of [the truth] being hidden from the congregation's eyes,* and they violate one of the [specified] prohibitory commandments of God, they shall incur guilt. ¹⁴ When the violation that they have committed becomes known, the congregation must bring a young bull as a sin offering, presenting it before the Communion Tent.

4:2   **certain specified.** Where the penalty is being "cut off" (*kareth*) (*Kerithoth* 2a; *Yad, Shegagoth* 1:1).

4:3   **anointed priest.** The High Priest (*Horayoth* 12b). See Exodus 29:7, 30:30.

—   **young bull.** In its second year (*Yad, Maaseh HaKorbanoth* 1:14). According to others, a three year old (*Parah* 1:1).

4:6   **toward.** Without the blood touching the partition (*Yoma* 57a; Rashi).

4:11   **food in its intestines** (Radak, *Sherashim*). See Exodus 29:14. According to some the food is left in the intestines (*Yoma* 68a).

4:12   **where the altar's ashes . . .** See 6:4.

4:13   **congregation's eyes.** This denotes the Sanhedrin (Rashi).

4   ¹⁵ The community elders* shall press their hands on the bull's head before
God, and it shall be slaughtered* before God.

   ¹⁶ The anointed priest shall bring some of the bull's blood into the Communion Tent, ¹⁷ and dipping his finger into the blood, he shall sprinkle [it]
seven times before God toward the cloth partition. ¹⁸ He shall then place
some of the blood on the horns of the [incense] altar that is before God in the
Communion Tent. He shall spill out all [the rest of] the blood at the base of
the sacrificial altar which is [in front of] the Communion Tent's entrance.

   ¹⁹ He shall then separate out all of its fat, and burn it on the altar, ²⁰ doing
with this bull exactly as he did with the bull sacrificed as a sin offering [for the
anointed priest].* The priest shall thus make atonement for [the community]
so that they will be forgiven.

   ²¹ He shall remove the bull to a place outside the camp, and burn it just as
he burned the first bull. This is the sin offering for the [entire] congregation.

[14. Sin Offerings for the King]

   ²² If the leader* commits a sin by inadvertently violating certain of God's
prohibitory commandments, he incurs guilt. ²³ When he is made aware of the
sin that he has committed, he must bring an unblemished male goat* as his
sacrifice. ²⁴ He shall press his hands on the goat's head, and have it slaughtered as a sin offering in the same place that the burnt offering* was slaughtered before God.

   ²⁵ The priest shall take the blood of the sin offering with his finger, and
place it on the protrusions* of the sacrificial altar. [The rest] of the blood shall
be poured out at the base of the sacrificial altar.

   ²⁶ All [the animal's] fat shall be burned on the altar, just like the fat of the
peace offerings. The priest shall thus make atonement for [the leader], and he
will be forgiven.

[15. Sin Offerings for Commoners]

   ²⁷ If a commoner commits an inadvertent violation by violating any one of
certain [specified] prohibitory commandments of God, he incurs guilt.
²⁸ When he is made aware of the violation he has committed, he must bring an

---

4:15   **elders.** Members of the Sanhedrin. See Exodus 3:16. Actually, three elders would place their hands on
       the bull's head (*Sanhedrin* 2a; *Yad, Maaseh HaKorbanoth* 3:10).
—   **it shall be . . .** Literally, "he shall."
4:20   **for the anointed priest** (Rashi).
4:22   **leader.** The king of Israel (*Horayoth* 10a, 11a).
4:23   **goat.** In its first year (*Yad, Maaseh HaKorbanoth* 1:14).
4:24   **burnt offering.** The north side of the altar; see 1:11.
4:25   **protrusions.** See Exodus 27:2.

unblemished female goat for the sin he committed. ²⁹ He shall press his   4
hands on the head of the sin offering, and have the sin offering slaughtered in
the same place as the burnt offering.*

³⁰ The priest shall take some of [the goat's] blood with his finger and place
it on the protrusions of the sacrificial altar, spilling out all [the rest] of the
blood at the altar's base. ³¹ He shall remove all the fat, as he did with the fat of
the peace offering, and the priest shall burn it on the altar, as an appeasing
fragrance to God. The priest shall thus make atonement for the individual,
and he will be forgiven.

[16. Sheep as Sin Offerings]

³² If he brings a sheep as a sin offering, it shall be an unblemished female.
³³ He shall press his hands on the head of the sin offering, and have it slaughtered in the same place that the burnt offering was slaughtered.

³⁴ The priest shall take some of the blood of the sin offering with his finger,
and place it on the protrusions of the sacrificial altar, spilling out all [the rest]
of the blood at the altar's base. ³⁵ He shall remove all its choice parts, just as
he removed all the choice parts of the sheep brought as a peace offering,* and
burn them on the altar along with the fire offerings dedicated to God. The
priest will thus make atonement for the sin the person committed and he will
be forgiven.

[17. The Adjustable Guilt Offering]

¹ [This is the law] if a person sins [in any of the following ways]:   5
If he is bound* by an oath* [to give evidence in court], where he was a witness who saw or knew [something], and he does not testify, he must bear his
guilt.

² [The same is true] if a person touches anything ritually unclean, whether
it is any dead non-kosher animal, wild or domestic, or any dead unclean
creeping animal,* and then commits a violation* while forgetting that he was
unclean. ³ Similarly, if he comes in contact with any ritual uncleanliness
stemming from a human being, which renders him unclean, and then forgets
about it, he may later discover that he has committed a violation.

4:29 **burnt offering.** The north side of the altar; see 1:11.
4:35 **peace offering.** Including the broad tail; see 3:9.
5:1 **bound.** Or, "accepts an oath;" literally "hears a dread oath" (see *Sifra; Shevuoth* 50a; *Yad, Shevuoth* 1:12).
— **oath.** *Alah* in Hebrew, a dread oath. See Genesis 24:41.
5:2 **creeping animal.** *Sheretz* in Hebrew. See below, 11:29, 30.
— **commits a violation.** By eating anything sanctified or going into a sanctified area (Rashi; *Yad, Shegagoth* 10:5).

5   ⁴ [This is also true] if a person makes a verbal oath* to do good or bad, no
matter what is expressed in the oath,* and then forgets about it.*

In any of these cases, the person is considered guilty as soon as he realizes
what he has done. ⁵ When he is guilty in any of these cases, he must confess the
sin that he has committed.

⁶ He must [also] bring his guilt offering* to God for the sin he has committed. It must be a female sheep or goat, [brought] as a sin offering. The priest
will then make atonement for [the person's] sin.

⁷ If he cannot afford a sheep, the guilt offering that he presents to God for
his sin shall be two turtle doves or two young common doves. One shall be a
sin offering and the other shall be a burnt offering.

⁸ He shall bring them to the priest, who shall first sacrifice the one for the
sin offering. He shall gouge through its neck from the back* without separating [the head from the body].* ⁹ He shall then drain some of the blood on the
side of the altar, and the rest of the blood at the altar's base. This one is the sin
offering.

¹⁰ Then he shall sacrifice the second [bird] as the law requires.* The priest
shall thus make atonement for the sin that [the person] committed, and he will
be forgiven.

[18. The Meal Offering for Guilt]

¹¹ If he cannot afford the two turtle doves or two common doves, the sacrifice that he must bring for his sin shall consist of 1/10 ephah* of wheat meal as
a sin offering. Since it is a sin offering, he shall not place any oil nor any
frankincense on it.

¹² He shall bring it to the priest, and the priest shall scoop up three fingers
full as a memorial portion. He shall burn [this portion] as a sin offering on the
altar along with God's [other] fire offerings.

¹³ The priest shall thus make atonement for [the person's] sin with one of
the above-mentioned offerings, and he will be forgiven. Just as in the case of

---

5:4   **verbal** . . . (Rashi; Radak, *Sherashim*). *Bata* in Hebrew.
—   **no matter** . . . This can also include an oath about something that already happened (*Shevuoth* 26a;
        Rashi).
—   **forgets about it.** And then violates the oath (*Yad, Shevuoth* 3:8). Specifically, "he is not aware that it incurs
        such a penalty" (*Shevuoth* 26a; *Yad, Shevuoth* 3:7).
5:6   **guilt offering.** *Asham* in Hebrew. In general, this sacrifice is known as an "adjustable sacrifice" or "a sac-
        rifice that can be more or less" (*korban oleh ve-yored*).
5:8   **he shall gouge** . . . Or, "nip through its neck" (see 1:15).
—   **without separating** . . . (Rambam; *Sefer HaMitzvoth*, Negative 112; *Chinukh* 124; Ralbag; see note on
        1:15). According to others, severing the gullet or windpipe, but not both (Rashi; Rashbam; Chizzkuni).
5:10   **as the law requires.** See 1:15.
5:11   **1/10 ephah.** Around 2 quarts. See Exodus 29:40.

the meal offering, [the unburnt portions of these sacrifices]* shall belong to   5
the priest.

[19. The Misappropriation Sacrifice]

¹⁴ God spoke to Moses saying:

¹⁵ If a person sins inadvertently by expropriating [for personal use]* something that is sacred to God, he shall bring as his guilt offering to God, an unblemished ram* with a prescribed value of [at least two]* shekels according to the sanctuary standard. It shall be [prepared as] a guilt offering.*

¹⁶ For misappropriating something that was sacred, he must make full restitution, adding one-fifth to it, and give it to the priest. The priest shall then* atone for him with the guilt offering ram, and he will be forgiven.

[20. The Offering for Questionable Guilt]

¹⁷ If a person sins by violating certain* of God's prohibitory commandments, without knowing [for sure]* he still bears responsibility. ¹⁸ He must bring an unblemished ram, with the prescribed value,* to the priest as a guilt offering. The priest shall then make atonement for the inadvertent sin that the person committed without definite knowledge, and he shall be forgiven. ¹⁹ It is a guilt offering that one must bring for his guilt toward God.

[21. Offerings for Dishonesty]

²⁰ God spoke to Moses saying:

²¹ [This is the law] if a person sins and commits a misappropriation offense against God by lying to his neighbor. [It can involve] an article left for safekeeping,* a business deal,* robbery, withholding funds* ²² or finding a lost object and denying it.* If the person swears falsely in any of these cases involv-

---

5:13   **the unburnt . . .** (*Zevachim* 53a; *Yad, Maaseh HaKorbanoth* 7:1; Rashi; Chizzkuni).
5:15   **expropriating for personal use** (*Meilah* 18a; Rashi).
—   **ram.** In its second year (*Zevachim* 90b).
—   **at least two** (*Zevachim* 90b; *Kerithoth* 27a; *Yad, Meilah* 1:3, *Pessuley Mukdashim* 4:22; *Chinukh* 127; Abarbanel).
—   **guilt offering.** *Asham* in Hebrew.
5:16   **then** (*Bava Kama* 111a; Raavad on *Yad, Meilah* 1:5). Or, "the priest shall have [previously]" (*Yad, loc. cit.*).
5:17   **certain.** Carrying a penalty of being "cut off". See 4:2.
—   **without knowing . . .** That is, if there is a question as to whether or not there was a violation (Rashi, etc.).
5:18   **prescribed value.** Two shekels, as in 5:15 (*Zevachim* 90b; Rashi). *Erkakha* in Hebrew; see below, 27:2.
5:21   **article left for . . .** See Exodus 22:10.
—   **business deal.** *Tesumath Yad* in Hebrew. Especially a loan (Rashi; Ralbag, Abarbanel) or partnership (Targum; Ibn Ezra). Also included is a claim of loss on security for a loan (*Bava Metzia* 48a).
—   **withholding funds.** *Ashak* in Hebrew. From someone to whom they are rightfully due (Rashi). This includes all illegal monetary cheating (Radak, *Sherashim*; Abarbanel). According to some, it denotes sneak thievery (Saadia; Ibn Ezra). See 19:13.
5:22   **and denying it** (Ralbag; Abarbanel). Or, "If he denies the truth" (Rashi). (See *Kerithoth* 2b, *Bava Kama* 103b; *Yad, Shevuoth* 7:1-4)

5   ing human relations,* he is considered to have sinned.

²³ When he becomes guilty of such a sin, he must return the stolen article, the withheld funds, the article left for safekeeping, the found article, ²⁴ or anything else regarding which he swore falsely.

He must make restitution of the principal,* and then add one-fifth to it. On the day [that he seeks atonement for]* his crime, he must give it to its rightful owner.

²⁵ He must then bring to the priest his sin offering to God. It shall be an unblemished ram, worth the prescribed amount, as a guilt offering. ²⁶ The priest shall make atonement for him before God, and he will then be forgiven for any crime that he has committed.

Tzav   צַו

[22. Ashes of the Burnt Offering]

6   ¹ God spoke to Moses, telling him ² to relate the following instructions* to Aaron and his descendants:

This is the law of the burnt offering. The burnt offering shall remain on the altar's hearth* all night until morning, so that the altar's fires can be ignited with it.* ³ The priest shall then put on his linen vestments,* including his linen pants. He shall remove the ashes* of the burnt offerings consumed by the fire that are on the altar, and place them near the altar.*

⁴ He shall then take off his vestments, and put on other garments.* He shall then take the ashes to a ritually clean place outside the camp.

—   **involving human relations** (Ralbag). Literally, "regarding one of these that a person may do to sin."

5:24   **principal** (Rashi). *Rosh* in Hebrew, literally "head." Or, "He must repay it by himself" (Ibn Ezra), or, "He must first make restitution" (Chizzkuni; Ralbag).

—   **that he seeks atonement** (Abarbanel; Rashbam), or, "on the day he brings his guilt sacrifice" (Chizzkuni). Or, "As [much as it was worth] on the day of his crime, he must return. . ." (*Sifra; Bava Metzia* 43b; *Yad, Gezelah* 3:1).

6:2   **following instructions.** Earlier, the laws relating primarily to the people bringing the sacrifices were given. Now the laws relating to the priest's follow-up are being given (Rashbam).

—   **altar's hearth** (Radak, *Sherashim*). *Mokdah* in Hebrew. This is the place where the sacrifices burn (*Yoma* 45a).

—   **the altar's fires** . . . (Ramban). Or, "the fires of the [incense] altar" (Rashi; *Yoma* 45a).

6:3   **vestments** (Targum; Ramban). Or, "fitted tunic" (Rashi). Some say that these were of a lower quality than the priest's usual vestments (*Yad, Temidim* 2:10). See note on 6:4.

—   **remove the ashes.** With a shovel; see Exodus 27:3. (*Tamid* 1:4; *Yad, Temidim* 2:12).

—   **near the altar.** To the southeast of the altar, some three handbreadths (9 inches) from the ramp (*Ibid.*). See 1:16.

6:4   **other garments.** Of lower quality (*Yoma* 23b; Rashi).However, some say that sacred vestments were not required here at all since this was not considered sacred service (*Yad, Temidim* 2:15; *Mishneh LaMelekh ibid.* 2:10).

⁵ The fire of the altar shall be ignited with [the remains of the offerings].   6
Each morning, the priest shall kindle wood on them. On [this wood] he shall
then arrange burnt offerings and burn the choice parts of the peace offerings.
⁶ Thus, there shall be a constant fire kept burning on the altar, without being
extinguished.

[23. Laws of the Meal Offering]

⁷ This is the law of the meal offering: [One of] Aaron's descendants shall
offer it before God, [near the place where one ascends*] to the altar. ⁸ With his
three middle fingers* he shall lift up some of the wheat meal and oil of the
offering, and [then remove] all the frankincense on the offering. He shall burn
[this] on the altar as an appeasing fragrance—it is the memorial portion to
God.

⁹ Aaron and his descendants shall then eat the rest of [the offering]. It must
be eaten as unleavened bread in a holy place. They must therefore eat it in the
enclosure of the Communion Tent. ¹⁰ It shall not be baked as leavened bread.

I have given this to them as their portion of My fire offerings, and it is holy
of holies, like the sin offering and the guilt offering. ¹¹ Every male among
Aaron's descendants may eat it. It is an eternal law for all generations [that it
be taken] from God's fire offerings. Any [food*] coming in contact with it shall
become holy.

[24. The High Priest's Offering]

¹² God spoke to Moses, saying:

¹³ This is the offering that Aaron and his descendants must bring from the
day* that [any one of them] is anointed [as High Priest].* It shall consist of
1/10 ephah* of wheat meal, and it shall be a daily meal offering, with one half
[offered] in the morning, and one half in the evening.*

6:7   **near the place** . . . (Rashi). Literally "face." This was at the south-west corner of the altar (Rashi; *Yad,
        Maaseh HaKorbanoth* 13:12; *Sotah* 14b).
6:8   **three middle fingers.** See note on 2:2
6:11   **food.** (Rashi). This is because any food touching the meal offering becomes holy by absorbing some of
        the offering's taste (*Sifra*; Rashi; cf. *Zevachim* 97a,b). This teaches that the mere taste of food has the same
        status as the food itself. It is for this reason that food cooked together with nonkosher food becomes
        nonkosher (see *Pesachim* 44b, 45a). Also see below 6:20. The same is true of any taste absorbed in a pot or
        the like, see Exodus 29:37.
6:13   **from the day** (Saadia). Literally "on the day." This is thus part of the inauguration ceremony of every
        priest (*Menachoth* 78a; Rashi; *Yad, Kley HaMikdash* 5:16). A common priest only brings this offering on the
        day he is installed, while the high priest brings it every day (*Yad, Temidim* 3:18).
—   **as High Priest** (*Targum Yonathan*; Rashbam. See 6:15).
—   **1/10 ephah.** Around 2 quarts. See Exodus 16:36, above, 5:11, 5:15.
—   **one half in the morning** . . . Twelve loaves were baked (see 6:14). According to some, they were broken
        in half, with the first halves offered in the morning, and the others in the evening (*Yad, Maaseh HaKor-*

6   ¹⁴ It shall be prepared with olive oil* on a flat pan* [after being] boiled* [and] baked.* It is then to be presented as an offering of [many] wafers of bread,* an appeasing fragrance to God.

¹⁵ It is a law for all time that the anointed priest* among [Aaron's] descendants shall prepare it.

It must be completely burned. ¹⁶ [Similarly], every meal offering brought by a priest must be completely [burned] and not eaten.

[25. Laws of Sin Offerings]

¹⁷ God spoke to Moses, telling him to ¹⁸ relate the following message to Aaron and his descendants:

This is the law of the sin offering*: The sin offering must be slaughtered before God in the same place that the burnt offering is slaughtered. It is holy of holies.

¹⁹ [Any] priest [fit]* to offer it may eat it. It must be eaten in a holy place, in the enclosure around the Communion Tent.

²⁰ Any [food] touching [the sin offering] shall become sanctified.*

If its blood splashes on any garment, it must be washed off in a sanctified area.*

²¹ Any clay pot in which it is cooked must be broken.* However, if it is cooked in a copper pot, [the pot] may be purged* and rinsed with water.

---

      banoth 13:4). According to others, 6 loaves were offered in the morning, and 6 in the evening (Raavad *ibid.*)

6:14   **olive oil.** 3 logs (around 1 quart). (*Sifra; Yad, Maaseh HaKorbanoth* 13:2).

—   **flat pan.** See 2:5.

—   **boiled.** (*Sifra;* Rashi; Radak; *Yad, Maaseh HaKorbanoth* 9:19; see note on Exodus 29:2). *Murbekheth* in Hebrew. Or, "fried" (*Targum Yonathan*); "prepared quickly" (Saadia; cf. Ibn Ezra); "soft" (Rashbam; Ibn Ezra); or, "well mixed" or "broken up" (Ibn Janach), or "well kneaded" (Septuagint).

—   **and baked** (*Menachoth* 50b; Rashi). "Baked slightly" (*Yad, Maaseh HaKorbanoth* 13:3).

—   **many wafers . . .** Twelve loaves were made. The meal was mixed with the oil, and the dough was cooked. It was divided into 12 wafers or rolls, and they were slightly baked. Each wafer was then fried in a *revi'ith* (2¼ oz.) of olive oil. (*Yad, Maaseh HaKorbanoth* 13:2,3; *Menachoth* 88b).

6:15   **anointed priest.** The High Priest.

6:18   **sin offering.** See above, 5:27-35.

6:19   **fit.** (See *Yad, Maaseh HaKorbanoth* 10:14).

—   **to offer** (Rashi). Or, "sprinkle its blood" (Ibn Ezra).

6:20   **Any food . . .** See note on 6:11.

—   **If its blood . . .** (See *Yad, Maaseh HaKorbanoth* 8:1).

6:21   **must be broken.** The taste is absorbed in the pot (see 6:11), and after the prescribed time, it becomes forbidden as food (Rashi; *Yad, Maaseh HaKorbanoth* 8:11). It is from here that we learn that a clay pot absorbs the taste of food and it cannot be purged (Rashi; *Zevachim* 95b). See 11:33, 15:12.

—   **purged.** In boiling water, to remove the taste of the offering (*Zevachim* 96b; *Yad, Maaseh HaKorbanoth* 8:12; Rashi). It is from here that we learn that pots contaminated with non-kosher food can be purged in boiling water. Also see Numbers 31:23.

²² [Although] it is holy of holies, any male priest may eat it. ²³ However, 6 any sin offering whose blood is brought into the Communion Tent to make atonement in the sanctuary* may not be eaten. It must be burned in fire.

[26. Laws of Guilt Offerings]

¹ This is the law of the guilt offering,* which is holy of holies. ² The guilt 7 offering must be slaughtered in the same place that the burnt offering is slaughtered, and its blood must be dashed on all sides of the altar. ³ All the choice parts, such as the broad tail and the fat covering the stomachs, must be presented. ⁴ The two kidneys and the fat on them along the flanks, and the lobe over the liver near the kidneys, must [also] be removed. ⁵ The priest must burn [all these] as a guilt offering on the altar, a fire offering to God.

⁶ All the male priests may eat [the rest]. It shall be eaten in a sanctified area, since it is holy of holies. ⁷ The sin offering and the guilt offering have exactly the same laws insofar as they can be given to [any] priest [fit] to offer them.*

⁸ [Similarly], any priest [fit] to sacrifice a person's burnt offering can [share] in the skin of the burnt offering [after] it is sacrificed.*

⁹ [The unburnt portion of] any meal offering which is baked in an oven, pan fried, or deep fried* shall [also] be given to [any] priest [fit] to offer it. ¹⁰ [Similarly],* any meal offering, whether mixed with oil or dry,* shall belong equally to all of Aaron's descendants.

[27. Laws of Peace Offerings]

¹¹ This is the law of the peace offering* that is sacrificed to God.

¹² If it is offered as a thanksgiving offering, then it must be presented along with unleavened loaves mixed with oil, flat matzahs saturated with oil,* and loaves made of boiled flour mixed with oil.* ¹³ The sacrifice shall [also] be

6:23 **whose blood is brought** . . . See above, 4:5,16.
7:1 **guilt offering.** *Asham.* See above, 5:16,19,25.
7:7 **any priest fit** . . . (*Sifra*; Rashi).
7:8 **Similarly** . . . (Rashi; *Yad, Maaseh HaKorbanoth* 5:19, 10:14).
7:9 **baked** . . . See above, 2:4,5,7.
7:10 **Similarly.** (See *Yad, Maaseh HaKorbanoth* 10:15).
— **dry.** Without oil, see above, 5:11 (Rashi).
7:11 **peace offering.** See above, 3:1-17.
7:12 **unleavened loaves** . . . See above, 2:4.
— **boiled flour** . . . See 6:14, Exodus 29:2.

7 presented along with loaves of leavened bread.* [All these] shall be presented
with one's thanksgiving peace offering.

¹⁴ He shall present some of* each [of the above four bread] offerings as an
elevated gift to God. This shall belong to the priest who sprinkles the blood of
the peace offering.

¹⁵ The flesh of the thanksgiving peace offering must be eaten on the day it
is offered. None of it may be left over until morning.

¹⁶ [However,] if one's sacrifice offering is meant [merely] to fulfill a general
vow or a specific pledge,* he shall eat it on the same day that he offers his sacrifice, but what is left over may also be eaten on the next day. ¹⁷ [Nevertheless,]
what is left over from the sacrifice's flesh on the third day, must be burned in
fire. ¹⁸ If the person bringing the offering [even plans]* to eat it on the third
day, [the sacrifice] will not be accepted. It is considered putrid,* and it will not
be counted in his favor. Any person who eats it will bear his guilt.*

¹⁹ Any [sacrificial] flesh* that comes in contact with something unclean
may not be eaten; it must be burned in fire. Otherwise, any ritually clean person may eat the flesh. ²⁰ But if any person eats the flesh of a peace sacrifice to
God while still in a state of ritual uncleanliness, his soul will be cut off from
his people.

²¹ Any person who comes in contact with human uncleanness, or with an
unclean mammal or other unclean creature, and then eats the flesh of a peace
offering to God, shall have his soul cut off from his people.

²² God spoke to Moses, telling him ²³ to relate the following to the Israelites:

Do not eat any of the hard fat* in an ox, sheep or goat. ²⁴ [Even if]* an
animal is improperly slaughtered or fatally wounded, you may use its hard fat
for any purpose you desire, as long as you do not eat it. ²⁵ But anyone who

---

7:13 **leavened bread.** Thus, four types of bread were presented. Ten loaves of each type, for a total of 40
loaves, were presented (*Yad, Maaseh HaKorbanoth* 9:17-22).
7:14 **some of . . .** One-tenth of the offering (*Sifra*; Rashi). Since ten of each loaf were made, one of each was
given to the priest (*Yad, Maaseh HaKorbanoth* 8:21).
7:16 **general vow or specific pledge.** (*Kinnim* 1:1). *Neder* or *nedavah* in Hebrew.
7:18 **even plans** (*Zevachim* 29a; Rashi).
—   **putrid** (Ibn Janach; Radak, *Sherashim*). *Piggul* in Hebrew. Or, "disgusting" (Saadia), or, "rejected"
(Targum).
—   **bear his guilt.** This involves being cut off spiritually (Rashi).
7:19 **sacrificial flesh.** (Rashi). The verse merely mentions "flesh," but in the desert, the only flesh eaten was
sacrificial flesh (see Deuteronomy 12:15).
7:23 **hard fat.** This is the fat offered in a sacrifice, see notes on 3:3,4.
7:24 **Even if** (cf. *Zevachim* 69b; *Pesachim* 23a).

eats the hard fat offered to God in any animal* shall have his soul cut off from 7
his people.

²⁶ Do not eat any blood, whether from a mammal or a bird, no matter
where you may live. ²⁷ Any person who eats blood shall have his soul cut off
from his people.

[28. The Priests' Portion]

²⁸ God spoke to Moses, telling him ²⁹ to convey the following to the Israelites:

When anyone brings a peace sacrifice to God, he must bring a special
offering to God from it. ³⁰ With his own hands, he must bring the choice
parts* presented as a fire offering to God on top of the [animal's] chest.* He
shall wave the chest in the prescribed motions* as a wave offering before God.

³¹ The priest shall then burn the choice parts on the altar. The chest [on the
other hand], shall belong to Aaron and his descendants.

³² The right hind leg of your peace offerings shall [also] be given as an
elevated gift to the priest. ³³ Any descendant of Aaron [fit to]* offer the blood
and fat of the peace offerings shall have the right leg as a portion.

³⁴ This is because I have taken the chest as a wave offering and the hind leg
as an elevated gift from the Israelites, from their peace sacrifices, and I have
given [these parts] to Aaron the priest and his descendants. It is a law for all
times [that this be taken] from the Israelites.*

³⁵ This is the [portion]* of God's fire offerings [that was given when] Aaron
and his sons were anointed, on the day that He brought them forth to be
priests to God. ³⁶ On the day that He anointed them, God commanded that
this be given to them by the Israelites. It is an eternal law for all generations.

³⁷ This then is the law of the burnt offering, the meal offering, the sin offering, the inauguration offering, and the peace offering, ³⁸ which God gave to

---

7:25 **the hard fat . . .** Literally, "the hard fat of any animal offered to God," (although both may be taken as
literal translations).
7:30 **choice parts.** The portions burned on the altar. See 3:9.
— **on top of the animal's chest.** The fat is initially placed on top of the chest. However, when given to the
priest, the fat is given first, and the chest is placed on it (Rashi). The hind leg is also placed on the chest
(*Sifra; Menachoth* 62a; *Yad, Maaseh HaKorbanoth* 9:6). See below, 10:15.
— **prescribed motions.** See Exodus 29:24. The priest would have his hands under the hands of the owner
(*Yad, Maaseh HaKorbanoth* 9:6).
7:33 **fit to** (*Zevachim* 98b; Rashi).
7:34 **It is a law . . .** See Exodus 29:27,28.
7:35 **This is the portion.** See Exodus 29:22,26.

7 Moses on Mount Sinai. [It was given] on the day that He commanded the Israelites to offer their sacrifices to God in the Sinai Desert.*

[29. Installation of the Priests]

8   ¹ God spoke to Moses, saying*: ² "Take Aaron along with his sons, the vestments, the anointing oil, the sin offering bull, the two rams, and the basket of unleavened bread. ³ Gather the entire community at the entrance of the Communion Tent."

⁴ Moses did as God commanded and the community was assembled at the Communion Tent's entrance. ⁵ Moses said to the community, "This is what God has commanded to be done."

⁶ Moses brought forth Aaron and his sons, and immersed them in a mikvah.*

⁷ He then dressed [Aaron] with the tunic, belted him with the sash, put the robe on him, and placed the ephod over it. He girded him with the ephod's belt, and tightened it on him.* ⁸ He then placed the breastplate on [the ephod],* and placed the Urim and Thumim* in the breastplate. ⁹ He placed the turban on [Aaron's] head, and toward his face just below* the turban, he placed the gold forehead plate as a sacred coronet. [It was all done] as God commanded Moses.*

¹⁰ Moses took the anointing oil* and anointed the tabernacle and everything in it, thus sanctifying them. ¹¹ He sprinkled some of [the oil] on the altar seven times.* He then anointed the altar and all its utensils, as well as the washstand and its base, thus sanctifying them.

¹² He poured some of the anointing oil on Aaron's head, and he anointed him to sanctify him.

7:38   **It was given** . . . See Exodus 24:5 (cf. Ibn Ezra). Or, "[in the Tabernacle] in the desert" (*Targum Yonathan*). Or,"It was given in the desert on the day. . ."
8:1   **God spoke** . . . Fulfilling the instructions given in Exodus 29:1-37.
8:6   **mikvah.** See Exodus 29:4.
8:7   **tightened** . . . (Saadia). *Aphad* in Hebrew. Or,"belted" (Radak, *Sherashim*) or, "fully, dressed him" (Targum).
          This is the middle verse of the Torah.
8:8   **the ephod.** or "him."
—   **Urim and Thumim.** See Exodus 28:30. According to some, these were divine names inside the breastplate (Rashi), while according to others, he placed the stones in the breastplate after putting it on Aaron (cf. Saadia). Or, "He placed the breastplate on the ephod, having previously placed in it the Urim and Thumim."
8:9   **just below** (Saadia). Literally, "on" or "near."
—   **It was all done.** Regarding the vestments see Exodus 28.
8:10   **anointing oil.** See Exodus 30:22-33.
8:11   **He sprinkled** . . . Not mentioned earlier (cf. Rashi; Ramban).

¹³ Moses then brought forth Aaron's sons, and he dressed them in tunics, **8** girded them with sashes, and fitted* them with hats. [It was all done] as God had commanded Moses.

¹⁴ He brought forth the bull for the sin offering, and Aaron and his sons pressed their hands on its head. ¹⁵ Moses* slaughtered it and collected the blood. With his finger, he placed [the blood] all around on the altar's protrusions, thus purifying* the altar. He poured the [rest of] the blood at the altar's base, thus sanctifying it so that atonement could be offered on it.*

¹⁶ He took the fat on the stomachs, the lobe of the liver, and the two kidneys along with their fat, and Moses burned them on the altar. ¹⁷ All [the rest of] the bull—its skin, flesh and insides—he burned in fire outside the camp. [It was all done] as God had commanded Moses.

¹⁸ He brought forth the ram for the burnt offering, and Aaron and his sons pressed their hands on its head. ¹⁹ He slaughtered it, and Moses dashed its blood on all sides of the altar. ²⁰ He cut the ram into pieces, and Moses burned the head, the cut pieces, and the intestinal membrane* [on the altar], ²¹ having [previously]* scrubbed the intestines and legs with water. Moses thus burned the entire ram on the altar as a burnt offering. It was an appeasing fragrance, a fire offering to God, [and it was all done] as God had commanded Moses.

²² He brought forth the second ram, which was the installation ram, and Aaron and his sons pressed their hands on the ram's head. ²³ He slaughtered it, and Moses took some of its blood and placed it on Aaron's right ear lobe,* on his right thumb, and on his right big toe.

²⁴ [Moses] brought forth Aaron's sons, and he placed some of the blood on their right ear lobes, their right thumbs, and their right big toes. Moses sprinkled [the rest of] the blood on all sides of the altar.

²⁵ He took the choice portions*: The broad tail, all the fat on the stom-

---

8:13 **fitted** (cf. Targum). *Chavash* in Hebrew. Or, "tied" (Rashi; Ibn Janach, Radak,*Sherashim*). See Exodus 29:36.
8:15 **Moses** (*Targum Yonathan*). Literally, "He slaughtered it and Moses took. . ."
— **purifying** (Targum; Rashi). See Exodus 29:36.
— **thus sanctifying** . . See Exodus 29:36.
8:20 **membrane**. See above, 1:8.
8:21 **having previously**. See Exodus 29:17.
8:23 **ear lobe**. See Exodus 29:20. Some say the upper part of the ear (Targum) (A), while others say the lower lobe of the ear (Saadia) (B), or the center of the ear (*Sifra*; cf. Raavad *ad loc.*) (C). According to some, the blood was placed on the cartilege just inside of the helix of the ear (Rambam on *Negaim* 14:9; *Yad, Mechuserey Kaparah* 5:1) (D). See below, 14:14.
8:25 **choice portions**. See above, 3:9.

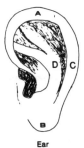

Ear
A. Helix B. Lobe

8   achs,* the lobe of the liver, the two kidneys along with their fat, and the right hind leg. [26] From the basket of unleavened bread, before God, he took one loaf of unleavened bread, one loaf of oil bread, and one flat loaf, and he placed them on the choice portions and the right hind leg.

[27] Moses placed all this in Aaron's hands and in his sons' hands, and he waved them in the prescribed motions as a wave offering before God. [28] Moses took it from their hands, and he burned it on the altar together with the burnt offering. This was the installation offering, an appeasing fragrance, a fire offering to God.

[29] Moses took [the ram's] chest, and made the prescribed motions for a wave offering before God. This was Moses' own portion of the installation ram. [It was all done] as God had commanded Moses.

[30] Moses took some of the anointing oil, [together with] some of the blood from the altar, and he sprinkled it on Aaron and his vestments, as well as on [Aaron's] sons and their vestments. He thus sanctified Aaron and his vestments as well as [Aaron's] sons and their vestments.

[31] Moses said to Aaron and his sons, "Cook the flesh at the Communion Tent's entrance. There you shall eat it, along with the bread in the installation basket. Do it, because I have given instructions that Aaron and his sons eat [these things]. [32] Whatever is left over of the flesh and bread, you must burn in fire.

[33] Do not leave the entrance of the Communion Tent for seven days, until your period of inauguration is complete. This is because your installation ceremony shall last for seven days. [34] God has commanded that whatever was done on this day must be done [all seven days] to atone for you. [35] Remain at the Communion Tent's entrance day and night for seven days. You will thus keep God's charge and not die, since this is what was commanded."

[36] Aaron and his sons did all these things, just as God had commanded through Moses.

Shemini   שְׁמִינִי

[30. The Eighth Day]

9   [1] On the eighth day,* Moses summoned Aaron, his sons, and the elders of Israel.* [2] He said to Aaron, "Take yourself a calf* for a sin offering and a

---

9:1   **eighth day.** After the seven days of installment (8:33-35).
—   **elders of Israel.** See Exodus 3:16. This may be because only the Sanhedrin had the authority to appoint a High Priest (*Tosefta, Sanhedrin* 3:2; *Yad, Kley HaMikdash* 4:15).Also see 4:13.
9:2   **calf.** Yearling (*Yad, Maaseh HaKorbanoth* 1:14; see below 9:3).

ram for a burnt offering, [both] unblemished, and sacrifice them before God. 9
³ Speak to the Israelites, and tell them to take unblemished [animals]: a goat
for a sin offering, a yearling calf and a lamb for a burnt offering, ⁴ and a bull
and a ram for peace offerings. They shall sacrifice these before God along with
a meal offering mixed with oil, because God will reveal Himself to you today."
⁵ They brought what Moses ordered to the front of the Communion Tent,
and the entire community came forth and stood before God.
⁶ Moses said, "This is what God has commanded. Do it and God's glory
will be revealed to you."
⁷ Moses [then] said to Aaron, "Approach the altar, and prepare your sin
offering and burnt offering, thus atoning for you and the people. Then prepare the people's offering to atone for them, as God has commanded."
⁸ Aaron went up to the altar, and he slaughtered the calf that he had for a
sin offering. ⁹ Aaron's sons brought forth the blood, and dipping his finger in
the blood, [Aaron] placed some on the altar's protrusions. He then spilled out
the rest of the blood at the altar's base. ¹⁰ He burned the fat, the kidneys and
the liver lobe of the sin offering. [It was all done] as God had commanded
Moses.
¹¹ He then burned the flesh and skin [of the sin offering] in fire outside the
camp.
¹² He slaughtered the burnt offering. Aaron's sons passed the blood to
him, and he dashed the blood on all sides of the altar. ¹³ They passed him the
cut up parts of the burnt offering, piece by piece, along with the head, and he
burned them on the altar. ¹⁴ He washed the entrails and the feet and burned
them on the altar along with [the rest] of the burnt offering.
¹⁵ He brought forth the people's offering. He took the goat that was the
people's sin offering, and slaughtered it, preparing it as a sin offering, just like
the first one.* ¹⁶ He brought forth the burnt offering, preparing it according to
the law.
¹⁷ He brought forth the grain offering. He took a handful* and burned it
on the altar. This was in addition to the morning [grain] offering.*
¹⁸ He slaughtered the bull and the ram that were the people's peace sacrifice. Aaron's sons passed the blood to him, and he dashed it on all sides of the
altar. ¹⁹ [They also passed him] the choice parts of the bull and ram: the broad
tail, the [fatty] membrane, the kidneys and the liver lobe. ²⁰ They placed the
choice parts on the chests [of the animals], and [Aaron] then burned the choice

9:15 first one. See 9:8-11.
9:17 handful. Or "partial handful," that is, three fingers full. See note on 2:2.
— morning grain offering (*Sifra*; Ramban). See Exodus 29:40 (Rashi).

9 parts on the altar. ²¹ Aaron [had first] waved the chests and right hind legs in the prescribed motions as a wave offering before God. [It was all done] as God had commanded Moses.

²² Aaron lifted his hands toward the people* and blessed them.* He then descended from [the altar* where he] had prepared the sin offering, the burnt offering, and the peace offerings.

²³ Moses and Aaron went into the Communion Tent, and when they came out, they blessed the people. God's glory* was then revealed to all the people.

²⁴ Fire came forth from before God* and consumed the burnt offering and the choice parts on the altar. When the people saw this, they raised their voices in praise* and threw themselves on their faces.

10 ¹ Aaron's sons, Nadav and Avihu,* each took his fire pan,* placed fire on it, and then incense on it. They offered it before God, [but it was] unauthorized fire,* which [God] had not instructed them [to offer]. ² Fire came forth from before God,* and it consumed them, so that they died before God.

³ Moses said to Aaron, "This is exactly what God meant when he said, 'I will be sanctified through those close to Me, and I will thus be glorified.'"* Aaron remained silent.

⁴ Moses summoned Mishael and Eltzafan, the sons of Aaron's uncle Uzziel,* and he said to them, "Come forth and remove your close relatives from inside the sanctuary. [Bring them] outside the camp."

⁵ They came forth and carried [Nadav and Avihu] outside the camp, in their tunics, as Moses had said.

9:22   **lifted his hands** . . . From this, we learn that the priests lift their hands for the priestly blessing (*Sotah* 38a).

—   **blessed them.** With the priestly blessing presented in Numbers 6:22-27 (Rashi). The commandment regarding the priestly blessing may have been given earlier, even though it is written later (Ramban).

—   **from the altar** (*Sifra*; Rashi).

9:23   **God's glory** . . . Prophetically (*Targum Yonathan*). Or, through the fire mentioned in 9:24 (Saadia; Rashbam).

9:24   **from before God.** From the Holy of Holies (Rashbam), or from the sky (*Sifra*). Some say that it came down like a flash of lightning (Josephus, *Antiquities* 3:8:6).

—   **raised their voices in praise** (Targum; Ibn Ezra); or "sang out" (Saadia) or "became ecstatic" (*Or Torah, MiKetz*, p. 37a. See *Meditation and the Bible*, p. 120).

10:1   **Nadav and Avihu.** See Exodus 6:23. They were Aaron's eldest sons who had been chosen for special status; Exodus 24:1,9.

—   **fire pan.** See Exodus 27:3.

—   **unauthorized** . . . See Exodus 30:9 (Ramban; Ralbag). Some say that they wanted to make use of sacrificial methods that had been in existence before Moses received God's instructions (Josephus, *Antiquities* 3:8:7).

10:2   **Fire came forth** . . . From the Holy of Holies (*Sifra*). Or, "the fire (in 9:24) that came forth from God . . ." (Rashbam). It began to burn them, and no one could quench it (Josephus 3:8:7).

10:3   **I will be sanctified** . . . See Exodus 19:22 (*Zevachim* 115b, Yehuda HaChasid; *Tur; Paaneach Raza*). Or, see Exodus 29:43 (Rashi).

10:4   **Mishael and Eltzafan** . . . (see Exodus 6:18,22).

⁶ Moses said to Aaron and his sons, Eleazar and Ithamar,* "Do not go   10
without a haircut* and do not tear* your vestments*; otherwise you will die,
bringing divine wrath upon the entire community. As far as your brothers are
concerned, let the entire family of Israel mourn for the ones whom God
burned. ⁷ Do not leave the entrance of the Communion Tent* lest you die,
because God's anointing oil is still upon you."
They did as Moses had said.

[31. Drunkenness]

⁸ God spoke to Aaron, saying: ⁹ When you enter the Communion Tent,
neither you nor your descendants may drink wine or any other intoxicant*;
otherwise you will die. This is an eternal law for all your generations. ¹⁰ [You
will thus be able]* to distinguish between the holy and the common, and
between the ritually unclean and the clean. ¹¹ [You will also be able] to render
decisions* for the Israelites in all the laws that God has taught you through
Moses.

[32. Completing the Service]

¹² Moses announced to Aaron and his surviving sons, Eleazar and Itha-

---

10:6 **Eleazar and Ithamar.** Aaron's younger sons (Exodus 6:23).
— **go without a haircut** (*Sifra*; Rashi; Saadia). This is because they were now like high priests; see below,
21:10 (Rashbam; Ramban). This indicates that they were not allowed to let their hair grow for 30 days
without being cut (*Sanhedrin* 22b; *Yad, Biyath HaMikdash* 1:11).
 This also teaches that it was forbidden for them to perform any divine service if they went without a
haircut for more than 30 days (Ramban on *Sefer HaMitzvoth*, Negative 73, 163). Some say that it was even
forbidden for them to enter the sanctuary without a haircut (*Yad, Biyath HaMikdash* 1:8; *Sefer HaMitzvoth*,
Negative 163). Others maintain that as long as the Temple stood, a priest could not go without a haircut
for more than 30 days under any conditions (Raavad, *Biyath HaMikdash* 1:9. from Ezekiel 44:20; cf. *Kesef
Mishneh ibid.*; *Sanhedrin* 22b).
 From here we learn that a mourner normally may not cut his hair for 30 days (*Moed Katan* 14b).
— **do not tear.** (Rashi; Ibn Ezra). *Param* in Hebrew. Or, "do not unravel stitches" (Rashi, *Makkoth* 22b, s.v.
VeNiframu; Radak, *Sherashim*; *Arukh*). According to others, *param* denotes pulling cloth apart so that its
weave unravels, rather than tearing it cleanly (Rambam on *Sotah* 1:5), or in general, tearing it very badly
(Rashi, *Sotah* 7a, s.v. *Velm*).
— **your vestments.** This is because a priest is forbidden to enter the temple with torn vestments (*Yad, Biyath
HaMikdash* 1:14; *Sefer HaMitzvoth*, Negative 164).
 It is from here that we see that a mourner must rend his garments (*Moed Katan* 15a).
10:7 **Do not leave . . .** Again, like a High Priest, who may not leave the Temple to mourn: see 21:12
(Ramban; Chizzkuni). According to some, this is a general prohibition for a priest not to leave the
Temple during the service (*Yad, Biyath HaMikdash* 2:5; *Sefer HaMitzvoth*, Negative 165; Ramban). Some
dispute this, and maintain that this commandment was only given to Eleazar and Ithamar, because they
had the anointing oil on their heads (Raavad on *Yad, loc. cit.*; also not counted in *Sefer Mitzvoth Gadol*).
10:9 **or any other intoxicant** (cf. Ibn Ezra; Saadia). Or, "Do not drink wine to make you drunk" (Rashi; cf.
Yad, Biyath HaMikdash 1:1,2,5).
10:10 **You will thus be able to . . .** (Saadia). Or, "This is to" (Rashi).
10:11 **to render decisions.** This teaches that a rabbi may not render decisions when drunk (*Kerithoth* 13b; *Yad,
Biyath HaMikdash* 1:3). According to some, this also implies a positive commandment for a duly qualified
rabbi to render decisions in Torah law (*Sefer Mitzvoth Katan* 111; *Cheredim*, Positive 4:20).

10   mar, "Take the remainder of the meal offering* that is before God, and eat it
as unleavened bread near the altar. Since it is holy of holies, ¹³ you must eat it
in a holy place. It is the portion for you and your descendants from God's fire
offerings, since I have thus been commanded.

·⁴ "However,* the chest taken as a wave offering and the hind leg taken as
an elevated gift, you may eat together with your sons and daughters. It is the
portion designated for you and your descendants from the peace sacrifices of
the Israelites.

¹⁵ "The hind leg for the elevated gift, and the chest for the wave offering,
shall be brought on top of* the choice parts designated as the fire offering. [It
is all] to be waved in the prescribed motions of the wave offering. [The leg and
chest] are meant to be a portion for you and your descendants for all time, as
God commanded."

¹⁶ Moses then inquired* about the goat [slaughtered] as a sin offering,* and
when he discovered that it had already been burned, he was angry with
Aaron's surviving sons, Eleazar and Ithamar. He said to them, ¹⁷ "Why did
you not eat the sin offering in a holy area?* It is holy of holies, and has been
given to you to remove the community's guilt and atone for them before God.
¹⁸ Since its blood was not brought into the inner sanctuary,* you [should have]
eaten it in a holy place, as I commanded you."

¹⁹ Aaron responded to Moses, "Today, when they sacrificed* their sin
offering and burnt offering before God, such a [terrible tragedy]* occurred to
me. If I had eaten the sin offering today, would it have been right in God's
eyes?"

²⁰ When Moses heard this, he approved.

[33. The Dietary Laws]

11   ¹ God spoke to Moses and Aaron,* telling them ² to speak to the Israelites,
and convey the following to them:
Of all the animals in the world, these are the ones that you may eat*:

10:12 remainder of . . . See 9:17.
10:14 However (Saadia).
10:15 on top of (Rashi). See note on 7:30.
10:16 inquired. This is the middle word of the Torah.
—   goat . . . See 9:15 (Baaley Tosafoth).
10:17 eat the sin offering . . . See 6:22.
10:18 Since its blood . . . See 6:23.
10:19 sacrificed . . . Helped sacrifice (Rashbam; see 9:8,12,15). Or, "Did they then offer. . ." (Rashi).
—   tragedy (Saadia).
11:1   God spoke . . . This explains 7:21. Narrative continues in 16:1.
—   Of all the animals . . . See Deuteronomy 14:3-21.

³ Among mammals, you may eat [any one] that has true hooves* that are   **11**
cloven and that brings up its cud.

⁴ However, among the cud-chewing, hoofed animals, these are the ones
that you may not eat:

The camel shall be unclean to you although it brings up its cud, since it
does not have a true hoof.*

⁵ The hyrax* shall be unclean to you although it brings up its cud, since it
does not have a true hoof.

⁶ The hare* shall be unclean to you although it brings up its cud, since it
does not have a true hoof.

⁷ The pig shall be unclean to you although it has a true hoof which is
cloven, since it does not chew its cud.

⁸ Do not eat the flesh of any of these animals. [At this time]* do not touch
their carcasses, since they are unclean to you.

⁹ This is what you may eat of all that is in the water:

You may eat any creature that lives in the water, whether in seas or rivers,*
as long as it has fins and scales.

¹⁰ [On the other hand], all creatures in seas and rivers that do not have fins

---

11:3   **true hooves** (Saadia; Rashbam; Ibn Ezra; Ibn Janach; Ralbag). *Maphreseth parsah* in Hebrew. Or, "that
has cloven hooves" (Targum; Rashi; Radak, *Sherashim*).

—   **that are cloven** (Saadia, etc.). Or, "completely split" (Rashi; Radak, *Sherashim*).

11:4   **does not have a true hoof** (see 11:3). The hooves of the camel are so reduced that they are like claws, and
the padded soles support most of the weight. Some, however, understand the padded sole to be the
"hoof" here, and translate it, "does not have a cloven hoof" (Rashi).

11:5   **hyrax.** *Hyrax syriacus* or *Procavia
capens syriaca.* Shafan in
Hebrew; *chiorogryllios* in Greek,
(Septuagint); *tafan* in Arabic.
The hyrax is a small mammal,
around 20 inches long, living
in the Negev mountains. It has
a flexible tail-less body, and
short feet, covered with elastic

           Hyrax   **Jerboa**

pads. It nests in the clefts of rocks (Psalms 104:18), and lives in small groups (Proverbs 30:26). Since it
has a maw like a ruminant, it is considered to "bring up its cud."

     Saadia similarly translates it into the Arabic *wabr,* denoting the hyrax or rock badger (cf. Malbim).
Other sources translate it as coney or jerboa.

11:6   **hare.** or rabbit. *Arneveth* in Hebrew. *Dasypous* in Greek (Septuagint), literally, "hairy foot," but translated
as *lepus,* a hare, in Latin (Vulgate). This is the angora rabbit (*Dryctolagus cuniculus*) whose wool is prized
(*Shabbath* 27a). It could be considered to "bring up its cud" since it regurgitates its food in the early
morning hours and then eats it again.

11:8   **At this time.** In the desert the Israelites had to maintain a standard of purity; cf. Numbers 5:2. Similarly,
during festivals when the people gathered in Jerusalem, they were forbidden to defile themselves (*Rosh
HaShanah* 16b; Rashbam). Although this was not actually a negative commandment, it would render a
person unclean (Ramban).

11:9   **seas or rivers.** Salt or fresh water (*Midrash HaGadol*; Ralbag).

11 and scales, whether they are small aquatic animals* or other aquatic creatures,* must be avoided* by you. ¹¹ They will [always]* be something to be
shunned. You must avoid them by not eating their flesh. ¹² Every aquatic creature without fins and scales must be shunned by you.

¹³ These are the flying animals that you must avoid. Since they are to be
avoided, do not eat any [of the following]:

The eagle,* the ossifrage,* the osprey,* ¹⁴ the kite,* the vulture* family,
¹⁵ the entire raven family,* ¹⁶ the ostrich,* the owl,* the gull,* the hawk* family,

---

11:10 small aquatic animals (Rashi). *Sheretz haMayim* in Hebrew. Some say that this expression denotes animals
that reproduce assexually (Ibn Ezra). It may possibly include all invertebrates.

— **other aquatic creatures.** Larger creatures (Rashi), or those that reproduce sexually (Ibn Ezra). This
includes aquatic mammals (*Sifra*).

— **avoided.** *Sheketz* in Hebrew. Also denoting vermin, or something that is abhorrent, detested, shunned,
repulsive, or loathesome.

11:11 always. Even when the laws of purity do not apply. (Cf. Ralbag; above, 11:8).

11:13 eagle. *Nesher* in Hebrew; *aetos* in Greek (Septuagint); *aigle* in French (Chizzkuni). It is described as having
large wings and long pinions (Ezekiel 17:2,3) and living long (Psalms 103:5).

Some sources, however, point out that the eagle does not fit the description of the *nesher* given in the
Talmud (*Tosafoth, Chullin* 63a, s.v. *Netz*). Moreover, the *nesher* is described in scripture as bald (Micah
1:16), and as a carrion-eating bird (Job 39:27-30). Therefore, some identify the *nesher* as the griffin vulture (*Gyps fulvus*), the largest carnivorous bird in Israel, with a wing span that often reaches as much as 10
feet.

— **ossifrage.** *Peres* in Hebrew; *grypha* in Greek (Septuagint); *gryphum* in Latin. Identified as the ossifrage
(King James), which is Latin for bone breaker (cf. *Toledoth Yitzchak*); *oscopla* in Old French (Chizzkuni);
akav in Arabic (Saadia; Ibn Ezra; Ibn Janach; Radak, *Sherashim*). The ossifrage (*Gypaetus barbatus grandis*)
is the largest European bird of prey, ranging in the mountainous regions from the Pyrenees to India, and
resembling both the eagle and the vulture. However, the Torah is not naming exact species, but
broad categories.

The Talmud describes the *peres* as living in uninhabited regions (*Chullin* 62b). Some identify it with
the bearded vulture (*Gypaetus barbatus*) that lives in the Holy Land.

— **osprey.** *Azniyah* in Hebrew; *aliaietos* in Greek (Septuagint); *orfraie* in French (Chizzkuni). The osprey, sea
eagle or fish hawk (*Pandion haliaetus*) is a large hawk that feeds on fish. It is found far from people (*Chullin*
62a), and in ancient times, dusters were made from its wings (*Kelim* 17:14; Rambam *ad loc.*)

Other sources identify the *azniyah* with the albatross (*abitroce* in Old Spanish; *Toledoth Yitzchak*).
Others say that is is the black vulture, of which two species live in the Holy Land, *Aegypius tracheliotus*,
which has a bright-colored belly, and the rare *Aegypius monachus*, which is dark brown.

— **kite.** *Da'ah* in Hebrew, *ra'ah* in Deuteronomy 14:13 (*Chullin* 63b; *Yad, Maakhaloth Assuroth* 1:14 Ralbag).
Iktinos in Greek (Septuagint); *milvus* in Latin (Vulgate); *chada* in Arabic (Saadia; Ibn Janach). The kite
(*Milvus migrans*) is a hawklike bird that eats mice, hares and carrion. It is thus described as flocking over
corpses (Isaiah 34:15), and grabbing meat from the hand (*Bava Metzia* 24b).

Other sources, however, identify the *da'ah* with the vulture (Ralbag; *Toledoth Yitzchak*), *vastoir* in Old
French (Chizzkuni).

— **vulture** *Ayah* in Hebrew; *gyph* in Greek (Septuagint); a bird like the vulture or buzzard, (cf. Ibn Janach).
Other sources translate it into Old Spanish as *agasa* (Radak, *Sherashim*), *ansa* (Ralbag) or *garsa*, which have
variously been identified with the goose, magpie or woodpecker. Saadia translates it as *tzadi*, a kind of
owl.

11:15 raven family. Or crow family. *Orev* in Hebrew; *corbeau* in French (*Tosafoth, Chullin* 62a, s.v. *Mipney*; Chizzkuni).

11:16 ostrich. *Bath yaanah* in Hebrew; *stouthion* in Greek (Septuagint); *autruche* in French (Chizzkuni). The Targum translates it as *naamitha*, and the Mishnah notes that vessels were made of its large eggs (*Kelim* 17:14;
Hai Gaon, Rosh, Bertenoro, *ad loc.*).

The scripture describes the *bath yaanah* as living in desolate places (Isaiah 34:13), and emitting a
mournful cry (Micah 1:8; cf. Radak, *Sherashim*; Ralbag; *Toledoth Yitzchak*). Therefore, some identify it

PLATE 24. NON-KOSHER BIRDS (A)

Little Owl   Cormorant   Fish Owl

Ibis   Long Eared Owl   Swan

Pelican   Magpie   Egyptian Vulture

Stork   Heron   Hoopoe

PLATE 25. NON-KOSHER BIRDS (B)

[17] the falcon,* the cormorant,* the ibis,* [18] the swan,* the pelican,* the   11
magpie,* [19] the stork,* the heron* family, the hoopoe,* and the bat.*
   [20] Every flying insect* that uses four legs for walking* shall be avoided by
you. [21] The only flying insects with four walking legs that you may eat are
those which have knees extending above their feet,* [using these longer legs] to

with the owl, particularly the dark desert eagle owls (*Bubo bubo ascalaphus*), which call back and forth, as if answering (*anah*) one another.

— **owl.** Tachmas in Hebrew; *glaux* in Greek (Septuagint); *yiyah* in Old French (Chizzkuni); *ofula* in Old Spanish (Ralbag); *kh'taf* in Arabic (Saadia).
   Others identify it with the falcon (*Falco tinnunculus kestrel*) which lives in the Holy Land.

— **gull.** Shachaf in Hebrew. *laros* in Greek (Septuagint); *moison* in Old French (Chizzkuni, equivalent to the modern French *mouette*). The gull is commonly found in the Holy Land.

— **hawk.** Netz in Hebrew; *ierax* in Greek (Septuagint); *osproir* in Old French (Rashi); *esparvel* in Old Spanish (Radak, *Sherashim*; Ralbag). Some sources question this (*Tosafoth, Chullin* 63a) and identify the *netz* with the gosshawk, *astoro* in Old Spanish (*Arukh*; Radak, *ibid.*).

11:17 falcon. (Radak, *Sherashim*; Ralbag; *Toledoth Yitzchak*). Kos in Hebrew; *onoraotalos* (one rattle) in Greek; *trua* in Latin. Others identify it with the owl, *chouette* in French (Rashi; Targum according to *Arukh*; Chizzkuni). Some identify it with the little owl (*Atene nocta glaux*) known in Arabic as the *bum* (Saadia; Ibn Janach).

— **cormorant.** Shalakh in Hebrew; *katarrakues* in Greek; *mergulus* in Latin; *cormoiesa* in Old French (Chizzkuni). The Talmud notes that the *shalakh* is a bird that catches fish from the sea (*Chullin* 63a). Other sources identify it with a species of owl, *hibou* or *chouette* in French (Rashi). This may be the fish owl (*Ketupa zeylonensis*) which feeds in the Kinnereth.

— **ibis.** Yanshuf in Hebrew; *ibis* in Greek. Other sources identify it as a falcon (*Arukh*, s.v. *Gaz*). Still others say that it is a species of owl (Radak, *Sherashim*), possibly the little owl, *chevenche* or *cavant* in French (Chizzkuni). According to other sources, it is the long-eared owl (*asio otus*) which lives in Edom (Isaiah 34:11), and winters in the Holy Land.

11:18 swan. Tinshemeth in Hebrew; *kuknos* in Greek; *cycnus* in Latin. Other sources identify it as a bat, *chauve-souris* in French (Rashi; Chizzkuni). Still others say that it is a kind of owl, *chouette* in French (Rashi, *Chullin* 63a); *suetta* in Old Spanish (Radak, *Sherashim*; Ralbag). This is thought to be the barn screech owl (*Tyto alba*).

— **pelican.** Ka'ath in Hebrew; *pelekon* in Greek; *kuk* in Arabic and Aramaic (*Chullin* 63a; Saadia; Radak, *Sherashim*). Also given as *kik* in Aramaic (*Shabbath* 21a), which is identified as a water bird (*Arukh*). However, some challenge this, since the *ka'ath* is seen as living in the desert (Psalms 120:7) and inhabiting ruins (Isaiah 34:11, Zechariah 2:14) (Ibn Janach). It is also seen as a bird that vomits up its prey (Chizzkuni; *Toledoth Yitzchak*), and this description fits the little desert owl (*Athena noctua saharae*).

— **magpie** or pie (Chizzkuni). Racham in Hebrew; *rachamah* in Deuteronomy 14:17; *porphorion* in Greek. Some sources identify it with the Egyptian vulture (*Neophron percnopterus*), *rakham* in Arabic (Saadia). This is the smallest vulture in the Holy Land, and it flocks on carrion and eats insects.

11:19 stork. Chasidah in Hebrew; *asida* in Septuagint; *cigogne* in French (Rashi; Chizzkuni; cf. *Teshuvoth HaRosh* 20:20). It is a bird that is known to live in juniper trees in Lebanon (cf. Psalms 104:17). According to some authorities, however, the *chasida* is not the stork, because the stork is a kosher bird (Rabbenu Yerocham, *Toledoth Adam VeChavah* 15:21, 132b).

— **heron.** (Rashi; Chizzkuni). Anapha in Hebrew; *cheradrois* in Greek.

— **hoopoe.** Dukhiphath in Hebrew; *epops* in Greek; *upupa* in Latin. The hoopoe is a bird with a large red and black crest, possibly *cresta* in Spanish (*Toledoth Yitzchak*) and *harupa* in Old French (Rashi; Chizzkuni); *hadhad* in Arabic (Saadia). It may also be identified with the mountain cock or capercaillie, the largest member of the grouse family (cf. Rashi, *Chullin* 63a, who translates it as *puaon chalbia*).

— **bat.** Atalef in Hebrew; *nukteris* in Greek; *khepash* in Arabic (Saadia); *grot* in Old French (Chizzkuni). However, see note on *tinshemeth*.

11:20 flying insect. (Rashi; Ramban; cf. *Makkoth* 16b). Sheretz ha-of in Hebrew.

— **that uses four legs for walking.** Or, "that walks like a quadruped." Insects have six legs, but members of the grasshopper family use four for walking and two for hopping (cf. *Ezrath Kohanim* on *Sifra*).

11:21 knees extending . . . Among grasshoppers, the knees of the hoppers protrude prominently above the rest of the foot.

11   hop on the ground. ²² Among these, you may [only] eat members of the red
locust* family, the yellow locust* family, the spotted grey locust* family, and
the white locust* family. ²³ All other flying insects with four feet [for walking]
must be avoided by you.*

²⁴ There are [also]* animals that will defile you so that anyone touching
their carcasses will be unclean until evening.* ²⁵ Furthermore, anyone lifting*
their carcasses will have to immerse [even]* his clothing, and then remain
unclean until evening. ²⁶ Thus, every animal that has true hooves, but is not
cloven-hoofed* and does not bring up its cud, is unclean to you, and anyone
touching [its flesh]* shall become unclean.

²⁷ [Similarly],* every animal that walks on its paws* among four-footed

11:22 **red locust.** *Arbeh* in Hebrew; *grad* in Arabic (Saadia). According to
Yemenite traditions, this reddish locust is permitted (Yosef Kapach,
Halikhoth Teimon, Jerusalem, 1968, p. 218). More generally, *arbeh*
denotes the Sudanese or desert locust (*Scistocerca gregaria*) which
reaches the Holy Land in large numbers.

Red Locust

—   **yellow locust.** *Sal'am* in Hebrew; *Rashona* in Aramaic (*Chullin* 65a);
daba or *dabai* in Arabic (Saadia; Ibn Janach). The yellow locust is
permitted according to Yemenite tradition (*Halikhoth Teimon*). The
Talmud describes the *sal'am* as having a head which is bald in front
(*gabachath*; see 13:42) and long (*Chullin* 65b; *Yad, Maakhaloth Assuroth* 1:22; cf. *Avodah Zarah* 37a). It is therefore sometimes translated
as "bald locust" or "long-headed locust." This locust, the *rashon*, is
said to resemble a human embryo in its first stages of development
(*Niddah* 25a; *Arukh*).

Yellow Locust

—   **spotted grey locust.** *Chargol* in Hebrew; *nippulah* in Aramaic; *chartziyiya* in Arabic, according to Yemenite
tradition (*Halikhoth Teimon*). The Talmud describes this locust as having a tail (*Chullin* 65a); some therefore identify it with the long-horned grasshopper (*tettigonidae*), since the female has a long protuberance
with which it lays eggs. The Septuagint translates *chargol* as *ophiomaches* which literally means "snake
fighter." It may have been given this name because of its long snake-like body or tail. The name also
denotes a large insect, perhaps a giant grasshopper, as is also suggested by its Aramaic name, *nippulah*,
which suggests a *nifla*, Hebrew for giant. Its large eggs were used as amulets (*Shabbath* 6:10).
    Some sources (King James; JPS) translate *chargol* as cricket, but this is incorrect, because the cricket is
wingless, and the Talmud clearly states that all permitted locusts have wings that cover the body (*Chullin*
59a).

—   **white locust.** *Chagav* in Hebrew; *gandav* in Arabic (Saadia). According to
Yemenite tradition, this is a small white locust (*Halikhkhoth Teimon*). From
scripture it also appears to be the smallest of the locusts (cf. Numbers 13:33).

11:23 **All other . . .** Even of the locust family. Since there are questions regarding
identification, most Jews do not eat locusts at all (*Turey Zahav, Yoreh Deah*
85:1). According to Yemenite tradition, only locusts that come in swarms (cf.
Proverbs 30:27) are permitted, but not those that live separately (*Halikhoth Teimon*). This would exclude
most ordinary grasshopper species.

White Locust

11:24 **There are also** (*Sifra*; Rashi). Literally, "and to these" (the following).

—   **until evening.** After immersing, as in next verse.

11:25 **lifting.** This imparts a greater degree of impurity, since touching a carcass merely defiles the body, while
lifting it also defiles the clothing (*Kelim* 1:2).

—   **immerse even.** And certainly his body. See Exodus 19:10, below 15:5.

11:26 **but is not . . .** Like the horse (Rashbam; Ralbag). Or, "that has cloven hooves, but they are not split
below", like the camel (Rashi). See 11:3,4.

—   **its flesh.** (*Sifra*; Ibn Ezra).

11:27 **Similarly** (cf. Ramban; *Yad, Avoth HaTumah* 1:2).

—   **paws** (Rashi). Or, " hands" like an ape (*Sifra*).

animals shall be unclean to you, and anyone touching its carcass shall be   11
unclean until evening. ²⁸ [Furthermore], one who lifts its carcass must
immerse [even] his clothing and then remain unclean until evening. They are
unclean to you [in this respect].*

[34. Smaller Animals]

²⁹ These are the smaller animals* that breed* on land which are unclean to
you: the weasel,* the mouse,* the ferret,* ³⁰ the hedgehog,* the chameleon,*
the lizard,* the snail,* and the mole.*

³¹ These are the small animals that are unclean to you; whoever touches

---

11:28 **in this respect** (Rashi).

11:29 **smaller animals** (Rashi on Genesis 1:20). Or, "creeping things" (Ramban on Genesis 1:20). See next
note. The Talmud notes that all these animals have usable hides (*Shabbath* 107a).

— **breed** (Radak, *Sherashim*; Ibn Ezra on Genesis 1:20). Or, "creep" (Targum).

— **weasel.** *Choled* in Hebrew; *galei* in Greek (Septuagint); *mustela* in Latin (Vulgate), Old French (Rashi;
Chizzkuni) and Old Spanish (Radak, *Sherashim*); *belette* in French (Chizzkuni). This is a predatory animal
(*Chullin* 52b). Some sources identify it as a martin or an ermine (*Arukh*, s.v. *glaksinin*).

Other sources, however, indicate that the *choled* or *chuldah* (cf. Targum) is a rat (*Pesachim* 1:2, *Tosefoth
Yom Tov ad loc.*) *khadar* in Arabic (Ramban *ad loc.*). Still others translate it as mole or mole-rat (*Arukh*), *khe-
lad* in Arabic (Saadia; Ibn Janach). The Talmud also notes that the *chulda* bores under ground and
undermines houses (*Bava Kama* 80a; *Bava Bathra* 19b; *Chullin* 20b). *Targum Yonathan* translates *choled* as
kirkushta, which means a field mouse (*Mossef LeArukh*).

— **mouse.** *Akhbar* in Hebrew; *mus* in Greek. Some sources appear to include also the rat (Chizzkuni; *MeAm
Lo'ez*). In Arabic, the word denotes the jerboa.

— **ferret.** *Tzav* in Hebrew; *huron* in
Spanish (Ralbag); *faruita* in Old
French (Chizzkuni; cf. Rashi).
This is an animal closely related
to the grison, *graisant* in Old
Spanish (Radak, *Sherashim*). We
have preferred this translation,
since it groups all the mammals
together.

Ferret   Salamander

The Septuagint translates *tzav* as *krokodelos chersaios*, literally, "land crocodile." This follows Talmudic
sources that liken it to a salamander or snake (*Sifra* 6:5; *Chullin* 127a), related to another large lizard, the
chardon (*Targum Yonathan*; *Yerushalmi, Berakhoth* 8:6). This is identified with the *chab* in Arabic (Saadia; Ibn
Janach), the dab lizard (*Uromastix aegyptius*). Others identify it with the thorntail lizard (*Uromastix spinipes*).

Other sources identify the *tzav* with the toad (Rashi), *kröte* in German (Hirsch). Some say that the *tzav*
is a tortoise (*MeAm Lo'ez*) since it is like a covered wagon, which is also called *tzav* (see Numbers 7:8;
Maharzav on *BeMidbar Rabbah* 12:17).

11:30 **hedgehog.** *Anakah* in Hebrew; *yala* in
Aramaic (Targum; *Bava Bathra* 4a);
herison in French (Rashi; Chizzkuni),
erizo in Spanish (Ralbag). Others
apparently identify it with the beaver
(Radak, *Sherashim*). The Septuagint
translates it as *mugale*, a mole, shrew
mouse or field mouse.

Other sources, however, translate
it as gecko, *warel* in Arabic (Saadia).

Hedgehog   Gecko

The gecko is a reptile of the order of *lacertilia*, up to 5″ long, with a soft speckled hide (cf. *Chullin* 9:2).
Anakah denotes groaning, and the gecko makes a groaning sound.

11   them when they are dead shall remain unclean until evening.*

    ³² If any of these dead animals falls on anything, such as wooden vessels, clothing, leather goods, sacks, or any other article with which work is done, then [that article] must be immersed in a mikvah, and remain unclean until evening, whereupon it becomes clean.

    ³³ If any of [these dead animals] falls on the inside* of a clay vessel, then anything inside it becomes unclean,* and [the vessel itself] shall be broken.*
³⁴ Thus,* any usual* food that has [once]* been wet with water* shall become

—   **chameleon.** *Ko'ach* in Hebrew; *chamaileon* in Greek (Septuagint). Other sources simply identify it as a lizard (Radak, quoting Rashi), possibly a poisonous one (Ralbag).

    Other sources translate it into Arabic as *charon* (Saadia; Ibn Janach; Radak, *Sherashim*); see note on *tzav*. This is said to be the monitor or monitor lizard (*Varanus griseus*), the largest reptile in the Holy Land, growing as long as 4 feet. Living on the coast, the Negev, and Arabah, it eats rodents and reptiles. Due to a transposition, it is possible that this is the "land crocodile" mentioned in the Septuagint.

Monitor

—   **lizard.** *Leta'ah* in Hebrew; *leisarda* in Old French (Rashi); or "a small lizard," *legartisa* (*Toledoth Yitzchak*), or *legramosa* in Spanish (Radak, *Sherashim*; cf. Ralbag; Chizzkuni). The Talmud notes that its tail moves when cut off (*Oholoth* 1:6) and then it is paralyzed by heat but revived with water (*Pesachim* 88b). It is probably a member of the family *lacertidae*, of which four species live in the Holy Land.

    In Arabic, it is translated as *echaya* (Saadia), the white lizard, or *abretz* (Ibn Janach; Rambam on *Oholoth* 1:7), the great gecko. The Septuagint translates it as *chalaboties*, from *chala*, a rock or claw, and hence the rock lizard or clawed lizard.

—   **snail.** *Chomet* in Hebrew; *limicon* or *limsa* in Old French (Rashi; Chizzkuni; Radak, *Sherashim*; cf. *Chaggigah* 11a; *Ikkarim* 3:1. However, see Bertenoro on *Shabbath* 14:1).

    Other sources, however, translate *chomet* as lizard, *saura* in Greek; *lacerta* in Latin. In Arabic it is rendered as *charba* (Saadia; Ibn Janach), most probably the skink. The skink is a lizard with small legs, of the family *scincidae*, of which there are four varieties in the Holy Land.

Skink

—   **mole.** *Tinshemeth* in Hebrew; *talpa* in Latin and Old French (Rashi; Chizzkuni; Ralbag; Radak, *Sherashim*. The Targum, too, translates it as *ashuth* which is a mole (cf. *Moed Katan* 6a).

    Other sources translate it as salamander (*Targum Yonathan*). In Arabic it is rendered as *sambratz* (Saadia), *sam abratz* (Ibn Janach), or *darbutz* (Ralbag), a large-headed lizard that burrows underground, probably a type of gecko.

11:31   **shall remain unclean** . . . After immersion in a mikvah.

11:33   **inside.** A clay vessel can become clean only if it is touched on the inside, not on the outside. Also, if it is not touched, the contaminating article is merely inside its space, it is still contaminated (Rashi; *Chullin* 24b; *Sifra*; *Yad, Kelim* 13:1).

—   **anything inside it** . . . Primarily food and drink, as below, but not other vessels (*Sifra*; *Pesachim* 20b; *Yad, Kelim* 13:3).

—   **shall be broken.** A clay vessel thus becomes clean when broken (*Yad, Kelim* 19:1). It cannot, however, be purified by immersion (*Sifra*; *Yad, Mikvaoth* 1:3). See above, 6:21.

11:34   **Thus.** If it is in a clay vessel (Rashi). Certainly if it is in contact with the dead animal itself.

—   **usual** Only human food can become contaminated (*Yad, Tumath Okh'lin* 1:1, 3:1).

—   **once.** Even if later dried off. However, food cannot become ritually unclean unless it was wet at some point after it was picked (*Yad, Tumath Okh'lin* 1:2).

—   **water.** The verse can also be translated, "Any usual food that has been wet with water or any other usual beverages. . ."(Rashi). The ambiguity teaches that as far as readying food to become ritually unclean, other liquids have the same status as water. The other liquids are: dew, olive oil, wine, milk, blood, and honey (*Makhshirim* 6:4; *Yad, loc. cit.*).

unclean. Any usual beverage in a vessel [likewise] becomes unclean.   11

³⁵ Thus, anything upon which their dead bodies fall shall be unclean. In such a case, even an oven or range* is unclean, and must be broken down, since it otherwise remains unclean to you.

³⁶ The only thing that shall [always] remain ritually clean* is a mikvah* of water, whether it is a [man-made] pit or a [natural] spring.* Any other [water]* that comes in contact with the dead bodies [of these animals] shall become unclean.

³⁷ If their dead bodies fall on any edible* seeds that are planted,* [the seeds] remain ritually clean. ³⁸ However, if water* has [once] been placed on [such unplanted]* seeds, and then the dead body of [any of these animals] falls on them, the [seeds] shall be unclean to you.

[35. Other Laws Involving Animals]

³⁹ If any animal that you may eat dies,* anyone touching its carcass shall be unclean until evening.

⁴⁰ Anyone eating something from such a carcass must immerse [even] his clothing, and then remain unclean until evening. Similarly, one who lifts such a carcass shall immerse [even] his clothing and then remain unclean until evening.

⁴¹ Every small animal that breeds on land shall be avoided by you and shall not be eaten. ⁴² Thus, you may not eat any creature that crawls on its belly, or any small animal with four or more feet* that breeds on land. They are [all] things that must be avoided.

11:35 **oven or range.** Made of clay (Rashi). Although other clay utensils cannot become ritually unclean until they are fired, an oven or range can become unclean as soon as it is used (Rash on *Kelim* 5:1). Furthermore, a building normally does not become defiled, but an oven or range can become defiled even though it is built up and attached to the ground; it does not have the status of a building (*Shabbath* 125a; Rash, *Kelim* 5:1).

11:36 **always remain ritually clean.** Therefore, it can be used for purification. As we see below, other water would become unclean upon contact with an unclean body (Malbim; Hirsch; cf. Rashi, *Pesachim* 16a, s.v. *Yihyeh*).

—   **mikvah.** See Isaiah 22:11. Here it is referred to as a "gathering (*mikveh*) of water.

—   **man made pit or...** (*Sifra*).

—   **Any other water...** (cf. Ibn Ezra; Ramban). Thus, no water other than that in a mikvah can be used for purification.

11:37 **edible** (cf. Rashi). If they are not edible, they cannot become unclean (*Yad, Tumath Okh'lin* 1:11, see above, 11:34).

—   **planted.** As long as food is rooted to the ground and has not been picked, it cannot become unclean (*Sifra*; Rashbam, Chizzkuni; *Yad, Tumath Okh'lin* 2:1). Moreover, even after it is picked, it cannot become unclean until at some point it becomes wet (Rashi). This is true even if it is touched by the dead animal itself (Ramban).

11:38 **water.** Or the other liquids mentioned in 11:34.

—   **unplanted...** (Rashi).

11:39 **dies.** Without being ritually slaughtered.

11:42 **or more feet.** Literally, "or many feet." Some say that this denotes the centipede (*Chullin* 67b; Rashi).

11   ⁴³ Do not make yourselves disgusting* [by eating] any small creature that
breeds. Do not defile yourselves with them, because it will make you spiritually insensitive.* ⁴⁴ For I am God your Lord, and since I am holy, you must
[also] make yourselves holy and remain sanctified. Therefore, do not defile
your souls [by eating] any small animal that lives on the land.

 ⁴⁵ I am God, and I brought you out of Egypt to be your God. Therefore,
since I am holy, you must [also] remain holy.

 ⁴⁶ This then is the law concerning mammals, birds, aquatic creatures and
lower forms of terrestrial animals. ⁴⁷ [With this law, you will be able] to distinguish between the unclean and the clean, between edible animals and animals
which may not be eaten.

Tazria   תַּזְרִיעַ

[36. Childbirth]

12   ¹ God spoke to Moses,* telling him ² to speak to the Israelites, relating the
following:

 When a woman conceives and gives birth to a boy, she shall be ritually
unclean for seven days, just as she is unclean during the time of separation
when she has her period.* ³ On the eighth day, [the child's] foreskin shall be
circumcised.* ⁴ Then, for 33 additional days,* she shall have a waiting period
during which her blood is ritually clean.* Until this purification period is
complete, she shall not touch anything holy and shall not enter the sanctuary.

 ⁵ If she gives birth to a girl, she shall have for two weeks the same ritually
unclean status as during her menstrual period. Then, for 66 days after that,*
she shall have a waiting period during which her blood is ritually clean.

 ⁶ When her purification period for a son or a daughter is complete, she
shall bring to the priest, to the Communion Tent entrance, a yearling sheep

---

11:43 **disgusting.** Or "shunned."

— **spiritually insensitive** (*Yoma* 39b). Or, "unclean."

12:1 **God spoke . . .** After discussing unclean animals, the Torah now discusses human uncleanness; see 7:21,
11:1.

12:2 **time of separation when she has her period** (Saadia; Rashbam). See below, 15:19-24. Or, "when she has
her periodic discharge" (Rashi); or, "when she has her periodic sickness" (Rashi; Ibn Ezra; Ramban).

12:3 **On the eighth day . . .** See Genesis 17:12

12:4 **for 33 additional days.** Making a total of 40.

— **her blood is ritually clean.** That is, even if the woman experiences vaginal bleeding during this time, she
does not have the status of a menstruant woman (*Niddah* 35b; *Yad, Issurey Biyah* 4:5; Rashbam). The current practice, however, is to consider the woman unclean if she bleeds, even during the latter 33 days
(*Yad, Issurey Biyah* 11:5-7; *Turey Zahav, Yoreh Deah* 194:1).

12:5 **for 66 days after that . . .** Making a total of 80 days.

for a burnt offering, and a young common dove, or a turtle dove* for a sin   12
offering. ⁷ [The priest] shall offer [the sacrifice] before God and atone for [the
woman], thus cleansing her of the blood coming from her womb. This law
applies whether a woman gives birth to a boy or to a girl.

⁸ If [the woman] cannot afford a sheep, she shall bring two turtle doves, or
two young common doves, one for a burnt offering and one for a sin offering.
The priest shall then make atonement for her, and she shall be clean.

[37. The Leprous Curse]

¹ God spoke to Moses and Aaron, saying: 13
² If a person has a [white] blotch,* discoloration* or spot* on the skin of

---

12:6 **a young common dove** . . . See note on 1:14.

13:2 **white blotch.** (cf. Saadia) *Se'eth* in Hebrew. This is a mark of leprosy (see 14:56), which is specifically
described as being white (13:10,19). According to Talmudic tradition, it is the color of clean white wool
(*Negaim* 1:1; *Yad, Tumath Tzaraath* 1:2). According to one opinion, it is the color of the membrane of an
egg (Rabbi Meir, *Negaim* 1:1).

According to many sources, the word *se'eth* comes from the root *nasa* meaning "raised" (cf. Genesis
4:7, 49:3). This is because it appears higher than the skin, even though it is not physically higher (*Sifra*;
cf. Gra *ad loc.*; *Yad, Tumath Tzaraath* 1:7; Rash, *Negaim* 1:1; Radak, *Sherashim*; Chizzkuni; Ralbag). Since
the skin is somewhat translucent, an opaque white patch will appear to be raised (see note on *bahereth*).

According to others, however, a *se'eth* is an actual swelling or raised spot (*Shevuoth* 6b; Raavad on
Tumath Tzaraath 1:7). It may thus be a sort of white wart or mole (Ibn Janach). The Septuagint translates
it as *oulie* which can denote a "barleycorn," hence, possibly, a subcutaneous nodule.

Later, we see that a *bahereth* can turn out to be a "*se'eth* due to a burn" (13:28). It is recognized as a
se'eth by the fact that it does not spread. Similarly, in other places where the *se'eth* is discussed, it is seen as
a mark that does not normally spread (13:10, 10, 43), but is declared unclean for other reasons. Nevertheless, however, if a *se'eth* spreads, it is a sign of uncleanness.

Since *se'eth* is associated with a burn (13:28), some authorities associate it with a burn of inflammation (Ibn Ezra; Radak, *Sherashim*; Ibn Janach; cf. Ramban). Some see the Septuagint's translation of *oulie*
as denoting a scar or cicatrix.

— **discoloration** (cf. Saadia). *Sapachath* in Hebrew. According to Talmudic tradition, this is a secondary type
of mark, of a slightly duller white than a *se'eth* (*Shevuoth* 6b; *Sifra*; Radak, *Sherashim*). According to tradition, it is the color of egg membrane (*Negaim* 1:1; *Yad, Tumath Tzaraath* 1:2). According to
some, it is the color of white wool, brighter than *se'eth* but duller than *bahereth* (Rabbi Meir, *Negaim* 1:1;
Tifereth Yisrael ad loc. 1:8).

According to some sources, *sapachath* denotes a scab (Ibn Ezra), a pustule (Radak, *Sherashim*), an erup-
tion (Ibn Janach), a birthmark (*Ibid.*; Septuagint, *siemasia* in Greek) or a cuticular crust. Although it is
seen as a leprous mark (14:56), it is not mentioned elsewhere in this section. The word *sapachath*, however, is related to *mispachath*, which is seen as a clean mark (13:6,7,8). Some interpret *sapachath* as a
secondary or external symptom (*HaKethav VeHaKabbalah*).

— **spot** (Saadia). *Bahereth* in Hebrew. Rashi also translates it as *chabarburah*, a spot (cf. Jeremiah 13:23), *tiar*
in Old French (*tache* in Modern French). It is a highly visible spot (Ibn Ezra), that can be seen from a
distance. The Septuagint thus translates it as *telaugema* which means a shiny or bright spot that can be
seen from a distance.

The Torah explicitly describes a *bahereth* as a spot (13:38,39), that is white (13:4) or bright pink
(13:19,24). According to Talmudic tradition, it is as white as snow, like Miriam's leprosy (Numbers
12:10; cf. Exodus 4:6; *Negaim* 1:1; See *Sifra* 2:2 on 13:4; Radak, *Sherashim*).

The Talmud describes a *bahereth* as appearing lower than the skin (see 13:4; *Shevuoth* 6b; *Sifra*, Rashi).
This appears to indicate that it is a spot that is more transparent than the surrounding skin, and hence
appears deeper (*Yerioth Sh'lomo* 2:46b; *HaKethav VeHaKabbalah*).

13 his body, and it [is suspected]* of being a mark of the leprous curse* on his
    skin, he shall be brought to Aaron, or to one of his descendants, who are the
    priests. ³ The priest shall examine the mark on [the person's] skin, and if the
    hair* on the mark has turned white, and the mark appears to have penetrated
    the skin,* then it is the leprous curse. As soon as the priest sees it, he shall
    declare it unclean.

    ⁴ However, if there is a [white] spot on the skin, but it does not appear to
    have penetrated the skin* and its hair has not turned white, then the priest
    shall quarantine* the affected person* for seven days. ⁵ The priest shall
    examine [the person] on the seventh day and if the mark has not increased in
    size, the priest shall quarantine [the victim] for an additional seven days. ⁶ The
    priest shall examine [him again] on the seventh day, and if the mark has
    faded* or* if it has not spread, the priest shall declare [the person] clean, since
    it is merely a white discoloration.* [The person] must immerse [his body and]
    clothing, and he is then clean.

    ⁷ However, if the white discoloration increases in size on the skin after it
    was shown to the priest, who purified it, [the person] must show it to the priest
    again. ⁸ If the priest sees that the rash has increased in size on the skin, [he]
    shall declare [the person] unclean, since it is the leprous curse.

—   **and it is suspected** . . . (Chizzkuni). Or, "[combining to] form a leprous mark on his skin" (*Sifra*, Hirsch).
       This teaches that the total area of the mark must be as great as a large bean (*garis*) (*Negaim* 6:1; *Yad,*
       Tumath Tzaraath 1:7). Thus, it must be approximately ¾ inch or 2 centimeters in diameter (*Darkey Teshuvah*
       190:40; cf. *Yad, Issurey Biyah* 9:6; *Yoreh Deah* 190:5).
—   **leprous curse.** *Tzara'ath* in Hebrew; *lepra* in Greek (Septuagint). The "leprosy" or "leprous curse" men-
       tioned in the Torah is not Hansen's disease caused by the germ *mycobacterium leprae.* Rather it was a physi-
       cal symptom of a spiritual defect, occurring primarily in individuals on a high spiritual level, whose
       body functions were subject to their spiritual state (cf. *Yad, Tumath Tzaraath* 16:10).Thus, a gentile having
       a leprous mark is not unclean (*Negaim* 3:1), and a bridegroom may delay having it examined (*Negaim*
       3:2). It is seen as resulting from slander (cf. Numbers 12:10).
13:3   **hair.** At least two hairs (*Sifra*; Rashi; *Yad, Tumath Tzaraath* 2:1; *HaKethav VeHaKabbalah*).
—   **to have penetrated the skin.** Literally, "deeper than the skin." Or, "in contrast to the skin" (*Sifra*; Rashi).
       Some say that this is true of all the above mentioned types of marks, *se'eth, sapachath* and *bahereth* (*Yad,*
       Tumath Tzaraath 1:7), while others say that it does not apply to *se'eth* which is a swelling (Raavad, *ibid.*;
       Ramban on 13:4).
13:4   **does not appear** . . . Or, "is not in strong contrast to. . ." (Chizzkuni; cf. *Targum Yonathan; HaKethav*
       VeHaKabbalah).
—   **quarantine** (Radak, *Sherashim*). See Numbers 12:14,15. In a separate house (Rashi). This is because the
       person is now unclean (*Yad, Tumath Tzaraath* 10:10; *Megillah* 8b; cf. *Tosafoth, Moed Katan* 7b, *Amar Rabbi*).
       According to others, the word *hisgir* here means that the priest shall suspend judgment regarding the
       case (Saadia; cf. Chizzkuni). Others translate it, "the priest shall encircle the mark" meaning that he
       should draw a line around the leprous mark to determine later whether or not it has expanded (Ibn
       Janach; Rosh, quoted in Tur on 13:8; *HaKethav VeHaKabbalah*). See 14:38.
—   **the affected person** (Ibn Ezra; see Saadia on 13:12). Or the mark (see previous note).
13:6   **faded** (Rashi). Or, "faded [but still a leprous mark] and. . ." (Ramban; see next note).
—   **or.** If it is not white enough to be considered leprosy, then even if it spreads, it is not unclean (*Yad,*
       Tumath Tzaraath 1:11; cf. Mizrachi).
—   **discoloration.** *Mispachath* in Hebrew. Some say that this is a type of psoriasis.

[38. Healthy Skin in a Spot]

13

⁹When a person [is suspected of] having the leprous curse, he shall be brought to the priest. ¹⁰ If the priest sees that there is a white blotch on the skin, and it has turned the hair white or* that there is an area of healthy skin* inside* the blotch, ¹¹ then it is a chronic leprosy* in his skin, and the priest must declare it unclean. He shall not quarantine it, since it is obviously unclean.

¹² [This is the law] if the leprous area spreads over the skin, so that it covers all the skin of the afflicted person from head to foot, wherever the priest can see it.* ¹³ When the priest sees that the leprous discoloration has covered all [the person's] skin, he shall declare the afflicted person clean. As long as he has turned completely white, he is clean.

¹⁴ However, on the day that healthy skin appears on [the person] he is unclean. ¹⁵ When the priest sees the healthy skin, he shall declare [the person] unclean. The healthy skin is a sign of uncleanness, since it is the leprous curse.

¹⁶ If the healthy skin turns white again, [the person] shall come back to the priest. ¹⁷ When the priest sees that the afflicted person has turned [completely] white, the priest shall declare him clean, and he is then ritually pure.

[39. Leprosy on an Infection]

¹⁸ [This is the law] when there is an infection* on the body and it heals. ¹⁹ If a white blotch or bright pink* spot then develops where the infection was, it must be shown to the priest. ²⁰ The priest shall examine it, and if it appears to have penetrated the skin and its hair has turned white, it is the leprous curse that has erupted over the infection.

²¹ However, if the priest examines it, and it does not have white hair, nor does it appear to have penetrated the skin since it is a dull white,* the priest

---

13:10 **or.** (Ramban).
— **healthy skin** (Ibn Janach). Some say it must be the original color of the skin (Rash, Bertenoro on *Negaim* 4:2), while other sources indicate that it can be any color but white (*Tosefta, Negaim* 1:2; *Bertenoro, on Negaim* 6:6; *Yad, Tumath Tzaraath* 3:2), even a dull white (*Tosefoth Yom Tov* on *Negaim* 6:6). The area of healthy skin must be as large as a lentil, approximately ⅓ inch in diameter (*Negaim* 6:5; *Yad, Tumath Tzaraath* 3:1).
— **inside.** (*Yad, Tumath Tzaraath* 3:3).
13:11 **chronic leprosy.** Or, "old leprosy" (Rashi).
13:12 **can see it.** But not in hidden places or crevices of the body (*Sifra*; cf. *Negaim* 2:4; *Yad, Tumath Tzaraath* 9:12).
13:18 **infection** (cf. Exodus 9:9). A pustule, boil or blister (Ibn Janach: *Tifereth Yisrael, Negaim* 9:1). This can be caused by anything other than a burn (*Negaim* 9:1).
13:19 **bright pink.** Like a cup of milk containing as much as 16 drops of blood (*Shevuoth* 6a; *Yad, Tumath Tzaraath* 1:4; cf. *Negaim* 1:2). The average cup is a *revi'ith*, which is 75 ml. while an average "drop" is 0.147 ml. (cf. *Tifereth Yisrael Mareh Cohen* 1:4). The color is therefore like a mixture of milk containing up to approximately 3% blood.
13:21 **dull white.** Or "faded."

13   shall quarantine the person for seven days. ²² If this spot then increases in size
      on the skin, the priest shall declare it unclean, since it is the curse.

      ²³ However, if the spot remains stable and does not expand, it is scar
      tissue* from the infection, and the priest shall declare it clean.*

[40. Leprosy on a Burn]

      ²⁴ [This is the law] when there is a burn on the body, and a bright pink or
      white spot appears where the burn has healed. ²⁵ The priest shall examine it,
      and if the hair on the spot has turned white, and [the spot] appears to have
      penetrated the skin, it is the leprous curse breaking out on the burn. Since it is
      the leprous curse, the priest shall declare it unclean.

      ²⁶ However, if the priest examines it, and the spot does not have white
      hair, and it is a dull white which does not appear to have penetrated the skin,
      then the priest shall quarantine it for seven days. ²⁷ On the seventh day, the
      priest shall examine it, and if it has increased in size on the skin, the priest
      shall declare it unclean, since it is the leprous curse.

      ²⁸ However, if the spot remains stable and does not increase in size, or if it
      has faded,* then it is a discoloration* due to the burn. Since it is merely scar
      tissue from the burn, the priest shall declare it clean.

[41. Bald Patches]

      ²⁹ [This is the law] if a man or woman has an affliction on the head or
      beard. ³⁰ The priest shall examine the affliction, and if it appears to have pene-
      trated the skin and has fine* blond* hairs in it, the priest shall declare it
      unclean. Such a bald mark* is a sign of the leprous curse on the head or
      beard.

13:23 **scar tissue** (Targum; Rashi; *HaKethav VeHaKabbalah*; Hirsch). Or, "inflammation" (Ibn Ezra; Ibn Janach; Radak, *Sherashim*).
—   **clean.** In such a case it need not be quarantined for a second week (*Negaim* 9:1; *Yad, Tumath Tzaraath* 5:4).
13:28 **or if it has faded.** Even if it expands in size.
—   **discoloration.** *Se'eth* in Hebrew. See 13:2.
13:30 **fine.** Short, fine hairs (*Yad, Tumath Tzaraath* 8:4).
—   **blond.** Or "gold" (Ibid).
—   **bald mark.** *Nethek* in Hebrew. This is a spot from which the hair has fallen out, and according to many,
no skin discoloration is required (*Yad, Tumath Tzaraath* 8:1; Raavad on *Sifra* 7:7; Ramban; Rash, *Negaim*
3:5; Sforno; cf. Ibn Ezra). According to others, however, there must be some skin discoloration as well
(Raavad on *Tumath Tzaraath* 8:1 from *Tosefta, Negaim* 1:2). Some require the discoloration to be white
(Ralbag), while others say that a *nethek* is a reddish black mark (Saadia), or a blackish mole (Radak,
Sherashim; Ibn Janach).The Septaugint translates *nethek* as *thrausma*, which may denote an area of broken-
off hair. Other sources indicate that it is somewhat like a herpes infection (*Pirkey Moshe* 23). It must be
obvious that the loss is due to a local cause, rather than simple male pattern baldness as below 13:40,41
(Rash on *Negaim* 10:9; *Kesef Mishneh, Tumath Tzaraath* 8:8).
      The *nethek* is a special case, since ordinary white spots do not constitute leprous marks on the head or
beard (*Sifra; Yad, Tumath Tzaraath* 6:1; Rash, Ramban, on *Negaim* 6:8).

³¹ However, if, when the priest examines the bald patch, [the affliction] **13** does not appear to have penetrated the skin, but it does not have black hair in it, the priest shall quarantine the person afflicted by the bald patch for seven days. ³² On the seventh day, the priest shall examine the mark. If the bald mark has not increased in size, and if there is no blond hair in it so that the mark does not appear to have penetrated the skin, ³³ [the person] shall shave himself, without shaving off the bald patch. The priest shall then quarantine [the person having] the bald patch for a second seven day period.

³⁴ The priest shall examine the bald patch on the seventh day, and if the area of fallen hair has not increased in size, or if [the affliction] does not appear to have penetrated the skin, the priest shall declare it clean. [The person] must then immerse his [body and] clothing, and he is clean.

³⁵ However, if the bald patch increases in size after he has cleansed himself, ³⁶ the priest must examine it [again]. If the bald patch has increased in size, the priest need not look for blond hairs, since it is [automatically] unclean.

³⁷ But if the bald patch remains the same, or* if the black hair grows on it, then the bald patch has healed and it is clean. The priest shall declare [the person] clean.

[42. Dull White Spots]

³⁸ If the skin of a man's or woman's body becomes covered with white spots,* ³⁹ the priest shall examine it. If the skin is [merely] covered with dull white spots, it is a simple rash* breaking out on the skin, and it is clean.

[43. Baldness]

⁴⁰ If a man loses the hair on his head,* it is simple baldness, and he is clean. ⁴¹ Similarly, if he loses hair near his face, it is merely a receding hairline and he is clean.

⁴² However, if he has a bright pink mark on his bald spot or where his hairline has receded, it may be* a sign of the leprous curse on his bald spot or hairless forehead. ⁴³ The priest shall examine it, and if the blotch* on his bald

---

13:37 **or** (Chizzkuni; *Yad, Tumath Tzaraath* 8:6).

13:38 **spots.** *Beharoth.* See note on 13:2.

13:39 **rash** (Rashi). *Bohak* in Hebrew. This teaches that no matter how many spots there are, if they are a dull white, and not bright like the marks mentioned in 13:2, then this is not considered a leprous mark (*Yad, Tumath Tzaraath* 1:1). There is, however, a question as to whether or not this is considered "healthy skin" as in 13:10 (*Tosefoth Yom Tov* on *Negaim* 6:6). Some identify *bohak* as vitiligo or leucodermy. The Septuagint translates it as *agopokia,* which seems to indicate a precursor of hair loss.

13:40 **on his head.** That is, toward the back of the head (*Negaim* 10:10).

13:42 **may be** (Saadia).

13:43 **blotch.** *Se'eth;* see note on 13:2.

13   spot or hairless forehead is bright pink, then [it is]* like leprosy on the skin of
his body. 44 The person is considered afflicted by the leprous curse, and he is
unclean. Since he is unclean, and the mark is on his head, the priest must
declare him unclean.

45 When a person has the mark of the leprous curse, his clothing must have
a tear in it,* he must go without a haircut,* and he must cover his head down
to his lips.* "Unclean! Unclean!" he must call out.

46 As long as he has the mark, he shall remain unclean. Since he is unclean,
he must remain alone, and his place shall be outside the camp.

[44. Discoloration of Garments]

47 [This is the law] when a garment has the mark of the leprous curse. It
can be woolen cloth, linen cloth,* 48 linen or wool [threads meant for] the
warp or woof,* leather, or anything made of leather. 49 If a bright green or
bright red* area appears in the cloth, leather, warp or woof [thread], or in any
leather article, [it may be] the mark of the leprous curse, and it must be shown
to the priest.

50 The priest shall examine the mark, and quarantine the affected [article]
for seven days. 51 On the seventh day, he shall examine the affected area, and if
the mark has increased in size on the cloth, the warp or woof [thread], the
leather, or the article crafted from leather, then it is a malignant* leprous
mark, and it is unclean. 52 The cloth, the warp or woof [thread], whether wool
or linen, or the leather article containing the spot must be burned. Since it is a
malignant leprosy, it must be burned in fire.

53 However, if, when the priest examines it, the mark has not expanded in
the garment, the warp or woof [thread], or the leather article, 54 the priest
shall order the article having the mark to be scrubbed and then quarantined

---

—   **it is** . . . (Saadia).

13:45   **must have a tear** . . . Like a mourner (*Moed Katan* 15a). See above, 10:6. This means that he must make a
tear or cut at least one handbreadth long in his garment (*Yad, Avel* 8:2).

—   **without a haircut.** Also like a mourner (*Moed Katan* 15a; above 10:6). He is forbidden to cut his hair until
he is purified (*Yad, Tumath Tzaraath* 10:6).

—   **must cover his head** . . . (*Moed Katan* 15a; Rashi; Ibn Ezra).

13:47   **woolen** . . . Only on wool and linen (*Kelayim* 9:1; *Yad, Tumath Tzaraath* 13:1). Moreover, the cloth must
be white (*Negaim* 11:3; *Yad, Tumath Tzaraath* 12:10).

13:48   **threads meant for** . . . (*Negaim* 11:8; *Yad, Tumath Tzaraath* 13:8; *HaKethav VeHaKabbalah*; Ralbag). It is
also true if the warp is white and the woof colored, or vice versa, and the visible part of the weave is dis-
colored (*Negaim* 11:4; *Yad, Tumath Tzaraath* 12:10). However, if the warp is wool or linen, and the woof is
another material, or vice versa, then the garment cannot become unclean; (*Tosefta, Negaim* 5:3 *Yad,
Tumath Tzaraath* 13:3).

13:49   **bright green or bright red** (*Negaim* 11:4). According to some sources, "green" also includes yellow here
(*Tosefta, Negaim* 1:3, HaGra, *Zer Zahav, Chasdey David* 1:5 *ad loc.* Cf. *Tosafoth Sukkah* 31b, s.v. *HaYarok*).

13:51   **malignant** (Saadia; cf. Rashi; Ibn Ezra). *Mam'ereth* in Hebrew.

for a second seven-day period. ⁵⁵ After the mark has been scrubbed [and quarantined], the priest shall examine the article, and if the mark has not changed in appearance, then [even if]* it has not expanded, it is unclean and must be burned. It is a mark of decay* [that can be] on the smooth or fluffy side* [of the cloth].

⁵⁶ If the priest examines it after it has been scrubbed [and quarantined], and the mark has faded* from the cloth, then he shall tear off [the mark] from the cloth, the leather, or from the warp or woof [threads]. ⁵⁷ If [the mark] then appears again in the [same] cloth, warp or woof [thread] or leather item, it is infected,* and [the article] having the mark must be burned in fire.

⁵⁸ If the mark is removed when the cloth, warp or woof [thread] or leather article is scrubbed, [the article] shall be immersed* this second time, and it is clean.

⁵⁹ This is the [entire]* law concerning the mark of the leprous curse in wool or linen cloth, in warp or woof [thread], or in any leather item, through which it is rendered clean or unclean.

Metzorah מְצֹרָע

[45. Purification of a Leper]

¹ God spoke to Moses, saying:

14

² This is the law concerning the leper when he is purified and placed under the jurisdiction of the priest.* ³ The priest shall go outside the camp,* where he shall examine the leper to determine that the leprous mark has healed. ⁴ The priest shall then order that for the person undergoing purification there be

---

13:55 **even if** (Ralbag; cf. *Negaim* 11:5; *Yad, Tumath Tzaraath* 12:1).

— **mark of decay** (Saadia; Ibn Janach; Radak, *Sherashim*; Rashbam; Ralbag). *Pechetheth* in Hebrew. Or, "penetrating blight" (*Targum Yonathan; Sifra;* Rashi). Or,"contrasting mark" (*Tosefta, Negaim* 1:3).

— **smooth or fluffy side** (Tur; Raavad on *Sifra*). *Karachath* or *Gabachath* in Hebrew; see 13:42. It thus indicates the inside or outside of the cloth (Saadia; Ibn Ezra; Rashi; *Ezrath Kohanim* on *Sifra*). According to others, it can denote "fluffy or worn" (Ramban on *Negaim* 11:11; *Korban Aaron* on *Sifra*; *Tosefoth Yom Tov* on *Negaim* 11:11), and hence, "new or worn" (Targum; Rashi). This teaches a law that if a cloth is fluffy or hairy, the discoloration must be both on the fluff and on the cloth itself (*Negaim* 11:11; *Sifra, Yad, Tumath Negaim* 12:9).

13:56 **faded** (cf. Raavad on *Tumath Tzaraath* 12:1). Or, "changed color," that is, from green to red or vice versa (*Yad, ibid.*).

13:57 **infected.** Or "spreading" (cf. Rashi).

13:58 **immersed** (Targum; *Sifra;* Rashi; *Yad, Tumath Tzaraath* 12:1; *HaKethav VeHaKabbalah*).

13:59 **entire.** Whenever the expression, "This is the law . . ." occurs at the end of a section, the law is not discussed anyplace else in the Torah (Yehudah HaChasid on 14:33).

14:2 **placed under the jurisdiction . . .** (Saadia; *HaKethav VeHaKabbalah*). Literally, "he shall be brought," or, "[the case] shall be brought."

14:3 **outside the camp.** See above, 13:46. The leper is not permitted to remain inside a walled city (*Yad, Tumath Tzaraath* 10:7).

14 taken two live kosher* birds,* a piece of cedar,* some crimson [wool],* and a hyssop branch.*

5 The priest shall give orders that one bird be slaughtered* over fresh spring water* in a clay bowl.* 6 He shall then take the live bird together with the piece of cedar, the crimson wool, and the hyssop.* Along with the live bird, he shall dip [the other articles] into the spring water mixed with the blood of the slaughtered bird. 7 He shall then sprinkle [this mixture] seven times on the person* undergoing purification from the leprous curse, thus

---

14:4   **kosher** (Rashi). Literally, "clean." See above, 11:13-19.
—   **birds.** *Tzipor* in Hebrew. According to Talmudic tradition, the bird used was the *deror* (*Negaim* 14:1; cf. Psalms 84:4, Proverbs 26:2). Some identify this as the swallow, *hirundo* in Latin, *hirondelle* in French (Rashi on Proverbs 26:2; Septuagint on Psalms 84:4). Nevertheless, among the swallows there are some varieties that are kosher and some that are not (cf. Radak, *Sherashim*, s. v. *Derar; Pri Chadash, Orach Chaim* 497:9; *Pri Megadim, Mishbetzoth Zahav, Yoreh Deah* 82:7).

    Other sources, however, identify the *deror* as the sparrow, *passer* in Latin, and *pasra* in Old Spanish (Radak on Psalms 84:4; *Tifereth Yisrael, Negaim* 14:4).

    The Talmud apparently identifies the *deror* with a bird known as the *senunith* (*Chullin* 62a; Ramban; cf. *Tosafoth Chullin* 139b, s. v. *Ta Sh'ma; Nekudoth HaKesef, Yoreh Deah* 82:7). The Talmud notes that only the white-breasted varieties of this bird are kosher, while the all black ones are not (*Chullin* 62a; cf. Rashba, *Torath HaBayith* 65a).

    The Targum identifies the *senunith* with the *agur* in Jeremiah 8:7, which some also identify as the swallow (Rashi, Radak ad. loc.), *rondenella* in Italian (Radak, *Sherashim*). Others, however, identify the *senunith* as a species of jay, *gayo* in Spanish, *gayt* in Old Spanish (Radak, *loc. cit.*). These were birds of the glandualia family, *glondrina* in Old Spanish (*Beth Yosef, Yoreh Deah* 82); *hadolo nadrina* in Provincial (Rabbenu Yerocham, *Toledoth Adam VeChavah* 15:21, 132b). As the Talmud notes, the jay is a bird closely related to the crow, but more colorful. To some degree, it can mimic human speech (cf. Radak, *loc. cit.*).

Swallow   Jay

—   **cedar.** The piece must be at least one cubit (18") long and one-fourth the cross section of a bedpost (*Negaim* 14:6; *Yad, Tumath Tzaraath* 11:1). Some say that the piece was the size of a hatchet handle (Raavad on *Sifra*). It appears that a bedpost in those times had approximately the same diameter as an egg (cf. *Betza* 3b).
—   **crimson wool.** See Exodus 25:4. This consisted of combed out unspun wool (Rashi; Bertenoro, *Tosefoth Yom Tov* on *Negaim* 14:1). According to tradition, one shekel (0.8 oz.) of wool would be used (*Yoma* 42a; *Yad, Tumath Tzaraath* 11:1).
—   **hyssop** ... See Exodus 12:22. The branch would have to be at least a handbreadth (3") long (*Niddah* 26a; *Yad, loc. cit.*) See Numbers 19:6.
14:5   **slaughtered.** The slaughtered bird is then buried (*Negaim* 14:1; *Yad, Tumath Tzaraath* 11:1).
—   **spring water.** *Mayim chaim* in Hebrew, literally, "living water." There must be a *revi'ith* (¼ *log* or 2¼ ounces) of water in the bowl (*Ibid.*)
—   **bowl.** It must be new (*Ibid.*).
14:6   **together with** ... The cedar and the hyssop are tied together with the end of the crimson skein of wool (Ibid.; cf. *Tifereth Yisrael, Negaim* 14:11). Some say that this must be prepared before the first bird is slaughtered (Rashi).
14:7   **on the person.** On the back of his hand (*Negaim, Yad, loc. cit.*). Some say that it is sprinkled on his forehead (*Negaim* 14:1; *Sifra*).

rendering him clean. He shall send the living bird away toward the fields.   14

⁸ The person undergoing purification shall then immerse his clothing, and [the priest]* shall shave off all the person's hair. He shall then immerse in a mikvah* and thus complete [the first part] of the purification process. He may return to the camp, but he must remain outside his tent* for seven days.

⁹ On the seventh day, [the priest] shall shave off all [the person's] hair. His head, beard, eyebrows and other [body] hair must all be shaved off. He shall then immerse his clothing and body in a mikvah and he is clean.

¹⁰ On the eighth day, he shall take two unblemished [male] sheep, one unblemished yearling female sheep, three-tenths [of an ephah]* of the best grade wheat flour mixed with oil* as a meal offering, and one log* of [olive] oil. ¹¹ The priest tending to the purification process shall stand [all these items] and the person undergoing purification before God at the Communion Tent entrance.*

¹² The priest shall take one [male] sheep and present it as a guilt offering* along with the log of oil. He shall wave them in the manner prescribed* for a wave offering before God. ¹³ He shall then slaughter the sheep in the same place where burnt offerings and sin offerings are slaughtered,* in a holy place. This guilt offering is holy of holies, and it is just like a sin offering to the priest.

¹⁴ The priest shall take some of the guilt offering's blood and place it on the right ear lobe, right thumb, and right big toe* of the person undergoing purification.

¹⁵ The priest shall take some of the log of oil* and pour it into the palm of [another]* priest's hand. ¹⁶ [This second] priest shall then dip his right forefinger into the oil in his left hand, and with his finger, sprinkle some oil before God* seven times. ¹⁷ The priest shall place some of the oil in his hand on the right ear, right thumb, and right big toe of the person undergoing purifica-

---

14:8 **the priest.** (*Yad, Tumath Tzaraath* 11:1, 3; cf. *Tosefta, Negaim* 8:6, HaGra *ad loc.* 12).
—   **mikvah.** See Exodus 29:4. Literally, "with the water."
—   **outside his tent.** That is, he may not be intimate with his wife (*Sifra; Negaim* 14:2; *Yad, Tumath Tzaraath* 11:1). During this period, too, he renders unclean anything with which he comes in contact (*Yad* 11:2).
14:10 **three-tenths . . .** Approximately 6 quarts. This is one-tenth for each animal.
—   **mixed with oil.** See above, 2:1.
—   **log.** Approximately 10 ounces.
14:11 **Communion Tent entrance.** But the leper still may not enter the sanctuary grounds, and must remain outside (Rashi; *Yad, Mechuserey Kapparah* 4:2).
14:12 **guilt offering.** *Asham.* See above, 7:1-7.
—   **manner prescribed.** See ʾodus 29:24.
14:13 **same place . . .** To the north of the altar; see above, 1:11, 4:33, 6:18, 7:2.
14:14 **right ear lobe ..** See above, 8:23.
14:15 **some of . . .** The rest of the oil could be used by the priests (*Yad, Mechuserey Kapparah* 4:2, 3).
—   **another . . .** (*Sifra; Negaim* 14:10; *Yad, Mechuserey Kapparah* 4:2).
14:16 **before God.** Toward the Holy of Holies (*Ibid.*).

14 tion, over the guilt offering's blood. [18] The priest shall then place the rest of
the oil in his hand on the head of the person undergoing purification. In this
manner, the priest shall make atonement for him before God.

[19] The priest shall then sacrifice the sin offering* to remove the defilement
for the person undergoing purification. After that, he shall slaughter the burnt
offering,* [20] and the priest shall present the burnt offering and the meal offering on the altar. The priest shall thus make atonement for him, and [the per-
son] is then ritually clean.

[46. The Poor Leper's Offering]

[21] If [the leper] is poor and cannot afford [the above sacrifices], he shall
take one [male] sheep as a guilt offering. This shall be the wave offering* to
atone for him. [He shall also take] one-tenth [ephah]* of the best grade wheat
meal mixed with oil as a meal offering, and a log of olive oil. [22] [In addition,
he shall bring] two turtle doves or two young common doves, as he can afford,
one for a sin offering, and one for a burnt offering.

[23] On the eighth day of his purification, he shall bring them to the priest,
to the Communion Tent entrance, before God. [24] The priest shall take the
guilt offering sheep and the log of oil, and wave them in the motions prescribed for a wave offering before God. [25] He shall slaughter the guilt offering
sheep. The priest shall take the blood of the guilt offering and place it on the
right ear lobe, the right thumb, and the right big toe of the person undergoing purification.

[26] The priest shall then pour some of the oil onto the left hand of [another]
priest. [27] With his right finger, [this second] priest shall sprinkle some of the
oil on his left hand seven times before God. [28] The priest shall place some of
the oil from his hand on the right ear lobe, right thumb and right big toe of
the person undergoing purification, right over the place where the blood of
the guilt offering [was put]. [29] The priest shall then place the rest of the oil that
is in his hand on the head of the person undergoing purification. [With all
this] he shall make atonement for [the person] before God.

[30] He shall then prepare one of the turtle doves or young common doves
that [the person] was able to afford. [31] [Taking this offering] that the person
could afford, [the priest] shall sacrifice one [bird] as a sin offering and one as a
burnt offering, [and then present] the meal offering. The priest shall thus make
atonement before God for the person undergoing purification.

14:19 **the sin offering.** The female sheep; see above 4:32.
—   **the burnt offering.** The second male sheep; see above 1:10.
14:21 **wave offering.** See above, 14:12.
—   **one-tenth ephah.** Approximately 2 quarts.

³² The above is the [entire]* law concerning the person who has the mark 14 of the leprous curse on him, and who cannot afford [more] for his purification.

[47. Discoloration in Houses]

³³ God spoke to Moses and Aaron, saying:

³⁴ When you come to the land of Canaan, which I am giving to you as an inheritance, I will place the mark of the leprous curse in houses in the land you inherit. ³⁵ The owner of the house shall come and tell the priest, "It looks to me as if there is [something] like a [leprous] mark in the house."*

³⁶ The priest shall give orders that the house be emptied out before [any] priest comes to see the mark, so that everything in the house will not become unclean. Only then shall a priest come to see the house.

³⁷ He shall examine the mark [to determine if] the mark on the wall of the house consists of penetrating streaks* that are bright green or bright red,* which appear to be below [the surface of] the wall.

³⁸ [If they are,] the priest shall leave the house [and stand just outside]* the entrance of the house. The priest shall then quarantine* the house for seven days. ³⁹ On the seventh day, he shall return and examine [it to determine] whether or not the mark has expanded on the wall of the house.

⁴⁰ [If it has], the priest shall give orders that [people]* remove the stones* having the mark, and that they throw [the stones] outside the city in an unclean place. ⁴¹ He shall then have the inside of the house* scraped off* all

---

14:33 entire. (Rabbi Yehudah HaChasid). See note on 13:59.

14:35 It looks . . . (*Sifra; Negaim* 12:5). Or, "[Something] like a [leprous] mark can be seen by me in the house," implying that the house is naturally illuminated so that the mark can be seen (*Sifra;* cf. *Negaim* 2:3; *Yad, Tumath Tzaraath* 14:5).

14:37 penetrating streaks. *Shekaruroth* in Hebrew. This is an area where the stain appears to have penetrated the wall (*Targum Yonathan; Sifra;* Rashi; *Yad, Tumath Tzaraath* 14:3). Some, however, say that it is an actual eroded area (Targum, according to Ibn Janach). Others say that it is an area of hairlike lines (Saadia; Ibn Ezra) or threadlike cracks (Ibn Janach; Radak, *Sherashim*). According to still other sources, it is simply a dark area (Radak, *Sherashim*).

The spot must be at least as large as two beans next to each other, around ¾" x 1½" in size (*Sifra; Yad, Tumath Tzaraath* 14:1). See note on 13:2, s. v. "and it is suspected."

Others translate this verse, "the mark on [the stones] imbedded in the walls of the house is bright red . . ." (*HaKethav VeHaKabbalah*).

— **bright green** . . . See note on 13:49.

14:38 just outside. (*Yad, Tumath Tzaraath* 14:5; *Sifra;* cf. *Tosefoth Yom Tov, Negaim* 12:6).

— **quarantine.** See above, 13:4.

14:40 people. Specifically, others owning an adjacent house sharing a common wall with the stricken house (*Sifra*).

— **stones.** From the plural, we see that at least two stones must be stained (*Negaim* 12:3; *Yad, Tumath Tzaraath* 14:7). Furthermore only normal building stone can render the house unclean, but if even a single wall in the house is made of brick, marble, or bedrock, the house cannot become unclean (*Negaim* 12:2, Bertenoro *ad loc.; Yad, Tumath Tzaraath* 14:8).

14:41 house. Or, "place from which the stone has been removed" (*HaKethav VeHaKabbalah;* cf. *Tosefta, Negaim* 6:7).

14 around [the mark], and [the people doing it] shall discard the removed dust
outside the city in an unclean place. ⁴² [The people] shall take other stones to
replace the [removed] stones. [The owner]* shall then plaster the [entire]*
*house with new clay.

⁴³ If, after the stones have been removed and the house has been scraped
and replastered, the mark comes back ⁴⁴ the priest shall return and examine it.
If the mark has spread in the house [again],* it is a malignant leprous mark
which is unclean. ⁴⁵ [The priest] must [order that] the house be demolished,
and its stones, wood* and all the clay from the house shall be brought outside
the city to an unclean place.

⁴⁶ As long as the house is in quarantine, anyone entering it shall be
unclean until evening.* ⁴⁷ If one [remains in the house long enough to] relax,*
he must immerse [both his body and] his clothing. [However] he must
immerse his clothing [only if he has remained] in the house [long enough] to
eat* [a small meal].*

⁴⁸ However, if the priest returns [at the end of the seven days] after the
house has been replastered, and he sees that the mark has not reappeared in
the house, then the mark has gone away and the priest shall declare the house
clean. ⁴⁹ To purify the house, he shall order two birds, a piece of cedar, some
crimson wool, and a hyssop branch.

⁵⁰ He shall slaughter one bird over fresh spring water in a clay bowl. ⁵¹ He
shall then take the piece of cedar, the hyssop, the crimson wool, and the live
bird, dip them in the blood of the slaughtered bird and fresh spring water and
sprinkle it on the house* seven times.

⁵² Thus, with the bird's blood and spring water, along with the live bird,
cedar wood, hyssop and crimson wool, he shall purify the house. ⁵³ He shall
then send the live bird outside the city toward the fields. [In this manner] he

—   **scraped off.** (Targum; Rashbam; Ibn Ezra). *Katza* in Hebrew. This implies that all the clay covering the
         stones must be scraped off (Radak, *Sherashim*). This teaches that for a house to become unclean, it must
         be covered with adobe or clay at least partially (*Yad, Tumath Tzaraath* 14:17).
14:42 **owner.** (Sifra; *Yad, Tumath Tzaraath* 15:4).
—   **entire.** (*Yad, Tumath Tzaraath* 15:2).
14:44 **again.** (cf. Rashi; Ramban; *HaKethav VeHaKabbalah*. See *Negaim* 13:1; *Yad, Tumath Tzaraath* 15:2).
14:45 **wood.** From this we see that the house must contain some wood (*Sifra; Negaim* 12:4; *Yad, Tumath Tzaraath*
         14:7).
14:46 **unclean until evening.** After immersing.
14:47 **long enough to relax.** (Sifra; *HaKethav VeHaKabbalah*; cf. Rash, Bertenoro on *Negaim* 13:9; *Yad, Tumath
         Tzaraath* 16:6). Literally, "One who lies down in the house . . ."
—   **However . . .** (*Ibid.* See Rambam on *Negaim* 13:9; *Eruvin* 4a).
—   **small meal.** This is called a *peras*, and it is a small amount of bread and a relish. According to some, the
         piece of bread must be the size of three eggs, while according to others, four eggs (cf. *Orach Chaim* 612:4;
         Tosefoth Yom Tov on *Negaim* 13:9).
14:51 **on the house.** On the *mashkof*, the beam over the door (*Negaim* 14:1; *Yad, Tumath Tzaraath* 15:8; see
         Exodus 12:22).

shall make atonement for the house, and it is then clean.   14

⁵⁴ The above is the [entire] law for every leprous mark, bald patch, ⁵⁵ leprous mark in a garment or house, ⁵⁶ and [white] blotch, discoloration or spot* [on the skin], ⁵⁷ so that decisions can be rendered as to* the day one is rendered clean and the day one is rendered unclean. This is the [entire] law concerning the leprous curse.

[48. Male Discharges]

¹ God spoke to Moses and Aaron, telling them ² to speak to the Israelites   15 and tell them [as follows]:

When a man has a discharge from his organ,* this discharge can render him unclean. ³ He becomes unclean through a discharge if his organ dribbles* with the discharge or if he has [some of it] stuck* to his organ.

This makes him unclean [so that] ⁴ any bed* upon which the man with the discharge lies is unclean, and any object upon which he sits is [also] unclean. ⁵ Any person who touches [the man's] bed must immerse his clothing and his body in a mikvah and [then] remain unclean until evening. ⁶ [Similarly,] anyone who sits on an object upon which the man with a discharge has been sitting must [also] immerse his clothing and his body in a mikvah, and [then] remain unclean until evening.

⁷ If anyone touches the body of the person with the discharge, he must [similarly] immerse his clothing and his body, and [then] remain unclean until evening.

⁸ If the saliva of the man with a discharge comes in contact with a ritually

---

14:56 blotch, discoloration or spot. See 13:2.

14:57 as to (Saadia; cf. Rashi).

15:2 organ. Male sex organ (*Sifra;* Rashi; Saadia).

15:3 dribbles. With clear liquid (Rashi), like saliva (Saadia), *baba* in Spanish (Radak, *Sherashim*). It can have the appearance of the egg white of a sterile (*Niddah* 35b, Rashi *ad loc.;* cf. *Chullin* 140b) or spoiled (*Arukh* s. v. *Zamar*) egg, in contrast with semen, which has the consistency of fresh egg white. It can also be a pus-like discharge, resembling the liquid from barley dough (*Niddah* 35b) or soft barley batter (*Yad, MeChuserey Kapparah* 2:1).

In order to render the man unclean, the discharge must continue running long enough for the man to immerse and then towel himself off (*Zavim* 1:4, *Yad, Mechuserey Kapparah* 2:10). If he discharges for a shorter time than this, then in order to become unclean, he must experience a second discharge on the same or the next day (*Zavim* 1:1, 1:3; *Yad, Mechuserey Kapparah* 2:6,8). He is, however, unclean to the same degree as one who experienced a seminal emission.

— **stuck** (Rashbam). This teaches that the discharge renders the man unclean no matter how little there is, even if there is not enough to run, but only to adhere to the organ (*Sifra; Yad, Mechuserey Kapparah* 2:9; Rambam on *Zavim* 1:4).

According to others, this teaches that a thick discharge renders the man unclean just like a thin one (Radak, *Sherashim;* cf. Saadia). Some say that if the discharge stops up the organ, it also renders the man unclean (Rashi; cf. *Niddah* 43b; Ibn Janach).

15:4 bed. Literally, "something upon which he lies", *mishkav* in Hebrew (see Rambam on *Kelim* 1:3).

15 clean person, [the latter] must immerse his clothing and his body, and [then] remain unclean until evening.

⁹ Every saddle upon which the person with the discharge rides shall be unclean. ¹⁰ [Thus]* anyone who touches something that has been under [the man with a discharge]* shall be unclean until evening. One who lifts [such an object] must immerse both his clothing and his body, and [then] remain unclean until evening.

¹¹ If anyone touches a man with a discharge who has not immersed [even]* his hands in a mikvah, then [that person] must immerse his clothing and his body in a mikvah, and [then] remain unclean until evening.

¹² If the man with a discharge touches the inside* of a clay vessel, it must be broken.* If it is a wooden vessel, it must be immersed* in a mikvah.

¹³ When the man is healed* of his discharge, he must count seven days for his purification. He shall then immerse his clothing and his body in a mikvah of running spring water.*

¹⁴ On the eighth day, he shall take two turtle doves or two young common doves, and coming before God to the Communion Tent entrance, he shall give them to the priest. ¹⁵ The priest shall prepare one [bird] as a sin offering, and one as a burnt offering. The priest shall thus make atonement before God for the person, [thus purifying him] of his discharge.

[49. Seminal Discharges]

¹⁶ When a man discharges semen, he must immerse his entire body* in a mikvah, and [then] remain unclean until evening.

¹⁷ If any cloth or leather gets any semen on it, it must be immersed in a mikvah and [then] remain unclean until evening.

¹⁸ If a woman has intercourse with a man, and he has a seminal discharge,

---

15:10 **Thus** (cf. Rashi).
—   **the man . . .** (Sifra; Rashi).
15:11 **even** (Sifra; Yad, Mikvaoth 1:2). As long as the man who had the discharge does not immerse, he remains unclean, even many years later (Sifra). This is true of all other cases of defilement as well. See below 15:13. The Torah specifies that even the person's hands must be immersed to teach that if any part of the body, even a hand, is not totally immersed, the entire person remains unclean (cf. Ralbag). He must also wash his hands and the rest of his body before immersing (Rashbam).
15:12 **inside** (cf. Sifra). See above, 11:33. If he moves the vessel, it becomes unclean even if he touches it only on the outside (Ibid.; Yad, Mishkav 8:3; see Rambam on Kelim 1:2).
—   **broken.** See above 6:21, 11:33.
—   **immersed** (Ralbag). Shataf in Hebrew, literally "rinsed" (cf. 6:21). This teaches that any dirt must be washed off the vessel before it is immersed (Rashbam).
15:13 **healed** (Megillah 8a). Literally, "cleansed."
—   **running spring water.** Literally, "living water" (Yad, Mikvaoth 1:5; see Rambam on Mikvaoth 1:8). Spring water can be brought from a distance through a canal (cf. Parah 8:11; Yad, Parah Adumah 6:16).
15:16 **his entire body.** This is a general rule, see 15:11. This also teaches that the mikvah must be large enough for him to immerse his entire body, namely 40 sa'ah or 80 gallons of water (Eruvin 4b). See Exodus 29:4.

[both of] them shall immerse in a mikvah and [then] remain unclean until 15
evening.

[50. Menstruation]

 ¹⁹ When a woman has a discharge, [it can consist] of [any]* blood that emerges from her body.* For seven days she is then [ritually unclean] because of her menstruation,* and anyone touching her shall be unclean until evening.

²⁰ As long as she is in her menstrual state,* anything upon which she lies shall be unclean, and anyone sitting on it is [likewise] unclean. ²¹ Whoever touches her bed must immerse his clothing and his body in a mikvah, and [then] remain unclean until evening. ²² [Similarly], anyone who sits on any article upon which she has sat must immerse his clothing and his body in a mikvah and [then] remain unclean until evening. ²³ Thus,* if he is on the bed or any other article upon which she sat, whether he touches it [or not], he is unclean until evening.

²⁴ If a man has intercourse with [such a woman], her menstrual impurity is transferred to him, and he shall be unclean for seven days. Any bed upon which he lies shall be unclean.

[51. Female Discharges]

²⁵ If a woman has a discharge of blood for a number of days* when it is not time for her menstrual period, or if she has such a discharge right after her period,* then as long as she has this discharge she is unclean, just as she is when she has her period.

²⁶ [Thus], as long as she has the discharge, any bed upon which she lies shall have the same status as it has while she is menstruating. Similarly, any article upon which she sits shall be unclean, just as it is unclean when she is menstruating. ²⁷ Anyone touching [these articles] must [similarly] immerse his clothing and his body in a mikvah, and [then] remain unclean until evening.

²⁸ When [the woman] is rid of her discharge, she must count seven days for herself, and only then can she undergo purification.*

²⁹ On the eighth day, she shall take for herself two turtle doves or two

---

15:19 **any.** (*Yad, Issurey Biyah* 5:1).
— **body.** That is, from her womb.
— **menstruation.** This section is speaking of menstruation (*Torah Temimah*; cf. *Niddah* 44a). The word *niddah* here, means "separation" (Rashi).
15:20 **As long as she is** . . . That is, until she immerses (*Yad, Issurey Biyah* 4:3).
15:23 **Thus** (cf. Rashi).
15:25 **number of days.** That is, 3 days (*Sifra; Yad, Issurey Biyah* 6:2,3, *Mechuserey Kapparah* 1:6).
— **right after** . . . (cf. *Yad, Issurey Biyah* 6:2; *Niddah* 73a).
15:28 **undergo purification.** By immersing.

young common doves, and bring them to the priest, to the Communion Tent entrance. ³⁰ The priest shall prepare one as a sin offering and one as a burnt offering, and the priest shall thus make atonement for her before God, [purifying her] from her unclean discharge.

³¹ You [Moses and Aaron] must warn the Israelites about their impurity, so that their impurity not cause them to die* if they defile the tabernacle that I have placed among them.*

³² This then is the [entire] law concerning the man who is unclean because of a discharge or seminal emission, ³³ as well as the woman who has her monthly period, the man or woman who has a [genital] discharge, and the man who lies with a ritually unclean woman.

Acharey Moth   אַחֲרֵי מוֹת

[52. The Yom Kippur Service]

16 ¹ God spoke to Moses right* after the death of Aaron's two sons,* who brought an [unauthorized] offering before God and died. ² God said to Moses:

Speak to your brother Aaron, and let him not enter the [inner] sanctuary* that is beyond the partition concealing the Ark, so that he may not die, since I appear over the Ark cover in a cloud.*

³ When Aaron enters [this inner] sanctuary, it must be with a young bull for a sin offering and a ram for a burnt offering. ⁴ He must put on a sanctified white linen tunic, and have linen pants on his body. He must [also] gird himself with a linen sash, and bind his [head] with a linen turban.* These are sacred vestments, and [therefore], before putting them on, he must immerse in a mikvah.

15:31 **not. . .die.** This is why the section from 11:1 to here is placed after the death of Aaron's sons (Ibn Ezra on 16:1).

— **if they defile . . .** The laws of purity thus deal with the Tabernacle and the Holy Temple. That is why today, when the Temple no longer stands, we are not careful regarding these rules. However, it is still forbidden to enter the area of the Temple Mount if one is ritually unclean. (*Shaarey Teshuvah, Orach Chaim* 561:1; cf. *Teshuvoth Radbaz* 691).

16:1 **right** (cf. Saadia).

— **death of Aaron's two sons.** Above, 10:2. The narrative is interrupted with the other laws of defilement, since it is important that the death of Aaron's sons serve as an object lesson for all Israel. After warning the other Israelites not to enter the sanctuary improperly, Aaron is also warned (cf. Ibn Ezra).

— **inner sanctuary.** The Holy of Holies (see Exodus 26:33).

16:2 **since I appear . . .** (Rashi; Rashbam; Ibn Ezra). Or, "Since I must [only] be seen in the smoke [of the incense] over the Ark cover. . ." (*Yoma* 53a; Rashi; Rashbam).

16:4 **He must put on . . .** On Yom Kippur, the High Priest wore four white linen vestments (*Yad, Kley HaMikdash* 8:3). The rest of the year, he would wear eight vestments (see Exodus 28:42).

⁵ From the Israelite community, he shall [also] take two goats for sin offer-   **16**
ings, and one ram for a burnt offering.

⁶ He shall [begin by]* presenting his own sin offering bull and atoning* for
himself and his family.

⁷ He shall then take the two goats, and stand them before God at the
Communion Tent entrance. ⁸ Aaron shall place two lots* on the two goats,
one lot [marked] "for God,"and one [marked] "for Azazel."*

⁹ Aaron shall present the goat that has the lot for God so that it will [later]
be prepared as a sin offering. ¹⁰ The goat (hat has the lot for Azazel shall
remain alive before God, so that [Aaron] will [later] be able to make atonement on it and send it to Azazel in the desert.

¹¹ Aaron shall present his sin offering bull, and make atonement for himself and his fellow [priests].* He shall then slaughter his bull as a sin offering.

¹² He shall take a fire pan* full of burning coals from [the side of]* the
altar* that is toward God, along with a double handful* of finely pulverized
perfume incense, and bring [them both] into the [inner sanctuary] beyond the
cloth partition. ¹³ There, before God, he shall place the incense on the fire, so
that the smoke from the incense covers the ark cover over the [tablets of]
testimony. Then he will not die.

16:6   **He shall begin by** . . . (*Yoma* 35b; *Yad, Avodath Yom HaKippurim* 4:1). This was done after the daily offering (Numbers 28:2-7) and the additional Yom Kippur offering (Numbers 29:7-10). (*Ibid.*).
—   **atoning** . . . Confessing their sins (*Ibid.; HaKethav VeHaKabbalah*).
16:8   **lots.** These were two pieces of boxwood (*Arukh*; Rambam on *Yoma* 3:10, *Negaim* 2:1), *ashkora* in Hebrew,
upon which the above words were written (*Yoma* 37a). These would be placed in a *kalpi* or small box
(*Ibid.*; *ascoran* or *ecrin* in French, Rashi). He would then mix up the two lots (*Arukh*, s.v. *Taraf*) and lift
them out of the box quickly without thinking about which one he is taking in which hand (*Yoma* 39a).
The box would be large enough to hold the High Priests two hands (*Ibid.*). Thus when he lifted them
out, one would be in his right hand and the other in his left hand. Since one goat would be to his right
and the other to his left, the hand in which each lot was lifted would determine which goat would be
designated for which part of the service (*Ibid.*).
—   **Azazel.** This is a proper noun (cf. Targum), and some say that it was the name of a known mountain
(Saadia; *Emunoth VeDeyoth* 3:10; Radak, *Sherashim*), possibly in the Sinai area (cf. Ibn Ezra). Others say
that it denotes a hard rocky cliff, indicating that this goat was pushed off a cliff to its death (*Yoma* 63a;
Targum Yonathan on 16:10; *Sifra*; Rashi; *HaKethav VeHaKabbalah*). Others say that *azazel* means "to be sent
away" (Septuagint), or "to carry away sins" (Symachus; Vulgate).
          There is another opinion that Azazel denotes the fact that this goat was designated for the forces of
evil (*Pirkey Rabbi Eliezer* 46; Ramban; Bachya; Chizzkuni; *Zohar* 3:63a). By making evil part of the service,
the evil of the people's sins is re-elevated to God.
          Others say that it is meant to atone for sexual crimes (Rashi, *Yoma* 67b, s.v. *Uza*), the sin of the fallen
angels, Uza and Uzael (*Yoma* 67b; cf. *Targum Yonathan* on Genesis 6:4; *Enoch* 10:4,5). Some say that
Azazel represents the forces of nature (Hirsch).
16:11 **fellow priests** (*Yoma* 41b; *Sifra*; Rashi). See 16:33. Literally, "for the household," here designating the
entire priestly family.
16:12 **fire pan.** See Exodus 27:3.
—   **side of.** The west side (*Sifra*; Rashi).
—   **altar.** The sacrificial altar (*Yoma* 45b; Rashi).
—   **double handful.** With both hands together. See Exodus 9:8.

16   ¹⁴ He shall take some of the bull's blood, and, with his forefinger, sprinkle
it [once]* above the east side* of the ark cover.* He shall [then] sprinkle with
his forefinger seven times [directly] toward the ark cover.*

    ¹⁵ He shall then slaughter the people's sin offering goat,* and bring its
blood into [the inner sanctuary] beyond the cloth partition. He shall do the
same with this blood as he did with the bull's blood, sprinkling it both above
the ark cover and directly toward the ark cover. ¹⁶ With this, he will make
atonement on the holy [ark] for the Israelites' defilement,* as well as for their
rebellious acts and all their inadvertent misdeeds.

    He shall then perform [exactly] the same [ritual] in the Communion Tent,*
which remains with the [Israelites] even when they are unclean.*

    ¹⁷ No one else shall be in the Communion Tent from the time that [Aaron]
enters the sanctuary to make atonement until he leaves. In this manner he
shall make atonement for himself, for his family, and for the entire Israelite
community.

    ¹⁸ He shall then go out to the altar that is before God,* and make atone-
ment on it. He shall [do this by] taking some of the bull's and goat's blood,
and placing [the mixture]* on the altar's horns all around.* ¹⁹ He shall
sprinkle the blood on it* seven times with his forefinger. Through this, he
shall purify and sanctify it from any defilement on the part of the Israelites.

    ²⁰ When he thus finishes making atonement in the [inner] sanctuary, in the
Communion Tent, and on the altar,* he shall present the live goat.

    ²¹ Aaron shall press both his hands on the live goat's head, and he shall

---

16:14 **once** (Rashi).

— **east side.** Since the Holy of Holies was to the west of the Tabernacle, the priest would be facing the east
side of the ark.

— **ark cover.** The "atonement device" (*kapporeth*); see Exodus 25:17. (Abarbanel; *HaKethav VeHaKabbalah*).

— **He shall then . . .** Thus, he would sprinkle once upward and seven times downward (*Sifra*; Rashi). He
would thus count "one, one and one, one and two. . ." until "one and seven" (*Yoma* 53b). He would not
actually sprinkle the blood upward or downward, but lift his hand and sprinkle with the downward
motion (*Arukh*, s.v. *Matzlif*). Others say that there was no sharp division between the "upper blood" and
the "lower," but the priest would begin sprinkling upward, and gradually sprinkle lower (Rashi, *Yoma*
55a). See *Yoma* 53b; *Yad, Avodath Yom HaKippurim* 3:5).

16:15 **sin offering goat.** The one chosen by lot for God.

16:16 **defilement.** That is, entering the sanctuary or eating sacrifice while unclean (Rashi; see above, 15:31).

— **He shall then perform . . .** (*Yoma* 56a). Thus he must sprinkle both the blood of the bull and that of the
goat (separately) toward the cloth partition, once upward and seven times downward (*Yoma* 53b; *Yad,
Avodath Yom HaKippurim* 3:5).

— **which remains . . .** Indicating that there is atonement even when the Israelites are defiled (*Midrash
HaGadol*). This may also indicate that there would be atonement even in the Second Temple, where
there was no ark or ark cover.

16:18 **altar that is before God.** The incense altar (*Yoma* 58b; Rashi).

— **mixture** (*Yoma* 53b; *Yad, Avodath Yom HaKippurim* 3:5).

— **all around.** North-east, north-west, south-west and then south-east (*Sifra*).

16:19 **on it.** On the center of the altar (*Sifra; Yoma* 58b).

16:20 **When he . . .** (cf. Saadia).

confess on it all the Israelites' sins, rebellious acts and inadvertent misdeeds.* 16
When he has thus placed them on the goat's head,* he shall send it to the
desert with a specially prepared man.* ²² The goat will thus carry all the sins
away to a desolate area when it is sent to the desert.

²³ Aaron shall then go into the Communion Tent, and take off the white
linen vestments that he wore when he entered the [inner] sanctuary. He shall
leave [these vestments] there. ²⁴ He shall immerse his body in a mikvah in the
sanctified area, and put on his [regular] vestments.

He shall then go out and complete his own burnt offering and the people's
burnt offering,* thus atoning for himself and the people. ²⁵ He shall [also]
burn the choice parts of the sin offering on the altar.

²⁶ The one who sends the goat to Azazel shall immerse his clothing and
body in a mikvah; only then can he enter the camp.

²⁷ The bull and goat presented as sin offerings, whose blood was brought
into the [inner] sanctuary to make atonement, shall be brought outside the
camp. There, their skin, flesh and entrails shall be burned in fire. ²⁸ The one
who burns them shall immerse his clothing and body in a mikvah, and he may
then come back into the camp.

²⁹ [All] this shall be an eternal law for you. [Each year] on the 10th day of
the 7th month* you must fast* and not do any work.* This is true of both the
native born and the proselyte* who joins you. ³⁰ This is because on this day
you shall have all your sins atoned, so that you will be cleansed. Before God
you will be cleansed of all your sins. ³¹ It is a Sabbath of Sabbaths to you, and
[a day upon which] you must fast. This is a law for all time.*

³² The priest who is anointed and installed to be [High] Priest in his ancestor's place* shall make [this] atonement, wearing the sacred vestments of
white linen. ³³ He shall be the one to make atonement in the holy [inner] sanctuary, in the Communion Tent, and on the altar. The atonement that he
makes shall be for the priests and for the people of the community.

16:21 **sins, rebellious acts** . . . (*Yoma* 36b).
— **When he has** . . . (cf. Saadia).
— **specially prepared man** (*Yoma* 66a; Rashi). *Iti* in Hebrew.
16:24 **burnt offering.** The rams mentioned in 16:3,5.
16:29 **the 10th day of the 7th month.** That is Yom Kippur, the tenth of Tishrei, counting from Nissan (*Targum Yonathan*; see Exodus 12:2). See below, 23:27.
— **fast** (Saadia; *Targum Yonathan*; cf. *Yoma* 77a). Literally, "afflict yourselves," or "afflict your souls." "Afflic-
tion" also includes refraining from washing, anointing, wearing shoes and sex (*Yad, Shevithath Assur* 1:5),
but many say that these are forbidden only by rabbinic legislation (*Tosafoth, Yoma* 7b).
— **work.** Like the Sabbath, see Exodus 20:9.
— **proselyte** (see *HaKethav VeHaKabbalah*).
16:31 **a law for all time.** Even when there is no temple (Sforno).
16:32 **ancestor's place.** That is, whoever is High Priest just as was Aaron, the father of all priests (cf. *Sifra*).

16   ³⁴ [All this] shall be for you as a law for all time, so that the Israelites [will
be able to] gain atonement for their sins once each year.
[Aaron later]* did exactly as God had commanded Moses.

[53. Slaughtering Animals]

17   ¹ God spoke to Moses,* telling him to ² speak to Aaron, his sons, and the
[other] Israelites, telling them that the following is literally what God commanded:
³ If any member of the family of Israel sacrifices* an ox, sheep or goat,
whether in the camp or outside the camp, ⁴ and does not bring it to the Communion Tent to be offered as a sacrifice to God before His sanctuary, that
person is considered a murderer.* That person has committed an act of
murder, and he shall be cut off [spiritually]* from among his people.
⁵ The Israelites shall thus take the sacrifices that they are offering in the
fields, and bring them to God, to the Communion Tent entrance, [where they
are given] to the priest. They can then be offered as peace offerings to God.
⁶ The priest will then dash the blood on God's altar at the Communion Tent's
entrance, and burn the choice parts as an appeasing fragrance to God.
⁷ The Israelites will then stop sacrificing to the demons* who [continue to]
tempt them. This shall be an eternal law* for them for all generations.
⁸ [Also] tell them that if any person, whether from the family of Israel or a
proselyte who joins them, prepares* a burnt offering or other sacrifice, ⁹ and
does not bring it to the Communion Tent to present it to God, that person
shall be cut off [spiritually] from his people.
¹⁰ If any person, whether of the family of Israel or a proselyte who joins
them, eats any blood, I will direct My anger* against the person who eats

---

16:34 **Aaron later** (Rashi; Rashbam).
17:1 **God spoke** . . . This completes the laws of sacrifice and the sanctuary.
17:3 **sacrifices** (Rashi). This commandment forbids any sacrifice outside the Tabernacle or Temple (*Sefer
HaMitzvoth,* Negative 90). In the desert, it was a general prohibition against killing any animal except as
a peace offering (Ramban; see Deuteronomy 12:15,21).
17:4 **murderer.** For killing the animal (Ramban; Bachya; *Chinukh* 186; cf. Rashi; *Targum Yonathan*). Literally,
"Blood shall be counted for that man; he has spilled blood." Some say that it is like eating blood (Abarbanel; *HaKethav VeHaKabbalah*).
—   **cut off spiritually.** See Genesis 17:14; Bachya on Leviticus 18:29).
17:7 **demons.** Even if the motive is not idolatrous, but merely to gain occult powers (Sforno). Since it was
permitted to send the goat to Azazel (above 16:8), the Torah specifically warned that this does not mean
that sacrifices to the forces of evil are permitted (cf. *Moreh Nevukhim* 3:46).
—   **eternal law.** Not to sacrifice to demons (Ralbag; Sforno). This also teaches that even when the Temple is
not standing, it is forbidden to sacrifice elsewhere. That is why, now that the Temple is destroyed, no sacrifices are offered.
17:8 **prepares.** Or "burns" (Saadia). This forbids the burning of a sacrifice (even a meal offering) any place
but in the Tabernacle or Temple (Rashi).
17:10 **direct my anger** (Targum; Saadia; *HaKethav VeHaKabbalah*). Literally, "I will set my face. . ."

blood and cut him off [spiritually] from among his people. [11] This is because the life-force of the flesh is in the blood*; and I therefore gave it to you to be [placed] on the altar to atone for your lives. It is the blood that atones for a life, [12] and I therefore told the Israelites, "Let none of you eat blood."* A proselyte who joins you shall [likewise] not eat blood.

[13] If any man, whether of the family of Israel or a proselyte who joins them, traps an animal or bird that may be eaten and spills its blood, he must cover [the blood] with earth.*

[14] [All this] is because every living creature has its blood associated with its life-force. Tell the Israelites not to eat any blood, since the life-force of all flesh is in its blood. Whoever eats it shall be cut off [spiritually].

[15] If any person, whether native born or a proselyte, eats a creature which has died on its own* and which [is forbidden only because it] has a fatal lesion,* he must immerse his clothes and his body in a mikvah. He then remains unclean until evening, whereupon he is clean. [16] If he does not immerse his clothing and body, then he can bear his guilt.*

[54. Sexual Laws]

[1] God spoke to Moses, telling him to [2] speak to the Israelites, and say to them: **18**

I am God. [3] Do not follow the ways of Egypt where you once lived, nor of Canaan, where I will be bringing you. Do not follow [any] of their customs.* [4] Follow My laws and be careful to keep My decrees, [for] I am God your Lord. [5] Keep My decrees and laws, since it is only by keeping them that a person can [truly] live.* I am God.

17 (upper right, marginal verse number for verse 11)

17:11 **the life force . . .** This is because the blood brings life to all parts of the body. The blood is also responsible for man's animal nature, through the hormones, as opposed to man's human nature, which is transmitted through nerve impulses. Since it is man's animal nature which leads him to sin, the blood is an atonement.

17:12 **I therefore told . . .** See above, 7:26.

17:13 **must cover . . .** This is a commandment to cover the blood of all birds and wild animals (*Chullin* 87a; *Sefer HaMitzvoth*, Positive 147).

17:15 **died on its own.** *Nevelah* in Hebrew. This is any animal that is not ritually slaughtered.

— **which is forbidden . . .** (*Sifra*; Rashi; *Yad, Avoth HaTumah* 3:1; *HaKethav VeHaKabbalah*). See above, 11:40. According to tradition, this is speaking of a kosher bird (which is forbidden only when *terefah*, with a fatal lesion) which was not ritually slaughtered. Above, there is no uncleanness associated with such a bird, and it does not defile unless swallowed (*Ibid.*).

17:16 **he can . . .** If he enters the sanctuary or eats any sacrifice (Rashi; see above, 15:31).

18:3 **Do not follow . . .** This is a specific commandment not to emulate gentiles (*Avodah Zarah* 11a; Rashi; *Yad, Avodath Kokhavim* 11:1). See Leviticus 20:23.

18:5 **truly live** (cf. Ralbag). This teaches that one may violate any commandment of the Torah to save a life (*Yoma* 88b). The only exceptions are the three cardinal sins: idolatry, murder, and sexual crimes (*Sanhedrin* 74a).

18   *[55. Incest]*

⁶ No person shall approach a close relative* to commit a sexual offense.* I
am God.

[56. Parents]

⁷ Do not commit a sexual offense against your father* or mother. [If a
woman is] your mother, you must not commit incest with her.

[57. A Stepmother]

⁸ Do not commit incest with your father's wife,* since this* is a sexual
[offense] against your father.

[58. A Sister]

⁹ Do not commit incest with your sister, even if she is the daughter of
[only] your father or mother. Whether she is legitimate or illegitimate,* you
must not commit incest with her.

[59. Grandchildren]

¹⁰ Do not commit incest with your son's daughter or your daughter's
daughter,* since this is a sexual crime against yourself.*

[60. A Half Sister]

¹¹ Do not commit incest with a daughter that your father's wife has borne
to your father.* She is your sister, and you must not commit incest with her.

18:6   **close relative** (Saadia). *Sh'er* in Hebrew. Or, "flesh," that is, one's flesh and blood (Ibn Janach; Radak,
          Sherashim).
—   **sexual offense.** Literally, "to uncover nakedness," since this is the first part of the sexual act (Ramban on
          20:17; Ralbag). The word *galah* here may also mean "be exiled", and hence *le-galoth ervah* may be trans-
          lated, "to exile nakedness" or "to pervert sexuality" (cf. *Targum Yonathan*).
18:7   **father.** By committing incest with his wife, as in 18:8 (Rashi). Others say that it also forbids homosexual
          relations with one's father, providing such an act with a double penalty (*Sanhedrin* 54a; Ramban; *Sefer
          HaMitzvoth*, Negative 351).
18:8   **father's wife.** Even if she is not one's mother, and even after one's father is dead or divorced from her
          (Rashi).
—   **since this . . .** (cf. Saadia).
18:9   **legitimate . . .** (cf. *Yevamoth* 23a; Rashi; Rashbam; Ibn Ezra; Ramban). Literally, "born in the house or
          outside" (cf. Saadia).
18:10 **daughter's daughter.** And certainly one's daughter herself (Rashi).
—   **against yourself.** Literally, "this is your own nakedness."
18:11 **with a daughter . . .** If a woman is one's sister borne by his father's wife, there is a double penalty
          (*Yevamoth* 22b; *Sefer HaMitzvoth*, Negative 333). This also teaches that a step-sister who is the daughter of
          a stepmother from another man, is permitted (*Yad, Issurey Biyah* 3:2).

[61. A Paternal Aunt]

¹² Do not commit incest with your father's sister, since she is your father's blood relative.

[62. A Maternal Aunt]

¹³ Do not commit incest with your mother's sister, since she is your mother's blood relative.

[63. An Uncle's Wife]

¹⁴ Do not commit a sexual offense against your father's brother by having [sexual] contact with his wife; she is your aunt.*

[64. A Daughter-in-Law]

¹⁵ Do not commit incest with your daughter-in-law. She is your son's wife; you must not commit incest with her.

[65. A Sister-in-Law]

¹⁶ Do not commit incest with your brother's wife, since this is a sexual offense against your brother.*

[66. Other Forbidden Relations]

¹⁷ Do not commit incest [by marrying]* a woman and her daughter. Do not even take her son's daughter or her daughter's daughter, since this constitutes incest. Since they are blood relatives, it is a perversion.*

¹⁸ Do not marry a woman and [then take] her sister as a rival to her as long as [the first one] is alive.

¹⁹ Do not come close to a woman who is ritually unclean because of her menstruation,* since this is a sexual offense.

²⁰ Do not lie carnally with your neighbor's wife, since this will defile her.*

²¹ Do not give any of your children* to be initiated to Molekh,* so that you not profane your God's name; I am God.

18:14 **aunt.** And she is forbidden even after the uncle's death.

18:16 **Do not . . .** Even after the brother's death. The only exception is if the brother dies without children, see Deuteronomy 25:5.

18:17 **by marrying** (*Yevamoth* 97a; Rashi).

— **perversion** (Saadia; Ramban). *Zimah* in Hebrew. Or, "perverted love" (*Targum Yonathan*), or, "a sinful plan" (Targum; Rashi; *HaKethav VeHaKabbalah*; cf. *Nedarim* 51a; Yehuda HaChasid).

18:19 **ritually unclean . . .** Who has not immersed in a mikvah (*Yad, Issurey Biyah* 4:3).

18:20 **will defile her.** So that she is forbidden to her husband henceforth (*Yerushalmi, Sotah* 5:1).

18:21 **children.** (see Deuteronomy 18:10) Literally, "seed." If one gives one's children away in this manner, then the semen with which the child was conceived is considered to have been emitted in vain (Abarbanel). This also forbids one to have intercourse with a gentile (*Megillah* 25a).

18   ²² Do not lie with a male as you would with a woman, since this is a disgusting perversion.

²³ Do not perform any sexual act with an animal, since it will defile you. A woman shall [likewise] not give herself to an animal and allow it to mate with her. This is an utterly detestable perversion.*

²⁴ Do not let yourselves be defiled by any of these acts. It was as a result of them that the nations that I am driving away before you became defiled. ²⁵ The land became defiled, and when I directed My providence at the sin committed there, the land vomited out its inhabitants.

²⁶ You, [however,] must keep My decrees and laws, and not become involved in any of these disgusting perversions—neither the native born nor any foreigner who settles among you.* ²⁷ The people who lived in the land before you did all these disgusting perversions and defiled the land. ²⁸ But [you shall not cause] the land to vomit you out when you defile it, as it vomited out the nation that was there before you.

²⁹ Thus, whenever anyone does any of these disgusting perversions, [all] the people involved* shall be cut off [spiritually] from the midst of their people.

³⁰ Keep My charge, and do not follow any of the perverted customs that were kept before you [arrived], so that you not be defiled by them. I am God your Lord.

Kedoshim   קְדשִׁים

[67. Holiness Laws]

19   ¹ God spoke to Moses, telling him to ² speak to the entire Israelite community and say to them:

—   **Molekh.** This was a ritual that related to many idolatrous religions, but was particular to Molekh, an Ammonite God (*Sanhedrin* 64a; 1 Kings 11:7). The ritual was an initiation whereby a man's sons and daughters would go through fire (2 Kings 23:10; cf. Deuteronomy 18:10, 2 Kings 16:3, 17:17, 21:6). Some say that the initiation rite consisted of crossing a platform between two large fires, while others say that it consisted of jumping over a fire (*Sanhedrin* 64b; Rashi; Radak, *Sherashim*; *Yad, Avodath Kokhavim* 6:3; cf. *Kesef Mishneh ad loc.*)
    In general, the Molekh ritual did not involve human sacrifice (*Yad, loc. cit.*). According to some, however, it was a trial by fire, in which the child could be killed (Ibn Ezra). In some cases, it actually did involve human sacrifice (Ramban; Rashi, Yalkut, on Jeremiah 7:31). Cf. Jeremiah 19:5, Ezekiel 23:37,39. This was associated with various occult practices (Ramban; Deuteronomy 18:10), possibly as an initiation rite for the father (Septuagint on Deuteronomy 18:10).
18:23   **an utterly detestable perversion** (Saadia). *Tebhel* in Hebrew. Or, "a destructive perversion" (Ibn Janach, s.v. *balal*), "a mixture of species" (Radak, *Sherashim*) or, "a spicy experience" (*Nedarim 51a*).
18:26   **foreigner . . .** (Ibn Ezra). Since a gentile must also keep most sexual laws. Or, "proselyte" (*Sifra*). Although the laws involving blood relatives do not apply to a proselyte (who has no blood relatives from the time he was a gentile), all the other laws apply to him.
18:29   **all the people involved.** Both the man and the woman (*Sifra*; Rashi).

You must be holy, since I am God your Lord [and] I am holy.   **19**

³ Every person must repect* his mother and father, and keep My Sabbaths.* I am God your Lord.

⁴ Do not turn aside to false gods, and do not make yourselves gods out of cast metal. I am God your Lord.

⁵ When you offer a peace sacrifice* to God, you shall do so of your own free will. ⁶ You can eat it on the day you sacrifice it and on the next day, but anything left over until the third ᵈay must be burned in fire. ⁷ If one [even plans to] eat it on the third day, it is considered putrid and it is not acceptable. ⁸ If one [then] eats it, he has desecrated that which is holy to God, and he shall bear his guilt. Such a person shall be cut off [spiritually] from his people.

⁹ When you reap your land's harvest, do not completely harvest the ends of your fields.* [Also] do not pick up individual stalks [that have fallen].* ¹⁰ [Furthermore,] do not pick the incompletely formed grape clusters* in your vineyards. [Also] do not pick up individual [fallen grapes]* in your vineyards. [All the above]* must be left for the poor and the stranger.* I am God your Lord.

¹¹ Do not steal.

Do not deny [a rightful claim].*

Do not lie to one another.

¹² Do not swear falsely by My name; [if you do so], you will be desecrating your God's name. I am God.

¹³ Do not [unjustly] withhold that which is due your neighbor.*

Do not let a worker's wages remain with you overnight until morning.*

19:3 **respect** (cf. *Kiddushin* 31a). Literally, "fear" or "reverence."

— **keep My Sabbaths.** Even if a parent tells one to violate it (*Yevamoth* 5b). The same is true of all other commandments (*Bava Metzia* 32a).

19:5 **peace sacrifice.** See above 3:1-17. This section repeats 7:11-19.

19:9 **do not completely harvest** . . . The portion left at the end of the field is known as *peah* (cf. *Yad, Matnoth Aniyim* 1:1). It must be left at the last edge of the field to be harvested (*Peah* 1:3; *Yad, Matnoth Aniyim* 2:12).

— **stalks that have fallen.** From the sickle or hand during harvest (*Peah* 4:10; *Yad, Matnoth Aniyim* 4:1). This is known as *leket*. If only one or two stalks fall, they may not be picked up, but if three or more stalks fall, they may be taken (*Peah* 6:5; Rashi).

19:10 **incompletely formed grape clusters.** Which do not have the grapes attached to a central stem, or do not have the grapes lying on one another (*Peah* 7:4; *Yad, Matnoth Aniyim* 4:17,18). *Oleleth* in Hebrew.

— **individual fallen grapes.** Which fall during harvest (*Peah* 7:3). Here too, if one or two grapes fall, they may not be picked up, but if a cluster contains three or more grapes, it may (*Peah* 6:5; *Yad, Matnoth Aniyim* 4:15). *Peret* in Hebrew.

— **All the above** (*Makkoth* 16b; *Yad, Matnoth Aniyim* 1:2; *Sefer HaMitzvoth*, Positive 120, 121).

— **stranger.** An Israelite (*Sifra*). A proselyte (Malbim).

19:11 **Do not deny** . . . (*Sefer HaMitzvoth*, Negative 248). *Kachash* in Hebrew. See above, 5:21.

19:13 **Do not unjustly withhold** . . . (*Yad, Gezelah* 1:4). *Ashak* in Hebrew; see above, 5:21. Also, "do not swindle" (*Sefer HaMitzvoth* Negative 247). This includes an injunction against refusing to pay wages due an employee (*Sifra*; Rashi).

— **Do not let a worker's wages** . . . See Deuteronomy 24:15. One must therefore pay wages on the agreed

19   ¹⁴ Do not curse [even]* the deaf.

Do not place a stumbling block before the [morally]* blind. You must fear your God. I am God.

¹⁵ Do not pervert justice. Do not give special consideration to the poor nor show respect* to the great. Judge your people fairly.

¹⁶ Do not go around as a gossiper among your people.

Do not stand still when your neighbor's life is in danger.* I am God.

¹⁷ Do not hate your brother in your heart.

You must admonish your neighbor, and not bear sin because of him.*

¹⁸ Do not take revenge nor bear a grudge against the children of your people.

You must love your neighbor as [you love] yourself. I am God.

¹⁹ Keep My decrees:

Do not crossbreed your livestock with other species.

Do not plant your field with different species of seeds.

Do not wear a garment that contains a forbidden mixture* of fabrics.

²⁰ If a man lies carnally with a slave woman* who is half married* to [another] man,* and she has not been redeemed* or given her freedom, she

---

upon day, without delay (*Yad, Sekhiruth* 11:1; *Sefer HaMitzvoth,* Negative 238).

19:14 even (*Sifra;* Rashi; cf. *Sanhedrin* 66a, *Shevuoth* 36a).

— **morally** (*Pesachim* 22b; Rashi). This means that it is forbidden to cause another person to commit a sin. Also "conceptually blind," by giving bad advice (*Sifra*). Some say that it is also to be taken in its literal sense, that it is forbidden to place something on the ground where it will cause damage (Ralbag; Sforno). According to others, however, this commandment is not to be taken in its literal sense (*Korban Aaron* on *Sifra; Mishneh LaMelekh, Malveh* 4:6, s.v. *Kathav; Minchath Chinukh* 232:4).

19:15 show respect. *Hadar* in Hebrew, see below 19:32. Or, "be impressed" (Saadia; Septuagint).

19:16 when your neighbor's life is in danger (*Sifra;* Rashi; *Sefer HaMitzvoth,* Negative 296). Expressed idiomatically as, "Do not stand still over your neighbor's blood."

19:17 and not bear sin . . . If one does not admonish, then he is responsible for the other's sin (*Sefer HaMitzvoth,* Positive 205; cf. *Shabbath* 54b). Or, "do not sin through him" by embarassing him publicly (*Arkhin* 16b; *Sefer HaMitzvoth,* Negative 305). This is also a general commandment not to embarrass a person publicly (*Ibid.*).

19:19 forbidden mixture. Of wool and linen (Deuteronomy 22:11). *Shaatnez* in Hebrew. It is forbidden whether the wool and linen are spun together, woven together, or sewn together (*Yad, Kelayim* 10:2,3).

19:20 slave woman. A woman who is half slave and half free (*Kerithoth* 11a; *Yad, Issurey Biyah* 3:13). Such a situation can arise if her freedom is partially bought (*Gittin* 41b; *Yad, Avadim* 7:4). Similarly, if a slave belongs to two partners, and is freed by one of them, the slave is half free (*Ibid.*). According to some, however, the Torah here is speaking of a woman who is fully a slave (Rabbi Yishmael, *Sifra, Kerithoth* 11a). According to all opinions, it is speaking of a born gentile, who was purchased as a slave by a Jew. A born Jewish woman cannot be a slave (except for a minor; see Exodus 21:7).

— **half married.** (cf. Ramban; *Yerushalmi, Kiddushin* 1:1; Radak, *Sherashim*). *Ne-cherefeth* in Hebrew. Since there is no marriage for a slave, only the "half" of the woman who is free is married. According to those who hold that this is speaking of a woman who is a total slave, the "marriage" is conditional, and is automatically nullified when the husband (see next note) is given his freedom (see Exodus 21:4).

— **man.** The only man that such a woman may marry is another slave. According to tradition, it is speaking of a case where she is married to a Hebrew slave (cf. Exodus 21:4).

— **redeemed.** When another person gives the slave's master money for his freedom (*Yad, Avadim* 5:2; *Kid-*

must be physically punished.* However, since she has not been freed, [the two] **19** shall not be put to death. ²¹ [The man] must bring his guilt offering* to God, to the Communion Tent entrance. It shall be a ram for a guilt offering. ²² The priest shall make atonement for him before God with the guilt offering ram, for the sin that he committed. He will thus gain forgiveness for his sin.

[68. Forbidden Practices]

²³ When you come to the [promised] land and plant any tree bearing edible [fruit], you must avoid its fruit as a forbidden growth.* For three years [the fruit] shall be a forbidden growth, and it may not be eaten. ²⁴ Then, in the fourth year, all [the tree's] fruit shall be holy,* and it shall be something for which God is praised.* ²⁵ In the fifth year, you may eat its fruit and thus increase your crops. I am God your Lord.

²⁶ Do not eat on blood.*

Do not act on the basis of omens.*

Do not act on the basis of auspicious times.*

²⁷ Do not cut off* the hair on the sides of your head.*

---

dushin 23a; Rashi). According to the majority opinion (above), it is speaking of the case where she was partially redeemed (*Kerithoth* 11a; Rashi; Malbim).

— **physically punished** (Septuagint). *Bakar* in Hebrew. She is flogged (*Yad, Issurey Biyah* 3:14; Rashi). Some say that this is because she is flogged with a lash made from the skin of a large animal (*bakar*) (Radak, *Sherashim;* cf. *Makkoth* 22b). Or, "she shall be disgraced" (Ibn Janach). Or, "she is public property" and not completely married (Radak, *Sherashim*).

19:21 **guilt offering**. *Asham.* See above, 7:1-7.

19:23 **avoid its fruit as a forbidden growth** (Ralbag). Literally, "you shall deem it uncircumcised." Such fruit is known as *Orlah*. Or, "You shall put it aside for destruction" (Targum); "You shall block it [from use]" (Rashi; Rashbam), "You shall consider it harmful" (Ibn Ezra); "You shall consider it forbidden" (Saadia; Ibn Janach); or "You shall purge its defilement" (Septuagint).

19:24 **holy**. Like the "second tithe" in Deuteronomy 14:23 (*Sifra;* Rashi; *Yad, Maaser Sheni* 9:1). It must therefore be eaten in Jerusalem or redeemed.

— **and something . . .** (Rashbam). Some derive from this the rule that a blessing must be recited before eating anything (*Berakhoth* 35a). See Deuteronomy 8:10.

19:26 **Do not eat . . .** This refers to occult practices (Ramban), perhaps a meal accompanying human sacrifice (Rashbam) or eaten on a murderer's grave (Chizzkuni). Some say that the blood of a slaughtered animal would be placed in a bowl for occult purposes, and a ritual meal would be eaten with it (Radak on 1 Samuel 14:32,33; *Torah Temimah*). This also includes a commandment not to eat an animal before it is completely dead (*Sanhedrin* 63a; Rashi; Chizzkuni), and not to eat a sacrifice before the blood has been sprinkled on the altar (*Ibid.*). This is particularly seen as a commandment not to eat like the rebellious son in Deuteronomy 21:20 (*Ibid.; Sefer HaMitzvoth,* Negative 195).

— **omens**. (*Sanhedrin* 65b; Rashi; *Yad, Avodath Kokhavim* 11:4; *Sefer HaMitzvoth,* Negative 23). It is therefore forbidden to be concerned (Saadia) or act on the basis of superstitious bad cmens (*Chinukh* 249). *Nachash* in Hebrew. Some say that this is a type of bird divination (Recanti; Septuagint, transposed).

— **auspicious times** (*Sanhedrin* 65b; Rashi; *Yad, Avodath Kokhavim* 11:8). *Me-onan* in Hebrew. It is particularly forbidden to seek out auspicious times astrologically (*Yad, loc. cit.*) Some include in this any action on the basis of good omens (Saadia). Also included in this is the presenting of magical illusions (*Sanhedrin* 65b; *Yad, loc. cit.* 11:9), possibly with smoke (Ibn Ezra; Recanti on Deuteronomy 18:10).

19:27 **cut off . . .** Some say that it is forbidden even to cut it off very close with a scissors (*Tur, Yoreh Deah* 181), while others maintain that the prohibition is primarily against shaving it off with a razor (*Yad, Avodath Kokhavim* 12:6).On the basis of this commandment, it is a Chassidic and Yemenite custom to let the side

19   Do not shave off the edges of your beard.*
²⁸ Do not make gashes in your skin for the dead.*

^28 Do not make gashes in your skin for the dead.*

Do not make any tattoo marks* on your skin. I am God.

²⁹ Do not defile your daughter with premarital sex.* You will then not make the land sexually immoral, and the land [will not] be filled with perversion.

³⁰ Keep My Sabbaths and revere My sanctuary. I am God.

³¹ Do not turn to mediums,* nor seek out oracles,* so as to defile yourselves through them. I am God your Lord.

³² Stand up before a white head, and give respect to the old. You shall thus fear your God. I am God.

³³ When a proselyte comes to live in your land, do not hurt his feelings. ³⁴ The foreigner who becomes a proselyte must be exactly like one who is native born among you. You shall love him as [you love] yourself, for you were foreigners in Egypt. I am God your Lord.

³⁵ Do not falsify measurements, whether in length, weight or volume. ³⁶ You must have an honest balance, honest weights, an honest dry measure,* and an honest liquid measure.*

I am God your Lord who took you out of Egypt. ³⁷ Safeguard My decrees and all My laws, and keep them. I am God.

---

hair grow as long *peyoth*. This is based on Kabbalistic teachings (*Shaar HaMitzvoth; Beth Lechem Yehudah on Yoreh Deah* 181).

— **sides of your head.** This is the area of the temples and upper sideburns, between the forehead and behind the ear (Rashi, *Makkoth* 20a, s.v. *chayav,* 20b, s.v. *ha-mashveh; Yoreh Deah* 181:9). Some translate this verse, "do not round off the edges of your hair", indicating that the prohibition is against producing a tonsured effect by removing the hair on the sideburns and temples (Rashi). However, it is forbidden to cut off any hair in this area completely (*Tosefta, Makkoth* 4:4; *Yoreh Deah* 181:9).

— **shave off . . . with a razor** (*Makkoth* 20a). However, some say that one should not even remove the beard with scissors or a depilatory, and from this is derived the prevalent custom of allowing the beard to grow.

19:28 **Do not make gashes** . . . As a sign of mourning (*Kiddushin* 35b; *Yad, Avodath Kokhavim* 12:12).

— **tatoo marks** (See *Sifethey Cohen, Yoreh Deah* 180:1).

19:29 **premarital sex.** Or any other sex outside of marriage (*Sifra*; Rashi).

19:31 **mediums.** *Ov* in Hebrew. This is a type of necromancy, often involving a human skull (*Sanhedrin* 65b; Rambam, Bertenoro on *Sanhedrin* 7:7). It was used to communicate with the dead (1 Samuel 28:3-9). In many cases, it may involve ventriloquism, *eggastrimuthos* in Greek (Septuagint). The medium makes a voice appear to come from under his arm (*Sanhedrin* 65a,b) or from the ground (Isaiah 29:4; Ralbag, Abarbanel on 1 Samuel 28:7). The methods can also involve meditation and incense drugs (*Yad, Avodath Kokhavim* 6:1; *Sefer HaMitzvoth,* Negative 9). He can also use these means to produce illusions and hallucinations (Saadia). Some identify the *ov* with pythonism, the methods of the Delphic oracle (*Sanhedrin* 65a). Pytho is the old name for Delphi (see *Odyssey* 8:79-81).

— **oracles.** *Yedoni* in Hebrew. They are described as chirping like a bird (Isaiah 8:19), perhaps a form of glossolalia. The Talmud likewise states that this involved the bone of a bird (*Sanhedrin* 65b), and most probably incense drugs and meditation (*Yad, Avodath Kokhavim* 6:2; *Sefer HaMitzvoth,* Negative 9; Ralbag). Here the Septuagint translates *yedoni* as *proskolliethiesesthe,* denoting one who seeks to open the mystical. Elsewhere, it is translated as *gnostas* (on 1 Samuel 28:9), one who seeks gnostic experiences.

19:36 **dry measure** (Rashi; Ibn Ezra). *Ephah* in Hebrew, a particular measure.

— **liquid measure** (*Ibid.*) *Hin* in Hebrew.

[69. Penalties]

¹ God spoke to Moses, telling him to ² say the following to the Israelites: **20**

If any person, whether a [born] Israelite or a proselyte who joins Israel, gives any of his children to Molekh, he must be put to death. The local people must pelt him to death with stones.* ³ I will direct My anger against that person, and will cut him off [spiritually] from among his people, since he has given his children to Molekh, thus defiling that which is holy to Me and profaning My holy name. ⁴ [Therefore,] if the people ignore the fact that this person has given his children to Molekh and they do not kill him, ⁵ I will direct My anger against that person and his family. I will cut him off [spiritually] from among his people, along with all those who are misled by him to prostitute themselves to Molekh.

⁶ If a person turns to the mediums and oracles* so as to prostitute himself to their ways, I will direct My anger against him, and cut him off [spiritually] from his people.*

⁷ You must sanctify yourselves and be holy, for I am God your Lord.
⁸ Safeguard My decrees and keep them, since I am God [and] I am making you holy.

⁹ Any person who curses his father or mother shall therefore be put to death. Since he has cursed his father or mother, he shall be stoned to death.*

¹⁰ If a man commits adultery with a married woman, [and] she is the wife of a fellow [Israelite],* both the adulterer and adulteress shall be put to death.*

¹¹ If a man has intercourse with his father's wife,* he has committed a sexual offense against his father. Therefore, both of them shall be put to death by stoning.*

¹² If a man has intercourse with his daughter-in-law, both of them shall be put to death. Since they have committed an utterly detestable perversion,* they shall be stoned to death.*

¹³ If a man has intercourse with another man in the same manner as with a

---

20:2 **pelt him to death** ... After trial by a duly ordained Sanhedrin. Since there is no such ordination today, death penalties are not imposed.
20:6 **mediums and oracles.** See above, 19:31.
—   **cut him off** ... See note on 20:27.
20:9 **he shall be stoned** ... (*Sanhedrin* 66a; Rashi; from 20:27). Expressed idiomatically by, "his blood is in him." This indicates that he shall be killed by a method that induces internal bleeding, and this is stoning. See Exodus 21:17.
20:10 **fellow Israelite** (*Sanhedrin* 52b; Rashi).
—   **put to death.** By strangulation (*Ibid.*). Whenever a death penalty is not specified, it is by strangulation.
20:11 **If a man** ... The Torah now gives the penalties for the sexual offenses outlined in 18:6-23.
—   **by stoning.** See 20:9.
20:12 **utterly detestable perversion.** *Tevel.* See 18:23.
—   **stoned to death.** See 20:9.

20   woman, both of them have committed a disgusting perversion. They shall be
      put to death by stoning.*
          14 If a man marries a woman and her mother, it is a perversion, and both
      he and [the second one taken]* shall be burned with fire.
          15 If a man performs a sexual act with an animal, he must be put to death,
      and the animal shall also be killed.
          16 If a woman presents herself to an animal and allows it to mate with her,
      you shall kill both the woman and the animal. They shall be put to death by
      stoning.*
          17 If a man takes his sister, even [a half-sister] who is [only] the daughter of
      his father or the daughter of his mother, and they both agree to a sexual act,*
      it is an extremely shameful perversion,* and they shall be cut off [spiritually]
      before their people. Since he has committed incest with his sister, he shall bear
      his guilt.
          18 If a man has intercourse with a woman who is [ritually impure from
      her]* menstruation, he has committed a sexual offense with her. He has
      violated* her womb, and she has revealed the source of her blood; [therefore]
      both of them shall be cut off [spiritually] from among their people.
          19 Do not commit incest with your mother's sister or with your father's
      sister. If one thus violates his blood relative, he shall bear his guilt.
          20 If a man has intercourse with his aunt, thus committing a sexual offense
      against his uncle, [both the man and woman] shall bear their guilt and die
      without children.
          21 If a man takes his brother's wife when she must be avoided,* he has
      committed a sexual offense against his brother, and both [the man and
      woman] shall be childless.
          22 Safeguard all My decrees and laws and keep them, so that the land to
      which I am bringing you to settle will not vomit you out. 23 Do not follow the
      customs* of the nation that I am driving out before you, since they did all the
      above mentioned [perversions] and I was disgusted with them.
          24 I therefore said to you, "Take over their land. I will give it to you so that

      20:13 by stoning. See 20:9.
      20:14 the second one taken (cf. Saadia). That is, if a man marries a woman legally, his wife's mother and
             daughter become forbidden to him. Either one who has intercourse with him then incurs the death
             penalty (*Yad, Issurey Biyah* 2:7; *Sanhedrin* 15:11; Rashi).
      20:16 by stoning. See 20:9.
      20:17 and they both agree . . . (cf. Ramban). Literally, "he sees her nakedness and she sees his nakedness."
      —   extremely shameful perversion. (Targum; Saadia; Rashbam; Ibn Ezra). *Chesed* in Hebrew.
      20:18 ritually impure . . . Who has not immersed in a mikvah; see 18:19.
      —   violated. Or, "penetrated" (*Yevamoth* 54a; Rashi).
      20:21 when she must be avoided. But sometimes she is permitted; Deuteronomy 25:5.
      20:23 Do not follow the customs . . . This is a specific commandment not to follow gentile customs (*Sefer
             HaMitzvoth*, Negative 30). See above, 18:3.

you can inherit it—a land flowing with milk and honey. I am God your Lord **20** who has separated you out from among all the nations. ²⁵ You must [likewise] separate out the clean animals and birds from the unclean. Do not make yourselves disgusting through animals, birds or other creatures that I have separated out for you as being unclean. ²⁶ You shall be holy to Me, for I, God, am holy, and I have separated you out from among the nations to be Mine."

²⁷ Any man or woman who is involved in [the practices of] the mediums or oracles* shall be put to death. They shall be pelted to death with stones, and thus stoned to death.*

אֱמוֹר
Emor

[70. Priestly Laws]

¹ God told Moses to declare the following to Aaron's descendants, the **21** priests:

Let no [priest] defile himself [by contact with] the dead among his people,* ² except for such close blood relatives as his mother, father, son, daughter or brother. ³ He may also allow himself to become ritually unclean for his [deceased] virgin sister, who is [also] close to him* as long as she is not married. ⁴ [However,] a husband may not defile himself for his [dead] wife* if she is legally unfit for him.*

⁵ Let no priest shave off patches of hair from his head.* Let them not shave the edges of their beards* and not make gouges in their skin.*

⁶ They must be holy to their God, and not profane their God's name. Since they present God's fire offerings, the food offering for their God, they must remain holy.

⁷ They shall not marry an immoral or profaned* woman. They [also] must not marry a woman who has been divorced from her husband.

[The priest] must thus be holy to his God. ⁸ You must [strive to] keep him

20:27 **mediums or oracles.** See above 19:31, 20:6.
— **stoned to death.** See note on 20:9. If there are witnesses and the person is condemned, there is a death penalty. Otherwise, the penalty is being "cut off" (above 20:6; Rashi).
21:2 **defile himself** . . . See Numbers 19:14.
21:3 **close to him.** This is a sister who has the same father as the priest (*Yevamoth* 22b; *Yad, Avel* 2:1).
21:4 **a husband may not** . . . (*Sifra*; Rashi). Or, "a man may not defile himself for a corpse among his people"—when there are others to care for it (Rashi). Or, "a man may not defile himself, even for the great" (Saadia; *Baaley Tosafoth*). Or, "[Since he is] a leader, he shall not be defiled among his people" (Targum).
— **if she is legally unfit** . . . See 21:7 (*Yevamoth* 22b; Rashi; cf. *Targum Yonathan*.) Or, "since it makes him unfit for service" (Rashi; Rashbam).
21:5 **let no priest** (*Sifra*; Rashi cf. *Yad, Avodath Kokhavim* 12:15). See Deuteronomy 14:1.
— **Let them not shave** . . . See above, 19:27.
— **and not make gouges** . . . Above, 19:28.
21:7 **profaned.** Born from a marriage between a priest and a woman forbidden to him (Rashi). See 21:15.

21 holy, since he presents the food offering to God. He must be holy, since I am
God—I am holy and I am making you holy.

⁹ If a priest's daughter defiles herself by committing adultery* she has
defiled her father's [position], and she must be burned with fire.

[71. The High Priest]

¹⁰ [These are the rules for] the High Priest* among his brothers, upon
whose head the anointing oil has been poured, and who has been inaugurated
to wear the [special priestly] vestments:

He shall not go without a haircut, and shall not allow his vestments to be
torn.*

¹¹ He shall not come in contact with any dead body. He shall thus not
defile himself, even for his father or mother. ¹² [In such a case]* he may not
[even] leave the sanctuary. He will then not profane his God's sanctuary, since
his God's anointing oil is upon him. I am God.

¹³ He must marry a virgin. ¹⁴ He must not marry a widow, a divorcée, or a
profaned or immoral woman. He may only marry a virgin from his own
people. ¹⁵ He will then not profane his children because of his wife.*

[He must do all this] because I am God, [and] I make him holy.

[72. Blemished Priests]

¹⁶ God spoke to Moses, telling him to ¹⁷ speak to Aaron as follows:

Anyone among your descendants who has a blemish may not approach to
present his God's food offering. ¹⁸ Thus, any blemished priest* may not offer
sacrifice.

[This includes] anyone who is blind* or lame,* or who has a deformed
nose* or a misshapen limb.* ¹⁹ [Also included] is anyone who has a crippled

---

21:9 **adultery.** If she is married (Rashi).
21:10 **High Priest.** *Cohen Gadol* in Hebrew.
—   **He shall not** . . . See above, 10:6.
21:12 **In such a case** . . . (Rashi).
21:15 **He will then not profane.** This defines the "defiled" woman of 21:7 (Rashi).
21:18 **priest.** Literally "man."
—   **blind.** Even in one eye (*Bekhoroth* 44a).
—   **lame.** Or, "paralyzed" (Saadia).
—   **deformed nose** (Septuagint; *Targum Yonathan*). *Charum* in Hebrew. This includes one whose nose is
abnormally long or short, or who has an unopened nostril (*Bekhoroth* 43a; *Yad, Biyath HaMikdash* 8:7;
Ramban). Or, "broken-nosed"(Saadia; cf. Chizzkuni). Some say that this is speaking specifically of a
deformity where the bridge of the nose between the eyes is sunken (Rashi; Radak, *Sherashim*). Others say
that it is speaking of one who has part of the lower septum missing (Ibn Janach).
      According to others, however, *charum* denotes a person who has a missing limb (Ralbag) or one that
is too short (Ibn Ezra; see next note).
—   **misshapen limb** (*Sifra*). *Sarua* in Hebrew. Some say that this includes anyone who has a limb that is dis-
proportionate, while others say that it denotes an oversized limb (Ibn Ezra; cf. Isaiah 28:20) or an extra

leg, a crippled hand, ²⁰ who is a hunchback* or a dwarf,* who has a blemish*   21
in the eye,* who has severe eczema* or ringworm,* or who has a hernia.*
   ²¹ Any descendant of Aaron the priest who has a blemish may not
approach to present God's fire offering. As long as he has a blemish, he may
not approach to present his God's food offering. ²² [Still] he may eat the food
offerings of his God, both from the holy of holies* and from the holy.* ²³ But
he may not come to the cloth partition [in the sanctuary], and he may not
approach the altar if he has a blemish. He shall thus not defile that which is
holy to Me, since I am God [and] I sanctify it.
   ²⁴ Moses told this to Aaron, his sons and all the Israelites.

[73. Priestly Purity]

¹ God spoke to Moses, saying: 22
² Speak to Aaron and his sons, and [tell them] to be careful* regarding the

---

limb (Ralbag). It includes such specific deformities as a club foot or an overly wide foot (*Sifra*) or eyes
that are unusually large or small (Rashi).
   According to some, *sarua* denotes a person who limps (Saadia), or who has a dislocated hip (*Targum
Yonathan*; *Yad, Biyath HaMikdash* 7:9; Ibn Janach, Radak, *Sherashim*). Some sources state that it denotes
one who has mutilated ears (Septuagint; cf. Ralbag).
21:20 **hunchback** (*Sifra*; *Bekhoroth* 43b; Saadia; Septuagint. Cf. Rambam on *Bekhoroth* 7:2; Ibn Janach, Radak,
Sherashim).*Gibben* in Hebrew. Or, "grossly fat" (Chizzkuni). According to others, the first three blemishes
mentioned in this verse are in the eye, and *gibben* denotes a person with misformed eyebrows (cf. Ralbag).
Some say that it denotes a person whose eyebrows are unusually long (*Targum Yonathan; Bekhoroth* 43b;
Rashi; Ramban; Radak, *Sherashim*), or whose eyebrows are attached to each other (*Bekhoroth* 43b). Others
say that it denotes one with missing eyebrows (*Ibid.*).
— **dwarf** (*Targum Yerushalmi*; Ibn Ezra; Chizzkuni). *Dak* in Hebrew. Here too, some say that this is relating
specifically to the eye. Some say that *dak* denotes a membrane or film over the eye, *tella* in Old French
and Latin (Rashi; Radak, *Sherashim*; cf. Septuagint). Others say that it denotes a white spot on the pupil
of the eye (*Yad, Biyath HaMikdash* 7:5; Rambam on *Bekhoroth* 6:2; Ralbag; cf. *Bekhoroth* 38b). Still others
describe the *dak* as a loss of eyebrows (*Targum Yonathan*) or as droopy eyelids (Ibn Janach).
— **blemish** (Chizzkuni). *Te-bhalul* in Hebrew. Some say that this specifically denotes one who has a streak of
white going into the iris (Rashi; *Targum Yonathan*; *Yad, Biyath HaMikdash* 7:5; *Bekhoroth* 38a) or pupil (Ibn
Janach; Radak, *Sherashim*) of the eye. Others see it as a growth in the eye (Saadia), or missing eyelashes
(Septuagint). It also includes a case where the eyes focus in abnormal directions (*Sifra*; *Bekhoroth* 44a).
— **in the eye.** As we have seen, there is a question as to whether just one term modifies "in the eye," or if all
three terms do. Thus, the verse can also be translated, "Who has misshapen brows, a film, or a blemish
in the eye." Although there is a dispute as to the precise meaning of the words here, all the blemishes are
known from tradition (Rambam on *Bekhoroth* 7:2).
— **severe eczema.** Or, "a hard dry rash," *garav* in Hebrew (*Bekhoroth* 41a; Saadia; Rashi). See Deuteronomy
28:27. Or, "an itch" (Radak, *Sherashim*) or, "a malignant skin ulcer" (Septuagint).
— **ringworm.** *Yalefeth* in Hebrew, *leichen* (lichen) in Greek (Septuagint). This is described as running sores,
pimples or scabs (*Bekhoroth* 41a; Saadia; Rashi; *Targum Yerushalmi*).
— **hernia.** Or "swollen testicles" (*Targum Yonathan*; Saadia). *Meroach ashekh* in Hebrew. Or, "crushed testicles" (Targum; Rashi; Radak, *Sherashim*; Chizzkuni), or "a missing testicle" (Septuagint; cf. *Targum Yerushalmi*). According to others, *meroach ashekh* denotes a person with abnormally dark skin coloration
(*Bekhoroth* 44b; Rambam on *Bekhoroth* 7:5).
21:22 **holy of holies.** The meal offering (above, 2:3,10), the sin offering (6:18), and the guilt offering (7:1).
— **holy.** Such as peace offerings.
22:2 **be careful** (Ibn Ezra; Septuagint). Or, "Withdraw" (Targum; Rashi).

22 sacred offerings that the Israelites consecrate to Me, so that they not desecrate My holy name. I am God.

³ Tell them that if any man among their* descendants is in an unclean state when he presents the sacred offerings that the Israelites consecrate to God, he shall be cut off [spiritually] from before Me. I am God.

⁴ Any descendant of Aaron who has a leprous mark* or a male discharge* may not eat any sacred offerings until he has purified himself. [The same is true] of one who touches anyone defiled by the dead,* who has had a seminal emmission,* ⁵ or who has touched any unclean small animal* or any person who can defile him.

⁶ A person who touches [any of the above]* shall be unclean until evening, and he shall not eat any sacred offering unless he has immersed in a mikvah.* ⁷ He then becomes ritually clean at sunset, and he can eat the sacred offerings which are his portion.

⁸ [The priest] shall not eat any creature that has died on its own, and which [is forbidden only because it] has a fatal lesion,* since this will defile him. I am God.

⁹ [The priests] shall thus keep My charge* and not profane [the sacred offering], which is a sin that can cause them to die. I am God [and] I am making them holy.

¹⁰ No non-priest may eat the sacred offering.* Even if a person resides with a priest or is hired by him,* that person may not eat the sacred offering.

¹¹ [However,] if a priest buys a slave* for money as his own property, then [the slave] may eat [the sacred offering]. Similarly, [a slave] born in his house may eat his food.

¹² When a priest's daughter marries a non-priest, she may no longer eat the sacred elevated gift.* ¹³ But if the priest's daughter has no children, and is

---

22:3 **their.** Literally, "your."

22:4 **leprous mark.** Above, 13:1-44.

— **male discharge.** Above, 15:1-15.

— **defiled by the dead** (Rashi). Literally, "unclean to a soul."

— **seminal emission.** Above, 15:16-18.

22:5 **small animal.** *Sheretz.* Above, 11:29,30.

22:6 **any of the above.** (Rashi).

— **immersed . . .** See Exodus 29:4.

22:8 **any creature . . .** This is speaking of a dead kosher bird, as in 17:15 (*Chullin* 100b; Rashi).

22:9 **keep My charge.** By not eating sacred offerings while unclean. This is also speaking of *terumah*, the priestly agricultural offering (Rashi).

22:10 **sacred offering.** The Torah here is specifically speaking of terumah, the priestly agricultural offering (*Sifra; Yevamoth* 70b; Rashi). See 22:12.

— **if a person . . .** Even a Hebrew slave, and even if his ear has been pierced as in Exodus 21:6 (*Yevamoth* 70a; Rashi).

22:11 **slave.** A gentile slave.

22:12 **elevated gift.** *Terumah* in Hebrew, the priestly agricultural offering.

widowed or divorced, she may return to her father's house [with the same   22
status] as when she was a girl, and she may eat her father's food.

No non-priest may eat [the elevated gift]. ¹⁴ If a person inadvertently eats
such a sacred offering, he must add one-fifth to it, and give it to the priest
along with [an appropriate substitute]* for the sacred offering.

¹⁵ [Non-priests]* thus shall not profane the sacred offerings which the
Israelites give as elevated gifts in God's [name]. ¹⁶ If they eat the sacred offerings, they will bear the guilt of sin, since I am God [and] it is I who make
[these offerings] holy.

[74. Blemished Animals]

¹⁷ God spoke to Moses, telling him to ¹⁸ speak to Aaron, to his sons and to
all the Israelites, saying to them:

[This is the law] if any person, whether of the family of Israel or of the
proselytes who join them, offers any [animal] that can be presented to God as
a burnt offering to fulfill a general or a specific pledge.* ¹⁹ To gain acceptance,*
it must be an unblemished male [taken] from the cattle, sheep or goats.* ²⁰ Do
not present any blemished animal, since it will not be accepted for you.

²¹ [Similarly], when a person presents a peace offering of cattle or sheep to
fulfill a general or specific pledge, it must be unblemished in order to be
acceptable. It shall not have any blemish on it.

²² Thus, you may not offer to God any animal that is blind,* broken-
limbed,* or gashed,* or that has warts,* mange* or ringworm.* You may not
place [such an animal] on the altar as a fire offering to God. ²³ [However, if] an
ox or sheep has an extra* or missing* limb, it can be offered as a gift [to the

---

22:14 substitute (*Sifra*; Rashi).

22:15 Non-priests. (Rashi).

22:18 general or specific pledge. *Neder* or *nedavah* (*Kinnim* 1:1).

22:19 To gain acceptance. (Saadia)

— **an unblemished . .** See above, 1:3,10.

22:22 blind. Even in one eye (Saadia).

— **broken-limbed.** Even if the tail is fractured (*Sifra*). Some say that the word *shabhur* here specifically
denotes a broken fore-foot (Ibn Ezra).

— **gashed** (Ralbag). *Charutz* in Hebrew. This includes a perforated or split eyelid, nose or lip (*Sifra; Bekhoroth*
38a, 39a). Some say that it specifically denotes a split eyelid (*Targum Yonathan*; Rashi; Ibn Janach; *Arukh*,
from *Bekhoroth* 38a,b, Gittin 56a). It also includes a gash anyplace where there is a bone (*Bekhoroth* 41a;
Yad, Biyath HaMikdash 7:11). Others say that it denotes a broken or crippled hind leg (Ibn Ezra). According to still others, it denotes a severed limb (Targum; Saadia; Chizzkuni), particularly a severed tongue
(Septuagint; cf. Exodus 11:7).

— **warts.** *Yabheleth* in Hebrew; *murmekionta* in Greek (Septuagint); *verrue* in French (Rashi); *verruga* in
Spanish (Radak, *Sherashim*; cf. *Sifra*; Saadia; *Yad, Biyath HaMikdash* 7:10). According to others, a *yabheleth*
is the same as a *te-bhalul* in 21:20, denoting white in the iris of the eye (*Targum Yonathan*; Ibn Ezra).

— **mange.** *Garav* in Hebrew, same as in 21:20. It is the animal equivalent of eczema.

— **ringworm.** *Yalefeth* in Hebrew, as in 21:20.

22:23 extra . . . (Targum; Ralbag). *Saru'a* in Hebrew, as in 21:18. Or, "an overgrown limb" (*Bekhoroth* 40a;
Rashi), "a limp" (Saadia), or, "ears cut off" (Septuagint).

22   sanctuary].* But [none of the above] shall be acceptable as a pledge [for the altar].*

²⁴ [Similarly,] you may not offer to God [any animal that has its testicles] crushed, whether by hand* or with an instrument,* pulled loose,* or severed. This is something that you must never do*, no matter where you live.*

²⁵ You may not offer any such animal, even if it is [presented by] a gentile. [Animals] that are maimed and blemished shall not be acceptable for you.

[75. Acceptable Animals]

²⁶ God spoke to Moses, saying:

²⁷ When a bull, sheep or goat is born, it must remain with its mother for seven days. Then, after the eighth day,* it shall be acceptable as sacrifice for a fire offering to God.

²⁸ Whether it is a bull, a sheep or a goat,* do not slaughter [a female animal]* and its child on the same day.*

²⁹ When you sacrifice a thanksgiving offering to God, you must do so in an acceptable manner. ³⁰ It must be eaten on the same day, with nothing left over until the [next] morning.* I am God.

³¹ Be careful regarding My commandments and keep them; I am God.

³² Do not desecrate* My holy name. I must be sanctified* among the Israelites.

I am God [and] I am making you holy ³³ and bringing you out of Egypt to be your God. I am God.

—   **missing limb** (Targum). Or, "an atrophied limb" (Ibn Ezra; Ibn Janach; Radak, *Sherashim*), "unsplit hooves" (*Bekhoroth* 40a; Rashi; Ralbag), "an abnormally long stride" (Saadia), or, "a lost tail" (Septuagint).
—   **gift to the sanctuary** (*Sifra; Temurah* 7b; Rashi; Ramban).
—   **for the altar** (cf. Ramban).
22:24 **crushed. . .by hand** (Rashi; Radak, *Sherashim*, from Ezekiel 23:3) *Ma'ukh* in Hebrew. Or, "pulled loose" (Ibn Janach), or, "ruptured" (Septuagint).
—   **with an instrument** (cf. Rashi; Radak, *Sherashim*).
—   **pulled loose** (Rashi). *Nathuk* in Hebrew. Or, "gelded" (Septuagint).
—   **you must never do.** This is a commandment forbidding any castration (*Shabbath* 110b; Rashi; *Sefer HaMitzvoth*, Negative 361; *Yad, Issurey Biyah* 16:10).
—   **no matter where you live** (Saadia; *Yad, loc.cit.*). Literally, "in your land." This is true even when there is no sacrifice (cf. Sforno).
22:27 **after the eighth day.** See Exodus 22:29.
22:28 **sheep or goat.** The Hebrew *seh* denotes both; see Exodus 12:3,5.
—   **a female animal** (Rashi).
—   **on the same day.** This is true of all animals, even those not slaughtered as sacrifices (*Chullin* 78a; *Sefer HaMitzvoth*, Negative 101; *Yad, Shechitah* 12:1,2).
22:30 **It must be eaten on the same day** . . . See above, 7:15.
22:32 **Do not desecrate.** This is a specific commandment not to do anything to give God or His Torah a bad name (*Sefer HaMitzvoth*, Negative 63).
—   **I must be sanctified.** This is the commandment of *kiddush ha-Shem*, to enhance the reputation of God and His Torah (*Sefer HaMitzvoth*, Positive 9).

[76. Special Days: The Sabbath]

¹ God spoke to Moses, telling him to ² speak to the Israelites and say to them:

There are special times that you must celebrate as sacred holidays to God. The following are My special times:

³ You may do work during the six weekdays, but Saturday* is a Sabbath of Sabbaths. It is a sacred holiday to God, when you shall do no work.* Wherever you may live, it is God's Sabbath.

[77. Passover]

⁴ These are God's festivals that you must celebrate as sacred holidays at their appropriate times:

⁵ The afternoon of the 14th day of the first month* is [the time that you must sacrifice] God's Passover offering.

⁶ Then, on the 15th of that month, it is God's festival of matzahs, when you eat matzahs for seven days. ⁷ The first day shall be a sacred holiday to you, when you may not do any service work.*

⁸ You shall then bring sacrifices to God for seven days.* The seventh day is a sacred holiday when you may not do any service work.

[78. The Omer]

⁹ God spoke to Moses, telling him to ¹⁰ speak to the Israelites and say to them:

When you come to the land that I am going to give you, and you reap its harvest, you must bring an omer* of your first reaping to the priest. ¹¹ He shall wave it in the motions prescribed* for a wave offering to God, so that it will be acceptable for you. The priest shall make this wave offering on the day after the first day of the [Passover] holiday.*

¹² On the day you make the wave offering of the omer, you shall prepare an unblemished yearling sheep as a burnt offering to God. ¹³ Its meal offering

---

23:3 **Saturday.** Literally, "the seventh day."
— **work.** See Exodus 20:10.
23:5 **first month.** Nissan. See Exodus 12:2.
23:7 **service work.** *Melekheth avodah* in Hebrew. This includes all work that is not necessary for preparing food, as in Exodus 12:16 (Ramban; Ralbag; Hirsch).
23:8 **bring sacrifice . . .** See Numbers 28:16-25.
23:10 **omer.** This is 1/10 ephah (Exodus 16:36), the daily measure of manna, and the usual measure for a meal offering (above, 5:11, 6:13, Numbers 15:4, etc.). It is about 2 quarts. The omer offering consisted of barley (see above, 2:14).
23:11 **prescribed.** See note on Exodus 29:24.
— **after the first day of the Passover holiday.** That is, the omer was offered on the second day of Passover (Rashi; *Yad, Temidim* 7:3; *Sefer HaMitzvoth*, Positive 44).

23 shall be two-tenths [of an ephah] of wheat meal, mixed with oil, a fire offering
to God. Its libation offering shall be one-fourth hin* of wine.

¹⁴ Until the day that you bring this sacrifice to your God, you may not eat*
bread, roasted grain* or fresh grain. This shall be an eternal law for all generations, no matter where you live.*

[79. Counting the Omer; Shavuoth]

¹⁵ You shall then count* seven complete weeks after the day following the
[Passover] holiday when you brought the omer as a wave offering, ¹⁶ until the
day after the seventh week, when there will be [a total of] 50 days. [On that
50th day]* you may present new grain* as a meal offering to God.

¹⁷ From the land upon which you live, you shall bring two loaves* of bread
as a wave offering. They shall be made of two-tenths [of an ephah] of wheat
meal, and shall be baked as leavened bread. They are the first-harvest* offering to God.

¹⁸ Together with this bread, you shall sacrifice seven unblemished yearling
sheep, one young bull, and two rams. These, along with their meal offerings
and libations* shall be a burnt offering to God, a fire offering as an appeasing
fragrance to God.

¹⁹ You shall also prepare one goat as a sin offering, and two yearling sheep
as peace sacrifices. ²⁰ The priest shall make the motions prescribed for a wave
offering before God with the bread for the first-harvest offering and the two
sheep. They belong to the priest* as something sacred to God.

²¹ This very day shall be celebrated as a sacred holiday when no service

23:13 **one-fourth hin.** A little less than a quart (0.8 liter).
23:14 **you may not eat . . .** This is the law of *chadash*, which forbids the eating of new grain until after the
second day of Passover (*Sefer Hamitzvoth*, Negative 189). Thus, any grain that has not begun to take root
before Passover is forbidden until the next Passover (*Yad, Maakhaloth Assuroth* 10:4; *Yoreh Deah* 293:3).
Therefore, if wheat is planted in the late spring after Passover, and harvested in the fall, it may not be
eaten until after the next Passover. See below.
— **roasted grain.** *Kali* in Hebrew. See above 2:14.
— **fresh grain.** *Karmel* in Hebrew. See above 2:14.
— **no matter where you live.** Even outside the Holy Land (*Orlah* 3:4; Rashi). However, others say that the
law of *chadash* does not apply outside the Holy Land (*Kiddushin* 37a; *Turey Zahav, Yoreh Deah* 293:4).
Others say that gentile grain is not included in the prohibition (*Beth Chadash, Yoreh Deah* 293). The chassidic custom is to follow the opinions that permit *chadash* outside the Holy Land (cf. *Zikhron Tov* 12b; *Sefer
Baal Shem Tov* 6). Many non-chassidim, however, regard it as forbidden.
23:15 **You shall then count . . .** This is the commandment to count the Omer (*Sefer HaMitzvoth*, Positive 161).
23:16 **50th day** (Rashi). *Pentacost* in Greek.
— **you may present new grain** (*Menachoth* 84b; *Sifra*; Rashi; *Yad, Issurey Mizbeach* 5:10). Or, "you shall bring
an offering of new grain," namely the two loaves mentioned in 23:17 (*Menachoth* 83b; *Yad, Temidim* 8:2).
23:17 **two loaves.** The loaves were rectangular, 4 x 7 handbreadths, and 4 fingerbreadths high (12" x 21" x 3")
(*Menachoth* 97a; *Yad, Temidim* 8:10).
— **first-harvest offering.** *Bikkurim* in Hebrew.
23:18 **meal offerings and libations.** See Numbers 15:1-12.
23:20 **to the priest** (Ralbag; cf. *Yad, Temidim* 8:11).

work may be done. This is an eternal law for all generations, no matter where 23
you may live.*

²² [Furthermore,] when you reap your land's harvest, do not completely harvest the ends of your fields.* [Also] do not pick up individual stalks that may have fallen. You must leave [all these] for the poor and the stranger. I am God your Lord.

[80. Rosh HaShanah]

²³ God spoke to Moses, telling him to ²⁴ speak to the Israelites and say:
The first day of the seventh month* shall be a day of rest for you. It is a sacred holiday for remembrance* [and] sounding [of the ram's horn].* ²⁵ Do not do any service work [on that day]. Bring a fire offering to God.*

[81. Yom Kippur]

²⁶ God spoke to Moses, saying:
²⁷ The 10th of this seventh month* shall be the Day of Atonement* for you. It is a sacred holiday when you must fast* and bring a fire offering to God.* ²⁸ Do not do any work* on this day; it is a day of atonement, when you gain atonement before God your Lord.

²⁹ If anyone does not fast on this day, he shall be cut off [spiritually] from his people. ³⁰ [Similarly,] if one does any work on this day, I will destroy him [spiritually] from among his people.

³¹ Do not do any work [on this day]. This is an eternal law for all generations, no matter where you may live. ³² It is a sabbath of sabbaths to you, [and a day] when you must fast. You must keep this holiday from the ninth of the month until [the next] night.

[82. Sukkoth]

³³ God spoke to Moses, telling him to ³⁴ speak to the Israelites, as follows:

23:21 **an eternal law** . . . To count the omer, even when there is no sacrifice (Sforno).
23:22 **when you reap** . . . See 19:9.
23:24 **seventh month.** This is Tishrei, the seventh month counting from Nissan (see above, 23:5). The Torah is speaking of Rosh HaShanah, the New Year.
— **remembrance** (Targum; Rashi; *Rosh HaShanah* 32a). Or, "commemorative sounding" (Chizzkuni). Others translate *zikhron* here as "sounding" (Saadia; Ibn Janach; cf. Numbers 10:9).
— **ram's horn** (*Sifra*; Ralbag; cf. *Rosh HaShanah* 26a).
23:25 **fire offering** . . . See Numbers 29:1-6.
23:27 **seventh month.** Tishrei.
— **Day of Atonement.** *Yom HaKippurim* in Hebrew. Usually abbreviated to Yom Kippur.
— **fast.** See above, 16:29.
— **fire offering** . . . See Numbers 29:7-11.
— **work.** See above, 16:29. Here the Torah says "work," rather than "service work," because on Yom Kippur, it is forbidden to do work to prepare food, just as it is on the Sabbath. See note on 23:7.

23   The 15th of this seventh month* shall be the festival of Sukkoth* to God,
[lasting] seven days. ³⁵ The first day shall be a sacred holiday when you may
not do any service work. ³⁶ For seven days then, you shall present a fire offering to God.*

        The eighth day* is a sacred holiday to you when you shall bring a fire
offering to God. It is a time of retreat* when you may do no service work.

        ³⁷ The above are God's special times which you must keep as sacred holi-
days. [They are times] when you must present to God a burnt offering, a meal
offering, a sacrifice and libations, each depending on the particular day.
³⁸ [This is in addition to] God's Sabbath [offerings],* and the gifts, and the
specific and general pledges that you offer to God.

        ³⁹ On the 15th of the seventh month, when you harvest the land's grain,
you shall celebrate a festival to God for seven days. The first day shall be a day
of rest, and the eighth day shall be a day of rest.

        ⁴⁰ On the first day, you must take for yourself a fruit of the citron tree,* an
unopened palm frond,* myrtle branches,* and willows [that grow near] the
brook.* You shall rejoice before God for seven days. ⁴¹ During these seven
days each year, you shall celebrate to God. It is an eternal law for all generations that you celebrate [this festival] in the seventh month.

        ⁴² During [these] seven days you must live in thatched huts.* Everyone
included in Israel* must live in such thatched huts. ⁴³ This is so that future
generations will know that I had the Israelites live in huts* when I brought
them out of Egypt. I am God your Lord.

        ⁴⁴ Moses related [the rules of] God's special times to the Israelites.

23:34 **seventh month.** Tishrei.
—   **Sukkoth.** Denoting "thatched huts." See 23:42.
23:36 **fire offering** . . . See Numbers 29:12-38.
—   **eighth day.** This is *Shemini Atzereth.* See next note.
—   **time of retreat.** *Atzereth* in Hebrew. It is a time when one must "hold back" from doing work (Saadia;
          Ibn Ezra; Radak, *Sherashim*) and maintain a level of holiness (Sforno). Others say it is a "holdover" for
          the holiday (Rashi; Ibn Ezra)
23:38 **offerings** (*Sifra*).
23:40 **citron** (Targum; Saadia). *Hadar* in Hebrew, usually referred to as Ethrog.
—   **unopened palm frond.** (*Sukkah* 32a; Rashi).
—   **myrtle branches** (cf. *Sukkah* 32b; Rashi). The practice is to place three such branches in the bunch.
—   **willows** . . . (cf. *Sukkah* 34a). Two are placed in the bunch, together with the palm frond and myrtle.
23:42 **thatched huts.** *Sukkoth* in Hebrew.
—   **Everyone included** . . . (cf. *Sifra*; Rashi).
23:43 **huts.** This was in the fall, when it generally begins to become cold, and Sukkoth is therefore celebrated in
          the fall (Ramban). Others say that after being in the desert, it is proper to thank God for the harvest at
          this time (Rashbam; see Exodus 23:16). Some say that the "huts" denote the clouds of glory that sur-
          rounded the Israelites in the desert (*Sukkah* 11b; Rashi).

[83. The Lamp]

¹ God spoke to Moses, telling him to ² instruct the Israelites to bring him* **24**
clear illuminating oil from hand-crushed olives, to keep the lamp burning
constantly.*

³ Aaron shall light [the lamp] consistently with [this oil]. [It shall burn]
before God, from evening to morning, outside the cloth partition in the
Communion Tent. This shall be an eternal law for all your generations. ⁴ He
shall consistently kindle the lamps on the pure [gold] menorah before God.

[84. The Showbread]

⁵ You shall take the finest grade of wheat flour and bake it into twelve
loaves. Each loaf shall contain two-tenths [of an ephah].* ⁶ Arrange [these
loaves] in two stacks, six loaves to each stack. This shall be on the undefiled
table* which is before God.

⁷ Place pure frankincense* alongside* these stacks. This will be the memorial portion* [presented as] a fire offering to God.

⁸ [These loaves] shall consistently be arranged before God each Sabbath. It
is an eternal covenant that this must come from the Israelites.

⁹ The [bread] shall be given to Aaron and his descendants, but since it is
holy of holies among God's fire offerings, they must eat it in a sanctified area.
This is an eternal law.

[85. The Blasphemer]

¹⁰ The son of an Israelite woman and an Egyptian man* went out* among
the Israelites and the Israelite woman's son had a quarrel* with an Israelite
man in the camp. ¹¹ The Israelite woman's son then blasphemed* God's name

---

24:2   **him.** Literally, "you."
—   **clear illuminating oil** . . . See Exodus 27:20.
24:5   **two-tenths** . . . Around one gallon.
24:6   **on the undefiled table.** See Exodus 25:30.
24:7   **frankincense.** See Exodus 30:34. This was placed in a bowl; see Exodus 25:29. There were three fingers
        full (a *kometz*) of this incense (*Yad, Temidim* 5:2).
—   **alongside** (*Menachoth* 97a; *Yad, Temidim* 5:2). Literally, "on."
—   **memorial portion.** *Azkara* in Hebrew; see above 2:9. Only the frankincense was burnt; the breads were
        eaten by the priests.
24:10 **Egyptian man.** This was the Egyptian who killed the Israelite (Exodus 2:11) and then took his wife
        (Rashi).
—   **went out.** This happened at the same time that a man was found gathering wood in Numbers 15:32
        (*Sifra; Chizzkuni*).
—   **had a quarrel.** Since he wanted to camp with the Danites (*Sifra; Tanchuma* 24).
24:11 **blasphemed** (Saadia; Radak, *Sherashim;* cf. 24:15). *Nakav* in Hebrew. Or, "pronounced" (Targum;
        Rashi).

24 with a curse. The [people] brought him to Moses. His mother's name was Shelomith daughter of Divri, of the tribe of Dan. ¹² They kept him under custody until the penalty could be specified by God.

[86. Penalties for Blasphemy]

¹³ God spoke to Moses, saying:

¹⁴ Take the blasphemer out of the camp, and let all who heard him place their hands on his head. The entire community shall then stone him to death.

¹⁵ Speak to the Israelites as follows:

Anyone who curses God shall bear his sin. ¹⁶ But if one actually blasphemes the name YHVH,* he shall be put to death. The entire community shall stone him. Whether he is a proselyte* or a native born [Israelite], he shall be put to death.

¹⁷ One who takes a human life must be put to death.

¹⁸ If one kills an animal, he must pay for it, [the value of]* a life for a life.

¹⁹ If one maims his neighbor, he must be penalized accordingly.* ²⁰ Thus, full compensation must be paid for* a fracture or the loss of an eye or a tooth. If one inflicts injury on another person, he must [pay as if the same injury were] inflicted on him.*

²¹ Thus, if one kills an animal, he must pay for it, but if one kills a human being, he must be put to death. ²² There shall be one law for you, for both the proselyte and the native born, for I am God, Lord of you [all].

²³ Moses related [all] this to the Israelites, and they took the blasphemer out of the camp, pelting him to death with stones. The Israelites thus did as God had commanded Moses.

BeHar   בְּהַר

[87. The Sabbatical Year]

25 ¹ God spoke to Moses at Mount Sinai,* telling him to ² speak to the Israelites and say to them:

24:16 **YHVH.** The Tetragrammaton, which may not be pronounced (see *Yad, Avodath Kokhavim* 2:7).
— **proselyte.** However, this is a prohibition for which even a gentile can be put to death, and hence, *ger* can be translated as "foreigner."
24:18 **the value of . . .** (obvious from context).
24:19 **penalized accordingly.** Idiomatically expressed as, "as he did, so shall be done to him."
24:20 **full compensation . . .** See Exodus 21:24,25.
— **pay as if . . .** (Rashi; *Bava Kama* 84a). That is, one must pay the amount a person would to avoid such an injury.
25:1 **at Mount Sinai.** At this time, the Israelites were still at the foot of Mount Sinai (cf. Numbers 10:11,12; see Josephus, *Antiquities* 3:12:3; *Baaley Tosafoth*). Or, "on Mount Sinai" (*Sifra*; Rashi). According to this,

When you come to the land that I am giving you, the land must be given a   25
rest period, a sabbath to God. ³ For six years you may plant your fields, prune
your vineyards, and harvest your crops, ⁴ but the seventh year is a sabbath of
sabbaths for the land.* It is God's sabbath during which you may not plant
your fields, nor prune your vineyards. ⁵ Do not harvest crops that grow on
their own* and do not gather the grapes on your unpruned vines,* since it is a
year of rest for the land.

⁶ [What grows while]* the land is resting may be eaten by you, by your
male and female slaves, and by the employees and resident hands who live
with you. ⁷ All the crops shall [also] be eaten by the domestic and wild animals
that are in your land.

[88. The Jubilee]

⁸ You shall count seven sabbatical years, that is, seven times seven years.
The period of the seven sabbatical cycles shall thus be 49 years. ⁹ Then, on the
10th day of the seventh month,* you shall make a proclamation with the ram's
horn. This proclamation with the ram's horn is thus to be made on Yom Kippur. ¹⁰ You shall sanctify the fiftieth year, declaring emancipation [of slaves]*
all over the world.* This is your jubilee year, when each man shall return to his
hereditary property and to his family.

¹¹ The fiftieth year shall [also] be a jubilee to you insofar as you may not
sow, harvest crops growing of their own accord, nor gather grapes from
unpruned vines during that [year]. ¹² The jubilee shall thus be holy to you.
You shall eat the crops from the field that [year].

¹³ In the jubilee year, every man shall return to his hereditary property.
¹⁴ Thus, when you buy or sell [land] to your neighbor, do not cheat one
another. ¹⁵ You are buying [only] according to the number of years after the

the section from here until the end of the book (see 27:34) was given before the tabernacle was erected
(Rashbam). Some say that it was given during Moses' first 40 days on the mountain, and was the "book
of covenant" (Exodus 24:7) that Moses read to the Israelites (Ibn Ezra; Chizzkuni). According to others,
it was given during the last 40 day period, while Moses was obtaining the second Tablets, and thus, it
constituted a new covenant (Ramban; Abarbanel). Some say that Moses declared it to the Israelites at
that time (*Ibid.*).
25:4 **but the seventh year** ... See Exodus 23:10,11.
25:5 **Do not harvest** ... (see *Yad, Shemitah* 4:1,2).
— **unpruned vines** (Ramban). *Nazir* in Hebrew. Or, "vines kept from others" (Rashi), "best vines" (Saadia),
"vines with which you have not worked" (Radak, *Sherashim*), or "vines you have left alone" (Ibn Janach).
25:6 **What grows** ... (Saadia; Ibn Ezra).
25:9 **seventh month.** Tishrei. See above, 23:27.
25:10 **slaves.** Hebrew slaves; see 25:46 (*Rosh HaShanah* 9b). See Exodus 21:6.
— **all over the world** (*Rosh HaShanah* 9b). Literally, "for the land and all who live on it." Jubilee was only in
force as long as the majority of tribes owned their hereditary lands; thus, it ceased to be in force after the
ten tribes were exiled (*Arukhin* 32b; *Yad, Shemitah* 10:8). The laws of Hebrew slaves and houses in walled
cities were also in force only as long as the jubilee (*Arkhin* 29a; *Yad, Shemitah* 10:9).

25 jubilee; [therefore], he is selling it to you for the number of years that [the land] will produce crops [until the next jubilee]. [16] Since he is selling it to you for the number of crops, you must increase the price if it will be for many years, and decrease it if there are few. [17] You will then not be cheating one another. You shall fear your God, since it is I who am God your Lord.

[18] Keep My decrees and safeguard My laws. If you keep them, you will live in the land securely. [19] The land will produce its fruit, and you will eat your fill, thus living securely in [the land].

[20] In the seventh year,* you might ask, "What will we eat [in the jubilee year]? We have not planted nor have we harvested crops."

[21] I will direct My blessing to you in the sixth year, and [the land] will produce enough crops for three years. [22] You will therefore be eating your old crops when you plant [after]* the eighth year. You will still be eating your old crops until the crops of the ninth year are ripe.

[23] Since the land is Mine, no land shall be sold permanently. You are foreigners and resident aliens as far as I am concerned, [24] and therefore, there shall be time of redemption for all your hereditary lands.

[89. Redemption of Land]

[25] If your brother becomes impoverished and sells some of his hereditary land, a close relative can come and redeem what his kinsman has sold.* [26] [The same is true] if a man does not have anyone to redeem it, but gains enough wealth to be able to redeem it himself. [27] He shall then calculate the number of years for which [the land] has been sold,* and return the balance to the buyer. He can then return to his hereditary land.

[28] If he does not have the means to retrieve [the land], then that which he has sold shall remain with the buyer until the jubilee year. It is then released by the jubilee, so that [the original owner] can return to his hereditary land.

[90. Houses in Walled Cities]

[29] When a man sells a residential house in a walled city* he shall be able to redeem it until the end of one year after he has sold it. He has one full year to

---

25:20 **In the seventh year** . . . (Ramban). Or, "You might ask, 'What will we eat in the seventh year?'"(Rashi).

25:22 **after.** (According to Ramban, *loc. cit.*). Because it is forbidden to plant in the jubilee year. According to Rashi, "in," since the eighth year is a regular year.

25:25 **a close relative** . . . (cf. *Kiddushin* 21b; *Yad, Shemitah* 11:18). This is true even against the buyer's will (Rashi). However, it can only be redeemed after two years have elapsed from the time of sale (*Yad, Shemitah* 11:9).

25:27 **the number of years** . . . From the time of sale until the jubilee year.

25:29 **walled city.** If it was already walled when Joshua first conquered the land (*Sifra; Arkhin* 33b; *Yad, Shemitah* 12:15).

the day* to redeem it. ³⁰ However, if it is not redeemed by the end of this year, 25
then the house in the walled city shall become the permanent property of the
buyer [to be passed down] to his descendants. It shall not be released by the
jubilee.

³¹ [On the other hand], houses in villages that do not have walls around
them shall be considered the same as open land. They shall thus be redeemable, and shall be released by the jubilee.

³² As far as the Levites' cities* are concerned, the Levites shall always have
the power to redeem the houses in their hereditary cities. ³³ Thus, if one buys*
a house or city from the Levites, it must be released by the jubilee. [This is
because] houses in the Levites' cities are their hereditary property among the
Israelites. ³⁴ Similarly, the open areas surrounding their cities* shall not be
sold [permanently],* because it is their hereditary property forever.

[91. Helping Others]

³⁵ When your brother becomes impoverished and loses the ability to sup-
port himself in the community,* you must come to his aid. Help him survive,*
whether he is a proselyte or a native [Israelite].*

³⁶ Do not take advance [interest]* or accrued interest* from him. Fear your
God, and let your brother live alongside you. ³⁷ Do not make him pay
advance interest for your money, and do not give him food for which he will
have to pay accrued interest. ³⁸ I am God your Lord, who brought you out of
Egypt to give you the land of Canaan, [and] to be a God for you.

[92. Slaves]

³⁹ If your brother becomes impoverished and is sold to you,* do not work
him like a slave. ⁴⁰ He shall be with you just like an employee or a resident
hand. He shall serve you only until the jubilee year, ⁴¹ and then he and his
children shall be free to leave you and to return to their family. He shall thus
return to the hereditary land of his ancestors.

—   **full year to the day** (*Arkhin* 31a; Rashi).
25:32 **Levites' cities.** See Numbers 35:6,7.
25:33 **buys** (Saadia; Rashi). Literally, "redeems."
25:34 **open area . . .** *Migrash* in Hebrew. This is an area of 3000 cubits (Numbers 35:4,5) or 0.85 mile around
    the city (*Sotah* 37b; *Yad, Shemitah* 13:2).
—   **permanently** (Saadia). Or, "for other than their original purpose" (*Arkhin* 33b; *Yad, Shemitah* 13:5;
    Ralbag).
25:35 **loses the ability . . .** Literally, "and slips down among you."
—   **Help him survive.** Literally, "he shall live with you." (cf. Rashi).
—   **native Israelite.** (Ibn Ezra; cf. *Bava Metzia* 71a,b; *Yad, Malveh* 5:1.
25:36 **advance [interest]** (*Bava Metzia* 60b). *Neshekh* in Hebrew.
—   **accrued interest.** *Tarbith* (or *ribith*) in Hebrew. (*Ibid.*).
25:39 **and is sold to you.** See Exodus 21:2.

25   **42** This is because I brought [the Israelites] out of Egypt, and they are My slaves. They shall not be sold [in the market]* as slaves. **43** Do not dominate [such a slave] to break his spirit,* since you must fear your God.

44 You can [also] have [other] male or female slaves. These are the male and female slaves that you buy from the nations around you. **45** You can also buy [such slaves] from the resident aliens who live among you, and from their families that are born in your land.

[All these] shall become hereditary property. **46** They are hereditary property that you shall pass down to your children, and you shall thus have them serve you forever.

However, where your fellow Israelites are concerned, you must not dominate one another to break one's spirit.

[93. Slaves of Gentiles]

47 [This is the law] if a foreigner or resident alien gains the upper hand, while your brother loses his means of support and is sold to a foreigner, a resident alien, or to [an idolatrous cult* which must] be rooted out from a foreigner's family.*

48 After he is sold, he must be redeemed, [and] one of his close relatives must redeem him [first].* **49** His uncle or cousin shall thus redeem him, or the closest [other] relative from his family shall redeem him.* If he obtains the means, he can also be redeemed [on his own].*

50 [In all such cases,] he shall make a reckoning with the one who bought him according to the number of years from the time he was sold until the jubilee. His purchase price shall then be counted for that number of years, as if he were hired [for that amount].

51 Thus, if there are still many years [until the jubilee], the redemption money that he returns [to his buyer] shall be in proportion to the money for which he was sold. **52** If only a few years remain until the jubilee year, he shall make a [similar] reckoning. [In either case], he shall return a sum of redemp-

---

25:42 **in the market** (*Sifra*; Rashi). Similarly, he may not be sold at auction or in any other public manner (*Sefer Hamitzvoth*, Negative 258).

25:43 **to break his spirit.** *Perekh* in Hebrew. See Exodus 1:13.

25:47 **an idolatrous cult** (*Bava Metzia* 7a; Rashi; *Yad, Avadim* 1:3).

—   **which must be rooted out . . .** (Ramban; Ralbag). *Eker* in Hebrew. Or, "the root of a foreigner's family" (Saadia; Ibn Janach); "the dedicated shrine of a foreigner's family (Radak, *Sherashim*); or, "the support of a foreigner's family" (Hirsch).

Or, "[an idolator] who must be rooted out of a foreigner's family (Targum according to Ramban); "a foreigner's family that is still rooted [in idolatry]" (Abarbanel); "an apostate foreign family" (Ibn Ezra; cf. Septuagint); or, "a distant foreign family" (Rashbam; Chizzkuni).

25:48 **first.** (see *Yad, Avadim* 2:7).

25:49 **shall redeem him.** The courts can force the relative to do so (*Ibid.*).

—   **If he obtains the means . . .** Even if he can borrow money (*Ibid.*).

tion money according to [the number of] years that he has [already worked].　**25**

⁵³ [Such a slave] shall thus be the same as an employee hired on a yearly basis. If you are aware of it,* [you may not let his master] dominate him so as to break his spirit. ⁵⁴ If [the slave] is not redeemed through any [of the above means], he and his children shall be freed in the jubilee year.

⁵⁵ [All this] is because the Israelites are [actually] My slaves. They are My slaves because I brought them out of Egypt. I am God your Lord.

¹ [Therefore,] do not make yourselves false gods. Do not raise up a stone　**26** idol or a sacred pillar for yourselves. Do not place a kneeling* stone in your land so that you can prostrate yourselves* on it. I am God your Lord.

² Keep My Sabbaths* and revere My sanctuary, I am God.

BeChuko-thai　　　　　　　　　　　　　　　　בְּחֻקֹּתַי

[94. Rewards for Obedience]

³ If you follow My laws and are careful to keep My commandments, ⁴ I will provide you with rain at the right time, so that the land will bear its crops and the trees of the field will provide fruit. ⁵ [You will have so much that] your threshing season will last until your grape harvest, and your grape harvest will last until the time you plant. You will have your fill of food, and [you will] live securely in the land.

⁶ I will grant peace in the land so that you will sleep without fear. I will rid the land of dangerous animals, and the sword will not pass through your land. ⁷ You will chase away your enemies, and they will fall before your sword. ⁸ Five of you will be able to chase away a hundred, and a hundred of you will defeat ten thousand, as your enemies fall before your sword.

⁹ I will turn to you, making you fertile and numerous, thus keeping My covenant with you.

¹⁰ You will continue eating the previous year's crops long after their time, and you will eventually have to clear out the old crops because of the new.

¹¹ I will keep My sanctuary in your midst, and not grow tired of you. ¹² I will make My presence felt* among you. Thus, I will be a God to you, and you will be a nation [dedicated]* to Me.

25:53　**If you are aware . . .** (see *Yad, Avadim* 1:6; *Sefer Hamitzvoth,* Negative 260). Literally, "before your eyes."

26:1　**kneeling** (*Targum; Yad, Avodath Kokhavim* 6:6; HaKethav VeHaKabbalah). *Evven maskith* in Hebrew. Or, "a decorated stone" (*Targum Yonathan*; Saadia; Rashbam); "a stone pavement" (Rashi; cf. *Megillah* 22b); "an indication stone" (Hirsch), *lithon opokon* in Greek (Septuagint). It may also indicate a stone having images for contemplation in order to see visions.

—　**prostrate yourselves.** Even to God (*Yad, loc. cit.*; *Sefer Hamitzvoth,* Negative 12).

26:2　**Keep My Sabbaths.** See above, 19:30.

26:12　**make My presence felt** (cf. Targum). Literally, "walk among you."

—　**dedicated . . .** (see *Moreh Nevukhim* 3:32).

26   ¹³ I am God your Lord. I brought you out from Egypt, where you were slaves. I broke the bands* of your yoke, and led you forth with your heads held high.

[95. Punishments for Disobedience]

¹⁴ [But this is what will happen] if you do not listen to Me, and do not keep all these commandments. ¹⁵ If you come to denigrate My decrees, and grow tired of My laws, then you will not keep all My commandments, and you will have broken My covenant.

¹⁶ I will then do the same to you. I will bring upon you feelings of anxiety,* along with depression* and excitement,* destroying your outlook* and making life hopeless.*

You will plant your crop in vain, because your enemies will eat it. ¹⁷ I will direct My anger* against you, so that you will be defeated by your foes, and your enemies will dominate you. You will flee even when no one is chasing you.

¹⁸ If you still do not listen to Me, I will increase the punishment for your sins sevenfold. ¹⁹ I will break your aggressive pride, making your skies like iron, and your land like brass.* ²⁰ You will exhaust your strength in vain, since your land will not yield its crops, and the trees of the land will not produce fruit.

²¹ If you are indifferent* to Me and lose the desire to obey Me, I will again increase the punishment for your sins sevenfold. ²² I will send wild beasts among you, killing your children, destroying your livestock, and reducing your population, so that the roads will become deserted.

26:13 bands (Rashbam; Radak, *Sherashim*; Septuagint). *Mototh* in Hebrew. Or, "pegs" or "bars" (Rashi).

26:16 anxiety (cf. Radak, *Sherashim*). *Behalah* in Hebrew. Also denotes trouble, trembling, disaster, sudden terror, and feelings of insecurity.

— **depression** (Hirsch). *Shachefeth* in Hebrew. Or, "tuberculosis" (Rashi; Saadia; Ibn Janach; Radak, *Sherashim*). Or, "scabs," "pox" or "impetigo," *psora* in Greek (Septuagint).

— **excitement** (cf. Radak, *Sherashim*). *Kadachath* in Hebrew. Or, "fever."

— **destroying your outlook** (Hirsch). Literally, "to destroy your eyes" (Septuagint), or "to make your eyes pine" (Rashi).

— **making life hopeless** (Hirsch). Or,"consuming your life" (Septuagint), "depressing your soul" (Radak, s.v. *D'ab*).

26:17 direct my anger. See above, 20:3. Literally, "I will set My face. . ."

26:19 brass. *Nechushah* in Hebrew.

26:21 If you are indifferent (cf. Hirsch). Literally, "If you walk with Me with *keri*." Variously translated, "If you make Me a temporary concern" (*Targum Yonathan*; *Sifra*; Rashi; Chizzkuni); "If you harden yourselves against Me" (Targum; *Tosafoth, Rosh HaShanah* 16a, s.v. *Keri*); "If you refuse to walk My way" (Menachem, quoted in Rashi, Rashbam); "If you become overconfident in your dealings with Me" (Ibn Ezra); "If you become rebellious against Me" (Saadia; Ibn Janach; Septuagint); "If you make it a burden to walk with Me" (Targum, according to Rashi); or, "If You treat My [acts] as accident" (*Arukh*; *Moreh Nevukhim* 3:36; Radak, *Sherashim*). The word *keri* can thus denote triviality, harshness, refusal, overconfidence, rebellion, a burden, or a natural accident.

²³ If this is not enough to discipline you, and you are still indifferent to Me, 26
²⁴ then I will also be indifferent to you, but I will again increase the punishment for your sins sevenfold. ²⁵ I will bring a vengeful sword against you to avenge [My]* covenant, so that you will huddle in your cities. I will send the plague against you, and give you over to your enemies.

²⁶ I will cut off your food supply* so that ten women will be able to* bake bread in one oven, bringing back only [a small] amount* of bread. You will eat, but you will not be satisfied.*

[96. Destruction and Repentance]

²⁷ If you still do not obey Me and remain indifferent to Me, ²⁸ then I will be indifferent to you with a vengeance,* bringing yet another sevenfold increase in the punishment for your sins. ²⁹ You will eat the flesh of your sons, and make a meal of the flesh of your daughters. ³⁰ When I destroy your altars* and smash your sun gods,* I will let your corpses rot on the remains of your idols.

I will thus have grown tired of you. ³¹ I will let your cities fall into ruins, and make your sanctuaries desolate. No longer will I accept the appeasing fragrance [of your sacrifices]. ³² I will make the land so desolate that [even] your enemies who live there will be astonished. ³³ I will scatter you among the nations, and keep the sword drawn against you. Your land will remain desolate, and your cities in ruins.

³⁴ Then, as long as the land is desolate and you are in your enemies' land, the land will enjoy* its sabbaths. The land will rest and enjoy its sabbatical years. ³⁵ Thus, as long as it is desolate, [the land] will enjoy the sabbatical rest that you would not give it when you lived there.

³⁶ I will bring such insecurity* upon those of you who survive in your enemies' land that the sound of a rustling leaf will make them flee from the sword. They will fall with no one chasing them. ³⁷ They will fall over one

26:25 **My** (Rashi; Rashbam; Ibn Ezra; Septuagint).
26:26 **I will cut off**... (Septuagint). Or, "take away the nourishing power..." (Rashi).
— **will be able to ...** (Rashbam). Or, "will have to" because of a shortage of fuel (Rashi).
— **small amount** (Ibn Ezra). Or, "by weight," since it will not rise (Rashi).
— **satisfied** (Rashbam). Or, "nourished" (Rashi). See 26:5.
26:28 **with a vengeance.** See 26:21. Or, "with the fury of chance" (*Moreh Nevukhim* 3:36), or, "as punishment for your rebellion" (Saadia).
26:30 **altars.** *Bamoth* in Hebrew. Or, "towers" (Rashi).
— **sun gods** (Rashi; Saadia; Radak, *Sherashim*). *Chaman* in Hebrew; see Isaiah 17:8, 27:8,9, Ezekiel 6:4,6, 2 Chronicles 34:4. Or, "hills dedicated to idolatry" (Saadia); "magical images" (*Targum Yonathan*), or, "wooden images" (Septuagint).
26:34 **enjoy** (cf. Septuagint). *Ratzah* in Hebrew. Or, "be appeased regarding its Sabbaths" (Rashi).
26:36 **insecurity** (Rashi). *Morekh* in Hebrew. Or, "slave mentality." *douleia* in Greek (Septuagint).

26   another as if [chased] by the sword, even when there is no one pursuing. You
     will have no means of standing up before your foes.
         38 You will thus be destroyed among the nations. The land of your enemies
     will consume you.
         39 The few of you who survive in your enemies' lands will [realize that] your
     survival is threatened* as a result of your nonobservance. [These few] will also
     [realize] that their survival has been threatened because of the nonobservance
     of their fathers. 40 They will then confess their sins and the sins of their fathers
     for being false* and remaining indifferent to Me. 41 [It was for this] that I also
     remained indifferent to them, and brought them into their enemies' land.
         But when the time finally comes that their stubborn spirit* is humbled, I
     will forgive* their sin. 42 I will remember My covenant with Jacob as well as
     My covenant with Isaac and My covenant with Abraham. I will remember the
     land. 43 [For] the land will have been left behind by them, and will have
     enjoyed its sabbaths while it lay in desolation without them. The sin [they had
     committed] by denigrating My laws and growing tired of My decrees, will
     [also] have been expiated.
         44 Thus, even when they are in their enemies' land, I will not grow so dis-
     gusted with them nor so tired of them that I would destroy them and break
     My covenant with them, since I am God their Lord. 45 I will therefore remem-
     ber the covenant with their original ancestors whom I brought out of Egypt in
     the sight of the nations, so as to be a God to them. I am God.
         46 These are the decrees, laws and codes that God set between Himself and
     the Israelites at Mount Sinai through the hand of Moses.

                              [97. Endowment Valuations]

27   1 God spoke to Moses, telling him to 2 speak to the Israelites and say to
     them:
         [This is the law] when a person expresses a vow* to donate to God the
     endowment valuation* of a person.

26:39 **survival is threatened** (Ralbag). *Yimaku* in Hebrew. Or, "deteriorate" (Rashi; Radak, *Sherashim*), or,
     "perish" (Septuagint).
26:40 **being false** *Ma'al* in Hebrew. Or, "transgressing and neglecting" (Septuagint).
26:41 **stubborn spirit**. Literally, "uncircumcised heart."
—   **forgive**. *Ratzah* in Hebrew. Literally, "desire," or, "be appeased for." See 26:34.
27:2 **vow**. *Neder* in Hebrew.
—   **endowment valuation**. *Erkakha* in Hebrew (Ibn Ezra). Or, "your endowment value," i.e. "your *erekh*"
     (Radak, *Sherashim*). See 27:23.
         Some say that this is speaking of a case where a person dedicates himself to God or to the Temple,
     and then wants to free himself (Josephus, *Antiquities* 4:4:4; cf. 1 Samuel 1:11,28). See 27:9. However, all
     Talmudic sources state that this is primarily a monetary endowment.

³ The endowment valuation of a 20 to 60 year old male shall be 50 shekels* **27** according to the sanctuary standard. ⁴ For a woman, this endowment valuation shall be 30 shekels.

⁵ For a person between 5 and 20 years old, the endowment valuation shall be 20 shekels for a male, and 10 shekels for a female.

⁶ For a person between one month and five years old, the endowment valuation shall be 5 silver shekels* for a male, and 3 silver shekels for a female.

⁷ For a person over 60 years old, the endowment valuation shall be 15 shekels for a man, and 10 shekels for a woman.

⁸ If [a person] is too poor to pay the endowment, he shall present himself before the priest, so that the priest can determine the endowment valuation. The priest shall then make this determination on the basis of how much the person making the vow can afford.

[98. Endowments of Animals and Real Estate]

⁹ If [the endowment] is an animal that can be offered as a sacrifice to God, then anything donated to God [automatically] becomes consecrated. ¹⁰ One may neither exchange it nor offer a substitute for it, whether it be a better [animal] for a worse one, or a worse [animal] for a better one. If he replaces one animal with another, both [the original animal] and its replacement shall be consecrated.

¹¹ If it involves any unfit* animal that cannot be offered as a sacrifice to God, [the owner] shall present the animal to the priest. ¹² The priest shall set the endowment value according to [the animal's] good and bad qualities,* and its endowment valuation shall be that which is determined by the priest. ¹³ If [the owner] wishes to redeem it, he must add 20% to its endowment value.

¹⁴ If a person consecrates his house as something sacred to God, the priest shall set its endowment value according to its good and bad points. The endowment value shall then remain that which is determined by the priest. ¹⁵ If the one who consecrates it wishes to redeem his house, he must add an additional 20% to its endowment value, and it then reverts to him.

¹⁶ If a man consecrates a field from his hereditary property to God, its endowment value shall be calculated according to the amount of seed [required to sow it], 50 silver shekels for each chomer* of barley seed.

27:3 **50 shekels.** Each shekel is 0.8 oz. silver.
27:6 **5 silver shekels.** The same as for redeeming a first-born boy (Numbers 3:47, 18:15).
27:11 **unfit.** Because of a blemish, as in 20:17-22 (*Sifra*; Rashi). Literally, "unclean."
27:12 **according to. . .good and bad qualities** (cf. *Sifra*). Literally, "whether good or bad." Or, "whether it is advantageous or disadvantageous" for the Temple (Ralbag).
27:16 **chomer.** A measure equal to 10 ephah or 30 sa'ah (*Yad, Arakhin* 4:4), that is, 220 liter, 58 gallons, or 7.96 cubic feet. It is the same as the Talmudic *kur* (*Arakhin* 25a). According to tradition, the area that can be

27   ¹⁷ This is the endowment valuation that must be paid if [the field] is consecrated [immediately after]* the jubilee year. ¹⁸ However, if one consecrates his
field later after the jubilee year, then the priest shall calculate the value on the
basis of how many years remain until the [next] jubilee year, and its endowment value shall be reduced accordingly.

¹⁹ If [the person] who has consecrated his field redeems it, he must add
20% to its endowment valuation, and it then reverts to him.

²⁰ However, if he does not redeem the field, or if [the sanctuary treasurer]*
sells it to someone else, it can no longer be redeemed. ²¹ When the field is then
released by the jubilee, it becomes consecrated to God, like a field that has
been declared taboo,* and it then becomes the hereditary property of the
priest.*

²² If the field that one consecrates to God is not his hereditary property but
a field he has bought, ²³ the priest shall calculate the proportion of its endowment valuation on the basis of the number of years remaining until the
[next] jubilee year. On that day, [anyone] can [redeem it by] giving its endowment valuation as something consecrated to God. ²⁴ [In any case],* on the
jubilee year, the field shall revert to the one from whom it was bought, the one
who had it as his hereditary property in the land.

²⁵ Every endowment valuation shall be according to the sanctuary standard, where the shekel is 20 gerahs.*

²⁶ A firstling animal which must be sacrificed as a first-born offering to
God may not be consecrated* by an individual. Whether it is an ox, sheep, or
goat,* it [automatically] belongs to God.

²⁷ If a non-kosher animal [is consecrated], it shall be redeemed for its
endowment valuation plus an additional 20%. If it is not redeemed, it shall be
sold for its endowment value.

²⁸ However, anything taboo,* that a person declares to be taboo to God,*

---

sown with one sa'ah is 2500 square cubits, half the area of the tabernacle enclosure (*Eruvin* 23b; *Yad,
Shabbath* 16:3). Therefore, the area that can be sown with a chomer of grain is a square measuring 274
cubits to a side, which is 75,000 square cubits, 168,750 square feet, or 3.87 acres. (*Yad, Arakhin* 4:4). It is
for each such measure that the evaluation is 50 shekels. This is the same as the evaluation for an adult
male (27:3).

27:17 **immediately after** (Rashi). Literally, "from."

27:20 **sanctuary treasurer** (*Arakhin* 25b; Rashi; cf. *Yad,Arakhin* 4:20).

27:21 **taboo.** *Cherem* in Hebrew. See below, 27:28,29. Such taboo property is the property of the priests (Numbers 18:14), as long as it is not dedicated specifically to the Temple.

—   **of the priest.** It is given to the priests serving on the new year of the jubilee (*Yad,Arakhin* 4:24).

27:24 **In any case . . .** (cf. *Arakhin* 26b).

27:25 **where the shekel is . . .** See Exodus 30:13.

27:26 **may not be consecrated.** For any other purpose (Rashi). Or, "need not be consecrated" (Ramban).

—   **sheep or goat.** *Seh* in Hebrew, which denotes both; see Exodus 12:3.

27:28 **taboo.** *Cherem* in Hebrew.

—   **taboo to God.** Either for the Temple or for the priests (*Yad, Arakhin* 6:1; see note on 27:21).

cannot be sold or redeemed. [This is true] of anything he owns, whether it is a   **27**
slave,* an animal, or his hereditary field. Everything that is taboo is holy of
holies to God. [29] If a human being is declared taboo,* he cannot be redeemed
and must be put to death.

[30] The land's tithes,* whether of the crops of the soil or the fruit of trees,
belong to God, and are thus consecrated to God. [31] If a person wishes to
redeem such tithes, he must add an additional 20%.

[32] All tithes of the herds and flocks shall be given when they are counted
under the rod, with every tenth one being consecrated to God. [33] No distinction may be made between better and worse animals, and no substitutions
may be made. If a substitution is made, then both [the original animal] and its
replacement shall be consecrated and not redeemable.

[34] These are the commandments that God gave Moses for the Israelites at
Mount Sinai.

—   **slave** (Rashi). A gentile slave. Literally, "a human being."

27:29 **declared taboo.** By a king or by the Sanhedrin (Ramban; Ralbag). Or, "If a human being [is sentenced to death and] must be declared taboo" (Saadia; Chizzkuni). Or, "If a human being is under the death penalty and is declared taboo, he need not be redeemed" (Rashi).

27:30 **tithes.** This is the "second tithe" (*maaser sheni*) and not the levitical tithe (*Sifra*; Rashi). See Deuteronomy 14:22-27.

בְּמִדְבַּר

NUMBERS

BeMidbar

בְּמִדְבַּר

[1. The Census]

¹ God spoke to Moses in the Sinai Desert, in the Communion Tent on the **1**
first [day] of the second month* in the second year of the Exodus, saying:
² Take a census of the entire Israelite community.* [Do it] by families
following the paternal line,* according to the names of each male, taken
individually.* ³ You and Aaron shall take a tally* of them by their divisions, [counting] every male over 20 years old who is fit for service.*
⁴ Alongside you there shall be [one] man from each tribe, [and] he shall
be the head of his paternal line. ⁵ These are the names of the men who will
assist you:*

For Reuben, Elitzur son of Shedey-ur.
⁶ For Simeon, Shelumiel son of Tzuri-shaddai.*
⁷ For Judah, Nachshon son of Aminadav.*
⁸ For Issachar, Nethanel son of Tzuar.
⁹ For Zebulun, Eliav son of Chelon.
¹⁰ For Joseph's sons:
For Ephraim, Elishama son of Amihud.*
For Manasseh, Gamliel son of Padah-tzur.

1:1 **first day of the second month.** According to most authorities, this was 1 Iyyar, two weeks after Passover (cf. *Seder Olam* 8). However, one source apparently indicates that is was 1 Marcheshvan, before
the Tabernacle was erected, and that this is the count mentioned in Exodus 30:12, 38:26 (*BeMidbar
Rabbah* 1:10; *Hadar Zekenim*). See next note.

1:2 **Take a census** ... According to most authorities, this was a second census, the first having been
taken before the Tabernacle was made; see Exodus 30:12, 38:26 (Rashi on Exodus 30:15,16; Ralbag;
Josephus, *Antiquities* 3:7:4). While the first census was to determine the population of Israel as a
whole, this was to determine the population of each tribe (*Baaley Tosafoth*). However, some sources
appear to indicate that there was only one census (*Tanchuma, Ki Thisa* 9; see previous note). See note
on 1:46.

— **paternal line** (cf. *Bava Bathra* 109b). The term *beth avoth* also denotes paternal extended families (see
Exodus 6:14, 12:3).

— **individually.** Literally, "by a head count."

1:3 **a tally.** Some say that this was done with a half shekel, as in Exodus 30:13, 38:26 (Rashi; *Midrash
Aggadah*). According to others, however, this census was made by name lists, where every Israelite
was listed separately (Ralbag; *Shaar HaPesukim; Adereth Eliahu;* cf. *Lekach Tov*).

— **fit for service.** Some say for military service (Saadia; Rashi). Some say that this was meant to exclude
those who were physically disabled (*Midrash HaGadol*). According to others, *tzava* does not denote
a military army, but the community as a whole, and "going out to *tzava*" denotes those who are full-
fledged members of the community (Ramban; *HaKethav VeHaKabbalah;* see 4:2). It may also denote
all who had participated in the building of the Tabernacle (see Exodus 38:8).

1:5 **These are** ... Also see chapters 2,7,10.

1:6 **Shelumiel** ... Some identify him with Zimri in 25:14 (*Sanhedrin* 82b; Chizzkuni).

1:7 **Nachshon** ... Aaron's brother-in-law (Exodus 6:23, q.v.).

1:10 **Elishama** ... Joshua's grandfather (see 1 Chronicles 7:26).

1   ¹¹ For Benjamin, Avidan son of Gid'oni.
         ¹² For Dan, Achiezer son of Ami-shaddai.
         ¹³ For Asher, Pag'iel son of Akhran.*
         ¹⁴ For Gad, Elyassaf son of D'euel.*
         ¹⁵ For Naphtali, Achira son of Eynan.
         ¹⁶ These are the communal representatives,* the princes of their pater-
nal tribes and leaders of Israel's thousands.
         ¹⁷ Moses and Aaron took aside these men whose names had been desig-
nated. ¹⁸ They assembled the entire community on the first day of the
second month,* and [all the people] were registered by ancestry* according
to their paternal families. [All] those over 20 years old were counted individually by name.
         ¹⁹ Moses thus took a tally of [the Israelites] in the Sinai Desert as God
had commanded him.

[2. Reuben]

²⁰ This was [the result] for the descendants of Reuben, Israel's first-
born. According to the records* of their paternal families, [this was] the
number of individual names for males over 20 years old, all fit for service.
²¹ The tally for the tribe of Reuben was 46,500.*

[3. Simeon]

²² For the descendants of Simeon: According to the records of their
paternal families, [this was] the number of individual* names in the tally*
for males over 20 years old, all fit for service. ²³ The tally for the tribe of
Simeon was 59,300.

[4. Gad]

²⁴ For the descendants of Gad: According to the records of their paternal families, [this was] the number of names for males over 20 years old, all
fit for service. ²⁵ The tally for the tribe of Gad was 45,650.

1:13   **Akhran.** Or Okhran.
1:14   **D'euel.** See 7:42,47, 10:20. However in 2:14 it is Reuel (cf. Septuagint).
1:16   **representatives.** Literally, "ones who are called" (Rashi). Or, "the most prominent" (Septuagint).
1:18   **first day of the second month.** See 1:1.
—   **registered by ancestry** (Septuagint). Some say that they actually had to bring proof of their ancestry
        (Rashi; Saadia).
1:20   **records.** Family records, *toledoth* in Hebrew. See Exodus 6:16.
1:21   **46,500.** All the numbers (except where a 50 is involved) are rounded out to the nearest hundred. But
        see below, 3:39.
1:22   **individual.** Literally, "by head count", see 1:2. This expression is only found concerning Reuben and
        Simeon (cf. Ibn Ezra on 1:19).
—   **tally.** This is only found regarding Simeon (see *Lekach Tov; Midrash HaGadol*; Bachya).

[5. Judah]

1

²⁶ For the descendants of Judah: According to the records of their paternal families, [this was] the number of names for males over 20 years old, all fit for service. ²⁷ The tally for the tribe of Judah was 74,600.

[6. Issachar]

²⁸ For the descendants of Issachar. According to the records of their paternal families, [this was] the number of names for males over 20 years old, all fit for service. ²⁷ The tally for the tribe of Issachar was 54,400.

[7. Zebulun]

³⁰ For the descendants of Zebulun: According to the records of their paternal families, [this was] the number of names for males over 20 years old, all fit for service. ³¹ The tally for the tribe of Zebulun was 57,400.

[8. Ephraim]

³² Among the sons of Joseph, for the descendants of Ephraim: According to the records of their paternal families, [this was] the number of names for males over 20 years old, all fit for service. ³³ The tally for the tribe of Ephraim was 40,500.

[9. Manasseh]

³⁴ For the descendants of Manasseh: According to the records of their paternal families, [this was] the number of names for males over 20 years old, all fit for service. ³⁵ The tally for the tribe of Manasseh was 32,200.

[10. Benjamin]

³⁶ For the descendants of Benjamin. According to the records of their paternal families, [this was] the number of names for males over 20 years old, all fit for service. ³⁷ The tally for the tribe of Benjamin was 35,400.

[11. Dan]

³⁸ For the descendants of Dan: According to the records of their paternal families, [this was] the number of names for males over 20 years old, all fit for service. ³⁹ The tally for the tribe of Dan was 62,700.

[12. Asher]

⁴⁰ For the descendants of Asher: According to the records of their paternal families, [this was] the number of names for males over 20 years old, all fit for service. ⁴¹ The tally for the tribe of Asher was 41,500.

1

[13. Naphtali]

⁴² The descendants* of Naphtali: According to the records of their paternal families, [this was] the number of names for males over 20 years old, all fit for service. ⁴³ The tally for the tribe of Naphtali was 53,400.

[14. The Total]

⁴⁴ These are the tallies made by Moses, Aaron, and the twelve men who were princes of Israel, one from each paternal family.

⁴⁵ The tally of Israelites according to their paternal families [included] those over 20 years old, all fit for service. ⁴⁶ The entire tally was 603,550.*

⁴⁷ [However,] the men who were Levites according to their father's tribe were not tallied together with [the other] Israelites.

[15. The Levites]

⁴⁸ God spoke to Moses, saying:

⁴⁹ Do not take a tally or census of the Levites together with the [other] Israelites.

⁵⁰ Put the Levites in charge of the Tabernacle of Testimony,* all its furniture, and everything pertaining to it. They shall carry the Tabernacle and all its furniture, and they will serve in it. They shall [therefore] camp around the Tabernacle.

⁵¹ When the Tabernacle is moved, the Levites shall take it down, and when it is to remain in one place, they shall set it up. Any non-Levite who participates* shall die.

⁵² When the Israelites camp, each individual shall be in his own camp, each one designated by the banner for its division. ⁵³ The Levites, however, shall camp around the Tabernacle of Testimony, so that there will not be any divine anger directed against the Israelites. It shall be the Levites who safeguard the trust of the Tabernacle of Testimony.

⁵⁴ The Israelites did all that God commanded Moses, [and] they did it exactly.

1:42 **The descendants.** The word "for" (le-) is omitted here (see *Shaar HaPesukim; Adereth Eliahu*).

1:46 **603,550.** The number is the same as that in Exodus 38:26. Some say that the population had stabilized, with deaths being approximately equal to the number of men celebrating their 20th birthday (Rashi on Exodus 30:15,16). According to others, age was determined by years beginning in Tishrei (Rosh HaShanah), and these were the same people counted in Exodus. From this we see that as long as the Tabernacle was being built, there were no deaths (*Lekach Tov*). See notes on 1:1, 1:2.

1:50 **Tabernacle of Testimony.** See Exodus 38:21. Fom this it appears that one of the main functions of the Tabernacle was to hold the Tablets of Testimony.

1:51 **participates** (Rashi). Literally, "approaches," or "comes close."

[16. The Camp: Judah to the East]

¹ God spoke to Moses and Aaron, saying: **2**

² The Israelites shall camp with each person near the banner having his paternal family's insignia. They shall camp at a specified distance* around the Communion Tent.

³ Camping to the east (the direction of sunrise) shall be the divisions under the banner of Judah.

The leader of Judah's descendants was Nachshon son of Aminadav. ⁴ The tally of his division was 74,600.

⁵ Camping near him shall be the tribe of Issachar, and the leader of Issachar's descendants was Nethanel son of Tzuar. ⁶ The tally of his division was 54,400.

⁷ [With them shall be] the tribe of Zebulun, and the leader of Zebulun's descendants was Eliav son of Chelon. ⁸ The tally of his division was 57,400.

⁹ The entire tally for the divisions in Judah's camp was thus 186,400.

On the march, they shall go first.

[17. Reuben to the South]

¹⁰ The divisions under the banner of Reuben's camp shall be to the south.

The leader of Reuben's descendants was Elitzur son of Shedey-ur. ¹¹ The tally of his division was 46,500.

¹² Camping near him shall be the tribe of Simeon, and the leader of Simeon's descendants was Shelumiel son of Tzuri-shaddai. ¹³ The tally of his division was 59,300.

¹⁴ [With them shall be] the tribe of Gad, and the leader of Gad's descendants was Elyassaf son of Reuel.* ¹⁵ The count of his division was 45,650.

¹⁶ The entire tally for the divisions in Reuben's camp was thus 151,450.

On the march, they shall go second.

[18. The Tabernacle on the March]

¹⁷ On the march, the Communion Tent [and] the camp of the Levites shall then proceed. [They] shall be in the middle of the [other] camps.

[The people] shall travel in the same manner as they camp. Each person shall be in his place, according to each one's banner.

2:2 **specific distance.** 2000 cubits (3000 feet or approximately 7/16 mile); see Numbers 35:5; Joshua 3:4 (*Tanchuma* 9; Rashi). *Neged* in Hebrew (cf. Ibn Ezra). Or, "near each other" (Septuagint).
2:14 **Reuel.** This is D'euel, see 1:14.

2

[19. Ephraim to the West]

[18] The divisions under the banner of Ephraim's camp shall be to the west.

The leader of Ephraim's descendants was Elishama son of Amihud. [19] The tally for his division was 40,500.

[20] Near him shall be the tribe of Manasseh, and the leader of Manasseh's descendants was Gamliel son of Padah-tzur. [21] The tally for his division was 32,200.

[22] [With them shall be] the tribe of Benjamin, and the leader of Benjamin's descendants was Avidan son of Gid'oni. [23] The tally for his division was 35,400.

[24] The entire count for the divisions of Ephraim's camp was thus 108,100.

On the march, they shall go third.

[20. Dan to the North]

[25] The divisions under the banner of Dan's camp shall be to the north.

The leader of Dan's descendants was Achiezer son of Ami-shaddai. [26] The tally of his division was 62,700.

[27] Camping near him shall be the tribe of Asher, and the leader of Asher's descendants was Pag'iel son of Akhron. [28] The tally for his division was 41,500.

[29] [With them shall be] the tribe of Naphtali, and the leader of Naphtali's descendants was Achira son of Eynan. [30] The tally for his division was 53,400.

[31] The entire tally for Dan's camp was thus 157,600.

On the march, they shall be the last of the banners.

[21. The Camp as a Whole]

[32] These then are the tallies of the Israelites according to their paternal families. The tally for all the camps in all divisions was 603,500. [33] The Levites were not registered among the [rest of the] Israelites, as God had commanded Moses.

[34] The Israelites did all that God had commanded Moses. They camped under their banners in the prescribed manner, and each person traveled in a similar manner with his family, according to his paternal line.

[22. Genealogy of Aaron]

3   [1] These are the chronicles of Aaron and Moses on the day that God spoke to Moses at Mount Sinai:

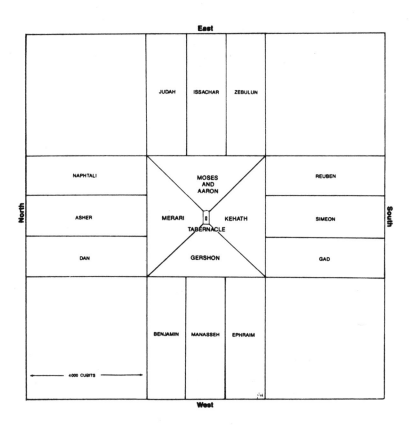

PLATE 26. THE CAMP

3   ² These are the names of Aaron's sons: Nadav (the first-born), Avihu, Eleazar and Ithamar.* ³ These are the names of Aaron's sons who were the anointed priests, installed to serve.

⁴ Nadav and Avihu died before God* when they offered unauthorized fire to God in the Sinai Desert. They had no children. Thus, [only] Eleazar and Ithamar served as priests during their father Aaron's lifetime.*

[23. Status of the Levites]

⁵ God spoke to Moses, saying:

⁶ Bring forth the tribe of Levi, and present it to Aaron the priest, so that [its members] shall serve him. ⁷ They shall safeguard My trust and the trust of the entire community involving the Communion Tent, performing any necessary service in the Tabernacle. ⁸ They shall guard all the Communion Tent's furniture, along with [everything else] that the Israelites have entrusted for the Tabernacle's service.

⁹ Give the Levites over to Aaron and his descendants. They are his gift from the Israelites.

¹⁰ Give special instructions to Aaron and his descendants that they safeguard their priesthood. Any non-priest who participates shall die.

[24. In Place of the First-Born]

¹¹ God spoke to Moses, saying:

¹² I have separated the Levites from the [other] Israelites so that they may take the place of all the first-born (who initiate the womb*) among the Israelites, and the Levites shall be Mine.

¹³ This is because every first-born became Mine on the day I killed all the first-born in Egypt. I then sanctified to Myself every first-born in Israel, man and beast alike, [and] they shall remain Mine. I am God.

[25. Census of the Levites: Gershon]

¹⁴ God spoke to Moses in the Sinai Desert [and] said, ¹⁵ "Take a tally of the Levites, family by family, according to their paternal lines. Count every male over one month old."

¹⁶ Moses numbered them at God's command, as he had been instructed.

¹⁷ By name, the sons of Levi were Gershon, Kehoth and Merari.*

3:2   **Nadav . . .** See Exodus 6:23.
3:4   **Nadav and Avihu died . . .** Leviticus 10:1,2.
—   **during . . .** (Rashi). Literally, "on the face of."
3:12   **who initiate the womb.** See Exodus 13:2.
3:17   **the sons of Levi were . . .** See Genesis 46:11, Exodus 6:16.

¹⁸ The sons of Gershon heading families were Livni and Shimi.*
¹⁹ The sons of Kehoth heading families were Amram, Yitzhar, Hebron,* and Uzziel.
²⁰ The sons of Merari heading families were Machli and Mushi.

These are the Levite families according to their paternal lines:
²¹ For Gershon there was the Livnite family and the Shimite family. These were the Gershonite families. ²² Numbering every male over one month old, their tally was 7500.
²³ The Gershonite family shall camp to the west, toward the back of the Tabernacle. ²⁴ Paternal leader of the Gershonites was Elyassaf son of La-el.
²⁵ The task of the descendants of Gershon involving the Communion Tent shall be the Tabernacle [tapestries],* the over-tent, its roof, the drapes at the Communion Tent entrance, ²⁶ the enclosure's hangings, the drape at the entrance of the enclosure surrounding the Tabernacle and altar, and the ropes,* as well as all the work involving [these items].*

[26. Kehoth and Merari]

²⁷ For Kehoth, there was the Amramite family, the Yitzharite family, the Hebronite family, and the Uzzielite* family. All these were the Kehothite families. ²⁸ The count of every male over one month old was 8600.

They were in charge of the sacred articles.* ²⁹ The family of Kehoth's descendants shall camp to the south side of the Tabernacle. ³⁰ Paternal leader of the Kehothite family is Eltzafan son of Uzziel.*
³¹ Their charge shall be the ark, the table, the menorah, the [two] altars, the sacred utensils for [all] these, the [partition] drape,* and all the work involving these [items].
³² The one in charge of the Levites' leaders shall be Eleazar, son of Aaron the priest. He shall be in charge of safeguarding the trust of the sacred articles.*
³³ For Merari, there was the Machli family and the Mushi family. These were the families of Merari. ³⁴ Their tally, numbering every male over one month old, was 6200.

3:18 **The sons of Gershon** . . . See Exodus 6:17-19.
3:19 **Hebron.** *Chevron* in Hebrew; same as the city name.
3:25 **tapestries.** See Exodus 26:1. (Rashi).
3:26 **ropes.** See Exodus 35:18.
— **all the work** . . . (see Ibn Ezra). Cf. 4:26.
3:27 **Uzzielite.** Literally, Azzielite or Ozzielite.
3:28 **sacred articles.** See 3:32.
3:30 **Eltzafan** . . . See Exodus 6:22.
3:31 **partition drape.** The cloth partition before the Holy of Holies (Rashi).
3:32 **sacred articles** (Septuagint). Or, "sanctuary."

3   **35** Paternal leader of the families of Merari was Tzuriel son of Avichail. They shall camp to the north side of the Tabernacle.

36 The appointed task of the descendants of Merari shall include the beams, crossbars, pillars and bases of the Tabernacle, all its utensils, and the associated work, **37** as well as the pillars, bases, stakes and ropes of the surrounding enclosure.

38 Camping to the east, in front of the Tabernacle, shall be Moses and Aaron and his sons, those who keep charge of the sanctuary as a trust for the Israelites. Any unauthorized person who includes himself shall die.

39 The entire tally of the Levites was made by Moses and Aaron by families. There were 22,000* males over one month old.

[27. Census of the First-Born]

40 God said to Moses, "Make a tally of the male first-born among the Israelites who are over one month old, and take a census of their names. **41** Take the Levites to Me (I am God) in place of all the Israelite male first-born. [Also take] the Levites' animals in place of the Israelites' first-born animals."

42 Moses made a tally of all the first-born male Israelites, as God had commanded him. **43** According to the number of their names, the tally of all the first-born over one month old was 22,273.*

[28. Substituting the Levites]

44 God spoke to Moses, saying:

45 Take the Levites in place of all the male first-born Israelites. [Also take] the Levites' livestock in place of [the Israelites' first-born] animals. The Levites shall thus become Mine. I am God.

46 [Also take] a redemption for the 273 individuals* by which the first-born outnumber the Levites. **47** This shall be 5 shekels* for each individ-

---

3:39 **22,000.** This is an exact count, as we see in 3:46. If the number from the sub-tribes of Gershon, Kehoth and Merari are added, however, the total is 22,300, so that 300 are missing. According to tradition, the 300 were first-born Levites, who could not redeem first-born Israelites (*Bekhoroth* 5a; Rashi).

3:43 **22,273.** It is significant to note that the first-born comprised only one out of 27 Israelites. If the fact that they were numbered from only one month is taken into account, while the count of 603,550 is for those over 20 years old, it comes out that the first-born were approximately one out of 45. This may be because the Israelites had huge families in Egypt (see Rashi on Exodus 1:7). It is also possible that many first-born did not observe the first Passover and died in Egypt. Another possibility is that the first-born of many families were girls.

3:46 **273 individuals.** Because there were 22,273 first-born and 22,000 Levites.

3:47 **5 shekels.** This is the amount for the redemption of a first-born son; see below, 3:47, 18:15; Leviticus 27:6.

ual, according to the sanctuary standard, where the shekel is 20 gerahs.* 3
⁴⁸ Give the silver* to Aaron and his sons as a redemption for [the first-born
who are] in excess [of the Levites].

⁴⁹ Moses took the redemption money for those who were left over [after
the majority of first-born]* had been redeemed by the Levites. ⁵⁰ The silver
that he took from the first-born Israelites consisted of 1365 sanctuary
shekels. ⁵¹ Moses gave the silver for those who were redeemed to Aaron
and his sons at God's command. [It was all done] as God had commanded
Moses.

[29. Duties for Kehoth]

¹ God spoke to Moses and Aaron, saying: 4
² Take a [special]* census of the descendants of Kehoth among the
Levites. [Take it] by families, following the paternal line. ³ [It shall include]
those from 30 to 50 years old, all who enter service to work in the Communion Tent.

⁴ The following is the service of Kehoth's descendants in the Communion Tent. It is holy of holies.

⁵ When the camp is about to travel, Aaron and his sons shall come and
take down the partition drape,* using it to cover the Ark of Testimony.
⁶ They shall then place a cover of blue-processed skins* over it, and on top
of that, a cloth of pure sky blue wool. They shall then put its carrying poles
in place.*

⁷ They shall spread a sky blue cloth over the inner table.* Then they
shall set in place on it the bread forms, incense bowls, half tubes, and
covering side frames,* so that the bread can remain [on the table] constant-

---

—	**the shekel is 20 gerahs.** See Exodus 30:13, Leviticus 27:25, Numbers 18:16, Ezekiel 45:12.
3:48	**the silver . . .** Or, "the redemption money."
3:49	**after the majority . . .** (cf. Rashi).
4:2	**special.** (Rashi). See below, 4:36.
4:5	**partition drape.** The drape over the Holy of Holies. See 3:31.
4:6	**blue processed skins.** *Tachash* in Hebrew. See note on Exodus 25:5.
—	**put its carrying poles in place.** See 4:8, 4:11, 4:14. In other cases, the Torah means that the poles had been removed, and replaced, but in the case of the ark, the poles were not to be removed (Exodus 25:15). Therefore, in the case of the ark, the poles were merely adjusted (*Baaley Tosafoth*; Ramban; Meiri on *Yoma* 72a). Others say that the rings were placed into slots in the poles, so that they would not slip (Chizzkuni). Others say that there was one set of decorative poles that could not be removed, and another set that were used to move the ark (*Tosafoth, Yoma* 72a, s.v. *Kethiv*; see note on Exodus 25:12). Others say that the poles were moved from the top rings to the bottom rings when the ark was carried (Ibn Ezra on Exodus 25:12). According to others, the poles were now set in place on the shoulders of the Levites (Ibn Ezra).
4:7	**inner table.** Since there were other tables outside for the sacrifices (Ibn Ezra; Chizzkuni). Or, "show-bread table" (Targum).
—	**bread forms . . .** See Exodus 25:29.

4   ly. **⁸** Over it all, they shall place a crimson wool cloth, and cover it with a case* of blue-processed skins. They shall then put its carrying poles in place.

⁹ They shall take a cloth of sky blue wool, and cover the menorah lamp along with its oil cups, wick tongs, ash scoops* and the oil containers used for it.* **¹⁰** [The menorah] and all its utensils shall be placed in a case of blue-processed skins, and placed on a carrying frame.*

¹¹ They shall spread a sky blue wool cloth on the golden altar, and then cover it with a case of blue-processed skins. They shall then set its carrying poles in place.

¹² They shall take all the sanctuary's service utensils, and place them on a sky blue wool cloth. They shall then be covered with a case of blue-processed skins, and placed on a carrying frame.

¹³ They shall remove all the ashes from the [sacrificial]* altar, and place a dark red* cloth over it. **¹⁴** They shall place on it all the utensils that are used for its service, such as the fire pans, flesh pokers, scoops, and sacrificial basins*—all the altar's utensils. They shall then cover it [all] with a case of blue-processed skins, and set its carrying poles in place.

¹⁵ Aaron and his sons shall thus finish covering the sacred [furniture]* and all the sanctuary utensils, so that the camp can begin its journey. [Only after the priests are finished] shall the Kehothites come to carry [these items], so that they not die when they touch the sacred objects.

The above is what the Kehothites must carry for the Communion Tent.

¹⁶ [This shall be]* under the direction of Eleazar, son of Aaron the priest, [along with] the illuminating oil, the perfume incense, the meal offerings for the daily sacrifice,* and the anointing oil. [He shall also be in] charge of the entire Tabernacle, and all its sacred furniture and utensils.

[30. Precautions for the Kehothites]

¹⁷ God spoke to Moses and Aaron, saying:

4:8   **case.** See 4:10. Or, "covering."
4:9   **wick tongs . . .** See Exodus 29:38.
—   **oil containers . . .** Mentioned here for the first time.
4:10 **carrying frame.** *Mot* in Hebrew. It was carried on the frame, not hanging from it (Chizzkuni). See Numbers 13:23.
4:13 **sacrificial.** (Rashi).
—   **dark red.** *Argaman* in Hebrew, see Exodus 25:4. This would appear to indicate that the dark red variety was less costly than the sky blue dye.
4:14 **fire pans . . .** See Exodus 27.3.
4:15 **furniture.** The ark and golden altar (Rashi).
4:16 **This shall be** (Rashi).
—   **daily sacrifice.** See Exodus 29:40, Numbers 28:5.

4

¹⁸ Do not cause the Kehothites to become extinct among the Levites.
¹⁹ This is what you must do so that they survive, and not die when they
come into the Holy of Holies. Aaron and his sons shall first come and
arrange each thing so that every [Kehothite] can perform his service, carrying his load. ²⁰ [The Kehothites] will then not come and see the sacred
[furniture] being packed,* and they will not die.

Naso

נָשֹׂא

[31. Duties of Gershon]

²¹ God spoke to Moses, saying:
²² Also take a census of Gershon's descendants by families, following
the paternal line. ²³ Take a tally of those from 30 to 50 years old, all who are
fit for duty in the Communion Tent's service.
²⁴ The Gershonite family shall serve by maintaining and carrying as
follows:
²⁵ They shall carry the Tabernacle's tapestries, the Communion Tent,*
the roof,* the over-roof of blue processed skins that is above it, the drape at
the Communion Tent entrance, ²⁶ the enclosure's hangings, the drape at the
entrance to the enclosure around the Tabernacle and altar, the guy-ropes,
all their appropriate tools, and everything necessary for their maintenance.
²⁷ All the carrying and maintenance service of the Gershonites shall be
under the supervision of Aaron and his sons. [The Gershonites] shall have
fixed appointments for everything they carry.*
²⁸ The above is the Gershonite family's service for the Communion
Tent. Their duties shall be under the supervision of Ithamar, son of Aaron
the priest.

[32. Duties of Merari; Tally of Kehoth]

²⁹ Take a tally of Merari's descendants by family, following the paternal
line. ³⁰ Take the tally of those from 30 to 50 years old, all who are fit for
duty in the Communion Tent's service.

4:20 **being packed** (Targum; Rashi; Saadia; Ibn Ezra). *Bala* in Hebrew, literally meaning "swallowed." Or,
"when the sanctuary is taken apart" (Ibn Ezra; Rashbam), "when the most holy is revealed" (Ibn
Ezra; Ramban); "if they take an instantaneous glance" (*BeMidbar Rabbah* 5:9; *Tanchuma, VaYakhel* 7; *HaKethav VeHakabbalah*; Septuagint); or, "steal a glance" (cf. Ramban; *Sanhedrin* 81b).
4:25 **Communion Tent.** The goats' wool over-tent (Rashi).
—   **roof.** Of reddened rams' skins (Rashi).
4:27 **fixed appointments . . .** By name (Septuagint). Or, "You keep a tally of everything they carry to safeguard it" (Saadia; Chizzkuni). Or, "Place them in charge, to entrust them with all that they carry."

4   ³¹ They shall be entrusted to carry and maintain the following items in
the Communion Tent: the beams, crossbars, pillars and bases of the
Tabernacle; ³² the pillars of the surrounding enclosure, their bases, stakes
and guy-ropes, all their tools, and all their maintenance equipment. They
shall be appointed by name to carry all the articles with which they are
entrusted.

³³ The above is the work comprising the entire service of Merari's
descendants in the Communion Tent. It shall be under the direction of
Ithamar, son of Aaron the priest.

³⁴ Moses, Aaron and the communal leaders took a tally of the descen-
dants of the Kehothites by family, following the paternal line, ³⁵ and
including everyone from 30 to 50 years old who was fit for duty in the
Communion Tent's service. ³⁶ Their tally by families was 2750.

³⁷ This was the complete tally of the Kehothite family, for all who
served in the Communion Tent, as taken by Moses and Aaron. It was done
as God had directed Moses.

[33. Tally of Gershon and Merari]

³⁸ [This was] the tally of Gershon's descendants by families, following
the paternal line ³⁹ and including everyone from 30 to 50 years old who was
fit for duty in the Communion Tent's service. ⁴⁰ Their tally by families,
following the paternal line, was 2630.

⁴¹ This was the complete tally of all who served in the Communion Tent
from the descendants of Gershon. The tally was taken by Moses and Aaron
as God had directed.

⁴² [This was] the tally of Merari's descendants by families, following the
paternal line ⁴³ and including everyone from 30 to 50 years old who was fit
for duty in the Communion Tent's service. ⁴⁴ Their tally by families was
3200.

⁴⁵ This was the complete tally of the families of Merari's descendants.
The tally was taken by Moses and Aaron as God had directed Moses.

⁴⁶ [This is] the entire tally that Moses, Aaron and the communal leaders
took of the Levites. [It was] by families following the paternal line,
⁴⁷ including everyone from 30 to 50 years old who was fit for duty in the
Communion Tent's service. ⁴⁸ Their tally was 8580.

⁴⁹ They were thus counted by Moses at God's bidding, each individual
according to his service, what he would carry, and his appointed task, as
God had commanded Moses.

[34. Purifying the Camp]

¹ God spoke to Moses, saying:*

² Instruct the Israelites to send out of the camp everyone who has a leprous mark* or a male discharge,* and all who are ritually defiled by the dead.* ³ Whether male or female, they must be sent out of the camp so that they not defile their camp where I dwell among them.

⁴ The Israelites did this, sending [all such people] out of the camp. The Israelites did exactly as God had told Moses.

[35. Offerings]

⁵ God spoke to Moses, telling him to ⁶ speak [as follows] to the Israelites:

If a man or woman sins against his fellow man, thus being untrue to God,* and becoming guilty of a crime, ⁷ he must confess the sin that he has committed.* He must [then] make restitution of the principle* plus a 20% surcharge, and give it to the victim of his crime.

⁸ If there is no relative* to whom the dishonest gain can be returned, it must be returned to God, [and given] to the priest.* This is in addition to the atonement ram* through which [the wrongdoer's] sin is expiated.

⁹ All the sacred offerings that the Israelites present as elevated gifts* to the priest shall become his property.

¹⁰ The sacred offerings of each individual remain his own property. When they are given to the priest, they become [the priest's] property.

5:1   **God spoke to Moses . . .** This occurred on the first of Nissan, the day the Tabernacle was erected; see Exodus 40:17 (*Gittin* 60a,b). According to some, this is true of everything in this section up to the Priestly Blessings (see note on 6:22). Thus, the narrative now goes back one month to the first of Nissan.

—   **leprous mark.** See Leviticus 13:1-46.

—   **male discharge.** See Leviticus 15:1-15.

—   **defiled by the dead** (Targum; Rashi; Septuagint). Literally, "unclean for a soul." See below, 19:14,16.

5:6   **If a man or woman . . .** See Leviticus 5:21.

5:7   **he must confess . . .** This is a commandment to confess a sin to God as part of one's repentance (*Yad, Teshuva* 1:1; *Sefer HaMitzvoth*, Positive Commandment 73). See Leviticus 5:5, 26:40.

—   **principle.** See Leviticus 5:24.

5:8   **relative.** Literally, "redeemer." It is speaking of the case where the victim has died. By tradition, it is speaking of the case where there can not be any heirs at all, which is only possible in the case of a proselyte (*Bava Kama* 109a; Rashi; *Yad, Gezelah* 8:6).

—   **and given . . .** (Sifri; Rashi).

—   **atonement ram.** Leviticus 5:24.

5:9   **elevated gifts.** *Terumah.*

5   *[36. The Suspected Adulteress]*

¹¹ God spoke to Moses, telling him to ¹² speak to the Israelites and say to them:

[This is the law]* if any man's wife is suspected of committing adultery* and being false to her husband. ¹³ A man may have lain with her carnally, keeping it hidden from her husband, and they may have acted secretly so that there could be no witness against [the woman]. [The woman] was not raped. ¹⁴ [This is a case where] the man [had previously*] expressed feelings of jealousy against his wife, and she then [may have been] defiled. [However,] he may have expressed such feelings of jealousy against his wife, and she [may have not been] defiled.

¹⁵ [The law is] that the man must bring [his wife] to the priest. When he brings her, he must also bring a sacrifice for her consisting of 1/10 ephah* of barley meal. He shall not pour oil on it, nor place frankincense on it, since it is a jealousy offering. It is a reminder offering to recall sin.

¹⁶ The priest shall bring forth [the woman] and have her stand before God.* ¹⁷ The priest shall take sanctified water* in a clay bowl.* He shall [also] take some earth from the Tabernacle floor and place it in the water. ¹⁸ The priest shall stand the woman before God and uncover her hair.* He shall place on her hands the reminder offering, the jealousy offering. In the priest's hand shall be the curse-bearing bitter* water.

¹⁹ The priest shall administer an oath to the woman, saying to her, "If a man has not lain with you, and you have not committed adultery so as to be defiled to your husband, you shall be unharmed by this curse-bearing bitter water. ²⁰ But if you have committed adultery against your husband

---

5:12   **This is the law ...** This ordeal, however, is only effective if the husband himself has never committed a sexual offense (*Sotah* 28a). Therefore, when such offenses became overly common, the ordeal ceased to be administered (*Sotah* 47a; *Yad, Sotah* 3:18,19).

—   **suspected of committing adultery** (cf. Rashi; Septuagint). Or, "goes astray" (Radak, *Sherashim*; cf. Proverbs 4:15, 7:25), or, "behaves foolishly" (*Sotah* 3a; Rashi)

5:14   **previously.** (Sotah 3a; Rashi). The law is that a woman becomes a *sotah* only if her husband had warned her not to be alone with a certain man, and she then violated the warning.

5:15   **1/10 ephah.** Approximately 2 quarts.

5:16   **before God.** At the entrance of the Communion Tent facing the Holy of Holies (*Sifri; Yad, Sotah* 3:3; Josephus, *Antiquities* 3:11:6).

5:17   **sanctified water.** From the washstand (Sifri; Rashi); cf. Exodus 30:17. This is because the washstand was made of the mirrors of the righteous women (Exodus 38:8; *BeMidbar Rabbah* 9:15; Rashi). One half log (around 5 oz.) water was used (*Menachoth* 88a; *Yad, Sotah* 3:9).

—   **clay bowl.** A new one (*Sotah* 15b; *Yad, Sotah* 3:9).

5:18   **uncover her hair** (Targum; *Sifri*). This teaches that a married woman's hair is normally covered (*Kethuvoth* 72a). Or, "he shall undo her hair (*Sotah* 7a; Rashi; cf. *Yad, Sotah* 3:11). The woman also had her clothing torn (*Ibid.*)

—   **bitter.** This indicates that a bitter substance was added to the water (*Sotah* 20a; *Yad, Sotah* 3:10; *Chizzkuni*), possibly a drug (see 5:27). According to others, it is water with a bitter after-effect (Sifri; Rashi). Or, "waters of conviction" (Septuagint).

and have become defiled, and if a man other than your husband has had   5
intercourse with you . . ."

²¹ [At this point] the priest shall administer to the woman [the part of]
the oath containing the curse. The priest shall say to the woman, "[In such
a case], God will make you into a curse and an oath among your people,
causing your sexual organs* to rupture* and your belly to blow up.* ²² This
curse-bearing water will enter your body and it will cause your belly to
blow up and your sexual organs to rupture."

The woman shall respond, "Amen. Amen."

²³ The priest shall then write these curses on a parchment,* and dissolve
[the writing] in the bitter waters. ²⁴ He shall then make the woman drink
the bitter curse-bearing waters,* and the curse-bearing waters shall begin
to take effect.

²⁵ The priest shall take the jealousy offering from the woman, and wave
the offering in the prescribed motions before God, bringing it near the altar.
²⁶ Thus after he makes the woman drink the water,* the priest shall scoop
out the memorial portion* of the meal offering and burn it on the altar.

²⁷ When the woman drinks the water, if she has been defiled and untrue
to her husband, the curse-bearing water will enter her body to poison her,
causing her belly to blow up and her sexual organs to rupture. The woman
will be a curse among her people.

²⁸ However, if the woman is pure and has not been defiled to her husband, she will remain unharmed and will become pregnant.*

²⁹ This is the [entire]* law regarding jealousy for the case when a

---

5:21 **sexual organs** (Chizzkuni). Expressed euphemistically as "thigh;" see note on Genesis 24:3, 32:26.
According to some, however, it literally denotes the thigh (Rashi, *Sotah* 8b, s.v. *yerekh*), particularly
the right thigh (Josephus, *Antiquities* 3:11:6).
—   **rupture.** Literally, "fall." Cf. Psalms 58:9, Ecclesiastes 6:3. Or, "become sterile" (Chizzkuni), or,
"rot" (*Targum Yonathan*; Septuagint). Or, "your thigh shall become dislocated" (Josephus). The
woman would also experience a menstrual discharge (*Niddah* 20b).
—   **blow up** (Targum; Septuagint; Radak, *Sherashim*). Or, "become distended with water" (Josephus).
There would be a tremendous build up of internal body pressure, and the woman would die (*Sotah*
20a; *Yad, Sotah* 3:16).
5:23 **parchment** (*Sotah* 17a; *Yad, Sotah* 3:8). It was a rolled up parchment, referred to here as a "book."
5:24 **He shall then make . . .** (*Sotah* 19a; *Yad, Sotah* 3:15). According to others, however, the offering
would be presented before the woman would drink (Ibid.; Rashi). This verse would then be translated, "These shall be the bitter curse-bearing waters that he shall make the woman drink . . ."
5:26 **Thus . . .** According to the first opinion in previous note. According to the second opinion, "The
priest shall scoop out . . . and he shall then make the woman drink the water."
—   **scoop out . . .** See Leviticus 2:2.
5:28 **become pregnant** (*Targum Yonathan*; Rashbam; Ibn Ezra; Josephus). She will also have a much better pregnancy than previously (*Sotah* 26a; Rashi). Or, "she is permitted to her husband" (Chizzkuni).
5:29 **entire.** See note on Leviticus 13:59.

5 woman commits adultery and becomes unclean [30] or when a man simply
has a feeling of jealousy against his wife. He shall stand the woman before
God, and the priest shall follow this entire procedure. [31] The man will then
be free of sin, but the woman will be punished if guilty.

[37. The Nazirite]

6 [1] God spoke to Moses, telling him to [2] speak to the Israelites and say to
them:
[This is the law] when a man or woman expresses a nazirite* vow to
God. [3] He must separate himself completely from wine and wine-brandy.*
He may not even drink vinegar made from wine and wine-brandy. He shall
not drink any grape beverage,* and he shall not eat any grapes or raisins.
[4] As long as he is a nazirite, he may not eat anything coming from the
grape, from its seeds to its skin.

[5] As long as he is under his nazirite oath, no cutting instrument* shall
touch [the hair on] his head. Until he completes his term as a nazirite to
God, the uncut hair that grows on his head is sacred.

[6] As long as he is a nazirite to God, he may not have any contact with
the dead. [7] He may not ritually defile himself even when his father, mother,
brother or sister dies, since his God's nazirite crown* is on his head. [8] As long
as he is a nazirite, he is holy to God.

[9] If a person dies in his presence suddenly, and renders his crowned
head ritually unclean, then, when he purifies himself on the seventh day,*
he must shave off the hair on his head. [10] On the eighth day, he must bring
two turtle doves or two young common doves* to the priest to the Communion Tent entrance. [11] The priest shall prepare one as a sin offering and
one as a burnt offering* to atone for his inadvertent [defilement] by the
dead. On that day, he shall resanctify his head. [12] He shall then begin

6:2 **nazirite.** This is unlike ordinary vows, since it involves a special protocol and ordinarily is for thirty
days (*Sifri; Yad, Nazir* 3:1). The word *nazir* denotes that which is set apart and consecrated (Rashi;
see notes on Genesis 49:26, Leviticus 25:5). It can also denote the "crown" of hair that the nazirite
wears (Ibn Ezra on 6:7; Ramban). According to Talmudic tradition, the main purpose of the nazirite
vow is to be a discipline against sexual temptation (*Sotah* 2a; Rashi) and to avoid pride (*Sotah* 4b).
However, it is also seen as a means of attaining spiritual gifts (cf. Judges 13:3; 1 Samuel 1:11), and
possibly as an initiation to prophecy (cf. Amos 2:11). By taking a nazirite vow, a layperson also to
some degree attains the status of a priest (Philo 1, *Legum Allegoriae* 249). Some say that it is an offering where one presents his hair to God (Josephus, *Antiquities* 4:4:4).

6:3 **wine-brandy** (*Nazir* 4a, 34b; Rashi). But not intoxicants in general.

—   **grape beverage** (Septuagint; Menachem, quoted in Rashbam). *Mishrah* in Hebrew. It includes any
liquid in which grapes have been soaked or steeped (*Nazir* 37a; Rashi; Radak, *Sherashim*).

6:5 **cutting instrument** (Saadia; *Sotah* 16a). Literally, "razor."

6:7 **nazirite crown.** His uncut hair (Targum: Ibn Ezra).

6:9 **seventh day.** See below, 19:12.

6:10 **two turtle doves . . .** See Leviticus 1:14.

6:11 **sin offering . . .** See Leviticus 5:7-10.

counting his nazirite days anew to God, and he shall bring a yearling sheep   6
as a guilt offering.* Since his nazirite crown was defiled, the first days must
be discounted.

¹³ The following is the law of what the nazirite must do when the term
of his nazirite vow is complete [and] of what* he must bring to the Communion Tent entrance:

¹⁴ The offering that he must present shall be one unblemished yearling
male sheep for a burnt offering, one unblemished yearling female sheep for
a sin offering, one unblemished ram for a peace offering, ¹⁵ and a basket
containing unleavened wheat loaves kneaded with oil and flat matzahs
saturated with oil,* along with the proper meal offerings and libations [for
the animal sacrifices].*

¹⁶ The priest shall come in before God and prepare [the nazirite's] sin
offering and burnt offering.* ¹⁷ He shall then [sacrifice] the ram as a peace
offering to God, to go with* the basket of unleavened bread. The priest
shall also present the meal offering and libation.

¹⁸ [After the service]* at the Communion Tent entrance, the nazirite
shall shave off the crown of hair on his head. He shall take the hair from the
nazirite crown on his head, and place it on the fire* that is under the peace
sacrifice.

¹⁹ After the nazirite has shaved, the priest shall take the cooked foreleg
of the ram along with one unleavened loaf and one flat matzah, and place
them on the nazirite's open hands. ²⁰ The priest shall wave them with the
motions prescribed* for a wave offering before God. These are sanctified to
[belong to] the priest, along with the animal's chest given as a wave offering, and the hind leg given as an elevated gift.*

After [all] this, the nazirite may* drink wine.

²¹ This is the [entire]* law concerning the nazirite, who has a vow obli-

6:12   guilt offering. Asham. See Leviticus 7:1-5.
6:13   and of what ... (Rashbam). Or, "he shall bring himself" (Rashi).
6:15   unleavened ... See Leviticus 2:4. The offerring was made of 2/3 ephah (3.2 gallons) of wheat meal
       (Menachoth 78a; Yad, Nazir 8:1). It was mixed with 1/4 log (2¼ oz) of olive oil (Ibid.). It consisted of
       twenty loaves, ten of each kind.
—   for the animal sacrifices. See below 15:1-11.
6:16   sin offering and burnt offering. In that order (Yad, Nazir 8:2).
6:17   to go with ... (Saadia; Septuagint). Or, "to sanctify" (Rashi).
6:18   After the service (Sifri; Targum Yonathan; Rashi). Or, "While the Communion Tent entrance [is
       open]" (Nazir 45a; Yad, Nazir 8:3). There was a special chamber in the Temple where Nazirites
       would shave (Ibid.).
—   place it on the fire. After soaking it in the juice from the cooked sacrifice (Nazir 45b; Yad, Nazir 8:2).
6:20   motions prescribed. See Exodus 29:24.
—   along with ... See Exodus 29:27, Leviticus 7:34.
—   may. (Yad, Nazir 8:4).
6:21   entire. See note on Leviticus 13:59.

6   gation* to bring his nazirite sacrifice to God. This is in addition to anything
else that he may wish to present to fulfill his vow,* which must be brought
above and beyond what the law requires for his nazirite vow.

[38—42. The Priestly Blessing]

²² God spoke to Moses,* telling him to ²³ speak to Aaron and his sons,
saying:
This is how you must bless the Israelites. Say to them:

²⁴ "May God bless you and keep watch over you.

²⁵ "May God make His presence* enlighten you and grant you grace.*

²⁶ "May God direct His providence toward you* and grant you peace."

²⁷ [The priests] will thus link My name with the Israelites and I will
bless them.

[43. The Leaders' Offering]

7   ¹ On the day that Moses finished erecting the Tabernacle,* he anointed
it and sanctified it along with all its furniture. He [also] anointed the altar
and all its utensils and thus* sanctified them.

² The princes of Israel, who were the heads of their paternal lines, then
came forward. They were the leaders of the tribes* and the ones who had
directed the census. ³ The offering that they presented to God consisted of
six covered* wagons and twelve oxen. There was one wagon for each two
princes, and one ox for each one. They presented them in front of the
Tabernacle.

⁴ God said to Moses, ⁵ "Take [the offering] from them, and let [the
wagons and oxen] be used for the Communion Tent's service. Give them to
the Levites, as appropriate for each [family's] work."

⁶ Moses took the wagons and oxen, and gave them to the Levites. ⁷ He

---

—   **vow obligation** (Ramban).
—   **This is in addition** . . . That is, he may stipulate to bring more (Rashi; Rashbam).
6:22   **God spoke** . . . This was also on the day the Tabernacle was erected (Ramban). See note on 5:1.
6:25   **presence** (cf. Targum). Literally "face."
—   **grace** (Sifri; Rashi). Or, "be kind to you" (Targum; Septuagint).
6:26   **providence** . . . (Saadia; Rashbam; Ibn Ezra; *Moreh Nevukhim* 1:37). Or, "bestow favor" (Rashi).
7:1   **On the day** . . . The first of Nissan (Exodus 40:17).
—   **thus.** (Chizzkuni).
7:2   **leaders of the tribes.** Even in Egypt (Sifri; Rashi).
7:3   **covered** (Targum; Sifri; Rashi; Septuagint). *Tzabh* in Hebrew. Or, "fully equipped" (Sifri; cf. *Targum Yonathan*); "full" (Ibn Ezra; Ramban); "ox wagons" (Ibn Ezra); two-ox wagons (Radak, *Sherashim*); "harnessed wagons" (Ibn Janach); or, "service wagons" (Chizzkuni).

gave two wagons and four oxen to the descendants of Gershon, as appro- 7
priate for their service. ⁸ To the descendants of Merari, he gave four wagons
and eight oxen. [Both were]* under the direction of Ithamar, son of Aaron
the priest.

⁹ He did not give [any wagons] to the descendants of Kehoth, [how-
ever,] since they had responsibility for the most sacred articles, which they
had to carry on their shoulders.

¹⁰ On the day that it was anointed, the princes presented their dedication offerings for the altar. The leaders placed their offerings before the altar.

¹¹ God said to Moses, "Let them present their offerings for the altar's
dedication, one prince each day."

[44. The Dedication Offerings: Judah]

¹² The one to bring his offering on the first day was Nachshon son of
Aminadav of the tribe of Judah. ¹³ His offering was as follows:

One silver bowl* weighing 130 shekels,* and one silver sacrificial
basin* weighing 70 shekels by the sanctuary standard, both filled with the
best grade wheat meal kneaded with olive oil for a meal offering.

¹⁴ One gold incense bowl* weighing 10 [shekels]* filled with incense.

¹⁵ One young bull, one ram and one yearling sheep for a burnt offering;
¹⁶ one goat for a sin offering; ¹⁷ and for the peace sacrifice, two oxen, five
rams, five male goats,* and five yearling sheep.

This was the offering of Nachshon son of Aminadav.

[45. The Second Day: Issachar]

¹⁸ On the second day, Nethanel son of Tzuar, prince of Issachar,
brought his offering. ¹⁹ The offering that he brought was one silver bowl
weighing 130 shekels and one sacrificial basin weighing 70 shekels by the
sanctuary standard, both filled with wheat meal kneaded with oil for a meal
offering; ²⁰ one gold incense bowl weighing 10 [shekels] filled with incense;
²¹ one young bull, one ram and one yearling sheep for a burnt offering;

7:8   **Both** . . . See above 4:28,33.
7:13   **bowl** . . . *Kaarah* in Hebrew. The Targum renders it as *megista*, a large tray or bowl, while the Sep-
       tuagint has it as *tryblion* in Greek, a large bowl or platter. See below.
—   **130 shekels.** 104 oz. or 6.5 lb.
—   **sacrificial basin.** *Mizrak* in Hebrew (see Exodus 26:3; Radak, *Sherashim*; cf. Amos 6:6). The bowl
       and the basin were both exactly the same size, except that the bowl had thicker walls (*Sifri; Ha-
       Kethav VeHaKabbalah*).
—   **70 shekels.** 56 oz. or 3.5 lb.
7:14   **incense bowl.** (Targum; Septuagint; cf. *Yerushalmi, Yoma* 5:1). *Kaf* in Hebrew. See Exodus 25:29.
—   **10 shekels.** 8 oz.
7:17   **male goats** (Radak, *Sherashim*; Septuagint). *Atudim* in Hebrew. See Genesis 31:12.

7   ²² one goat for a sin offering; ²³ and for the peace sacrifice, two oxen, five
rams, five male goats, and five yearling sheep. This was the offering of
Nethanel son of Tzuar.

[46. The Third Day: Zebulun]

²⁴ On the third day, it was the leader of Zebulun's descendants, Eliav
son of Chelon. ²⁵ His offering was one silver bowl weighing 130 shekels and
one sacrificial basin weighing 70 shekels by the sanctuary standard, both
filled with wheat meal kneaded with oil for a meal offering; ²⁶ one gold
incense bowl weighing 10 [shekels] filled with incense; ²⁷ one young bull,
one ram and one yearling sheep for a burnt offering; ²⁸ one goat for a sin
offering; ²⁹ and for the peace sacrifice, two oxen, five rams, five male goats,
and five yearling sheep. This was the offering of Eliav son of Chelon.

[47. The Fourth Day: Reuben]

³⁰ On the fourth day, it was the leader of Reuben's descendants, Elitzur
son of Shedey-ur. ³¹ His offering was one silver bowl weighing 130 shekels
and one sacrificial basin weighing 70 shekels by the sanctuary standard,
both filled with wheat meal kneaded with oil for a meal offering; ³² one gold
incense bowl weighing 10 [shekels] filled with incense; ³³ one young bull,
one ram and one yearling sheep for a burnt offering; ³⁴ one goat for a sin
offering; ³⁵ and for the peace sacrifice, two oxen, five rams, five male goats,
and five yearling sheep. This was the offering of Elitzur son of Shedey-ur.

[48. The Fifth Day: Simeon]

³⁶ On the fifth day, it was the leader of Simeon's descendants, Shelumiel
son of Tzuri-shaddai. ³⁷ His offering was one silver bowl weighing 130
shekels and one sacrificial basin weighing 70 shekels by the sanctuary
standard, both filled with wheat meal kneaded with oil for a meal offering;
³⁸ one gold incense bowl weighing 10 [shekels] filled with incense; ³⁹ one
young bull, one ram and one yearling sheep for a burnt offering; ⁴⁰ one goat
for a sin offering; ⁴¹ and for the peace sacrifice, two oxen, five rams, five
male goats, and five yearling sheep. This was the offering of Shelumiel son
of Tzuri-shaddai.

[49. The Sixth Day: Gad]

⁴² On the sixth day, it was the leader of Gad's descendants, Elyassaf son
of Deuel. ⁴³ His offering was one silver bowl weighing 130 shekels and
one sacrificial basin weighing 70 shekels by the sanctuary standard, both
filled with wheat meal kneaded with oil for a meal offering; ⁴⁴ one gold

incense bowl weighing 10 [shekels], filled with incense; ⁴⁵ one young bull,   **7**
one ram and one yearling sheep for a burnt offering; ⁴⁶ one goat for a sin
offering; ⁴⁷ and for the peace sacrifice, two oxen, five rams, five male goats,
and five yearling sheep. That was the offering of Elyassaf son of Deuel.

[50. The Seventh Day: Ephraim]

⁴⁸ On the seventh day, it was the leader of Ephraim's descendants,
Elishama son of Amihud. ⁴⁹ His offering was one silver bowl weighing 130
shekels and one silver sacrificial basin weighing 70 shekels by the sanctuary standard, both filled with wheat meal kneaded with oil for a grain offering; ⁵⁰ one gold incense bowl weighing 10 [shekels], filled with incense;
⁵¹ one young bull, one ram and one yearling sheep for a burnt offering;
⁵² one goat for a sin offering; ⁵³ and for the peace sacrifice, two oxen, five
rams, five male goats, and five yearling sheep. That was the offering of
Elishama son of Amihud.

[51. The Eighth Day: Manasseh]

⁵⁴ On the eighth day, it was the leader of Manasseh's descendants,
Gamliel son of Padah-tzur. ⁵⁵ His offering was one silver bowl weighing
130 shekels and one silver sacrificial basin weighing 70 shekels by the
sanctuary standard, both filled with wheat meal kneaded with oil for a
grain offering; ⁵⁶ one gold incense bowl weighing 10 [shekels] filled with
incense; ⁵⁷ one young bull, one ram and one yearling sheep for a burnt
offering; ⁵⁸ one goat for a sin offering; ⁵⁹ and for the peace sacrifice, two
oxen, five rams, five male goats, and five yearling sheep. This was the offering of Gamliel son of Padah-tzur.

[52. The Ninth Day: Benjamin]

⁶⁰ On the ninth day, it was the leader of Benjamin's descendants,
Avidan son of Gid'oni. ⁶¹ His offering was one silver bowl weighing 130
shekels and one silver sacrificial basin weighing 70 shekels by the sanctuary standard, both filled with wheat meal kneaded with oil for a grain offering; ⁶² one incense bowl weighing 10 [shekels] filled with incense; ⁶³ one
young bull, one ram and one yearling sheep for a burnt offering; ⁶⁴ one goat
for a sin offering; ⁶⁵ and for the peace sacrifice, two oxen, five rams, five
male goats, and five yearling sheep. That was the offering of Avidan son of
Gid'oni.

[53. The Tenth Day: Gad]

⁶⁶ On the tenth day, it was the leader of Dan's descendants, Achiezer

7   son of Ami-shaddai. [67] His offering was one silver bowl weighing 130
shekels and one silver sacrificial basin weighing 70 shekels by the sanctuary standard, both filled with wheat meal for a grain offering; [68] one gold
incense bowl weighing 10 [shekels] filled with incense; [69] one young bull,
one ram and one yearling sheep for a burnt offering; [70] one goat for a sin
offering; [71] and for the peace sacrifice, two oxen, five rams, five male goats,
and five yearling sheep. That was the offering of Achiezer son of Ami-
shaddai.

[54. The Eleventh Day: Asher]

[72] On the eleventh day, it was the leader of Asher's descendants, Pagiel
son of Akhran. [73] His offering was one silver bowl weighing 130 shekels
and one silver sacrificial basin weighing 70 shekels by the sanctuary standard, both filled with wheat meal kneaded with oil for a grain offering;
[74] one incense bowl weighing 10 [shekels] filled with incense; [75] one young
bull, one ram and one yearling sheep for a burnt offering; [76] one goat for a
sin offering; [77] and for the peace sacrifice, two oxen, five rams, five male
goats, and five yearling sheep. That was the offering of Pagiel son of
Akhran.

[55. The Twelfth Day: Naphtali]

[78] On the twelfth day, it was the leader of Naphtali's descendants,
Achira son of Eynan. [79] His offering was one silver bowl weighing 130
shekels and one silver sacrificial basin weighing 70 shekels by the sanctuary standard, both filled with wheat meal kneaded with oil for a grain offering; [80] one incense bowl weighing 10 [shekels] filled with incense; [81] one
young bull, one ram and one yearling sheep for a burnt offering; [82] one goat
for a sin offering; [83] and for the peace sacrifice, two oxen, five rams, five
male goats, and five yearling sheep. That was the offering of Achira son of
Eynan.

56. [The Altar's Dedication]

[84] That was the dedication offering for the altar given by the princes of
Israel on the day that it was anointed.

There were twelve silver bowls, twelve silver sacrificial basins, and
twelve gold incense bowls. [85] Since each bowl weighed 130 shekels and
each sacrificial basin weighed 70, all the silver in the utensils amounted to
2400 sanctuary shekels.*

7:85   **2400 shekels.** 1920 oz, or 120 lb.

⁸⁶ There were twelve gold incense bowls full of incense, each weighing   7
ten sanctuary shekels. Therefore, all the gold in the incense bowls
amounted to 120 [shekels].*

⁸⁷ The total of all the animals for burnt offerings was 12 oxen, 12 rams,
and 12 yearling sheep, along with their meal offerings. There were also 12
male goats for sin offerings.

⁸⁸ The total of all the animals for peace sacrifices was 24 bulls, 60 rams, 60
male goats, and 60 yearling male sheep.

That was the dedication offering for the altar after it was anointed.

⁸⁹ When Moses came into the Communion Tent to speak with [God], he
would hear the Voice speaking to him from between the two cherubs on the
ark cover over the Ark of Testimony. [God] thus spoke to him.

BeHa'alothekha   בְּהַעֲלֹתְךָ

[57. Lighting the Lamp]

¹ God spoke to Moses, telling him to ² speak to Aaron and say to him,   8
"When you light* the lamps, the seven lamps shall illuminate the
menorah."*

³ Aaron did that, lighting the lamps to illuminate the menorah, as God
commanded Moses.

⁴ The menorah was made of a single piece of beaten gold. Everything
from its base to its blossom* consisted of a single piece of beaten metal. The
menorah was thus made exactly according to the vision that God showed
Moses.

[58. Inaugurating the Levites]

⁵ God spoke to Moses, saying:

⁶ Take the Levites from among the Israelites and purify them. ⁷ In order
to purify them, you must sprinkle the water of the sin offering* on them
after* they have shaved their entire bodies with a razor. They shall then
immerse [their bodies and] their clothing* and they will be clean.

7:86   **120 shekels.** 96 oz., or 6 lb.
8:2   **light** (Targum; Saadia). Or, "set in order" (Septuagint). Literally, "raise up."
—   **illuminate** . . . Or, "Shall shine toward the center of the menorah" (Rashi; Rashbam). See Exodus
       25:37.
8:4   **blossom.** At the top of the center shaft. According to tradition, however, there was also a flower
       directly above the base (see note on Exodus 25:31).
8:7   **water of the sin offering** (Ibn Ezra; see below, 19:19). Or, "water of purification" (Ibn Ezra; Septu-
       agint).
—   **after** (Ibn Ezra; Chizzkuni). Some say that they did not shave the sides of the head and beard, as
       deliniated in Leviticus 19:27 (Ibn Ezra; Bachya).
—   **immerse** . . . See Exodus 19:10.

8   ⁸ They shall then take a young bull* along with its grain offering* consisting of the best grade wheat meal mixed with olive oil. You shall also present a second bull as a sin offering.

⁹ Bring the Levites to the front of the Communion Tent, and assemble the entire Israelite community. ¹⁰ Present the Levites before God, and have the Israelites* lay their hands* on the Levites. ¹¹ Aaron shall then designate* the Levites as a wave offering to God from the Israelites, and [the Levites] shall become the ones to perform God's service.

¹² The Levites shall then lay their hands on the heads of the bulls, and you shall prepare one [bull] as a sin offering and one as a burnt offering to God, to atone for the Levites. ¹³ You shall stand the Levites before Aaron and his sons and designate them as a wave offering to God. ¹⁴ In this manner you will separate the Levites from the other Israelites, and the Levites shall become Mine.

¹⁵ After you have purified them and designated them as a wave offering, the Levites shall come to perform the service in the Communion Tent. ¹⁶ They are given to Me from among the Israelites in place of the first-born (that initiate the womb) of all the Israelites. I have taken them for Myself.

¹⁷ This is because all first-born of the Israelites are Mine, man and beast alike. I sanctified them for Myself on the day that I killed all the first-born in Egypt. ¹⁸ I have now taken the Levites in place of all the first-born Israelites ¹⁹ and I have given the Levites as a gift from the Israelites to Aaron and his descendants. They shall [henceforth] perform the service for the Israelites in the Communion Tent and atone for the Israelites. The Israelites will then not be subject to divine wrath when they approach the sanctuary.

²⁰ Moses, Aaron, and the entire Israelite community did for the Levites all that God had instructed Moses regarding the Levites. The Israelites did it for them exactly.

²¹ The Levites purified themselves through a sin offering* and they immersed [their bodies and] their clothing. Aaron designated them as a wave offering before God and made atonement for them to purify them. ²² After that, the Levites came to perform the Communion Tent's service under the direction of Aaron and his sons. [It was all done] exactly as God had commanded Moses regarding the Levites.

8:8   **bull.** For the burnt offering (Rashi; see 8:12).
—   **grain offering.** Three-tenths of an ephah (6 quarts) as in 15:9 (Ibn Ezra; Abarbanel).
8:10   **Israelites.** Some say that this denoted only the first-born (Chizzkuni).
—   **lay their hands.** Or, "ordain" (Lekach Tov).
8:11   **designate.** Literally, "lift up" (Targum; Rashbam; Abarbanel). Or, "make them pass by" (Saadia; Lekach Tov); or, "separate . . . as a gift" (Septuagint).
8:21   **purified themselves through . . .** See 8:7. Or, "purified" (Targum; Saadia; Septuagint).

[59. Levitical Terms of Service]   **8**

²³ God spoke to Moses, saying:

²⁴ This is [the rule] regarding the Levites: Beginning at the age of 25, they shall participate in the work force engaged in the Communion Tent's service. ²⁵ Then, when they are 50 years old, they shall retire from the work force and not serve any more.

²⁶ [During their duty period]* they shall perform their appointed tasks, serving their brethren [the priests] in the Communion Tent. They shall not, however, participate in the divine service. This is what shall be done for the Levites as far as their appointed tasks are concerned.

[60. Passover in the Desert]

¹ God spoke to Moses in the Sinai Desert, in the second year of the **9** Exodus from Egypt, in the first month,* saying, ² "The Israelites shall prepare the Passover offering at its proper time. ³ The proper time for its preparation shall be the 14th day of this month in the afternoon. They must prepare it in accordance with all its decrees and laws."

⁴ Moses spoke to the Israelites, [telling them] to prepare the Passover offering. ⁵ They prepared the Passover offering in the Sinai Desert, on the 14th of the first [month] in the afternoon. The Israelites did exactly as God had instructed Moses.

⁶ There were, however, some men who had come in contact with the dead, and were therefore ritually unclean, so that they could not prepare the Passover offering on that day. During the course of that day, they approached Moses and Aaron.

⁷ "We are ritually unclean as a result of contact with the dead," the men said to [Moses]. "But why should we lose out and not be able to present God's offering at the right time, along with the other Israelites?"

⁸ "Wait here," replied Moses. "I will hear what orders God gives regarding your case."

[61. Making Up the Passover Offering]

⁹ God spoke to Moses, telling him to ¹⁰ speak to the Israelites, saying:

If any person is ritually unclean from contact with the dead, or is on a distant journey, whether among you [now] or in future generations, he shall still have the opportunity to prepare God's Passover offering. ¹¹ He

---

8:26 **During their duty period** . . . Or, "They shall then perform their appointed tasks with their brethren in the Communion Tent, but they shall not do any [physical] labor" (Rashi; Rashbam).

9:1 **first month.** Nissan, the month of Passover. This appears to be before the events described in 1:1.

9 shall prepare it on the afternoon of the 14th of the second month,* and
shall eat it with matzahs and bitter herbs.* [12] He shall not leave any of it
over until morning, and not break any bone in it.* He shall thus prepare it
according to all the rules of the [regular] Passover offering.

[13] However, if a man is ritually clean, and not on a distant journey, and he
neglects to prepare the Passover offering, that person shall be cut off [spiri-
tually] from his people. He shall bear his guilt for not offering God's sacrifice
at the prescribed time.

[14] If a proselyte joins you, he must also prepare God's Passover offering,
presenting it according to the rules and laws governing the Passover offering. There shall thus be a single law for [all of] you, the proselyte and
native born [alike].

[62. Divine Signs to Move On]

[15] On the day that the Tabernacle was erected, the cloud covered the
Tabernacle, the Tent of Testimony. Then, in the evening, there was something that appeared to be like fire on the Tabernacle, [remaining there] until
morning. [16] From then on it remained that way. There was a cloud covering
it [by day],* and a fire-like apparition by night.

[17] Whenever the cloud rose up from the Tent, the Israelites would set
out on the march. The Israelites would then camp in the place where the
cloud rested. [18] The Israelites would thus move on at God's bidding, and at
God's bidding they would remain in one place for as long as the cloud
remained on the Tabernacle.

[19] If the cloud remained over the Tabernacle for a long time, the Israelites would keep their trust in God and not travel on. [20] In some cases, the
cloud would remain on the Tabernacle for just a few days, and they would
similarly remain camped at God's word, and then move on at God's word.
[21] There were even cases where the cloud remained [only] from evening to
morning; when the cloud then rose in the morning, they would travel on.
[At other times, it might be] for a day and night, and they would then move
on when the cloud rose.

[20] Thus, whether it was for two days, a month, or a full year, no matter
how long the cloud remained at rest over [the Tabernacle], the Israelites
would remain in one place and not move on. Then, when [the cloud] rose,
they would continue on their travels. [23] They thus camped at God's word

---

9:11 **14th of the second month.** 14 Iyyar, one month after the regular Passover.
—   **shall eat it . . .** See Exodus 12:8.
9:12 **not break any bone . . .** See Exodus 12:46.
9:16 **by day** (Targum Yonathan; Septuagint). However, it is possible that the cloud was there also at night.

and moved on at God's word, keeping their trust in God. [It was all done]   9
according to God's word through Moses.

[63. The Trumpets]

¹ God spoke to Moses, saying: 10
² Make yourself two silver trumpets.* Make them out of beaten metal.*
They shall be used by you to assemble the community and to make the
camps break camp for their journeys.
³ When [both* of the trumpets] are sounded with a long note, the entire
community shall assemble at the Communion Tent entrance. ⁴ If a long note
is sounded on [only] one of them, the princes, who are leaders of thousands
in Israel, shall come together to you.
⁵ When you sound a series of short notes,* the camps to the east shall
begin the march. ⁶ Then, when you sound a second series of short notes,
the camps to the south shall set out.*

Thus, when [the Israelites] are to move on, you are to signal it with a
series of short notes. ⁷ However, when the community is to be assembled,
[the trumpets] shall be sounded with a long note, and not with a series of
short notes.
⁸ The priests who are Aaron's descendants shall be the ones to sound
the trumpets. This shall be an eternal law for future generations.
⁹ When you go to war against an enemy who attacks you in your land,
you shall sound a stacatto on the trumpets. You will then be remembered
before God your Lord, and will be delivered from your enemies.
¹⁰ On your days of rejoicing, on your festivals, and on your new-moon
celebrations, you shall sound a note with the trumpets for your burnt offerings and your peace offerings. This shall be a remembrance before your God.
I am God your Lord.

[64. The Journey from Sinai]

¹¹ In the second year [of the Exodus], on the 20th of the second month,*

10:2   **trumpets.** Josephus describes them as a little less than one cubit (18") long,
        a little thicker than an ordinary flute, with a bell-like end (*Antiquities*
        3:12:6).
—   **beaten metal.** See Exodus 25:18,31.   **Trumpet**
10:3   **both** (Rashi).
10:5   **short notes** (Targum). In the Talmud there is a dispute as to whether the *teruah* mentioned here was a
        stacatto note or a series of three short notes (*Rosh HaShanah* 33b). It is also noted that the series of
        short notes was preceded and followed by a single long note (*Sifri; Rosh HaShanah* 34a; Rashi).
10:6   **the camps to the south ...** The Tabernacle would then move on. See below, 10:17,21. Some say that
        a third blast would signal the beginning of the march for the western camp, and a fourth for the
        northern camp (Ramban; Josephus, *Antiquities* 3:12:6; Septuagint). In other sources, however, this
        is debated (*Sifri*).
10:11   **20th of the second month.** 20 Iyyar, 36 days after the Passover.

10   the cloud rose from the Tabernacle of Testimony. [12] The Israelites thus
      began their travels, [moving on] from the Sinai Desert, [until] the cloud
      came to rest in the Paran Desert.* [13] This was the first journey* at God's
      word through Moses.

      [14] The divisions in the banner camp of Judah's descendants set out
      first.* Heading that division was Nachshon son of Aminadav.* [15] Heading
      the tribal division of Issachar's descendants was Nethanel son of Tzuar,
      [16] and heading the tribal division of Zebulun's descendants was Eliav son of
      Chelon.

      [17] The Tabernacle was then dismantled, and the descendants of Gershon
      and Merari, who carried the Tabernacle, began the march.*

      [18] The divisions in the banner camp of Reuben then began to march.
      Heading that division was Elitzur son of Shedey-ur. [19] Heading the tribal
      division of Simeon's descendants was Shelumiel son of Tzuri-shaddai,
      [20] and heading the tribal division of Gad's descendants was Elyassaf son of
      Deuel.

      [21] The Kehothites, who carried the sacred furniture,* then began their
      march. The Tabernacle would be set up before they arrived [at the destina-
      tion].

      [22] The divisions in the banner camp of Ephraim's descendants then
      began the march. Heading their division was Elishama son of Amihud.
      [23] Heading the tribal division of Manasseh's descendants was Gamliel son
      of Padah-tzur, [24] and heading the tribal division of Benjamin's descendants
      was Avidan son of Gid'oni.

      [25] Then the divisions in the banner camp of Dan's descendants, the last*
      of the camps, began the march. Heading their division was Achiezer son of
      Ami-shaddai. [26] Heading the tribal division of Asher's descendants was
      Pagiel son of Akhran, [27] and heading the tribal divisions of Naphtali's
      descendants was Achira son of Eynan.

      [28] When they set out, this was the marching order of the Israelites,
      according to their divisions.

      10:12 **Paran Desert.** The exact location where they arrived was *Kibhroth HaTaavah* (Graves of Craving),
      see below, 11:34, 33:16. This was a three day journey (100 miles) from Sinai (below, 10:33; *Sefer
      HaYashar*, p. 215). Some identify *Kibhroth HaTaavah* with Kadesh Barnea (Ibn Ezra on 33:16). See
      note on 13:1.
      10:13 **This was the first** . . . (*Midrash HaGadol*). Or, "The first rank departed . . ." (Septuagint).
      10:14 **The divisions** . . . The order is that given above in 2:1-31.
      —   **Nachshon** . . . See 1:6-15.
      10:17 **began the march** (*Lekach Tov*; Ralbag; cf. Ramban). This is a detail not mentioned in 2:17. Or, "they
      would prepare to march" but not march until after Reuben's division (*Bareitha deMelekheth
      HaMishkan* 13; quoted in Ramban)
      10:21 **sacred furniture** (Rashi; Septuagint). Or, "the ark" (Ibn Ezra).
      10:25 **last** (Septuagint). Or, "gatherer" (Rashi; Chizzkuni).

[65. Chovev]

²⁹ Moses said to his* father-in-law,* Chovev son of Reuel* the Midian-ite, "We are now on our way to the place that God promised to give us.* Come with us and we will let you share the benefit of all the good things* that God has promised Israel."

³⁰ "I would rather not go," replied [Chovev]. "I wish to return to my land and my birthplace."

³¹ "Do not abandon us," said [Moses]. "After all,* you are familiar with the places where we are going to camp in the desert, and you can be our guide.* ³² If you go with us, we will share with you whatever good God grants us.*"

³³ [The Israelites] marched [the distance of] a three day journey* from God's mountain. The Ark of God's covenant* traveled three days ahead of them in order to find them a place to settle. ³⁴ When they began traveling from the camp by day, God's cloud remained over them.

[66. The Ark Goes Forth]

³⁵ When the Ark went forth,* Moses said, "Arise, O God, and scatter your enemies! Let your foes flee before You!"

³⁶ When it came to rest, he said, "Return, O God, [to]* the myriads of Israel's thousands."

[67. Complaints]

¹ The people began to complain, and it was evil* in God's ears. When **11** God heard it, He displayed His anger, and God's fire flared out, consuming

---

10:29 **his.** Literally, "Moses."
— **father-in-law** (Rashi; Septuagint). Some identify him with Jethro, mentioned in Exodus 3:1, 18:1 (Rashbam; Ramban). According to others, Chovev was Moses' brother-in-law (Ibn Ezra).
— **Reuel.** See Exodus 2:18.
— **promised to give us.** Literally, "That God said, 'I will give it to you.'"
— **benefit of all the good things** (cf. Saadia).
10:31 **After all.** See Genesis 18:5, 19:8, 33:10.
— **and you can be our guide** (cf. Ibn Ezra). Literally, "you shall be like eyes for us." Or, "you shall be an advisor" (Septuagint). Or, "You have been our guide" (Rashi; Ibn Ezra).
10:32 **whatever good . . .** Some sources indicate that Chovev eventually agreed to this (Sifri; Rashi). However, some say that he first went home (Sifri; see Exodus 18:27).
10:33 **three day journey.** 100 miles, to Paran as in 10:12 (Ramban; Ibn Ezra).
— **Ark of God's covenant.** Some say that there were two arks, and this was the one containing the broken tablets (Sifri; Rashi).
10:35 **When the ark . . .** In the Torah scroll, this section is preceded and followed by inverted letters Nun. It is said in the synagogue when the Torah is taken from the ark and returned.
10:36 **to.** Saadia. Or, "Rest Your presence on . . ." (Targum). Or, "O God, let the myriads . . . of Israel return" (Baaley Tosafoth).
11:1 **and it was evil . . .** Or, "The people had evil complaints for God's ears" (Saadia).

11   the edge of the camp. ² The people cried out to Moses, and when Moses
prayed to God, the fire died down. ³ He named the place "Burning"
(*Tabh'erah*), for God's fire had burned them.

⁴ The mixed multitude* among [the Israelites] began to have strong
cravings, and the Israelites once again began to weep. "Who's going to give
us some meat to eat?" they demanded. ⁵ "We fondly remember the fish that
we could eat in Egypt at no cost, along with the cucumbers, melons, leeks,
onions and garlic. ⁶ But now our spirits are dried up, with nothing but the
manna before our eyes."

⁷ The manna was like coriander seed* with a pearl-like* luster. ⁸ The
people could simply go for a stroll and gather it. They would then grind it
in a hand-mill or crush it in a mortar, cooking it in a pan and making it into
cakes. It tasted like an oil wafer.* ⁹ At night, when the dew would fall on
the camp, the manna would descend on it.

¹⁰ Moses heard the people weeping with their families near the
entrances of their tents. God became very angry, and Moses [also] considered it wrong.

¹¹ "Why are You treating me* so badly?" said Moses to God. "Don't
you like me any more? Why do You place such a burden upon me? ¹² Was I
[the woman] who was pregnant with this nation [in my belly]? Did I give
birth to them? But You told me that I must* carry them in my bosom, as a
nurse carries an infant [until we come]* to the land that You swore to their
ancestors.

¹³ "Where can I get enough meat to give all these people? They are
whining to me to give them some meat to eat. ¹⁴ I cannot be responsible for
this entire nation! It's too hard for me! ¹⁵ If You are going to do this to me,
just do me a favor* and kill me! Don't let me see myself get into such a terrible predicament!"

[68. The Promise of Meat]

¹⁶ God said to Moses, "Assemble seventy of Israel's elders*—the ones

---

11:4   **mixed multitude.** See Exodus 12:38. However, in Exodus it is referred to as an *erev rav*, while here it
is called the *asafsuf.*
11:7   **coriander seed.** See Exodus 16:31.
—   **pearl-like.** *Bedolach* in Hebrew, translated as pearl (Saadia). See Genesis 2:12. Or, "crystal" (Rashi;
Septuagint).
11:8   **wafer** (Septuagint). *Leshad* in Hebrew. Or, "oil-saturated loaf" (Donash, quoted in Rashi). See
Exodus 16:31.
11:11   **me.** Literally, "Your servant."
11:12   **that I must.** Literally, "You told me, 'Carry them . . .'"
—   **until we come** (Ibn Ezra).
11:15   **do me a favor.** See note on Genesis 47:29. Literally, "If I have found favor in your eyes."
11:16   **seventy of Israel's elders.** See Exodus 24:1.

you know to be the people's elders and leaders. Bring them to the Com- **11**
munion Tent, and let them stand there with you. [17] When I lower My
essence* and speak to you there, I will cause some of the spirit that you
possess to emanate, and I will grant it to them. You will then not have to
bear the responsibility all alone.

[18] "Tell the people as follows: Prepare yourselves for tomorrow, for you
will then have meat to eat. You have been whining in God's ears, saying,
'Who's going to give us some meat to eat? It was better for us in Egypt!'

"Now God is going to give you meat, and you will have to eat it. [19] You
will eat it not for one day, not for two days, not for five days, not for ten
days, and not for twenty days. [20] But for a full month [you will eat it] until
it is coming out of your nose and making you nauseated. This is because
you rejected God [now that He] is among you, and you whined before Him,
'Why did we ever leave Egypt?' "

[20] Moses said, "Here I am among 600,000 men on foot* [alone], and
You are saying that You will give them enough meat to eat for a full month!
[21] Even if all the cattle and sheep were slaughtered, could there be enough
for them? If all the fish in the sea were caught, would it be sufficient?' "

[69. The Quail]

[23] God said to Moses, "Has My power then become limited?* You will
now see whether or not My word will come true!"

[24] Moses went out* and told the people what God had said. He gathered
seventy of the people's elders, and stood them around the Tent. [25] God
descended in the cloud, and spoke to [Moses]. He caused the spirit that had
been imparted on [Moses] to emanate, and He bestowed it upon the seventy
elders. When the spirit descended on them, they gained the gift of prophecy and did not lose it.*

[26] Two men remained in the camp, and the spirit [also] rested on them.
The name of one was Eldad, and the name of the second was Medad.*
Although they were among those registered,* they did not go out to the

---

11:17 **lower My essence.** See Exodus 19:11.
11:20 **on foot.** See Exodus 12:37.
11:23 **Has My power** . . . Literally, "Has God's hand become short?"
11:24 **went out.** Of the Communion Tent (Ibn Ezra).
11:25 **did not lose it.** (Targum). Or, "did not keep it" (Sifri; Ralbag; Septuagint).
11:26 **Eldad ... Medad.** Some say that they were the sons of Eltzafan son of Parnach (Numbers 34:25),
    born to Yocheved while she was divorced from Amram, and hence, half-brothers to Moses (*Targum
    Yonathan*). Others say that Eldad was Elidad son of Chislon of Benjamin (34:21) and that Medad was
    Kemuel son of Shiftan of Ephraim (34:24) (*BeMidbar Rabbah* 15:19).
— **registered.** There were six from each of the twelve tribes, making a total of 72, and these two were
    then excluded by lot (*Sifri*; Rashi).

11   [Communion] Tent, but they spoke prophetically in the camp.

²⁷ A young man ran to tell Moses. "Eldad and Medad are speaking prophecy in the camp!" he announced.

²⁸ Joshua son of Nun, Moses' chosen* attendant, spoke up. "My lord Moses," he said. "Stop them!"*

²⁹ "Are you jealous for my sake?" replied Moses. "I only wish that all of God's people would have the gift of prophecy! Let God grant His spirit to them [all]!"

³⁰ Moses then returned to the camp along with the elders of Israel.

³¹ God caused a wind to start blowing, sweeping quail* up from the sea.* They ran out of strength over the camp, and [were flying]* only two cubits above the ground for the distance of a day's journey* in each direction. ³² The people went about all that day, all night, and the entire next day, and gathered quail. Even those who got the least had gathered ten chomers.* [The people] spread them out around the camp.

³³ The .meat was still between their teeth* when [the people] began to die.* God's anger was displayed against the people, and He struck them with an extremely severe plague.

³⁴ [Moses]* named the place "Graves of Craving" (Kivroth HaTaavah), since it was in that place where they buried the people who had these cravings.

³⁵ From Graves of Craving, the people traveled to Chatzeroth.* They were to remain in Chatzeroth [longer than planned].

11:28 **chosen** (Ibn Ezra; Septuagint). Or, "young attendant" (Ibn Ezra); "from among his students" (Saadia); or, "from his youth" (Targum; Rashbam; Radak, *Sherashim*).

—   **Stop them** (Radak, Sherashim; Septuagint). Or, "Imprison them" (Targum; Sifri; Rashi; Rashbam); or, "destroy them" (*Sifri*; Ibn Janach).

11:31 **quail.** See Exodus 16:13.

—   **sea.** The Red Sea (Sforno), or the Mediterranean Sea (*Targum Yonathan*).

—   **flying . . .** (Sifri; *Targum Yonathan*; Rashi). Or, "they were piled two cubits (3') on the ground" (Saadia; Ibn Ezra; Ralbag; Septuagint).

—   **day's journey.** Around 34 miles; see note on Genesis 30:36.

11:32 **chomers.** See Leviticus 27:16. *Kor* in Greek (Septuagint. Cf. *Targum Yonathan*). Since a chomer is 30 sa'ah, each one had ten sa'ah per day (Chizzkuni). The ten chomers was around 80 cubic feet, or around 1000 pounds of meat.

11:33 **between their teeth.** It is from here that we learn that meat retains its status even when it is between the teeth, and that therefore one must wait six hours between meat and dairy (*Chullin* 105a). According to others, they were still eating the meat during the designated month (Sforno).

—   **began to die** (Rashi). Literally, "were (or was) cut off." Or, "before it was used up" (Sforno; cf. Targum; Septuagint); or, "and was not yet digested" (*Sifethey Chakhamim*); "was not yet totally eaten" (*Gur Aryeh*); "was not yet chewed" (Hirsch), or, "before they swallowed it" (Saadia).

11:34 **Moses.** (Ibn Ezra)

11:35 **Chatzeroth.** See below, 33:17, Deuteronomy 1:1. Some say that this can be identified with Ain Khadra, some 37 miles north-east of Sinai. The Israelites arrived in Chatzeroth on 22 Sivan (*Taanith* 29a; Chizzkuni). Some say that Korach's rebellion occured in Chatzeroth (Rashi on Deuteronomy 1:1), see below, 16:20.

[70. Miriam and Aaron Complain]

¹ Miriam and Aaron began speaking against Moses because of the **12** dark-skinned* woman he had married. The woman that [Moses] had married was indeed dark-skinned.* ² They [then went on to]* say, "Is it to* Moses exclusively that God speaks? Doesn't He also speak to us?"

God heard it. ³ Moses, however, was very humble, more so than any man on the face of the earth.

[71. Miriam's Punishment]

⁴ God suddenly said to Moses, Aaron and Miriam, "All three of you go out to the Communion Tent!"

When the three of them went out, ⁵ God descended in a pillar of cloud and stood at the Tent's entrance. He summoned Aaron and Miriam, and both of them went forth.

⁶ [God] said, "Listen carefully to My words. If someone among you experiences divine prophecy,* then when I make Myself known to him in a vision, I will speak to him in a dream. ⁷ This is not true of My servant Moses, who is like a trusted servant* throughout My house. ⁸ With him I speak face to face,* in a vision not containing allegory, so that he sees a true picture of God. How can you not be afraid to speak against My servant Moses?"

⁹ God displayed anger against them and departed. ¹⁰ When the cloud left its place over the Tent, Miriam was leprous, white like snow. When Aaron turned to Miriam [and saw] her leprous, ¹¹ Aaron said to Moses, "Please, my lord, do not hold a grudge against us for acting foolishly and sinning. ¹² Let [Miriam] not be like a stillborn child, who comes from the womb with half its flesh rotted away."*

¹³ Moses cried out to God, "O God, please heal her!"

12:1 **dark-skinned.** Tzipporah was a dark-skinned Midianite (Ibn Ezra; Radak, *Sherashim*). Kushite in Hebrew, literally Ethiopian (cf. *Targum Yonathan*; Rashbam; Septuagint). It is from here that the tradition is derived that after he escaped from Egypt, Moses was a ruler in Ethiopia, and married an Ethiopian princess (Rashbam; *Sefer HaYashar*; *Divrey Yamim DeMoshe*; *Yalkut Shimoni* 168; Rashbam; Josephus, *Antiquities* 2:10:2). Or, "a beautiful wife" (Targum; Saadia; Rashi; *HaKethav VeHaKabbalah*); or, "a distinguished wife" (Rashi).

— **the woman ...** Or, "for he had divorced his beautiful wife" (Targum; Saadia; Rashi).

12:2 **then went on to ...** (Rashbam).

— **to.** Or, "through" (Rashbam).

12:6 **experiences divine prophecy.** Literally, "experiences prophecy to God" (Ibn Ezra; Septuagint). Or, "experiences prophecy, then I, God, make ..." (Targum; Saadia; Rashi).

12:7 **like a trusted servant** (Rashbam; Ibn Ezra). Or, "trusted in all ..." (Targum; Saadia; Septuagint).

12:8 **face to face** (Saadia). Literally, "mouth to mouth." See Exodus 33:11.

12:12 **Let Miriam not be ...** (Saadia).

12   *[72. Miriam Quarantined]*

¹⁴ God said to Moses, "If her father had spit in her face, would she not have been embarrassed for seven days? Let her remain quarantined* for seven days outside the camp, and then she can return home."

¹⁵ For seven days, Miriam remained quarantined outside the camp, and the people did not move on until Miriam was able to return home. ¹⁶ The people then left Chatzeroth, and they camped in the Paran Desert.*

Sh'lach   שְׁלַח

[73. Exploring the Promised Land]

13   ¹ God spoke to Moses, saying, ² "Send out men for yourself to explore the Canaanite territory that I am about to give the Israelites. Send out one man for each patriarchal tribe. Each one shall be a person of high rank."

³ Moses sent them from the Paran Desert* at God's bidding. All the men were leaders of the Israelites. ⁴ Their names were as follows:

From the tribe of Reuben, Shamua* son of Zakur.

⁵ From the tribe of Simeon, Shaphat son of Chori.

⁶ From the tribe of Judah, Caleb son of Yefuneh.*

⁷ From the tribe of Issachar, Yig'al son of Joseph.*

⁸ From the tribe of Ephraim, Hoshea son of Nun.*

⁹ From the tribe of Benjamin, Palti son of Raphu.

¹⁰ From the tribe of Zebulun, Gadiel son of Sodi.

¹¹ From the tribe of Manasseh (from Joseph), Gaddi son of Susi.

¹² From the tribe of Dan, Amiel son of Gemalli.

12:14 **quarantined.** See Leviticus 13:4.

12:16 **Paran Desert.** The next move was to Rithma; see 33:18. The Israelites left Chatzeroth on 29 Sivan (*Taanith* 29a; *Seder Olam Rabbah* 8).

13:3 **Paran Desert.** Some say that they were then in Rithma, which was the next stop after Chatzeroth as we see in 33:18 (Sforno on 12:16). Other sources, however, indicate that they were in Kadesh Barnea, as evident from 13:26 (Chizzkuni on 12:16; *Lekach Tov* on 13:17). See below 32:8; Deuteronomy 1:19,22, 9:23, Joshua 14:7. However, it appears that Kadesh Barnea is simply another name for Rithmah (Chizzkuni on 33:16). Kadesh Barnea is not to be confused with the Kadesh to which the Israelites came at the end of the 40 years (Below, 20:1; Ramban, Chizzkuni, *ad loc.*).

13:4 **Shamua.** Possibly a form of Samuel or Sh'muel (cf. Septuagint). See 1 Chronicles 4:26.

13:6 **Caleb son of Yefuneh.** See below, 13:30, 14:6, etc. He was 40 years old at the time (Joshua 14:6,7). According to tradition, he is the same as Caleb son of Chetzron mentioned in 1 Chronicles 2:9 (*Yerushalmi, Yevamoth* 10:7), and was thus a great-grandson of Judah (cf. Genesis 46:12). He was the step-brother of Othniel son of Kenaz (Joshua 15:17; *Sotah* 11b). Caleb married Miriam and was the father of Chur (1 Chronicles 2:19,20; Targum *ad loc.*; *Sifri*). He also married Bithia, the daughter of Pharaoh who raised Moses (*Megillah* 13a, from 1 Chronicles 4:18; see note on Exodus 2:5). Also see 1 Chronicles 2:42-50, 4:15.

13:7 **Joseph.** Yosef in Hebrew. Possibly named after Jacob's son Joseph.

13:8 **Hoshea . . . Joshua,** see below 13:16. See note on Exodus 17:9.

¹³ From the tribe of Asher, Sethur son of Michael.*   **13**
¹⁴ From the tribe of Naphtali, Nachbi son of Vafsi.*
¹⁵ From the tribe of Gad, Geu'el son of Makhi.
¹⁶ These are the names of the men Moses sent to explore the land.
[However,] Moses gave Hoshea son of Nun the [new] name Joshua (*Yeho-shua*).*
¹⁷ When Moses sent [the men] to explore the Canaanite territory, he
said to them, "Head north* to the Negev,* and then continue north to the
hill country. ¹⁸ See what kind of land it is. Are the people who live there
strong or weak, few or many? ¹⁹ Is the inhabited area good or bad? Are the
cities where they live open or fortified? ²⁰ Is the soil rich or weak? Does [the
land] have trees or not? Make a special effort to bring [back] some of the
land's fruits."

It was the season when the first grapes begin to ripen.* ²¹ The men
headed north and explored the land, from the Tzin Desert* all the way to
Rechov* on the road to Chamath.* ²² On the way through the Negev, they*
came to Hebron, where [they saw] Achiman, Sheshai and Talmi,* descendants of the Giant.* Hebron had been built seven years before Tzoan* in
Egypt.

13:13 **Michael.** Like the angel.
13:14 **Vafsi.** Or Vofsi.
13:16 **Moses gave Hoshea** . . . Some say that Moses renamed him Joshua earlier, when he first became
  Moses' servant, so the name Joshua is used earlier in Exodus 17:9, etc. (Rashbam; Chizzkuni).
  Others say that his true name was Joshua, but he used the anonym Hoshea because he would be
  passing dangerously near Amalekite territory (Chizzkuni). Other sources, however, indicate that he
  was given the name of Joshua at this time (Rashi; Ralbag), but the Torah uses the name Joshua
  earlier because this became his final name (Sforno).
13:17 **Head north.** Literally, "go up." See note on Genesis 12:10.
  — **Negev.** "Drylands" to the south of the Holy Land.
13:20 **It was the** . . . According to tradition, it was 29 Sivan (*Targum Yonathan*; *Taanith* 29a; *Seder Olam
  Rabbah* 8). This was the early summer.
13:21 **Tzin Desert.** This is in the southern Negev, north of Kadesh.
  — **Rechov.** This is to the north-west of the Holy Land (Chizzkuni). Some say that it is in Asher (cf.
  Joshua 19:28,30, 21:31, Judges 1:31, 2 Samuel 10:8, 1 Chronicles 6:60). Some identify it with Beth
  Rechov (Judges 18:28). Other sources, however, translate it as "the highway heading to Chamath"
  (*Targum Yonathan*).
  — **Chamath.** A large city, some 160 miles north of the Holy Land on the Orontes River. It was a major
  city in ancient times (cf. Numbers 34:8). Some sources identify it with Antioch (*Targum Yonathan*).
13:22 **they.** Literally, "he." Some say that only Caleb went to Hebron (*Sotah* 34b; Rashi; Rashbam). He
  was therefore given Hebron as his inheritance, see below 14:24.
  — **Achiman** . . . See note on Genesis 23:2. They were later driven out by Caleb (Joshua 15:14), and
  killed (Judges 1:10).
  — **Giant.** (Targum; Saadia). Some say that Anak is a proper name (*Targum Yonathan*; Septuagint).
  — **Tzoan.** This is identified with Tanis (Targum; Septuagint), a city south of the Delta. According to
  tradition, Hebron was built at the time of the Tower of Babel in 1996 or 1764 b.c.e. (*Seder HaDoroth*
  1996). This would indicate that Tanis was built in 2003 or 1757 b.c.e. However, if we allow for the
  163 year discrepancy (see Genesis 12:15, Exodus 2:23), then Tanis was built in 1920 b.c.e. Tanis was
  the capital of the Hyksos.

13 ²³ When they came to Cluster Valley (*Nachal Eshkol*),* they cut a branch and a cluster of grapes, which two men caried on a frame.* [They also took] some pomegranates and figs. ²⁴ Because of the grape-cluster that the Israelites cut there, the place was named Cluster Valley.

²⁵ At the end of forty days* they came back from exploring the land. ²⁶ When they arrived, they went directly to Moses, Aaron and the entire Israelite community, [who were] in the Paran Desert near Kadesh.* They brought their report to [Moses, Aaron,] and the entire community, and showed them fruit from the land.

²⁷ They gave the following report: "We came to the land where you sent us, and it is indeed flowing with milk and honey, as you can see from its fruit. ²⁸ However, the people living in the land are aggressive, and the cities are large and well fortified. We also saw the giant's descendants there. ²⁹ Amalek* lives in the Negev area, the Hittites, Yebusites and Amorites* live in the hills, and the Canaanites* live near the sea* and on the banks of the Jordan."

³⁰ Caleb tried to quiet the people for Moses. "We must go forth and occupy the land," he said. "We can do it!"

³¹ "We cannot go forward against those people!" replied the men who had gone with him. "They are too strong for us!"

³² They began to speak badly about the land that they had explored. They told the Israelites, "The land that we crossed to explore is a land that consumes its inhabitants. All the men we saw there were huge!* ³³ While we were there, we saw the titans. They were sons of the giant, who descended from the [original] titans.* We felt like tiny grasshoppers*! That's all that we were in their eyes!"

14 ¹ The entire community raised a hubbub and began to shout. That night,* the people wept. ² All the Israelites complained to Moses and Aaron. The entire community was saying, "We wish we had died in Egypt!

13:23 **Cluster Valley . . .** See 32:9.
— **frame.** See above, 4:10. Some say that the frame was made out of the branch that they cut (Chizzkuni). Talmudic sources state that the frame consisted of two poles, carried by eight men (*Sotah* 34b).
13:25 **At the end of 40 days.** 8 Av (*Taanith* 29b; *Seder Olam* 8). See below, 14:1.
13:26 **Kadesh.** See above 13:3. Also see Genesis 14:7, 16:14, 20:1.
13:29 **Amalek.** See Exodus 17:8.
— **Hittites . . .** See Genesis 10:15, 15:20.
— **Canaanites.** The other tribes. See Genesis 15:21.
— **sea.** The Mediterranean.
13:32 **huge** (Rashi; Ibn Ezra; Septuagint). Literally, "men of measure."
13:33 **titans.** *Nefilim* in Hebrew. See Genesis 6:4.
— **tiny grasshoppers.** *Chagavim* in Hebrew, the smallest kosher species of locust (see Leviticus 11:22).
14:1 **That night.** The eve of 9 Av, better know as Tisha B'Av. (See note on 13:25). It hence became a day of tragedy.

We should have died in this desert! ³ Why is God bringing us to this land to die by the sword? Our wives and children will be captives! It would be best to go back to Egypt!"

⁴ The people started saying to one another, "Let's appoint a [new] leader and go back to Egypt."

⁵ Moses and Aaron fell on their faces before the whole assembled Israelite community. ⁶ Among the men who had explored the land, Joshua son of Nun and Caleb son of Yefuneh tore their clothes in grief. ⁷ They said to the whole Israelite community, "The land through which we passed in our explorations is a very, very good land! ⁸ If God is satisfied with us and brings us to this land, He can give it to us—a land flowing with milk and honey. ⁹ But don't rebel against God! Don't be afraid of the people in the land! They have lost their protection* and shall be our prey!* God is with us, so don't be afraid!"

¹⁰ The whole community was threatening to stone them to death, when God's glory suddenly appeared at the Communion Tent before all the Israelites.

[74. Threat of Destruction]

¹¹ God said to Moses, "How long shall this nation continue to provoke Me? How long will they not believe in Me, despite all the miracles that I have done among them? ¹² I will kill them with a plague and annihilate them.* Then I will make you into a greater, more powerful nation than they."

¹³ Moses replied to God, "And what will happen when the Egyptians hear about it? You have brought this nation out from among them with Your great power! ¹⁴ And what if they tell the people who live in this land? They have heard that You, God, have been with this nation [Israel]. You, God, have revealed Yourself to them face to face,* and Your cloud stands over them. You go before them in a pillar of cloud by day, and a pillar of fire at night.

¹⁵ "Now you want to kill this [entire] nation like a single man! The nations who hear this news about You will say that ¹⁶ God was not able to bring this nation to the land that He swore to them, so He slaughtered them in the desert.

14:9 **They have lost their protection** (Rashi; Rashbam; Ibn Ezra). Or, "[God] will take away their protection" (Saadia), or, "Their time is over" (Septuagint).

— **prey.** Literally "bread."

14:12 **annihilate . . .** (Rashi; *Targum Yonathan*; Septuagint). Or, "disown."

14:14 **face to face.** Literally, "eye to eye."

14   ¹⁷ "Now, O God, is the time for You to exercise even more restraint.* You once declared,* ¹⁸ 'God is slow to anger, great in love, and forgiving of sin and rebellion. He does not clear [those who do not repent], but keeps in mind the sins of the fathers for their children, grandchildren, and great-grandchildren.'

¹⁹ "With Your great love, forgive the sin of this nation, just as You have forgiven them from [the time they left] Egypt until now."

²⁰ God said, "I will grant forgiveness as you have requested. ²¹ But as I am Life,* and as God's glory fills all the world, ²² [I will punish] all the people who saw My glory and the miracles that I did in Egypt and the desert, but still tried to test Me these ten times by not obeying Me. ²³ They will therefore not see the land that I swore to their ancestors. All those who provoked Me will not see it.   .

²⁴ "The only exception will be My servant Caleb, since he showed a different spirit and followed Me wholeheartedly. I will bring him to the land that he explored,* and his descendants will possess it.

²⁵ "The Amalekites and Canaanites are living in the valley. Tomorrow you will have to leave this place and strike out into the desert toward the Red Sea."

[75. The Decree of Forty Years Wandering]

²⁶ God spoke to Moses and Aaron, saying, ²⁷ "How long shall this evil group exist, complaining against Me? I have heard how the Israelites are complaining about Me. ²⁸ Tell them as follows:

"As I am Life, it is God's solemn declaration that I will make your accusations against Me come true. ²⁹ Because you complained about Me, your corpses will fall in this desert. [This will happen to] your complete tally, everyone over twenty years old who was counted. ³⁰ [My oath is that] you will not come into the land regarding which I swore with a raised hand that I would let you live in it undisturbed. The only exceptions will be Caleb (son of Yefuneh) and Joshua (son of Nun).

³¹ "You said that your children will be taken captive, but they will be the ones I will bring [there], so that they will know the land that you rejected.   .

³² "You, however, will fall as corpses in the desert. ³³ Your children will

---

14:17 **restraint** (Rashbam). Literally, "strength."
—   **declared.** Exodus 34:6.
14:21 **as I am Life.** (see *Yad, Yesodey HaTorah* 2:10).
14:24 **explored.** Literally, "to which he came." See note on 13:22. Caleb was thus subsequently given Hebron as his inheritance (Joshua 15:13).

be herded [from place to place] in the desert for forty years, paying for your **14**
indiscretion until the last of your corpses lie here in the desert.
³⁴ "[The punishment] shall parallel the number of days you spent
exploring the land. There were forty days, and there shall be one year for
each day, a total of forty years until your sin is forgiven. You will then
know how I act.* ³⁵ I, God, have spoken, and [there is no way] that I will
not do this to the entire evil community that has banded against Me. They
will end their lives in this desert, and here is where they will die."

³⁶ The men whom Moses sent to explore the land, and who returned
and complained about it to the entire community, slandering the land, [were
punished immediately]. ³⁷ The men who had given a bad report about the
land thus died before God in the plague. ³⁸ Among the men who went to
explore the land, only Joshua (son of Nun) and Caleb (son of Yefuneh)
remained alive.

³⁹ Moses related [God's] words to all the Israelites, and they were over-
come with terrible grief. ⁴⁰ When they got up early in the morning, they
began climbing toward the top of the mountain,* declaring, "We are now
ready! We shall go forward to the place that God described. We [admit
that] we were mistaken."

⁴¹ "Why are you going against God's word?" said Moses. "It won't
work! ⁴² Do not proceed; God is not with you. Don't be killed by your
enemies! ⁴³ Up ahead of you are the Amalekites and Canaanites, and you
will fall by the sword. You have gone away from God, and [now] God will
not be with you."

⁴⁴ [The people] defiantly climbed toward the top of the mountain, but
the Ark of God's covenant* and Moses did not move from the camp. ⁴⁵ The
Amalekites and Canaanites who lived on that mountain swooped down,
and defeated [the Israelites], pursuing them with crushing force all the way
to Chormah.*

[76. Meal Offerings for Sacrifices]

¹ God spoke to Moses, telling him to ² speak to the Israelites and say to **15**
them:

14:34 **how I act** (Saadia). Literally, "My motions." Or, "My absence." (Rashi; Sforno); "the results of complaining against Me" (Targum); "that I can change [an oath]" (Ibn Ezra), "how I destroy your plans
(Radak, *Sherashim*); "My fierce anger" (Septuagint); or, "how I can stop you" (Ibn Janach).
14:40 **mountain.** About 12 miles south-east of Kadesh Barnea there is a mountain some 3300 feet high.
14:44 **Ark of God's covenant.** See note on 10:33.
14:45 **Chormah.** Some identify this with Tel Esh-Sheri'ah, which is the same as Zepheth, between Beer
Sheba and Gaza. See below, 21:3, Deuteronomy 1:44, Joshua 12:4, 15:30, 19:4, 1 Samuel 30:30,
Judges 1:17, 1 Chronicles 4:30. Some identify Chormah with Safed. Others identify it with Mount
Hermon or a city in the area (Septuagint). Other sources translate this verse, "pursuing them . . .
until they were destroyed" (*Targum Yonathan*; Ibn Ezra).

15   When you come to your homeland* that I am giving you, ³ you will be presenting fire offerings to God. They may be burnt offerings,* or other sacrifices, either for a general or specific pledge,* or for your festivals. Taken from the cattle or smaller animals, they shall be meant to provide an appeasing fragrance to God.

⁴ The one bringing the sacrifice to God must then present a grain offering consisting of 1/10 [ephah]* of the best grade wheat meal* mixed with 1/4 hin* olive oil. ⁵ The wine for the libation shall [also] be 1/4 hin. This shall be for each sheep offered as a burnt offering or [peace]* sacrifice.

⁶ For a ram, you shall prepare a grain offering of 2/10 [ephah]* wheat meal mixed with 1/3 hin* oil. ⁷ The wine for the libation shall [also] be 1/3 hin, presented as an appeasing fragrance to God.

⁸ If you prepare one of the cattle as a burnt offering or [other] sacrifice, to fulfill a vow, or as a peace offering* to God, ⁹ then together with each animal one must present a grain offering of 3/10 [ephah]* of wheat meal mixed with 1/2 hin* oil. ⁷ The wine presented as a libation shall [also] be 1/2 hin, as a fire offering, an appeasing fragrance to God.

¹¹ You must follow this prescription for each bull or ram, or, among the smaller animals, for sheep and goats. ¹² Regardless of the number prepared, you must present [the prescribed meal offering] for each one.

¹³ In order to present a fire offering that is an appeasing fragrance to God, every native born [Israelite] must present it in this manner, along with the prescribed [grain offerings]. ¹⁴ If a proselyte joins you, or lives among you in future generations, and he prepares a fire offering as an appeasing fragrance to God, he must do it in exactly the same manner.

¹⁵ Among the group that may marry one another,* the same rule shall apply both to you and to the proselyte who joins. It is an eternal law for future generations that the proselyte shall be the same as you before God.

15:2   **When you come to your homeland.** Grain offerings (*menachoth*) were not offered together with sacrifices until after the Israelites entered the promised land (Sifri; Ramban).
15:3   **burnt offerings.** See Genesis 8:20, Leviticus 1:3.
—   **general or specific pledge.** See Leviticus 7:16.
15:4   **1/10 ephah.** This is an omer, a day's worth of food (Exodus 16:36). It is around 2 quarts.
—   **wheat meal.** See note on Leviticus 2:1.
—   **1/4 hin.** Around one quart.
15:5   **peace.** (See *Yad, Maaseh HaKorbanoth* 2:2,3; *Menachoth* 90b).
15:6   **2/10 ephah.** Around 4 quarts.
—   **1/3 hin.** Around 1-1/3 quarts.
15:8   **peace offering.** See Leviticus 3:1.
15:9   **3/10 ephah.** Around 6 quarts.
—   **1/2 hin.** Around 2 quarts.
15:15 **the group that may marry one another.** *Kahal* in Hebrew. See Deuteronomy 23:2-4.

[16] There shall thus be one Torah and one law for you and for the proselyte   **15**
who joins you.

[77. The Dough Offering]

[17] God spoke to Moses, telling him to [18] speak to the Israelites and say
to them:

When you come to the land to which I am bringing you, [19] and you eat
the land's produce, you must separate an elevated gift* for God. [20] You
must separate the first portion of your kneading as a dough offering.* It
must be separated very much like the elevated gift that is taken from the
threshing floor.* [21] In future generations, you must thus give the first of
your kneading as an elevated gift to God.

[78. Communal Sin Offerings for Idolatry]

[22] [This is the law] if you inadvertently [commit an act of idolatry,*
which is equivalent to] violating all these commandments that God gave to
Moses. [23] [It is like a violation of] all that God commanded you through
Moses, from the day that God gave His commandments, as well as [what
He will command you] later in future generations.

[24] If [such a sin] is committed inadvertently by the community [because
of their] leadership,* the entire community must prepare one young bull
for a burnt offering as an appeasing fragrance to God, along with its prescribed grain offering and libation. [They must also present] one goat for a
sin offering.*

[25] The priest shall then make atonement for the entire Israelite community, and they will be forgiven. It was inadvertent, and they brought
their sacrifice as a fire offering to God along with their sin offering before

---

15:19 elevated gift. *Terumah* in Hebrew.
15:20 dough offering. *Challah* in Hebrew. This offering must be separated from an *omer* of dough, about
8 cups (*Eruvin* 83b; Rashi). In the codes, this is given as the volume of 43.2 eggs (*Yad, Bikkurim*
6:15; *Yoreh Deah* 324:1). Since the volume of an average egg is 50 cc., 1.69 fl. oz., or 3.05 cu. in., the
amount of dough that must be kneaded so that there is an obligation to separate *challah* is 2160 cc.,
73 fluid ounces, 9-1/8 cups, or 131.8 cubic inches. [Incidentally, the codes give the volume as 311 cubic
finger-breadths (*Yad, loc. cit.*). A simple calculation shows that if a finger-breadth is 3/4 inch, this is 131.8
cubic inches.]
—   **threshing floor.** The elevated gift (*terumah*) taken from crops. This was given to the priest; see below
18:12.
15:22 idolatry . . . (*Horayoth* 8a; Rashi; Rashbam). Some say that it also includes any other situation
where the entire Israelite nation would violate the entire Torah (Ramban).
15:24 leadership. Literally, "eyes." See Leviticus 4:13.
—   **one goat . . .** This was only true of idolatry; for other sins, only the bull had to be presented (Leviticus 4:14; see *Yad, Shegagoth* 12:1).

15   God, for their misdeed. ²⁶ Since all the people acted without knowledge, the
entire Israelite community along with the proselytes who join them shall thus
be forgiven.

[79. Individual Sin Offerings for Idolatry]

²⁷ If a single individual* commits [such a sin] inadvertently, he must
bring a yearling female goat* for a sin offering.
²⁸ The priest will then make atonement before God for the individual
who sinned inadvertently, to expiate his sin, and he will be forgiven.
²⁹ There shall be a single law for one who does such an inadvertent act,
whether he is a native born Israelite or a proselyte who joins them.
³⁰ However, if a person commits [such an act of idolatry] highhandedly,
whether he is native born or a proselyte, he is blaspheming God, and that
person shall be cut off [spiritually] from among his people. ³¹ Since he has
denigrated God's word and violated His commandment, that person shall
be utterly cut off [spiritually and] his sin shall remain upon him.

[80. The Man Gathering Sticks]

³² While the Israelites were in the desert,* they discovered a man*
gathering* sticks on the Sabbath. ³² The ones who found him gathering
sticks brought him to Moses, Aaron and the entire community. ³⁴ Since it
was not specified what must be done to him,* they placed him under guard.

[81. The Penalty for Sabbath Violation]

³⁵ God said to Moses, "That man must die. Let the entire community
pelt him with stones outside the camp."

15:27 individual. Even a high priest or king. In this respect also, idolatry is different from other sins (see
   Leviticus 4; *Horayoth* 7b; *Yad, Shegagoth* 1:4).
—   **yearling female goat.** Not like the other sins where one can also bring a lamb (Leviticus 4:32; Rashi;
   Yad, loc. cit.).
15:32 in the desert. Some say that they were still in the Sinai Desert (Ibn Ezra). This follows the opinion
   that all the Israelites only kept one Sabbath after it was given with the Manna and this Sabbath violation
   occurred on the very next Sabbath (Sifri; Rashi; cf. Chizzkuni). The date given for this event is then 22
   Iyyar of the first year of the Exodus (*Sifri Zuta; Yalkut Shimoni*). According to tradition, it occurred around
   the same time as the act of blasphemy recorded in Leviticus 24:11 (q.v.; see Chizzkuni).
      Others, however, maintain that this event occurred after the return of the spies, or around the
   same time (cf. Ramban). There is thus an opinion that it occurred on 21 Iyyar of the second year of
   the Exodus (*Midrash HaGadol*).
—   **man.** Some say that he was Tzeloph'chad, mentioned in 27:3 (*Shabbath* 96a; Sifri).
—   **gathering** (Radak, *Sherashim*; Ibn Janach; Septuagint). Some say that the violation consisted of
   carrying on the Sabbath. According to others it was cutting the sticks, or binding them (*Shabbath*
   96b; Sifri).
15:34 not specified ... The death penalty was specified (Exodus 31:14, 35:2). However, the form of the
   penalty had not been specified (*Sanhedrin* 78b; Sifri; Rashi).

³⁶ The entire community took him outside the camp, and they pelted   15
him to death with stones. It was done as God had commanded Moses.

[82. Tassels]

³⁷ God spoke to Moses,* telling him to ³⁸ speak to the Israelites and
have them make tassels* on the corners of their garments for all generations. They shall include a twist* of sky-blue wool* in the corner tassels.

³⁸ These shall be your tassels, and when you see them, you shall remember all of God's commandments so as to keep them. You will then not
stray after your heart and eyes, which [in the past] have led you to immorality. ⁴⁰ You will thus remember and keep all My commandments, and be
holy to your God.

⁴¹ I am God your Lord, who brought you out of Egypt to be your God. I
am God your Lord.

Korach   קרח

[83. Korach's Rebellion]

¹ Korach son of Yitz'har (a grandson of Kehoth and great-grandson of   16
Levi*) began a rebellion* along with Dathan and Aviram (sons of Eliav*)

15:37 God spoke to Moses . . . This is the third paragraph of the Sh'ma.

15:38 tassels. *Tzitzith* in Hebrew. Also see Deuteronomy 22:12. The tzitzith-tassels consist of four strings doubled over so that eight strings appear to hang from each corner (*Menachoth* 39b). There is also an area where a single string is wound around the other seven, consisting of one-third of the tassel (*Menachoth* 39a). This must be held in place by a knot (*Yevamoth* 4a,b). The custom is that there be five knots and four areas of winding on each tzitzith-tassel (*Targum Yonathan*). The prevailing custom is that these wound areas have respectively 7, 8, 11 and 13 windings.

— **twist.** Some say that this denotes a single thread made of two strands twisted together (Sifri; *Targum Yonathan*). According to this, only one of the seven strings would be dyed blue (*Yad, Tzitzith* 1:6). This was done by dying half of one of the strings before it was inserted (*Teshuvoth Ramban, P'er HaDor* 21).

A second opinion is that the word *pethil* here denotes a doubled-over string (*Tosafoth, Menachoth* 38a, s.v. *HaTekheleth*, end, 39b, s.v. *U'Posle-hah*). This may agree with the opinion that an entire thread was dyed blue, so that when it was doubled over, two out of the eight strings were blue (Raavad on *Yad, Tzitzith* 1:6).

There is a third opinion that the word *pethil* denotes the thread that is wound around the others (Rashi, *Menachoth* 39b, s.v. *U'Posle'hah*; Rashi on Deuteronomy 32:5). Thus, it was the blue thread that was wound around the others. According to this opinion, the number of blue threads is not defined, and may be equal to the number of white threads. There were thus four blue and four white strings in the tassel (Rashi, Tosafoth, *Menachoth* 38a, s.v. *HaTekheleth*).

If the special blue wool is not available, the fringes can be made entirely white (*Menachoth* 38a).

— **sky blue wool.** See note on Exodus 25:4.

16:1 Korach . . . See Exodus 6:18,21. According to tradition, he was one of Pharaoh's officials (*BeMidbar Rabbah* 18:1). He was extremely wealthy (*Pesachim* 119a; *Sanhedrin* 110a; *Targum Yonathan* on 16:19; Josephus, *Antiquities* 4:2:2).

— **began a rebellion** (Targum; Rashi). Literally, "took." According to some, he "took" Dathan, etc, (Chizzkuni), the 250 men (Ramban; Sforno), or a mob (Rashbam). Others translate it as, "took the

16 and On son of Peleth,* descendants of Reuben. ² They had a confrontation with Moses along with 250 Israelites who were men of rank in the community, representatives* at the assembly,* and famous.*

³ They demonstrated against Moses and Aaron, and declared to them, "You have gone too far!* All the people in the community are holy, and God is with them. Why are you setting yourselves above God's congregation?"

⁴ When Moses heard this, he threw himself on his face. ⁵ Then he spoke to Korach and his whole party. "[Tomorrow] morning,"* he said, "God [will show that He]* knows who is His and who is holy, and He will bring them close to Him.* He shall choose those who shall [be allowed to] present [offerings]* to Him.

⁶ "This is what you must do: Let Korach and his entire party take fire pans.* ⁷ Tomorrow, place fire* on them, and offer incense* on them before God. The man whom God chooses shall then be the holy one. You sons of Levi have [also] gone too far!"

⁸ Moses tried to reason with Korach. "Listen [to what I have to say], you

---

initiative" (Ramban); "committed himself" (Ibn Janach); "plotted" (Radak, *Sherashim*), "came forward" (Saadia, see above 8:6), or "spoke up" (Septuagint).

Many authorities state that the Torah is in chronological order here, and that the rebellion took place after the episode of the spies (Ramban; *Sefer HaYashar*; Josephus, *Antiquities* 4:2:2). The motivation for the rebellion may have been the decree that they would die in the desert (Abarbanel; see 16:14).

Others, however, maintain that the rebellion occurred before the episode of the spies. Some say that it took place when the Levites were substituted for the first-born (Ibn Ezra). The Midrash states that the motivation was the appointment of Eltzaphan son of Uzziel over the Kehothites (above 3:30; *BeMidbar Rabbah* 18:1; Bachya). Others say that it took place in Chatzeroth (above, 11:35, 12:16; Rashi on Deuteronomy 1:1). According to these opinions, nothing is recorded in the Torah of what happened between the episode of the spies and Miriam's death (20:1).

—   **Dathan and Aviram** . . . See Numbers 26:9. See notes on 2:13. Aviram was a son of Palu and a grandson of Reuben (26:5,8).

—   **On son of Peleth.** He did not stay with Korach and was therefore not killed (*Sanhedrin* 109b; Abarbanel; *Midrash HaGadol* on 16:32; *Lekach Tov* on 16:12).

16:2   **representatives.** See 1:16 (*Tanchuma*; Bachya).

—   **assembly** (Targum). Or, "Communion [Tent]" (Ibn Ezra); or, "chosen counselors" (Septuagint).

—   **famous.** Literally, "men of name." See Genesis 6:4.

16:3   **You have gone too far.** Literally, "Much to you." May mean, "You have taken too much upon yourself." See below, 16:7.

16:5   **Tomorrow morning** (Targum; Rashi). Or, "God has examined and knows . . ." (Septuagint).

—   **will show** . . . (cf. Targum; *Hakethav VeHaKabbalah*).

—   **He will bring them close** . . . (Targum; *Tanchuma*; Rashi). Or, "and he can present offerings to Him (*Targum Yonathan*; Sforno; Septuagint).

—   **present offerings** (Targum).

16:6   **fire pans.** See Exodus 27:3, Leviticus 10:1, 16:12.

16:7   **fire.** From the altar (Ralbag).

—   **incense.** The regular incense described in Exodus 30:34-36 (*BeMidbar Rabbah* 18:7; *Tanchuma* 5; Ralbag). According to others, however, it was a simple incense spice, such as frankincense (Targum according to Ramban).

sons of Levi. ⁹ Isn't it enough that the God of Israel has separated you from **16**
the community of Israel? He has brought you close to Him, allowing you to
serve in God's Tabernacle and to minister as the community's leaders.
¹⁰ Although He gave this privilege to you and all your fellow Levites, you
are now also demanding the priesthood! ¹¹ It is actually* against God that
you and your party are demonstrating! After all, who is Aaron that you
should have grievances against him?"

¹² Moses then sent word to summon Dathan and Aviram, the sons of
Eliav.

"We won't come!"* was their response. ¹³ "Isn't it enough that you
brought us out of [Egypt], a land flowing with milk and honey*—just to kill
us in the desert! What right do you have to set yourself above us? ¹⁴ You
didn't bring us to a land flowing with milk and honey, or give us an inheritance of fields and vineyards. Do you think that you can pull something
over our eyes?* We will definitely not come!"

¹⁵ Moses became very angry. He prayed to God, "Do not accept their
offering. I did not take a single* donkey* from them! I did not do any of
them any harm!"

¹⁶ Moses then said to Korach, "You and all your party will have to
present yourselves before God. You and [your party] will be there tomorrow along with Aaron. ¹⁷ Each man shall take his fire pan and place incense
on it, and each one shall then present it before God. [There shall thus be]
250 fire pans [besides] the pans that you and Aaron will have."

¹⁸ Each one took his fire pan, placed fire on it, and then offered incense.
They stood at the Communion Tent entrance along with Moses and Aaron.
¹⁹ Then, when Korach had rallied his whole party to the Communion Tent
entrance, God's glory suddenly became visible to the entire community.

[84. Moses Intercedes for Israel]

²⁰ God spoke to Moses and Aaron, saying, ²¹ "Separate yourselves from

16:11 **actually.** *Lakhen* in Hebrew. See Genesis 4:13.
16:12 **come.** Literally "go up." Some say that this teaches that the Tabernacle was built on high ground (Bachya).
16:13 **a land flowing . . .** This was because Dathan and Aviram were wealthy leaders in Egypt (*Lekach Tov*).
16:14 **pull something over our eyes.** (Ibn Ezra; Ramban). Literally, "put out the eyes of those men." Or, "blind a man [such as Korach]" (Chizzkuni). Or, "Are you trying to satisfy us with illusions?" (Ibn Ezra), or, "Are you threatening to put out our eyes?" (Rashi; Ibn Ezra). Cf. Judges 15:21, 2 Kings 25:4-7, Jeremiah 52:7-11.
16:15 **single** (Rashbam). Or, "I did not take a donkey from any one of them" (Targum; Rashi).
— **donkey.** The Septuagint substitutes "desirable thing" for donkey, changing the reading from *chamor* to *chamud*. The Talmud notes that this change was deliberate (*Megillah* 9a).

16 this community, and I will destroy them in an instant."

²² [Moses and Aaron] fell on their faces. They prayed, "Omnipotent God of all living souls. If one man sins, shall You direct divine wrath at the entire community?"

[85. Korach's Punishment]

²³ God spoke to Moses, telling him to ²⁴ announce to the entire community, "Withdraw from the pavillion* of Korach, Dathan and Aviram."

²⁵ Moses took the .initiative, and followed by the elders of Israel,* went over to Dathan and Aviram. ²⁶ He announced to the community, "Get away from the tents of these evil men. Do not touch anything that is theirs, lest you be swept away because of all their sins."

²⁷ [The people] withdrew from around the pavillion of Korach, Dathan and Aviram. Dathan and Aviram went out and stood defiantly at the entrance of their tents, along with their wives, sons and infants.

²⁸ Moses announced, "This shall demonstrate to you that God sent me to do all these deeds and I did not make up anything myself. ²⁹ If these men die like all other men, and share the common fate of man, then God did not send me. ³⁰ But if God creates something entirely new,* making the earth open its mouth and swallow them and all that is theirs, so that they descend to the depths alive, then it is these men who are provoking God."

³¹ Moses had hardly finished speaking when the ground under [Dathan and Aviram]* split. ³² The earth opened its mouth, and swallowed them and their houses, along with all the men who were with Korach* and their property. ³³ They fell into the depths along with all that was theirs. The earth then covered them over, and they were lost to the community.

³⁴ [Hearing] their cries, all the Israelites around them screamed that the earth would also swallow them up, and they began to run away. ³⁵ Fire* then came down from God, and it consumed the 250 men who were presenting the incense.

16:23 **pavillion** (cf. Ibn Ezra). The Hebrew word is *mishkan,* and it is possible that Korach had already erected a competing sanctuary. Or, "Place of assembly" (Septuagint).

16:25 **elders of Israel.** The 70 elders (Bachya).

16:30 **creates something entirely new** (Rashi; Rashbam; Chizzkuni). Or, "causes destruction" (Ibn Ezra), or, "produces a miracle" (Septuagint).

16:31 **Dathan and Aviram.** From context. See next note.

16:32 **men who were with Korach.** According to some, Korach himself was not swallowed up (*Sanhedrin* 110a) but was killed in the plague (Rashi *ad loc.*) or by the divine fire (Josephus, *Antiquities* 4:3:4). The Torah, however, appears to indicate that Korach actually was swallowed up, but that his children survived (below, 26:10,11). However, elsewhere it seems that only Dathan and Aviram were swallowed up (Deuteronomy 11:6).

16:35 **Fire.** Josephus notes that this fire was supernaturally bright and fierce (*Antiquities* 4:3:4).

[86. The Incense Pans]

17 [1] God spoke to Moses, saying, [2] "Tell Eleazar (son of Aaron the priest) that the fire pans have been sanctified, and he must gather them up from the burned area. He shall then scatter the burning coals far and wide. [3] The fire pans belonging to the men who committed a mortal sin have been presented before God and thus sanctified, so he shall make them into beaten plates to cover* the altar. Let this be a sign for the Israelites."

[4] Eleazar took the copper fire pans that the victims of the fire had presented, and he beat them flat as a covering for the altar. [5] It was to be a reminder for the Israelites, so that no one other than a descendant of Aaron shall bring unauthorized fire* and burn incense before God. They shall then not be like Korach and his party. [Eleazar thus did]* as God had told him through Moses.

[87. Fear and Complaint]

[6] The next day the entire Israelite community began to complain to Moses. "You have killed God's people!" they exclaimed.

[7] The people were demonstrating against Moses and Aaron, when they turned toward the Communion Tent. It was suddenly covered with the cloud, and God's glory appeared. [8] Moses and Aaron went to the front of the Communion Tent.

[88. Aaron Saves the People]

[9] God spoke to Moses, saying, [10] "Stand clear of this community and I will destroy them in an instant."

[Moses and Aaron] threw themselves on their faces. [11] Moses then said to Aaron, "Take the fire pan and place on it some fire from the altar. Offer incense and take it quickly to the community to make atonement for them. Divine wrath is coming forth from God. The plague has already begun!"

[12] Aaron took [the pan] as Moses had told him, and he ran to the middle of the assembled masses, where the plague had already begun to kill people. He offered the incense to atone for the people. [13] He stood between the dead and the living, and the plague was checked.

[14] The number of people who died in that plague was 14,700. These were in addition to the ones who died because of Korach's rebellion.

17:3 **to cover.** The literal meaning (cf. *Menachoth* 99a). Josephus, however, states that they were made into ornamental plates that were placed *near* the altar (*Antiquities* 4:3:4).
17:5 **unauthorized . . .** See Exodus 30:9, Leviticus 10:1.
— **Eleazar thus did.** (Rashbam).

17   ¹⁵ When the plague had been stopped, Aaron returned to Moses at the
Communion Tent entrance.

[89. The Test of Staffs]   .

¹⁶ God spoke to Moses,* telling him to ¹⁷ speak to the Israelites and take
a staff from each paternal tribe. "Twelve staffs shall thus be taken from all
the leaders, [one] for [each] of their paternal tribes. Let each man write his
name* on his staff. ¹⁸ Since there shall be only one staff for the head of each
paternal tribe, write Aaron's name on Levi's staff. ¹⁹ Place [the staffs] in the
Communion Tent, before the [Ark of] Testimony where I commune with
you. ²⁰ The staff of the man who is My choice will then blossom. I will thus
rid Myself of the complaints that the Israelites are directing at you."

²¹ Moses spoke to the Israelites, and each of the leaders gave him a staff
for his paternal tribe. There were twelve staffs, with Aaron's staff among
them. ²² [Moses] placed the staffs before God in the Testimony Tent. ²³ The
next day, when Moses came to the Testimony Tent, Aaron's staff, repre-
senting the house of Levi, had blossomed. It had given forth leaves,* and
was [now]* producing blossoms* and almonds were ripening on it.

²⁴ Moses brought all the staffs out from before God, and let all the
Israelites see them. Each man took his own staff.

[90. Aaron's Staff]

²⁵ God said to Moses, "Put Aaron's staff back there before the [Ark* of]
Testimony as a keepsake. Let it be a sign for anyone who wants to rebel.
This should put an end to their complaints to Me, and then they will not
die."

²⁶ Moses did exactly as God had instructed him.

[91. Fear of the Sanctuary]

²⁷ The Israelites said to Moses, "We're going to die! We will be
destroyed! We are all lost! ²⁸ Whoever approaches God's Tabernacle dies!
Are we then doomed to die?"

17:16 **God spoke to Moses.** Some say that this occurred before Korach's rebellion (Yehudah HaChasid).
The majority opinion, however, is that it was afterward (cf. Josephus, *Antiquities* 4:4:2).

17:17 **Let each man write his name.** Or, "let each [tribe] write its name" (Josephus, *Antiquities* 4:4:2).

17:23 **leaves** (Saadia, Radak, *Sherashim*; cf. Rambam on *Shevi'ith* 7:5, *Kelayim* 6:9). Or, "buds and
branches" (Josephus, *Antiquities* 4:4:2), or, "buds" (Septuagint), or "blossoms" (Rashi).

—   **now** (Rashbam; cf. *HaKethav VeHaKabbalah*).

—   **blossoms** (Radak, *Sherashim*; Septuagint). Or, "unripe fruit" (Rashi), or, "ripe fruit" (Josephus).

17:25 **Ark.** (*Midrash HaGadol*). According to some, however, it was actually placed inside the ark (Ralbag).

[92. Duties of Priests and Levites]

18

¹ God said to Aaron: You, along with your sons and your paternal tribe shall expiate* any sin associated with the Sanctuary. You and your descendants will [also] expiate any sin associated with your priesthood.

² Also bring close to you your brothers, the members of your father's tribe, Levi. Let them be your associates and minister to you and your descendants before the Testimony Tent. ³ [The Levites] shall thus be entrusted with their responsibilities toward you and the Tent, but they shall not approach the sacred furniture or the altar, so that you and they not die.

⁴ [The Levites] shall be your associates and they shall be entrusted with responsibility for the Communion Tent [and] all the Tent's service. Let no unauthorized person join them. ⁵ Let them be entrusted with responsibility for the sanctuary and the altar, so that there not be any more divine wrath directed at the Israelites.

⁶ I have thus taken your brethren the Levites from among the [other] Israelites as a gift to you. They are given over to God to perform the Communion Tent service.

⁷ You and your sons shall be entrusted with your priesthood, so that your service shall include everything that pertains to the altar and to anything inside the cloth partition.* This is the gift of service that I have given you as your priesthood. Any unauthorized person who participates shall die.

[93. The Priestly Share]

⁸ God announced to Aaron: I have given you responsibility for My elevated gifts. I am thus giving you all the sacred gifts of the Israelites as part of your anointment.* These shall be an eternal portion for your descendants.

⁹ Among the fire [offerings] that are holy of holies,* the following shall be yours: All [the Israelites'] sacrifices,* all their grain offerings,* all their sin offerings,* all their guilt offerings,* [and] everything that they return to Me. These shall be holy of holies to you and your descendants. ¹⁰ Every

---

18:1   **expiate** (Targum). Or, "bear the sin" (*Targum Yonathan*; Rashi).
18:7   **cloth partition.** See Leviticus 21:23.
18:8   **anointment.** See Leviticus 7:35.
18:9   **holy of holies.** See Leviticus 2:3, 2:10, 6:10, 6:18, 6:22, 7:1, 7:6, 14:13, 24:9.
—   **sacrifices.** Such as communal peace offerings (Rashi).
—   **grain offerings.** See Leviticus 2:3,10, 6:10.
—   **sin offerings.** Leviticus 6:18.
—   **guilt offerings.** Leviticus 7:1.

18   male [priest] may eat [these offerings], but you must eat them in a most
holy area,* since they must remain holy to you.

¹¹ This is what shall be bestowed as an elevated gift to you:

All the Israelites' wave offerings* are given to you, along with your sons
and daughters, as an everlasting portion. Everyone in your household who
is ritually clean may eat them.

¹² The dedicated portion* of oil, wine and grain that must initially be
presented to God* is now given to you.

¹³ The first fruit of all that [grows] in your land, which is presented to
God, shall be yours. Everyone in your household who is ritually clean may
eat it.

¹⁴ Everything that the Israelites declare taboo* shall be yours.

¹⁵ The first fruits of the womb, that must be presented to God, among
man and beast, shall be yours. However, you must redeem first-born
humans, as well as the first-born of unclean animals.* ¹⁶ The redemption
[of a first-born human male] from one month old, shall be made with [the
usual] endowment* of 5 shekels by the sanctuary standard, where [the
shekel] is 20 gerahs.*

¹⁷ You must not, however, redeem the first-born of an ox, sheep or goat,
since [such first-born] are sacred. You must therefore dash their blood on
the altar, and burn their choice parts* as an appeasing fragrance to God.
¹⁸ Their flesh shall then belong to you like the chest [presented as] a wave
offering and the right thigh [of peace offerings].*

¹⁹ I have thus* given you, together with your sons and daughters, as an
eternal portion, the elevated gifts* from the sacred offerings that the Israelites present to God. For you and your descendants, this is a covenant that
shall be preserved* forever before God.

²⁰ God [then] said to Aaron, "You will not have any inheritance in the

---

18:10 **most holy area.** Within the enclosure; see Leviticus 6:19.
18:11 **wave offerings.** See Leviticus 7:30, 14:12, 14:24, 23:17, 23:20, Numbers 6:20 (Rashi).
18:12 **dedicated portion.** *Chelev* in Hebrew, which usually denotes "fat," or the portion dedicated to the
altar (see Leviticus 3:9). Here it refers to the portion dedicated to the priest.
— **initially be presented . . .** This is the *terumah* offering that must be given to the priest (Rashi).
18:14 **taboo.** See Leviticus 27:21.
18:15 **unclean animals.** Actually, only the donkey, as in Exodus 13:13 (*Bekhoroth* 8b).
18:16 **endowment.** See Leviticus 27:6.
— **20 gerahs.** See Exodus 30:13, Leviticus 27:25.
18:17 **choice parts.** See Leviticus 3:9.
18:18 **chest . . . and the right thigh . . .** See Exodus 29:27, Leviticus 7:31, 10:15.
18:19 **thus** (Rashi).
— **elevated gifts.** *Terumah* in Hebrew.
— **covenant that shall be preserved** (Saadia; cf. Rashi). Literally, "covenant of salt." See Leviticus 2:13;
2 Chronicles 13:5.

land [of the Israelites], and you will not have a portion among them. I
Myself shall be your portion and inheritance among the Israelites."

[94. The Levitical Share]

²¹ To the descendants of Levi, I am now giving all the tithes in Israel as
an inheritance. This is in exchange for their work, the service that they perform in the Communion Tent.

²² The [other] Israelites shall therefore no longer come forth to the Communion Tent, since they can then become guilty of sin and die. ²³ Instead,
the necessary service in the Communion Tent will be performed by the
Levites, and they will expiate the sins [of the Israelites].*

It shall be an eternal law for future generations that [the Levites] not
have any [land] inheritance. ²⁴ Instead, the inheritance that I am giving the
Levites shall consist of the tithes of the Israelites, which they separate as an
elevated gift. I have therefore told [the Levites] that they shall not have any
[land] inheritance among the Israelites.

[95. The Levites' Priestly Gifts]

²⁵ God spoke to Moses, telling him to ²⁶ speak to the Levites and say to
them:

When you take from the Israelites the tithe that I have given you as
your inheritance from them, you must separate from it an elevated gift to
God, a tithe of the tithe.* ²⁷ This [tithe given to you by the Israelites]* is
your own elevated gift, and it is exactly like grain from the threshing floor
or wine* from the vat. ²⁸ You must therefore separate an elevated gift from
all the tithes that you take from the Israelites, and you must give it as God's
elevated gift to Aaron the priest. ²⁹ Thus, from all that is given to you, you
must separate God's elevated gift, [taking] a sanctified portion as its dedicated [tithe* for the priest].

³⁰ Say to [the Levites]: After you have separated out the dedicated [tithe
for the priest, the rest] shall be for [all] the Levites exactly like [ordinary]*
produce from the threshing floor and wine vat. You and your household

---

18:23 **of the Israelites** (Rashi).
18:26 **a tithe of the tithe.** The Levites had to take a tenth of their tithe which in turn was one tenth of the
   Israelite's produce. Hence this *"terumath maaser"* was 1% of the produce.
18:27 **This tithe . . .** Or, "That which you give as an elevated gift [to the priest] shall be considered like [the
   elevated gift] taken from . . . (Rashi).
—   **wine.** *Meleah* in Hebrew, see Exodus 22:8. Or, "best wine" (Saadia; cf. *Targum Yonathan*), or,
   "offerings" (Septuagint).
18:29 **dedicated tithe** (cf. Ibn Ezra). See 18:12.
18:30 **ordinary.** (cf. Ralbag).

18 can eat it anywhere [you desire], since it is your wage for your service in the
    Communion Tent. ³² Therefore, after you have separated out the dedicated
    [tithe], you will not bear any sin because of it. You will thus not profane the
    sacred offerings of the Israelites, and you will not die.

Chukath   חֻקַּת

[96. The Red Cow]

19   ¹ God spoke* to Moses and Aaron, telling them that ² the following is
      declared to be the Torah's decree as commanded by God:
      Speak to the Israelites and have them bring you a completely red* cow,*
      which has no blemish,* and which has never had a yoke on it. ³ Give it to
      Eleazar the priest,* and he shall have it brought outside the camp. It shall
      then be slaughtered* in his presence.*
      ⁴ Eleazar the priest shall take the blood with his finger* and sprinkle it*
      toward the Communion Tent seven times. ⁵ The cow shall then be burned*
      in [Eleazar's] presence. Its skin, flesh, blood and entrails must be burned.
      ⁶ The priest shall take a piece of cedar wood,* some hyssop,* and some crim-
      son [wool],* and throw it into the burning cow.*

19:1   **God spoke . . .** According to tradition, this was said on 1 Nissan of the second year of the Exodus,
       the day when the Tabernacle was erected (*Gittin* 60a,b). It is mentioned now because it was used to
       purify the people after Miriam's death (below, 20:1; Josephus, *Antiquities* 4:4:6).
19:2   **completely red.** If it has two or more hairs that are not red, it is invalid (*Parah* 2:5).
—   **cow.** At least three years old (*Parah* 1:1; *Yad, Parah Adumah* 1:1).
—   **blemish.** See Leviticus 22:18-22.
19:3   **Eleazar the priest.** This indicates that it could be made by a common priest (*Yoma* 42b; *Yad, Parah
       Adumah* 1:11; Ramban). According to some, however, it had to be prepared by the *segan,* the assis-
       tant to the High Priest (Rashi; cf. *Sifri*).
—   **then be slaughtered.** By anyone, even a non-priest (*Yoma* 43b; Rashi; *Yad, Pesuley Mukdashin* 1:2).
       Others, however, maintain that it must be slaughtered by a priest (*Targum Yonathan; Midrash
       HaGadol; Adereth Eliahu*).
—   **in his presence.** This indicates that the supervising priest must be present and attentive (*Yoma* 42a;
       Midrash HaGadol).
19:4   **with his finger.** Directly from the cow's neck, and therefore, the blood could not be collected in a
       vessel (*Sifri; Yad, Parah Adumah* 4:4), but some may dispute this (Raavad on *Yad,* ibid. 3:2). The
       priest would therefore collect the blood in his left hand and sprinkle it with his right forefinger (*Yad,*
       ibid. 3:2; *Sifri*).
—   **sprinkle it.** From where he is outside the camp (*Yad, Parah Adumah* 3:2).
19:5   **burned.** By a priest (*Yad, Parah Adumah* 1:11).
19:6   **cedar wood.** See Leviticus 14:4. This had to be taken from the trunk of the tree (*Sifri Zuta; Adereth Eliahu*).
       Some say that it had to be at least one handbreadth long (*Midrash HaGadol*).
—   **hyssop.** See Exodus 12:22. It also had to be at least one handbreadth long (*Niddah* 26a; *Yad, Parah
       Adumah* 3:2). Some sources appear to indicate that three branches were required (*Sifri; Toledoth
       Adam ad loc.*; Malbim).
—   **crimson wool.** See Exodus 25:4, Leviticus 14:4. The piece of wool had to weigh at least 5 shekels (4
       oz.). It was used to tie the hyssop and cedar together (*Yoma* 42a; *Yad, Parah Adumah* 3:4).
—   **burning cow.** When the heat of the fire caused the belly of the cow to burst, the above articles would
       be thrown into the body cavity (*Targum Yonathan; Parah* 3:10; *Sifri; Yad, Parah Adumah* 3:4).

⁷ The priest must then immerse his vestments and his body in a mik- **19**
vah,* and remain unclean until evening,* after which he may come into the
camp.* ⁸ The one who burns [the cow] must also immerse his clothing and
body in a mikvah, and then remain unclean until evening.

⁹ A ritually clean person* shall gather up the cow's ashes,* and place
them outside the camp in a clean place. They shall be a keepsake for the
Israelite community to be used for the sprinkling* water, as a means of
purification.* ¹⁰ The one who gathers up the cow's ashes must immerse [his
body and] his clothing, and remain unclean until evening.

[All] this shall be an eternal law for the Israelites and for any proselyte
who joins them:

¹¹ If one has contact with any dead human being,* he shall become
ritually unclean for seven days. ¹² [In order to become] clean, he must have
himself sprinkled* [with the purification water]* on the third day and the
seventh day.* If he does not have himself sprinkled on the third day and the
seventh day, he cannot become clean.

¹³ Any person who touches the corpse of a human being who has died,
and does not have himself sprinkled, shall be cut off [spiritually] from
Israel if he defiles God's Tabernacle [by entering it].* Since the purification
water was not sprinkled on him, he remains unclean and is pervaded by his
defilement.

¹⁴ When a man* dies in a tent, this is the law: Everything that comes

19:7 **immerse** ... See Exodus 19:10.
— **until evening.** See Leviticus 11:24, 14:26, 15:5, 17:15, 19:23, 22:6.
— **after which** ... (Rashi).
19:9 **ritually clean person.** Anyone, even a woman (Yoma 43a; Yad, Parah Adumah 43a). Other sources, however, apparently require a priest (Targum Yonathan; cf. HaKethav VeHaKabbalah).
— **ashes.** They were ground up into fine dust (19:17; Parah 3:11; Midrash HaGadol; Yad, Parah Adumah 3:3).
— **sprinkling** (Targum; Rashi; Saadia; Septuagint). Niddah in Hebrew. Or, "purification water," that is, water that separates man from defilement (Ibn Janach); or, "restricted water" (Ibn Ezra; Radak, Sherashim).
— **purification** (Rashi; Septuagint). See 19:17. Or, "it is a sin offering" (Targum), or, "it is like a sin offering" (Avodah Zarah 23b; Rashi).
19:11 **human being.** Even a gentile (Yad, Tumath Meth 1:12).
19:12 **have himself sprinkled** (Targum). Yith-chata in Hebrew. Or, "purify himself" (Ibn Janach; Septuagint), or, "have himself expiated (Radak, Sherashim). From here is derived the custom of washing the hands after a funeral (Bachya; Paaneach Raza on 20:2).
— **with the purification water.** See 19:9,18.
— **third day and the seventh day.** From the time that he became unclean (Yad, Parah Adumah 11:2). One can begin counting three days at any time and then begin the process. However, if one then delays the second sprinkling until after the seventh, some say that he must begin the count again (Raavad ibid.), while others maintain that he can be sprinkled after the seventh day as well (Yad, ibid.).
19:13 **if he** ... (Rashi).
19:14 **man.** Only an Israelite. Although even a gentile defiles on contact, only an Israelite can defile the entire tent or house (Yad, Tumath Meth 1:13; see above, 19:11).

19 into the tent or was [originally] in the tent shall be unclean for seven days. ¹⁵ Every open vessel* that does not have an airtight* seal* shall be unclean.

¹⁶ [Similarly], anyone who touches a victim of the sword, [any other] corpse, a human bone, or a grave, [even] in the open field, shall be unclean for seven days.

¹⁷ Some of the dust* from the burnt purification offering* shall be taken for such an unclean person. It shall be placed* into a vessel* that has been* [filled with water directly*] from a running spring.*

¹⁸ A ritually clean person shall then take some hyssop* and dip it into the water. He shall sprinkle [the water] on the tent, on all the vessels and persons who were in it, and on anyone who touched a bone, a murder victim or any other corpse, or a grave. ¹⁹ The ritually clean person shall sprinkle [the water] on the unclean person on the third day and on the seventh day. The purification process is completed on the seventh day, when [the person undergoing purification] must immerse his clothing and body in a mikvah, and then become ritually clean in the evening.

²⁰ If a person is unclean and does not purify himself, and then defiles God's sanctuary [by entering it], that person shall be cut off [spiritually]

19:15 vessel. Only a vessel that cannot become unclean if touched on the outside, and therefore, a clay vessel (*Sifri; Yad, Tumath Meth* 5:6; see Leviticus 11:33). This rule also applies in the case of vessels that cannot be ritually defiled at all, such as those made of stone or aquatic animals. In such cases, if they are sealed, articles inside them do not become unclean (*Kelim* 10:1; *Yad, Tumath Meth* 21:1).

— **airtight.** (See *Yad, Tumath Meth* 22:9). This seems to be required by the law (cf. *Ohaloth* 10:2,4; *Ha-Kethav VeHaKabbalah*). *Tzamid* in Hebrew, denoting a bracelet and an airtight seal. In general, *tzamad* denotes tight attachment (Numbers 25:3, 2 Samuel 20:8, Psalms 50:19), and hence, *tzamid* denotes something that is tightly attached (Saadia, Radak, *Sherashim*; Ibn Janach; Bertenoro on *Kelim* 10:2; Eliahu Rabbah, *Kelim* 9:7; *Adereth Eliahu*). Some say that it denotes something that is sealed tightly to something else, such as when two things are melted together (Rashi, *Sanhedrin* 64a, s.v. HaNitzmadim; Rash, *Kelim* 10:2; *Yad, Tumath Meth* 22:8; cf. *Bava Kama* 105a). According to others, it denotes "tight" (Rashi, *Chullin* 25a, s.v. Hah Yash). Some sources, however, indicate that a *tzamid* is a cap or stopper (*Sifri*; Septuagint).

— **seal** (Rashi; Ibn Janach; Rambam on *Kelim* 10:2). *Pethil* in Hebrew, which denotes a thread or a cap (cf. Genesis 38:18, Exodus 28:37). Or, "tight" (Rosh, *Kelim* 10:2); "'stopper" (Rashi, *Chullin* 25a, s.v. Pethil); "all around it" (*Sifri*; Saadia); "bound to it" (Septuagint); or "cloth" (Radak, *Sherashim*; but see *Kelim* 10:4).

Tzamid Pethil can thus denote "a tight cover," "a tight stopper," "a sealed-on cover," "a seal all around it," "a covering bound on it," "a cloth attached to it," or, as we have it, "an airtight seal."

If a clay vessel has a *tzamid pethil* on it, it does not become defiled if it is in the same tent or house as a corpse. Moreover, anything inside it also does not become defiled.

19:17 dust. This teaches that the ashes are ground into dust. See note on 19:9.

— **purification offering.** *Chatath* in Hebrew; see note on 19:15.

— **shall be placed.** By anyone (*Yad, Parah Adumah* 6:2).

— **vessel.** Any vessel (*Sifri; Yad, Parah Adumah* 6:3).

— **that has been.** The water must be put in first (*Sotah* 16b; *Yad, Parah Adumah* 9:1).

— **directly** (*Yad, Parah Adumah* 6:1, 6:9).

— **running spring.** Literally, "living water." See Leviticus 14:4, 15:13. There is a question as to whether river water is good for this (*Yad, Parah Adumah* 6:10, Raavad *ad loc.*).

19:18 hyssop. 3 branches (*Sifri; Yad, Parah Adumah* 11:1). See Exodus 12:22, Leviticus 14:4).

from the community. As long as the purification water has not been sprin-   **19**
kled on him, he shall remain unclean.

²¹ This shall be to you a law for all times.

One who sprinkles the purification water [other than when it is done
for the purification ritual]* must immerse [both his body and] his clothing.
However, if he [merely] touches the purification water, [he must only
immerse his body]* and then be unclean until evening.

²² Anything that a person* unclean [by contact with the dead]* touches
shall become unclean. [Moreover] any person touching [him] shall be
unclean until evening.

[97. Miriam's Death; Lack of Water]

¹ In the first month,* the entire Israelite community came to the Tzin   **20**
Desert,* and the people stopped in Kadesh.* It was there that Miriam died*
and was buried.

² The people did not have any water, so they began demonstrating
against Moses and Aaron. ³ The people disputed with Moses. "We wish
that we had died together with our brothers before God!" they declared.
"Why did you bring God's congregation to this desert? So that we and our
livestock should die? ⁵ Why did you take us out of Egypt and bring us to
this terrible place? It is an area where there are no plants, figs, grapes or
pomegranates. [Now] there is not even any water to drink!"

⁶ Moses and Aaron moved away* from the demonstration to the Communion Tent entrance, and fell on their faces.* God's glory was revealed to
them.

19:21 **other than** ... (*Yoma* 14a; Rashi; *Yad, Parah Adumah* 15:1). This is true no matter how one lifts that
amount of water.
—   **must only immerse** ... (*Ibid.*).
19:22 **person.** An Israelite.
—   **by contact with the dead** (Rashi).
20:1   **first month.** Nissan of the 40th year (Rashbam; Josephus, *Antiquities* 4:4:7), after the entire generation of the Exodus had died (Rashi; Bachya; Abarbanel; but see Deuteronomy 2:16). There is no
information about what happened during the 38 intervening years, other than the travels mentioned
in 33:19-36 (Ibn Ezra).
—   **Tzin Desert.** To the south-west of the Dead Sea. Some translate it as "Desert of Palms" (*Adereth Eliahu*).
—   **Kadesh.** See 33:36. Also see Genesis 14:7; 16:14, 20:1. This is not to be confused with Kadesh Bar-
nea, from which the spies were sent (Ramban; Bachya).
—   **Miriam died.** Some day that she died on 1 Nissan (*Seder Olam* 9; *Midrash HaGadol*; Josephus,
Antiquities 4:4:6), while others say that she died on 10 Nissan (*Megillath Taanith* 13; *Targum
Yonathan*; *Orach Chaim* 580:2). Some say that the Israelites arrived in Kadesh on 1 Nissan, and
Miriam died on 10 Nissan (*Shalsheleth HaKabbalah*; *Seder HaDoroth*). It was about the same time
that the message was sent to the king of Edom (*Seder Olam* 9). Josephus, however, has the encounter
with Edom before Miriam's death (*Antiquities* 4:4:5).
20:6   **moved away** (Saadia; Ibn Ezra; Septuagint). Literally, "came."
—   **fell on their faces.** To pray (Ibn Ezra; Ralbag; Bachya), or to try to appease the demonstrators (Ralbag). Some say that they fell on their faces to seek prophecy (Ibn Ezra; see Genesis 17:3, Ezekiel

[98. Water from the Rock]

20   ⁷ God spoke to Moses, saying, ⁸ "Take the staff,* and you and Aaron assemble the community. Speak to* the cliff* in their presence,* and it will give forth its water. You will thus bring forth water from the cliff, and allow the community and their livestock to drink."

⁹ Moses took the staff from before God* as he had been instructed. ¹⁰ Moses and Aaron then assembled the congregation before the cliff. "Listen now, you rebels!" shouted Moses. "Shall we produce water for you from this cliff?"

¹¹ With that, Moses raised his hand, and struck the cliff twice* with his staff. A huge amount of water gushed out, and the community and their animals were able to drink.

[99. Punishment of Moses and Aaron]

¹² God said to Moses and Aaron, "You did not have enough faith* in Me to sanctify Me* in the presence of the Israelites! Therefore, you shall not bring this assembly to the land that I have given you."

¹³ These are the Waters of Dispute (*Mey Meribhah*)* where the Israelites disputed with God, and where He was [nevertheless]* sanctified.*

1:28). This may have been the first time that God spoke to Moses after a 38 year hiatus (*Taanith* 30b; *Sifra* on Leviticus 1:1). See Deuteronomy 2:16.

20:8 staff. Some say that this was Aaron's staff, which was placed in the Holy of Holies (see 20:9, 17:25; *Chizzkuni*; *K'li Yekar*; *Zera Berakh* 2). According to others, it was Moses' staff, which had been kept in the Tabernacle (*Lekach Tov*; Abarbanel; cf. *Targum Yonathan*). This was the staff with God's name engraved on it (*Midrash Aggadah*). According to one opinion, God had told Moses to take his own staff, but Moses took Aaron's (*Tzafanath Paaneach*).

— **Speak to.** Or, "Speak to [the Israelites] regarding. . ." (Ramban; Ralbag; Tur).

— **cliff.** The hebrew word *sela* denotes a cliff or any other bedrock that protrudes from the ground, and not a loose rock on the surface. Some say that he was to speak to the nearest rock available (Ramban).

— **in their presence** (see *HaKethav VeHaKabbalah*). Or, "to the first one they see" (Ramban).

20:9 from before God. See note on previous verse.

20:11 twice. Or, "a second time," referring to Exodus 17:6 (*HaKethav VeHaKabbalah*; *Mekhilta de Rashbi*).

20:12 enough faith. Or, "You did not work to make [the Israelites] have faith" (Saadia; Ralbag).

— **sanctify Me.** See note on 20:13.

20:13 Waters of Dispute . . . See 20:24, Psalms 81:8, 95:8, 106:32. Also see 27:14, Deuteronomy 32:51; Ezekiel 47:19, 48:28. Cf. Exodus 17:7

— **nevertheless** (Rashbam). Or, "sanctified through [Moses and Aaron]" (Ibn Ezra; cf. Leviticus 10:3). Or, "He was profaned" (*HaKethav VeHaKabbalah*). Or, "showed His power against them" (Saadia; cf. *Targum Yonathan*).

— **sanctified.** *Kadesh* in Hebrew. Some say that it was for this reason that the place was named Kadesh (*BeMidbar Rabbah*; *Tanchuma* 11; *Chizzkuni*).

[*100. Encounter with Edom*] 20

¹⁴ Moses sent envoys from Kadesh* to the King of Edom* [with the following message]: "This is what your brother* Israel declares: You know about all the troubles that we have encountered. ¹⁵ Our fathers migrated to Egypt and we lived in Egypt for a long time. The Egyptians mistreated both our fathers and us. ¹⁶ When we cried out to God, He heard our voice and sent a representative to take us out of Egypt. We are now in Kadesh, a city at the edge of your territories. ¹⁷ Please let us pass through your land. We will not go through any fields or vineyards, and we will not drink any water from your wells. Until we pass through your territories, we will travel along the King's Highway,* not turning aside to the right or to the left."

¹⁸ Edom's response was, "Do not pass through my [land], or I will greet you with the sword!"

¹⁹ The Israelites said, "We will keep on the beaten path.* If we or our cattle drink any of your water, we will pay the full price. It is of no concern.* We only want to pass through on foot.*"

²⁰ "Do not come through!" was Edom's response. Edom came forth to confront [the Israelites] with a large number of people and a show of force.* ²¹ Edom thus refused to allow Israel to pass through its territories, and Israel had to go around [the area].*

[*101. Aaron's Death*]

²² Moving on from Kadesh, the entire Israelite community came to Hor Mountain.* ²³ At Hor Mountain, God said to Moses and Aaron, ²⁴ "Aaron

---

20:14 from Kadesh. Apparently right after Miriam's death (cf. *Seder Olam* 9). Josephus, however, has this before Miriam's death (see note on 20:1). See Deuteronomy 2:4-8.

— **King of Edom.** This is Hadar, mentioned in Genesis 36:39 (*Seder HaYashar*, p. 217). Edom lived in the area south of the Dead Sea (cf. *Adereth Eliahu*).

— **brother.** Edom consisted of the descendants of Jacob's brother Esau (see Genesis 25:30, 36:1, 36:8, 36:9, 36:19).

20:17 King's Highway. An important highway running north along the plateau to the east of the Dead Sea. It was later improved by the Romans, and stretches are still discernable. Or, "the way the king goes" (Bachya), or, "the route specified by the king" (Ibn Ezra; Sforno; Abarbanel).

20:19 beaten path (Targum). *Mesilla* in Hebrew. Or, "cleared path" (Radak, *Sherashim*), or, "mountain route" (Septuagint; cf. 2 Chronicles 9:11).

— **It is of no concern** (*Tur*; *HaKethav VeHaKabbalah*; Septuagint) Or, "It will cause no harm" (Rashi), or, "we have no bad intentions" (Targum).

— **on foot.** Or, "with my foot troops" (Bachya; see Exodus 12:37).

20:20 show of force. Literally, "strong hand." See Exodus 3:19.

20:21 had to go around the area. Since God had told the Israelites not to fight with Edom (Deuteronomy 2:5; *BeMidbar Rabbah*).

20:22 Hor Mountain. Some identify this with Jebel Nebi Harun, 50 miles south of the Dead Sea, and just

20 will [now die and] be gathered up to his people. He will not come to the land that I am giving the Israelites because you rebelled against My word at the Waters of Dispute.*

²⁵ "[You Moses] take Aaron and his son Eleazar, and bring them up to Hor Mountain. ²⁶ Divest Aaron of his vestments and place them on his son Eleazar. Aaron will then be gathered up [to his ancestors] and die there."

²⁷ Moses did as God commanded him. [The three of them] climbed Hor Mountain in the presence of the entire community. ²⁸ Moses divested Aaron of his vestments, and placed them on [Aaron's] son Eleazar. Aaron died* there on the top of the mountain. When Moses and Eleazar descended from the mountain, ²⁹ the people realized that Aaron had died. The entire family of Israel* mourned Aaron for thirty days.*

[102. Confrontation with Canaan]

21   ¹ When the Canaanite* king of Arad,* who lived in the Negev,* heard that the Israelites were traveling along the Atharim* Highway, he attacked them and took some captives. ² The Israelites* made a vow to God, and said, "If You give this nation into our* hand, we will render their cities taboo.*"

³ God heard Israel's voice, and He allowed them to defeat the Canaanites. [The Israelites] declared them and their cities taboo. The place was therefore named Taboo (*Charmah*).*

---

south of Petra in an area known as Acre (cf. Josephus, *Antiquities* 4:5:7). It is thus described as being on the border of Edom (19:23, 33:37). Others identify it with Jebel Madurah, north-west of the Dead Sea, or Jebel Akkar (cf. Josephus). *Hor HaHar* can also be translated "mountain of the mountain," and some say that it was a mountain with a protrusion (like a second mountain) on top of it (*BeMidbar Rabbah* 19:16; Rashi). Some sources translate it as Mt. Umanos (*Targum Yonathan*), which may be identified with Amanah, a mountain to the north of the Holy Land (cf. Song of Songs 4:8; *Shevi'ith* 6:1). See Deuteronomy 10:6.

20:24 **Waters of Dispute.** See above 20:13.
20:28 **Aaron died.** On 1 Av, at the age of 123 years; below 33:38,39.
20:29 **family of Israel.** Literally, "House of Israel;" see Exodus 16:31.
—   **thirty days.** See Genesis 50:3; Deuteronomy 34:8. A number of the events recorded subsequently occurred during these 30 days; see note on 21:12. It was when the period of mourning was over that Israel fought against Sichon; see 21:21.
21:1   **Canaanite.** Some say that he was an Amalekite (*BeMidbar Rabbah* 19:20; Rashi).
—   **Arad.** This is identified with Tel Arad, 13 miles west of the Dead Sea, about half way between the Dead Sea and Beer Sheba. See 33:40, Joshua 12:4. Also see Judges 1:16, and some say that the war described there occurred in Moses' time.
—   **Negev.** Southern part of Holy Land.
—   **Atharim.** A proper noun (Saadia; Septuagint). Probably the main highway leading through the Negev toward Beer Sheba. Or, "the route of the spies" (Targum; Rashi; Rashbam), or, "a roundabout route" (Chizzkuni).
21:2   **The Israelites.** Literally, "Israel."
—   **our.** Literally, "my." Entire sentence is in the singular.
—   **taboo.** *Cherem.* See Leviticus 27:21,29.
21:3   **Charmah.** Or Chormah. See above 14:45. This was some 27 miles directly west of Arad. Some say that Chormah here is not the same as the one in 14:45 (Chizzkuni).

Numbers 20:25   *441*

[103. The Snakes: Further Journeys]   21

⁴ [The Israelites] moved on from Hor Mountain, going by way of the South Sea* so as to skirt* the territory of Edom. The people began to become discouraged* along the way. ⁵ The people spoke out against God and Moses, "Why did you take us out of Egypt to die in the desert? There is no bread and no water! We are getting disgusted with this insubstantial* food."

⁶ God sent* poisonous snakes against the people, and when they began biting the people, a number of Israelites died. ⁷ The people came to Moses* and said, "We have sinned by speaking against God and you. Pray to God, and have Him take the snakes away from us."

When Moses prayed for the people, ⁸ God said to Moses, "Make yourself [the image of] a venomous snake, and place it on a banner. Everyone who is bitten shall look at it and live."*

⁹ Moses made a copper snake* and placed it on a high pole. Whenever a snake bit a man, he would gaze at the copper snake and live.

¹⁰ The Israelites then moved on and camped in Ovoth.*

¹¹ From Ovoth they moved on and camped in the desolate passes* along Moab's eastern border.* ¹² They then continued and camped along the Zered Brook.*

21:4 **South Sea.** *Yam Suf* in Hebrew, usually denoting the "Red Sea," but here most probably the Gulf of Aqaba.

— **to skirt.** According to tradition, after Aaron's death, the Israelites went back seven stages, finally going from Beney Yaakan to Moserah (comparing Deuteronomy 10:6 and Numbers 33:31; *Seder Olam* 9; *Yerushalmi, Yoma* 1:1, 2a,b; *BeMidbar Rabbah* 19:20; Rashi on 26:13). It was therefore in Moserah that Aaron was mourned (Bachya). The Israelites then came back, and stopped in Tzalmona and Ponan (33:42; *Baaley Tosafoth; Lekach Tov; Chizzkuni*, on, 21:10).

— **discouraged.** *Katzar nefesh* in Hebrew; see Exodus 6:9. The discouragement began in Tzalmonah, and the snakes began biting them in Punon (*Targum Yonathan* on 33:41,42; cf. *Lekach Tov* on 21:10).

21:5 **insubstantial** (Rashi; Ibn Ezra; Radak, *Sherashim*; Septuagint). Or, "weightless" (Saadia; Ibn Janach); or "wasteless" (Rashi). Speaking of the Manna.

21:6 **God sent.** Some say that the people left the camp to get other food and they were bitten (Yehudah HaChasid).

21:7 **The people came . . .** Some say that Moses went out to find out what was wrong (*Lekach Tov*).

21:8 **shall look at it and live.** They would then think of God and repent (*Targum Yonathan; Rosh HaShanah* 29a; Rashi). Some say that they would meditate on the copper serpent (*HaKethav VeHaKabbalah*). According to others, the snake would be a reminder for the people not to leave the camp (Yehudah HaChasid), or not to speak against God (Ralbag).

21:9 **copper snake.** Snake is *nachash* and copper is *nechosheth*. The Israelites later called it Nechushtan and served it, so it was destroyed by Hezekiah (2 Kings 18:4).

21:10 **Ovoth.** See below 33:43. Ovoth is identified with el-Weiba, 30 miles due south of the Dead Sea, or Ein Hosob, 15 miles south of the Dead Sea.

21:11 **desolate passes** (Saadia; Rashi; Rashbam). Or, "travelers' passes" (Targum). Or, "ruins of Avarim," speaking of the area of Mount Nebo (see 27:12, 33:47, Deuteronomy 33:49; Rashi; Chizzkuni). The Septuagint has Achal Ai.

— **along Moab's eastern border.** They did not enter Moab's land, because God had told them not to fight against Moab (Deuteronomy 2:9). See Judges 11:17.

21:12 **Zered Brook.** This is the river that flows into the south-east end of the Dead Sea. It forms the south-

21   ¹³ They traveled further and camped in the desert extending from the
Amorite border,* on the opposite side* of the Arnon [River].* The Arnon is
the Moabite border, separating Moab from the Amorites.
           ¹⁴ It is therefore told in the Book of God's Wars,* "As an outermost
bou⌐dary,* I have given [you]* the streams of Arnon,* ¹⁵ as well as the

ern border of Moab. The area of the Zered was most probably conquered earlier by Edom and taken
from Moab (see Genesis 36:35). From the context, it appears that the Israelites were at the eastern
extreme of the Zered. Some say that the crossing of the Zered is not recorded in Numbers 33 (*Lekach Tov*),
but others identify the place of crossing with Divon Gad in Numbers 33:45 (*Baaley Tosafoth*; Chizzkuni).
This may have been Divon (21:30), which later became a city of Gad (32:34). Some say that this stop
along the Zered is also to be identified with Vahabh and Matanah (21:14,18; *Adereth Eliahu*).
    It was while the Israelites were on the Zered that the last of the generation of the Exodus died, as we
see in Deuteronomy 2:14 (*Adereth Eliahu*). According to tradition, this was on 15 Av, just 15 days after
Aaron's death (33:38,39; *Taanith* 30b). According to some, none of these people died during the last
year, but it was not until 15 Av that they realized that the decree had come to an end (*Eikhah Rabbah*,
Introduction 33; Rashi, *Taanith* 30b; *Tosafoth ibid.*, s.v. *Yom*). See above, 20:1.

21:13 **in the desert extending . . .** (Septuagint). Or, "extending beyond the Amorite border" (Saadia). This
    may have been a strip of land along the eastern end of the Arnon, on the north shore, to the south of
    the Ammonite territory (Rashi; Chizzkuni).

—   **opposite side.** That is, to the north, so as not to enter Moabite territory, which had been forbidden in
    Deuteronomy 2:9.

—   **Arnon River** (*Baaley Tosafoth*). The Arnon is an enormous trench across the plateau of Moab, some
    1700 feet deep and two miles broad. Some say that Arnon here is a city (Ramban), possibly identified
    with Almon Divlathaymah in 33:46 (Chizzkuni *ad loc.*; *Adereth Eliahu*). See 24:18. Some say that
    Arnon is the same as Nachaliel in 21:19 (*Adereth Eliahu*).

21:14 **Book of God's Wars.** An ancient lost book (*Baaley Tosafoth*; Ramban; Chizzkuni). Some say that it
    existed among the gentiles (Abarbanel), while others say that it was a book of records kept from
    Abraham's time (Ibn Ezra; Bachya). Others, however, identify this book with the Torah as a whole
    (*Targum Yonathan*), or, in particular, the book of Exodus (*Midrash Aggadah*) or Deuteronomy
    (Yehudah HaChasid). To some degree, this depends upon the meaning of the quotation, as we shall
    see below.
        According to others, it is not actually a book, but "the telling of God's wars" (Rashi; Rashbam;
    Lekach Tov; Bachya). Or, "It is therefore written in this book, 'God's wars . . .'" (Targum; *Lekach
    Tov*; Septuagint).

—   **As an outermost boundary** (Chizzkuni; Malbim). *Be-Sufah* in Hebrew. Others say that *sufah*
    denotes "whirlwind" (*Baaley Tosafoth*; Abarbanel; cf. Isaiah 29:6, Amos 1:14), and hence, "quick-
    ly" (*Baal HaTurim*). Or, "in the reeds" (Ralbag; *Adereth Eliahu*; cf. Exodus 2:3), and thus, possibly
    denoting the Red Sea, *Yam Suf* in Hebrew (Targum; Saadia; Rashi). Others say that Sufah is a place
    name, denoting a location on the Arnon River (*Midrash HaGadol*; Ibn Janach; cf. Septuagint). See
    Deuteronomy 1:1. In the Hebrew, *be-sufah* comes after the word *vahev*.

—   **I have given . . .** Following the authorities that have *eth-vahev* as a single word (Radak, *Sherashim*;
    Chizzkuni). Some indicate that as a reflexive form it means "I have given Myself" (*Baaley Tosafoth*).
    Others take *vahev* as a separate word related to the root *yahav*, and hence denoting a gift (Rashi;
    Lekach Tov) or a "burden" to be cast upon God (Rashbam, cf. Psalms 55:23). Others see *vahev* as
    denoting a whirlpool (Saadia), or, on the basis of Semitic cognates, a pool in the desert. According to
    other ancient sources, *vahev* is related to the word *lahav*, and denotes a fire (Septuagint).
        According to a number of sources, however, Vahev is a place name, denoting a town along the
    Moabite border (*Midrash HaGadol*; Ibn Janach; Abarbanel). Since it means "gift," some identify it
    with Matanah in 21:18 (*Adereth Eliahu*; Malbim). This in turn is identified with Divon Gad (see
    note on 21:12).
        Others see the word *eth* here as a separate word rather than a preposition. Hence, it can also be
    translated as "come" (*Lekach Tov*). A Talmudic source states that Eth and Hav are the names of two
    lepers (*Berakhoth* 54a,b; cf. *Baaley Tosafoth* on 26:59).
        Therefore, the very difficult expression *eth vahev be-sufah* can be translated as we have it, "As
    an outermost boundary, I have given you . . ." (Chizzkuni on 21:17); "I have given Myself in the

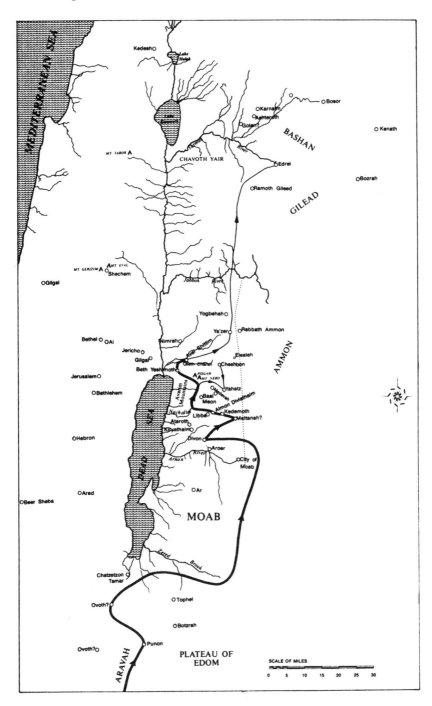

PLATE 27.   LAST JOURNEYS OF THE EXODUS

21 valley's rapids* that hug* Moab's borders, turning aside at the fortress* settlement."

¹⁶ From there* [the Israelites traveled] to the well.* This is the well regarding which God said to Moses, "Gather the people, and I will give them water."

whirlwind" (*Baaley Tosafoth*); "a gift in the whirlwind" (*Lekach Tov*; *Baal HaTurim*); "a gift at the Red Sea" (Rashi; Hirsch); "a whirlpool was in the Red Sea" (Saadia); "God's wars were a fire in Sufah" (Septuagint).

If Vahev is taken as a place name, the verse can be translated, "Vahev is on [Moab's] border" (Chizzkuni; Malbim); "God's wars were against Vahev in a whirlwind" (Tur); "Vahev is in the reeds" (Ralbag) "Vahev in Sufah . . . hugs the border of Moab" (Ibn Janach; cf. *Midrash HaGadol*); "[The Israelites traveled through] Vahev in Sufah" (Rashbam; *Adereth Eliahu*); "God's wars were fought against Vahev in Sufah" (Ibn Ezra); "[The Amorites conquered] until Vahev in Sufah" (Abarbanel).

If *eth* is taken as a separate word, the verse is, "[God] came and gave [miracles] at the Red Sea" (*Lekach Tov*); or, "written by Eth and Hav who were at the edge [of the camp]" (*Berakhoth* 54a,b).

We have chosen the first translation cited, since it flows from the context of the verse. The Torah states that the Arnon was Moab's border (21:13; 22:36). God, however, had told the Israelites not to attack Moab (Deuteronomy 2:9). However, since the Amorites had conquered the Moabite territory as far as the Arnon (21:26), this was permitted to the Israelites (Deuteronomy 2:24). The Israelites therefore conquered as far as the Arnon (21:24, Deuteronomy 3:8,12), and their borders extended from Arnon to Mount Hermon (Deuteronomy 3:8, Joshua 12:1).

— **the streams of Arnon.** The streams in the Arnon valley. Some identify this with Almon Divlathaymah in 33:46 (*HaKethav VeHaKabbalah*). See note on 21:13.

21:15 rapids. Or "waterfall"; *eshed* in Hebrew (Targum; Rashi; Saadia). See Deuteronomy 3:17, Joshua 10:40, 12:3. Or, "spilling," alluding to the blood of the Amorites who were miraculously killed on the cliffs of the Arnon (Rashi; *Berakhoth* 54b). Other sources translate *eshed* as projections (*Tanchuma* 20) or "appointed" (Septuagint). Some identify this with Mount Abarim (*HaKethav VeHaKabbalah*; see note on 21:11).

— **hug.** Literally, "lean on." Or, "They relied [on God] at Moab's borders (*Baal HaTurim*).

— **fortress** (Targum). Ar in Hebrew. Other sources have Ar as a place name (Saadia; Chizzkuni), and indeed some have *Shebheth Ar* as a place name (Ralbag). As we see here, it was on the Arnon, most probably on the southern branch. It was attacked by the Amorites (21:28), but apparently retained by Moab or inhabited by them (Deuteronomy 2:9,29, Isaiah 15:1). Therefore, although the Israelites passed through Ar, they did not conquer it (Deuteronomy 2:18; *Midrash HaGadol*). Some say that Ammon's borders extended as far south as Ar (*Lekach Tov*).

The Septuagint translates this verse, "[God] has appointed brooks to cause Ar to dwell there."

21:16 From there. According to many commentaries, this is not part of the quotation, but merely a continuation of the description of the Israelites' travels, interrupted with 21:14,15 (Ibn Ezra; Ramban; *Adereth Eliahu*). According to this, the Israelites came to the well after Aaron's death (20:28), and the well was dug by Moses and Eleazar (*Lekach Tov*). Indeed, according to some, the well was dug at the Israelites' final stop in the Western Plains of Moab (22:1; *Adereth Eliahu*; *HaKethav VeHaKabbalah*). On the basis of this, some say that the well was dug after the wars with Sichon and Og (Yehudah HaChasid). However, the main Israelite camp may have arrived at the well in the Western Plains of Moab before the battles, and only the fighting men may have left the area to fight.

According to other sources, the sentence, "and from there to the well" is still part of the quotation. The song may thus be saying, "the valley's rapids . . . turning aside at the fortress settlement, and from there [providing water] for the well" (Rashi; *Lekach Tov*; Chizzkuni). According to this, the well may have been dug before Aaron's death, and indeed, according to some, it was dug by Moses and Aaron (Rashi; Rashbam on 21:18). Some say that this "well" thus refers to the rock that Moses struck (20:11; *Baaley Tosafoth*; Chizzkuni; Abarbanel).

According to others, the Torah is saying that there on the banks of the Arnon, they were given a well (Targum).

— **to the well.** *B'erah* in Hebrew. Possibly a place name (cf. Isaiah 15:8).

[104. Song of the Well]   **21**

¹⁷ It was then that Israel sang this song:*

Rise, O well,* respond to [this song].*
¹⁸ A well was dug by princes*
Sunk by the people's leaders*
Carved out* with their staffs.

From the desert,* [the Israelites went to] Matanah,* ¹⁹ from Matanah to Nachaliel,* and from Nachaliel to Bamoth.* ²² From Bamoth [they went] to

---

21:17 **this song.** (see *Rosh HaShanah* 31a). Or, "a song," and some say that it was Psalm 136 (Yehudah HaChasid). See next notes. Some say that the entire song is not written (Ibn Ezra).

— **Rise, O well** (Rashi). Or, "Israel sang this song at the well," (Septuagint), or, "about the well" (Ralbag).

— **respond to this song** (*Lekach Tov*). Or, "sing of the well" (Ralbag; Septuagint); "responding to one another" (Saadia).

21:18 **princes.** And not slaves (*Baaley Tosafoth*; *HaKethav VeHaKabbalah*). Some say that the "princes" were Moses and Aaron (Rashi; Rashbam), while others say that they were Moses and Eleazar (*Lekach Tov*); see note on 21:16. According to others, the "princes" were the Patriarchs (*Targum Yonathan*).

— **leaders.** *Nadiv* in Hebrew. Or, "volunteers."

— **Carved out** (Saadia; Ibn Ezra; Septuagint). *Mechokek* in Hebrew. Some say that this indicates that they dug a trench bringing the well's water from the desert to Matanah, etc. (*Baaley Tosafoth*; Chizzkuni). Some see *mechokek* as a noun, indicating a lawgiver, namely Moses (Rashi), a scribe (Targum), or God (*HaKethav VeHaKabbalah*). See Genesis 49:10.

— **From the desert.** Some say that this is not part of the song (Rashbam; Abarbanel). According to others, however, it is part of the song. See next note.

— **Matanah.** A place name (Saadia; Rashbam; *Midrash HaGadol*). Some identify it with Vahev (see note on 21:14), Almon Divlathaymah in 33:47 (Ibn Ezra) or the Avarim Mountains in 33:48 (Chizzkuni; see note on 21:11). It may also be the Bashan, which the Targum translates as Mathnan (on 21:33). The Septuagint renders Mathan as Mantanaim. See Deuteronomy 2:26.

Some say that Matanah was a place from which the Israelites retreated after the encounter with Edom (Abarbanel), while others say that it represents the next stage on their journey (Chizzkuni). Others say that the Israelites carved a trench or canal, causing the well's water to flow to Matanah (Yehudah HaChasid; Chizzkuni). Some identify Matanah with Khirbet el-Medeiyineh.

The word *matanah*, however, also denotes a "gift," and some render the verse, "[The well] was a gift from the desert"(Targum; *Baaley Tosafoth*).

21:19 **Nachaliel.** Some commentators take this as a proper name (Ibn Ezra; Rashbam; Septuagint). Indeed, some say that it is the stream Arnon (*HaKethav VeHaKabbalah*). Some sources identify it with Divon Gad and Almon Devlathaymah (*Lekach Tov*; see note on 21:12,14). According to others, it is the area filled with streams and wadis on the east bank of the Jordan (*Midrash Aggadah*).

Others take *nachaliel* to be a common noun, meaning "mighty stream" (Saadia). Some say that the well increased from a mere "gift" to a "mighty stream" (*Baaley Tosafoth*). Others translate *nachaliel* as "God's inheritance" (Targum; Rashi).

Geographically, Nachaliel appears to be the large stream some 11 miles north of the Arnon. This would indicate that the Israelites were proceeding along the eastern shore of the Dead Sea.

— **Bamoth.** Also a place name. Some identify it with the Avarim mountains in 33:47, which are the mountains to the east of the Dead Sea (*Lekach Tov*; see notes on 21:11,15). Some say that Nachaliel was a stream that flowed from Bamoth (Chizzkuni).

According to others, *bamoth* simply means "high places" or "high altars" (*Targum*; Rashi). Thus, those who maintain that the verses are speaking about the well (rather than the Israelites' travels) say that the stream flowing from the well eventually covered "high places" (*Baaley Tosafoth*). Others translate *bamoth* as "idolatrous altars" (Saadia).

21 Hagai* in the field of Moab. It is on the top of the cliff* that overlooks the Wastelands.*

[105. Confrontations with Sichon and Og]

21 Israel* sent emissaries to Sichon* king of the Amorites* with the following message, **22** "Let us* pass through your land. We will not turn aside to the fields and vineyards, and we will not drink any well water. We will follow the King's Highway until we have passed through your territories."

23 Sichon, however, did not let Israel pass through his territories. Instead, Sichon mustered up all his people, and went out to confront Israel in the desert. When he came to Yahatz,* he attacked* Israel. **24** Israel struck him down with the sword,* and occupied his land from the Arnon to the

---

Some identify Bamoth with Bamoth Baal (22:41, Joshua 13:17), which may be identical with Bamoth Moab (Isaiah 16:2). Also see 21:28. Looking at a detailed map of the area, it appears that the Israelites passed by the edge of the Aravah range that juts out to within 3 miles of the Dead Sea, some 10 miles from its northern end.

— **Hagai.** Also a place name (cf. Septuagint). See Deuteronomy 34:6, Ezekiel 39:11. Some sources identify this with Avel HaShittim in 33:49 (Chizzkuni); cf. 25:1, Joshua 2:1, 3:1. The Targum translates it as "the plain," and some say that it is the same as the Western Plains of Moab (*HaKethav VeHaKabbalah*), west of the Pisgah cliff in Deuteronomy 3:17 (*Lekach Tov*). Others say that it was the top of the Pisgah cliff, where Moses died (Ibn Ezra; cf. Deuteronomy 34:6).

Geographically, it appears to be the depression in the heights just to the south of Mount Nebo. This is the source of the present Ujami stream, which flows into the northern end of the Dead Sea, about 3 miles east of the Jordan. See Deuteronomy 3:29.

— **cliff.** (Targum; Rashi). *Pisgah* in Hebrew. Some have it as a proper name (cf. Psalms 48:14). Others translate *pisgah* as "quarry" (Septuagint).

Pisgah may be a generic term for the cliffs overlooking the eastern shore of the Dead Sea. However, it is usually thought to denote the cliff that juts out some 8 miles directly east of the Dead Sea's northern shore, 2 miles due west of Mount Nebo (cf. Deuteronomy 3:27).

— **Wastelands** (Rashi; Ibn Ezra). Some take Yeshimon here to be a proper name (Targum); see Deuteronomy 32:10. Some identify it with Beth HaYeshemoth in Numbers 33:48 (see Chizzkuni *ad loc.*). Cf. Joshua 12:3, 13:20, Ezekiel 25:9. Also see 23:28, 1 Samuel 23:19,24, 26:1,3.

Geographically, it appears that the Yeshimon is the desolate area to the northeast of the Dead Sea.

21:21 Israel. See Judges 11:19. Some say that Moses sent them; see Deuteronomy 2:26 (*BeMidbar Rabbah* 19:28; Rashi). According to tradition, the encounter with Sichon occurred in Elul, about one month after Aaron's death (*BeMidbar Rabbah* 19:32).

— **Sichon.** According to ancient tradition, Sichon and Og were brothers, and were both over 800 years old at the time. They were both giants, but Og was the greater (*Niddah* 61a; Bachya).

— **Amorites.** See Genesis 10:16, 14:7.

21:22 us. Literally, "me" (cf. *HaKethav VeHaKabbalah*).

21:23 Yahatz (Targum) or Yahatzah (Septuagint). Yahatz is found in Isaiah 15:4, Jeremiah 48:34, while Yahatzah is in Deuteronomy 2:32, Judges 11:20, Jeremiah 48:21. It was assigned to Reuben (Joshua 13:18), and was a Levitical city (1 Chronicles 6:63). It can be identified with Jalul or Khirbet el-Teim, some 15 miles east of the Dead Sea's northern end, and 7 miles south of Cheshbon.

— **attacked.** Some say that Moses provoked the battle at God's command (Josephus, *Antiquities* 4:5:2; cf. Deuteronomy 2:24).

21:24 Israel struck . . . Josephus states that Sichon did not have the courage to battle the Israelites, and when the Amorites tried to stop for water, they were killed (*Antiquities* 4:5:2).

Jabbok,* as far as the [borders of] the Ammonites.* The borders of the 21
Ammonites, however, remained firm.*

²⁵ Israel thus took all these cities. They [later]* settled in Cheshbon* and
all its tributary towns, all the Amorite cities.

²⁶ Cheshbon was the capital of Sichon king of the Amorites. He had
fought against the first king of Moab* and taken all his land as far as the
Arnon.

²⁷ The minstrels* therefore say:

> Come to Cheshbon*!
> Let Sichon's city be built and established*!
> ²⁸ For a fire has come out of Cheshbon;
>   a flame from Sichon's capital,
> And it has consumed Ar* of Moab,
>   the masters* of the Arnon's altars
> ²⁹ Woe is to you, Moab;
>   you are destroyed, nation of Kemosh.*
> Your* sons have become refugees,
>   your daughters are captives
> To Sichon, king of the Amorites.

— **Jabbok.** See Genesis 32:23. The Jabbok runs parallel to the Arnon, some 50 miles to the north of it.

— **Ammonites.** See Genesis 19:38. Their territory was to the east of Sichon's land, beginning some 20 miles east of the Jordan. Ammon and Moab were cousins (Genesis 19:37,38), and hence their lands were originally next to each other. Some say that the Ammonites also had lands to the north of the Jabbok (Chizzkuni). The modern city of Aman, Jordan derives its name from Ammon.

— **remained firm** (Targum). This was because God told the Israelites not to attack Ammon (Deuteronomy 2:19; *Sefer HaYashar*; *Lekach Tov*; Bachya). Others see Az here as a proper noun, which the Septuagint renders as Y'azer, see below 21:32. The Torah is thus saying, "Az was the border of Ammon." Other sources apparently identify Az with Ar (21:15, *Lekach Tov ad loc.*)

21:25 **later.** See 32:2, Joshua 13:17.

— **Cheshbon.** The Amorite capital. It was some 15 miles to the east of the Dead Sea's northern tip.

21:26 **He had fought . . .** Some say that this war had occurred four years earlier (*Sefer HaYashar*). Because Sichon had conquered Moab, it was permissible for the Israelites to occupy it (*Chullin* 60b).

21:27 **minstrels.** Poets, or makers of parables (*Targum Yonathan*; Rashbam; Bachya), possibly denoting prophets (Rashbam), women who make up parables (*Lekach Tov*), or people who speak in parables (Septuagint). *Mosh'lim* in Hebrew. Or, "rulers" (Radak, *Sherashim*; Tur), possibly the governors under Sichon mentioned in Joshua 13:21 (Yehudah HaChasid). Some say that they were Balaam and his father Beor (22:5; *BeMidbar Rabbah* 19:30; Rashi; *Sefer HaYashar*). See Jeremiah 48:45.

— **Come to Cheshbon.** "Come and conquer Cheshbon" (Ralbag), "Come and defend Cheshbon" (Sforno), or, "Come and see Cheshbon" (*Adereth Eliahu*).

— **Let . . .** Or, "Sichon's city has been built . . ."

21:28 **Ar.** Or, "the fortress of . . ." See 21:16.

— **masters.** Or, "plains" (Chizzkuni). See 21:19.

21:29 **Kemosh.** Moabite deity, possibly a war god; see Judges 11:24; 1 Kings 11:7, 2 Kings 23:13; Jeremiah 48:7,13. It is said to be a natural formation of black rock in the form of a woman (*Paneach Razah*, quoting *Sekhel Tov*). Its worship included shaving the head (*Midrash HaGadol* on Exodus 20:5; *Sefer HaMitzvoth*, Negative Commandment 6; cf. Jeremiah 9:25).

— **Your.** Literally, "his."

21

³⁰ [Moab's] kingdom* was obliterated [from] Cheshbon as far as Divon,* and was laid waste as far as Nofech* near Medeva.*

³¹ Israel thus settled in the Amorite territory. ³² Moses sent out men to reconnoiter Ya'azer,* and they* captured its surrounding villages, driving out the Amorites who lived there.

³³ [The Israelites]* then went on* and headed north toward the Bashan.* At Edrei,* Og* king of the Bashan came out with all his people to engage [the Israelites] in battle.

³⁴ God said to Moses, "Do not be afraid of him. I have given him, along with all his people and territory, into your hand. I will do the same to him as I did to Sichon, king of the Amorites who lived in Cheshbon."

³⁵ [The Israelites] killed [Og] along with his sons and all his people, leaving no survivors, and they occupied his land.

21:30 kingdom (Targum). *Niram* in Hebrew, from the root *nir*. Or, "power" (Saadia), or, "heir" (*Baaley Tosafoth*; Chizzkuni; Septuagint). Others see the word *ve-niram* here as coming from the root *yarah,* and meaning, "and we cast them down, destroying Cheshbon," and said by Moses (Rashbam; Ibn Ezra).

— **Divon.** A city some 3 miles north of the Arnon, and 12 miles east of the Jordan. This was later occupied by Gad (32:34, 33:45); see note on 21:12. Also see Joshua 13:9,17, 48:18,22, Isaiah 15:2. Cheshbon was to the north of Sichon's kingdom, while Divon was to the south of his conquered territory.

— **Nofech.** A place name (Targum; Saadia). Or, "It was laid waste until bodies rotted as far as Medebha" (*Targum Yonathan*); or, "Their women have further kindled a fire as far as Medebha" (Septuagint). Here, *nofech* is seen as meaning "blown up" or "swollen," or, "blown upon" to kindle a fire.

— **Medeva.** A city 4 miles south of Cheshbon, on the King's Highway. See Joshua 13:9,16, Isaiah 15:2, 1 Chronicles 19:7. It appears that Sichon destroyed Moab's power as far south as Divon, but in the area immediately around Cheshbon, he killed all the inhabitants.

21:32 Ya'azer. A city just west of Rabbath Ammon, later on the eastern border of Gad (Joshua 13:25). It was built up by Gad (31:35), and later became a Levitical city (Joshua 21:37, 1 Chronicles 6:66). See 21:24. It was apparently on the eastern boundary of Og's kingdom, near the Ammonite border (cf. 1 Maccabees 5:8).

— **they.** The spies (Rashi; Sforno; *Sefer HaYashar*). Some say that these were led by Caleb and Pinchas (*Targum Yonathan*). This occurred after the festival of Sukkoth, that is, around 23 Tishrei, some six weeks after the defeat of Sichon (*BeMidbar Rabbah* 19:33). According to some sources, it occurred somewhat after the defeat of Og (*Sefer HaYashar*).

21:33 The Israelites (*Sefer HaYashar*). Some say that only the fighting men went to Bashan, while the rest of the camp remained in Aravoth Moab (Chizzkuni on 22:1).

— **went on** (Ibn Ezra here and on Exodus 10:6). Literally, "turned around." It might mean, however, that the expeditionary force turned back from Ya'azer and headed toward Og's kingdom.

— **Bashan.** This is the area to the east of the Sea of Kinnereth. Josephus identifies it with Gilead and Golan (*Antiquities* 4:5:3), the present Golan Heights.

21:33 Edrei. The capital of Og, some 32 miles southeast of the Kinnereth Sea. Cf. Deuteronomy 3:1,10. It was some 14 miles southeast of Ashteroth, and was later given to Manasseh (Joshua 13:31). This was the land of the Raphaim who had been decimated by Chedorlaomer and his allies (Genesis 14:5). See next note.

— **Og.** A giant, who is described as among the survivors of the Raphaim, a race of giants (Joshua 12:4, 13:12). He is described as having a bed that was over 13 feet long (Deuteronomy 3:11). According to tradition, he was over 800 years old, and survived the flood in the time of Noah. He was either a brother of Sichon (see 21:21), or his close friend (Josephus, *Antiquities* 4:5:3). Other sources, however, indicate that Og was just over 500 years old (*BeMidbar Rabbah* 19:32).

¹ The Israelites then moved on,* and they camped in the western plains* **22** of Moab, across the Jordan from Jericho.*

Balak   בָּלָק

[106. Balak and Balaam]

² When Balak* son of Tzippor* saw all that Israel had done to the Amorites,* ³ the Moabites became deathly afraid* because the [Israelite] people were so numerous. Dreading* the Israelites, ⁴ Moab said to the elders of Midian,* "Now the [Israelite] community will lick up everything around us, just as a bull licks up all the vegetation in the field." Balak son of Tzippor was then king of Moab.* ⁵ He sent emissaries to Balaam* son of Beor,* to his native land* in Pethor* on the [Euphrates]*

22:1 **moved on.** Headed back south (Chizzkuni; see 21:33).

— **western plains** (Septuagint). Aravoth Moab in Hebrew.

— **across the Jordan from Jericho.** They were just north-east of the Dead Sea. More specifically, they were in the Shittim area (25:1, Micah 6:5). This consisted of a plain, Avel Shittim (33:49), and the stream or wadi that flows into the north-east end of the Dead Sea, "the stream of Shittim" (Joel 4:18). The Israelites were to remain there until Joshua brought them across the Jordan (Joshua 2:1, 3:1) (See Ibn Ezra on 25:1).

22:2 **Balak.** See Joshua 24:9, Judges 11:25, Micah 6:5. Balak was a descendant of Lot (*BeMidbar Rabbah* 20:19). According to tradition, he was the ancestor of Ruth (*Sotah* 47a; *Nazir* 23b). See notes on 22:4,5.

— **Tzippor.** Hebrew for bird. It is similar to Tzipporah, the name of Moses' Midianite wife (Exodus 2:21). Some say that he was called Tzippor because he practiced bird divination (*Zohar* 3:184b).

— **Amorites.** Sichon, see above, 21:21 ff.

22:3 **deathly afraid** (*HaKethav VeHaKabbalah*; Rashi; Ibn Ezra; cf. I Samuel 18:15, Psalms 22:24). Or, "huddled [in their cities]" (*Paneach Raza*; cf. Psalms 59:4, 149:3).

— **Dreading.** Or, "distressed at" (Ibn Ezra; Radak, *Sherashim*). See Exodus 1:12. Or, "grieved at" (Ibn Janach; Septuagint), or, "disgusted with life" (Rashi; Rashbam).

22:4 **Midian.** Descendants of Abraham through Keturah; Genesis 25:2. Midian's territories were to the south of Edom, just northeast of the Gulf of Aqaba. At this time, Moses was already making plans to attack Midian (Josephus, *Antiquities* 4:6:1). Although Midian and Moab were hereditary enemies, they made peace out of fear of Israel (Sanhedrin 105a).

— **then** . . . Some say that Balak had been one of Sichon's generals, and now that Sichon had been killed, he had just been appointed king over Moab (*Tanchuma* 4; Sh'muel HaChasid). Other sources indicate that kings of the area would come from Midian and Moab on an alternating basis (*Targum Yonathan*).

22:5 **Balaam.** Bil'am in Hebrew. See Deuteronomy 23:5, Joshua 24:9, Michah 6:5, Nehemiah 12:3. See note on Genesis 36:32. Some say that Balaam was descended from Abraham's nephew Kemuel (*Lekach Tov*; see Genesis 22:21). Others say that he was a descendant of Laban (Sanhedrin 105a; *Torah Temimah*).

— **Beor.** See Genesis 36:32.

— **his native land.** Balaam's land (Ramban; Chizzkuni). Others say that Balak and Balaam were both from Pethor, and the verse refers to Balak's native land (*BeMidbar Rabbah* 20:7; Rashi; Midrash HaGadol).

— **Pethor.** In Aram Naharaim; see Deuteronomy 23:5. Some identify this with Padan Aram (*Targum Yonathan*; see Genesis 25:20). From the context it appears to be in the mountainous regions of Aram (see below, 23:7). Some identify it with Pitru, or the Egyptian Pedru, on the upper Euphrates. Thus, it must have been at least a 300 mile journey from Moab. See next note.

— **Euphrates.** (*Targum Yonathan*; Saadia; Josephus, *Antiquities* 4:6:2). The only mountainous region

22   River. They were to summon him with the following message: "A nation
that covers the land's surface has left Egypt, and is now staying right near
us.* ⁶ This nation is too powerful for us [alone], so if you would, come and
curse this nation for me. Then, we may be able to defeat them and drive
them from the area. I know that whomever you bless is blessed, and whomever you curse is cursed."*

⁷ The elders of Moab and Midian, versed in occult arts,* went to
Balaam, conveying to him Balak's message. ⁸ "Spend the night here," he
replied to them, "and when God speaks to me, I will be able to give you an
answer."

The Moabite* dignitaries remained with Balaam. ⁹ God appeared* to
Balaam and asked, "Who are these men with you?"

¹⁰ Balaam replied to God, "Balak son of Tzippor, king of Moab, has
sent me a message: ¹¹ 'A nation that covers the earth's surface has left
Egypt. Come and curse them for me, so that, hopefully, I will be able to
fight against them and drive them away.'"

¹² God said to Balaam, "Do not go with them. Do not curse the nation
[in question], because it is a blessed [nation]."

¹³ When Balaam got up in the morning, he said to Balak's dignitaries,
"Go home! God refuses to let me go with you."

¹⁴ The Moabite dignitaries set out, and when they came to Balak, they
said, "Balaam refuses to go with us."

¹⁵ Balak sent another delegation, this time with a larger number of dignitaries, higher in rank than the first. ¹⁶ When they came to Balaam, they
gave him the following message in the name of Balak son of Tzippor:* "Do
not refuse to come to me. ¹⁷ I will give you great honor, doing anything you
say. But please come and curse this nation for me."

¹⁸ Balaam interrupted Balak's servants and said, "Even if Balak gave me
his whole palace full of gold and silver, I would not be able to do anything
great or small that would violate the word of God my Lord. ¹⁹ But now,
you, too, remain here overnight. Then I will know what God shall declare
to me."

---

near the Euphrates is that in the vicinity of As Sukhnah or Dayr az Zawr, in what is now central
Syria. It is also possible that Pethor was in the vicinity of Palmyra.

—   **us.** Literally, "me."

22:6   **I know** . . . See note on 21:27.

22:7   **versed in occult arts** (Ibn Ezra). Or, "with magical devices in hand" (*Tanchuma* 5; Rashi; Rashbam;
Septuagint), or, "with mystical text" (*Baaley Tosafoth*; Chizzkuni), "fees for magic" (*Ibid.*; Bachya),
or, "magical tests" (*Lekach Tov*).

22:8   **Moabite.** But the Midianites did not remain (*Sanhedrin* 105a).

22:9   **appeared** (Saadia). Literally, "came."

22:16   **in the name of** . . . Literally, "Thus says . . ."

20 That night, God appeared* to Balaam and said to him, "If the men **22** have come to summon you, set out and go with them. But only do exactly as I instruct you."

21 When Balaam got up in the morning, he saddled his female donkey,* and went* with the Moabite dignitaries. **22** God displayed anger because [Balaam was so anxious to]* go, and an angel of God planted himself in the road to oppose him. [Balaam] was riding on his donkey, accompanied by his two boy servants.

23 When the donkey saw God's angel standing in the road with a drawn sword in his hand, the donkey went aside from the road into the field. Balaam beat the donkey to get it back on the road.

24 God's angel then stood in a narrow path* through the vineyards, where there was a fence on either side. **25** When the donkey saw God's angel, it edged over to the side, crushing Balaam's foot against the wall. [Balaam] beat it even more.

26 God's angel continued ahead [of Balaam], and he stood in a narrow place, where there was no room to turn right or left. **27** When the donkey saw God's angel, it lay down [refusing to budge] for Balaam. Balaam lost his temper, and beat the donkey with a stick.

28 God then gave the donkey the power of speech,* and it said to Balaam, "What have I done to you that you beat me these three times?"

29 "You have been playing games* with me!" shouted Balaam at the donkey. "If I had had a sword in my hand just now, I would have killed you!"

30 The donkey replied to Balaam, "Am I not your [old] donkey? You have been riding on me as far back as you remember.* Have I ever been in the habit* of doing this to you?"

"No," replied [Balaam].

31 God then gave Balaam the ability to see,* and he perceived the angel

22:20 **appeared.** See 22:9.
22:21 **female donkey.** See note on Exodus 22:18.
— **and went.** At a distance (Chizzkuni).
22:22 **was so anxious to** (see *Lekach Tov*; *HaKethav VeHaKabbalah*).
22:24 **narrow path** (Targum; Saadia; *Lekach Tov*; Septuagint). Wide enough for a single man (Radak, *Sherashim*).
22:28 **gave the donkey ...** Literally, "opened the donkey's mouth." However, some say that the donkey did not actually speak, but that this was a prophetic vision (*Moreh Nevukhim* 2:42).
22:29 **playing games.** (Radak, *Sherashim*). *Hith-olal* in Hebrew; see Exodus 10:2. Or, "embarrassed" (Rashi), "insulted" (*Lekach Tov*). Or, "rebelled" (Saadia).
22:30 **as far back as you remember.** Literally, "From when you first started until now."
— **been in the habit** (Saadia; Ibn Ezra; Radak, *Sherashim*). Or, "have I ever been unmindful" (Septuagint). Also, possibly, "have I ever endangered you."
22:31 **gave ... ability to see** (Saadia). Literally, "opened the eyes of."

22 standing in the road, with a drawn sword in his hand. [Balaam] kneeled and prostrated himself on his face.

³² God's angel said to him, "Why did you beat your donkey these three times? I have come out to oppose you, because your errand is obnoxious to me. ³³ When the donkey saw me, it turned aside these three times. If it had not turned aside before me, as it did now, I would have killed you and spared [the donkey]."

³⁴ Balaam said to God's angel, "I have sinned! I did not know that you were standing on the road before me. If you consider it wrong [for me to go], I will go back home."

³⁵ God's angel said to Balaam, "Go with the men. But do not say anything other than the exact words that I declare to you."

Balaam thus continued with Balak's dignitaries. ³⁶ When Balak heard that Balaam had arrived, he went out to meet him in the City of Moab,* which was at the extreme end of his territory, on the edge of the Arnon.* ³⁷ Balak said to Balaam, "I had to make so much effort to get you. Why did you not come to me [right away]? Did you think that I couldn't honor you?"

³⁸ "And now that I have come to you," replied Balaam to Balak, "do you think that I can say anything? I can only declare the words that God places in my mouth."

³⁹ Balaam went with Balak, and they came to the city's suburbs.* ⁴⁰ Balak sacrificed* cattle and sheep, sending some to Balaam and the dignitaries who were with him.

⁴¹ In the morning, Balak took Balaam, and brought him to the High Altars of Baal,* where he could see [as far as]* the outer edges of the [Israelite] people.

22:36 **City of Moab.** The capital of Moab (Rashi). Some identify this with Ar, see 21:15, 21:28. It was some 23 miles from the dead sea.

— **Arnon.** The northern border of Moab, since Balaam was coming from the north. See 21:13.

22:39 **city's suburbs** (cf. Targum). Or, "the city's outer markets" (Rashi; *Tanchuma* 11). Others see Kiryath Chutzoth here as a proper noun (Ibn Ezra).

22:40 **sacrificed.** For food (*Lekach Tov*).

22:41 **High Altars of Baal.** *Bamoth Baal* in Hebrew. See 23:9. Some identify this with Baaley Bamoth Arnon in 21:28 (Ibn Ezra). Others say that this was an idolatrous temple (*Lekach Tov; Midrash Hagadol*), possibly that of Baal Peor in 25:3 (*Targum Yonathan; BeMidbar Rabbah* 20:18). Others say that it was the plain of altars (Chizzkuni).

Josephus states that it was a mountain some 60 furlongs or 5.5 miles from the Israelite camp (*Antiquities* 4:6:4). This would appear to indicate that Bamoth Baal was the same as Bamoth in 21:19. Geographically, this would appear to indicate that Balaam was on the mountain spur directly to the south of the one containing Mount Nebo, which would be a little over 5 miles from the Israelite camp. This may be the site of the present Um Juresa.

— **as far as** (*Baaley Tosafoth; Paaneach Raza*; cf. Ramban). Now he saw the entire camp, because later he saw only part of it (23:13; *Lekach Tov*). Others, however, maintain that he only saw "the edge of

¹ "Build seven altars for me here," said Balaam to Balak, "and prepare **23** for me seven bulls and seven rams."

² When Balak did as Balaam had requested, Balak and Balaam sacrificed a bull and ram as a burnt offering on each altar. ³ Balaam said to Balak, "Keep a vigil beside your burnt offerings, and I will go. Hopefully, God will appear to me, and declare that He will show me something that I can relate to you." With that, [Balaam] went off to meditate.*

⁴ God appeared to Balaam. "I have set up seven altars," said [Balaam] to [God], "and I have sacrificed a bull and ram as a burnt offering on each altar."

⁵ God placed a message in Balaam's mouth and said, "Go back to Balak, and declare exactly [what I have told you]." ⁶ When [Balaam] returned, Balak was still standing in vigil over his burnt offering, along with all the Moabite dignitaries.

⁷ [Balaam] declared his oracle, and said, "Balak, king of Moab, has brought me from Aram,* from the hills of the east,* [telling me] to come curse Jacob and conjure divine wrath against Israel. ⁸ But what curse can I pronounce if God will not grant a curse? What divine wrath can I conjure if God will not be angry?

⁹ "I see [this nation] from mountain tops, and gaze on it from the heights. It is a nation dwelling alone at peace, not counting itself among other nations. ¹⁰ Jacob [is like] the dust;* who can count his [hordes]? Who can number the seed* of Israel? Let me die the death of the upright, but let my end be like his!"

¹¹ Balak said to Balaam, "What have you done to me? I brought you to curse my enemies, but you have made every effort to bless them!"

¹² [Balaam] interrupted and said, "Didn't [I tell you that] I must be very careful to say only what God tells me?"

¹³ "If you would," replied Balak, "come with me to another place. There

---

the camp" (*Tur*; cf. Ramban). Some say that he saw the camp's outcasts (*Midrash HaGadol*; cf. *Targum Yonathan*).

23:3 **to meditate** (Saadia). *Shefi* in Hebrew. Also, "alone" (Targum; Rashi). Or, "to an isolated peak" (Ibn Ezra; Ibn Janach; Radak, *Sherashim*; cf. Jeremiah 3:20); "broken and depressed" (*Targum Yonathan*; Ibn Ezra; from Psalms 109:16); "limping" (*Targum Yerushalmi*; Ibn Ezra; Rashbam; from Job 33:21); "with a dislocated leg" (*Paneach Raza*; Sotah 10a); "straight ahead (Septuagint); "like a snake" (*Shefifon*, Genesis 49:17; *Lekach Tov*). Others say that Shefi here is the name of an unclean angel (*Zohar*; *Kav HaYashar* 29; *MeAm Lo'ez*).

23:7 **Aram.** See note on 22:5.

— **hills of the east.** Ibid. Some identify these with the hills of Gilead, through which Baalam had to pass (*Tur*).

23:10 **like the dust.** See Genesis 13:16, 28:14.

— **seed** (Saadia; Rashi; Hirsch). *Robha* in Hebrew, cf. Leviticus 19:19, 20:16. Or, "even a fourth" (Targum; Ibn Ezra; Radak, *Sherashim*); or, "families" (Septuagint).

23 you will be able to see only a small section of [the Israelite camp], and you will not have to see them all. From there you may be able to curse them for me."

¹⁴ With that, he took [Balaam] to Lookout Field* at the top of the cliff.* There he built seven altars and offered* a bull and a ram on each altar. ¹⁵ "Keep a vigil here with your burnt offering," said [Balaam] to Balak, "and I will go yonder and seek a vision."

¹⁶ God appeared to Balaam, and placed a message in his mouth. He said, "Return to Balak, and declare exactly [what I have told you]."

¹⁷ When [Balaam] returned, [Balak] was standing vigil over his burnt offering, along with the Moabite dignitaries. "What has God declared?" asked Balak.

¹⁸ [Balaam] proclaimed his oracle and said, "Rise, Balak, and listen: pay close attention to my insight,* son of Tzippor. ¹⁹ God is not human that He should be false,* nor mortal that He should change His mind.* Shall He say something and not do it, or speak and not fulfill? ²⁰ It is a blessing that I have taken, and when there is such a blessing,* I cannot reverse it.

²¹ "[God] does not look* at wrongdoing* in Jacob, and He sees no vice* in Israel. God their* Lord is with them, and they have the King's friendship.* ²² Since God brought them out of Egypt, they are like His highest expression of strength.*

23:14 **Lookout Field.** (cf. Rashi). *Sedeh HaTzofim* in Hebrew. Or, "Field of the Seers" or "Prophets" (*Or HaGanuz* on *Bahir* 62; cf. *Megillah* 2b, end).

— **cliff.** *Pisgah.* See note on 21:19. It is possible that he took him somewhat behind Mount Nebo, where he could only see part of the camp.

— **offered.** It appears that only Balak offered sacrifice this time. (see *Tzafanath Paaneach*).

23:18 **insight.** *Ad* in Hebrew. Or, "my words" (Targum; Saadia; Radak, *Sherashim*). Or, "testimony" (Septuagint), or, "listen to me" (Hirsch).

23:19 **false.** *Kazav* in Hebrew. Or, "waver" (Septuagint).

— **change His mind.** *Yith-nachem* in Hebrew. Or, "be threatened" (Septuagint).

23:20 **and when there is such blessing . . .** Or, "since God has blessed them . . ."(Rashi; Ibn Ezra; *Baaley Tosafoth*); "I will bless them and not reverse it" (Targum; Saadia; Septuagint); "I will not return unless I bless them" (*Lekach Tov*); or, "I will not hold back a blessing from them" (*Targum Yonathan*).

23:21 **God does not look** (*Tanchuma* 14; Rashi; Rashbam; Ibn Ezra). Or, "One cannot see" (Bachya; Septuagint); or "I do not see" (*Targum Yonathan*).

— **wrongdoing.** *Aven* in Hebrew. Or, "falsehood" (Ramban; Radak, *Sherashim*); or, "trouble" (Septuagint).

— **vice.** *Amal* in Hebrew. See Psalms 10:7. Or, "sorrow" (Septuagint). Thus, according to the Septuagint, "No trouble or sorrow shall be seen in Israel."

— **their.** Literally, "his." The entire verse is in the collective singular.

— **friendship.** (Rashi; Saadia). *Teruah* in Hebrew; cf. Psalms 27:6, Job 33:26. Or, "divine presence" (Targum; Rashbam); "trumpet blast" (Ibn Ezra; Chizzkuni; see above 10:9); "power" (Bachya); "homage to the king" (Hirsch); or, "glory of kings" (Septuagint).

23:22 **His highest expression of strength** (Rashi; Targum). *Toafoth R'em* in Hebrew; see below 24:8. Also see Psalms 95:4. Or, "like the horns of the *r'em*" (Saadia; Ibn Ezra) where the *r'em* is a unicorn or rhinocerous (Radak, *Sherashim*; Septuagint); the white antelope (Saadia), the wild ox, aurochs, or

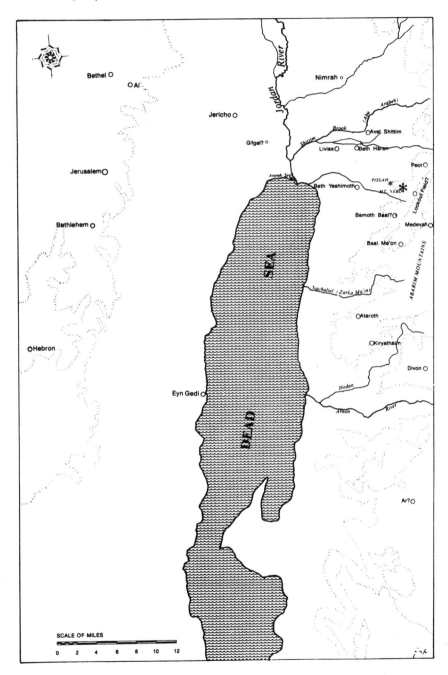

PLATE 28.   AREA OF THE FINAL CAMP

23   ²³ "No black magic can [be effective] against Jacob, and no occult powers against Israel. 'How is God acting?' is the only question pertinent to Jacob and Israel. ²⁴ This is a nation that rises like the king of beasts*, and lifts itself like a lion. It does not lie down until it eats its prey and drinks the blood of its kill."

²⁵ Balak said to Balaam, "If you can't curse them, at least don't bless them!"

²⁶ Balaam interrupted and said to Balak, "My exact words to you were, 'I will do precisely what God declares,' weren't they?"

²⁷ "If you would, let's go on," said Balak to Balaam. "I will take you somewhere else. Hopefully, God will consider it proper* to let you curse them for me there."

²⁸ Balak took Balaam to the top of the peak* that overlooks the Wasteland.* ²⁹ Balaam said to Balak, "Build me seven altars here, and prepare for me here seven bulls and seven rams." ³⁰ Balak did as Balaam said, and he sacrificed a bull and ram as a burnt offering on each altar.

24   ¹ When Balaam realized that God desired to bless Israel, he did not seek out the occult forces as he had done before. Instead, he set his gaze toward the desert.* ² When Balaam raised his eyes, and saw Israel dwelling at peace by tribes, God's spirit was on him. ³ He proclaimed his oracle and said, "This is the word of Beor's son Balaam, the word of the man with the enlightened* eye. ⁴ It is the word of one who hears God's sayings, who sees a vision of the Almighty,* falling [into a meditative trance]* with mystical insight.*

---

bison. See Deuteronomy 33:17, Psalms 22:22, 29:6. Or, "like the *r'em's* power." (Radak, *Sherashim*; Ibn Janach), "like the glory of a unicorn" (Septuagint); "like the mighty mountains" (*Lekach Tov*); "like the angels [and] demons" (*Gittin* 68b); "like the power of demons" (Rashi).

23:24 king of beasts. *Lavi* in Hebrew. See below, 24:9, Genesis 49:9.

23:27 proper (Targum; Septuagint). *Yashar* in Hebrew. Or, "easy." (Saadia).

23:28 peak (Targum; Saadia). Others take Peor here as a proper noun (Septuagint), possibly associated with Baal Peor in 25:3 (cf. Rashi). This overlooked the valley where the Israelites were camped (cf. Deuteronomy 3:29). One ancient source states that Peor is between Livias and Esbus (Cheshbon) (Eusebius, s.v. Aravoth Moab). This would place it to the north of Mount Nebo, possibly in the area of the present Mushakar. From there, he would be able to look east toward the desert (24:1).

—   **Wasteland.** See note on 21:20.

24:1   desert. Some say the Western Plains of Moab (Chizzkuni). It is also possible that he stood contemplating the Syrian Desert, which would have been visible toward the east.

24:3   enlightened (Ramban; *Midrash Aggadah*). *Shethum* in Hebrew. Or, "future seeing eye" (*Lekach Tov*), "seeing eye" (Targum; Saadia); "open eye" (Rashbam; Radak, *Sherashim*; Rashi); "truesighted eye" (Septuagint); "sleepless" (Ibn Janach), "evil eye" (*Zohar* 1:68b); "dislocated" (Rashi); "blinded" (*Sanhedrin* 105a; *Niddah* 31a).

24:4   Almighty. *Shaddai* in Hebrew. See Genesis 17:1; Exodus 6:3.

—   **falling into a meditative trance** (Targum; Rashi; Ibn Ezra); involving meditation (Ralbag; cf. Abarbanel). Some say that this involved sexual practices (*Sanhedrin* 105a; see note on 22:21). Some sources maintain that Balaam would actually fall to the ground during prophecy (*Lekach Tov*; Josephus, *Antiquities* 4:6:5); cf. 1 Samuel 19:24, Ezekiel 1:28, Daniel 8:18. Some say that he fell

⁵ "How good are your tents, Jacob, your tabernacles, Israel. ⁶ [They] **24** stretch out like streams,* like gardens by the river; they are like the aloes* God has planted, like cedars by the water. ⁷ His dipper* shall overflow, and his crops shall have abundant water.*

"When their kingdom is established, their king shall be greater than Agag.* ⁸ Since God brought them out of Egypt, they are like His highest expression of strength.* [God]* shall devour His enemy nations, grinding* their bones and piercing them with His arrows.* ⁹ [Israel] crouches, lies like a lion, like an awesome lion, who will dare rouse him?* Those who bless you are blessed, and those who curse you are cursed.*'"

¹⁰ Furious at Balaam, Balak struck his hands together. "I brought you to curse my enemies," said Balak to Balaam, "but you blessed them these three times! ¹¹ Now go home as fast as you can!* I promised to honor you, but God won't let you get any honor!"

¹² Balaam said to Balak, "My exact words to the mesengers you sent me were, ¹³ 'Even if Balak gives me his whole palace full of gold and silver, I cannot do anything good or bad on my own that would violate God's word.' Isn't that true? I must proclaim whatever God declares. ¹⁴ Now I am returning to my people, but first I will advise you about what this nation will do to your people in the final days."

¹⁵ He then proclaimed his oracle and said, "This is the word of Beor's son Balaam, the word of the man with the enlightened eye. ¹⁶ It is the word of the one who hears God's sayings and knows the Highest One's will; who

---

because he was uncircumcised (*Midrash Aggadah*; cf. Genesis 17:3). Or, "the one who sees a vision of God in a trance and has open eyes" (Septuagint).

— **mystical insight.** Literally, "uncovered eyes."

24:6 **They stretch out . . .** Or, "like shady groves" (Septuagint).

— **aloes** (Targum; Rashi; Rashbam; Ibn Ezra). *Ahalim* in Hebrew; see Psalms 45:9, Proverbs 7:17, Song of Songs 4:14. See note on Exodus 30:23, s.v. "fragrant cinnamon." Or, "tents" (Rashi; Saadia; Ralbag; Septuagint).

24:7 **dipper** (cf. Rashi, Ibn Ezra). *Dal* in Hebrew. Or, "branches" (Chizzkuni), "poor" (*Nedarim* 81a), or, "power" (*Baaley Tosafoth*; see next note).

— **and his crops . . .** (cf. Ibn Ezra). Or, "his power will overflow, and his offspring against the mighty waters" (*Baaley Tosafoth*). This is thus rendered, "A king shall come forth from his children, and he shall rule many nations" (Targum; Septuagint). The agreement here between the Targum and the Septuagint is highly significant.

— **Agag.** A generic name for the kings of Amalek (Rashbam; Ramban); see notes on Genesis 12:15, 20:2. See 1 Samuel 15:8; Esther 3:1. The Septuagint identifies Agag with Gog; cf. Ezekiel 38:2.

24:8 **God brought . . .** See above, 23:22.

— **God** (Ralbag). Or, "they shall" (Targum).

— **grinding . . .** (Rashi). Or, "draining their marrow." (Septuagint).

— **piercing them . . .** (Saadia, Radak, *Sherashim*; Septuagint). Or, "dipping his arrows [in their blood]" (Rashi), or, "Taking away their portion" (Targum).

24:9 **Israel . . . lies . . .** See Genesis 49:9.

— **Those who bless . . .** See Genesis 12:3.

24:11 **Now go home . . .** (Bachya; Radak, *Sherashim*). Literally, "flee."

24 sees a vision of the Almighty while fallen [in a meditative trance] with mystical insight.

¹⁷ "I see it, but not now; I perceive it, but not in the near future. A star* shall go forth from Jacob, and a staff shall arise in Israel, crushing all of Moab's princes,* and dominating* all of Seth's* descendants. ¹⁸ Edom shall be demolished,* and his enemy Seir destroyed,* but Israel shall be triumphant. ¹⁹ Out of Jacob shall come an absolute ruler* who will obliterate the city's last survivors.*"

²⁰ When [Balaam] saw* Amalek,* he proclaimed his oracle and said, "First among nations is Amalek, but in the end he will be destroyed forever."

²¹ When he saw the Kenites,* he proclaimed his oracle and said, "You live in a fortress,* and have placed your nest* in a cliff. ²² But when the time comes to destroy the Kenites,* how long will Assyria* hold back from you*?"

²³ He then declared his oracle and said, "Alas! Who can survive God's devastation? ²⁴ Warships* shall come from the ports* of the Kittim,* and they will lay waste Assyria and Eber.* But in the end they too shall be destroyed forever."

24:17 star. A person who rises high above the others (cf. Ramban). This is a messianic prophecy, (see *Yad, Melachim* 11:1).

— **princes** (Targum; Septuagint). Or, "corners" (Saadia; Radak, *Sherashim*).

— **dominating** (Targum). *Karkar* in Hebrew. Or, "devastating" (Rashi; Radak, *Sherashim*; Septuagint).

— **Seth.** The ancestor of Noah, and hence, the father of all mankind (Rashi; cf. Targum). Or, "the sons of incest," denoting Ammon and Moab (Chizzkuni; see Genesis 19:37,38).

24:18 demolished (Saadia; Ibn Ezra). Or, "occupied" (Septuagint).

— . **and his enemy . . .** Or, "he shall be destroyed by his enemy Seir" (cf. Ramban).

24:19 absolute ruler (Rashi; Radak, *Sherashim*), *Yerd* in Hebrew. Or, "come down" (Targum), or, "one who rises up" (Septuagint).

— **the city's last survivors** (Ramban). Or, "those who escape the city" (Septuagint).

24:20 saw. Literally, because Amalek's territories are visible from the Moabite heights (Ramban). Or, "saw in prophecy" (Rashi; Ibn Ezra).

— **Amalek.** See Genesis 36:12, Exodus 17:8, Deuteronomy 25:19.

24:21 Kenites. See Genesis 15:19. This was a tribe that lived near Amalek, perhaps on the western bank of the Dead Sea (Rashi; cf. 1 Samuel 15:6). Some identify them with Ammon (Chizzkuni). Others say that they were the people of Jethro's family (*Targum Yonathan*; Ibn Ezra; cf. *Sanhedrin* 106a). See Joshua 15:22, 1 Chronicles 2:55.

— **You live in a fortress** (Bachya). Or, "Live in a fortress" as advice (Ramban; *Midrash Aggadah*).

— **nest.** *Kin* in Hebrew, a play on Kenite (Bachya).

24:22 the Kenites. Literally, Kain, the same as Cain. Here it is a place name (cf. Chizzkuni).

— **Assyria.** See Genesis 2:14, 10:11. Assyria eventually dominated the entire middle east, and exiled many of its inhabitants, as described in 2 Kings 16 ff.

— **hold back from you.** Or, "How long will Assyria hold you in captivity!" (Rashi).

24:24 Warships . . . See Daniel 11:30. Also see Isaiah 33:30, Ezekiel 30:9. *Tzim* in Hebrew. Or, "one shall come forth" (Septuagint).

— **ports** (Saadia). *Yad* in Hebrew.

— **Kittim.** See Genesis 10:4. Also see Isaiah 23:1,12, Jeremiah 2:10, Ezekiel 27:6. These are identified with the Romans (Targum), the Greeks (Ibn Ezra), or the Cypriots (Saadia).

— **Eber . . .** A grandson of Shem (Genesis 10:21,24), and hence, the Semitic nations (*Targum Yona-*

²⁵ With that, Balaam set out* and returned home. Balak also went on his **24** way.

[107. Israel Sins with Moab]

¹ Israel was staying in Shittim* when the people began to* behave **25** immorally with the Moabite* girls. ² [The girls] invited the people to their religious sacrifices, and the people ate and worshiped the [Moabite] gods. ³ Israel thus became involved* with Baal Peor,* and God displayed anger against Israel.*

⁴ God said to Moses, "Take the people's leaders, and [have them] impale* [the idolators]* publicly* before God. This will reverse God's display of anger against Israel."

⁵ Moses said to Israel's judges, "Each of you must kill your constituents* who were involved with Baal Peor."

⁶ [The judges] were still weeping [in indecision]* at the Communion Tent entrance, when an Israelite* brought forth a Midianite* woman to his brethren before the eyes of Moses and the Israelite community. ⁷ When Pinchas,* a son of Eleazar and a grandson of Aaron the priest, saw this, he rose up from the midst of the assemblage and took a spear in his hand. ⁸ He

---

than). However, Eber also denotes the Hebrews, and hence, the Israelites (Ramban). Others have, "all who live on the other side [of the Euphrates]" (Targum).

24:25 **Balaam set out.** See below, 31:8.

25:1 **Shittim.** This is the "stream of Shittim" mentioned in Joel 4:18 (*Sefer HaYashar*). This can also be translated "Acacia Grove" (cf. Saadia); see Exodus 25:4. The Israelites remained here until they crossed the Jordan (Joshua 2:1, 3:1). See note on 22:1.

— **began to** (Targum). Or, "desecrated themselves" (Septuagint). This was done at Balaam's advice (below, 31:16; *Sanhedrin* 106a; *Tanchuma* 18; *Josephus*, 4:6:6).

— **Moabite girls.** The Moabite girls may have initiated this, but it was the Midianite girls who were primarily involved; see below 25:6, 31:2,15,16 (Josephus, *Antiquities* 4:6:7; cf. *Bava Kama* 38a,b; Ramban on 25:18; Abarbanel; Malbim).

25:3 **became involved.** *Tzamad* in Hebrew; literally, "paired off" (Bachya).

— **Baal Peor.** An idol associated with Peor (see 23:28). According to Talmudic tradition, the worship of this idol involved scatological practices (*Sifri*; *Sanhedrin* 60b, 64a; Rashi).

— **God displayed anger . . .** This involved the plague mentioned below, 25:9 (Rashi).

25:4 **impale.** *Hoka* in Hebrew, from the root *yaka*. Related to *taka*, to impale. Or, "hang" (*Sanhedrin* 34b; Rashi); "kill" (Targum); or, "judge" (Septuagint).

— **the idolators** (Targum; Rashi; Ibn Ezra; cf. *Sanhedrin* 35b). This was never accomplished (Ramban; see 25:6).

— **publicly** (Rashi; Ibn Ezra; *Lekach Tov*). Literally, "before the sun." Or, "through witnesses" (*Lekach Tov*). Cf. note on Exodus 22:2. Josephus also notes that Moses assembled all the people (*Antiquities* 4:6:10).

25:5 **constituents** (cf. *Yerushalmi, Sanhedrin* 10:2). Literally, "his men". Or, "his neighbors" (Saadia).

25:6 **in indecision** (cf. Ramban; *Sanhedrin* 82a). Or, "the people were weeping in prayer" (Ibn Ezra), because the plague had begun (Bachya), or because they had been commanded to kill (Chizzkuni).

— **an Israelite.** See 25:14. The man, Zimri, publicly confronted Moses (Josephus, *Antiquities* 4:6:11), pointing out that Moses was vulnerable because Moses had married a Midianite woman (Exodus 2:16,21; above 12:1; *Sanhedrin* 82a; *Targum Yonathan*; *BeMidbar Rabbah* 20:25).

— **Midianite.** See 25:1, 25:15.

25:7 **Pinchas.** See Exodus 6:25.

25 followed the Israelite man into the tent's inner chamber,* and ran them
through, [driving the spear] through the Israelite man and the woman's
groin.*

With that, the plague that had struck the Israelites was arrested. ⁹ In
that plague, 24,000 people had died.

Pinchas   פִּינְחָס

[108. Pinchas' Reward]

¹⁰ God spoke to Moses, saying, ¹¹ "Pinchas (a son of Eleazar and grandson of Aaron the priest) was the one who zealously took up My cause
among the Israelites and turned My anger away from them, so that I did not
destroy them in My demand for exclusive worship.* ¹² Therefore, tell him
that I have given him My covenant of peace. ¹³ This shall imply a covenant
of eternal priesthood* to him and his descendants after him. It is [given to
him] because he zealously took up God's cause and made atonement for the
Israelites."

¹⁴ The name of the man who was killed along with the Midianite
woman was Zimri son of Salu,* a prince of the Simeonite* paternal line.
¹⁵ The name of the Midianite woman who was killed was Kazbi,* the
daughter of Tzur,* governor* of a paternal line in Midian.

[109. Orders to Attack Midian]

¹⁶ God spoke to Moses, saying, ¹⁷ "Attack the Midianites and kill them
¹⁸ since they attacked you through their plot with Peor,* as well as through

---

25:8 **inner chamber.** *Kubbah* in Hebrew, like the womb of a woman, which is also called *kubbah* (cf. Radak, *Sherashim*; Septuagint).
— **groin.** Also *kubbah*. (see Radak; *Lekach Tov*; Chizzkuni). Or, "in her tent" (Ibn Ezra).
25:11 **exclusive worship.** See Exodus 20:5 (cf. Ibn Ezra).
25:13 **eternal priesthood.** This implies that his line of descendants would never die out (Ralbag). It was descendants of Pinchas who served as high priests in the first and second Temples (1 Chronicles 5:30-40, 6:34-38; Ibn Ezra; Ralbag; Chizzkuni).
25:14 **Zimri son of Salu.** The Talmud identifies him with Shelumiel son of Tzuri-Shaddai in 1:6 (*Sanhedrin* 82b). He was head of the Saulite family in the tribe of Simeon (26:13; Sanhedrin ibid.; *HaKethav VeHaKabbalah* on Genesis 46:10).
— **Simeonite.** See note on 26:14.
25:15 **Kazbi.** Or Kozbi. Talmudic sources state that her name was also Sh'vilani (*Sanhedrin* 82b), Shelonai (*Targum Yonathan*) or Shulani (*Arukh*).
— **Tzur.** a king of Midian; see below 31:8, Joshua 13:21 (*Lekach Tov*). There is a Midrashic teaching that Kazbi was a daughter of Balak (22:2; *Targum Yonathan*; *BeMidbar Rabbah* 20:24; *Midrash Aggadah* on 25:6). Some say that Kazbi was a grand-daughter of Tzur on her mother's side (cf. *Tzafanath Paneach*). It is also possible that Balak was her maternal grandfather.
— **govenor.** Literally, "head of nations."
25:18 **Peor.** Although Peor was a Moabite god, it was the Midianites' idea to use it as a means of harming the Israelites (*Tzafanath Paneach*).

their sister, Kazbi, daughter of a Midianite prince, who was killed on the 25
day of plague that resulted from Peor."

¹ It was now after the plague.* 26

[110. The New Census: Reuben]

God spoke to Moses and Eleazar (son of Aaron the Priest), saying,
² "Take a census of the entire Israelite community by paternal lines, [count-
ing] every male over 20 years old who is fit for duty."

³ Moses and Eleazar the priest spoke to [the Israelites] in the Western
Plains of Moab near the Jordan [opposite] Jericho, saying, "[Count] those
over 20 years old, just as God commanded Moses and the Israelites who
had left Egypt."

⁵ Reuben was Israel's first-born. The descendants of Reuben* were the
Enochite family from Enoch,* the Paluite family from Palu, ⁶ the Chetzronite family from Chetzron, and the Karmite family from Karmi. ⁷ These were
the Reubenite families, and their tally was 43,730.*

⁸ The sons of Palu: Eliav.

⁹ The sons of Eliav: Nemuel, Dathan and Aviram.* Dathan and Aviram
were the communal leaders who led a revolution against Moses and Aaron as
part of Korach's rebellion against God. ¹⁰ The earth opened its mouth and
swallowed them and Korach when the [rebellious] group died and* fire
annihilated 250 men. This involved a divine miracle. ¹¹ The sons of Korach,*
however, did not die.

[111. Simeon]

¹² By families, the descendants of Simeon* were the Nemuelite family
from Nemuel,* the Yaminite family from Yamini, the Yakhinite family from

---

26:1 **after the plague.** The Midianites were not attacked until later, see below 31:2 (*Lekach Tov*).
26:5 **Reuben.** See Genesis 46:9, Exodus 6:14.
26:5 **Enoch.** Chanokh in Hebrew.
26:7 **43,730.** In the first census, their number was 46,500 (1:21), so they suffered a net loss of 2770 (*Lekach Tov*).
26:9 **Dathan and Aviram.** See Numbers 16:1, Deuteronomy 11:6.
26:10 **and** (Saadia).
26:11 **sons of Korach.** Assir, Elkana and Aviasaph (Exodus 6:24).
26:12 **Simeon.** Of Simeon's sons, Ohad, mentioned in Genesis 46:10 and Exodus 6:15, is missing here. Some say that it is because he died childless (*Lekach Tov*). Others say that this family was wiped out in the desert (Rashi on 26:13; *Midrash Aggadah*; from *Yerushalmi, Yoma* 1:1, 2a), or during the plague that had just occurred (Rashi). According to others, this family became extinct in Egypt (*Midrash Aggadah*). The same is true of the other families mentioned in Genesis but not here.
— **Nemuel.** Yemuel in Genesis 46:10 (*Lekach Tov*).

26   Yakhin, [13] the Zarchite family from Zerach,* and the Saulite family from
Saul. [14] These are the families of Simeon, [numbering] 22,200.*

[112. Gad]

[15] By families, the descendants of Gad* were the Tzefonite family from
Tzefon,* the Chaggite family from Chaggi, the Shunite family from Shuni,
[16] the Aznite family from Azni,* the Erite family from Eri, [17] the Arodite
family from Arod,* and the Arelite family from Areli. [18] These are the families of Gad's descendants, their tally being 40,500.*

[113. Judah]

[19] The [first] sons of Judah were Er and Onan, but Er and Onan died in
the land of Canaan.* [20] By families, then, the descendants of Judah* were
the Shelanite family from Shelah, the Partzite family from Peretz, and the
Zarchite family from Zerach.

[21] The descendants of Peretz were the Chetzronite family from Chetzron, and the Chamulite family from Chamul.*

[22] These are the families of Judah, their tally being 76,500.*

[114. Issachar]

[23] By families, the descendants of Issachar* were the Tolaite family from
Tola, the Punite family from Puva.* [24] the Yashuvite family from Yashuv,*
and the Shimronite family from Shimron. [25] These are the families of
Issachar, their tally being 64,300.*

[115. Zebulun]

[26] By their families, the descendants of Zebulun* were the Sardite

---

26:13 **Zerach.** Tzohar in Genesis (Rashi).
26:14 **22,200.** In the first census, they were 59,300 (1:23), so they suffered a loss of 37,100. Some say that
since Zimri was of the tribe of Simeon, all 24,000 who died in the plague (25:9) were from Simeon
(Rashi; *Lekach Tov*). Thus, Simeon was the instigator of most of the rebellion in the desert (Ralbag).
26:15 **Gad.** See Genesis 46:16.
—   **Tzefon.** Tzefion in Genesis.
26:16 **Azni.** Or Ozni. Etzbon in Genesis.
26:17 **Arod.** Arodi in Genesis.
26:18 **40,500.** Down by 5150 from the first census, which showed 45,650. Reuben, Simeon and Gad were
on the south side (2:10-16), and this side suffered a net loss of 45,020.
26:19 **Er and Onan died . . .** Genesis 38:7,10.
26:20 **Judah.** See Genesis 46:12.
26:21 **Chetzron . . . Chamul.** *Ibid.*
26:22 **76,500.** Up by 1900 from the first census where it was 74,600.
26:23 **Issachar.** See Genesis 46:13.
—   **Puva.** Puah in 1 Chronicles 7:1, and hence, "the Punite."
26:24 **Yashuv.** Yov in Genesis (q.v.).
26:25 **64,300.** Up 9900 from 54,400 in the first census (1:27).
26:26 **Zebulun.** See Genesis 46:14.

family from Sered, the Elonite family from Elon, and the Yachliélite family **26**
from Yachliel. ²⁷ These are the families of Zebulun, their tally being
60,500.*

[116. Manasseh]

²⁸ By their families, the descendants of Joseph were Manasseh and
Ephraim.

²⁹ The descendants of Manasseh consisted of the Makhirite family from
Makhir.* Makhir's son was Gilead,* and from Gilead came the family of the
Gileadites.

³⁰ These were the descendants of Gilead: The Iyezerite family from
Iyezer,* the Chelekite family from Chelek,* ³¹ the Asrielite family from
Asriel,* the Shikhmite family from Shekhem,* ³² the Shemidaite family
from Shemida,* and the Chefrite family from Chefer.*

³³ Chefer's son, Tzelafchad,* did not have any sons, only daughters.*
The names of Tzelafchad's daughters were Machla, No'ah, Chaglah, Milkah and Tirtzah.*

³⁴ These are the families of Manasseh, and their tally was 52,700.*

[117. Ephraim]

³⁵ By their families, the descendants of Ephraim* were the Shuthalchite
family from Shuthelach,* the Bakhrite family from Bekher,* and the
Tachanite family from Tachan.*

26:27 60,500. Up 3100 from 57,400 in the first census (1:31). Judah, Issachar and Zebulun were on the east
side (2:3-9) and this side had a net gain of 14,900.
26:29 Makhir. See Genesis 50:23.
—   **Gilead.** See Joshua 17:3, 1 Chronicles 2:21,23, 7:14,17.
26:30 Iyezar. Aviezer in Joshua 17:2, Judges 6:11,24,34, 8:2,32; Septuagint. Also see 1 Chronicles 7:18,
2 Samuel 23:27.
—   **Chelek.** See Joshua 17:2.
26:31 Asriel. See Joshua 17:2, 1 Chronicles 7:14.
—   **Shekhem.** See Joshua 17:2, 1 Chronicles 7:19. He may have been named after the city Shechem
which was given to Joseph; Genesis 12:6, 48:22, Joshua 24:32. In Chronicles he is seen as a son of
Shemida. Some, however, maintain that there were two different individuals with the name Shemida
(Radak on Chronicles).
26:32 Shemida. See Joshua 17:2, 1 Chronicles 7:19.
—   **Chefer.** See below, 27:1, Joshua 17:2,3, 1 Chronicles 11:36.
26:33 Tzelafchad. Or, Tzelofchad. See 1 Chronicles 7:15.
—   **daughters.** See below, 27:11, 36:2,6, Joshua 17:3, 1 Chronicles 7:15.
—   **Machla ...** See 27:11, 36:11, Joshua 17:3.
26:34 52,700. Up 20,500 from 32,200 in the first census (1:35).
26:35 Ephraim. He had other sons who were killed; 1 Chronicles 7:21. Also see Septuagint, Genesis 46:20.
—   **Shuthelach.** An ancestor of Joshua; 1 Chronicles 7:20,21.
—   **Bekher.** See note on Genesis 46:21.
—   **Tachan.** A possible ancestor of Joshua, see 1 Chronicles 7:25.

26   ³⁶ The descendants of Shuthelach consisted of the Eranite family from Eran.*
³⁷ These are the families of Ephraim's descendants, their tally being 32,500.*

All these were the descendants of Joseph by their families.

[118. Benjamin]

³⁸ By their families, the descendants of Benjamin* were the Bal'ite family from Bela, the Ashbelite family from Ashbel, the Achiramite family from Achiram,* ³⁹ the Shefufamite family from Shefufam,* and the Chufamite family from Chufam.*

⁴⁰ The sons of Bela were Ard and Naaman.* These gave rise to the Ardite family, and the Naamite family from Naaman.

⁴¹ These are Benjamin's descendants by their families, and their tally was 45,600.*

[119. Dan]

⁴² By their families the descendants of Dan consisted of the Shuchamite family from Shucham.* This was the only family of Dan. ⁴³ The tally of all the families of the Shuchamites was 64,400.*

[120. Asher]

⁴⁴ By their families, the descendants of Asher* were the Yimnah family from Yimnah, the Yishvite family from Yishvi, and the Beri'ite family from Beriah.

⁴⁵ The descendants of Beriah consisted of the Chevrite family from Chever,* and the Malkielite family from Malkiel.*

26:36 **Eran.** Some identify him with Beriah in 1 Chronicles 7:23 (Malbim).
26:37 **32,500.** Down 8000 from 40,500 in the first census (1:33).
26:38 **Benjamin.** See Genesis 46:21.
— **Achiram.** Echi in Genesis.
26:39 **Shefufam.** Muppim in Genesis.
— **Chufam.** Chuppim in Genesis.
26:40 **Ard and Naaman.** Although they are listed as sons of Benjamin, the Septuagint in Genesis amends the text, having them as Bela's sons. Others say that Benjamin actually had sons Ard and Naaman, but that those families became extinct; the families Ard and Naaman here are not the same as those in Genesis (*HaKethav VeHaKabbalah*).
26:41 **45,600.** Up 10,200 from 35,400 in the first census (1:37). Manasseh, Ephraim and Benjamin were on the west side (2:18-24), and their number increased by 22,700.
26:42 **Shucham.** Chushim in Genesis 46:23.
26:43 **64,400.** Up 1700 from 62,700 in the first census (1:39).
26:44 **Asher.** See Genesis 46:17.
26:45 **Chever.** See 1 Chronicles 7:31,32.
— **Malkiel.** See 1 Chronicles 7:31.

⁴⁶ The name of Asher's daughter was Serach.*   **26**
⁴⁷ These are the families of Asher's descendants, their tally being 53,400.*

[121. Naphtali; Total]

⁴⁸ By their families, the descendants of Naphtali* consisted of the Yachtzielite family from Yachtziel, the Gunite family from Guni, ⁴⁹ the Yitzrite family from Yetzer, and the Shilemite family from Shilem. ⁵⁰ These are the families* of Naphtali, their tally being 45,400.*
⁵¹ The total tally of the Israelites was thus 601,730.*

[122. Dividing the Land]

⁵² God spoke to Moses, saying:
⁵³ Among these [people] you shall divide the land as an inheritance, following the number of names [recorded]. ⁵⁴ To a larger [group]* you shall give a larger inheritance, while to a smaller group, you shall give a smaller inheritance. Each one shall thus be given his hereditary property according to its tally.
⁵⁵ However, hereditary property shall be granted to paternal families through a lottery system.* This is how the land shall be divided. ⁵⁶ Whether a group is large or small, its hereditary property shall be divided by a lottery system.

[123. Tally of the Levites]

⁵⁷ These are the tallies of the Levites by their families: the Gershonite family from Gershon, the Kehothite family from Kehoth, and the Merarite family from Merari.
⁵⁸ These are the sub-families of Levi: The Libnite* family, the Chev-

---

26:46 **Serach.** She is mentioned in Genesis 46:17 as one of the people who came to Egypt. According to Talmudic tradition, she was still alive at this time (cf. *Targum Yonathan*).
26:47 **53,400.** Up 11,900 from 41,500 in the first census (1:41).
26:48 **Naphtali.** See Genesis 46:24.
26:50 **families.** There are a total of 57 families mentioned here (Chizzkuni).
—   **45,400.** Down 8000 from 53,400 in the first census (1:43). Dan, Asher and Naphtali were on the north side (2:25-31), and they had a net gain of 5600.
26:51 **601,730.** Down 1820 from 603,550 in the first census (1:46). From all four camps, we have, −45,020 + 14,900 + 22,700 + 5,600 = −1820.
26:54 **group.** Family (Chizzkuni) or tribe (Rashi; Saadia).
26:55 **lottery system.** There were two baskets of slips, one with the names of tribes, and the other with the names of land areas. These would be chosen in pairs to determine which area went to each tribe (*Bava Bathra* 120a; Rashi). Some say that the land was originally divided into 12 equal parts for the lottery, and then each portion was increased or decreased, depending upon the tribes' populations (HaGra on Joshua 17:14; *HaKethav VeHaKabbalah*). Also see below, 33:54, Joshua 14:2, 19:51.
26:58 **Libnite.** From Gershon, 3:18.

26 ronite* family, the Machlite* family, the Mushite* family, and the Korchite* family.

Kehoth had a son Amram. ⁵⁹ The name of Amram's wife was Yokheved,* a daughter* of Levi, who had been born* to Levi in Egypt. She bore Amram's children, Aaron and Moses, as well as their sister Miriam.

⁶⁰ Born to Aaron were Nadav, Avihu, Eleazar and Ithamar. ⁶¹ Nadav and Avihu, however, died* when they offered unauthorized fire before God.

⁶² Counting every male over one month old, the tally of [the Levites] was 23,000.* They were not tallied among the other Israelites because they were not to be given hereditary property among the [other] Israelites.

⁶³ The above was the census that Moses and Eleazar the priest took of the Israelites in the Western Plains of Moab, on the Jericho section of the Jordan. ⁶⁴ Among those [counted now] there was no one [previously] counted by Moses and Aaron the priest, who had taken a census of the Israelites in the Sinai Desert.* ⁶⁵ This was because God had decreed to them that they would all die in the desert, and that not a single man would survive, with the exception of Caleb son of Yefuneh, and Joshua son of Nun.

[124. Tzelafchad's Daughters]

27 ¹ A petition was presented by the daughters of Tzelafchad,* son of Chefer, son of Gilead, son of Makhir, son of Manasseh, of the family of Joseph's son Manasseh. The names of these daughters were Machlah, No'ah, Chaglah, Milkah and Tirtzah. ² They now stood before Moses, Eleazar the priest, the princes, and the entire community* at the Communion Tent entrance with the following petition:

— **Chevronite.** From Chevron (Hebron), son of Kehoth; 3:19.
— **Machlite.** From Merari; 3:20.
— **Mushite.** From Merari; 3:20.
— **Korchite.** From Korach, son of Yitzhar, son of Kehoth; Exodus 6:21 (Ibn Ezra). Missing are the families of Shimi from Gershon (3:18), and Uzziel from Kehoth (3:19), and the other sons of Yitzhar (Exodus 6:21) (Rashi). It is possible that these families became extinct in the desert (*Yerushalmi, Yoma* 1:1, 2a).
26:59 Yokheved. See Exodus 6:20.
— **daughter.** Or, "granddaughter" (see *ibid.*).
— **who had been born.** Or, "whom Othah had born to Levi" (*Baaley Tosafoth*).
26:61 died. Leviticus 10:2.
26:62 23,000. Up 1000 from 22,000 in the first census (3:39).
26:64 Sinai Desert. See 1:1,2.
27:1 Daughters of Tzelafchad. See 26:33. Josephus states that this took place after the battle against Midian (*Antiquities* 4:7:5).
27:2 the princes, and ... Some say that they had previously brought their case to all the lower courts, who now came with them to Moses (*Tanchuma* 9; cf. *Tosefta, Sanhedrin* 7:1). Some say that the question was actually asked by the elders (Josephus, *Antiquities* 4:7:5).

³ "Our father died in the desert. He was not among the members of **27**
Korach's party who protested against God, but he died because of his own
sin* without leaving any sons. ⁴ Why should our father's name be dis-
advantaged in his family merely because he did not have a son? Give us a
portion of land along with our father's brothers."

⁵ Moses brought their case before God.

[125. Inheritance for Daughters]

⁶ God spoke to Moses, saying:

⁷ The daughters of Tzelafchad have a just claim. Give them a hereditary portion of land alongside their father's brothers. Let their father's
hereditary property thus pass over to them.

⁸ Speak to the Israelites and tell them that if a man dies and has no son, his
hereditary property shall pass over to his daughter. ⁹ If he has no daughter,
then his hereditary property shall be given to his brothers. ¹⁰ If he has no
brothers, you shall give his property to his father's brothers. ¹¹ If his father
had no brothers, then you shall give his property to the closest relative in
his family, who shall then be his heir.

This was the decreed law for the Israelites, as God had commanded
Moses.

[126. Moses Told to Prepare for Death]

¹² God said to Moses, "Climb up to the Avarim Mountain* where you
will be able to see the land that I am giving to the Israelites. ¹³ After you see
it, you will be gathered up to your people, just as your brother Aaron was.*
¹⁴ When the community disputed God in the Tzin Desert,* you disobeyed
My commandment [when you were] to sanctify Me before their eyes with
the water."

27:3 **own sin.** Some say that he was the one cutting wood on the Sabbath (15:33). Others say that he was
among those who tried to invade the Holy Land's hill country (14:45) (*Sifri* on 15:33; *Shabbath* 96b,
97a; Rashi).

27:12 **Avarim Mountain.** This is the mountain range to the east of the Dead Sea, particularly at its northern end. They are in front of Mount Nebo (33:47; Deuteronomy 32:49). Some say that they were
called Avarim because they were opposite the crossing point to Jericho (*Tur*; cf. Josephus, *Antiquities*
4:8:48). See Deuteronomy 32:49. This would indicate that Mount Nebo was on the site of the
present Mount Sh'anab, some 8 miles north of its traditional site. However, the stream Abu Arabeh
flows into the Jordan almost exactly west of the traditional site of Mount Nebo. Some say that it was
called Avarim because from its peak one could see the burial places of Aaron and Miriam (*Zohar*
3:183b; Bachya on 20:28, Deuteronomy 32:49).

27:13 **Aaron was.** Above, 20:28.

27:14 **Tzin Desert.** See 13:21, 20:1.

27   [God was speaking] of the Waters of Dispute (*Mey Meribhah*)* at
Kadesh in the Tzin Desert.

[127. Joshua Chosen to Replace Moses]

¹⁵ Moses spoke to God, saying, "Let the Omnipotent God of all living
souls* appoint a man over the community. ¹⁶ Let him come and go before
them, and let him bring them forth and lead them. Let God's community not
be like sheep that have no shepherd."

¹⁸ God said to Moses, "Take Joshua son of Nun, a man of spirit, and lay
your hands on him.* ¹⁹ Have him stand before Eleazar the priest and before
the entire community, and let them see you commission him. ²⁰ Invest him
with some of your splendor* so that the entire Israelite community will
obey him. ²¹ Let him stand before Eleazar the priest, who shall seek the
decision of the Urim* before God on his behalf. By this* word [Joshua],
along with all the Israelites and the entire community shall come and go."

²² Moses did as God had ordered him. He took Joshua and had him
stand before Eleazar the priest and before the entire community. ²² He then
laid his hands on him and commissioned him. [It was all done] as God had
commanded Moses.

[128. The Daily Sacrifice]

28   ¹ God spoke to Moses, telling him to ² give the Israelites instructions
and tell them: Be careful to offer My fire-offering food sacrifice to Me in its
proper time as My appeasing fragrance.

³ Tell them that the fire offering that they must offer to God shall consist
of two yearling sheep* without blemish each day as a regular daily* burnt
offering. ⁴ Prepare one sheep in the morning, and the second sheep in the
afternoon.* ⁵ There shall also be 1/10 ephah* of wheat meal for the grain

---

—   **Waters of Dispute.** See 20:13.
27:15   **Omnipotent . . .** See 16:22.
27:18   **lay your hands . . .** See Deuteronomy 34:9. Some say that this "laying of hands" actually denoted
         ordination (*Sanhedrin* 13b). According to others, Moses actually laid his hands on Joshua, but in
         later generations, it was not required for ordination (*Yad, Sanhedrin* 4:1,2).
27:20   **splendor.** That is, authority (Ibn Ezra; Sforno). Others say that Moses gave Joshua a radiance similar
         to his own (Exodus 34:29; *Targum Yonathan*). The Talmud states that Moses' face gleamed like the
         sun, while Joshua's shone like the moon (*Bava Bathra* 75a).
27:21   **Urim.** See Exodus 28:30.
—   **this.** (Ibn Ezra). Or, "Eleazar's" (Rashi).
28:3   **yearling sheep.** A male (*Yad, Maaseh HaKorbanoth* 1:15).
—   **regular daily.** *Tamid* in Hebrew.
28:4   **Prepare . . .** See Exodus 29:39. Also see below, 28:6.
28:5   **1/10 ephah.** Around 2 quarts.
—   **wheat meal.** See Exodus 29:2, Leviticus 2:1 (*Sifri*).

offering, mixed with 1/4 hin* hand pressed* olive oil.   **28**

⁶ This is the regular daily burnt offering, [the same as that] presented at Mount Sinai* as an appeasing fragrance, a fire offering to God. ⁷ Its libation shall be 1/4 hin* wine for each sheep, poured in the sanctuary as a libation, a drink offering to God.

⁸ Present the second sheep in the afternoon. You shall present it [with the same] meal offering and libation as the morning [sacrifice]; it is a fire offering, an appeasing fragrance to God.

[129. The Additional Sabbath Offering]

⁹ On the Sabbath* day, [you shall present] two [additional] yearling sheep without blemish, 2/10 [ephah] wheat meal mixed with oil as a grain offering, and its libation. ¹⁰ This is the burnt offering presented each Sabbath in addition to the regular daily burnt offering and its libation.

[130. The New Moon Offering]

¹¹ On your new moon festivals* you shall present as a burnt offering to God, two young bulls, one ram, and seven yearling sheep, [all] without blemish. ¹² There shall be a grain offering* of 3/10 [ephah] wheat meal mixed with oil for each bull, a grain offering of 2/10 [ephah] wheat meal mixed with oil for the ram, ¹³ and a grain offering of 1/10 [ephah] mixed with oil for each sheep. This shall be the burnt offering [presented] as an appeasing fragrance to God.

¹⁴ Their wine libations* shall consist of 1/2 hin for each bull, 1/3 hin for the ram, and 1/4 hin for each sheep. This is the new moon burnt offering, for the year's lunar months.

¹⁵ There shall also be one goat [presented] as a sin offering to God. [All this] shall be presented in addition to the regular daily burnt offering and its libation.

[131. The Passover Offering]

¹⁶ The 14th day of the first month* is God's Passover. ¹⁷ Then, on the

---

—   **1/4 hin.** Around a quart.
—   **hand pressed.** See Exodus 27:20 (*Sifri*).
28:6   **at Mount Sinai.** See Exodus 24:5, 29:39. Some say that the Israelites began bringing a daily sacrifice
       at Mount Sinai even before the Tabernacle was erected (*Chagigah* 6a).
28:7   **1/4 hin.** See above, 15:5.
28:9   **Sabbath.** All the following are called *Mussaf* offerings.
28:11 **new moon festivals.** The first of every lunar month.
28:12 **grain offering.** See above 15:4,6,9.
28:14 **wine libations.** See above, 15:5,7,10.
28:16 **14th day of the first month.** 14 Nissan.

28 15th day, a festival shall begin, when matzahs shall be eaten for seven days.

¹⁸ The first day shall be a sacred holiday when you shall do no mundane* work. ¹⁹ As a burnt fire offering to God, you shall offer two young bulls, one ram, and seven yearling sheep, making sure that [all] are without blemish. ²⁰ The grain offering that you must present shall consist of wheat meal mixed with oil, 3/10 [ephah] for each bull, 2/10 for the ram, ²¹ and 1/10 for each of the seven sheep.

²² [There shall also be] a sin offering goat to make atonement for you. ²³ [All] these shall be presented in addition to the morning burnt offering that [is offered as] the regular daily sacrifice.

²⁴ On each of the seven days, you shall prepare a similar [sacrifice] as a consumed fire offering, an appeasing fragrance to God. This shall be in addition to the regular daily burnt offering and its libation.

²⁵ The seventh day shall be a sacred holiday to you, when you shall not do any mundane work.

[132. The Shavuoth Offering]

²⁶ The day of first fruits is when you bring a new grain offering* to God as part of your Shavuoth* festival. It shall be a sacred holiday to you when you may not do any mundane work.

²⁷ As an appeasing fragrance to God, you shall then present a burnt offering consisting of two young bulls, one ram and seven yearling sheep. ²⁸ Their grain offering consisting of wheat meal mixed with oil shall be 3/10 [ephah] for each bull, 2/10 for the ram, ²⁹ and 1/10 for each of the seven sheep.

³⁰ There shall also be one male goat to atone for you. ³¹ You must present [all this] in addition to the regular daily burnt offering and its meal offering. These [sacrifices] and their libations* must be without blemish for you [to present them].

[133. The New Year Offering]

29   ¹ The first day of the seventh month* shall be a sacred holiday to you

---

28:18 **mundane.** Or, "service work;" see Leviticus 23:7.
28:26 **new grain offering.** See Leviticus 23:16.
—   **Shavuoth.** Or, "Weeks." The Targum renders this *Atzereth* (Retreat), another name for Shavuoth (cf. Chizzkuni).
28:31 **libations.** They must also be without blemish, that is, the wine must be without taint (*Sifri*; *Menachoth* 86b; Rashi).
29:1 **first day of seventh month.** This is 1 Tishrei, which is Rosh HaShanah, the Hebrew New Year. See Leviticus 23:24.

when you may not do any mundane work. It shall be a day of sounding the [ram's] horn. 29

² As an appeasing fragrance to God, you must present a burnt offering consisting of one young bull, one ram, and seven yearling sheep [all] without blemish. ³ Their grain offering of wheat meal mixed with oil shall be 3/10 [ephah] for the bull, 2/10 for the ram, ⁴ and 1/10 for each of the seven sheep.

⁵ [There shall also be] one goat as a sin offering to make atonement for you. ⁶ [All this] is in addition to the new moon offering,* the regular daily offering, and their required meal offerings and libations, [which are] an appeasing fragrance, a fire offering to God.

[134. The Yom Kippur Offering]

⁷ The 10th of this month* shall be a sacred holiday to you when you must fast* and not do any work.*

⁸ As a burnt offering for an appeasing fragrance to God, you shall present one young bull, one ram, and seven yearling sheep, making sure that [all] are without blemish. ⁹ Their grain offering of wheat meal mixed with oil shall be 3/10 [ephah] for the bull, 2/10 for the ram, ¹⁰ and 1/10 for each of the seven sheep.

¹¹ There shall also be one goat as a sin offering, in addition to the [special] Atonement sin offering.* [All these sacrifices] and their libations are in addition to the regular daily burnt offering and its meal offering.

[135. The Sukkoth Offering: First Day]

¹² The 15th day of the seventh month* shall be a sacred holiday to you when no mundane work may be done. You shall celebrate a festival* to God for seven days.

¹³ As an appeasing fragrance to God, you shall present a burnt offering consisting of 13 young bulls, 2 rams, and 14 yearling sheep, all without blemish. ¹⁴ Their grain offering of wheat meal mixed with oil shall be 3/10

29:6 **in addition to . . .** Since Rosh HaShanah is also the first day of a lunar month, the new moon offering is also presented. The new moon offering comes before the Rosh HaShanah offering, because that which is brought the most often has precedence (*Yad, Temidim* 9:2).

29:7 **10th of this month.** 10 Tishrei, Yom Kippur. See Leviticus 16:29, 23:27.

— **fast.** See Leviticus 16:29, 23:27.

— **work.** See Leviticus 23:27.

29:11 **Atonement sin offering.** The goat chosen by lot in Leviticus 16:9 (Rashi). The *Mussaf* offering mentioned here preceded the service described in Leviticus 16.

29:12 **15th day of the seventh month.** 15 Tishrei, which is Sukkoth. See Leviticus 23:34-36, 39-43.

— **celebrate a festival.** *Chag* in Hebrew. Or, "prepare a sacrifice" (see Exodus 23:14).

29   [ephah] for each of the 13 bulls, 2/10 for each of the 2 rams, [15] and 1/10 for each of the 14 sheep.

[16] There shall also be one goat as a sin offering. This is in addition to the regular daily burnt offering, its grain offering and its libation.

[136. Second Day of Sukkoth]

[17] On the second day there shall be 12 young bulls, 2 rams and 14 yearling sheep, [all] without blemish, [18] along with the grain offerings and libations appropriate for the number of bulls, rams and sheep. [19] There shall also be one goat as a sin offering. [These offerings] and their libations* shall be in addition to the regular daily burnt offering and its grain offering.

[137. Third Day of Sukkoth]

[20] On the third day there shall be 11 young bulls, 2 rams, and 14 yearling sheep, [all] without blemish, [21] along with the grain offerings and libations appropriate for the number of bulls, rams and sheep. [22] There shall also be one goat as a sin offering. [All this] is in addition to the regular daily burnt offering, its grain offering and its libation.

[138. Fourth Day of Sukkoth]

[23] On the fourth day there shall be 10 young bulls, 2 rams, and 14 yearling sheep, [all] without blemish, [24] along with the grain offerings and libations appropriate for the number of bulls, rams and sheep. [25] There shall also be one goat as a sin offering. [All this] is in addition to the regular daily burnt offering, its grain offering and its libation.

[139. Fifth Day of Sukkoth]

[26] On the fifth day, there shall be 9 young bulls, 2 rams, and 14 yearling sheep, [all] without blemish, [27] along with the grain offerings and libations appropriate for the number of bulls, rams and sheep. [28] There shall also be one goat as a sin offering. [All this] is in addition to the regular daily burnt offering, its grain offering and its libation.

[140. Sixth Day of Sukkoth]

[29] On the sixth day, there shall be 8 young bulls, 2 rams, and 14 yearling sheep, [all] without blemish, [30] along with the grain offerings and libations appropriate for the number of bulls, rams and sheep. [31] There shall

29:19 **and their libations.** See 29:11 (cf. *Taanith* 2b).

also be one goat as a sin offering. [All this] is in addition to the regular daily   29
burnt offering, its grain offering, and its libations.*

[*141. Seventh Day of Sukkoth*]

³² On the seventh day, there shall be 7 young bulls,* 2 rams, and 14
yearling sheep, [all] without blemish, ³³ along with their appropriate* grain
offerings and libations for the number of bulls, rams and sheep. ³⁴ There
shall also be one goat as a sin offering. [All this] is in addition to the regular
daily burnt offering, its grain offering and its libation.

[*142. The Shemini Atzereth Offering*]

³⁵ The eighth day shall be a time of retreat* for you when you shall do
no mundane work.
³⁶ As a burnt fire offering for an appeasing fragrance to God, you shall
present one bull, one ram, and seven yearling sheep, [all] without blemish,
³⁷ along with their* appropriate number of meal offerings and libations.
³⁸ There shall also be one goat as a sin offering. These are in addition to the
regular daily burnt offering, its grain offering and its libation.
³⁹ [All] these are what you must present to God on your festivals, in
addition to your burnt offerings, grain offerings, libations, and peace offerings [presented as] a general or specific pledge.*
¹ Moses spoke to the Israelites [telling them] all that God had com-   30
manded him.*

Mattoth   מַטּוֹת

[*143. Vows*]

² Moses spoke* to the tribal heads of the Israelites, telling them that this
is the word that God had commanded:

29:31 libations. The plural here alludes to the special water libation that was offered on Sukkoth (*Taanith* 2b; *Targum Yonathan*).

29:32 7 young bulls. Thus the total number of bulls offered on Sukkoth was 13 + 12 + 11 + 10 + 9 + 8 + 7 = 70. These 70 bulls were offered for the 70 nations of the world (*Sukkah* 55b). See note on Genesis 10:32.

29:33 their appropriate. A somewhat different wording (cf. *Taanith* 2b).

29:35 time of retreat. *Atzereth* in Hebrew; see Leviticus 23:36. Hence, this festival is known as Shemini Atzereth, "the eighth day of retreat."

29:37 their. See 29:33.

29:39 general or specific pledge. See Leviticus 7:16.

30:1 him. Literally, "Moses." This ends God's word to Moses (Rashi; cf. Ramban).

30:2 Moses spoke. Some say that this was given after the war with Midian (31) (Ibn Ezra; Chizzkuni).

30   ³ If a man makes a vow to God, or makes an oath to obligate himself,* he
must not break his word.* He must do all that he expressed verbally.
     ⁴ [This is the law] when a woman makes a vow to God or binds herself
by an obligation while still a girl* in her father's house. ⁵ If her father
remains silent when he hears* her vow or self-imposed obligation, then all
her vows and self-imposed obligations must be kept. ⁶ However, if he
obstructs* her on the day* he hears [it], then any such vow or self-imposed
obligation of hers shall not be fulfilled. Since her father has obstructed her,
God will forgive her.
     ⁷ [This is the law] if she is [betrothed]* to a man and is bound by her
vows and self-imposed verbal* obligations. ⁸ If the men in her life* hear
about it and remain silent on the day they hear, then her vows and self-
imposed obligations must be kept. ⁹ However, if the men in her life obstruct
her on the day they hear about it, they can annul her vows and self-
imposed verbal obligations, and God will forgive her.
     ¹⁰ The vow of a widow or divorcée must be kept, no matter what obliga-
tion she takes upon herself.
     ¹¹ [This is the law] if [a woman] makes a vow or an oath for a self-
imposed obligation in her husband's house.* ¹² If her husband hears* it and
remains silent without obstructing her, then all her vows and self-imposed
obligations must be kept. ¹³ However, if her husband annuls them on the
day he hears them, then all her verbally expressed vows and self-imposed
obligations need not be kept. Since her husband has annulled them, God
will forgive her.

30:3   **obligate** (*Yerushalmi, Nedarim* 9:1; Septuagint). *Assar* in Hebrew. Or, "forbid" (*Sifri*).
—   **he must not . . .** This is a commandment (*Sefer HaMitzvoth,* Negative Commandment 157).
30:4   **girl.** From age 11 until 12-1/2 (*Yad, Nedarim* 11:7). Before that age, her vows are not binding, and
       later, her father can no longer annul them.
30:5   **hears.** There is a question as to whether this means that he must actually hear the vow, or if he
       merely hears *of* it (*Yoreh Deah* 334:25).
—   **obstructs** (Rashi). *Heyni* in Hebrew. Or, "breaks" (Ibn Ezra), "annuls" (*Sifri;* cf. *Mizrachi*); or
       "countermands" (Septuagint). Any wording that negates the vow is effective (*Nedarim* 77b; *Yad,
       Nedarim* 13:1,2).
—   **on the day.** Until nightfall of that day; below 30:15 (*Nedarim* 76b; *Yad, Nedarim* 12:15).
30:7   **betrothed** (*Nedarim* 67a; Rashi). See Exodus 22:15.
—   **verbal** (Malbim). *Bata* in Hebrew. Or, "oath" (*Shevuoth* 20a). See Leviticus 5:4.
30:8   **men in her life.** That is, both her father and her husband together (*Nedarim* 66b, 67a; *Yad, Nedarim*
       11:9). Although the Torah literally says, "her man," it denotes both (*Yad, Nedarim* 12:17; *Tzafanath
       Paneach*). Or, "If her husband [also]" (Rashi, Ran, *Nedarim,* 67a).
30:11 **in her husband's house.** Once a woman enters her husband's house, she is considered fully married,
       and is no longer under her father's control. The wedding canopy (*chupah*) is a symbolic "home" into
       which the husband brings her. The husband can annul the vows of his wife even when she is an
       adult (cf. *Yad, Nedarim* 11:8).
30:12 **hears.** Here too there is a question as to whether he must actually hear it (see 30:5).

¹⁴ Thus, in the case of every vow or oath involving self-denial,* [a **30** woman's] husband can uphold them, and her husband can annul them. ¹⁵ If her husband remains silent for the entire day,* then he has [automatically] upheld any vow or obligation that she has assumed. He has upheld them simply by remaining silent on the day he heard them. ¹⁶ However, if he annuls them after hearing them, he removes any guilt that she may have [for violating them].

¹⁷ These are the rules that God commanded Moses regarding the relationship between a man and his wife, [and] between a father and his daughter as long as she is a girl in her father's house.

[144. Attacking the Midianites]

¹ God spoke to Moses, saying, ² "Take revenge for the Israelites against **31** the Midianites. Then you shall [die and] be gathered to your people."

³ Moses spoke to the people, saying, "Detach* men for armed service against Midian, so that God's revenge can be taken against the Midianites. ⁴ One thousand from each of Israel's tribes shall be sent into armed service."

⁵ From the thousands of Israel, 1000 volunteered* from each tribe, [a total of] 12,000 special troops. ⁶ Moses sent forth the 1000 men from each tribe as an army* along with Pinchas* son of Eleazar the priest, who was in charge* of the sacred articles* and signal* trumpets.*

⁷ They mounted a surprise attack* against Midian as God had com-

---

30:14 self-denial. While the father of a young girl can annul any vow, a husband can only annul a vow that involves self-denial (*Nedarim* 79b; *Yad, Nedarim* 12:1). It does not matter how minor the self-denial is (*Yad* 12:4). Any self-denial on the part of the wife will ultimately affect the husband (*HaKethav VeHaKabbalah*). Others, however, maintain that the father also can annul only vows that involve self-denial (Ran, *Nedarim* 68a, s.v. *Lomer*: Rosh, *Nedarim* 79a, s.v. *VeElu*; *Yoreh Deah* 234:58).

30:15 entire day (*Nedarim* 76b; Rashi). Literally, "from day to day."

31:3 detach (Radak, *Sherashim*; Hirsch). *Chalatz* in Hebrew. Or, "alert" (*Targum*; Saadia); "arm" (Ibn Ezra; Ibn Janach; Septuagint); "draft" (*Yevamoth* 102b); or "mount a special force" (Malbim).

31:5 volunteered (Abarbanel). Or, "were given over" (*Sifri*; Malbim).

31:6 as an army. Or, ". . . along with Pinchas sons of Eleazar, the army priest" (*HaKethav VeHaKabbalah*). See next note.

— **Pinchas.** He was sent out as the priest anointed for war (*Sotah* 43a; Rashi). See Deuteronomy 20:2 (*Yad, Melakhim* 7:1). He was also the one who had begun the battle against Midian (above, 25:7; Rashi).

— **in charge** (*Sifri*; Rashi). Literally, "who had in his hand."

— **sacred articles.** The ark (*Sifri*; *Sotah* 43b; Rashi). See note on 10:33. Others say that it was the priestly forehead plate (*tzitz*) mentioned in Exodus 28:36 (Rashi; *Midrash Aggadah*), or the Urim and Thumim (Exodus 28:30; *Targum Yonathan*). Or, "the sacred vessels which were the trumpets" (Ralbag).

— **signal** (Septuagint). *Teruah* in Hebrew, literally staccato.

— **trumpets.** See above, 10:9 (*Midrash HaGadol*). Others say that these were ram's horns (*Sotah* 43b; *Tzafanath Paneach*).

31:7 mounted a surprise attack (Saadia). Or, "set themselves in battle array" (Septuagint), or, "sieged"

31   manded Moses, and killed all the [adult]* males. ⁸ Along with the other victims,* they also killed the five kings of Midian:* Evi, Rekem,* Tzur,* Chur, and Reva, the five Midianite kings. They also killed Balaam son of Beor* by the sword.

⁹ The Israelites took captive all the women of Midian and their children. They took as booty all their animals, all their possessions,* and all their wealth.* ¹⁰ [The Israelites] also set fire to all their residential cities and fortresses,* ¹¹ taking all the booty and plunder, both man and beast.

¹² They brought the captives, the plunder, and the spoils to Moses, Eleazar the priest, and the entire Israelite community, [who were] in the Western Plains of Moab, on the Jericho Jordan. ¹³ Moses, Eleazar and all the community princes went out to greet them outside the camp. ¹⁴ However, Moses was angry at the generals and captains,* who were the officers returning from the military campaign.

¹⁵ "Why have you kept all the women alive?" demanded Moses. ¹⁶ "These* are exactly the ones who were involved with the Israelites at Balaam's instigation, causing them to be unfaithful to God in the Peor incident, and bringing a plague on God's community. ¹⁷ Now kill every male child, as well as every woman who has been involved intimately with a man. ¹⁸ However, all the young girls who have not been involved intimately with a man, you may keep alive for yourselves.

¹⁹ "You must now remain outside the camp for seven days. Whoever killed a person or touched a corpse must purify himself on the third and seventh days.* As far as you and your captives* are concerned, ²⁰ every gar-

---

(Sifri). Josephus writes that the Midianites assembled an army and set up a fortified line on their borders (*Antiquities* 4:8:1).

—   **adult** (Ibn Ezra). See 31:9.

31:8   **Along with . . .** (Chizzkuni). Literally, "on top of" (Rashi; cf. *Midrash HaGadol*).

—   **five kings of Midian.** For each of the five Midianite nations; see note on Genesis 25:4. Also see Joshua 13:21.

—   **Rekem.** Some say that the city Rekem, otherwise known as Kadesh and Petra, was named after him (Josephus, *Antiquities* 4:8:1). See note on Genesis 14:7. Also see Joshua 18:27.

—   **Tzur.** Kazbi's father; see 25:15 (Ibn Ezra).

—   **Balaam son of Beor.** Although he was heading home (24:25), he went to Midian to try to collect his fee (*Sanhedrin* 106a; *Targum Yonathan*; Rashi). He felt that it was his due because of the plague that had come as a result of his advice (25:9, 31:16).

31:9   **possessions** (Septuagint). Or, "livestock" (Targum).

—   **wealth** (Targum; Ibn Ezra). Or, "and spoiled their forces" (Septuagint).

31:10   **fortresses.** Or, "fortified cities" (Ralbag). *Tirah* in Hebrew; see Genesis 25:16. Ezekiel 25:4, 49:23, Psalms 69:26. Or, "palaces" (Saadia; Rashi; Ibn Janach; Ibn Ezra); "temples" (*Targum*; *Sifri*; Rashi); "observatories" (Malbim), "open villages" (Septuagint).

31:14   **generals and captains.** Literally, "commanders of thousands and commanders of hundreds."

31:16   **These.** (cf. Abarbanel). See above, 25:3.

31:19   **third and seventh days.** See above, 19:12,19.

—   **As far as you and your captives . . .** (Ramban). Or, "this is true of both you and your captives." Actually, gentiles do not become unclean upon contact with the dead (cf. Rashi). However, as soon

ment, every leather article, anything made of goat products,* and every   31
wooden article, must undergo such purification.*"

[145. Purification After the War]

²¹ Eleazar the priest said to the soldiers returning from the campaign:
This is the rule that God commanded Moses:

²² As far as the gold, silver, copper, iron, tin and lead are concerned,
²³ whatever was used over fire* must be brought over fire and purged, and
[then] purified with the sprinkling water.* However, that which was not
used over fire need only be immersed in a mikvah.*

²⁴ You yourselves must also immerse [your bodies and]* your garments
on the seventh day, and you will then be clean so that you can enter the
camp.

[146. Dedicating a Portion of the Spoil]

²⁵ God spoke to Moses, saying, ²⁶ "Together with Eleazar the priest and
the community's paternal leaders, you must take an accounting of the men
and animals plundered as spoil. ²⁷ Then divide the plunder equally,* giving
half to the warriors who went out to battle and the other half to the community.

²⁸ "From the soldiers who participated in the campaign, levy a tax to
God consisting of one out of 500 of the humans, cattle, donkeys and sheep.
²⁹ Take this from their half, and give it to Eleazar the priest as an elevated
gift to God.

³⁰ "From the half that is going to the other Israelites, take one part out

---

as the prisoners were taken captive, they acquired the status of slaves, and thus had a status similar
to that of true Israelites (Ralbag; cf. *Sifri*; *Tzafanath Paneach*). Some say that there were Israelite
apostates included among the prisoners (*Midrash Aggadah*).

31:20 **goat products.** Even from the horns and hooves (*Sifri*; Rashi).

— **such purification.** See above, 19:18.

31:23 **over fire . . .** This teaches that any vessels used for cooking must first be purged to remove any taint
of forbidden food. If it is used for cooking with water, it must be boiled out with water (see Leviticus
6:21). If it is used directly over fire without water, it must be burned out (*Targum Yonathan*; Rashi).
Others say that this is speaking specifically of articles used in fire without water, such as baking pans
and spits (*Sifri*; Ramban).

— **sprinkling water.** *Mey Niddah*; see above, 19:9.

— **immersed in a mikvah** (*Targum Yonathan*; Rashi). From here, the law is derived that metal vessels
procured from a gentile must be immersed before they can be used (*Avodah Zarah* 75b). This is like a
"conversion" process, very much like the immersion of a proselyte (*Yerushalmi, Avodah Zarah* 5:15).
Some say that this teaches that cooking vessels that are used with water need merely be purged, and
not burnt out, and hence translate the verse, "must be brought through [boiling] water" (*Sifri*;
Ramban).

31:24 **bodies and . . .** (Chizzkuni). See Exodus 19:10.

31:27 **divide the plunder equally.** This set the pattern that any spoils would be divided equally between
those who went to battle and those who remained behind to stand guard (1 Samuel 30:24; Ralbag).

31 of 50* of the humans, cattle, donkeys, sheep and other animals,* and give it
to the Levites who are entrusted with God's Tabernacle."

³¹ Moses and Eleazar the priest did as God had commanded Moses.

³² In addition to the goods* that the troops had taken as booty, the
plunder consisted of 675,000 sheep, ³³ 72,000 head of cattle, ³⁴ 61,000
donkeys, ³⁵ and 32,000 humans (women who had never experienced intimacy with a man).

³⁶ The half-portion for those who went out in the army was as follows:
The number of sheep was 337,500, ³⁷ and the tax for God from the
sheep consisted of 675 sheep.

³⁸ There were 36,000 cattle, out of which the tax for God was 72.

³⁹ There were 30,500 donkeys, out of which the tax for God was 61.

⁴⁰ There were 16,000 humans, out of which the tax for God consisted of
32 individuals.

⁴¹ Moses gave the tax to Eleazar the priest as an elevated gift to God, as
God had commanded Moses.

⁴² The half that Moses took from the military men for the [other] Israelites as ⁴³ the community's portion consisted of 337,500 sheep, ⁴⁴ 36,000
cattle, ⁴⁵ 30,500 donkeys, ⁴⁶ and 16,000 humans.

⁴⁷ From the humans and beasts that were the Israelites' half, Moses took
one out of fifty and gave them to the Levites, who are entrusted with God's
Tabernacle. [It was all done] as God had commanded Moses.

⁴⁸ The generals and captains, who were officers over the army's divisions, approached Moses. ⁴⁹ They said to Moses, "We* have taken a census
of the warriors under our command and not a single man has been lost!
⁵⁰ We therefore want to bring an offering to God. Every man who found
any gold article [such as] an ᵊnklet,* a bracelet,* a finger ring,* an earring,*

31:30 **one part out of 50.** This is taken as a standard for the average priestly *terumah* gift (*Yerushalmi,
Terumah* 6:2). Some say that a part of the spoils must be set aside in all wars of revenge (*Halakhoth
Gedoloth; Tzafanath Paneach;* cf. *Sefer HaMitzvoth, Shoresh* 3, 39a), although it is definitely not
required in the case of ordinary wars (*Menachoth* 77b).

— **other animals.** Such as camels (Chizzkuni).

31:32 **goods . . .** Inanimate goods (Rashi; cf. *Midrash HaGadol;* Bachya, on 31:12). Specifically, gold and silver
(*Lekach Tov;* see below, 31:53). Or, "besides what was destroyed in the war" (*Lekach Tov*), or,
"besides what was eaten" (Ibn Ezra; Chizzkuni).

31:49 **We.** Literally, "your servants." See note on Genesis 44:18.

31:50 **anklet** (Rashi; *Yerushalmi, Shabbath* 6:4), *Etz'adah* in Hebrew, from the root *tza'ad,* "to walk"
(*Lekach Tov;* Radak, *Sherashim;* Bachya). Or, "arm band" from 2 Samuel 1:10 (Saadia; Ibn Ezra;
Septuagint).

— **bracelet** (Saadia; Rashi; Ibn Ezra). *Tzamid* in Hebrew, see Genesis 22:24. Or, "chain" (Septuagint).

— **finger ring** (Saadia). *Tabaath* in Hebrew. See Exodus 35:22.

— **earring.** (Saadia; Rashi; Ibn Ezra). *Agil* in Hebrew; see Ezekiel 16:12. (cf. *Yerushalmi, Shabbath*
6:4). Or, "brassiere" (*Mesekhta Kallah* 1; *Midrash HaGadol*); or, "bracelet" (Septuagint). However,
it is possible that there is a transposition in the Septuagint, and *agil* should be translated as "chain."

or a body ornament* [wishes to bring it] to atone for our souls before God."   31
⁵¹ Moses and Eleazar the priest took all the gold articles from them.
⁵² The entire elevated gift of gold that was offered to God [totalled] 16,750 shekels.* This was given by the generals and captains. ⁵³ The other soldiers, however, took their plunder for themselves.

⁵⁴ Moses and Eleazar the priest took the gold from the generals and captains, and brought it to the Communion Tent as a remembrance for the Israelites before God.

[147. The Petition of Reuben and Gad]

¹ The descendants of Reuben and Gad had an extremely large number   32
of animals, and they saw that the Ya'azer* and Gilead* areas were good for livestock. ² The descendants of Gad and Reuben therefore came and presented the following petition to Moses, Eleazar the priest, and the community princes:

³ "Ataroth,* Divon,* Ya'azer,* Nimrah,* Cheshbon,* El'aleh,* Sevam,* Nebo* and Be'on* ⁴ [in] the land that God struck down before the Israelite community is livestock land—and what we have is livestock."

—   **body ornament** (Saadia). *Kumaz* in Hebrew. Or, "hair clasp" (Septuagint).
        See note on Exodus 35:22.
31:52   **16,750 shekels.** 837.5 pounds.
32:1   **Ya'azer.** See above 21:32. This most probably denotes the land to the east of
        the Jordan and Dead Sea and to the south of the Jabbok River.
—   **Gilead.** See Genesis 31:21. The area to the east of the Jordan to the north of
        the Jabbok. See 32:39.
32:3   **Ataroth.** This was later built up by Gad (32:34). This is identified with the   **Kumaz**
        modern Attaruth, 7 miles east of the Dead Sea, 8 miles north of the Arnon, and 8 miles n.n.w. of Divon.
        Although it was built up by Gad, it eventually became part of Reuben's territory; see next note.
—   **Divon.** See above 21:30. Although it was built up by Gad (32:34), it eventually became part of
        Reuben's territory (Joshua 13:17).
—   **Ya'azer.** See above 21:32. It was built up by Gad (32:35), and became the border of their territory
        (Joshua 13:25) and a Levitical city (Joshua 21:37; 1 Chronicles 6:66).
—   **Nimrah.** Or Beth Nimrah. This was built up by Gad (32:36), and became part of their territory (Joshua
        13:27). It was also known as Nimrim (Isaiah 15:6, Jeremiah 48:35). In Roman times, it was called
        Bethennabris (Septuagint on Joshua 13:27; Eusebius), and in Talmudic times, Beth Nimrin (Targum)
        or Beth Namar (*Peah* 4:5). It is the modern Tel el-Bleibil or Tel Nimrin, on the Nimrin River near the
        modern Shunath Nimrin, 11 miles east of Jericho.
—   **Cheshbon.** The capital of Sichon; above, 21:25.
—   **El'aleh.** A city built up by Reuben (32:27), and part of the Reubenite territory. It is the present el-Al,
        around 2 miles northeast of Cheshbon (Eusebius; cf. Isaiah 15:4, 16:9, Jeremiah 48:34).
—   **Sevam.** Also known as Sivmah (cf. Septuagint), a city built by the Reubenites (32:38), and part of
        their territory (Joshua 13:19). A town near Cheshbon (cf. Isaiah 16:8,9; also see Jeremiah 48:32).
—   **Nebo.** *N'bho* in Hebrew. This was the mountain upon which Moses died (Deuteronomy 32:49;
        Targum). See above, 27:12. It is the modern Neba at the northwest corner of the Dead Sea. It was
        built up by Reuben (32:38).
—   **Be'on.** Changed to Baal Meon and built by the Reubenites (32:38), and known as Beth Baal Meon, part
        of their territory (Joshua 13:17). It is the modern Ma'in, 6 miles south of Mount Nebo (cf. 1 Chronicles
        5:8), and midway between Nebo and Kiryathaim (cf. Jeremiah 48:23, Ezekiel 25:9). The Septuagint
        (on Ezekiel 25:9) translates it a "Fountain City."

32   *[148. Moses Objects]*

⁵ They said, "If you would grant us a favor,* let this land be given to us as our permanent property, and do not bring us across the Jordan."

⁶ Moses said to the descendants of Gad and Reuben, "Why should your brothers go out and fight while you stay here? ⁷ Why are you trying to discourage the Israelites from crossing over to the land that God has given them?

⁸ "This is the same thing your fathers did when I sent them from Kadesh Barnea* to see the land. ⁹ They went as far as Cluster Valley* to see the land, but then they discouraged the Israelites from coming to the land that God gave them. ¹⁰ God displayed His anger that day and swore, ¹¹ 'None of the men over 20 years old who left Egypt will see the land that I swore to Abraham, Isaac and Jacob, since they did not follow Me wholeheartedly. ¹² The only exceptions shall be Caleb son of Yefuneh the Kenizite* and Joshua son of Nun, because they followed God wholeheartedly.' ¹³ God displayed anger against Israel, and He made them wander forty years in the desert, until the generation that had done evil in God's eyes had died out.

¹⁴ "Now you are trying to take your fathers' places as a band of sinners, and bring yet more of God's wrath against Israel. ¹⁵ You will dissuade them from following Him, and He will once again leave us in the desert. Then you will have destroyed this nation completely!"

                          [149. A Pledge of Aid]

¹⁵ [The Reubenites and Gaddites] approached [Moses] and said, "We will build enclosures for our sheep here and cities for our children. ¹⁷ But we will then arm ourselves and go as an advance guard* before the [other] Israelites, [fighting] until we have brought them to their homeland. Because of the area's inhabitants, our children will remain in fortified cities, ¹⁸ but we ourselves will not return home until every Israelite has taken possession of his hereditary property. ¹⁹ We, however, will not take possession with

---

32:5   **grant us a favor.** Literally, "if we have found grace in your eyes." See note on Genesis 47:29.

32:8   **Kadesh Barnea.** See above, 13:26, Deuteronomy 1:19, 9:23. See note on 13:3.

32:9   **Cluster Valley.** Nachal Eshkol. See above, 13:23. From here, it appears that this is as far as they went.

32:12 **Kenizite.** See Joshua 14:6,14; also note on 13:6. He was called a Kenizite because he was the stepson of Kenaz, that is, the son of Kenaz's wife (Rashi here and *Sotah* 11b, end). He was thus the step-brother of Othniel; cf. Joshua 15:17, Judges 1:13, 1 Chronicles 4:13. Also see Genesis 15:19, 36:11. The Septuagint translates *Kenizi* as "the one set apart," or "the independent one." On the basis of Semitic roots, Kenizi denotes a hunter or lone warrior.

32:17 **advance guard** (Septuagint). Or, literally, "quickly" (Rashi; Saadia; Ibn Ezra).

them on the far side of the Jordan, since our inheritance shall come to us on 32
the Jordan's eastern bank."

[150. Moses' Conditions; Conquests]

²⁰ Moses said to them, "If you do that and go forth as a special force
ahead of your brothers, [your petition will be granted]. ²¹ Your entire special force must cross the Jordan before God, [and fight] until He has driven
His enemies before Him. ²² When the land is then conquered before God,
you may return [home], and you will be free of any obligation* before God
and Israel. This land will then be yours as your permanent property before
God.

²³ "But if you do not do that, you will have sinned to God, and you
must realize that your sin will be your undoing. ²⁴ Now build yourself cities
for your children and folds for your sheep—but keep your promise!"

²⁵ The descendants of Gad and Reuben said to Moses, "We will do as
you have ordered. ²⁶ Our children, wives, property and livestock will
remain here in the cities of Gilead. ²⁷ Meanwhile, all our special forces shall
cross over for battle before God, as you have said."

²⁸ Moses then gave instructions to Eleazar the priest, Joshua son of
Nun, and the paternal heads of the Israelite tribes. ²⁹ Moses said to them,
"If the entire special force of the Gaddites and Reubenites crosses the
Jordan to fight with you, then when the land is conquered, you shall give
them the Gilead area as their permanent property. ³⁰ But if they do not go
as a special force before you, then they shall have their property alongside
you in the land of Canaan."

³¹ The descendants of Gad and Reuben responded, "We will do what-
ever God has told us. ³² We will cross over as a special force to the land of
Canaan, and we shall then have our permanent hereditary property on
[this] side of the Jordan."

³² To the descendants of Gad and Reuben, and to half the tribe of
Manasseh* (son of Joseph), Moses then gave the kingdom of Sichon* (king
of the Amorites) and the kingdom of Og* (king of the Bashan). [He gave

---

32:22 free of any obligation. Or, literally, "innocent."
32:32 half of the tribe of Manasseh. Some say that although the original request came from Gad and
Reuben, they did not have enough population to occupy the land, and therefore invited Manasseh to
join them (Ramban; Abarbanel). The rest of Manasseh took land by lot with the other tribes (Joshua
17:2). According to others, however, Manasseh was involved in the original request (Josephus,
Antiquities 4:7:3). See below 32:39-42.
— **Sichon.** See above 21:21.
— **Og.** Above, 21:33.

32 them] the land along with the cities along its surrounding borders.*

³⁴ The descendants of Gad built up Divon, Ataroth,* Aro'er,* ³⁵ Atroth Shofan,* Ya'azer,* Yagbehah,* ³⁶ Beth Nimrah,* and Beth Haran.* [These were built] into fortress cities and enclosures for flocks.

³⁷ The descendants of Reuben built up Cheshbon, Elaleh,* Kiryathaim,* ³⁸ Nebo,* Baal Meon* (these names had been changed),* and Sivmah.* They gave these cities the names that they had when they were built.*

³⁹ The sons of Makhir* (son of Manasseh) went to Gilead* and captured it, expelling the Amorites who were there. ⁴⁰ Moses gave the Gilead to Makhir son of Manasseh, and he lived there.

⁴¹ Ya'ir, a grandson of Manasseh,* went and conquered the villages* [in this district],* and he named them Ya'ir's Villages (*Chavvoth Ya'ir*).*

—   **the land . . .** Literally, "the land to its cities, in the cities and the cities on its surrounding borders" (Septuagint; cf. Abarbanel).
32:34 **Divon, Ataroth.** See above, 32:3.
—   **Aro'er.** The modern Ara'ir, just north of the Arnon, some 13 miles east of the Dead Sea (cf. Deuteronomy 2:36, etc.). It formed the southern boundary of Sichon's kingdom (Joshua 12:2), and of Reuben (Joshua 13:16), although it was actually in Gad's territory (Joshua 13:25).
32:35 **Atroth Shofan.** Unknown. The Septuagint has Shefer; see 33:23.
—   **Ya'azer.** See 32:3.
—   **Yagbehah.** Or Yogbehah. A place name (Targum), cf. Judges 8:11. This is a city some 19 miles east of the Jordan, 18 miles north of the Dead Sea, the modern Jubeihat. The Septuagint, however, translates this, "and raised it (Ya'azer) up."
32:36 **Beth Nimrah.** Also known as Nimrah, see 32:3.
—   **Beth Haran.** Also known as Beth Haram. It was in the Abu Araba valley, half way between Cheshbon and the Jordan (cf. Joshua 13:27). In Roman times it was known as Betharamptha and Livias, and Herod renamed it Julias (Josephus, *Antiquities* 18:2:1). It is the site of the modern Tel Iktanu. See Genesis 11:26.
32:37 **Cheshbon, Elaleh.** See 32:3
—   **Kiryathaim.** In the mountain leading to the valley (Joshua 13:19). See Genesis 14:5. It is the modern el Qereiyat, 7 miles north of the Arnon, and 8 miles east of the Dead Sea.
32:38 **Nebo.** See 32:3.
—   **Baal Meon.** Be'on in 32:3. Some say that this was Balak's capital (*Targum Yonathan*).
—   **these names had been changed.** By Sichon when he took this territory from Moab (Ramban; Chizzkuni). Or by the Israelites when they conquered the territory (Rashi). Or, a proper name, "Musaboth Shem," so named because its heroes' names were engraved on its surrounding walls (*Targum Yonathan*). Or, "Baal Meon, surrounded with walls" (Septuagint).
—   **Sivmah.** This is Sevam in 32:3 (Rashi).
—   **They gave these cities . . .** (Ramban; Ralbag). Or, "they gave [new] names to the cities that they built" (Rashi; Saadia); or, "they named these cities after their builders." (*Targum Yonathan*; cf. Septuagint).
32:39 **Makhir.** See above 26:29. The sons involved were probably Peresh and Sheresh (1 Chronicles 7:16).
—   **Gilead.** See above, 32:1. It is possible that Gilead was named after Makhir's son. According to some, Gilead had died by now (*Midrash Aggadah*).
32:41 **Ya'ir, a grandson of Manasseh.** Actually a great-grandson. Chetzron (son of Peretz and grandson of Judah), married a daughter of Makhir and had a son Seguv, who was Ya'ir's father (1 Chronicles 2:22; Ibn Ezra; Ramban).
—   **villages.** *Chavoth* in Hebrew. Consisting of small clusters of houses (Ibn Janach; Radak, *Sherashim*, s.v. *Chayah*). These were in the Argov region, to the south of the Yarmok (Deuteronomy 3:14). There were a total of 23 villages (1 Chronicles 2:23).
—   **in this district.** Literally, "their villages." Or, "villages of Ham," see Genesis 14:5.

⁴² Novach* went and captured Kenath* and its surrounding towns, and   **32**
he gave [the area] his own name, Novach.*

Massey   מַסְעֵי

[151. Journeys: The Exodus to Aaron's Death]

¹ These are the journeys of the Israelites, who had left Egypt in organ-   **33**
ized groups* under the leadership of Moses and Aaron. ² Moses recorded
their stops* along the way at God's command. These were their stops along
the way:

³ [The Israelites] left Ra'meses* on the 15th of the first month.* On the
day after the Passover [sacrifice]* the Israelites left triumphantly* before the
eyes of the Egyptians. ⁴ Egypt was still burying all their first-born,* who
had been killed by God, and God had destroyed their idols.*

⁵ The Israelites left Ra'mses and camped in Sukkoth.*

⁶ They left Sukkoth, and camped in Etham* at the edge of the desert.

⁷ They left Etham, and returned to Freedom Valley facing Lord-of-the-
North, camping near Tower.*

⁸ They left Freedom Valley and crossed the Red Sea* toward the desert.

—   **Chavvoth Ya'ir.** See Deuteronomy 3:14, Joshua 13:30, 1 Kings 4:13. Some say that he named the
area after himself because he had no sons, only daughters (*Midrash Aggadah*).

32:42   **Novach.** A descendant of Manasseh (Chizzkuni). He had been born in Egypt (*Seder Olam Rabbah*
9).

—   **Kenath.** See 1 Chronicles 2:23. This is the modern Qanawat, some 42 miles east of the Kinnereth. In
Roman times, it was known as Canatha (Josephus, *Wars* 1:19:2; Ptolemy, *Geography* 5:15, p. 139;
Pliny 5:16).

—   **Novach.** See Judges 8:11. This name, however, did not stick (*Ruth Rabbah* 5:5; Rashi). Some say
that he gave it this name because he only had daughters, and no sons to carry his name (*Midrash
Aggadah*).

33:1   **organized groups.** See Exodus 12:51. Also see Exodus 6:26, 7:4, 12:1, 12:17.

33:2   **stops.** Or, "starting points," literally, "goings out" (Targum; Ibn Ezra; *HaKethav VeHaKabbalah*).
Or, "events," "these are the events along the way" (Radak, *Sherashim*; *HaKethav VeHaKabbalah*;
cf. Joshua 2:23). Since most of the place names here occur nowhere else in the Bible, it appears that
they were given by the Israelites to commemorate specific events (Abarbanel).

33:3   **left Ra'meses.** See Exodus 12:37.

—   **15th of the first month.** 15 Nissan. See Exodus 12:6. This was 15 Nissan, 2448, or, according to
Jewish tradition, March 25, 1313 b.c.e.

—   **Passover sacrifice.** (cf. *Yerushalmi, Challah* 2:1). See Leviticus 23:4, Numbers 28:16.

—   **left triumphantly.** Exodus 14:8.

33:4   **burying all their first-born.** Exodus 12:29.

—   **had destroyed their idols.** Exodus 12:12, 18:11, Isaiah 19:1.

33:5   **Sukkoth.** "Shelters;" Exodus 12:37. It was there that they were first protected by the Clouds of
Glory (*Targum Yonathan*).

33:6   **Etham.** Exodus 13:20.

33:7   **Freedom Valley . . .** See Exodus 14:1. From here we see that they actually camped at Migdal (Tower).

33:8   **crossed the Red Sea.** Exodus 14:22. This was on 21 Nissan, 2448. (March 31, 1313 b.c.e.)

33 They then traveled for three days in the Etham Desert* and camped in Marah.*

⁹ They left Marah and came to Elim.* In Elim there were twelve water springs and seventy palms, and they camped there.

¹⁰ They left Elim and camped near* the Red Sea.*

¹¹ They left the Red Sea and camped in the Sin Desert.*

¹² They left the Sin Desert and camped in Dofkah.*

¹³ They left Dofkah and camped in Alush.*

¹⁴ They left Alush and camped in Rephidim,* where there was no water for the people to drink.

¹⁵ They left Rephidim and camped in the Sinai Desert.*

¹⁶ They left the Sinai Desert and camped in Graves-of-Craving.*

¹⁷ They left Graves-of-Craving and camped in Chatzeroth.*

¹⁸ They left Chatzeroth and camped in Rithmah.*

¹⁹ They left Rithmah and camped in Rimmon Peretz.*

— **Etham Desert.** See 33:6. Apparently the Etham Desert encompassed both sides of the northern Red Sea.

— **Marah.** Exodus 15:23. This was 24 Nissan, 2448 (April 3, 1313 b.c.e.)

33:9 **Elim.** Exodus 16:27.

33:10 **near.** On the shore of . . . (*Targum Yonathan*).

— **Red Sea.** See Exodus 15:27. However, some say that the Israelites actually returned to the place where they had crossed the Red Sea (see *HaKethav VeHaKabbalah*).

33:11 **Sin Desert.** Exodus 16:1.

33:12 **Dofkah.** Not mentioned in Exodus; see note on Exodus 17:1. This is possibly Serabith el-Khadim, an oasis south of the ridge that runs across the Sinai.

33:13 **Alush.** Not mentioned in Exodus; see note on Exodus 17:1. Some say that this is where the manna began to fall; see note on Exodus 16:1 (*Bereshith Rabbah* 48:12; *Sh'moth Rabbah* 25:5). The Israelites therefore arrived there on 15 Iyyar, 2448 (April 24, 1313 b.c.e.). It was therefore in Alush that they were given the first Sabbath (Exodus 17:29; *Yerushalmi, Betza* 2:1, 9b).

Some sources translate Alush as "powerful city" (*Targum Yonathan*). The Talmud notes that it was built by Sheshai, one of the giants of Hebron (above, 13:22; *Yoma* 10a).

33:14 **Rephidim.** Exodus 17:1. They arrived in Rephidim on Sunday, 23 Iyyar, 2448 (May 3, 1313 b.c.e.; *Seder Olam* 5).

33:15 **Sinai Desert.** Exodus 19:1. They arrived on 1 Sivan, 2448 (May 9, 1313 b.c.e.), and remained almost a year, until 20 Iyyar, 2449 (May 17, 1312 b.c.e.); above, 10:11 (*Seder Olam* 8).

33:16 **Graves of Craving.** Kivroth HaTaavah; above 11:34.

33:17 **Chatzeroth.** "Courtyard." Above, 11:35. This is where Miriam was struck (above, 12:16). Some say that it also was where Korach rebelled (Rashi on Deuteronomy 1:1; see below 33:22). They arrived in Chatzeroth on 22 Sivan, 2449 (June 17, 1312 b.c.e.; *Taanith* 29a).

33:18 **Rithmah.** This is Kadesh Barnea, the place from which the spies were sent; see note on 13:3 (Rashi; *Midrash Aggadah*; *Baal HaTurim*; cf. Psalms 120:4). Some say that this was a place where many broom (*rothem*) trees grew (*Targum Yonathan*; cf. 1 Kings 19:4, Job 30:4). The Israelites arrived here on 29 Sivan, 2449 (June 14, 1312 b.c.e.; see note on 12:16).

Some say that they remained here for 19 years (*Seder Olam* 8, from Deuteronomy 1:46, according to Ramban on 20:1; Chizzkuni). See below, 33:36. They were thus in Rithmah until 2468 (1293 b.c.e.).

33:19 **Rimmon Peretz.** Or Rimmon Paretz (Septuagint). "Spreading Pomegranate Tree," or "Heavy-fruited Pomegranate" (*Targum Yonathan*). They arrived here in 2468 (1293 b.c.e.); above note. They were now heading south toward the Gulf of Aqaba (see 14:25, 33:35); circumscribing the Seir Mountains (Deuteronomy 2:1). The Israelites were therefore most probably traveling east of the mountains in

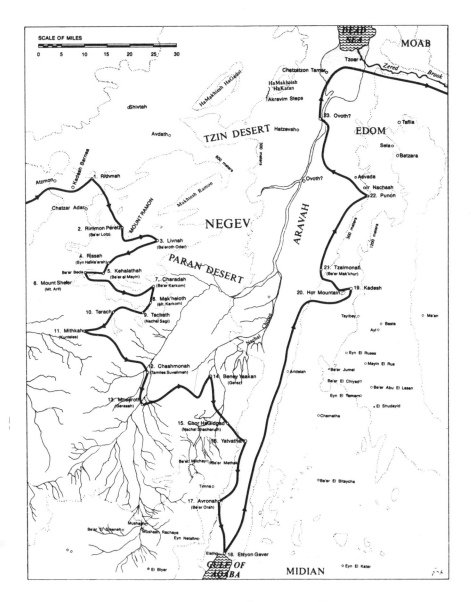

PLATE 29. WANDERINGS THROUGH THE DESERT

33   ²⁰ They left Rimmon Peretz and camped in Livnah.*

²¹ They left Livnah and camped in Rissah.*

²² They left Rissah and camped in Kehelathah.*

²³ They left Kehelathah and camped at Mount Shefer.*

²⁴ They left Mount Shefer and camped in Charadah.*

²⁵ They left Charadah and camped in Mak'heloth.*

²⁶ They left Mak'heloth and camped in Tachath.*

²⁷ They left Tachath and camped in Terach.*

²⁸ They left Terach and camped in Mithkah.*

²⁹ They left Mithkah and camped in Chashmonah.*

³⁰ They left Chashmonah and camped in Moseroth.*

³¹ They left Moseroth and camped in Beney Yaakan.*

the Negev. It may be possible to identify Rimmon Peretz with Mount Ramon in the Negev. Some say that they traveled through the Moab Desert (*Sefer HaYashar, Sh'lach*).

33:20 Livnah. "Bricks;" a place where the boundaries were marked with building bricks (*Targum Yonathan*). See Deuteronomy 1:1.

33:21 Rissah. Or, "Beth Rissah" (*Targum Yonathan*); "Ressan" (Septuagint). In Arabic, "rissah" denotes a well stopped up with stones.

33:22 Kehelathah. Or, "Mak'helath" (*Targum Yonathan*; Septuagint; see 33:25. See *Ketoreth HaSamim*). Some say that this was the place of Korach's rebellion (16:1; *Targum Yonathan*; *Baal HaTurim*). Since there were 18 stops between Rithmah and Kadesh, the Israelites spent on the average of one year at each stop (see 33:18,36). Therefore, this occurred approximately in 2471 (1290 b.c.e.).

33:23 Mount Shefer. Or, "Shafer" (cf. Septuagint). Literally, "beautiful mountain." Some say that it was a mountain with beautiful fruit (*Targum Yonathan*).

33:24 Charadah. "Trembling." This is where they trembled because of the plague (17:12; *Targum Yonathan*).

33:25 Mak'heloth. This is said to be a place of assembly (*Targum Yonathan*), possibly where the miracle of Aaron's rod occurred (17:17, 17:24). It might have also been a place of praising God (cf. Psalms 68:27, 26:12). Some say that it was the place where a demonstration occurred (*Baal HaTurim*; cf. 16:3, 20:2).

33:26 Tachath (Targum). Identified with "Kataath" (Septuagint). Some say that *tachath* is an improper noun, denoting the lowlands of Mak'heloth (*Targum Yonathan*). It is possibly the area south of Mount Karkom or Ram el-Parudi in the Sinai.

33:27 Terach. Or Tarach. This was the name of Abraham's father (Genesis 11:25). Following Semitic cognates, *terach* denotes a kind of ibex, and this was possibly a place where such animals were found.

33:28 Mithkah. "Sweetness." This was a place with good fresh water (*Targum Yonathan*). Possibly Beer el-Mayin or Beer Bedah in the Sinai.

33:29 Chashmonah. See Psalms 68:32, Joshua 15:27. The Chashmonian family, which included Mattathias, may have had their origins here (cf. *Middoth* 1:6, *Shabbath* 21b). In Psalms 68:32, the Septuagint translates *chashman* as "ambassador." Chashmonah is identified with Selmonah (Septuagint).

33:30 Moseroth. From the word *mussar*, "chastisement." It is thus seen as a place of chastisement or rebellion (*Targum Yonathan*; see Targum on 1 Samuel 20:30). In Deuteronomy 10:6 we find the Israelites going from Beney Yaakan to Moserah; and according to tradition, the Israelites returned as far as Moserah after Aaron's death. This was an act of rebellion, and a large number of Israelites were killed (*Yerushalmi*, *Yoma* 2:2, 2a; see note on 26:12). Some say that Aaron was buried in Moserah (Malbim on 20:29).

33:31 Beney Yaakan. Beeroth Beney Yaakan, "Wells of the Sons of Yaakan" in Deuteronomy 10:6; Banaea in Septuagint. Yaakan was a Horite; see Genesis 36:27, 1 Chronicles 1:42. Others render this, "wells of distress" (*Targum Yonathan*), or "wells of the narrow pass" (Commentary on *Targum Yonathan*). Possibly Beeroth Oded in the Sinai.

³² They left Beney Yaakan and camped in Chor HaGidgad.*

³³ They left Chor HaGidgad and camped in Yatvathah.*

³⁴ They left Yatvathah and camped in Avronah.*

³⁵ They left Avronah and camped in Etzyon Gever.*

³⁶ They left Etzyon Gever and camped in Kadesh in the Tzin Desert.*

³⁷ They left Kadesh and camped at Hor Mountain* at the edge of the land of Edom. ³⁸ Aaron the priest climbed Hor Mountain at God's command, and he died there on the first day of the fifth month,* in the 40th year of the Israelites' exodus from Egypt. ³⁹ When he died on Hor Mountain, Aaron was 123 years old.*

[152. Final Journeys]

⁴⁰ The Canaanite king of Arad,* who lived in the Negev in the land of Canaan, heard that the Israelites had arrived.

⁴¹ They left Hor Mountain and camped in Tzalmonah.*

⁴² They left Tzalmonah and camped in Punon.*

⁴³ They left Punon and camped in Ovoth.*

⁴⁴ They left Ovoth and camped in the Desolate Passes* on Moab's borders.

⁴⁵ They left the passes and camped in Divon Gad.*

33:32 Chor HaGidgad. "Hole of Gidgad," or "Clefts of Gidgad" (*Targum Yonathan*). Gudgad in Deuteronomy 10:7. The Septuagint had "Gadgad Mountain."

33:33 Yatvathah. Yatbah in Deuteronomy 10:7, a place described as having flowing brooks. It is rendered, "a good, calm place" (*Targum Yonathan*).

33:34 Avronah. This is translated as a "river crossing" or "ford," *megisathah* in Aramaic (*Targum Yonathan*; cf. Targum on 21:11, Jeremiah 22:20). This may be where they crossed the Aravah wadi on the way to Elath (cf. Deuteronomy 2:8).

33:35 Etzyon Gever. "Rooster's Crow!" *K'rakh Tarngul* in Aramaic (*Targum Yonathan*; Commentary *ad loc.*) or, "Rooster City." It is a town on the Gulf of Aqaba (cf. 1 Kings 22:49, 2 Chronicles 8:17), some 2 miles east of Elath (cf. Deuteronomy 2:8, 1 Kings 9:26). The Israelites therefore had headed south from Kadesh Barnea to the Gulf of Aqaba.

33:36 Kadesh . . . This is where Miriam died (20:1). They arrived there on 1 Nissan, 2484 (March 17, 1273 b.c.e.), or according to some, 10 Nissan (March 26), see note on 20:1. According to some, however, it was in this Kadesh that they remained for 19 years (Ibn Ezra on 20:1). Therefore they would have arrived here in 2468. The Israelites were now heading north again.

33:37 Hor Mountain. See 20:22,26, 21:4. Also see below, 34:6.

33:38 first day of the fifth month. 1 Av, 2488 (July 13, 1273 b.c.e.). See Deuteronomy 10:6, 32:50.

33:39 123 years old. He was three years older than Moses (Exodus 7:7; Abarbanel).

33:40 king of Arad. See 21:1.

33:41 Tzalmonah. This is where the people began complaining again (21:5; *Targum Yonathan*). They were again heading south toward the Gulf of Aqaba (21:4, Ibn Ezra, Chizzkuni *ad loc.*).

33:42 Punon. This is where the people were bitten by poison snakes (21:6; *Targum Yonathan*; cf. Ramban).

33:43 Ovoth. See 21:10.

33:44 Desolate Passes. See 21:11. Or, "crossing fords" (Targum), or, "desolate mounds" (Rashi).

33:45 Divon Gad. This is seen as a place of good fortune (*Targum Yonathan*; see Genesis 30:11). Some say that this was on the Zered Brook (see notes on 21:12), which is where the decree that the Israelites would die in the desert for 40 years came to an end (Deuteronomy 2:14). According to tradition, this

33   ⁴⁶ They left Divon Gad and camped in Almon Divlathaymah.*

⁴⁷ They left Almon Divlathaymah and camped in the Avarim mountains* in front of Nebo.*

⁴⁸ They left the Avarim mountains and camped in the West Plains of Moab on the Jericho Jordan.* ⁴⁹ There they camped along the Jordan from Beth HaYeshimoth* to Avel Shittim* in the West Plains of Moab.

[153. Occupying the Land]

⁵⁰ God spoke to Moses in the West Plains of Moab on the Jericho Jordan, telling him to ⁵¹ speak to the Israelites and say to them:

When you cross the Jordan into the land of Canaan, ⁵² you must drive out the land's inhabitants ahead of you. You must destroy all their carved stones* and demolish all their cast metal idols and high altars. ⁵³ Clear out* the land and live in it, since it is to you that I am giving the land to occupy.

⁵⁴ It is by a lottery system* that you shall distribute the land to your families. To a large [family] give a large portion; to a smaller one, give a smaller portion. Distribute the land to the paternal tribes, and each one shall have what the lottery system dictates.

⁵⁵ If you do not drive out the land's inhabitants before you, those who

---

was on 15 Av, 2488 (July 27, 1273 b.c.e.; *Taanith* 30b), two weeks after Aaron's death (33:38).

Some identify Divon Gad with Vahev (see 21:14) and Matanah (21:18; *Adereth Eliahu*). Some say that it is on Nachaliel, a stream some 11 miles north of the Arnon (*Lekach Tov* on 21:19).

33:46 Almon Divlathaymah. Some say that this is also on the Zered Brook (Ramban). Others identify it with Matanah (Ibn Ezra), where Eshed Nachal, Beer, Matanah and Nachaliel are all in the Almon Divlathaymah area (Ibn Ezra on 21:18). Others say that it is on Nachaliel (*Lekach Tov* on 21:19), or the far side of the Arnon in 21:13 (Chizzkuni). It may be related to Almon in Joshua 21:18, Beth Divlathayim in Jeremiah 48:22, or Divlah in Ezekiel 6:14.

33:47 Avarim Mountains . . . See 27:12. Some identify this with Matanah (21:18; Chizzkuni) or Bamoth (*Lekach Tov* on 21:18).

—   **Nebo.** *N'vo* in Hebrew. This is where Moses died (Deuteronomy 32:49, 34:1). Also see above, 32:3, 32:38).

33:48 West Plains of Moab . . . Aravoth Moab. See 22:1

33:49 Beth HaYeshimoth. Some identify it with the Wasteland (*yeshimon*) in 21:19 (Chizzkuni) or with Hagai (Ibn Ezra). Others say that it is the stream running down from the Wasteland (Abarbanel). It is thought to be an area some 3 miles north of the Dead Sea's northeast corner, possibly on the Abu Arabah stream, which might be Nachaliel. Some note that Nachaliel, Bamoth and Hagai might all be in this area (Chizzkuni). See next note.

—   **Avel Shittim.** Shittim Plain (Targum; Saadia; Rashi). Some say that an *avel* is a desolate plain (Ramban on Genesis 14:6). This is Shittim mentioned in 25:1; and was the last stop before crossing the Jordan (Joshua 2:1, 3:1). It may be related to Avel Mitzraim in Genesis 50:11.

The Talmud notes that Avel Shittim is 12 miles from Beth HaYeshimoth (*Eruvin* 55b; *Yerushalmi, Shevi'ith* 6:1; Rashi). It would therefore appear that the Israelites were camped between the Ujemi Brook, just north of the Dead Sea, and the Abu Araba stream, some 5 miles to the north. The plain between the Jordan and the Aravah mountains there is approximately 12 miles wide.

33:52 carved stones. *Maskith* in Hebrew; see Leviticus 26:1 (Ibn Ezra). Or, "temples" (Targum; Rashi).

33:53 Clear out. Or, "occupy." Some see this as a commandment for the Israelites to conquer the Holy Land (Ramban, here and on *Sefer HaMitzvoth*, Additional Positive Commandment 4; Tur).

33:54 lottery system. See above, 26:55.

remain shall be barbs in your eyes and thorns in your sides, causing you troubles in the land that you settle. [56] I will then do to you what I originally planned to do to them. 33

[154. The Land's Boundaries]

[1] God spoke to Moses, telling him to [2] give the Israelites instructions and say to them: 34

When you come to the land of Canaan, this is the land within the borders of the land of Canaan that shall be your hereditary territory.

[3] Your southern sector shall begin* in the Tzin Desert* alongside Edom. The southern border to the east shall be the edge of the Dead Sea.* [4] The border shall then turn to pass to the south of the Akrabim Steps.* It shall then pass toward Tzin* with its southernmost point at* Kadesh Barnea,* and then extend to Chatzar Adar* and reach as far as Atzmon.* [5] From Atzmon the border shall turn [north] and follow the Egyptian Wadi* which shall be its far boundary to the west.

[6] The western boundary shall be the Mediterranean Sea* and [its]* shores. This shall be your western border.

[7] This shall be your northern boundary. From the Mediterranean Sea, draw a line* to Hor Mountain. [8] From Hor Mountain* draw a line along the

34:3 **begin** (cf. Saadia).
— **Tzin Desert.** See above 13:21, 20:1. The Tzin Desert is the area to the southwest of the Dead Sea. This also formed the southern border of Judah (Joshua 15:1).
— **edge of the Dead Sea.** Apparently this is the southern shore of the Dead Sea; see Joshua 15:2.
34:4 **Akrabim Steps.** Or, "Ascent of Scorpions;" see Joshua 15:3, Judges 1:36. This denotes the mountains to the southwest of the Dead Sea. It is one of the passes that lead to the northern slope of Wadi el-Fikreh.
— **Tzin.** See note on 34:3.
— **its southmost point at . . .** (Saadia). Or, "to the south of" (Rashi).
— **Kadesh Barnea.** See above, 32:8. It is thought to be some 63 miles southwest of the Dead Sea, either at the present Eyn Kadis, or Eyn el-Kuderath. Others say that it is in the area of Petra, some 48 miles due west of the Dead Sea.
— **Chatzar Adar.** Rendered as "Temples of Adarya" (*Targum Yonathan*), or, "Village of Arad" (Septuagint). Saadia translates it as Rapiach, the same as he does *chatzeroth* in Deuteronomy 2:23. It is thought to be Khirbet el-qudeirat, 5 miles northwest of Kadesh Barnea (Eyn Kadis). In Joshua 15:3, the points are given as Chetzron, Addar and Karka.
— **Atzmon.** This is identified as Kesam (*Targum Yonathan*), which is Queseimah or Kutzemah, 5 miles west of Chatzar Adar. Saadia renders it Menazel.
34:5 **Egyptian Wadi.** Wadi el Arish (Saadia; *Kaftor VaPherach* 11, 41b). See note on Genesis 15:18, Exodus 23:31. This is some 80 miles west of the Dead Sea, in the middle of the Sinai Peninsula.
34:6 **Mediterranean Sea.** Literally, "Great Sea."
— **its** (Saadia). This includes offshore islands (Rashi) and promontories (*Targum Yonathan*).
34:7 **draw a line** (Targum; Bachya). Or, "mark a boundary" (Saadia; Radak, *Sherashim*), or, "turn around" (Rashi).
34:8 **Hor Mountain.** This is not the same Hor Mountain as in 33:37 (Abarbanel; Paaneach Razah). This is identified with Amanah mountains (*Targum Yonathan*; Rashi, *Gittin* 8a, s.v. *Eyzehu*), which are usually identified with Jebel Zebedani, the range passing through Lebanon and Syria. See Song of Songs (Rashi *ad loc.*), 2 Kings 5:12. It may also be Mount Amanus, the modern Giaour Dagh. Other

34 Chamath Highway,* so that the extreme edge of the boundary is toward Tzedad.* ⁹ The border shall then extend through Zifron,* with its extreme end at Chatzar Eynan.* This shall be your northern border.

¹⁰ For your eastern boundary, you shall draw a line from Chatzar Eynan to Shefam.* ¹¹ The boundary shall then run southward* from Shefam to Rivlah* to the east of Eyin.* Continuing to the south, the boundary shall run along* the eastern shore of the Kinnereth Sea.* The boundary shall then continue south along the Jordan, continuing until the Dead Sea.

All these shall be your boundaries on all sides.

¹³ Moses gave the Israelites the following instructions:

This is the land that God commanded you to give to nine tribes and a half tribe,* and which you must distribute as hereditary property through a lottery system.* ¹⁴ However, the tribe of the Reubenite descendants, the Gaddite descendants, and half the tribe of Manasseh have already taken their hereditary property. ¹⁵ These two and a half tribes have already taken their hereditary property across the Jordan from Jericho, to the east.

---

sources identify it with Banas, possibly associated with the modern Baniyas on the Syrian Coast. Some say that it is the mountain El Hori Adah, some 15 miles south of Latakia, on the Syrian Coast due west of Chamath (*Kaftor VaPherach* 11, 42a). It would be some 160 miles south of the present Israeli border.

— **Chamath Highway.** See above, 13:21; 2 Kings 14:25. Chamath is a city in Syria, some 50 miles from the Mediterranean; the modern Hamah.

Some sources note that Chamath is near Antioch (*Targum Yerushalmi*; Rashi). Others note that the boundary line runs approximately from the Amanah Mountains to Tiberias (*Targum Yonathan*).

— **Tzedad.** See Ezekiel 47:15. The Septuagint renders it as Saradac. Tzedad is thought to be Sedad, some 70 miles east of Byblos, and 55 miles south of Chamath. This would indicate that the border turns sharply south at Chamath. Others identify Tzedad with the Baghche Pass.

Other sources identify Tzedad with Khirbet Serada, north of Abil, East of Merj Ajun, toward Hermon. Ancient sources state that Tzedad is Avlas of Kilka'ey (*Targum Yerushalmi*), which is probably Avlas in Cilicia, or Pylae Ciliciae on the northeast corner of the Mediterranean.

34:9 Zifron. This is possibly Zifran, which is northeast of Damascus, or Zaferane between Chums and Chamath. The Septuagint renders it as Defrona. Some say that this is Afrin, on the river of the same name.

— **Chatzar Eynan.** See Ezekiel 47:17, 48:1. This is the northeast border (Rashi). Some identify this with Al Qaryatein, 80 miles northeast of Damascus. Classic sources identify it with Chatzan Alakrat, some 30 miles southwest of Chamath (*Kaftor VaPherach* 11, 42b). Others identify it with Aintab.

34:10 Shefam. Identified as Sepphamar (Septuagint), Paamia (Saadia), or, Afmia (*Targum Yonathan*). Some say that this is Apamea, east of the lower Orontes valley, now known as Kulat el-Mudik.

34:11 southward. Literally, "down."

— **Rivlah.** This is identified as Dafne (*Targum Yonathan*; Saadia), the current Khirbet Dafne, 10 miles north of Lake Hulah. The Septuagint renders it as Bela. It appears obvious that the border veers sharply toward the west, most probably at Shefam.

— **Eyin.** A proper name (Targum; Rashi), or, "the spring" (Septuagint).

— **run along.** Or, "strike" (Radak, *Sherashim*; Bachya), or, "become obliterated" (*HaKethav VeHa-Kabbalah*).

— **Kinnereth . . .** That is, the Sea of Galilee.

34:13 half tribe. The other half of Manasseh; see above 32:33.

— **lottery system.** Above, 26:55.

PLATE 30. BIBLICAL BOUNDARIES OF THE HOLY LAND

34   *[155. New Leadership]*

¹⁶ God spoke to Moses, saying:

¹⁷ These are the names of the men who shall parcel out* the land. [First, there shall be] Eleazar the priest and Joshua son of Nun. ¹⁸ You shall also appoint one leader from each tribe to help parcel out the land.

¹⁹ These are the names of the men:

For the tribe of Judah, Caleb son of Yefuneh.*

²⁰ For the tribe of Simeon's descendants, Shemuel* son of Amihud.*

²¹ For the tribe of Benjamin, Elidad* son of Kislon.

²² For the tribe of Dan's descendants, the leader is Bukki son of Yagli.*

²³ Among Joseph's sons, for the tribe of Manasseh's descendants, the leader is Chaniel son of Ephod.

²⁴ For the tribe of Ephraim's descendants, the leader is Kemuel son of Shiftan.*

²⁵ For the tribe of Zebulun's descendants, the leader is Elitzafan son of Parnakh.*

²⁶ For the tribe of Issachar's descendants, the leader is Paltiel son of Azzan.

²⁷ For the tribe of Asher's descendants, the leader is Achihud son of Shelomi.

²⁸ For the tribe of Naphtali's descendants, the leader is Pedah-el son of Amihud.

²⁹ These are the [men] whom God commanded to distribute to the Israelites their hereditary property in the land of Canaan.

                                       [156. Levitical Cities]

35   ¹ God spoke to Moses in the West Plains of Moab on the Jericho Jordan, saying:

² Give orders to the Israelites, and have them give the Levites residential cities* from their hereditary holdings. Also provide the Levites suburbs*

34:17 **parcel out** (Saadia). Or, "make inherit."

34:19 **Caleb** . . . See above, 13:6.

34:20 **Shemuel.** The same as the name of the prophet, known in English as Samuel.

—   **Amihud.** A common name, see 1:10, 34:28.

34:21 **Elidad.** Some identify him with Eldad in 11:26 (q.v.; *Baal HaTurim*; cf. Septuagint).

34:22 **Yagli.** Or, Yogli.

34:24 **Kemuel** . . . Some identify him with Medad in 11:26 (q.v.; *BeMidbar Rabbah* 15:19).

34:25 **Elitzafan** . . . Some say that when Amram divorced Yocheved for a short time, Elitzafan married her, and she gave birth to Eldad and Medad (*Targum Yonathan* on 11:26). See Exodus 6:22, 1 Chronicles 15:5, 2 Chronicles 29:13.

35:2 **residential cities.** See Leviticus 35:32, Joshua 14:3, 21:2, Ezekiel 45:1; 1 Chronicles 6:42-66.

—   **suburbs.** *Migrash* in Hebrew. Or, "pasture," or, "common land." See Leviticus 25:34.

around their cities. ³ The cities shall be their residence, while the suburbs 35
shall be for their animals, property, and other amenities.*

⁴ The suburbs that you shall give the Levites shall extend outward 1000
cubits* from the city wall. ⁵ You shall measure off outside the city, 2000
cubits on the eastern side, 2000 cubits on the southern side, 2000 cubits on
the western side, and 2000 cubits on the northern side. This shall constitute
the city's suburbs, with the city in the exact center.

⁶ Along with the cities that you shall give to the Levites shall be the six
refuge cities, which you shall provide as [places] to which a murderer can
flee. Besides these [six] you shall provide an additional 42 cities. ⁷ Therefore, the total number of cities that you shall give the Levites shall be 48
cities* along with their suburbs.

⁸ These cities shall be given from the holdings of the Israelites, more
from a larger holding, and fewer from a smaller one. ⁹ Each [tribe] shall
therefore give the Levites cities in proportion to the hereditary property
that it has been given.

[157. Refuge Cities; Murder]

⁹ God spoke to Moses, telling him to ¹⁰ speak to the Israelites and say to
them:

Now that you are crossing the Jordan into the land of Canaan, ¹¹ you
must designate towns which shall serve you as refuge cities* to which a
murderer, who killed a person accidentally, can flee. ¹² These cities shall
serve you as a refuge from the avenger, so that a murderer not die until he
can stand trial before the courts.*

¹³ The towns that you provide for yourselves shall be six cities in all.
¹⁴ As refuge cities, you shall provide three towns on [this] side of the Jordan,
and three in the land of Canaan. ¹⁵ These cities shall be a place of refuge for
both proselytes and residents* among the Israelites, so that anyone who

---

35:3 **amenities** (see *Nedarim* 81a).
35:4 **1000 cubits.** In the next verse, the Torah says that 2000 cubits shall be measured. Some say that of
the 2000 cubits around the city, 1000 shall be clear land, and an additional 1000 shall be fields and
vineyards (*Sotah* 27b, according to Rashi, Rashbam). Others say that 1000 cubits shall be clear land,
and an additional 2000 cubits, fields and vineyards (*Yad, Shemitah* 13:2; *Chinukh* 342). There is also
a question as to whether this area is round or square (*Eruvin* 49b, 51a; *Midrash HaGadol*; *Paaneach
Razah*; cf. *Ramban*).
35:7 **48 cities.** Joshua 21:41, 1 Chronicles 6:42-66.
35:11 **refuge cities.** See Exodus 21:13.
35:12 **until he can stand trial . . .** Thus, all murderers were brought to the refuge cities before trial (*Makkoth* 9b; *Yad, Rotzeach* 5:7).
35:15 **residents.** Resident aliens; that is a resident alien gentile who kills another gentile (*Makkoth* 9a; *Yad,
Rotze'ach* 5:3). See Leviticus 25:6,35,47, Genesis 23:4.

35   accidentally kills a person shall be able to escape there.

   ¹⁶ [Of course,] if one strikes [his victim purposely] with an iron weapon,
killing him, then he is a murderer, and he must be put to death for murder.
¹⁷ [Similarly,] if he strikes with a hand-held* stone that can be a deadly
weapon, and [the victim] dies, he is a murderer and must be put to death for
murder. ¹⁸ Likewise, if he strikes with a deadly wooden hand weapon, and the
victim dies, he is a murderer and must be put to death for murder.

   ¹⁹ [In such cases, after the trial],* the blood avenger shall kill the murderer, and he can kill him wherever he finds him.*

   ²⁰ [The same law applies] if [the killer] pushes down [his victim] or
throws [something] down on him with hatred, causing [the victim] to die.
²¹ [This is also true] if he maliciously strikes him with his hand, causing
[the victim] to die. The person dealing the blow is a murderer and he must be
put to death. [Once he has been tried,] the blood avenger shall kill him
wherever he finds him.

   ²² [This is not true, however,] if [the killer] pushes down [his victim]
accidentally and without malice, or throws any object at him without planning to kill him. ²³ Even if it is a stone that can kill, if he did not see [the
victim], and it killed him by falling on him, [he is not a murderer], since he
was not an enemy and did not bear [his victim] any malice.

   ²⁴ [In such cases,] the court* shall follow these laws and judge between
the killer and the blood avenger. ²⁵ The court shall protect the [accidental]
murderer from the blood avenger, and return him to the refuge city to
which he fled. [The killer] must live there until the death of the high priest
anointed with the sacred oil.*

   ²⁶ If the killer goes outside the boundaries of the refuge city to which he
fled, ²⁷ and the blood avenger finds him outside the borders of his refuge
city, then if the blood avenger puts the killer to death, it is not an act of
murder.* ²⁸[The killer] is thus obligated to live in his refuge city until the
high priest dies. After the high priest dies, the killer may return to his hereditary land.

   ²⁹ These shall be the rules of law for you for all generations, no matter
where you may live.

   ³⁰ If anyone kills a human being, the murderer shall be put to death on

---

35:17 **hand-held.** Or, "a stone that fits in the hand" (Targum); or, "a fist-sized stone" (*Sifri*; Rashi).
35:19 **after the trial.** See 35:12 (*Yad, Rotze'ach* 1:5).
—   **wherever he finds him.** (cf. Rashi; *Yad, Sanhedrin* 14:8).
35:24 **court.** *Edah* in Hebrew, literally, "community" or "assembly." The court, however, acts as a repre-
       sentative of the entire community.
35:25 **sacred oil.** See Exodus 29:7, 30:30. Cf. Leviticus 4:3, 21:10.
35:27 **not an act of murder.** Literally, "there is no blood [liability]."

the basis of eyewitness testimony. However, a single eyewitness may not 35 testify against a person where the death penalty is involved.

[31] Do not take ransom for the life of a murderer who is under the death penalty, since he must be put to death. [32] Similarly, if one has fled to his refuge city, do not take ransom to allow him to return and live in the land before the high priest dies.

[33] Do not pollute the land in which you live; it is blood that pollutes the land. When blood is shed in the land, it cannot be atoned for except through the blood of the person who shed it. [34] You must not defile the land upon which you live and in which I dwell, since I, God, dwell among the Israelites.

[158. Intermarriage Between Tribes]

[1] The paternal leaders of the family of Gilead,* son of Makhir, son of 36 Manasseh (which was one of the families from Joseph's sons), came forth and spoke before Moses and the leaders who were the paternal heads of the Israelites.

[2] They said, "God has commanded you* to give the land to the Israelites as hereditary property through a lottery system.* You have also been commanded by God to give the hereditary property of Tzelafchad our brother to his daughters.*

[3] "But if they marry a member of another Israelite tribe, then the hereditary property coming to us from our fathers will be diminished, since it will be added to the tribe into which they marry. Our hereditary property from the lottery system will thus be diminished. [4] Even if the Israelites have the jubilee, their hereditary property will be added to the property of the tribe into which they marry, and it will be subtracted from the property of our fathers' tribe."

[5] Moses gave the Israelites instructions at God's command, saying, "The tribe of Joseph's descendants have a just claim.* [6] This is the word* that God has commanded regarding Tzelafchad's daughters: You may marry anyone you wish as long as you marry within your father's tribe.

36:1 **Gilead.** See above, 26:29-33.
36:2 **you.** Literally, "my lord."
— **lottery system.** Above, 26:55.
— **to his daughters.** Above, 27:7.
36:5 **just claim.** See 27:7.
36:6 **This is the word** . . . The rule that the tribes were not allowed to intermarry was only true for the generation that entered the Holy Land (*Bava Bathra* 120a). On 15 Av it was finally permitted for the tribes to intermarry, and that day was made into a festival (*Taanith* 30b). This was the anniversary of the day that the 40 year decree in the desert ended (see note on 33:45).

36   ⁷ The hereditary property of the Israelites will thus not be transferred from one tribe to another, and each person among the Israelites will remain attached to the hereditary property of his father's tribe.

⁸ "Thus, every girl who inherits property among the Israelite tribes shall marry a member of her father's tribe. Each Israelite will then inherit his fathers' hereditary property, ⁹ and the hereditary property will not be transferred from one tribe to another. Each of the Israelite tribes will then remain attached to its hereditary property."

¹⁰ Tzelafchad's daughters did exactly as God had commanded Moses. ¹¹ Machlah, Tirtzah, Chaglah, Milcah and No'ah,* the daughters of Tzelafchad, married their cousins.* ¹² They thus married into the families of Manasseh son of Joseph, and their hereditary property remained with their father's family.

¹³ These are the commandments and laws* that God instructed the Israelites through Moses in the West Plains of Moab on the Jericho Jordan.

36:11 Machlah, Tirtzah ... Here Tirtzah is listed before No'ah, since Tirtzah was older. However, in 27:1, No'ah is listed first, because she was more intelligent (*Bava Bathra* 120a; Rashi).
—   **cousins.** Literally, "uncles' sons." See above, 26:30-32.
36:13 These are the commandments ... From 26:52 to here (Chizzkuni).

דְּבָרִים

DEUTERONOMY

[1. Introduction]

1 These are the words that Moses spoke to all Israel* on the east bank* **1**
of the Jordan, in* the desert,* [and] in the Aravah,* near Suf,* in the vicinity of* Paran,* Tofel,* Lavan,* Chatzeroth* and Di Zahav.* ² [This is in the
area]* which is an eleven day journey* from Ḥoreb* to Kadesh Barnea* by
way of the Seir highlands.

1:1 **to all Israel.** Although Moses taught the Israelites many things, most were taught through Aaron and the
elders (*Eruvim* 54b). From here until 4:49, however, there are presented orations that Moses himself
delivered to all Israel (Ramban; Chizzkuni; *Adereth Eliahu*; Malbim; *HaKethav VeHaKabbalah*). These
orations were stated in the places mentioned in this verse.

— **east bank.** Literally, "far side."

— **in.** Or, "regarding" (Targum; Rashi; Ralbag). Some say that Moses named areas around the Israelite
camp after events that had happened to them earlier (Hirsch).

— **the desert.** See 1:9-14, 1:16,17.

— **Aravah.** This is the deep valley running to the north and south of the Dead Sea. Specifically, it usually
denotes the valley to the south, leading to the Gulf of Aqaba (see below 2:8; Chizzkuni).

— **Suf.** Many sources identify this with the *Yam Suf,* the "Reed Sea," the "Southern Sea," or the "Red Sea,"
possibly identified here with the Gulf of Aqaba (Targum; Rashi; Saadia; Septuagint). It may also be
identified with Sufah in Numbers 21:14.

— **vicinity of.** Or, literally, "between." Or, "[and] in the vicinity."

— **Paran.** The area to the north of Sinai and west of the Aravah, now known as the wilderness of el-Tih.
The reference is most probably to Rithmah (Number 33:18), or Kadesh Barnea (Numbers 13:3), the
place from which the spies were sent (Rashi). The reference would then be to 1:20,21, 1:29-33.

The context then seems to indicate that the Aravah and Suf were places between Sinai and Kadesh
Barnea. It appears that instead of heading directly north, the Israelites took a roundabout way to Kadesh
Barnea through the Aravah passing by the Gulf of Aqaba (Suf). Some say that this was when Moses
appointed judges in 1:16,17 (cf. *Adereth Eliahu ad loc.*). Suf might have been near Kivroth HaTaavah
(Numbers 11:34) along the west shore of the Gulf of Aqaba. See below.

— **Tofel.** Some say that Suf was between Paran and Tofel, where Tofel is identified with the Kivroth Ha-
Taavah area (*Sifri*; Rashi). Others say that it is in the area of Shittim, perhaps where the Tabernacle stood
(Ralbag). Others identify it with Marah (*Paaneach Razah*). The Septuagint notes that Tofel was in the
Paran Desert. Some sources identify it with el Tafile, a village about 15 miles southwest of the Dead Sea.

— **Lavan.** Some say that this was the place of Korach's rebellion (Ralbag). Others identify it with the place
where there were complaints about the Manna (*Sifri*; Rabbi; cf. Numbers 11:6). It is also possibly identified with Livnah in Numbers 33:20.

— **Chatzeroth.** See Numbers 11:35, 33:17. Some say that this was the place of Korach's rebellion (Rashi;
Lekach Tov; Chizzkuni).

— **Di Zahav.** A place name (Ibn Ezra; Abarbanel). Some say that it was the area where the Golden Calf was
built (*Targum*; *Sifri*; *Berakhoth* 32a; Rashi). Others identify it as the area where the Tabernacle stood
(*Paaneach Razah*). The Septuagint translates it as *katachrusea,* literally, "the gold works."

There are a number of possible interpretations regarding these place names: 1. That they are places
surrounding the Aravoth Moab where the Israelites were now camped. 2. That they were places along
the way, where Moses presented these orations to Israel (the interpretation favored in our translation).
3. That they were places regarding which Moses spoke in his orations.

1:2 **This is in the area.** Following the second interpretation above, all these places were in that area. (cf.
Chizzkuni; Abarbanel).

— **eleven day journey.** The distance between Sinai and Kadesh Barnea is actually 150 miles.

— **Ḥoreb.** Sinai, see note on Exodus 3:1.

— **Kadesh Barnea.** See note on Numbers 13:3.

1   ³ On the first of the eleventh month* in the fortieth year, Moses [also]*
spoke to the Israelites regarding all that God had commanded him for them.
⁴ This was after he had defeated Sichon king of the Amorites who lived in
Cheshbon,* and Og, king of the Bashan,* who lived in Ashtaroth, [who
was defeated in]* Edre'i.*

       ⁵ Moses began* to explain this law on the east bank of the Jordan, in the
land of Moab,* saying:

       ⁶ God our Lord spoke to us at Ḥoreb, saying, "You have remained near
this mountain too long. ⁷ Turn around and head toward the Amorite highlands and all its neighboring territories in the Aravah, the hill country, the
lowlands, the Negev, the seashore, the Canaanite territory, and Lebanon, as
far as the Euphrates River. ⁸ See! I have placed the land before you. Come,
occupy the land that God swore He would give to your fathers, Abraham,
Isaac and Jacob, and to their descendants after them."

       ⁹ I then* said to you, "I cannot lead you all by myself. ¹⁰ God your Lord
has increased your numbers until you are [now] as many as the stars of the
sky. ¹¹ May God, Lord of your fathers, increase your numbers a thousandfold,
and bless you as He promised. ¹² But how can I bear the burden, responsibility and conflict that you present if I am all by myself? ¹³ Designate for yourselves men who are wise, understanding, and known to your tribes,* and I will
appoint them* as your leaders."

       ¹⁴ You answered me, "Yours is a good suggestion."

       ¹⁵ I selected wise and well known men from among your tribal leaders,
and appointed them as your leaders—captains of thousands, captains of
hundreds, captains of fifties,* captains of tens, and police* for your tribes.

1:3   **first of eleventh month.** 1 Shevat, 2488 (January 18, 1273 b.c.e.).
—   **also** (cf. *Adereth Eliahu*; Ramban). See 5:1 ff.
1:4   **Sichon** . . . Numbers 21:21-24, below, 3:33.
—   **Og** . . . Numbers 21:31-35, below, 3:3.
—   **who was defeated in** (Ramban). Or, "Ashtaroth in Edre'i" (Rashi).
—   **Edre'i.** See Numbers 21:33.
1:5   **began** (Rashi). Or, "spoke at length" (Saadia). See note on Genesis 18:27.
—   **land of Moab.** The former land of Moab, which had been taken by Sichon.
1:9   **then.** Some say that this occurred after they left Sinai (*Adereth Eliahu*). Others say that it was before
       (Ramban).
1:13   **known to your tribes** (Rashi). Or, ". . . men from your tribes who are wise, understanding and well
       known" (Ramban), or, "knowledgeable" (*Adereth Eliahu; HaKethav VeHaKabbalah*), or, "prudent men"
       (Septuagint).
—   **I will appoint them.** Although this was Jethro's suggestion (Exodus 18:24), here the Torah only records
       Moses' oration (see note on 1:1). Some say that Moses did not discuss the appointment until after Jethro
       had left (Abarbanel).
1:15   **captains of thousands** . . . Some say that the captains of thousands and hundreds were primarily military
       leaders (cf. Numbers 31:14), while the captains of fifties were primarily Torah teachers and elders (cf.
       Isaiah 3:3; *Adereth Eliahu; HaKethav VeHaKabbalah*).
—   **and police.** Or, "who are police" (*Ibid.*). See below, 16:18.

¹⁶ I then gave your judges instructions, saying, "Listen [to every dis-   1
pute] among your brethren, and judge honestly between each man and his
brother, [even] where a proselyte [is concerned].* ¹⁷ Do not give anyone
special consideration when rendering judgment. Listen to the great and
small alike, and do not be impressed* by any man, since judgment belongs
to God. If any case is too difficult, bring it to me, and I will hear it."

¹⁸ At that time, I gave you instructions regarding everything that you
must do.

¹⁹ We then moved on from Ḥoreb* and traveled all through that great,
terrifying desert that you have seen, [going] by way of the Amorite highlands, as God our Lord commanded us. We finally came to Kadesh Barnea.*

²⁰ I said to you, "You have come to the Amorite highlands, which God
our Lord is giving us. ²¹ See! God has placed the land before you. Head
north and occupy it, as God, Lord of your fathers, has told you. Do not be
afraid and do not be concerned."

²² All of you then approached me and said, "Send men ahead of us to
explore the land. Let them bring back a report about the way ahead of us
and the cities that we shall encounter."

²³ I approved* and appointed twelve men, one for each tribe. ²⁴ They set
out* and headed north toward the hill country, going as far as Cluster Valley* and exploring the territory. ²⁵ They took samples of the area's fruit and
brought it back to us. The report that they brought back was, "The land
that God our Lord is giving us is good."

²⁶ You did not want to head north, however, and you rebelled against
God your Lord. ²⁷ You protested* in your tents, and said, "God brought us
out of Egypt because He hated us! He wanted to turn us over to the
Amorites to destroy us! ²⁸ Where are we heading? Our brothers took away
our courage by telling us that they* saw there a race that was larger and

---

1:16   **proselyte . . .** (Targum; *Yevamoth* 46b, 47a; Septuagint). Or, "resident alien" (Saadia), "impressive
        speaker" (*Sifri*; Rashi), or, "common property" (*Sanhedrin* 7b; Rashi).
1:17   **be impressed** (Septuagint), or, "fear" (Rashi; Targum; Ibn Ezra from Genesis 15:13), or, "be con-
        cerned" (Saadia). This is a commandment that a judge not be impressed by the litigants (*Sefer HaMitz-
        voth*, Negative 277).
1:19   **moved on from Ḥoreb.** See Numbers 10:33 (Chizzkuni).
—   **Kadesh Barnea.** See 1:2.
1:23   **I approved.** At God's word; Numbers 13:2.
1:24   **set out.** Literally, "turned around."
—   **Cluster Valley.** Nachal Eshkol; see Numbers 13:23.
1:27   **protested** (Ralbag). *Ragan* in Hebrew; see Proverbs 16:28, 26:22. Or, "complained" (Rashi), "spread
        false rumors" (Saadia; Rashi); "became agitated" (Hirsch); "became confused" (Ibn Janach); Or,
        "spread hypocritical rumors" (Radak, *Sherashim*).
1:28   **by telling us that . . .** Literally, ". . . saying, 'We saw . . .'"

1 taller than we, with great cities fortified to the skies, as well as children of the giants.*"

²⁹ I said to you, "Don't be so impressed*! Don't be afraid of them! ³⁰ God your Lord is going before you. He will fight for you, just as you watched Him do in Egypt. ³¹ In the desert, you [also] saw that God your Lord carried you along the road you traveled to this place, just as a man carries his son. ³² But now, here, you have no faith in God your Lord! ³³ He goes before you in fire by night and in cloud by day to show you the path to follow, just like a scout finding you a place to camp."

³⁴ When God heard what you said, He angrily swore, ³⁵ "No man* of this evil generation will see the good land that I swore to give your fathers. ³⁶ The only exception will be Caleb son of Yefuneh.* Since he followed God wholeheartedly, not only will he see it, but I will give him and his descendants the land he walked.*"

³⁷ God also displayed anger* at me because of you [and] He said, "You too will not enter [the land]. ³⁸ Joshua son of Nun,* who stands before you, will be the one to enter, and he will give Israel their hereditary property. ³⁹ The ones to enter the [land] will be the children whom you feared would be taken captive and your little ones who even now do not know good from bad. To them I will give [the land] and they will occupy it. ⁴⁰ You must now turn around and head into the desert toward the Southern Sea.*"

⁴¹ Your answer to me was, "We have sinned to God! We will head north and fight, just as God our Lord commanded us." Each of you took his weapons, and you made every effort* to head north to the highlands.

⁴²God said to me, "Tell them not to go* and not to fight, since I will not be with them. Let them not be killed by their foes."

⁴³ I spoke to you, but you would not listen. You rebelled against God's word, and willfully headed north to the highlands. ⁴⁴ The Amorites who

---

—   **giants.** Anakim.
1:29   **impressed** (*HaKethav VeHaKabbalah*; Hirsch). *Aratz* in Hebrew. Or, "don't let your spirit be broken" (Radak, *Sherashim*; Ibn Janach).
1:35   **No man.** Literally, "If any man," an oath form. See Numbers 14:22, 32:11.
1:36   **Caleb** . . . See Numbers 13:6.
—   **the land he walked** . . . See Numbers 14:24.
1:37   **displayed anger** (*Targum Yonathan*; *HaKethav VeHaKabbalah*). See Numbers 20:12 (Ralbag).
1:38   **Joshua** . . . Numbers 27:18.
1:40   **Southern Sea.** *Yam Suf* in Hebrew, here denoting the Gulf of Aqaba. See Numbers 14:25, below, 2:8.
1:41   **made every effort** (*Tzafenath Paaneach* from *Avodah Zarah 66b*). *Hin* in Hebrew. Or, "were prepared" (Rashi), "hurried" (Saadia), "agreed" (Ibn Ezra), "considered it enough" (Hirsch), or, "desired" (Radak).
1:42   **not to** . . . Actually a direct quote.

lived in the highlands came out to confront you, and chased you like bees. **1**
They struck you down in Seir as far as Chormah.*

⁴⁵ You came back and wept before God, but God would neither listen to
you nor pay attention to you. ⁴⁶ You remained in Kadesh Barnea for a long
time, as long as you remained [in all the other places].*

¹ We then turned around and headed into the desert toward the South- **2**
ern Sea* as God had told me. We traveled around in the Seir highlands* for
a long time.

[2. Encountering Esau]

² God said to me, ³ "You have traveled around these highlands long
enough. Turn around [and head] north. ⁴ Give the people the following
instructions:

"You are passing by the borders of your brothers, the descendants of
Esau, who live in Seir.* Although they fear you, be very careful ⁵ not to
provoke them. I will not give you even one foot of their land, since I have
given Mount Seir as Esau's inheritance.

⁶ "You may purchase* from them with money food to eat and drinking
water. ⁷ God your Lord is blessing you in everything you do. He knows
your way in this great desert, and for these forty years, God your Lord has
been with you, so that you lacked nothing."

⁸ We passed by our brothers, the descendants of Esau who lived in Seir,
and headed through the Aravah* from Elath and Etzyon Gever.*

[3. Encountering Moab]

We turned around* and passed through the Moab desert.* ⁹ God said to
me, "Do not attack Moab and do not provoke them to fight. I will not give

---

1:44   **Chormah.** See Numbers 14:45. Here it appears that Chormah was in Seir.
1:46   **in all the other places** (Saadia; Rashi). Some say that the Israelites were in Kadesh Barnea for 19 years
      (*Seder Olam* 8; Rashi; *Lekach Tov*), while others indicate that they were there for 18 (*Moreh Nevukhim* 3:50;
      Midrash HaGadol). See note on Numbers 33:18.
2:1   **Southern Sea.** See 1:40.
—   **Seir highlands.** See Genesis 14:6, 36:8.
2:4   **Esau . . .** See Genesis 36:8. This is the encounter with Edom, in Numbers 20:14-21.
2:6   **You may purchase.** Or, "Do you then have to purchase" (Ramban).
2:8   **through the Aravah.** The deep valley to the south of the Dead Sea, see note on 1:1. Or, "the Aravah
      Highway."
—   **Elath and Etzyon Gever.** See note on Numbers 33:35. Both are on the Gulf of Aqaba. The Israelites thus
      headed north from the Gulf of Aqaba directly toward the Dead Sea.
—   **turned around.** Toward the east (Rashi), to go around the Moabite territory.
—   **Moab desert.** To the east of Moab; see Numbers 21:11, 33:43.

2   you their land as an inheritance, since I have already given Ar* to Lot's
descendants* as their heritage.

¹⁰ "The Emim* lived there originally, a powerful and numerous race, as
tall as giants.* ¹¹ As giants, they might be considered Rephaim,* but the
Moabites called them Emim. ¹² It was like Seir, where the Horites* lived
originally, but were driven out by Esau's descendants, who annihilated
them and lived there in their place. This is also what Israel is to do in the
hereditary land that God gave them.

¹³ "Now get moving and cross the Zered Brook*!"

We thus crossed the Zered Brook. ¹⁴ From the time that we left Kadesh
Barnea until we crossed the Zered Brook, 38 years had elapsed, during
which the generation of warriors had died out from the camp, as God had
sworn. ¹⁵ God's hand had been directed specifically against them, crushing
them* so that they would be finished. ¹⁶ It was at this time that all the men
of war among the people finished dying.*

[4. Encountering Ammon]

¹⁷ God then* spoke to me, saying, ¹⁸ "You are now about to pass
through Ar, which is Moabite territory. ¹⁹ You will be coming close to the
Ammonites,* but do not attack or provoke them. I will not let you occupy
the land of the Ammonites, since I have given it as a heritage to the descendants of Lot.*

²⁰ "This might also be considered the territory of the Rephaim,* since
the Rephaim lived there originally. The Ammonites refer to them as Zamzumim.* ²¹ The [Rephaim] were a powerful and numerous race, as tall as

---

2:9   **Ar.** The name of the area where Moab lived (Rashi). See Numbers 21:15,28; below 2:18.
—   **Lot's descendants.** Moab was Lot's illegitimate son (Genesis 19:37).
2:10 **Emim.** They lived in Shavah Kiryathaim but were killed by the four kings (Genesis 14:5).
—   **giants.** *Anakim* in Hebrew.
2:11 **As giants, they might be considered . . .** (cf. Ramban; Septuagint). Or, "The Rephaim consider them
      Anakim . . ." (cf. Rashi). See 2:20.
2:12 **Horites.** See Genesis 14:6, 36:20.
2:13 **Zered Brook.** See Numbers 21:12.
2:15 **crushing them** (Radak, *Sherashim*). *Hamam* in Hebrew, see Esther 9:24. Or, "agitate" (Rashi, Saadia),
      "kill" (Septuagint), or, "kill suddenly" (Hirsch).
2:16 **finished dying.** See note on Numbers 33:45.
2:17 **God then.** Only after the previous generation had died out (*Taanith* 30b; Rashi). See note on Numbers
      20:6.
2:19 **Ammonites.** See Numbers 21:24.
—   **descendants of Lot.** See Genesis 19:38.
2:20 **Rephaim.** Who lived in Ashteroth-Karnayim (Genesis 14:5), and whose land was promised to Abraham
      (Genesis 15:20; Rashi; *Midrash Aggadah*).
—   **Zamzumim.** Some say that these are the Zuzim in Genesis 14:5 (Rashi *ibid.*). Others translated *Zam-
      zumim* as "plotters" (Targum; Chizzkuni; *Tur*), or, "strong nations" (Septuagint). In Arabic, *zamzam*

the giants, but God annihilated them before [the Ammonites] who drove   2
them out and lived [there] in their place.

²² "This was the same as God had done for Esau's descendants who
lived in Seir, when he annihilated the Horites* before them, allowing
[Esau's descendants] to drive them out and live in their place to this very
day. ²³ This was also true of the Avvim* who lived from Chatzerim* to
Gazza*; the Kaftorim* came from Kaftor and defeated them, occupying
their territories.

²⁴ "Now set out and cross the Arnon Brook.* See! I have given over
Sichon, the Amorite king of Chesbon,* and his land, into your hands. Begin
the occupation! Provoke him into war! ²⁵ Today I am beginning to make all
the nations under the heavens fear and dread you. Whoever hears of your
reputation will tremble* and be anxious* because of you."

²⁶ I sent emissaries from the Kedemoth Desert* to Sichon king of
Cheshbon with a peaceful message, saying, ²⁷ "We* wish to pass through

---

means to speak gibberish, so that *zamzumim* may be the equivalent of the Greek-based "barbarian,"
which means "gibberish speaker."

2:22   **Horites.** See 2:12. Some say that they were descended from the Rephaim (Ramban).

2:23   **Avvim.** Some say that they were a Canaanite tribe (*Targum Yonathan*) and hence identify them with the
Chivites (Genesis 10:17; *Baaley Tosafoth*; Ramban). They are said to be related to the Rephaim (*Bereshith
Rabbah* 26:16), who in turn may have been descendants of the Nefilim (Ramban).
    Others, however, maintain that the Avvim were a Philistine tribe (*Chullin* 60b; Rashi) since the Avvim
were later found to be one of the divisions of the Philistines (Joshua 13:3). However, if the Kaftorim (see
next note) were a Philistine tribe, they might have taken the name of the Avvim from their geographic
location. Indeed, there is a city in Benjamin by the name of Avvim, (Joshua 18:23), possibly identified
with Ai. There was also Avith in Edom (Genesis 36:36), and Avvah (2 Kings 17:24).

—   **Chatzerim.** Asedoth in the Septuagint, identified with Dafiach (Targum) or Rafiach (Saadia), the modern
Rafah, some 16 miles southwest of Gazza on the Mediterranean coast. This was the southernmost border
town in the Holy Land (cf. *Tosefta, Shevi'ith* 4:5. However, there was also a Rafiach to the south of the
Dead Sea (*Targum Yerushalmi* on Numbers 34:15). Other sources, however, translate *chatzerim* as "courtyards" or, "open villages" (*Targum Yonathan*; Ramban; *Paaneach Razah*). See Leviticus 15:31, Genesis
25:16.

—   **Gazza.** Azza in Hebrew. This was originally Canaanite territory (Genesis 10:19). In Abraham's time,
Gerar, which was between Rafah (Chatzerim) and Gazza was a Philistine capital (Genesis 20:2), although
it was also originally a Canaanite city (Genesis 10:19).

—   **Kaftorim.** These were a Philistine people (Genesis 10:14). Some of them may have taken the name Avvim
from the previous dwellers of their area (Joshua 13:3, see previous notes). Some identify the Kaftorim
with the Capacodians (Targum; Septuagint). Others identify them with the Demiatim (Saadia), the
group living in Demat on the eastern delta of the Nile, near El Arish and west of the modern Port Said.
Still other sources state that their place of origin was Cyprus or Crete.

2:24   **Arnon Brook.** See Numbers 21:13.
—   **Sichon . . .** Numbers 21:21 ff.

2:25   **tremble.** (Hirsch from Genesis 12:5). *Ragaz* in Hebrew.
—   **be anxious.** (Hirsch from Exodus 15:14). *Chul* in Hebrew.

2:26   **Kedemoth Desert.** Kedemoth was an eastern city given to Reuben (Joshua 13:18) and designated as a
Levitical city (Joshua 21:37, 1 Chronicles 6:64). Since *kedem* means "east," some call this the "eastern
desert" (Chizzkuni), while others identify it with Matanah in Numbers 21:18 (Ibn Ezra). It is thought to
be the present Ez Zafaran, some 16 miles east of the Dead Sea and 13 miles north of the Arnon, near
Matanah and Almon Divlathaymah. Hence, the Israelites were then to the east of Sichon's territory.

2:27   **We.** Literally, "I." See Numbers 21:22.

2 your land. We will travel along the main highway,* not turning to the right or the left. ²⁸ We will buy the food we eat for cash, and will pay for the drinking water you give us. We only wish to pass through on foot, ²⁹ just as we passed by the territory of Esau in Seir* and Moab in Ar. We only wish to ross the Jordan to the land that God our Lord is giving us."

But Sichon, King of Cheshbon, would not let us pass through his land. God had hardened his spirit and made his heart firm, so that He could give [his land] over to our hands, as it is today.

[5. Last Episodes in the Desert]

³¹ God said to me, "See! I have begun to place Sichon and his land before you. Begin the occupation and take possession of his land."

³² Sichon and all his troops came out to meet us in battle at Yahatz.* ³³ God our Lord gave him over to us, so that we killed him along with his sons and all his troops. ³⁴ We then captured all his cities, and we annihilated* every city, including the men,* women and children, not leaving any survivors. ³⁵ All that we took as our plunder were the animals and the goods of the cities we captured.

³⁶ Thus, in [the entire territory] from Aro'er* on the edge of the Arnon Gorge and the city in the valley itself, to the Gilead,* there was no city that could defend itself* against us, since God had placed everything at our disposal. ³⁷ The only land that we did not approach was the Ammonite territory,* which included the area around the Jabbok,* the cities of the highlands, and all the other [areas] that God our Lord had commanded us [to avoid].

3 ¹ We then turned and traveled along the road to the Bashan, where Og* and his troops came to confront us in battle at Edre'i. ² God said to me, "Do not be afraid of him, since I have turned him over to you along with all his people and his land. You will do the same to him as you did to the Amorite king Sichon, who lived in Cheshbon."

—   **main highway.** Literally, "the road the road." "King's Highway" in Numbers 21:22.
2:29   **Just as we passed by . . .** (Ibn Ezra), without fighting (*Lekach Tov*), and with them selling us food (Rashi; cf. Ramban on 23:5). Literally, "as they did to me." However, Edom (Esau) did not actually let the Israelites pass through their land (Numbers 20:21).
2:32   **Yahatz.** See Numbers 21:23
2:34   **annihilated.** *Charam* in Hebrew. Or, "declared taboo" (see Leviticus 27:29). See 20:16.
—   **men** (Targum; Rashi; Radak, s.v. *Mathath*). Cf. Genesis 34:30. Or, "in succession" (Septuagint).
2:36   **Aro'er.** An important city in Ar, the Moabite territory (above 2:9). It is just north of the Arnon, some 13 miles east of the Dead Sea.
—   **Gilead.** To the north. See Genesis 31:21, Numbers 32:1.
—   **defend itself** (Hirsch). *Sagav* in Hebrew. Or, "was stronger than" (Targum, Ibn Ezra); "remained above (Radak, *Sherashim*); or, "escaped" (Septuagint).
2:37   **Jabbok.** See Genesis 32:23, Numbers 21:24.
3:1   **Og.** Numbers 21:33.

³ God thus also turned Og, king of the Bashan, and all his people over   3
to us, and we defeated him, not leaving any survivors. ⁴ We then captured
all his cities, not leaving a single city that we did not take from [his people].
These included the entire Argov group* of 60 cities that constituted Og's
kingdom in the Bashan. ⁵ They were all cities fortified with high walls,
gates and bars, and there were also very many open towns.*

⁶ We destroyed [these cities] just as we had done to those of Sichon,
king of Cheshbon, annihilating every man, woman and child. ⁷ For ourselves, we took as plunder all the animals and all the spoils of the cities.

⁸ At that time we thus took the lands of the two Amorite kings who
lived to the east* of the Jordan, in the area between the Arnon Brook and
Mount Hermon.* ⁹ (The people of Sidon* refer to Hermon as Siryon,* while
the Amorites call it Senir.*) ¹⁰ [The occupied territory included] all the cities
of the flatlands, the entire Gilead, and the entire Bashan as far as Salkhah*
and Edre'i;* the cities of Og's kingdom in the Bashan.

¹¹ Of all the Rephaim, only Og had survived. His bed* was made of
iron. It is in the Ammonite city of Rabbah,* nine standard* cubits long and
four cubits wide.*

3:4   **Argov group.** *Chevel Argov* in Hebrew. (cf. Ibn Ezra; Septuagint). See 3:14, 1 Kings 4:13; cf. 2 Kings
15:25. Saadia identifies the Argov as Almogav, the land between the Arnon and the Jabbok. The Targum
renders Argov as *Tarkhona*, which Rashi interprets as "royal cities," but which others see as a place name
(*Arukh*). Others see Argov as coming from the root *ragav* (cf. Job 21:33, 38:38), a swamp (Ibn Janach), a
mound, or a river tributary (Radak, *Sherashim*), a canal (Ibn Ezra on Job 21:33) or a gully (Ibn Ezra on
Job 38:38). Some say that the Argov area is around Suwet, south of the upper Yarmuk, while others
identify it with el-Leja, east of Lake Kinnereth (see *Menachoth* 8:3).

3:5   **open towns** (Targum; Rashi). Or, "Perizite towns" (Septuagint; cf. Genesis 13:7, 15:20).

3:8   **east.** Literally, "other side."

—   **Mount Hermon.** The large mountain to the north of the Holy Land. At 9232 feet high, it is the highest
mountain of the southern Lebanon range.

3:9   **Sidon.** Tzidon in Hebrew; see Genesis 10:15,19, 49:13. This was a city on the Mediterranean, just north-
west of Hermon.

—   **Siryon.** See Psalms 29:6. Some say that it denotes "falling fruit" (*Targum Yonathan*) or "much fruit" (*Targum Yerushalmi*) or it can possibly be related to Shiryon, armor. See 4:48.

—   **Senir.** See Ezekiel 27:5, Song of Songs 4:8, 1 Chronicles 5:23. This denotes "snow mountains" (Targum;
Rashi). The eastern peaks are known as Siryon, while the northern peaks are known as Senir (cf. Malbim).

3:10   **Salkhah.** Identified with the present Salkhad, 70 miles east and 20 miles south of the Kinnereth Sea and
some 40 miles east of Edre'i. It forms the extreme southeast of Bashan, and is situated on very high
ground, providing a natural fortress.

—   **Edre'i.** See Numbers 21:33. It is approximately halfway between Salkhah and the Kinnereth.

3:11   **bed.** *Eres* in Hebrew. Or, "cradle" (Rashbam; *HaKethav VeHaKabbalah*).

—   **Rabbah.** Cf. Joshua 13:25. Or, Rabbath, cf. 2 Samuel 12:26, Jeremiah 49:2, Ezekiel 21:25 (Targum).
This was the capital city of Ammon, some 22 miles east of the Jordan, and 18 miles north of the Dead
Sea. In Roman times it was known as Philadelphia (cf. Josephus, *Wars* 1:6:3), and it is the present
Amman, capital of Jordan. The Septuagint translates *Rabbah* as *akra*, Greek for a chief city, citadel or
extremity.

—   **standard.** Literally, (at the end of the verse), "the cubit of a [normal] man."

—   **and four cubits wide.** The bed was thus 13½′ × 6′. Since a bed is usually one third longer than the person, this would indicate that Og was some 6 cubits or 9 feet high (*Moreh Nevukhim* 2:47).

3   ¹² Of the land that we* then captured, I gave the Reubenites and Gaddites [the territory] between Aro'er on the Arnon Gorge and the [southern]
half of the Gilead highlands, along with the cities there.

¹³ The rest of the Gilead and the entire Bashan which had been Og's
kingdom, I gave to half of the tribe of Manasseh. This included the entire
Argov group and the entire Bashan, which was known as the land of the
Rephaim. ¹⁴ Yair,* a descendant of Manasseh, took the Argov group as far
as the borders of the Geshurites* and Maakhathites,* and he gave that area
in the Bashan the name Chavvath Yair, [a name] which is still used today.
¹⁵ To Makhir* I gave the Gilead region.

¹⁶ To the Reubenites and Gaddites, I gave [the territory] between the
Gilead and the Arnon Gorge, including the interior of the gorge and its
boundary.* [The territory extended] as far as the gorge of the Jabbok,* the
border of the Ammonites. ¹⁷ [It also included] the Aravah,* the Jordan, and
its boundary, from the Kinnereth* as far as the Aravah Sea,* which is [the
portion of] the Dead Sea under the rapids* on the cliff to the east.

¹⁸ At that time I gave you* instructions, saying, "God your Lord has
given you this land as a heritage. Let every able-bodied man among you go
forth ahead of your fellow Israelites as a special force. ¹⁹ I know that you
have much livestock; your wives, children and livestock can remain in the
cities I have given you ²⁰ until God gives your brethren the same haven that
He has given you. When they occupy the land that God your Lord is giving
them across the Jordan, each man will be able to return to his inheritance
that I have given you."

3:12   **Of the land . . .** (Saadia; Ramban). Or, "We thus occupied that land at that time" (Rashi).
3:14   **Yair.** See Numbers 32:41.
—   **Geshurites.** An Aramaic nation (cf. 2 Samuel 15:8), possibly identified with Gether son of Aram (Genesis
        10:23). Others identify them with the Girgashites (Septuagint; cf. Genesis 10:6, 15:21, Joshua 3:10).
        They later lived with the Israelites (Joshua 13:13), inhabiting the city of Geshur (Joshua 12:5, 13:11, 2
        Samuel 3:3). This is the area between Gilead and Hermon, particularly that to the east and northeast of
        the Kinnereth. Some identify it with the present Jaulan, or Jisre in Ledjah, to the east of Jaulan. Ancient
        sources identify it with Kirvah (*Targum Yonathan*; cf. *Shabbath* 45b).
—   **Maakhathites.** Maakhah was a son of Nachor (Genesis 22:24), and the city Maakhah was near Aram
        Tzovah (2 Samuel 10:9), usually identified with Aleppo, Syria. Also see 2 Samuel 20:14, 1 Kings 15:20.
        See note on Genesis 22:24.
3:15   **Makhir.** Numbers 32:40.
3:16   **its boundary** (Saadia). Or, "far bank" (Rashi).
—   **Jabbok.** See Genesis 32:23, Numbers 21:24. The Jabbok formed the northwest border of Ammon.
3:17   **Aravah.** See 1:1.
—   **Kinnereth.** See Numbers 34:11.
—   **Aravah Sea.** See below 4:49, Joshua 3:16, 12:3, 2 Kings 14:25. This may be the small bay at the north
        end of the Dead Sea, just to the west of the point where the Jordan flows into it.
—   **rapids.** Or, "waterfall," *ashdoth* in Hebrew. See Numbers 21:15.
3:18   **you.** Speaking to Reuben and Gad (Rashi; Ibn Ezra).

²¹ At that time, I gave instructions to Joshua,* saying, "Your own eyes **3** have seen all that God your Lord has done to these two kings. God will do the same to all the kingdoms [in the land] to which you will be crossing. ²² Do not fear them, since God your Lord is the One who will be fighting for you."

VaEthChanan   וָאֶתְחַנַּן

[6. Moses' Plea to Enter the Holy Land]

²³ At that time I pleaded with God, saying, ²⁴ "O God, Lord! You have begun to show me* Your greatness and Your display of power.* What Force is there in heaven or earth who can perform deeds and mighty acts as You do? ²⁵ Please let me cross [the Jordan]. Let me see the good land across the Jordan, the good mountain* and the Lebanon."

²⁶ But God had turned Himself against* me because of you, and He would not listen to me. God said to me, "Enough! Do not speak to Me any more about this! ²⁷ Climb to the top of the cliff, and gaze to the west, north, south and east. Let your eyes feast on it, since you will not cross the Jordan. ²⁸ Give Joshua instructions, strengthening him and giving him courage, since he will be the one to lead these people across, and he will parcel out to them the land that you will see."

²⁹ At that time we were staying in the valley* facing Beth Peor.*

[7. Foundations of the Faith]

¹ Now, Israel,* listen to the rules and laws that I am teaching you to do, **4** so that you will remain alive and come to occupy the land that God, Lord of your fathers, is giving you. ² Do not add to the word that I am commanding you, and do not subtract from it. You must keep all the commandments of God your Lord, which I am instructing you.

³ You have seen with your own eyes what God did at the Baal Peor*

3:21 **Joshua.** See Numbers 27:23 (Chizzkuni).
3:24 **me.** Literally, "Your servant."
—   **display of power.** Literally, "mighty hand."
3:25 **good mountain.** Some say that the reference is to Jerusalem (*Sifri*; *Berakhoth* 48b; Rashi).
3:26 **turned Himself against** (Hirsch; Septuagint). *Hith-avar* in Hebrew. Or, "made Himself angry" (Targum; Rashi; Radak, *Sherashim*). See Zephaniah 1:15, Psalms 78:49 (Bachya).
3:29 **valley.** (Targum; Septuagint). *Gai* in Hebrew. Or, "plateau" (Ibn Ezra). Some identify this with the Avarim Mountains (Numbers 27:12; Ibn Ezra). See Numbers 21:20.
—   **Beth Peor.** "The house of Peor." See Numbers 23:28, 25:3.
4:1   **Now, Israel . . .** This was said in the valley (Ibn Ezra). See 4:41. This marks the beginning of the commandments (Ramban).
4:3   **Baal Peor.** See Numbers 25:3 ff.

4 episode. God your Lord annihilated every person among you who followed Baal Peor. ⁴ Only you, the ones who remained attached to God your Lord, are all alive today.

⁵ See! I have taught you rules and laws as God my Lord has commanded me, so [that you] will be able to keep them in the land to which you are coming and which you will be occupying. ⁶ Safeguard and keep [these rules], since this is your wisdom and understanding in the eyes of the nations. They will hear all these rules and say, "This great nation is certainly a wise and understanding people."

⁷ What nation is so great that they have God close to it, as God our Lord is, whenever we call Him? ⁸ What nation is so great that they have such righteous rules and laws, like this entire Torah that I am presenting before you today?

⁹ Only take heed and watch yourself very carefully, so that you do not forget the things that your eyes saw. Do not let [this memory] leave your hearts, all the days of your lives. Teach your children and children's children about ¹⁰ the day you stood before God your Lord at Horeb.

It was then that God said to me, "Congregate the people for Me, and I will let them hear My words. This will teach them to be in awe of Me as long as they live on earth, and they will also teach their children."

¹¹ You approached and stood at the foot of the mountain. The mountain was burning with a fire reaching the heart of heaven, with darkness, cloud and mist.*

¹² Then God spoke to you out of the fire. You heard the sound of words, but saw no image; there was only a voice. ¹³ He announced to you His covenant, instructing you to keep the Ten Commandments,* and He wrote them on two stone tablets.* ¹⁴ At that time, God commanded me to teach you rules and laws, so that you will keep them in the land which you are crossing [the Jordan] to occupy.

¹⁵ Watch yourselves very carefully, since you did not see any image on the day that God spoke to you out of the fire at Horeb. ¹⁶ You shall therefore not become corrupt and make a statue depicting any symbol.* [Do not make] any male or female image, ¹⁷ or the image of any animal on earth, any winged creature* that flies in the sky, ¹⁸ any lower form of land animal, or

---

4:11   mist. *Arafel.* See Exodus 20:18. Or, "storm" (Septuagint).
4:13   **Ten Commandments.** Literally, "Ten Words" or "Ten Statements."
—   **tablets.** See Exodus 31:18.
4:16   **symbol.** *Semel* in Hebrew; see Ezekiel 8:3, 2 Chronicles 33:7. Or, "visible form" (*Chothem Takhnith*); "imaginary form" (Hirsch), or, "four-sided form" (Malbim).
4:17   **winged creature** (cf. *Chullin* 139b).

any animal that lives in the water below the earth.   **4**

¹⁹ When you raise your eyes to the sky, and see the sun, moon, stars and other heavenly bodies, do not bow down to them or worship them. It was to all the [other] nations under the heavens that God made them a portion. ²⁰ But you, God Himself took, and He brought you out of the iron crucible that was Egypt, so that you would be His heritage nation, as you are today.

²¹ God displayed anger at me because of your words, and He swore that I would not cross the Jordan, and that I would not come to the good land that God your Lord is giving you as a heritage. ²² I will die in this land and will not cross the Jordan, while you will be the ones to cross and occupy this good land.

²³ Be careful that you not forget the covenant that God your Lord made with you. [Do not] make for yourself any statue image that is forbidden by God. ²⁴ God your Lord is [like]* a consuming fire, a God demanding exclusive allegiance.*

[8. Allegiance to God]

²⁵ When you have children and grandchildren, and have been established in the land for a long time, you might become decadent and make a statue of some image, committing an evil act in the eyes of God your Lord and making Him angry. ²⁶ I call heaven and earth as witnesses for you today that you will then quickly perish from the land that you are crossing the Jordan to occupy. You will not remain there very long, since you will be utterly destroyed.

²⁷ God will then scatter you among the nations, and only a small number will remain among the nations to which God will lead you. ²⁸ There you will serve gods that men have made out of wood and stone, which cannot see, hear, eat or smell. ²⁹ Then you will begin to seek God your Lord, and if you pursue Him with all your heart and soul, you will eventually find Him.

³⁰ When you are in distress and all these things have happened to you, you will finally* return to God your Lord and obey Him. ³¹ God your Lord is a merciful Power, and He will not abandon* you or destroy you; He will not forget the oath He made upholding your fathers' covenant.

³² You might inquire about times long past, going back to the time that

---

4:24   **like** (Chizzkuni). Or, "God's . . . [punishment] is a burning fire" (Saadia).
—   **demanding exclusive allegiance.** See Exodus 20:5.
4:30   **finally.** Literally, "in the end of days," possibly a Messianic prophecy.
4:31   **abandon** (Targum, Rashi; Septuagint). *Raphah* in Hebrew. Or, "turn you away" (Saadia), or, "weaken you" (Ibn Ezra).

4 God created man on earth, [exploring] one end of the heavens to the other. See if anything as great as this has ever happened, or if the like has ever been heard.

³³ Has any nation ever heard God speaking out of fire, as you have, and still survived? ³⁴ Has God ever done miracles* bringing one nation out of another nation with such tremendous miracles, signs, wonders, war, a mighty hand and outstretched arm,* and terrifying phenomena, as God did for you in Egypt before your very eyes?

³⁵ You are the ones who have been shown, so that you will know that God is the Supreme Being,* and there is none besides Him.

³⁶ From the heavens, He let you hear His voice admonishing you, and on earth He showed you His great fire, so that you heard His words from the fire.

³⁷ It was because He loved your fathers, and chose their* children after them, that [God] Himself* brought you out of Egypt with His great power. ³⁸ He will drive away before you nations that are greater and stronger than you, so as to bring you to their lands, and give them to you as a heritage, as [He is doing] today.

³⁹ Realize it today and ponder it in your heart: God is the Supreme Being in heaven above and on the earth beneath—there is no other.

⁴⁰ Keep His decrees and commandments that I am presenting to you today, so that He will be good to you and your children after you. Then you will endure for a long time in the land that God your Lord is giving you for all time.

[9. Refuge Cities]

⁴¹ Moses then* designated three cities on the east* of the Jordan, toward the rising sun, ⁴² where a murderer could escape.* If a person killed his

---

4:34 **done miracles** (Targum; Rashi). *Nissah* in Hebrew. Or, "lifted a banner" (Saadia), or, "attempted" (Septuagint).
— **mighty hand** . . . See Exodus 6:6, 13:3.
4:35 **Supreme Being.** Literally, "*The* God." Possibly denoting the sum total of everything ascribed to all deities. *Ha-Elohim* in Hebrew.
4:37 **their** (Saadia). Literally, "his." Some say that this denotes Jacob in particular (*Targum Yonathan*; Rashi).
— **Himself** (*Lekach Tov* from 2 Samuel 17:11; Septuagint). *Be-phanav* in Hebrew, literally, "with His presence," "with His 'face', " or "before Him." See Exodus 33:14. Or, "face," can denote desire (Saadia), anger (Ibn Ezra), or "the angel of the face" (Isaiah 63:9; *Tur*). Or, "before" [Egypt]" (Chizzkuni).
4:41 **then.** (Ramban; cf. Ibn Ezra). Or, "Then I designated" (Chizzkuni). Some say that Moses designated these cities after he had been told that he would not see the promised land (*Devarim Rabbah* 2:26; Malbim), or after he saw it from afar (*Tzafenath Paaneach*).
— **east.** Literally, "other side."
4:42 **where a murderer** . . . See Numbers 35:14.

neighbor without intent and without prior enmity, he would be able to   **4**
escape to one of these cities and live.

⁴³ [The cities were] Betzer* in the desert flatlands for the Reubenites,
Ramoth* in the Gilead for the Gaddites, and Golan* in Bashan for the
Manassites.

⁴⁴ This* is the law that Moses presented before the Israelites.

⁴⁵ These* are the rituals,* rules and laws that Moses discussed with the
Israelites when they left Egypt. ⁴⁶ [They were now] on the east bank of the
Jordan, in the valley opposite Beth Peor* in the land of Sichon, king of
Cheshbon, whom Moses and the Israelites had defeated when they left
Egypt.

⁴⁷ [The Israelites] occupied [Sichon's] land, as well as the land of Og,
king of Bashan. [These were] the two Amorite kings to the east of the Jordan. ⁴⁸ [The land] extended from Aro'er on the edge of the Arnon Gorge,*
to Mount Siyon,* also known as Hermon, ⁴⁹ as well as the entire flood
plain* on the east bank of the Jordan, as far as the Aravah Sea under the
rapids* flowing from the cliff.

[10. Review of the Ten Commandments]

¹ Moses summoned* all Israel, and said to them: **5**

Listen, Israel, to the rules and laws that I am publicly* declaring to you
today. Learn them and safeguard them, so that you will be able to keep
them.

4:43   **Betzer.** See Joshua 20:8, 1 Chronicles 6:63. Although its exact location is unknown, the Talmud (*Makkoth* 9b) states that it was parallel to Hebron, and it was therefore probably near Divon (see Numbers 21:30). Some identify it with Bosor in 1 Maccabees 5:26,28. It is also identified with Kevathirim (*Targum Yona-than*), which is also unknown.

—   **Ramoth.** Usually identified with Ramoth Gilead; see Joshua 21:36, 1 Kings 22:3. This is the modern Tell Remith or es-Salt, 25 miles east of the Jordan, and 12 miles south of the Kinnereth. However, according to the Talmud, Ramoth parallels Shechem, while Tell Remith is considerably to its north.

—   **Golan.** See Joshua 20:8, 21:27, 1 Chronicles 6:56. It was later known as Gaulon (Eusebius, *Omonastica Sacra* 242), and Gaulanitis (Josephus, *Antiquities* 8:2:3, *Wars* 1:4:4, 3:3:1, 4:1:1, 4:1:5). This is the modern Jaulan or Sachem el Jolan, some 18 miles east of the Kinnereth. Other sources identify it with an unknown city, Dabra (*Targum Yonathan*). The Talmud states that it parallels Kadesh in Naphtali.

4:44   **This.** All the above (*Lekach Tov*; cf. Bachya). Or, the following (Rashi).

4:45   **These.** The following (Chizzkuni).

—   **rituals.** *Edoth* in Hebrew. Actually, "commemorative rituals."

4:46   **valley opposite Beth Peor.** See 3:29.

4:48   **Aro'er on the edge . . .** See 2:36, 3:12.

—   **Siyon.** See 3:9. Cf. Psalms 133:3.

4:49   **flood plain.** *Aravah* in Hebrew.

—   **Aravah Sea . . .** See above 3:17.

5:1   **summoned.** To repeat the Ten Commandments to the younger generation that had not been at Sinai (Chizzkuni; cf. Bachya).

—   **publicly.** Literally, "in your ears." See Genesis 20:8, 23:10.

5   [2] God your Lord made a covenant* with you at Horeb. [3] It was not with
your ancestors that God made this covenant, but with us—those of us who
are still alive here today. [4] On the mountain, God spoke to you face to face*
out of the fire. [5] I stood between you and God at that time, to tell you God's
words, since you were afraid* of the fire, and did not go up on the mountain.

[God then] declared [the Ten Commandments]

[11. The First Two Commandments]

[6] I am God your Lord, who brought you out of Egypt, from the place of
slavery.

[7] Do not have any other gods before Me. [8] Do not represent [such gods] by
a statue or picture of anything in the heaven above, on the earth below, or in
the water below the land. [9] Do not bow down to [such gods] and do not worship them. I, God your Lord, am a god who demands exclusive worship.
Where My enemies are concerned, I keep in mind the sin of the fathers for
[their] descendants for three and four [generations]. [10] But to those who love
Me, and keep My commandments, I show love for thousands [of generations].

[12. The Third Commandment]

[11] Do not take the name of God your Lord in vain. God will not allow
the person who takes His name in vain to go unpunished.

[13. The Fourth Commandment]

[12] Observe* the Sabbath to keep it holy, as God your Lord commanded
you.* [13] You can work during the six weekdays, and do all your tasks, [14] but
Saturday is the Sabbath to God your Lord, so do not do anything that constitutes work. [This includes] you, your son, your daughter, your male and
female slave, your ox, your donkey, your [other] animals, and the foreigner
who is in your gates.

5:2   **covenant.** See Exodus 19:5, 24:8, 34:27 (cf. *Lekach Tov*). Also see above, 4:23, below 28:69.
5:4   **face to face.** See Exodus 33:11 (Bachya).
5:5   **you were afraid.** See Exodus 20:15,16.
—   **the Ten Commandments.** Given earlier in 20:2-14.
5:12   **Observe.** Or, "safeguard." "Remember" in Exodus 20:8. The earlier generation had experienced the
         Sabbath with the Manna (Exodus 16:26), and therefore merely had to remember it. However, the
         generation that would enter the promised land, whom Moses was addressing, would henceforth have to
         'safeguard' the Sabbath (cf. Chizzkuni). According to tradition, the Ten Commandments were given
         prophetically, and at Sinai the people heard the words "remember" and "observe" simultaneously
         (*Mekhilta* on Exodus 20:8; Rashi).
—   **as God . . . commanded you.** At Sinai (Ibn Ezra; Bachya; *Tur*). Or, according to tradition, at Marah
         (*Sanhedrin* 56b; Rashi; see Exodus 15:25).

Your male and female slaves will then be able to rest just as you do. 5
¹⁵ You must remember that you were slaves in Egypt, when God your Lord brought you out with a strong hand and an outstretched arm. It is for this reason that God your Lord has commanded you to keep the Sabbath.

[14. The Fifth Commandment]

¹⁶ Honor your father and mother as God your Lord commanded you.* You will then live long and have it well on the land that God your Lord is giving you.

[15. The Sixth Commandment]

¹⁷ Do not commit murder.

[16. The Seventh Commandment]

Do not commit adultery.

[17. The Eighth Commandment]

Do not steal.

[18. The Ninth Commandment]

Do not testify as a perjurous witness against your neighbor.

[19. The Tenth Commandment]

¹⁸ Do not desire your neighbor's wife.

[20. Desire]

Do not desire your neighbor's house, his field, his male or female slave, his ox, his donkey, or anything else that belongs to your neighbor.

[21. After the Revelation]

¹⁹ God spoke these words in a loud voice to your entire assembly from the mountain, out of the fire, cloud and mist, but He added no more.* He wrote [these words] on two stone tablets, and [later] gave them to me.

²⁰ When you heard the voice out of the darkness, with the mountain burning in flames, your tribal leaders and elders approached me. ²¹ You said, "It is true that God our Lord has showed us His glory and greatness,

---

5:16 **as God . . . commanded you.** See above note.
5:19 **but He added no more** (Chizzkuni; Septuagint; cf. Ibn Ezra). Or, "in a loud voice that did not hesitate" (Targum; Rashi). See Numbers 11:25.

5   and we have heard His voice out of the fire. Today we have seen that when God speaks to man, he can still survive. ²² But now, why should we die? Why should this great fire consume us? If we hear the voice of God our Lord any more, we will die!

²³ "What mortal has heard the voice of the living God speaking out of fire as we did and has survived? ²⁴ You approach God our Lord, and listen to all He says. You can transmit to us whatever God our Lord tells you, and when we hear it, we will do it."

²⁵ God heard what you said, and God told me, "I have heard what this nation has said to you. They have spoken well. ²⁶ If only their hearts* would always remain this way, where they are in such awe of Me. They would then keep all My commandments for all time, so that it would go well with them and their children forever.

²⁷ "Go tell them to* return to their tents.* ²⁸ You, however, must remain here with Me.* I will declare to you all the rules and laws that you shall teach them, so they will keep them in the land that I am giving them to occupy."

²⁹ Be careful to do what God your Lord has commanded you, not turning to the right or left. ³⁰ Follow the entire way that God your Lord has commanded you, so that you may live and do well, enduring for a long time on the land that you are going to occupy.

6   ¹ This is the mandate, the rules and the laws that God your Lord commanded [me] to teach you, so that you shall keep them in the land you are crossing over to occupy. ² Remain in awe of God your Lord, so that you will keep all His rules and laws that I am prescribing to you. You, your children and your children's children [must keep them] as long as they live, so that you will long endure.

³ Listen, Israel, and be careful to do [it]. Things will then go well for you and you will increase very much [in]* the land flowing with milk and honey, just as God, Lord of your fathers, promised you.

5:26   **If only their hearts . . .** Here we see what absolute free will God gives man (Bachya). That generation was therefore called "the enlightened generation," *dor de'ah* in Hebrew (*Lekach Tov*).

5:27   **to.** Actually a direct quotation.

—   **return to their tents.** A euphemism for marital relations (*Betza* 5b; see Exodus 19:15).

5:28   **remain here with Me.** Indicating that Moses would henceforth always remain on the level of prophecy (*Yad, Yesodey HaTorah* 7:6; cf. *Shabbath* 87a).

6:3   **in . . .** (Ibn Ezra). Or, ". . . and you will increase very much, since God . . . promised you a land flowing with milk and honey (Ramban).

6

[22. The Creed]

⁴ Listen,* Israel, God is our Lord, God is One.

⁵ Love God your Lord with all your heart, with all your soul, and with all your might.

⁶ These words which I am commanding you today must remain on your heart. ⁷ Teach them to your children and speak of them* when you are at home, when traveling on the road, when you lie down and when you get up.

⁸ Bind [these words] as a sign on your hand, and let them be an emblem* in the center of your head ⁹ [Also] write them on [parchments affixed to] the doorposts* of your houses and gates.

[23. Dangers of Prosperity]

¹⁰ When God your Lord brings you to the land that He swore to your fathers, Abraham, Isaac and Jacob, that He would give to you, [you will find] great, flourishing cities that you did not build. ¹¹ [You will also have] houses filled with all good things that you did not put there, finished cisterns that you did not quarry, and vineyards and olive trees that you did not plant.

You will eat and be satisfied, ¹² but be careful that you do not forget God, who is the One who brought you out of Egypt, the place of slavery.

¹³ Remain in awe of God, serve Him, and swear by His name.

¹⁴ Do not follow other deities, such as the gods of the nations around you. ¹⁵ God your Lord is a God demanding exclusive allegiance from you. Do not cause God's anger to be unleashed against you, since it will destroy you from the face of the earth.

[24. Keeping the Commandments]

¹⁵ Do not test God your Lord, as you tested Him in Massah.* ¹⁶ Be very careful to keep the commandments of God your Lord, as well as the rituals

---

6:4   **Listen.** *Sh'ma* in Hebrew, and hence the name of this reading that is said twice each day. Also known as *Keriath Sh'ma.* Since the Sh'ma is in the tefillin, which were mandated much earlier (Exodus 13:9,16), it seems probable that the Sh'ma was given immediately after the Exodus or after the Ten Commandments. Alternatively, until this point, the parchment containing the Sh'ma did not have to be put into the tefillin. See 6:8. Also see note on 7:12.

6:7   **speak of them . . . when you lie down . . .** This is a commandment to recite the Sh'ma twice daily.

6:8   **emblem.** The tefillin. See Exodus 13:9,16. The Sh'ma is the third parchment in the tefillin.

6:9   **doorposts.** *Mezuzah* in Hebrew, and hence the name given to the parchment. Both the Sh'ma and Deuteronomy 11:13-21 are written on the parchment in the Sh'ma; see below, 11:20.

6:15   **Massah.** See Exodus 17:7.

6 and decrees that He commanded you. [17] Do what is upright and good in God's eyes, so that He will be good to you. You will then come and occupy the good land that God promised your fathers. [19] As God promised, He will repulse* all your enemies before you.

[25. Recalling the Exodus]

[20] In the future, your child may ask you, "What are the rituals, rules and laws that God our Lord has commanded you?"

[21] You must tell him, "We were slaves to Pharaoh in Egypt, but God brought us out of Egypt with a mighty hand. [22] God directed great and terrible miracles against Pharaoh and all his household before our very eyes. [23] We are the ones He brought out of there, to bring us to the land He promised our fathers, and give it to us.

[24] God commanded us to keep all these rules, so that [we] would remain in awe of God for all time, so that we would survive, even as [we are] today. [24] It is our privilege to safeguard and keep this entire mandate before God our Lord, as He commanded us."

[26. Warnings Against Assimilation]

7 [1] When God your Lord brings you to the land you are entering, so that you can occupy it, He will uproot many nations before you—the Hittites, Girgashites, Amorites, Canaanites, Perizites, Hivites and Yebusites—seven nations more numerous and powerful than you are. [2] When God your Lord places them at your disposal and you defeat them, you must utterly destroy them, not making any treaty with them or giving them any consideration.*

[3] Do not intermarry with them.* Do not give your daughters to their sons, and do not take their daughters for your sons. [4] [If you do], they will lead your children away from Me, causing them to worship other gods. God will then display His anger against you, and you will quickly be destroyed.

[5] What you must do to them is tear down their altars, break their sacred pillars, cut down their Asherah trees,* and burn their idols in fire.

[6] You are a nation consecrated to God your Lord. God your Lord chose you to be His special people* among all the nations on the face of the earth.

6:19 **repulse** (Radak, *Sherashim*). *Hadaf* in Hebrew, literally, "push;" see Numbers 35:22. Or, "chase" (Septuagint), or, "break" (Targum).
7:2 **consideration** (*Avodah Zarah* 20a; Rashi). Or, "mercy" (Septuagint).
7:3 **intermarry.** This prohibition includes all gentiles (*Avodah Zarah* 36b; *Yad, Issurey Biyah* 12:1). The above mentioned seven nations, however, are forbidden even if they convert to Judaism (*Yevamoth* 76a).
7:5 **Asherah trees.** See Exodus 34:13.
7:6 **special people.** *Am segulah* in Hebrew. See Exodus 19:5.

⁷ It was not because you had greater numbers than all the other nations **7** that God embraced* you and chose you; you are among the smallest of all the nations. ⁸ It was because of God's love for you, and because He was keeping the oath that He made to your fathers. God therefore brought you out with a mighty hand, liberating you from the slave house, [and] from the power of Pharaoh king of Egypt.

⁹ You must realize that God your Lord is the Supreme Being. He is the faithful God, who keeps in mind* [His] covenant and love for a thousand generations when it comes to those who love Him and keep His commandments. ¹⁰ But He pays back His enemies to their face* to destroy them. He does not delay the payment that He gives His enemies to their face.

¹¹ So safeguard the mandate, the rules and laws that I am teaching you today, so that you will keep them.

Ekev

עֵקֶב

[27. Rewards for Obedience]

¹² If only* you listen to these laws, safeguarding and keeping them, then God your Lord will keep in mind the covenant and love* with which He made an oath to your fathers. ¹³ He will love you, bless you and make you numerous. He will bless the fruit of your womb, the fruit of your land, your grain, your wine, your oil, the calves of your herds, and the lambs of your flocks, in the land that He promised your fathers that He would give to you.

¹⁴ You will be blessed above all nations. Among you and your livestock, there will not be any sterile or barren. ¹⁵ God will take all sickness from you. He will not allow any of the terrible Egyptian afflictions that you experienced to affect you; instead, He will direct them against all your enemies.

¹⁶ When you consume all the nations that God your Lord is giving you, do not show them any pity. Do not worship their gods, since this will be a deadly trap for you.

7:7 **embraced** (Ramban; Radak, *Sherashim*). *Chashak* in Hebrew. Or, "preferred" (Septuagint).

7:9 **keeps in mind** (*HaKethav VeHaKabbalah*; see Genesis 37:11).

7:10 **pays back . . .** Or, "grants reward" (Targum; Rashi), that is, God gives them their reward in this world so as to destroy them in the next.

7:12 **If only.** *Ekev* in Hebrew; literally, "because" (Rashi); "as a reward, if" (Radak, *Sherashim*; Ibn Janach; Saadia; cf. Ramban); "as a final result, if," (Ibn Ezra; Chizzkuni;*HaKethav VeHaKabbalah*); or, "it shall come to pass if" (Septuagint).
       Some say that this section was said soon after the Exodus (*Sifri*). See note on 6:4.

— **love.** Some say the love the Israelites expressed toward God; cf. Jeremiah 2:2 (*Midrash HaGadol*).

7

[28. Confidence]

¹⁷ You might say to yourself, "These nations are more numerous than we* are. How will we be able to drive them out?"

¹⁸ Do not be afraid of them. You must remember what God did to Pharaoh and all the rest of Egypt. ¹⁹ [Recall] the great miracles that you saw with your own eyes—the signs, the wonders, the mighty hand and the outstretched arm* with which God your Lord brought you out of Egypt.

God will do the same to all the nations whom you fear. ²⁰ God your Lord will also send deadly hornets* to attack them, so that the survivors hiding from you will also be destroyed.

²¹ Do not cringe before [these nations]. God your Lord is with you—a great and awesome God.

²² God will uproot these nations before you little by little. You will not be allowed to finish them off too quickly, so that the wild animals not overwhelm you.

²³ God will place [these nations] in your power. He will throw them into utter panic until they are destroyed. ²⁴ He will place their kings in your power, and you will obliterate their names from under the heavens. No man will stand up before you until you destroy them.

²⁵ You must burn their idolatrous statues in fire. Do not desire the gold and silver on [these statues]* and take it for yourselves. Let it not bring you into a deadly trap, since it is something offensive to God your Lord. ²⁶ Do not bring any offensive [idol] into your house, since you may become just like it. Shun it totally and consider it absolutely offensive, since it is taboo.

[29. Dangers of Overconfidence]

8

¹ You must safeguard and keep the entire mandate that I am prescribing to you today. You will then survive, flourish, and come to occupy the land that God swore to your fathers.

² Remember the entire path along which God your Lord led you these forty years in the desert. He sent hardships to test you, to determine* what is in your heart, whether you would keep His commandments or not. ³ He made life difficult for you, letting you go hungry, and then He fed you the Manna, which neither you nor your ancestors had ever experienced. This

---

7:17   **we.** Literally, "I."
7:19   **mighty hand . . .** See 4:34.
7:20   **hornets.** See Exodus 23:28.
7:25   **on these statues** (Ramban; *Yad, Avodath Kokhavim* 8:7).
8:2   **determine.** Or, "show others" (Bachya).

was to teach you that it is not by bread alone that man lives, but by all that   8
comes out of God's mouth.

⁴ The clothing you wore did not become tattered, and your feet did not
become bruised* these forty years. ⁵ You must thus meditate on the fact
that just as a man might chastise his child, so God your Lord is chastising
you. ⁶ Safeguard the commandments of God your Lord, so that you will
walk in His ways and remain in awe of Him.

⁷ God your Lord is bringing you to a good land—a land with flowing
streams, and underground springs* gushing out in valley and mountain.
⁸ It is a land of wheat, barley, grapes, figs and pomegranates—a land of oil-
olives and honey-[dates].* ⁹ It is a land where you will not eat rationed*
bread, and you will not lack anything—a land whose stones are iron, and
from whose mountains you will quarry copper.

¹⁰ When you eat and are satisfied, you must therefore bless God your
Lord* for* the good land that He has given you.

¹¹ Be careful that you not forget God your Lord, not keeping His commandments, decrees and laws, which I am prescribing to you today.

¹² You may then eat and be satisfied, building fine houses and living in
them. ¹³ Your herds and flocks may increase, and you may amass much
silver and gold—everything you own may increase. ¹⁴ But your heart may
then grow haughty, and you may forget God your Lord, the One who
brought you out of the slave house that was Egypt.

¹⁵ It was He who led you through the great, terrifying desert, where
there were snakes, vipers, scorpions and thirst. When there was no water, it
was He who provided you water from a solid cliff.* ¹⁶ In the desert He fed
you Manna, which was something that your ancestors never knew. He may
have been sending hardships to test you, but it was so He would eventually
do [all the more] good for you.

¹⁷ [When you later have prosperity, be careful that you not] say to
yourself, "It was my own strength and personal power that brought me all
this prosperity."

¹⁸ You must remember that it is God your Lord who gives you the

---

8:4   **become bruised** (*Lekach Tov*). *Batzak* in Hebrew. Or, "swell" (Targum; Rashi; Ibn Ezra); "lacked shoes"
        (Saadia; Radak, *Sherashim*; cf. Septuagint); or, "become painfully hardened" (Septuagint).
8:7   **underground springs.** Or, literally, "springs and subterranean waters."
8:8   **dates.** (Rashi, *Berakhoth* 41b, s.v. *Devash*). See note on Leviticus 2:11.
8:9   **rationed** (*Targum Yonathan*; Saadia). Or, "in poverty" (Rashbam; Ibn Ezra).
8:10   **bless** . . . This is a commandment to recite the grace after meals (*Berakhoth* 21a).
—   **for.** Or, "on," or "for the fruit of" (*Targum Yonathan*).
8:15   **solid cliff** (Targum; Ibn Janach; Radak, *Sherashim*). *Chalamish* in Hebrew. Or, "flint" (Septuagint), or,
        "diamond-hard stone") *Targum Yonathan*; *Arukh*, s.v. *Shamir*).

8   power to become prosperous. He does this so as to keep the covenant that
He made with an oath to your fathers, even as [He is keeping it]* today.

[30. Warning Against Idolatry]

¹⁹ If you ever forget God your Lord, and follow other gods, worshiping
them and bowing to them, I bear witness to you today that you will be
totally annihilated. ²⁰ You will be destroyed just like the nations that God is
destroying before you—that will be the result if you do not obey God your
Lord.

[31. Warnings Against Self-Righteousness]

9   ¹ Listen, Israel, today you [are preparing to]* cross the Jordan. When
you arrive, you will drive out nations greater and more powerful than you,
with great cities, fortified to the skies. ² They are a great nation, as tall as
giants. You know that you have heard the expression, "Who can stand up
before a giant?"

³ But you must realize today that God your Lord is the One who shall
cross before you. He is [like]* a consuming fire, and He will subjugate
[these nations] before you, rapidly driving them out and annihilating them,
as God promised you.

⁴ When God repulses them before you, do not say to yourselves, "It was
because of my virtue that God brought me to occupy this land."

It was because of the wickedness of these nations that God is driving
them out before you. ⁵ It was not because of your virtue and basic integrity* that you are coming to occupy their land, but because of the wickedness of these nations whom God is driving out before you. It is also because
God is keeping the word that He swore to your ancestors, Abraham, Isaac
and Jacob.

⁶ Therefore, realize that it is not because of your virtue that God your
Lord is giving you this land to occupy, since you are a very stubborn
nation.

⁷ Remember and never forget how you provoked God your Lord in the
desert. From the day you left Egypt until you came here, you have been
rebelling against God.

8:18   **as He is keeping it** (*Adereth Eliahu*; *HaKethav VeHaKabbalah*). Or, "so even today, [you cannot say that it
is your own strength]" (Abarbanel).
9:1   **preparing to** (Chizzkuni).
9:3   **like** (Chizzkuni). Or, "God your Lord will send a consuming fire across before you" (*HaKethav VeHa-
Kabbalah*).
9:5   **basic integrity.** Literally, "uprightness of heart."

⁸ Even at Horeb you provoked God! And God was ready to display 9 anger and destroy you.

⁹ I had climbed the mountain to get the stone tablets—tablets of the covenant that God had made with you. I remained on the mountain forty days and forty nights* without eating food or drinking water. ¹⁰ God gave me the two stone tablets written with God's finger.* Upon them were written all the words that God declared to you on the mountain out of the fire, on the Day of Assembly.

¹¹ At the end of the forty days and forty nights, God gave me the two stone tablets as tablets of the covenant. ¹² But God then said to me, "Get moving and hurry down from here! The nation that you brought out of Egypt has become corrupt. They have been quick to turn aside from the path that I prescribed for them, and they have made themselves a cast statue."

¹³ God then said to me, "I see that this is a very stubborn nation. ¹⁴ Just leave Me alone,* and I will destroy them, obliterating their name from under the heavens. I will then make you into a nation greater and more numerous than they."

¹⁵ I turned around and went down from the mountain. The mountain was still burning with fire, and the two tablets of the covenant were in my two hands.

¹⁶ I immediately saw that you had sinned to God your Lord, making a cast calf. You were so quick to turn from the path that God your Lord had prescribed! ¹⁷ I grasped the two tablets, and threw them down from my two hands, breaking them before your eyes.

¹⁸ I then threw myself down before God,* and just as during the first forty days and forty nights, I did not eat any food or drink water. This was because of the sin you committed, doing evil in God's eyes to provoke Him. ¹⁹ I dreaded the anger and rage that God was directing at you, which had threatened to destroy you. But God also listened to me this time.

²⁰ God also expressed great anger toward Aaron, threatening to destroy him, so, at that time, I also prayed for Aaron.

²¹ I took the calf, the sinful thing* that you had made, and I burned it in

9:9　**forty days** . . . See Exodus 24:18.
9:10　**written with** . . . Exodus 31:18.
9:14　**leave Me alone.** By not interceding (Targum), or by ceasing your prayer (Saadia). See Exodus 32:10.
9:18　**I then threw** . . . This took place between 17 Tammuz and 1 Elul (*Seder Olam* 7). Some say that Moses was on the mountain during this period, while others maintain that he was in his tent (cf. Radak on *Pirkey Rabbi Eliezer* 46:12).
9:21　**sinful thing** (Chizzkuni).

9   fire. I then pulverized it,* grinding it well, until it was as fine as dust, and I
threw the dust into the stream flowing down from the mountain.

²² At Tav'erah,* Massah,* and Graves-of-Craving,* you also provoked
God. ²³ And at Kadesh Barnea,* God sent you forth and said, "Head north
and occupy the land that I have given you," but you rebelled against the
word of God your Lord, and did not have faith in Him or obey Him.

²⁴ You have been rebelling against God since the day I knew you!

²⁵ [In any case,] because God said He would destroy you, I threw myself
down before God [and] lay prostrate for forty days and forty nights. ²⁶ My
prayer to God was,* "God! Lord! Do not destroy Your nation and heritage,
which You liberated with Your greatness, and which You brought out of
Egypt with a mighty hand. ²⁷ Remember Your servants, Abraham, Isaac
and Jacob. Do not pay attention to the stubbornness of this nation, or to
their wickedness and sin.

²⁸ "Do not let the land from which You took them say, 'God brought
them out to kill them in the desert because He hated them and could not
bring them to the land He promised them.' ²⁹ After all, they *are* Your people
and Your heritage. You brought them out with Your great power and with
Your outstretched arm!'"

[32. The Second Tablets]

10   ¹ At that time, God said to me, "Carve out two stone tablets* like the first
ones, and come up to Me on the mountain. Make yourself a wooden ark.* ² I
will write on the tablets the words which were on the first tablets* that you
broke, and you shall place them* in the ark."

³ I made an ark out of acacia wood* and carved out two tablets like the
first. I then climbed the mountain with the two tablets in my hand. ⁴ [God]
wrote on the tablets the original script of the Ten Commandments which He

---

—   **pulverized it.** Exodus 32:20.
9:22   **Tav'erah.** See Numbers 11:3.
—   **Massah.** Exodus 17:7.
—   **Graves-of-Craving.** Numbers 11:34.
9:22   **Kadesh Barnea.** When the spies were sent out; see Numbers 13:26.
9:26   **My prayer.** See Exodus 32:11.
10:1   **Carve out . . .** Exodus 34:1. This was on 1 Elul, after Moses had prayed for the people forty days (Rashi).
—   **ark.** Some say that this was a temporary ark, that was used until the golden ark mentioned in Exodus
         25:10 was made (Ramban; Bachya). According to others, this ark was used for the broken tablets, and it
         was taken out in war (Rashi; see Numbers 10:33). Some say that Moses made the basic ark out of acacia
         wood, and then Betzalel covered it with gold (Malbim; cf. Ibn Ezra; *Yoma* 3b, 72b).
10:2   **the words which were on . . .** Hence, both the first and second tablets had exactly the same wording.
—   **place them.** Some say that this denotes the second tablets, while others say that it denotes the first. See
         note on 10:1.
10:3   **acacia wood.** See Exodus 25:4.

declared to you from the mountain out of the fire on the Day of Assembly. 10
God gave them to me, [5] and I turned around and went down from the mountain. I placed the tablets in the ark I made, and they remained there as God
had commanded.

[6] [Later],* after the Israelites had left the wells of Beney Yaakan* [and]*
Moserah, Aaron died* and was buried there, so that Eleazar his son became
priest in his stead. [7] From those areas, they had traveled to Gudgodah,* and
from Gudgodah to Yatvath,* an area of flowing brooks.*

[8] [After I came down from the mountain]*, God designated the tribe of
Levi to carry the ark of God's covenant,* to stand before God and serve Him,*
and to offer blessing in His name.* [9] It is for this reason that Levi was not
given any portion or inheritance along with his brethren. God is his heritage,
as God promised him.

[10] I had thus remained on the mountain* forty days and forty nights, just
like the first time, and God listened to me this time as well, agreeing not to
destroy you.

[11] God then said to me,* "Get moving and resume the march at the head
of the people. Let them come and occupy the land that I swore to their fathers
that I would give to them."

10:6   **Later** (Rashbam; cf. Saadia). Moses was stressing that Aaron had survived forty years because of his
       prayer (Ibn Ezra).

—   **wells of Beney Yaakan.** Some say that this is identical with Beney Yaakan in Numbers 33:31 (*Yerushalmi,
       Yoma* 1:1, 2a; Ralbag). In Numbers, however, we see that the Israelites traveled from Moserah to Beney
       Yaakan. Therefore, some say that after Aaron's death they turned back and went as far as Beney Yaakan
       to Moserah (*Yerushalmi loc. cit*). Others say that while Beney Yaakan (sons of Yaakan) lived to the north of
       Moserah, the *wells* of Beney Yaakan were to the south of Moserah (Ramban). According to others, "Wells
       of Beney Yaakan" is in no way related to Beney Yaakan (Ibn Ezra; *Baaley Tosafoth*).

—   **and** (Ralbag). Others have, "had left the wells of Beney Yaakan toward Moserah; see above note. Since
       Aaron died on Mount Hor, which was several stages later (Numbers 20:22, 33:38), we would then have
       to say that "Wells of Beney Yaakan" is distinct from Beney Yaakan, or that the Israelites had turned back.
       According to the translation followed here, however, there is no contradiction.

—   **Aaron died.** See Numbers 20:22, 33:38.

10:7   **Gudgodah.** Or, "Hagudgodah," or "Gudgod." Possibly Chor HaGidgod in Numbers 33:32. See note
       on 10:6.

—   **Yatvath** (Targum). Or, "Yatvathah" (Septuagint). Possibly the same as in Numbers 33:33.

—   **flowing brooks.** But when they came to Kadesh (Numbers 20:1,2), there was a shortage of water
       (Ralbag).

10:8   **After I came down from the mountain** (Ralbag); cf. Numbers 8:6,14. Or at the time of the golden calf;
       cf. Exodus 32:26,29 (Rashbam). Literally, "at that time." Possibly, after Aaron's death, when the priests
       were given special status (cf. Ramban).

—   **to carry the ark** . . . See Numbers 4:15.

—   **to stand** . . . Numbers 8:19. Some say that this denotes the Levites' song (*Arakhin* 11a). See next note.

—   **to offer blessing** . . . Some say that this denotes the levitical song during the service (Ralbag). Others say
       that it denotes the priestly blessing in Numbers 6:22-27 (Rashi; Ibn Ezra).

10:10 **I had thus remained** . . . This was a third 40 day period, during which Moses received the second tablets;
       cf. Exodus 34:28 (Rashi). Others say that this was the second period (Ibn Ezra).

10:11 **God then said** . . . See Exodus 33:1, Numbers 10:11. This was after the Levites had been separated
       (Rashi).

[33. Following God's Way]

¹² And now, Israel, what does God want of you? Only that you remain in awe of God your Lord, so that you will follow all His paths and love Him, serving God your Lord with all your heart and with all your soul. ¹³ You must keep God's commandments and decrees that I am prescribing for you today, so that good will be yours.

¹⁴ The heaven, the heaven of heaven, the earth and everything in it, all belong to God! ¹⁵ Still, it was only with your ancestors that God developed a closeness. He loved them and therefore chose you, their descendants, from among all nations, just as the situation is today.

¹⁶ Remove the barriers from your heart* and do not remain so stubborn any more!

¹⁷ God your Lord is the ultimate Supreme Being* and the highest possible Authority.* He is the great, mighty and awesome God, who does not give special consideration* or take bribes.* ¹⁸ He brings justice to the orphan and widow, and loves the foreigner, granting him food and clothing. ¹⁹ You must also show love toward the foreigner,* since you were foreigners in the land of Egypt.

²⁰ Remain in awe of God, serve Him, cling* to Him, and swear by His name. ²¹ He is your praise* and your God, the One who did for you these great and awesome deeds that you saw with your very eyes.

²² Your ancestors emigrated to Egypt with only seventy individuals,* but now God your Lord has made you as numerous as the stars of the sky.

11 ¹ So love God your Lord, and safeguard His trust, His decrees, laws and commandments, for all time.

10:16 **Remove the barriers . . .** (Rashi). Literally, "circumcise the foreskin of your heart." That is, remove the barriers keeping you from the truth (Ibn Ezra; Ramban). Or, "remove from your hearts' foolishness" (Targum), "the evil urge" (*Sukkah* 52a), "thoughts of sin" (Saadia), "coarse desires" (Ibn Ezra), or, "bad traits" (Bachya).

10:17 **ultimate Supreme Being.** Literally, "God of Gods," *Elohey HaElohim* in Hebrew. See above 4:35, 7:9. Or, "God of judges" (Targum), or, "God of the angels" (*Midrash HaGadol*; *Moreh Nevukhim* 3:6; Ramban).

— **highest possible Authority.** Literally, "Master of masters." Or, "Master of kings" (Targum), or, "master of all natural forces" (Bachya; cf. *Moreh Nevukhim* 3:6).

— **does not give special consideration.** Even to the perfectly righteous (Bachya). Or, "who does not automatically forgive sin" (Rashi).

— **take bribes.** Even of good deeds (Rambam on *Avoth* 4:22; Ramban). Thus, when a person does good deeds, it does not diminish the punishment for his sins (cf. *Sotah* 21a).

10:19 **show love . . .** This is a special commandment to show love toward a proselyte (*Sefer HaMitzvoth*, Positive 207).

10:20 **cling . . .** See below, 13:5.

10:21 **praise.** The reason you are praised (Ramban), or the object of your praise (Saadia). Or, "your pride" (Chizzkuni).

10:22 **seventy individuals.** Genesis 46:27, Exodus 1:5.

² You must now realize that [I am not speaking]* of your children, who did   11
not know and did not see the lesson that God your Lord [taught] through His
greatness, His mighty hand and His outstretched arm.

³ [There were] the signs and deeds that He did in Egypt, to Pharaoh king
of Egypt and all his land. ⁴ There was what He did to Egypt's forces, to their
horses and chariots, when He swamped them with the water of the Red Sea as
they were pursuing you. God destroyed them so that even now [they have not
recovered].* ⁵ There was what He did in the desert, until you came to this area.
⁶ There was what He did to Dathan and Aviram,* the sons of Reuben's son
Eliav, when in the midst of all Israel the earth opened its mouth* and swallowed them, along with their houses,* their tents, and all the living things*
that were with them.*

⁷ Thus, your own eyes have seen all the great deeds that God has done.

⁸ Safeguard the entire mandate that I am prescribing to you today, so that
you will be strong and come to occupy the land which you are crossing to
occupy. ⁹ You will then long endure on the land that God swore to your
fathers that He would give to them and their offspring, a land flowing with
milk and honey.

[34. A Demanding Land]

¹⁰ The land which you are about to occupy is not like Egypt, the place you
left, where you could plant your seed and irrigate it by yourself,* just like a
vegetable garden. ¹¹ But the land which you are crossing to occupy is a land of
mountains and valleys, which can be irrigated only by the rain. ¹² It is therefore a land constantly under God your Lord's scrutiny; the eyes of God your
Lord are on it at all times, from the beginning of the year until the end of the
year.

[35. Yoke of the Commandments]

¹³ If you* are careful to pay heed to my commandments, which I am pre-

---

11:2   **I am not speaking** . . . (Rashi; cf. Bachya). Or, "it is not your children [who will be punished]" (*Baaley
        Tosafoth*), or, "[From now on it depends] on no one but your children" (Saadia).
11:4   **they have not recovered** (Ibn Ezra).
11:6   **Dathan and Aviram.** See Numbers 16:1.
—   **earth opened its mouth.** Numbers 16:32. Here it appears that only Dathan and Aviram were swallowed;
        see note *ibid.*
—   **houses** (Targum; Septuagint). Or, "families" (households) (*Targum Yonathan*; Ibn Ezra; Chizzkuni).
—   **living things.** (Radak, *Sherashim*). *Yekum* in Hebrew, cf. Genesis 6:23). Or, "property" (Targum; *San-
        hedrin* 110a; Rashi; Septuagint); "that which exists" (Ibn Janach).
—   **that were with them** (Targum; Saadia). Or, "because of them" (Ibn Ezra). Literally, "at their feet."
11:10   **by yourself** (*Targum Yonathan*). Or, "with your feet" (Rashi; Septuagint).
11:13   **If you** . . . This is the second paragraph of the Sh'ma, see 11:10. This is known as the "Yoke of the Com-
        mandments" (*Berakhoth* 13a).

scribing to you today, and if you love God your Lord with all your heart and soul, [then God has made this promise]:* ¹⁴ "I will grant the fall and spring* rains in your land at their proper time, so that you will have an ample harvest of grain, oil and wine. ¹⁵ I will grant forage in your fields for your animals, and you will eat and be satisfied."

¹⁶ Be careful that your heart not be tempted* to go astray and worship other gods, bowing down to them. ¹⁷ God's anger will then be directed against you, and He will lock up the skies so that there will not be any rain. The land will not give forth its crops, and you will rapidly vanish from the good land that God is giving you.

¹⁸ Place these words of mine on your heart and soul. Bind them* as a sign on your arm, and let them be an insignia in the center of your head. ¹⁹ Teach your children to speak of them, when you are at home, when traveling on the road, when you lie down and when you get up.* ²⁰ [Also] write them on [parchments affixed to] the doorposts* of your houses and gates.

²¹ [If you do this,] you and your children will long endure on the land that God swore to your ancestors, [promising that] He would give it to them as long as the heavens are above the earth.

[36. Promise of Victory]

²² If you carefully safeguard and keep this entire mandate that I prescribe to you today, [and if you] love God, walk in all His ways, and cling to Him, ²³ then God will drive out all these nations before you. You will expel nations that are greater and stronger than you are.

²⁴ Every area upon which your feet tread shall belong to you. Your boundaries shall extend from the desert* [to]* the Lebanon,* from a tributary* of the Euphrates River* as far as the Mediterranean Sea.* ²⁵ No man will

---

—   **then God has made this promise.** Since the person changes from Moses to God (cf. *Midrash HaGadol*). See 29:4.
11:14   **fall and spring.** (cf. *Targum Yonathan*; *Taanith* 6a). In the Holy Land, the growing season is during the winter, which is the rainy season. Therefore, *yoreh* is the rain at the beginning of the planting season, and *malkosh* is at the end.
11:16   **tempted** (Radak, *Sherashim*). *Pathah* in Hebrew. Or, "err" (Targum), "become foolish" (Chizzkuni), or, "become puffed up" (Septuagint). See Genesis 9:27.
11:18   **Bind them** . . . This section is also in the tefillin. See Exodus 13:9,16, above, 6:8.
11:19   **when you lie down** . . . Some say that there is also a Biblical commandment to read this section each day (*Pri Chadash, Orach Chaim* 67).
11:20   **doorposts.** This section is the second writing in the mezuzah; see above, 6:9.
11:24   **desert.** To the south. See Numbers 34:3.
—   **to.** Literally, "and."
—   **Lebanon.** To the north.
—   **a tributary.** Or, literally, "the river, the Euphrates river."
—   **Euphrates river.** See Genesis 15:18.
—   **Mediterranean Sea** (Saadia). Literally, "final sea."

stand up before you. God your Lord will place the fear and dread of you upon   11
the entire area you tread, just as He promised you.

Re'eh   רְאֵה

[37. The Choice]

²⁶ You can therefore see that I am placing before you both a blessing and a
curse. ²⁷ The blessing [will come]* if you obey the commandments of God
your Lord, which I am prescribing to you today. ²⁸ The curse [will come] if
you do not obey the commandments of God your Lord, and you go astray
from the path that I am prescribing for you today, following other gods to
have a novel spiritual experience.*

[38. Unified Worship]

²⁹ When God your Lord brings you to the land which you are about to
occupy, you must declare the blessing* on Mount Gerizim,* and the curse on
Mount Ebal.* ³⁰ They are across the Jordan, just beyond the Sunset Highway*
on the way to Gilgal,* near the Plains of Moreh,* in the territory of the
Canaanites who live in the flood plain.*

³¹ [You must do this] because you are crossing the Jordan to come to the
land which God your Lord is giving you and occupy it. When you have
occupied it and you live there, ³² you must carefully keep all the rules and laws
that I am prescribing to you today.

11:27 **will come** (Ibn Ezra; cf. Rashi). Or, "The blessing is obeying . . ." (Abarbanel).

11:28 **to have a novel spiritual experience.** Literally, "which you have not known;" see below, 13:3, 13:7,
13:14. To "know" God is interpreted as knowing Him in a mystical sense, especially among the
Kabbalists. See 1 Chronicles 28:9. (cf. *HaKethav VeHaKabbalah*).

11:29 **declare the blessing** (Ibn Ezra; Ramban). Or, "Place the blessers" (Targum; Rashi). See below, 27:12,
Joshua 8:33.

— **Mount Gerizim.** About one mile to the west of Shechem, currently known as Jebel et-Tor, 2849 feet
high.

— **Mount Ebal.** Or Eival. A mountain 3077 feet high (the highest point in Samaria), some two miles northeast of Mount Gerizim (cf. Ramban).

11:30 **Sunset Highway.** From context, this appears to be the ancient highway running from north to south
through the mountains. This highway passed just to the east of Mount Gerizim and Mount Eival, they
were "beyond this mountain." It may have been called "Sunset Highway" (*Derekh Mavo HaShemesh*),
because from where the Israelites were, the sun appeared to set on the mountains through which the
road ran.

— **Gilgal.** (cf. *Sotah* 33b). This is not Gilgal mentioned in Joshua 4:19, 5:9 (Ibn Ezra; *HaKethav VeHa-
Kabbalah*), but a city some 20 miles west of Shechem, now known as Jiljulieh, possibly in Joshua 12:23
(cf. Septuagint *ad loc.*), and perhaps also in, 2 Kings 2:1, Nehemiah 12:29. In ancient times, a road led
from Shechem to this Gilgal.

— **Plains of Moreh.** Abraham's first stop in the Holy Land, near Shechem (Genesis 12:6).

— **flood plain.** *Aravah* in Hebrew. This would indicate that although the Canaanites' main base was in the
Jordan flood plain, their territory extended some 20 miles east toward Shechem.

12 ¹ These are the rules and laws that you must carefully keep in the land that God, Lord of your fathers, is giving you so that you will be able to occupy it as long as you live on earth:

² Do away with all the places where the nations whom you are driving out worship their gods, [whether they are] on the high mountains, on the hills, or under any luxuriant* tree. ³ You must tear down their altars, break up their sacred pillars, burn their Asherah trees,* and chop down the statues of their gods, obliterating their names from that place.

⁴ You may not worship God your Lord in such a manner.* ⁵ This you may do only on the site that God your Lord will choose* from among all your tribes, as a place established in His name. It is there that you shall go to seek His presence.*

⁶ That shall be the place to which you must bring your burnt offerings and eaten sacrifices, your [special] tithes,* your hand-delivered elevated gifts,* your general and specific pledges,* and the first-born of your cattle and flocks.* ⁷ You and your families shall eat there* before God your Lord, and you shall rejoice in all your endeavors, through which God your Lord shall bless you.

⁸ You will then not be able to do everything that we are now doing, [where each] person does what is right in his eyes.* ⁹ Now you have not yet come to the resting place and hereditary land that God your Lord is giving you. ¹⁰ But you shall soon cross the Jordan and live in the land that God your Lord is

---

12:2 **luxuriant.** *Ra'anan* in Hebrew. "Heavily branched" (Targum), "beautiful" (*Targum Yonathan*), "thick" (Septuagint), or "Green" (Hirsch).

12:3 **Asherah trees.** See Exodus 34:13, above, 7:5.

12:4 **You may not worship . . .** That is, in places such as those mentioned in 12:2 (Rashi; Rashbam; Ibn Ezra; Bachya). Literally, "Do not do this to God your Lord" (cf. 12:31). However, the Talmud attaches this to verse 12:3, and cites this as a commandment not to destroy anything associated with God's worship (*Sifri*), and not to erase God's name (*Makkoth* 22a).

12:5 **site that God . . . will choose.** Mentioned a number of times in this section. Ultimately, of course, this "place" turned out to be Jerusalem. However, the "place" could not be named before the royal line had been established in Israel (*Moreh Nevukhim* 3:45).

— **seek His presence** (Targum; Ramban). Or, "seek [prophetically] to establish His sanctuary, and come there" (*Sifri*).

12:6 **special tithes.** Not the Levitical tithes (Numbers 18:24), but animal tithes (Numbers 27:32) and the second tithe (below, 14:22; *Bekhoroth* 53a; Rashi). Some say that the Levitical tithes were also to be brought to Jerusalem if they could not be given to the Levite locally (Ramban).

— **hand-delivered elevated gifts.** *Terumah* in Hebrew. The reference is to the first fruits, which were hand-delivered (Deuteronomy 26:4; *Yevamoth* 73b; Rashi). This might also be referring to the priestly *terumah*, if there were no local priests to whom it could be given (Ramban). See 12:10.

— **general and specific pledges.** Sacrifices (cf. *Kinim* 1:1).

— **first-born . . .** See Exodus 13:2, below, 15:20.

12:7 **eat there.** Because sacrifices could be eaten only in Jerusalem (*Zevachim* 55a).

12:8 **You will then . . .** In the desert, non-priests could eat sacrifice any place in the camp (*Zevachim* 112b). See Leviticus 7:15.

allotting you. When He has granted you safety* from all your enemies around   12
you, and you live in security, ¹¹ there will be a site that God will choose as the
place dedicated to His name.*

It is there that you will have to bring all that I am prescribing to you as
your burnt offerings, eaten sacrifices, [special] tithes, hand-delivered elevated
gifts, and the choice general pledges* that you may pledge to God. ¹² You
shall rejoice before God your Lord along with your sons, your daughters,
your male and female slaves, and the Levites from your settlements, who have
no hereditary portion with you.

¹³ Be careful not to offer your burnt offerings in any place that you may see
fit.* ¹⁴ It must be done only in the place that God shall choose in [the territory
of] one of your tribes. Only there shall you sacrifice burnt offerings, and only
there shall you prepare all [the offerings] that I am prescribing to you.

¹⁵ [Elsewhere] in all your settlements,* you may only slaughter animals to
satisfy your own wants, so that you will be able to eat the meat that God gives
you as His blessing. There the clean and unclean may eat it,* like the deer and
the gazelle.* ¹⁶ The only thing you must not eat is the blood,* which you must
spill on the ground* like water.

¹⁷ However, in your own settlements, you may not eat the tithes* of your
grain, wine and oil, the first-born of your cattle and flocks, any general
pledges you make, your specific pledges, or your hand-delivered elevated
gifts.* ¹⁸ These you may eat only before God your Lord, in the place that God
your Lord shall choose. You [shall eat them] along with your son, your
daughter, your male and female slave, and the Levite from your settlements,
and you shall rejoice before God your Lord for everything you have.

¹⁹ As long as you are in the land, you must be careful not to abandon the
Levite.

[39. Non-Sacrificial Flesh]

²⁰ When God expands your borders as He promised you, and your natural

---

12:10 **When he has granted you safety.** Only then could Jerusalem be chosen (cf. *Sanhedrin* 20b).
12:11 **dedicated to His name.** Literally, "for His name to rest there."
— **general pledges.** See above 12:6.
12:13 **Be careful . . .** See Leviticus 17:4.
12:15 **settlements** (*Targum*; Radak, *Sherashim*). Or, "gates."
— **clean and unclean . . .** Unlike sacrifice, which is forbidden to the unclean; Leviticus 7:20. By allowing
the unclean to eat it, one shows that the animal was not offered as a sacrifice.
— **deer and the gazelle.** See below, 14:5. These were animals that could not be offered as sacrifices. See
Leviticus 17:13.
12:16 **not eat is the blood.** See Leviticus 7:26, 17:10; below, 12:23,24, 15:23.
— **spill on the ground.** As distinguished from sacrificial blood, as in 12:27 (Ralbag).
12:17 **tithes.** The second tithe, below 14:22 (*Sefer HaMitzvoth*, Negative 141).
— **hand-delivered elevated gifts.** The first fruits (*Makkoth* 17a). See 12:6.

12 desire to eat meat asserts itself, so that you say, "I wish to eat meat," you may eat as much meat as you wish. ²¹ Since the place chosen by God your Lord to be dedicated to His name is far, you need only slaughter your cattle and small animals that God will have given you in the manner that I have prescribed.* You may then eat them in your settlements in any manner you desire. ²² However, you must eat them as you would a deer or gazelle, with the clean and unclean eating together.

²³ Be extremely careful* not to eat the blood, since the blood is [associated] with the spiritual nature,* and when you eat flesh, you shall not [ingest] the spiritual nature along with it.* ²⁴ Since* you must not eat [the blood], you can pour it on the ground like water. ²⁵ If you do not eat it, you and your descendants will have a good life, since you will be doing what is morally right* in God's eyes.

²⁶ However, when you have any sacred offerings and pledges, you must take them and bring them to the place that God shall choose. ²⁷ Then, when you prepare your burnt offerings, both the flesh and blood shall be placed on the altar of God your Lord. In the case of eaten sacrifices, the blood shall be poured on the altar of God your Lord, and the flesh shall be eaten.

²⁸ Carefully listen to all these words that I prescribe to you, so that you and your descendants will have a good life forever, since you will be doing that which is good and morally right in the eyes of God your Lord.

[40. Worshiping God with Idolatrous Practices]

²⁹ When God excises the nations to which you are coming, and drives them away before you, you shall expel them and live in their land. ³⁰ After they have been wiped out before you, be very careful not to fall into a deadly trap by trying to follow them.

Do not try to find out about their gods, saying, "Now, how did these nations worship their gods? I would also like to try [such practices]." ³¹ Do not worship God your Lord with such practices.* In worshiping their gods,

---

12:21 **in the manner that I have prescribed.** This alludes to all the many rules of ritual slaughter (*Chullin* 28a; Rashi).

12:23 **Be extremely careful** (Septuagint). Literally, "be strong," or, "restrict your desires" (*Targum Yonathan*). There was a temptation to eat blood, since it was used in many mystical occult practices (Bachya).

— **blood is . . . spiritual nature.** Or "life-force", literally, "soul." See Leviticus 17:11,14.

— **you shall not ingest . . .** Or, "Do not eat flesh with life in it," prohibiting flesh from a living animal (*Chullin* 102b; *HaKethav VeHaKabbalah*; Rashi). See Genesis 9:4.

12:24 **Since.** (Saadia).

12:25 **morally right** (cf. *Sifri* on 12:28). *Yashar* in Hebrew. Here we see that even in ritual laws there is an element of divine morality. Or, "the straight way toward your calling" (Hirsch).

12:31 **Do not worship . . .** (Ibn Ezra; Ramban; Bachya). Literally, "Do not do this to God your Lord;" see above, 12:4.

[these nations] committed all sorts of perversions hated by God. They would **12** even burn their sons and daughters in fire as a means of worshiping their gods!

¹ [It is enough that you] carefully observe everything that I am prescribing **13** to you. Do not add to it and do not subtract from it.*

[41. The Idolatrous Prophet]

² [This is what you must do] when a prophet or a person who has visions in a dream arises among you. He may present you* with a sign* or miracle, ³ and on the basis of* that sign or miracle, say to you, "Let us try out a differ-ent god. Let us serve it and have a new spiritual experience.*"

⁴ Do not listen to the words of that prophet or dreamer. God your Lord is testing you to see if you are truly able to love God your Lord with all your heart and all your soul.* ⁵ Follow God your Lord, remain in awe of Him, keep His commandments, obey Him and serve Him, and you will then be able to have a true spiritual experience through Him.*

⁶ That prophet or dreamer must be put to death for having spoken rebel-liously* against God your Lord, who brought you out of Egypt and liberated you from the place of slavery. He was trying to make you leave the path that God your Lord commanded you to walk, and you must destroy such evil from your midst.

[42. Idolatrous Missionaries]

⁷ [This is what you must do] if your blood brother,* your son, your daughter, your bosom wife, or your closest friend* secretly tries to act as a

---

13:1   **Do not add . . .** This is a commandment not to add or subtract from any observance prescribed by the Torah (Rashi; *Sifri*; *Sefer HaMitzvoth*, Negative 313). There is also a commandment not to try to increase or diminish the number of commandments (Deuteronomy 4:2; *Adereth Eliahu*; *HaKethav VeHaKabbalah*). In simplest terms, the Torah here is saying that we should not try to "improve" the Torah by borrowing gentile practices.

13:2   **present you** (cf. Ramban). Literally, "give." Or, "predict" (Rashbam).

—   **sign.** A prediction of the future (Ramban; *Adereth Eliahu*). Such a sign is usually required of a prophet; below 18:21 (see *Yad, Yesodey HaTorah* 10:1.

13:3   **on the basis of . . .** (Ramban). Literally, "the sign or miracle comes." Or, "If the [predicted] sign or miracle comes true" (Saadia; Rashbam).

—   **new spiritual experience.** See above, 11:28.

13:4   **with all your heart . . .** Here we see the extent of the desire for new spiritual experiences (cf. *Yoma* 69b).

13:5   **have a true spiritual experience . . .** (Bachya). Literally, "cling to" or "attach yourself to Him;" see above 10:20.

13:6   **rebelliously** (Ibn Janach; Bachya). *Sarah* in Hebrew, from the root *sur*; see below, 19:16, Isaiah 59:13, Jeremiah 28:16, 29:32. Or, "falsely" (Saadia; Rashi; Hirsch); "perversely" (Targum), "to lead you astray" (Ibn Ezra; Radak, *Sherashim*; Septuagint) or, "deistically" (*HaKethav VeHaKabbalah*).

13:7   **blood brother.** Literally, "your brother, son of your mother."

—   **closest friend.** Literally, "your friend, who is like yourself."

13   missionary* among you, and says, "Let us go worship a new god. Let us have
      a spiritual experience* previously unknown by you or your fathers." [8] [He
      may be enticing you with] the gods of the nations around you, far or near, or
      those that are found* at one end of the world or another.

      [9] Do not agree with* him, and do not listen to him. Do not let your eyes
      pity him, do not show him any mercy, and do not try to cover up for him,
      [10] since you must be the one to put him to death. Your hand must be the first
      against him to kill him, followed by the hands of the other people. [11] Pelt him
      to death with stones, since he has tried to make you abandon God your Lord,
      who brought you out of the slave house that was Egypt.

      [12] When all Israel hears about it, they will be afraid, and they will never
      again do such an evil thing among you.

                              [43. The Apostate City]

      [13] [This is what you must do] if, with regard to one of your cities that God
      your Lord is giving you as a place to live, you hear a report, stating that
      [14] irresponsible* men among you have been successful in leading the city's
      inhabitants astray by saying, "Let us worship another god and have a novel
      spiritual experience.*"

      [15] You must investigate and probe, making careful inquiry.* If it is estab-
      lished to be true, and such a revolting thing has occurred in your midst,
      [16] then you must kill all the inhabitants of the city by the sword. Destroy it and
      everything in it as taboo, and [kill] all its animals by the sword.

      [17] Gather all [the city's] goods to its central square, and burn the city along
      with all its goods, [almost] like a sacrifice* to God your Lord. [The city] shall
      then remain an eternal ruin, never again to be rebuilt. [18] Let nothing that has
      been declared taboo there remain in your hands.

      God will then have mercy on you, and reverse any display of anger that
      might have existed. In His mercy, He will make you flourish, just as He prom-

---

—   **to act as a missionary** (Radak, *Sherashim*; *Sifri*, from 1 Samuel 26:19). *Sith* in Hebrew, and one who does it
         is called a *mesith*. Or, "try to convince" (Targum; Ibn Janach; Septuagint), "try to mislead" (*Targum
         Yonathan*; *Sifri*), or, "give bad advice" (Rashbam).
—   **Let us have a spiritual experience** . . . See note on 11:28.
13:8   **those that are found** . . . (Ralbag; *Adereth Eliahu*).
13:9   **agree with** (*Targum Yonathan*; Septuagint). *Abhah* in Hebrew. Or, "accept" (Ramban), or, "be tempted
         by" (Rashi; Radak, *Sherashim*).
13:14   **irresponsible.** Or, "undisciplined," that is, "without a yoke" (*Sanhedrin* 111b; *Sifri*; Rashi). *Beli ya'al* in
         Hebrew. Or, "worthless" (*beli ya'al*; Radak, *Sherashim*; Hirsch); "wicked" (Targum; Septuagint); "non-
         believers" (Saadia), "wicked scholars" (*Targum Yonathan*).
—   **novel spiritual experience.** See note on 11:28. It is understood that they were successful in convincing
         the majority of the city (*Sanhedrin* 111b; *Yad, Avodath Kokhavim* 4:2).
13:15   **making careful inquiry.** Of witnesses (*Sanhedrin* 40a).
13:17   **almost like a sacrifice** (cf. *Sanhedrin* 111b).

ised your fathers. ¹⁹ You will have obeyed God your Lord, keeping all the   **13**
commandments that I prescribe to you today, and doing what is morally right
in the eyes of God your Lord.

[44. Responsibility as a Chosen People]

¹ You are children of God your Lord. Do not mutilate yourselves and do   **14**
not make a bald patch in the middle of your head* as a sign of mourning.*

² You are a nation consecrated to God your Lord. God has chosen you
from all nations on the face of the earth to be His own special nation.*

[45. Forbidden Animals]

³ Do not eat any abomination.

⁴ These are the mammals that you may eat: the ox,* the sheep, the goat,
⁵ the gazelle,* the deer,* the antelope,* the ibex,* the chamois,* the bison,* and
the giraffe.*

⁶ You may thus eat every animal that has a true hoof that is cloven* into
two parts, and which brings up its cud.

⁷ However, among the animals that bring up their cud or have a true
cloven hoof, there are some that you may not eat. These include the camel,

---

14:1   **middle of your head.** Idiomatically expressed by the expression, "between your eyes" (*Menachoth* 37b).
See Exodus 13:9.

—   **sign of mourning.** Literally, "for the dead."

14:2   **special . . .** See above 7:6.

14:4   **the ox.** That is, all kinds of cattle.

14:5   **gazelle.** *Ayal* in Hebrew. The Septuagint translates it as *elaphon*, a deer, but possibly transposed with *tz'vi*,
below. It would then be *dorkada* in the Greek, literally, "bright eyes." The gazelle is distinguished by its
lustrous eyes. Some identify the *ayil* as the roe deer or red deer, *cerf* in French (Chizzkuni). It is described
as an animal with branched antlers (Rashi, *Yoma* 29a, s.v. *Lamah*).

—   **deer.** *Tz'vi* in Hebrew. *Elaphon* in Greek (Septuagint, transposed); *cevral* in Provançal (Chizzkuni),
equivalent to the Latin *cervus*, a deer.

—   **antelope.** *Yachmur* in Hebrew; see 1 Kings 5:3. *Pygargon* in Greek (Septuagint), literally, "white rumped,"
that is, the white rumped antelope. Others identify the *yachmor* as a large white goat (Radak, *Sherashim*; cf.
Saadia; Ibn Janach) or a buffalo (Abarbanel on 1 Kings 5:3). See *Bekhoroth* 7b. Others identify it as the
roe deer or fallow deer.

—   **ibex.** The wild goat (*Caora segagrus*). *Akko* in Hebrew; *yaalah* in Aramaic, equivalent to the Hebrew *ya'el* in
1 Samuel 24:3, Psalms 104:18, Job 39:1 (Radak, *Sherashim*). Asstanbok in Old French (Rashi; Chizzkuni);
Wa'al in Arabic (Saadia; Ibn Janach). See *Shabbath* 152a.

—   **chamois.** A small goatlike antelope (*Rupicapra rupicapra*); *Dishon* in Hebrew; *arvi* in Arabic (Saadia),
shagoin or *shagla* in Provançal (Chizzkuni). Or, possibly, the addax, a large light colored antelope with
twisted horns. Others identify it with the *re'em* in Numbers 23:22, *rim* in Aramaic (Targum; Radak,
Sherashim; Ibn Janach). In Arabic, the *rim* is the white antelope.

—   **bison.** *Te'o* in Hebrew; cf. Isaiah 4:5. That is, the "wild ox" (*Targum Yonathan*; *Sifri*; Rashi; Ibn Janach;
Radak, *Sherashim*). The Septuagint translates it as *oruga* or *orux*, either the oryx, a large straight horned
antelope, or the aurochs, the "wild ox." Saadia also identifies it with oryx, *tethal* in Arabic. Chizzkuni
renders it as *shulia*.

—   **giraffe.** *Zemer* in Hebrew. *Zarafa* (from which the English word is derived) in *Arabic* (Saadia; Ibn Janach;
Radak, *Sherashim*; *Shiltey Gibborim* 53); *camelepard* in Greek (Septuagint), also used in English for giraffe
(camelopard). *Ditza* in Aramaic (see Targum on Proverbs 5:19).

14:6   **every animal . . .** See Leviticus 11:3.

14 hyrax and hare,* which may bring up their cud, but do not have true hooves, and are therefore unclean to you. **8** Also included is the pig, which has a true hoof, but does not have a cud, and is therefore unclean to you.

Do not eat the flesh of these [animals] and do not touch their carcasses.*

[46. Aquatic Creatures]

9 Among that which is in the water,* you may eat anything that has fins and scales. **10** But those which have no fins and scales, you may not eat, since they are unclean to you.

[47. Birds]

11 You may eat every kosher bird.

12 The birds that you may not eat are the eagle, the ossifrage, the osprey,* **13** the white vulture,* the black vulture,* the kite,* **14** the entire raven family, **15** the ostrich, owl, gull and hawk families, **16** the falcon, the ibis, the swan,* **17** the pelican, the magpie, the cormorant, **18** the stork, the heron family, the hoopoe, and the bat.

19 Every flying insect that is unclean to you shall not be eaten. **20** However, you may eat every kosher flying creature.*

21 Since you are a holy nation to God your Lord, you may not eat any [mammal or bird] that has not been properly slaughtered.* You may give it to the resident alien in your settlements so that he can eat it, or you may sell it to a foreigner.*

Do not cook meat in milk [even that] of its mother.*

[48. The Second Tithe]

22 Take a [second] tithe* of all the seed crops* that come forth in the field

---

14:7 **camel, hyrax, and hare.** See Leviticus 11:4-6.
14:8 **Do not touch . . .** See Leviticus 11:8. Or, "do not touch [to eat]" (*Baaley Tosafoth*).
14:9 **in the water.** Leviticus 11:10-12.
14:12 **the eagle . . .** Leviticus 11:13-19.
14:13 **white vulture** (*Targum Yonathan*). *Ra'ah* in Hebrew. This is seen as a species of *ayah* (Chullin 63b; cf. Ibn Janach). Others see the *ra'ah* as the kite, the same as the *da'ah* in Leviticus 11:14 (*Chullin* 63b).
—   **black vulture** (*Targum Yonathan*). *Ayah* in Hebrew, translated as "vulture" in *Leviticus* 11:14.
—   **kite.** *Daya* in Hebrew, the same as the *da'ah* in Leviticus 11:14 (Saadia; Onkolos translates both as *deitha*).
14:16 **ibis . . . swan . . .** The order is somewhat different than in Leviticus.
14:20 **flying creature.** Including kosher locusts in Leviticus 11:22 (*Sifri*; Ibn Ezra). Or, "birds" (Abarbanel).
14:21 **that has not been . . .** *Nevelah* in Hebrew. (see *Sefer HaMitzvoth* Negative 180).
—   **You may give it to . . .** (cf. *Pesachim* 22b; Abarbanel).
—   **Do not cook . . .** See Exodus 23:19, 34:26 (cf. Targum; Saadia; Bachya).
14:22 **second tithe** (Rashi; *Yad, Maaser Sheni* 1:1). This was in addition to the first tithe given to the Levites (Numbers 18:24). It was given in all years of the Sabbatical cycle except the third and sixth (see below 14:28).
—   **seed crops** (see *Yerushalmi, Maaser Sheni* 1:1; *Yad, Terumoth* 2:6; *HaKethav VeHaKabbalah*; cf. Ramban)

PLATE 31. KOSHER MAMMALS

14   each year. [23] You must eat this before God your Lord in the place that He will
      choose as dedicated to His name. [There you shall eat] the [second] tithe of
      your grain, wine and oil, as well as the first-born of your cattle and smaller
      animals. You will then learn* to remain in awe of God your Lord for all time.

      [24] If the journey is too great for you, and God your Lord has blessed you
      so that the place that God your Lord has chosen as a site dedicated to His
      name is too far for you to carry it there, [25] you may redeem [the tithe] for
      silver. The silver in your hand must consist of coinage,* which you can bring
      to the place that God your Lord will choose.

      [26] You may then spend the money on anything you desire, whether it be
      cattle, smaller animals, wine, brandy,* or anything else for which you have an
      urge.* Eat it there before God your Lord, so that you and your family will be
      able to rejoice.

      [27] This, however, does not mean that you can abandon the Levite in your
      settlements. [You must give him your first tithe]* since he has no hereditary
      portion with you.

[49. Tithes for the Poor]

      [28] At the end of each three year period,* you must bring out all the tithes of
      that year's crop, and place them in your settlements. [29] The Levite,* who does
      not have a hereditary portion with you shall then come, along with the for-
      eigner, orphan and widow in your settlement, and they will eat and be satis-
      fied. God your Lord will then bless you in everything that you do.

[50. The Remission Year]

15   [1] At the end of every seven years, you shall celebrate the remission year.*
      [2] The idea of the remission year is that every creditor shall remit any debt
      owed by his neighbor and brother when God's remission year comes around.

      [3] You may collect from the alien, but if you have any claim against your
      brother for a debt, you must relinquish it. [4] God will then bless you in the

---

14:23 **You will then learn . . .** By coming in contact with priests and scholars in Jerusalem (Ramban; Sforno).
14:25 **must consist of coinage** (cf. *Sifri; Bava Metzia* 54a; *Yad, Maaser Sheni* 4:9). Or, "take the silver wrapped in
       your hand" (*Sifri; Bava Metzia* 42a).
14:26 **brandy.** Or, "old wine" (Targum). *Shekher* in Hebrew. Or, "fruit wine" (Radak, *Sherashim*), "mead" (Ibn
       Ezra), or any other "intoxicating beverage" (Ibn Janach; Septuagint).
—   **have an urge.** Literally, "for which your soul asks."
14:27 **You must give him your first tithe** (Rashi). See Numbers 11:24.
14:28 **each three year period.** (*Rosh HaShanah* 12b; *Yad, Matnoth Ani'yim* 6:4). This is the tithe that is given to the
       poor on the third and sixth year of the Sabbatical cycle, in place of the "second tithe." See below, 26:12.
14:29 **the Levite.** For the first (Levitical) tithe (*Rosh HaShanah* 12b).
15:1   **remission year.** *Shemitah* in Hebrew. See Exodus 23:10, Leviticus 25:2.

land that God your Lord is giving you to occupy as a heritage, and there will 15
not be any more poor* among you.

⁵ This, however, will be true only if you obey the word of God your Lord,
carefully keeping this entire mandate that I am prescribing to you today.
⁶ God your Lord will then bless you as He promised you, so that you will
extend credit* to many nations, but you will not need any credit for yourselves. You will thus dominate many nations, but none will dominate you.

[51. Lending Money]

⁷ When, in a settlement in the land that God your Lord is giving you, any
of your brothers is poor, do not harden your heart or shut your hand against
your needy brother. ⁸ Open your hand generously, and extend to him any
credit he needs to take care of his wants.

⁹ Be very careful that you not have an irresponsible* idea and say to yourself, "The seventh year is approaching, and it will be the remission year." You
may then look unkindly at your impoverished brother, and not give him anything. If he then complains to God about you, you will have a sin.

¹⁰ Therefore, make every effort to give him, and do not feel bad about giving it, since God your Lord will then bless you in all your endeavors, no matter what you do. ¹¹ The poor will never cease to exist in the land, so I am commanding you to open your hand generously to your poor and destitute
brother in your land.

[52. The Israelite Slave]

¹² When your fellow Hebrew man or woman is sold to you, he may serve as
much as six years, but in the seventh year you must send him away free.*
¹³ When you send him away free, do not send him empty-handed. ¹⁴ Give him
a severance gift* from your flocks, from your threshing floor, and from your
wine vat, so that he will have a share of all the things through which God your
Lord has blessed you. ¹⁵ You will thus remember that you were a slave in
Egypt and God your Lord liberated you. It is for this reason that I am commanding you today to do this.

¹⁶ If [the slave] likes you and your family,* and has it so good with you that
he says, "I do not want to leave you," ¹⁷ then you must take an awl,* and place

---

15:4 **and there will not be . . .** (Ibn Ezra; Bachya).
15:6 **extend credit.** *Abat* in Hebrew. Or, "exact a pledge for a loan," see Deuteronomy 24:10. (cf. Bachya).
15:9 **irresponsible.** See note on 13:14.
15:12 **but in the seventh year . . .** See Exodus 21:2.
15:14 **severance gift.** Of 30 shekels (*Kiddushin* 17a).
15:16 **family.** (Targum). Or, literally, "house" (Septuagint).
15:17 **awl.** See Exodus 21:6.

15   it through his ear and the door. He will then become your permanent slave. You must also [grant a severance gift]* to your female slave.

¹⁸ Do not think it difficult to send [your slave] away free. He has done double the work of a hired hand* during the six years, and God your Lord will bless you in all you do.

[53. First-Born Animals]

¹⁹ You must consecrate to God every male firstling born among your cattle and flocks. Do not work with your first-born ox, and do not shear your first-born sheep. ²⁰ You and your family must eat them before God your Lord each year in the place that God shall choose.

²¹ If [the animal] has a blemish, such as when it is crippled or blind, or afflicted with any other serious blemish,* you may not sacrifice it to God your Lord. ²² The clean and unclean may then eat it in your settlements, just like the deer and gazelle.* ²³ Do not eat its blood, but spill it on the ground like water.*

[54. Passover]

16   ¹ Safeguard* the month of standing grain so that you will be able to keep the Passover to God your Lord, since it was in the month of standing grain that God your Lord brought you out of Egypt at night.

² In the place that God will choose to be dedicated to His name, you shall sacrifice the Passover offering to God your Lord [along with other] sheep and cattle.* ³ Do not eat any leaven with it. As part of [the celebration] you shall eat matzah for seven days. This shall be hardship bread, since you left Egypt in a rush. You will then remember the day you left Egypt all the days of your life.

⁴ No leavening shall be seen with you in all your borders for seven days. Do not let the flesh that you sacrificed in the evening of the first day remain overnight until morning.

⁵ You may not slaughter the Passover offering in any of your settlements which God your Lord is giving you. ⁶ The only site where you may sacrifice the

---

—   grant a severance gift (*Kiddushin* 17b; Rashi; *Yad, Avadim* 3:13).
15:18 double the work . . . (Rashi; cf. Targum). Or, "He has worked for you at the yearly wage of a hired hand" (Septuagint).
15:21 serious blemish. See Leviticus 22:22-24.
15:22 The clean and unclean . . . See above, 12:15.
15:23 spill it on the ground . . . See above, 12:16.
16:1   Safeguard. Adjusting the lunar calendar so that Nissan remains in the spring (*Rosh HaShanah* 21a; *Yad, Kiddush HaChodesh* 1:1).
16:2   along with other sheep and cattle (Ramban). Or, "sacrifice sheep as the Passover offering, along with the cattle (Targum; *Sifri*; Rashi). The other animals are the special festival offering, known as the Chagigah. This consisted of a peace offering (*Yad, Chagiga* 1:1).

Passover offering is in the place that God will choose as a site designated in 16
His name.

There you shall sacrifice it in the evening, as the sun is setting, at the time
of year that you left Egypt. ⁷ You shall cook it* and eat it in the place chosen
by God your Lord, and then you may turn around in the morning and return
to your tents.*

⁸ For six [additional]* days you shall then eat matzah, with the seventh day
as a retreat* dedicated to God your Lord, when you may not do any work.

[55. Shavuoth]

⁹ Then count seven weeks for yourself.* From the time that you first put the
sickle* to the standing grain, you must count seven weeks.

¹⁰ You shall then celebrate the festival of Shavuoth* to God your Lord,
presenting a hand-delivered offering according to* the extent of the blessing
that God your Lord has granted you. ¹¹ You shall rejoice before God your
Lord in the place that God your Lord shall choose to be designated in His
name. You [shall rejoice along] with your sons, your daughters, your male and
female slaves, the Levites from your settlements, and the proselytes, orphans
and widows among you.

¹² You must remember that you were a slave in Egypt, and thus carefully
keep all these rules.

[56. Sukkoth]

¹³ When you bring in the products of your threshing floor and wine vat,
you shall celebrate the festival of Sukkoth* for seven days. ¹⁴ You shall rejoice
on your festival along with your son and daughter, your male and female
slave, and the Levite, proselyte, orphan and widow from your settlements.
¹⁵ Celebrate to God your Lord for seven days in the place that God will

---

16:7 **cook it.** That is, roast it, as in Exodus 12:9 (Ibn Ezra; Bachya).

— **return to your tents.** Around Jerusalem (Ibn Ezra). Or, on the morning of the second day of Passover (*ibid.*).

16:8 **additional.** After the first day (Chizzkuni; Abarbanel). Or, "For six days . . . eat matzah, and then the seventh . . ." (Ralbag; Abarbanel).

— **retreat.** See Leviticus 23:36; Numbers 29:35.

16:9 **Then count . . .** See Leviticus 23:15.

— **sickle.** *Chermash* in Hebrew; see Deuteronomy 23:26 (Ibn Janach; Radak, *Sherashim*; Septuagint). This is the sickle used to cut the omer (Targum; *Sifri*; Rashi).

16:10 **Shavuoth.** "Weeks." See Exodus 23:16, 34:22, Leviticus 23:15, Numbers 28:26.

— **according to . . .** Or, "sufficient for" (Rashi; Rashbam; Radak, *Sherashim*). *Missah* or *missath* in Hebrew. Or, "as a donation" (Ibn Ezra; Bachya). Or, "as a tax," indicating that the Chagigah must be taken from an animal that is the absolute property of the person bringing it, and not an animal that has been previously sanctified (*Chagigah* 8a).

16:13 **Sukkoth.** "Shelters." See Exodus 23:16, Leviticus 23:34, Numbers 29:12.

16 choose, since God will then bless you in all your agricultural and other endeavors, so that you will be only happy.

[16] Three times each year, all your males shall thus be seen in the presence of God your Lord in the place that He will choose: on the festival of Matzahs, on the festival of Shavuoth, and on the festival of Sukkoth. [In those times] you shall not appear before God empty-handed. [17] Each person shall bring his hand-delivered gift, depending on the blessing that God your Lord grants you.

Shof'tim   שֹׁפְטִים

[57. Judges and Justice]

[18] Appoint yourselves judges and police* for your tribes* in all your settlements that God your Lord is giving you, and make sure that they administer honest judgment for the people.

[19] Do not bend justice* and do not give special consideration [to anyone]. Do not take bribes, since bribery makes the wise blind and perverts the words of the righteous.* [20] Pursue perfect honesty, so that you will live and occupy the land that God your Lord is giving you.

[58. Sacred Trees and Pillars]

[21] Do not plant for yourself an Asherah* [or any other]* tree near the altar that you will make yourselves for God your Lord.

[22] Do not erect a sacred pillar,* since this is something that God your Lord hates.*

16:18 **police.** Shot'rim in Hebrew. Officers to enforce the dictates of the courts and judges (Sifri; Rashi). See above, 1:15. Also see Exodus 5:6.
— **for your tribes.** Since members of one tribe may not go to the court of another (Sanhedrin 16b). Therefore, even if there are two tribes in a city, each must have its own court (Tosafoth ibid. s.v. Shoftim). Some translate this verse, "for all your tribes [and] in all your settlements" indicating that besides the city courts, there must also be tribal courts (Ramban). Others translate it, "in all the settlements that God . . . is giving you for your tribes" (Saadia).
16:19 **Do not bend justice.** See Exodus 23:6, Leviticus 19:15.
— **perverts the words . . .** See Exodus 23:8.
16:21 **Asherah.** See Exodus 34:13. Or, "grove" (Septuagint; cf. HaKethav VeHaKabbalah). Some say that any tree planted at the entrance to a house of worship is called an Asherah (Lekach Tov; Ramban).
— **or any other.** (Mizrachi; cf. Yad, Avodath Kokhavim 6:9).
16:22 **sacred pillar.** Some say that it is a monolith used for sacrifices (Rashi; Radak, Sherashim; Ibn Janach; Sefer Mitzvoth Gadol, Negative 44). Others say that it is a structure built as a focus for worship (Yad, Avodath Kokhavim 6:6; Ralbag; Chinukh 493). See Leviticus 26:19.
— **that God your Lord hates.** Although it was common in the time of the patriarchs (Genesis 28:18, 31:34, 35:14, Exodus 24:4), by this time, such sacred pillars had become identified with idolatrous practices (Sifri; Rashi). However, some say that the patriarchs did not use the pillars for sacrifices, but merely as a sign (Abarbanel). It is for this reason that it is permitted to erect a monument for the dead (Midrash HaGadol).

[59. Blemished Sacrifice]

¹ Do not sacrifice to God your Lord any ox, sheep or goat* that has a| **17**
serious blemish,* since to do so before God your Lord is considered revolting.

[60. Penalties for Idolatry]

² [This is what you must do] when you discover a man or woman doing evil
in the eyes of God your Lord in one of the settlements that God your Lord is
giving you. [That person] will have violated [God's] covenant ³ by going and
worshiping or bowing down to the sun, moon or other heavenly bodies,
whose [worship]* I prohibited.

⁴ When it is told to you, you must listen and carefully interrogate [the wit-
nesses]. If the accusation is established* to be true, and this revolting practice
has been done in Israel, ⁵ you shall take that man or woman who did the
wicked act out to your gates.* You shall then pelt the man or woman to death
with stones.

⁶ The accused shall be put to death only through the testimony of two or
three* witnesses. He shall not be put to death through the testimony of one
witness. ⁷ The hand of the witness shall be against him first to put him to
death, and only then shall the hand of all the other people [be set against
him]. You shall thus rid yourselves of evil.

[61. The Supreme Court]

⁸ If you are unable to reach a decision* in a case involving* capital punishment,* litigation, leprous marks,* [or any other case] where there is a dispute
in your territorial courts,* then you must set out and go up to the place that

---

17:1   **sheep or goat.** The Hebrew *seh* denotes both.
—   **serious blemish.** See Leviticus 22:22-24.
17:3   **whose worship I prohibited.** (Septuagint; *Megillah* 9a; Rashi). Literally, "which I did not command."
17:4   **established.** *Nakhon* in Hebrew; see above 13:15. Or, "if the testimony [of the two witnesses] matches"
          (Rashi; *HaKethav VeHaKabbalah*).
17:5   **gates.** That is, the gate of the city where the sin was committed. However, if the majority of the city's
          population were gentile idolators, the penalty would be carried out within the confines of the court
          (*Kethuvoth* 45b; *Yad, Sanhedrin* 15:2; cf. Targum; Rashi; *Sifri*; *HaKethav VeHaKabbalah*).
17:6   **two or three.** This indicates that if there are three witnesses they must be interrogated the same as two
          (Ralbag). Moreover, if the testimony of the third witness does not agree with the two, the entire testi-
          mony must be rejected (*Makkoth* 5b; Rashi).
17:8   **unable to reach a decision** (cf. Malbim). *Pala* in Hebrew. Or, "if it is concealed" (Targum; Rashi),
          "separated" (*Targum Yonathan*), "with a hidden answer" (Saadia), or, "too difficult" (Septuagint).
—   **involving** (cf. *HaKethav VeHaKabbalah*).
—   **capital punishment** (Rashbam; Ibn Ezra). Literally, "blood." Or, "[clean and unclean] blood" (*Sanhedrin*
          87a; *Niddah* 19a; *Targum Yonathan*; Rashi; Ramban); cf. Leviticus 15:19,25.
—   **leprous marks** (Targum; Rashi; Rashbam).*Nega* in Hebrew. Or, "damages for injury" (Ibn Ezra; Sep-
          tuagint).
—   **where there is a dispute . . .** (Targum; Rashi). Or, "or any other dispute in your settlements" (Ramban;
          Septuagint).

17 God your Lord shall choose. ⁹ You must approach the Levitical priests* [and other members of] the supreme court* that exists at the time. When you make inquiry, they will declare to you a legal decision.

¹⁰ Since this decision comes from the place that God shall choose, you must do as they tell you, carefully following their every decision. ¹¹ [Besides this, in general,] you must keep the Torah as they interpret it for you, and follow the laws that they legislate for you.* Do not stray* to the right or left from the word that they declare to you.

¹² If there is any man* who rebels* and refuses to listen to the priest or other judge who is in charge of serving God your Lord there [as leader of the supreme court],* then that man must be put to death, thus ridding yourselves of evil in Israel. ¹³ When all the people hear about it, they will fear and will not rebel again.

[62. The Monarch]

¹⁴ When you come to the land that God your Lord is giving you, so that you have occupied it and settled it, you will eventually say, "We would like to appoint a king, just like all the nations around us." ¹⁵ You must then appoint the king whom God your Lord shall choose.* You must appoint a king from among your brethren; you may not appoint a foreigner who is not one of your brethren.

¹⁶ [The king,] however, must not accumulate many horses,* so as not to

---

— **Levitical priests** (Rashi; Ibn Ezra). Or, "Levites [and] priests," indicating that both should preferably be members of the supreme court (*Sifri; Yad, Sanhedrin* 2:2). Cf. 2 Chronicles 19:8. Or, "the supreme court [associated with] the Levitical priests," indicating that for the court to have full authority, the priesthood must also be functioning (*Sanhedrin* 52b; *Yad, Sanhedrin* 14:11). The priests were associated with the court because they were supported by the community (see 18:1), and could therefore devote their entire time to Torah study (Abarbanel).

— **supreme court.** Or, literally, "judge." However, by tradition, this is speaking of the council of 70 elders, the first of which was appointed by Moses; cf. Numbers 11:16,24 (*Yad, Sanhedrin* 1:3). Also see Exodus 24:1. In Talmudical times, this supreme court was known as the Sanhedrin. Besides being a court, this body also had legislative powers, see 17:11

17:11 **Besides this . . .** (*Sefer HaMitzvoth*, Positive 174; *Chinukh* 495).

— **Do not stray.** This is a negative commandment, that also includes legislation (*Berakhoth* 19b; *Shabbath* 23a; *Sefer HaMitzvoth*, Negative 312; *Chinukh* 496). However, some say that these commandments apply only to decisions and not to legislation (Ramban on *Sefer HaMitzvoth, Shoresh* 1, 4a ff.)

17:12 **any man.** Actually, only a man who is duly ordained and fit to sit on the supreme court, and is thus normally able to reach a decision as in 17:8 (*Sanhedrin* 87a). Such a person is known as a "rebellious elder" (*zaken mamre*).

— **rebels.** *Zyd* in Hebrew. Or, "acts wickedly" (*Targum*), "acts purposely" (*Targum Yonathan*); or, "acts in haughtiness" (*Septuagint*).

— **as leader . . .** (cf. Hirsch; *Sifri*).

17:15 **shall choose.** Prophetically (*Sifri; Yad, Melakhim* 1:3).

17:16 **many horses.** It is thus forbidden for an Israelite king to have more horses than he needs for transportation and war. He may not have any horses merely for pomp (*Sanhedrin* 21b; *Yad, Melakhim* 3:3).

bring the people back to Egypt to get more horses. God has told you that you **17**
must never again return on that path.

¹⁷ He [also] must not have many wives,* so that they not make his heart go
astray. He shall likewise not accumulate very much* silver and gold.

¹⁸ When [the king] is established on his royal throne, he must write a copy
of this Torah as a scroll* edited by the Levitical priests.* ¹⁹ [This scroll] must
always be with him, and he shall read from it all the days of his life. He will
then learn to be in awe of God his Lord, and carefully keep every word of this
Torah and these rules. ²⁰ He will then [also] not begin to feel superior to his
brethren, and he will not stray from the mandate to the right or the left. He
and his descendants will thus have a long reign in the midst of Israel.

[63. The Levitical Priests]

¹ The Levitical priests [and]* the entire tribe of Levi shall not have a terri- **18**
torial portion with [the rest of] Israel, and they shall [therefore]* eat God's fire
offerings* and [their] hereditary gifts.* ² Since God shall be their heritage, as
He promised them, they shall not have any [territorial] heritage among their
brethren.

[64. The Priestly Portion]

³ This shall be the law* [of what the] priests [receive] from the people:
When any ox* sheep or goat* is slaughtered as food, you must give the
priest the foreleg,* the jaw* and the maw.*

⁴ You must [also] give him the first portion* of your grain, wine and oil,
and the first of your shearing.*

⁵ This is because God your Lord has chosen him and his descendants out
of all your tribes to stand and serve in God's name for all time.

17:17 **many wives.** Although polygamy was permitted, and was common for kings, an Israelite king was forbidden to have more than eighteen wives (*Sanhedrin* 21b; *Yad, Melakhim* 3:2).
— **very much.** That is, the king is forbidden to build up a personal fortune (*Yad, Melakhim* 3:4).
17:18 **scroll.** Literally, "book," but all books were then written as scrolls.
— **Levitical priests.** That is, by the Sanhedrin (*Tosefta, Sanhedrin* 4:4; *Yad, Melakhim* 3:1). See note on 17:9.
18:1 **and** (Saadia; cf. *Sefer HaMitzvoth, Negative* 169, 170).
— **therefore** (Saadia).
— **fire offerings.** Portions of sacrifices eaten by priests.
— **hereditary gifts.** Agricultural offerings (*Sifri*; Rashi).
18:3 **This shall be the law ...** See Numbers 18:8-19.
— **ox.** A cow or bull.
— **sheep or goat.** The Hebrew *seh* includes both.
— **foreleg.** The right foreleg (*Chullin* 134b; *Yad, Bikkurim* 9:18; *Yoreh Deah* 61:2).
— **jaw.** The lower jaw (*Yad, Bikkurim* 9:18).
— **the maw.** *Kebhah* in Hebrew. This is the last of a cow's four stomachs (Rashi, *Chullin* 42a, s.v. *Beth*; *Yoreh Deah* 48:1).
18:4 **first portion.** This is the "elevated gift" (*Terumah*) in Numbers 18:11 (Rashi).
— **first ... shearing.** That is, the first wool shorn from one's sheep (*Yad, Bikkurim* 10:4; *Chullin* 137a).

18   *[65. Special Service]*

⁶ The Levitical [priest],* no matter where he lives among all the Israelites, can come to the place that God shall choose on a festival,* [or]* whenever else he wishes to [bring his own sacrifice]. ⁷ He can then serve* before God his Lord just the same as any of his fellow Levitical [priests] whose turn it is* to serve before God. ⁸ [On the festivals], he shall receive the same portion that they do to eat.* The only exception is that which [is theirs] by ancestral right.*

[66. Divination and Prophecy]

⁹ When you come to the land that God your Lord is giving you, do not learn to do the revolting practices of those nations. ¹⁰ Among you, there shall not be found anyone who passes his son or daughter through fire,* who practices stick divination,* who divines auspicious times,* who divines by omens,* who practices witchcraft,* ¹¹ who uses incantations,* who consults mediums and oracles,* or who attempts to communicate with the dead.*

18:6 **Levitical priest** (*Sifri*; Rashi; Rashbam; Ralbag; cf. *Yevamoth* 86b). Some, however, say that it literally denotes a Levite (*Arakhin* 11a; Saadia; Chizzkuni; *Adereth Eliahu*).

—   **on a festival** (*Sifri*; *Yad, K'ley HaMikdash* 4:4). Literally, "from one of your gates," or "settlements," indicating the time that all the Israelites are together in one settlement; i.e. on a festival pilgrimage.

—   **or . . .** (see *Yad, K'ley HaMikdash* 4:7).

18:7 **serve**. Priestly service. Or, if the verse is speaking of a Levite, singing (*Arakhin* 11a).

—   **whose turn it is.** Literally, "who stand." The priests were divided into different shifts, with each having a different day to serve (*Yad, K'ley HaMikdash* 4:3).

18:8 **On the festivals . . .** (*Yad, K'ley HaMikdash* 4:4; *Sukkah* 55b).

—   **The only exception . . .** That is, sacrifices that are not brought especially for the festival (*Yad, K'ley HaMikdash* 4:5). However, some intepret this verse, "The Levitical priest who lives in any of your Israelite settlements can come to the place that God shall choose whenever he desires. ⁷ He can then serve before God his Lord, just the same as any of his fellow Levitical priests who stand and serve before God. ⁸ He shall then receive the same portion to eat as they do, with the exception of those portions that have been sold as an ancestral right" (Ramban on *Sefer HaMitzvoth*, Positive 36). This is actually a more literal translation.

18:10 **through fire.** For Molekh; see Leviticus 18:21 (*Sanhedrin* 64b).

—   **stick divination.** *Kasam* in Hebrew. Some say that this denotes tapping a stick to produce a meditative state so as to be able to predict the future (*Yad, Avodath Kokhavim* 11:6). Others describe it as peeling one side of a stick and seeing on which side it falls (*Sefer Mitzvoth Gadol*, Negative 52; *Paaneach Razah*), or grasping a stick and measuring off to the end with one's fingers, calling off positive and negative responses (Chizzkuni; cf. *Sifri*; Rashi).

        Some say that the *kesem* includes all sorts of meditative methods used to predict the future (Ralbag; *Chinukh* 510). It may also include geomancy (*Yad, loc. cit.*; *Sefer HaMitzvoth*, Negative 31), and divination by lots in general (Rashi on Ezekiel 21:27; cf. Septuagint).

—   **divines auspicious times.** See Leviticus 19:26.

—   **divines by omens.** *Ibid.*

—   **witchcraft.** See Exodus 22:17.

18:11 **uses incantations.** *Chover chaver* in Hebrew. This denotes incantations in general (*Yad, Avodath Kokhavim* 11:10; Septuagint). In particular, it denotes using incantations to gather demons (Ibn Ezra), or animals (*Targum Yonathan*; Radak, *Sherashim*; *Sefer Mitzvoth Gadol*, Negative 64; cf. *Sanhedrin* 65b). It can also involve incantations to cure snakebites and the like, and, possibly, those used in alchemy (Saadia; *Sefer HaMitzvoth*, Negative 35; *Yad, loc. cit.*).

—   **mediums and oracles.** See Leviticus 19:31.

—   **communicate with the dead.** Through fasting (*Sanhedrin* 65b) and meditation (Ralbag).

¹² Anyone involved in these practices is repulsive to God, and it was **18** because of repulsive practices such as these that God your Lord is driving out [these nations] before you. ¹³ You must [therefore] remain totally faithful to God your Lord. ¹⁴ The nations that you are driving out listen to astrologers and stick diviners, but what God has given you is totally different.

¹⁵ In your midst,* God will set up for you a prophet like me from among your brethren, and it is to him that you must listen.

¹⁶ This is a result of the request that you made of God your Lord at Horeb on the Day of Assembly,* [when you] said, "We cannot listen to the voice of God our Lord any more! We cannot look at this great fire any more! We do not want to die!"*

¹⁷ God then said to me, "They have spoken well. ¹⁸ I will set up a prophet for them from among their brethren, just as you are. I will place My word in his mouth, and he will declare to them all that I command him. ¹⁹ If any person does not listen to the word that he declares in My name, I will punish [that person].* ²⁰ Conversely, if a prophet presumptuously makes a declaration in My name when I have not commanded him to do so, or if he speaks in the name of other gods, then that prophet shall die."

²¹ You may ask yourselves, "How shall we recognize that a declaration was not spoken by God?"

²¹ If the prophet predicts something in God's name, and the prediction does not materialize or come true, then the message was not spoken by God. That prophet has spoken deceitfully, and you must not fear him.

[67. Refuge Cities]

¹ When God your Lord excises the nations in the land that God your Lord **19** is giving you, so that you can occupy it and live in their cities and houses, ² you must separate three cities* in the land which God your Lord is giving you to occupy. ³ Establish yourself a road,* and divide the land area that God your Lord is allotting you into three parts. [The cities in each of these parts] shall be places where a murderer can find refuge.

⁴ The murderer who seeks refuge [in these cities] shall be allowed to live if he accidentally killed his neighbor, without prior hatred. ⁵ [Thus for example,] one may join his friend in the forest to cut wood, and as his hand

---

18:15 **In your midst.** That is, in the Holy Land (*Sifri*).
18:16 **Day of Assembly.** See above, 9:10, 10:4.
—   **We cannot listen . . .** See Exodus 20:16, above, 5:22.
18:19 **I will punish . . .** This is death by God's hand (*Yad, Yesodey HaTorah* 9:2).
19:2 **three cities.** See Numbers 35:14. Also see Exodus 21:13, Joshua 20:2.
19:3 **a road.** Joining the refuge cities (*Makkoth* 9b). These roads were 32 cubits (48 feet) wide (*Bava Bathra* 100b).

19   swings the ax to cut the wood, the head slips off the handle, striking the friend and killing him. In such a case, [the accidental killer] shall find refuge in one of these cities and live.

⁶ If the journey were too far, however, the blood avenger would be able to pursue the killer in hot anger and catch up to him. He could then kill him, even though [the killer] did not previously hate his victim, and therefore could not lawfully be put to death. ⁷ It is for this reason that I am commanding you to separate three cities.

⁸ God will [eventually] expand your borders,* as He swore to your fathers, and He will give you all the territory that He promised them.* ⁹ He will do so because you will carefully keep the entire mandate that I am prescribing for you today, loving God your Lord, and constantly walking in all His paths. [When your borders are thus expanded] you will have to add an additional three cities to the above-mentioned three.

¹⁰ Thus, innocent blood will not be spilled in the land which God your Lord is giving you as a heritage. [But if you do not do this, then] you yourselves will be guilty of murder.

[68. Murder]

¹¹ [This is what you must do] if a person hates his neighbor, and lays a trap for him, doing something to wound him mortally. If [the victim] then dies and [the killer] seeks refuge in one of these cities, ¹² the elders of his city shall send messengers and take him from there. They shall then place [the murderer] in the hand of the blood avenger, and he shall die.

¹³ Do not have pity on the [killer]. If you rid Israel of [those who have shed] innocent blood,* things will go well for you.

[69. Preserving Boundaries]

¹⁴ Do not move your neighbor's boundary marker, which was set in place by the first settlers who were allotted hereditary property in the land that God your Lord is giving you to occupy.

[70. Witnesses]

¹⁵ One witness must not testify against a person to inflict any punishment or penalty for a crime that he may have committed. A case must be established

---

19:8 **expand your borders.** In the Messianic age (*Yad, Melakhim* 11:2).

—   **all the territory that He promised them.** This includes the lands of the Kenites, Kenizites and Kadmonites mentioned in Genesis 15:19 (*Sifri; Yad, Rotze'ach* 8:4). Some say that this is the land extending as far as the Euphrates (Genesis 15:18) (Bachya).

19:13 **those who have shed . . .** (Saadia; Cf. *HaKethav VeHaKabbalah*).

through the testimony of [at least] two or three witnesses.   **19**

¹⁶ [This is what you must do] if a corrupt witness acts to testify falsely against a person. ¹⁷ Two men who have testimony to refute [the false witnesses]* shall stand before God, before the priests and judges who are involved in that case.* ¹⁸ The judges shall carefully interrogate [the refuting witnesses], and if the [first] two witnesses are found to have testified falsely against their brother, ¹⁹ you must do the same to them as they plotted* to do to their brother, thus removing evil from your midst.

²⁰ When the other people hear about this, they will have fear and never again do such an evil thing in your midst. ²¹ Do not have pity in such a case, [since you must take] a life for a life, a tooth for a tooth, a hand for a hand, and a foot for a foot.

[71. Preparing for War]

¹ When you go to battle against your enemies, and see horses, war chariots   **20** and an army larger than yours, do not be afraid of them, since God your Lord, who brought you out of Egypt, is with you.

² When you approach [the place of] battle,* the priest* shall step forward and speak to the people. ³ He shall say to them, "Listen, Israel, today you are about to wage war against your enemies. Do not be faint-hearted,* do not be afraid, do not panic,* and do not break ranks* before them. ⁴ God your Lord is the One who is going with you. He will fight for you against your enemies, and He will deliver you."

⁵ The lower officers* shall then speak to the people, and say, "Is there any man among you who has built a new house, and has not begun to live in it? Let him go home, so that he will not die in war and have another man live in it.

⁶ "Is there any man among you who has planted a vineyard and has not redeemed its first crop?* Let him go home so that he not die in war and have another man redeem its crop.

19:17 **to refute the false witnesses.** By testifying that they were elsewhere at the time that they supposedly saw the act regarding which they testified (Ramban; *Makkoth* 5a).
— **involved in the case.** Literally, "who are in those days."
19:19 **plotted.** That is, where the sentence has not yet been carried out on the basis of their testimony. However, if it has, the witnesses are not punished, since the punishment is an atonement (*Makkoth* 5b; Ramban).
20:2 **place of battle** (*Yad, Melakhim* 7:3).
— **priest.** A priest anointed especially for war (*Sotah* 42a).
20:3 **fainthearted.** See below, 20:8.
— **panic.** *Chaphaz.* See 2 Samuel 4:4.
— **break ranks** (cf. Targum; Ibn Ezra; Septuagint). *Aratz* in Hebrew. See above, 7:21.
20:5 **lower officers.** *Shotrim* in Hebrew. See above 1:15.
20:6 **redeemed . . .** On the fourth year, as in Leviticus 19:24. (Rashi; Saadia). Or, "enjoyed" (Chizzkuni).

20   ⁷ "Is there any man among you who has betrothed* a woman and not married her? Let him go home, so that he not die in war and have another man marry her."

⁸ The lower officers shall then continue speaking to the people and say, "Is there any man among you who is afraid or faint-hearted?* Let him go home rather than have his cowardliness demoralize his brethren."

⁹ When the lower officers have finished speaking to the people, then they shall appoint senior officers* to lead the people.

[72. Taking Captives]

¹⁰ When you approach a city to wage war against it, you must propose a peaceful settlement. ¹¹ If [the city] responds peacefully and opens [its gates] to you, all the people inside shall become your subjects and serve you.

¹² If they reject your peace offer and declare war, you shall lay siege to [the city]. ¹³ when God your Lord gives it over into your hand, you shall then strike down its [adult] males by the sword. ¹⁴ However, the women, children, animals, and all the goods in the city, you shall take as your spoils. You shall thus consume the spoils that God your Lord gives you from your enemies.

¹⁵ That is what you must do to the cities that are very far from you, and which do not belong to the nations that are here.

¹⁶ However, when dealing with the cities of these nations, which God your Lord is giving you as hereditary territory, you shall not allow any people to remain alive.* ¹⁷ Where the Hittites, Amorites, Canaanites, Perizites, Hivites, and Yebusites are involved, you must wipe them out completely, as God your Lord commanded you.* ¹⁸ This is so that they will not teach you all the revolting practices with which they worship their gods, causing you to sin to God your Lord.

[73. Conducting a Siege]

¹⁹ When you lay siege to a city and wage war against it a long time to capture it, you must not destroy its trees, wielding an ax against any food producing tree. Do not cut down a tree in the field, unless it is being used by the men who confront you in the siege.*

20:7   **betrothed.** See note on Exodus 22:15.
20:8   **fainthearted.** By nature (Ramban) afraid of weapons (*Sotah* 44a), and unable to kill (Ibn Ezra, Chizzkuni).
20:9   **senior officers.** See note on Deuteronomy 1:15 (cf. *Yad, Melakhim* 7:4).
20:16   **you shall not allow ...** If they do not make peace as in 20:10 (*Yad, Melakhim* 6:1; Ramban). Others maintain that one can only make peace with distant nations, but nearby nations must be annihilated (Rashi).
20:17   **commanded you.** Numbers 21:2, 33:52, above 7:1,2.
20:19   **unless it is being used ...** (Chizzkuni; Abarbanel). Or, "Is a tree of the field then a man who will come against you in the siege" (Rashi; Septuagint).

²⁰ However, if you know that a tree does not produce food, then until you 20
have subjugated [the city], you may destroy [the tree] or cut off [what you
need] to build siege machinery against the city waging war with you.

[74. The Unsolved Murder]

¹ [This is what you must do] when a corpse is found fallen in the field in the 21
land that God your Lord is giving you to occupy, and it is not known who the
murderer is. ² Your elders and judges* must go out and measure the distance
to the cities around the corpse.

³ The elders of the city closest to the corpse must then bring a female calf,*
which has never been worked, and which has never drawn a load with a yoke.
⁴ The elders of that city shall bring the calf to a swiftly flowing* stream,* [the
land around which]* must never be* worked or sown. There at the stream,
they shall decapitate* the calf.

⁵ The priests from the tribe of Levi shall then come forth. (It is these
[priests] whom God has chosen to serve Him and to pronounce blessings in
God's name, and who are entrusted to decide in cases of litigation and leprous
signs.) ⁶ All the elders of the city closest to the corpse shall wash their hands
over the decapitated calf at the stream.

⁷ [The elders]* shall speak up and say, "Our hands have not spilled this
blood, and our eyes have not witnessed it."

⁸ [The priests* shall then say,] "Forgive* Your people, whom You, God,
have liberated. Do not allow [the guilt for] innocent blood to remain with
your people Israel."

The blood shall thus be atoned for.* ⁹ You shall thus rid yourself of [the

---

21:2 **elders and judges.** A total of five members of the Sanhedrin (*Yad, Rotze'ach* 9:1).

21:3 **calf.** Under two years old (*Yad, Rotze'ach* 10:2).

21:4 **swiftly flowing** (*Yad, Rotze'ach* 9:2; Ralbag; *HaKethav VeHaKabbalah*) *Ethan* in Hebrew; cf. Exodus 14:27, Psalms 74:15 (Chizzkuni). Or, "harsh" (*Sotah* 45b; Rashi; cf. Numbers 21:24), "fertile" (Radak, *Sherashim*; cf. Amos 5:24), or, "rough" (Septuagint).

— **stream.** (*Yad, Rotze'ach*; Radak, *Sherashim*; cf. *Midrash Aggadah*). *Nachal* in Hebrew. Or, "valley" (Rashi; Septuagint), "field" (*Targum Yonathan*), or, "wadi" (Ibn Janach). See above note.

— **the land around which.** (Chizzkuni; cf. *Minchath Chinukh* 531).

— **must never be** (*Sefer HaMitzvoth*, Negative 309; *Makkoth* 22a). There is a question as to whether the forbidden distance around the place where the calf was killed must be four cubits or fifty cubits (*Yerushalmi, Sotah* 9:5).

— **decapitate.** *Araph* in Hebrew (see *Yerushalmi, Sotah* 9:5). See note on Exodus 13:13. However, there is a Midrashic opinion, that the calf is merely struck on the back of the neck so that it will run away and find the house of the murderer (*Midrash Aggadah*; Bachya).

21:7 **The elders** (*Sotah* 46a; *Yad, Rotze'ach* 9:3).

21:8 **The priests** . . . (*Ibid.*; *Targum*).

— **forgive.** Or, "reveal the truth" (*Midrash Aggadah*; Bachya).

— **The blood** . . . (see note on 21:7).

21 guilt of]* innocent blood in your midst, since you will have done that which is morally right in God's eyes.

Ki Thetze   כִּי־תֵצֵא

[75. Women Captives]

¹⁰ When you wage war against your enemies, God will give you victory over them, so that you will take captives. ¹¹ If you see a beautiful woman among the prisoners and desire her, you may take her as a wife.*

¹² In such a case,* when you bring her home, she must shave off her head* and let her fingernails grow.* ¹³ She must take off her captive's garb* and remain in your house a full month,* mourning for her father and mother.* Only then may you* be intimate with her and possess her, making her your wife.*

¹⁴ If you do not desire her, however, you must send her away free.* Since you have had your way with her,* you may not sell her for cash or keep her as a servant.*

21:9 **the guilt of** (Ibn Ezra).

21:11 **as a wife.** He can marry her immediately if she agrees to convert to Judaism (*Yevamoth* 47b; *Yad, Melakhim* 8:5). However, some maintain that he must still wait three months before being intimate with her (*Kesef Mishneh ad loc.*). See note on 21:13.

21:12 **In such a case.** That is, if she does not immediately wish to convert (*Yad, ibid.*).

—   **shave off her head.** To make her less attractive (Ibn Ezra). Also as a sign of purification and new status; see Leviticus 14:8, Numbers 8:7 (Chizzkuni).

—   **let her fingernails grow** (*Targum*; Rashi; *Yad, Melakhim* 8:5). Literally, "make her nails." Or, "cut her fingernails" (Chizzkuni; Septuagint). Both opinions are found in the Talmud (*Yevamoth* 48a; *Sifri*; cf. *HaKethav VeHaKabbalah*).

21:13 **take off her captive's garb.** To remove from her any taint of idolatry (*Midrash Aggadah*). Also to make her less attractive (Rashi; Rashbam; Ibn Ezra).

—   **a full month.** Actually, the man could not marry her for 90 days (*Yevamoth* 48b; *Yad, Melakhim* 8:5). He thus would have to wait an additional two months after her mourning period was over.

—   **her father and mother.** As well as their idolatrous religion, which she must abandon (*Yevamoth* 48b; *Yad, Melakhim* 8:5; Ramban). This is an act of mercy (*Moreh Nevukhim* 3:41). This delay also gives the girl a chance to accustom herself to Judaism and refrain from mentioning idolatrous deities (*Midrash Aggadah*). Thirty days is a normal mourning period; see Numbers 20:29.

—   **Only then . . .** After converting her to Judaism. She is given 12 months to make up her mind to convert, after which she is sent away (*Yad, Melakhim* 8:7). However, others maintain that she may be converted against her will (Ramban).

—   **making her your wife.** Some say through a regular marriage ceremony (*Yad, Melakhim* 8:6), while others maintain that she becomes his wife through intercourse alone (Ramban). In either case, she has the full rights of a wife, as in Exodus 21:10 (*Sifri*).

21:14 **away free.** However, she must agree not to return to idolatry (Ramban; Ralbag). Some also maintain that she cannot be forcibly sent back to her parents (Ramban). If she is married, she requires a divorce like any other woman (*Lechem Mishneh* on *Yad, Melakhim* 8:6). However, those who maintain that she is forcibly converted and married by intercourse alone maintain that she might not need a formal divorce (Ramban; *Tur*).

—   **had your way with her.** Or, "violated;" see below, 22:24.

—   **keep her as a servant.** Or, "enjoy her services" (*Sifri*; Rashi; Radak, *Sherashim*; *Yad, Melakhim* 8:6). Hith-

[76. The First-born's Share]   **21**

¹⁵ [This is the law] when a man has two wives, one whom he loves and one whom he dislikes, and both the loved and unloved wives have sons, but the first-born is that of the unloved one. ¹⁶ On the day that [this man] wills his property to his sons, he must not give the son of the beloved wife birthright preference over the first-born, who is the son of the unloved wife.

¹⁷ [Even if]* the first-born is the son of the hated wife, [the father] must recognize him so as to give him a double portion of all his property. Since [this son] is the first fruit of [his father's] manhood,* the birthright is legally his.

[77. The Rebellious Son]

¹⁸ When a man has a wayward, rebellious son,* who does not obey his father and mother, they shall have him flogged.* If he still does not listen to them, ¹⁹ then his father and mother must grasp him* and bring him to the elders of his city, to that area's supreme court.* ²⁰ [The parents] must declare to the elders of his city, "Our son here is wayward and rebellious. He does not listen to us, and is an [exceptional*] glutton* and drunkard.*"

²¹ All the men of his city shall then pelt him to death with stones, so that you will rid yourself of the evil in your midst. When all Israel hears about it, they will fear.

[78. Hanging and Burial]

²² When a man* is legally sentenced to death and executed, you must then

---

amar in Hebrew; see below 24:7. Or, "lord over her" (Ramban; Saadia); "do business with her" (Targum; Rashbam; Ibn Janach); "deceive her" (Ibn Ezra), or, "treat her contemptuously" (Septuagint).

21:17 Even if. Since this is the law for all first-born (*Yad, Nachaloth* 2:1).

— **manhood.** See Genesis 49:3.

21:18 son. This rule applies only to a boy between the ages of 13 and 13¼ (*Sanhedrin* 68b; *Yad, Mamrim* 7:5). It does not apply to a girl (*Yad, Mamrim* 7:11).

— **flogged.** With 39 lashes (*Yad, Mamrim* 7:7). The boy is flogged only if he eats the "meal of a rebellious son" (see note on 21:20), which is forbidden by Leviticus 19:26 (*Hagahoth Maimonioth ad loc.; Sanhedrin* 63a).

21:19 grasp him. That is, both must agree to bring him (Bachya).

— **supreme court** (*Targum*). Literally, "gate." This is the local supreme court of 23 judges. There must be two witnesses to the "meal of the rebellious son" besides the parents (*Yad, Mamrim* 7:7).

21:20 exceptional (Saadia). See Proverbs 23:20,21 (*Midrash HaGadol*).

— **glutton.** This alludes to the "meal of the rebellious son." By tradition he must steal money from his father, and buy 50 dinars of meat, eating it rare outside his father's property and in bad company. This is the act that must be witnessed for the son to be put to death (*Yad, Mamrim* 7:2; *Sanhedrin* 70a).

— **drunkard.** He must also drink 1/2 log (5 oz.) of wine with the meal (*Ibid.*). It is therefore forbidden for a boy of this age to eat such a meal at any time (*Sefer HaMitzvoth*, Negative 195).

21:22 man. But not a woman (*Sifri*). Hanging is imposed only in the case of a blasphemer (Leviticus 24:16) and an idolator (*Yad, Sanhedrin* 15:6). Some say that it is true of all who incur the penalty of stoning (Rashi). Both opinions are found in the Talmud (*Sanhedrin* 45b).

21 hang him* on a gallows.* ²³ However, you may not allow his body to remain on the gallows overnight, but you must bury it on the same day.* Since a person who has been hanged is a curse to God,* you must not [let it] defile the land that God your Lord is giving you as a heritage.

[79. Returning Lost Articles]

22   ¹ If you see your brother's ox or sheep going astray, you must not ignore them. You must return them to your brother.*

² If your brother is not near you, or if you do not know who [the owner is], you must bring [the animal] home and keep it until your brother identifies it,* whereupon you must return it to him.

³ You must do the same to a donkey, an article of clothing, or anything else that your brother loses and you find. You must not ignore it.

[80. The Fallen Animal]

⁴ If you see your brother's donkey or ox fallen [under its load]* on the road, you must not ignore it. You must help him pick up [the load].*

[81. Transvestism]

⁵ No male article* shall be on a woman, and a man shall not wear a woman's garment. Whoever does such practices is revolting to God your Lord.

[82. The Bird's Nest]

⁶ If you come across a bird's* nest on any tree or on the ground, and it contains baby birds or eggs, then, if the mother is sitting on the chicks or eggs, you must not take the mother along with* her young. ⁷ You must first* chase

---

- **hang him.** After he is put to death, he is hung up by his hands. He is hung up just before sunset and immediately taken down again (*Yad, Sanhedrin* 15:7).
- **gallows.** (Targum; Saadia). Cf. Esther 5:14 (Chizzkuni). The gallows consisted of a pole sunk into the ground, with a beam projecting from its side (*Sanhedrin* 47a,b).
- **21:23 bury it on the same day.** If this is true of a criminal, it is all the more true of an innocent person. Immediate burial is therefore the Jewish norm (*Sanhedrin* 46b; *Yerushalmi, Nazir* 7:1).
- **a curse to God** (literally). Or, "an extraordinarily great curse" (*Adereth Eliahu; HaKethav VeHaKabbalah*).
- **22:1 You must return them . . .** See Exodus 23:4.
- **22:2 identifies it** (*Bava Metzia* 28a).
- **22:4 under its load** (*Bava Metzia* 32a; Ralbag). See Exodus 23:5.
- **pick up the load.** (*Sefer HaMitzvoth*, Positive 203; Rashi).
- **22:5 male article.** Clothing (Septuagint). But this also includes weapons (*Nazir* 59a), and, according to some, tefillin and tzitzith (*Targum Yonathan*; cf. *Eruvin* 96a; *Orach Chaim* 38:3 in Hagah).
- **22:6 bird's.** Only a kosher bird (*Chullin* 139b).
- **along with** (*Sefer HaMitzvoth*, Negative 306; *Chinukh* 544; *Chakham Tzvi* 83; Septuagint; Bachya; Chizzkuni; cf. *Chullin* 141a). Or, "from on" (*Targum Yonathan*; *Sifri*; *Tur, Yoreh Deah* 292. Cf. *HaKethav VeHaKabbalah*; *Minchath Chinukh* 544).
- **22:7 first.** (see *Chiddushey HaRan, Chullin* 139a; *Teshuvoth Rashba* 18, 3:283). However, some maintain that it is a

away the mother, and only then may you take the young. [If you do this] you   **22**
will have it good, and will live long.

[83. Guard-rails; Mixed Agriculture]

⁸ When you build a new house,* you must place a guard-rail* around
your roof. Do not allow a dangerous situation to remain in your house, since
someone can fall from [an unenclosed roof].

⁹ Do not plant different species* in your vineyard. [If you do so] the yield
of both the crops you planted and the fruit* of the vineyard will be forfeit.*

[84. Forbidden Combinations]

¹⁰ Do not plow with an ox and donkey together.

¹¹ Do not wear a forbidden mixture,* where wool and linen* are together
[in a single garment].*

[85. Bound Tassels]

¹² Make yourself bound tassels* on the four corners of·the garment with
which you cover yourself.

[86. The Defamed Wife]

¹³ [This is the law in a case] where a man marries a woman, cohabits with

---

meritorious deed to send away the mother even if one does not wish to take the young (*Teshuvoth Chavvoth Yair* 67; cf. *HaKethav VeHaKabbalah*).

22:8   new house. The same is true if one buys a house (*Sifri*), or rents one (*Yad, Sekhiruth* 6:3). However, some maintain that the latter cases are obligations only by rabbinical legislation (*Hagahoth Maimonioth*, on *Yad, Rotze'ach* 11:1; *Tzafenath Paaneach*).

—   **guard-rail.** At least 10 handbreadths (30″) high (*Bava Bathra* 61a; *Yad, Rotze'ach* 11:1,3).

22:9   different species. See Leviticus 19:19 (*Berakhoth* 22a; *Sefer HaMitzvoth*, Negative 216; *Yad, Kelayim* 5:1; *Chinukh* 548). The mixtures forbidden in the vineyard are primarily the same as those forbidden otherwise, but if they are planted in a vineyard they become forbidden, for any use at all (*Yad, Kelayim* 5:4, *Maakhaloth Assuroth* 10:6). See below.

—   **fruit** (*HaKethav VeHaKabbalah*).

—   **forfeit** (Rashbam; Ralbag). Literally, "sanctified." Or, "an abomination" (Targum), or, "fit to be burned" (*Kiddushin* 56b; *Targum Yonathan*). See above note.

22:11 forbidden mixture. *Shaatnez* in Hebrew; see Leviticus 19:19.

—   **wool and linen.** Some say that this was forbidden because such mixtures were reserved for the priests (*Baaley Tosafoth*; Chizzkuni; Josephus, *Antiquities* 4:8:11). Others say that it is forbidden because such mixtures were worn by gentile priests (*Moreh Nevukhim* 3:37; *Chinukh* 551). Other sources indicate that it is forbidden because sheep were the sacrifice of Abel while linen was the sacrifice of Cain (*Pirkey Rabbi Eliezer* 21; Tanchuma, Bereshith 9; Chizzkuni).

—   **in a single garment** (Bachya).

22:12 bound tassels. *Gedilim* in Hebrew (cf. 1 Kings 7:17; Targum on Exodus 28:22). See Numbers 15:38. The ritual tzitzith-tassels are made by doubling over four threads so that eight appear to be coming from each corner. One of these threads is longer than the rest, and this is wound aroung the rest. This section, around which a thread is wound, constitutes one third of the length of the tassel, and is called the *gedil* (*Menachoth* 39a; Rashi *ibid.* 39b, s.v. *U'Pothli-hu;* Rashi on Deuteronomy 32:5). Or, "doubled tassels" (*Sifri; Menachoth* 39b).

22 her, and then finds himself hating her. ¹⁴ He therefore invents charges against
her, framing her and saying, "I have married this woman and have consummated the marriage. But I have found evidence that she has not been faithful.*"

¹⁵ The girl's* father and mother, however, then obtain evidence of their
daughter's virtue,* and present it to the city elders in court.* ¹⁶ The girl's
father shall then declare to the elders, "I have given my daughter to this man
as a wife, but he has grown to hate her. ¹⁷ He has therefore invented charges
against her, and claims that he has evidence that she has not been faithful to
him. But here is evidence of my daughter's virtue." With that, [the girl's
parents] shall present their case* before the city elders.

¹⁸ The city elders shall then take the man and flog him.* ¹⁹ They shall fine
him 100 [shekels]* of silver [as a penalty] for defaming an Israelite virgin, and
give it to the girl's father. [The man] must then keep [the girl] as his wife, and
may not send her away as long as he lives.

[87. If the Accusation is True]

²⁰ If the accusation is true, however, and the girl does not have evidence*
of her innocence, ²¹ then they shall take her out to the door of her father's
house,* and the people of her city shall put her to death by stoning. She has
brought sexual immorality to her father's house, doing a shameful thing in
Israel. You must therefore rid yourself of the evil in your midst.

[88. Penalty for Adultery]

²² If a man is found* lying with a married woman, both the woman and

---

22:14 **evidence that . . .** That is, two witnesses who saw the girl committing adultery (*Sifri; Yad, Naarah Bethulah* 3:6; Ralbag from 17:6). Literally, "I have not found tokens of virginity" (cf. Ramban).

22:15 **girl's.** This law applies primarily in the case of a girl between 12 and 12½ years old (*Yad, Naarah Bethulah* 3:7).

—   **evidence . . .** That is, two witnesses to refute those of the husband (*Sifri; Yad, Naarah Bethulah* 3:6, 3:12). See above, 19:18.

—   **court.** A local supreme court of 23 judges.

22:17 **their case** (*Kethuvoth* 46a; *Yad, Naarah Bethulah* 3:12; Ralbag). Literally, "the garment." (cf. Ramban).

22:18 **flog.** 39 lashes. (*Kethuvoth* 46a). Some say that even if the husband merely falsely accuses his bride of not being a virgin, he is also flogged, but he is not given the full penalty of 39 lashes (Chizzkuni).

22:19 **100 shekels** (*Bekhoroth* 49b; Ralbag). This is twice the 50 shekels (below, 22:29), which is the normal dowry of a bride (*Moreh Nevukhim* 3:49; see Exodus 22:2,16).

22:20 **evidence.** Witnesses to refute those who accuse her of committing adultery (*Sifri; Yad, Naarah Bethulah* 3:6).

22:21 **of her father's house.** But only if she was living at home when she committed adultery (*Yad, Issurey Biyah* 3:9).

22:22 **found.** By two eyewitnesses (*Sifri*).

the man lying with her shall be put to death.* You shall thus rid Israel of evil. 22

[89. The Betrothed Maiden]

²³ [This is the law] where a virgin girl* is betrothed* to one man, and another man comes across her in the city and has intercourse with her. ²⁴ Both of them shall be brought to the gates of that city,* and they shall be put to death by stoning. [The penalty shall be imposed on] the girl because she did not cry out [even though she was]* in the city, and on the man, because he violated his neighbor's wife. You shall thus rid yourselves of evil.

[90. Rape]

²⁵ However, if the man encountered the betrothed girl in the field and raped her, then only the rapist shall be put to death. ²⁶ You must not impose any penalty whatsoever upon the girl, since she has not committed a sin worthy of death. This is no different from the case where a man rises up against his neighbor and murders him. ²⁷ After all, [the man] attacked her in the field, and even if the betrothed girl had screamed out, there would have been no one to come to her aid.

[91. The Unmarried Girl]

²⁸ If a man* encounters a virgin girl* who is not betrothed and is caught raping her, ²⁹ then the rapist must give the girl's father 50 [shekels]* of silver. He must then take* the girl he violated as his wife, and he may not send her away as long as he lives.

[92. A Father's Woman]

¹ A man must not take his father's woman.* He must not pervert that 23
which is private to his father.

— **to death.** By strangulation. See Leviticus 20:10.
22:23 **girl.** Between 12 and 12¼ years old (*Sanhedrin* 66b; *Yad, Issurey Biyah* 3:4). If she is older, the penalty is no longer stoning, but strangulation, as in all cases of adultery.
— **betrothed.** See note on Exodus 22:15).
22:24 **gates of that city.** See note on 17:5. (cf. *Yad, Issurey Biyah* 3:11).
— **did not cry out . . .** This is considered *prima facie* evidence that she was not raped (Ramban; Ralbag; see Yehuda HaChasid).
22:28 **If a man . . .** See Exodus 22:15,16.
— **virgin girl.** Only if she is between 12 and 12¼ (*Kethuvoth* 38a).
22:29 **50 shekels.** The normal dowry of a bride (see note on Exodus 22:15).
— **he must take . . .** But only if the girl consents (*Yad, Naarah Bethulah* 1:3).
23:1 **A man must not . . .** See Leviticus 18:8, 20:11. Some say that this includes any woman that his father seduced or raped (*Kethuvoth* 97a; Ibn Ezra), but this is not the law (*Yad, Issurey Biyah* 2:11). It also includes the father's wife after the father's death (*Midrash Aggadah*).

23

[93. Mutilated Genitals]

² [A man] with crushed testicles or a cut member may not enter into God's marriage group.*

[94. The Bastard]

³ A bastard* must not enter God's marriage group. Even after the tenth generation, he may not enter God's marriage group.

[95. Ammonites and Moabites]

⁴ An Ammonite or Moabite* [man]* may not enter God's marriage group. They may never enter God's marriage group, even after the tenth generation.

⁵ This is because they did not greet you* with bread and water when you were on the way out of Egypt, and also because they hired Balaam son of Beor* from Pethor* in Aram Naharaim* to curse you. ⁶ Of course, God did not consent to listen to Balaam, and God your Lord transformed the curse into a blessing for you, since God your Lord loves you.

⁷ You must never seek peace* or anything good [with these nations], as long as you exist.

[96. Edomites and Egyptians]

⁸ Do not despise the Edomite, since he is your brother.*
Do not despise the Egyptian, since you were an immigrant in his land.

⁹ [Therefore,] children born to [members of these nations] in the third generation [after becoming proselytes]* may enter God's marriage group.

[97. The Army Camp]

¹⁰ When you go out as a camp against your enemies, you must avoid everything evil.* ¹¹ Therefore, if a man is unclean because of a nocturnal emission,*

23:2 marriage group. This denotes all native born Israelites who may freely intermarry with each other. They may, however, marry a proselyte or a freed slave (*Yevamoth* 76a).

23:3 bastard. *Mamzer* in Hebrew. A person has the status of a *mamzer* only if he is born of an adulterous or incestuous union, not if he is merely born out of wedlock.

23:4 Ammonite or Moabite. See Genesis 19:37,38.

—   **man.** But not a woman (*Yevamoth* 69a). See Ruth 1:4, 4:13.

23:5 they did not greet . . . Even though Abraham showed special kindness to their ancestor Lot (Genesis 12:5, 19:29; *Midrash Aggadah*; Abarbanel).

—   **Balaam . . .** Numbers 22:5.

—   **Pethor.** *Ibid.*

—   **Aram Naharaim.** See Genesis 24:10.

23:7 You must never seek peace. Even when encountering them in battle, as above, 20:10 (*Sifri*).

23:8 your brother. Since the Edomites are descendants of Esau.

23:9 after becoming proselytes (*Yevamoth* 78a).

23:10 everything evil. The usual immorality that is prevalent in an army camp (Ramban; Bachya). Also excessive cruelty (Josephus, *Antiquities* 4:8:42).

23:11 nocturnal emission. See Leviticus 15:16.

he must leave the camp and remain outside. [12] Toward evening, he must immerse in a mikvah,* and then, when the sun sets, he can enter the camp.

[13] You must designate a place outside the camp to use as a lavatory.* [14] You must also keep a spike* with your weapons,* so that when you have to sit down to relieve yourself, you will first dig a hole with it, and then sit down, [and finally,] cover your excrement.

[15] This is because God your Lord makes His presence known* in your camp, so as to deliver you and grant you victory over your enemy. Your camp must therefore be holy. Let Him not see anything lascivious among you,* and turn away from you.

[98. Sheltering Slaves]

[16] If a slave seeks refuge with you from his master,* you must not turn him back over to his master. [17] He must be allowed to live alongside you wherever he chooses in your settlements. You must do nothing to hurt his feelings.

[99. Prostitution]

[18] There must not be any prostitutes* among Israelite girls. Similarly, there must be no male prostitutes* among Israelite men.

[19] Do not bring a prostitute's fee or the price of a dog to the temple of God your Lord, since both are repugnant to God your Lord.

[100. Deducted Interest]

[20] Do not deduct advance interest* from your brother, whether it is interest for money, interest for food, or interest for anything else for which interest is normally taken.* [21] Although you may take such interest from a gentile, you may not do so from your brother. [If you keep this rule,] God will

---

23:12 **immerse in a mikvah.** *Ibid.*
23:13 **lavatory.** Even to urinate (*Berakhoth* 25a).
23:14 **spike.** *Yathed* in Hebrew. Or, "trowel" (Septuagint).
— **weapons.** (*Sifri*) *Azen* in Hebrew. Some say that it was worn to the left (*Lekach Tov*).
23:15 **makes His presence known.** Literally, "walks among you."
— **anything lascivious. . .** Or "any nakedness" (cf. *Berakhoth* 25b).
23:16 **from his master.** Specifically, if the slave of a Jew escapes to the Holy Land (*Gittin* 45a; *Yad, Avadim* 8:10). Some also include a circumcised slave who escapes from his gentile master (*Sifri*; *Targum*; cf. Bachya). Others also include a slave who escapes to the army camp (Ibn Ezra; Chizzkuni; Abarbanel).
23:18 **prostitutes.** According to some, this includes all forms of premarital intercourse (*Yad, Ishuth* 1:4, *Naarah Bethulah* 2:17, *Issurey Biyah* 18:2). Others say that this only prohibits intercourse with a true prostitute (Raavad, *Naarah Bethulah* 2:17). According to others, this is primarily a prohibition against a woman having premarital intercourse (Bachya). Others say that it is a commandment incumbent on the courts and community leaders (Ramban).
— **male prostitutes.** For homosexual (*Sanhedrin* 54b) and heterosexual purposes (cf. Ramban; Abarbanel).
23:20 **advance interest.** See Exodus 22:24, Leviticus 25:36,37.
— **normally taken.** That is, where the borrowed articles are normally repaid with substitutes.

23   bless you in all your endeavors on the land to which you are coming to occupy.

[101. Keeping Vows]

²² When you make a pledge to God your Lord, do not be late in paying it,* since God will then demand it, and you will have committed a sin.

²³ If you refrain from making vows completely, then you will not sin. ²⁴ But when you have spoken, be careful of your word and keep the pledge that you have vowed to God your Lord.

[102. The Worker in a Vineyard]

²⁵ When you come [to work]* in your neighbor's vineyard, you may eat as many grapes as you desire to satisfy your hunger.* However, you may not put any into a receptacle that you may have.

[103. The Field Worker]

²⁶ When you come [to work]* in your neighbor's standing grain, you may take the ears with your hand. However, you may not lift the sickle* [for your own benefit]* in your neighbor's grain.

[104. Divorce and Remarriage]

24   ¹ When a man marries a woman or possesses her,* if she is displeasing to him [or] if he has evidence* of sexual misconduct on her part,* he shall write her a bill of divorce* and place it in her hand, thus releasing her from his household. ² When she thus leaves his household, she may go and marry another man.

³ However, if her second husband hates her, and therefore writes her a bill of divorce, placing it in her hand and releasing her from his household, or if her second husband dies, ⁴ then her first husband who divorced her cannot

---

23:22 **do not be late . . .** Delaying over three festivals (*Rosh HaShanah* 4b).
23:25 **to work** (*Bava Metzia* 87b; Saadia; Rashi).
—   **to satisfy your hunger.** But not to fill yourself up (*Bava Metzia* 87b).
23:26 **to work** (*Sifri*; *Yerushalmi, Maasroth* 2:4).
—   **sickle.** *Chermash* in Hebrew; see above, 16:9.
—   **for your own benefit** (*Sefer HaMitzvoth*, Negative 268; *Yad, Sekhiruth* 12:3). According to this, the commandment here prohibits the worker from stopping work in order to eat. Others say that it forbids him to make a full meal during his working time (*Raavad ibid.*).
24:1 **or possesses her.** For the purpose of marriage (Bachya).
—   **or if he has evidence** (Saadia; cf. *Gittin* 90a).
—   **sexual misconduct . . .** In which case he must divorce her. Or, "immodesty" (*Gittin* 90b).
—   **bill of divorce.** *Get* in Aramaic (*Targum*).

remarry her, since she is now forbidden* to him. To do so would be repulsive **24** to God, and you must not bring immorality to the land that God your Lord is giving you as a heritage.

[105. The New Bridegroom; The Millstone]

⁵ When a man takes a new bride, he shall not enter military service or be assigned to any associated duty. He must remain free for his family for one year, when he can rejoice with his bride.*

⁶ Do not take an upper or lower millstone as security for a loan, since that is like taking a life as security.

[106. Kidnapping]

⁷ If a man kidnaps a fellow Israelite,* forces him to serve* and then sells him, when the kidnapper is caught, he shall be put to death. You shall thus rid yourself of the evil in your midst.

[107. Leprosy]

⁸ Be careful with regard to leprous signs* and carefully keep [the rules]. Be very careful to do all that the Levitical priests* decide for you, as I have commanded them.

⁹ Remember what God did to Miriam* on your way out of Egypt.

[108. Security for Loans]

¹⁰ When you make any kind of loan to your neighbor, do not go into his house to take something as security. ¹¹ You must stand outside, and the man who has the debt to you shall bring the security outside to you.

¹² If the man is poor, you may not go to sleep holding his security.

24:4 **forbidden** (*HaKethav VeHaKabbalah*). Literally, "defiled." Or, "[The same is true] if she is defiled to him [by committing adultery]" (Rashi; Bachya; *Sotah* 11b).
24:5 **with . . .** (*Targum Yonathan*). Or, "he shall gladden his wife" (Targum; Rashi; Septuagint).
24:7 **kidnaps . . .** See Exodus 21:16.
— **forces him to serve** (*Sanhedrin* 85b; Rashi; *Yad, Genevah* 9:3). *Hith-amer* in Hebrew; see above, 21:14. Or, "does business" (Targum).
24:8 **Be careful . . .** This is a specific prohibition against removing a leprous sign from one's body (*Sanhedrin* 132b; *Makkoth* 22a). It also mandates that one abide by the priest's decision, and maintain the quarantine (Abarbanel). Some say that it is also a commandment to the priest not to give anyone special consideration, just as Miriam was not given any such consideration (*Baaley Tosafoth*; Chizzkuni).
— **Levitical priests . . .** See Leviticus 13:9, etc.
24:9 **to Miriam.** Numbers 12:10. Despite her high status (Ralbag). This is a specific commandment to refrain from such slander as that committed by Miriam (Numbers 12:1; *Sifri*; Ramban). It also tells us not to suspect religious leaders (*Midrash HaGadol*).

24   ¹³ Return it to him at sundown, so that he will be able to sleep in his garment and bless you. You will then have charitable merit before God your Lord.

[109. Paying Wages on Time]

¹⁴ Do not withhold the wages due to your poor or destitute hired hand, whether he is one of your brethren or a proselyte* living in a settlement in your land. ¹⁵ You must give him his wage on the day it is due,* and not let the sun set with him waiting for it. Since he is a poor man, and his life depends on it, do not let him call out to God, causing you to have a sin.

[110. Testimony of Close Relatives]

¹⁶ Fathers shall not die [through the testimony]* of their sons, and sons shall not die [through the testimony] of their fathers, since [in any case]* every man shall die for his sins.

[111. Widows and Orphans]

¹⁷ Do not pervert justice for the proselyte* or orphan.*
Do not take a widow's* garment* as security for a loan.
¹⁸ You must remember that you were a slave in Egypt, and God your Lord then liberated you. It is for that reason that I am commanding you to do this.

[112. Forgotten Sheaves]

¹⁹ When you reap* your grain harvest and forget a sheaf in the field, you must not go back to get it. It must be left for the foreigner, orphan and widow, so that God your Lord will bless you, no matter what you do.

[113. Leftover Fruit]

²⁰ When you beat* the fruit from your olive tree, do not pick the last remaining fruit,* since it must be left for the foreigner, orphan and widow.

24:14 **proselyte** (*Bava Metzia* 110a; Rashi).
24:15 **give him his wage** . . . See Leviticus 19:13.
24:16 **through the testimony** (*Sanhedrin* 27b; Rashi; *Sefer HaMitzvoth*, Negative 287). In a literal sense, also, that the courts should not punish a parent for a child's crime (Ralbag).
—   **since in any case** (Rashbam). That is, even if they are not punished by the courts.
24:17 **proselyte** (Ralbag).
—   **or orphan.** See Exodus 23:6.
—   **widow's.** Some say that this same law also applies to a divorcee (*Sema, Choshen Mishpat* 97:22; cf. Shakh 97:1).
—   **garment.** Some say only a garment (*Shiltey Gibborim*, Rif, *Bava Metzia* 70a #2), while others say that it includes all articles (*Chinukh* 591; cf. *Pith'chey Teshuvah, Choshen Mishpat* 97:2).
24:19 **When you reap** . . . See Leviticus 19:9,10, 23:22.
24:20 **beat** (Saadia; Radak, *Sherashim*). *Chabat* in Hebrew. Or, "gather" (Septuagint).
—   **pick the last remaining fruit** (Rashi; from *Chullin* 131b; *HaKethav VeHaKabbalah*). *Pa'ar* in Hebrew. Or,

²¹ When you gather the grapes in your vineyard, do not strip the last **24** grapes,* but let them remain for the foreigner, orphan and widow.

²² I am commanding you to do this because you must remember that you were a slave in Egypt.

[114. Flogging]

¹ A trial shall be an adversary proceeding* where a verdict is handed **25** down, acquitting the innocent and convicting the guilty. ² If the guilty man has incurred the penalty of flogging, the judge shall make him lean over,* and have him flogged with a fixed number of lashes for his crime.

³ Do not go beyond the limit and give him forty lashes.* You may not give him a more severe flogging, striking him any more than this, since your brother will then be degraded in your presence.

⁴ Do not muzzle an ox when it is treading grain.

[115. The Childless Brother-in-Law]

⁵ When brothers live together, and one of them dies childless, the dead man's wife shall not be allowed to marry an outsider. Her husband's brother* must cohabit with her, making her his wife, and thus performing a brother-in-law's duty to her. ⁶ The first-born son whom she bears will then perpetuate* the name of the dead brother, so that his name will not be obliterated from Israel.

"do not remove the highest branch" or "crown" (Radak, *Sherashim*; Hirsch); "do not re-inspect it" (Targum; Septuagint); "do not carefully pick it over" (*Targum Yonathan*; Saadia; Ibn Janach); "do not harvest the smaller branches" (Ibn Ezra; Radak, *Sherashim*; Ibn Janach), or, "Do not go back over it" (*Yad, Matnoth Aniyim* 1:6). If only two clusters of olives remain on a branch, it is forbidden to go back and harvest them (*Yad, Matnoth Aniyim* 5:15).

24:21 do not strip . . . (*Chullin* 131a; cf. *Yad, Matnoth Aniyim* 5:16). *Alal* in Hebrew. Or, "do not glean" (Saadia; Septuagint), or, "do not pick immature clusters (*Sifri*; Rashi; Josephus, *Antiquities* 4:8:21).

25:1 A trial shall be . . . The adversary proceeding is between the accused and the witnesses (*Midrash HaGadol*). Literally, "When there is a dispute between men and they go to judgment." Others say that the dispute is between the accused and the witnesses who must first warn him and try to dissuade him from committing the crime (*HaKethav VeHaKabbalah*).

25:2 make him lean over (*Makkoth* 22b; Rashi; Septuagint). Literally, "make him fall," or "make him lie down." Or, "throw him down" (Targum).

25:3 Do not go beyond the limit . . . Thus, in practice, no more than 39 lashes could be given (*Makkoth* 22a; *Sifri*; *Targum Yonathan*; Josephus, *Antiquities* 4:8:21). Some dispute this, however, and maintain that a full 40 lashes are given (Rabbi Yehudah, *Makkoth* 22a).

25:5 husband's brother. *Yabham* in Hebrew, a specific term denoting a childless man's brother, who has an obligation to marry his dead brother's wife.

25:6 perpetuate (Ramban). Expressed idiomatically by, "shall stand up upon the name of his dead brother." This does not, however, mean that he shall be named after the dead brother; cf. Ruth 3:13, 4:17, where the firstborn was not named after the dead husband (Ralbag; cf. *Yevamoth* 24a). The dead brother's property also eventually becomes that of the children born of this levirate union (*Ibid.*; *Targum Yonathan*; *Midrash HaGadol*; Bachya).

25   ⁷ If the man does not wish to take his brother's wife, the sister-in-law shall
go up to the elders in court, and declare, "My brother-in-law refuses to perpetuate his brother's name in Israel, and will not consent to perform his
brotherly duty with me."

⁸ The elders of his city shall summon him and speak to him. If he remains
firm, he must say,* "I do not want to take her." ⁹ His sister-in-law shall then
approach him before the elders, take off his shoe* and spit toward* his face.
She shall then declare, "This is what shall be done to the man who will not
build up a family for his brother."

¹⁰ The name of [that place]* shall then be known in Israel as, "the house
[where] the shoe was removed."

[116. The Assailant]

¹¹ If a man is fighting with his brother,* and the wife of one comes to
defend her husband, grabbing his attacker by his private parts,* ¹² you must
cut off her hand [if necessary, to save her victim]* and not have any pity.*

25:8 He must say . . . (see *Evven HaEzer* 169:29).

25:9 shoe. The right shoe (*Yevamoth* 104a).
There are many laws regarding exactly
how the special shoe used in this ceremony must be constructed (See *Evven
HaEzer* 169:14-23).

Some say that the reason that his shoes
are removed is so that he shall be like a
mourner or one who is excommunicated
(*Hagahoth Maimonioth, Yibbum* 4:8 #9; *Beth
Sh'muel* 169:43). Others say that was
done in order to humiliate the man (*Moreh
Nevukhim* 3:49). According to others, it
was to release any claim the brother may
have had to the dead one's inheritance
(Rashbam; Chizzkuni; cf. *Ruth* 4:7). Still
another opinion states that it was to show
that the woman was not free to remarry
up to this time, and therefore had to perform such services for the man (*Chinukh*
599). Others say that it is as if she is plead-
ing for the man to marry her (*Paaneach Razah*).

— **toward** (*Yevamoth* 106b; Rashi).

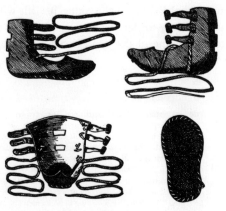

Chalitzah Shoe

25:10 that place (*Gur Aryeh*; cf. *Yad, Yibbum* 4:2). Or, "That family shall be known . . . as, 'the family of the one
whose shoe was removed.'" (Abarbanel). Or, "That man's name shall be known as, 'the family man
whose shoe was removed.'" (*Paaneach Razah*). Some say, "Let the name . . ." making it part of the
woman's statement (Abarbanel; *Yad, Yibbum* 4:7; cf. *Yevamoth* 106b).

25:11 with his brother. So that there is no deadly intent. See below.

— **private parts.** Testicles (Ibn Ezra). The same is true if she does any act that might endanger the man's life.

25:12 if necessary . . . (*Sifri; Yad, Rotze'ach* 1:7,8). The same is true in any case where a person is attacking
another with deadly intent. Anyone witnessing the act must maim or kill the assailant to save the victim
(*Ibid.*).

According to others, however, it is speaking of a case where the woman has no deadly intent, and
"cutting off her hand" denotes that she must pay for the humiliation she caused her victim (*Bava Kama*

[117. Weights and Measures]
25

¹³ You must not keep* in your pouch* two different* weights, one large and one small. ¹⁴ [Similarly], you must not keep in your house two different measures, one large and one small.

¹⁵ You must have a full honest weight and a full honest measure. If you do, you will long endure on the land that God your Lord is giving you. ¹⁶ Conversely, anyone who is dishonest and [has dishonest weights or measures] is repulsive to God your Lord.

[118. Remembering Amalek]

¹⁷ Remember what Amalek* did to you on your way out of Egypt. ¹⁸ When they encountered you on the way, and you were tired and exhausted, they cut off those lagging to your rear, and they did not fear God.

¹⁸ Therefore, when God gives you peace from all the enemies around you in the land that God your Lord is giving you to occupy as a heritage, you must obliterate* the memory of Amalek from under the heavens. You must not forget.

Ki Thavo
כִּי־תָבוֹא

[119. First Fruits]

¹ When you come to the land that God your Lord is giving you as a heritage, occupying and settling it, ² you shall take the first* of every fruit of the ground* produced by the land that God your Lord is giving you. You must place it in a basket,* and go to the site that God will choose* as the place associated with His name. ³ There you shall go to the priest officiating at the
26

27a; Rashi). Some translate it, "You shall reckon the cost of her act (hand)" (*HaKethav VeHaKabbalah*).
— **and not have any pity.** This is a negative commandment, not to have pity on an assailant (*Sefer HaMitzvoth,* Negative 293).
25:13 You must not keep . . . See Leviticus 19:35,36. See Ezekiel 45:10–1ż, Micah 6:1¹ ˙roverbs 11:1.
— **pouch** (*Targum Yonathan*; Septuagint). *Kis* in Hebrew. Or, "Place of scales" (Ibn ⌐ra; *Tur*).
— **different** (cf. *HaKethav VeHaKabbalah*).
25:17 Amalek. See Exodus 17:8.
25:18 you must obliterate. See Exodus 17:16.
26:2 first. The owner would mark the first fruit to ripen by tying a piece of papyrus reed around it (*Bikkurim* 3:1).
— **fruit . . .** Only the seven species mentioned above 8:8 (*Menachoth* 84b; Rashi). The first-fruits could only be brought to the Temple after Shavuoth, which is called the "feast of first-fruits" (Exodus 23:16, Numbers 28:26; *Bikkurim* 1:3).
— **basket.** A food basket (below 28:5), *tenè* in Hebrew. The baskets were made of peeled willow twigs (*Bikkurim* 3:8), but the main law here is that the first-fruits must be brought in a vessel (*Sifri*).
— **the site . . .** See above, 12:5.

26 time,* and say to him,* "Today I am affirming to God your Lord that I have come to the land that God swore to our fathers to give us."

⁴ The priest shall then take* the basket from your hand and place it* before the altar of God your Lord.

⁵ You shall then* make the following declaration before God your Lord: "My ancestor* was a homeless Aramaean.* He went to Egypt with a small number of men and lived there as an immigrant, but it was there that he became a great, powerful, and populous nation. ⁶ The Egyptians were cruel to us, making us suffer and imposing harsh slavery on us. ⁷ We cried out to God, Lord of our ancestors, and God heard our voice, seeing our suffering, our harsh labor, and our distress.

⁸ "God then brought us out of Egypt with a strong hand and an out-stretched arm, with great visions* and with signs and miracles. ⁹ He brought us to this area, giving us this land flowing with milk and honey. ¹⁰ I am now bringing the first fruit of the land that God has given me."

With that, you shall set* the basket down before God* your Lord, and you shall then bow down* before God your Lord. ¹¹ You, the Levite,* and the

---

26:3 officiating at the time. That is, in the shift (*mishmor*) officiating at the time (Abarbanel).

— **and say to him . . .** At that time, the owner is holding the basket on his shoulder (*Bikkurim* 3:6; *Yad, Bikkurim* 3:12).

26:4 take. As God's agent (Chizzkuni). Some say that the priest now takes it to wave it in the prescribed manner; see note on Exodus 29:24. (Rashi; see *Sukkah* 47b, *Makkoth* 18b; *Menachoth* 61b).

— **place it.** Some say that at this point the basket is placed before the altar, and then it is put down a second time as mentioned in 26:10 (*Sifri*; *Midrash HaGadol*; Rash, *Bikkurim* 3:6; Abarbanel). Others translate "place" here as "wave" (*Sukkah* 47b) and render the verse, "The priest shall take the basket . . . and wave it before the altar . . ." (cf. *Tosafoth, Makkoth* 18b, s.v. *U'Man*). Or, "The priest shall then wave the basket from your hand, and before placing it before the altar . . . ⁵ you shall make the following declaration (*Tosefoth Yom Tov, Bikkurim* 3:6; cf. *Yad, Bikkurim* 3:12). Or, "Before the priest takes the basket from your hand and places it before the altar . . . ⁵ you shall make the following declaration" (*Shenoth Eliahu, Bikkurim* 3:6).

26:5 You shall then . . . After taking the basket back from the priest (Rashi on 26:10). Or while waving the basket (cf. *Yad, Bikkurim* 3:12; *Tosafoth Yom Tov* on Bikkurim 3:6). Or before the priest takes the basket (*Shenoth Eliahu, Bikkurim* 3:6).

— **ancestor.** Jacob. Or, Abraham (Rashbam).

— **homeless Aramaean.** (Rashbam; Sforno; cf. Chizzkuni on 11:17). Or, "a poor Aramaean" (Ibn Ezra, Chizzkuni; Bachya), or, "a persecuted Aramaean" (Radak, *Sherashim*). Jacob is referred to as an Aramaean because this was the homeland of his ancestors. Or, "my ancestor was exiled to Aramaea" (*Targum Yonathan*; Ralbag), or, "my ancestor abandoned Aramaea" (Septuagint). Or, "An Aramaean [tried to] destroy my ancestor [Jacob]," where the Aramaean is Laban (cf. Genesis 31:22,29; *Targum*; *Sifri*; Saadia; Rashi).

26:8 visions (*Targum*; Chizzkuni; Septuagint). Or, "terror" (Abarbanel).

26:10 set. Literally (*Yad, Bikkurim* 3:12). Or, "wave" (*Sukkah* 47b). Thus, some say that it was waved twice (*Sifri*; Rash on *Bikkurim* 3:6; *Tosafoth, Makkoth* 18b), or put down twice (*Shenoth Eliahu* on Bikkurim 3:6; *Lekach Tov*; *Midrash HaGadol*).

— **before God.** On the southwest corner of the altar (*Yerushalmi, Bikkurim* 3:4; *Yad, Bikkurim* 3:12). See Leviticus 6:7 (Malbim).

— **bow down.** Literally, "prostrate yourself" (Ralbag; *Tifereth Yisrael* on *Shekalim* 6:1).

26:11 Levite. Who must also bring first fruits of his produce (Rashi).

proselyte* in your midst shall thus rejoice in all the good that God your Lord has granted you and your family.

[120. Declaration For Removing Tithes]

¹² When you have finished taking all the tithes of your grain for* the third year,* which is the special tithe year, you must give them to the Levite,* and to the foreigner,* orphan and widow, so that they will eat their fill in your settlements. ¹³ You must then make the following declaration before God your Lord:

"I have removed all the sacred portions from my house. I have given the appropriate ones to the Levite and to the orphan and widow, following all the commandments You prescribed to us. I have not violated your commandment, and have forgotten nothing.

¹⁴ "I have not eaten [the second tithe]* while in mourning.* I have not separated* any of it while unclean, and I have not used any for the dead.* I have obeyed [You], God my Lord, and have done all that You commanded me.

¹⁵ "Look down from Your holy habitation in heaven,* and bless Your people Israel, and the land that You have given us, the land flowing with milk and honey that You swore to our fathers."

[121. Concluding the Commandments]

¹⁶ Today* God your Lord is commanding you to obey all these rules and

---

— **proselyte.** Who has the same status as any other Israelite, and can even make the above declaration, since he is a spiritual descendant of Abraham (*Yerushalmi, Bikkurim* 1:4; *Yad, Bikkurim* 4:3).

26:12 **for.** (see *HaKethav VeHaKabbalah*).

— **the third year.** Thus, on the eve of Passover of the fourth and seventh years, one would have to rid himself of all tithes and priestly gifts (*Maaser Sheni* 5:6). See above, 14:28. Then, on the seventh day of Passover in the afternoon, one would make the declaration below (*Maaser Sheni* 5:10).

— **to the Levite.** This is the Levitical tithe (*Maaser Sheni* 5:10).

— **to the foreigner** ... This is the tithe for the poor, given in the third and sixth years, as in 14:29 (*Ibid.*; Rashi).

26:14 **the second tithe** (*Sefer HaMitzvoth*, Negative 151; Ramban).

— **mourning** (*Maaser Sheni* 5:12; Targum; Rashi; Septuagint). Or, "dishonestly" (Rashbam; *Paaneach Razah*; cf. Abarbanel).

— **separated** (*Maaser Sheni* 5:12; *Targum Yonathan*). Or, "consumed" (Rashi; *Sefer HaMitzvoth*, Negative 150).

— **for the dead.** Such as to buy shrouds and a casket (*Sifri*; Rashi; *Maaser Sheni* 5:12). Actually, the second tithe cannot be used for any non-food purpose. Some say that even use for non-food purposes other than the dead does not prevent one from making this statement, even though it is forbidden (Ramban; *Shenoth Eliahu* on *Maaser Sheni* 5:12). Others say that although fruits of the second tithes that have become unclean may be used for non-food purposes, they still may not be used for the dead (Rash on *Maaser Sheni* 5:12 from Yevamoth 74a). Others interpret "dead" as denoting any use that does not sustain life, that is, any non-food use (*Yad, Maaser Sheni* 3:10; *Sefer HaMitzvoth*, Negative 152).

26:15 **heaven.** That is, a realm beyond. The Hebrew word for "heaven" is *shamayim*, from the word *sham* meaning "there." Thus, *shamayim* denotes that which is not here. Or, it can come from the root *shamam* meaning "unimaginable" (see *HaKethav VeHaKabbalah* on Genesis 1:1, Deuteronomy 1:28).

26 laws. You must carefully keep them with all your heart and with all your soul.

¹⁷ Today you have declared allegiance* to God, making Him your God, and [pledging to] walk in His paths, keep His decrees, commandments and laws, and to obey His voice.

¹⁸ God has similarly declared allegiance to you today, making you His special nation* as He promised you. If* you keep all His commandments, ¹⁹ He will make you the highest of all the nations He brought into existence, [so that you will have]* praise, fame and glory. You will remain a nation consecrated to God your Lord, as He promised.

[122. The Written Stones]

27   ¹ Moses and the elders of Israel* gave the following instructions to the people:

Keep the entire mandate that I am prescribing to you today.

² On the day* that you cross the Jordan to the land that God your Lord is giving you, you must erect large stones* and plaster them with lime.* ³ When you then cross over, you shall write on them all the words* of this Torah. In this manner you shall come to the land that God your Lord is giving you, the land flowing with milk and honey that God, Lord of your fathers, promised you.

26:16 **Today.** Now that Moses has finished declaring all the commandments to the Israelites (Ramban; Abarbanel). They are also about to enter into the covenant; below, 29:11 (Sforno). This concludes the second part of Deuteronomy, from 12:1 to here, where Moses clarifies the last commandments given to the Israelites (*HaKethav VeHaKabbalah*; Malbim; cf. 1:3).

26:17 **declared allegiance.** Or, "betrothed" (Malbim; cf. *Gittin* 57b). *He-emar* in Hebrew. Or, "distinguished" (Rashi) "raised" (Rashi; Ibn Janach; Radak, *Sherashim*; Sforno), "raised to the top" (*Lekach Tov*; Ralbag); "given fame to" (Ibn Janach, quoting Sherira Gaon, *Shabbath* 105a); "accepted the uniqueness of" (Rashi, *Chagigah* 3a, *Gittin* 57b; *Arukh*, s.v. *Amar*); "granted praise and importance to" (Rashi, *Berakhoth* 6a, s.v. *Chativa*; cf. Targum); "exchanged everything for" (Chizzkuni; *Paaneach Razah*); "brought God to declare" (Ibn Ezra, quoting Rabbi Yehuda HaLevi), *fais dire* in French (Rashbam; Chizzkuni); "caused it to be said of God" (Hirsch); "recognized God" (Saadia), or, "chosen" (Septuagint).

26:18 **special nation.** *Am Segulah.* See above, 7:6, 14:2, Exodus 6:7, 19:5. This day was therefore like Sinai (Ramban).

—   **If.** Literally, "and." Or, "Therefore, keep . . ." (*Targum Yonathan*).

26:19 **that you will have** (Ramban; *Midrash HaGadol*).

27:1 **the elders** . . . The 70 elders (*Lekach Tov*; see Exodus 24:1, Numbers 11:16)

27:2 **On the day** . . . Some sources indicate that this was not done until after the blessings (*Sotah* 32a). Other sources indicate that it was before the blessings (cf. *Lekach Tov*). See Joshua 8:33.

—   **large stones.** Twelve stones; Joshua 4:3. They were like the 12 pillars erected by Moses (Exodus 24:4), and served as a sort of *mezuzah* for the Holy Land (Abarbanel).

—   **plaster them** . . . To give them a surface for writing. However, in the Talmud there is an opinion that the lime was placed over the writing to preserve it (*Sotah* 35b). Others maintain that these stones were made into an altar, and the plaster was to hold them together (Chizzkuni). Others say that they were set in lime so as to keep them standing (Ibn Ezra).

27:3 **words** (Ramban). Some say that it was a synopsis, or parts of Deuteronomy (Abarbanel). Or, "commandments" (Saadia; Ibn Ezra; cf. 4:13). See Joshua 8:32.

⁴ When you cross the Jordan, you shall set up the stones that I am now   **27**
describing to you on* Mount Ebal,* and you shall plaster* them with lime.
⁵ There you shall then* build an altar to God your Lord. It shall be a stone
altar, and you shall not lift up any iron to it.* ⁶ The altar that you build shall
thus be made of whole stones. It is on this [altar] that you shall sacrifice burnt
offerings. ⁷ You shall also sacrifice peace offerings and eat there, rejoicing
before God your Lord.
⁸ On the stones, you shall write all the words of this Torah in a clear
script.*

[123. Becoming a Nation]

⁹ Moses and the Levitical priests spoke to all Israel, saying:
Pay attention* and listen, Israel. Today you have become a nation* to God
your Lord. ¹⁰ You must therefore obey God your Lord and keep His commandments and decrees, as I am prescribing them to you today.

[124. Blessings and Curses]

¹¹ On that day, Moses gave the people the following instructions:
¹² When you cross the Jordan, the ones who shall stand on* Mount Gerizim*
for the people's blessing* shall be Simeon, Levi,* Judah, Issachar, Joseph and
Benjamin.

27:4 **on.** (Septuagint). Or, "near" (*cf.* Rashi).

— **Mount Ebal.** See above, 11:29. This was the mountain of the curse, and the stones were placed there as a
consolation for the tribes associated with this mountain (Chizzkuni). They were also to indicate that the
curse would come for violating the Torah (Abarbanel).

— **plaster.** Some say that they were plastered after having been written on (*Sotah* 35b; see 27:2). Others
maintain that they were re-plastered (Malbim).

27:5 **you shall then.** Some say out of different stones (Malbim), while others maintain that the altar was made
out of the stones with the writing (*Lekach Tov*; Ralbag; Bachya; Abarbanel). Both opinions are found in
Talmudical sources (*Tosefta, Sotah* 8:5; Yerushalmi, Sotah 7:5; *Tosafoth, Sotah* 35b, s.v. *Ketza*). See Joshua
8:32.

— **not lift up any iron . . .** See Exodus 20:22, Joshua 8:31.

27:8 **clear script** (Ibn Ezra; Septuagint); cf. Habakkuk 2:2. *Ba'er Hetiv* in Hebrew. Or, "in clear language"
(Targum; Radak, *Sherashim*; cf. 1:5), indicating that the Torah was written on the stones in 70 languages
(*Sotah* 32b; *Targum Yonathan*; Rashi). Some say that the stones were plastered, inscribed, replastered and
then inscribed again (Malbim).

27:9 **Pay attention** (Targum; Saadia; Radak, *Sherashim*; cf. *Berakhoth* 16a). *Hasketh* in Hebrew. Or, "accept
this" (Ibn Janach), "be silent" (Septuagint; cf. *Berakhoth* 63b); "form groups" or "push yourselves to the
limit" (*Ibid*).

— **you have become a nation.** With the giving of all the commandments (Ramban), and the sealing of the
covenant (below, 29:11,12; Chizzkuni).

27:12 **on** (*Sotah* 32a; Rashi). Or, "near" (*Sotah* 37a; Chizzkuni). The Hebrew word *al* has both connotations.

— **Mount Gerizim.** See above, 11:29.

— **for the people's blessing.** Or, "when the blessing is given" (*HaKethav VeHaKabbalah*). Some say that the
blessings were the precise opposite of the curses given below (*Sotah* 37b). However, others indicate that
the blessings might be 28:1-14 (Ibn Ezra). See Joshua 8:34.

— **Levi.** The younger ones, or those not fit for service (see Numbers 4:47; *Sotah* 37a). The other Levites pronounced the blessings (below 27:14).

27   [13] The ones who shall stand on Mount Ebal for the curse shall be Reuben, Gad, Asher, Zebulun, Dan and Naphtali.

[14] The Levites shall then speak up and say the following to every individual Israelite in a loud voice:

[125. The First Curse]

[15] "Cursed is the person who makes a sculptured or cast idol, which is repulsive to God your Lord even if it is a piece of fine sculpture, and places it in a hidden place."

All the people shall respond and say, "Amen."

[126. The Second Curse]

[16] "Cursed is he who shows disrespect for his father and mother."*
All the people shall say, "Amen."

[127. The Third Curse]

[17] "Cursed is he who moves his neighbor's boundary marker."*
All the people shall say, "Amen."

[128. The Fourth Curse]

[18] "Cursed is he who misdirects the blind* on the way."
All the people shall say, "Amen."

[129. The Fifth and Sixth Curses]

[19] "Cursed is he who perverts justice* for the foreigner, orphan and widow."
All the people shall say, "Amen."

[20] "Cursed is he who lies with his father's wife,* thus violating his father's privacy."*
All the people shall say, "Amen."

[130. The Seventh Curse]

[21] "Cursed is he who lies with any animal."*
All the people shall say, "Amen."

27:16 **shows disrespect . . .** See Exodus 20:12, 21:17, Leviticus 19:3.
27:17 **moves** . . . Above 19:14.
27:18 **who misdirects . . .** Leviticus 19:14.
27:19 **perverts justice . . .** Exodus 22:21,22; above, 10:18, 24:17.
27:20 **lies with his father's wife . . .** Leviticus 18:8, 20:11.
—   **his father's privacy.** See above 23:1.
27:21 **animal.** Leviticus 18:23, 20:15.

[131. The Eighth Curse]   27

²² "Cursed is he who lies with his sister,* whether she is the daughter of his father or of his mother."
All the people shall say, "Amen."

[132. The Ninth Curse]

²³ "Cursed is he who lies with his mother-in-law."*
All the people shall say, "Amen."

[133. The Tenth Curse]

²⁴ "Cursed is he who strikes down his neighbor in secret."
All the people shall say, "Amen."

[134. The Eleventh Curse]

²⁵ "Cursed is he who takes a bribe* to put an innocent man to death."
All the people shall say, "Amen."

[135. The Twelfth Curse]

²⁶ "Cursed is he who does not uphold and keep this entire Torah."*
All the people shall say, "Amen."

[136. The Blessing for Obedience]

¹ If you obey God your Lord,* carefully keeping all His commandments   28
as I am prescribing them to you today, then God will make you highest of all
the nations on earth. ² As long as you listen to God your Lord, all these blessings will come to bear on you.

³ Blessed will you be in the city, and blessed in the field.

⁴ Blessed will be the fruit of your womb, the fruit of your soil, and the fruit
of your livestock, the calves of your herds and the lambs of your flock.*

⁵ Blessed will be your food basket* and your kneading bowl.

⁶ Blessed will you be when you come and blessed when you go.

27:22 **with his sister.** Leviticus 18:9, 20:17.

27:23 **mother-in-law** (Targum; Rashbam; Radak, *Sherashim*; Ibn Janach). *Chotheneth* in Hebrew. See Leviticus 18:17, 20:14. Or, "daughter-in-law" (Septuagint).

27:25 **takes a bribe.** See Exodus 23:7,8, above, 10:17, 16:19. Some say that this is directed to the judges, while others say that it includes a witness (Ibn Ezra).

27:26 **who does not uphold ...** This is an oath to keep the entire Torah (Rashi; *Shevuoth* 37a), and not to abandon any commandment (Ramban).

28:1 **If you obey ...** See Leviticus 26:3-13.

28:4 **calves ...** see above, 7:13.

28:5 **food basket.** *Tĕnè.* See above 26:2.

28   ⁷ If any enemies attack you, God will make them flee from you in panic. They may march against you on one road, but they will flee from you in seven directions.

⁸ God will grant a blessing in your granaries and all your [other] endeavors. He will bless you in the land that He, God your Lord, is giving you.

⁹ If only you keep the commandments of God your Lord and walk in His paths, God will establish you as His holy nation, as He promised you.* ¹⁰ All the nations of the world will realize that God's name is associated with you, and they will be in awe of you.

¹¹ God will grant you good surplus* in the fruit of your womb, the fruit of your livestock, and the fruit of your land. [You will thus flourish] on the good land that God promised your ancestors to give you. ¹² God will open His good treasury in heaven to give your land rain at precisely the right time, and to bless everything you do. You will lend many nations, but you will not have to borrow.

¹³ God will make you a leader and never a follower.* You will be on the top and never on the bottom. You must merely obey the commandments of God your Lord, as I am prescribing them to you today, carefully keeping them.

¹⁴ Do not stray to the right or left from all the words that I am commanding you today. [Be especially careful not to] follow other gods or serve them.

[137. The Curse of Disobedience]

¹⁵ If you do not obey God your Lord and do not carefully keep all His commandments and decrees as I am prescribing them for you today, then all these curses will come to bear on you.

¹⁶ Cursed will you be in the city and cursed in the field.

¹⁷ Cursed will be your food basket and your kneading bowl.

¹⁸ Cursed will be the fruit of your womb, the fruit of your land, the calves of your herd and the lambs of your flock.

¹⁹ Cursed will you be when you come, and cursed when you go.

²⁰ God will send misfortune,* confusion* and frustration* against you in

---

28:9 **as He promised you.** Exodus 19:6.

28:11 **grant you good surplus** (Saadia; Septuagint). Or, "will allow you to survive well through" (Ibn Ezra; Ralbag).

28:13 **a leader . . .** (cf. Ramban). Literally, "a head and not a tail." See below 28:44.

28:20 **misfortune.** *M'erah* in Hebrew. "Attrition" (Rashi; Ibn Ezra), "shortages" (Septuagint), "curse" (*Targum Yonathan*); "failure" (Saadia); "destruction" (Ibn Janach), or, "pain" (Radak, *Sherashim*).

—   **confusion** (Rashi; Rashbam). *Mehumah* in Hebrew. Or, "restlessness" (Saadia; Hirsch); "inability to finish a job" (Ibn Ezra); or, "famine" (Septuagint).

—   **frustration** (Saadia). *Migereth* in Hebrew. Or, "guilt feelings" (Hirsch); "attrition" (Septuagint; Ibn Janach); "destruction" (Radak, *Sherashim*); or, "famine" (Rashbam).

all you undertake. It will destroy you and make you rapidly vanish because of   28
your evil ways in forsaking my [teachings].

²¹ God will make disease attach itself to you, until it* wipes you out from
on the land which you are about to occupy. ²² God will strike you with consumption,* fever,* delerium,* paralysis,* the sword,* the black blight* and
the yellow blight,* and [these calamities] will pursue you until they destroy
you.

²³ The skies above you will be like brass, and the earth below you like iron.
²⁴ God will turn your rain into powder and dust, and it will come down from
the skies to destroy you.

²⁵ God will make you panic before your enemies. You will march out in
one column, but flee from them in seven. You will become a terrifying
example* to all the world's kingdoms. ²⁶ Your corpses will be food for all the
birds of the sky and beasts of the land, and no one will chase them away.*

²⁷ God will strike you with the Egyptian boil,* and with incurable
tumors,* running sores* and itch.* ²⁸ God will strike you with insanity, blind-

---

28:21 **it** (Bachya). Or, "He" (Septuagint).

28:22 **consumption.** Tuberculosis (Saadia; Ibn Janach; Radak, *Sherashim*), *sachaf* in Arabic. *Shachefeth* in Hebrew; see Leviticus 26:16, 11:15. Or, "debilitating disease" (*Midrash HaGadol*); "acute fever" (Ralbag); "depression" (Hirsch on Leviticus 26:16); or, "a disease that debilitates and causes swelling" (Rashi).

— **fever** (Rashi; Ibn Janach; Septuagint). *Kadachath* in Hebrew; see Leviticus 26:16; below 32:22, Isaiah 3:11, 64:1, Jeremiah 17:4. Specifically, chronic fever (Saadia; Ibn Ezra; Ralbag), "inflammation" (Radak, *Sherashim*), or "excitement" (Hirsch on Leviticus 26:16). In medieval medical texts, the word often denotes malaria.

— **delerium** (*Targum Yonathan*). *Daleketh* in Hebrew. Or, "burning fever" (Radak, *Sherashim*; cf. Ralbag); "recurring fever" (Saadia), "chills" (Septuagint), possibly malaria; "chest inflammation" (*Midrash HaGadol*), or, "excitement" (Ibn Janach; cf. Genesis 31:36).

— **paralysis** (Saadia). *Charchur* in Hebrew. Or, "burning fever" (Radak, *Sherashim*); "inflammation" (Septuagint); "angina" (*Targum Yonathan*); or, *"astronment,"* a disease where one thirsts for water (Rashi); probably typhoid fever.

— **the sword** (*Targum Yonathan*; Rashi). *Cherev* in Hebrew. Or, "dryness," possibly drought (Saadia; Ibn Ezra; Chizzkuni; Hirsch).

— **black blight** (from Arabic cognates). *Shiddafon* in Hebrew; see 1 Kings 8:37, Amos 4:9. Some interpret it to denote the damage to crops caused by the searing, hot east wind (Saadia; Rashi; Radak, *Sherashim*; cf. Genesis 41:6). Or, "grain with empty husks" (Ibn Janach). Others speak of it as a human affliction, "swelling" or "shriveling" (Ibn Ezra), or, "wasting away" (Ralbag; Hirsch). The Septuagint translates it as *erithismo* which can denote "blighting" or "excitement."

— **yellow blight** (Saadia; Rashi; Ibn Janach). *Yerakon* in Hebrew. Or, "wind destruction," *anemophthoria* in Greek (Septuagint; but possibly transposed with the above); "jaundice" (Ralbag; Hirsch; cf. *Berakhoth* 25a; *Shabbath* 33a); or, "terror" (Radak, *Sherashim,* cf. Jeremiah 30:6).

28:25 **terrifying example** (Rashi). *Zaavah* in Hebrew. Or, "example" (Saadia), "something terrible" (Ibn Ezra; Ibn Janach; cf. Isaiah 28:19); "a trembling group" (Radak, *Sherashim*), "a pariah" (*Targum Yonathan*); or, "a dispersed group (Septuagint).

28:26 **chase them away** (*Targum Yonathan*; Saadia; Rashbam; Ibn Ezra; Septuagint). *Macharid* in Hebrew. Or, "none will be concerned" (Chizzkuni).

28:27 **boil.** *Shechin* in Hebrew; see Exodus 9:9. It is described as being wet inside and dry outside (*Bekhoroth* 41a; Rashi).

— **tumors.** Or, "hemorrhoids" (Ibn Ezra; Radak, *Sherashim*; Chizzkuni; Ralbag; cf. Septuagint). *Afolim* in

28 ness* and mental confusion.* ²⁹ You will grope about in broad daylight just like a blind man gropes in the darkness, and you will have no success in any of your ways. You will be constantly cheated and robbed, and no one will help you.

³⁰ When you betroth a woman, another man will sleep with her. When you build a house, you will not live in it. When you plant a vineyard, you will not enjoy its fruit.* ³¹ Your ox will be slaughtered before your eyes, but you will not eat from it. Your donkey will be stolen right in front of you, but you will not be able to get it back. Your sheep will be given to your enemies, and no one will come to your aid.

³² Your sons and daughters will be given to a foreign nation. You will see it happening with your own eyes, and will long for them all day long, but you will be powerless. ³² A strange nation will consume the fruit of your land and all your toil. You will be constantly cheated and crushed.*

³⁴ You will go insane from what you will have to witness. ³⁵ God will then strike you with a malignant skin disease on your knees and thighs, and you will not be able to find a cure for it until it [covers you]* from head to toe.

³⁶ God will bring you and your elected king to a nation unknown to you and your fathers, and there you will serve idolators* who worship wood and stone. ³⁷ You will be an object of horror, a by-word and an abject lesson among all the nations where God will lead you.

³⁸ You will bring much seed out to the field, but the locusts will devour [the crop] and you will bring little back. ³⁹ You will plant vineyards and work hard, but the worms will eat [the grapes], so you will not drink wine or have a harvest. ⁴⁰ You will have olive trees in all your territories, but the olives will drop off and you will not enjoy their oil.

⁴¹ You will have sons and daughters, but they will not remain yours, since

---

Hebrew, read as *Tachorim* (see *Megillah* 25b); cf. 1 Samuel 5:9. A type of swelling; see Numbers 14:44. Since these are associated with mice (1 Samuel 6:4), some say that it may be bubonic plague (cf. Abarbanel).

— **running sores** (Rashi; *Midrash HaGadol*; cf. *Bekhoroth* 41a), wet inside and out. *Garav* in Hebrew; see Leviticus 21:20. Or, "malignant scabs," *psora agria* in Greek (Septuagint). Possibly eczema.

— **itch** (*Targum Yonathan*; Saadia; Ibn Ezra; Radak, *Sherashim*; Ralbag; Septuagint). *Cheres* in Hebrew. Or, "dry scab" (Targum; Rashi), or, "sunstroke" (Ibn Ezra; Bachya).

28:28 **blindness.** Some say that this is hysterical blindness (Ibn Ezra; Ralbag) or blindness due to terror (Abarbanel).

— **confusion** (Ralbag; Septuagint). *Timhon* in Hebrew. Or, "dullness," *shamimuth* in Aramaic (Targum), "hallucinations" (Hirsch), or, "numbness of heart," *astordison* in Old French (Rashi).

28:30 **enjoy its fruit.** See above, 20:6. In general, the three things mentioned here are those for which a man can return from war, above 20:5-7 (*Lekach Tov*).

28:32 **crushed** (see *HaKethav VeHaKabbalah*).

28:35 **until it covers you** (Ralbag).

28:36 **idolators** (Targum). Literally, "You will serve foreign gods of wood and stone." Or, "you will serve the temples of . . ." (Rashi on 28:64).

they will be taken into captivity. ⁴² All your trees and the fruit of your land will **28**
be reduced* by the cricket.*

⁴³ The alien among you will rise higher and higher over you, while you
will descend lower and lower. ⁴⁴ He will make loans to you, but you will not
be able to lend him anything. He will become the master, while you will be the
vassal.*

⁴⁵ All these curses will thus have come upon you, pursuing you and catch-
ing you so as to destroy you, all because you did not obey God your Lord, and
[did not] keep the commandments and decrees that He prescribed to you.
⁴⁶ [These curses] will be a sign and proof to you and your children forever.

⁴⁷ When you had plenty of everything, you would not serve God your Lord
with happiness* and a glad heart. ⁴⁸ You will therefore serve your enemies
when God sends them against you, and it will be in hunger, thirst, nakedness
and universal want. [Your enemy] will place an iron yoke on your neck so as to
destroy you.

⁴⁹ God will bring upon you a nation from afar, from the end of the earth,
swooping down like an eagle. It will be a nation whose language you do not
understand, ⁵⁰ a sadistic* nation, that has no respect for the old and no mercy
for the young.

⁵¹ [That nation] will eat the fruit of your livestock and the fruit of your land
so as to destroy you. It will leave you nothing of your grain, wine, oil, calves in
your herds and lambs in your flocks,* so as to annihilate you. ⁵² It will lay
siege* to you in all your settlements, until it has brought down* all your high
fortified walls, in which you trust, throughout your land. [That nation] will
then persecute* you in all the settlements throughout the land which God
your Lord has given you.

⁵³ You will then eat the fruit of your womb. When your enemies are besieg-
ing you* you will become so desperate that you will actually eat the flesh of
your sons and daughters. ⁵⁴ The most tender-hearted and dainty man among

---

28:42 **reduced** (Rashi). Or, "taken away" (Bachya); or, "stricken" (Septuagint).
— **cricket.** A noisy member of the locust family (Rashi; Radak, *Sherashim*; cf. *Taanith* 8b). *Tzelatzal* in
Hebrew. Cf. Isaiah 18:1, Job 40:31. Or, "moth" (Saadia); "caterpillar" (Ralbag); "blight" (Septuagint),
erisubie in Greek; or, "marauders" (Ramban; Bachya; cf. *Bava Kama* 116b).
28:44 **the master . . .** Literally, "he will be the head, and you will be the tail." See above, 28:13.
28:47 **with happiness.** From here we see that one must serve God with joy and gladness (*Yad, Lulav* 8:15;
Bachya). This can include song (*Arakhin* 11a).
28:50 **sadistic.** *Az panim* in Hebrew. Or, "arrogant," or, "aggressive."
28:51 **calves . . .** See above, 7:13, 28:4.
28:52 **lay siege** (Saadia; cf. Radak, *Sherashim*). *Hetzar* in Hebrew. Or, "crush" (Septuagint; cf. Targum).
— **brought down** (*Targum Yonathan*; Radak, *Sherashim*; Septuagint). *Redeth* in Hebrew. Or, "conquered"
(*Targum*; Rashi).
— **persecute** (Saadia).
28:53 **besieging.** Or, "persecuting."

28 you will begrudge his brother, his bosom wife, and his surviving children, [55] not giving them the flesh of his children that he is eating. This will be because nothing will remain for you, and you will be desperate when your enemies besiege all your settlements.

[56] The most pampered, delicate woman, who is so refined that she does not let her foot touch the ground, will then begrudge her bosom husband, her son, and her daughter, [57] when she secretly eats the afterbirth* that comes out from between her legs and the infant she has born. So great will be her lack of all things and her desperation when your enemies besiege your settlements.

[58] If you are not careful to keep all the words of this Torah, as written in this book, so as to fear this glorious, awesome name of God your Lord, [59] then God will strike you and your descendants with unimaginable plagues. The punishments will be terrible and relentless,* and the diseases will be malignant and unyielding.

[60] God will bring back on you all the Egyptian diseases that you dread, and they will cling to you. [61] God will also bring upon you every punishment that is not written in this book of the Torah, so as to destroy you.

[62] Where you were once as numerous as the stars of the sky, the survivors among you will be few in number, all because you did not obey God your Lord. [63] As happy as God was to be good to you and increase you, so will He be happy to exile you and destroy you. You will be torn up from the land which you are about to occupy.

[64] God will scatter you among the nations, from one end of the earth to the other. There you will serve idolaters who worship gods of wood and stone, unknown to you and your fathers. [65] Among those nations you will feel insecure,* and there will be no place for your foot to rest. There God will make you cowardly,* destroying* your outlook and making life hopeless.

[66] Your life will hang in suspense. Day and night, you will be so terrified that you will not believe that you are alive.* [67] In the morning, you will say, "If it were only night,"* and in the evening you will say, "If it were only

---

28:57 afterbirth (Targum Yonathan; Septuagint; cf. Chullin 77a; Niddah 26a). Shilyah in Hebrew. Or, "newborn" (Targum; Rashi), or, "stillborn child" (Ibn Janach; Radak, Sherashim).

28:59 relentless (Saadia; Ibn Ezra). Literally, "faithful."

28:65 feel insecure. "You will find no security" (Saadia), or, "no rest" (Rashi).
—   cowardly (Targum; Rashi; Midrash HaGadol).
—   destroying . . . See Leviticus 26:16.

28:66 you will not . . . Literally, "you will not believe in your life."

28:67 If it were only night. Or, "if it were only last night" (Sotah 49a; Rashi). Or, "If I will only survive until evening" (Saadia).

morning." Such will be the internal terror that you will experience and the   28
sights that you will see.

⁶⁸ God will bring you back to Egypt in ships,* along the way that I promised you would never see again.* You will [try to]* sell yourselves as slaves and
maids, but no one will want to buy you.

[138. The Covenant]

⁶⁹ The above* are the words of the covenant that God instructed Moses to
make with the Israelites in the land of Moab, besides the covenant that was
made with them at Horeb.*

[139. Moses' Final Discourse]

¹ Moses summoned* all Israel, and said to them: **29**

You have seen all that God did in Egypt before your very eyes, to Pharaoh,
to all his servants, and to all his land. ² Your own eyes saw the great miracles,*
signs and wonders. ³ But until this day, God did not give you a heart to know,
eyes to see and ears to hear.

⁴ [God is now declaring to you,]* "I brought you through the desert for
forty years, during which your clothes did not wear out on you, and the shoes
on your feet did not become tattered. ⁵ You neither ate bread nor drank wine,
so that you would know that I am God your Lord."*

⁶ When you came to this area, Sichon king of Cheshbon* and Og king of
the Bashan* came out to fight us, but we defeated them. ⁷ We took their land,
and gave it as a heritage to the Reubenites, the Gaddites and half the tribe of
the Manassites.

28:68 **ships.** *Aniyoth.* Or, "misery" (*HaKethav VeHaKabbalah*).
—   **that I promised** ... See Exodus 14:13, above, 17:16 (*Yerushalmi, Sukkah* 5:1; *Midrash HaGadol*).
—   **try to.** (Bachya).
28:69 **The above.** (Rashi; *Midrash HaGadol*). Literally, "These." Some, however, say that "these" refers to the
    next section, particularly to the covenant mentioned in 29:11 (cf. *Tanchuma, Netzavim* 3).
—   **at Horeb.** See Leviticus 25:1, 26:3-46 (Rashi; Rashbam; see note on Exodus 24:7). Others identify it
    with the covenant mentioned in Exodus 24:7,8 (Abarbanel). However, from 5:2, it appears that the
    covenant at Horeb was the Ten Commandments.
29:1 **Moses summoned** ... To make the covenant (Ibn Ezra). Or, after the covenant (Ramban).
29:2 **miracles** (Targum). *Massoth* in Hebrew. Or, "tests" (Malbim; Septuagint).
29:4 **God is now declaring** ... From context in verse 5 (Chizzkuni; Abarbanel; Malbim). See above, 11:13.
    Others, however, see this as Moses' statement; see note on 29:5.
29:5 **that I am God your Lord.** Assuming that these are God's words, as in previous notes. Or, "[and God
    said that this would be] so that you would know that I am God your Lord" (Saadia). Or, "so that you
    would know that 'I am God' is your Lord" (Hirsch; *HaKethav VeHaKabbalah*; cf. *Sukkah* 45a).
29:6 **Sichon** ... Numbers 21:21-24.
—   **Og** ... Numbers 21:33-35.

29   **8** If you safeguard the words of this covenant* and keep them, you will be
successful* in all you do.

Netzavim   נִצָּבִים

[140. The Covenant Renewed]

9 Today* you are all standing before God your Lord*—your leaders, your
tribal chiefs,* your elders, your law enforcers, every Israelite man, **10** your
children, your women, and the proselytes in your camp—even your woodcutters and water drawers.*

11 You are thus being brought into the covenant* of God your Lord, and
[accepting] the dread oath* that He is making with you today. **12** He is estab-
lishing you as His nation, so that He will be a God to you, just as He promised
you, and as He swore to your ancestors, Abraham, Isaac and Jacob.

13 But it is not with you alone that I am making this covenant and this
dread oath. **14** I am making it both with those who are standing here with us
today before God our Lord, and with those who are not [yet]* here with us
today.

15 You know full well that we lived in Egypt, and that we also passed
through [the territories of] the nations you encountered. **16** You saw the disgusting, putrid idols that they have, made of wood and stone, gold and silver.
17 Today, there must not be among you any man, woman, family or tribe,
whose heart strays from God, and who goes and worships the gods of those

---

29:8 **covenant.** Above, 28:69 or below, 29:11.
— **successful** (Targum; *Avodah Zarah* 19b; Saadia; Ibn Ezra; Ibn Janach). *Haskel* in Hebrew. Or, "act intelli-
gently" (Radak, *Sherashim*; *Paaneach Razah*; Hirsch).
29:9 **Today.** But in the future, you will be scattered throughout the Promised Land (*Baaley Tosafoth* on 29:11;
Abarbanel). See 29:1 (Rashbam).
— **before God . . .** Some say that this denotes the area around the Ark (Ibn Ezra).
— **your leaders, your tribal chiefs** (*Targum Yonathan*; *Lekach Tov*; cf. Ibn Ezra). Some say that the tribal chiefs
are the ones who were to supervise the division of the land (Numbers 34:18-28; *Lekach Tov*). Or, "the
leaders of your tribes" (Rashi; Septuagint). Or, "Your leaders, your tribes—" (Ramban).
29:10 **even your woodcutters . . .** Some say that these were Canaanites who came to embrace Judaism, just as
in the time of Joshua (*Tanchuma* 2; Rashi); cf. Joshua 9:21-27. Others say that they were the mixed multitude (Exodus 12:38; Ramban), or the Israelites' slaves (*Baaley Tosafoth*; Chizzkuni).
29:11 **covenant.** In addition to the covenant at Sinai. Some say that a new covenant was needed because the
original one was violated with the Golden Calf (*Tanchuma* 3; Bachya). Others say that this covenant was
to make the Israelites into a nation (Ralbag; Sforno; see above, 27:9). Others say that it was a covenant
with regard to the Promised Land (Abarbanel). According to another opinion, it was to prevent the
Israelites from assimilating the idolatrous practices of the Canaanites (Rashi, Ramban on 29:17). Some
say that this covenant involved the same elements as that in Exodus 24:4-8 (Ramban).
— **dread oath.** (*Yerushalmi, Sotah* 2:5; *Lekach Tov*). *Alah* in Hebrew. Or, "curse" indicating the curse at Sinai
(cf. Leviticus 26:18; *Midrash HaGadol*) or that on Mount Ebal (Chizzkuni).
29:14 **yet.** That is, to future generations (Rashi).

nations. There must not be among you a root whose fruit is gall* and worm-   **29**
wood.*

¹⁸ When [such a person] hears the words of this dread curse, he may
rationalize* and say, "I will have peace, even if I do as I see fit.* Let me add*
some moisture* to this dry* [practice]!"

29:17 gall (Septuagint;
xole in Greek).
Rosh in Hebrew;
see below, 32:32,
Jeremiah 9:14,
Hosea   10:4,
Psalms   69:22,
Lamentations
3:19. Or, "poi-
son,"   or
"venom"
(Saadia; Radak,
Sherashim;
Bachya);   cf.

Hemlock   **Gall**   **Wormwood**

below, 32:33, Amos 6:12. Some sources identify *rosh* with hemlock (*Conium maculatum*), a dark poisonous
plant. Others identify it with gall poppy (*Papaver somniferum*), a species of opium poppy that grows in the
Holy Land. The person described can bring about the same mental confusion as opium.

— **wormwood.** *Laanah* in Hebrew; *aklam* in Arabic (Saadia; Ibn Janach), *exenjos* in Old Spanish (Radak,
Sherashim). Wormwood (*Artemisia absinthium*) is an herb yielding a bitter, dark green oil. A paradigm of
bitterness, and hence translated merely as "bitterness" (*pikra*) by the Septuagint.

29:18 rationalize (Saadia). *Hith-barekh* in Hebrew. Literally, "bless himself" (*Lekach Tov*; Yehudah HaLevi in
Ibn Ezra; Chizzkuni; Sforno). Or, "conclude" (Targum; Ibn Janach); "give up hope" (*Targum Yonathan*);
"think that he will have blessing" (Rashi); or, "flatter himself" (Septuagint).

— **as I see fit.** Literally, "in the vision of my heart" (Rashi; Radak; *Sherashim*). *Sheriruth* in Hebrew, see
Jeremiah 3:17, Psalms 81:13. Or, "follow my own ideas" (Targum; Ibn Janach); "follow my heart's
desires" (*Targum Yonathan*; Saadia); "remain free in my heart" (*Lekach Tov*); "maintain my strong position" (*Lekach Tov*; Radak, *Sherashim*); "follow my stubborn desires" (Ramban); "annul it in my heart"
(Sforno); or, "follow my own error" (Septuagint).

— **add.** (Targum; Rashi; Radak, *Sherashim*; Ramban). *Sefoth* in Hebrew; see Isaiah 30:1, Psalms 4:15. Or,
"destroy" (Yehudah HaLevi in Ibn Ezra; Ibn Janach; Chizzkuni; Septuagint); "annul" (Ibn Ezra),
"water" (Abarbanel), or, "join" (Rashi, *Sanhedrin* 76b).

— **moisture.** *Ravah* in Hebrew, denoting the moist, well watered, or unthirsty. Some say that this is an allegory for the righteous (Ibn Ezra; Ibn Janach; Radak, *Sherashim*), or one who has no desires (Ramban),
while others say that it denotes the wicked (Septuagint), who have slaked their thirst by following their
desires (Ramban; Ralbag; Radak; Sforno). Others say that it denotes the accidental sinner,
who acts like a drunkard (Rashi; cf. Targum), while some say that it denotes the spiteful sinner, who sins
even though he has no real desire (Rashbam).

— . **dry.** Or, "thirsty," the opposite of *ravah*. Here again, some say that this denotes the "dry" wicked person
(Ibn Ezra; Ibn Janach; Radak, *Sherashim*), while others say that it denotes the person who "thirsts"
because he controls his desires (Radak, *Sherashim*; Septuagint). Others say that the "thirsty" denotes those
who have desires (Ralbag), or the desire itself (Chizzkuni; Bachya). Some would translate "thirsty" as
"sober," indicating one who sins with full knowledge (Rashi; cf. Targum), while others say that it indicates the one who sins because of his "thirst" and desire (Rashbam).

   This verse can then be translated, "to rid thirst with wetness" (Saadia); "to join the thirsty to the
unthirsty" (Rashi, *Sanhedrin* 76b); "to liken the thirsty to the unthirsty" (*Ibid.*); "Let the righteous be
included with the wicked [and save them]" (Radak, *Sherashim*); "to destroy the righteous with the
wicked" (Ibn Ezra; Ibn Janach); "to join the righteous with the wicked" (Chizzkuni); "shall the righteous then be destroyed with the wicked?" (Bachya); "[in any case,] the moist are watered with the dry"
(Abarbanel); "Lest the sinner destroy the guiltless [with him]!" (Septuagint); "to annul the words of the

29 ¹⁹ God will not agree to forgive such a person. God's anger and demand for exclusive worship* will be directed like smoke against that person and the entire dread curse written in this book will lie [at his door],* so that God will blot out his name from under the heavens. ²⁰ God will separate him so that he will have more evil than any of the Israelite tribes, and he will be subject to all the dread curses of the covenant, which are written in this Torah scroll.

²¹ A future generation, consisting of your descendants, who rise up after you, along with the foreigner* from a distant land, shall see the punishment directed against that land, and the plague with which God has struck it, and they will say,* ²² "Sulphur and salt has burned all its soil. Nothing can be planted and nothing can grow—not even grass can grow on it. It is like the destruction of Sodom, Gomorrah, Adma and Tzevoyim,* [the cities] that God overturned in His anger and rage."

²³ All the nations will ask, "Why did God do this to the land? What was the reason for this great display of anger?"

²⁴ They* shall answer, "It is because they abandoned the covenant that God, Lord of their fathers, made with them when He brought them out of Egypt. ²⁵ They went and served foreign gods, bowing down to them. These were gods alien to them, something that was not their portion. ²⁶ God displayed anger against this nation, bringing upon it the entire curse written in this book. ²⁷ God drove them from their land with anger, rage and great fury, and He exiled them to another land, where they remain even today."

²⁸ Hidden things may pertain to God our Lord, but that which has been revealed applies to us and our children forever. [We must therefore] keep all the words of this Torah.

[141. Repentance and Restoration]

30 ¹ There shall come a time when you shall experience all the words of bless-

---

righteous with the wicked" (Yehudah HaLevi in Ibn Ezra); "so that accidental sins be added to purposeful ones" (Targum; Rashi; *Lekach Tov*); "so that spiteful sins be added to those of desire" (Rashbam); "to add undesired sins to sins of lust" (*Baaley Tosafoth*); "to fulfill the desires of my freethinking" (Ralbag); "to add desire even when he is satisfied" (Rambam; Chizzkuni); "to let his desires satisfy his craving" (Sforno); "to let his desires be added to his intellect" (Radak, *Sherashim*); "to graft my well watered [root] to the dry one" (Ramban); or, "to graft my well watered [wormwood] to the unwatered one" (*Ibid.*).

29:19 demand for exclusive worship. See Exodus 20:5.
— **at his door.** See Genesis 4:7. Or, "rest upon him" (Hirsch), or, "attach itself to him" (Targum; Saadia; Septuagint).
29:21 foreigner. Or, "proselyte" (*Lekach Tov*).
— **will say.** Or, "will speak of it" (Abarbanel). Others say that "will say" is attached to and repeated in 29:23 (Ralbag).
29:22 Sodom, Gomorrah ... See Genesis 19:24.
29:23 They. The descendants; or, the nations.

ing and curse* that I have presented to you. There, among the nations where 30
God will have banished* you, you will reflect* on the situation. ² You will then
return to God your Lord, and you will obey Him, doing everything that I am
commanding you today. You and your children [will repent] with all your
heart and with all your soul.

³ God will then bring back your remnants* and have mercy on you. God
your Lord will once again gather you from among all the nations where He
scattered you. ⁴ Even if your diaspora is at the ends of the heavens, God your
Lord will gather you up from there and He will take you back.*

⁵ God your Lord will then bring you to the land that your ancestors occupied, and you too will occupy it. God will be good to you and make you
flourish even more than your ancestors. ⁶ God will remove the barriers from
your hearts* and from the hearts of your descendants, so that you will love
God your Lord with all your heart and soul. Thus will you survive.

⁷ God will then direct all these curses against your enemies and against the
foes who pursued you.

⁸ You will repent and obey God, keeping all His commandments, as I
prescribe them to you today. ⁹ God will then grant you a good surplus* in all
the work of your hands, in the fruit of your womb, the fruit of your livestock,
and the fruit of your land. God will once again rejoice in you for good, just as
He rejoiced in your fathers.

¹⁰ All this will happen when you obey God your Lord, keeping all His
commandments and decrees, as they are written in this book of the Torah, and
when you return to God your Lord with all your heart and soul.

[142. Availability of the Torah]

¹¹ This mandate that I am prescribing to you today is not too mysterious*
or remote from you. ¹² It is not in heaven,* so [that you should] say, "Who
shall go up to heaven and bring it to us so that we can hear it and keep it?"
¹³ It is not over the sea so [that you should] say, "Who will cross the sea and

---

30:1 **blessing and curse.** Some say above, 11:26-28; 27:9:14 (*Yerushalmi, Sotah* 7:4).
— **banished.** Or, "scattered" (Septuagint).
— **reflect.** See above, 4:39.
30:3 **bring back your remnants.** Or, "captives" (Targum; Radak, s.v. *Shavah*). Or, "accept your repentance"
(*Targum Yonathan*); "grant your exiles rest" (*HaKethav VeHaKabbalah*); "return to your exiles" (Hirsch);
"return to your repenters" (Malbim); "heal your iniquities" (Septuagint); or, "restore your fortunes."
30:4 **take you back.** As His people (*HaKethav VeHaKabbalah*).
30:6 **remove the barriers . . .** See above, 10:16.
30:9 **good surplus.** See above, 28:11.
30:11 **mysterious** (Saadia). Or, "hidden" (Targum; Rashi); or, "difficult" (Ibn Ezra; Septuagint). *Pala* in
Hebrew. See above, 17:8.
30:12 **not in heaven.** Requiring new prophetic insight (*Bava Metzia* 59b; *Temurah* 16a; Ralbag).

30 get it for us, so that we will be able to hear it and keep it?" ¹⁴ It is something
that is very close to you. It is in your mouth and in your heart, so that you can
keep it.

[143. Free Choice]

¹⁵ See! Today I have set before you [a free choice] between life and good
[on one side], and death and evil [on the other].

¹⁶ I have commanded you today to love God your Lord, to walk in His
paths, and to keep His commandments, decrees and laws. You will then survive and flourish, and God your Lord will bless you in the land that you are
about to occupy.

¹⁷ But if your heart turns aside and you do not listen, you will be led astray
to bow down to foreign gods and worship them. ¹⁸ I am warning you today,
that [if you do that] you will be utterly exterminated. You will not last very
long in the land which you are crossing the Jordan and coming to occupy.

¹⁹ I call heaven and earth as witnesses!* Before you I have placed life and
death, the blessing and the curse. You must choose life, so that you and your
descendants will survive.

²⁰ [You must thus make the choice] to love God your Lord, to obey Him,
and to attach yourself to Him. This* is your sole means of survival and long
life when you dwell in the land that God swore to your fathers, Abraham,
Isaac and Jacob, [promising] that He would give it to them.

VaYelekh   וַיֵּלֶךְ

[144. Preparation for New Leadership]

31   ¹ Moses went* and spoke the following words to all Israel, ² saying to
them:

Today I am 120 years old* and I can no longer come and go.* God has
[also]* told me that I would not cross the Jordan.

30:19 **heaven and earth** . . . See 32:1.
30:20 **This** (Septuagint). Or, "He (God)" (Ibn Ezra).
31:1   **went.** To each tribe (Ibn Ezra), to each individual tent, to the Israelite camp (Ramban; Malbim), to the
study hall (*Targum Yonathan*; see Exodus 33:7), from the Communion Tent (Chizzkuni). Or, Moses went
to the Israelites instead of assembling them to him as usual (Hirsch). Or, "Moses took the initiative"
(Sforno), or, "Moses finished speaking" (Septuagint).
31:2   **Today I am 120 years old.** This was actually Moses' 120th birthday, and it was the day he died; see below
34:7 (*Sotah* 13b).
—   **come and go.** Literally, "go out and come." See Numbers 27:17. Some say that this denotes leadership
in Torah learning (*Sotah* 13b; Ramban) or in war (Ibn Ezra).
—   **also** (*Baaley Tosafoth*; cf. Ramban). Or, "[because] God told me . . ." (Rashi).

³ God your Lord will be the One who will go across before you. It is He 31
who will destroy these nations before you, so that you will expel them. Joshua
will be the one who will lead you across, as God has promised.

⁴ God will do the same to [these nations] that He did to the Amorite kings,
Sichon and Og.* [As you know,] He annihilated them and their land. ⁵ When
God gives you power over [these nations], you must do to them everything
required by this mandate* that I have prescribed to you.

⁶ Be strong and brave.* Do not be afraid or feel insecure before them. God
your Lord is the One who is going with you, and He will not fail you or forsake you.

[145. Joshua; The Torah]

⁷ Moses summoned Joshua, and in the presence of all Israel, said to him,
"Be strong and brave, since you will be the one to bring this nation to the land
that God swore to their fathers that He would give it to them. You will be the
one to parcel it out to them. ⁸ But God will be the One who will go before
you, and He will be with you. He will never forsake you or abandon you, so
do not be afraid and do not let your spirit be broken.*"

⁹ Moses then wrote down this Torah.* He gave it to Levi's descendants, the
priests in charge of* the ark of God's covenant, and to the elders of Israel.

¹⁰ Moses then gave them the following commandment:

"At the end of each seven years, at a fixed time on the festival of Sukkoth,*
after* the year of release,* ¹¹ when all Israel comes to present themselves
before God your Lord, in the place that He will choose,* you must read*
[from] this Torah* before all Israel, so that they will be able to hear it.

31:4 **Sichon ... Og.** See Numbers 21:21-24, 33-35.
31:5 **by this mandate.** See above 20:10-18 (Chizzkuni).
31:6 **strong and brave** (cf. *Adereth Eliahu*; *HaKethav VeHaKabbalah*).
31:8 **let your spirit be broken** (cf. *Targum*).
31:9 **Moses then wrote ...** Up to 31:13 (Ramban; Abarbanel). See 31:24. Other sources, however, indicate
    that he wrote the entire Torah (*Lekach Tov*).
— **in charge of** (Chizzkuni). Literally, "who carry." Some say that this indicates their initial packing of the
    ark as outlined in Numbers 4:5. Others say that this alludes to the fact that the priests would carry the
    ark across the Jordan (Joshua 3:13,17; Chizzkuni).
31:10 **Sukkoth.** Some say that it was read on the second day of Sukkoth (the first intermediate day) (*Minchath
    Chinukh* 612); while others maintain that it was read at night, on the eve of the second day (*Tifereth Yis-
    rael, Sotah* 7:48). (See *Sotah* 41a; *Yad, Chagigah* 3:3).
— **after.** That is, at the beginning of the first year of the Sabbatical Cycle (*Sotah* 41a; *Yad, Chagigah* 3:1). See
    Exodus 23:16.
— **release.** *Shemitah* in Hebrew; see above, 15:1.
31:11 **place that He will choose.** Jerusalem; see above, 12:5.
— **you must read.** A wooden platform was erected and the king would read the sections (*Sotah* 41a).
— **from this Torah.** According to tradition, the reading was Deuteronomy 1:1-6:9, 11:13-21, 14:22-28:69
    (*Yad, Chagigah* 3:3; *Lechem Mishneh ad loc.*; *Tosafoth Yom Tov, Sotah* 7:8). Others say that it was Deuteron-
    omy 1:1-6:9, 11:13-21, 14:22-27, 26:12-15, 27:11-28:69, 17:14-20. In most editions of the Talmud,

31   ¹² "You must gather together the people, the men, women, children and proselytes* from your settlements, and let them hear it. They will thus learn to be in awe of God your Lord, carefully keeping all the words of this Torah. ¹³ Their children, who do not know, will listen and learn to be in awe of God your Lord, as long as you live in the land which you are crossing the Jordan to occupy."

[146. Final Preparations]

¹⁴ God said to Moses, "The time is coming for you to die. Summon Joshua and let him stand in meditation* in the Communion Tent, where I shall give him orders.*"

Moses and Joshua went, and they stood in meditation in the Communion Tent. ¹⁵ God appeared in the Tent in* a pillar of cloud. The pillar of cloud stood at the Tent entrance.

¹⁶ God said to Moses, "When you go and lie with your ancestors, this nation shall rise up and stray after the alien gods of the land* into which they are coming. They will thus abandon Me and violate the covenant that I have made with them. ¹⁷ I will then display anger against them and abandon them. I will hide My face from them* and they will be [their enemies'] prey.*

"Beset by many evils and troubles, they will say, 'It is because my God is no longer with me that these evils have befallen us.' ¹⁸ On that day I will utterly hide My face because of all the evil that they have done in turning to alien gods.

¹⁹ "Now write* for yourselves this song* and teach it to the Israelites.

---

however, the order is, Deuteronomy 1:1-6:9, 11:13-21, 14:22-27, 26:12-15, 17:14-20, 27:11-28:68.
31:12 proselytes (*Lekach Tov*)
31:14 stand in meditation (see *Mekhilta* on Exodus 14:13)
— **give him orders** (Ramban). Or, "appoint him" (Saadia), or "give him encouragement" (Rashi).
31:15 in (Ramban). Or, "near" (Ibn Ezra).
31:16 alien gods of the land (Ramban; Septuagint). Or, "gods of the aliens of the land" (Targum; Rashi).
31:17 hide My face . . . Taking away providence and divine protection (*Moreh Nevukhim* 1:23, 3:51; Ralbag). Or, as a sign of love, as if God cannot bear to see Israel being punished (*Baaley Tosafoth*; Chizzkuni; *Paaneach Razah*).
— **their enemies' prey** (Ibn Ezra). Or, "devoured" (Septuagint); "despoiled" (*Targum Yonathan*); or, "destroyed" (Ralbag).
31:19 write. The commandment was to Moses and Joshua together, so as to initiate Joshua (Ramban; cf. *Sotah* 13b).
— **this song.** The song known as *HaAzinu*, below, 32:1-43 (Rashi; Ramban). Others say that it denotes the entire Torah (Ralbag), possibly because the special Torah that Moses wrote contained vowel points and cantellation (cf. *Tzafenath Paaneach*). From this verse is derived the commandment for each Jew to write (or have written for him) a Torah scroll (*Sanhedrin* 21b; *Yad, Sefer Torah* 7:2). Some say that this is because with the writing of the song of *HaAzinu*, the Torah was completed; see 31:24 (*Torah Temimah*).

Make them memorize it,* so that this song will be a witness for the Israelites.   31

²⁰ "When I bring them to the land flowing with milk and honey that I promised their ancestors, they will eat, be satisfied, and live in luxury. They will then turn to foreign gods and worship them, despising Me and violating My covenant. ²¹ When they are then beset by many evils and troubles, this song shall testify for them like a witness, since it will not be forgotten by their descendants. I know their inclinations through what they are doing right now, even before I have brought them to the promised land."

²² On that day, Moses wrote down this song, and he taught it to the Israelites.

²³ [God also]* gave Joshua orders, saying, "Be strong and brave, since you will bring the Israelites to the land that I promised them, and I will be with you."

²⁴ Moses finished writing the words of this Torah in a scroll* to the very end.* ²⁵ Moses then gave orders to the Levites who carried the Ark of God's covenant, saying, ²⁶ "Take this Torah scroll and place it to the side* of the ark of God your Lord's covenant, leaving it there as a witness. ²⁷ I am aware of your rebellious spirit and your stubbornness. Even while I am here alive with you, you are rebelling against God. What will you do after I am dead?

²⁸ "Gather* to me all the elders of your tribes and your law enforcers, and I will proclaim these words to them. I will bring heaven and earth as witnesses for them. ²⁹ I know that after I die, you will become corrupt and turn away from the path that I have prescribed to you. You will eventually* be beset with evil, since you will have done evil in God's eyes, angering Him with the work of your hands."

³⁰ Moses then proclaimed the words of this song to the entire assembly of Israel until it was completed.

—   **Make them memorize it** (cf. *Eruvin* 54b; Ibn Ezra). Literally, "place it in their mouth." See Numbers 23:5.
31:23 **God** . . . (Saadia; Rashi; Ramban). Cf. 31:14. Or, "[Moses] gave Joshua orders [in God's name], saying . . ." (Ibn Ezra on 31:15).
31:24 **scroll.** Or, "book."
—   **to the very end.** Completing the Torah from 31:14 until the end (Sforno). Some say that the section from 32:44 had already been written, and with the song *HaAzinu* the Torah was completed (Ibn Ezra on 31:1; Ramban; see note on 31:19). In the Talmud there is a question as to whether Moses or Joshua wrote 34:5-12 which describes Moses' death (*Bava Bathra* 15a).
31:26 **to the side.** On a shelf attached to the ark (*Bava Bathra* 14b; Rashi). Others say that it was inside the ark, to the side of the tablets (*Bava Bathra* 14a). According to the first opinion, the Torah was later placed on the chest of gold sent by the Philistines, which was placed near the ark (*Ibid.*; see 1 Samuel 6:8).
31:28 **Gather** . . . Personally, without using the trumpets, as in Numbers 10:3 (Rashi; *Tanchuma, Vayechi* 2).
31:29 **eventually.** Literally, "in the end of days;" see Genesis 49:1, 4:3.

HaAzinu   הַאֲזִינוּ

[147. Moses' Song]

32 ¹ Listen heaven!* I will speak! Earth! Hear the words of my mouth!

² My lesson* shall* drop* like rain, my saying shall flow down like the dew—like a downpour* on the herb, like a shower* on the grass. ³ When I proclaim God's name,* praise God for His greatness.

⁴ The deeds of the Mighty One* are perfect, for all His ways are just. He is a faithful God,* never unfair; righteous and moral is He. ⁵ Destruction is His children's fault, not His own,* you warped* and twisted generation.

⁶ Is this the way you repay God, you ungrateful,* unwise nation? Is He not your Father, your Master,* the One who made* and established* you?

32:1 **heaven.** Literally, (Ibn Ezra; Ramban). Or, "angels in heaven" (Saadia); or, "the soul" (*Paaneach Razah*; cf. *Sanhedrin* 91a).

32:2 **lesson.** *Lekach* in Hebrew. Wise teaching (Ibn Janach), or, in particular, "oral teaching" (cf. Radak, *Sherashim*). Some say from the root *lakach*, "to take," since it is taken from on high (Bachya), is taken up by the student (Hirsch), or brings the soul to good (Ralbag; Abarbanel).

— **shall . . .** Or, "May my lesson drop as rain . . ." (both in Chizzkuni).

— **drop** (Ibn Ezra). *Araf* in Hebrew, possibly related to *oref,* the back of the neck, or *araf,* to decapitate (cf. Exodus 13:13). Variously translated as, "flow down" (Saadia; Rashi; Radak, *Sherashim*; Ibn Janach); "be pleasant" (Targum), "be sought as" (Septuagint), "be gathered" (*Sifri*), "penetrate" (Hirsch); "strike" (*Targum Yonathan; Sifri; Taanith* 7a; Malbim); "strike its target" (*Midrash HaGadol*); or, "strike from behind" (*Sifri*; Chizzkuni).

— **downpour.** Or, "rainstorm" (Targum; Rashi; Bachya). Or, "mist" (Ibn Ezra; Ibn Janach; Radak, *Sherashim*). *Se'irim* in Hebrew.

— **shower** (Rashi). *Revivim* in Hebrew. Or, "heavy rains" (Ibn Ezra; Ibn Janach; Radak, *Sherashim*); "late rains" (Targum; cf. 11:14); or, "snow" (Septuagint).

32:3 **God's name.** Or, "God's teaching" (*HaKethav VeHaKabbalah*; cf. *Berakhoth* 21a).

32:4 **Mighty One.** (*Targum; Sifri;* Ibn Ezra; Bachya). *Tzur* in Hebrew, usually denoting "rock," or "bedrock." The Septuagint simply translates it as "God" (cf. *Berakhoth* 5b). Some see this as indicating that God is permanent like a rock (Ibn Ezra). Others see it denoting that God is the bedrock of our existence (*Moreh Nevukhim* 1:16). Others see the word *tzur* as coming from *yatzar*, "to form," denoting that God is the creator (*Sifri*). Or, from *tzayar*, "to draw," that He is the divine artist (*Berakhoth* 10a). Or, from *tzarar*, "to bind together," indicating that He is the unifying force in the universe, and the one to whom all are bound (*HaKethav VeHaKabbalah*).

— **faithful God.** Or, "true Omnipotent One" (Ibn Ezra).

32:5 **Destruction is . . .** (Ralbag; Malbim; *HaKethav VeHaKabbalah*). Literally, "Destruction to Him no His children their defect." Or, "They have hurt themselves, not Him, faulted children" (Targum); "The defect of His non-children is that they have been corrupt to Him" (Ibn Ezra; Ramban; Sforno); "They were corrupt to Him, not [like] children; this is the defect of the warped and twisted generation" (Saadia; cf. *Lekach Tov*); "They have been corrupt, not Him, it is His children's defect" (Ralbag); "The ones who have corrupted His [name] are not His children because of their defect" (Abarbanel); "Is destruction His? No! It is the fault of His children" (*Moreh Nevukhim* 3:12; Chizzkuni); "Have they corrupted Him? No. It is [merely] their own defect" (Abarbanel); "He destroyed His non-children, but it was their own fault" (Chizzkuni); "Their defect has corrupted it so that they are no longer His children" (Hirsch); or, "They were corrupt, not [pleasing] Him, defective children" (Septuagint).

— **you warped.** Or, "a warped."

32:6 **ungrateful** (Rashi; Ramban on 32:15; Abarbanel). *Nabhal* in Hebrew. Or, "foolish" (*Targum Yonathan*; Septuagint); "degraded" (Radak, *Sherashim*); or, "non-believing" (Abarbanel).

— **Master.** *Koneh* in Hebrew; (see Genesis 14:19). "The One who made us His" (Abarbanel). Or, "the one who rectified us" (Chizzkuni).

⁷ Remember days long gone by. Ponder the years of each generation. Ask   32
your father and let him tell you, and your grandfather, who will explain it.

⁸ When the Most High gave nations their heritage and split up the sons of
man,* He set up the borders of nations to parallel the number* of Israel's
descendants. ⁹ But His own nation remained God's portion; Jacob was the
lot* of His heritage.

¹⁰ He brought them into being* in a desert region, in a desolate, howling*
wasteland.* He encompassed* them and granted them wisdom, protecting
them like the pupil of His eye. ¹¹ Like an eagle arousing its nest, hovering over
its young, He* spread His wings and took them, carrying them on His
pinions. ¹² God alone guided* them; there was no alien power with Him.

¹³ He carried* them over the earth's highest places, to feast on the crops of
the field.* He let them suckle honey from the bedrock, oil from the flinty*
cliff. ¹⁴ [They had] the cheese* of cattle, milk of sheep, fat of lambs,* rams of
the Bashan,* and luscious* fat wheat. They drank the blood of grapes for
wine.

¹⁵ Jeshurun* thus became fat and rebelled. You grew fat, thick and gross.*
[The nation] abandoned the God who made it, and spurned* the Mighty One

—   **made.** By teaching you the Torah (Ralbag; Abarbanel; cf. Genesis 12:5).
—   **established you.** With a land (Abarbanel).
32:8   **man.** (Targum). Or, "Adam" (Septuagint). Referring to the Tower of Babel (Genesis 11).
—   **the number.** Seventy nations (note on Genesis 10:32), paralleling the seventy individuals who went to
          Egypt with Jacob (Genesis 46:27; *Targum Yonathan*; Rashi).
32:9   **lot** (*Sifri*). *Chevel* in Hebrew. Or, "group" (*HaKethav VeHaKabbalah*; cf. *Sifri*; Rashi); "portion" (Chizz-
          kuni); "line" (Septuagint), or, "rope" (cf. Rashi).
32:10   **brought them into being** (Malbim). Or, "found them," or, "sustained them" (Targum). Or, "They
          found Him" (Ralbag).
—   **howling** (*Targum Yonathan*; Rashi; Ibn Ezra; Radak, *Sherashim*). *Yelel* in Hebrew. Or, "parched" (Targum;
          Septuagint).
—   **wasteland.** *Yeshimon.* See Numbers 21:19.
—   **encompassed them.** Or, "led them around" (Ralbag).
32:11   **He . . .** (Sifri). See Exodus 19:4. Or, "spreading its wings . . ." (Ibn Ezra; Septuagint).
32:12   **guided.** Or, "led" (Rashi; Septuagint). Or, "gave them rest" (Chizzkuni; cf. Ibn Ezra).
32:13   **carried.** Literally, "made them ride."
—   **field** (*Targum Yonathan*; Rashi; Septuagint). *Sadai* in Hebrew. Or, "their spoilers" (Targum).
—   **flinty.** *Chalamish* in Hebrew. See above 8:15.
32:14   **cheese.** *Chemah* in Hebrew. See Genesis 18:8. Or, "meat" (Ibn Ezra).
—   **fat of . . .** Or, "the best parts of" (see Leviticus 3:9).
—   **Bashan.** The best place for livestock; see Numbers 32:4.
—   **luscious** (Chizzkuni). *Kilyoth* in Hebrew. Or, "fat kidneys of wheat" (*Ketuvoth* 111b; Septuagint).
32:15   **Jeshurun.** "The one who sees" (Ibn Ezra; Bachya; Sforno). Or, "the upright one" (Ibn Ezra; Abarbanel;
          Hirsch), or, "the beloved one" (Septuagint). A poetic name for Israel.
—   **gross** (Saadia; Radak, *Sherashim*). *Kasah* in Hebrew. Or, "covered with fat" (Rashi; Ibn Ezra), or,
          "broad" (Septuagint).
—   **spurned** (Rashi). *Nabhal* in Hebrew. Or, "profaned" (Ibn Ezra); "ignored" (Ralbag); or, "was ungrateful
          to" (Ramban). See 32:6.

32   who was its support. [16] They provoked His jealousy with alien practices; made
Him angry with vile deeds.*
      [17] They sacrificed to demons who were non-gods, deities they never knew.
These were new things, recently arrived, which their fathers would never consider.* [18] You thus ignored the Mighty One who bore you; forgot the Power
who delivered you.*
      [19] When God saw this, He was offended,* provoked by His sons and
daughters. [20] He said:
      I will hide My face from them,* and see what will be their end.* They are a
generation which reverses itself* and cannot be trusted.* [21] They have been
faithless* to Me with a non-god,* angering Me with their meaningless acts.
Now I will be unfaithful to them with a non-nation,* provoking them with a
nation devoid of gratitude.*
      [22] My anger has kindled a fire, burning to the lowest depths. It shall con-
sume the land and its crops, setting fire to the foundations of mountains. [23] I
will heap* evil upon them, striking* them with My arrows. [24] [They will be]*
bloated* by famine, consumed* by fever,* cut down* by bitter plague.* I will

---

32:16 **vile deeds** (Sifri; Rashi). Or, "idolatry" (Ibn Ezra).
32:17 **consider** (Saadia; Ibn Janach; *Paaneach Razah*). *Sa'ar* in Hebrew. Or, "dread" (*Sifri*; Ibn Ezra; Hirsch);
       "worship" (Radak, *Sherashim*); "be involved with" (Targum); "appraise" (*Lekach Tov*); "imagine" (Ral-
       bag); "even grasp by a hair" (Ralbag); or, "knew" (Septuagint).
32:18 **delivered you** (Rashi). *Chalal* in Hebrew. Or, "gave birth to" (Ibn Ezra; Chizzkuni); "began" or "made"
       (*Targum*; Ralbag); "suffered for you" (*Sifri*); "placed His name on you" (*Sifri*); "forgives your sins"
       (*Sifri*); who made you dance" (Chizzkuni); "who fed you" (Septuagint); or, "who is still forming you"
       (*Targum Yonathan*; Hirsch).
32:19 **offended.** *Na'atz.* Angry (*Targum*). Or, "disgusted with them"(*Adereth Eliahu*; *HaKethav VeHaKabbalah*; cf.
       Numbers 14:11).
32:20 **hide My face** . . . See above, 31:18.
—   **and see** . . . (*Targum Yonathan*; Rashi). Or, "because I see their end" (Targum; Ibn Ezra); or, "because I
       see they have no future" (Sforno; *HaKethav VeHaKabbalah*).
—   **reverses itself** (Abarbanel; Hirsch). *Tah'pukhoth* in Hebrew. Or, "easily changed" (Radak, *Sherashim*;
       Chizzkuni); "turns the wrong way" (Ibn Ezra); or, "that seeks contradictions" (Ralbag).
—   **cannot be trusted.** Or, "has no faith" (*Sifri*). Or, "that has no one to raise them correctly" (Rashi).
32:21 **faithless.** That is, "violated My demand for exclusiveness" (see Exodus 20:5). Or, "provoked Me to
       jealousy."
—   **non-god** (Rashi). Or, "non-power" (Ibn Ezra). Or, "by [saying that I am] not [their] God" (see below).
—   **non-nation** (Rashi; Ramban). Or, "by [declaring that they] are not [My] nation" (Ibn Ezra).
—   **devoid of gratitude.** See note on 32:6.
32:23 **heap.** Or, "gather" (Targum; *Sifri*; Ibn Ezra; Septuagint). *Aspeh* in Hebrew. Or, "join" (Rashi), "add"
       (Saadia); "make sweep down" (Ibn Ezra); "send destruction through" (Radak, *Sherashim*; Ralbag), or,
       "use up" (Rashi; *Sifethey Chakhamim*; Ibn Janach).
—   **striking** (Targum; Septuagint). *Kalah* in Hebrew. Or, "using up" (Rashi; Hirsch), or, "scattering"
       (Saadia).
32:24 **They will be** . . . Or, "I will send against them, bloating famine . . ."
—   **bloated** (Targum). *Mezey* in Hebrew. Or, "burned," or "consumed" (Saadia; Ibn Ezra; Radak, *Sherashim*;
       Septuagint); "melted away" (Ralbag; cf. *Chullin* 45b); "feverish from" (Abarbanel); or, "cast about"
       (*Lekach Tov*).
—   **consumed.** Or, "eaten" (Targum; Ibn Janach; Chizzkuni). *Lechum* in Hebrew, possibly from *lechem*,
       bread; *lacham* to battle; or *chum*, heat. Or, "attacked" (Rashi), "fever" (Saadia), or, "flesh" (Ralbag).

send against them fanged beasts, with venomous* creatures who crawl* in the 32 dust. ²⁵ Outside, the sword shall butcher boys, girls, infants, white-headed elders, while inside, there shall be terror.

²⁶ I was prepared* to exterminate them,* to make their memory vanish from among mankind. ²⁷ But I was concerned* that their enemies would be provoked, and their attackers alienated,* so that they would say, "Our superior power* and not God, was what caused all this."

²⁸ But they* are a nation who destroys* good advice, and they themselves have no understanding. ²⁹ If they were wise, they would contemplate this, and understand what their end will be. ³⁰ How could one [man] pursue a thousand,* or two [men], ten thousand, if their Mighty One had not given them over,* and God had not trapped* them? ³¹ Their powers* are not like our Mighty One, although our enemies sit in judgment.*

— **fever** (Saadia; Radak, *Sherashim*; Ralbag). *Reshef* in Hebrew. See Habbakuk 3:5, Job 5:7. Also see Psalms 76:4, 78:48, Song of Songs 8:6. Or, "birds" (Targum; Ibn Ezra; *Lekach Tov*; Septuagint); "demons" (*Berakhoth* 5a; Rashi); "suffering" (*Berakhoth* 5a); "burning fire" (Ibn Ezra; Chizzkuni); "hot coals," "firebolts," or, "meteorites?" (*Baaley Tosafoth*; Rashbam); "arrows" (Chizzkuni).
  Hence, "consumed by fever," "with burning flesh," "eaten by birds" "stricken by firebolts," "attacked by demons."

— **cut down** (Rashi; *Baaley Tosafoth*; Ralbag). *Ketev* in Hebrew; see Isaiah 28:2, Hosea 13:14, Psalms 91:6. Or, "plague," *al-chalaf* in Arabic (Saadia; Ibn Janach; Ibn Ezra; Bachya; Radak, *Sherashim*); "destruction" (Septuagint); "crushed" (Targum).

— **bitter plague** (Saadia; Ralbag), or "bad air," possibly "malaria" (Ibn Ezra; Ralbag). *Meriri* in Hebrew. Or, "unquenchable destruction" (Septuagint); "robbers" (Rashbam); "evil spirits," or, "bad vapors" (Targum); "demons" (*Sifri*; Rashi); or, "madness" (*Tzafenath Paaneach*; cf. *Sifri* on 21:18).

— **venomous.** See 32:33. Literally, "anger of," *chamath* in Hebrew. Or, "bites of" (Ibn Ezra).

— **crawl** (Rashi; Ibn Janach; Radak, *Sherashim*). *Zachal* in Hebrew. Or, "who are terrifying" (Ibn Ezra; cf. Job 32:6).

32:26 **I was prepared.** Literally, "I said that I would . . ."

— **exterminate them** (Ibn Ezra; *Baaley Tosafoth*; Abarbanel), *Pa'ah* in Hebrew, possibly from *pe'ah*, a corner. Or, "destroy their every corner (Chizzkuni); "banish them from the world" (Rashbam); "scatter them to every corner" (Ibn Ezra; Radak, *Sherashim*, Ibn Janach; Ralbag; Septuagint); "put them in a corner" (Abarbanel; Hirsch); "banish them to the ends of the earth" (Ramban); "rid Myself of them" (Rashi); "let out My anger against them" (Targum; Malbim); "be exacting" (Saadia); "take away their Divine Spirit" (*Targum Yonathan*); or, "Where are they" (*Sifri*).

32:27 **concerned** (Saadia; Ibn Ezra; *Baaley Tosafoth*; Radak, *Sherashim*; Ralbag; Sforno). *Agur* in Hebrew. Or, "gathering," making the sentence, "Except that the enraged enemy might form a gathering" (Targum; *Sifri*; Rashi; Abarbanel); or, "might be annoyed" (Hirsch), or, "might live long" (Septuagint).

— **alienated** (*Sifri*; Ibn Ezra). *Ye-nakru* in Hebrew. Or, "deny the truth" (Saadia; Radak, *Sherashim*); "misunderstand it" (Hirsch); or, "combine against them" (Septuagint).

— **power.** Literally, "hand." (Septuagint). Or, "Our power is superior. It was not God . . ." (Targum).

32:28 **they.** The gentile nations (Rabbi Nechemiah in *Sifri*; Rashi; Rashbam; Ibn Ezra; Chizzkuni; Bachya). Or, the Israelites (Rabbi Yehudah in *Sifri*).

— **destroys** (cf. *HaKethav VeHaKabbalah*). Or, "lost."

32:30 **one man pursue** . . . See Leviticus 26:8.

— **given them over.** (Rashi; Saadia). Or, "sold them" (Septuagint). "Them" can refer to Israelites or gentiles; see note on 32:28.

— **trapped.** Literally, "closed them in."

32:31 **powers.** *Tzur* in Hebrew. Literally, "their 'mighty one.'" That is, "their god."

— **even though** . . . (Targum; Rashi). Or, "Their god is not like our Mighty One, as even our enemies admit (Ibn Ezra), or, more literally, "even in our enemy's own judgment" (Hirsch). Or, "but our enemies will

32

³² But their* vine is from the vine of Sodom and the shoot* of Gomorrah. Their grapes are poison* grapes; their grape cluster is bitterness to them. ³³ Their vine is serpents' venom,* like the poison* of the dreadful* cobra.*

³⁴ But it* is concealed with Me for the future,* sealed up in My treasury. ³⁵ I have vengeance and retribution, waiting for their foot to slip. Their day of disaster is near, and their time is about to come. ³⁶ God will then take up the cause* of His people, and comfort* His servants. He will have seen that their power is gone,* with nothing left to keep or abandon.*

³⁷ [God] will then say*: Where is their god, the power in which they trusted? ³⁸ [Where are the gods] who ate* the fat of their sacrifices and drank the wine of their libations? Let them now get up and help you! Let them be your protector!

³⁹ But now see! It is I! I am the [only] One! There are no [other] gods with Me! I kill and give life! If I crushed, I will heal! But there is no protection from My power!

⁴⁰ I lift My hand to heaven* and say: I am Life forever.* ⁴¹ I will whet My

---

not admit it" (Saadia; Septuagint). Or, "Although their god is not like ours, our enemies judge us" (Chizzkuni); "Their god is not like ours, and not fit to be our judge" (Bachya); or, "When our enemies judge us, [it seems that] our God is not like theirs" (Bachya).

32:32 their. The gentiles' or Israel's (see note on 32:28). Or, "Is [Israel's] . . . then . . .?" (Chizzkuni).

— **shoot.** Or, "vine branch" (Saadia; Radak, *Sherashim*; Ibn Janach; Septuagint). *Shedemah* in Hebrew; see Isaiah 16:8, Habakkuk 3:16. Or, "field" (Rashi; cf. Radak, *Sherashim*). Or, "stream" (cf. Targum on 2 Kings 23:4, Jeremiah 31:40).

— **poison.** *Rosh* in Hebrew; see note on 29:17. Or, "gall" (Septuagint), or, "bitter herb" (Rashi).

32:33 venom. *Chamath.* See 32:23.

— **poison.** *Rosh.* See 32:32.

— **dreadful** (cf. Ibn Ezra). *Akhzar* in Hebrew. Or, "sadistic" (Rashi); or, "rage" (Septuagint).

— **cobra.** *Pethen* in Hebrew; cf. Isaiah 11:8, Psalms 48:8, a venomous snake (Ibn Janach; Radak, *Sherashim*), possibly an asp (Septuagint) or cobra. *Pethen* may be cognate to the Greek *Python*, a huge mythical snake.

32:34 it. The deeds of man (Targum); their sins (Malbim); their pride (Rashbam), what they did to Israel (Abarbanel), their punishment (*Baaley Tosafoth*), their poison (Ibn Ezra; Ramban), the day of reckoning (Chizzkuni), the Messianic age (Abarbanel).

— **for the future** (*HaKethav VeHaKabbalah*). Or, "Is it not stored up with Me . . ."

32:36 take up the cause (cf. Ibn Ezra). Or, "judge."

— **comfort** (cf. Septuagint). *Hith-nachem.* Or, "reconcile Himself" (Rashi), or, "regret what He has done" (Radak, *Sherashim*).

— **their power is gone** (Sifri; Ibn Ezra; Ralbag). Or, "their hand is paralyzed" (Septuagint). Or, "[the enemy's] power grows" (Targum; Rashi).

— **nothing to keep or abandon** (Radak, *Sherashim*; Ralbag; Abarbanel; Hirsch). *Atzur* and *azuv* in Hebrew. Or, "no protection or help" (Rashi); "no leader or helper" (Abarbanel), "none left to set free or take captive" (Ibn Ezra), "no inhabited or abandoned [city]" (Ibn Janach), "wiped out because of captivity and abandonment" (Saadia), or, "failed in invasion" (Septuagint).

32:37 God will then say . . . regarding the gentile enemies (Rashi; Septuagint). Or, to Israel (Ralbag). Or, Israel will say of the gentiles (Rabbi Yehudah in *Sifri*). Or, the gentiles will say to Israel, "where is their God . . ." (Rabbi Nechemiah in *Sifri*; *Targum Yonathan*; Saadia; Ibn Ezra; Ramban).

32:38 the gods who ate . . . Or, "Their worshipers ate . . ." (Ralbag).

32:40 lift My hand . . . See Genesis 14:22.

— **I am life forever** (Ramban; Abarbanel; cf. *Yad, Yesodey HaTorah* 2:10). Or, "as I live forever" (Ibn Ezra).

lightning sword* and grasp judgment in My hand. I will bring vengeance   32
against My foes, and repay those who hated Me. ⁴² I will make My arrows
drunk with blood, My sword consuming flesh. The enemy's first punishment*
will be the blood of the slain and wounded.*

⁴³ Let the tribes of His nation* sing praise,* for He will avenge His servants' blood. He will bring vengeance upon His foes, and reconcile* His
people [to] His land.*

[148. Presenting the Song]

⁴⁴ Moses came and proclaimed all the words of this song* to the people,
along with Hoshea* son of Nun.

⁴⁵ When Moses had finished speaking all these words to all Israel, ⁴⁶ he
said to them, "Pay close attention to all the words through which I warn* you
today, so that you will be able to instruct your children to keep all the words
of this Torah carefully. ⁴⁷ It is not an empty teaching for you. It is your life,
and with it you will long endure on the land which you are crossing the
Jordan to occupy."

[149. Moses Told to Die]

⁴⁸ On that very day,* God spoke to Moses, saying:

32:41 **lightning sword** (*Targum Yonathan*; Saadia). Or, "my sword like lightning" (Septuagint; cf. Targum); or,
"with lightning" (Bachya); or, "the blade of My sword" (Rashi; Ralbag).

32:42 **The enemy's first punishment** (*Targum Yonathan*; Rashi; Radak, *Sherashim*). Literally, "from head *par'oth*
enemy," where *par'oth* can denote punishment, long hair, or be related to Pharaoh. Thus, alternatively,
"of the heads of the enemies who rule over them" (Septuagint); "from the locks on the head of the
enemy" (Hirsch); or, "from the heads of the most bitter enemy" (Saadia; cf. Targum).

— **wounded** (Ibn Ezra). Or, "captive."

32:43 **tribes of His nation** (Radak, *Sherashim*; Chizzkuni). Or, "Let the nations sing praise to His people."

— **sing praise** (Targum; *Sifri*; Rashi; Rashbam; Ibn Ezra). *Harnin* in Hebrew. Or, "make His people
rejoice" (Ibn Janach, "rejoice with His people" (Septuagint); or, "announce" (Ibn Ezra); or, "wail in
regret" (Chizzkuni).

— **reconcile** (Chizzkuni; cf. Genesis 32:21). *Kapper* in Hebrew. Or, "atone for" (Targum; Ibn Ezra);
"purify" (Ibn Ezra; Ralbag); "purge" (Septuagint).

— **His people to His land** (Chizzkuni). Or, "He will atone for His land [and] His people" (Targum; Saadia;
Ibn Ezra); "His Land will atone for His people" (*Sifri*; *Kethuvoth* 111a; Ibn Ezra); "His people will atone
for all His world" (Hirsch); "He will purify His people's land" (Ralbag); "He will purge His land of His
people" (Septuagint).

32:44 **and proclaimed . . .** Some say that Moses proclaimed this song three times, first to those around him
(31:22); second to the elders (31:28), and third to the entire nation (31:30) (Abarbanel).

— **Hoshea.** See Numbers 13:16. He was called by the name Hoshea because he considered himself as small
as when he was sent as an explorer (*Sifri*; Bachya; Ralbag; Abarbanel); because this was his popular
name among the people (Ibn Ezra); because he was now a leader in his own right (Chizzkuni; *Paaneach
Razah*); since he is now being compared to Moses (*Or HaChaim*), or, because the generation of the spies
was now dead (*Kley Yekar*).

32:45 **warn.** See Exodus 19:21. Literally, "bear witness."

32:48 **that very day.** When the song was proclaimed (Ibn Ezra). Or, "at midday" (*Sifri*; Rashi); see Genesis
7:11.

32   49 Climb the Avarim Mountain* here to Mount Nebo,* in the land of
Moab facing Jericho,* and see the land of Canaan that I am giving the Israelites as a holding. 50 Die* on the mountain that you are climbing, and be
gathered up to your people, just as your brother Aaron died on Hor Mountain* and was gathered to his people.

      51 This is because you broke faith with me in the midst of the Israelites at
the Waters of Dispute* at Kadesh in the Tzin Desert, and because you did not
sanctify Me among the Israelites. 52 You will therefore see the land from afar,*
but you will not come there to the land I am giving the Israelites.

      VeZoth HaBerakhah   וְזֹאת הַבְּרָכָה

                  [150. Blessing of the Tribes; Reuben]

33   1 This is the blessing* that Moses, man of God,* bestowed on the Israelites
just* before his death. 2 He said:
      God came* from Sinai,* shone forth* to them from Seir,* and made an
appearance from Mount Paran.* From the holy myriads, He brought* the fire
of a religion* to them from His right Hand.

32:49 **Avarim Mountains.** See Numbers 27:12 (Abarbanel). Also see Numbers 33:47,48.
—   **Mount Nebo.** See Numbers 32:38, 33:47.
—   **facing Jericho.** The mountain was across the Jordan from Jericho.
32:50 **Die.** (Bachya; *Adereth Eliahu; HaKethav VeHaKabbalah*). Or, "prepare to die" (Ibn Ezra).
—   **Aaron died on Hor Mountain.** See Numbers 20:22-28, 33:38.
32:51 **Waters of Dispute.** See Numbers 20:13.
32:52 **afar** (Rashi). Or, "before you" (Septuagint).
33:1   **This is the blessing** . . . See Genesis 49:1-27.
—   **man of God.** See Psalms 90:1. Also see 1 Samuel 2:27, 9:6, 1 Kings 12:22, 13:1, 2 Kings 1:13, 4:9,
       Nehemiah 12:24, 2 Chronicles 25:7 (cf. *Sifri; Midrash HaGadol*). This indicates that the blessing is from
       God (*Paaneach Razah*) and would be fulfilled (Ramban). Or, "prophet of God" (Targum; Ibn Ezra;
       Ralbag), or, "messenger of God" (Saadia).
—   **just.** (*Sifri;* Ibn Ezra).
33:2   **came.** Or, "revealed Himself" (Targum; Saadia).
—   **from Sinai.** (Ibn Ezra; Bachya).
—   **shone forth** (Targum). *Zarach.* Or, "appeared" (Septuagint; possibly as in *ezrach*).
—   **Seir.** The territory of Esau (Genesis 14:6, 32:4, 36:8). See Judges 5:4. Some say that Seir is near Sinai
       (*Emunoth VeDeyoth* 3:8; Ibn Ezra; see note on Exodus 3:1). Others say that God appeared from the *direc-
       tion* of Seir (Chizzkuni; cf. *Sifri*). Another opinion is that God appeared to them again at Seir after they
       left Sinai (Ramban; Ralbag; Abarbanel). See next note. Midrashically, this teaches that God offered the
       Torah to Esau before giving it to Israel (*Sifri; Avodah Zarah* 2b; *Targum Yonathan;* Rashi).
—   **Mount Paran.** Near Seir (see Genesis 14:6). This was Ishmael's territory (Genesis 21:21). Paran was the
       Israelites first stop after Sinai (Numbers 10:12). Some say that this represents the revelation of Deuteron-
       omy; see above 1:1 (*Adereth Eliahu; Ophan Sheni; HaKethav VeHaKabbalah*). Midrashically, this indicates
       that the Torah was offered to Ishmael (see above).
—   **From the holy myriads** . . . (Ibn Ezra; Sforno; *HaKethav VeHaKabbalah*). Or, "He came from the holy
       myriads . . ." (Ramban). "He came to the holy myriads" (Ralbag); "He brought to the holy myriads"
       (Saadia); "He brought with Him myriads of holy beings" (Targum); "He brought some of His holy
       myriads" (*Sifri;* Rashi); or, "He came with the myriads of Kadesh" (Septuagint).
—   **fire of a religion** (Rashi; Ibn Ezra). *Esh dath* in Hebrew. Or, "fire become law" (Hirsch); "a law of fire"

³ Although there is love* for nations, all Your holy ones are in Your **33**
hand.* They follow* Your footsteps,* and uphold Your word.*

⁴ Moses prescribed the Torah to us, an eternal heritage* for the congregation of Jacob. ⁵ He* was king in Jeshurun* when the people's leaders
gathered* themselves together, [and] the tribes of Israel were united.

⁶ May Reuben live and not die, although his ranks are numbered.*

[151. Judah]

⁷ The same goes for Judah.* [Moses also] said, "May God hear* Judah's
voice and bring him to his people. Although his power* suffices him,* may
You* help him against his enemies."

(Ramban), or "a Torah of light" (Saadia). Some see *eshdath* as a single word, indicating a waterfall as in
Numbers 21:15, above, 3:17 (Eliahu Levitas; cf. Ibn Janach who rejects this), and hence, "from His right
hand a waterfall to them." Or, "from the fire at His right hand, a law to them" (Targum); or, "at His
right hand, His angels were with Him" (Septuagint). Or, "Although He came with the holy myriads, His
fiery law was given to them by His right hand" (Abarbanel).

33:3 love (Targum; Rashi; Radak, *Sherashim*). *Chovev* in Hebrew. Or, "bestows duty" (Hirsch), "shelters"
(Ramban; Ralbag); or, "spares" (Septuagint).

— for nations ... (*Sifri; Lekach Tov*; Rashi; Chizzkuni; Sforno). Or, "Although beloved by nations, ..."
(*Targum Yonathan*; Chizzkuni); "Although He loves gentiles [who become proselytes]" (Rashbam;
Paaneach Razah); "He also loves them above all nations" (*Sifri*; Bachya); "He also loves the tribes [of
Israel]" (Targum; Saadia); "Although He loves the tribes, all Your holy ones (Levi) are in Your hand"
(Ibn Ezra); "Although He shelters the tribes" (Ramban; Ralbag); "He spared His people, [and] all His
holy ones are in His hands" (Septuagint); or, "Also to take nations to duty, you take all Your holy ones
in Your hand" (Hirsch).

— follow (Saadia; Ibn Ezra; Radak, *Sherashim*). *Tuku* in Hebrew. Or, "under your feet" (Septuagint; cf.
Exodus 24:10); gather (Targum; Rashi); "subjugated" (Malbim); "conscious of their powerlessness"
(Hirsch); or, "they are beaten for Your sake" (*Sifri*; Ramban; Chizzkuni; see next note).

— Your footsteps. Or, "Your feet," denoting Sinai (Rashi), or the clouds of glory (Targum). Or, "for Your
sake" (see Genesis 30:30; Chizzkuni). Also possibly, "your pilgrimage."

— uphold ... Or, "bear burden of" (Chizzkuni); "accepted" (Rashi); "spread" (Ibn Ezra); "speak" (Ramban; *Tur*). Or, "He received the words of the Torah that Moses ..." (Septuagint; cf. Sforno). Or, "lifted
eyes to Your word" (Rashi); "Passed on" (Saadia) or, "it bears Your word expressing itself" (Hirsch).

33:4 eternal heritage (*HaKethav VeHaKabbalah*). Or, "inheritance" (Targum; Septuagint). *Morashah* in Hebrew ·

33:5 He. (Saadia; Ibn Ezra). Or, "God" (Rashi; Ramban; Abarbanel); or, "Joshua" (Malbim). Or, "There
shall be a king ..." speaking of Saul (Ralbag). Others say that the Torah is the king (Yehudah HaLevi, in
Ibn Ezra).

— Jeshurun. See 32:15.

— gathered. See 31:28 (Ibn Ezra). Or, "When the people gather themselves together, [God] will be king in
Jeshurun" (*Baaley Tosafoth*).

33:6 although his ranks are numbered (Ralbag; cf. Ramban). Or, "may his ranks be many in number (*Tur*;
Septuagint); "may he retain his full number" (*Baaley Tosafoth; Paaneach Razah*; Abarbanel); "may he not
be few in number" (Saadia; Ibn Ezra); "may those unfit for battle be few" (Malbim); "may he be
counted with the others" (Rashi), or, "may his men have power" (*Sifri*).

33:7 The same goes for Judah (Ibn Ezra; Chizzkuni; Sforno). Or, literally, "This is for Judah" (Ramban; cf.
Saadia; Septuagint).

— hear. *Sh'ma* in Hebrew, possibly alluding to Simeon (*Shimeon*), who is omitted (*Sifri*).

— power. (Malbim). Literally, "hand."

— suffices him (Ibn Ezra; Malbim). *Rav* in Hebrew. Or, "fights" (Rashi; Ibn Ezra; Septuagint); "takes
revenge" (Targum; Saadia); "shoots [arrows]" (Ibn Ezra, from Genesis 49:23, Psalms 18:15). Or, "with
his power he fights for them" (Hirsch); or, "[You are] the power fighting for him" (Saadia; Sforno).

— You (Saadia; Septuagint). Or, "It" (his hand) (Targum; Sforno).

33

[152. Levi]

⁸ To Levi,* he said: Your Urim and Thumim* belong to Your* pious one.*
You tested him at Massah,* and contended with him at the Waters of Dispute.*

⁹ He was the one who said of his father and mother, "I do not see them,"*
not recognizing brother or child. They thus kept Your word and safeguarded
Your covenant.*

¹⁰ They shall [therefore] teach your law to Jacob, and your Torah to Israel.
They shall place incense in Your presence* and consume sacrifices on Your
altar.

¹¹ May God bless his effort* and favor the work of his hands. May He
smash the loins of those who rise up against him, so that his enemies rise no
more.*

[153. Benjamin]

¹² To Benjamin he said: God's beloved one shall dwell securely beside
Him.* [God] protects* him all day long and dwells among his slopes.*

[154. Joseph]

¹³ To Joseph he said: His land is a blessing of God, with the sweetness* of

---

33:8 **To Levi** (*Targum Yonathan*; Saadia; Ramban; Septuagint). Or, "Regarding Levi" (Rashi; Ibn Ezra).
—   **Urim and Thumim.** See Exodus 28:30.
—   **Your.** God's (Rashi; cf. Saadia). Or, Levi's (Ramban).
—   **pious one.** The tribe of Levi (Ralbag), or, Aaron (*Targum Yonathan*; Sforno).
—   **Massah.** See Exodus 17:7 (Saadia; Ramban; cf. Rashi). Or, "tests" (Targum; Ibn Ezra).
—   **Waters of Dispute.** Numbers 20:13.
33:9 **who said . . .** See Exodus 32:27-29 (*Sifri*; Rashi; Ibn Ezra). Or, abandoning family to serve God (Ibn
         Ezra), possibly relating to those outside the proper age of Levitical service (see *Targum Yonathan*; see
         Numbers 4:47). Or, if relating to the High Priest, not to defile himself for a dead relative (Leviticus
         21:11; Chizzkuni; *Paaneach Razah*).
—   **safeguarded Your covenant.** By not worshiping the Golden Calf (Exodus 32:26; Abarbanel), or by not
         worshiping idols in Egypt (*Midrash HaGadol*); by keeping circumcision in Egypt (*Yad, Issurey Biyah* 13:2;
         Bachya), and in the desert (Rashi; cf. *Sifri*). Or, covenant of the priesthood (Chizzkuni; cf. Numbers
         25:13), or the covenant of the Torah in general (Ralbag).
33:10 **in Your presence** (Targum; Saadia). Literally, "in Your nostrils." Or, "to [assuage] Your anger" (Abar-
         banel; Malbim; Septuagint; cf. Numbers 17:11).
33:11 **effort** (Septuagint). *Chayil* in Hebrew. Or, "brigade" (Saadia; Ramban); "wealth" (*Sifri*; Targum); or,
         "spirit" (Malbim).
—   **so that . . .** (Targum; Saadia; Rashi). Or, "of the enemies who rise against him" (Ibn Ezra).
33:12 **securely beside Him** (Ibn Ezra; Ramban; Chizzkuni).
—   **protects** (Targum; Rashi). *Chafaf* in Hebrew. Or, "overshadows" (Septuagint; cf. Radak, *Sherashim*); or,
         "oversees" (Chizzkuni). Or, "[Benjamin] longs for [God] all day long" (*Yoma* 12a).
—   **dwells among his slopes** (Targum; Saadia; Rashi; cf. Genesis 48:22). This may allude to the fact that the
         Holy of Holies was destined to be in Benjamin's portion (*Sifri*; *Zevachim* 54b). Or, "[Benjamin] dwells
         between His shoulders" (Septuagint), or, "boundaries" (Chizzkuni).
33:13 **sweetness** (Ramban). *Meged* in Hebrew; see Genesis 24:53, Song of Songs 4:13. Or, "best" (Radak,
         Sherashim), or, "seasons" (Septuagint).

the heaven's dew, and the waters that lie below,* [14] the sweetness of the sun's 33
yield, the sweetness of the moon's* crop,* [15] the best* of the ancient mountains, the sweetness of the eternal hills, [16] the sweetness of the land and its fullness, and the favor of the One who dwells in the thornbush.* It shall come*
upon Joseph's head, on the brow of the elect of his brothers.*

[17] His glory* is like a first-born* ox,* and his horns are the horns of the
aurochs.* With both of them he shall gore nations to the end of the earth.
They* are the myriads of Ephraim and the thousands of Manasseh.

[155. Zebulun, Issachar]

[18] To Zebulun he said: Rejoice Zebulun in your excursions,* and Issachar
in your tents.*

[19] They shall summon* nations to the mountain,* and there they shall
offer righteous sacrifice. They will be nourished by the bounty of the sea, and
by what is* hidden* in* the secret treasures of the sands.

—   **the waters . . .** See Genesis 49:25.
33:14 **moon's** (Rashi). *Yerachim* in Hebrew. Or, "of each month's crop" (Targum; Rashi; Septuagint).
—   **crop** (Septuagint). *Geresh* in Hebrew. From *garash*, meaning "to drive out," denoting what the moon
causes the earth to bring forth (Radak, *Sherashim*; Chizzkuni; cf. Ibn Ezra, from Isaiah 57:20). Or, "what
follows the moon" (Ibn Janach). Others relate it to *sheger* with a transposition of letters, denoting young
animals as in Exodus 13:12, above, 7:13 (*Paaneach Razah*).
33:15 **best.** (*Targum Yonathan*). Or, "top" (Septuagint).
33:16 **the One who dwells in the thornbush.** See Exodus 3:2-5 (Targum; *Sifri*; Rashi; Septuagint). Or, "He
who dwells in heaven" (Saadia; Ibn Ezra; cf. Targum). Or, "favor even [in areas] inhabited by thorn-
bushes (wastelands)" (*Paaneach Razah*).
—   **It shall come** (Targum; Ramban; Ralbag; Septuagint). *Tavothah* in Hebrew. Or, "Its grain" (cf. Ibn Ezra).
—   **on the brow . . .** See Genesis 49:26.
33:17 **glory** (Targum; Saadia; Ralbag; Septuagint). *Hadar* in Hebrew. Or, "given" (Rashi), or, "multitude"
(Ibn Ezra).
—   **first-born.** Or, "ruler" (Rashi).
—   **ox.** *Shor* in Hebrew. Or, "fitting" (*Targum Yonathan*). See Genesis 49:6. In general, denoting a powerful
person (cf. Ramban), or a ruler (Radak, *Sherashim*).
        Thus, "His glory is as a first-born bull" (Septuagint); "His firstling ox-like leader shall have the
glory of royalty" (Ramban); "The firstling of his bull will have glory" (Hirsch); "There will be glory to
the one who will rule his firstling bull" (Saadia); "His bull-like king is given to him" (Rashi); "the
advantage of birthright is glory to him" (*Paaneach Razah*; cf. *Targum Yonathan*); or, "His first-born ruler is
a glory to him."
—   **aurochs.** *Re'em.* See Numbers 23:22.
—   **They.** The two horns (Ramban; Chizzkuni). Or, "[Those nations] are the myriads [killed by]
Ephraim . . ." (*Targum Yonathan*; *Sifri*; Rashi; cf. 1 Samuel 18:7).
33:18 **excursions.** Doing business by the sea (Ramban; cf. Genesis 49:13). Or, to war (Ibn Ezra; Ralbag).
—   **in your tents.** Since their land is so fertile, no work is needed (*Paaneach Razah*), cf. Genesis 49:15 (Ibn
Ezra). Or in tents of study, supported by Zebulun (Rashi).
33:19 **summon.** *Kara* in Hebrew. Or, "assemble" (Saadia; Rashi).
—   **to the mountain** (*Sifri*; Sforno; cf. Targum). Or, "Nations shall assemble at your mountain" (*Targum
Yonathan*; Saadia); "Nations shall call that place a mountain (temple)" (Ralbag); or, "They shall utterly
destroy the nations and shall call men there" (Septuagint; translating *har* the same as *haras*, "destroy").
—   **and by what is . . .** Or, "and have enough to hide . . ." (Ibn Ezra; Bachya).
—   **hidden** (Ibn Ezra; Radak, *Sherashim*; Hirsch). *Safan* in Hebrew, related to *tzafan*. Or, "covered" (Ibn

33

[156. Gad]

²⁰ To Gad he said: Blessed is the one* who helps Gad expand. He dwells at peace like a dread lion,* tearing as prey the arm and head. ²¹ He saw the first portion for himself,* for that is where the portion of the lawgiver is hidden.* He* came with the first of his people, doing what is just with God, and lawful with Israel.

[157. Dan, Naphtali]

²² To Dan he said: Dan is a young lion, springing* from the Bashan.*

²³ To Naphtali he said: Naphtali shall be totally satisfied* and filled with God's blessing. He shall occupy the [land] to the southwest [of Dan].*

[158. Asher; All Israel]

²⁴ To Asher he said: Blessed among the sons* is Asher. He shall be

---

Janach). Or, "stored up" (Saadia), "markets" (Septuagint), "shipwrecked boats" (Chizzkuni; *Paaneach Razah*), from *sefinah,* a ship.

—   **in.** Or, "and" (*Sifri; Megillah* 7a). Hence, "and by what is hidden in the secret treasures of the sands" (Radak, *Sherashim;* Hirsch), "what is hidden and the secret treasures . . ." (*Sifri; Megillah* 7a); "they will assemble treasuries of what is hidden in the sand" (Saadia); "They will have to hide their wealth [and] conceal it in the sand" (Ibn Ezra), "and from the shipwrecked boats hidden in the sand (Chizzkuni); or, "and from the markets of those who dwell by the sea coast" (Septuagint).

33:20   **the one** (*Paaneach Razah*). Or, "Blessed is [God] who . . . (Hirsch).

—   **dread lion.** *Labhi* in Hebrew. See Genesis 49:9.

33:21   **He saw the first portion for himself** (Rashi; Ibn Ezra; *Baaley Tosafoth*). Or, "He took the first portion . . ." (Targum), or, "He saw himself as the first one" (Hirsch); or, "When he saw at the beginning of his land . . ." (Saadia), or, "He saw his first fruits" (Septuagint).

—   **for that is where . . .** Some say that this indicates that Moses was buried in Gad's territory (Targum; Rashi). Or, "that is where the lawgiver's treasures were" (*Targum Yonathan;* cf. 33:19). Or, "that is where the palaces of the mighty were" (Ibn Ezra); or, "there are the lands of the princes" (*Paaneach Razah;* cf. Septuagint).

—   **He.** Gad (Rashi; Ibn Ezra; *Baaley Tosafoth*). Or, Moses (Rashi; *Sotah* 13b; *Avoth* 5:18).

33:22   **springing** (Ibn Ezra; Radak, *Sherashim;* Septuagint). *Zanak* in Hebrew. Or, "drawing water" (Targum); "spurting" or "dividing" (*Sifri;* cf. *Niddah* 59b; *Chullin* 38a); or, "indolent" (Ibn Janach).

—   **from the Bashan.** Since Dan's territory is directly to the west of the Bashan.

33:23   **totally satisfied** (Rashi; cf. Ibn Ezra). *Seva Ratzon* in Hebrew. Or, "has the fullness of good things" (Chizzkuni; Septuagint); "Shall be satisfied with [God's] will" (Ramban), or, "has the desire to be satisfied" (Abarbanel).

—   **to the southwest of Dan** (cf. Ibn Ezra). This is actually where Naphtali was. Or, "He shall occupy the sea and [the area to its] south," where the sea is the Kinnereth (Targum; *Sifri; Bava Kama* 81b; Rashi).

33:24   **Blessed among the sons . . .** (Ramban; Sforno). Or, "Blessed by the [other] sons . . ." (Ramban; Chizzkuni); "Increased by the [other] sons" (Ramban). Or, "Blessed with sons" (*Sifri;* Rashi; Septuagint), cf. 1 Chronicles 7:40 (Ramban). Possibly because Asher already had grandchildren when they went to Egypt (Genesis 46:17; *Tzafenath Paaneach*), or because of their increase during the 40 years in the desert (Numbers 27:47; *Aravey Nachal*).

PLATE 32.   PORTIONS OF THE TRIBES

33   accepted by his brothers, and dip his foot in oil.* ²⁵ Iron and copper are your doorbolts,* and your strength* shall increase each day.*

²⁶ There is none like God, Jeshurun.* Your Helper is He who controls* the heavens and has His majesty in the skies.*

²⁷ The eternal* God is a shelter* [above],* with [His] everlasting arms beneath.* He shall drive the enemy before you, and shall proclaim, "Destroy!" ²⁸ Israel shall thus dwell securely, alone* in a land of grain and wine, just like* Jacob. Your heavens shall also drip* with dew.

²⁹ Happy* are you Israel! Who is like you? [You are] a nation delivered by God, the Shield who helps you, and your triumphant Sword.* Your enemies

---

—   **in oil.** See Genesis 49:20, which can be translated, "His bread shall be oil."

33:25   **doorbolts.** (Saadia; *Lekach Tov*). *Min'al* in Hebrew. Or, "locks" (Chizzkuni; cf. Nehemiah 3:3); "treasuries" (Radak, *Sherashim*); "closed cities" (*Targum*; Rashi; Hirsch); "shoes" (Radak, *Sherashim*; Chizzkuni; Malbim; Septuagint); "sinews" (*Baaley Tosafoth*). Or, "you are a lock [to the Holy Land] of iron and copper" (Sifri). Or, "Your [land] is filled with iron and copper" (Ibn Janach).

—   **strength** (Targum; Saadia; Ibn Ezra; Septuagint). *Dabha* in Hebrew. Or, "energy" (Malbim); "youth" (Rashi; *Lekach Tov*; cf. Targum); "overflow" (*Sifri*; Ramban); "old age" (Ibn Janach; Radak, *Sherashim*; Chizzkuni); "weakness" (Hirsch); or "troubles" (Paaneach Razah).

—   **shall increase each day** (Septuagint). Or, "as in the days of your youth" (Rashi); or, "Even in the days of your old age" (Radak, *Sherashim*).

33:26   **There is none like God, Jeshurun** (Rashi; *Or HaChaim*). Or, "There is none like the God of Jeshurun" (Targum; Septuagint); "The God of Jeshurun, who has none like Him, is the one . . ." (Saadia); "None has the power of Jeshurun" (*Tur*); or, "None has the power [of Asher] in Jeshurun" (Abarbanel).

—   **controls** (*Moreh Nevukhim* 1:70). Literally, "rides." Or, "dwells" (Saadia), or, "has His Divine Presence in" (Targum).

—   **and has His majesty . . .** (Targum). Or, "and who controls the spheres in His majesty" (*Moreh Nevukhim* 1:10; cf. Rashi); Or, "who supports the skies in His majesty" (Ibn Ezra).

33:27   **eternal** (*Emunoth VeDeyoth* 2:12; Sforno). *Kedem* in Hebrew.

—   **is a shelter** (*Bereshith Rabbah* 68:10; Saadia; Ibn Ezra; Radak, *Sherashim*; Bachya). *Meonah* in Hebrew; cf. Psalms 90:1. Or, "Is the support of all existence" (Ibn Janach). Or, "[The heavens] are the abode of the eternal God" (Targum; Rashi).

—   **above** (Ibn Ezra).

—   **with His everlasting arms beneath** (Ibn Ezra). Or, "under [His] eternal arms" (Septuagint); "and below [Him] are the arms of the universe" (*Lekach Tov*; cf. *Sefer HaYetzirah* 5:1); "and under [His] arms is the world" (*Yerushalmi, Chagigah* 2:1); "[and the support] of the arms of the universe below" (Bachya); "[and who rides] the arms of the universe below" (Chizzkuni; Ralbag); "and below [the heavens] are [His] eternal arms" (*Baaley Tosafoth*); "the eternal arms [lifting] from the depths below" (Hirsch); "and below are the arms of the universe" (Radak, *Sherashim*); "and [subjugated] below Him are the mighty of the world" (Saadia; Rashi; Ibn Janach); or, "And down below are the mighty of the world" (*Midrash HaGadol*).

33:28   **alone.** See Numbers 23:9. (*Baaley Tosafoth*).

—   **just like** (Targum; *Sifri*; Saadia; Rashi; Radak, *Sherashim*). *Eyn* in Hebrew. Or, "those who come from Jacob's well" or "fountain" (Ibn Ezra; *Baaley Tosafoth*; Hirsch; Ibn Janach; cf. Psalms 68:27); denoting "children" (Chizzkuni), or, "land" (Septuagint). Or, "eye of Jacob," denoting prophecy (*Midrash HaGadol*).

—   **drip.** *Araf*, see above, 32:2. Or, "shall be misty with dew" (Septuagint).

33:29   **Happy.** *Ashrey* in Hebrew. *Makarios* in Greek (Septuagint), denoting happiness, good fortune, or having things go just right. Or, "You have it good" (Targum), or, "all progress is yours" (Hirsch). See Genesis 30:13. Or, "the greatest success" (Sforno).

—   **and your triumphant Sword** (Rashi; Ibn Ezra; Hirsch). Or, "Your Helper shall hold His shield over you,

shall come cringing* to you, and you shall crush their high altars underfoot.   **33**

[159. Moses Dies]

34 ¹ Moses climbed up* from the western plains* of Moab to Mount Nebo,* to the top of the cliff* facing Jericho. God showed him all the land of the Gilead as far as Dan,* ² all of Naphtali, the land of Ephraim and Manasseh, the land of Judah as far as the Mediterranean Sea,* ³ the Negev, the flat plain,* and the valley of Jericho, city of dates,* as far as Tzoar.*

⁴ God said to him, "This is the land regarding which I made an oath to Abraham, Isaac and Jacob, saying, 'I will give it to your descendants.' I have let you see it with your own eyes, but you will not cross [the river] to enter it."

⁵ It was there in the land of Moab that God's servant* Moses died* at God's word.* ⁶ [God]* buried him in the depression* in the land of Moab, opposite Beth Peor.* No man knows the place that he was buried, even to this day.*

⁷ Moses was 120 years old when he died,* but his eyes* had not dimmed,

and [His] sword is your boast" (Septuagint). Or, "For you the sword is merely a proud ornament" (*Paaneach Razah*).

— **come cringing.** (Targum; Ibn Janach; Radak, *Sherashim*). *Kachash* in Hebrew; see 2 Samuel 22:45 (*Midrash HaGadol*). Or, "will deny [their hatred]" (Chizzkuni); "will speak falsely" (Septuagint), "will renounce their principles" (Hirsch). Or, "[God] will subjugate your enemies" (Saadia).

34:1 **Moses climbed up.** Some say that this was written by Joshua (Ibn Ezra; see 34:5).
— **western plains.** See Numbers 22:1.
— **Mount Nebo.** See Numbers 33:47, above, 32:49. This was in Reuben's territory (Numbers 32:38), but Moses was buried in Gad's territory, as in 33:21 (*Sifri*; *Sotah* 13b).
— **cliff.** *Pisgah.* See Numbers 21:20, 23:14, above, 3:17, 3:27, 4:49.
— **Dan.** The territory of Dan. Or the city of Dan mentioned in Genesis 14:14, identified with Banias (Saadia).
34:2 **Mediterranean Sea.** "Final sea" literally. See above, 11:24.
34:3 **flat plain.** *Kikar* in Hebrew. See Genesis 13:10.
— **city of dates.** Or, "city of palm trees." See Judges 1:16.
— **Tzoar.** See Genesis 13:10, 19:22.
34:5 **God's servant.** During his entire lifetime (Ralbag) and even in death (Ibn Ezra). He was not called this until after he had died (Bachya). Cf. Joshua 1:1.
— **died.** There is a dispute in the Talmud as to whether this was written by Joshua, or prophetically by Moses (*Bava Bathra* 15a; *Sifri*; Rashi). See Joshua 24:26.
— **at God's word** (Targum). Or, "with God's mouth," that is with the divine kiss (*Sifri*; Rashi; *Moreh Nevukhim* 3:51).
34:6 **God** (*Sotah* 9b, 14a; Rashi; Ralbag). Or, "He buried himself" (*Lekach Tov*; Ibn Ezra; Bachya; Sforno). Or, "they buried him" (Septuagint).
— **depression.** *Gey* in Hebrew. See Numbers 21:19.
— **Beth Peor.** See Numbers 23:28, Joshua 13:20.
— **to this day.** Some say that this was written by Joshua (Ibn Ezra). See note on 34:5.
34:7 **120 years old . . .** According to tradition, on 7 Adar, 2488 (February 23, 1273 b.c.e.) (*Seder Olam* 10; *Kiddushin* 38a). Other sources indicate that he died on 1 Adar (*Esther Rabbah* 7:11; Josephus, *Antiquities* 4:8:49).
— **his eyes** (Targum; Septuagint). Or, "his appearance;" cf. Exodus 34:29 (Chizzkuni; Bachya).

34   and his natural powers had not left him. ⁸ The Israelites mourned Moses in the west plains of Moab for thirty days.*

The wailing period of Moses' mourning came to an end. ⁹ Joshua son of Nun was filled with a spirit of wisdom, because Moses had laid his hands* on him. The Israelites therefore listened to him, doing as God had commanded Moses.

¹⁰ No other prophet like Moses has arisen in Israel,* who knew God face to face.* ¹¹ [No one else could reproduce]* the signs and miracles that God let him* display in the land of Egypt, to Pharaoh and all his land, ¹² or any of the mighty acts* or great sights* that Moses displayed* before the eyes of all Israel.

34:8   **thirty days.** See Numbers 20:29.
34:9   **lay his hands.** Or, "ordained." See Numbers 27:18, 8:10.
34:10   **No other prophet . . .** It is therefore a basic principle of the Jewish Faith that no other human being ever had a revelation equal to that of Moses (Thirteen Principles of Faith 7).
—   **face to face.** See Exodus 33:11, Numbers 12:8.
34:11   **No one else could reproduce . . .** (cf. Ramban; Ralbag. Also see *Moreh Nevukhim* 2:33). Or, "There never has existed . . ." (Saadia).
—   **let him.** Literally, "sent him to . . ."
34:12   **mighty acts.** Literally, "mighty hand." Or, "all in his hand" (Septuagint).
—   **great sights.** *Mora'oth* in Hebrew; see above, 4:34. Some interpret this word as sights (Targum; Chizzkuni), while others interpret it to denote fearsome acts (Ralbag; see *HaKethav VeHaKabbalah*).
—   **displayed** (Ramban). Literally, "did."

חזק חזק ונתחזק

Completed 3 Tammuz, 5740
June 17, 1980

BIBLIOGRAPHY

BIBLIOGRAPHY

Abarbanel, Rabbi Yitzchak (ben Yehudah) (1437–1508). Extensive commentary on the Torah, first published in Venice, 1579. (We have used the Jerusalem, 1964 edition). The author was one of the leaders of Spanish Jewry at the time of the 1492 expulsion. His Torah commentaries were begun around 1503 in Venice.

Abudarham, Rabbi David (ben Yosef) (1420–1494). Laws and commentary on prayers for the entire year, first published in Lisbon, 1490. (We have used the Jerusalem, 1963 edition). The author was a student of Rabbi Yaakov ben Asher (see *Baal HaTurim*) and a rabbi in Seville. The work, which is considered an important classic of Jewish law, was written in 1450.

Adereth Eliahu, Commentary on the Torah by Rabbi Eliahu (ben Sh'lomo Zalman) (1720–1897), better known as the Vilner Gaon. The greatest genius of his time, he was the acknowledged leader of all non-Chassidic Jewry in Eastern Europe.

Aelian, also known as Claudius Aelianus (circa 210 c.e.). Roman author and teacher of rhetoric. His major work, *De natura animalium* (Of the Nature of Animals), contains important material on ancient zoology. It was published by Schneider in 1784 and by Jacobs in 1832.

Aggadath Bereshith. A midrash on Genesis, compiled from earlier ancient sources around 950 c.e. In ancient times it was also known as *Chuppath Eliahu.* It was first published as part of *Sh'tey Yadoth* by Rabbi Menachem di Lonzano in Venice, 1618, and separately in Vilna, 1802. A critical edition was published by Shlomo Buber in Cracow, 1903.

Akedath Yitzchak. An encyclopedic philosophical commentary on the Torah consisting of 105 chapters by Rabbi Yitzchak (ben Moshe) Arama (1420–1494), first printed in Salonika, 1522. The author was a rabbi in Spain, and after the 1492 expulsion, settled in Naples.

Alexander Polyhistor (circa. 100–40 b.c.e.). A Greek scholar, born in Miletus in Asia Minor. His work, *Concerning the Jews,* is preserved by Eusebius (q.v.) in *Prepataria evangelica* 9. He is quoted by Josephus (see note on Genesis 25:4).

Alshekh, Rabbi Moses (ben Chaim) (1521–1593). Important Torah commentary, properly known as *Torath Moshe,* first published in Venice 1601. The author was a preacher in Safed, as well as an eminent authority on Jewish law.

Aquila (circa 120 c.e.). Author of a Greek translation of the Torah, mentioned in the Talmud and Midrash. It is related that his translation was praised by Rabbi Eliezer and Rabbi Yehoshua (*Yerushalmi, Megillah* 1:9). He was a native of Pontus, a disciple of Rabbi Akiba, and a proselyte who was a relative of the Emperor Hadrian (Epiphanius, *Di pondus et Mensura,* chapter 15). His translation, which was very literal, was incorporated as the third column in the *Hexapla* by Origen (184–253 c.e.). Only fragments of it survive. (See note on Genesis 2:12).

Arakhin. Tract of the Talmud (q.v.) dealing with endowment valuations (see Leviticus 27).

Aristotle (384–322 b.c.e.). The most important ancient Greek philosopher and naturalist. His work, *Historia Animalium* (History of Animals) sheds important light on ancient processes (see note on Exodus 25:4).

Arrian or Flavius Arrianus (96–180 c.e.). Greek historian, living in Nicomedia in Bithynia. His work, *Indica,* a description of India in the Ionian dialect, sheds light on ancient geography. His complete works, edited by F. Duebner, was published in 1846, and an English translation of *Indica* by E.J. Chinnock was published in 1893. (See note on Exodus 10:19).

Artapanus (circa 120 b.c.e.). Hellenistic Jewish author, whose work *On the Jews* demonstrates how the foundations of Egyptian culture were laid by the Patriarchs and Moses. He is quoted by Alexander Polyhistor (q.v.). (See notes on Exodus 2:5, 2:10).

Artscroll. Contemporary anthology of commentaries on the Torah in English, edited by Rabbi Meir Zlotowitz. The first volume of the series, which is currently in progress, was published in New York, 1977. The series has received wide acclaim and popularity.

Arugath HaBosem. A commentary on liturgical poems (*piyyutim*) by Rabbi Avraham ben Azriel (circa. 1230). A two volume edition, edited by Rabbi Ephraim Ohrbach was published in Jerusalem, 1939, 1947. (See note on Exodus 28:20).

Arukh. One of the earliest and most popular Talmudic dictionaries, by Rabbi Nathan (ben Yechiel) of Rome (1035-1106), first printed in Rome, 1472. The author was a colleague of Rabbenu Gershom (q.v.) and corresponded with Rashi (q.v.). The work is extremely valuable in translating the Aramaic in the Targum (q.v.).

Arukh HaShalem. A greatly expanded version of the *Arukh* (q.v.) by Chanokh Yehudah (Alexander) Kohut (1842-1894), first published as a multivolume set in Vienna and New York, 1878-92.

Avodah Zarah. Tract of the Talmud (q.v.) dealing with idolatrous practices.

Avodath HaKodesh. Important kabbalistic classic by Rabbi Meir ibn Gabbai (born 1480), first published in Venice, 1567. Born in Spain, the author also lived in Egypt and Safed.

Avoth. Tract of the Talmud (q.v.) dealing with moral and ethical teachings.

Avoth deRabbi Nathan. A commentary on *Avoth,* by the Babylonian sage, Rabbi Nathan (circa. 210 c.e.). It is printed in all editions of the Talmud. We follow the paragraphing of the 1833 Romm Vilna edition of the Talmud.

Avraham ben HaRambam (1186-1237). Arabic commentary on the Torah, of which the sections on Genesis and Exodus were published with Hebrew translation by E. Weisenberg, in 1958. The author was the son of the famed Maimonides (Rambam), and was leader (*naggid*) of the Jews in Egypt.

Baal HaTurim. Commentary on the Torah by Rabbi Yaakov ben Asher (1268-1340), famed as the author of the *Tur* (q.v.). The popular work, first printed in Constantinople, 1514, was actually the author's introduction to each portion, written in the form of word plays (see Tur on Torah). It was later published in many editions of the Torah.

Baaley Tosafoth or *Daath Zekenim,* midrashic commentary on the Torah attributed to the authors of the Tosafoth (q.v.). Edited by Rabbi Yehudah ben Eliezer and first printed in Livorno, 1783. It is included in many editions of the Torah.

Bachya ben Asher, Rabbenu (1263-1340), also known as Rabbenu Bachayay. Torah commentary, written in 1291, and first published in Naples, 1492. The author lived in Saragoss, Spain, where he was a rabbinical judge (*dayyan*) and preacher. He was a student of Rabbi Shlomo Adreth, the Rashba (q.v.).

Bahir. An important, ancient kabbalistic classic attributed to the school of Rabbi Nechunia ben HaKana (circa. 80 c.e.), first printed in Amsterdam, 1651. An English translation by Rabbi Aryeh Kaplan was published in New York, 1979.

Baraitha. See *Baraitha Melekheth HaMishkan.*

Baraitha Melekheth HaMishkan. An ancient work, from around 220 c.e., dealing with the building of the Tabernacle in the desert. First printed in Offenbach, 1802, with a critical edition by Meir Ish Shalom (Friedman), Vienna, 1908.

Baraitha of 49 Middoth. An ancient work dealing with the Tabernacle, quoted in full in *Yalkut Shimoni* (q.v.).

Batey Midrashoth. A collection of ancient midrashim and the like from manuscript by Sh'lomo Aaron Wertheimer (1866-1935), first published in Jerusalem, 1893-97, and with additions, Jerusalem, 1950.

Bava Bathra. Tractate of the Talmud (q.v.) dealing with the laws involving real property.

Bava Kama. Tractate of the Talmud dealing with torts and damages.

Bava Metzia. Tractate of the Talmud dealing with movable property and wages. *Bava Kama, Bava Metzia,* and *Bava Bathra* denote the "first," "middle," and "final gates" of the tract that deals with general civil law.

Bayith Chadash, often referred to as *Bach,* after its initials. Major commentary on the Tur (q.v.) by Rabbi Yoel Sirkes (1561–1640). One of the important classics of Jewish Law. The author was one of the greatest sages of his time in Poland.

Bekhor Shor, Rabbi Yosef ben Yitzchak (circa 1150). Commentary on the Torah, first published in Constantinople, 1520. The author was a member of the school that compiled the Tosafoth (q.v.), and was a student of Rabbenu Yaakov Tam.

Bekhoroth. Tractate of the Talmud (q.v.) dealing with first-born animals.

BeMidbar Rabbah. Part of the collection known as *Midrash Rabbah,* dealing with the Book of Numbers. It consists of homolies on various verses, rather than a commentary on the text.

Ben Sirah. An ancient work comprising part of the Apocrypha, written around 320 b.c.e. According to tradition, Ben Sirah was a son of the prophet Jeremiah. A Greek version of the book is found in the Septuagint (q.v.), and is otherwise known as Ecclesiasticus. A Hebrew edition was published in Breslau, 1798. A better Hebrew edition, based on ancient manuscripts was published in Cambridge, 1899, and is included in Avraham Kahana's *HaSefarim HaChitzoni'im* (Tel Aviv, 1936).

Berakhoth. Tractate of the Talmud (q.v.) dealing with prayers and blessings.

Bereshith Rabbah. The most important part of the collection known as *Midrash Rabbah,* (q.v.) dealing with the Book of Genesis. It is written as a running commentary, based on material from Talmudic times, and serves as the basis for much later interpretation.

Bereshith Rabbathai. A midrash on Genesis based on the teachings of Moshe HaDarshan (circa 1050), first published in Jerusalem, 1940. The author makes use of *Yov'loth* (q.v.) and *Tzavaath HaShevatim* (q.v.). Moshe HaDarshan is often quoted by Rashi (q.v.).

Bertinoro, Rabbi Ovadiah (ben Avraham Yare) (1445–1515). Most important commentary on the Mishnah, first published in Venice, 1548, and in many subsequent editions. The author came from northern Italy, and later settled in the Holy Land.

Beth Lechem Yehudah. Commentary on Yoreh Deah (q.v.), by Rabbi Tzvi Hirsch ben Azriel of Vilna (died 1733). An important work on Jewish law, first published in Zolkiev, 1733, and later in editions of *Yoreh Deah.* The author was rabbi in Alik, Lublin and Vienna.

Beth Sh'muel. Major commentary on *Evven HaEzer* (q.v.), by Rabbi Sh'muel ben Uri Shraga Feivish of Vadislav (1630–1690). An important work on Jewish law, first published alone in Dyhernfurth, 1689, and with the *Shulchan Arukh* in Furth, 1726, and most subsequent editions. The author was a leading rabbi in Poland and Germany.

Beth Yosef. Major commentary on the Tur (q.v.) by Rabbi Yosef (ben Ephraim) Caro (1488–1575). A monumental classic of Jewish law, it was first published in Venice, 1555, and in many subsequent editions. Born in Toledo, Spain, the author was exiled in 1492, and lived in Portugal, Turkey, and eventually in Safed, where he served as rabbi. As author of the *Shulchan Arukh* (q.v.), the author is considered one of the foremost authorities on Jewish law.

Betza. Tractate of the Talmud (q.v.) dealing with festival laws.

Bikkurim. Tractate of the Talmud dealing with first fruits.

Buber, Sh'lomo (1827–1906). Scholar and authority on Midrashic literature. He published critical editions of sixteen major midrashic works, and helped edit the Romm Vilna edition of the Talmud.

Chagigah. Tractate of the Talmud dealing with festival offerings.

Challah. Tractate of the Talmud dealing with dough offerings.

Chamra VeChayay. Commentary on the Talmudic tractate of Sanhedrin (q.v.) by Rabbi Chaim (ben Yisrael) Benveniste (1603–1673), first published in Livorno (Leghorn), 1802. The author was acting chief rabbi of Izmir (Smyrna), and one of the leading authorities on Jewish law in his time. He is best known as the author of *Kenesseth HaGedolah,* a major classic on Jewish law.

Chananel. See Rabbenu Chananel.

Charedim. Important work on the commandments and kabbalistic theology, by Rabbi Eleazar (ben Moshe) Azikri or Azkari (1533–1600), first published in Venice, 1601. The author was an important kabbalist and a leader of the Safed school.

Chasdey David. The most important commentary on the Tosefta (q.v.) by Rabbi David Sh'muel (ben Yaakov) Pardo (1718–1790), first published in Livorno (Leghorn), 1776–90, Jerusalem, 1890, Jerusalem, 1970. Also included in the Romm Vilna edition of the Talmud. The author was born in Venice, and served as rabbi in Jerusalem.

Chidushey HaRan. Important commentary on Talmud (q.v.) by Rabbi Nissim (ben Reuven) Gerondi (1308–1376), first published (on Sanhedrin) as part of *Chamesh Shittoth,* Sultzbach, 1762. The author was one of the most important early authorities (*rishonim*) living in Gerona and Barcelona, Spain.

Chinukh. An anonymous work on the 613 commandments, following their order in the Torah, first published in Venice, 1523. The author is believed to be Rabbi Aaron (ben Yosef HaLevy) of Barcelona (1233–1300). The work is the subject of a number of commentaries (see *Minchath Chinukh*).

Chizzkuni. Important Torah commentary by Rabbi Chezekiah ben Manoach (circa 1250), published with the Torah in Venice, 1524, and separately in Cremona, 1559. The work quotes many midrashim of which it is the only source, and translates many obscure Hebrew words into French or Provencal.

Chokhmath HaMishkan. Work dealing with the construction details of the Tabernacle, by Rabbi Yosef Shallith (ben Eliezer) Richietti (flourished circa 1650–1670), first published in Mantua, 1676. The author came from Mantua, but eventually settled in Safed.

Choshen Mishpat. The fourth part of the *Tur* (q.v.) and *Shulchan Arukh* (q.v.) dealing with the courts, witnesses, legal documents, torts and business law.

Chothem Tokhnith. An important book on Hebrew synonyms and linguistic analysis, by Rabbi Avraham (ben Yitzchak) Bedarsi (circa 1230–1300), first published in Amsterdam, 1865. The author was a poet and linguist living in Beziers in southern France.

Chullin. Tractate of the Talmud (q.v.) dealing with Kashruth.

Conciliator. A work reconciling all contradictions in the Bible, by Rabbi Menasheh ben Yisrael (1604–1657), first published in Spanish as *Conciliador* in Amsterdam, 1632, 1641–51, and an English translation by E.H. Lindo was reprinted in New York, 1972. Although written in the vernacular, the book was widely respected (see *Shem HaGedolim, Sefarim,* Nun 48). The author was a rabbi and leader of the Amsterdam Jewish community. He petitioned Cromwell to allow Jews to resettle in England. He was a friend of Rembrandt, who painted his portrait.

Damai. Tract of the Talmud (q.v.) dealing with produce purchased from the unschooled, concerning which there is a question as to whether proper tithes were separated. .

Darkey Teshuvah. Encyclopedic commentary on *Yoreh Deah* (q.v.) by Rabbi Tzvi Hirsch (ben Sh'lomo) Shapira of Munkatch (1850–1913). This major work in Jewish law, which anthologizes hundreds of responsa works, was first published in Vilna, Munkatch (Munkacs) and Pressburg, 1893–1934. The author was an important Chassidic leader in Hungary.

Demetrius. The earliest known Greco-Jewish writer, living during the reign of Ptolemy IV (221–204 b.c.e.). He wrote a chronology of the Torah, quoted by Alexander Polyhistor (q.v.), and cited by Eusebius (q.v.). He is also quoted by Josephus. (See note on Exodus 13:18).

Devarim Rabbah. A midrash on Deuteronomy, comprising part of the collection known as *Midrash Rabbah* (q.v.). It is written in a homeletic style, resembling that of the Tanchuma (q.v.).

Dio Cassius or Cassius Dion (circa 150-235 c.e.). Roman historian, born in Nicaea in Bithynia. His history of Rome, *Romaika,* contains important geographical information regarding the ancient world. It was published by H.S. Reimer in 1750-52, F.G. Struz in 1824-36, and in English translation by E. Cary as part of the Loeb Series, 1912. It is quoted in the Conciliator (q.v.). (See note on Exodus 10:19).

Diodorus Siculus (died circa 20 b.c.e.). Greek historian, born at Agyrium, Sicily. His history, *Bibliotheca historica* (Historical Library) contains much important information regarding the ancient world, and is quoted in the Conciliator (q.v.). His 40 volume work was published by H. Stephanus in 1559, and by P. Wesseling in 1746. (See notes on Genesis 25:5, 50:2).

Dioscrodides, Pedanios (flourished circa 50 c.e.). Greek pharmacologist who served in Nero's army. His *Materia Medica,* which was very popular in the middle ages, contains much important information about ancient botany and processes. The Greco-Latin text, edited by K. Sprengel, was published in Leipzig, 1829, and a German translation by J. Berendes was published in Stuttgart, 1902. (See note on Exodus 30:24).

Divrey HaYamim DeMoshe or *Divrey HaYamim LeMoshe Rabbenu.* An ancient account of Moses' life, first published in Constantinople, 1517. It is cited by the *Arukh* (q.v.; s.v. Aaron), Rashbam (q.v.; on Numbers 12:1), and Ibn Ezra (q.v.; on Exodus 2:22, 4:20). It was reprinted in *Beth HaMidrash* 2:1-11, and in *Otzar Midrashim,* pp. 356-361.

Divrey Shalom. Collection of 30 sermons on the Torah by Rabbi Yitzchak Adarbi (1510-1577), first published in Salonika, 1580. The author was a rabbi in Salonika.

Divrey Sh'lomo. Discussions regarding the Torah, by Rabbi Sh'lomo ben Yitzchak HaLevi, first published in Venice, 1596.

Douai-Rheims. The first Catholic English translation of the Bible, first published in Douai, France in 1609-10. It is a translation of the Latin Vulgate (q.v.), and not the Hebrew original. It is, however, valuable for its analysis of the Vulgate, especially where obscure terms are concerned.

Eduyoth. Tract of the Talmud (q.v.) dealing with various rulings cited as testimony by various sages.

Eikhah Rabbah. Midrash on Lamentations comprising part of the collection known as Midrash Rabbah (q.v.).

Eliezer of Garmiza (Worms) (1164-1232), Commentary on *Sefer Yetzira* (q.v.). Mystical and philosophical work, first published with the *Sefer Yetzirah* in Mantua, 1562. A leader of the *Chasidey Ashkenaz,* the author was a leading authority on Jewish law and one of the foremost kabbalists in his time. He is best known as the author of the *Rokeach,* an important work in Jewish law.

Emunoth VeDeyoth. One of the most important works on Jewish philosophy, originally written in Arabic as *Amanat wa-i'tiqadat* by Saadia Gaon (882-942 c.e.). It was translated into Hebrew by Rabbi Yehudah ibn Tibbon in 1186, and first printed in Constantinople, 1562. The author was the greatest scholar of the gaonic period, and as head of the yeshiva in Pumbedita, Babylonia, was the leader of world Jewry.

Enoch. An ancient mystical work, probably written in Aramaic around 160 b.c.e. It was translated into Greek, and then into other languages. The Ethiopic version is known as 1 Enoch and the Slavonic version as 2 Enoch. The Ethiopic Enoch was published by R.H. Charles in 1906, and the Slavonic version by the same person in 1913 as part of the Apocrypha 2:425-69. It was published in Hebrew translation by Avraham Kahana in *HaSefarim Ha-Chitzoni'im* (Tel Aviv, 1936), pp. 19-141. There was also a book of Enoch (Chanokh) published as part of *Divrey HaYamim Shel Moshe Rabbenu,* Constantinople, 1516. The book is apparently mentioned in the Zohar (1:37b, 1:72b, 2:55a, 3:10b).

Eruvin. Tractate of the Talmud (q.v.) dealing with the various domains with regard to carrying on the Sabbath, and how such domains can be "blended" to permit carrying.

Etz Chaim. The major classic of Kabbalah based on the teachings of the Ari (Rabbi Yitzchak

Luria, 1534–1572). The work was written by the Ari's foremost disciple, Rabbi Chaim Vital (1542–1620), and first published in Koretz, 1782. Both the Ari and Chaim Vital were leaders of the Safed school of Kabbalah. The Ari is considered by many to be the greatest kabbalist who ever lived.

Eusebius of Caeseria (circa 260–340). Bishop of Caeserea and ecclesiastical historian. His *Praeparatio evangelica* in 15 books, quotes from many otherwise lost works, most notably, the writings of Alexander Polyhistor (q.v.). It was published in Oxford, 1843. His *Onomasticon sacra* deals with place names in Scripture, and since he lived in Talmudic times, it can be expected that he had access to traditions and information that has since been lost. This work was published in Leipzig, 1912–14. (See notes on Exodus 2:10, Numbers 23:28, Deuteronomy 4:43).

Evven HaAzel. Commentary on the *Yad* (q.v.) by Rabbi Isser Zalman Meltzer (1870–1953), first published in Jerusalem, 1935–1947. The author was a disciple of Rabbi Chaim Soloveichik, Rabbi Naftali Tzvi Yehudah Berlin (see *HaAmek Davar*) and Rabbi Yisrael Meir HaCohen, the Chafetz Chaim (see *Likutey Halakhoth*), and was a leading rabbi and *rosh yeshiva* in Jerusalem. He was the father-in-law of Rabbi Aaron Kutler, one of the most important leaders of American Jewry, and founder of the Beth Midrash Gavoah in Lakewood.

Evven HaEzer. The third section of the *Tur* (q.v.) and *Shulchan Arukh* (q.v.) dealing with the laws of marriage, divorce and related topics.

Eyn Tekheleth. Research involving the "blue wool" used in tzitzith-tassles, by Rabbi Gershon Henach Leiner of Radzyn (1839–1891), first published in Warsaw, 1890. The author was a Chassidic leader and an important Torah scholar. His conclusions regarding the source of the "blue wool" (*tekheleth*) were highly controversial, however. (See note on Exodus 25:4).

Eyn Yaakov. A collection of the non-legal portions of the Talmud (q.v.) by Rabbi Yaakov (ben Sh'lomo) ibn Chabib (1433–1516). A popular classic, first published in Salonika, 1515–22, and in many subsequent editions. Born in Zamora, Spain, the author headed the yeshiva in Salamanca, the largest in Spain. After the 1492 expulsion, he moved to Portugal and then to Salonika. He exchanged halakhic correspondence with the leading figures of his time.

Ezrath Kohanim. Commentary on Sifra (q.v.) by Rabbi Tzvi Hirsch (ben Naftali Hertz) Rappaport of Dubno (died 1865), first published in Vilna, Zhitamar, 1845–66. The author was a rabbi in Dubno.

Get Pashut. Work on the laws of divorce and related topics, by Rabbi Moshe ibn Chabib (1654–1696), first published in Ortokoi (near Constantinople), 1719. A leading figure in Jerusalem, the author was appointed chief rabbi of the Holy Land (*rishon le-Tzion*). He was a descendant of Rabbi Yaakov ibn Chabib (see *Eyn Yaakov*), and grandfather of Rabbi Yaakov Culi (see *MeAm Lo'ez*).

Ginath Veradim. Responsa (*teshuvoth*) involving Jewish law and related topics, by Rabbi Avraham (ben Mordecai) HaLevi (1642–1710), first published in Constantinople, 1717. The author succeeded his father as head of the Egyptian rabbinate.

Gittin. Tract of the Talmud (q.v.) dealing with divorce.

God, Man and Tefillin. A detailed study of the underlying philosophy of tefillin, by Rabbi Aryeh Kaplan, first published in New York, 1973.

Gra on Mekhilta. Notes on the *Mekhilta* (q.v.) by Rabbi Eliahu ben Sh'lomo, the Vilner Gaon (see *Adereth Eliahu*); first published together with the Malbim (q.v.) in 1874.

Gra on Seder Olam. Notes on *Seder Olam* (q.v.) by Rabbi Eliahu ben Sh'lomo, the Vilner Gaon; first published in Warsaw, 1862.

Gra on Sifra. Notes on Sifra (q.v.) by Rabbi Eliahu ben Sh'lomo, the Vilner Gaon; first published together with notes by Rabbi Yisrael Meir HaCohen, the Chafetz Chaim (see *Likutey Halakhoth*), Pieterkov, 1918.

Gur Aryeh. Supercommentary on Rashi's Torah commentary, by Rabbi Yehudah Liva (ben Betzalel), the Maharal of Prague (1525–1609), first published in Prague, 1578–9. The author was one of the foremost thinkers of his time, and was credited with making a golem.

Ha'amek Davar. Torah commentary by Rabbi Naftali Tzvi Yehudah Berlin (1817–1893), commonly known as the Netziv; first published in Vilna, 1879–80, Jerusalem, 1937. The author was son-in-law of Rabbi Chaim Voloziner (see *Nefesh HaChaim*) and head of the yeshiva in Volozhin for some forty years.

Hadar Zekenim. Torah commentary by the *Tosafoth* (q.v.) school and the Rosh (q.v.), first published in Livorno (Leghorn), 1840.

Hagah. Gloss on the *Shulchan Arukh* (q.v.) presenting Ashkenazic customs, by Rabbi Moshe (ben Yisrael) Isserles (1525–1572). Originally known as *HaMappah,* it was first published together with the *Shulchan Arukh* in Cracow, 1578, and in virtually every subsequent edition. The author was a leading sage in Cracow, and one of the greatest halakhic authorities of his time.

Hagahoth Bayith Chadash. Better known as *Hagahoth HaBach,* textual corrections on the Talmud, by Rabbi Yoel Sirkes (see *Beth Chadash*). First published separately in Warsaw, 1824, and later included on the page in the Romm Vilna edition of the Talmud.

Hagahoth Maimonioth. Notes on the *Yad* (q.v.) presenting Ashkenazic practices, by Rabbi Meir HaCohen of Rothenberg (1237–1299), first published with the *Yad* in Constantinople, 1509, and in virtually every subsequent edition. The author lived in Rothenberg, where he was a leading disciple of the famed Rabbi Meir of Rothenberg.

Haggadah, Minhag Teiman. Passover Haggadah according to the Yemenite custom, edited by Rabbi Yosef Kafach and published in Jerusalem, 1952.

HaGra. See Gra.

Hai Gaon (ben Sherira) (939–1038). Head of the yeshiva in Pumbedita, Babylonia, and the most prominent Jewish figure in his time. His commentary on the Mishnah is included on the page in the Romm Vilna edition of the Talmud (1887).

HaKethav VeHaKabbalah. Torah commentary using an in-depth linguistic approach, by Rabbi Yaakov Tzvi Meklenburg (1785–1865), first published in Leipzig, 1839. The author was rabbi of Koenigsberg.

Halikhoth Teiman. Work describing the customs and practices prevailing in the Yemenite Jewish community, by Rabbi Yosef Kafach (1917–   ), published in Jerusalem, 1961 and 1968.

Handbook of Jewish Thought. Concise, encyclopedic work on basic Jewish theology, by Rabbi Aryeh Kaplan, published in New York, 1979.

HaNothen Imrey Shefer. Analytic essays on the Torah, by Rabbi Eliahu ibn Chaim (1530–1610), first published in Venice, 1630. The author, known as the Raanach, was rabbi of Constantinople, and an important expert on Jewish law and Talmud.

Herodianus (flourished circa 200 c.e.). Greek historian. His historical work deals with the period between 180–238 c.e., published by G.W. Irmisch in 1789–1805 and by I. Bekker, 1855. An important source for information on ancient culture (see note on Exodus 34:13).

Herodotus (circa 484–425 b.c.e.). The greatest of the ancient Greek historians. His History is an important source for information on ancient geography and culture. He lived at the close of the Biblical era, and is quoted by Josephus (q.v.).

Herzog, Yitzchak Isaac HaLevi, Rabbi (1888–1959). Chief Rabbi of the Holy Land. His unpublished doctoral thesis, *The Dyeing of Purple in Ancient Israel* (1919) contains important research on the "blue wool" (*techeleth*) used in tzitzith-fringes (see note on Exodus 25:4).

Hirsch, Rabbi Samson Raphael (1808–1888). Monumental commentary on the Torah, first published in German as *Der Pentateuch uebersetzt und erklaert* in five volumes, Frankfurt am Main, 1867–78, and in English translation, 1956–62. The author was one of the greatest thinkers and Hebrew philologists of his time. He served as rabbi of the Orthodox community in Frankfort am Main, and was the spiritual leader of all German Jewry.

Horayoth. Tractate of the Talmud (q.v.) dealing with decisions by the Sanhedrin.

Ibn Caspi, Yosef ben Abba Mari (1279–1340). His Torah commentary, *Metzaref LeKesef* was published as part of *Mishneh Kesef* in Cracow-Pressberg, 1905–06. The author, who lived in Spain, was a leading philosopher and grammarian.

Ibn Ezra, Avraham (ben Meir) (1080–1164). His Torah commentary was printed separately in

Naples, 1488, and with the Torah text, Constantinople, 1522. A shorter, possibly earlier version, on Exodus (*Perush HaKatzar*) was published in Prague, 1848. It appears that the author rewrote the commentary a number of times, and other versions from manuscripts were published in London, 1877 and Shtersberg, 1894 (*Chilufey Girsaoth*). The author was born in Toledo, Spain, and was an expert in grammar, philosophy, astronomy, mathematics, and medicine, as well as an accomplished poet. After 1140, he lived the life of a wandering scholar, and it was during this period that he composed most of his works.

Ibn Janach, Rabbi Yonah, also known as Abu al-Walid Marwan (circa 990–1050). One of the most important Biblical dictionaries and grammars. The work, written in Arabic as *Kitab al-Tanqich* was translated by Yehudah ibn Tibbon (circa 1120–1190) as *Sefer HaDikduk*. It consists of two parts, *Kitab al-Luma*, translated as *Sefer HaRikmah*, and *Kitab al-Usal*, translated as *Sefer HaSherashim*. The *Sefer HaSherashim* was published in Berlin, 1896, and reprinted in Jerusalem, 1966. A contemporary of Rashi (q.v.), the author lived in Cordova and Saragossa, Spain, where he practiced as a physician.

Ikkarim. A major work on Jewish philosophy and theology, by Rabbi Yosef Albo (1357–1445), first printed in Soncino, 1485. The author was rabbi of Daroca and Soria in Spain.

Iliad. An epic poem of the battle of Troy, by Homer. One of the key classics of ancient literature, valuable for information on early geography and culture. According to Herodotus (q.v.), Homer lived around 830 b.c.e., while others maintain that he lived as early as 1159 b.c.e. (Philostratus) or as late as 685 (Theopompus). He is quoted by Josephus.

Jastrow, Marcus Mordecai (1829–1903). His *Dictionary of the Targumim, the Talmud Babli and Yerushalmi and the Midrashic Literature* was based on earlier works by Yaakov Levi and S. Kraus, and published in 2 volumes in 1886–1903, with numerous subsequent editions. The author served as a rabbi in Philadelphia. Although he was a traditionalist, who opposed radical changes, he was swayed by his congregation toward Reform. Nevertheless, his dictionary is considered, for the most part, reliable, and is used in yeshivahs.

Jerusalem, Eye of the Universe. Detailed analysis and philosophy of Jerusalem as spiritual capital of Judaism, by Rabbi Aryeh Kaplan, New York, 1979.

Josephus, Flavius, also known as Yosef ben Mattashyahu ben Gurion (circa 38–100 c.e.), Jewish scholar and historian, and main source of much of our knowledge of ancient Jewish history. His main works are *Antiquities* dealing with Jewish history from Biblical times; *Contra Apion*, defending the status of the Jews as an ancient and noble people; and *Wars*, describing the wars between the Jews and Romans. The Greek text was published by B. Niese (Berlin, 1887–1895). The author served as a military commander during the war against the Romans until he was captured in 67 c.e. A follower of the Talmudic tradition, he is considered reliable even when he seems to dispute the Talmud (see *Tzemach David* 3829; *Seder HaDoroth* 3829). He is occasionally quoted by Rashi (see *Bava Bathra* 3b end).

JPS. Bible translation by the Jewish Publication Society of America, Philadelphia, 1917. Produced by Reform and Conservative scholars, it often follows the King James (q.v.) translation rather than traditional Jewish sources. Although it is largely unreliable, it remains a standard even in many Orthodox Jewish sources.

Judith. Book of the Apocrypha.

Kaftor VaPherach. Work on the geography and laws of the Holy Land, by Rabbi Yitzchak Estori (ben Moshe) HaParchi (1280–1355), first published in Venice, 1549, with a critical edition published in Jerusalem, 1897. The author's family came from Florenza, Andalusia, Spain, and hence the name HaParchi (flower). He lived in Touraine or Tours, France, and was hence known as Estori or *ish Touri* (man of Tours).

Kalir, Eleazar. Author of much of the synagogue liturgy, he lived in Tiberias around 600 c.e. However, some earlier sources identified him with Rabbi Eleazar son of Rabbi Shimeon bar Yochai (*Tosafoth, Chagigah* 13a, s.v. *VeRagley*) or with Rabbi Eleazar ben Arakh (*Teshuvoth Rashba* 449).

Kav HaYashar. Ethical classic by Rabbi Tzvi Hirsch (ben Aaron Sh'muel) Kaidanover (1648–1712), first published in Frankfurt am Main, 1705. The author lived in Frankfurt am Main.

Kedushath Levi. Chassidic teachings on the Torah, by Rabbi Levi Yitzchak (ben Meir) of Berdichev, first published in Slavita, 1798. The author was one of the most important Chassidic leaders of the third generation, and was renowned as a sage, saint, and defender of the masses. He served as rabbi of Berdichev in the Ukraine.

Kelim. Tract of the Talmud dealing with the ritual impurity of vessels and utensils. The Tosefta (q.v.) is divided into three parts, *Bava Kama, Bava Metzia* and *Bava Bathra.*

Kenzil. Popular name for *Perushim LeRashi,* a collection of supercommentaries on Rashi's Torah commentary, because it contains a commentary by Rabbi Yaakov Canizal. Very important is the supercommentary by Rabbi Aaron (ben Gershon) Alrabi or Abulrabi (circa 1376–1430). The work was first published in Salonika, 1525. Abulrabi was a rabbi in Sicily. (See note on Exodus 35:22).

Kerithoth. Tract of the Talmud dealing with offenses for which the punishment is excision or being "cut off."

Kesef Mishneh. Important commentary on *Yad* (q.v.) by Rabbi Yosef Caro (see *Beth Yosef*), first published in Venice, 1574–76.

Kesseth HaSofer. Torah commentary including much archeological and geographical material, by Rabbi Aaron Marcus (1843–1916), first published in Cracow, 1913. The author was born and educated in Hamburg, but studied in the yeshiva at Boskovice and joined the Chassidic community.

Ketoreth HaSamim. Commentary on Targum Yonathan (q.v.) by Rabbi Mordecai ben Naftali Hirsch of Kremsier (died circa 1670), first published in Amsterdam, 1671–77. Born in Kremsier, the author was a famous preacher and Kabbalist in Cracow.

Kethuboth. Tractate of the Talmud (q.v.) dealing with marriage contracts.

Kiddushin. Tractate of the Talmud dealing with marriage.

Kilayim. Tractate of the Talmud dealing with forbidden mixtures.

King James. The most popular Protestant English translation of the Bible, first published in 1611. Although the translation was based on the Hebrew text, it made extensive use of the Septuagint and Vulgate for technical terms, and made use of extensive classical scholarship to understand the Greek and Latin. The translation, however, is heavily Christian orientated, and often goes against Jewish traditions.

Kinnim. Tractate of the Talmud dealing with bird sacrifices.

K'li Yekar. Torah Commentary by Rabbi Sh'lomo Ephraim (ben Aaron) of Luntschitz (1550–1619), first published in Lublin, 1602, and later in many editions of the Torah. The author was an important rabbinical leader in Poland.

Korban Aaron. Commentary on Sifra (q.v.) by Rabbi Aaron (ben Avraham) ibn Chaim (1545–1632), first published in Venice, 1609–11. The author was a member of the rabbinical court (*beth din*) in Fez, North Africa, and eventually settled in Jerusalem.

Kuzari. One of the most important works on Jewish philosophy and theology, by Rabbi Yehudah HaLevi (1074–1141). The work was originally written in Arabic with the title *Kitab al-Hujja wa'al Dalil fi Nasr al-Din al-Dhalil,* and translated into Hebrew by Rabbi Yehudah ibn Tibbon (circa 1120–1190). It was first printed in Constantinople, 1506. The author was one of the most important Jewish poets and philosophers, born in Toledo, Spain, where he practiced medicine and served kings and nobles. The Kuzari is written as a dialogue between the king of the Khazars (*Kuzari*) and a Jewish scholar.

Lechem Mishneh. Important commentary on *Yad* (q.v.) by Rabbi Avraham (ben Moshe) di Boton (1545–1588), first published in Venice, 1609, and in most subsequent editions of the *Yad.* The author lived and taught in Salonika.

Lekach Tov, also known as *Pesikta Zutratha,* a Midrashic work by Rabbi Tovia (ben Eliezer)

HaGadol (1036–1108), and first printed in Venice, 1546. This work incorporates many earlier midrashim that were circulating in fragmentary manuscripts. The author lived in Bulgaria and Serbia.

Likutey Halakhoth. Abridgement and halakhic commentary on the sections of the Talmud dealing with sacrifice, by Rabbi Yisroel Meir HaCohen (or Kagan; Poupko) (1838–1933), first published in Warsaw, 1899, 1903. The author, popularly known as the Chafetz Chaim, was one of the most saintly figures in modern Judaism. He lived and taught in Radun.

Likutey Moharan. Mystical, chassidic work, by Rabbi Nachman (ben Simcha) of Breslov (1772–1810), first published in Ostrog, 1806. A great-grandson of the Baal Shem Tov (founder of Chassidism), the author was one of the greatest original thinkers in the Chassidic world.

Livy or Totus Livius (59 b.c.e. - 17 c.e.). Roman historian, whose *Ab urbe condita libri,* a history of Rome, consisted of 142 books, 35 of which are still extant. They were published in Rome, 1469, and in a number of subsequent editions. The work sheds important light on ancient life (see note on Exodus 10:13).

Maaseh Choshev. Important work, describing the building of the Tabernacle in detail, by Rabbi Raphael Immanuel (ben Avraham) Chai Ricchi (1688–1743), first published in Venice, 1716. A rabbi and an important kabbalist, the author lived in Italy.

Maaseh HaShem. Running analytic commentary on the Torah, by Rabbi Eliezer (ben Eliahu) HaRofé Ashkanazi (1513–1586), first published in Venice, 1583. Born in Salonika, the author served as rabbi in Egypt, Cyprus and Poland.

Maaseh Tovia. Encyclopedia of science and medicine, by Rabbi Tovia (ben Moshe) Narol of Metz (1652–1729), first published in Venice, 1707. The author lived in Germany.

Maaser Sheni. Tractate of the Talmud dealing with the "second tithe."

Maas'roth. Tractate of the Talmud dealing with tithes.

Maccabees. Two books of the Apocrypha, dealing with the events surrounding the story of Chanukah, around 142 b.c.e.

Maharsha. Abbreviation of Morenu HaRav Sh'muel Eliezer, denoting Rabbi Sh'muel Eliezer (ben Yehudah HaLevi) Aidel's (1555–1631), an important Talmudic commentator. His *Chidushey Halakhoth* on the legal sections of the Talmud was first published in Lublin, 1612–1621, and his *Chiddushey Aggadoth,* on the non-legal sections, in Lublin, 1627, and Cracow, 1631. They were included in the Prague, 1739–1746 edition of the Talmud, and in virtually every subsequent edition. The author was one of the most important rabbis and Talmudic scholars in Poland in his time.

Makhshirim. Tractate of the Talmud dealing with wetting that predisposes foods to become ritually unclean (see Leviticus 11:34).

Makkoth. Tract of the Talmud dealing with the penalty of flogging.

Malbim, Abbreviation of Meir Leib ben Yechiel Michael (Weiser) (1809–1879), author of HaTorah VeHaMitzvah, a monumental, analytic commentary on the Torah, first published in Warsaw, 1860–1876. The author was considered one of the great intellects of his time, and served as chief rabbi of Roumania.

Maskil LeDavid. Supercommentary on Rashi's Torah commentary, by Rabbi David Sh'muel Pardo (1718–1790), first published in Venice, 1761. The author is best known for his *Chasdey David* (q.v.).

Massa Rabbi Ovadiah Bertinoro. Letters describing the journeys of Rabbi Ovadiah Bertinoro (q.v.) that took place in 1487–90, published in *Otzar Massa'oth* (New York, 1927) pp. 106–124. Published earlier *Darkey Tzion* (Kolomea, 1886) and *HaMassa LeEretz Yisrael* (Berlin, 1922). Contains much important geographical information.

Mass'oth Binyamin. Journal describing the travels of Rabbi Binyamin of Tudela, between 1160 and 1172, first published in Constantinople, 1543, and in Otzar Massa'oth, pp. 15–44. Contains much important geographical material.

Matnoth Kehunah. Commentary on *Midrash Rabbah* (q.v.) by Rabbi Yessachar Ber ben Naphtali Katz (circa 1580), first published in Cracow, 1597. The author lived in Poland, and was a student of Rabbi Moshe Isserles (see *Hagah*).

MeAm Lo'ez. Monumental running commentary on the Torah, written in Ladino (Judeo-Spanish) by Rabbi Yaakov (ben Makhir) Culi (1689–1732), first published in Constantinople, 1730–33. A Hebrew translation by Rabbi Sh'muel Yerushalmi (Kreuser) was published under the title *Yalkut MeAm Lo'ez* in Jerusalem, 1967–71, and an English translation, by Rabbi Aryeh Kaplan, under the title *The Torah Anthology* (q.v.) is being published in New York, 1977– . Rabbi Yaakov Culi was born in Jerusalem, and later moved to Constantinople, where he was the leading disciple of Rabbi Yehudah Rosanes (see *Mishneh LaMelekh*).

Mebhaser HaBavli. Criticisms (*hassagoth*) on the translation of Saadia Gaon (q.v.) on the Torah by Mebhaser ben Nissi HaLevi, published by Moshe Zucker as part of *Hassagoth al Rav Saadia Gaon.*

Meditation and the Bible. Analysis of the meditative state and its relationship to the prophetic experience, by Rabbi Aryeh Kaplan, New York, 1978.

Megillah. Tractate of the Talmud dealing with Purim.

Megillath Taanith. Compendium of important dates in Jewish history, when fasting was forbidden, by Chanania ben Chezekiah (circa 70 c.e.; cf. *Shabbath* 13b). Mentioned in the Talmud. First printed in Amsterdam, 1659.

Meilah. Tractate of the Talmud dealing with forbidden use of consecrated articles.

Meiri, Menachem ben Sh'lomo (1249–1316). Author of *Beth HaBechirah,* an encyclopedic commentary on the Talmud, digesting much earlier work. The author lived in Provence.

Mekhilta. The earliest commentary on the Book of Exodus, by the school of Rabbi Yishmael (circa 120 c.e.), often quoted in the Talmud. First printed in Constantinople, 1515.

Mekhilta deRashbi. Mekhilta of Rabbi Shimeon bar Yochai, so named because he is the first sage mentioned in the work. A different version of the ancient commentary on Exodus, published by David Tzvi Hoffman, Berlin, 1905.

Melekheth Sh'lomo. Commentary on the Mishnah encompassing the full range of Talmudic literature, by Rabbi Sh'lomo (ben Yehoshua) Adeni (1567–1625). First published in the 1905 Vilna edition of the Mishnah. Born in Yemen, the author moved to the Holy Land where he studied under Rabbi Chaim Vital (see *Etz Chaim*) and Rabbi Betzalel Ashkenazi.

Menachem (ben Yaakov) ibn Seruk (circa 965 c.e.), author of *Machbereth Menachem,* an early Biblical dictionary, first printed in London, 1854. The work is often quoted by Rashi (q.v.). The author lived in Spain.

Menachoth. Tractate of the Talmud dealing with meal offerings.

Meor Eynayim. Analysis of Jewish history, by Rabbi Azariah ben Moshe Die Rossi (Min Ha-Adumim) (1511–1578), first published in Mantua, 1574. The author was the greatest scholar of Hebrew letters of his time, but since he quotes many gentile and Christian authors, his work was very controversial. It is, however, quoted in histories such as *Seder HaDoroth* (q.v.).

Mitzpeh Ethan. Talmudic commentary by Rabbi Avraham (ben Yehudah Leib) Maskil LeEthan (1788–1848), first published in the Zhitomar Talmud, 1858–64, and with additions, in the Romm Vilna Talmud, 1880–1886. The author was rabbi of Novograd and Minsk.

Midrash. A generic term, usually denoting the non-legalistic teachings of the Rabbis of the Talmudic era. In the centuries following the final redaction of the Talmud (around 505 c.e.), much of this material was gathered into collections known as Midrashim.

Midrash Aggadah. A midrashic collection based on the works of Moshe HaDarshan (see *Bereshith Rabathai*) compiled around 1150, and published by Sh'lomo Buber in Vienna, 1893–94.

Midrash HaGadol. A Midrashic collection, used extensively by the Yemenite community, written by Rabbi David ben Amram Adani (circa 1250). Printed as a set, Jerusalem, 1975.

Midrash Ne'elam. A mystical Midrash comprising part of the Zohar (q.v.).

Midrash Or HaAfelah or *Meor HaAfelah,* Midrashic collection by the Yemenite scholar, Rabbi Naftali ben Yeshiah, published by Rabbi Yosef Kafach, Jerusalem, 1957. Often quoted in Torah Sh'lemah (q.v.) from manuscript.

Midrash Rabbah. A major Midrashic collection on the Torah, assembled during the early Gaonic period. The component Midrashim vary widely, some being almost pure commentary, while others are pure homily. The *Midrash Rabbah* on the Torah was first printed in Constantinople, 1512.

Midrash Tadshe. An ancient Midrash attributed to Rabbi Pinchas ben Yair (circa 130 c.e.). Published in Beth HaMidrash 3:164, and in Otzar Midrashim p. 475 ff. It is cited by the Rokeach (see Eliezer of Garmiza).

Midrash Talpioth. A dictionary of Midrashic and kabbalistic concepts by Rabbi Eliahu (ben Sh'lomo Avraham) HaCohen of Izmir (1654–1729), first published in Izmir, 1736. The author was a preacher in Izmir, and is best known as the author of the moralistic classic, *Shevet Mussar*.

Midrash Tehillim. Also known as *Midrash Shocher Tov*. An ancient Midrash on the Psalms, first printed in Constantinople, 1515. A critical edition based on manuscript was published by Sh'lomo Buber, Vilna, 1891.

Midrash VaYisau. Midrash describing the wars of Jacob's sons, quoted in full in *Yalkut Shimoni* 1:133 (q.v.), and printed separately in Constantinople, 1519. It is also cited by the Ramban (q.v., on Genesis 34:13), and in *Sefer HaYashar* (q.v.). The story is based on an account in *Yov'loth* (q.v.) and *Tzavaath Yehudah* (q.v.).

Midrash VaYosha. Ancient Midrash cited by Bachya (q.v.), first printed in Constantinople, 1519, with a critical edition by S. Munk, in *Divrey Chakhamim*, Metz, 1849. It is also included in *Beth HaMidrash* 1:35–57, and Otzar Midrashim pp. 146 ff.

Middoth. Tract of the Talmud dealing with the dimensions of the Temple.

Milchamoth HaShem. Important philosophical work by Rabbi Levi ben Gershom (1288–1344), best known by his initials as the Ralbag (q.v.). It was printed in Riva di Trento, 1560, and Leipzig, 1863.

Minchah Belulah. Torah commentary based on Midrashim, by Rabbi Avraham Menachem HaCohen Rapa Porto (1520–1594), first published in Verona, 1594, and together with the Torah, Hamburg, 1795. The author was rabbi of Verona, Italy.

Minchath Chinukh. Commentary on the Chinukh (q.v.) by Rabbi Yosef (ben Moshe) Babad (1800–1874), first printed in Lvov, 1869. The author lived in Poland. The work frequently discusses questions found nowhere else in the literature. It has been the subject of an entire literature.

Mishneh LaMelekh. Commentary on the Yad (q.v.) edited by Rabbi Yaakov Culi (see *MeAm Lo'ez*) from the writings of Rabbi Yehudah Rosanes (1658–1727), chief rabbi of Constantinople, and leader of world Jewry. Printed in Constantinople, 1731 as a separate volume, and together with the Yad in Jessnitz, 1739–42 and most subsequent editions.

Mizrachi, Rabbi Eliahu (1448–1526), author of a supercommentary on Rashi's Torah commentary, first published in Venice, 1527. One of the greatest rabbis in the Ottoman Empire in his time, the author served as chief rabbi (*chakham bashi*) of Constantinople.

Moed Katan. Tract of the Talmud dealing with the intermediate days of a festival.

Moreh Nevukhim. One of the most important Jewish philosophical works, written in Arabic as *Delalah al-Charin,* by Rabbi Moshe Maimonides (see Rambam) in 1200. It was translated into Hebrew by Rabbi Sh'muel ibn Tibbon in 1204, and first printed in Rome, 1475.

Moshe of Narbonne (died 1362), author of a commentary on *Moreh Nevukhim* (q.v.), first published in Berlin, 1791, and edited by J. Goldenthal, Vienna, 1852 (Reprinted in *Shelosha Kadmone Mefarshey HaMoreh*, 1961). The author was a philosopher and physician in Narbonne.

Musaf HeArukh. Commentary on the Arukh (q.v.) by Rabbi Binyamin (ben Immanual) Mussafia (1606–1675), first published in Amsterdam, 1655. The author made use of the *Lexicon Chal-*

daicum Talmudicum by Johannes Buxtorf (Basle, 1604) to show how many Talmudic words are derived from Greek and Latin. The author was a physician in Hamburg.

Nazir. Tractate of the Talmud dealing with the Nazirite vow.

Nechmad VeNaim. An important work on astronomy by Rabbi David (ben Sh'lomo) Gans (1541–1613; see *Tzemach David*), first published in Jesnitz, 1743.

Nedarim. Tractate of the Talmud dealing with vows.

Nefesh HaChaim. Kabbalistic work by Rabbi Chaim (ben Yitzchak Berlin) Volozhiner (1749–1821), first published in Vilna, 1824. The author was a leading disciple of the Vilner Gaon (see *Adereth Eliahu*), the foremost Talmudist of his time, and the leader of non-Chassidic Jewry in Eastern Europe.

Negaim. Tractate of the Talmud dealing with leprous marks.

Nekudath HaKesef. Critical gloss on the *Turey Zahav* (q.v.) by Rabbi Shabathai ben Meir Ha-Cohen, author of *Sifethey Cohen* (q.v.); first published in Frankfurt am Main, 1677, and in later editions of the *Shulchan Arukh* (q.v.).

Niddah. Tractate of the Talmud dealing with the laws involving menstruation.

Odyssey. Epic poem about Ulysses' travels after the Trojan war, by Homer. See Iliad.

Oholoth. Tractate of the Talmud dealing with the defilement of things in houses and tents where human remains are found.

Onkelos. See Targum.

Or HaAfelah. See Midrash Or HaAfelah.

Or HaChaim. Commentary on the Torah by Rabbi Chaim (ben Moshe) ibn Attar (1696–1743), first published in Venice, 1742, and with many editions of the Torah. Born in Salé, Morocco, the author migrated to the Holy Land, where he established an important yeshiva.

Or Torah or *Torah Or.* Chassidic commentary on the Torah by Rabbi Shneur Zalman of Lyadi (1745–1813), first published in Kapust, 1837. The author was a leading Chassidic figure, and founder of the Lubavicher dynasty.

Or Yashar. Prayer book of Rabbi Moshe Cordevero (1522–1570), first published in Amsterdam, 1709, and as *Tefillah LeMoshe*, Przemysl, 1892. The author was one of the most important kabbalists, and a head of the Safed school.

Orach Chaim. First section of the *Tur* (q.v.) and *Shulchan Arukh* (q.v.), dealing with prayers and holy days.

Orlah. Tractate of the Talmud dealing with immature trees.

Orosius, Paulus (385–415 c.e.). Historian and theologian, born in Spain. His *Historiae adversum Paganos,* which contains important information regarding the ancient world, was first published in Augsburg, 1471. (See note on Exodus 10:13).

Otzar HaGeonim. Encyclopedic collection of Gaonic responsa and other writings, following the order of the Talmud, by Rabbi Binyamin Manasheh Lewin (1879–1944), published in Haifa and Jerusalem, 1928–1942.

Paaneach Raza. Allegorical commentary on the Torah, by Rabbi Yitzchak ben Yehudah HaLevi (circa 1300), first printed in Prague, 1607. The author was a grandson of Rabbi Sh'muel ben Sh'lomo of Falaise, teacher of Rabbi Meir of Rothenberg.

Pachad Yitzchak. A major encyclopedia of Talmud and Jewish law, by Rabbi Yitzchak Chezekiah (ben Sh'muel) Lampronti (1679–1756), published in Venice, Reggio and Livorno, 1750–1840. A graduate of the University of Padua, the author was rabbi of Ferrara, Italy.

Parah. Tractate of the Talmud dealing with the red heifer (see Numbers 19).

Peah. Tractate of the Talmud dealing with the portions of the harvest that must be left over for the poor.

Peliah. Kabbalistic classic attributed to the school of Rabbi Nechunia ben Hakana (see *Bahir*), thought to have been written by Rabbi Elkana ben Yerochem, first published in Koretz, 1784.

Pesachim. Tractate of the Talmud dealing with Passover and its sacrifices.

Peshitta. Eastern Aramaic or Syriac translation of the Bible, thought to have been made at the request of King Izates II of Abiabene (died 55 c.e.) who converted to Judaism. In many places it follows Talmudic interpretation rather than the literal meaning of the text, and may be alluded to in the Talmud (*Shabbath* 10b; *Rosh HaShanah* 33b; *Megillah* 10b; see *Jeshurun* 2:10; *Otzar Yisrael* 4:322). The name Peshitta was first used by Moshe ben Kefa (died 913). It was first published in the Paris Polyglot Bible in 1645, and in a critical edition in London, 1826.

Pesikta Zutratha. See Lekach Tov.

Philo Judaeus (circa 20 b.c.e. - 50 c.e.). Jewish philosopher and leader of the Alexandria community. His works are quoted by Josephus and in *Midrash Tadshé* (q.v.), and according to tradition, his Hebrew name was Yedidya HaAlexandri (*Meor Eynayim Imrey Binah* 3-6). His known works include *De opificio mundi* on creation; *Legum allegoriarum* (Allegorical Interpretation), an allegorical commentary on the Torah; *De Vita Mosis* (Life of Moses); *De Decalogo* (On the Decalogue); *Quaestiones et solutiones in Genesin* (Questions and Answers on Genesis); *Quaestiones et solutiones in Exodum* (Questions and Answers on Exodus); and *De Nominum Matetisae.* They were published in Greek with English translation by the Loeb Classical Library Series in 10 Volumes, 1929-62.

Philostratus (circa 170-245 c.e.). Author of the *Life of Apollonius of Tyana* which contains important geographical information (see note on Exodus 10:19), published by Aldus, 1502. The author was born in Lemnos, taught in Athens, and settled in Rome.

Photius (circa 820-891). Patriarch of Constantinople. His *Bibliotheca* or *Myriobiblon,* published by I. Bekker in 1824-25, is a collection of extracts from 280 classical volumes, the originals of which are for the most part lost. The work therefore contains much information regarding the ancient world (see note on Exodus 10:19).

Pinto, Yoshiah ben Yosef (1565-1648), author of *Meor Eynayim* on the *Eyn Yaakov* (q.v.), published in Amsterdam, 1643, Mantua, 1743, and as the "Riph" in the 1883 Vilna edition of *Eyn Yaakov.* An important Talmudist and kabbalist, the author lived in Damascus, and then migrated to Jerusalem and Safed.

Pirkey Moshe. Medical work by Rabbi Moshe Maimonides (see Rambam). Originally written in Arabic as *Fusal Musa,* the work was translated into Hebrew by Rabbi Nathan HaMe'ati (circa 1250), and published in Lemberg, 1824. (See note on Leviticus 13:30).

Pirkey Rabbi Eliezer. Important Midrashic work by the school of Rabbi Eliezer (ben Hyrcanus) HaGadol (circa 100 c.e.). First published in Constantinople, 1514. See Radal.

Pith'chey Teshuvah. Commentary on *Yoreh Deah* (q.v.), by Rabbi Avraham Tzvi (ben Yaakov) Eisenstadt (1813-1868), first published with *Yoreh Deah* in Vilna, 1836, and in many subsequent editions. A compilation of material from earlier legal responsa. The author was born in Bialystok, and served as rabbi in the Kovna (Kaunas) district.

Pliny the elder, or Gaius Plinius Secundus (circa 23-79 c.e.). Roman polymath. His *Natural History,* one of the most important ancient works on the subject, is extant in 37 books, and was first published in Venice, 1469. The work sheds much light on the ancient world.

Pri Chadash. Commentary on the *Shulchan Arukh* (q.v.) by Rabbi Chizkeya (ben David) da Silva (1659-1695), first published in Amsterdam, 1706. The author was the head of a major yeshiva in Jerusalem.

Pri Megadim. Encyclopedic commentary on the *Shulchan Arukh* (q.v.) by Rabbi Yosef (ben Meir) Teomim (circa 1727-1792), first published in Berlin, 1771. The author was a rabbi in Poland.

Ptolemy, or Claudius Ptolemaeus of Alexandria (circa 100-178 c.e.), mathematician, astronomer and geographer. His *Geographike uphegesis* (Guide to Geography), an important source of information about the ancient world, was published in Latin translation in 1462, and in the original Greek in Basle, 1533.

Raavad. Acronym for Rabbi Avraham ben David of Posquires (1125–1198), author of critical notes on the *Yad* (q.v.), first printed with the Yad in Constantinople, 1509. The author headed a school in Posquires in southern France, which was famous throughout Europe.

Raavad on Sefer Yetzirah. Commentary on *Sefer Yetzirah* (q.v.) attributed to the Raavad in the first edition (Mantua, 1562) and in subsequent editions, but actually written by a later sage (see introduction to *Etz Chaim*; *Shem HaGedolim*). It is thought to have been written by Rabbi Yosef (ben Shalom) Ashkenazi (circa 1310), known as Yosef HaArokh (the tall). The work combines kabbalah, mysticism, medicine and philosophy.

Raavad on Sifra. Commentary on *Sifra* (q.v.) by the Raavad (q.v.), first published in Constantinople, 1523, with a critical edition by I.H. Weiss, in Vienna, 1862.

Rabbenu Chananel ben Chushiel (died circa 1056). His commentary on the Talmud, one of the earliest, is included in the margin of the Romm Vilna edition of the Talmud (1880–86). His commentary on the Torah, which is quoted in many early sources, was published in *Migdal Chananel*, Berlin, 1876; by J. Gad in *Shelosha Meoroth HaGedolim*, 1950, and by Rabbi Chaim Dov Chavel, Jerusalem, 1972. Rabbenu Chananel was the head of the yeshiva in Kairouan, North Africa.

Rabbenu Ephraim ibn Avi Alragan (circa 1100), author of a commentary on the Talmud. He lived in North Africa, where he was a student of Rabbi Yitzchak Alfasi (see Rif).

Rabbenu Gershom (ben Yehudah) Meor HaGolah (circa 960–1028). Author of a commentary on the Talmud, published on the margins of the Romm Vilna edition of the Talmud (1880–86). He was one of the first great Talmudic scholars in Germany, and spiritual molder of German Jewry. He is best known for his ban on polygamy.

Rabbenu Meyuchas ben Eliahu (circa 1300), author of a commentary on the Torah. The commentary on Genesis was published in London, 1909, and the commentary on Exodus in Budapest, 1929.

Radak. Acronym for Rabbi David Kimchi (1157–1236), author of one of the most important commentaries on the Bible, first printed with the *Mikra'oth Gedoloth*, Venice, 1517. His commentary on Genesis was first published in Pressburg, 1842. The author, who lived in Narbonne, Provence, sought to ascertain the precise meaning of the scripture.

Radak, Sherashim. An extremely important dictionary of Biblical word roots by Rabbi David Kimchi (see above). It is especially useful in presenting the author's interpretation on verses where he has no formal commentary. The work was first published in Naples, 1490.

Radal. Acronym of Rabbi David (ben Yehudah) Luria (1798–1855), author of an important commentary on *Pirkey Rabbi Eliezer* (q.v.), first published in Warsaw, 1852. The author lived in Lithuania, and was considered as one of the spiritual leaders of his generation.

Ralbag. Acronym for Rabbi Levi ben Gershom (1288–1344), author of one of the most important commentaries on the Bible, first published in the *Mikraoth Gedoloth*, Venice, 1523. His commentary on the Torah was first published in Mantua, 1475. The author lived in Orange and Vignot, and also wrote on mathematics, philosophy, and astronomy.

Rambam. Acronym for Rabbi Moshe ben Maimon (1135–1204), also known as Maimonides. It denotes his commentary on the Mishneh, written in Arabic as *Kitab al-Saraj* (Book of Illumination), and translated into Hebrew by Rabbi Yehudah al Charizi (1170–1235) and others. It was published together with the first edition of the Mishnah, Naples, 1492. The author is considered one of Judaism's leading Torah authorities and philosophers. One of the greatest minds of his time, he served as personal physician to Saladin the Great, Sultan of Egypt and Syria.

Rambam, Kafach edition. A new Hebrew translation of Maimonides' commentary on the Mishnah by Rabbi Yosef Kafach (1917–   ), first published in Jerusalem, 1964.

Ramban. Acronym for Rabbi Moshe ben Nachman (1194–1270), denoting his commentary on the Torah, first printed in Rome, 1472. The author was one of the leading spiritual leaders of his time, writing over fifty works on Bible, Talmud, Jewish law, philosophy, Kabbalah and medicine, all of which are considered major classics. He lived in Gerona, Spain, where he maintained a yeshiva.

Ramban on Sefer HaMitzvoth. Critical commentary on Maimonides' *Sefer HaMitzvoth* (q.v.), disputing many major points, by the Ramban (see above). First published in Constantinople, 1510. We have used the Vilna, 1883, edition, which has been reprinted a number of times.

Ran. Acronym of Rabbenu Nissim (ben Reuven Gerondi) (1308–1376), author of important commentaries on the Talmud and Rif. His commentary on the Talmudic tract of *Nedarim* (q.v.) is published in virtually all editions of the Talmud. His commentary on the Rif (q.v.) was also published in virtually all editions. See *Chidushey HaRan*.

Rashbam. Acronym for Rabbi Sh'muel ben Meir (circa 1080–1174), author of an important commentary on the Torah, dealing with the precise simple meaning of the text. It was first printed together with the Torah in Berlin, 1705, with a critical edition (from the same manuscript used in the first printed edition) by David Rosin, Breslau, 1882. The author was a grandson of Rashi (q.v.) and elder brother of Rabbenu Yaakov Tam. He earned a livelihood from sheep farming and viticulture. Besides his commentary on the Torah, he also wrote commentaries on portions of the Talmud.

Rash. Acronym of Rabbenu Shimshon (ben Avraham of Sens) (died circa 1220), author of an important commentary on parts of the Mishnah, published in most editions of the Talmud. The author was a brother-in-law of Rabbi Yaakov Tam, leader of the school that produced the Tosafoth (q.v.).

Rashi. Acronym of Rabbenu Sh'lomo (ben Yitzchak) Yarchi (see *Shem HaGedolim*) (1040–1105), author of the most important commentaries on the Bible and Talmud, printed in most major editions. His commentary on the Torah was the first known Hebrew book to be printed (Rome, circa 1470). He headed yeshivos in his native Troyes and Worms in France. His commentaries are known to be extremely terse, immediately bringing forth the main idea of the text.

Ravya. Acronym of Rabbi Eliezer ben Yoel HaLevi (of Bonn) (1140–1225), author of a commentary on the Talmud, published by Rabbi Avigdor Aptovitzer, Berlin, 1913–1930, Jerusalem, 1935–38. The author was rabbi of Mintz, and an important leader of German Jewry.

Raziel HaMalakh. An anonymous Kabbalistic classic, actually consisting of three parts, *Sefer Raziel, Raziel HaGadol,* and *Raziel HaMalakh:* first published in Amsterdam, 1701. It is mentioned by Ibn Ezra (q.v.) in his commentary on Exodus 14:19.

Recanti, Rabbi Menachem (ben Binyamin) (1217–1305), author of a kabbalistic commentary on the Torah, first published in Venice, 1523 (we have used the edition with *Levush Evven Yekara* by Rabbi Mordecai Yaffe, Lvov, 1880). The author was one of the leading kabbalists of his time, and one of the first to quote the Zohar (q.v.).

Reshith Limudim. Geographical work by Rabbi Barukh Lindau (1759–1849), first published in Berlin, 1798.

Rif. Acronym of Rabbi Yitzchak (ben Yaakov) Al-fasi (1013–1103) author of an abridgement of the Talmud meant to serve as a practical legal code; first printed as *Hil'khoth Rav Al-fasi,* Hijer, Spain, circa 1485. (We have used the version in the Romm, Vilna Talmud). The author was born in Algeria, but settled in Fez, and is hence known as Al-fasi (the person of Fez). His code, which was the most important before the writing of Maimonides' *Yad,* brought the Gaonic period to a close.

Ritva. Acronym for Rabbi Yom Tov ben Avraham Ishbili (1248–1330), author of an important commentary on the Talmud. His commentary on the non-legalistic portions of the Talmud was first published with the *Eyn Yaakov* (q.v.), Salonika, 1515–22. The author was rabbi of Saragossa, Spain, and after the death of his teachers, was considered the spiritual leader of all Spain.

Rosh. Acronym for Rabbenu Asher (ben Yechiel) (1250–1327), author of *Piskey HaRosh,* an important legal work, following the style of the Rif (q.v.), first published with the Talmud, Venice, 1523, and in most subsequent editions. His commentary, *Perush HaRosh* on the Talmudic tract of Nedarim (q.v.) was also published in virtually every edition of the Talmud. His commentary on the Torah was printed as part of *Hadar Zekenim* (q.v.), Livorno, 1840. The Rosh was the leading talmudist in Germany, but after a time of persecution, became rabbi of Toledo, Spain.

Rosh HaShanah. Tract of the Talmud dealing with the New Year and the calendar.

Saadia. Arabic translation of the Torah by Saadia (ben Yosef) Gaon (882–942 c.e.). It was first published in Paris, 1893, and as the *Kether Torah* or *Taj,* Jerusalem 1894–1901. A Hebrew translation of key parts was published by Rabbi Yosef Kafach, Jerusalem, 1963. The author was the greatest scholar of the Gaonic period, and as head of the yeshiva in Pumbedita, was the leader of world Jewry. His *Emunoth VeDeyoth* (q.v.) is considered one of the most important works on Jewish philosophy.

Saadia on Sefer Yetzirah. A commentary on *Sefer Yetzirah* (q.v.) by Saadia Gaon (see previous note), translated from Arabic into Hebrew by Rabbi Yosef Kafach, and first published in Jerusalem, 1972.

Sanhedrin. Tractate of the Talmud (q.v.) dealing with the judiciary system.

Seder HaDoroth. One of the most comprehensive Jewish histories, based entirely on traditional sources, by Rabbi Yechiel (ben Sh'lomo Heilprin) (1660–1746), first published in Karlsruhe, 1769. The author was head of the yeshiva in Minsk.

Seder Olam, or *Seder Olam Rabbah.* The earliest comprehensive Jewish history based on Talmudic traditions, by Rabbi Yosi ben Chalafta (circa 130 c.e.), first printed in Mantua, 1514.

Sedey Chemed. Encyclopedia of Jewish law, by Rabbi Chaim Chezekiah (ben Raphael Eliahu) Medini (1832–1904). One of the most monumental halakhic works ever written, it was first published in Warsaw, 1890–1911. The author lived in Jerusalem.

Sefer Baal Shem Tov. An anthology of the teachings of Rabbi Yisrael, known as the Baal Shem Tov (1698–1760), compiled by Rabbi Shimeon Menachem Mendel Vednik, and first published in Lodz, 1938. The Baal Shem Tov was the founder of the Chassidic movement.

Sefer Chasidim. Laws and customs of the *Chasidey Ashkenaz* (German pietists) by Rabbi Yehudah (ben Sh'muel) HaChasid (1148–1217), first printed in Bologna, 1538. A different edition, based on an early manuscript, was published by the *Mekitzey Nirdamim* society in Berlin, 1891. The author, who lived in Speyer and Regensburg, was master of the *Chasidey Ashkenaz* movement, and a leading rabbinical authority of his time.

Sefer HaAtzamim. A work about man and his world, by Rabbi Avraham Ibn Ezra (q.v.), first published in London, 1901.

Sefer HaIttur. Important early work on Jewish law, by Rabbi Yitzchak ben Abba Mari of Marseilles (circa 1120–1190), first published in Venice, 1608. (We have used the Vilna-Warsaw edition of 1874–85).

Sefer HaMitzvoth. Work on the 613 Commandments by the Rambam (q.v.), first published in Constantinople, 1510.

Sefer HaYashar. Anonymous history of the Torah, written in story form, first printed in Venice, 1525. (We have used the Alter Bergman edition, Tel Aviv). Some consider the work to have been written in Talmudic times or earlier, while others consider it a medieval work.

Sefer HaYov'loth. See *Yov'loth.*

Sefer Mitzvoth Gadol, also known as the *S'mag.* Halakhic work on the 613 commandments, by Rabbi Moshe (ben Yaakov) of Coucy (1198–1274), first printed in Rome, 1474. (We have used the Venice, 1547, edition.) The author preached in Spain, and taught in the spirit of the *Chasidey Ashkenaz* (see *Sefer Chasidim*).

Sefer Mitzvoth Katan. Halakhic work on the commandments, also known as *Amudey HaGolah,* by

Rabbi Yaakov (ben Yosef) of Corbeil (1206–1280), first printed in Constantinople, 1510. The work follows the *Sefer Mitzvoth Gadol* (see above) but is in a different order. The author was a member of the school that compiled the Tosafoth (q.v.).

Sefer Yereyim. Compilation of laws based on the 613 commandments, by Rabbi Eliezer (ben Sh'muel) of Metz (1114–1189). An abridgement of this work was first published in Venice, 1566, and a complete work, based on a Paris manuscript, in Vilna, 1902. The author, who earned a living as a moneylender, was a member of the Tosafoth school. The work was highly important insofar as it bridged the gap between the French and Spanish schools of halakhah.

Sefer Yetzirah. One of the most important and ancient mystical works, thought to be from Talmudic times or earlier. First published in Mantua, 1562. It has been the subject of over one hundred commentaries.

Sekhel Tov. A midrashic work by Rabbi Menachem ben Sh'lomo (circa 1120), first published by Sh'lomo Buber, Berlin, 1900.

Septuagint. Greek translation of the Bible by 70 scholars, prepared for King Ptolemy Philadelphus (309–246 b.c.e.) (see *Letter of Aristeas*; *Megillah* 9a). The most ancient translation of the Torah. While the text has not been as carefully preserved as the Hebrew, it is valuable in the case of obscure words. In many places, however, the translators deliberately altered the text (*Megillah* 9a; see note on Numbers 16:15). In other cases, the Septuagint is followed by Talmudic sages such as Rabbi Nechemiah (see note on Exodus 8:17) and Rabbi Yehudah (note on Exodus 25:5), as well as the Targum of Onkelos (note on Numbers 24:7). It was included in the Hexapla by Origen (245 c.e.), and first printed in the *Biblia Sacra Poliglotta Complectentia*, London, 1655.

Sforno, Rabbi Ovadia (ben Yaakov) (circa 1470–1550, author of a Torah commentary, first published with the Torah in Venice, 1567. The author, who often follows the Ralbag (q.v.), lived in Italy.

Shaar HaMitzvoth. Portion of the "Eight Gates," presenting the teachings of the Ari (see *Etz Chaim*) regarding the commandments, first published in Salonika, 1852.

Shaar HaPesukim. Portion of the "Eight Gates" presenting the Biblical interpretations of the Ari (see above), first published in Solonika, 1863.

Shaarey Teshuvah, commentary on Orach Chaim (q.v.), begun by Rabbi Chaim Mordecai Margolioth of Dubnow (died 1823), and completed by his brother Rabbi Ephraim Zalman Margolioth; first published in Dubnow, 1820. The authors were important rabbis in Poland.

Shabbath. Tractate of the Talmud dealing with the Sabbath.

Shalsheleth HaKabbalah, Jewish history based on traditional sources, by Rabbi Gedaliah (ben Yosef) ibn Yachya (1515–1587), first published in Venice, 1587. The author lived in Italy and Alexandria.

Shekalim. Tractate of the Talmud dealing with the half-shekel donations given to the Temple.

Shemoth Rabbah. Midrash on Exodus comprising part of the collection known as *Midrash Rabbah* (q.v.).

Shenoth Eliahu. Commentary on the Midrash by Rabbi Eliahu ben Shlomo, the Vilner Gaon (see *Adereth Eliahu*), first published in Lvov, 1799.

Shevi'ith. Talmudic tractate dealing with the Sabbatical year.

Shevuoth. Talmudic tractate dealing with oaths.

Shiltey Gibborim. Work on the construction of the Tabernacle and Temple, by Rabbi Avraham (ben David) Portaleone (Shaar Aryeh) (1542–1612), first published in Mantua, 1612. The author makes a scientific inquiry into the stones, spices, and other materials used in the Tabernacle, using the Septuagint (q.v.), Vulgate (q.v.), and other ancient Greek and Roman sources. He was a rabbi and physician in Italy. The work was the first Hebrew book to use European punctuation.

Shiltey Gibborim. Halakhic work on the Rif (q.v.) by Rabbi Yehoshua Boaz ben Shimon Barukh (circa 1550), first published with *Hil'khoth Alfasi,* Sabbioneta, 1554.

Shir HaShirim Rabbah. Midrash on the Song of Songs, comprising part of the general collection known as *Midrash Rabbah* (q.v.).

Sh'moth Rabbah. Midrash on Exodus comprising part of the collection known as *Midrash Rabbah* (q.v.).

Sh'muel ben Chofni Gaon (died 1013), Gaon of Sura, and author of a Torah commentary, published in Jerusalem, 1979. The author was one of the most prolific writers of the Gaonic era.

Shulchan Arukh, the standard code of Jewish law, by Rabbi Yosef (ben Ephraim) Caro (1488–1575), first published in Venice, 1564. Like the Tur (q.v.), the *Shulchan Arukh* is divided into four parts, *Orach Chaim, Yoreh Deah, Even HaEzer* and *Choshen Mishpat.* Born in Spain, the author migrated to Turkey and then to Safed, where he served as chief rabbi. With the addition of the *Hagah* (q.v.) the *Shulchan Arukh* became the standard halakhic work for all Jews.

Siddur Rav Amram Gaon. The oldest surviving prayerbook, compiled by Rav Amram (ben Sheshna) Gaon (died circa 875 c.e.), Gaon of Sura, and leader of world Jewry. First published by N. Coronel, Warsaw, 1865. (We have used the 1971, Jerusalem, edition, edited by Daniel Goldsmidt.).

Siddur Rav Saadia Gaon. Another important ancient prayerbook by Saadia Gaon (q.v.) (882–942 c.e.), first published in Jerusalem, 1941. The Yom Kippur Service by the poet Yosi ben Yosi (around 450 c.e.) contains much information about the priestly vestments (see note on Exodus 28:6).

Sifethey Chakhamim. Supercommentary on Rashi's Torah commentary by Rabbi Shabathai (ben Yosef Streimer Meshorer) Bass (1641–1718), first published in Frankfort am Main, 1712, and reprinted in many editions of the Torah. The author was a cantor in Prague, and also wrote *Sifethey Yeshenim,* the first major Hebrew bibliography.

Sifethey Cohen. Commentary on *Yoreh Deah* and *Choshen Mishpat* (q.v.) by Rabbi Shabbethai (ben Meir) HaCohen (1621–1662), first published alone in Cracow, 1646, and later with standard editions of the *Shulchan Arukh* (q.v.). One of the important works on Jewish law. The author was a leading rabbi in Poland.

Sifra. Also known as *Torath Cohanim,* one of the earliest commentaries on Leviticus, written by Rav (circa 220 c.e.), and often quoted in the Talmud. First published (with commentary of Raavad, q.v.) in Constantinople, 1530.

Sifri. The oldest commentary on Numbers and Deuteronomy, written by Rav, and often quoted in the Talmud. First published in Venice, 1546.

Sifri Zuta. A somewhat different, shorter, version of *Sifri,* first published in Breslau, 1917.

Sotah. Talmudic tractate dealing with a suspected adulteress (see Numbers 5:11–31).

Strabo (born circa 63 b.c.e.). Greek geographer, important for information regarding the ancient world. His Geography consists of 17 books and was first published in Venice, 1516, with subsequent editions in Geneva, 1587 and Paris, 1815–19. An English translation by H.L. Jones was published as part of the Loeb Classical Library, 1922–28.

Sukkah. Talmudic tractate dealing with the festival of Sukkoth.

Symachus. Author of a Greek translation of the Torah, included in Origen's *Hexapla,* compiled around 245 c.e. (see Aquila). The translation is precise but idiomatic.

Syriac. See Peshitta.

Taanith. Talmudic tractate dealing with fasts.

Tacitus, Cornelius (circa 55–120 c.e.), Roman historian, whose works shed important light on the ancient world. His *Annals* consists of 14 books (some only in fragments) covering the period from 14–68 c.e., while his *Histories* consists of 12 books, covering the period from 69–97 c.e.

Talmud. The embodiment of the Oral Torah, as taught by the great masters between around 50 b.c.e. and 500 c.e. The first part to be codified was the Mishnah, set in its present form by Rabbi Yehudah the Prince around 188 c.e. Subsequent discussions were redacted as the Gemara by Rav Ashi and Ravina in Babylonia around 505 c.e., and it is therefore referred to as the *Babylonian* Talmud. Next to the Bible itself, it is the most important text for the Jew, furnishing the basis for all Jewish law practice and theology. Individual volumes of the Talmud were printed in Soncino as early as 1482, but the entire Talmud was first printed by Daniel Bomberg in Venice, 1523, along with the commentary of Rashi (q.v.) and *Tosafoth* (q.v.). (Also see Yerushalmi).

Tamid. Tractate of the Talmud dealing with the daily Temple service.

Tanchuma. An early homiletical Midrash on the Torah, attributed to Rabbi Tanchuma bar Abba (circa 370 c.e.) but added to until around 850. First printed in Constantinople, 1522.

Tanchuma B. A different version of the Tanchuma, containing many teachings cited from the Tanchuma in early sources, but not found in the other version. Published from manuscript by Sh'lomo Buber, Vilna, 1885.

Tanna DeBei Eliahu, Rabba and **Zuta.** An early Midrash attributed to the teachings of the prophet Elijah, first printed in Venice, 1598.

Targum. Authorized Aramaic translation of the Torah by the proselyte Onkelos (around 90 c.e.). In Talmudic times, it was read along with the Torah, so that the congregation could understand what was being read. In many cases, however, the Targum renders the text homiletically rather than literally.

Targum Yerushalmi. Ancient Aramaic translation of the Torah, usually included alongside the *Targum Yonathan* and probably written around the same time or somewhat earlier.

Targum Yonathan. Aramaic translation of the Torah, attributed to Yonathan ben Uzziel (circa 50 c.e.) (see *Tosafoth Avodah Zarah* 59a, s.v. *Ikla, Chagigah* 27a, s.v. *Salamandra*; but see Maharatz Chajas *ad loc.*). Other sources, however, merely refer to this translation as *Targum Yerushalmi* (Jerusalem Targum) (cf. *Arukh,* s.v. *Karkashta*), and Hai Gaon writes that it is of unknown origin (*Otzar HaGeonim, Megillah* 3a). Many later authorities write unequivocally that it was not written by Yonathan ben Uzziel (Rabbi Yaakov Chagiz, *Korban Mincha* 54; *Idem., Halakhoth Katanoth* 2:170; *Shem HaGedolim,* Tav 96; *Netzutzey Oroth* on Zohar 1:89a). From the text itself, it appears that some portions were written around the time of Yonathan ben Uzziel, while others were written a few centuries later.

Temurah. Tractate of the Talmud dealing with exchanged sacrifices.

Terumah. Tractate of the Talmud dealing with priestly offerings.

Teshuvoth Chavath Yair. Halakhic responsa by Rabbi Yair Chaim (ben Moshe Shamshon) Bacharach (1638–1702), first published in Frankfort am Main, 1699. The author was a leading Talmudic scholar in Germany.

Teshuvoth HaGeonim, Harkavy. Collection of Gaonic responsa edited by Avraham Eliahu (Albert) Harkavy (1835–1919), published in Berlin, 1887. Also known as *Zikhron LeRishonim*.

Teshuvoth HaGeonim, Shaarey Teshuvah. Collection of Gaonic responsa, edited by Rabbi David Luria (see Radal), first published in Leipzig, 1858.

Teshuvoth HaRosh. Responsa of the Rosh (q.v.), first published in Constantinople, 1517.

Teshuvoth Kenesseth Yechezkel. Responsa by Rabbi Yechezkel (ben Avraham) Katzenellenbogen (1688–1749), first published in Altona, 1732. The author was rabbi of Hamburg, Altona and Wandsbeck.

Teshuvoth Meir Nethivim. Responsa by Rabbi Meir (ben Tzvi Hirsch) Margolioth of Ostrog (died 1790), first published in Polonnoye, 1791. The author was a disciple of the Baal Shem Tov (see *Sefer Baal Shem Tov*).

Teshuvoth Radbaz. Responsa of Rabbi David (ben Sh'lomo) ibn Abi Zimra (1479–1573), first published in Livorno, 1652. Born in Spain, the author was Rabbi of Egypt, and was reported to have been the master of the Ari (see *Etz Chaim*) in Kabbalah.

Teshuvoth Rambam, P'er HaDor. Responsa of the Rambam (q.v.), first published in Amsterdam, 1765.

Teshuvoth Rashba. Responsa by Rabbi Sh'lomo ben Avraham Adreth (circa 1235-1310), published in Rome, 1475, Constantinople, 1516, Jerusalem, 1901. The author was rabbi of Barcelona, Spain, and was considered the foremost Jewish scholar of his time.

Teshuvoth Tashbatz. Responsa of Rabbi Shimon ben Tzemach Duran (1361-1444), first published in Amsterdam, 1738-41. Born in Majorca, Spain, the author moved to Algiers, where he served as a member of the rabbinical court (*beth din*).

Theophrastus (372-287 b.c.e.). A native of Eresus in Lesbos, he was the successor of Aristotle (q.v.) as head of the Peripatetic School. His works include *History of Plants* in 9 books, *Enquiry into Plants* in 6 books, and *On Stones*. They provide insight into ancient science, and can often be used to help translate Greek words in the Septuagint (q.v.).

Thucydides (circa 460-400 b.c.e.). Athenian historian. His *History of the Peloponnesian War* is a major classic, and sheds important light on ancient geography and culture.

Tifereth Yisrael. Important commentary on the Mishnah by Rabbi Yisrael (ben Gedaliah) Lipshutz (1782-1860), first published in Hanover, 1830. The author was a rabbi in Germany.

Tikkuney Zohar. Part of the Zoharic literature, consisting of seventy chapters on the first word of the Torah, by the school of Rabbi Shimeon bar Yochai (circa 120 c.e.). It was first printed in Mantua, 1558, but the second edition (Orotkoi, 1719) provided the basis for all subsequent editions. The work contains some of the most important discussions on the Kabbalah, and is essential for understanding the *Zohar* (q.v.).

Tohoroth. Tract of the Talmud dealing with ritual cleanliness with regard to food.

Toledoth Adam. Commentary on Sifri (q.v.) by Rabbi Moshe David Avraham Troyes Ashkenazi (circa 1710), published in Jerusalem, 1974. Some say that the author was the mysterious Adam Baal Shem (from his initials), who was the teacher of the Baal Shem Tov (see *Sefer*).

Toledoth Adam VeChavah. Important halakhic work by Rabbi Yerocham ben Meshulam (1287-1350), first published in Constantinople, 1516. The work consists of two parts describing the life cycle, *Adam,* from birth to marriage, and *Chava* from marriage to death. The author was a colleague of Rabbi Yaakov ben Asher (see *Tur*), and a student of the Rosh (q.v.) and Rashba (see *Teshuvoth*). He lived in Toledo, Spain.

Toledoth Yitzchak. Torah commentary by Rabbi Yitzchak (ben Yosef) Caro (1458-1535), first published in Constantinople, 1518. The author lived in Spain, and after the 1492 expulsion, in Portugal, Constantinople, Egypt and Jerusalem. He was an uncle of the famed Rabbi Yosef Caro (see *Beth Yosef*).

Torah Anthology, The. Translation of *MeAm Lo'ez* (q.v.) by Rabbi Aryeh Kaplan, first published in Brooklyn, 1977. The notes contain much original material.

Torah Sh'lemah. Encyclopedic anthology of Midrashim and early commentaries on the Torah by Rabbi Menachem Kasher (1895-). The first volume was published in Jerusalem, 1926, with over thirty subsequent volumes. The author was born in Poland, and migrated to Israel.

Torah Temimah. Encyclopedic Torah commentary by Rabbi Barukh Epstein (1860-1942), first published in Vilna, 1904. The work is noteworthy for quoting all the main Talmudic references to a verse, and offering extensive commentary on them. The author lived in Russia, and was the son of Rabbi Yechiel Michel Epstein, author of the *Arukh HaShulchan.*

Torath HaBayith. Important halakhic work by the Rashba (see *Teshuvoth*) first published in Venice, 1608. (We have used the Jozefov, 1883, edition.)

Tosafoth. A collection of teachings, using the method of the Talmud on the Talmud itself. It is the product of the yeshivah academies of France and Germany between around 1100 and 1300, begun by the students of Rashi (q.v.) and his grandsons, most notably Rabbi Yaakov Tam (circa 1100–1171). It is printed in virtually all editions of the Talmud.

Tosefoth Yom Tov. Important commentary on the Mishnah by Rabbi Yom Tov Lipman (ben Nathan HaLevi) Heller (1579–1654), first published in Prague, 1614–17, and in many subsequent editions of the Mishnah. The work was a supplement to the commentary of Bertenoro (q.v.), much as the *Tosafoth* was a supplement to the Talmud. The author was a student of the Maharal (see *Gur Aryeh*), and served as a rabbi in Prague and Poland.

Tosefta. Additions to the Mishnah (see Talmud) by Rabbi Chiyya and Rabbi Oshia (circa 230 c.e.), published together with most editions of the Talmud. The *Tosefta* is also often quoted in the Talmud. (We have used the ordering found in the Romm Vilna (1880–1886) edition of the Talmud).

Tur or *Arba'a Turim*. Monumental code of Jewish law by Rabbi Yaakov ben Asher (1268–1340), first printed in Piove di Sacco, 1475. The work is divided into four parts, *Orach Chaim, Yoreh Deah, Evven HaEzer,* and *Choshen Mishpat* (q.v.), and is the subject of numerous commentaries. A son of the famed Rosh (q.v.), the author was a leader in Toledo, Spain.

Tur on Torah. Torah commentary by Rabbi Yaakov ben Asher (see above), first published in Zolkiev, 1806. The author seeks to derive the simple meaning of the text, especially as found in the commentary of the Ramban (q.v.). Also see *Baal HaTurim*.

Turey Zahav or Taz. Major commentary on the *Shulchan Arukh* by Rabbi David (ben Sh'muel) HaLevi (1586–1667), first published together with the *Shulchan Arukh* in Dyherenfurth, 1692. This commentary on the *Shulchan Arukh* helped establish it as the definitive work on Jewish law. Son-in-law of Rabbi Yoel Sirkes (see *Bayith Chadash*), the author served as rabbi and yeshiva head in a number of communities in Poland.

Tzafnath Paaneach. Torah commentary by Rabbi Yosef Rozin or Rogachov (1858–1936), published in Jerusalem, 1960. One of the greatest geniuses of his time, the author was rabbi of Dvinsk.

Tzavaath Binyamin. The "Testament of Benjamin." See Tzavaath HaShevatim.

Tzavaath HaShevatim. A work written as the last testament of Jacob's twelve sons, authored around 137 b.c.e. The work, which was probably written originally in Hebrew (see *Tzavaath Naftali*) is now extant only in Greek translation, with a number of Christian interpolations. The Greek edition, with English translation was published by R.H. Charles, 1908, while a Hebrew translation was published by Avraham Kahana in *HaSefarim HaChitzoni'im*, Tel Aviv, 1936, pp. 142 ff.

Tzavaath Levi. The Testament of Levi. See *Tzavaath HaShevatim*.

Tzavaath Naphtali. The Testament of Naphtali; see *Tzavaath HaShevatim*. An original Hebrew version is found in *Batey Midrashoth* (q.v.), Volume 1, p. 187 ff.

Tzavaath Reuven. The Testament of Reuben.

Tzavaath Yehudah. The Testament of Judah.

Tzavaath Yissachar. The Testament of Issachar.

Tzavaath Yosef. The Testament of Joseph.

Tzavaath Zevulun. The Testament of Zebulun.

Tzemach David. An important Jewish history by Rabbi David (ben Sh'lomo) Gans (1541–1613), first published in Prague, 1592. The author was a student of Rabbi Moshe Isserles (see *Hagah*) and the Maharal (see *Gur Aryeh*). His work also contains a section on general history.

Tzeror HaMor. Torah commentary, drawing heavily on the *Zohar* (q.v.) by Rabbi Avraham (ben Yaakov) Seba HaSephardi (1440–1508), first published in Venice, 1522. The author was driven from Spain in the 1492 expulsion, and settled in Morocco and Algeria.

Tzioni. Kabbalistic Torah commentary by Rabbi Menachem (ben Meir) Tzioni (circa 1380), first published in Cremona, 1559. The author lived in Cologne.

VaYikra Rabbah. Homiletic midrash on Leviticus, compiled around 450 c.e., comprising part of the collection known as *Midrash Rabbah* (q.v.).

Vulgate. Latin translation of the Bible by Jerome or Eusebius Sophronius Hieronymus (circa 340–420 c.e.). The translation is useful for determining obscure words in the text and in the Septuagint. It is reported that the author consulted with Jewish scholars in making the translation.

Wisdom of Solomon. A book of the Apocrypha, written around 170 b.c.e. Extant only in the Greek translation found in the Septuagint. A Hebrew translation of the Greek was published by Avraham Kahana in *HaSefarim HaChitzoni'im*, Tel Aviv, 1936, pp. 463 ff.

Yad. Short for *Yad HaChazakah*, otherwise known as *Mishneh Torah*. The monumental code of the Rambam (q.v.). It was so named because the numerical value of *yad* is 14, the number of divisions in the work. It was the first systematic codification of Jewish law, and the only one that encompasses every aspect of the Torah. It is considered one of the greatest classics of Torah literature. It was first printed in Rome, 1475, and in many subsequent editions, and it has been the subject of many commentaries.

Yalkut Shimoni, or simply, *Yalkut*. One of the most popular early collections of Midrashic material, compiled by Rabbi Shimon Ashkenazi HaDarshan of Frankfort (circa 1260), first published in Salonika, 1521–27. Many Midrashim are known only because they are cited in this work. The author was a preacher in Frankfort.

Yehudah HaChasid, Rabbi (1148–1217). Torah commentary, quoted in many early sources, and published in Jerusalem, 1975. The author is best known as the author of *Sefer Chasidim* (q.v.).

Yelam'denu. A midrash compiled around 800 c.e. and often quoted in the *Yalkut Shimoni* (q.v.) and *Arukh* (q.v.). Fragments were published in *Beth HaMidrash* 6:79–90; *Batey Midrashoth* 1:136; and *Otzar Midrashim* p. 222 ff.

Yereyim. See *Sefer Yereyim.*

Yerioth Sh'lomo. Monumental work on Hebrew synonyms and language by Rabbi Sh'lomo (ben Zelligman) Pappenheim (1740–1840), published in Dyherenfurth, 1784, 1811, Redelheim, 1831. The work is often quoted (as the Rashap) in *HaKethav VeHaKabbalah* (q.v.) and is said to have influenced Hirsch (q.v.). The author served as a rabbinical judge (*dayyan*) in Breslau.

Yerushalmi or *Talmud Yerushalmi*. An earlier version of the Talmud, which according to tradition was redacted around 240 c.e. by Rabbi Yochanan (182–279 c.e.) and his disciples in Tiberias, with the concurrence of the sages of Jerusalem. The Babylonian Talmud was the more accepted, however, since it was compiled later, and was assumed to include the accepted opinions of the *Yerushalmi*. The *Yerushalmi*, conversely, contains many important earlier opinions that are omitted in the Babylonian Talmud. The *Yerushalmi* was first published in Venice, 1523. We have used the pagination of the Vilna edition of 1922–28.

Yetziath Mitzraim U'Mattan Torah. A contemporary analysis of the Exodus and revelation at Sinai, based on traditional sources, by Rabbi Avraham Korman, published in Tel Aviv, 1978.

Yevamoth. Talmudic tractate dealing with a widowed sister-in-law.

Yitzchak ben Malkhi-tzedek (circa 1090–1160), author of a commentary on parts of the Mishnah, first published in the 1880–86 Romm Vilna edition of the Talmud. The author lived in southern Italy, and often translated Hebrew words into the vernacular, making use of Greek, Italian and Arabic.

Yoma. Talmudic tractate dealing with Yom Kippur.

Yoreh Deah. Second section of the *Tur* (q.v.) and *Shulchan Arukh* (q.v.), dealing with the dietary laws and other areas requiring rabbinical decision.

Yosippon. Anonymous work on the history of the Second Temple, based on the work of Josephus (q.v.). A manuscript exists copied by Rabbenu Gershom (q.v.), and it was used by Rashi (q.v.). The text was expanded around 1160, and this was edited around 1340 by Rabbi Yehudah Leon Mosconi, serving as the basis for the first printed edition in Constantinople, 1510.

Yov'loth or *Yov'lim*. A history of the periods covered in the Books of Genesis and Exodus, written around 110 b.c.e. It is the earliest source for much material found in *Pirkey Rabbi Eliezer,*

Sefer HaYashar, Bereshith Rabathai, Midrash Tadshe, and _Midrash VaYisau_ (q.v.), and is quoted by name in _Yosippon_ (q.v.). It was also used by the school of Saadia Gaon (q.v.) (see _Perush LeDivrey HaYamim HaMeyuchas LeTalmid Rasag,_ Frankfurt am Main, 1874, p. 36). It is evident that Saadia had a Hebrew version of the text, and such a version apparently was also in the hand of Jerome (see Vulgate). All that survives are Greek, Syriac and Ethiopic versions. The Greek and Syriac were published by R.H. Charles in his _Apocrypha and Pseudopigrapha_ (Volume 2, 1913), and the question of authorship, in _The Book of Jubilees or the Little Genesis,_ 1902. The Ethiopic text was published by A. Dillman in 1850, and a Hebrew translation, under the title _Bereshith Zutratha_ by Sh'lomo Rubin, Vienna, 1870. A Hebrew version is also in Avraham Kahana's _HaSefarim HaChitzoni'im,_ pp. 216–313. Although the work occasionally is at odds with halakhah, it is clearly evident that the author was a firm believer in the tradition that would be embodied in the Talmud, and not a Saduccee. He thus holds the strictest views on circumcision, the Sabbath, and belief in immortality. (For numerous parallels in the Talmud and Midrash, see _Beth HaMidrash_ 3:xii.)

Zavim. Talmudic tractate dealing with bodily discharges (see Leviticus 15).

Zer Zahav. Commentary on the Tosefta (q.v.) by Rabbi Eliahu, the Vilner Gaon (see _Adereth Eliahu_), compiled by Rabbi Meir ben Eliezer of Vilna, published in the Romm Vilna edition of the Talmud (1880–86).

Zera Berakh. Torah commentary by Rabbi Berakhia Berakh (ben Yitzchak) Spira (1598–1666, published in Cracow, 1646 and Amsterdam, 1662.) The author was a son-in-law of Rabbi Yom Tov Lipman Heller (see _Tosefoth Yom Tov_), and he served as preacher and rabbinical judge (_dayyan_) in Cracow.

Zevachim. Tractate of the Talmud dealing with sacrifices.

Zikhron Tov. Collections of teachings of Rabbi Yitzchak (ben Mordecai) of Neskhiz (1798–1868), and debates regarding the customs of the Baal Shem Tov, edited by Rabbi Yitzchak ben Leib Landau, first published in Pieterkov, 1892. The debate was reprinted as _Vikucha Rabba,_ New York, 1898.

Zohar. The primary classic of Kabbalah, from the school of Rabbi Shimon bar Yochai (circa 120 c.e.), compiled by his disciple Rabbi Abba. It is written as a running commentary on the Torah. After being restricted to a small, closed circle of Kabbalists and hidden for centuries, it was finally published around 1380–90 by Rabbi Moshe (ben Shem Tov) de Leon (1239–1305). It was first printed in Mantua, 1558–1560, and in over sixty subsequent editions. It is the subject of dozens of commentaries.

INDEX

(the suffix "n" denotes a footnote)